D0952759

THE AGE OF CATASTROPHE

HEINRICH AUGUST WINKLER

THE AGE OF CATASTROPHE

A HISTORY OF THE WEST, 1914–1945

Translated by Stewart Spencer

YALE UNIVERSITY PRESS
NEW HAVEN AND LONDON

First published in English by Yale University Press in 2015

English language translation copyright © 2015 Stewart Spencer

Originally published under the title *Geschichte des Westens: Die Zeit der Weltkriege, 1914–1945* by Heinrich August Winkler © 2011 Verlag C. H. Beck oHG, Munich, the second volume in the author's trilogy *Geschichte des Westens*

For information about this and other Yale University Press publications, please contact:
U.S. Office: sales.press@yale.edu   www.yalebooks.com
Europe Office: sales@yaleup.co.uk   www.yalebooks.co.uk

Typeset in Minion Pro by IDSUK (DataConnection) Ltd
Printed in Great Britain by TJ International Ltd, Padstow, Cornwall

Library of Congress Cataloging-in-Publication Data

Library of Congress Control Number: 2015947312

ISBN 978-0-300-20489-6

A catalogue record for this book is available from the British Library.

The translation of this work was funded by Geisteswissenschaften International – Translation Funding for the Humanities and Social Sciences from Germany, joint initiative of the Fritz Thyssen Foundation, the German Federal Foreign Office, the collecting society VG WORT and the Börsenverein des Deutschen Buchandels (German Publishers & Booksellers Association).

10 9 8 7 6 5 4 3 2 1

For Dörte

CONTENTS

3. Democracies and Dictatorships: 1933–9

4. Fault Lines in Western Civilization:
The Second World War and the Holocaust

INTRODUCTION

THE PRECURSOR TO THIS BOOK, *Geschichte des Westens: Von den Anfängen in der Antike bis zum 20. Jahrhundert*, published in German in the autumn of 2009, covered the history of the West from its earliest manifestations through Jewish monotheism, late antiquity and Christianity to the outbreak of the First World War. Central to my narrative in that work and in this is the evolution of what I call the normative project of the West, by which I principally mean the ideas of the two revolutions – the American and the French – of the late eighteenth century. These are ideas that the old European West struggled either to assimilate or to reject until well into the twentieth century. These are also ideas that the 'inventor nations' repeatedly violated, and yet they continue to provide the yardstick by which the West must be judged whenever it seeks to validate its values vis-à-vis the non-western world.

The current work deals with an exceptional period in world history, for the three decades between 1914 and 1945 were dominated by conflicts, crises and catastrophes in a way practically unprecedented in modern times – only the Thirty Years War of 1618 to 1648 had a remotely comparable impact. Throughout the first half of the twentieth century Germany was central to developments taking place over a far wider area, just as it had been in the first half of the seventeenth century. Indeed, its role was so central between 1914 and 1945 that this period can with some justification be described as the German chapter in the history of the West. It was also the most terrifying chapter in the history of humankind. It ended with the annihilation of European Jews, the most rigorously implemented mass murder in the history of the twentieth century – a period already particularly well stocked with state-organized crimes. And it brought with it the downfall of the Third Reich.

Many writers, including the sociologist Zygmunt Bauman, have seen the Holocaust as the result of a specifically modern quest for 'unambiguousness', a quest aimed at a functional rationality and concerned with the avoidance of 'ambivalence'. As such, it is seen as a borderline instance of the technological 'social engineering' that occupied a significant place in the thinking of the interwar period. Moreover, a large number of observers have long drawn attention to the basic experience of boundless violence of the First World War, violence practised hitherto only in colonial wars and described by the American historian and diplomat George F. Kennan as the 'seminal catastrophe' of the twentieth century. Visions of what might be possible in terms of social policies and an increasing willingness to accept mechanical methods of killing other human beings were phenomena that no longer admitted of national boundaries. Many of the developments that took place after 1918 can be viewed from this perspective, and yet this still does not explain why the Holocaust was a *German* crime against humanity. The present examination of the course of German history between 1914 and 1945 should be seen as an attempt to explain how a country that is culturally a part of the West could so obstinately refuse to respect the West's normative project and the idea of inalienable human rights that it plunged not only itself but the rest of the world into a state that can be described only as catastrophic.

If Woodrow Wilson had had his way, the period after 1918 would have resulted in the European triumph of western democracy, and yet by 1925 the German economist Moritz Julius Bonn was already referring to a 'crisis in European democracy'. Central to his analysis were the social and intellectual changes brought about by the First World War: the workers' increase in power and the resultant fears on the part of the bourgeoisie, and the militarization of thinking and the ensuing loss of faith in a civilian solution to conflicts on the basis of uncontested norms and within the framework of acknowledged institutions.

Of the new Continental European states that came into existence in the wake of the First World War on the strength of democratic constitutions, only two could still be described as western democracies two decades later: Czechoslovakia and Finland. The others were by then being ruled by more or less dictatorial regimes that had adopted those aspects of the western legacy that reflected their rulers' interests, while rejecting the idea of democracy in the form of the principle of a 'nation une et indivisible'. To the extent that these new states were not pure nation states but in many cases clearly based on the notion of nationality, this reception of western and, specifically, French ideas contained within it the germ of serious conflict.

One novel aspect of the political systems of the interwar years was the appearance of a new type of dictatorship in the form of totalitarian regimes. The contentious term 'totalitarian' is intended to refer to states in which the monopoly on power and the degree of repression go far beyond that normally found in conventional dictatorships such as overt or covert military regimes. What was new about these totalitarian regimes was the claim that they made on every aspect of their inhabitants' lives and the political aim of producing a new kind of individual. No matter how much they may have differed on every other point, the dictatorships established by Lenin, Mussolini and Hitler were very similar in this regard. Western democracies saw in Russian Bolshevism a far greater threat than they did in Fascism, which first came to power in Italy in 1922 and which conservative politicians and liberal journalists long regarded with a certain sympathy. It needed the experience of a far more radical, far more aggressive and far more 'totalitarian' Fascist regime – that of National Socialist Germany – before the Anglo-Saxon powers could be persuaded to revise their view of Communism and form an alliance with its principal representative, the Soviet Union.

It was National Socialist Germany that unleashed the Second World War. With its end came the emergence of that 'bipolar' world that was to leave its mark on the post-war period in general. Germany paid for its second attempt to gain control of Europe by having to capitulate unconditionally, losing a quarter of its pre-war lands and having its entire country occupied by the Allies. The largest European colonial powers, Britain and France, were so weakened by the war that they were no longer able to resist the progressive loss of their overseas territories. Whereas the first of the two world wars had led to a particularization of European states, the second resulted in their polarization: the United States and the Soviet Union were the leading powers in the blocs that waged a 'Cold War' with one another after 1947.

My plan is to deal with the history of the West after 1945 in a further volume. The fact that I was able to publish the current volume only two years after the earlier work is thanks to several institutions and individuals: the Robert Bosch Foundation, the Hans Ringier Foundation and the Ebelin and Gerd Bucerius ZEIT Foundation, all of which have supported my work since 2007; the Humboldt University in Berlin, which placed a room at my disposal, together with all the necessary technical equipment; my colleague of many years' standing, Monika Roßteuscher, and my student assistants, Angela Abmeier, Sarah Bianchi, Felix Bohr and Rahel Marie Vogel, without whose tireless help I would never have been able to write this book. I am grateful to Gretchen Klein, Monika Roßteuscher and Felix Bohr for the care with which they turned my handwritten manuscript into a printable format.

The editor in chief at C. H. Beck, Dr Detlef Felken, has lavished the same amount of care and attention on the present volume as he did on the first. Janna Rösch, Tabea Spieß and Alexander Goller proved a great help at the proofreading and indexing stages. I am grateful to all of them for their labours. My final debt of gratitude should in fact have come first: I have been able to discuss with my wife all the questions that have arisen in the context of my work on this volume. Her advice, her encouragement and her criticisms have left their mark on this book, too. That is why I have dedicated it to her.

Heinrich August Winkler, Berlin, March 2011

1

The Twentieth Century's Seminal Catastrophe: The First World War

Battles and War Crimes: Military Action: 1914–16

THE WAR WOULD BE short and would end with their country's victory. On this point, at least, everyone was agreed as they cheered their departing front-line troops in August 1914. And this was true whether the cheering crowds were in Berlin, Vienna, Paris, London or St Petersburg. But within weeks a mood of sobriety had descended on them all, and by the end of 1914 it was clear that the enemy would not be quickly defeated. From the outset, this war assumed different, greater, proportions from any that had previously been waged in Europe, wars in which many older contemporaries had themselves played an active part.

During the first four weeks of the war the forces drawn up against each other were, on the one hand, the two Central Powers of Germany and Austria-Hungary and, on the other, the Triple Entente of Russia, France and Great Britain, together with Serbia, Montenegro and Japan. Neutral Belgium became Germany's enemy when it refused to bow to an ultimatum from Berlin and opposed Germany's violation of international law. Turkey entered the war in October 1914, Bulgaria in October 1915, in both cases siding with the Central Powers. The Triple Entente was strengthened in May 1915, when Italy entered the war, and in 1916, when Portugal, Romania and Greece followed suit.

During the early weeks of the war, nothing inspired public revulsion as much as the German atrocities committed in neutral Belgium. The Belgian army put up unexpectedly stiff resistance, and it is possible that non-uniformed members of the Civil Guard were also involved in the fighting. Whatever the facts of the matter, the German military quickly developed a fear of 'franctireurs' that led to the same degree of panic that had been felt during the Franco-Prussian War of 1870–71. They responded by destroying private and public buildings, taking hostages and indiscriminately executing civilians falsely accused of shooting German soldiers. At the end of August large parts of the medieval town of Louvain, including the Catholic University's priceless library, were burnt to the ground. A total of 5,521

Belgian civilians were killed in the course of the massacres that took place between August and October 1914. Countless Belgian women were raped by German soldiers. It has also been claimed, but never proved, that children's hands were cut off and that other forms of mutilation were perpetrated, but these reports are almost certainly invented, their psychological origins lying in the colonial practices known to have taken place in the Belgian Congo during the reign of King Leopold II, who died in 1909.

John Horne and Alan Kramer, the authors of what is still the most thorough investigation of the atrocities perpetrated by the Germans in 1914, describe the Germans' mistaken belief that the Belgians were conducting a 'popular war' as an exceptional case of autosuggestion unique in any modern army. The actual atrocities committed by German soldiers were so terrible that in Belgium, France and England events that sprang, rather, from an overexcited imagination were taken to be true: as Horne and Kramer suggest, the severed hands became 'an allegory of the invasion, the enemy, and the war'.[1] The brutality of the German troops in Belgium and shortly afterwards in northern France was seen as a typical expression of Prussian militarism, impossible to reconcile with the Hague Convention signed by Germany in 1907 or with German claims to be one of the world's leading centres of civilization. From then on it was easy for the Allies' wartime propaganda machine to portray the barbaric enemy as twentieth-century Huns and Kaiser Wilhelm II as a latter-day Attila.

In early October 1914, ninety-three well-known German academics, artists and intellectuals signed an officially inspired 'Appeal to the World of Culture' protesting at such attacks. The signatories included the zoologist and social Darwinian Ernst Haeckel, the philosopher and Nobel laureate for literature Rudolf Eucken, the chemist Fritz Haber, the immunologist and Nobel laureate for medicine Paul Ehrlich, the historians Eduard Meyer and Karl Lamprecht, the painter Max Liebermann and the poet Gerhart Hauptmann. In putting their names to this document, they not only denied that the Germans were guilty of war crimes but even ignored the fact that Belgium's neutrality had been criminally violated, claiming that the lives and property of Belgian citizens had not been affected, except in cases of extreme necessity; they denied the destruction caused by German troops in Leuven; and they even found it in themselves to state that 'without German militarism, German culture would long since have been wiped from the face of the earth'.[2] The impact of this appeal in countries that were hostile to Germany and even in those that maintained their neutrality was devastating: Germany's cultural elite seemed to have parted company with the 'cultural world' at which its patriotic manifesto was primarily directed.

By September 1914 German advances in northern France had stalled, and for no compelling reason a profoundly pessimistic chief of the general staff, Count Helmuth von Moltke ('the Younger'), abandoned the Battle of the Marne as lost, ordering a precipitate retreat and finding himself replaced on 14

September by Prussia's minister of war, Erich von Falkenhayn. This marked the end of the 'Schlieffen plan', according to which the German army would break through enemy lines in Belgium and Lorraine and defeat the French forces, after which the bulk of the German troops would be sent to Russia. The Germans failed to win control of the most important Channel ports, including Dunkirk and Boulogne, where reinforcements of the British Expeditionary Force were in consequence able to land. The battles fought in the autumn of 1914 brought successes to both sides in turn, but both suffered appalling losses in the process. In the end the western front between Flanders and Upper Alsace could best be described as a standoff.

To the east, by contrast, Germany reported a military triumph during the early months of the war that it was never able to repeat in the west. At the end of August 1914 the Eighth Army under the nominal command of the infantry general Paul von Hindenburg – brought out of retirement for the occasion – but under the actual command of the chief of the general staff, General Erich Ludendorff, who had recently taken the city of Liège, succeeded in defeating the Russian army at Ortelsburg following the latter's incursion into East Prussia. For reasons of historic symbolism the battle was named after the nearby town of Tannenberg, where Poles and Lithuanians had defeated the army of the Teutonic Order in 1410.

At the First Battle of the Masurian Lakes in September 1914, German forces drove back the occupying Russian troops, but it was in February 1915 at the Winter Battle of Masuria that the Russians suffered their worst and definitive defeat in East Prussia. On the Polish front, too, the German and Austrian units that were deployed there were able to make substantial territorial gains in the autumn of 1914. But in the spring of 1915 an attempt by Austro-Hungarian forces to drive the Russians back into Carpathia proved ineffectual, and the Danube Monarchy, which had already lost 1.2 million soldiers in 1914 alone, suffered further losses of 800,000 men, a blow from which Germany's leading ally had still not recovered by the end of the war.

In spite of this, the Central Powers were able to place immense pressure on tsarist Russia, capturing Lithuania, Courland and Russian Poland between May and October 1915, and driving the Russians from Galicia. In the course of their retreat, the Russian troops deported more than 1.6 million Lithuanians, Latvians, Jews and Poles, claiming that in doing so they were acting in the interests of their own safety and security but in fact anticipating the even crueller fate that was to be meted out to Turkmen and Kirghiz nomads in 1916 after both of these groups had refused to accept the decision to call up all the Muslims living in tsarist Russia. Some half million Turkmen and Kirghiz nomads were robbed of their herds and property and driven into the mountains or deserts, where they died a pitiful death. By the autumn of 1915 a tenacious standoff had developed along the eastern front, too, albeit one that was broken in the summer of 1916 by the Russians' Brusilov offensive. The

Austro-Hungarian army suffered a devastating defeat at Bukovina, and between then and the Russian February Revolution of 1917, the front remained largely unchanged.

On 5 November 1916 the military situation made it possible for the two Central Powers in the persons of Kaiser Wilhelm II and Kaiser Franz Joseph to proclaim the establishment of a Polish state – the 'Kingdom of Poland' – on the territory formerly occupied by Russian Poland, although the real executive power lay not in the newly formed Polish National Council in Warsaw but in the hands of the German governor general in Warsaw and the Austrian governor general in Lublin. In consequence there could be no talk of an 'independent' Poland, still less of a secure frontier: Germany retained the right to annex a 'border strip' that was also to include Polish parts of the Upper Silesian industrial region. The future of two other areas occupied by German troops also remained open: Lithuania and Courland. Among the voices raised in favour of the annexation of the Baltic States were not only the Pan-Germans but also, and above all, the upper strata of German Balt society and many of the German Balts who were living and working in Germany.

Meanwhile on the western front there were repeated attempts in 1915 and 1916 to end the military stalemate. At the end of April 1915 German troops used poison gas for the first time at Ypres, and at the end of February 1916 Erich von Falkenhayn launched an offensive aimed at capturing Verdun. By June the German and French armies had each lost more than 200,000 men in sustained and bitter fighting. Falkenhayn broke off the battle in mid-July in order to repel the British offensive on the Somme. By November the British, German and French armies had between them lost more than one million men here, the end result being only the most insignificant gains for the Allies. Falkenhayn paid for his failure by being replaced as chief of the general staff, and in August 1916 the Third Army High Command was appointed, with Hindenburg as chief of the general staff and Ludendorff as quartermaster-general.

From now on, Ludendorff was the 'strong man' in the German military, Hindenburg its popular figurehead. In the face of all the historical facts, Ludendorff was even hailed as the 'victor of Tannenberg' by the army's propaganda machine and soon assumed the role of substitute Kaiser, Wilhelm II being wholly unsuited to such a role – from August 1914 he rarely appeared in public at all. True, neither of the two army commanders was able to bring about an improvement in the situation on the western front, and between October and December 1916 the French regained control of the fortifications at Verdun that the Germans had previously wrested from them.

At sea, too, the stalemate between Germany and the two western powers remained largely unchanged during the first two years of the war. At the instigation of Winston Churchill, then the first lord of the Admiralty, Britain imposed a blockade in the North Sea from the Shetland Islands to southern Norway, cutting off Germany from supplies of raw materials and food and also preventing the country from exporting its own produce overseas. Germany responded by deploying submarines and mine ships, whereas its surface fleet was kept on standby at the insistence of its commander in chief, Germany's secretary of state for the navy, Admiral Alfred von Tirpitz.

In March 1915 the German High Command gave orders for an unrestricted submarine war, enabling its vessels to attack even neutral ships without warning. The first fatal outcome of this new strategy was the sinking of the British liner the *Lusitania* in May 1915, with the loss of 1,200 passengers and crew, including 120 American citizens. The government in Washington responded by issuing a series of ultimatums, leading in September 1915 to a reduction in the scope of German submarine attacks. Not until late May 1916, at the Battle of Jutland, was the surface fleet used to any greater extent. Although the British fleet suffered more serious losses than its German equivalent, it was none the less able to prevent the Germans from breaking through the naval blockade. And while Germany's naval leaders demanded a return to full-scale submarine warfare, they were unable to persuade either Wilhelm II or his chancellor, Theobald von Bethmann Hollweg, to accept their proposal. Tirpitz responded to his defeat by resigning as secretary of state for the navy.

When compared with France and Russia, south-east Europe and the Mediterranean were sideshows of the First World War. By the end of 1914 the Central Powers had overrun the whole of Serbia. Montenegro capitulated in January 1915. And in the autumn of 1916 large tracts of Romania fell into the hands of the Germans and Austrians. But these successes were overshadowed by Italy's decision in May 1915 to enter the war on the side of the Entente. Prior to taking this step, Italy had been in negotiations with Austria-Hungary and had demanded that in compensation for its claims to the Balkans, Austria-Hungary would cede Trentino, Görz, Gradisca, Istria (including Trieste) and several Dalmatian islands, demands to which Austria, under pressure from Berlin, largely agreed, but they stopped short of the concessions that Britain, France and Russia had made in secret negotiations that were conducted in parallel. The result was the secret Treaty of London of April 1915, under the terms of which the Entente agreed that at the end of the war, Italy would receive reparations in the form of the South Tyrol, Trieste and Istria (but without the Hungarian port of Rijeka, or Fiume), north and central Dalmatia and the islands off its coast and, finally, complete sovereignty over the Dodecanese Islands. Italy was also to acquire an area of influence on the Turkish Mediterranean coast and would be given a protectorate over a reduced Albania.

The Italian prime minister, Antonio Salandra, and his foreign minister, Sidney Sonnino, supported intervention on the side of the Allies, but they had the majority of members of parliament against them, and so Salandra resigned on 21 May 1915. His predecessor, Giovanni Giolitti, had championed Italian neutrality and could count on a parliamentary majority but he had no desire to govern himself. Ultimately, the decisive factor proved to be pressure from the overwhelmingly middle-class demonstrators on the streets of Rome and other large cities, many of whom were students. Among them were several leaders emphatically on the side of intervention, including the nationalist poet Gabriele D'Annunzio and the former radical Marxist and syndicalist Benito Mussolini, who since his break with the decidedly anti-interventionist Socialist Party in November 1914 had edited his own *Popolo d'Italia*, a newspaper financed by industry and by the French government. King Victor Emanuel III aligned himself with the vociferous nationalist minority, refused to accept Salandra's resignation and persuaded him to continue to run the country. In turn, this meant that the liberal majority in parliament took the interventionist line and granted the government the extraordinary powers that it demanded. Italy declared war on Austria-Hungary on 23 May 1915, but waited until August 1916 to declare war on Turkey and Germany. The first of a total of eleven Battles of Isonzo began in June, leading to serious casualties and only minimal territorial gains.

The Ottoman Empire had already been drawn into the war by this date. The Turkish fleet had moved out of port at the end of October 1914 in order to mine and attack Russian Black Sea ports in keeping with the terms of an agreement signed with Germany on 2 August. Tsarist Russia replied on 3 November by declaring war on Turkey. Two days later Britain and France took the same step. By January 1915 the Russians had inflicted a serious defeat on the Turkish army in the southern Caucasus, although the Turks were successful on another front and in late April thwarted an Allied attempt to occupy the peninsula of Gallipoli to the north of the Dardanelles. (It may be mentioned in passing that the majority of the Allied troops comprised soldiers from the British dominions of Australia and New Zealand.)

Meanwhile, on 24–5 April 1915, Turkey began to arrest and deport more than 200 prominent Armenians, almost all of whom were murdered shortly afterwards in what was arguably the worst chapter in the history of the First World War: this was the Armenian genocide. Even under Sultan Abdul Hamid II the Armenians had already been subjected to brutal terror, up to 200,000 men, women and children having lost their lives in pogroms between 1884 and 1896. Up to 20,000 more Armenians died during the pogroms of early 1909, which coincided with the Young Turk revolution. Although there was a feeling of kinship between the Armenians living in the Ottoman Empire and those who were living in Russia, there could be no question of any collective Armenian resistance to Turkish rule, even though there had been numerous revolutionary groupings, some of them supported by Russia, which since the end of the nineteenth century had fought against the oppressive rule of the Turkish Islamists.

Under Talaat Pasha, the ruling party of the Young Turks, Ittihat ve Terakki (Unity and Progress), was from the outset keen to do more than merely intimidate an ostensibly unreliable section of the population and destroy any remaining independence enjoyed by the non-Muslim religious communities. Ittihat ve Terakki wanted to create a homogenous Turkish state out of the multiracial Ottoman Empire, and this could be done only by driving out or annihilating the 2.1 million Armenians, who had been the largest Christian minority since the loss of almost all the European part of Turkey in the Balkan Wars of 1912–13. Their hatred was aimed not only at the Armenians who lived in eastern Anatolia in regions bordering Russia but at every Armenian in the whole of the Ottoman Empire. The war offered the best possible opportunity to carry out this murderous plan.

Some 1.5 million Armenian men, women and children were massacred in 1915. They died on forced marches through deserts and as a result of torture and executions. Others starved to death or were drowned or burnt alive. In many respects, including their banishment to the wilderness, the eradication of the Armenians resembled the annihilation of the Herero by the Germans in South-West Africa in 1904 and 1905, the first systematic genocide of the twentieth century. The German diplomats and military leaders who lived and worked in Turkey were fully aware of the Armenian massacres, and they duly passed on this information to their superiors in Berlin. Although individual eyewitnesses such as Johannes Lepsius, an Evangelical theologian from Potsdam, repeatedly urged the German government to lodge a complaint in Istanbul, both the chancellor and his Foreign Ministry declined to register a formal protest, being reluctant to antagonize an ally on whose assistance the Reich was more than ever dependent. Instead, they merely made polite requests that extreme violence be avoided.

The German colonies remained on the fringes of the war, during the early months of which New Guinea and the Samoan Islands were occupied by Australian and New Zealand troops respectively, while the Marshall Islands, the Marianas, the Palau Islands and the Caroline Islands were taken by Japanese forces. In November 1914 Japan also forced Qingdao to capitulate. In Africa Togo fell into Allied hands as early as 1914, followed in 1915 by German South-West Africa and in 1916 by Cameroon. The bitterest and most protracted battles were fought in German East Africa. In September 1916 forces of the British Empire captured Dar es Salaam, but even by the end of the war the German colonial army under General Paul von Lettow-Vorbeck was able to maintain its grip on the greater part of the colony and also to make incursions into the Portuguese part of East Africa.

War Aims, Ideological Warfare, Opposition to the War

'We are not driven by the love of conquest,' Kaiser Wilhelm II had told the Reichstag in his speech from the throne on 4 August 1914, thereby making it possible for the Social Democrats to vote for the war loans demanded by the country's leaders. And yet the assertion that Germany was merely defending itself was quickly called into question by a number of influential circles. Any public discussion of the aims of the war was banned in Germany until November 1916, but behind the scenes there was a lively debate in word and print on the subject of the territorial gains, resources and power that might accrue to Germany as a result of the war.

In September 1914 the chancellor, Theobald von Bethmann Hollweg, summed up his ideas in a programme that amounted to a German-dominated central Europe and, hence, German hegemony on the Continent. The annexation of Longwy-Briey, with its ore mines in northern Lorraine, was as much a part of this plan as the integration into a greater Germany of the fortified town of Belfort, the annexation of Luxembourg and the reduction of Belgium to a vassal state. As for Russia, the chancellor's aims were for the present couched in only the most general terms: the country should be 'driven back from the German border and its dominion over non-Russian vassal states broken'. Neighbouring states, including Austria-Hungary, France and perhaps even 'Poland', should join a central European economic union 'under the superficial equality of all its members but de facto under German leadership'.[3]

For the most part, the chancellor's 'September programme' incorporated ideas held to be necessary by the Deutsche Bank and by those sections of German industry that were dependent on exports. Far more extreme notions were proposed by the ultra-nationalist Pan-Germans and individual leaders of the country's heavy industries. Even as early as late August 1914, Heinrich Claß, the president of the Pan-German League, was already demanding that Russia should be driven back to the lands held by Peter the Great and that the Baltic states, together with parts of Russian Poland, White Russia and north-west Russia, should be occupied by German settlers, while Russian Jews should be resettled in Palestine. In September 1914 the industrialist August Thyssen insisted that Belgium, several of the *départements* of eastern France and Russia's Baltic provinces should all be part of a greater Germany. And in order to safeguard the supply of raw materials for the future, the Reich should also take control of the Crimea, of the areas around Odessa and Azov and, finally, of the Caucasus.

During the early months of 1915 leading business associations, together with numerous German academics, civil servants and artists, came together under the banner of the Berlin theologian Reinhold Seeberg, who hailed, coincidentally, from the Baltic, and aligned themselves with the Pan-German programme, while a significantly smaller number of more moderate intellectuals grouped around the editor of the *Berliner Tageblatt*, Theodor Wolff, and the historian Hans Delbrück argued in July 1915 that while 'politically independent nations used to their own independence to the west of Germany' should not be 'incorporated and annexed', the country should not rule out territorial acquisitions to the east.[4] The most detailed expression of the aspirations of these moderate imperialists was a book published in 1915 by the liberal left-wing politician Friedrich Naumann, *Central Europe*. In it, Naumann, who had studied theology, harked back to ideas associated with the Pan-German legacy of 1848 and with the Holy Roman Empire that had finally come to an end in 1806, painting a picture of an essentially German central Europe organized around the German and Austro-Hungarian economic bloc, which should work together as a confederation of states. On one point the more moderate and the more radical imperialists were in agreement: the German colonies should be expanded, especially in central Africa, otherwise Germany's claim to be regarded as a world power was impossible to sustain.

The contemporary debate on Germany's war aims has been better researched than that of the other leading participants in the war, not least because Germany's aims were the most far-reaching. In France, there was widespread agreement on at least one such aim: Alsace and Lorraine, which had been annexed by Germany in 1871, should be returned to France. Equally uncontroversial was the need to restore Belgium's sovereignty and France's right to German reparations. Leading military figures, together with nationalist politicians and intellectuals, went beyond this modest programme, as did the Comité des Forges and its secretary general, Robert Pinot. At the top of their agenda was the annexation of the Saarland, with its rich reserves of coal. In 1916 the chief of the general staff, Joseph Joffre, also demanded as guarantees against any future threat to France that Germany should cede the left bank of the Rhine, an area that would be divided into several smaller states dependent on France, and that a series of French bridgeheads be built on the right bank of the river. The radically nationalist Action Française refused to content itself with this neutralization of the left bank of the Rhine but demanded its annexation. In 1916, when France's wartime aims were first debated in public, these demands of Action Française met with fierce resistance from the Socialists.

The president of the French Republic, Raymond Poincaré, shared the position of the nationalist right and, like the right, wanted to see Germany broken up into smaller states. But out of regard for divided public opinion and the views of his British allies, he refrained from setting down his ideas in writing. On 10 March 1917 – only days before the February Revolution in Russia – the French prime minister Aristide Briand signed a secret treaty with the tsarist government enshrining Russia's approval of France's annexation of the Saarland and the transformation of the left bank of the Rhine into a neutral state independent of the Reich. In return Russia was to be allowed to expand its territories in the west at the expense of Poland and the Central Powers and in that way be given a free hand in annexing East Prussia. France and Britain had already agreed in March 1915 that once Turkey was defeated, Russia could lay claim to Constantinople and the Straits of Bosporus.

Britain and France were basically in agreement on the way in which the Ottoman Empire might be divided up, and they staked out their intended post-war spheres of influence in the Sykes–Picot Agreement of May 1916. Those parts of the Ottoman Empire that were Arab-held were to become nominally independent states or a confederation of states under Arab leadership but with Franco-British control, France acquiring control of the Lebanon, Syria and the area around Mosul, while Britain took over the rest of Mesopotamia and Egypt. For Palestine, an international administration was envisaged. But the most important document affecting the future of Palestine was the Balfour Declaration, named after the British foreign minister and dated 2 November 1917: in keeping with Zionist aspirations it supported the creation of a national homeland for the Jewish people in Palestine, while respecting the rights of existing non-Jewish communities. There was no doubting the ulterior tactical motives of the British government, which hoped that in this way it would gain the support of American Jews in its attempts to persuade the United States to enter the war.

As for Europe, the Foreign Office limited itself in the autumn of 1916 to drawing up a memorandum demanding the restoration of Belgian sovereignty and the fulfilment of France's wishes with regard to Alsace-Lorraine. Otherwise, the national principle should be upheld, the whole of Poland should form an alliance with Russia, and German Austria should be united with Germany in compensation for Germany's territorial losses. Although this last-named demand ran counter to French interests, the memorandum merely reflected the old maxim whereby a victorious France should not be too powerful or a defeated Germany too weak. For the rest, Britain and France agreed that Prussia's military might should be curtailed and the German economy held in check.

Germany's ideological warfare was conducted in the spirit of the 'ideas of 1914', a term coined in 1915 by the Münster economist Johann Plenge, although it was the Swedish constitutional lawyer and expert in the field of geopolitics, Rudolf Kjellén, who put the phrase into wider circulation, not least on the strength of the considerable popularity that he enjoyed in Germany as a champion of the German cause. The 'ideas of 1914' amounted to a rejection of liberalism and individualism, of democracy and universal human rights – in short, a repudiation of western values. German values, conversely, were duty, order and justice, all of which could be guaranteed only by a powerful state acting in the interests of the community as a whole. 'Not since 1789 has there been a revolution to compare to the German revolution of 1914,' wrote Plenge:

> The twentieth-century revolution of the building up and unification of all state powers vs. the destructive liberation of the nineteenth century. [. . .] The pressure of war has driven the socialist idea into German economic life. Its organization grew together in a new spirit, and in this way the self-assertion of our nation gave birth to the new idea of 1914 for humanity, the idea of German organization, the people's cooperative of national socialism.[5]

'Capitalist' England was seen as the true antithesis of 'socialist' Germany. Germany had been 'socialist' since the days of Bismarck's national insurance laws, while England was still said to hold the laissez-faire attitudes of Manchester liberalism. There were two reasons why Britain began to assume an increasingly central position in terms of ideological warfare. In the first place, Britain, as a world power, differed from France in that it was not Germany's historic archenemy but an admired and envied model, resulting in a love–hate relationship and in a dramatization of the relations between the two countries that culminated in the greeting 'God punish England!' And, second, Russia no longer had a part to play as Germany's most dangerous foe following the German victories of 1914 and 1915. Nothing, on the other hand, suggested that the English would be defeated as quickly.

The Catholic philosopher Max Scheler was one of the first to advance the claim that the war was 'first and last a German-English war'.[6] In his 1915 book *Shopkeepers and Heroes*, the economist Werner Sombart drew a comparison between English commercialism and German militarism, describing the latter as 'the spirit of heroism raised to the spirit of war' and as 'Potsdam and Weimar in ultimate union'. That spirit was '*Faust* and *Zarathustra* and Beethoven's score in the trenches, for the "Eroica" and the *Egmont* Overture are arguably expressions of the purest militarism'.[7]

Perhaps the most sophisticated account of the 'ideas of 1914' is Thomas Mann's *Reflections of a Nonpolitical Man*, which appeared in the final year of the war. In it the author of *Buddenbrooks* described the war as the struggle between German culture and western civilization. Mann defended the authoritarian German state on the grounds that it afforded protection for the country's deepest and innermost essence as expressed in music, poetry and philosophy. In consequence the war was essentially designed to fend off the 'trois pays libres' of the West – France, Great Britain and the United States – and to protect against their democracy. 'The politicization of the German concept of art would mean its democratization, an important feature of the democratic levelling and realignment of Germany.'[8]

British and French intellectuals did not need persuading that their own political systems were superior to their German equivalent. On the other hand, their countries' alliance with tsarist Russia prevented them from describing the war as a struggle for democracy. And in the case of Great Britain, there was a further obstacle: there was not yet universal male suffrage, a right that had existed throughout Germany since 1871. In ideological debates with Germany, therefore, pride of place was given to a point that from the perspective of western intellectuals was specifically German: Prussian militarism, which was felt to be profoundly reactionary. In England, the three leading representatives of this militaristic outlook were repeatedly quoted as being the writer on military history, Friedrich von Bernhardi, whose study *Dentschland und der Nächste Krieg* (Germany and the Next War) had appeared in 1912; the historian Heinrich von Treitschke, who had coined the oft-cited description of the war as an 'examen rigorosum of states'; and, rather more questionably, Friedrich Nietzsche, who was not a German nationalist at all. From 1914 onwards, there were also repeated sightings of the old topos of two Germanys: one the idealistic land of poets and thinkers, the other the power-hungry military state of the Hohenzollerns that had dominated Germany since 1871.

One of the prominent writers to promote this view was the London-based philosopher and sociologist L. T. Hobhouse whose book *The World in Conflict*, first published in 1915, was based on a series of articles that had appeared in the liberal *Manchester Guardian*. In it, Hobhouse explored the question of Germany's intellectual development and its deviation from the main current in western thought. Germany, he wrote, had produced its own self-referential culture based on a particular idea of the state and of its claims on the individual and its rights vis-à-vis the rest of the world. But this was an idea of the state that western civilization abhorred: 'The whole movement of the reaction as we see it expressed as early as Hegel is to the reassertion of the old ideal. The State is master of the man, and it knows no laws of God or humanity to bind it in its dealings with others.'[9]

But it was in France, far more than in England, that the old cliché of the Germans as 'barbarians' was revived, especially in the wake of the atrocities in Belgium and, shortly afterwards, the destruction of Reims Cathedral. The philosopher Henri Bergson – famous for his theory of the élan vital – was one of the first to refer to the Germans as barbarians in August 1914. The following year the historian and journalist Ernest Lavisse and the Germanist Charles Andler co-authored a volume titled *Pratique et doctrine allemandes de la guerre*, in which Lavisse, taking issue with the wartime lectures of the Leipzig historian Karl Lamprecht, wrote that German militarism was a 'terrible set of material interests, greed, natural and barbaric brutality, patriotism made worse by insane arrogance and a multilayered and powerful mysticism in which every-thing conspires to raise "Deutschland über alles" to new heights'. Two years later, Lavisse expressed the hope that the world would recognize that in having resisted the 'barbarian onslaught', France had made the common victory possible. 'In defending its own life, it will liberate humankind from the hated yoke with which it is threatened by a power that places pride and its appetites above justice and right.'[10]

Much the same tenor informed a publication, *L'Allemagne au-dessus de tout* (Germany above all), by the famous sociologist Émile Durkheim. Heinrich von Treitschke's posthumously published lectures on politics were seized on by Durkheim as a key to understanding a Pan-Germanism that was obsessed with the pursuit of power and which he analysed as a case of social pathology. Treitschke had taught that the state was synonymous with power and that it had a duty to be strong. It was bound by international agreements only in the sense of 'clausula rebus sic stantibus' – in other words, only as long as the conditions that obtained when the agreement was signed remained in force. In the eyes of the state no nation had the right of self-determination. And middle-class society had to submit to it.

For Durkheim, the mentality championed and influenced by Treitschke was a morbid will to power. Germany, he argued, had created for itself a mythology that persuaded it to think that it was superior to all other nations and 'the supreme embodiment of divine power on earth'.[11] But the world, he went on, would never be enslaved by Germany:

> Germany cannot fulfil its self-appointed task without preventing human-kind from leading a life of freedom, but life cannot be fettered for ever. Although it may be possible to restrict and paralyse our lives for a time by means of some mechanical action, ultimately those lives will resume their course and sweep aside the obstacles that prevent them from freely unfolding.[12]

One of the most original contributions to the intellectual debate with Germany came from the United States. *Imperial Germany and the Industrial Revolution* was published in 1915 and was the work of the sociologist and economist Thorstein Veblen, who was born in Wisconsin in 1857 to Norwegian immigrants. One of the most eloquent voices of the 'progressive era', Veblen had already made a name for himself in 1899 with his *Theory of the Leisure Class*, a trenchant and largely satirical critique not only of a leisured upper echelon of society addicted to luxury but of society in general. In 1915 he turned his sights on the authoritarian and militaristic Prussian state and the Germany that that state had produced, while at the same time trumpeting the love of freedom of the English-speaking peoples of the world. For all its exaggerations and distortions, Veblen's study offers a perceptive and even brilliant analysis of the particular course taken by Germany, a concept that was to gain acceptance, of course, only in the wake of the Second World War.

According to Veblen, Germany provided contemporaries with the paradoxical example of a country that combined the most modern technological developments with an extremely backward system of government. In terms of its industrialization, Germany had taken its cue from England, but the libertarian ideas and institutions that England had produced were not adopted by the Germans, who inhabited a country that had never had a successful revolution, a land in which the Middle Ages lived on in the form of Junkers from the east of the Elbe and their belligerent brand of feudalism: 'The case of Germany is unexampled among western nations both as regards the abruptness, thoroughness and amplitude of its appropriation of this technology, and as regards the archaism of its cultural furniture at the date of this appropriation.'[13] With Prussia as a leading power, Germany had no other means of holding itself together apart from blood and iron, while its only ideals were dynastic.

As a result, the Germans and the English had a different attitude to the military:

> The German ideal of statesmanship is [. . .] to make all the resources of the nation converge on military strength; just as the English ideal is, *per contra*, to keep the military power down to the indispensable minimum required to keep the peace.[14]

The English and all other English-speaking peoples thought in the categories of 'popular autonomy', while the Germans thought in those of the state and, specifically, the dynastic state. In turn this meant that the English concept of freedom was radically different from its German counterpart. From a German standpoint, freedom meant giving orders and willingly obeying them, whereas the English interpreted freedom in an almost anarchical spirit as the option of not having to follow orders in case of doubt.

According to Veblen, the creation of the Reich under Bismarck meant that Germany had fallen under the 'hegemony of the most aggressive and most irresponsible – substantially the most archaic' of the German states,[15] a state incapable of denying its bellicose nature. Under Bismarck's successors, it had been able to rely on its great industrial potential and become a danger not only to its neighbours but to the West in general. Veblen did not even need to speak out explicitly in favour of the United States' entry into the war, for his account of the 'Prussian-Imperial system' as 'the type-form and embodiment of this reaction against the current of modern civilisation'[16] could have only one logical conclusion: the English-speaking nations of the world must stand together and protect the achievements of the West from the threat that was posed by a Prussian Germany.

Veblen was a radical liberal, but no Marxist. Marxist writers were bound to find the deeper causes of the war in the contradictions inherent in the capitalist system. Capitalism had entered an imperialist phase at the end of the nineteenth century. As the leader of the Russian Bolsheviks, Vladimir Ilyich Lenin, had noted in an essay written in exile in Zurich in the early part of 1916 and published in Petrograd – the new name for St Petersburg – in April 1917, imperialism was 'the highest stage of capitalism', a stage characterized by the convergence of banking capital and industrial capital as finance capital, by the replacement of free competition by monopolies and international cartels and by the export of capital to underdeveloped parts of the world which, rich in raw materials, were now subjected to the rule of capital.

Hand in hand with the transition from capitalism to monopoly capitalism and finance capitalism went a struggle to divide up the world. If one agreed with Lenin, then the exploitation of the developing world produced high profits that allowed capitalists in major cities to lead parasitical lives and

became known as the 'Zimmerwald Left'. In a final communiqué agreed by all the parties, all those present spoke out in support of a rapid end to the war, peace without annexations or war reparations and the right of self-determination on the part of all nations.

At the next international socialists' meeting in Kienthal in the Bernese Oberland in April 1916, Lenin and his supporters once again found themselves in a minority. But on two points the resolutions agreed at Kienthal went further than those at Zimmerwald. First, the delegates demanded 'the rejection of all support for war policies by the representatives of socialist parties' and refusal to agree any more war loans. And, second, they criticized the offices of the International for having failed miserably and for being 'complicit in policies of the denial of principles, betrayal of the fatherland and of the party truce'.[21] Although this did not lead to a schism in the Second International and to the foundation of a new, revolutionary Third International, as Lenin hoped, it was still symptomatic of the worsening situation within the international workers' movement.

The French equivalent of Germany's party truce was the 'union sacrée', which meant that French Socialists were also formally involved in government from the end of August 1914 – Marcel Sembat became the minister for public works and Jules Guesde the minister without portfolio. There was less opposition to the war in the French Socialist Party – the Section Française de l'Internationale Ouvrière (SFIO) – than in its German counterpart. The Zimmerwald conference was attended by two leaders of the metalworkers' union within the Confédération Générale du Travail (CGT), Albert Bourderon and Alphonse Merrheim, but none of the French parliamentarians. The SFIO's annual conference in December 1915 produced broad agreement for the 'patriotic' line adopted by the party's leaders. A small minority aligned itself with the Zimmerwald resolutions, while a more moderate and conciliatory position was taken by a group associated with Jean Longuet, a grandson of Karl Marx. This was a group that in April 1916 chose a third of the delegates for the SFIO's national council. At the end of December 1916 only a narrow majority of the national council supported the proposal that the new defence minister, Albert Thomas, the only socialist in Briand's cabinet, should remain in his post.

Members of the British Labour Party were prevented from attending the Zimmerwald conference by the government's refusal to grant them passports. But there was socialist opposition to the war in Britain. Indeed, it was from the outset even more vocal than in Germany. On 3 August 1914 the *Daily Citizen*, the Labour Party's official newspaper, described the mere idea of Britain fighting alongside reactionary Russia as 'simply appalling'. On the morning of 4 August the Labour Party executive issued a declaration stating that it was the duty of the working class to end the war as quickly as possible by means of a peace that would allow 'the re-establishment of amicable feelings between the workers of Europe'.[22]

Shortly afterwards the Labour MPs in the lower house voted by a large majority to agree to the war loans demanded by Asquith's government, precipitating the resignation of the most prominent opponent of the war, the party's leader, Ramsay MacDonald, who was also a leading member of the International Labour Party. The International Labour Party maintained its pacifist position until the end of the war, while avoiding any disciplinary measures on the part of the majority. In mid-October the Labour Party justified voting in favour of war loans and enlisting voluntary recruits by insisting that Germany was to blame for the war not least by invading neutral Belgium and, more generally, by reference to the need to prevent Germany's military despotism from triumphing.

The Labour Party went on to support the government of the Liberal prime minister, Herbert Asquith, in all its executive decisions, starting with the Defence of the Realm Act of 8 August 1914, which conferred emergency powers on the government. By the end of May 1915 the military situation in the Balkans and the Dardanelles had led to the formation of an all-party cabinet with the Labour leader Arthur Henderson as education minister. At the beginning of 1916 Labour even agreed to what in the context of English history seems a positively revolutionary step: the introduction of conscription. In the spring of 1916 Britain had to deal with its most testing internal challenge of the war, its bloody suppression of the German-backed Easter Rising, mounted by the nationalist Sinn Féin movement and which began with the proclamation of the Irish Republic in Dublin on 24 April. Over 500 people were killed, including 300 civilians, and around 2,000 were injured. The leaders of the uprising were executed. Among them was Sir Roger Casement, a former British diplomat and international critic of the appalling treatment of the indigenous population of the Belgian Congo under King Leopold II of the Belgians. It was a German submarine that brought Casement back to his native Ireland four days before the rising.

Nine months later, on 7 December 1916, the bullish war secretary, David Lloyd George, replaced his Liberal colleague Herbert Asquith as prime minister. From then on the true centre of power was a five-man cabinet committee made up of the prime minister, three Unionists, including the far-right Viscount Milner, and Labour's Arthur Henderson, now minister without portfolio. As Lloyd George began to move ever further to the Tory right, Henderson resigned from the government in August 1917, but in spite of this, Labour remained a part of the wartime coalition, and its members continued to hold ministerial posts in the government of national unity.

Apart from the British Independent Labour Party, there were only two other socialist parties among the countries engaged in hostilities that refused to support the war. One was the Serbian Labour Party, whose two elected representatives were the only members of the Skupština to vote against war loans on 31 July 1914, and the other was the Russian Socialist Party. Both of the groups that made up the Russian Social Democrats – the relatively moderate Mensheviks and the far more radical Bolsheviks – had agreed to abstain in the vote of confidence in the Duma on 8 August and to refuse to consent to any war loans. Instead, they both agreed to issue a joint declaration protesting against the war and to demonstrate their international solidarity with the working class. The sharply worded declaration was read out by a Menshevik deputy, after which the socialist members left the plenary meeting and took no further part in the vote.

This attitude on the part of the socialist deputies did not reflect the mood of patriotism among Russian workers. Nor did it conform to the line adopted by leading exiled politicians, including the Menshevik Georgy Valentinovich Plekhanov, all of whom wanted to support the war on the side of the Western Powers. At the same time, Lenin's catchphrase to the effect that the imperialist war should be turned into a civil war was rejected by the majority of the Bolsheviks. In the autumn of 1914 the mood in Russia was far from revolutionary, and another two years were to pass before conditions had deteriorated to the point where Lenin's radical ideas began to gain widespread support.

A Year to Remember: The Russian Revolution; the United States Enters the War

Nowhere did the initial euphoria sparked by the war vanish as swiftly as it did in Russia. The defeats that the tsar's armies suffered at the hands of the Germans in 1914 and 1915 caused growing discontent with existing political and social conditions, leading in turn to strikes, first in the textile industries in the summer of 1915, then in the metal industry, in mining and in oil-rich areas around Baku and in the Urals. In August 1915 all the parties in the Duma with the exception of the extreme right and left joined a 'Progressive Bloc' that demanded a new government based on the trust of the people. Tsar Nicholas II had become supreme commander of the Russian armies following his dismissal of Grand Duke Nikolai Nikolayevich in September 1915 and was strenuously opposed to any greater degree of parliamentary democracy. During the tsar's long absences from Petrograd, his wife, Alexandra Fyodorovna, exerted a decisive influence on all important appointments, including even ministerial posts, but for years she had been superstitiously dependent on the suggestions of her favourite, the Siberian monk Grigori Rasputin. Rasputin's murder by two members of the aristocracy and a right-wing member of the Duma on 30 December 1916 afforded dramatic evidence of the fact that even in the upper echelons of Russian society support for the tsar was waning.

This period also witnessed an increase in social unrest that assumed distinctly alarming proportions. During the first two months of 1917 food supplies practically ran out in the major cities and industrial centres. By January the price of consumer goods had risen sixfold in Petrograd and fivefold in the provinces when compared to pre-war prices. That same month the police warned that famine riots could break out at any time. By early March protest demonstrations were already gathering pace in the capital. On 8 March a demonstration by women held to mark International Women's Day was joined by workers from the Putilov metalworks, quickly developing into a strike and two days later into a general strike. In vain the president of the Duma, Mikhail Rodzianko, urged the tsar to form a new constitutional government that would enjoy the confidence of the country, but Nicholas continued to oppose the idea and instead prorogued the Duma, an act of provocation that served to exacerbate an already tense situation. During the night of 11/12 March large sections of the Petrograd garrison, including a number of officers, fired on demonstrating workers and students, thereby marking the beginning of the February Revolution, so called because according to the old Julian calendar it began on 23 February. Above all, the events that followed led to the collapse of a system that had proved increasingly incapable of functioning efficiently.

In order to assert itself in the face of pressure from the streets, the majority of members of the Duma took the revolutionary step of setting up a provisional committee made up of representatives of the Progressive Bloc as well as Mensheviks and Socialist Revolutionaries. On 13 March 1917 this committee in turn appointed a provisional government under the liberal Prince Georgy Yevgenyevich Lvov as prime minister and the historian Paul Milyukov, the leader of the Constitutional Democrats ('Cadets'), as his foreign minister. The previous day, adopting the model established in 1905, a provisional executive committee of the Petrograd Soviet of Workers' and Soldiers' Deputies had been formed in the Taurian Palace, the building where the Duma met. Its deputy chairman, Alexander Kerensky, who was the leader of the socialist Trudoviks, joined the Provisional Government as justice minister and for a while acted as intermediary between the two centres of power. Urged to step down by the Provisional Government and ultimately by his own headquarters, Nicholas abdicated on 15 March in favour of his brother Mikhail, only for the latter to decline the crown, bringing to an end not only the 300-year rule of the Romanovs but also the thousand-year rule of the Russian monarchy.

Working together with the Provisional Committee of the Duma, the Petrograd Soviet settled a number of the most pressing matters immediately after it was constituted, the agreements between the two groups extending to preparations for elections to a body that would lay the foundations for Russia's democratic future, an immediate and comprehensive amnesty for all political prisoners and exiles, complete freedom of speech, freedom of the press, freedom of worship, freedom of assembly, the right to strike, the replacement of the police by a national militia and democratic elections at a regional level. The Soviet organized food supplies for the capital and formed a people's militia. Order no. 1 of 14 March placed troops under the political control of the Soviet. Its officers had to seek legitimization from the newly formed committees, and soldiers were instructed to obey only those orders that did not contradict the decrees of the Petrograd Soviet. The aim was to do away with the old officer caste and, hence, with the existing form of military discipline.

On 27 March there followed a manifesto addressed to the world's proletarian masses, in which the Petrograd Soviet hailed the victory of Russian democracy as 'the great victory of international freedom and democracy',[23] a victory that had destroyed 'the main pillar of international reaction and the gendarme of Europe'. Democratic Russia could not pose a threat to freedom and civilization. An appeal was being made, therefore, to the proletarian masses to cast off the 'imperious yoke', just as the Russian workers had done. No longer should they allow themselves to be used as 'a weapon of annexation of brute force in the hands of kings, landowners and bankers'.[24] A congress of local workers' and soldiers' soviets met in Petrograd between 11 and 16 April and summed up this appeal in the memorable phrase about universal peace 'without annexations and indemnities'.

The establishment of the Provisional Government and the Petrograd Soviet marked the beginning of what was known even at the time as a Dual Authority, the contradictory character of which has been aptly described by the German historian Dietrich Geyer, who writes that the soviets

> did not try to penetrate the state bureaucracy. Instead they were satisfied with tight, outside control. They could reduce it to paralysis, but they had no intention of overthrowing it. [. . .] While the revolutionaries waited for the Constituent Assembly to be convened, their determination to remould Russia was held in abeyance. [. . .] The result of this *attentisme* was a curious mutual dependence between the government and the Soviet. The term 'dual power', coined to describe this situation, is rather misleading. Those who were supposed to rule did not have the support of the masses and never really held power while those on whom the Revolution had conferred power did not want to exercise it.[25]

When the February Revolution broke out, most of the leading Bolsheviks were still living in exile: Lenin, Zinoviev and Karl Radek were in Switzerland, Bukharin in New York, where he was editing an émigré newspaper with Trotsky, a former left-wing Menshevik who was by then growing closer to the position taken by Lenin. Other leading Mensheviks, including Stalin, Kamenev and Sverdlov, were living in exile in Siberia. They were the first to return to Petrograd at the end of March, when they immediately took control of the party newspaper, *Pravda*, and used it to forge a closer link between the Petrograd Soviet and the Provisional Government and to demand immediate peace talks with all sides in the war. Until then the soldiers were to remain at their posts.

Lenin held a radically different view. Writing from his exile in Switzerland at the end of March, he penned two 'Letters from Afar' addressed to the two most important members of the Provisional Government, the foreign minister Paul Milyukov and the war minister Alexander Guchkov, accusing them of having been coerced into seizing power by the Anglo-French imperialists in order to prolong the imperialist war. He demanded that all treaties with the Allies be abandoned, that all secret negotiations be made public and that all colonies be liberated. The workers of every country were urged to overthrow their governments and transfer their powers to workers' councils. In short, it amounted to a call to the world's proletarian masses to rise up in revolution.

In the specific case of Russia, Lenin was keen to see a clear division between Communist and international elements on the one hand and petty-bourgeois elements on the other. With the help of the Communist and international elements, Soviets of the Workers' and Farmers' Deputies would be transformed into the organs of a revolutionary force along the lines of the Paris Commune of 1871. (In making this proposal, Lenin appealed directly to Marx's essay, *The Civil War in France.*) This meant destroying the old state machinery and replacing it with a new body in which police, army and bureaucracy would be 'merged [. . .] with *the entire armed people*'. The proletariat must 'organise and arm *all* the poor, exploited sections of the population in order that they *themselves* should take the organs of state power directly into their own hands, in order that *they themselves should constitute* these organs of state power'.[26]

If he was to exert any real influence on the subsequent course of events in Russia, Lenin first needed to bring his own Bolshevik party into line, an aim he could not achieve in exile but only in Russia itself. Since France refused to grant him a transit visa and declined to facilitate his journey back to Russia, he was able to return home only with German assistance. The army's supreme command and the government of Theodor von Bethmann Hollweg had the greatest possible interest in helping the most determined opponent of the war among all the Russian émigrés in whatever way they could – not only by enabling Lenin to return home through Germany but also by offering his subversive movement generous financial support. From a German point of view, the aim of using Lenin to bring an end to the war in the east in order to be able to concentrate all the country's forces on the western front justified the extremely dangerous policy of bringing revolution to Russia under the leadership of a man who was effectively a German agent at this period. On 8 April Lenin left Zurich in the legendary and allegedly lead-lined train in the company of a number of loyal supporters, including his wife Nadezhda Krupskaya, Grigory Zinoviev and Karl Radek. The party travelled via Sweden and Russia-controlled Finland, arriving in Petrograd's Finland Station on 16 April, where they were greeted by a large crowd.

Lenin's radical ideas initially encountered incredulous astonishment and tremendous opposition among the Bolsheviks in Petrograd and more especially among the Mensheviks, and the situation was no different on the Petrograd Soviet, on which the Bolsheviks were far less powerfully represented than the Mensheviks and Socialist Revolutionaries. But Lenin refused to be discouraged by their combined opposition and on 22 April published a piece in *Pravda* headed 'The Tasks of the Proletariat in the Present Revolution'. These 'April Theses' rapidly became famous. Without the overthrow of capital, he argued here, it was impossible to end the war by means of a truly democratic peace. The first stage of the revolution was to bring the bourgeoisie to power, but its second stage must be to place that power in the hands of the proletariat and the poorest sections of the peasantry. The immediate task in hand was to explain to the masses that the soviets were the only possible form of revolutionary government.

Lenin's new watchword was 'Not a parliamentary republic [. . .] but a republic of Soviets of Workers', Agricultural Labourers' and Peasants' Deputies throughout the country, from top to bottom'.[27] It was a slogan that could be reduced to the cry of 'All power to the soviets'. Police, army and bureaucracy were to be abolished, all landed estates were to be confiscated and '*all* lands in the country' were to be nationalized, control over them passing to the local Soviets of Agricultural Labourers' and Peasants' Deputies. At the same time, all the country's banks were to be merged into a single national bank controlled by the Soviet of Workers' Deputies. According to Lenin, these measures still fell short of the 'introduction' of socialism but were designed simply 'to bring social production and the distribution of products under the *control* of the Soviets of Workers' Deputies'.[28]

In a more detailed text on the 'Tasks of the Proletariat in Our Revolution' that Lenin wrote in April but did not publish until September 1917, he explained that 'State power in Russia has passed into the hands of a new *class*, namely, the bourgeoisie and landowners who had become bourgeois. *To this extent* the bourgeois-democratic revolution is completed.' The present situation was characterized by a unique interlocking of two dictatorships, the dictatorship of the bourgeoisie and that of the proletariat. Lenin held up the February Revolution as an example of the metamorphosis of an imperialist war into a civil war. Each and every concession to 'revolutionary defencism' was a betrayal of socialism and tantamount to the total abandonment of internationalism. In order to point up the break with the opportunistic Socialist Democrats, Lenin invited the party to rename itself the Communist Party. Its principal task, he argued, was to end the imperialist world war by means of a genuinely democratic peace, but this could be achieved only through the most violent overthrow in the whole history of humankind: 'The *only* way out is through a proletarian revolution.'[29]

Within a matter of only a few weeks, Lenin had already managed to persuade the Bolsheviks to adopt this line. In the middle of May *Pravda* published a resolution on the agricultural question agreed to by the party's April Conference, demanding the immediate transfer of all the confiscated estates into the hands of the peasants and the nationalization of the land. A further resolution on the national question demanded that all the nations that made up Russia should have the right to break free and form their own independent states. This right did not mean, however, that it was advisable for any nation to adopt this course either now or in the future. Rather, the question must invariably be solved by the proletariat taking account of every social change and must be approached from the standpoint of the class struggle's impact on socialism. In the case of the agricultural question, Lenin's concern was to win over to the Bolshevik cause the largest section of the population – the peasants who owned very little land. In the case of the nationalist question he banked on the support of all the non-Russian peoples who lived in Russia. Even if they took advantage of their right to break away from Russia, he expected that in the wake of a successful proletarian revolution they would want to rejoin the new Russia.

In Lenin's view, the 'dual power' that had existed since March 1917 could be no more than a transitional stage that must be ended as quickly as possible. As he had noted in *Pravda* on 22 April, the Provisional Government was a government of and for the bourgeoisie, while the soviets of the Workers' and Soldiers' Deputies in Petrograd and elsewhere represented a government of the proletariat that was still too weak to be effective. The human race had yet to produce a higher and better type of government. In order to achieve power, the class-conscious workers needed to gain a majority. As long as force was not used against the masses, there was no other route to power. 'We are not Blanquists [followers of the French socialist Louis-Auguste Blanqui who advocated armed insurrection], we do not stand for the seizure of power by a minority. We are Marxists, we stand for proletarian class struggle against petty-bourgeois intoxication, against chauvinism-defencism, phrase-mongering and dependence on the bourgeoisie.'[30] Only when the class-conscious workers united to form a proletarian Communist Party and could rely on the support of the majority of the poor peasants could they ensure the undivided power of the Soviets. This meant bringing clarification to proletarian minds and emancipating them from the influence of the bourgeoisie.

This 'dual power' quickly proved fraught with conflict. On 1 May 1917 the foreign minister, Paul Milyukov, assured the Allies that Russia would continue to fight the war, prompting violent protests among the left-wing parties. Three days later, under pressure from the Petrograd Soviet, the Provisional Government was obliged to explain that it was making no territorial claims. Within days, the minister of war, Alexander Ivanovich Guchkov, had resigned, followed by Milyukov two weeks later. On 18 May the Provisional Government was joined by six men who enjoyed the trust of the Mensheviks and Socialist Revolutionaries, a move roundly criticized by Lenin and the Bolsheviks at the First All-Russian Congress of the Soviets in the middle of June. At the end of the month, Guchkov's successor as minister of war, Alexander Kerensky, ordered a military offensive by Russian troops, an order supported by the Soviets' executive committee. Within three weeks – and in spite of General

Alexei Brusilov's initial successes on the Galician front – this offensive had proved an unmitigated disaster.

On 16 July an uprising broke out in Petrograd in which the leading Bolsheviks were far from being the driving force. (Lenin was on holiday, some distance from the capital.) They were unable to control the rabble and the anarchists or even their own military organization and received insufficient support from the soldiers. Fighting broke out between, on the one hand, sailors from Kronstadt, a pro-Bolshevist regiment from the Petrograd garrison, workers from the Putilov Plant, supporters of the Bolsheviks and anarchists and, ranged against them, pro-government troops. The skirmishes left 400 dead and injured and led to looting, arbitrary arrests by Bolshevik supporters and finally an assault on the Taurian Palace, where the Petrograd Soviet met. The uprising lasted three days and effectively ended with the storming of the palace, after which the Soviet appealed to the workers to return home peacefully, an appeal that was largely heeded.

The following day – 19 July – the Provisional Government ordered the arrest of the leading Bolsheviks. Lenin and Zinoviev were able to evade capture by fleeing to autonomous Finland. Their flight coincided with reports in Russian newspapers about the continuing high level of payments to Lenin by the German general staff. The events of mid-July marked a serious setback for the Bolsheviks, and for a few days they seemed to disappear from the scene completely.

On 21 July the leader of the Provisional Government, Prince Georgy Yevgenyevich Lvov, resigned and was succeeded by the energetic and eloquent Kerensky. On 22 August it was announced that elections to the Constituent Assembly that had been repeatedly postponed were finally to take place on 25 November 1917, but this announcement failed to calm the mood within the country. There were ever more instances of soldiers either refusing to carry out orders or deserting, and since there was still no sign of the land reform that had been promised, peasants occupied land that was not their own. Meanwhile, the supply situation was growing worse. In August, Kerensky convened a national conference attended by more than 2,000 representatives of every class and every party with the exception of the Bolsheviks, but it failed to achieve any practical results. The response by the nationalist right to the Provisional Government's lurch to the left was an attempted putsch by General Kornilov, the army's supreme commander, on 9 September – six days after German troops had taken Riga. The putsch failed as a result of the passive resistance of the railway and telegraph workers. Kornilov and his generals were arrested. On 14 September Kerensky officially declared Russia a republic.

It was the extreme left wing in the shape of the Bolsheviks that benefited most from the September crisis. In the Petrograd and Moscow Soviets their successful deployment in the battle with Kornilov meant that they were able to win over the majority of deputies. Leon Trotsky had joined the Bolsheviks following his return from exile in America and now proceeded to build up an armed paramilitary organization – the 'Red Guard' – with the active support of the factory committees of workers that had been elected in the spring.

Lenin was still in Finland at this date. In mid-September he wrote to the Central Committee of the Social-Democratic Workers' Party of Russia – in other words, the Bolshevik leadership – and advanced the bold claim that the Bolsheviks now had 'the majority of a class, the vanguard of the revolution, the vanguard of the people' and, indeed, the majority of the people behind them, which had not been the case in July. 'All the objective conditions exist for a successful revolution.' Power must now be transferred to 'revolutionary democrats, headed by the revolutionary proletariat.'[31] Under pressure from the masses it was now a question of offering a choice to the 'Democratic Conference' that had been convened by Kerensky and that was intended as a kind of provisional parliament. Either there should be an unequivocal acceptance of the Bolshevik programme, which included first and foremost a peace without annexations, an immediate break with the Entente imperialists and, indeed, with all imperialists, or there should be an insurrection. As Marx had already observed, insurrection was an art, hence Lenin's detailed instructions for carrying it out by occupying Petrograd's central telephone exchange. As a result, the history of the Russian Revolution was about to enter a new, second phase: the aim of Lenin's appeal was to make this clear to the Bolsheviks.

Lenin's involuntary sojourn in Finland bore fruit in the form of his essay 'The State and Revolution', which he wrote in August and September 1917 and published in early 1918. His central thesis was directed at the 'opportunistic' Social-Democrats and reads: 'A Marxist is solely someone who *extends* the recognition of the class struggle to the recognition of the *dictatorship of the proletariat*.'[32] In advancing this notion, Lenin was able to appeal to Marx who in a letter of March 1852 had expressed the view that the class struggle must necessarily lead to the dictatorship of the proletariat, a dictatorship that was no more than a transitional phase culminating in the abolition of all classes and the formation of a classless society. As such, it had always been central to Marxist thinking. Another witness for the prosecution to whom Lenin was able to appeal was Friedrich Engels, who had described the Paris Commune as an example of the 'dictatorship of the proletariat' in his 1891 introduction to Marx's *The Civil War in France*.

For Marx, the Commune's decision to abandon the distinction between legislative and executive power in favour of a single 'working body' and to deprive the judges of their 'apparent' independence was a great historical and even revolutionary step. Lenin relied on this view in declaring war on the 'venal and rotten parliamentarism of bourgeois society'.[33] He defined the dictatorship of the proletariat as the 'organisation of the vanguard of the oppressed as the ruling class for the purpose of suppressing the oppressors'. The dictatorship of the proletariat was not a simple expansion of democracy but 'democracy for the poor, democracy for the people, and not democracy for the money-bags'. 'Democracy for the vast majority of the people, and suppression by force, i.e., exclusion from democracy, of the exploiters and oppressors of the people – this is the change democracy undergoes during the *transition* from capitalism to communism.'[34]

Freedom had not yet been achieved. 'So long as the state exists there is no freedom. When there is freedom, there will be no state.'[35] Only in the 'higher' phase of communist society could the state 'wither away', to quote Engels's famous expression, and the administration of objects and control of production processes would replace control over people. Before that could happen, equality must be achieved not just on a formal level, and a classless society would become a reality. 'By what stages, by means of what practical measures humanity will proceed to this supreme aim we do not and cannot know.'[36] But Lenin did think that it was possible to predict events closer to hand: the time was ripe for the revolution of the proletariat, a revolution that would begin in Russia and then spread to the rest of the world.

The idea that Russia – a backward and still predominantly agricultural country – could be seen as the vanguard of a proletarian world revolution was in stark contrast to the assumption of Marx and Engels that only the working class in a largely industrialized society could defeat capitalism by means of a revolution and build a socialist society in its place. After the 1905 Revolution, Lenin, too, had assumed that Russia would have to go through a series of stages involving capitalism and a bourgeois democracy, but in the summer of 1917 he announced that the bourgeois-democratic revolution was for the most part complete and in his 'April Theses' even claimed that Russia was at that time 'the freest of all the belligerent countries in the world'.[37] The fact that following the Kornilov Putsch the Bolsheviks were able to persuade most of the deputies in the Petrograd and Moscow Soviets to join them was enough for him to announce that his party was now the executive organ of the will of the majority. Decisive throughout all of this was his will to power: he regarded the conditions for an armed insurrection as given precisely because he was determined to delay no longer in mounting the revolution that he himself regarded as necessary.

While Russia's tsarist regime was witnessing its final crisis, relations between Germany and the United States were taking a dramatic turn for the worse. On 12 December 1916 the leaders of the German Reich announced their willingness to enter into peace negotiations, but without going into detail about their ideas on a post-war order. The declaration was addressed in particular to the president, Woodrow Wilson, who had been re-elected with a narrow majority only a few weeks earlier. Wilson was asked to inform the Entente powers about the German initiative, and he responded by inviting all the countries involved in the war to discuss a negotiated peace.

On 11 January 1917 Great Britain, France, Italy and Romania set out their common war aims, including a restructuring of Europe along nationalist lines, the removal of foreign troops from occupied territories and reparations for damage caused by enemy action. More particularly, they demanded the restoration of Belgium, Serbia and Montenegro, 'the liberation of Italians, of Slavs, of Rumanians, of Czecho-Slovaks from foreign domination; the enfranchisement of populations subject to the bloody tyranny of the Turks' and the 'expulsion from Europe of the Ottoman Empire, decidedly foreign to western civilisation'.[38] For their part, the Central Powers initially preferred not to clarify their own position. In a note dated 26 December 1916 the leaders of the German Reich informed Washington that they had no desire to see the American president involved in the actual peace negotiations. In neither of the opposing camps could there be any talk of a willingness to end the fighting.

Wilson refused to be disheartened, and in a speech to the Senate on 22 January 1917 he set out his ideas on a future world order. His aim was nothing less than the restoration of peace to the entire world and the formation of an international League for Peace designed to secure that peace. 'Only a tranquil Europe can be a stable Europe. There must be, not a balance of power, but a community of power; not organized rivalries, but an organized common peace.' The precondition for all of this was 'a peace without victory':

> No peace can last, or ought to last, which does not recognize and accept the principle that governments derive all their just powers from the consent of the governed, and that no right anywhere exists to hand peoples about from sovereignty to sovereignty as if they were property.

Wilson attributed an equally great importance to the 'freedom of the seas' and the 'moderation of armaments'. These, he concluded, were American principles and practices, but at the same time they were the common property of all 'forward-looking men and women everywhere, of every modern nation, of every enlightened community. They are the principles of mankind and must prevail'.[39]

The French politician Georges Clemenceau reacted to Wilson's speech with a degree of sarcasm not meant to reach a wider public: 'Never before has any political assembly heard so fine a sermon on what human beings might be capable of accomplishing if only they weren't human.'[40] There is no doubt that Wilson's programme sounded extremely idealistic, but his speech reflected his own Democratic views and was expressed in such a way so as to gain the approval of the American people. In Europe his words echoed the sentiments of all who were working for the self-determination of their respective nations, no matter whether they were currently ruled by Austria–Hungary, Germany, Turkey or Russia. True, the governments of Great Britain and France had no intention of granting the right of self-determination to their various colonies, whereas it was in London's interest to ensure that the nations of the Habsburg Empire and Poland gained a greater degree of autonomy, the details of which remained vague. In Paris everything depended on whether right- or left-wing forces had the ultimate say in peace negotiations. Wilson could expect far more support from the left than from the right. Conversely, the Central Powers' actions were in such stark contrast to Wilson's principles that Berlin and Vienna would simply not have been believed if they had accepted a peace framework similar to the one proposed by the president.

Nor had Germany's leaders any intention of doing so. On 19 January 1917 – three days before Wilson's Senate address – Arthur Zimmermann, the Foreign Office's secretary of state, had written to the Mexican government to suggest that if the United States declined to remain neutral, Germany and America should form an alliance, promising at the same time to help Mexico regain New Mexico, Texas and Arizona, which Mexico had lost in 1848. The British navy's secret service managed to intercept and decode the relevant telegram, the contents of which were brought to the attention of the State Department on 24 February. Its publication on 1 March triggered an outcry of indignation in the United States. By this date, diplomatic relations between Germany and the United States had already been broken off, Washington having taken this step on 3 February in response to a German note of 31 January announcing a resumption of its policy of unrestricted submarine warfare, which it justified by reference to Great Britain's naval blockade, claiming that the latter was in contravention of international law.

Germany could hardly have taken a more disastrous decision. The country's naval commanders had never accepted the ending of unrestricted submarine warfare, which Germany had temporarily abandoned in September 1915 only under massive pressure from the United States. On 9 January 1917 the chancellor, Theobald von Bethmann Hollweg, had given in to the demands of the army and navy supreme command as well as the Kaiser and agreed to the resumption of unrestricted submarine warfare. On that occasion he had been persuaded to act by an assurance on the part of the admiralty staff that with the help of submarines England would be defeated within a matter of only five months. In 1917 the decision to resume such attacks could be taken only because Germany grotesquely underestimated America's economic strength, military potential and moral resolve. That the chancellor not only informed Wilson of the resumption of unrestricted submarine warfare but at the same time confided in him a list of Germany's war aims was bound to be taken as an additional affront by the president.

In November 1916 Wilson had sought re-election not least by arguing that he was the president who had kept the United States out of the war. His Senate address on 22 January 1917 contained a passage in which he clearly distanced himself from all 'entangling alliances' with European powers – the phrase picks up the famous formulation from Thomas Jefferson's first inauguration speech on 4 March 1801. Following Germany's resumption of unrestricted submarine warfare and the publication of the 'Zimmermann telegram', there could no longer be any serious question of the United States remaining neutral. Germany even snubbed Wilson in rejecting his request that American ships be allowed to sail to England. By February the first American merchant vessels had been sunk by German U-boats, leaving Wilson with no alternative but to ask both houses of Congress to declare war on Germany, which they did on 6 April. The Senate voted 82–6 in favour, the House of Representatives 373–50. It was not until eight months later, on 7 December 1917, that the United States declared war on Austria-Hungary.

Wilson's speech on 2 April was one of the most important of his presidency. Germany's submarine war against merchant shipping, he declared, was a war on humanity and on every nation. And he left his fellow Americans in no doubt about the consequences for his country: the war that Germany was waging against the government and people of the United States would oblige the country to introduce universal conscription. In the war that had now become inevitable, America's goal was to defend the principles of peace and justice in the world against selfish and autocratic power. Under the truly free and self-governed peoples of the world, the United States should 'set up such a concert of purpose and of action as will henceforth ensure the observance of those principles'.

Wilson's 'War Message to Congress' culminated in his vision of a future world without war and oppression. America, he insisted, was fighting for a state of definitive peace in the world and for the liberation of all its peoples, including the German nation. It was also fighting for the rights of nations great and small, for the

> privilege of men everywhere to choose their way of life and of obedience. The world must be made safe for democracy. Its peace must be planted upon the tested foundations of political liberty. [. . .] We seek no indemnities for ourselves, no material compensation for the sacrifices we shall freely make. We are but one of the champions of the rights of mankind. We shall be satisfied when those rights have been made as secure as the faith and the freedom of nations can make them.[41]

If tsarist Russia had not fallen on 15 March 1917, Wilson would not have been able to appeal only two and a half weeks later for the democratization of the world, an appeal that allowed his speech to Congress to enter the history books. Only since March 1917 had it been possible to see the First World War as an ideological struggle between freedom and oppression, and only because of this did the decision to go to war enjoy such widespread support in the United States. American politics had always been powerfully fuelled by a desire to realize the ideals of 1776 on a universal scale and in that way to assume a leading role in the world. But this need had been hampered by the equally long-standing realization that the United States would be seriously harmed by becoming involved in dealings with the Old World.

The situation would change only if and when a European power or coalition were to challenge the United States in such a way that a response became inevitable. And this was the situation that resulted from Germany's resumption of its unrestricted submarine warfare in early 1917. Wilson responded by mobilizing a resource without which the Central Powers could never have been defeated: America's moral resolve. Moreover, his profession of faith not only in the right of all nations to self-determination but in human rights and democracy in general had every prospect of finding a powerful echo in the Poles and all the Slav nations that were a part of the Danube Monarchy. Not least, Wilson could hope that the Germans, too, would be impressed when he assured them that the United States was not waging war on the German people but seeking, rather, to liberate them.

But even before the United States succeeded in promoting the cause of freedom in Europe, its own internal freedoms were drastically curtailed, and they were restricted, moreover, in a way that made the German Reich seem positively liberal at this time. The press was instructed to reprint all the government's anti-Germany war propaganda and to exercise self-censorship; and non-English-language newspapers – especially those that were published in German – were required to submit all articles dealing with the war to the censor for approval. The Espionage Act of June 1917 and the Sedition Act of May 1918 contained definitions that could be extended at will and used to stifle any form of opposition to the war and even to the president and his government. Among the organizations affected were the left-wing Industrial Workers of the World and the Socialist Party, whose chairman and presidential candidate Eugene V. Debs was sentenced to ten years' imprisonment in 1918, a sentence commuted by President Warren Harding in 1921. Many German Americans had sided with the Central Powers in 1914 and now found themselves at the receiving end of a particularly vicious hate campaign. Anti-German sentiments even extended to the American language, sauerkraut being renamed 'liberty cabbage' and bratwurst 'liberty sausage'.

Employers and consumers also had to endure restrictions on their traditional liberties. The trade embargos that were designed as a means of putting pressure on neutral states and that began to take effect in June 1917 hit the export industry and agriculture hardest of all. The Lever Food Control Act of August 1917 created measures to regulate the supply of foodstuffs in such a way as to meet the needs of the American troops and their allies first and foremost. From July 1917 the armaments industry was subjected to the controls of the War Industries Board, a means of corporative self-administration in which the representatives of major concerns should have the final say in all contentious matters. The National War Labor Board was established in April 1918 with the task of using arbitration to prevent strikes in the armaments industry, in return for which employers were forced to accept an eight-hour day, minimum wages and the principle of equal pay for men and women, together with the right to collective bargaining of wage agreements and the right to strike. The financing of the war, including supplies to America's European allies on credit, was achieved largely by war loans ('Liberty Bonds') but also by new contributions and taxes. By the end of the war in November 1918 the Allies had run up debts of ten thousand million dollars.

Militarily speaking, the United States was far from being prepared to enter the war in the spring of 1917. In May 1917 Congress voted to support Wilson's Selective Service Act introducing universal conscription. Almost three million conscripted soldiers would find themselves fighting alongside professional soldiers and volunteers – in 1917–18, 4.8 million Americans served in the army, navy and the recently founded air force. Initially, the most important contribution to the war was made by American destroyers that helped the British navy to sink German submarines and to mine the North Sea, with the result that the Germans, with their U-boats, were denied any further lasting successes.

The United States began transporting a total of forty-two infantry divisions to Europe in October 1917, and by the spring of 1918 more and more American troops were being deployed on the front line in France. The words 'Lafayette, we are here!' became something of a catchphrase. Often wrongly attributed to General Pershing, the commander of the American Expeditionary Forces, they were in fact first spoken by Colonel Charles E. Stanton of the Sixteenth Infantry Division at the Paris grave of the Marquis de Lafayette on Independence Day 1917. Both France and the United States still remembered the help that France had offered America in its War of Independence. Indeed, it was felt appropriate to recall the legacy of the two revolutions of the eighteenth century and to counter Germany's 'ideas of 1914' with the far more attractive concepts of 1776 and 1789.

The Prussian version of 'socialism' that Germany's wartime ideologues sought to present as an alternative to western 'capitalism' acquired a legal form on 5 December 1916, when the Auxiliary Service Law was passed, obliging all men between seventeen and sixty who had not already enlisted in the armed forces to work in the armaments industry and other organizations that were crucial to the war effort. In return, companies employing more than fifty workers were required to agree to an early kind of worker participation in the form of workers' and employees' committees and arbitration panels made up equally of employers and employees. The Auxiliary Service Law was a part of Ludendorff's 'Hindenburg programme' designed to force German industry to switch to supplying armaments. Although the trade unions gained greater influence under the new law, they were also brought increasingly under the control of the state, the military and employers, with the result that in the eyes of many they forfeited their claim to represent proletarian interests.

The Auxiliary Service Law was passed at a time of extreme hardship and even widespread famine: this was the so-called 'turnip winter' of 1916/17. Social deprivation increased the sense of political discontent on the left wing of the Social Democratic Party, and the February Revolution in Russia provided opponents of the party's leadership, including those eighteen members of the Social Democratic Workers' Union who had been excluded from the Reichstag party in March 1916, with their final incentive to break away from their old roots: in April 1917 they formed the Independent Social Democratic Party in Gotha and immediately launched an outspoken attack not only on the prevailing system of government and the current policies of the country's leaders vis-à-vis the war but also on war loans and the truce between the different political parties.

Wildcat strikes followed in many major cities, marking the first appearance in Berlin's metal industry of the Revolutionary Representatives who hailed from the left wing of the Independent Social Democratic Party. The revolt was ostensibly aimed at raising the level of bread rations but was in fact a part of a much wider workers' protest at the conduct of the war. It was the first great protest of its kind. Nor was it only workers who protested, but soldiers too. From June 1917 onwards there had been a noticeable increase in the number of hunger strikes and unauthorized shore leaves among members of the navy. The military courts reacted with draconian punishments, handing down sentences on the 'ringleaders' that could not be legally justified. Ten sailors were sentenced to death, and in two cases those sentences were carried out.

Germany's rulers did little to calm the internal political situation. Although the chancellor, Theobald von Bethmann Hollweg, was able to persuade the Kaiser, on 7 April 1917, to deliver his 'Easter Message' in which Wilhelm II announced constitutional reforms for the period after the war, including a reform of voting rights in Prussia, it was impossible to interpret this as a promise to introduce universal suffrage for men and women. This period also witnessed increasing signs of a crisis among Germany's leading allies. Kaiser Karl, the grand-nephew and successor of Franz Joseph, who had died in November 1916, had spent the months between January and April 1917 seeking a negotiated settlement with France and raising the possibility that Germany might renounce its claims to Alsace-Lorraine, an offer vehemently opposed by Berlin. The demarche came to nothing, its failure serving only to make the Habsburg monarchy even more dependent on Germany, while doing nothing to lessen Vienna's desire to end the war as quickly as possible in order to preserve the multiracial monarchy.

For Bethmann Hollweg the situation grew increasingly difficult during the summer of 1917. On the one hand, two of the parties that had supported him until then were urging him to break with the right, with its desire for annexation. These were the Catholic Centre Party, which was then being influenced by the Württemberg deputy Matthias Erzberger, who had previously advocated extensive territorial conquests, and the Majority Social Democrats, who were responding to pressure from the Independent Social Democratic Party. In June 1917, at an international conference held in Stockholm at the instigation of Dutch and Scandinavian socialists, the SPD claimed for itself the phrase 'peace without annexations and indemnities' that had first been formulated by the Petrograd Congress of local Workers' and Soldiers' Soviets. Soon afterwards the Social Democrats responded to a new demand for war loans by inviting the chancellor to provide a clear account of Germany's war aims and internal political intentions. Bethmann Hollweg refused to meet their demand and in doing so lost the parliamentary majority on which he had relied since 4 August 1914.

But Bethmann Hollweg also found himself under pressure from a very different quarter as the army's supreme command felt that he was far too indecisive in implementing measures that the military regarded as necessary. It was in order to persuade the Kaiser to dismiss Bethmann Hollweg and appoint a chancellor acceptable to the army's supreme command that Hindenburg and Ludendorff offered their own resignations on 12 July. Wilhelm II bowed to their demands and on 14 July appointed Georg Michaelis, a former lawyer with no political experience and hitherto responsible for the distribution of Prussia's crops, as Bethmann Hollweg's successor. The army supreme command could be confident that he would not pursue any independent policies of his own.

Two days previously, three parties in the Reichstag agreed on a 'peace resolution'. They had already worked together on the recently formed Cross-Party Committee and were the Majority Social Democrats, the Centre Party and the left-wing, liberal Progressive People's Party. From now on, these were known as the 'majority parties', their avowed aim being a peace of 'understanding and lasting reconciliation' between peoples. Such a peace, they went on, was incompatible with 'forcible territorial expansion' and with 'other kinds of political, economic, and financial rape'. Such a formulation left scope for an increase in Germany's sphere of influence but was still far too 'soft' when viewed from the standpoint of those parties that were even further to the right, parties that ranged from the National Liberals to the German Conservatives. The army high command protested vociferously at this resolution but was unable to prevent the Reichstag from agreeing to it on 19 July by 212 votes to 126, with seventeen abstentions. The new chancellor had declared in advance of the vote that the aims of the country's leaders could be 'achieved within the framework of your resolution, as I interpret it'.[42]

The nationalist right reacted to the Reichstag vote by founding the German Fatherland Party in September 1917, a party that was designed to bring together all the 'patriotic' forces in the country and that drew its greatest support from those parts of Prussia that lay to the east of the Elbe. Its more active members came largely from the Evangelical, educated middle classes and from the region's equally Evangelical landowning class, while its supporters in general were drawn from the ranks of the Conservatives and National Liberals. By attracting numerous 'nationalist' associations, the new party rapidly grew in size and is said to have numbered 450,000 members by March and 800,000 by September 1918. In its inaugural appeal, it claimed that German freedom 'stands sky-high above sham democracy with all its supposed blessings, which English hypocrisy and Wilson seek to wheedle the Germans into accepting, so as to destroy Germany, which is invincible in arms'.[43] The 'peace without annexations and indemnities' advocated by the majority parties and described by the right as the 'Scheidemann peace' after one of the two chairmen of the Social Democratic Party was contrasted with a 'Hindenburg peace' by the Fatherland Party, a peace that would be bought 'at the price of tremendous sacrifices and efforts' but which would ultimately end in victory.

The founding of the German Fatherland Party was far from being an expression of widespread enthusiasm for the war but, quite the opposite, was an attempt to counter the growing sense of weariness occasioned by the conflict. Disenchantment at the unexpectedly protracted hostilities found expression at this time in the search for scapegoats who could be accused of illicit trading and profiteering, of exacerbating class differences and of creating signs of subversion in the military. From the standpoint of the extreme right, no one was better suited to playing this role than the Jews, who without exception were suspected of being secretly in league with enemy forces. The Gießen professor of chemistry, Hans von Liebig, a prominent Pan-German, even went so far as to brand Bethmann Hollweg 'the chancellor of German Jewry' in December 1915.[44] In October 1916 the routine reproach, expressed in nationalist circles, that there was a significantly increased number of Jews among the 'cowards' who had refused to do military service persuaded the Prussian Ministry of War to order a set of 'Jewish statistics' to be drawn up for the army. The results comprehensively refuted the defamatory charge but were not published until after the war. And yet the mere fact that the exercise had been conducted at all already signified an official recognition and legitimization of anti-Semitism.

In the autumn of 1917 Germany suffered its second change of chancellor in four months. Michaelis's fall from power was triggered by the immoderate attacks launched against the leaders of the Independent Socialist Party on 9 October by Eduard von Capelle, secretary of state to the Reich's Navy Department, accusing them of supporting plans for a mutiny in the ocean-going fleet. Together with the Majority Socialists' leader Philipp Scheidemann, Friedrich Ebert declared open war on the chancellor, who had by then lost the support of the Centre Party, the Progressive People's Party and, finally, the National Liberals.

Michaelis was succeeded as chancellor and Prussian prime minister by the Bavarian prime minister, Georg von Hertling, who took up his new post on 1 November 1917. Hertling was a committed federalist and fiercely opposed to the parliamentarianism of the Reich, but in spite of this he accepted as his vice-chancellor a politician from the ranks of the Progressive People's Party, Friedrich von Payer, while Robert Friedberg, a Reichstag member of the National Liberal Party, was appointed vice-president of the Prussian State Ministry. Although Hertling gave no reason to assume that he would be any better disposed to the Reichstag's peace resolution than Michaelis, his allegiance to the Centre Party meant that the right did not regard him as one of their own. Indeed, those Conservatives, National Liberals and members of the Fatherland Party who held staunchly Evangelical views felt that the appointment of a Catholic chancellor was a deliberate act of political provocation in a year when the country was marking the 400th anniversary of Martin Luther's Reformation.

While the political truce was coming under pressure in Germany in 1917, a similar situation was developing with the 'union sacrée' in France. Although there had been increasing numbers of strikes since 1916, the workforce remained for the most part 'patriotic'. On 20 March, only days after the fall of Nicholas II, Alexandre Ribot replaced Aristide Briand as prime minister. Ribot had been the architect of the Franco-Russian alliance of 1891–2, with the result that the majority of members of the National Assembly expected him to pursue policies more energetic than those of his predecessor. The only Socialist member of the cabinet was the armaments minister, Albert Thomas, who had been appointed by Briand in December 1916. Shortly before this, General Robert Nivelle, who became commander in chief of the French armed forces on 26 December 1916 following General Joseph Joffre's setbacks in the Battle of the Somme, had put forward his ideas on an attack strategy that were approved by the Supreme War Council in spite of misgivings not only on the part of the government but also on the part of General Pétain and Field Marshal Haig. As a result, a new offensive began to the north of Reims on 16 April. Within three days it had been stopped in its tracks by the Germans at the Chemin des Dames, the French having sustained heavy losses in making only the smallest of advances.

This failure of so badly prepared a venture resulted in mutinies in some 160 regiments. In some cases socialist slogans were heard. Nivelle, who by now was known to his soldiers and to the workers' movement as a 'leech', was relieved of his post by the minister of war, Paul Painlevé, on 15 May and replaced by the popular figure of General Pétain, a convinced supporter of a defensive strategy. The mutinies led to 3,400 convictions, including 554 death sentences, forty-nine of which were carried out. This was also a time of more widespread strikes, but thanks to the intervention of the country's minister of the interior, Louis Malvy, these were soon brought to an end.

When Painlevé replaced Ribot as prime minister in September 1917, the French Socialists were no longer involved in government. (It is significant that Thomas's successor as armaments minister was a leading industrialist, Louis

Loucheur.) The decision to quit on the part of the French Section of the Workers' International reflected the growing influence of the left wing of the party, which had always been opposed to the war. But its departure from the government did not spell the end of the 'union sacrée', for the vast majority of members of the French Section of the Workers' International continued to vote in favour of war loans by relying on the support of the largest trades union, the CGT. For the most trivial of reasons, the government of Paul Painlevé was toppled on 18 November 1917. His successor – the middle-class radical Socialist Georges Clemenceau – was a man who towered above all his predecessors in terms of his political stature and resolve. Known – respectfully – as 'the Tiger', he remained in office until January 1920 and during the final year of the war proved an outstanding political leader worthy of standing alongside David Lloyd George in England and Woodrow Wilson in the United States. Of Germany's wartime chancellors, none enjoyed a degree of prestige that came anywhere close to theirs.

In England, as in Germany and France, social unrest grew appreciably in the course of 1917. The first major strikes had already taken place in February 1915, when the first elected shop stewards had come to prominence, organizing walkouts and challenging business leaders to respond. Like the Revolutionary Representatives in the Berlin metal industry and the Independent Socialist Party of Germany, they worked closely with the emphatically anti-militarist Independent Labour Party, accusing the trade unions and the majority of members of the Labour Party of increasingly neglecting workers' interests. Their criticisms grew even more vocal when in July 1915 the Labour Party and the trade unions voted for a Munitions Act that curtailed workers' freedoms in the same way that the Auxiliary Service Law was to do in Germany in December 1916. In 1916 76,000 men and women went on strike in the mechanical engineering industry, in the shipyards and in metal processing, resulting in the loss of 346,000 working days. In 1917 the number of striking workers rose to 386,700, and the number of days lost to strikes was reckoned to be some three million.

Lloyd George's government took the protests so seriously that in February 1917 it undertook a close inspection of profits in the coal industry and in June established several commissions to examine the causes of the recent social unrest. It was clear that the February Revolution in Russia had contributed in no small way to the radicalization of the British workers' movement. In July 1917 the miners' union demanded the introduction of a six-hour day and a five-day week. In October 1917 the war cabinet felt obliged to award certain groups of specialized workers a wage increase of 12.5 per cent, but this did little to calm the situation, and following a further major strike in Coventry, one of the centres of the mechanical engineering industry, Winston Churchill, then the minister of munitions, threatened the strikers with conscription if they failed to return to work forthwith. A committee of inquiry set up by Churchill noted that 'It is obvious from the evidence before us that the great body of workers are anxious to reduce, and, as soon as possible, to remove the war-time regulations of labour conditions which at present exist.'[45]

The British army did not suffer from mutinies to the same extent as its French counterpart in the spring of 1917, and this remained true even during the fiercest fighting in the third Battle of Ypres at Passchendaele between June and October 1917, when thousands of New Zealand and Canadian soldiers fell alongside their British comrades. The offensive began only after Lloyd George, under pressure from Field Marshal Haig, had abandoned his resistance to it. Like the French offensive in the spring, it turned into a catastrophic disaster. The total number of Allied soldiers who fell in Flanders between the end of July and the beginning of November 1917 was 245,000 – the losses on the German side can hardly have been any less serious.

Between February and December 1917 the number of desertions in the British Expeditionary Force grew considerably, and that number continued to increase in 1918, while still remaining relatively modest: in 1917 the number of charges of desertion remained almost constantly well below 0.015 per cent of the British military strength on the western front. British military justice was meted out in more arbitrary and draconian ways than in the German army, a situation reflected in the number of deserters who were executed. The most obvious reason for this discrepancy is clear, for whereas compulsory military service had long been the norm in Germany, it was only after 1914 that the British army changed from a professional army to one of volunteers and finally to one of conscripts, without any attempt being made to adapt the old disciplinary laws to the new situation. It is a German historian, Christoph Jahr, who has best summed up the deeper reasons for the difference in attitudes between Germany and Great Britain:

> In Germany, with its tradition as an authoritarian state based on the rule of law, civilian society and the army were in many ways a reflection of one another, whereas in England there were two different normative systems, one for civilian society, the other for the army.[46]

From a military point of view, the Central Powers were more successful than the Triple Entente at this time. German troops entered Riga in January 1917 and in October, assisted by the ocean-going fleet, they captured the Baltic islands of Ösel, Moon and Dagö. Only a few days later the two Central Powers inflicted a devastating defeat on the Italians at Caporetto (now Kobarid in Slovenia) on the upper Isonzo. The defeat was notable not least for mass desertions and the capture of 275,000 Italian soldiers. In the Middle East, conversely, the British were able to chalk up a number of victories: in March 1917 they captured Baghdad; in October they advanced on Palestine from the direction of the Suez Canal; and in early December the Turks vacated Jerusalem.

The Triple Entente was also able to report a political victory in the Balkans, where in June France and Britain forced King Constantine I of Greece to abdicate. He had been a staunch supporter of his country's neutrality and was replaced by his son Alexander, under whom a new government was formed by the former prime minister Eleftherios Venizelos, whom Constantine had dismissed in 1915 and who in the wake of regional uprisings had formed a provisional government in Thessaloníki in 1916. At the end of June 1917 Venizelos broke off diplomatic relations with the Central Powers. The Triple Entente had won a new ally.

The most important event in the second half of 1917 was one that had international repercussions: the Russian October Revolution. (According to the western Gregorian calendar, it was in fact a November Revolution.) A strictly secret meeting of the Bolshevik Central Committee took place in Petrograd on 23 October and was attended by Lenin, who had only recently returned to Russia from his hideaway in Finland and who proposed that his comrades should waste no more time but start an armed insurrection at once. After a tempestuous debate, Lenin's proposal was adopted in the face of opposition from two of the most prominent Bolsheviks, Grigory Zinoviev and Leonid Kamenev. Following the meeting, Lenin again went to ground. The preparations for the uprising were placed in the hands of Leon Trotsky, who had been elected chairman of the Petrograd Soviet on 5 October, returning to a position that he had already occupied at the time of the 1905 revolution. From 22 October he spearheaded the newly formed Military Revolutionary Committee of the capital's Soviet.

On 4 November the committee assumed command of the Petrograd garrison, a step that proved decisive on the Bolsheviks' road to power. The government signalled the start of the revolution on 6 November, when it occupied the Neva bridges and closed down the Bolsheviks' official newspaper. By the evening of the following day most of Petrograd was in the hands of revolutionary troops and of the Red Guard, a workers' militia armed by the Bolsheviks. At the second All-Russian Congress of Soviets on 7 November, the Bolsheviks and their allies, the left-wing Socialist Revolutionaries, had a clear majority. The Bolsheviks demanded that delegates should approve the *coup d'état* as a fait accompli, and following the walkout of the Mensheviks and the majority of the Socialist Revolutionaries, the remaining delegates duly fell into line the very next day. The decrees relating to peace and the land question submitted by Lenin in the name of the newly formed Council of People's Commissars – the new revolutionary government – were unanimously approved. The first decree provided for the immediate resumption of negotiations for a truce to be followed by peace without annexations or reparations, while the second demanded that all landowners be dispossessed without redress, all their lands to be transferred to regional committees and the Soviets of Peasants' Deputies, the ultimate decision over property rights remaining the preserve of the Constituent Assembly.

That same day – 8 November 1917 – pro-Bolshevik troops supported by sailors from the cruiser *Aurora*, who provided covering cannon fire, stormed the Winter Palace, and the members of the Provisional Government who were meeting there were arrested. Absent from the meeting were the prime minister and the minister of war, Alexander Kerensky, who had fled the city and was currently seeking support from generals still loyal to the government. The storming of the Winter Palace left six people dead – the only fatalities of the October Revolution in the capital. In Moscow, conversely, the number of dead was far higher, armed officer cadets resisting the Bolshevik forces for an entire week. Elsewhere in the country the Bolsheviks rarely encountered any determined resistance, the only real exceptions being Siberia and the agricultural south and south-east of central Russia, where the soviets – to the extent that they existed at all – were controlled by the 'right-wing' Socialist Revolutionary Party.

Lenin had advocated an armed uprising, but the events that unfolded in November 1917 scarcely deserve that name. As in the previous March, the existing order simply collapsed. Although it was no longer the order of the tsarist regime, it was a weak republican transitional order that was overthrown by the forces of the revolution without any great effort or the mobilization of large crowds of people. The Provisional Government had delayed dealing with the more pressing internal problems, foremost among which was the agricultural question. And far from seeking to end the war, it had ordered the Kerensky offensive at the end of June that had failed miserably and by the middle of July had brought Russia to the brink of military collapse. Kerensky's government survived September's Kornilov putsch only with the help of revolutionary workers and, not least, the Bolsheviks, who were able to enlist the support of the majority of deputies in the Petrograd and Moscow Soviets at this time. By November the Provisional Government enjoyed little support among the population at large as a result of the increasing tendency of the metropolitan proletariat to side with the Bolsheviks, while the peasants were ever more inclined to solve the agricultural problem by means of illegal land occupations. For their part, the soldiers were no longer willing to obey their superiors' orders. The Bolsheviks were in this way able to seize power in a situation that could be described, with little exaggeration, as amounting to a power vacuum.

Seizing power was one thing. Holding on to it was another. Lenin was convinced that in a country as backward as Russia the proletariat could prevail only if there were follow-up revolutions in central and western Europe. He therefore appealed at the Second All-Russian Congress of Soviets on 8 November to 'the class-conscious workers of the three most advanced nations of mankind and the largest states participating in the present war, namely, Great Britain, France, and Germany' to acknowledge their duty 'to save mankind from the horrors of war and its consequences' by coming to the aid of Russian workers and, by their 'comprehensive' and 'determined' action, 'help us to conclude peace successfully, and at the same time emancipate the labouring and exploited masses of our population from all forms of slavery and all forms of exploitation.'[47] Lenin envisaged a process that began with a proletarian revolution in Russia before taking in central and western Europe and finally the rest of the world. It was a process that had already started in Petrograd in the spring of 1917.

From this point of view the October Revolution was the logical extension of the February Revolution, namely, the second and decisive phase of the Russian revolution when radical forces would succeed in liberating the people, something that they could not have done under a more moderate regime. The Bolsheviks hoped that they would find allies not only in the proletariat of other powers involved in the war but also among the non-Russian nationalities that made up the former Russian Empire. On 15 November the Council of People's Commissars issued a declaration concerning the rights of Russia's constituent nations, granting them the right to independence and hence to secession and sovereignty. The wording reflected a resolution passed at the Bolsheviks' April Conference and repeated the position that Lenin had adopted in 1914 in his article 'The Right of Nations to Self-Determination'. A week later Georgia responded by declaring its independence, and on 28 November the Estonian parliament took a similar step. For the present, it remained unclear how an independent Georgia and Estonia would view the new Russia under Bolshevik control.

This question also gave rise to widespread debate in Finland, which until the fall of the tsars had been a grand duchy under Russian control and which was still a part of Russia under international law. In the middle of November 1917 the Finnish trade union had joined forces with the more leftist Social Democrats and Otto Kuusinen's Finnish Bolsheviks to trigger a general strike aimed at seizing power. The armed Red Guards were resisted by paramilitary organizations supporting the middle-class independence movement. On 6 December the country's parliament decided that with the agreement of the new, purely middle-class government of Pehr Evind Svinhufvud, it would declare Finnish independence. Civil war broke out in January 1918, a war in which Russian Bolshevik forces stationed in Finland fought alongside the Red Guards, capturing Helsinki almost without a fight at the end of January and forming a Council of People's Representatives that met in Vaasa. Svinhufvud had remained in Helsinki and managed to flee to Tallinn on an icebreaker. From there he made his way to Berlin. German intervention in the Finnish civil war on the side of the 'White Guards' under their military leader Carl Gustav Mannerheim was now only a question of time.

There was also a nationalist independence movement in the Ukraine, especially in the western half of the country. Ukrainian nationalism was actively supported by the Central Powers, the Foreign Office in Berlin offering generous financial help to the 'League to Liberate the Ukraine', an organization of socialist émigrés eager to establish an autonomous, democratic and socialist Ukraine, a desire to which they coupled the demand for comprehensive land reform. Ukrainian prisoners of war were also recruited by the Germans, who saw in them future participants in a national revolutionary uprising. In the event, there was no such insurrection, not even after German troops had occupied a part of western Ukraine. But in the course of the war the desire for greater autonomy continued to grow until the Provisional Government saw itself obliged in the summer of 1917 to grant the Ukraine the right of self-rule. From August onwards the Central Council – a kind of provisional parliament formed in the wake of the February Revolution – was acknowledged by Petrograd as the legitimate representative of the Ukrainian People's Republic. Such concessions to Ukrainian autonomy were far too little in the minds of Ukrainian nationalists, but the Central Council was also placed under tremendous pressure by the Ukrainian Bolsheviks whose principal strongholds lay in the industrial east of the country. After a failed attempt to topple the government in Kiev, they declared a Ukrainian Socialist Soviet Republic in Kharkov in December. Bolshevik troops marched into eastern Ukraine from Russia to lend them their support.

The Bolsheviks continued to hope that central and western Europe would be overrun by revolution, but until the end of 1917 there was no basis for any such optimism. The German Majority Social Democrats had long been Lenin's most vocal critics among the parties of the Second International. Although they welcomed his decree on peace on the grounds that it promised to bring the end of the war a stage closer, they still had no intention of abandoning the parliamentary truce that obtained in the Reich. The Independent Socialist Party welcomed the Bolshevik revolution but declined to go any further than calling for a general armistice and a peace without annexations.

In France the Socialists were no less concerned than the bourgeois parties that Russia might sign a separate peace treaty with the Central Powers, with the result that in the wake of the October Revolution the Section Française de l'Internationale Ouvrière moved a little further to the right and would, indeed, have drifted even further in the same direction if the nationalist policies of Clemenceau's new cabinet had not placed a barrier in the way of such inclinations. Only the extreme left adopted a pro-Bolshevik position, but they represented no more than a tiny minority whose radical rejection of the 'imperialist war' came close to Lenin's attitude. Among the British labour movement, there was even less support for the October Revolution than there was in France, only the shop stewards evincing any sympathy for the Bolshevik cause. The Independent Labour Party, which had always been opposed to the war, was too indebted to the whole idea of parliamentary democracy to be able to accept either the theory or the practice of the Leninists, and this was even truer of the vast majority of members of the Labour Party.

Back in Russia, elections for the new constitutional assembly began on 25 November. Planned by the Provisional Government, they were conducted on the basis of universal suffrage for men. The winners were the Socialist Revolutionary Party, which presented a united front even though it had been no such thing since early November, when its left wing had broken away from the main party. If the right-wing Socialist Revolutionaries from all parts of the country were counted together, they held an absolute majority of seats, with 380 out of a total of 703. Thirty-nine members of the Constituent Assembly belonged to the left-wing Socialist Revolutionaries. The Bolsheviks received barely a quarter of the votes and had 168 representatives. The Constitutional Democratic Party and the Mensheviks fared even worse, with only seventeen and sixteen seats respectively.

Lenin refused to be sidetracked by his party's defeat, for he had never interpreted the term 'majority' in a literal sense. What mattered for him was that the Bolsheviks had maintained their support among the metropolitan proletariat, that they were the only party with a proper organization and a revolutionary strategy and that thanks to their radical anti-war policies and agricultural plans they did not have to fear the opposition of the mass of poor peasants.

As long as they could, the Bolsheviks found ways of delaying the constitutive meeting of the Constituent Assembly and carried on as if the elections had not taken place at all. On 27 November the Council of People's Commissars issued a decree on workers' control that was interpreted in many quarters as a licence to place the running of the factories in the hands of workers' committees, an idea that had never been part of Lenin's thinking. On 3 December revolutionary troops captured the headquarters of the Russian forces in Mogilev, and the chief of the general staff, Nikolay Nikolayevich Dukhonin, who had refused to obey the country's new rulers, was murdered. Two days later, on 5 December, the Council of People's Commissars abolished the country's legal system and ordered the election of new judges either by the soviets or by a popular vote. By 15 December a negotiated armistice had been agreed in Brest-Litovsk (now in Belarus) after twelve days of deliberations. German and Russian delegates began peace negotiations on 22 December, again in Brest-Litovsk. The Germans were joined for these negotiations by their allies, Austria-Hungary, Bulgaria and Turkey, but not – as the Bolsheviks had hoped – the Central Powers *and* the Western Powers. The result could only be a special, separate peace, not a comprehensive one.

The truce allowed the Bolsheviks to extend their power base within the country. A decree dated 16 December and calling for the democratization of the army placed all sections of the armed forces under the control of the corresponding soldiers' committee or soviet. All existing insignia of rank were to be abolished and officers elected by means of a universal vote within their units. The internal organization of the army had already been permanently weakened by mass desertions following the overthrow of the tsar and was now effectively destroyed altogether by this latest decree. On 15 December the Central Economic Council was established to run the economy, followed on

20 December by the creation of a 'special commission' – the infamous Cheka, or secret police – under Felix Edmondovich Dzerzhinsky or, to give him his Polish name, Feliks Dzierżyński. Banks were nationalized a week later. If Lenin had had his way, the nationalized banks would have overseen all the industrial concerns that were still in private hands, but his plans were thwarted by the decree on workers' control of 27 November and by the urge to act on the part of the local soviets and factory committees. This 'socialization from below' led to a massive drop in discipline in the workplace and to an equally disastrous reduction in productivity and industrial output.

In many places land reform had already been taken in hand by the peasants even before the October Revolution, and by the end of 1917 it was complete in parts of central Russia. Not until much later, conversely, were other regions affected. On average the landless peasants and those who owned very little land received 80 per cent of the land available for redistribution, while the rest went to the state, the communes and the cooperatives. But land distribution on its own was not enough to solve the problems of the peasants, not least because hunger and famine had driven innumerable city-dwellers into the countryside during the war, swelling the numbers entitled to a share in the land to around three million. In consequence, the peasants' share in the land was reduced to the point at which we can speak of a levelling of rural ownership structures to a low and often unprofitable level. The creation of private ownership among the peasants was not 'socialist' in the sense normally understood by that term, but in Russia in 1917 this kind of land reform represented a precondition for the seizure and maintenance of power on the part of the most radical socialists: the Bolsheviks.

At the insistence of the Bolsheviks, the peace negotiations that were launched in Brest–Litovsk on 22 December included a novel aspect in that they were conducted in public. The Council of People's Commissars had already made public all the secret treaties between tsarist Russia and the Triple Entente at the end of November, so that it was only logical to open up the peace negotiations in this way. It also allowed the representatives of the new Russia to use the negotiating table as a platform for revolutionary propaganda and to expose the Central Powers as imperialists. On 18 December Germany's privy council, meeting at Kreuznach, had agreed on a wide-ranging programme that included granting the right of self-determination to Poland, Lithuania and Courland. Both Berlin and Vienna were keen to see the Ukraine gain its independence not least in order to ensure that it would provide German heavy industry with ores low in phosphorus and high in manganese, while Austria–Hungary was interested primarily in Ukrainian grain supplies.

On 25 December the Austrian foreign minister Ottokar Czernin, after consulting with the Germans and agreeing on a conciliatory approach, reacted to the speech of the head of the Russian delegation, Adolf Joffe, with an impassioned plea for a peace without annexations and reparations and for the right of self-determination for all nations, including colonial nations. In reacting in this way, he caused general confusion, and it was not until the following day that Max Hoffmann, the German chief of the Oberost general staff, brought any clarity to the situation, arguing that the Russian negotiators evidently had a different understanding of the renunciation of violent annexations from the Central Powers, who were insisting on the voluntary breaking away from Russia of particular regions, namely, Poland, Lithuania and Courland. The Russian delegation was outraged and threatened to break off the negotiations. On 28 December they obtained a ten-day delay in order to obtain new instructions. This period was also to be used by the other powers to explain whether they were willing to agree to a peace without annexations and reparations, the Central Powers having linked their agreement to this condition. For a time it was uncertain whether the negotiations would be resumed at all.

The Russian delegation returned to Brest–Litovsk on 8 January 1918, this time under the leadership of Leon Trotsky, who had been people's commissar for foreign relations since the October Revolution. He seized the opportunity to attack the Central Powers' plans for annexation and to insist that the right to self-determination of the Lithuanians, Latvians and Poles should be real and not just specious and manipulated. Finally he appealed to the desire for peace on the part of all nations, especially the Germans. By now Hoffmann's demand had become public knowledge, and this, coupled with Trotsky's emotive views on world revolution, resulted in mass demonstrations in Germany and Austria that filled the Bolsheviks with feelings of the greatest optimism. In Vienna the Austrian Social Democrats called for large-scale demonstrations on 14 January. The wave of strikes that began that day soon affected large sections of the country.

By 18 January the strike had spread to Budapest. That same day Czernin received a deputation from the recently elected Vienna Workers' Council and assured its members that his government had no desire to make any territorial gains at the expense of Russia and that it recognized without reservation Poland's right to self-determination. The following day Czernin confirmed these statements in writing. Only then did the leaders of the Social Democrats suggest that the strike be brought to an end, a suggestion seconded by the Workers' Council and finally implemented a few days later.

Reports of the strike in Austria encouraged the Revolutionary Representatives in the Berlin metal industry to proclaim a general strike of their own, and by 28 January more than half a million workers had already walked out. Berlin was particularly badly affected, with several hundred thousand workers in the metal industry – important for the armaments sector – going on strike. In addition to leaders of the Independent Socialist Party, several prominent Majority Social Democrats, including its two leaders, Friedrich Ebert and Philipp Scheidemann, allowed themselves to be elected to the strike committee in the hope of bringing an end to the walkout, in which the trade unions were not involved. This aim had been achieved by 4 February. Had the strike lasted any longer, it would have threatened the country's military power. The countermeasures undertaken by the military authorities, police and judiciary were correspondingly draconian, and large numbers of striking workers were arrested or conscripted.

Meanwhile, there had been another setback to the negotiations in Brest-Litovsk, where Max Hoffmann had added to his previous demands by insisting that the Russians should withdraw from Livonia and Estonia, even banging his fist on the table in order to underline his point. As Joffe had done before him, so Trotsky reacted by requesting a break in the talks and returned to Petrograd with his delegation.

That same day the Russian Constituent Assembly met for its first and, as it turned out, its only constitutional meeting. The Bolsheviks confronted the non-Bolshevik majority by issuing an ultimatum and demanding that state power be transferred forthwith to the soviets. The motion was defeated, where-upon the Bolsheviks walked out of the meeting, leaving the remaining members to pass laws affecting the abolition of property and the convening of a peace conference. They also solemnly declared that Russia was a democratic federal republic. Demonstrators seeking to show their support for the Constituent Assembly were prevented from doing so by armed Bolshevik elite troops, resulting in many dead and injured. When the deputies tried to continue their deliberations the following day, they found their way to the Taurian Palace barred by soldiers armed with rifles, machine guns and two field artillery guns. Newspapers that had reported the previous day's meeting were impounded and either shredded or burnt by members of the Bolshevik troops.

The violent dissolution of the Constituent Assembly was entirely in line with a decree issued by the All-Russian Executive Committee of Soviets drafted by Lenin himself. It claimed that

> To relinquish the sovereign power of the Soviets, to relinquish the Soviet Republic won by the people, for the sake of the bourgeois parliamentary system and the Constituent Assembly, would now be a step backwards and would cause the collapse of the October workers' and peasants' revolution. [...] It was inevitable that the Bolshevik group and the Left Socialist-Revolutionary group, who now patently constitute the overwhelming majority in the Soviets and enjoy the confidence of the workers and the majority of the peasants, should withdraw from such a Constituent Assembly. [...] It is obvious that under such circumstances the remaining part of the Constituent Assembly could only serve as a screen for the struggle of the counter-revolutionaries to overthrow Soviet power.[48]

The breaking-up of the Constituent Assembly on 19 January 1918 marked nothing less than the definitive break between the Bolsheviks and the democratic majority of the European workers' movement. The appeal to a higher will than the one that found expression in elections represented Lenin's variation on Rousseau's distinction between the true 'volonté générale' and the relatively unimportant 'volonté de tous'. It was a dialectical trick designed to invest the assumption of power with a semblance of theoretical legitimacy. The Bolsheviks' *coup d'état* had a compelling inner logic when seen from the standpoint of their premises and in the light of their situation in January 1918. Their policies were a radical reaction to Russia's extreme backwardness and to its social and political culture. All of this helps to explain why their January putsch initially encountered little real resistance in Russia. But wherever workers were used to more freedom and more legal safeguards than in Russia, the Bolsheviks could count on strenuous opposition to their ideas. Nor was it long before such opposition made itself felt, finding its clearest and most fundamental expression in the country on which the Bolsheviks had pinned their greatest hopes: Germany.

Here it was not only the Majority Social Democrats but also the more moderate members of the Independent Social Democratic Party who were outraged by the events of 19 January. Karl Kautsky, who had joined the Independent Social Democrats in protest at the Majority Social Democrats' decision to support war loans, told Lenin in no uncertain terms that a dictatorship by one of several parties was not the same as a 'dictatorship of the proletariat' in the sense understood by Marx and Engels but 'the dictatorship of one section of the proletariat over another section'. But the dictatorship of a minority found its most powerful support in a dedicated army, and the more the minority replaced the majority by force of arms, 'the more it forces the opposition to seek salvation by appealing to bayonets and fists, rather than to the electoral system from which it is excluded: at that point *civil war* becomes the only way in which political and social conflicts can be resolved'.[49]

For Kautsky, civil war was the most terrible form of war and as such a disaster:

> In a civil war every party fights for its own existence, threatening the defeated with total destruction. [...] Some people confuse civil war with social revolution, considering it its formal expression and tending to excuse the acts of violence that are inevitable in such a war by claiming that no revolution is possible without them. [...] If we were to adopt the example of bourgeois revolutions and say that revolution is synonymous with civil war and dictatorship, we should have to draw the logical conclusion and say that revolution necessarily ends in the rule of a Cromwell or a Napoleon.[50]

Even in the far left Spartacus League, opinions were divided. Clara Zetkin, a pioneer of the socialist women's movement, and the historian Franz Mehring were unreserved in their support of the violent suppression of the Constituent

Assembly, Zetkin even commenting that not to have destroyed it 'would have been a crime coupled with an act of folly'.[51] On the other hand, Rosa Luxemburg, who had been in 'protective custody' since July 1916, felt that it was indefensible that the Bolsheviks failed to call for new elections immediately after they had abolished the Constituent Assembly, an action which in itself she too had justified. 'Freedom only for the followers of the government, only for the members of a particular party – no matter how numerous they may be – is no freedom. Freedom is only ever the freedom of the person who thinks differently.'[52] These oft-cited sentences are taken from a piece, 'The Russian Revolution', that was not published until after Rosa Luxemburg's death. They were intended not as a profession of faith in some liberal pluralism but in a revolutionary, socialist pluralism. She was not thinking of 'class traitors' and bourgeois 'revolutionaries' when referring to the 'freedom of the person who thinks differently'.

As for the abolition of the Constituent Assembly, Lenin could count on the backing of the leading Bolsheviks, but in terms of the question of peace, the situation was rather different, for Lenin was resolved to accept only the sort of peace that would ensure the survival of the Bolshevik regime, which is why he pleaded for the peace treaty to be signed without delay. Stalin expressed a similar sentiment. Bukharin and Dzierżyński regarded the acceptance of Germany's conditions as a political disaster. Trotsky demanded that the Russian delegation refuse to sign but also refuse to stop fighting and encourage the subversion of the Central Powers' armies: 'neither war nor peace' was his motto. There were violent disagreements on the Central Committee, but in the end a majority of its members adopted Trotsky's line. By 10 February Trotsky was back in Brest–Litovsk, where he declared that the war was over and broke off all further negotiations. The German delegation responded on the 16th with an ultimatum to the Soviet government that the latter simply ignored. Within two days the Germans had gone on the offensive. Lenin continued to use all his influence to press for an acceptance of the peace terms, and this time he prevailed with seven of the thirteen votes on the Central Committee. The German government was informed by telegram that the Council of People's Commissars was willing to accept the peace terms and to respond at once to any new conditions.

The German answer of 22 February went further than ever. Russia was required not only to abandon the whole of the Baltic region, including Finland, but also to acknowledge the independence of the Ukrainian People's Republic proclaimed by its Central Rada on 22 January, a step that Germany had already taken by means of a separate treaty dated 10 February. (This demand also included the withdrawal of the Bolshevik troops that had occupied Kiev on 9 February.) The Ukraine was now a German protectorate. During their offensive, German troops occupied not only the rest of the Baltic states but also large tracts of White Russia and the Ukraine, including the capital, Kiev, which they entered on 2 March.

The following day the peace treaty was signed in Brest-Litovsk after Lenin had threatened to resign as party leader and chairman of the Council of People's Commissars. The terms were brutal. Russia lost a third of its population and arable land, more than half of its total industry, including three-quarters of its heavy industry, four-fifths of its iron reserves and nine-tenths of its coal mines. The creation of an independent Ukrainian state and the handing over of parts of Georgia and Armenia to Turkey meant that its position on the Black Sea was considerably weakened. And following the occupation of the entire Baltic region by German troops it had only limited access to the Baltic Sea.

Once Russia had been defeated, the Central Powers, disregarding the Treaty of Brest-Litovsk, continued their march on the Caucasus, resulting in a race between the German Reich and the Ottoman Empire. German troops occupied Tbilisi in June 1918, while Turkish forces captured Baku and its oilfields in the September of that year. The humiliation of the defeated country continued in other areas, too: as a result of further treaties Russia had to agree to the payment of six thousand million gold marks at the end of August 1918 and renounce for good the northern Baltic provinces of Livonia and Estonia. As had already been the case with Courland, it was again the German-Baltic upper stratum of society and its representatives in the Reich who were particularly insistent that 'their' lands should be handed over and Germanicized.

Even without this pressure, public opinion in Germany would easily have been convinced of the need to create a buffer zone of eastern central European states to keep Soviet Russia at bay. One of these border states was Finland, where German troops and a specially created Mannerheim auxiliary force came to the aid of the 'White Guards' and helped them to victory in May 1918. In another border state, the Ukraine, the German protectorate authority dissolved the Socialist-dominated Central Rada in April 1918, replacing it with a Conservative government under the hetman Pavlo Skoropadsky and changing its name from the Ukrainian People's Republic to the Ukrainian State. Skoropadsky's regime showed its gratitude for the Central Powers' support by providing them with large quantities of grain.

The Brest-Litovsk peace treaty brought Germany closer to its aim of dominating central Europe than would otherwise have been thought possible in early 1918. Although this aim could hardly have been further removed from the Reichstag's peace resolution of 19 July 1917, the representative body of the people voted for the treaty by a large majority on 22 March 1918. Among those who supported it were the two middle-class majority parties: the Centre Party and the Progressive People's Party. The Majority Social Democratic Party was divided, and abstained. Only the Independent Social Democratic Party voted against it. The Majority Social Democrats had previously joined forces with the two other majority parties to pass a resolution expressing the hope that the Reich would take account of the right of self-determination of Poland, Lithuania and Courland.

Two months later, on 7 May 1918, the Central Powers signed a peace treaty with Romania in Bucharest that was entirely comparable to the one foisted on the Russians at Brest-Litovsk. The conquered country was required to hand over the whole of Dobrudja, of which the Central Powers' ally, Bulgaria, received only the southern half, while the northern half was placed in the hands of the victorious powers. Germany and Austria-Hungary were granted special rights to the oil reserves in the region, and the two countries also ensured that they would receive all of Romania's surplus agricultural produce for a period of two years. By way of compensation, Romania was allowed to keep Bessarabia, which had previously belonged to Russia and which had been annexed in April 1918. Richard von Kühlmann, the secretary of state at the Foreign Office, was entirely right to tell the Foreign Committee of the Bundesrat that from an economic standpoint the principal result of the Bucharest treaty was to reduce Romania to a colony of the Central Powers.

On 7 March 1918, four days after the signing of the peace treaty at Brest-Litovsk, the Seventh Party Congress of the 'Communist Party of Russia (Bolsheviks)', as the party now called itself, agreed to Russia's capitulation. Lenin was able to persuade the delegates that it was necessary to submit to Germany's conditions in order to give the Soviet system breathing space. As he told the party conference, true salvation could come only from 'revolution in the whole of Europe', beginning with Germany, but this was not happening with the speed desired by the Bolsheviks. Even so, it was undoubtedly true, he went on, that Russia would perish without a revolution in Germany. Inasmuch as this revolution had not taken place and to the extent that Russia had no deployable army (the decree founding a new Red Army had been issued only on 20 February), the country had no choice but to accept a 'Tilsit Peace' of the kind that Napoleon had imposed on a vanquished Prussia in 1807. It was now necessary to build up a new army, to learn the art of warfare from the very first principles and to create order on the railways. They could learn much from the Germans. 'Learn from the Germans their discipline, otherwise we are a doomed people and shall forever be prostrate in slavery.'[53]

If need be, discipline had to be achieved by brute force and terrorism. On 21 February 1918, as the German offensive reached its climax, the Council of People's Commissars had issued a decree drawn up by Trotsky, the new war commissar, and signed by Lenin, 'The Socialist Fatherland is in Danger!', a title that alluded specifically to the famous appeal of the French National Assembly on 11 July 1792. In it workers and peasants from Petrograd, Kiev and all the regions close to the new front were required to form battalions and dig trenches under the guidance of military experts. 'These battalions are to include all able-bodied members of the bourgeois class, men and women, under the supervision of Red Guards; those who resist are to be shot.' The appeal ended with the words: 'Enemy agents, profiteers, marauders, hooligans, counter-revolutionary agitators and German spies are to be shot on the spot.

The socialist fatherland is in danger! Long live the socialist fatherland! Long live the international socialist revolution!'[54]

Even after the treaty had been signed at Brest-Litovsk, the feeling of threat did not recede, for it was well founded. On 9 March British forces landed at the port of Murmansk on the Barents Sea, where war materials supplied by the Western Powers were being stored, materials that the Triple Entente had no wish to fall into the hands of its former ally. On 12 March the Council of People's Commissars moved its headquarters from the strategically threatened city of Petrograd to the relative safety of Moscow, which was restored to its former status as Russian capital, a title it had forfeited in 1712. The Fourth (Extraordinary) All-Russian Congress of Soviets met here in the middle of March and voted for the peace treaty in the face of embittered opposition from the left wing of the Bolsheviks under Bukharin and the left-wing Socialist Revolutionaries, who responded by walking out of the Council on which they had been represented by two members since 22 December 1918. The Bolsheviks thus lost an important ally that still enjoyed a mass following, especially in the vicinity of the Volga. Other pockets of resistance were the Cossack region on the Don and Transcaucasia, where the Bolsheviks had practically no support at all and where the Mensheviks were more powerful than Lenin's party, at least within the socialist movement. The danger of an all-encompassing civil war continued to grow, therefore, and with it came the danger of western interference in Russia's internal power struggles. The Brest-Litovsk treaty had given the Soviet regime no more than a brief respite to catch its breath.

Of course, the Bolshevik reign of terror was more than just a reaction to the extremely difficult situation in early 1918 both inside Russia and beyond its borders, for it necessarily resulted from Lenin's plan to create a new communist society within a backward country. The weakness of the bourgeoisie had led him to conclude that the Russian proletariat or, rather, its vanguard in the form of the Communist Party needed to shoulder the bulk of the burden that Marx had seen as the historic task of the bourgeoisie, namely, the removal of the bases of the older society and its type of rule, which had been dominated for centuries by 'tsarist autocracy' and the 'Asiatic tyranny of the authorities'.

Lenin was a westerner to the extent that for him the West embodied scientific, technological and industrial progress, in which regard it held up a mirror in which Russia might glimpse its own future. The change from the Julian to the Gregorian calendar that was decreed by the Council of People's Commissars on 6 February 1918 (New Style) and that came into force on 14 February was thus an act of supreme symbolic significance that served notice of revolutionary Russia's desire to raise itself up to the level of more advanced nations. Nor was it any accident that Lenin appealed by preference to the example of Germany: the German Reich was emblematic of an authoritarian, rather than a liberal, variant of western rule. For Lenin, learning from Germany meant modernizing without liberalizing. From his point of view, the normative project of the West that had taken shape in the two revolutions of 1776 and 1789 could offer nothing from which Russia could take its cue. As had already been the case with Marx, the only aspect of the French Revolution that interested him was its second, Jacobin phase notorious for its Reign of Terror, rather than its first, more moderate phase. As Marx had observed in 1847, the Reign of Terror of 1793–4 could 'by its mighty hammer-blows only serve to spirit away, as it were, the ruins of feudalism from French soil. The timidly considerate bourgeoisie would not have accomplished this task in decades.'[55]

It was on the strength of a historical analogy that Marx and Engels both drew the conclusion that they did: just as the bourgeoisie had replaced a class – the feudal aristocracy – that had ceased to have any function, so the proletariat must now drive the bourgeoisie from power after the latter had served its purpose in society. In fact, the 'fourth estate', or working class, had never become the 'universal class' in developed societies in the West that the 'third estate' had been entitled to feel it was in 1789, and this was even more true of the Russian proletariat. Only the structural weakness of the Russian bourgeoisie gave the Bolsheviks – a group of professional revolutionaries largely drawn from the intelligentsia – a chance to seize power in the name of the proletariat.

The Jacobin Reign of Terror had been a transitional stage that was to be followed by Thermidor, a modern government of a more moderate hue, and then by Napoleon's rule. In order to prevent anything similar from happening in Russia, the Bolsheviks, whom Lenin had dubbed the 'Jacobins of modern socialist democracy' as long ago as 1905, were resolved to adopt an incomparably stricter and more consistent approach to dealing with their enemies than their historical predecessors had done. They also felt that they were justified and, indeed, obliged to act in this way because, when judged by contemporary standards, Russia in 1917–18 was far more backward as a country than France had been in 1793–4 – so backward, in fact, that it was impossible to see the new reign of terror ending. In the longer term, the Jacobins' Reign of Terror had been unable to obscure the ideas of 1789, whereas the Russian Revolution of 1905 and the February Revolution of 1917 had produced no ideas that could have eclipsed those of October 1917. The Bolsheviks represented these new ideas, and their reign of terror was therefore a part of their project from the outset: it was to be the most radical alternative conceivable to the normative project of the West.

Freedom for Civilized Nations: Woodrow Wilson's New World Order

The events that took place in Russia itself and between Russia and the Central Powers from October 1917 represented a threefold challenge to the Western Powers. In the first place, the Bolshevik victory meant that the Central Powers no longer had to fight a war on two different fronts: Germany could now concentrate its forces entirely on the western front, Austria-Hungary on its war with Italy. Second, Bolshevik propaganda demanded a response, and one, moreover, that confronted its talk of a general peace rather than its call for a proletarian revolution. The Russian revolutionaries had turned the peace talks at Brest-Litovsk into a political platform, a move that could well have unwanted consequences for western European workers and even for workers in America. London, Paris and Washington all had to reckon on that possibility. Third, the mere fact that the negotiations in Brest-Litovsk ignored one of the fronts in the war was not without danger for the Western Powers, for the Central Powers were giving the impression that they were the only countries that took seriously the Bolsheviks' appeal for peace.

Britain's Liberal prime minister, David Lloyd George, was the first western statesman to respond to the Bolsheviks' demand that all the countries involved in the war should publicly state their conditions for peace. At a trade union congress in London on 5 January 1918, he first set out his government's war aims in detail. Great Britain, he explained, was not waging an offensive war against the German people and had no intention of destroying either Germany itself or its imperial constitution,

> much as we consider the military, autocratic constitution a dangerous anachronism in the Twentieth Century. Our point of view is that the adoption of a really democratic constitution by Germany would be the most convincing evidence that in her the old spirit of military domination had indeed died in this war, and would make it much easier for us to conclude a broad democratic peace with her. But, after all, that is a question for the German people to decide.

Nor had Great Britain any wish to destroy Austria-Hungary or to drive Turkey from those parts of Asia Minor and Thrace that were then inhabited by Turks. What mattered was the right of self-rule of the peoples of the Danube Monarchy, including the Italians who lived there. As for the Ottoman Empire, 'Arabia, Armenia, Mesopotamia, Syria and Palestine are in our judgment entitled to a recognition of their separate national conditions.'

At the head of Britain's demands were the 'complete restoration, political, territorial and economic, of the independence of Belgium' and France's insistence on 'reconsideration of the great wrong of 1871, when, without any regard to the wishes of the population', the provinces of Alsace and Lorraine were 'torn from the side of France and incorporated in the German Empire'. Turning his attention to Russia, Lloyd George pilloried Prussia for seeking to annex the Russian provinces that it had occupied.

> The democracy of this country means to stand to the last by the democracies of France and Italy and all our other Allies. We shall be proud to fight

to the end side by side with the new democracy of Russia. [. . .] But if the present rulers of Russia take action which is independent of their Allies we have no means of intervening to arrest the catastrophe which is assuredly befalling their country. Russia can only be saved by her own people.[56]

Lloyd George went on to profess his faith in an independent Poland incorporating all truly Polish elements. He demanded international agreement on the question of the German colonies respecting the wishes and interests of their inhabitants. He further announced that Great Britain would insist on reparations for the damage caused by Germany in violating international law. And he ended by pleading for the establishment of an international organization that would prevent wars by settling international conflicts, limiting arms and facilitating a just and lasting peace. The British Empire was fighting for these goals, and in order to secure the conditions necessary for such a peace, its peoples were ready to make even greater sacrifices than they had already done.

In making his speech, Lloyd George was not only anxious to ensure the continuing support of the British workers' movement, an aim in which he was successful, as was clear from the friendly response of the trade unions and the Labour Party; he was also keen to build bridges with America by more or less repeating Woodrow Wilson's insistence on the right of nations to self-government and demand for a League of Nations. Since December 1917, Wilson's closest advisers, including Colonel Edward M. House, had been encouraging him to declare his country's war aims. In House's eyes, such a declaration was all the more pressing in that he had failed in the face of French and Italian opposition to persuade the parties at an Allied conference in Paris in November 1917 to agree to a generally worded Allied communiqué. The start of peace talks at Brest-Litovsk was a further reason for clarifying the American position without any further delay. Wilson responded by listing his famous 'Fourteen Points' in a speech to both Houses of Congress on 8 January 1918. It was consciously formulated in such a way that it was Wilson's speech, not Lloyd George's, that has gone down in history as the West's answer to the Bolsheviks' appeal for peace, turning Wilson into Lenin's true adversary.

Wilson's address to Congress differed from Lloyd George's speech not least by flattering the Bolsheviks:

> Their conception of what is right, of what is humane and honorable for them to accept, has been stated with a frankness, a largeness of view, a generosity of spirit, and a universal human sympathy which must challenge the admiration of every friend of mankind.

Whether Russia's then-leaders believed him or not, it was America's 'heartfelt desire and hope that some way may be opened whereby we may be privileged to assist the people of Russia to attain their utmost hope of liberty and ordered peace'.

Wilson proceeded to set out fourteen points demanding 'open covenants of peace' without any 'private international understandings of any kind'; absolute freedom of navigation; the removal of all economic barriers; universal disarmament; a free, open-minded and absolutely impartial adjustment of all colonial claims that would take account of the interests of the populations concerned as well as those of the colonial powers; and the evacuation of all Russian territory by foreign troops and a settlement of all questions affecting Russia that would enable the country to decide its own future and 'assure her of a sincere welcome into the society of free nations under institutions of her own choosing'. Belgium must be evacuated and its sovereignty restored, and the same was true of those parts of France that were currently occupied by foreign troops. The injustice that Prussia had caused France in 1871 must be righted. Italy's borders must be redrawn 'along clearly recognizable lines of nationality'. The peoples of Austria-Hungary should be 'accorded the freest opportunity to autonomous development'. Romania, Serbia and Montenegro were to be evacuated, and Serbia should additionally be 'accorded free and secure access to the sea'.

As for the Turks, Wilson demanded a secure sovereignty, whereas the other nationalities then under Turkish rule should be assured an undoubted security of life and an absolutely unmolested opportunity of autonomous development, while the Dardanelles should be permanently open as a free passage to the ships and commerce of all nations under international guarantees. Turning to Poland, Wilson asked that an independent Polish state be established, one that should include 'the territories inhabited by indisputably Polish populations, which should be assured a free and secure access to the sea, and whose political and economic independence and territorial integrity should be guaranteed by international covenant'. Wilson finally suggested setting up a 'general association of nations' with the aim of 'affording mutual guarantees of political independence and territorial integrity to great and small nations alike'.

Towards the end of his speech, Wilson turned his attention to the Germans. 'We have no jealousy of German greatness', he insisted, and 'we grudge her no achievement or distinction.' America had no wish 'to block in any way her legitimate influence or power':

We do not wish to fight her either with arms or with hostile arrangements of trade if she is willing to associate herself with us and the other peace-loving nations of the world in covenants of justice and law and fair dealing. We wish her only to accept a place of equality among the peoples of the world, – the new world in which we now live, – instead of a place of mastery. Neither do we presume to suggest to her any alteration or modification of her institutions. But it is necessary, we must frankly say, and necessary as a preliminary to any intelligent dealings with her on our part, that we should know whom her spokesmen speak for when they speak to us, whether for the Reichstag majority or for the military party and the men whose creed is imperial domination.

Wilson ended by striking a note of entreaty: 'The moral climax of this the culminating and final war for human liberty has come, and they [the United States] are ready to put their own strength, their own highest purpose, their own integrity and devotion to the test.'[57]

Wilson could not have given his speech on 2 April 1917, in which he announced his desire 'to make the world safe for democracy', if the regime of Tsar Nicholas II had not been toppled two and a half weeks earlier. And his speech of 8 January 1918 was able to assume the form that it did only because it was not until the 19th that the Bolsheviks forcibly disbanded the freely elected Constituent Assembly. Wilson's praise for the still young Russian democracy and what he referred to as the sympathetic openness of its leaders attests to scant knowledge of what was actually happening in Russia but was dictated by his desire to point up a clear distinction between Russia and Germany. Whether or not the Bolsheviks were pleased at Washington's recognition of their achievements, they had no hesitation in exposing the president's misconception by their act of brutality only a few days later.

But Wilson's illusions with regard to the new Russia were not the only questionable aspect of his speech, for several of his points ran roughshod over the true facts of the matter. He can hardly have been unaware that if it was applied indiscriminately, the principle of the rule of the democratic majority could easily lead to violence against ethnic minorities in states made up of several nationalities. He also made strategic demands such as free access to the sea for Serbia and Poland without asking if this could be squared with the principle of nationality. And his remarks on the legitimate interests of colonial peoples, finally, were couched in such general terms that they will scarcely have troubled the colonial powers, of which the United States had also been a member since the Spanish-American War of 1898. Wilson came from the southern state of Virginia and shared the American south's prejudices against blacks. Like most Americans and Europeans, he ultimately regarded only white nations as truly 'civilized', so that against this background he could hardly be a credible advocate of colonial freedom.

But none of this detracted from his speech in terms of its international historical importance. He added to the controversial nature of his Fourteen Points when, on 11 February 1918, he spoke in no less vague but equally inflammatory terms of the right of 'self-determination'. Wilson's vision of a community of self-governing nations living at peace with each other echoed ideas already found in Thomas Paine's Common Sense and Kant's Eternal Peace and was ultimately aimed at calling into question the 'Westphalian system' that prohibited interference in the internal affairs of a country by appealing to the sovereignty of the state in question. (The term 'Westphalian system' is in fact something of a misnomer.) Wilson's vision was also a response to Lenin's revolutionary variant of a nation's right of self-determination, and although Wilson meant nothing more than 'self-government' when he spoke of 'self-determination', his phrase could also be interpreted as propagating the right of 'civilized' nations to secede and form their own states. Together with his message of 11 February 1918, Wilson's Fourteen Points contained within them the power to explode the old order, a power felt as early as 1918 in the case of those European nations – primarily the Poles, Czechs and the South Slavs living in the Habsburg Empire – that strove for national independence. The same forces were also seen in the desire for greater democratization within the German Reich.

In Berlin Wilson's Fourteen Points were rightly interpreted as a call for a radical democratization of the country as a whole, with the result that the reaction in right-wing parties was correspondingly negative, but the same was true of the country's leaders, and on 24 January 1918 the chancellor emphatically rejected those of Wilson's specific demands that were addressed to Germany, arguing that any new order in the east concerned Russia and the Central Powers alone. The 'violent annexation' of Belgium, he went on, had never been a part of Germany's political agenda. And he categorically refused to countenance any territorial sacrifices to the west or to the east. As for the freedom of the seas, Hertling made it dependent on Britain's willingness to relinquish Gibraltar, Malta, Aden, Hong Kong, the Falkland Islands and other strategic bases.

In France the Socialists were grateful to Wilson for spelling out America's war aims or, rather, its peace goals. The persistent refusal of France's prime minister, Georges Clemenceau, to specify France's war aims merely served to deepen the rift between government and opposition. In France, the Section Française de l'Internationale Ouvrière became the true 'Wilson party', a claim that could also be made for the moderate majority of the Independent Social Democratic Party in Germany and for the Labour Party in Great Britain. Clemenceau's obstinacy was due not just to his determination to reincorporate Alsace-Lorraine without a plebiscite. (Neither Wilson nor Lloyd George nor the French Socialists had as yet made any specific demands on this point.) He also had no interest whatsoever in speaking publicly about his far-reaching demands with regard to the Saarland and the Rhineland, demands supported by the chief of his general staff, Joseph Joffre. In Italy, too, there was an equally determined refusal to explain the country's war aims on the part of the prime minister Vittorio Emanuele Orlando and his foreign minister Sidney Sonnino: there was too clear a discrepancy between Wilson's advocacy of the principle of nationality and Italy's insistent claims to the Brenner frontier, to Istria and to large parts of Dalmatia.

Orlando had succeeded Paolo Boselli in October 1917. It was under Boselli's administration that the two Reform Socialists, Leonida Bissolati and Ivanoe

Bonomi, had assumed ministerial positions. Bissolati was the most eloquent champion of the 'Democratic Interventionists' who supported the nation's right of self-determination in the Wilsonian spirit and who were opposed, therefore, to demands for the annexation of the German-, Slav- and Greek-speaking parts of the region. At least from a tactical standpoint, Orlando came closer to the views held by the Democratic Interventionists when, at the insistence of the chief of his general staff and in the face of opposition from Sonnino, he began to work together with the South Slavs, a move that required a certain restraint in terms of Italian demands for territorial expansion in the eastern Adriatic. The semi-official Patto di Roma that was passed at a Congress of Oppressed Nationalities in April 1918 took account of this new line in Italian foreign policy. Conversely, no attempt was made, then or later, to revoke the corresponding parts of the secret Treaty of London that had been drawn up with the Entente in April 1915, the contents of which were made public by the Soviet authorities in November 1917.

Among the émigrés from the Habsburg monarchy who championed the independence of their own countries, none was as close to Wilson's ideas as the Czech philosopher Tomáš Masaryk, who was born in Moravia in 1850 as the son of a Slovak carter and a German-Moravian peasant girl and who went on to found the Realistic Party, which he represented in the Austrian parliament from 1900 to 1914. But both he and his colleague Edvard Beneš took exception to certain aspects of Wilson's Fourteen Points, especially to the fact that in order not to drive Austria–Hungary even further into the arms of Germany, Wilson had avoided any calls for the dissolution of the Danube Monarchy. (Much the same was true of Lloyd George, both men being motivated by their hope of signing a separate peace treaty with Vienna.) From this point of view, they had closer allies in Clemenceau and his foreign minister Stéphen Pichon, neither of whom made any secret of the fact that they were keen to see the unconditional capitulation and, with it, the end of Austria-Hungary. In 1918 they adopted a more active approach to the question and in doing so reflected Masaryk's wishes by encouraging aspirations for national independence within the Habsburg Empire.

Masaryk and Beneš were both able to contribute to this struggle, for together they had founded the Czechoslovak National Council in Paris in 1916. Set up with the agreement of the French government, this council worked for Czech and Slovak independence, an aim initially agreed to by Czech and Slovak exiles in Cleveland, Ohio, in October 1915 and later, in a more binding form, in the Pittsburgh Agreement of May 1917. Under the terms of this last-named treaty, Masaryk granted the Slovaks far-reaching autonomy. Following the February Revolution, he travelled to Russia, where he organized the Czechoslovak Legion made up of prisoners of war and deserters from the Austro-Hungarian army and turned them into an army of liberation that was to be deployed on the French side on the western front. Unable to travel directly through lands held by the Central Powers, the army was forced to make a major detour via Vladivostok, where Japanese troops had landed on 5 April 1918.

The Soviet government had initially approved of this plan but after several untoward incidents it withdrew its support. Trotsky's order that the legion be disarmed could not be implemented, however, because of the resistance offered by the soldiers, who now numbered over 40,000. Within weeks it had succeeded in seizing control of a large part of the central Volga, the area around Ufa in the southern Urals, part of south-western Siberia and a considerable stretch of the Trans-Siberian Railway almost as far as Irkutsk. Their gains were made possible only with the help of Russian opponents of the Bolsheviks, including the Socialist Revolutionaries from the Volga region. The Legion entered Samara on 8 June 1918, prompting the local committee of Socialist Revolutionary members of the Constituent Assembly to declare the Bolshevik government defunct and to appoint itself the provisional government instead. Far from travelling to France, as planned, the Czechoslovak Legion found itself actively engaged in the early stages of the Russian civil war and is known to have committed a number of atrocities, including looting from the civilian population and murdering German and Austro-Hungarian officers who fell into its soldiers' hands.

During the summer of 1918 the fall of the Bolshevik government seemed for a time to be only a matter of days. In early July the left-wing Socialist Revolutionaries triggered an uprising in Moscow and central Russia, in the course of which the German ambassador, Wilhelm von Mirbach-Harff, was murdered on 6 July. At around the same time the White Army under Generals Anton Denikin and Pyotr Krasnov, the hetman of the Don Cossacks, succeeded in driving the Bolsheviks from the floodplains of the Kuban and the Don. In western Siberia Admiral Alexander Kolchak – a supporter of the tsar – collected a band of counterrevolutionary forces that captured Kazan with the help of the Czechoslovak Legion. The Bolsheviks responded by murdering the royal family at Ekaterinburg (later Sverdlovsk) on 16 August 1918. Shortly beforehand the White Army had driven the Bolsheviks from the ruling council in Archangelsk in the far north of Russia. The following day, 1 August, the city was handed over to the British and French who had marched there from Murmansk in order to prevent Allied war materials stored in the city from falling into German hands. (In Murmansk there had for some time been the same sort of cooperation between the Allies and the local soviet, which had broken off relations with the Council of the People's Commissars in Moscow on 29 June.) An act that had originally been directed at the Germans gradually became an Allied intervention in the Russian civil war.

Seconded by Great Britain, France was particularly keen that the Allies should take steps to oust the Bolsheviks: France, after all, had been imperial Russia's principal creditor and leading foreign investor. The plan was to invade Russia from Vladivostok in eastern Siberia, where there were even greater supplies of Allied war material than in Murmansk and Archangelsk. Hitherto controlled by the Bolsheviks, Vladivostok was overrun on 29 June by an isolated section of the Czechoslovak Legion that had reached this part of Russia during the previous months. But it was only with the help of their allies in the form of the United States and Japan that the soldiers who made up this section of the Legion would be able to return to western Siberia and support their comrades in their fight against the Bolsheviks.

Sympathy for the Czech cause was one of the main reasons why Woodrow Wilson finally gave in to pressure from the French and British and agreed to send a total of 7,000 American troops to Siberia. In the event, these American units were rarely involved in any fighting with the Red Army, their principal task consisting in guarding sections of the Trans-Siberian Railway that had previously been controlled by the Bolsheviks. But in spite of holding back in this way, it was clear by August 1918 whose side the United States was on in the Russian civil war: the side of the White Army that was seeking to overthrow the rule of the Bolsheviks whom Wilson had courted as recently as the January of that year.

Two Countries Lie in Ruins; One is Reborn: Germany, Austria–Hungary and Poland at the End of the First World War

The separate peace treaty signed with the Bolsheviks allowed the Germans to move the bulk of their forces to the western front. In March 1918, 192 of the country's 240 divisions were based here, numbering 3.5 million men, and during the weeks that followed these were joined by a further twenty-eight divisions from the east, briefly giving the Germans a slight numerical advantage over the Western Powers. 'Operation Michael' began on 21 March, a large-scale offensive against the British and French in Picardy. The offensive was briefly successful, but by the first week of April it had developed into a stalemate. Further offensives in Flanders, on the Chemin des Dames and on the Marne likewise failed to achieve the hoped-for breakthrough.

The Allied counter-offensive began on 18 July under General – or, from 6 August, Marshal – Foch. This was also the first time that larger numbers of American troops under General Pershing took part in the fighting. The decisive factor proved to be the massive deployment of British tanks, allowing them to break through enemy lines along a broad front at the Battle of Amiens on 8 August, a day that Ludendorff is said to have described as a 'black day for the German army'. From 20 August the German lines were repeatedly driven back by the hammer-blows of French, British and American assaults, leading to a palpable decline in German morale.

This period also witnessed a series of serious setbacks for Germany's allies. During the second half of June an Austrian offensive on the Altipiano dei Sette Comuni and on the lower reaches of the River Piave came to nothing. There were also increasing signs of friction among non-German-speaking sections of the army, so that from August 1918 Austria-Hungary became more insistent in its demands that Germany bring the war to a rapid conclusion. When these demands failed to achieve their desired result, Austria approached the United States with a proposal on 14 September, suggesting a general peace conference, only to be rebuffed by Wilson. During the second half of September the Bulgarian army capitulated in Macedonia under the sustained assault of the British, French, Italians, Serbs and Greeks, and on 30 September a truce was agreed, forcing Bulgaria to demobilize and to consent to vacating all those parts of Serbia and Greece that its troops had previously occupied. (Bulgaria had been an independent kingdom since 5 October 1908, when Prince Ferdinand I had declared himself tsar.)

Also in September, the British succeeded in breaking through the Turkish and German front at Jaffa in Palestine, and in the course of the weeks that followed British troops under Sir Edmund Allenby advanced to Aleppo, Damascus and Beirut with the help of Arab forces assembled by T. E. Lawrence – the legendary 'Lawrence of Arabia'. The German army corps managed to retreat to Anatolia, while fighting a rearguard action. The Ottoman Empire laid down its arms on 30 October, the terms of its capitulation dictated by the armistice agreement signed on a battleship in the port of Mudros on the island of Lemnos.

Ludendorff – the strong man in the army's supreme command – had by now come to realize that Germany had lost the war and needed to approach Wilson with a peace offer without delay, a realization due less to the fact that his own troops had been forced to retreat than to the losses suffered by Germany's allies. But responsibility for this approach was to be assumed not by the army's supreme command but by a new government made up of the majority parties in the Reichstag. On 29 September, the day of the armistice in Bulgaria, Ludendorff and Hindenburg informed the Kaiser of their assessment of the military situation and of the conclusions that this invited: 'I have asked His Majesty to bring into government those circles whom we mostly have to thank for getting us into the present situation,' the first quartermaster-general informed a gathering of high-ranking officers on 1 October. 'We shall now see these gentlemen moving into the country's ministries. Let them conclude the peace that must now be concluded. Let them lie in the bed they made for us.'[58] In this way Ludendorff promulgated the myth that he and his army had been stabbed in the back.

In July 1917 the majority parties in the Reichstag had declared their willingness to enter into peace talks that involved no compulsory territorial losses or any other acts of political, economic or financial violation. By the early months of 1918 there was an increasing readiness on their part to take upon themselves the responsibility for ending the war. Although there had been violent debates on this score within the largest of the German parties, the Social Democrats, by 23 September Friedrich Ebert, who with Philipp Scheidemann was co-chairman of the party, had persuaded the leadership committees to accept that it was the

Social Democrats' 'damned duty and obligation' to reach an agreement with the middle-class parties and the government, because without such an agreement the country was threatened by the same kind of chaos, violence, terror and civil war as were then laying waste to Russia. The left-wing liberal Progressive People's Party was of the same opinion, whereas the conservative wing of the Catholic Centre Party still had serious reservations about a shift to a parliamentary system, which was the logical consequence of having a share in government. The Centre Party came round only after the National Liberals had spoken out in favour of a complete change to a parliamentary system on 29 September.

If Germany was to become a parliamentary democracy, there was a better chance that the peace terms imposed on it would be less severe than would otherwise have been the case under the old authoritarian regime that was effectively run by the army supreme command. Such terms, it was hoped, would be in the spirit of Wilson's Fourteen Points. This, then, was one of the hopes that brought together the moderate middle-class parties and the Majority Social Democrats in the autumn of 1918. And there was another point on which these parties were in agreement: the parliamentarization of Germany by the constitutional bodies of the Reichstag and Bundesrat would take the ground from under a revolution of a kind that Ebert and others feared would quickly lead to the sort of situation that had developed in Russia.

Parliamentarization meant a change of chancellor first and foremost. The present incumbent, Count Hertling, was unwilling to usher in the new system himself. Nor would the Social Democrats have accepted him as head of the new government. And so he resigned on 30 September. As his successor, Wilhelm II appointed Prince Max of Baden, a man regarded as a moderate and one whom Ludendorff and the majority parties had already agreed was acceptable. The new government included members of the Centre Party, the Progressive People's Party, the National Liberals and, for the first time, two Social Democrats: Gustav Bauer, the deputy chairman of the General Commission of Free Trade Unions, who headed the newly formed government Employment Exchange, and Philipp Scheidemann, who was one of four secretaries of state without a portfolio.

The change from constitutional to parliamentary democracy was sealed on 28 October 1918 by the necessary alteration to the country's 1871 constitution. From then on, the chancellor depended on the trust of the Reichstag: if the Reichstag had no confidence in him, then he would have to step down. His responsibilities extended to all actions of a political significance that the Kaiser traditionally undertook in exercising his constitutional authority. As a result, the Kaiser's military power of command was now subject to parliamentary control at least to the extent that acts of 'political significance' were involved. Another change to the constitution was scarcely less significant: without the agreement of the Reichstag it was no longer possible to declare war or to conclude a peace deal.

As a result of these 'October reforms' and the retention of its existing form as a monarchy, Germany became a traditional western democracy and, as such, comparable to Great Britain, Belgium, the Netherlands and the Scandinavian monarchies. Unlike these other constitutional monarchies, it had introduced universal suffrage for men at a relatively early date (in 1867 in the North German League and four years later in the new German Reich). Half a century later, the German system of government was democratized in the narrower sense, finally putting an end to the basic contradiction inherent in the Reich: the clash between economic and cultural progress on the one hand and the regressive nature of its pre-democratic form of government on the other.

For the present, however, the country's parliamentarization was no more than a formal act. Whether it would change the face of politics depended on the old elite, foremost among whom was the military. The mere fact that the parliamentarization of Germany was closely bound up with the country's military defeat meant that reforms, although long overdue, were compromised from the outset. Even before the constitutional changes had come into force, the extreme right had countered the formation of Germany's first de facto parliamentary government by declaring war on democracy and on the Jews. On 3 October, the president of the Pan-German League, Heinrich Claß, demanded the foundation of a 'great, bold and dashing national party and the most ruthless war on the Jews, at whom our good and misled people's all too righteous anger must now be directed'. Two and a half weeks later at a conference of the League's leadership and executive committee on 19 and 20 October, Claß called on his audience to 'use the situation to hold up Jewry and the Jews as lightning rods for all injustices'. Towards the end of his speech he assured his listeners that he would shrink from nothing but heed the words of the poet Heinrich von Kleist: 'Strike them all dead! On Judgement Day / No court will ever make you pay!'[59]

On 4 October 1918 and under pressure from the army high command, the new government of Prince Max of Baden lost no time in asking Woodrow Wilson for a truce. After various notes had been passed to and fro, the definitive answer came on 23 October. Drawn up by Robert Lansing, the chief of the State Department, it demanded nothing less than the abdication of Wilhelm II, prompting the army high command to request that negotiations with the United States be broken off and that the fighting be continued 'until the bitter end'. The following day it provoked a conflict with the new parliamentary government by asking army commanders in a joint telegram to fight on. Given the situation on the ground, this can only have been an attempt on Ludendorff's part to avoid all responsibility for the subsequent course of events. On the 26th he was relieved of his duties by the Kaiser at the government's request. General Wilhelm von Groener was appointed the new first quartermaster-general and de facto head of the army high command. A native of Württemberg, he was regarded as a level-headed leader.

In order to remove the Kaiser from the immediate sphere of influence of the government and of the Reichstag, Hindenburg advised Wilhelm II to leave Berlin for Spa in Belgium, the army's current headquarters. On 29 October, a day after signing the new laws altering the constitution, Wilhelm did as he had been bidden by the popular general. The Evangelical theologian and religious philosopher Ernst Troeltsch, who was a keen-eyed observer of contemporary events, saw in this an important constitutional development: 'The monarchical and military power was now completely separated from the parliamentary bureaucratic power, and the two were now in conflict.'[60]

An even greater challenge to the new parliamentary system came from the navy high command. Germany had suspended submarine warfare on 20 October, giving the navy high command an excuse to announce that it had won back its right to operate freely. When the chancellor received this news from Admiral Reinhard Scheer, he was unable to appreciate its scope. Nor was it intended that he should do so. The fleet had seen practically no operational duties since the Battle of Jutland in late May 1916, but now it saw a chance to inflict serious losses on England and in this way maintain its 'honour'. That it would suffer serious losses in turn was accepted as a price worth paying. The inevitable conflict with the government and its majority in the Reichstag was welcomed by the navy's leaders, for if the new parliamentary system were to be brought down by this move, this would be a gratifying side-effect of its English escapade. The navy's leaders were playing politics on their own initiative – and in a way that invites us to speak of an attempted putsch.

The navy's leaders had not expected any resistance on the part of their sailors, but the first mutinies took place on 29 October on a number of ships anchored off Wilhelmshaven. The naval command took drastic countermeasures, but this merely fuelled the protest, and on 1 November a further mutiny broke out in Kiel. Within two days shipyard workers had joined the action. On the 4th the government intervened at the request of the local governor, Admiral Wilhelm Anton Souchon. In an attempt to bring the situation under control as quickly as possible, the government dispatched the state secretary without portfolio, Conrad Haussmann of the Progressive People's Party, and the Social Democrats' spokesman on naval affairs, Gustav Noske, who was able to calm the sailors by promising them an amnesty, but he was incapable of containing the situation. On the 4th only Kiel had been in the hands of the sailors, but by the 6th they had seized control of Lübeck, Brunsbüttel, Hamburg, Bremen and Cuxhaven.

By the 7th the mutiny had become a full-scale revolution. The first German throne to be toppled was that of the Wittelsbachs. As chairman of the Munich Workers' and Soldiers' Council, Kurt Eisner – a journalist from Berlin who represented the Independent Social Democrats – took control in Bavaria and on 8 November declared it a 'free state'. That same day a Workers' and Soldiers' Council in Cologne seized power, and on the evening of 8 November the

Prussian Ministry of War declared nine other cities to be 'Red', including Halle, Leipzig, Düsseldorf, Osnabrück and Stuttgart.

In Berlin, meanwhile, the Social Democrats were trying to persuade the Kaiser, who was also the king of Prussia, to abdicate. A few successes could be recorded by this date, and some of the measures required by the war had been lightened at the request of the majority parties. Karl Liebknecht, sentenced to four years' imprisonment for treason in July 1916, was released on 23 October, while Rosa Luxemburg's house arrest was lifted on 8 November, the day on which sailors convicted of mutinying in 1917 were also released from prison. On 7 November the Social Democrats responded to a ban on meetings by the Independent Social Democrats imposed by the regional commander by issuing an ultimatum to the war cabinet. Central to their demands was a reorganization of the Prussian government to reflect the state of the parties in the Reichstag, an increase in the Social Democrats' influence within government, the abdication of the Kaiser and a promise by the crown prince that he would not ascend the vacant throne. If its conditions were not met, the Majority Social Democratic Party threatened to withdraw its members from government with immediate effect.

On the evening of 8 November the Social Democrats extended their ultimatum until such time as the armistice was signed. (The German negotiators headed by the secretary of state Matthias Erzberger of the Centre Party had left Berlin on 6 November and accepted the victors' conditions at the Allied headquarters at Compiègne to the north of Paris on the morning of the 8th.) Important concessions by the middle-class majority parties made it easier for the Social Democrats to put their names to the agreement: in Prussia and all the other German states, universal suffrage was to be introduced on the basis of proportional representation; Prussia would adopt a parliamentary system of government without any further delay; and the Social Democrats' influence within government would be increased. At the very last moment the Progressive People's Party and the Centre Party agreed to the introduction of women's suffrage. In turn both parties also demanded the abdication of the Kaiser, and even the National Liberals made it known that they would welcome it if Wilhelm II were to step aside.

Revolution reached the streets of Berlin on 9 November, prompting the capital's Majority Social Democrats under their district secretary Otto Wels to call a general strike at nine in the morning, a move designed to place their own party in the vanguard of the movement for greater reform. An hour later Philipp Scheidemann stepped down as secretary of state, and at the same time the leaders of the Majority Social Democrats entered into negotiations with the Independent Social Democrats, but the latter felt unable to negotiate as their chairman, Hugo Haase, had gone to Kiel to see the insurrection at first hand and had not yet returned to Berlin. For their part, the Revolutionary Stewards on the left wing of the Independent Social Democrats had not wanted to make their first move until the 11th. The temporary power vacuum to the left of the Majority Social Democrats gave Ebert's and Scheidemann's party a chance that they seized with both hands. In the course of an inflammatory speech, Wels was able to persuade the battalion of the Naumburg Riflemen stationed in Berlin that it was their duty to side with the people and with the Social Democrats.

When the chancellor, Prince Max of Baden, learnt that soldiers hitherto deemed implacably loyal to the Kaiser had defected to the opposition, he knew that the tide had turned. At around eleven o'clock that morning he had been informed by telephone that the Kaiser had decided to abdicate, and although there was as yet no official confirmation, he revealed the Kaiser's decision in a communiqué to Wolff's Telegraph Office, adding that he himself was keen to step down as soon as the question of his successor had been resolved. He was planning to recommend that the new regent appoint Ebert as chancellor and to propose elections for a national assembly that would provide the country with a new constitution that would in turn decide on the type of state that Germany should in future be.

But the attempt to salvage the monarchy by means of a regency was doomed to fail, for shortly after 12:30 on 9 November a delegation from the SPD turned up at the chancellor's office and demanded that he and his assembled secretaries of state hand over power without further ado. Ebert justified his demand by arguing that only in this way could law and order be maintained and bloodshed avoided. He went on to explain that the Majority Social Democratic Party had the backing of the Independent Social Democratic Party, which might have a part to play in the new government, as could representatives of the middle-class parties. But the preponderance of the Social Democrats had to be safeguarded. When Prince Max remarked that the question of the regency still needed to be addressed, Ebert replied that it was already too late, prompting Max to invite Ebert to take over as chancellor, an invitation that had the backing of all the secretaries of state. After hesitating briefly, Ebert agreed. For the first time in its history, Germany had 'a man of the people' at its helm. A native of Heidelberg, Ebert was then forty-seven. After working as a saddler, he had gone on to edit the local paper of the Bremen SPD.

At two o'clock – an hour or so after this revolutionary change of government – Philipp Scheidemann, the co-chairman of the Majority Social Democrats, declared the foundation of the 'German Republic' from a balcony of the Reichstag building. He had not been authorized by Ebert to do so. Two hours later, the end of the monarchy was once again announced by a politician with far more extreme left-wing views: Karl Liebknecht. From his position in the main gateway to the Berlin Stadtschloss he proclaimed the 'free Socialist Republic of Germany'. Ebert had wanted to leave it to the Constituent Assembly to decide on the form that the new state would adopt. The frenzied applause that greeted Scheidemann's brief speech and the events that took place during the hours that followed fully justified Scheidemann. Liebknecht, as the leader of the Spartacus League, was too late to influence the course of events.

Scheidemann graphically underlined the break with the old authoritarian state, whereas Ebert stressed the sense of continuity, appealing to all German men and women to respect the rule of law and calling on civil servants, judges and army officers to continue to carry out their duties. He also tried to persuade the Independent Social Democratic Party to agree to a form of government in which the two Social Democratic parties were equally represented, while the middle-class parties provided only junior ministers. When Liebknecht asked the Independent Social Democrats to demand that 'all executive, legislative and legal power' be handed over to the Workers' and Soldiers' Councils, the Majority Social Democrats refused: 'If this demand means the dictatorship of one section of a class that does not have a popular majority, then we must reject it since it does not accord with our democratic principles.'[61] The Majority Social Democrats also turned down the Independent Social Democrats' demand that the middle-class parties be excluded from government, arguing that it would be difficult, if not impossible, to feed the nation in consequence.

The position of the Independent Social Democrats initially bore all the hallmarks of Liebknecht and his Revolutionary Stewards. Following the return of the party's chairman, Hugo Haase, from Kiel late on the evening of 9 November, more moderate voices were able to assert themselves. The Independent Social Democrats no longer opposed the election of a Constituent Assembly on principle, but wanted political power to be placed in the hands of the Workers' and Soldiers' Councils, who were to be invited to attend a plenary meeting drawn from representatives from the entire country. In the expectation that they would have a majority there, the Majority Social Democrats agreed to this demand and also accepted the three members of the new Council of People's Deputies proposed by the Independent Social Democrats. Two of these members, Hugo Haase and Wilhelm Dittmann, were moderates, while the third, Emil Barth, was a Revolutionary Steward. For their part, the Majority Social Democrats nominated Ebert, Scheidemann and the Breslau lawyer Otto Landsberg, who had been a member of the Reichstag since 1912.

The new government had not yet been formally constituted when, at noon on 10 November, the three Majority Social Democrat members of the Council of People's Deputies held their first meeting with almost all the secretaries of state from the old government and a handful of members of the Prussian government. The only item on the agenda was the conditions for an armistice, conditions that Marshal Foch had handed to the German delegation under Matthias Erzberger in the forest at Compiègne on 9 November. Among the victorious powers' demands was the handing back of occupied lands in Alsace-Lorraine, France, Belgium and Luxembourg as well as the left bank of the Rhine. As a result of the October Revolution in Russia, German troops were not yet to be withdrawn from the former Russian territories. The peace treaties of Brest–Litovsk and Bucharest were declared invalid. Germany also had to hand over all its submarines and most of its airplanes, ships, weapons and munitions as well as locomotives, railway carriages and lorries. The ocean-going fleet was also to be disarmed. Hindenburg had already let it be known that if easier terms could not be negotiated, he recommended acceptance of these conditions. To this the participants at the meeting in Berlin agreed. The three Independent Social Democrats on the Council of People's Deputies were subsequently informed of these developments, and they too consented to the Allies' terms. At six o'clock on the morning of 11 November the German delegation signed the truce in a railway carriage at Compiègne. For the present, it was to last thirty-six days and come into force at eleven o'clock that same morning.

Before it could begin work and in keeping with its agreement with the two Social Democratic parties, the new government had to seek confirmation of its mandate from a meeting of some 3,000 representatives of the Workers' and Soldiers' Councils from Greater Berlin that was held in the Busch Circus on the afternoon of 10 November. Emil Barth's demand that the government be moni-tored by an action committee appointed by the Revolutionary Stewards almost led to the break-up of the meeting, as did a physical threat to Ebert by members of the Spartacus League, a threat that the soldiers' representatives managed to avert. Wels was able to persuade them to adopt the Majority Social Democrat line, with the result that in the end they too demanded the principle of parity for the action committee. The Revolutionary Stewards then fell into line. Seven representatives of the Majority Social Democrats and seven Independent Social Democrats were then elected to the Workers' Council of the Executive Committee. The fourteen-man Soldiers' Council that was elected the following day was dominated, conversely, by representatives who belonged to none of the mainstream parties. Late on the evening of 10 November the Majority Social Democrats and the Independent Social Democrats confirmed their coalition agreement. Germany again had a government.

Until the evening of 10 November revolution had been largely bloodless in Germany. On the previous day there had been a handful of skirmishes on the Marstall and at the University. And on the 10th, Theodor Wolff, the editor in chief of the left-wing, liberal *Berliner Tageblatt*, felt able to speak of 'the greatest of all revolutions', a superlative justified, in his view, by the fact that 'never had a Bastille so solidly built and surrounded by such stout walls been taken in a single attack'.[62]

Neither on the 9th nor the 10th could it be claimed that everything belonging to the old order had been ruthlessly swept away. Public authorities continued to function as before. True, they had been taken over by local Workers' and Soldiers' Councils, most of which were controlled by the Majority Social Democrats, but this tended to confer a new legitimacy on them, rather than preventing them from operating. The judiciary, grammar schools and universities had yet to be affected by the revolution. By the evening of 10 November the army's supreme command had reached the point where it could be described as a partner of the revolutionary government. In the course of a telephone conversation that has been the source of many a later legend, it has been claimed that the new first quartermaster-general, Wilhelm Groener, suggested to Ebert, as the chairman of the Council of People's Deputies, that they enter into an anti-Bolshevik alliance, a suggestion to which Ebert is said to have agreed. Whatever Ebert may in fact have said, he certainly needed the help of the army's supreme command in ensuring that German troops were brought home as soon as possible in an orderly and expeditious manner. Demobilization was a precondition of a rapid shift in the German economy, allowing it to switch as smoothly as possible from wartime needs to those dictated by peacetime. For that reason if for no other the People's Delegates were keen to ensure that Germany's military collapse was not followed by a collapse of the country's military.

It was the political system associated with an authoritarian state that collapsed in November 1918, a system that found expression above all in the princes of the realm and of individual states. By the end of 1918 the old order was held together only by minorities, and the number of people willing to defend the monarchy by force of arms was infinitesimally small. But royalists did still exist. They were more numerous among Protestants than among Catholics, and nowhere more so than in Prussia to the east of the Elbe. True, regional rulers had also been Church leaders in every German state, but the sense of an inner bond with the idea of the unity of Church and state and with the local prince as the 'summus episcopus' was a feature more especially of Lutheranism in northern and eastern Germany. It was no accident that in what was probably his final wartime sermon on 27 October 1918 Berlin's court preacher Bruno Doehring described Woodrow Wilson's demand that Wilhelm II should abdicate as a 'satanic suggestion'. 'The monarchy in Prussia', he confessed, 'means infinitely more to us Evangelicals than any political question, for to us it is a question of faith.'[63]

Shortly after the end of the war, the sociologist Max Weber observed with reference to Germany that

> the history of the dissolution of the old system of domination legitimate in Germany up until 1918 is instructive in this connection. The War, on the one hand, went far to break down the authority of tradition; and the German defeat involved a tremendous loss of prestige for the government. These factors combined with systematic habituation to illegal behavior, undermined the amenability to discipline both in the army and in industry and thus prepared the way for the overthrow of the older authority.[64]

Weber's findings may be summed up in his argument that by the autumn of 1918 the German Reich had largely forfeited 'the belief in legality' that he regarded as 'the most common form of legitimacy' and that he defined as 'the compliance with enactments which are *formally* correct and which have been made in the accustomed manner'.[65]

According to Weber's succinct analysis, there were three factors above all that contributed to the collapse of the German Reich: the war had undermined traditional values; the military defeat of the Central Powers was becoming increasingly evident; and there was a growing black market as a result of the failure of the existing economic system and of the policies associated with its currency. And it was the German Kaiser and king of Prussia who most clearly embodied the old system. In the eyes of the workers as well as members of the lower middle class and the peasant class, it was he who bore the ultimate responsibility for the duration and catastrophic outcome of the war as well as for the privations suffered by the nation as a whole, and because of his refusal to see this, he had to go. Wilson's Fourteen Points had fuelled the belief that Germany could hope for a just peace if it introduced a more democratic form of government, with the result that the desire for peace encouraged Germans to hanker after a democratic constitution. By the autumn of 1918 a broad majority backed these goals, forming the nucleus of a consensus that may not have been all-encompassing but which certainly included every social class and religious denomination, bringing the country together on the eve of 9 November and for the weeks that were to follow.

Germany had been a de facto parliamentary monarchy since 3 October 1918 – by 28 October it was also legally so. And yet the autonomous actions of the Kaiser and of the army and naval command in the days that followed the country's constitutional reforms made it clear that the new parliamentary system existed only on paper. Revolution broke out from below because revolution from above had foundered on military obstruction, making it impossible to uphold the institution of the monarchy. The collapse of the existing system, the obstruction of the military and revolutionary insurrection led to the proclamation of the German Republic on 9 November 1919. But this did not mean the end of revolution, for it was merely a new chapter in the history of the German revolution that began on this day.

Germany was not the only country to be rocked by national upheavals in the autumn of 1918. On 12 November, three days after the German Republic had been proclaimed, the German members of the Austrian Reichsrat proclaimed the Republic of German Austria that they insisted was an 'integral part of the German Republic'. The history of the dissolution of the Habsburg monarchy stretches back to the years before the outbreak of the First World War. The Reichsrat was prorogued on 16 March 1914 after the Czech Agrarians had obstructed its workings and rendered it ineffectual. Not until 30 May 1917 did the government reconvene it, a decision inspired in part by the fear that the Russian February Revolution might encourage imitators within the Danube Monarchy.

The three years during which emergency decrees remained in force contributed in no small way to the radicalization of the Austrian opposition, and this was true not only of the nationalist opposition, especially those who supported the Czechs, but also of the left wing of the Social Democrats. On 21 October 1916 Friedrich Adler, the son of the party's founder, Victor Adler, shot the prime minister, Count Karl Stürgkh, in protest not only at the war but also at the 'Socialist patriotism' of his own party. He was sentenced to death by a special court, but the sentence was commuted to eighteen years' hard labour. On 1 November 1918 he was released from prison under the terms of an imperial amnesty. His actions made him a martyr in the eyes of his political friends, but the hoped-for impact of those actions and of his speech to the court failed to materialize, and there was neither a mass strike nor even any protest demonstration.

The earliest instance of nationalist resistance to the government in Vienna was a secret organization calling itself the 'Mafie' that was founded in Prague in early 1915. At the heart of its circle of conspirators were the Russophile leaders of the Young Czechs, Karel Kramář and Alois Rašin, together with the sociologist Edvard Beneš, who was a close colleague of Tomáš Masaryk. Their principal aim was to establish an independent Czech – and, if possible, Czechoslovak – state. (As a representative of the Realist Party in the Reichsrat Masaryk had yet to advocate a completely independent Czech state that would have spelt the dissolution of the Habsburg Empire.) Beneš left the country in early September on a forged passport and together with Masaryk worked on his great project in exile in France. Kramář and Rašin had already been arrested for high treason in July 1915 but were released in July 1918 under the terms of the amnesty decreed by Kaiser Karl. A third beneficiary of the Kaiser's act of clemency was the leader of the National Socialists, Václav Klofáč.

As long as Russia seemed to have any chance of defeating the Central Powers, the pro-Russian supporters of Czech nationalism were more powerful than the pro-western groups who supported Masaryk and Beneš. Kramář and the Russophiles could appeal to the fact that as early as 16 September 1914 the commander in chief of the Russian army, Grand Duke Nikolay Nikolayevich, had informed the nations of the Habsburg Empire in the name of Tsar Nicholas II that Russia had entered the war to liberate the nations of Austria-Hungary and ensure that their nationalist aspirations were met. In the wake of the February Revolution of 1917, staunchly nationalist circles hoped that the Western Powers would now be more vocal in their support for the right of national self-determination.

But for the vast majority of leading Czech politicians, it was not until 1918 that their catalogue of demands included the dissolution of the Habsburg

Empire: only then did they come to hold views similar to those advocated by the Empire's émigrés and nationalist prisoners. Most Czech political parties set up a National Committee in November 1916, while their representatives in the Reichsrat formed a Czech Union. The first declaration by the National Committee on 18 November 1916 included an acknowledgement of the signal importance of the 'monarchy and of the great historical task of the Empire' and of the 'complete equality of all its nationalities'. In an open letter dated 21 January 1917 and addressed to the foreign minister, Ottokar Czernin, the Czech Union pilloried the western European allies for the fact that the 'liberation of the Czechs from foreign rule' that they themselves demanded was an 'insinuation based entirely on the wrong premises'. Just as it always had done in the past, the Czech nation continued to see its future and the basis of its development 'only under the rule of the house of Habsburg'.[66]

Following the first of the two Russian revolutions of 1917 and America's entry into the war, the more moderate nationalists struck a rather more defiant note. A 'Manifesto of Czech Authors' inspired by the 'Mafie' and signed by 222 writers in May 1917 described a 'democratic Europe consisting of autonomous and free states' as 'the Europe of the future'.[67] The Czech members of the Reichsrat were invited to show themselves equal to the historic situation or else resign their seats.

On 29 May, a day before the Reichsrat reconvened after an enforced break lasting more than three years, the Czech delegates agreed on the wording of a declaration that was read out the next day at the plenary session to the dismay of the government and of the German members of the Reichsrat. In it, the Czechs voiced more fundamental criticisms of the dualistic structure of the dual monarchy than at any previous point in their history, arguing that it had created ruling and subject nationalities and demanding

> the transformation of the Habsburg monarchy into a federal state consisting of free and equal national states. [. . .] Relying at this historic moment on the natural rights of nations, on self-determination and free development, [. . .] we shall demand the unification of all the branches of the Czechoslovak nation in one democratic state; we must not forget the Slovak branch, which forms a close historical unity with the Czech lands.[68]

The Slovaks spoke a language which, although very similar to Czech, was not the same. Historically speaking, by contrast, the two nations had developed along very different lines. Slovakia was a part of the Transleithanian, Hungarian half of the Danube Monarchy, whereas Bohemia and Moravia – the home of the Czechs – was a part of the Cisleithanian half. Bohemia had always been regarded as a part of the Holy Roman Empire, and the same was true of Moravia, which had been united to Bohemia since 1029 by feudal law. The kings of Bohemia belonged to the Empire's electoral curia, and in the fourteenth and fifteenth centuries, following the union of the house of Przemyśl with that of Luxembourg, they served as German Kaiser on more than one occasion. Bohemia and Moravia fell to the Habsburgs in 1526, and from 1815 to 1866 the two Habsburg crown lands – unlike Hungary and Galicia – were part of the German League. During the First World War Czech and Slovak politicians living in exile in America agreed on the constitution of a common state, although for the present it remained unclear to what extent they spoke for their respective peoples. And there was another problem that had still to be resolved. In their dealings with Vienna and the rest of the world the Czech nationalists appealed to the natural right of national self-determination. But historical Bohemian constitutional law was to apply to the Germans living in Bohemia and Moravia, most of whom were confined to self-contained settlement areas, resulting in the insistence that the territory in question could not be divided up.

The declaration of 29 May 1917 had not gone as far as demanding the dissolution of the Habsburg Empire, but nor had it advocated its preservation. In the Reichsrat the Czech deputies worked closely with the South Slav – mostly Slovenian – members from Carinthia, Styria, Carniola, Istria and the coastal region around Trieste. These members of parliament formed the South Slav Club and on 30 May they demanded that all the regions inhabited by Serbs, Croats and Slovenes be united, a demand that spelt the end of Austro-Hungarian dualism, since the Habsburg Serbs and most of the Croats – except for those in Istria – lived in Transleithania. Outside the Reichsrat, too, there were attempts to unite the South Slavs, attempts actively encouraged by Masaryk. The exiled Serbian prime minister, Nikola Pašić, and the exiled Croat politician Ante Trumbić, who was chairman of the South Slav Committee, signed the Corfu Declaration on 27 July 1917, demanding a unified kingdom of Serbia, Croatia and Slovenia, while not accepting the Croats' suggestion that the state be constructed along federalist lines.

The Ruthenian deputies in the Reichsrat shared these aspirations. On 30 May 1917 they expressed their conviction that the crown land of Galicia was 'an artificial administrative unit' at odds with the region's historical and national rights. It must be replaced, therefore, by a union of Ukrainian lands independent of Poland but including the areas of Russian Poland and White Russia settled by Ukrainians. The Polish parliamentarians refrained from expressing so extreme a view and contented themselves with announcing that they would comment in due course on national questions in the light of the unanimous agreement made in Kraków on 28 May. In this resolution, the Polish-Galician members of the Reichsrat had declared their support for a powerful Polish state with access to the sea.

With the start of 1918 the internal crisis in the Habsburg Empire began to grow increasingly acute. On 6 January – Twelfth Night – the Czech Union demanded a peace based on the nations' right of self-determination, a peace that would liberate all nations groaning beneath a foreign yoke. (This demand enjoyed the support of the Socialists, a party now dominated by forces hostile to the Habsburgs.) The January strikes to which we have already referred were followed on 1 February by a mutiny on the part of the Fifth Fleet in the Gulf of Kotor, when the navy band played the 'Marseillaise' and red flags were hoisted on every vessel. In the words of the Czech historian Zbyněk A. Zeman, the demands of the leaders were 'a mixture of Bolshevik slogans and the programmes of the political exiles'.[69] The uprising was not merely the result of a spontaneous protest caused by hunger but was a carefully planned political demonstration. The mutiny collapsed when the Third Fleet arrived in the Gulf of Kotor on 3 February and the sailors refused to follow their leaders. Among the forty sailors who were hauled before the courts following the suppression of the uprising, the Czechs were the largest national group with seven members. The others were German Austrians, Italians, South Slavs and Poles.

Subsequent developments were largely a consequence of the German spring offensive in 1918 and of the closer cooperation between Germany and Austria–Hungary, as agreed to by Kaiser Wilhelm II and Kaiser Karl when the latter visited the German high command at Spa. The Western Powers responded by demanding the full right of self-determination of the nations that made up the Danube Monarchy, a demand tantamount to the dissolution of the Habsburg Empire. In April exiled politicians from the whole of the dual Monarchy met in Rome at the Congress of Oppressed Nationalities that was supported by Italy and France and that demanded the end of the multiracial state that was said to be an instrument of German domination. The representatives of the Italian and 'South Slav' nation agreed on the wording of a declaration – the 'Patto di Roma' – demanding the liberation of the Adriatic, an amicable settlement of all territorial disputes and the protection of all minorities. (Conversely, there was no mention of Italy's claim to Trieste, Istria, several Istrian islands and large sections of the Dalmatian coast, a claim acknowledged by the Entente in the secret London Treaty of April 1915.) After hesitating at length, Woodrow Wilson finally added his voice to these demands on 28 June 1918, when he insisted that all nations of Slavic origin be liberated from the 'Austrian yoke'.[70]

Meanwhile, the economic situation in Austria-Hungary had taken a dramatic turn for the worse. By the middle of 1918 real incomes among the Empire's workers were only around half of their pre-war level, whereas prices had risen immeasurably. The whole population was suffering from hunger, nowhere more so than in Cisleithania. The harvest of 1918 was less than 50 per cent of the 1913 figure, while industrial production – leaving aside war items – was around 40 per cent of its pre-war equivalent. Between 1914 and 1917 coal production had dropped by 95 per cent. There was renewed discontent among the working population; and such was the social hardship that revolutionary slogans fell on fertile ground.

In Hungary the situation was complicated by local political conditions that fostered radicalization. Until the final year of the war aristocratic land-owners and the political forces close to them obstinately resisted the introduction of universal suffrage. In May 1917 Kaiser Karl finally forced the resignation of one of the principal enemies of reform, the prime minister István Tisza, but it was not until July 1918 that Tisza's successor, Sándor Wekerle, managed in the face of considerable parliamentary opposition to force through a modest democratization of the electoral system: 13 per cent of the population was now allowed to elect deputies to the national assembly. The industrial proletariat, which until then had not been represented in parliament at all, remained unimpressed by the prime minister's plans, and on 20 June 1918, shortly before the electoral law was passed, workers in the state-owned locomotive engineering works in Budapest went on strike. When the city's military commander gave orders for the striking workers to be shot, the workers at all of Budapest's factories joined the revolt, which lasted nine days and ended only with the intervention of the Social Democrats. The protesters' principal demands were political and included, first and foremost, an immediate peace deal and the resignation of Wekerle's government.

Austro-Hungarian dualism ended three months later. On 16 October 1918, barely two weeks after Vienna had added its voice to Germany's request for an armistice, Kaiser Karl issued the Imperial Manifesto drawn up and counter-signed by his last prime minister but one, Max Hussarek-Heinlein. In it he called for the creation of national councils made up of the relevant members of the Reichsrat and announced that the monarchy would be turned into a federal state. As Adam Wandruszka has written, he had unwittingly 'legitimized the violent overthrow of the existing order and triggered the dissolution of the monarchy'.[71]

Although Wekerle's government had insisted that the integrity of the Transleithanian half of the Empire should not be violated, it was unable to prevent the Romanians, South Slavs and Slovaks from becoming more vocal in their secessionist demands. On 24 October it was reported in Budapest that Croatian troops had mutinied. That same day Hungarian officers demonstrated for peace and for a new government under Count Mihály Károlyi, who was regarded as a reformer, prompting Károlyi's party – the Independents – to join forces with the bourgeois Radicals and Social Democrats to form a National Committee that began its work by demanding an independent Hungary and acknowledging other countries' right of self-determination, while at the same time insisting on Hungary's territorial integrity. On 29 October the Budapest garrison swore an oath of allegiance to the National Committee. Two days later Archduke Josef named Károlyi prime minister at the behest of Kaiser Karl. Károlyi formed a government that included Social Democrats. That same day the former prime minister, Count Tisza, was murdered. On 16 November Károlyi's government announced that all legal ties between Hungary and

Austria were officially severed: the house of Habsburg no longer had a throne; and Hungary was now a people's republic. Károlyi was appointed the republic's interim president on 11 January 1919.

The change of government in Budapest could do nothing to prevent the break-up of historical Hungary. A National Council was convened in Czernowitz – the capital of the duchy of Bukovina – on 17 November, its aim being to promote union with Romania. In their final declaration to the Budapest parliament on 18 October, the Romanian deputies issued a similar demand for Transylvania. On 5 and 6 October representatives of the South Slav parties from both halves of the Empire had met in Zagreb and turned the existing National Council that had been formed with Czech support into an expanded council that proposed the union of all Serbs, Croats and Slovenes. On 20 October the Croatian parliament passed a draft law declaring null and void all constitutional ties between Croatia, Slavonia, Dalmatia and Fiume on the one hand and the Austro-Hungarian monarchy on the other. From now on these lands were to be part of 'the state of Serbs, Croats and Slovenes'. Slovenian independence was proclaimed in Ljubljana on 29 October. And on 1 November the National Council took over administrative control of Bosnia and Herzegovina from the regional military commander.

The desired union with Serbia took longer to bring about. Prince Regent Alexander, who had been living in exile on the island of Corfu, returned in state to Belgrade on 6 November, and on 1 December he proclaimed the Kingdom of Serbs, Croats and Slovenes. His ability to prevail over the National Council in Zagreb was due in part to Italy, which, appealing to the secret Treaty of London of April 1915, laid claim to large stretches of the Dalmatian coast and which had in the meantime occupied Fiume, even though this was not part of the London agreement. Italian advances along the eastern Adriatic were also a consequence of the country's military victory over the troops of the Danube Monarchy in the nine-day Battle of Vittorio Veneto that had begun on 24 October – the first anniversary of Austria–Hungary's annihilating defeat at Caporetto – and ended on 3 November with the capitulation of the Austrian and Hungarian units and agreement to the terms of a ceasefire between the Western Powers and the Danube Monarchy that was reached at Padua. Also on 3 November Trento fell into the hands of Italian troops. Italy's victory over its Habsburg archenemy seemed finally to offer the country the chance to carry out its programme of integrating into a united Italy all of those 'unredeemed' borderline territories that had been omitted from the Unification settlement, a programme known as Irredentism.

For the Czech protectors of South Slavic unity, the road to independence was now a little easier. In Prague the National Council was dominated by middle-class nationalists, whose desire for total severance from the house of Habsburg received substantial support from a whole series of declarations acknowledging a willingness to accept a future Czechoslovak state: Italy and France on 30 June,

Great Britain on 13 August and the United States on 3 September. When, on 27 October, the foreign minister in Heinrich Lammasch's cabinet, Count Julius Andrássy the Younger, approached the United States with a request for an immediate ceasefire on the basis of an American note of 18 October, this approach was interpreted by the National Council as precisely what it was: a declaration of the end of the alliance with the German Reich and an acknowledgement of the claim of the Czechs and South Slavs to national independence. That same day – 27 October – the army's commander in chief in Bohemia asked the National Council to press Czech soldiers to remain at their posts at least until such time as a ceasefire had been agreed. On 28 October the National Council noted that an independent Czechoslovak state was a reality and assumed command of the military in Prague, Plzeň and Litomeričě. And on 30 October, Lammasch acknowledged the new situation by welcoming an emissary from the National Council to Vienna as the 'ambassador from the Czechoslovak state'.

At this date it was in fact not yet clear if the Slovaks were willing to form a union with the Czechs, a union which hitherto had been a predominantly intellectual concern. On 30 October, immediately after it had been established, the Slovak National Council had declared that 'linguistically, culturally, and historically' the Slovaks were 'a part of the Czechoslovak nation',[72] but at the same time it had insisted on the Slovaks' right of self-determination. The leader of the Slovak National Party, Vavro Šrobár, became head of the first Slovak government. He had only recently been released from prison in Hungary and was the only Slovak member of the Prague National Council to take part in the vote establishing an independent Czechoslovak state. But it was more difficult to get from Prague to Bratislava than Šrobár and his Czech supporters had imagined: since the Slovak capital was still in Hungarian hands, his government had to hold its first session in Skalica in Moravia.

Resistance to the establishment of a Czechoslovak state came from the Germans in Bohemia and Moravia, most of whom lived in areas bordering on Austria or the German Reich. Since it was now the Social Democrats who set the tone in Vienna, the middle-class deputies from Bohemia and Moravia turned to the Workers' Party in the hope of winning its support in their attempt to oppose the formation of a new Czech state. In their response of 3 October, the Social Democrats recognized the right of the Slav nations to form their own national states, while adding that

> we resist, resolutely and for good, the subjection, to these national states, of German territories. We demand that all German territories in Austria should be unified in one state which would regulate its relations to other nations of Austria and to the German Empire according to its needs.[73]

This laid out the line that was to be adopted by the representatives of German Austria during the ensuing months. On 21 October representatives of the

German-speaking parts of the Cisleithanian half of the empire met to constitute themselves as a 'Provisional National Assembly of the Independent
German Austrian State'. On the 30th it passed a provisional constitution. That
same day the Social Democrat Karl Renner was appointed chancellor, heading
a provisional government that included Social Democrats, Christian Socialists
and Pan-German German Nationalists. The Foreign Ministry was placed in
the hands of Victor Adler, the chairman of the Social Democratic Party, who
died suddenly on 11 November at the age of sixty-six.

The defeat of the imperial army at Vittorio Veneto and the resultant capture
of 400,000 prisoners by the Italian army was greeted with dismay in Austria and
this circumstance, coupled with the collapse of the monarchy in Germany, played
a leading role in promoting republican views in Austria, too. On 11 November,
at the urging of his advisers and of representatives of the Provisional National
Assembly, Kaiser Karl announced his decision to forgo all further involvement in
the affairs of state and his willingness to accept whatever decision German
Austria might take in respect of its future form of state. The following day the
Provisional National Assembly passed the aforementioned law declaring German
Austria a democratic republic and 'part of the German Republic'.

With the abdication of Karl as Austrian Kaiser (he remained king of
Hungary, albeit in name alone), the history of the Habsburg Empire came to
an end. For four centuries it had exerted considerable influence on the old
Continent and throughout that time had intermittently enjoyed the status of a
major European power. In Germany the house of Habsburg (or, to give it its
official name, the house of Habsburg-Lorraine, a title acquired in 1736 with the
marriage of Maria Theresa and Duke Francis Stephen of Lorraine) was regarded
as the enemy of freedom, initially in its struggle with Protestantism, later in its
war on liberalism. The Germans could not achieve unity and freedom with
Austria – this was one of the reasons why the revolution of 1848–9 had ended
in failure. The impact of Habsburg rule on its own more immediate sphere of
influence was more lasting and not entirely negative, for the Danube Monarchy
had left its mark on the whole of east central Europe from Galicia to Dalmatia
and from the Sudetenland to Carpathia, an influence apparent in its administration, its courts of justice and schools, its postal services and railway network,
its police and army and, not least, the dark yellow of its official buildings, a
colour known as 'Habsburg yellow'.

The Habsburg Empire was not the 'dungeon of peoples' that the Czech and
South Slav nations claimed to see in it. But the Slav nations had suffered at its
hands since the dual monarchy was created in 1867, for they were granted only
inferior rights by the German Austrians and Magyars. From the late nineteenth
century onwards, the sense of bitterness caused by this situation progressively
undermined the Empire's very foundations. So terrified was Austria that the
dual monarchy might fall apart that following the assassination of the Grand
Duke Franz Ferdinand and his wife at Sarajevo it reacted with exaggerated

severity to the challenge posed by pan-Serbian nationalism and, aided and abetted by the government in Berlin, it pursued policies that were to lead inexorably to the First World War.

In the crisis of July 1914 a leading role in Vienna's 'war party' was played by the elderly Kaiser Franz Joseph, whose immense popularity would in fact have allowed him to play the part of a peacemaker. The federalist reforms that his successor attempted to implement at the last minute came too late to save the monarchy, the desire for independence being more powerful than the last Kaiser's statesmanship. Whether the new states that called themselves nation states, even though, strictly speaking, they were no such thing, would be better placed than the old monarchy to deal with the problems of a mix of nationalities was one of many questions that remained open during the turbulent months of 1918–19.

For much of the war, the Polish question, too, remained unresolved. Of its three regions, the Austrian crown land of Galicia, together with the free city of Kraków, which had been autonomous until 1846, felt the least threatened in terms of its national identity. The Poles who lived there were Catholic, like the Austrians, a denominational singularity that distinguished this part of Poland from the other two regions and which had to deal with partitioning powers in thrall to other faiths: Protestant in the case of Prussian Germany and Orthodox in that of Russia. It was the local landed gentry in Galicia who set the tone, forming part of the Habsburg's ruling elite and in general proving 'Austrian' in their thinking. Only the introduction of universal equal suffrage in Cisleithania in 1907 gave members of the middle class as well as the region's workers and peasants the chance to express their interests within a political forum. The government in Vienna regarded with mistrust the attempts on the part of Ukrainian-speaking Ruthenians to gain their independence. Whereas the 'old Ruthenians' felt an affinity with Greater Russia and Russian Orthodoxy and were actively encouraged by pan-Slavic and militantly Orthodox circles in Russia, most of the younger and predominantly Greek-Catholic Ukrainians championed a national union of all Ukrainians and were therefore as implacably anti-Russian as they were hostile to Austria. ('Greek-Catholic' implies a Greek Orthodox rite but a commitment to the ecclesiastical laws of Rome.)

The Prussian part of historical Poland consisted of the Grand Duchy of Posen and Western Prussia and was the most heavily industrialized, the most affluent and most 'middle-class' of the three parts of Poland. (In 1921, following the restoration of an independent Polish state, the number of people over the age of ten who could not read or write was 4.2 per cent in the former Prussian voivodeships, whereas the national average was 33.1 per cent. Ten years later 60.6 per cent of the entire Polish population capable of working was employed in agriculture, whereas in Posen that figure was under 50 per cent.) The Poles were represented by their own party in the Prussian Chamber of Deputies as well as in the German Reichstag, and there were many family ties between the Prussian aristocracy and its Polish counterpart. But Berlin politicians had been increasingly eager to Germanize Poland since the 1880s, placing greater pressure not only on the Polish language but also on major landowners in Poland. There could be no question of the Poles growing closer to the German Reich, at least if we ignore those Polish workers who had emigrated to the Ruhr Basin.

The part of Poland that had been incorporated into the Russian Empire was divided into two very different regions: the historical Eastern Marches, which were inhabited for the most part by Lithuanian, White Russian and Ukrainian peasants, and the Kingdom of Poland that had been created in 1815 in the wake of the Congress of Vienna and that was inhabited in the main by ethnic Poles, with smaller minorities of Germans, Jews, Lithuanians and Ukrainians. The Eastern Marches had been exposed to a systematic policy of Russification since the 1860s, Congress Poland since the mid-1880s, and it was only with the Russian Revolution of 1905 that the policy became less extreme. In the wake of the region's industrialization, a powerful workers' movement had arisen, more especially in the area around Warsaw and Lodz. This movement was made up of two different parties: the first, strident in its Polish nationalism, was the Polish Socialist Party under Józef Piłsudski, while the second, far more internationalist in character, was the Social Democratic Party of the Kingdom of Poland and Lithuania, the party of Rosa Luxemburg and, following her move to Germany in 1899, of Feliks Dzierżyński. This second-named party exerted a powerful influence on the left wing of the first-named party. The Polish Social Democratic Party worked closely with the right wing of the Polish Socialist Party in Galicia and Silesia under Ignacy Daszyński. The Polish Social Democratic Party had considerable weight within the Cisleithanian Social Democratic movement.

In the bourgeois camp, the most important group was the Democratic League that had been formed in 1886 and six years later was turned into the National League by the young Roman Dmowski, who saw Germany as the true enemy of Polish aspirations. What was needed, in his view, was reconciliation between Poland and Russia. Piłsudski was a member of the lower Polish aristocracy from the region around Vilnius and belonged to the 'Jagiellonian' tradition of a great Polish-Lithuanian federation similar to the one that had existed before the first partition of Poland in 1772. Dmowski, conversely, represented the 'Piastic' school of thought that wanted to take up and develop the ostensible heritage of the Polish-Silesian family of rulers and expand Poland to the west, at the expense of Germany.

The National Democratic Party, or Endecja, that Dmowski founded after the 1905 Revolution and which proved extremely successful in the elections to the Duma that were held the following year, was opposed not only to Germany but also to the Jews, who were accused of dominating the urban crafts and in that way preventing a healthy Polish middle class from evolving. They were additionally at odds with the Socialists, the enemies of private property and hence of bourgeois order. The increase in authoritarianism in tsarist Russia after 1905 led many disillusioned National Democrats to break with Dmowski's party and join Piłsudski, who in the meantime had begun to organize a movement for Polish independence that went far beyond the programme of the Polish Socialist Party.

Writing about Russian Poland, the German historian Hans Roos has described the internal political fronts: 'An anti-Russian camp was confronted by an anti-German one; a socialist intelligentsia by a *bourgeois* group; a group aiming at independence by one aiming at autonomy; a revolutionary one by one favouring legal methods.'[74] In Galicia the contrast between the National Democrats and the Socialists was no less pronounced than in Russian Poland. But there was a third force here in the form of the Kraków school that sought closer cooperation with the most moderate of the partitioning powers, Austria. The younger adherents of this movement in particular regarded Galicia as a 'Polish Piedmont': in the event of a war between Russia and Austria-Hungary, which in the light of the growing conflicts between them seemed a distinct possibility, Galicia was to play a role in the struggle for Polish independence similar to the one taken by the Kingdom of Sardinia-Piedmont in the war of Italian unification. Piłsudski likewise placed his hopes in a war between the partitioning powers. As early as June 1914, he had revealed remarkable foresight in predicting that in the event of such a conflict the Central Powers would first defeat Russia, after which the Western Powers would defeat the Central Powers. Piłsudski was fifty-six when he made this prediction. As Roos puts it, the supporters of the idea of a Polish state

> should therefore first ally themselves with the Central Powers, and then, when the change in fortunes occurred, go over to the West. [. . .] For him August 1914 was the answer to the prayer which the famous poet Adam Mickiewicz [. . .] had once addressed to God for a universal war to free the oppressed Poles.[75]

In terms of Poland's future course, two of the partitioning powers entered the First World War with no clear aims. In August 1914 the German chancellor, Theobald von Bethmann Hollweg, drew up plans for a formally independent Congress Poland that would none the less be closely allied to Germany, while the Russian government hesitated to back Dmowski's programme and agree to a Congress Poland bound to Russia and enlarged to include Galicia and the German provinces in the east. Only Austria-Hungary already had a clear idea of what it wanted at the start of the war, namely, the union of Galicia and Congress Poland, which would then become a crown land of the Habsburg Empire. In Berlin, where the Baltic states were a matter of greater concern than Poland, the 'Austro-Polish' solution for a time enjoyed some support, but the military successes of the Germans and the defeat of the Austrians quickly led the government in Berlin to turn its back on this model. As we have already had occasion to remark, the German governor general in Warsaw and his Austrian counterpart in Lublin declared the Kingdom of Poland to be a constitutional monarchy on 5 November 1916. Essentially, this consisted of Congress Poland. Politically, economically and militarily, it was a puppet state dependent on the Central Powers.

Among Polish politicians, 'passivists' such as Dmowski were ranged against activists such as Piłsudski after 1914. Even the former group became active when it seemed likely that the Central Powers would be defeated, whereas the latter were determined from the outset to become involved in the war in order to defend Poland's interests. Militarily speaking, Piłsudski was self-taught. On 6 August 1914 he crossed the border into Congress Poland to the north-east of Kraków with a small army of volunteers but was unable to achieve anything either politically or militarily. A week later an Austrian ultimatum persuaded him to submit to the newly formed Supreme National Committee in Kraków.

Piłsudski's Western Legion of Polish volunteers was able to report a number of impressive military victories in the winter of 1914/15 and in the spring of 1915. The previous autumn he had established an underground movement, the Polish Military Organization, with the help of some friendly officers in Warsaw. By the autumn of 1916 his legion numbered around 1,000 officers and some 20,000 men. He refused to see it turned into a Polish Auxiliary Corps of the Central Powers and when this move went ahead in spite of his protestations, he resigned as its commander in chief. In January 1917 he decided to join the provisional State Council convened by the German governor general, Hans Hartwig von Beseler, and to take over the portfolio of military affairs. He had no intention of submitting to Germany's leaders but wanted to strengthen Poland's military might to the point where, following Russia's anticipated defeat, Poland could join the Western Powers in overthrowing the Central Powers.

For Poland, too, the Russian Revolution of February 1917 proved to be an important turning point. On 30 March 1917 the Provisional Government in Petrograd declared its support for an independent Poland embracing all the regions inhabited by Poles and united with Russia in a free military union. In early June, in the wake of the intended federalization of the Russian Empire, the Provisional Government decided to incorporate all non-Russian soldiers in the Russian armed forces into national units. The newly formed Supreme Polish Army Committee immediately gained the support of the National Democrats, whom Dmowski had in the meantime persuaded to work closely with the Western Powers. Dmowski travelled to London in early 1916 in order to enlist the support of the Western Allies for his ideas for an independent Poland enlarged at Germany's expense. In Lausanne in August 1917 he formed the Polish National Committee as a government in exile and placed himself at its head. The internationally acclaimed pianist Ignacy Jan Paderewski promoted Dmowski's ideas in the United States, appealing personally to Woodrow Wilson and to the latter's closest advisers.

For a time the Polish Socialist Party and Polish Military Organization cooperated with the Warsaw State Council but in early May 1917 they joined the opposition and by June were in open conflict with the Central Powers. At the same time Piłsudski formed an alliance between his own close supporters and the Polish Socialist Party and the peasants' People's Party, naming his new party the Democratic League. On 24 July 1917 he resigned from the provisional State Council and instructed those of his volunteers in the Polish Auxiliary Corps who were loyal to him to refuse to swear an oath of allegiance to the German Kaiser. Some 4,000 out of 6,500 legionaries respected his wishes, as did 164 of their 275 officers. All were immediately interned by the German occupying power. Piłsudski himself was arrested on 22 July and taken to the Prussian fortress at Magdeburg, where he remained until early November 1918, unable to influence political events in Poland. But his enforced absence left his political authority unaffected, and internment helped, rather, to turn him into a national hero of positively mythical dimensions.

Shortly after Piłsudski's arrest, the governments in Berlin and Vienna decided to give the Kingdom of Poland a provisional head in the form of a Regency Council, a development accelerated by the demonstrative resignation of the State Council on 25 August 1917 in protest at the way in which its workings were constantly overseen and hampered by the occupying forces. On 12 September the two Kaisers, Wilhelm II and Karl, jointly introduced a provisional constitution, or patent, under the terms of which legislation, the dispensation of justice and all administrative matters were largely placed in Polish hands. On 27 October, a three-man Regency Council was appointed, made up of the archbishop of Warsaw, Aleksander Kakowski, the mayor of Warsaw, Prince Zdzisław Lubomirski, and the landowner Józef Ostrowski. On 7 December a Polish government was installed under the premiership of the lawyer Jan Kucharzewski.

The Kingdom of Poland had barely become an autonomous state when the second Russian Revolution of 1917 altered the international situation in an altogether radical way. The Bolsheviks' seizure of power dashed the hopes of the 'passivists' that Russia would continue to work alongside the Western Powers and help defeat the Central Powers. As part of the moves to dispossess all the major landowners, Polish landowners in the Eastern Marches likewise lost their estates. The First Polish Corps that was stationed there under General Józef Dowbor-Muśnicki took up arms against the Bolsheviks in order to protect Polish possessions both in the countryside and in the towns and cities. In January 1918 the fortress at Bobruisk fell into the hands of the Polish units that were, objectively speaking, the allies of the Central Powers at this time. The city of Minsk fell to them in February. The National Democrats likewise switched sides, and one of their most prominent representatives, Jan Stecki, became foreign minister in Kucharzewski's government. Hans Roos has described the influence of Russian events on Poland in the following terms: 'If the February revolution had alienated the Polish left-wing parties from the policy of the Central Powers, the October revolution brought considerable numbers of the right-wing closer to the occupation authorities and the Government set up by them.'[76]

But this large measure of agreement between Poland and the Central Powers proved to be of short duration. On 9 February 1918 Germany and Austria-Hungary signed a separate peace treaty with the Ukraine, granting the latter all those regions that were largely settled by Ukrainians, including the Chelm region, which was a part of Congress Poland. A week later the Lithuanian Regional Council installed by the German Supreme Command in the East proclaimed an independent Lithuanian state that was officially recognized by the Reichstag on 23 March. In this way the Germans were able to prevent a restitution of the old Lithuanian-Polish union, or 'Jagiellonian' Poland, desired by Piłsudski and his supporters and latterly also by Dmowski's National Democrats. Poles of all shades of opinion were particularly unhappy at the fact that Vilnius, a city largely inhabited by Poles, and the eastern half of Galicia, with its Polish and Ukrainian populations, were not a part of the new Polish state. On 14 February 1918 the Regency Council protested at the new division of Poland, and Kucharzewski's government resigned, as did the Austrian governor general in Lublin, Count Stanislaus Maria von Szeptycki.

But there was no open breach between Poland and the Central Powers. On 4 April a new government was formed in Warsaw under the Galician lawyer and economist Jan Steczkowski and Prince Janusz Radziwiłł, who ran the Political Department. What united their government with the occupying forces was their common interest in resisting the onrush of Bolshevism, although such an 'alliance' was highly controversial in Poland, where the Socialists, and especially the left wing of the Polish Socialist Party, were sympathetic towards Lenin and his party. And so the left boycotted the (indirect) elections to the State Council in June. (Only some of its members were elected by the regional and municipal councils, the others being nominated by the Regency Council.)

By this stage of the war, few Poles still believed that the Central Powers might win, and the military developments of August 1918 dispelled any remaining doubts. At the end of September an army of volunteers in France under the command of General Józef Haller and comprising around 20,000 men was recognized by a Franco-Polish military convention as an Allied army. On 8 October Roman Dmowski, acting on behalf of the Polish National Committee which the Allies had not previously recognized as a government in exile, submitted to Woodrow Wilson a memorandum proposing the formation of an independent Polish republic as a 'buttress against the German drive towards the east'.[77] The new Polish state would include not only Congress Poland but also Posen, West Prussia, Upper Silesia and parts of East Prussia, in the south, Galicia and the small Silesian duchy of Teschen (Polish Cieszyn, Czech Těšin), which was partly Polish-speaking, partly Czech-speaking, and in the east large tracts of the historical Grand Duchy of Lithuania and Western Ukraine. The previous day, and without seeking the consent of the two governors general, the Regency Council had issued an appeal to the Polish people, invoking the right of self-determination of all nations proclaimed by Woodrow Wilson and announcing the formation of an all-party government and elections for a constituent national assembly.

Events then came thick and fast. On 12 October, in an attempt to pre-empt a feared insurrection by the Polish Military Organization, the Regency Council put the Polish Defence Force under its own authority, a force that until then had been under the control of the German governor general, and also called for volunteers for this now purely Polish army. On the 26th a cabinet was formed that was made up for the most part of National Democrats and that was to offer the still interned Piłsudski the post of minister of war. The following day a Polish Liquidation Commission was established in Kraków on the basis of Kaiser Karl's 'People's Manifesto'. Made up of Socialists, National Democrats and members of the Peasants' Party, it was effectively the government of Western Galicia. In L'viv and eastern Galicia, a Ukrainian National Council assumed power on 30 October and 1 November respectively, in each case with the help of Ukrainian rifle clubs. Having failed in its attempt to overthrow the Regency Council, the new Warsaw government was forced to resign. On the night of 6/7 November, the Polish Military Organization mounted a coup in Lublin under the command of Edward Rydz-Śmigły, one of Piłsudski's most loyal supporters. The following day a Provisional People's Government of the Polish Republic was formed under the Galician Socialist leader Ignacy Daszyński, while Rydz-Śmigły was appointed commander of all the Polish troops. The Regency Council was declared null and void.

Two days later, on 9 November, Józef Piłsudski was released from prison on the basis of orders issued by the last imperial government in the person of Prince Max of Baden. He arrived in Warsaw by special train on the morning of the 10th, and on the 11th declared the date on which the new state was founded. The Regency Council placed him in charge of the army, entrusting him with political power on the 14th. It was the Council's final official action before its resignation. In order to avoid any conflict with the government in Lublin, the 'chief of state' – a title last borne by Tadeusz Kościuszko during the 1794 uprising – named Daszyński his prime minister, only to replace him on the 17th by a more moderate Socialist, Jedrzej Moraczewski, who formed a government of Socialists and members of the Peasants' Party. The move was designed to silence protests from the right. A joint decree by the chief of state and the government on 22 November, delimiting their respective areas of competence, completed the process of creating the new state.

In November 1918 it was still completely unclear where the frontiers of the new Poland would lie. What mattered for the present was that for the first time since the third partition of Poland on 3 January 1795, there was again an independent Polish state, a state that had not existed for almost 124 years. All three partitioning powers – Russia, Prussia and Austria – were losers in the First World War. Their defeat was necessary in order to make good, as far as possible, the injustices brought about by the partitions of 1772, 1792 and 1795. A world war was the precondition for Poland's national liberation: Polish patriots from Mickiewicz to Piłsudski were convinced of this connection. The First World War had not started because of Poland, but its outcome represented an example of poetic justice for the country. Poles regained their freedom, a freedom for which they had fought in vain, not only under Napoleon but in the insurrections of 1830/31, 1848 and 1863. If there can ever be a triumph of historical nemesis, then Poland witnessed it in November 1918.

Trust Gambled Away and Violence Unleashed: The Legacy of the First World War

At least sixty-five million soldiers were mobilized; 8.5 million were killed and more than twenty-one million wounded. There were also 7.8 million prisoners of war and missing persons, and more than five million civilian fatalities in Europe, not including Russia. By the time that the First World War came to an end with the ceasefire agreed at Compiègne on 11 November 1918, the victors were no less profoundly affected than the nations that had been defeated. 'La Grande Guerre', or the 'Great War', as the First World War continues to be called in France and Great Britain, had proved to be very different from any of the wars that had been fought in Europe in the nineteenth century. Between 1914 and 1918 the civilian population had suffered far more than in the struggles to unify either Italy or Germany between 1859 and 1871. According to the latest research, it remains unclear whether famine and wartime privations were the immediate cause of the pandemic of 'Spanish flu' that killed between twenty-five and fifty million civilians and soldiers between 1918 and 1923.

The First World War was the first in which human beings were destroyed anonymously and in vast numbers by the resources of modern technology: flamethrowers and mustard gas, torpedoes launched from submarines and bombs dropped from aircraft. But most victims were killed by machine guns, which had first been used in the American Civil War between 1861 and 1865 and afterwards in the colonial wars in Africa. The horror of automatic weapons continued to haunt the survivors no less than the fascination of what massed resources and technology were capable of achieving when allowed to strip away the veneer of civilization and unleash hitherto unknown forces.

There was not just one experience of war, but several. Soldiers had a different experience from civilians; those who served on the front reported different reactions from those who served behind the lines; academics responded differently from 'ordinary' people; men differently from women; women who worked in factories and offices in place of their menfolk serving in the armed forces differently from women who were not in gainful employment; and adults, finally, reacted differently from adolescents and children. And the way in which people perceived the war and assessed it retrospectively depended also on their own political standpoint. Those who had refused to be carried along on the initial tide of enthusiasm or who in the course of the war had come to oppose it could in the end adopt the most radical of left-wing positions and respond to the war with the civil war necessary to remove the capitalist social order that was ostensibly to blame for the 'imperialist' war. Those who accepted the war as a necessity and who continued to hold the view that their own country was in the right were scarcely willing to accept defeat as definitive: for them, peace could only be an interim stage before the next armed conflict erupted between nations. This was the position of the extreme right and, like that of the extreme left, it was a minority view in 1918. In every country, the vast majority had had enough of war without, however, converting to pacifism as a point of principle. How lasting the peace would be depended above all on how just or unjust it was felt to be.

Nations such as the Poles, Finns and Czechs who owe their longed-for national independence to the First World War naturally look back on it with feelings markedly different from those of the Germans, French and British, none of whom can forget the terrible mass killings on the battlefields of Flanders and northern France and who know that two decades later the First World War was to be followed by a second global conflict. The famous remark of the American historian and diplomat George F. Kennan, who referred to the First World War as '*the* great seminal catastrophe' of the twentieth century, reflects the dominant view of those countries that made up the Central and Western Powers. But there is no single phrase that represents a consensus view in Europe of the present day.

The longer the war lasted, the less the parliaments of the period enjoyed the trust of the broad mass of voters, the only exceptions being the lower house in Great Britain and the United States Congress. In most of the countries involved in the war the elected assemblies lost influence after 1914. The Austrian Reichsrat was unable to meet between March 1914 and May 1917; the French Chamber of Deputies met only in private until the end of 1917; and the Italian Chamber met only rarely and was in any case denied control of the way in which the resources it sanctioned were used: there were no longer any budgetary debates. And in Germany the concentration of executive power – especially the military power that was vested in the army's high command – did little to inspire confidence in the state and its institutions. The authorities were held responsible for shortages in foodstuffs, for inflation and for the black market; omnipresent censorship encouraged a belief in rumours; and even more than in peacetime the judiciary had to contend with the suspicion that in the eyes of the law not everyone was equal any longer.

In the longer term, one of the biggest dangers was the undermining of faith in the stability of the world's currencies. Public debt mounted inexorably in all the countries fighting the war, and the Western Powers in Europe were able to finance their war effort only with war loans from the United States. (Concern over repayment of these loans must have been one of the reasons why Woodrow Wilson's decision to enter the war proved so uncontentious at home.) In the expectation that they would be victorious, all states took out war loans with their citizens, particularly Germany. Even as early as August 1914 the Reichsbank was issuing treasury bonds and bills – purely financial transactions like commercial bills of exchange and, like these, used together with gold to cover the Reichsmark. From then on there was effectively no limit on how much money the Reichsbank could create: the country's war loans could have been repaid only by reparations by the country's enemies. The Austro-Hungarian Bank likewise contributed to the country's inflation by issuing huge numbers of banknotes.

Everywhere countries were turning their backs on the monetary systems of the pre-war period. In the words of the German economic historian Wolfram Fischer:

> The gold standard, with its legally fixed parities, had provided stable conditions for private finance. These were now lost. In terms of a country's domestic economy, people had to get used to increasing rates of inflation, and in foreign trade they had to accept foreign exchange controls and allocations and even import and export bans. At the very start of the war most countries suspended their central banks' obligation to redeem gold – only Great Britain retained this obligation, at least on a formal level, while making things more difficult for its citizens. They also banned the export of gold – although, once again, there was no such ban in Britain, all such dealings came to a virtual end. In France such exports were allowed only in exceptional circumstances until July 1915. [...] Foreign trade, which prior to the war had lain entirely in the hands of private firms, increasingly became a matter of international agreements, especially of loan agreements that no longer involved private bankers as creditors but which were reached with central banks and state treasuries. Here Britain led the way, later followed above all by America. In this way the international loan business passed from private into public hands and was politicized in the process, a development that was to have considerable implications after the war.[78]

The nationalization of foreign trade was in no small measure a result of the dramatic shift in international trade routes caused by the British naval blockade and the German U-boat war. As such, it was merely a particularly crass example of a phenomenon described by the Marxist thinker Rudolf Hilferding as 'organized capitalism'. Hilferding was born in Vienna in 1877, becoming editor in chief of the Berlin Social Democratic newspaper *Vorwärts* in 1907. It was in 1910, in his book *Finance Capital*, that he first developed his ideas on the way in which a mere handful of banks dominated industry, which was organized along the lines of a monopoly. In 1915 he took these ideas a stage further, arguing that 'the tremendous increase in the power of the state' that had been produced by finance capital and its policies tended 'to mitigate the anarchy of production' and contained within it

> the seeds for a transformation of an anarchically capitalist economic order into one marked by organized capitalism. [. . .] Instead of socialism, it seems possible to have a society in which the economy is organized not democratically but powerfully, a society at the head of which would be the combined forces of capitalist monopolies and of the state, under which the working masses would be active as the civil servants of production structured according to a particular hierarchy. Instead of the defeat of capitalist society by socialism we would have a society of organized capitalism better suited to meeting the immediate needs of the different social classes.[79]

In Hilferding's view this development gave capitalism a chance of survival and could even have provided an alternative to socialism. Nor was this necessarily the same as the downfall of the proletariat. To the extent that the proletariat had organized itself and learnt to fight for its own concerns, it had altered the face of capitalism and made it more bearable: 'The counterrevolutionary effects of the workers' movement weakened the revolutionary tendencies of capitalism.'[80] Although the transition to a qualitatively new socialist society remained a task for politicians, the fact that the workers' movement had made it impossible for capitalism to commit its worst excesses and impoverish the population clearly removed all the essential preconditions for a revolutionary transformation of society in the spirit of Marx and Lenin. Indeed, Hilferding's remarkably optimistic analysis could be taken to mean that the rights that the workers had acquired by means of their class struggle increased the prospects of an evolutionary realization of socialism.

Hilferding's 'organized capitalism' was described by his enemies in less flattering terms as 'state socialism', 'wartime socialism' or simply 'socialism'. In every country involved in the war, including even the most liberal, the state interfered in the economic life of the nation with increasing importunity after 1914, regulating and organizing it in ways not seen until then. The British Defence of the Realm Act of August 1914, the establishment of a Department for Wartime Raw Materials at the Prussian Ministry of War under the leadership of Walther Rathenau, the president of AEG, that same month, the formation of wartime industrial committees in Russia in May 1915, the establishment of a State Secretariat for Weapons and Munitions under General Alfredo Dallolio in Italy in May 1915, which two years later became a full Ministry, and the creation of the American War Industries Board in July 1917 are only a few examples of the way in which state and industry grew closer to one another during the war years. Not only did state bodies influence business undertakings, but the latter in turn left their mark on political decisions.

The organized workforce also became involved in the wartime economy: in France, for example, the socialist Albert Thomas was appointed secretary of state for artillery and munitions in May 1915, becoming armaments minister in December 1916, while in Germany a similar development stemmed from the enactment of the Patriotic Auxiliary Service Law in December 1916. The relations between trade unions and the state also proved reciprocal, although labour was invariably subordinated to the demands of the wartime economy. (These priorities were especially clear in France, where the industrialist Louis Loucheur replaced Albert Thomas as armaments minister in September 1917, after the Socialists had turned their back on government.) When Hilferding committed his thoughts to paper in 1915, it was still unclear which elements of this 'state socialism' or 'organized capitalism' would survive the war, and it was also extremely doubtful if state control of the economy and society, as practised during the war, would make capitalism less prone to periods of crisis than had been the case prior to 1914, even though Hilferding and many other Social Democrats expected to see improvements in this regard.

Of all the experiences of the war years, arguably the most shocking was the realization that the accustomed norms of bourgeois life so quickly lost their validity. The killing of thousands of Belgian civilians and the destruction of medieval Louvain by German soldiers in the late summer and early autumn of 1914, the murder of at least 1,000 Serbian civilians by Hungarian troops in September 1914, the first use of poison gas by German troops at Ypres in April 1915, the mass deportation of Poles, Latvians, Lithuanians and Jews by the Russian army and the genocide of the Armenians in the Ottoman Empire in 1915: the number of times that expectations of wartime 'normality' were transgressed was legion.

For many 'civilized' Europeans, the atrocities committed during the two Balkan Wars of 1912–13 still seemed specifically Balkan or oriental, but in 1914 it became clear that even nations that had contributed to the Age of Enlightenment were capable of unspeakably barbaric acts in waging war on their fellow Europeans, acts hitherto visited only on colonial nations. In November 1914, fifteen months before he was killed at Verdun on 4 March 1916, the German Expressionist painter Franz Marc wrote an essay to which he gave the title 'Secret Europe'. For him, the claims made for the war by nationalists in every country were no more than a tissue of lies. He, too, believed that the war was a historical necessity, but he was also convinced that it had a deeper meaning, a meaning hidden from its main actors:

In this war it is not – in spite of what is written in the newspapers and notwithstanding all that our politicians tell us – the Central Powers that are fighting an external enemy, nor even is one race at war with another. Rather, this great war is a *European civil war, a war with the inner, invisible enemy of the European spirit.*[81]

But this war had to be fought not just by Europeans – and this was true well before the United States of America entered the conflict. The great colonial nations deployed troops brought to Europe from across the seas: France, in particular, drew heavily on soldiers from North Africa, with 175,000 coming from Algeria alone. (Algeria, it is true, was not an actual colony but a part of the motherland.) Great Britain's army was strengthened by 500,000 Canadians, 332,000 Australians and 112,000 New Zealanders, most of them volunteers of British extraction. On all the fronts there were 1.5 million members of the Indian volunteer army, together with 90,000 Chinese recruits from Weihai who were forced to dig trenches in France for the Allies. Equally unwillingly, countless black African porters had to serve in the army. Of these, around 100,000 are believed to have been killed in the fighting in German East Africa.

But the most extreme eruption of violence in Continental Europe after 1917 was the Russian civil war, which would not have been possible at all without the First World War and which in many respects represented its continuation with only partly different means. The tendency to think in the categories of friend and foe, of self-assertion and destruction, was now directed first and foremost at an internal enemy, which it generally required little effort to make objectively complicit with the external enemy. Nor was it only in Russia that a war between nations turned into an internal civil war, for such a development became a sign of the times, a hallmark of the era that began with the signing of the armistice at Compiègne on 11 November 1918.

From the Armistice to the World Economic Crisis: 1918–33

The Pace of Revolution Slows: Germany on the Way to the Weimar Republic

TOWARDS THE END of the First World War, Europe underwent three different kinds of upheaval. First, there was the nationalist, revolutionary break-up of three multiracial states, namely, the Russian, Habsburg and Ottoman Empires, of which only the first was to be reborn in a radically altered form as the Union of Socialist Soviet Republics. Second, there were the socio-revolutionary upheavals, of which only that of the Bolsheviks was to prove enduring. And, third, there was the revolutionary reconstitution of existing states that made the change from a monarchy to a republic while retaining their existing social order.

The third type of upheaval, involving a mere change of the state's form, was felt only by Germany. From the outset it was clear that the Majority Social Democrats, the principal force for change here, were keen to avoid a civil war of the kind seen in Bolshevik Russia. When they spearheaded the revolutionary movement, Friedrich Ebert's Social Democrats remained an established party: it's leaders leapt aboard a runaway train and brought it under control. If the Social Democrats had behaved any differently at that time, they would have jeopardized their party unity. They acted in the interests of self-preservation and out of a sense of responsibility towards the country as a whole.

The Social Democrats may have been wary of unleashing the forces of revolution, but they had an essential role to play in any democratic revolution in Germany. The fear of chaos and civil war was well founded, as was the concern that if civil war were to break out, the Allies would intervene, turning Germany into the plaything of the victorious powers. It was a danger that could be exorcised only if by far the largest of the workers' parties in Germany could steer the movement along well-ordered lines. The leaders of the Social Democrats were able to avoid their own worst fears, and yet they achieved very little of what they had hoped for. It was a high price that they had to pay for an orderly transition of power, and within only a few months of the events of 9 November 1918 even large sections of the Social Democratic Party found it hard to recognize themselves in the republic that had emerged from all the upheavals that had taken place in Germany.

Dubbed 'the father of revisionism', Eduard Bernstein, who had joined the Independent Socialist Party in 1916 only to return to the bosom of the parent party in December 1918, was one of the first to draw attention to the link between social complexity and fear of the violent overthrow of existing conditions. He published his analysis in 1921 under the title *Die deutsche Revolution, ihr Ursprung, Verlauf und Werk* (The German Revolution: Its Origins, Course and Work), arguing that the more a society is based on the principle of the division of labour, the less it can sustain a radical restructuring. According to Bernstein, a further reason for the political restraint of the weeks after 9 November 1918 lay in the advanced, if partial, democratization of Germany: although the Reich had no government that was responsible to parliament until October 1918, it had none the less had universal equal suffrage for men for half a century.

In 1918, therefore, the only way forward was greater democracy in the form of the extension of the democratic right to vote to women and to individual states right down to the level of district councils and local communities, together with a complete parliamentarization of the existing system of government. The Social Democrats had been the most decisive champions of greater democracy in the Reich and would have lost their credibility if they had deviated from that line in 1918 and returned to the orthodox Marxist slogan of a 'class struggle'. It was for the same reason that the Majority Social Democrats responded with a clear and emphatic 'no' to the call 'All power to the Councils', a call that amounted to a dictatorship of a minority.

The moderate Independent Social Democrats, including Hugo Haase and Wilhelm Dittmann, both of whom were members of the Reichstag, and the theorist Rudolf Hilferding, who was not, had no objections to a Constituent Assembly but wanted to postpone the elections and use the delay to provide democracy with a firmer social and political basis. As Hilferding noted in his party newspaper, *Freiheit*, on 18 November 1918:

> Democracy must be anchored in such a way that reaction is impossible. The administration must not become a playground for counterrevolutionary aspirations. Above all, however, we must prove that we are not just democrats but socialists, too. The implementation of a whole series of important transitional measures is possible without further ado; these must be carried out in order to create positions unassailable by any capitalist countermove.[1]

There were good reasons for adopting a policy aimed at the cautious establishment of a parliamentary democracy, but this did not mean that the elections had to be postponed, and this was the view taken by the vast majority of delegates at the First General Congress of the Workers' and Soldiers' Councils of Germany, which met in Berlin between 16 and 21 December 1918. Of the 514 delegates representing local councils, some 300 Majority Social Democrats and around 100 Independent Socialists were inclined to hold this view. The remainder were either left-wing liberals or independent. Rosa Luxemburg and Karl Liebknecht had not been elected, and the proposal that they be allowed to attend the proceedings in an advisory capacity was rejected by a large majority on the very first day of the congress. The key decision was taken on 19 December: by 344 to 98 votes, the delegates rejected a proposal that the constitution of the Socialist Republic be based on the system of councils. Conversely, the proposal that elections to the Constituent National Assembly be held on 19 January 1919 was adopted by 400 votes to 50. This was even earlier than the Council of People's Deputies had agreed to on 29 November, namely, 16 February.

Two other votes made it clear that the majority of members of the Congress were to the left of the provisional revolutionary government. By a large majority, the Council of People's Deputies was invited to nationalize all those branches of industry, especially mining, that were deemed ready for such a move. And the delegates unanimously approved the 'Hamburg Points' that transferred the military command initially to the Council of People's Deputies and then to the still to be elected Central Council of Workers' and Soldiers' Councils. Moreover, all badges of rank were to be abolished and officers elected by their men. The Soldiers' Councils were to ensure discipline. And a people's militia would replace the standing army.

The Hamburg Points were a reaction to the failings of the People's Delegates. True, they had to work together with the army high command in the interests of a speedy demobilization, but it was by no means necessary to treat the country's military leaders as equal partners in the revolutionary government. If the People's Delegates had not accepted some of the Soldiers' Councils' more moderate demands for reform such as the closure of officers' clubs and the abolition of the need to salute officers when not on duty, it is unlikely that the Hamburg Points would have been adopted at all: some, after all, were positively utopian in character. It would certainly have been difficult to create a republican militia since most workers would have found it profoundly abhorrent to fire on their own comrades in the event of a putsch. But there were no moves on the part of the Council of People's Deputies to create a force loyal to the Republic in spite of demands by a number of younger officers associated with the newly formed Republican Leaders' Union. The guidelines for implementing the Hamburg Points passed by the Council of People's Deputies on 19 January 1919 already bore the imprint of the army high command, and in the law governing the formation of a provisional army that was passed by the National Assembly on 6 March 1919, it was no longer possible to detect any signs of the military resolution of the Congress of Councils.

In terms of the country's nationalization programme, the Majority Social Democrats did not want to act unduly hastily during the difficult transitional period between a wartime and a peacetime economy and, in spite of their fundamental support for the idea of common property, they were willing to leave the Constituent Assembly to decide on the exact nature of the future distribution of property. They were also afraid that the Allies might treat any nationalized industries as a security to be offset against any demands that might be made in terms of reparations. A way out of their dilemma was the formation of a nationalization commission made up of experts from both Social Democratic parties and also from the middle classes. The Council of People's Deputies took this decision on 18 November 1918, and for the present this delayed the need for any more immediate action. By the time that Karl Kautsky's commission had reported in the middle of February 1919 and offered a majority view that coal-mining should be nationalized as a matter of economic and political necessity, the National Assembly had already been elected, but it did not enjoy the sort of majority that would have made it possible to implement the type of policy recommended by the commission.

An even more cautious approach was taken by the Free Trade Unions, which were likewise Social Democratic in their outlook. They reached an agreement with the employers' leaders on 15 November aimed at establishing a Central Cooperative Union of the Industrial and Commercial Employers' and Employees' Federations of Germany. Known as the Stinnes–Legien Agreement after its two main signatories, the leading heavy industrialist Hugo Stinnes and the chairman of the General Commission of Free Trade Unions, Carl Legien, it accepted that salary agreements should be worked out by both unions and management, that an eight-hour day should be regarded as the norm, although this would be a permanent measure, of course, only if all civilized countries were to follow the German example, and that workers' committees be set up in all firms with more than fifty employees. The Central Cooperative Union sprang from a common interest on the part of both trade unions and employers, for neither side wanted the economy to be subjected to the dictates of the state; and both were keen to avoid any kind of 'unofficial' nationalization from below. For the time being, then, there could be no possibility of the kind of change to the distribution of property envisaged by the majority of members of the Congress of Councils.

A final conflict that arose at the Congress of Councils and that was to leave a lasting legacy concerned the division of responsibilities between the Council of People's Deputies and the future Central Council. The Majority Social Democrats proposed that the Council of People's Deputies be given legislative and executive powers and that the Central Council should be entrusted with the role of parliamentary watchdog. Hugo Haase was in full agreement with this proposal. All laws should be submitted to the Central Council, which should also be consulted on the most important ones. But the Independent Social Democrats wanted more: the Central Council should have the full right to accept or reject laws before they were promulgated. The Majority Social Democrats felt that if this were to happen, the Council of People's Deputies would find its ability to act compromised, and so it issued an ultimatum: if the Independents' motion were accepted, then the Majority Social Democratic delegates would resign, together with their secretaries of state and Prussian ministers. Once the Congress had agreed to the term 'parliamentary watchdog' in the sense that Haase intended it, the extreme left wing of the Independent Social Democrats carried out its threat to boycott the elections to the Central Council, with the result that the twenty-seven members who made up the Central Council of the German Socialist Republic were without exception Majority Social Democrats.

The delegates from the Independent Social Democratic Party had thus lost all basis for their work. The 'Berlin Christmas Struggles' led to the formal abandonment of the coalition of 10 November. These struggles were the dramatic high point of a conflict that had been smouldering for two weeks and that concerned payment of the People's Navy Division, a group of revolutionary sailors that had occupied the Stadtschloss in Berlin. The mutinous sailors detained the government on 23 December and 'arrested' Otto Wels, the city's commander, in the Marstall. The ensuing bloody fighting around the Stadtschloss and the Marstall ended with the military defeat of the regular troops and the political defeat of the government. The Independent Social Democrats complained quite rightly that their Majority Social Democrat colleagues had given a blank cheque to the minister of war whom they had called on to help them and in doing so placed Wels's life in jeopardy. When the Central Council none the less approved the actions of Ebert and his party associates on 28 December, the three representatives of the Independent Social Democratic Party, Haase, Dittmann and Barth, took this as their excuse to resign from the Council of People's Deputies.

Two days later the inaugural meeting of the German Communist Party opened in the Prussian House of Representatives. The new party was made up of members from two different schools of thought: on the one hand, there was the Spartacus League, which until then had formed the extreme left wing of the Independent Social Democrats, and the International Communists of Germany, a grouping drawn from left-wing radicals in Hamburg and Bremen. The delegates' mood could hardly have been more radical. Rosa Luxemburg attempted in vain to persuade the conference that it was senseless and even dangerous to agree to a motion committing the party to boycott the elections to the Constituent National Assembly. The delegates passed the motion by 62 votes to 23. There was no escaping the anti-parliamentary thrust of the decision. The Marxist historian Arthur Rosenberg, who left the Communist Party in 1927 after having been an active member for seven years, was quite right to note in 1935 that the resolution was 'indirectly a invitation to indulge in putschist activities of an altogether foolhardy kind'.[2]

The impulse to overthrow existing conditions was strong and it did not take long to find an excuse upon which to act. On 4 January 1919, three days after the Communist Party's inaugural congress had ended, the Prussian prime minister, Paul Hirsch, who was a member of the Majority Social Democrats, dismissed the Berlin chief of police, Emil Eichhorn, who was on the left wing of the Independent Social Democrats. During the Christmas struggles, Eichhorn's force had sided with the mutinous sailors, so that his dismissal was inevitable. No government could entrust the capital's police force to a man who had worked for the overthrow of that government. Left-wing radicals saw this differently. For them, Eichhorn's removal from office was a deliberate challenge, and by the evening of 4 January the executive committee of Berlin's Independent Social Democrats had consulted the Revolutionary Stewards from the city's metal industry and decided to hold a day of action in protest at Eichhorn's dismissal. The corresponding call to workers to demonstrate on the 5th was also signed by the central committee of the German Communist Party.

The number of demonstrators and the belligerence that they evinced went far beyond anything that the organizers had expected, and within hours events had got out of control. The Berlin Independent Socialists, the Communist Party and the Revolutionary Stewards met at the city's police headquarters to discuss what they should do next, but even while they were doing so, armed workers were occupying the printing works of the Social Democratic *Vorwärts* and the left-wing liberal *Berliner Tageblatt* as well as the premises occupied by the publishing houses of Mosse, Ullstein and Scherl, the Büxenstein printing works and Wolff's Telegraph Office. It was rumoured – inaccurately – that all the army regiments in Berlin and even garrisons from out of town, including one from Frankfurt an der Oder, were ready to rise up in armed insurrection, prompting Karl Liebknecht to give the fatal signal: 'Down with the Ebert–Scheidemann government.' In the face of individual protests, the majority of members decided to support the occupation of the newspaper offices, to call out Berlin's workers on a general strike and to bring the government to the point of collapse.

The January uprising in Berlin continues – with questionable legitimacy – to be called the 'Spartacist revolt'. From the outset it was leaderless, but it was not without a purpose. The watchword 'Down with the Ebert–Scheidemann government' meant nothing less than the prevention of elections to the Constituent National Assembly and the establishment of a dictatorship of the proletariat. Even before elections for a Constituent Assembly could be held, the German followers and sympathizers of the Russian Bolsheviks were keen to achieve what the Russians had done in January 1918 when they had brought their country's freely elected Constituent Assembly to a brutal end. In this way the Council of People's Deputies was forced to take up the gauntlet thrown down by the most radical minority of the Berlin proletariat and counter their assault on democracy.

The man responsible for carrying out this task was Gustav Noske, who had joined the Council of People's Deputies as recently as 29 December, the day after the Independent Social Democrats had walked out. He was a trained woodcutter who had later become the Social Democrats' spokesman on naval affairs in the Reichstag. In dealing with the present putsch, he was able to rely on only a handful of replacement battalions in the city, together with sections of the Republican Militia, the Charlottenburg security troops and, finally, the recently formed auxiliaries of the Social Democratic Party. They were joined by the right-wing volunteer corps that was formed on 7 January in response to the government's appeal for volunteers, and, from 8 January, by volunteer troops from the army high command.

It was initially unclear whether there would be any armed fighting at all. At the insistence of the executive committee of the Independent Socialists, the government began negotiations with the rebels on 6 January. The Majority Socialists demanded the immediate evacuation of the newspaper offices occupied by the insurgents, while Karl Kautsky proposed a compromise to the more moderate members of the Independent Socialists: the negotiations were to be deemed a failure if they did not lead to the complete restoration of the freedom of the press. It seems unlikely that those occupying the buildings in question would have been prepared to cross this bridge. Their counter-demand, that Eichhorn be reinstated, was impossible to meet. But the attempt was not even made since the Majority Social Democrats rejected it, as did the Central Council when it met on 7 January. The die had been cast for a violent resolution of the conflict.

Given the situation on the ground, there could be no doubt about the eventual outcome. The demonstrators who had occupied the *Vorwärts* building were driven from the premises on 11 January, and later that same day government troops regained control of the other press offices that had been occupied. Also on 11 January the volunteer corps assembled by the army high command on Noske's instruction and placed under the orders of General Walther von Lüttwitz began to march on Berlin. There was no compelling military reason for them to do so since the uprising had for the most part been put down by then, but Noske and the army high command were eager to make an example in the hope of averting any further attempts at insurrection. Early victims of the volunteer corps' actions were Karl Liebknecht and Rosa Luxemburg, the two most prominent members of the Central Committee of the German Communist Party. They were murdered by Freikorps officers on 15 January.

The uprising in Berlin in January 1919 was an attempted coup by a radical minority. If it had not been put down, civil war would have spread to the whole of Germany and triggered an Allied intervention. But there was no justification for the violent excesses, which opened up an unbridgeable chasm between the moderate and the radical elements in the German workers' movement. The ruling Majority Social Democrats had relied unduly on volunteer troops, most of whom were as keen to foment a civil war as the Communists. The young officers and students who set the tone in these units were not concerned with saving the Republic. What drove them on was their hatred of the 'left'. From their point of view, it was only logical to continue the war that had previously been waged against an external enemy and transfer the fighting to the country's interior. After all, it was the extreme left that they blamed most of all for Germany's defeat.

The suppression of the January revolt opened up the way for elections to the Constituent National Assembly, elections that were contested not only by the two Social Democrat parties but also by several bourgeois parties. The Catholic German Centre Party must have hoped that it could exploit the indignation provoked by the Prussian minister of culture, the Independent Socialist Adolph Hoffmann, with his radically anti-clerical policy for schools. Formerly known as the Bavarian Centre Party, the Bavarian People's Party also took part in the elections. The German Democratic Party inherited the mantle of the left-wing liberal Progressive People's Party, while the German People's Party under its chairman Gustav Stresemann, who had demanded extensive German annexations during the war, took over from the more right-wing National Liberal Party. The Reich's two conservative parties had been the German Conservatives and the Free Conservatives. Together with the various anti-Semitic parties, they formed the German National People's Party, which was even more strident in its advocacy of the restoration of the monarchy than the German People's Party. Among the younger conservatives, especially members of the Prussian aristocracy, there were, of course, many who felt aggrieved that the last Hohenzollern ruler had not fought for his crown but decamped to the Netherlands on 10 November 1918 in order to live in exile.

In the elections on 19 January 1919, when all women over the age of twenty-five were allowed to vote for the first time, the turnout was 83 per cent. (In 1912 it had been 84.9 per cent.) It was above all the Majority Socialists who profited from the introduction of proportional representation, winning 37.9 per cent of the vote – 3.1 per cent more than seven years earlier, when the present two Social Democrat parties had still been a single party. The Independent Socialists won 7.6 per cent of the vote. Of the bourgeois parties, the German Democratic Party was the most successful with 18.5 per cent of the vote – 6.2 per cent more than the Progressive People's Party had polled in 1912. The two Catholic parties, the Centre Party and the Bavarian People's Party, together polled 19.7 per cent. (In 1912 the undivided Centre Party had received 16.4 per cent of the total number of votes cast.) The still relatively disorganized German People's Party had to settle for 4.4 per cent in contrast to the 13.6 per cent polled by the National Liberals in the earlier elections. With 10.3 per cent, the German National People's Party also came out of the elections with a poorer showing than the conservative and anti-Semitic parties, which in 1912 had polled 15.1 per cent of the total. Support for those parties that still championed the monarchy was relatively weak, therefore. No doubt this was due in part to the loss of personal esteem already suffered by the Kaiser before 1914 but more especially during the war. The principal beneficiaries of women's suffrage were the German Democratic Party and those parties with strong links to the Church that had previously been most obstinate in resisting the demands of the suffragettes. In the case of Protestant women, especially in the German territories to the east of the Elbe, it was the German Nationals who benefited, whereas in the case of Catholic women, it was the Centre Party and the Bavarian People's Party.

All the decisions affecting the task of laying the foundations of the German Republic were taken in Weimar between February and August 1919. A city known popularly as a 'Temple of the Muses', Weimar was felt to be safer than Berlin, which was wracked by unrest. And the principal actors hoped that as the epitome of German classicism, it would meet with a positive response abroad if it became the meeting place of the National Assembly. On 6 February 1919, Friedrich Ebert addressed the National Assembly in his capacity as the former chairman of the Council of People's Deputies and submitted a report in which he explained that he and his colleagues were 'the bankruptcy trustees of the old regime'.[3] This was both honest and apt. If the ruling Social Democrats had felt that they were the founding fathers of a democracy, they would undoubtedly have preserved less of the old regime and changed far more of it. Their scope for action was limited, but not as restricted as they thought. They could have shown more self-assurance in their dealings with the military and with senior civil servants and they could have ensured that obvious opponents of the new state did not remain in key positions, as was the case above all in Prussia in every area of the administration right down to the level of the regional councils.

Even as recently as November 1918 it was by no means certain that Prussia would survive as a state. In the Catholic Rhineland there was a strong desire to break free from the former Hohenzollern state – and also from the Reich. The new secretary of state at the Ministry of the Interior was the left-wing liberal constitutional lawyer Hugo Preuß, who, asked by the Council of People's Deputies to draw up a new constitution for the Reich, expressed the wish to break up Prussia into several smaller states 'in order to prevent one state from becoming predominant and producing a new dualism' between Prussia and the Reich. Among the most vocal detractors of this proposal were the ruling Prussian Social Democrats headed by the prime minister, Paul Hirsch. Their arguments were compelling: only a united Prussia could form a buffer between east and west and effectively resist, on the one hand, the secessionist aspirations of the Rhineland that were being encouraged by France and, on the other, the pressure exerted by Poland on East Prussia. Only in this way was it possible to preserve the unity of the Reich and prevent any further politicization of the denominational differences between Protestants and Catholics. In the end, it was the 'pro-Prussians' who prevailed, much to the relief not only of the Prussian Social Democrats but also of their most bitter opponents, the Prussian conservatives and the latter's most reliable supporters, the local major landowners.

After November 1918 there could no longer be any serious question of dividing up the estates of larger landowners in favour of farmers and agricultural workers who owned little or no land since the revolutionary governments in Prussia and in the country as a whole had no desire to jeopardize food supplies, which were in any case extremely precarious as a result of the Allies' continuing blockade of Germany. The People's Delegates even allowed landowners to the east of the Elbe to form joint councils made up of larger landowners and farmers, a move that was tantamount to guaranteeing the existing distribution of land in the countryside. Other long-standing elite groups also took advantage of the political restraint of the new government: the judiciary, universities and grammar schools were largely untouched by the revolution. Even in 1918 it was well known that these institutions harboured many opponents of the Republic. But a large-scale political 'purge' would have antagonized the entire middle class, something that the Social Democrats refused to contemplate.

As a result, the elite groupings in the German Empire were able to salvage more of the social bases of their power than was good for the new Republic. For Ebert and his political friends, avoiding civil war was a categorical imperative. This demonstrated their sense of responsibility as clearly as their resultant willingness to work closely with moderate middle-class elements, for this was the only way to create a German democracy. That this would result in a democracy characterized by the legacy of the old authoritarian state and in consequence handicapped in advance was recognized more clearly by moderate Independent Social Democrats like Haase and Hilferding than by Majority Social Democratic practitioners such as Ebert and Scheidemann.

The National Assembly passed Hugo Preuß's law on the new provisional constitution on 10 February, and the following day the delegates elected Friedrich Ebert as the country's provisional president. That same day Ebert asked Philipp Scheidemann to form a government. By the 13th the cabinet, made up of ministers from the Social Democrats, Centre Party and German Democratic Party, was able to begin work. The only member of the cabinet who did not belong to any party was the foreign minister Ulrich von Brockdorff-Rantzau.

In terms of its domestic policies, the government's greatest challenge was the series of strikes that shook Germany to its very foundations during the early months of 1919. They had begun in the Ruhr Valley in late December 1918 and by February 1919 had spread to central Germany. Their aim was the nationalization of the mining industry, although the exact path this process would take was far from clear. The strikes in central Germany ended on 8 March after Scheidemann's government had promised legislation introducing employees' organizations and the nationalization of the coal and potash syndicates. In the

Ruhr Valley the strike turned into a general strike, to which the government responded by sending in troops. The most violent clashes took place in Berlin in early March. On the 9th the new minister for the armed forces, Gustav Noske, gave orders to shoot on sight anyone who was found holding a weapon while fighting government troops. He had no legal backing for his measure, which resulted in the deaths of around one thousand strikers in the city during the March uprising.

The major strikes in the spring of 1919 were part of the second phase of the German revolution, a phase that ended in early May. During this time the radical section of the proletariat tried to use force to bring about the social changes that the first phase had failed to achieve. The results lagged far behind the expectations of the extreme left. The 'nationalization' that took shape and form in a series of laws enacted in March and April 1919 did nothing to change the way in which property was distributed in the coal- and potash-mining industries. The principal achievement of the spring of unrest in 1919 and the only lasting result of this whole period was the highly controversial law of February 1920 governing the creation of factory committees, a move contested by both the right and the extreme left. Works committees, or employee organizations, were introduced in companies with at least twenty employees. Not only did they have a say in hiring and firing workers, they also had far-reaching claims to information about operational practices. This law became the Magna Carta of worker participation and played an important role in turning Germany into a pioneering home of economic democracy.

Another element in the second phase of the German revolution was the creation of the two Munich soviet, or council, republics. The history of the first can be traced back to the murder of the Bavarian prime minister Kurt Eisner on 21 February 1919. He was shot by Count Anton von Arco-Valley, a law student currently on leave from the army, while on his way to the Bavarian parliament, where he was planning to hand in his resignation following the annihilating defeat of his Independent Socialists in the elections on 12 January. His murder resulted in a radicalization of politics that also affected sections of the Majority Socialist Party. On 3 April the Augsburg Councils urged the creation of a council republic for Bavaria, a move prompted by the proclamation of the Hungarian Soviet Republic under Béla Kun, and on the night of 6/7 April the Central Council of the Bavarian Republic under the left-wing Social Democrat Ernst Niekisch responded to this demand. The government of the Majority Social Democrat Johannes Hoffmann, Eisner's successor as prime minister, was declared to be at an end.

The first Munich Soviet Republic was dominated by literati from Schwabing, one of the city's bohemian quarters, and within days had managed to make itself the object of general ridicule. Breaking off diplomatic relations with Germany, sending a message to Lenin informing the latter of the unification of the proletariat in Upper Bavaria and announcing that 'free money' would be issued in order to abolish capitalism – these were only three of the highlights of this short-lived regime, which the Communists dismissed as a sham. On Palm Sunday (13 April) Hoffmann's government, which had in the meantime moved to Bamberg, sent in the Republican Militia to quell the putsch, leading the Communists to side with the 'Red Army' that had been formed by the Central Committee of the Bavarian Republic. Together, they inflicted a serious defeat on the militia. That same evening Eugen Leviné, the Russian leader of the Bavarian Communist Party, assumed control of what was now the second Munich Soviet Republic, a move undertaken without consultation with the party headquarters in Berlin.

The attempt to impose a dictatorship by a small revolutionary clique on a largely agrarian, Catholic and conservative country like Bavaria was doomed from the outset. During the first week of May the 'Red' terror of the Communists was followed by the 'White' terror of the Württemberg Volunteer Corps that at Noske's bidding came to the aid of the legitimate Bavarian government. By the time that the second soviet republic was overthrown on 3 May, there had been 606 fatalities, including thirty-eight government soldiers and 335 civilians. Leviné was indicted for high treason, condemned to death and executed on 5 June 1919.

The fact that Kurt Eisner was a Prussian Jew, that Eugen Leviné and his party colleague Max Levien were east European Jews and that many of the intellectual leaders of the first and second soviet republics, including the writers Ernst Toller, Erich Mühsam and Gustav Landauer, who was murdered by soldiers from the Volunteer Corps, all came from Jewish families gave powerful impetus to what was already a particularly virulent form of anti-Semitism not only in Munich and Bavaria but in the country as a whole. The most gifted and ruthless of these anti-Jewish agitators, Adolf Hitler, began his political career as an informant of the Bavarian Reichswehr's group command. For him, the conditions in post-revolutionary Munich, a city currently traumatized by the experience of two soviet republics, proved seminal: nowhere else would he have found such fertile soil for his slogans.

The impoverished son of a customs inspector from the Austrian town of Braunau am Inn, he had left school with no qualifications and had received no subsequent professional training but earned a pittance painting postcards and doing odd jobs. In May 1913, when he was twenty-four, he had moved from Vienna to Munich in order to avoid having to do military service in the Danube Monarchy but in August 1914 he joined the Bavarian army as a volunteer and worked on the western front as a dispatch runner, rising to the rank of corporal and being awarded the Iron Cross. In September 1919 he joined a radical right-wing organization, the German Workers' Party, which changed its name in February 1920 to the National Socialist German Workers' Party (NSDAP). By then, his anti-Semitic view of the world was already fully formed, as he explained to Adolf Gremlich in June 1919:

For the Jew, everything that makes people strive for higher things, be it religion, socialism or democracy, is merely a means to an end, that end being the satisfaction of his greed for money or domination. In its consequences, its impact is the racial tuberculosis of nations, and this produces the following: anti-Semitism for purely emotional reasons will find its ultimate expression in the form of programs [sic], but the anti-Semitism of reason must inevitably lead to the systematic legal battle to combat and remove those privileges that the Jews, unlike all the other foreigners who live among us, are allowed to enjoy (legislation governing foreigners). There is absolutely no doubt that the ultimate goal of this legislation must be the removal of all Jews. Only a government of national potency is capable of achieving both these aims, not a government of national impotency.[4]

Scheidemann's cabinet met in March – after the street fighting in Berlin and before the first soviet republic was proclaimed in Munich – to discuss the response that Germany would adopt at the forthcoming peace talks to the question of the country's guilt for causing the war. As early as the previous November, the Council of People's Deputies had asked the Independent Social Democrat Karl Kautsky, who was then working as a councillor at the Foreign Office, and the Majority Social Democrat Max Quarck, a councillor in the Department of the Interior, to redact the relevant documents. By the end of March, Kautsky was nearing the completion of his task. In his capacity as president of Germany, Ebert attended the cabinet meeting and recommended that 'the sins of the old regime be condemned in the strongest possible terms'[5] and asked that the new government's position be presented in the form of a memorandum. Most of the ministers present at the meeting agreed with Ebert, whereas the finance minister, Eugen Schiffer of the German Democratic Party, who had been a member of the National Liberals until 1918, warned his colleagues in no uncertain terms not to admit to their guilt, for such an admission would rob the Germans of all their remaining self-respect and allow their enemies to triumph. Scheidemann did not consider it necessary to join in the debate.

By the time that the cabinet returned to the question of Germany's war guilt at its meeting on 18 April 1919, Kautsky's redaction of the relevant documents was already available. It left no doubt that in the crisis in July 1914 the country's leaders had driven Austria-Hungary into war with Serbia and were therefore chiefly to blame for triggering the First World War. Eduard David, the Social Democrat minister without portfolio, spoke out in favour of publication, whereas the justice minister Johannes Bell of the Centre Party opposed it. Scheidemann once again refused to become involved in the debate. In the end he advised his colleagues to refrain from publishing the documents in the shorter term, a recommendation opposed by Eduard David.

Publication would have meant a moral break with the old regime, which is what Ebert demanded, but we can now only speculate on the political impact that such a bold course of action would have had. The nationalist right would have reacted to the admission that Germany was not only complicit in the war but largely responsible for it with an outcry of indignation, while it would have been difficult to claim that the Triple Entente had forced the war on Germany. A public display of self-criticism by the Germans would presumably have strengthened the hand of the forces on the left that were willing to show understanding, but it would scarcely have impressed the government representatives who were advising on the peace treaty in Paris.

But there was another reason why there was no moral break with the Kaiserreich: most Social Democrats were afraid of the reproach that they had betrayed their country and of the critical debate that their policy of a party truce would inevitably entail. Their silence had serious consequences. Left in the dark by Scheidemann's government as to Germany's policies in July 1914, the German public was in no way prepared for the outcome of the Paris deliberations on the Allies' peace terms in early May 1919.

A Blighted New Beginning: Austria and Hungary in 1918/19

The early months of the immediate post-war period were no less turbulent in Austria than they were in Germany. Here the government was made up of Social Democrats, Christian Socialists and Pan-German German Nationalists. Since 30 October 1918 the country's chancellor had been the Social Democrat Karl Renner, one of whose first official actions had been to receive submissions from the regional assemblies, declaring their intention of joining the Republic of German Austria. Following the death on 11 November of Victor Adler, the Social Democrats' long-standing chairman and the country's foreign minister, a new secretary of state was appointed on the 21st in the person of Otto Bauer, a leading voice in Austrian Marxism, a left-wing advocate of the Slav nations' right of self-determination and a vocal supporter of the policy of a union between German Austria and Germany as unanimously agreed to by the Provisional National Assembly at its meeting on the 12th.

On one important point, Austria differed from Germany in that the transitional period between the fall of the monarchy and the election of a new Constituent National Assembly witnessed a fundamental reform of the military. As early as 8 November the Social Democrat Julius Deutsch, a former artillery officer employed in the War Ministry, had proposed the relevant guidelines, which he implemented as soon as he became minister for the army on the 15th. A defence law passed by the Provisional Government on the 18th provided for universal conscription for all men between the ages of eighteen and forty-one. The new defence force also included officers from the Habsburg army who were sympathetic to the Social Democrats, and in 1918/19 these officers played an active and, indeed, decisive role in the fighting in southern Carinthia, an area largely settled by Germans and currently occupied by units of South Slav troops. They were also instrumental in putting down several attempted Communist putsches.

The Communist Party of German Austria was founded on 3 November 1918 with substantial political and financial support from the Bolsheviks and the participation of left-wing radical intellectuals and soldiers returning from Russia, but neither then nor later was the party able to build up a base in the proletariat, with the result that the Social Democrats remained the party of Austrian workers. This state of affairs was due above all to the enforced proro-gation of the Reichsrat between 1914 and 1917: unlike the German Social Democrats, their Austrian counterparts had no possibility of arguing over the approval of war loans. Also in Austria, an organ of the soviet councils survived the elections to the Constituent Assembly in February 1919, when the Central Workers' Council became one of the principal representatives of the Austrian workforce. It was headed by Victor Adler's son Friedrich, who, as we have already noted, shot the prime minister, Karl Stürgkh, in October 1916 in protest at the war and was released from prison on 1 November 1918. Together with Otto Bauer, he set the Austrian Social Democrats on an emphatically left-wing course at odds with the policies not only of an Austrian 'Social Democrat patriot' like Karl Renner but also of the German Social Democrats.

At the time that Austria proclaimed itself a republic on 12 November, it was still far from clear which regions would be a part of German Austria. Earlier that month the Germans in Bohemia and Moravia had tried in their various ways to assert their desire to enter into a union with German Austria. The regions next to the border with Austria wanted to join as the Bohemian Forest Gau and German South Moravia, while regional governments for German Bohemia and the Sudetenland were formed in Reichenberg and Troppau. Passed on 22 November 1918, an Austrian law confirmed German claims to the whole of the self-contained area settled by Germans within the king-doms and regions previously represented by the Reichsrat. On the 14th the Provisional National Assembly elected Tomáš Masaryk in his absence as presi-dent of the Czechoslovak Republic – not until 21 December did he return home from exile. In the meantime the leader of the 'Young Czechs', Karel Kramář, took on the post of prime minister. In December his government sent troops into the Sudetenland. It remained unclear how Vienna's claims to the annexation of the German-speaking parts of Bohemia and Moravia could be implemented in the face of opposition from the new leaders in Prague as well as from the Allies.

The same was true of the demand that German Austria become a part of the German Reich. In Germany itself, the call for a realization of the pan-German idea had widespread support, especially among Social Democrats, who saw themselves as the true heirs and executors of the revolution of 1848–9. When the Austrian ambassador in Berlin, Ludo Hartmann, stated Vienna's wish to join a greater Germany at a conference of the German regions on 25 November, his request, although supported by a unanimous vote on the part of the National Assembly, met with an emphatic rejection from Wilhelm Solf, the secretary of state at the Foreign Office, who had retained his post from the previous administration and who backed up his objection by drawing his audience's attention to the forthcoming peace talks. He received support from the delegates who were present, with Ebert at their head. In his speech to the German National Assembly on 6 February 1919 Ebert was warmly applauded when he welcomed German Austria's wish to become a part of Germany and expressed the hope that the Assembly would invite the future government to enter into negotiations with German Austria as soon as possible with a view to bringing such a union to fruition. Although Solf had retired in December 1918, his objection remained valid: the plans for a Greater Germany could not be allowed to jeopardize the peace talks with the victorious powers.

The elections for the Constituent National Assembly were held on 16 February. The Social Democrats won seventy-seven seats, the Christian Socialists sixty-one and the German Nationalists twenty-six. The Germans living in the Sudetenland were unable to vote and so they organized demonstrations in all their towns and cities on the day when the Constituent Assembly met for the first time, 4 March. Acting on the orders of Kramář's government, the Czechoslovak police responded with particular brutality, even going so far as to fire at demonstrators and killing fifty-two protesters in Kaaden (now Kadaň).

On 14 March the Constituent National Assembly passed two laws concerning the representation of the people and the government that served as a provisional constitution and at the same time repeated its belief that German Austria was a part of the German Reich. The next day the chancellor, Karl Renner, was able to name his new cabinet, which was made up of Social Democrats, Christian Socialists and other ministers who belonged to no particular political party. Among the latter was the eminent economist Joseph Schumpeter as head of the finance department. One of the new government's most pressing tasks was to deradicalize the workers' soviets, with their profound sympathy for the soviet republics that had been proclaimed by Béla Kun in Budapest on 21 March and by the Central Council of the Bavarian Republic in Munich on 6/7 April. An attempted putsch on 17 April triggered by Kun's agents was put down by the army, but it was two Social Democrat politicians who played the biggest part in calming the workers: the chairman of the Central Council of Workers, Friedrich Adler, and Ferdinand Hanusch, who was the minister, or secretary of state, responsible for social administration and who steered through parliament a number of important socio-political laws, including those governing an eight-hour day, the right to time off, the right of wage agreements, a limit on the work that could be undertaken by women and children and at night, health insurance, welfare for the disabled and the creation of chambers of commerce.

As with Austria, so with Hungary, the local Communist Party was for the most part founded by prisoners of war returning from Russia. Among them was Béla Kun, a Jewish journalist who had previously been active in the trade union movement. The Social Democrats joined Mihály Károlyi's coalition government in late October. Károlyi assumed the office of provisional president on 11 January 1919, by which date Hungary had already lost more than half its territory and population following the secession of large areas of land that were mostly settled by South Slavs, Slovaks and Romanians and occupied by troops from neighbouring states. The Entente actively encouraged this development, persuading an embittered Károlyi to throw in his lot with Soviet Russia, resulting in a change of direction in terms of Hungary's foreign and domestic policy. Internally, this meant a transfer of power to the workers. The decisive factor proved to be a note handed to Károlyi by the Allies on 19 March, when the victorious powers demanded a new demarcation line in Transylvania and the creation of a neutral zone there.

In the meantime Kun had succeeded in gaining a considerable number of supporters among workers who were not organized into trade unions and in calling on both them and the country's soldiers to rise up in armed rebellion against the government and the latter's principal bulwark, the Social Democrats. After a number of bloody clashes he was arrested on 21 February 1919, together with several other Communist leaders – not that this prevented him from establishing a party secretariat in his prison cell, a move tolerated by the government he was seeking to overthrow. On 21 March the Social Democrats responded to pressure from Károlyi and the bourgeois parties to work together with the Communists and decided that in order to avoid civil war and the threatening hegemony of the Communists they should agree to Kun's demands for a merger between the two parties as the Hungarian Socialist Party and also to the establishment of a council dictatorship and the formation of a government in which each party would be equally represented. Its nominal head was appointed that same evening in the person of the Social Democrat Alexander Garbai, although the effective leader was the recently released Béla Kun in his role as people's commissioner for foreign affairs. The people's commissioner for education was the young Marxist philosopher György Lukács.

The Bolsheviks, who were then holding their eighth party conference in Moscow, reacted enthusiastically: Kun was their representative, and Hungary the first central European country to follow the Russian example. On 27 May 1919 Lenin wrote to congratulate the Hungarian workers on their success – by this date the new Hungarian regime had been in power for over two months: 'You have set the world an even better example than Soviet Russia by your ability to unite all socialists at one stroke on the platform of genuine proletarian dictatorship.'[6] The Hungarian soviet government had indeed spent the intervening period nationalizing large numbers of industrial concerns and dispossessing major landowners, without, however, redistributing their lands among the peasantry, but allowing their existing owners to administer them on behalf of the state, leading to feelings of rank disaffection among the country's peasants.

On the other hand, the government's emphatically 'national Bolshevik' policies proved popular with most Hungarians, for they aimed to re-establish a Greater Hungary under the banner of a war on western imperialists and on those of Hungary's neighbours that supported them. Suggestions for a peaceful resolution of border conflicts that were made by the British general (and later prime minister of South Africa) Jan Christiaan Smuts in the name of the victorious powers at their meeting in Paris in early April were rejected by Kun. On 20 April the Central Council of Soldiers, Workers and Peasants agreed to wage a defensive war in order to protect the attainments of the proletarian dictatorship and ordered that half the workforce of all companies should take up arms against Czech, Romanian and South Slav troops. In May the Red Army under the command of the Social Democrat delegate Wilhelm Böhm succeeded in defeating Czech units under French command, leading to the temporary capture of large parts of Slovakia.

But this victory exhausted the military strength of the revolutionary army, and in early June a 'White' counter-government was formed in Szeged in southern Hungary, which was then under French military rule. Its leader was Count Gyula Károlyi, a close relative of the former president, with Count Pál Teleki as his foreign minister and Admiral Miklós Horthy, the former commander in chief of the Austro-Hungarian navy, as his minister of war. Romanian troops that had already started to invade southern Hungary in April continued to advance on Budapest during the summer of 1919. Kun appealed to Lenin to attack Romania in order to relieve the pressure on him, but his appeal fell on deaf ears. At the end of July, the Red Army, routed by the Romanians, was disbanded, and on 1 August Kun abandoned the system of councils, inviting the Workers' Council to transfer power to a cabinet made up of moderate trade union leaders and attributing the failure of the proletarian dictatorship to those workers who were not sufficiently revolutionary and who would now have to learn from the cruel dictatorship of the bourgeoisie what it meant to be revolutionary. On stepping down, Kun and a number of his followers left for Austria, where thanks to the mediation of the Social Democrats he was given political asylum.

On 3 August Budapest was occupied by Romanian troops, and the following day the trade union government was toppled by a right-wing group, prompting the government in Szeged to resign in favour of the new bourgeois cabinet. On 5 August a mission from the Entente began work in Budapest, and although it did not officially recognize the new government, it entered into negotiations with Admiral Miklós Horthy, the commander in chief of the national army that had been established in Szeged.

In the middle of November the Allies ordered the Romanian troops to leave Budapest, allowing Horthy's units to march into the city soon afterwards. Over the months that followed, they and a number of volunteer corps officers brought a reign of terror to the city, attacking real and imagined supporters of the old regime, while reserving their most brutal fury for Jews of all political persuasions. More than half of the people's commissars had been Jewish, a state of affairs that lent particular virulence to the anti-Semitism that was in any case widespread in Hungary. The 'Red terror' of the revolutionary tribunals had caused some 120 deaths, whereas around 2,000 men and women fell victim to the terror of the units commanded by Horthy. Another 70,000 individuals were imprisoned or interned. Hungary was not only the sole country in central Europe to see the Communists come to power; it was also the only one to move in the direction of a right-wing authoritarian regime in the wake of the First World War.

The Struggle for Independence: Estonia, Latvia, Lithuania and Finland

The overthrow of the Hungarian Soviet Republic was not the only political setback that the Bolsheviks had to endure in 1919. Following the defeat of the Central Powers, the Council of People's Commissars in Moscow had declared as early as 13 November 1918 that it no longer felt obliged to uphold the terms of the Treaty of Brest-Litovsk. The first nations to appreciate what this meant in practice were the Baltic peoples. In Estonia, which included not only the historical region of Estonia but also northern Livonia, the Maapäev – the regional council formed in the wake of the Russian February Revolution – had declared the country independent on 24 February 1918, only for the country to be overrun by German troops a short time afterwards. Following the fall of the monarchy, Germany recognized Estonia's independence in November 1918, Great Britain and France following suit in March 1919.

Scarcely had German troops left, however, when the Red Army marched into Estonia. A handful of 'Red' Estonian units joined them. With the help of weapons from Finland and the Triple Entente, the Provisional Government of the prime minister, Konstantin Päts, was able to build up an effective national army. The government gained the support of the country's peasants by promising to distribute among them the lands owned by German Balts. By February 1919 the whole of Estonia was rid of its invaders from Soviet Russia.

Latvia at this date comprised the southern part of Livonia, Courland and the region around Dünaburg (now Daugavpils) known as Latgale. Here the Bolsheviks found more support among the peasant population than they had done in Estonia. On 18 January 1918, the Latvian National Council that had been formed at the time of the German occupation proclaimed the independent Republic of Latvia and invited the chairman of the Farmers' Union, Kārlis Ulmanis, to form a government. This was recognized by the Council of People's Deputies in Berlin at the end of November 1918, but from the outset it was placed under intolerable pressure by the local pro-Bolshevik movement and by the Red Army, which marched into Latvia in January 1919 and occupied the capital, Riga. Although Ulmanis was sympathetic to the Entente, he felt obliged to ask for help from a military organization set up by the German Balts and also from a number of German volunteer corps that were operating in the Baltic region with the tacit approval of the victorious powers and that received a promise from Ulmanis's government that if they so desired their dependants would be granted Latvian nationality and be allowed to settle permanently in the country.

But Ulmanis's refusal to allow the German Balts to play a significant role in running the country led to the 'Libau putsch' that was undertaken on 18 April by shock troops from the Baltic Land Defence. Ulmanis's government was deposed and replaced by a government loyal to the German Balts under the nominal leadership of the Latvian pastor Andrievs Niedra. In May the Land Defence recaptured Riga with the help of Latvian and German units. But Ulmanis, who had in the meantime sought protection from the British, was in no mood to quit the political stage, the violence of the Libau putsch having assured him of the national solidarity of the Latvians that he had previously lacked, and at the end of June Latvian troops loyal to him and his government were able to defeat the combined forces of the German volunteer corps and the Baltic Land Defence. An attempt by the German commander, General Rüdiger von der Goltz, to use a counterrevolutionary army of German and Russian volunteers to reverse the situation and to support the White army in the Russian civil war was thwarted in October 1919 by the concerted efforts of Latvian, Lithuanian and Estonian troops supported in turn by an Allied squadron.

Latvia's southern neighbour, Lithuania, had declared its independence in February 1918, a declaration that had had the support of the German occupying power. (Conversely, the June election of the Catholic Duke Wilhelm von Urach as King Mindaugas II did not have the approval of Germany's leaders or of the eastern military command and was reversed by the Lithuanian parliament, the Taryba, in the wake of Germany's defeat.) On 28 October 1918 the Taryba approved a provisional constitution, and on 5 November the philologist and historian Augustinas Voldemaras formed the first Lithuanian government.

The Lithuanian supporters of the Bolsheviks responded on 8 December by establishing a Revolutionary Workers' and Peasants' Government in Dünaberg that was formally recognized two weeks later by Soviet Russia but which did not exercise any real power until the German troops left on 1 January 1919. The official government had in the meantime been reorganized under Mykolas Sleževičius and met at Kaunas (Kovno). The Red Army overran Vilnius and the surrounding area on 5 January and began work on forming the Socialist Republic of Lithuania and White Russia. 'Litbel', as it was known for short, was proclaimed on 27 February 1919.

In the event, Communist rule over even a small part of Lithuania proved to be short-lived. At the end of April Polish units captured the capital without a major struggle, not least because there were more Poles living there than Lithuanians. Kaunas turned down an offer from the Polish prime minister, Józef Piłsudski, to cede Vilnius to Lithuania if the country was willing to enter into a federation with Poland. By August 1919 the Red Army had – with the help of German troops – been driven from those areas that it had occupied in the north-east of the country. In November 1919 the Lithuanian army – by now a fully operational fighting force – defeated anti-Bolshevik Russian troops under the command of the 'White' general Prince Pavel Bermondt-Avalov, which had entered Lithuania from Latvia the previous month. With this there began a period of gradual stabilization for the new state, even though it continued to be governed from the provisional capital Kaunas, rather than from Vilnius.

Like Estonia, Latvia and Lithuania, Finland, too, had been part of the Russian Empire until 1917. Here the local 'Reds' and their Russian supporters had been defeated with German assistance in the civil war of early 1918. From May 1918 the 'Reich administrator' of the new independent Finland was the monarchist Pehr Evind Svinhufvud, while the Conservative government was headed by Juho Kusti Paasikivi. Svinhufvud was intended merely to stand in for a king who would come from Germany. The proposed candidate was Prince Friedrich Karl of Hesse, but he withdrew following Germany's defeat in the war. In the wake of the withdrawal of all German troops, General Mannerheim, who had defeated the 'Reds', became Reich administrator and on 17 June 1919 signed the constitution that turned Finland into a republic with a strong president elected by the people and a government responsible to parliament. The following month, the true father of the Finnish constitution, Kaarlo Juho Ståhlberg, was elected the country's first president. In October 1920 Soviet Russia signed a peace treaty with Finland. It had been preceded by similar treaties with Estonia in February, with Lithuania in July and with Latvia in August 1920.

The East Remains Red: The Russian Civil War and the Foundation of the Third International

If the Bolsheviks had prevailed in the Baltic region, they would have found it much easier to export their particular brand of revolution to central Europe and above all to Germany, but the defeats in Estonia, Latvia and Lithuania caused the Soviet Union serious difficulties, not least because this was not the only major setback that the Bolsheviks had to endure in the area covered by the former Russian Empire during the spring and summer of 1919. Once the Treaty of Brest-Litovsk had been torn up, the Red Army had felt free to march into the eastern Ukraine in December 1918 and to take Kiev the following February. The government of the Ukrainian 'Directorate' under Volodymyr

Vynnychenko that had seized power in December 1918 fled to Podolia, where it organized resistance to the Bolsheviks under the leadership of Symon Petlura. By the summer of 1919 the Red Army had been driven from the Ukraine by units under the 'White' general, Anton Ivanovich Denikin. The following October 'White' units under General Nikolai Nikolayevich Yudenich advanced from the Baltic as far as the gates of Petrograd. The former capital could be held only thanks to Trotsky's iron will and to organized resistance on the part of the city's population. In the south the 'White' units under Denikin and Krasnov advanced as far as Kursk and from there to Orel, so that the road to Tula and Moscow seemed to lie open to them. In the east the opponents of Bolshevism succeeded in advancing almost as far as the Volga under Admiral Kolchak, who since June had been commander in chief of all the 'White' troops.

An additional factor was the intervention of the Western Allies who, following the defeat of the Central Powers, were able to increase the number of their troops operating on Russian soil. In November and December 1918 new units were sent to Murmansk and Vladivostok. Marshal Foch drew up a plan for an anti-Bolshevik 'crusade', and although this was rejected by the Allied Supreme Council in Paris on 27 March 1919, the 'Whites' continued to receive financial and technical support. The Western Powers recognized Kolchak's government in May 1919, several months after he had declared himself the Reich administrator on 18 November 1918. The Allies imposed an economic blockade on Soviet Russia on 10 October 1919, and yet the Bolsheviks' fortunes improved only a short time afterwards when the British fleet failed to intervene in the Gulf of Finland and Yudenich's offensive in the north-west collapsed. His retreat was followed by that of Kolchak, who, under pressure from the Red Army and Bolshevik partisans, was forced back to Irkutsk. Denikin, meanwhile, was driven back in the south, and in the west the Ukraine was recaptured. On 4 January 1920 Kolchak stepped down as Reich administrator, and on the 16th the Allied Supreme Council lifted the economic blockade. Although this did not mean the end of the Russian civil war, the outcome had for the most part already been decided in favour of the 'Reds'.

The Russian civil war was waged by both sides not only with extreme military rigour but also with all the resources of political terror, the only difference being that the 'Red' terror was more systematic than its 'White' counterpart. On 31 August 1918 – a day after Lenin had been seriously injured in an assassination attempt by the social revolutionary Fanny Kaplan – the Bolsheviks' official newspaper, *Pravda*, announced that the time had come 'for the destruction of the bourgeoisie'. On 5 September the 'decree for the Red terror' declared that it was absolutely vital that the Cheka, or secret police, be strengthened, that the class enemies of the Soviet republic be sent to concentration camps and that all who were involved in organizations such as the White Guards or in other conspiracies and uprisings were to be shot on sight. A few days later this policy was summed up by Grigory Zinoviev, a prominent member of the party leadership: 'In order to liberate us from our enemies, we need our own socialist terror. Some 90 million of the 100 million inhabitants of Soviet Russia need to be brought round. There is nothing we have to say to the others. They must be destroyed.' Zinoviev told the soldiers of the Red Army: 'The bourgeoisie kills individuals, but we kill entire classes.' This policy was confirmed by Martyn Latsis, one of the Cheka leaders, in early October 1918 when he declared that 'We are in the process of rooting out the bourgeoisie as a class.'[7]

Nor was it long before his words were matched by actions, and the taking and execution of hostages became a routine occurrence. On 31 August 1918 141 hostages were executed in Nizhny Novgorod alone, with another 700 being taken into custody over a three-day period. The revolutionary sailors in Kronstadt murdered around 500 of the men and women whom they took prisoner. In September 1918 the Petrograd Cheka shot 512 hostages within a matter of days. In the early autumn of 1918 the Cheka Association of the Urals reported the execution of twenty-three former police officers, 154 'counter-revolutionaries', eight monarchists, twenty-eight 'Cadets', 186 officers and ten Mensheviks and right-wing social revolutionaries, all within the space of a week. A further thirty-nine executions were reported by the Tver Cheka and fifty by that at Perm. In total it is believed that between 10,000 and 15,000 men and women fell victim to the 'Red' terror in the autumn of 1918. The number of 'class enemies' held in concentration camps had risen to 16,000 by May 1919 and to 70,000 by September 1921.

On 24 January 1919 the Central Committee of the Russian Communist Party decided to embark on what it termed an 'implacable war on the wealthy Cossacks who must be rooted out and physically destroyed right down to the very last man, this being the only politically correct measure'.[8] Between the middle of February and the middle of March 1919 more than 8,000 Cossacks were executed. Reliable estimates suggest that the number of Cossacks who were either executed or deported in 1919–20 was between 300,000 and 500,000 out of a total population of less than three million. The fact that most of the Cossacks who were liquidated were by no means 'wealthy' was of no consequence to their persecutors.

The 'White' terror was directed above all at the Jews whom the Cossacks and many 'Whites' lumped together with the Bolsheviks. Divisions of Denikin's 'White Army' and other Ukrainian units under the command of Symon Petlura were responsible for pogroms that cost the lives of some 150,000 men, women and children. In the Ukraine alone at least 30,000 Jews were killed in the course of the civil war in 1919 and 1920. A far greater number were seriously injured and robbed of all their possessions.

Anti-Bolshevism and anti-Semitism were especially rife among the well-to-do peasants, the Kulaks, who were particularly numerous in the Ukraine. Their protests were directed against the Red Army and its requisitioning or seizure of corn, potatoes, meat, milk and eggs, all of them measures of 'war-time Communism'. In August 1918 Lenin demanded 'civil war in the villages' and 'pitiless war on the Kulaks', whom he described as 'rabid enemies of the Soviet power'. He threatened them not only with being taken hostage and put to death but also made it clear in a telegram that he sent to the Penza Soviet on 11 August exactly how he imagined their deaths: 'You need to hang (hang without fail, so that the people see) no fewer than 100 of the notorious Kulaks, the rich and the bloodsuckers. [...] Telegraph us concerning receipt and implementation.'9 In the ten provinces for which complete figures have survived, it is clear that in September 1919 there were almost 49,000 deserters, mostly peasants, more than 700 imprisoned 'bandits', 1,826 deaths and 2,230 shootings. Among party and state officials and the military there were 430 reported deaths.

There were widespread strikes in the spring of 1919, starting on 10 March in the Putilov Works in Petrograd, which until 1917 had been a stronghold of Bolshevism. The strikes were for the most part a desperate protest at the rampant famine, low wages and the government ban on such actions. When Lenin and Zinoviev appeared at the Putilov Plant on 12 and 13 March, they were booed and greeted with shouts of 'Down with the Jews and Commissars!' (Some of the most prominent Bolsheviks, including Trotsky, Zinoviev, Kamenev, Rykov and Karl Radek, were Jews.) The Putilov strike was put down by Cheka units, 900 workers were arrested and around 200 summarily executed. Mutinous soldiers joined the strikers in Orel, Bryansk, Gomel and Astrakhan. Here, too, anti-Semitic chants were heard. In every case the Cheka responded with violent reprisals and withdrew the strikers' ration cards. In Tula, where the head of the Cheka, Feliks Dzierżyński, intervened personally, twenty-six alleged ringleaders were executed at the beginning of April 1919. Workers who wanted to be reinstated had to sign agreements stating that going on strike was tantamount to deserting and as a result was punishable by death. The following year the Cheka even resorted to drowning convicts in the Dvina which ran past the Kholmogory Camp. It was a practice that had been used by the Jacobins during the French Revolution.

If the Reds ultimately defeated the Whites, this was due not only to the effectiveness of the Communist reign of terror and to the – at best – half-hearted support of the counterrevolution by the Western Powers. The decisive factor was the attitude of the peasants, in whose eyes the counterrevolutionary forces were the agents of the aristocratic landowners who were hoping for a return to earlier property conditions. Such peasants represented the vast majority of the Russian population and were grateful to the Bolsheviks for this redistribution of the land. When compared with the Whites, the Reds were thus the lesser of two evils. This assessment of the situation allowed the peasant class to overlook its sense of bitterness at the requisitioning of crops and other agricultural produce and its compulsory military service in the Red Army, where it represented by far the largest group.

Only a few days before the start of the strike at the Putilov Plant, the first congress of the Third or Communist International met at the Kremlin between 2 and 6 March 1919. Lenin believed that the Second International had betrayed the cause of Marxism and, hence, of the working class, with the result that for him it went without saying that a completely new, truly revolutionary International needed to be created. The decision was ultimately triggered by the convening of the first post-war conference of the Second International at Berne on 27 January 1919. In view of the threat that was posed to them by both counterrevolutionary forces in Russia itself and by the military intervention of the Allies, the Bolsheviks had to do everything in their power to prevent the European proletariat from being led down an anti-Bolshevik road by right-wing 'social-chauvinists' or by 'Centrist' politicians like Kautsky.

Some fifty-four delegates attended the first Congress of the Communist International. Five of them came from abroad: from Germany, Austria, the Netherlands, Sweden and Norway. A handful of other countries were represented by former prisoners of war or by revolutionaries who happened to be in Russia. The euphoric mood of the participants was in stark contrast to the Soviet state's current situation, which was nothing if not desperate. Lenin and the other leading Bolsheviks believed that revolution would very soon sweep across Europe, bringing with it the victory of the international revolution. Germany, they were convinced, would play a key role in this process. As soon as the soviet republic had triumphed there, the Third International would transfer its headquarters and offices from Moscow to Berlin in keeping with a decision taken at the congress. The German Communists, who were represented by Hugo Eberlein in Moscow in March 1919, were initially opposed to the foundation of a new International, a view that reflected the thinking of the murdered Rosa Luxemburg, who had been afraid that an International dominated by the Russian Bolsheviks would soon be entirely dependent on Moscow. In the end Eberlein abstained. Following the foundation of the 'Comintern', as the Communist International soon became known, the German Communist Party joined the International at Eberlein's request. It was the first party to do so.

In the congress's resolutions, the 'social patriots' or 'social-chauvinists' on the right wing of the socialist movement, together with the centre around the Independent Labour Party as well as the new majority of the SFIO under Jean Longuet and the moderate wing of the Independent Socialist Party of Germany under Haase, Hilferding and Kautsky, were attacked with far greater virulence than the capitalists and imperialists. According to the 'guidelines' drawn up by Bukharin, the essential requirement for the victory of the working class was a clean break not only with the right-wing Social Democrats, with 'the outright lackeys of capital and the hangmen of the Communist revolution', but also with the 'centre' of the 'Kautskyites', a centre that abandoned the proletariat at critical moments. In a resolution that he submitted to the congress,

Zinoviev – elected president of the Communist International in Moscow – even declared the centrists to be more dangerous than the 'social-chauvinists' who, he claimed, had murdered Karl Liebknecht and Rosa Luxemburg, because the former were in fact striving for unity with the social-chauvinists and attempting to hoodwink the revolutionary elements. 'The organizational break-away from the centre is an absolute historical necessity.'[10]

The decisive factor in establishing the Communist International had been the Berne Conference of Socialist Parties that had met in the Swiss capital between 27 January and 9 February 1919. On that occasion the German Majority Socialists – in the eyes of Lenin and Zinoviev the most dangerous of all the 'social-chauvinists' – had found themselves hard pressed. The workers' parties of the victorious powers and also those of most of the countries that had remained neutral during the war accused them of betraying the cause of the international proletariat, whereas the Independent Socialist Party of Germany was regarded as the guardian of the socialist tradition. Although the French socialist Albert Thomas met with no agreement when he demanded the exclusion of the Majority Socialists, Kurt Eisner received substantial backing when he invited the Majority Socialists to acknowledge the error of their ways. The representatives of the Majority Socialists duly conceded their mistake, albeit only half-heartedly, demanding the publication of all the relevant documents relating to the outbreak of the war in every country involved and admitting merely that the German invasion of Belgium had been a breach of international law.

In the end the desire to achieve a compromise proved decisive. Allowances were made for the German Social Democrats, and the International's verdict on the 'world-historical question as to responsibility' for the war was reserved for a later congress. The agreement was made easier by the universal hostility to Communism. The left-wing socialists may have been able to prevent the congress from voting on a resolution in favour of democracy and, hence, against the Bolshevik dictatorship, but the majority left observers in no doubt as to its rejection of the Russian road to socialism. This attitude was underlined by the election of the Swedish party chairman, Hjalmar Branting, as president of the Second International. The central point of the new programme was by no means non-controversial, involving, as it did, the approval of a League of Nations that would not be a debating club for the representatives of the world's governments but an international parliament with an international government invested with the power to settle international conflicts by peaceful means.

The Bolsheviks rightly saw in the resurrected Second International an obstacle to their plans for world revolution. On 6 February 1919 *Pravda* published an article expressing the Bolsheviks' anger at the participants in the conference, whom it upbraided as 'lackeys' and 'social obscurantists': 'One feeling unites them: a furious hatred for Bolsheviks. One slogan unites them:

the slogan of war against the Bolsheviks. The first words of the Yellow International were "Fight the Bolsheviks!""[11]

The Victors Move to the Right: The Western Powers on the Eve of the Paris Peace Talks

Whereas it was the left-wing centre parties that came to power in the defeated countries of Germany, Austria and Hungary, three of the four most important victorious powers – the United States, Great Britain and Italy – underwent a shift to the right at this time. In France the move to the right had taken place a year earlier, in November 1917, when the 'Jacobin' nationalist Georges Clemenceau was elected prime minister. In the United States the Republicans, previously the party of opposition, won a resounding victory in the 'off-year elections' of November 1918, when the House of Representatives and a third of senators were elected. In the Senate, where the Democrats had previously had six seats more than the Republicans, the latter now had a two-seat majority, while in the House of Representatives they turned a minority of five into a majority of forty-five seats. What counted most of all for the 'Grand Old Party' was its ferocious attacks on the 'weak' internationalism of the Democrat Woodrow Wilson, who was accused of having been unduly lenient towards the Germans.

Great Britain's elections in December 1918 were a repeat of the 'khaki elections' of 1900, which had been overshadowed by the Boer War. On both occasions, a jingoistic note was struck not only by the nationalistic mass-circulation papers such as the *Daily Mail* and *Morning Post* but also by the Conservatives. The most demagogic slogan came from a member of David Lloyd George's war cabinet, the minister without portfolio George N. Barnes, who at the end of November demanded: 'Hang the Kaiser!' In a speech in Cambridge on 9 December the first lord of the Admiralty, Sir Eric Geddes, recommended that Germany be stripped of all its gold and silver, together with its jewels, paintings and libraries, all of which should be handed over to the Allies and to the neutral powers. On another occasion Geddes demanded that his country 'squeeze the German lemon until the pips squeak'.[12] Rising above party politics, Lloyd George contented himself with demanding that Germany pay the entire cost of the war.

The elections to the lower house were the first since December 1910 and were three years overdue. This was also the first time that elections had been held according to the new electoral law of February 1916, whereby all men over the age of twenty-one and all women over thirty were entitled to vote. The Conservatives – officially known since May 1912 as the Conservative and Unionist Party following their merger with the Liberal Unionists, the party of Joseph Chamberlain, who had died in 1914 – agreed to a national electoral pact with the majority of the Liberals who were loyal to the government. This pact was possible only because Lloyd George had declared his willingness to tone down the Liberal demand for home rule for Ireland. A minority of Liberals under the former prime minister, Herbert Henry Asquith, had voted against the government in the vote of confidence proposed by Lloyd George on 9 May 1918 in protest at the prime minister's policies, which were felt to be too 'right-wing'. As a result, the British Liberals entered the elections a divided and weakened force.

The Labour Party, too, was internally divided. The Independent Labour Party was an important grouping within the main party. Under Ramsay MacDonald, it had opposed the war from the outset. During the final year of the war the main party had moved significantly to the left. In February 1918 a party conference adopted a new statute according to which the Labour Party officially acknowledged itself as a socialist party and demanded the reform of society on the basis of property held in common by every member of that society. In a programme agreed to at the same conference, the party also spoke out in favour of nationalizing not only all land but also the railways, mines, power stations, the armaments industry, canals, ports and shipping companies. The influence of the Russian October Revolution was unmistakable, and responses from the right were correspondingly hostile, the Labour Party being accused of Bolshevik tendencies. In spite of its change of direction, it remained a decidedly reformist party.

The elections on 14 December 1918 produced a clear victory for the right, the Conservative and Unionist Party alone winning 382 seats, three-fifths of the total. To their number may be added 136 coalition Liberals under the former and future prime minister Lloyd George and a handful of nationalists. Asquith's Liberals won only thirty-three seats, while the Labour Party won fifty-nine, or 20.8 per cent of the total votes cast. Almost all the well-known Labour leaders left the lower house and were replaced by largely unknown trade union officials with no parliamentary experience. Labour was no longer represented in Lloyd George's new cabinet.

Of the 105 members of the lower house who were elected in Ireland, seventy-three were members of the republican Sinn Féin, which had been founded in 1905, six were Irish Nationalists and twenty-six were Unionists from the predominantly Protestant Ulster. The representatives from areas outside Ulster did not take up their seats at Westminster, thereby continuing the boycott that had started in April 1918 in protest at the introduction of conscription in Ireland. On 21 January 1919 the elected Irish Nationalists met in Dublin as a revolutionary constituent assembly, or Dáil Eireann, for Ireland. It immediately declared an independent Irish Republic and on 1 April 1919 appointed Eamon de Valera the leader of its illegal government. De Valera had been born in New York in 1882 to a Spanish father and an Irish mother and had recently escaped from prison. Shortly afterwards the IRA – the successor of the Irish Republican Brotherhood that had been formed by the nationalist Fenians in the 1850s – began its armed struggle against British troops and agents of the law in Ireland, a struggle that had been narrowly averted twice before during the previous five years: first by the outbreak of the war in the summer of 1914 and, second, by the Easter Uprising in Dublin in 1916, when British troops were deployed on a massive scale.

On 13 December 1918 – the eve of the elections to the lower house – Woodrow Wilson had arrived in the French port of Brest in Brittany on the first leg of what was the first visit to Europe ever undertaken by an American president. His visit had only one aim: to ensure that the United States exerted the greatest possible influence in shaping the international order in the wake of the First World War. No political welcome was as warm and, indeed, as enthusiastic as that extended by Socialist workers and their leaders, who saw in Wilson an ally in their struggle for a peace based on understanding and for more democracy and greater social justice.

The French Socialists did everything they could to persuade Clemenceau to agree to Wilson's Fourteen Points as the basis for a lasting peace, but in vain. Clemenceau did not want to pre-empt the peace negotiations and concentrated instead on securing America's support for a cordon sanitaire – a buffer zone of independent central and south-east European states that would help to provide a bulwark against Bolshevism. In a speech to the Chamber of Deputies on 29 December Clemenceau steadfastly refused to specify any concrete peace aims. In doing so he could be sure of broad parliamentary support. As early as the end of October most of the middle-class parties to the right and left of the centre had joined the Entente Républicaine Démocratique with whose help Clemenceau won a decisive vote on 29 December, when the budget was accepted by 414 votes to six. The divided Socialists had agreed to abstain.

Wilson had meanwhile travelled on to England, where he received an overwhelmingly warm reception for a speech in Manchester on 30 December, four days after his arrival. He also found himself in far more agreement with Lloyd George than he had with Clemenceau, although he was under no illusions about the effect of the recent elections, for the advocates of a tougher line against Germany, primarily the Conservatives, were now more powerful, whereas the British 'Wilsonians' who supported a negotiated peace found that their position had been weakened.

Wilson then passed through Paris, where he made no secret of his disappointment at Clemenceau's speech to the Chamber of Deputies, before heading for Italy, a country that had not entered the war until 1915, when enthusiasm for armed conflict had been markedly less pronounced than elsewhere and which was now on the brink of economic and financial bankruptcy. In Rome Wilson's opposite number in his talks was the right-wing liberal prime minister, Vittorio Emanuele Orlando, who had taken office in October 1917 and whose government included several ministers with conflicting views:

whereas his right-wing liberal foreign minister, Sidney Sonnino, demanded the annexation of large tracts of land, especially Dalmatia, thereby winning the backing of the nationalist right wing, there were others, such as the deputy prime minister Leonida Bissolati, a reform socialist, and the left-wing middle-class finance minister Francesco Nitti, who advocated a peaceful settlement with the South Slavs.

The right's most vocal mouthpiece was Mussolini's *Il Popolo d'Italia* which demanded the annexation of a large part of the Dalmatian coast and South Tyrol as far as the Brenner Pass. A moderate left-wing politician like Bissolati wanted the border with Austria to be drawn just to the north of Bolzano, while on the eastern side of the Adriatic he hoped to gain possession of Gorizia and Istria and to see the border with the South Slav state drawn close to Trieste; Fiume would acquire the status of a free city under an Italian protectorate, but otherwise few territorial claims would be made on Dalmatia. Unable to persuade Sonnino to accept this relatively modest programme, Bissolati resigned as deputy prime minister. Shortly afterwards, Nitti too asked to step down on 4 January 1919, but out of respect for Wilson, whose state visit had started the previous day, he remained in office at Orlando's request until the 15th. Although the cabinet still included a number of moderate left-wing politicians such as the reform socialist Ivanoe Bonomi, the right emerged from the crisis of 1918/19 with its strength significantly increased.

Throughout his visit to Italy Wilson was cheered whenever he appeared in public, whether in Rome or Milan. He spoke not only to Orlando and Sonnino, both of whom struck him as men of limited vision, but also to Bissolati and Luigi Albertini, the liberal editor of the Milan-based *Corriere della sera*. In Italy, too, the most outspoken 'Wilsonians' were left-wing politicians, including the leaders of the Socialists in parliament, Filippo Turati and Claudio Treves, who in spite of their opposition to Italy's entry into the war had helped to maintain the country's war effort, albeit with a demonstrable lack of enthusiasm. But the Socialist Party and its officials had shifted to the left in the wake of the Russian October Revolution, and since its conference in Rome in September 1918 the party leadership was dominated by the left-wing 'Maximalists' under Giacinto Serrati, whose aim was the establishment of a socialist republic and the dictatorship of the proletariat, with the result that they refused to attend the Berne congress of the Second International. In their eyes, Wilson was a bourgeois politician whom the proletariat should treat with due reserve and caution.

The most prominent of the middle-class 'Wilsonians' was the Catholic priest Don Luigi Sturzo, a Sicilian who in January 1919 founded the Christian Democratic Partito Popolare Italiano, a move that had the backing of the Vatican. It supported Wilson's idea of a League of Nations and advocated far-reaching social reforms, an improvement in conditions in the south of the country and the introduction of votes for women. Sturzo's party thus came close to the position held by Bissolati, who after January 1919 was increasingly targeted by Mussolini and his *Popolo d'Italia*. From the standpoint of the nationalist right, Bissolati was the most dangerous of the *rinunciatori*, who advocated a policy of renunciation. A meeting organized by the Reform Socialists at La Scala was disrupted by Mussolini and his supporters, including the Futurist Filippo Tommaso Marinetti, their shouts and chanting effectively preventing Bissolati from speaking.

On 15 January 1919 the writer Gabriele D'Annunzio published an 'Open Letter to the Dalmatians' in *Il Popolo d'Italia*. It was a manifesto of Irredentism and, being incompatible with a nation's right of self-determination, it ended in a declaration of war on the 'Wilsonians' of all countries, especially those of D'Annunzio's native Italy. The writer hailed his country as the most triumphant of all nations because it had triumphed not only over its enemies but also over itself. It should not allow any peace to be imposed on it, whether those terms be Gallic, British or American. Rather, it should establish a 'Pax Romana' over the Alps and the sea. 'If necessary we will meet the new plot in the fashion of the Arditi, a grenade in each hand and a knife between our teeth.'[13] The 'Arditi' were a volunteer force made up of former elite soldiers. On 16 April 1919, the day of a general strike called by the Socialist trade unions, the Arditi stormed the building containing the offices of the Socialist *Avanti* in Milan, setting it on fire and provoking clashes that resulted in five deaths and numerous injuries. They then decamped to the offices of *Il Popolo d'Italia* and offered a public tribute to Mussolini. A new age was dawning in Italy, its long shadows already casting their pall over the coming period.

A Fragile Peace: From Versailles to the League of Nations

The Paris peace conference began on 18 January 1919, the forty-eighth anniversary of the day on which King Wilhelm I of Prussia had been proclaimed the German Kaiser. Thirty-two states – the 'Allies and associated powers' – were represented with full voting rights. The 'Allies' were the powers that made up the Entente Cordiale, namely, Great Britain and France, while the 'associated powers' included the United States, Japan, Belgium and Italy. Also present with full voting rights were the 'additional members of the British Empire' – Canada, Australia, New Zealand, South Africa and India – as well as new states such as Poland and Czechoslovakia and others that had merely broken off diplomatic relations with the Central Powers, and Romania, which had entered the war on the side of the Allies in November 1918, six months after the Treaty of Bucharest. Conversely, the countries that had been defeated were not represented. Nor was Russia, which had cut itself off from the Central Powers in the spring of 1918 as a result of the Bolshevik revolution.

There were only eight plenary sessions attended by all the participating states. Until 24 March 1919 the decisions were taken by the Council of Ten, on which the major powers of the United States, Great Britain, France, Italy and Japan were represented by their heads of state or government and by their foreign ministers. After 24 March an even smaller committee, the Council of Four, had a say. It consisted of the United States, Great Britain, France and Italy, although not even Italy was involved in the talks between 23 April and 6 May 1919, when open disagreement broke out between the victorious powers over the future of Fiume, and the Italian prime minister and his foreign minister, responding to pressure from the nationalist right, decided to lend dramatic expression to their demand for the annexation of the Adriatic port by returning home. One of the most important participants in the negotiations, Woodrow Wilson, was unable to attend the conference between 14 February and 14 March as he had to return to Washington to fight for his survival in Congress. During this time he was represented by his secretary of state, Robert Lansing. The heads of state and government chiefs were assisted by some sixty committees, only one of which could report directly to the plenary sessions. This was the committee set up to discuss the League of Nations.

The League of Nations was intended to provide the organizational framework necessary to safeguard peace and security in the world, hence its insistence that in the case of disagreements between them, member states should be obliged to appeal to the Permanent International Court in The Hague or to a court of arbitration set up by the parties in question. The Assembly should include all member states, each of which would have a single vote and as many as three delegates. With a two-thirds majority, it would have the power to impose sanctions on its members. The same was true of the Council of the League of Nations, which was made up of permanent and non-permanent members. Permanent members were the major powers, assuming they joined the League: the United States, Great Britain, France, Italy and Japan. Non-permanent members were elected for a term of three years, their number being open. The Assembly could exclude members and accept new ones, again with a two-thirds majority.

The Assembly had at its disposal a Permanent Secretary General's Office under a secretary general. Its headquarters were in Geneva. It appointed the commission which was to oversee the mandated territories, namely, the former German colonies and the Arab parts of the former Ottoman Empire, including Palestine. It also set up the High Commission for Refugees and special organizations such as the one that dealt with all matters of health. It also oversaw the International Labour Office, the Institute for Intellectual Cooperation in Paris and other international bodies. The Assembly additionally gave a direct mandate to the Government Commission for the Saar region and to the High Commission for the newly created Free City of Gdańsk.

Whether the League of Nations could really help establish peace and settle disputes in the way that Wilson envisaged was debatable from the very outset. The member states of this system of collective security remained absolutely sovereign. And in the light of their divergent interests, especially those of the larger states, it was hard to see how any consensus could be reached on the question of sanctions. Among the privileged permanent members of the Council of the League of Nations, the larger European colonial powers had the upper hand. (In the spring of 1919 no one could have suspected that the United States would not become a member of the League of Nations.)

If the League of Nations could be expected to make any significant contribution at all, then it would most likely be in the field of humanitarian endeavour, whereas it was inherently unlikely that a body from which the colonial nations were by definition excluded would ever be able to form a single representative 'world government' or even a 'federation of free states' of the kind that Kant had envisaged as the basis of a new type of international law that he had advocated in 1795 in his essay *Eternal Peace*. The League of Nations began life as an assembly of victors of the First World War and of states that had remained neutral during that conflict. For the present the defeated powers were excluded. At best, they could hope that things would soon change, a state of affairs that applied not only to Germany, Austria, Hungary, Bulgaria and Turkey but also to Soviet Russia.

While in Paris, Wilson had urged his fellow leaders to contain the revolution in Russia by sending in food supplies and at the same time holding talks not only with the Allies, but also with the Communist government in Moscow and the counterrevolutionary governments set up by the 'Whites'. The attempt initially foundered in February 1919 on the Whites' refusal to sit down at the same table as the Reds. Then, in April 1919, following clandestine contacts between the Americans and the Bolsheviks, when the question of food supplies seemed almost to have been resolved, further problems arose, the Bolsheviks finding themselves unable to meet western conditions, including the Allies' demand that the Russian transport network be taken out of the control of the government in Moscow. Germany, by contrast, received substantial shipments of corn and fats after the French had ended their opposition to Anglo-Saxon proposals in this regard. As a result the Allied blockade was lifted, although this was the consequence not so much of humanitarian considerations as of the fear that the starving Germans might turn to Russia and embrace Bolshevism.

The main bone of contention at the Paris Peace Conference was Germany. It soon became clear that France held very different views from those of the Anglo-Saxon delegates and that there were in turn differences of opinion between Washington and London. Although his demands were couched in less strident terms than those of Marshal Foch, Clemenceau none the less insisted that the Saarland and the rest of Germany situated along the left bank of the

Rhine be partitioned off from Germany and form an autonomous state dependent on France. In the interest of a 'balance of power' Lloyd George had no wish to see France become unduly powerful and so he resisted France's expansionist ambitions in the west, just as he resisted Polish expansionism in the east. Wilson was all in favour of punishing Germany, a desire in which he drew little distinction between the old Kaiserreich and the new government. But he had no wish to come into conflict with his own principle of self-determination and not least as a result of this he felt unable to bow to French pressure.

The result of this tenacious struggle was a compromise that respected both France's need for national security and the principles of the Anglo-Saxon delegates. In order to satisfy France's need for national security the United States and Great Britain agreed to a treaty guaranteeing France against an unprovoked German attack. Alsace-Lorraine was handed back to France without a plebiscite, a move that had previously been far from uncontroversial among the victorious powers. The Saarland was not ceded to France but was placed under the administration of the League of Nations for a period of fifteen years, at the end of which term the local population would have the right to determine its own future. France also had to backtrack in respect of its claims to the Rhineland. The area to the west of the Rhine was not partitioned off from Germany. Instead the peace terms provided for Allied occupation of the area, which was divided into three parts to be administered for periods of five, ten and fifteen years respectively. There would also be a number of bridgeheads on the right bank of the Rhine and a permanent 'demilitarization' of those parts of Germany that lay on the left bank. In partial recompense for the political and material wrong that it had suffered at Germany's hands, Belgium was handed the region of Eupen-Malmedy, with its predominantly German-speaking population. The ballot that was organized to this end involved public lists inviting voters to state whether or not they wanted to remain part of Germany. This was hardly an appropriate way of establishing the will of the population, and the result was correspondingly compromised.

Incomparably more painful for the Germans were their territorial losses in the east. It was widely anticipated that Poland would fall heir to the former grand duchy of Posen, but Poland was also to receive the whole of Upper Silesia and – as a result of Wilson's promise in his Fourteen Points that the country would have free and secure access to the Baltic – most of West Prussia, together with a port to the west of Gdańsk, meaning that East Prussia was now cut off from the rest of the country. Gdańsk became a free city governed by a commissar appointed by the League of Nations, while the area of Memel bordering on Lithuania fell under the administration of the Entente.

In two regions – Masuria in East Prussia and in the area of West Prussia around Marienburg (modern Malbork) and Marienwerder (now Kwidzyn) to the east of the Vistula – the population was left to decide whether it wanted to remain part of Germany or to become a part of Poland. A further referendum was planned for the largely Danish-speaking Northern Schleswig. This duly took place in February and March 1920 and led to the region's being divided between Denmark and Germany along linguistic lines. In Masuria and in the area around Marienburg and Marienwerder the population decided almost unanimously in favour of remaining a part of Germany in July 1920.

At the insistence of France the peace treaty firmly closed the door on any attempt to compensate Germany for its territorial losses by sanctioning the union of Germany and Austria. According to Article 80 of the Treaty of Versailles, Germany had to recognize Austrian independence. A change was possible only with the agreement of the Council of the League of Nations. Under the terms of the peace treaty Germany lost a seventh of its lands and a tenth of its population. And it also lost its colonies. Economically speaking, the reduction in the country's size meant that, if we also take into account the division of Upper Silesia in 1921, Germany lost a third of its income from coal and three-quarters of its iron ore revenue. The victorious powers were unable to agree on a sum that might be paid by way of reparations. For the present, Germany had to hand over its trunk cables and nine-tenths of its cattle. For the next ten years it also had to provide France, Belgium, Luxembourg and Italy with forty million tons of coal annually.

The military terms that the Allies imposed on Germany were even more draconian. Conscription was abolished and the army reduced to 100,000 men, the navy to 15,000 professionals with several years' service. The country was no longer permitted to maintain an air force or a submarine fleet, while tanks and gas weapons were likewise banned. The general staff was disbanded. And, with few exceptions, the ocean-going fleet had to be handed over, a provision that the navy pre-empted by scuttling its fleet at Scapa Flow on 21 June.

No article in the peace treaty met with such impassioned opposition as Article 231, which was drawn up by John Foster Dulles, a legal adviser to the American delegation who became secretary of state between 1953 and 1959. Under its terms, Germany was obliged to accept 'responsibility for causing all the loss and damage to which the Allied and Associated Governments and their nationals have been subjected as a consequence of the war imposed upon them by the aggression of Germany and her allies'. Neither Dulles nor the Americans were interested in condemning Germany from a moral point of view but wanted only to find a binding legal title for the Allies' claims to reparations. The terms 'war guilt' and 'sole responsibility' do not occur in this article, but this is exactly how it was interpreted in Germany, an interpretation that was all the easier to read into the clause in that the idea that Germany and its allies had led a war of aggression also lay behind the demand that Germany must hand over its war criminals and those statesmen who were responsible for the outbreak of the war.

The peace terms of the Allies and their associated governments were presented to the German peace delegation on 7 May 1919 in Versailles. As president of the peace conference Clemenceau gave a short introductory speech, to which the German foreign minister, Count Ulrich von Brockdorff-Rantzau, felt the need to respond with a deliberately arrogant address of his own, which he delivered from his seat, in contrast to Clemenceau, who had stood. He rejected the claim that Germany was solely to blame for the war and accused the victors of having cold-bloodedly murdered hundreds of thousands of non-combatants even after the Armistice of 11 November as a result of their blockade. The effect was devastating: Wilson regarded the speech as a personal affront and felt that his negative opinion of Prussian Junkers was fully justified.

The Germans as a nation had still been hoping for a 'Wilson peace' on the basis of every nation's right to self-determination and reacted to the announcement of the peace terms with outrage and indignation. In the camp that consisted of the ruling parties of the 'Weimar Coalition', namely, the Majority Social Democrats, the Centre and the German Democratic Party, the initial response was to declare the terms unacceptable. At a rally held by the National Assembly in the Great Hall of the University of Berlin on 12 May, the prime minister Philipp Scheidemann asked the rhetorical question: 'What hand shall not wither that binds itself and us in these fetters?' The Prussian prime minister, Paul Hirsch, who like Scheidemann was a Majority Social Democrat, coined the phrase: 'Better dead than a slave!' And the president of the National Assembly, Konstantin Fehrenbach, who was a member of the Centre Party, called the treaty a 'perpetuation of the war' and threatened the Allies with a second world war: 'In the future, too, German women will give birth to children, and these children will smash the chains of bondage and cleanse the disgrace that is to be smeared on our German face.'[14]

But only one of the three ruling parties was more or less resolved to reject the peace treaty: the German Democratic Party. The Social Democrats and the Centre were both internally divided. The proponents of Realpolitik, including three ministers, Matthias Erzberger of the Centre party and Gustav Noske and Eduard David of the Social Democrats, were aware that if the Germans rejected the treaty, the Allies would occupy Germany which, with its weakened military resources, would be unable to prevent them, a view shared by the acting first quartermaster-general, Wilhelm Groener. But the German negotiators were still able to achieve a number of concessions after they had submitted their 'observations' on the treaty in Versailles on 29 May: on 16 June the victorious powers, acting at the instigation of Lloyd George, agreed to a plebiscite in Upper Silesia, allowing the local population to decide whether it preferred to be a part of Germany or Poland. As for the Rhineland, the Allies accepted that the occupation of the region might end prematurely if the Germans behaved themselves. But the Allies rejected the German account of the question of who was guilty of causing the war, a rejection couched in terms as unequivocal as they were exhaustive.

As a result of these concessions and the arguments put forward by Erzberger, the following few days witnessed the emergence of a majority consensus in the National Assembly and, with it, a willingness to sign the Treaty of Versailles on two conditions: neither the article on the question of war guilt nor the obligation to hand over war criminals was to be regarded as binding. But both Scheidemann and Brockdorff-Rantzau were so implacably opposed to acceptance that Scheidemann saw no alternative but to resign, which he did on 26 June. He was succeeded by Gustav Bauer, a politically colourless Majority Social Democrat who had previously been labour minister and, before that, the co-chairman of the General Commission of Free Trade Unions. The new foreign minister was the multilingual Hermann Müller, who had only just been elected chairman of the Social Democrats. Unlike the Centre Party, the German Democratic Party was no longer a part of Bauer's government.

On 22 June the National Assembly voted to sign the treaty by a majority of 237 votes to 138, with six abstentions. Again, it refused to accept sole culpability for the war and to extradite German war criminals. The Allies responded swiftly with an ultimatum: Germany had to sign the treaty unconditionally within twenty-four hours. In short, the National Assembly had to decide again on 23 June, this time definitively.

Everything now depended on the Centre. The members of the Catholic party found it easier to agree to an unconditional acceptance of the terms of the peace treaty in that Groener, in a telegram, had stressed the hopelessness of military action, while the right-wing opposition parties – the German Nationals and the German People's Party – expressly declared their acquiescence in the 'patriotic' motives of those delegates who voted in favour of acceptance. The two Social Democratic parties, the majority of the Centre Party and a minority of the German Democrats finally voted in favour of acceptance, while the German National People's Party, the German People's Party, a majority of the German Democratic Party and a minority of the Centre Party voted against. Five days later the treaty was signed in the Hall of Mirrors at Versailles, where Wilhelm I had been proclaimed the German Kaiser in 1871. The German signatories were the foreign minister Hermann Müller of the Social Democrats and the transport minister Johannes Bell of the Centre Party.

The profound and long-lasting sense of outrage at the 'diktat of Versailles' stemmed not least from the refusal of Scheidemann's government to publish the German documents collected by Kautsky on the outbreak of the war and in that way to prepare the German people for what they could expect from the victorious Allies. It was a refusal that flew in the face of President Ebert's entreaties. During the spring and summer of 1919 the majority of Social Democrats were reluctant to confront the question of the country's guilt in an open, self-critical way. When Eduard Bernstein, at the Social Democrats' first post-war party conference in Weimar between 10 and 15 June 1919, appealed to his fellow delegates to face up to the question of guilt and responsibility and to stop being prisoners of the vote of 4 August 1914, when the Social Democrats in the Reichstag had voted in favour of war loans, he was severely criticized, especially so by Hermann Müller, whose putdown was manifestly anti-Semitic in tone. But Scheidemann trumped Müller by calling Bernstein an 'advocate of the devil' who in his overdeveloped sense of justice would defend even the country's imperialist enemies.

The reluctance to consider the policies of the German leadership during the July crisis of 1914 in a remotely impartial way soon turned into a denial on the part of the political right to accept any responsibility at all for Germany's culpability in causing the war. In an attempt to deny the Allies' 'lie' about the country's guilt, the Germans began to promote a legend about their innocence which, like its twin sister, the legend of the stab in the back, proved to be a dangerous weapon in the struggle not only with Versailles but also with Weimar. The claim that the Germans were 'undefeated on the field of battle' had been promoted by Ebert when, as chairman of the Council of People's Deputies, he had told the returning troops on 10 December 1918: 'No enemy has defeated you!' The legend of the stab in the back was given classic expression on 18 November 1919, when Hindenburg, who together with Groener had stepped down as chief of the army supreme command at the end of June, had addressed a parliamentary committee examining the causes of the country's collapse and quoted an unnamed English general as having said that the German army had been 'stabbed in the back'. For the German right, this inevitably meant the German left, the 'Marxists' and 'Bolsheviks' and, even more simplistically and frequently, the Jews.

It was not only the question of Germany's complicity in causing the war that most Germans chose to repress, however, but also the diktat imposed on Russia by the Reich in 1918. In terms of the economic and territorial losses that it inflicted, Versailles was less severe in its impact than Brest-Litovsk. Of course, neither peace treaty was just or astute. While working on the Paris treaties, the representatives of the victorious powers were under pressure from their own citizens, who demanded that the former Central Powers, and principally Germany, should be punished and that they be compensated for the losses that they had endured. In order to punish the vanquished, the victors violated individual nations' right of self-determination, notably in the case of the 'Polish corridor' that henceforth divided East Prussia from the Reich. In the northern part of West Prussia it was the German-speaking population, rather than its Polish counterpart, that was in the majority. But had the Germans not done exactly the same when they were the victors? Had they not contested Poland's claim to be treated as an independent state ever since the late eighteenth century? And was it possible to imagine a viable Polish state without access to the Baltic – in other words, at the expense of those areas settled by Germans?

As soon as the peace terms became known in Germany, Wilson, on whom so many hopes had been placed, was accused of betraying his own highest principle, that of a nation's right of self-determination, and from then on he was as hated a figure in Germany as Clemenceau. He had had to make concessions to France, but France had had to make far greater ones. Great Britain and America protected Germany from many of the indignities that it would have suffered if the peace had been dictated by France alone. Throughout the negotiations in Paris, Wilson had to take account of the American public and especially of the Republican-dominated Senate, for only if the latter agreed to the treaty by a two-thirds majority could this and other international treaties be ratified. If Wilson had returned to Washington prematurely by way of protest, he would have abandoned the field to Clemenceau, and the result would have been chaos in Europe. During the final weeks of the conference, the alternative facing Wilson was, in the words of the historian Klaus Schwabe, no longer either a 'compromise peace' or a 'Wilson peace' but a 'compromise peace or no peace at all'.[15]

The Treaty of Versailles was harsh, but few people in Germany realized that it could all have turned out very much worse. The Reich was preserved, and the Rhineland remained a part of Germany. Germany was still the most heavily populated country to the west of the Russian border and, economically speaking, the most powerful force in Europe. In certain ways it could even be argued that the country's external situation had improved when compared with the period before 1914, for the conflict between the Western Powers and Soviet Russia meant that Germany no longer had any reason to feel encircled. And even in Versailles the first cracks had already appeared in the relations between the Western Allies, with France on one side and Great Britain and the United States on the other. For the present Germany was denied membership of the League of Nations, but this was a situation that would surely change with time, and Germany had a good chance of once again becoming a major European power. It needed only a sober assessment of the new situation to see 'Versailles' from a realistic standpoint.

Germany was not the only country to criticize the peace treaty. In the victorious states it was above all left-wing parties and newspapers that expressed dissent. Once the terms of the peace treaty had been made known, the *Daily Herald* – the official paper of the British Labour Party – argued that those terms violated every pledge and that the planned League of Nations was 'a mechanical League of Victors without a soul'. For its part, the *Labour Leader*, the organ of the Independent Labour Party, felt that Wilson's Fourteen Points had been treated with 'callous contempt'. The leader of the majority of French Socialists, Jean Longuet, compared the draft treaty to Tilsit in 1807 and Brest–Litovsk in 1918, two other peace treaties imposed by diktat. The mouthpiece of the Partito Socialista Italiano, *Avanti*, described the draft treaty as a 'diplomatic Caporetto', a reference to the humiliating defeat of the Italian army in October 1917, and it pronounced the collapse of the democratic ideology which capitalist governments had used to justify a world cataclysm that had cost twelve million lives. In the United States, the left-wing liberal *Nation* claimed that Wilson had accepted terms that betrayed all his promises, thereby proving himself to be no more than an 'arrogant autocrat and a compromising politician'. The *New Republic* declared 'this Punic treaty' 'the prelude to quarrels in a deeply divided and hideously embittered Europe'.

But there was also criticism from the political right among the victorious nations, even if such criticism was radically different from that expressed by the left. The historian Jacques Bainville, one of the leading figures of Action Française, argued that the peace was 'too soft for being too hard'. Germany, he went on, would survive as a major power and could some day hope to free itself from the conditions that military defeat had compelled the country to accept. After fifteen years – by 1934 – Germany would demonstrate its newfound strength by wreaking vengeance on Poland and Czechoslovakia rather than on France. The British right-wing press was relatively restrained in comparison: the *Morning Post*, the *Daily Mail* and the *News Chronicle* all conceded that on the whole the naval, military, territorial and colonial terms were better than expected, whereas only the financial provisions fell short of the promises made at the time of the elections to the lower house in December 1918.[16]

The economist John Maynard Keynes came to a very different conclusion. A financial expert, he represented the British chancellor of the exchequer at the deliberations of the Great Economic Council in Páris, only to resign in early June 1919 in protest at the Treaty of Versailles. The following year he published *The Economic Consequences of the Peace*, in which he justified his critique of the peace conference's work. The book was quickly translated into German and encountered widespread support in Germany. According to Keynes, 'Paris was a nightmare, and every one there was morbid.' Turning to Clemenceau, whom he saw as the evil genius of the peace conference, he noted wryly that 'he had one illusion – France; and one disillusion – mankind, including Frenchmen, and his colleagues not least'.[17] The aim of the French prime minister and, hence, of France had been to turn back the clock as far as possible and invalidate all the progress that Germany had made since 1870. Keynes portrayed Wilson as an unworldly realist who from the outset was browbeaten by Clemenceau and Lloyd George, two intellectually volatile and astute power politicians who ensured that the American president was the conference's real loser.

Keynes's principal aim was to show that 'the Carthaginian Peace is not *practically* right or possible'.[18] In his view, the reason for this impossibility was the flagrant contradiction inherent in the peace treaty's goals: on the one hand it contained everything that could rob Germany in the short term and everything that might prevent it from evolving in the future, while on the other the country was required to pay reparations that in Keynes's eyes were an expression of mere wishful thinking. He ascribed the participants' politico-economic illusions to their manifest lack of interest in a viable international economic and financial order:

> The Council of Four paid no attention to these issues, being preoccupied with others, – Clemenceau to crush the economic life of his enemy, Lloyd George to do a deal and bring home something which would pass muster for a week, the President to do nothing that was not just and right. [. . .] Reparation was their main excursion into the economic field, and they settled it as a problem of theology, of politics, of electoral chicane, from every point of view except that of the economic future of the States whose destiny they were handling.[19]

Keynes castigated the French for the enormous shortfall in their budget, a result, he argued, of their failure to raise taxes and a cause of the continuing devaluation of the franc. In comparison, the British had financed the war along far sounder lines. The misguided policy on reparations on the part of the Allies affected not only the vanquished nations but sooner or later would also have consequences for the victors: 'An inefficient, unemployed, disorganised Europe faces us, torn by internal strife and international hate, fighting, starving, pillaging, and lying. What warrant is there for a picture of less sombre colours?'[20]

Keynes went beyond mere criticism and made a number of suggestions aimed at remedying the situation, including the demand that Germany should pay a lump sum of forty million gold marks as a realistic contribution to the war reparations. He also proposed an international loan combined with international currency reform. The Allies should also work with Germany to ensure Russia's economic recovery. No less revolutionary was Keynes's suggestion that the Allies' war debts be written off completely. The United States and Great Britain would have to make sacrifices: the former as a pure creditor nation whose financial contributions had made it possible for the Western Powers to win the war at all, Great Britain as a state that had given more war credits to its European allies than it had received from America.

Keynes believed that Great Britain should refuse to accept German reparations and that these should be channelled instead into the new states of eastern central and south-east Europe. This, he was convinced, was a precondition for a forward-looking solution to the problem of the Allies' debts that had been caused by the war, a problem that weighed on Italy no less than on France. Keynes regarded the economy of the United States as strong enough to be able to afford to forgo the repayment of what it was owed by the Allies. Whether Washington would share this conclusion was doubtful in the extreme, and Keynes could do little more than hope that time would work in his favour and that his insight would ultimately gain acceptance: 'Europe, if she is to survive her troubles, will need so much magnanimity from America, that she must herself practise it.'[21]

The keenest criticism of the peace treaty with Germany came from Moscow, where in July 1919 the executive committee of the Communist International that had been formed four months earlier compared Versailles with Brest-Litovsk in an appeal to the workers of the world. The full weight of the treaty, it argued, fell primarily on Germany's working class. 'If the Peace of Versailles were to prove at all long-lasting, this means that the working class of Germany would have to groan beneath a double yoke: beneath that of its own bourgeoisie and beneath that of foreign slave owners.' The German government may have protested verbally at the peace treaty, but in fact it was helping the imperialists of the Entente to carry out its diabolical plan with regard to Germany's working class:

> In Germany the henchman Clemenceau has no more faithful servants than Scheidemann and Ebert. [. . .] The proletarian world revolution is the only salvation for the downtrodden masses of the world. [. . .] As long as capitalism lives, there can be no lasting peace. A lasting peace will be built on the ruins of the bourgeois order. Long live the uprising of the workers against their oppressors! Down with the Peace of Versailles! Down with Brest! Down with the government of the social traitors! Long live the soviet power of the whole world![22]

The peace treaties drawn up in the wake of the pioneering treaty with Germany paid no heed to Keynes's warning. The second of the Paris suburban treaties was signed in St-Germain on 10 September 1919 and was a peace treaty with Austria. According to Article 80 of the Versailles Treaty, Austria could not be annexed by Germany, a point underscored by Article 88 of the St-Germain Treaty, which decreed that the name 'German Austria' had to be changed to the 'Republic of Austria'. The principle of a nation's right to self-determination was also undermined by the decision to draw the border at the Brenner Pass, dividing the Tyrol and apportioning the German-speaking South Tyrol to Italy. The same was true of the Allies' earlier decision to create a Czechoslovak state that would include the whole of Bohemia and Moravia, thereby incorporating those regions where the population spoke German.

The Western Powers attempted to secure the rights of national minorities such as the Germans and the Hungarians living in Slovakia by means of a treaty with Czechoslovakia that was signed on the same day as the peace treaty with Austria: 10 September 1919. Two plebiscites were held to decide two other border disputes: the first took place in October 1920 in Carinthia, which had previously endured a violent struggle between German and Slovene nationals, resulting in the intervention of Serbian troops and ending with the region remaining Austrian, while the second took place in December 1920 in Ödenburg (now Sopron), which opted to be a part of Hungary. Those parts of western Hungary that bordered Austria and that were settled by Germans fell to Austria at the insistence of the Italians and were thenceforth known as 'Burgenland'. It was a move that prevented the establishment of a 'Slav corridor' between Czechoslovakia and the new Kingdom of Serbs, Croats and Slovenes, a corridor that had been one of the aspirations of Czech and South Slav nationalists and based on scattered Croat settlements in western Hungary.

The peace with Hungary was signed at Trianon on 4 June 1920. The Kingdom of Hungary had been an agglomeration of different nationalities, but the enforced loss of parts of its territory to Romania, Czechoslovakia and Yugoslavia meant that it now became a largely Magyar national state, albeit one that was far from providing a home for all ethnic Magyars, some 3.5 million of whom were obliged to become citizens of Romania, Czechoslovakia and Yugoslavia. Hungary also lost two-thirds of its historic lands and population, a loss far more serious than the reduction in size of its territory as demanded by the Treaty of Versailles. Predictably, the result was a radical form of nationalism aimed at revising the Treaty of Trianon and destined to shape the country's fortunes throughout the interwar period.

When compared to Hungary's, the territorial losses suffered by Bulgaria appeared to be less dramatic. The peace treaty signed at Neuilly on 27 November 1919 meant not only that Bulgaria had to relinquish all the lands that it had won during the First World War but also that it no longer had any access to the Aegean Sea: the region in question – Southern Thrace with the port of Alexandroupoli (Dedeagatch) – initially fell under the control of the Allies, who in turn passed it on to Greece in April 1920 under the terms of the Treaty of San Remo. Turkey and Bulgaria agreed to a reciprocal exchange of populations in those regions that were ethnically mixed.

As a result of the Treaty of Neuilly, Bulgaria was reduced in size from 44,000 square miles in 1915 to 39,000 square miles in 1919. In future the country was allowed to maintain only a small army of 10,000 men and had to pay reparations of £100 million. The peace treaty was signed by a coalition government led by the Agrarian Union and also including the Socialists. The prime minister at this time was Alexander Stamboliyski, whose Agrarian League remained the most powerful force during the immediate post-war period in a country that was still predominantly agrarian. Its most powerful opponents were, on the political left, the Communist Party which enjoyed growing support among the poorest peasants and, on the right, the army, which was the most important ally of all the forces that urged a renegotiation of the terms of the Treaty of Neuilly.

The negotiations leading to a peace agreement with Turkey proved to be the most protracted. The truce that was signed at Mudros on 30 October 1918 turned out to be a mere intermezzo. In the middle of May 1919 Greek troops, supported by the British and armed with a mandate from the Supreme Council of the Allied and Associated Powers in Paris landed in Smyrna (Izmir), where they caused a terrible bloodbath among the fez-wearing inhabitants and used the city as a base from which to launch an invasion of western Anatolia. The troops had only recently belonged to an anti-Bolshevik interventionist force in southern Russia and were allegedly intended to pre-empt an Italian attack on southern Anatolia but were in reality an instrument in the far more ambitious policies of the Athens government, the aim of which was to ensure Greek control over the coastal region of Asia Minor that was partly Greek and partly Turkish, its ultimate goal being the creation of a Greater Greece.

This Greek intervention soon met with stout resistance on the part of General Mustafa Kemal, the most successful military commander of the war years and later the founder and leader of the Turkish Republic. The government of Sultan Mehmed VI had entrusted him with the task of demobilizing sections of the Ottoman army. In the summer and early autumn of 1919 two national congresses in Erzurum and Sivas elected him their chairman. His programme was the 'national pact' concluded in Sivas on 22 September 1919, the aim of which was the formation of a Turkish national state that was to include not only those regions inhabited by ethnic Turks but also those parts of Anatolia and Thrace populated by Armenians, Kurds and Greeks.

With its headquarters in Ankara, Mustafa Kemal's Representative Committee may have claimed to be protecting the Sultanate and the Caliphate, but it was in fact an alternative government to that of the sultan. Mustafa Kemal's principal concern was the organization of the struggle for independence, a struggle waged against the Greeks in the west of Anatolia, against the British-protected 'peace-keepers' or 'Caliphate's army' in the north, against the Armenian independence movement in the east and against the French troops that had occupied Cilicia in the south. When Sultan Mehmed VI began to draw closer to the line adopted by Mustafa Kemal in early 1920 and the parliament that had been newly elected at his behest decided to adopt the national pact, the British reacted decisively and on 16 March placed Istanbul under their military control. Mustafa Kemal then ordered the election of a new Grand National Assembly with extraordinary powers. Meeting in Ankara, it declared itself the provisional instrument of Turkish sovereignty on 23 April and asked Mustafa Kemal to form a new government, the sultan having been effectively interned. In a truce intended to last twenty days and to lead to the evacuation of Cilicia, France was the first foreign power to recognize the government in Ankara. On 18 July the Grand National Assembly swore a solemn oath upholding the national pact and in doing so declared an end to the peace terms proposed by the Allies in Sèvres on 10 June.

In spite of this, the sultan's representatives signed the Treaty of Sèvres on 10 August 1920, albeit under protest. This document confirmed the loss of all non-Turkish – in other words, Arab – parts of the Ottoman Empire, a loss already agreed to by the Allies during the war. Mesopotamia – later the kingdom of Iraq – and Palestine were handed over to Great Britain as mandated territories of the League of Nations, while Syria and Lebanon fell to France on similar terms. Greece was to receive south-eastern Thrace as far as the Chatalja line some thirty miles from Istanbul and also, for an initial period of five years, Smyrna. Armenia was for the present to become independent, while Kurdistan was to become an autonomous region. The Straits of Bosporus were placed under international administration and control, which represented a profound infringement of Turkish sovereignty. International military courts were to prosecute Ottoman war crimes, especially the mass deportation and murder of Armenians in 1915–16, and in that way bring to an end the work started with the 'Young Turk trials' in April 1919, trials undertaken under extreme pressure from the Entente and in the absence of the leading defendants. (The former Grand Vizier Talaat Pasha, the former war minister Enver Pasha and the former navy minister Djemal Pasha had all fled to Germany in order to escape the death sentences handed down to them. Talaat Pasha was murdered in Berlin on 15 March 1921 by an Armenian student who belonged to a group of nationalist conspirators.)

The Treaty of Sèvres did not mark a new beginning or herald an age characterized by the idea that every nation had the right of self-determination. Instead, it represented a reversion to the heyday of European imperialism. It was the last of the treaties signed in Paris and its environs – and the only one that never came into force, for the Grand National Assembly refused to ratify it. In order to counter the Entente in an effective way, Mustafa Kemal had in the meantime sought a tactical alignment with Soviet Russia, the tedious negotiations for which were made even more difficult by the fact that for a time Moscow supported the Democratic Republic of Armenia that had been proclaimed in May 1918 and against which the Turkey of Mustafa Kemal began to wage war in 1920. By March 1921 Soviet Russia and Turkey were ready to sign a friendship agreement that led to the partition of Armenia between the two countries and brought to an abrupt end the brief period of Armenian independence. (The agreement also provided for Russia to supply gold to Turkey.)

This period also witnessed a number of important military successes for the Turkish national army under the chief of the general staff, Ismet Pasha. On two occasions – in January and March 1921 – the Turkish army defeated the Greek troops that had in the meantime captured a third of the country. Both victories were won at a small town halfway between Ankara and Istanbul called Inönü, allowing Mustafa Kemal to grant Ismet Pasha the name Inönü in 1934, when family names became obligatory in Turkey. Ismet Pasha was later three times the country's prime minister and, from 1938 to 1950, its president.

Mustafa Kemal could pride himself on a major political victory in October 1920, when France saw itself obliged to sign a treaty with the government in Ankara that was effectively a special peace treaty. Italy, too, openly sided with

Mustafa Kemal – under the terms of the secret Treaty of London of April 1915, it had acquired an area of influence in southern Anatolia. In September 1922 the Turkish national army under Mustafa Kemal advanced as far as Smyrna, which fell on the 12th of that month. So precipitate, indeed, was the Turkish advance that the fleeing Greek soldiers and civilians were driven into the sea, many of them drowning before they could reach the safety of boats and escape to the nearby Greek islands of Chios and Mytilene.

The Greek presence in Asia Minor that had lasted for three millennia thus came to a bloody end. In the wake of revolutionary unrest in Greece itself, King Constantine I was forced to abdicate in favour of his son George II on 27 September. (This was in fact the second time that he had abdicated, the Entente having already obliged him to do so in June 1917, but he had returned to the throne in December 1920 following the death of his son and successor Alexander and an ensuing plebiscite.) There had almost been a direct clash between Turkish and British troops in early September 1922, when the former approached Chanak in the neutral zone of the Dardanelles, but it was averted thanks to the circumspection of the British commanding officer, General Charles Harrington, and the deliberate restraint of the Turks. Lloyd George, who had until recently been urging the Greeks to attack the Turks, had to pay a high price for his obstinacy when the Conservatives abandoned the wartime coalition and emerged as victors from the elections to the lower house on 15 November.

The Turkish victory in Asia Minor was followed on 10 October by the Truce of Mudanya and, nine days later, by the occupation of eastern Thrace by the national army. Peace talks began in Lausanne on 1 November 1922. Since the Allies had invited the sultan's government to take part in the negotiations, the Grand National Assembly declared the abolition of the Sultanate that very same day. Following Mehmed VI's flight from Istanbul, the Assembly elected Abdülmecid his successor on 18 November and, hence, made him leader of the Muslim world, while denying him all political powers.

Mustafa Kemal's government was able to achieve its main political objectives at the Lausanne conference, and in the peace treaty signed on 24 July 1923 the Allies recognized Turkey's independence and sovereignty, the 'capitulations' were abolished, and foreign troops were withdrawn from Istanbul. On only two points was Mustafa Kemal unable to get his way: full sovereignty over the Straits of Bosporus and the restitution of the oil-rich province of Mosul. For its part, Turkey agreed to grant the same rights to non-Muslim Turks as to Muslims, including the right of religious freedom.

As for Greece, agreement had already been reached in January 1923 with regard to an exchange not only of civilian prisoners and prisoners of war but also of almost the whole of the Muslim population of Greece and the Greek Orthodox population of Turkey, the only exceptions being the Greeks in Istanbul and the Turks in western Thrace. The agreement was formally ratified by the Treaty of Lausanne. In total, some 1.5 million Greeks and 400,000 Turks were resettled. Four years earlier, a similar exchange of populations between Turkey and Bulgaria had been provided for in the Treaty of Neuilly of November 1919.

This kind of mass relocation of ethnic minorities, rendered compulsory by the state, enshrined in a treaty, internationally sanctioned and riding rough-shod over the will of the individuals concerned, was a new feature of international politics and international law. The agreement reached between Turkey and its south-east European neighbours with the consent of the western European major powers was intended to facilitate the creation of ethnically homogeneous states but was in fact an early example of what was later to become known as 'ethnic cleansing', a concept already adumbrated in the mass expulsions during the Balkan War of 1912–13 and the annihilation of the Armenians in 1915–16 and, as the history of the second half of the twentieth century was to demonstrate, it set a dangerous precedent.

On 13 October 1923, eleven days after the Allied troops had left Istanbul, Mustafa Kemal declared Ankara the Turkish capital. On 29 October the Grand National Assembly proclaimed the country a republic and elected Mustafa Kemal its president, marking the start of a historically unique modernization process involving the fundamental social, political and mental reform of an Islamic country. The former Ottoman Empire had been made up of numerous peoples, while at the same time reigning supreme over the Muslim world. It was now to become a western state and, as its founder declared at the economic conference in Izmir in March 1923, the 'most modern nation' in the world.

The fall of the Ottoman Empire and the end of its dominion over the Arab world were necessary if Turkey was to free itself from its Arab past, a legacy that Mustafa Kemal saw as reactionary, hence not only the abolition of the Caliphate on 3 March 1924 but also the closure of faith schools and Islamic courts, the gradual extension of women's rights, progressive industrialization, the Europeanization of clothing, including headgear, the ban on dervish seminaries, the conversion of monasteries into museums, the introduction of the Christian calendar and Latin script, the purification of the language by removing Arab and Persian elements and, last but not least, the abandonment of Islam as the state religion under the constitution of 20 April 1924, which described the Turkish state as 'republican, national, populist, statist, reformist and laic'.[23]

In many ways the regime of Mustafa Kemal, on whom the National Assembly bestowed the honorary title of 'Atatürk' (Father of the Turks) in 1934, recalls the systems of government associated with the age of enlightened absolutism. Although Turkey could not be described as a fully fledged dictatorship, neither was it a fully developed democracy. Mustafa Kemal's party, the Republican People's Party, maintained a dominant position in parliament, only briefly tolerating rival parties. And Atatürk's Turkey systematically adopted

European ways, taking over Swiss civil law, German commercial law and
Fascist Italy's criminal law, while ignoring the West's normative project in the
form of the inalienable human rights of individualism and pluralism.

In the words of the American political scientist Samuel P. Huntington, the
end of the Ottoman Empire 'left Islam without a core state'.[24] Kemal Atatürk's
Turkey was neither able nor willing to assume this role, its official ideology
being that of a secular nationalism aimed at homogeneity in terms of both
politics and philosophy. And in spite of the provisions of the Treaty of Lausanne,
this nationalist philosophy was opposed to any religious or linguistic deviation
from the majority's cultural norm. The Christians, few of whom were left
after 1923, the Kurds and the Alawites were repeatedly made to feel just how
different they were. But not even Muslims enjoyed any religious freedoms:
although Islam was no longer the state religion after 1924, religious practices
were subjected to strict state control. The persecution and murder of the
Armenians affected the very foundations of the new state no less than the
expulsion of the Greeks. The politicians and military leaders who stood accused
of the genocide of 1915–16 were granted a political amnesty in March 1923.
From then on, the period running up to the foundation of the new state was
surrounded by a taboo for the genocide contradicted the idealized picture of
Kemal Atatürk's revolution.

In modernizing the country from the top, the main support came from the
military, which served as a bulwark against all attempts to reimpose Islam on
the country and against all that might threaten the new state's rigid centralization. A powerful state was necessary to bridge the gulf between the developed
urbanized western half of Turkey and the backward agrarian eastern half of the
country. The willingness to learn from Europe was more highly developed in
Turkey than in any other society marked by Islam. The result was impressive,
but ultimately it amounted to no more than a partial westernization of the
country, for the Turkey of Kemal Atatürk took over from the West everything
that could be reconciled with the goals and ideals of Kemalism, while rejecting
everything that might have presented a serious challenge to the country's new
understanding of itself.

Turkey could balk at the Treaty of Sèvres without having to fear any armed
intervention on the part of the Allies. If Germany, by contrast, had decided
against ratifying the Treaty of Versailles, it would immediately have been
overrun by troops from the Allied and associated powers, an occupation
already planned in case of just such an eventuality. This war did not take place
in central Europe in the wake of the First World War. Another war that did take
place was the Russo-Polish War of 1920. On 23 November 1918, shortly after
the end of the Great War, Józef Piłsudski's army had wrested L'viv (Lemberg)
from the Ukrainians, and by the end of December the city of Poznan (Posen)
and the Polish-speaking parts of the province of the same name had likewise

been captured with little in the way of a struggle. On 31 July 1919, as a precondition for the annexation of the new areas in the west of the region, the Polish lower house – the Sejm – ratified a treaty guaranteeing protection for the minorities living there and promising the Germans and other minorities the right to a minimum of teaching in their own languages in school. (Many of the National Democrats in the national assembly voted against this move.) With the acceptance of the peace treaty by Germany, Poland's western border was now fixed, the only exceptions being those regions where plebiscites were still planned.

Conversely, the question of the country's eastern border was still unresolved, but the Russian Civil War gave Poland the chance to extend its territory eastwards by engaging with one or other of the two sides in the conflict. Piłsudski initially saw the pan-Russian 'Whites' as a far greater danger than the Bolsheviks, who advocated a country's right of national self-determination, for all that that support was manifestly tactically motivated. As a result, the first marshal of Poland, as Piłsudski was known after being acclaimed as such by his legionaries on 14 November 1918, refused to answer Denikin's appeal for help in November 1919. But this situation changed during the winter of 1919/20, when it seemed increasingly likely that the 'Reds' would win. Piłsudski assumed that the Red Army would soon be launching a western offensive: in February 1920 the general staff of the Soviet Russian army did indeed work on a plan to attack Poland. In order to pre-empt the assault, Piłsudski decided to attack the Red Army, in spite of warnings from the Grand Council in Paris.

Piłsudski's only possible ally was Symon Petlura's Ukrainian People's Republic, and on 21 April 1920 the two men signed a deal that handed the People's Republic of the Ukraine to the east of the Dnieper to Petlura's government, which for its part declared its willingness to enter into a federation with Poland, a move that would have left Poland covering almost the same area as it had done before the first partition of Poland in 1772. Five days later the offensive was launched under Piłsudski's personal leadership. The Polish and Ukrainian troops quickly advanced as far as Kiev but failed to find the support that they had hoped for among the local population, and by June the Red Army was on the march. So successful was its advance that by the middle of June they had already taken Vilnius and Grodno. It was a development that seemed to prove Lenin right: against Trotsky's advice he had urged a Bolshevik offensive that would take the Communist revolution to Warsaw and from there to Germany and to the whole of central and western Europe.

The situation became so serious that Poland's new prime minister, the National Democrat Władysław Grabski, travelled to Spa to ask for the Allies' help. But the latter were willing to assist the Poles only on certain conditions: Poland was required to accept in advance the terms of the Supreme Council with regard to the frontiers with Lithuania and Czechoslovakia; it had to cede Vilnius to Lithuania; and it had to withdraw its troops to a line that was essentially that of Congress Poland in 1815. This line, which was also to form Poland's future eastern border, was communicated by telegram to the Soviet Russian government by the British foreign minister, George Curzon, on 11 July after Poland had given its agreement. Termed the Curzon Line by the Bolsheviks, it began in the north with the railway line linking Dünaburg, Vilnius and Grodno, then passed via Brest along the Bug to Kryłów, before cutting through Galicia to the west of Lemberg and to the east of Przemyśl. Only if the Red Army were to cross this line would Poland receive western help.

Only a short time afterwards the terms of the treaty had to be invoked, but in the event western help, especially in the form of the provision of war goods, was thwarted by various factors, including protests from the political left and the organized workforce not only in Great Britain, where the Labour Party and the unions even threatened a general strike, but also in France, Italy and Germany, all of which were opposed to the idea of a war with the Soviet Union. Dockworkers in Gdańsk refused to unload munitions from Allied vessels. And the governments in Berlin and Prague both declined to allow troops and war materials to be transported across their respective territories. As a result, Poland was largely left to its own devices. A new 'government of national defence' under the peasants' leader Wincenty Witos that included politicians from all parties except for the Communists mustered a volunteer army of 80,000 men armed with scythes adapted to be used as weapons. For a time the Polish army numbered 900,000 men in total.

It was Piłsudski who, with the help of a French contingent under General Weygand, turned the fortunes of war in favour of Poland. (Among Weygand's troops was the young Charles de Gaulle, who had been serving as a staff officer in the Polish army since 1919.) Piłsudski decided to mount an offensive on 6 August. The battle for Warsaw lasted from 13 to 25 August 1920 and has gone down in the history books as the 'miracle on the Vistula'. It ended with victory for the Poles, followed a few days later with a further victory on the Njemen, forcing the Red Army to retreat. By September Polish troops had already advanced far into White Russia and the Ukraine and by 9 October they had captured Vilnius without a struggle, consciously – and with Piłsudski's approval – disregarding an agreement signed only two days previously between Poland and Lithuania, under the terms of which Vilnius was to remain a part of Lithuania.

Cowed by the Polish advance, Soviet Russia agreed to a preliminary peace treaty that was signed in Riga on 12 October 1920, bringing the war to an end. The definitive peace treaty that was signed on 18 March 1921, again in Riga, granted Poland an eastern border more than 125 miles to the east of the Curzon Line. Pinsk, L'viv and Ternopil were now a part of Poland, as were areas with a White Russian and Ukrainian population that were members of the Orthodox or Greek United Church. 'Central Lithuania' – the area around Vilnius inhabited by Poles, Lithuanians and Jews – was united with Poland in March 1922, after attempts to mediate on the part of the Council of the League of Nations had failed to produce any results. Lithuania, which regarded Vilnius as its historic capital, refused to recognize this unilateral action, with the result that there were no diplomatic ties between the two states, a situation that both parties aptly described as 'neither war nor peace'.

Of the twenty-seven million men, women and children living within Poland's borders in 1922/3, only nineteen million – or around 70 per cent – regarded themselves as Polish nationals. Four million were ethnic Ukrainians, and more than two million were Germans and White Ruthenians, not to mention the smaller groups of Russians, Czechs and Tartars. The Poland of 1923 was no longer a 'national state' but, to quote the historian Hans Roos, a 'conglomeration of minorities' and 'a multi-national state with a uni-nationalist ideology'.[25] And it was surrounded by enemies keen to change all this. On this one point, at least, there was agreement between three of Poland's neighbours: Germany, Soviet Russia and Lithuania. Czechoslovakia, too, looked askance at the present balance of power: Poland refused to accept a decision taken by the Allied Ambassadors' Conference at the end of July 1920 that divided the disputed region of Teschen along the River Olsa between Poland and Prague, leaving some 70,000 Poles citizens of Czechoslovakia.

The 'miracle on the Vistula' was a historical turning point not only for Poland, for Poland's victory dramatically reduced the chances that revolution would be carried from East to West. France, which had taken upon itself the role of Continental Europe's pre-eminent power and Soviet Russia's principal enemy, was able to reap the rewards of its military support for Piłsudski, and Poland now became the cornerstone of the cartel of medium- and small-sized states that served as a cordon sanitaire designed to prevent both Bolshevik Russia and Germany from extending their influence to central and southern *Zwischeneuropa* – the states in eastern and south-east Europe situated between Germany and Russia.

On 20 March 1921, two days after the Peace of Riga was signed, the plebiscite demanded by the Treaty of Versailles was held in Upper Silesia. Just 60 per cent voted for Germany, 40 per cent for Poland. There were 597 communes with a Polish majority as against 664 with a German majority. Germany immediately demanded the whole of Upper Silesia for itself, whereas Poland and the Allies were in favour of partition. In order to lend weight to its demands, the Warsaw government secretly supported an uprising led by the former Reichstag deputy Adalbert Korfanty, in the course of which Polish insurgents occupied large sections of the area covered by the plebiscite.

The German and Prussian governments responded by arming the Upper Silesian Self-Defence League, a paramilitary organization that had existed since 1920 and that joined forces with the Bavarian free corps Oberland to storm the Annaberg – the region's highest point – on 23 May. The Inter-Allied Commission persuaded the armed parties in the conflict to withdraw at the end of June. On 20 October 1921 the Supreme Council of the League of Nations settled the question of the division of Upper Silesia in a way that reflected the Council's own report: four-fifths of Upper Silesia's industrial region, including the cities of Kattowitz (Katowice) and Königshütte (Chorzów), went to Poland in spite of the large majorities in both cities that had voted on 20 March to be a part of Germany. Germany could do no more than register its objection to this interpretation of the right of self-determination, for it had no means to insist on a more equitable solution.

Poland was not the only country in the victors' camp to dispute the Allies' decisions. Italy did so too. Although it had received the South Tyrol, the Julian March (Julijska Krajina), Trieste, Istria and the Dodecanese Islands, it had not been granted the former Venetian lands on the Dalmatian coast as far south as the Bay of Cattaro, an area demanded by the radical Irredentists but given instead to the new Kingdom of Serbs, Croats and Slovenes. Equally unrealized was the goal of turning Albania into an Italian protectorate and of acquiring a stake in the former German colonies. The more vocal among the nationalists also regarded it as particularly humiliating that the eastern Adriatic port of Fiume (Rijeka), in which there were more Italians than Croats and which Italian troops had occupied in early November 1918, was not ceded to Italy but made an independent free city. The bitterness felt by the radical right found expression in the term *vittoria mutilata* – a mutilated victory.

On the Italian side, responsibility for the outcome of the peace talks was taken by the prime minister Francesco Nitti, the successor of Vittorio Emanuele Orlando, who had been toppled from power on 19 June 1919, and the foreign minister Tommaso Tittoni, who had succeeded Sidney Sonnino. When Nitti ordered the withdrawal of a number of army units stationed in Fiume following clashes between Italian and French occupying troops in September, the units in question mutinied and joined the irregular volunteers under the leadership of the poet Gabriele D'Annunzio, who marched into Fiume on 12 September and persuaded the Italian commander to hand over control of the town and surrounding area. Nitti's initial reaction was outrage, but he was eventually forced to realize that the army's leaders were not prepared to act against a man described as the Garibaldi of the early twentieth century. It was not long before Nitti was supporting D'Annunzio's government with financial aid and food supplies.

In the parliamentary elections in November 1919 both the Socialists and the new Christian Democratic 'Popolari' achieved excellent results, together holding more than half the seats in the Chamber of Deputies. The grand old man of pre-war Italian liberalism, Giovanni Giolitti, formed the new government and initially continued to give undercover help for D'Annunzio. In November 1920 Giolitti signed a treaty with the Kingdom of Serbs, Croats and Slovenes in Rapallo, granting Fiume the status of a free city and allowing the town of Zara (Zadar) and four of the Dalmatian islands to pass into Italian hands. After serious clashes between the Italian military and units loyal to D'Annunzio, Giolitti's government gave the army an official order to attack in December 1920, whereupon D'Annunzio capitulated. Three years later the status of Fiume was changed yet again when Mussolini, in the second year of his rule, signed a friendship agreement with the Kingdom of Serbs, Croats and Slovenes, granting them control over parts of the port and the whole of its hinterland, while the city of Fiume became a part of Italy.

It was Woodrow Wilson's wish that the creation of the League of Nations should be the most positive signal to emerge from the Paris peace conference. On 10 January 1920 the act establishing the League of Nations came into force with the Treaty of Versailles, and that same day the League began work in Geneva. A good two months later, on 19 March, the American Senate failed to ratify the treaty, falling seven votes short of the required two-thirds majority, a development that will not have surprised attentive observers after a majority had voiced American 'reservations' about the treaty when it was discussed there on 18 November 1919. The vote was taken, of course, on a bill that contained the 'reservations' rejected by Wilson, so that even a two-thirds majority would not have helped the president. It was not the parts of the treaty that affected Germany that caused Wilson's great plan to fail but the charter for the League of Nations that was also contained in the treaty. The defeat of the president was the work of 'isolationists' led by Republican senators such as William E. Borah from Idaho and Henry Cabot Lodge from Massachusetts, whose main argument was their concern that if the United States were to become a member of the League of Nations, it would be increasingly drawn into the 'entangling alliances' that Thomas Jefferson had decried in his first inauguration address on 4 March 1801. But Wilson's enemies saw the danger of involvement in European affairs not only in the United States' entry into the League of Nations but also in the guarantee treaty that Wilson and Lloyd George had agreed to at the Paris peace conference in order to save France from an unprovoked German attack. This treaty, too, was invalidated by the vote on 19 March 1920.

In the wake of his return to Washington from the Paris peace conference, Wilson sought to elicit support for the League of Nations both in the Senate on 8 July 1919 and in countless nationwide rallies. Following a speech in Pueblo, Colorado, on 25 September he collapsed with exhaustion, and the rest of his tour was cancelled. A few days later he suffered a stroke in Washington, with the result that for eight weeks he was unable to carry out his duties at all. Although he recovered, the final eighteen months of his presidency were over-shadowed by illness.

It is questionable whether concessions to his critics in the Senate might have helped to turn over a new leaf. Wilson refused to compromise, arguing that this would lead to other unilateral changes to the wording of the treaty. In keeping with current practice he would in any case have been unable to contest the 1920 presidential elections as he had already completed two terms in office. Although he had won the Nobel Peace Prize in 1919, he was regarded as a failed president by March 1920, having foundered in an almost tragic manner on the yawning gulf between his own high ideals and the reality of the situation on the ground in both Europe and the United States.

The role of global leader that Wilson hoped that his country would assume, ultimately ensuring a Pax Americana, was not accepted by large sections of the American public, especially the country's political and financial elite. With its war loans, supplies and troops, America had helped Britain and France to defeat Germany and its allies but was not prepared to assume the political responsibility on the world's stage that this victory required it to assume. In refusing to join the League of Nations, America did not turn its back completely on Europe for it continued to maintain a powerful economic and financial presence in the Old World. In doing so, the United States to a certain extent made up for the greater weakness of Great Britain, which until then had been the world's banker but which both during the war and afterwards had grown dependent on American aid. But no European power could close the gap opened up by the Senate's veto on joining the League of Nations.

Before 1914 a Pax Britannica had existed only on the colonial margins, not in Continental Europe, where France was now the most powerful country. But once France had failed to achieve its two main aims along the Rhine, it had banked on receiving guarantees of assistance and security from both Anglo-Saxon powers. When America voted against joining the League of Nations and rejected the Treaty of Versailles, it was obliged to abandon this hope. As Theodor Schieder has concluded, France's outwardly powerful position within the international system was no more than a 'sham hegemony'[26] that was threatened in part by the appalling state of the country's finances and in part by the possibility that Germany might recover and join forces with another 'revisionist' state – Soviet Russia – that would likewise call into question the status quo in the rest of Europe, a nightmare that Lloyd George had already foreseen at the Paris peace conference.

In short, France did not feel secure after 1919 even though it was one of the victorious powers. And the fact that it did not feel secure meant that it tried to achieve that sense of security by means of German reparations. Throughout the post-war period, French nationalism was so pronounced that there could be no thought of a Pax Gallica. A French-influenced peace framework would have required Paris's willingness to subordinate its own national interest to a larger, overriding concern, and this willingness was lacking.

France would also have had to find sufficiently powerful allies to share the feeling of a genuine partnership. Prior to 1917, Russia had been one such partner, but since the time of the October Revolution it was no longer available to fulfil this function. After 1918, Great Britain, its partner in the 1904 Entente Cordiale, no longer had any interest in making France even stronger and Germany yet weaker. France's partners were now Poland and the states of the 'Little Entente' made up of Czechoslovakia, Romania and the Kingdom of Serbs, Croats and Slovenes, all of whom joined forces under French patronage in order to counter Hungarian revisionism. Poland concluded a mutual assistance pact with France in February 1921, but even after the Peace of Riga it remained a revisionist state, at least in terms of its western border and, above all, its border with Czechoslovakia, while the states of the Little Entente with whom the Quai d'Orsay signed alliances and friendship agreements between 1924 and 1927 were in greater need of French help than the other way round. Italy was embittered at the *vittoria mutilata* and far too preoccupied with its own affairs to be seriously considered as an ally. In short, the post-war situation in Europe was precarious and peace was fragile, a state of affairs regarding which French politicians could be under no illusions.

The task facing the peace conference of 1919–20 differed fundamentally from the one that had confronted the Congress of Vienna in 1814–15. On that occasion France, although defeated, had taken its place at the negotiating table and was invited to accept peace terms that had nothing to do with vengeance and retribution but were aimed at achieving stability and balance. The politicians responsible for restoring peace in 1814–15 did not have to take account of their peoples' sensitivities. With the exception of Great Britain, they were all agreed that a nation's right to having a political say could largely, if not entirely, be ignored. A century later democratic ideas had become so firmly entrenched that it was impossible for politicians to sign peace treaties that disregarded the will of their people. The peoples who made up the victorious powers wanted to punish the country – Germany – that they blamed for the war and to demand the maximum possible compensation for the suffering, damage and privations that the war had caused them. Any government that rejected this demand by appealing to reasons of state would have been toppled without further ado. As a result, Germany could not take part in the peace conference and had to accept conditions that the victorious powers had worked out among themselves.

With regard to eastern central Europe, the Paris peace conference had to deal with a number of problems that had already been on the agenda during the revolutions of 1848–9. At that date few of the Slav nations that formed part of the Habsburg monarchy had aspired to sovereign statehood but had insisted, instead, on an appropriate place within the empire, turning them into the enemies of all those forces that were either eager to see its dissolution or at the very least content to accept that consequence. These groupings included the Austrian Germans, at least to the extent that they supported the creation of a unified German state; the Poles who were seeking an end to their country's partition and working for an independent Poland; and the Hungarians who rebelled against the role of the Kaiser in Vienna. This opposition led to the formation of an alliance with the Habsburg counterrevolution and contributed in no small way to the failure of the revolution in the whole of central Europe.

Seven decades later not a single Slav nation wanted to retain the Habsburg Empire any longer. Their aim was now the creation of independent nation states, an aim that revived problems that had first emerged in 1848–9, when the Magyars had set out to create an autonomous state independent of Vienna and in the process provoked resistance on the part not only of the Slav nations but also of the Romanians and Germans who did not belong to the Hungarian titular nation. The western, or, to be more precise, the French idea of a 'nation une et indivisible' presupposed a large measure of national homogeneity, and where this quality did not exist, then it was brought about by force. In eastern central and south-east Europe, conversely, a national mix was not so much the exception as the rule. Here the unconditional application of the majority principle was bound to mean that the most powerful nationality would assert itself at the expense of the others and in that way threaten their very identity.

The Western Allies saw this problem and tried to solve it by means of treaties designed to protect minorities. Their ratification was a precondition for full recognition under international law of the states in eastern central and south-east Europe that were either new or reborn or territorially much enlarged. The first of the treaties intended to safeguard a minority was signed with Poland on 28 April 1919, and in the course of the months that followed, similar treaties were signed with the Kingdom of Serbs, Croats and Slovenes, with Czechoslovakia and with Romania. A treaty with Greece was concluded in August 1920. All of the countries concerned saw these treaties as serious infringements of their sovereignty and did all they could to oppose them. Certainly, these treaties contained only the most minimal demands with regard to the equal rights of all citizens and demanded certain cultural rights for those who did not belong to the titular nation, including – under certain conditions – the right to be taught at school in the minority's mother tongue.

Few of the treaties contained a collective right to national identity. The Romanian treaty enshrined certain exceptions that favoured the region's Hungarian and German minorities. And in the Memel Convention of 8 May 1924, Lithuania was required to grant autonomous status to the Memel region, together with its own parliament and government, as a price for international recognition of its de facto annexation of the region in January 1923. Estonia went the furthest down this particular road and in 1925, on its own initiative, granted full cultural autonomy to its national minorities, allowing them to form associations recognized under public law and enjoying the right to levy their own taxes. Both the German and the Jewish minorities took advantage of this right, but the Estonian example did not set a trend, and most of the new national states were content to meet the minimum conditions guaranteed by the League of Nations. In their own 'mother countries' the German and

Hungarian minorities had protectors who ensured that the subject of minority protection was not forgotten, but other nationalities did not have such influential protecting powers to assist them.

The historian Theodor Schieder has distinguished between three different phases in the formation of nation states. During the first phase, existing states are reshaped by integrating their territories into centrally governed national states. The two classic examples of this phase are England following the revolutions of the seventeenth century and France after the French Revolution of 1789. The second phase is best illustrated by Italy after 1859 and by Germany after 1866: in these cases the nation state came into existence as a result of the merger of several smaller states, a development aided by liberal unification movements and a single historical state – Piedmont in the case of Italy, Prussia in that of Germany. In the first phase the geographical focus was western Europe, in the second central Europe. The creation of a further series of nation states in 1918 and 1919 belongs to the third phase in Schieder's system. Its beginnings can be traced back to the liberation of Greece and Serbia from the hands of the Ottoman Empire in the first half of the nineteenth century. The new nation states all arose as a result of secessionist movements directed against a multiracial state, whether it be the Ottoman, Habsburg or Romanoff Empire. This third and final phase was centred on eastern central and south-eastern Europe.

The western or, rather, the French principle, according to which a nation rests on the political decision of many individuals, so that its existence is – to quote the famous remark made by Ernest Renan in 1882 – 'un plébiscite de tous les jours', becomes increasingly unimportant the further east one goes. Even in Germany there had been a predominant belief since Herder's day that membership of a particular nation was based on objective factors such as a common language, culture and tradition, rather than subjective expressions of an individual's will. And this was even truer in the new nation states that were to be found further to the east.

During the interwar years, the deeper cause of the crisis of the nation state in eastern central and south-east Europe was to be found in this widespread view of the way the individual and the nation regarded themselves. No matter what the treaties designed to protect minorities may have said, anyone who did not belong to the titular nation was less 'equal' than the members of the hegemonic or principal nation. The whole idea of taking over the western principle of the democratic majority decision was from the outset associated with the danger that national minorities would be discriminated against. In order for it to survive in the new nation states, this principle had to be restricted, and national minorities had to be protected in ways that prevented them from being exploited by the majority. In fact, almost all the new states lacked this insight to a greater or lesser extent, impeding the progress of democracy in most.

Only the most cursory examination could make it appear as if the First World War had produced the world of which the extreme left had dreamt during the revolutions of 1848–9. The 'prisons of nations' had been abolished, including the most reactionary of the European powers, tsarist Russia; there were free democratic nation states in most of Europe, and over them was a League of Nations whose very creation was influenced by the idea of a nation's right of self-determination. But even on the left, few could see a progressive or libertarian system in the Communist regime that had come to power in Soviet Russia in November 1917, while the rest of the left, often in league with conservative forces, did everything in its power to prevent Soviet Communism from spreading westwards, incurring the same reproach as the one that had been levelled at moderate liberals in 1848, namely, that they had betrayed the revolution. Even as early as 1919–20 there were already good reasons to doubt whether freedom rested on firm foundations in the states that had come into being in the wake of the dissolution of the multiracial Ottoman, Habsburg and Russian Empires, with the result that it was equally unclear whether these states could support a new peace framework that would encompass the whole of the world, an aim enshrined in the charter of the League of Nations.

One of the fathers of the League of Nations was the South African politician General Jan Christiaan Smuts, who from 1917 represented the Dominions in the newly established Imperial War Cabinet. He had originally suggested that the new nation states in eastern central and south-east Europe be mandated territories of the League of Nations, a suggestion which, if realized, would have dramatically curtailed the sovereignty of these new states, with the result that the states in question vigorously rejected the idea. But Smuts's notion of mandated territories was applied to the Arab parts of the Ottoman Empire and to the former German colonies.

The notion of a mandate by the League of Nations was also a concession to the powerful anti-colonial lobby in the United States, a lobby that Woodrow Wilson had only reluctantly taken into consideration in Paris out of regard for his European allies and out of personal indifference. If the League of Nations were to entrust one of its members with guardianship over a dependent territory, this might be viewed as a milder form of colonialism and imperialism than colonialism pure and simple. In principle the mandate was conceived as a transitional phase leading to eventual independence, but in reality this prospect was likely to be achieved only in the first of the three categories into which the regions in question were divided. This category, A, included the Arab parts of the former Ottoman Empire, of which three – Iraq, Transjordan and Palestine – were mandated to Great Britain, while two others – Syria and Lebanon – were entrusted to France. Mandated territories in category A were regarded as sufficiently developed to allow them to be granted independence within a relatively short period of time. The first of these territories to be granted its independence was Iraq, which since 1921 had been a kingdom under Faisal I, the son of Hussein ibn Ali, the sharif of Mecca, and which became independent in October 1932.

Category B included countries whose independence lay some distance away in the unforeseeable future. With the exception of German South-West Africa, it was made up of the German Empire's former African colonies. Togo and Cameroon were divided up between Great Britain and France. Most of German East Africa fell to Great Britain, while Belgium received the provinces of Rwanda and Burundi, and the Kionga Triangle passed to Portuguese East Africa – present-day Mozambique. At the urging of General Smuts, German South-West Africa was assigned to category C, a category with even less prospect of ever achieving independence than category B. As such, it was entrusted to the Union of South Africa, which pursued the same policy of discriminating against the country's black population as that which obtained in its own territory. Also included in category C were the German colonies in Polynesia. Those which lay to the south of the equator were assigned to Australia and New Zealand, while the ones to the north fell to Japan, which also acquired Germany's former rights in China, albeit with the proviso that Jiaozhou be later returned to China. This was agreed to in the wake of an international disarmament conference organized by the United States and held in Washington between November 1921 and February 1922. There Japan accepted not only a reduction in the strength of its fleet (in a proportion of 5 to 5 to 3 when related to the capacities of the United States, Great Britain and Japan) but also recognized Chinese independence and agreed to an open-door policy which in the eyes of many Japanese nationalists and members of the military amounted to a humiliating concession to the Western Powers.

The League of Nations' actions with regard to the former colonies and the Arab parts of the former Ottoman Empire were a continuation of the earlier practices of colonialism and imperialism. With the exception of the mandated territories in the Middle East, the 'new' colonies had practically the same chance of becoming independent as the 'old' colonies of the victorious and neutral powers. As a result of the relative privileges granted to the mandated territories in category A and the discrimination shown to all the other colonies, the European colonial powers unwittingly fostered the desire for independence on the part of all the territories dependent on them, most of all in those countries such as India and Egypt where nationalism had already gained a considerable following before 1914.

By 1919 Egypt was already suffering from revolutionary unrest that was fomented by the Wafd Party and triggered by Britain's refusal to allow an Egyptian delegation ('wafd') to attend the Paris peace conference. By the following year the anti-colonial unrest had spread to other mandated territories in the Middle East: in Syria and Iraq the Arabs protested at the decision by Britain, France and the League of Nations to prevent the formation of a larger Arab state, while Palestine objected to plans to create a national homeland for the Jews envisaged by the Balfour Declaration of November 1917. In 1921 the Rif began an insurrection first in Spanish Morocco, then in French Morocco, that was not definitively put down until 1926.

In India, bloody clashes broke out between the colonial power and the local population within six months of the end of a war to which the country had made a huge military contribution. In April 1919 Gurkha troops under the command of a British general fired on an unarmed crowd in Amritsar protesting at the Rowlatt Act, so called after a British judge, Sir Sidney Rowlatt, that had made the wartime curtailment of civil liberties a permanent feature of India's peacetime constitution. The confrontation resulted in the deaths of 379 protesters and some 1,200 injuries. The events in Amritsar and other places in the Punjab, where aircraft and machine guns were used against the local population, left India profoundly shaken and led to a radicalization of the independence movement. After 1920 its hitherto moderate leader, Mahatma Gandhi, was likewise radicalized by these events. British rule was now placed under a greater threat than at any time since the uprising of 1857–8, a warning sign to all who believed that it was possible to pursue the same imperialist policies in Asia and Africa after 1918 as those that had been adopted before the First World War.

When the war began in August 1914 the English writer H. G. Wells – a member of the socialist Fabian Society – had spoken of a 'war that will end war', unwittingly taking up a remark by the Young Hegelian Arnold Ruge, who in a speech in St Paul's Church in Frankfurt on 22 July 1848 had referred to what he and his listeners hoped would be a European war of liberation against autocratic Russia as 'the last war, the war against war, the war against the barbarism that is war'.[27] Wells's interpretation of the war found a powerful response not only in Britain and France but also on the other side of the Atlantic, in the United States. As such, it chimed with the ideas of bringing peace to the world that Woodrow Wilson had invoked in his attempts to persuade American voters that their country needed to enter the war and to persuade Europe that America had a mission to perform. The post-war order that emerged from the Paris peace talks offered little hope that an era of lasting peace was about to dawn.

Protest, Prohibition, Prosperity: The United States in the 1920s

The United States lost 115,000 soldiers in the First World War, a figure far lower than that for the European powers: Germany lost 1.8 million, Russia 1.7 million, France 1.4 million, Austria-Hungary 1.2 million and Great Britain one million. Even so, the war represented a significant turning point in American lives, for in 1917–18 Americans broke with much that until then they had taken for granted: not only had they fought in Europe but for a time had abandoned their traditional principles of free enterprise and freedom of expression, including freedom of the press. With the end of hostilities, therefore, nothing seemed more pressing than to return as quickly as possible to pre-war normality.

For employers, normalization meant first and foremost an end to the concessions that they had had to make to workers and their trade unions during the war. For their part, the workers who had been called up wanted their old jobs back, jobs that had in the meantime been done by women and by the blacks who as part of the Great Migration had moved from the rural south to the industrial north. In 1919–20 all workers suffered the economic consequences of the war in the form of rampant inflation. Prices rose by up to 15 per cent, far in excess of the modest wage increases of 1917–18.

In 1919 several waves of strikes swept across the whole country from west to east. In Seattle a walkout by dockworkers in January turned into a general strike lasting several days and was supported by the radical Industrial Workers of the World – known for short as the 'Wobblies' or IWW – but not by Samuel Gompers's umbrella organization, the American Federation of Labor (AFL). Following the intervention of federal troops, it was brought to a rapid and bloodless end. In September even the Boston police refused to work in protest at their low salaries, resulting in riots and looting that persuaded the Republican governor of Massachusetts, Calvin Coolidge, to call in the National Guard. When Gompers suggested that the wage demands of the striking policemen be met, Coolidge responded with a remark that earned him the approval of many conservative Americans: 'There is no right to strike against public safety by anybody, anywhere, anytime.'[28]

Within days of the end of the Boston police strike, 365,000 workers in the steel industry in the Midwest went on strike. As in Seattle, their action was backed by the IWW but not by the AFL. Bloody clashes between striking workers and the military in Gary, Indiana, in early October resulted in nineteen deaths among the strikers. But steel production was unaffected because an unorganized – mainly black – workforce was drafted in to take over from the striking workers. The strike collapsed in January 1920 without the workers achieving any of their demands.

Black Americans had fought just as bravely as their white comrades during the war, but their goal of equal rights remained as remote as ever. Blacks who had found work in industry after 1917 were quickly replaced by returning white veterans after the end of 1918. The fact that black workers generally earned far less than their white counterparts meant that they were accused by the latter of keeping wages artificially low, fuelling the increasing resentment at the country's black minority. The number of blacks who were lynched by white Americans rose from forty-eight in 1917 to sixty-three in 1918 and to seventy-eight in 1919. In Chicago, where there had already been several bomb attacks in black districts of the city during the early months of 1919, racial tensions boiled over in July and assumed the proportions of a civil war, with 537 injuries and thirty-eight deaths, most of them blacks. The race riots of the summer of 1919 cost a total of 120 lives.

The largest organization that represented black Americans was the National Association for the Advancement of Colored People. It concluded from the escalation of violence against blacks that the latter could no longer be content to call on the authorities for help but must defend themselves against the white mob. Radical blacks associated with Jamaican-born Marcus Garvey went further and advocated a complete break with white society and a return to Africa. A few years later the 'Harlem Renaissance' began in New York, a movement of black writers and artists that sought to raise black awareness by recalling their African roots and their cultural identity as black Americans.

In April 1919 the American public was alarmed by a series of parcel bombs sent to prominent economists and politicians, although nearly all were intercepted by the postal services before they could reach their intended recipients. (The parcel that did get through blew off the hands of a senator's domestic servant.) On 2 June, conversely, bombs went off almost simultaneously in eight different towns and cities. One of them caused considerable damage to the front of the house occupied by Woodrow Wilson's justice minister, A. Mitchell Palmer. The press immediately began to inveigh against a large-scale and complex conspiracy led by the Communist International in Moscow and designed to overthrow the existing political and social order in the United States. Most of the country's states responded to this 'Red Scare' by passing anti-sedition laws, and in many cities, schools and universities political purges were launched against alleged or actual revolutionaries.

As justice minister, Palmer reacted to the 'Red Scare' with extreme rigour and in early November gave orders for 250 members of a Union of Russian Workers to be arrested and deported by sea to Soviet Russia. But it was in January 1920 that Palmer, aided and abetted by his young assistant J. Edgar Hoover, struck his most decisive blow, when he ordered the newly established Federal Bureau of Investigation to arrest and interrogate over 6,000 'radicals', including strike agitators, members of two small Communist parties and a number of self-declared anarchists. Some 500 foreigners were deported, even though there was no evidence that they had committed any criminal acts or even that they held extreme views. And around 250 individuals who had come to America from tsarist Russia were sent back to its Soviet successor.

These 'Palmer raids' initially met with widespread support among the American public, with only a handful of liberal and left-wing protests at such a crass violation of civil rights and liberties. Among the most notorious victims of this general suspicion of left-wing 'aliens' were two Italian immigrants, the shoemaker Nicola Sacco and the fishmonger Bartolomeo Vanzetti, neither of whom made any secret of his anarchist leanings. In May 1920 they were accused of jointly robbing and murdering the chief accountant of a shoe factory in Braintree, Massachusetts, and on 14 July 1921 condemned to death on the basis of highly questionable evidence. Liberals, socialists and Communists organized worldwide demonstrations in their support. Many prominent intellectuals, including Bernard Shaw, H. G. Wells and Albert Einstein, all expressed their sympathy. But all they achieved was a temporary stay of execution, and on 23 August 1927, in spite of international protests, Sacco and Vanzetti were executed in the electric chair. Not until July 1977, half a century later, were they rehabilitated, when the governor of Massachusetts, the Democrat Michael Dukakis, formally pardoned them.

If there was any subject that exercised the American public more than the 'Red Scare' in 1919–20, it was prohibition. The Eighteenth Amendment to the 1787 constitution came into force on 16 January 1920 after the necessary majorities had been achieved in both Congress and the individual state assemblies. It banned the manufacture, sale and shipment of alcoholic drinks in the United States. Prohibition was a long-standing aim not only of the members of the Anti-Saloon League and of Evangelical fundamentalists, especially in the rural south and Midwest, but also of many women's associations and, finally, of the Progressive Movement, the great reform movement of the late nineteenth and early twentieth centuries. The required majorities could be achieved at national and state level only because senators and representatives were placed under tremendous pressure by the anti-alcohol lobby.

In practice the ban proved unworkable as the vast majority of the population rejected and ignored it and the banned saloons were replaced by illegal bars – 'speakeasies' – disguised as private clubs. Organized crime profited from illicit stills and from smuggling alcohol across the Mexican and Canadian borders. The German political scientist and jurist Ernst Fraenkel judged prohibition to be 'perhaps the greatest act of political stupidity in the whole of American history', a judgement as severe as it is apt. In Fraenkel's view it undermined 'the nation's legal morality, encouraged gangsterism, corrupted the state apparatus and brought the country to the brink of administrative chaos'.[29] Prohibition came to an end in 1933 with the start of the presidency of Franklin D. Roosevelt, when public opinion forced the adoption of the Twenty-first Amendment, rescinding the Eighteenth Amendment, while allowing individual states to pass laws banning the shipment or importation of alcoholic drinks.

In August 1920, eight months after the Eighteenth Amendment had passed into the statute books, the Nineteenth Amendment came into force. This finally brought women the right for which American suffragettes had fought for decades and which they had already won in eleven states: to vote in elections under the same conditions as men. The first presidential elections in which women were able to vote were held in November 1920, when the Republicans emerged as victors, even though their candidate, the conservative senator from Ohio, Warren G. Harding, was politically undistinguished and inexperienced. His running mate for the office of vice-president was the governor of Massachusetts, Calvin Coolidge, the 'hero' of the Boston police strike of September 1919. The Democratic candidates – the governor of Ohio, James M. Cox, and, as his vice-presidential running mate, Franklin D. Roosevelt, who was then the assistant secretary of the navy – received only 34 per cent of the votes cast, the lowest percentage ever polled until then by a presidential candidate of either of the two main parties. The Republicans' triumph was the expression of an overwhelming desire to return to normality: the American 'normalcy' of which Harding was fond of speaking and which amounted to a rejection of the idealistic internationalism of the Woodrow Wilson years.

Harding's term of office lasted only a little over two years, ending with his death on 2 August 1923 as a result of two heart attacks. The period was overshadowed by scandals over fraud and corruption involving both the Department of the Interior and the Justice Department. The most spectacular case was that of the secretary of the interior, Albert B. Fall, who had previously been the senator for New Mexico and to whom Harding had given control over the navy's oil reserves in Wyoming and California, which he had then secretly leased to private contractors in return for substantial bribes. The case came to light in the summer of 1923, shortly after Harding's death, and earned Fall a year's imprisonment. Harding was succeeded by Coolidge, who in November 1924 easily won the presidential election in his own right, polling 54 per cent of the votes cast, while the Democratic candidate, John W. Davis, a financial lawyer from New York, polled 29 per cent and Senator Robert M. La Follette from Wisconsin, standing for the League for Progressive Political Action, won 17 per cent.

During the 1924 election campaign the Democrats had considered going on the offensive against the Ku Klux Klan but decided against doing so out of consideration for their voters in the south. The secretive and racist KKK dated back to the time of the American Civil War but had died out in the 1870s, only to be resurrected in 1915. Its violence was directed not only against blacks but also against Jews, Catholics and 'left-wing' foreigners. After the war it found increasing support not only in the south itself but also in smaller towns in the Mid- and far west, Indiana becoming its new stronghold. Its followers were for the most part heavily indebted farmers, small shopkeepers and other independent and self-employed individuals. At its height, in 1924, it is said to have had four million members. Its preferred methods of intimidation included beatings, tarring and feathering, and whipping and lynching. During the years of American prosperity in the mid-1920s it lost some of its appeal, while remaining the most powerful organization of its kind among extreme rightwing groups. By 1928 it had abandoned all pretence at secrecy.

The Ku Klux Klan represented the most extreme expression of American 'nativism' during the post-war period, turning itself into the mouthpiece of widespread fears and resentment that were also reflected in the country's legislative programme. In 1921 Congress passed a law limiting immigration: no more than 3 per cent of people of the same nationality as those who had lived in the USA in 1910 could enter the United States from another country. The number of immigrants who were admitted officially sank from 800,000 to 300,000, although nativists regarded this figure as no more than a step in the right direction.

A further law followed in 1924: the National Origins Act went even further than Canada's Chinese Exclusion Act of 1923 and prohibited all immigrants from eastern Asia from entering the United States, reducing the quota from European countries from 3 per cent in 1921 to 2 per cent. But the base figure was now that for 1880, rather than for 1910, a change that discriminated in particular against Jewish immigrants from eastern and central Europe. Immigration was further curtailed in 1929, when the upper limit of immigrants was reduced to 150,000 a year. Throughout the years that followed the number of immigrants admitted to the country was generally well below this limit. There is no doubt that such a policy was rooted in racist motives. One of the 'experts' to whom the House of Representatives appealed when drafting the legislation in 1924 was the eugenicist Harry H. Laughlin, who never tired of warning his fellow Americans of the dangers of 'mongrelization'. One of the law's principal champions was the Democrat R. E. Allen from West Virginia, who in a speech to a plenary session of the House on 5 April 1924 even went so far as to speak of 'purifying and keeping pure the blood of America' as the only way of saving the country from the threat of Bolshevism.[30]

In no other western country was the fear of Communism less well founded than it was in the United States. In 1919 two Communist parties had broken free from what was already a tiny Socialist Party: the Communist Labor Party had 60,000 members, nine-tenths of whom were immigrants, while the Communist Party had around 10,000 members, most of whom had been born in America. In May 1921, at the urging of the Communist International, the two groups merged to form the Communist Party of America, which was repeatedly shaken by violent internal arguments until Trotsky's supporters were expelled in 1928. Even then the Communist Party of America was never anything more than a splinter group – in 1929, for example, it had fewer than 10,000 members. Only the bomb attacks by anarchists and the sympathy for the Bolshevik cause initially shown by members of the IWW suggested that they may have posed a revolutionary threat in 1919–20.

The Socialist Party strenuously rejected the brutal methods of the Bolsheviks but it, too, remained no more than a marginal phenomenon, enjoying its greatest support among voters at the 1920 presidential election, when it polled almost one million votes for its candidate, Eugene V. Debs, who was still in prison at that date. The vast majority of American workers continued to be indifferent to any fundamental changes to the existing capitalist system. What they wanted were higher wages and shorter working hours: to them 'bread and butter' were more important than placing the means of production in public ownership.

The way in which large sections of the American public reacted to the challenge of Communism can be explained by reference to their past history. In no other large country was democracy as firmly rooted in everyday culture as it was in the United States, and nowhere was private property as sacrosanct as it was here. A system that sought to establish a completely new society based on common property and run in the name of the 'dictatorship of the proletariat' was tantamount to the most radical declaration of war on the American way of life. Even worse: such a system seemed to call into question the divine order of things. For the Christian right, the militant atheism of the Bolsheviks turned them and their followers into a modern manifestation of the Antichrist. It was no accident, therefore, that those who were the most outspoken in their anti-Communist views were Evangelical fundamentalists.

It was not necessary, of course, to be a Communist or a socialist to draw down the concentrated hatred of this profoundly religious minority. Such hostility could be incurred by anyone expressing doubts in the literal truth of the Biblical story of the Creation, no matter whether such doubts were voiced by liberal theologians or by the supporters of Darwin's theory of evolution. In March 1925 the fundamentalists in Tennessee scored a spectacular victory in their battle against what they saw as a heretical doctrine, passing a law that banned teachers from promoting any view of the Creation that departed from the one set forth in the Bible. This declaration of war on enlightenment and free thinking prompted the American Civil Liberties Union to act. This organization, that had been formed in 1917, encouraged a young biology teacher from Dayton, John T. Scopes, who was unwilling to abide by the new law, to mount a challenge in the form of a test case for which the Union provided the defence in the form of the famous lawyer Clarence Darrow and paid for the cost of the proceedings. The fundamentalists' case was represented by William Jennings Bryan, who repeatedly stood for election as a presidential candidate, first for the Democrats, later as a progressive.

Scopes, who had in the meantime been dismissed from his teaching post, was fined $100, although this was later quashed by a higher court on the grounds of a procedural error. The exchange of blows between Darrow and Bryan was followed with tremendous interest both in America and further afield, Darrow emerging as the clear victor. Even though a number of other southern states followed Tennessee's example, the advocates of freedom of expression had won a clear moral victory with the Scopes case and put the fundamentalists firmly on the defensive.

Material conditions also left a mark on the development of the social, political and intellectual climate of post-war America. The social unrest of 1919 was a reflection of the devaluation that to a greater or lesser extent affected all the countries that had been involved in the war and that had run up debts in financing it. Inflation initially stimulated the economy, but by the end of 1920 the growing gap between high prices and low wages had caused the market for consumer goods to collapse, marking the start of a period of post-war depression that quickly enveloped the entire world, the only notable exception – as we shall see in due course – being Germany. In the United States the gross national product fell by almost 10 per cent between 1920 and 1921; some 100,000 companies filed for bankruptcy; and around five million workers lost their jobs. Only in the second half of 1922 did the economy start to recover.

During the next seven years, the United States enjoyed a period of higher growth that was due above all to two factors: the building industry, where, as a result of the war, there was a tremendous need to catch up on investment, and the car industry which thanks to immense technological progress during the previous decade could now produce vehicles so cheaply that the market for new cars grew in ways that no one had previously seen. In 1917 1.7 million cars were produced; by 1929 that figure had risen to 4.5 million. In 1929 – the last of America's boom years – there were twenty-six million private cars and lorries on the country's roads. The car had become a luxury item that most households could afford. In the country of Ford, General Motors and Chrysler, one person in five owned a car by the end of the decade, whereas in Great Britain the figure was one in forty-three, in Italy one in 325 and in Russia one in 1,000. In the 1920s America became a pioneering country in terms of mass consumption, a development that had already begun before 1914 but which was able to unfold along a broad front only after the war, encouraging contemporaries to speak enthusiastically of a 'new era'.

The boom in the car industry stimulated other areas of the economy, including road building, the construction industry, the steel industry, tyre manufacturing and numerous other supply industries, oil companies, petrol stations and restaurants. The car reduced distances and brought Americans closer together, facilitating commuting between the suburbs and the cities, increasing individual mobility and, together with long-distance coaches and the country's ever-faster trains, giving a boost to mass tourism. Scarcely less dramatic was the triumphant progress of another means of mass communication, the radio, which in America – unlike Europe – was run by private broadcasters rather than by the state. In 1925 there were around two million radios in the United States. Within five years almost every American household had one. Newspapers remained a competitive force thanks to the speed with which they were able to disseminate news, while radio stations vied with theatres, opera houses and music halls for their audience's favours.

But radio was unable to compete with the cinema in terms of popularity and entertainment value. In 1922 American cinemas had a combined audience of forty million; eight years later that figure had climbed to 100 million. After 1927 talking pictures gradually replaced the silent film. Hollywood used the temporary weakness of the European film industry that resulted from the war to assert its claims to global domination. However much America may have learnt from Europe in this regard, stars such as Buster Keaton, Charlie Chaplin, Laurel and Hardy and Rudolph Valentino and the cartoon films of Walt Disney helped the United States' own particular brand of popular culture to triumph all over the world, a triumph that no other country could contest. Hollywood also allowed European film stars such as Pola Negri and Greta Garbo to enjoy international careers. Sound films additionally proved an excellent vehicle for exporting another American product, jazz from New Orleans as embodied by Louis Armstrong and Duke Ellington. The 1927 film *The Jazz Singer* with Al Jolson in the title role was the first talkie ever made. Jazz finally conquered Europe in the 1920s, while dividing opinion there between admirers and contemptuous critics of this revolutionary kind of American music.

The 'roaring twenties' began in America and soon gripped the whole of the world, but nowhere were the 1920s as 'golden' as in the United States. Not only big business profited from the prosperity of the new era after 1923, so too did the bulk of the population. Henry Ford, the head of the Ford Motor Company, stuck rigidly to the philosophy of Fordism that included passing on the benefits of rationalization in the form of increased wages and shorter working hours. Ford's welfare capitalism included social insurance and trade unions but no salary agreements with independent unions. Instead, big business was increasingly able to implement an open-shop policy after 1919, meaning that no member of their workforce was obliged to join a trade union. In turn the number of trade union members fell from over five million to under three million between 1920 and 1929, a development also due, of course, to the fact that the AFL continued for the most part to represent the interests of white skilled workers and did relatively little for unskilled workers and for the blacks who made up the bulk of this group.

Calvin Coolidge's administration was as business-friendly as any Republican government was expected to be. A practising Protestant from New England, he adopted the maxim, 'The man who builds a factory builds a temple, the man who works there worships there.'[31] His trade minister, Herbert Hoover, systematically encouraged the voluntary merger of whole branches of industry to form associations linked by shared interests and, he hoped, conducive to stabilizing prices.

In keeping with Republican tradition, the economic policies of the 1920s were liberal within the country and protectionist in terms of America's dealings with the outside world. Even during Harding's presidency, the Republican majority in Congress had introduced the highest import tariffs in American history in the form of the Fordney–McCumber Tariff Act in an attempt to protect the rural economy as well as the chemical and metal industries from what they feared would be the dumping of foreign goods on America. Farmers were by now suffering from massive over-production as a result of progressive mechanization and demanded far greater protection, a demand that met with widespread support in the Senate and the House of Representatives. Under the impact of the international decline in farm prices Congress voted for the McNary–Haugen Bill in 1927 and 1928, providing for the government purchase of wheat, cotton, tobacco, rice and maize, which would then be sold on at the lower international prices. On both occasions, however, Coolidge used his veto to prevent the bill from becoming law as he was afraid of sweeping retaliatory measures on the part of the overseas countries affected.

Even without the McNary–Haugen Bill, America's policy on foreign trade throughout the Republican administrations of the 1920s would still deserve to be labelled highly protectionist. The country's protective tariffs encouraged economic nationalism in those countries that were particularly harmed by the isolation of the American market. Germany was especially badly affected because it was forced to finance its reparations bill by means of exports. The United States had signed a separate peace treaty with Germany in August 1921. This was a logical consequence of the Senate's refusal to ratify the Treaty of Versailles. Both as a trading partner and as the scene of American investments, Germany was far too important for the United States to regard its development with indifference – another reason why Coolidge twice stood up to Congress over the McNary–Haugen Bill.

American isolationism would in any case have prevented the country from joining the League of Nations, but it was clear to those responsible in Washington that the economic interests of the United States needed a supporting policy in Europe and especially Germany. The question of German reparations was closely associated with the problem of Allied debts, a problem that could be solved only by the United States. A stable Germany in a stable Europe was of supreme importance for the United States, a view that imposed certain limits on its isolationist policies and ensured that the protectionists did not overreach themselves. America was to maintain a far greater presence in post-war Europe than Wilson's enemies expected in 1919/20.

The International Revolution is Delayed: The Rise of the Soviet Union and the Divisions within Left-wing Parties in Europe

The country that most Americans would almost certainly have described as the most dangerous in the world – Soviet Russia – could not be certain that it would overcome its internal enemies until the end of 1919. The Red Army had been advancing on all fronts since October of that year. Admiral Kolchak, for a time the most dangerous of the 'White' leaders, was forced to retreat to Irkutsk, where he was handed over to Bolshevik supporters by war-weary members of the Czechoslovak Legion and shot on 7 February 1920. In April, following several major defeats, General Denikin stepped down as the commander in chief of the 'Whites' in southern Russia and was succeeded by Pyotr Nikolayevich Wrangell, whose autumn offensive, supported by the British and launched from the Crimea, ended in disaster. The evacuation of his remaining troops on Allied ships in November 1920 effectively marked the end of the Russian civil war and, with it, the end of the half-hearted intervention on the part of the Allies, who had sided with the 'Whites' in 1918.

The defeat of the disorganized 'Whites' was due mainly to the inability of the counterrevolutionaries to gain broad support among the Russian population. The industrial proletariat more or less closed ranks against them; they were hated by the peasants, who regarded them as hangers-on of the old order, keen to overturn the recent redistribution of the land; and as pan-Russian chauvinists they could never be reliable allies of the Ukrainian nationalists. All that harmed the 'Whites' benefited the Reds, who enjoyed their greatest support among the workers and who, compared with the 'Whites', seemed the lesser of two evils to most peasants, complaints about the impounding of corn and foodstuffs being more than offset by gratitude towards the Reds for ending large-scale landownership; and non-Russian nationalities, finally, expected the Bolsheviks to safeguard their interests more than the 'Whites', who had always advocated a powerful central state.

The year 1920 witnessed not only the end of the Russian civil war but also Soviet Russia's recognition of the independence of Estonia, Lithuania and Latvia, the cessation of hostilities in the Russo-Polish War in October and peace with Finland. In March 1921, as we have already noted, Russia concluded the Peace of Riga with Poland. The western border of the Russian Soviet Federative Socialist Republic, as the country officially became known in July 1918, together with that of the independent White Russian and Ukrainian Republics, now ran much further east than that of tsarist Russia but incorporated the greater part of the Ukraine, including the areas on the right bank of the Dnieper that Russia had acquired in the second half of the seventeenth century under the terms of the Russo-Polish Truce of Andrusovo in January 1667. This region was predominantly Russian in character.

In the Caucasus, conversely, the Bolsheviks were able to add considerably to their Soviet Russian territories, and Soviet regimes were imposed on both Azerbaijan and Armenia after the British troops withdrew in 1920. In Georgia the Mensheviks had established an independent state in 1918, and this had been officially recognized by Moscow in May 1920, only for it to be overrun by the Red Army in February 1921. In spite of widespread international protests, especially on the part of the non-Communist left, the country was declared the Georgian Soviet Socialist Republic which, subsumed into the Transcaucasian Federation the following year, played a role in the foundation of the Union of Soviet Socialist Republics in December 1922. The USSR made further territorial gains in the Far East in November 1922 when it incorporated two states that had come into existence during the Japanese occupation but which were now vacated by the Japanese: the Far Eastern Republic and the Coastal Republic. For the present the two central Asiatic soviet republics that had been created with Bolshevik assistance in 1920 in the form of the khanate of Khiva and the emirate of Bukhara remained independent.

Soviet Russia's civil war may have been over, but the country was still far from having achieved a state of internal stability. On 10 July 1918 the Fifth All-Russian Soviet Congress had approved a constitution that enshrined the soviet system, but constitutional reality looked very different. During the civil war the eastern soviets had lost much of their existing authority to extraordinary bodies armed with comprehensive powers. One such body was the All-Russian Extraordinary Commission for Combating Counterrevolution and Sabotage, known as the Cheka for short. Its measures were very soon aimed at all suspicious members of the soviets. For a time the coordination of all political, military and economic tasks was entrusted not to the Council of People's Commissars but to the Council for Workers' and Peasants' Defence, an organization established in November 1918. All ordinary and extraordinary bodies were controlled by the Communist Party, which dictated the revolutionary process on every level. By March 1921 it had 730,000 members, of whom workers represented an ever smaller percentage, while the number of white-collar workers and other professionals grew.

The civil war witnessed a period of 'War Communism', a primitive form of controlled economy that forced workers, peasants and tradesmen to perform the tasks imposed on them, where necessary with the resources of terror. The government had to do all it could to make up for the dramatic fall in industrial production. Not least as a result of the nationalization of large farms in the early summer of 1918, production at the end of 1918 was only a fifth of what it had been in 1913. Where necessary, the workforce was recruited by force. Since inflation had largely destroyed the purchasing power of incomes, workers were paid in kind, including rations. In the Urals 37 per cent of workers returned to the countryside in 1920. By the following year metalworking plants had lost up to half of their employees. There was no longer any private commerce after the autumn of 1918.

In the course of the civil war the granaries in southern Russia had fallen into the hands of the 'Whites'. The subsequent requisitioning of corn in the areas controlled by the Bolsheviks was implemented by the newly formed Committees of Poor Peasants (kombedy) and by the Red Army and meant that the farmers stopped ploughing their land and produced only what they needed for their own personal use. By 1921 the area of land under cultivation had shrunk to 62 per cent, the harvest yield to 37 per cent of its pre-war total. The logical consequence of the enforced measures undertaken both in cities and in the countryside was a growing bureaucratization that paralysed individual initiative.

But the end of the civil war did not mean the end of War Communism. This end was closely bound up with the growing protests at the continuation of a controlled economy and of terror. During the first half of 1921 there were innumerable peasants' revolts and hunger strikes by workers, especially in Moscow and Petrograd. In January distribution of bread was cut by a third in the towns and cities; and in Petrograd 60 per cent of the largest factories had to close through lack of fuel. On 22 February workers at other major concerns in Petrograd held a demonstration at which a number of Mensheviks and Social Revolutionaries spoke, demanding the abolition of the Bolshevik dictatorship and the restoration of basic freedoms and calling for a general strike in pursuit of these aims. The Cheka responded two days later by firing on the participants in a second demonstration, leaving twelve people dead. Mass arrests followed. Even so, thousands of soldiers joined the striking workers. Russia seemed to be on a brink of a new revolution.

On 2 March 1921 Moscow's worst fears were realized when 15,000 sailors mutinied in Kronstadt on the island of Kotlin in the Gulf of Finland – effectively at the very gates of Petrograd. In 1917 the sailors at Kronstadt had been the Bolsheviks' most loyal and radical supporters. Three and a half years later they were demanding not only far-reaching material improvements but a return to the constitution of July 1918, secret new elections for the soviets, the restoration of the freedoms fought for during the Revolution, including freedom for the supporters of the anarchists and left-wing Socialist parties, and, finally, the removal of all Communist commissars from the army and navy.

Lenin saw this as a counterrevolutionary attack and gave orders for an assault on Kronstadt on 7 March. Trotsky, who had been defence commissar since March 1918, ordered General Mikhail Nikolayevich Tukhachevsky to turn his heavy artillery on the island and then to take it with land troops. The result was a bloodbath that ended the mutiny on 18 March, the fiftieth anniversary of the Paris Commune. Three months later, in June 1921, Tukhachevsky adopted equally brutal tactics in suppressing the largest and longest of the peasants' revolts in the province of Tambov. Its leader, Alexander Antonov, was taken prisoner and murdered, while 15,000 of his supporters were imprisoned or deported.

While Kronstadt was under siege and under fire, the Tenth Party Congress of the Russian Communists was held in Moscow. In the face of considerable opposition, Lenin forced through a motion that banned the formation of factions within the party, thereby putting a definitive end to the phase of relative internal democracy that had been introduced a year earlier in the wake of violent arguments. The ban – for which Trotsky, Bukharin, editor in chief of *Pravda*, and, ultimately, Lenin were jointly responsible – was directed in the main at the 'Workers' Opposition' supported by trade union officials and distinguished by its outspoken critique of the 'militarization of work'.

An equally far-reaching decision affected the transition to the New Economic Policy, as it came to be called only after the Tenth Party Conference had ended in late May 1921. The change of policy represented Lenin's response to the failure of War Communism. From now on farmers were no longer to be obliged to give up their corn and other produce but paid a tax in kind and were allowed to keep everything they had produced that exceeded that amount. The nationalization of small businesses that had been agreed to only a short time earlier, in late November 1920, was effectively reversed by this measure and the economic scope of manual work was extended. The main areas of the economy – the major banks, large businesses, foreign trade and transport – all remained under state control: from February 1921 this meant the state planning commission, or Gosplan.

Crucial to Gosplan were the members of the State Commission for the Electrification of Russia, a committee largely made up of 'bourgeois' – non-Communist – experts that had submitted its ambitious project in time for the Eighth Soviet Congress at the end of December 1920. 'Communism is Soviet power plus electrification of the whole country,' Lenin famously declared.[32] As the historian Heiko Haumann has noted, his words were carefully chosen:

> Electrification was understood not just in the narrow technological sense, it was also intended to simplify the running of the economy and speed up the growth of the forces of production. Before them was the goal of removing the difference between town and country and turning the executive function of the worker into an organizational function. Not least of their aims was the promotion of 'education through light', especially in the countryside.[33]

The partial return to capitalist economic methods helped to smooth the path to trade deals with western nations. The first to be signed was with Great Britain on 16 March 1921, followed in May by a trade agreement with Germany and shortly afterwards one with Italy and with most of the other European states. Only France and the United States turned down the Soviet demarche. Currency was stabilized in the wake of the New Economic Policy, and industrial production rapidly increased. But the party and government were powerless in the face of the failed harvest of 1920 and the widespread drought of 1921. The result was a catastrophic famine that reached its climax during the winter of 1921/2 and according to reliable estimates cost the lives of between four and five million men, women and children. The number of victims would have been much higher if Fridtjof Nansen, the famous polar explorer and League of Nations' commissioner for refugees, together with the American trade minister Herbert Hoover and the Communist and non-Communist workers' parties in Europe, had not organized generous relief action in support of Soviet Russia's famine-stricken population.

In April 1921 Lenin wrote a pamphlet in which he described the recent introduction of the tax in kind as marking a transition from War Communism to a regulated socialist exchange of products and the reintroduction of free trade as 'capitalism', which, he went on, would help the Communists by preventing the fragmentation of small producers and to a certain extent also help to combat bureaucracy. He quoted at length from an earlier pamphlet, 'On Russia's Present Economy' (1918), in which he had hailed state capitalism as a transitional phase between the capitalism of private industry and socialism. He continued to regard socialism without the techniques of big business as unthinkable. War Communism had been forced on the country by war and by financial ruin but was not a policy that reflected the economic tasks of the proletariat as it was merely a temporary measure:

> The correct policy of the proletariat exercising its dictatorship in a small-peasant country is to obtain grain in exchange for the manufactured goods the peasant needs. That is the only kind of food policy that corresponds to the tasks of the proletariat, and can strengthen the foundations of socialism and lead to its complete victory.[34]

The Bolsheviks' mass terror, which was the dominant feature of War Communism, shared many of the characteristics of the Reign of Terror perpetrated by the French Jacobins. Indeed, Lenin, an ardent pupil of Marx, regarded the Jacobins as his historical model. In 1793–4, as in 1918–20, the connection between counterrevolution inside the country and intervention from outside had a radicalizing effect, challenging the most decisive revolutionaries to engage in a struggle in which the very existence of the new order was at stake. In each case the dynamics of terror led to a point where the terror threatened to become self-destructive. The Jacobin Terror was followed by Thermidor, when more moderate voices prevailed. But the New Economic Policy was not the Thermidor of the Bolshevik Revolution, for the previous revolutionary leaders remained in control, fine-tuning their own policies and declining to turn their backs on terror. Instead, they merely limited its scope and applied it only in those cases where the situation seemed to them to require it, legalizing actions that had previously been outside the law in order to remove what they termed 'class enemies'. In short, the Bolshevik terror was not a transitional stage in their revolution but remained their means of ruling the country even after the immediate internal and external threat had passed. It could be reactivated at any time, whenever the centre of power deemed it necessary to do so.

The centre of power of the Communist Party of Russia – the Bolsheviks – was the Politburo. It was elected by the Central Committee, which in turn was appointed by the party conference. Within the Politburo, the members who wielded the greatest power after Lenin were the leaders of the party organizations in Petrograd and Moscow, Grigory Yevseyevich Zinoviev and Lev Borisovich Kamenev. To their names must be added that of Stalin, whom the Central Committee appointed its secretary general in April 1922. Trotsky had no firm organizational support within the party, whereas Bukharin, experienced as an economist and a theorist, gradually acquired this support for himself. Lenin suffered a stroke in May 1922, followed by a second one in the December of that same year and by a third in March 1923, after which he effectively quit the political stage in Russia.

The Russian Communist Party grew in size in 1920 when it merged with a number of rival groups, including large sections of the 'maximalist' Social Revolutionaries, the General Jewish Workers' League and the Revolutionary Communists. The most active Menshevik officials were arrested for their part in the workers' protests in 1921, and their party was banned, as was that of the Social Revolutionaries. A show trial of forty-seven Social Revolutionaries was held in July 1922, when they were accused of counterrevolutionary activities in connection with the peasants' uprisings. Fourteen of the accused were sentenced to death, although following international protests from the non-Communist left, the sentences were not carried out. Instead, the accused were sent to the Solovki labour camp on the Solovetsky Islands in the White Sea. By then, Russia's one-party state felt sufficiently strong to meet its critics halfway.

The Communist Party of Russia also set the tone in the soviets that had had only minimal influence during the first two years after the October Revolution but which were granted extended rights at the Seventh All-Russian Soviet Congress in December 1919. Its newly formed executive committee gradually usurped the influence of the Extraordinary Commissions, including the one set up to combat counterrevolution and sabotage, and created the new organization of the Workers' and Peasants' Inspection that was intended to replace the People's Commissariat for State Control. Since the peasants were more powerfully represented in the soviets than in the Communist Party, the soviets were better suited to implementing the New Economic Policy, central to which was a new approach to agriculture that favoured the peasants. The soviets could claim some success in abolishing the death penalty in January 1920, only for it to be reintroduced in May 1922 in time for the trial of the Social Revolutionaries. In the future, too, the Soviet state was keen to be able to draw upon the ultimate sanction in dealing with its political enemies and with others whom it branded 'criminals'.

For many years the role of the trade unions remained controversial. The 'Workers' Opposition' sought an independent role in representing the proletariat's interests, whereas Trotsky and Bukharin wanted the trade unions to be dependent on state institutions. At the Communist Party's Ninth Party Conference in late March and early April 1920 a moderate line represented by Vyacheslav Molotov gained support: the trade unions were to remain independent organizations and form a 'transmission belt' between workers and party. In other words, they would inform the Communist Party of workers' wishes and convey the party's instructions to the workers. In practice this concept placed the trade unions in a subservient position: their task was to educate the proletarian masses and train them to be good Communists, while at the same time working for greater productivity. Lenin had initially been inclined to adopt Trotsky's position, but by the end of 1920 he had come round to Molotov's way of thinking, at which point the question of the trade unions ceased to be contentious. In March 1921 the Tenth Party Conference defined the new role of the trade unions as a 'transmission belt'.

The logic of the New Economic Policy also concealed within it a more elastic policy towards nationalities that did not detract from the supremacy of the central power. The constitution of July 1918 had made no reference to the reciprocal relations between the individual Soviet Republics, whether Russian, White Russian or Ukrainian. Once the Bolsheviks had brought Azerbaijan and Armenia under their control in 1920–21, followed by Georgia in 1922, and merged them all in the Transcaucasian Federation, the way was open for the formation of the Union of Socialist Soviet Republics, or USSR, known for short as the Soviet Union. A state treaty between the Ukrainian, Byelorussian and Transcaucasian Soviet Republics on the one hand and the Russian Soviet Federated Socialist Republic on the other was ratified at the First All-Union Soviet Congress on 30 December 1922. (This congress was in fact nothing more than the expanded and renamed Seventh All-Russian Soviet Congress.)

The two central Asian soviet republics of Khiva and Bukhara were still sovereign states at this date, but in the wake of 'national delimitation', as it was called, they were merged with the general governorships of the Steppe and Turkestan and turned into the Union Republics of Uzbekistan and Turkmenistan. The Tajik part of the former general governorship of Turkestan was granted the status of an autonomous republic in 1924. Five years later Tajikistan became a union republic in its own right.

The constitution of the USSR was worked out in the first half of 1923 and was approved by the Central Executive Committee in July and ratified at the Second All-Union Soviet Congress at the end of January 1924. It did not contain a single article that defined or guaranteed human and civil rights and no division of powers that could be characterized as 'bourgeois'. Protests at decisions by the supreme court could be lodged with the Central Executive Committee of the Soviets, which grew out of the All-Union Soviet Congress and consisted of two chambers, the Soviet of the Union and the Soviet of Nationalities.

Foreign policy and foreign trade were in the hands of the central authority, as were the military, transport, postal services and telegraphy. In terms of state control over the economy and the nation's finances, welfare and work, the central authority's powers were so comprehensive when compared with those of the individual republics that there was no question as to the relative weighting: formally, the Soviet Union may have been a federalist state, but in practice it was centralized. If we ignore the territorial losses in the west, its land mass was similar to that of tsarist Russia. Both were multinational states.

Whether the Soviet Union would be more just towards the needs of non-Russian nationalities than the monarchy had been was a question that only the reality of the constitution could answer.

The early years of the Soviet Union were dominated by the principles of *korenizacija* (taking root) and 'national reconstruction'. Members of non-Russian ethnic groups were to be won over to the new revolutionary state and, hence, to Communism by express consideration of their unique cultural values. In the Islamic republics, for example, the Arabic alphabet was replaced not by Cyrillic but by the Latin alphabet, and regional administrative posts and party offices were filled by local forces, except in the case of the very highest positions.

In the Ukraine this new policy led to a revival of the Ukrainian language in those regions that had spoken a mixture of Russian and Ukrainian. Having suffered oppression at the hands of the Romanoffs, many Jews had thrown in their lot with the Bolsheviks, and it was Jews who now made up many of the leading Bolshevik officials, including Zinoviev, Kamenev and Trotsky. All enjoyed the right, granted to them in the wake of the 1917 February Revolution, to settle anywhere in the Soviet Union, including areas outside the 'settlement area' in thirteen western governorships of the old tsarist empire. The policy relating to individual nationalities between 1922 and 1926 was in theory geared to the principle of cultural self-determination, but in practice it came into conflict even at this early date with the pan-Russian traditions of the party apparatus, a problem that became progressively worse with the passage of time.

Aspects of this policy that seemed at this time to be liberal were in keeping with the relative pluralism of the pre-Stalinist period. Only in the case of the Soviet Union's policy towards the Church does the label 'liberal' seem undeserving. Its relation to the Orthodox Church was compromised from the outset by the Church's own reactionary tradition and by the militant atheism of the Bolsheviks. During the revolution Church lands had been confiscated and a radical division between Church and state was implemented. The violent attacks on godless Bolshevism by Tikhon, the Metropolitan of Moscow and Patriarch of the Russian Orthodox Church, merely provoked the revolutionary regime into closing churches and persecuting priests through the courts. During the civil war, thousands of Orthodox Christians and at least twenty-eight bishops were murdered, and in 1922 and 1923 the total number of Orthodox priests who were killed amounted to over 8,000.

In 1922 a bitter power struggle broke out between the 'reformers', who were loyal to the regime, and the patriarch, who had almost the entire clergy behind him. In April 1923 a council dominated by the 'reformers' voted to abolish the office of patriarch, prompting Tikhon to intervene and to publish a declaration of loyalty in the government newspaper *Izvestiya*, with the result that in June 1923 the house arrest under which he had been placed since May 1922 was lifted, ushering in a period during which the Russian Orthodox Church was tolerated by the state. But in the wake of Tikhon's death in April 1925 a further power struggle broke out between the state and the Church. It ended only when the Metropolitan of Novgorod, Sergey Stragorodski, swore comprehensive allegiance to the Soviet state.

The position adopted by Alexandra Kollontai, an early champion of women's rights, on the questions of marriage and the family was regarded as unduly radical not only by devout Christians but even by many Bolsheviks. She defended the right of free love, which was also to be practised in the communes that she proposed. As people's commissar for social welfare between November 1917 and March 1918, she was the world's first female government minister. Both in this function and as head of the women's section of the Central Committee, she strove to relax marital and family law, to improve the legal protections available to expectant and nursing mothers and to fight for the right to terminate a pregnancy. Conversely, she was unable to achieve her demand for the collective upbringing of children, while her views on marriage and the family were not shared by Lenin and other leading Bolsheviks. Her political influence waned when she joined the left-wing 'Workers' Opposition' and demanded greater democracy within the party. The Central Committee tried to exclude her, but its attempts were thwarted by the resistance of the delegates at the Eleventh Party Congress in March 1922. The following year she was appointed the Soviet Union's ambassador to Norway, which proved to be the first stage in a long diplomatic career. The liberal marriage and family laws that she had championed in 1918 were ratified in 1926.

Early Soviet cultural politics were also comparatively liberal. From 1917 to 1929 they bore the imprint of the people's commissar for education, Anatoly Lunacharsky. Lenin had charged him with eradicating illiteracy, and although the lack of suitable teachers prevented him from introducing universal compulsory education, which the Central Committee did not enact until July 1930, he was none the less able to reduce the rate of illiteracy from between 60 and 70 per cent in 1919 to 49 per cent in 1926. An important role in this development was played by workers' faculties ('Rabfak') established not only in colleges but also in factories and intended to teach reading and writing and the basic elements of a general education in three-year courses.

Schooling was also extended. Even during the period of the civil war from 1918 to 1921, some 8,500 new schools were built. As part of the National Economic Plan, Lunacharsky placed greater importance on teaching basic knowledge than on ideological indoctrination, for all that the latter was not for a moment neglected, for teachers were regarded as the principal mediators of socialism in the country's villages. Lunacharsky could not, of course, prevent the number of primary schools dropping from 76,000 to 50,000 in the wake of the economic crisis of 1921–3, when the number of pupils fell from 6.1 to 3.6 million, and it was not until 1926 that the figure was restored to its pre-war level. By 1927 the number of children attending school was around three million more than it had been in 1914.

The struggle to combat illiteracy was only one aspect of Lunacharsky's work, for in October 1920 the Politburo placed him in charge of 'Proletkult', a cultural movement for workers that until then had been independent and which the philosopher and physician Alexander Alexandrovich Bogdanov had summoned into existence with Lunacharsky's help before the war. Bogdanov's aim had been to introduce workers to 'middle-class' culture through their own clubs, libraries and theatres and at the same time to turn them into the representatives of a new proletarian culture. During the civil war anti-bourgeois feelings grew within the movement and eventually demanded a radical break with tradition. Proletkult inherited all manner of avant-garde ideas, from Expressionism to Cubism and Futurism. It also produced a significant kind of poster art and a sophisticated type of political theatre, influencing the work of writers and film directors, notably Sergei Eisenstein, whose film *Battleship Potemkin* of 1925 did much to invest the October Revolution with quasi-mythical status in the eyes of the rest of the world.

If it was to be innovative, then Proletkult needed to be artistically independent, and Lunacharsky was prepared to grant it a considerable degree of freedom even after it had been disbanded as an independent organization, but in the longer term he was unable to prevail over Lenin and the Politburo. When Proletkult was placed under the additional control of the trade unions in 1926, its decline was inevitable, and under Stalin the movement lost everything that until then had constituted its international fascination. This development also marked the end of the period when Bolshevism and avant-garde art had seemed to be two sides of the same coin, a time when 'fellow travellers' and even émigrés returning from abroad had found it possible to contribute to Soviet art without the fear of censorship and the secret police, and the Academy of Science had still been able to enrol declared critics of the teachings of Marx and Lenin.

But even the early Soviet Union already had its secret police, the Gosudarstvennoye Politicheskoye Upravleniy (GPU), which was created in 1922 under the overall control of the Ministry of the Interior and replaced the earlier Cheka. By 1923 the GPU had in turn been replaced by the OGPU, the Joint State Political Directorate, which enjoyed the status of a supreme authority, having a seat and a vote on the Council of People's Deputies. Like the Cheka, it was run by Polish-born Felix Dzerzhinsky. The OGPU also shared its headquarters with its predecessor, the notorious Lubyanka in Moscow. As Manfred Hildermeier has written, the OGPU had the authority to combat

'counterrevolution', espionage and banditry throughout the entire country. It was able to establish branches in every Soviet Republic and also station troops and open camps. It was responsible solely to the Council of People's

Delegates and the Executive Committee of Soviets but to no regional authority. By enhancing the status of what had once been the quintessential makeshift organization, the constitution granted normalcy to the exceptional in the central area of securing both power and the newer order. The OGPU became the third pillar of the revolutionary regime alongside the monopolistically authoritarian party and the increasingly loyal and elitist army, which was notable for its awareness of the needs of the state as a whole.[35]

By the time the Soviet Union was founded, the Bolsheviks were by no means as isolated with regard to other states and within the international workers' movement as they had been in 1918–19. This became clear at the Second World Congress of the Communist International, which met in Petrograd on 19 July 1920 and in Moscow between 23 July and 7 August. The Third International had grown considerably in size since its inaugural meeting in March 1919 and was now attended by 217 delegates from thirty-six different countries representing 152 Communist parties and organizations. The most important delegations were not Communist, however, but left-wing socialists with widespread support among their countries' voters: the Italian Socialist Party, the French Socialist Party, the Independent Social-Democratic Party of Germany, which had only recently won a sensational 18.6 per cent of the vote in the Reichstag elections on 6 June 1920, and the Norwegian Workers' Party. Two of these parties – the German Independents and the French Socialists – were not even members of the Comintern but had sent negotiators in an advisory role and with the authority to discuss the conditions under which their parties might join the International.

There were many reasons why the workers' movement in Europe lurched to the left: among them were disenchantment at the course of the revolutions in central Europe, where in the view of more extreme thinkers, there had been a noticeable lack of any real change to social and political conditions; the failure of the great strikes of 1919 and 1920; anger at the ineffectual nature of the Second International in the war and an unwillingness on the part of many of its members to examine the reasons for this ineffectuality in a self-critical manner; and, not least, admiration for the one party that had achieved a proletarian revolution, managing to hang on to power in its struggle against the counter-revolution and the intervention of the Allies and which now, at the start of the Second World Congress that coincided with the climax of the Russo-Polish War, was apparently on the point of carrying Communism into the heart of central Europe.

At their party conference in Bologna in the autumn of 1919, the Italian Socialists voted to join the Third International, the majority of members under Serrati carrying the day in the face of opposition from the reformists under Turati and Treves, who none the less remained in the party. At their own conference in Strasbourg at the end of February 1920 the French Socialists, it is true, had come out against joining the Communist International, but they had voiced their agreement with its basic principles, especially the dictatorship of the proletariat, and they had severed their links with the Second International. In Germany the Independent Social Democrats had already met in Berlin in March 1919 and asserted their allegiance to the soviet system, to the dictatorship of the proletariat and to an uncompromising class struggle, but its members were deeply divided between sympathizers and opponents of Bolshevism.

Lenin prepared for the Second World Congress by writing 'Left-Wing Communism: An Infantile Disorder' in April and May 1920. It was not only a sharply worded critique of putschist, syndicalist and, principally, anti-parliamentary deviations from the true spirit of Marxism but also a manifesto in which Lenin raised the doctrines of the Bolshevik revolution to the level of universals. One of its central theses runs:

> The experience of the victorious dictatorship of the proletariat in Russia has clearly shown even to those who are incapable of thinking or have had no occasion to give thought to the matter that absolute centralisation and rigorous discipline of the proletariat are an essential condition of victory over the bourgeoisie.[36]

This doctrine found practical application in twenty-one conditions for membership of the Comintern that were largely drafted by Zinoviev and that the Congress passed practically unanimously on 6 August, only two delegates voting against it. It provided for a state of total subordination of all its members to the decrees of the Congress and Executive Committee of the Third International. All Communist parties – this name, too, now became obligatory – were to assume the Soviet principle of 'democratic centralism':

> The Communist party will be able to fulfil its duty only if its organization is as centralized as possible, if iron discipline prevails, and if the party centre, upheld by the confidence of the party membership, has strength and authority and is equipped with the most comprehensive powers.

Regular purges of party organizations must be undertaken in order to prevent the spread of aberrant ideas. 'Reformist' politicians and moderate left-wing socialists – so-called 'Centrists' – must be replaced by 'reliable Communists'. In addition to the legal party apparatus, an illegal party organization must also be set up in order to pave the way for the revolution. 'Notorious opportunists' such as Kautsky and Hilferding as well as socialist leaders like Turati, Longuet and MacDonald could not be members of any Communist party. An 'unyielding struggle' must be waged against reformist trade unions. Propaganda and political agitation must reflect the programme of the Communist International, with the result that new or revised party programmes must be ratified by the Congress or the Executive Committee of the Comintern.

In keeping with the decrees passed by the Second Congress, the Executive Committee, or ECCI, was the leading organ of the Comintern between its world congresses. Its principal burden of work was to be shouldered by the 'party of that country where, by the decision of the world congress, the Executive Committee has its seat': in other words, the Russian Communists. In consequence, that country was entitled to send five representatives to the ECCI and to appoint Zinoviev their secretary general. They would be joined by representatives of the 'ten to thirteen most important Communist parties, the list to be ratified by the regular world congress'.[37] Each representative would have a casting vote. The other Communist parties could each send a representative to the Executive Committee, but they would attend only in an advisory capacity.

The aim of these twenty-one points and of the Second Congress's statutes was clear: all Communist parties were to accept the directives of the ECCI in Moscow. But this committee was controlled by Bolsheviks, which meant that anyone accepting these twenty-one points was obliged to make a radical break with the democratic traditions of the western workers' movement and accept the privileged position of a party whose structure and policies could be explained only by reference to the specific conditions in Russia. Tsarist Russia had been largely unaffected by the great movements in European emancipation from the Renaissance and Reformation to the Enlightenment, to the 'bourgeois' revolutions of the eighteenth and nineteenth centuries and, finally, the classic liberalism of the later period. In Russia there was no bourgeoisie in the European sense but only millions of peasants who, lacking any land of their own, were only too keen to acquire some and who had ceased to be serfs only in the 1860s. A brutal police state had driven the early workers' movement underground and encouraged the formation of a secret alliance of conspirators.

The Bolshevik party was the expression of extreme economic and political backwardness. Before 1917 it would never have occurred to a socialist to be ruled by the ideas and by the battle strategies of such a party, and even as late as 1919 the Russian leaders had assumed that the centre of the coming world revolution would shift westwards to Germany as soon as the proletariat seized power there. It required the failure of the revolutionary movements outside Russia and the Bolsheviks' own powers of self-assertion to make the non-Russian movements see that in 1920 there was only one way to achieve a proletarian revolution, and that was to follow the course that they themselves had adopted.

Many workers' parties in the west were torn apart by their inability to decide whether or not to accept the twenty-one points. The first of these parties to confront the problem was the Independent Social Democratic Party of

Germany. Most of its officials and the majority of its newspapers were emphatically opposed to the idea of being subject to the dictates of the Moscow party, but its members saw things differently, and a decision was taken at the primary election of the delegates to the party conference, which was held in Halle in October 1920. The delegates of both camps were elected by members meeting according to the principle of proportional representation, who travelled to Halle with an imperative mandate. The advocates of acceptance of the twenty-one points received not quite 58 per cent of the vote, its opponents 42 per cent. The former owed their majority in the main to workers who were not born into the social-democratic tradition but had been politicized only during the war and its aftermath.

At the party conference the delegates witnessed a dramatic exchange between Grigory Zinoviev and Rudolf Hilferding and a moving indictment of the Bolsheviks' bloody terror by one of the most respected leaders of the persecuted Mensheviks, Julius Martov. But the outcome of the vote was clear even before it had been taken: there were 236 votes for acceptance of the twenty-one points, 156 against. In December 1920 the left-wing majority of the German Communist Party joined the United Communist Party of Germany at a conference in Berlin. The defeated minority initially remained an independent party and retained its existing name.

In the case of the left-wing majority of the French Socialists, the twenty-one points found less unquestioning support than they did with the left wing of the Independent Social Democrats in Germany. The party's secretary general, Ludovic-Oscar Frossard, and the editor in chief of the party's official newspaper, *L'Humanité*, Marcel Cachin, had both attended the Second World Congress and at the party conference in Tours in December 1920 initially refused to exclude representatives of the recalcitrant minority, including 'Centrists' such as Jean Longuet and Paul Faure. But a telegram signed by Lenin, Zinoviev and other members of the ECCI made it clear to delegates that Moscow would not tolerate such a violation of the Comintern edict. The party therefore agreed to join the Communist International by a clear majority of 3,028 votes to 1,022. The Parti Communiste (Section Française de l'Internationale Communiste) had around 140,000 members, Longuet's SFIO only around 30,000. But the relative figures changed in the course of the following years, and by 1924 the SFIO had almost 100,000 members, the Parti Communiste only 68,000. At the parliamentary elections in May 1924 the Socialists also proved to be the stronger party, polling almost 1.7 million votes against the Communists' 800,000.

Some six months after the old Socialist Party split, the Confédération Générale du Travail (CGT), the umbrella organization of all the socialist trade unions in France, had to decide on its future course. At its congress in Lille in July 1921, shots were fired before a relatively small majority decided not to join the Red Trade Union International that had been founded only a short time earlier in Moscow at the same time as the Comintern's Third World Congress.

The minority under the leadership of the rail and construction workers refused to accept defeat and declared the CGT a divided organization. In St-Étienne in June 1921 an independent Communist trades union was founded, the Confédération Générale du Travail Unitaire (CGTU), which joined the Red Trade Union International in 1922. The split involved a massive loss of members: in 1920 the socialist trade unions had had around two million members, but by 1924 the CGT and CGTU combined had fewer than half that number, of whom around two-thirds belonged to socialist trade unions, the remaining third to their Communist counterpart.

In many ways developments in Italy resembled those in France. Like Frossard, Serrati refused to exclude more moderate members from his party. Lenin, who thought that Italy was on the eve of a proletarian revolution, insisted on unconditional acceptance of all twenty-one points and also demanded the expulsion from the party not only of Turati but also – in the event of his remaining obdurate – Serrati. Lenin's message was relayed to their Italian comrades by a delegation from the ECCI under the Hungarian Communist Mátyás Rákosi, a former member of Béla Kun's government, and the leading Bulgarian party theorist Christo Kabakchiev.

Apart from Serrati and his allies, the principal negotiators were the Pure Communists within the Socialist Party. But these were divided into three groups: to the left stood the anti-parliamentarian forces ranged around Amadeo Bordiga, the editor of Il Soviet; in the middle was the group associated with L'Ordine Nuovo and its founder Antonio Gramsci, who whole-heartedly supported the twenty-one points and agreed that the Communists should take part in the elections and work in parliament; and the third group of Andrea Marabini and Antonio Graziadei, who largely agreed with Gramsci but felt that a split in the party was premature. Ranged against the Pure Communists were the Unitarian Communists around Serrati and the Concentrationists around Turati, Treves and Modigliani, who also commanded the support of the secretary general of the Trade Union Federation, Ludovico d'Aragona. The emissaries of the ECCI were able to persuade the Pure Communists to agree to unconditional acceptance of the twenty-one points, whereas they had no success with Serrati's Unitarian Communists.

The decision was taken at the party conference in Livorno in January 1921. Serrati won 98,000 votes, the Pure Communists 59,000 and Turati around 15,000. Delegates casting a total of 981 votes abstained. When the result of the vote was announced, the representatives of the Pure Communists left the conference hall and went with Kabakchiev and Rákosi to the Teatro San Marco, where they constituted themselves into the Partito Comunista Italiano.

Lenin saw in the split in the party a major success for the revolutionary cause, but in the parliamentary elections in May 1921 it emerged that the Communists had the support of only a tiny minority of the Italian proletariat, winning only thirteen seats against 128 for the Socialists. (At the previous elections in November 1919 the undivided Socialist Party had won 156 seats.) But unlike their French counterparts, the Italian trade unions were not split, and from now on the Communists were a part of the Confederazione Generale del Lavoro. At the same time the split in the Socialist Party was enough to prevent them from offering any joint resistance to Mussolini's Fascists, who were resorting to ever more extreme forms of violence. Lenin had won no more than a pyrrhic victory in Livorno.

The attempt to split the British labour movement proved a total failure. At the Labour Party's annual conference in Scarborough in July 1920 a proposal by the small British Socialist Party, which was affiliated to the Labour Party, that the party should join the Third International was rejected by an over-whelming majority. Later that same year another grouping within the Labour Party, the Independent Labour Party, voted by a large majority not to join the Comintern; and in March 1921 the party conference, meeting in Southport, rejected the twenty-one points by 618 to 97 votes. For the Labour Party as a whole, it went without saying that its members would refuse to be subjected to the dictates of Moscow. At its party conference in 1923, its president, the Fabian Sidney Webb, declared that it was not Karl Marx who had founded British socialism but Robert Owen, 'who preached not the class struggle but the time-honoured doctrine of the brotherhood of all mankind'.[38]

In his *History of the International* Julius Braunthal drew attention to the evolutionary nature of English history since the Glorious Revolution of 1688–9, seeing in this quality the main reason why the British workers' movement aligned itself with neither Marx nor, at a later date, Lenin. The concentration of all power in parliament and the extension of suffrage ultimately opened the gates to power to the working class as well:

> The British labour movement was imbued with the spirit of humanitarian pacifist Socialism. The idea of civil war as a means of furthering the struggle of Socialism was alien to the minds of British Socialists. Bolshevik theories, which idealized violence as a creative force of Socialism, civil war as an inevitable stage in the struggle for Socialism, and terroristic dictatorship as an inexorable instrument for its realization, could awake no sympathetic echoes among British Socialists. Such ideas ran counter to their traditional feelings and ideas.[39]

In the light of all this, it is unsurprising that the British Communist Party, which was founded in 1920, never rose above the status of a left-wing splinter group.

For those members of the socialist left who were unwilling to submit to the twenty-one points, the events of 1920 left them feeling the need to close ranks. There was no question, therefore, of their joining the Second International – sometimes described as the London International on account of the leading role of the Labour Party and the seat of its secretariat. At its congress in Geneva in early August 1920 the Second International had given its unconditional backing to the idea of parliamentary democracy and branded the Communist system the tyranny of a small minority. It was above all the Independent Labour Party, the German Independent Social Democrats and the Swiss Social Democrats who urged closer cooperation between those parties that belonged to neither the Moscow nor the London International. (In the spring of 1920 the Independent Labour Party had severed its links with the Second International at its Glasgow conference.)

A preliminary conference was held in Berne in December 1920 and attended not only by the foregoing parties but also by the Socialist parties from France, Austria and Czechoslovakia, together with the Russian Mensheviks, who at that date were not yet merely a party in exile. They formed their own International – the International Working Union of Socialist Parties, mockingly dismissed by the Comintern as 'International 2½' – in Vienna in February 1921. The meeting was attended by twenty Socialist parties from thirteen different countries represented by seventy-one delegates. At the head of the Vienna International, as it has come to be called, was the Austrian Socialist, Friedrich Adler, who came to prominence as its secretary. The new International distanced itself from 'reformist ministerialism' as emphatically as it did from the sectarianism of the Comintern parties but later did not exclude the possibility of working with the two rival Internationals, whenever the situation demanded.

By the date of its Third World Congress, which was held in Moscow between 22 June and 12 July 1921, the Comintern, for its part, had abandoned all attempts at working with its rivals. Forced on to the defensive in almost every country apart from Soviet Russia, the Bolsheviks insisted that in December 1921 the ECCI pass a series of guidelines for a 'united front policy' involving Communists, Social Democrats and trade unions, the new tactics inevitably involving continuing attacks on the 'reformists' of all shades of opinion, their main aim being to persuade the mass of workers who were currently members of the parties belonging to the two other Internationals to switch their allegiance to the various Communist parties. In mid-January 1922, the Vienna International invited the executive committees of the Moscow and London Internationals to attend a joint conference, but the items on the agenda were not the ideological differences between Social Democrats and Communists but, first, the economic situation in Europe and the political actions of the working class and, second, the proletariat's resistance to the politics of reaction.

The conference convened by the Vienna International took place in early April 1922 in the Reichstag building in Berlin. The Third International attended since it hoped to muster support for its united front policy, while the Second International took part in order to avoid giving the impression that it was seeking to sabotage the attempts to find common ground. But in accepting the invitation, it made clear its reservations, insisting that the conference should also discuss the fate of political prisoners in Soviet Russia and the fate of Georgia, where the Bolsheviks had toppled the Menshevik regime the previous year as a result of their military intervention and installed a Communist system. The Communists were also to give their guarantee that in future they would not attempt to form cells within the trade unions.

In spite of all attempts to mediate by the two Austrian Socialists Friedrich Adler and Otto Bauer, the Berlin conference became little more than an arena in which the Social Democrats were able to trade blows with the Communists who were present. The principal spokesman of the Third International was Karl Radek, who was unwilling to jeopardize his main aim of using a major congress of international workers as a platform for international Communist propaganda, and so he was ready to compromise with the reformers. On the Georgian question he agreed to the setting up of a commission of inquiry appointed by the executive committees of the three Internationals. As for the forty-seven Social Revolutionaries currently in Soviet prisons awaiting trial and facing the death sentence, the two other Internationals were allowed to send defence counsels to Moscow; no prisoners would be executed. The conference then decided to form a Committee of Nine whose principal task was to prepare the way for a 'general conference'. The workers of all countries were invited to organize mass demonstrations in support of an eight-hour day, the 'Russian revolution', famine-struck Russia, the 'restoration by all countries of political and economic relations with Soviet Russia' and 'a united front of the workers in every country and in the International'. At the same time they would protest at the 'capitalist offensive'.[40]

On their return to Moscow, the Comintern delegates faced a severe dressing down by Lenin, who accused them of making concessions to the 'shrewd bourgeois diplomats' and to the 'representatives of the Second and Two-and-a-Half Internationals' without receiving any concessions in return.[41] By agreeing that representatives from all three Internationals would be admitted to the trial of the Social Revolutionaries and that no death sentences would be passed, the Comintern delegation had, in Lenin's view, paid too high a price. As a result, the ECCI's ratification of the Berlin agreement was of dubious value at best.

The first meeting of the Committee of Nine was held in Berlin on 23 May 1922 under the chairmanship of Friedrich Adler. It was also the committee's last meeting. By way of an ultimatum, Radek demanded the immediate convening of a world labour congress, a demand rejected by the representatives of the two other Internationals, who argued that the Comintern had failed to keep its promises. At that point the Moscow delegates announced that they had done what they had come to do. The following day the Comintern accused the London and Vienna Internationals of deliberately sabotaging the Committee of Nine. The new watchword for the workers of all countries was 'Form the united front from the ground upwards.' If necessary, then, they were to oppose the leaders of the 'reformist' parties and trade unions.

The Comintern had clearly lost interest in a world labour congress now that Soviet Russia had found another way of overcoming its external isolation. Only a few days after the Berlin conference of the three Internationals had ended, a world economic conference opened in Genoa, the first international congress to which the Western Powers had invited Soviet Russia. From Moscow's standpoint it was useful to represent its own interests on all levels. In Soviet eyes there was no irreconcilable contradiction between Realpolitik in the relationship between the Soviet government and the capitalist powers and revolutionary subversion which, massively supported by Moscow with both money and manpower, did not shy away from violent attempts to overthrow the governments of the countries with which it was currently dealing: the two, after all, could be seen as dialectically linked. And however important Europe may have been for the cause of world revolution, there were other parts of the globe where the capitalist system could – and should – be challenged: in the colonies and half-colonies of Asia, Africa and Latin America, where there was an even more urgent need for national bourgeois revolutions than for any Communist overthrow.

As early as September 1920 the ECCI had organized a 'congress of oppressed peoples of the East' in Baku, where Zinoviev had taken the opportunity to declare a 'holy war' on imperialist England. In January 1922 the First Congress of the Communist and Revolutionary Organizations of the Far East met in Moscow and then in Petrograd. Among the delegates were representatives of the Communist parties of China, Japan, Korea and the Dutch East Indies as well as revolutionary groups from Mongolia and the revolutionary Kuomintang from southern China. They passed a resolution that added an anti-colonial dimension to the classic slogan from the Communist Manifesto: 'Proletarians of all lands and oppressed peoples of the whole world, unite!' The appeal culminated in what amounted to a declaration of war on Japanese, American, British, French and sundry other imperialists:

> We declare a life-and-death war on the venal imitators and lackeys of our subjugators in China. We declare a life-and-death war on hypocritical American imperialism and the rapacious British robbers. Get out of China and Korea, get out of Indochina and the Dutch East Indies! Get your hands off the islands of the Pacific! Down with all intruders in the Far East![42]

The Fourth World Congress of the Communist International met in Moscow in November 1922 at a time when the country was celebrating the fifth anniversary of the October Revolution. In his address to the conference, Lenin, who had barely recovered from his first stroke, defended the New Economic

Policy, criticized a resolution of the Third World Congress concerning the organizational structure of the Communist parties as being too permeated by the Russian spirit, and drew conclusions from post-revolutionary events that were notable for their lack of revolutionary euphoria. Their foe, he insisted, could easily provoke the Communists into attacking them and in that way set back their cause by many years:

> For this reason, I think, the idea that we must prepare for ourselves the possibility of retreat is very important, and not only from the theoretical point of view. From the practical point of view, too, all the parties which are preparing to take the direct offensive against capitalism in the near future must now give thought to the problem of preparing for a possible retreat.[43]

Lenin had not abandoned his goal of world revolution, which he continued to advocate even in his final Comintern conference speech, but he had by now come to see that the journey there would be longer and more difficult than he had thought at the time of the October Revolution.

Three Elections and a Secession: Post-war Britain

When Zinoviev called on all Communists to rise up in a 'holy war' in September 1920, he was declaring hostilities not only on the British presence in the Near East but on the Empire in general. In Europe, France, too, might have been deemed a leading enemy of Soviet Russia, but there was an additional reason why Soviet ire was directed at Britain first and foremost: the City of London remained the world's chief financial centre, which in Moscow's eyes made Great Britain the leading force in the capitalist world.

In Britain itself the First World War left the people wondering if the country's international standing had been undermined for good. Although it had taken over control of most of Germany's colonial possessions in Africa, Indian and Arab nationalists had been radicalized in consequence, so that the very existence of the Empire seemed to be threatened. During the war 1.3 million Indian soldiers had been deployed on all fronts, making it highly unlikely that the survivors would be satisfied with their country's continuing colonial status in the longer term.

Unlike the colonies, the white Dominions had on their own initiative provided soldiers to support the mother country. Canada had sent half a million, 57,000 of whom were killed in action, while Australia sent 332,000 and New Zealand 112,000. The number of those killed was 59,000 in the case of Australia, 17,000 in that of New Zealand. After 1917 representatives of the Dominions were able to influence the newly created Imperial War Cabinet, which also included three representatives for India, one for Newfoundland, the five members of the British war cabinet and the minister for the colonies and secretary of state for India.

Four years after the war had ended Britain was forced to realize that it would never again be able to count on such a willingness for self-sacrifice. In early September 1922, when Turkish troops fighting in the Greek-Turkish War approached Chanak in the Dardanelles neutral zone, there was the very real threat of a military escalation and even of war between Turkey and Great Britain. (France and Italy had already withdrawn their units from the neutral zone during the Chanak Crisis.) In London Winston Churchill, then the minister for the colonies, was particularly insistent that the British government should act decisively against Turkey, and he knew that he had the backing of the prime minister, Lloyd George. The Canadian prime minister, William Lyon Mackenzie King, who ran his country from 1921 to 1930 and again from 1935 to 1948, immediately announced that if Britain declared war on Turkey, Canada would not automatically regard itself as also at war, as it had in 1914. The South African prime minister, General Smuts, expressed himself in similar terms. These warnings did much to weaken the 'party of war' in London and contributed to a peaceful solution to the conflict between Britain and Turkey.

A year later Canada took a further step in the direction of emancipation and in March 1923 signed a fishing agreement with the United States without consulting the British Embassy in Washington. Meeting in London shortly afterwards, the Imperial Conference confirmed the right of the Dominions to sign treaties with third parties. For the white Dominions, this opened the way to their establishing missions in all those countries with which they wanted to have diplomatic relations, a right that Australia and New Zealand, unlike Canada, initially ignored. For its part, Great Britain created a new government department, the Dominions Office, which enjoyed equal rights to those of the Colonial Office. For the present they shared a common head.

In terms of the country's internal politics, the early post-war period in Britain was overshadowed by bitter labour disputes and social unrest. At the end of January 1919 70,000 shipyard workers, dockworkers and miners in the Clyde industrial area and in Belfast held a wild-cat strike to demand a forty-hour week. In the course of violent unrest in Glasgow workers unfurled the Red flag on the city's town hall, prompting the government to declare a state of siege and to send in 10,000 heavily armed troops backed up by tanks. When hundreds of thousands of miners and railway workers threatened to strike in the rest of the country and the miners' union additionally demanded the nationalization of the coal mines, a nationwide general strike seemed inevitable.

The army soon restored order in Glasgow and elsewhere, but threats of force were insufficient to stem the tide of social unrest. The Liberal–Conservative coalition under Lloyd George responded by setting up a royal commission under the chairmanship of Sir John Sankey, a High Court judge entrusted with the task of examining the mining industry. Not only employers and experts but the trade unions and the Labour Party took part in this commission as they did in the National Industrial Conference convened in late February 1919. Sankey's preliminary report, submitted in March 1919, bore the imprint of all these groups whilst meeting many of the demands of the miners in respect of their working hours and wages. The final report came out in June 1919 and by a majority of one – Sankey's own vote – recommended the nationalization of the mines. But the government declined to accept the recommendations, although it met some of the miners' demands, leading to a brief period of calm.

In June 1919 the workers in the cotton factories went on strike, followed in July by the Welsh miners, prompting the government to send in the army in Wales, too. The autumn months saw strikes among railway workers and among workers employed in the armouries of both the army and the navy. Whenever the government negotiated directly with the trade unions, it did what it could to accommodate the workers' demands concerning higher wages and shorter working hours. But it remained obdurate on the question of nationalization and turned down the recommendations of the Royal Commission.

During the war the mines had been placed under state control, but when they reverted to their former ownership in the spring of 1921 – a year of depression – their owners seized the opportunity to announce lower wages. The Miners' Federation responded by demanding state supervision of earnings and a national wage pool, a demand that also had the support of the railway unions and transport workers, the two unions that had formed a 'Triple Alliance' with the miners in 1914. A general strike was threatened in response to the swift rejection of this demand by the government and employers alike, but in the event this was averted when, faced by the government's threat to send in troops, the general secretary of the Miners' Federation, Frank Hodges, agreed to a suggestion that wages be increased at least temporarily, while describing the day – 15 April 1921 – as the 'Black Friday' of the British trade union movement. Although his own executive rejected the proposal, it was accepted by the railway and transport workers, who no longer felt bound by any feelings of solidarity, bringing the Triple Alliance to an end.

Isolated, the miners went on strike, a strike that ended only in July 1921 with an agreement that for the individual mining regions there would be a link between minimum wages and output. The Miners' Federation paid for its failure with a dramatic drop in its membership figures and the loss of the leading position that it had held until then at the Trades Union Congress.

In general, the trade union movement had gained in strength in the course of the war, membership rising from four million in 1914 to 6.5 million in 1920 and 8.3 million in 1926. And just as the trade union movement grew in size, so, too, did the Labour Party, numbering 1.6 million members in 1914, 3.5 million in 1919 and almost 4.4 million by 1920. The number of votes that it received increased from half a million in the last pre-war election in 1910 to 2.2 million in December 1918 and 4.2 million in the elections to the lower house in November 1922.

Even after it had left Lloyd George's all-party government in December 1918, the Labour Party continued to exert considerable influence on politics and legislation. The two most important socio-political laws of the early post-war period would probably not have been passed without pressure from the Labour Party and the trade unions. The Housing and Town Planning Act of July 1919, often named after Christopher Addison, the first minister of health, introduced council houses for working-class people. And in 1920 a law was passed covering unemployment insurance, extending to every branch of industry the provisions of the 1911 National Insurance Bill that required employers in the construction, machine-building and ship-building industries to insure their employees. It provided for contributions from employers and employees alike where the latter earned less than £50 a year. Once they had paid their contributions for at least twelve weeks, they could, in the event of their becoming unemployed, claim unemployment benefit for fifteen weeks. When the economy collapsed shortly after the law had been passed and the number of unemployed men and women rose dramatically, the state had to intervene, which it continued to do even after the period of support required by law had elapsed.

The most explosive problem faced by British politicians between 1919 and 1921 was the struggle for Irish independence, which began on 21 January 1919 with the proclamation of the Irish Republic by the revolutionary Irish parliament, the Dáil Éireann. The Sinn Féin government under Eamon de Valera managed to build up powerful support among the Catholic population, a development in which they received considerable help from the new Dáil Courts. Ranged against the Irish Volunteers of the Irish Republican Army (IRA) in their war of independence were the United Kingdom police and the Royal Irish Constabulary and their volunteers, most of whom were ex-officers who had fought in the First World War. The bloody guerrilla war was waged with great brutality by both sides in the conflict and lasted until well into 1921.

London hoped that the Government of Ireland Act of December 1920 would bring a political solution to the conflict. This provided for a division of the island into two states, the larger of which would also include three of Ulster's predominantly Catholic counties. Under the Act the king of England would be the head of both states. The two-chamber system provided for in the legislation was also designed to ensure that the Protestant landowners in the south were represented in the upper house of the new state. But the Act was ratified only by the new parliament in Ulster, whereas in the south Sinn Féin, having won 124 of the 128 seats in the lower house, refused to carry out its mandate, with the result that parliament was unable to operate. Instead of seeking a military solution to the conflict, London decided to negotiate with the Irish Republicans.

The initial outcome of the talks between the governments of Lloyd George and Eamon de Valera was an armistice agreed to on 11 July 1921. It was particularly hard to find common ground between the Republican creed of the Irish and the British insistence that Ireland should be granted the status of a dominion. (Ulster, if it so wished, could remain a part of the United Kingdom.) At the head of the Dublin delegation that in the autumn of 1921 held talks concerning the links between Ireland and the Empire were the moderate Arthur Griffith and one of the leaders of the armed uprising, Michael Collins. On 6 December both men agreed to the wording of a treaty stipulating that Ireland, as a dominion, would remain a part of the Empire and that the king of England would continue to be king of Ireland. Britain also secured a number of navy bases in Ireland but granted the free state independence, including fiscal autonomy.

In Ireland the agreement encountered violent opposition on the part of staunch Republicans. The greatest cause of indignation was the oath of allegiance that civil servants, judges, ministers and members of parliament would be required to swear to the British throne as supreme head of the nations that together formed the British Commonwealth of Nations. Following a heated debate, the Irish parliament passed the treaty by a narrow majority of sixty-four votes to fifty-seven on 7 January 1922, whereupon de Valera, who had always opposed full membership of the Empire and, hence, ratification of the treaty, resigned as prime minister and was replaced by Griffith. The general public, the Catholic bishops and the majority of the Irish Republican Brotherhood – the political umbrella organization of the Irish Republicans – welcomed the treaty as it brought Ireland as close to independence as was possible in the present circumstances.

The radical minority remained unimpressed. In April 1922 a group of IRA officers occupied a number of public buildings in Dublin, thereby signalling the start of the Irish civil war. De Valera formed an alternative government, while Collins placed himself at the head of the government troops. With the help of cannons loaned by the British Collins was able to suppress the rebellion in the capital, albeit only after a series of bloody confrontations. He himself was killed in a Republican ambush in August 1922. After the radical Republicans had suffered a number of crippling defeats, de Valera finally ordered a ceasefire on 24 May 1923.

But divisions within the independence movement continued. The first free elections took place in the summer of 1923 when, in keeping with the constitution of December 1922, women had the same voting rights as men. Those opposed to the treaty won thirty-five of the 128 seats but refused to take their seats. The moderate wing of Sinn Féin, which formed an independent party under the name of Cumann na nGaedheal, won fifty-eight seats, while the remaining supporters of the treaty, including the Irish Labour Party, together won thirty-five. The new prime minister, replacing the late Arthur Griffith, was the moderate William T. Cosgrave. In 1926 a group of staunch Republicans formed a new party under de Valera, Fianna Fáil, and in 1927 backed the Anglo-Irish Treaty. The forty-four representatives of Fianna Fáil who were elected to the Dáil in 1927 swore an oath of allegiance to the king of England, arguing that this was a mere formality, and the Irish Free State now began to develop in the direction of a 'normal' western democracy.

Relations between the Irish Free State and the largely Protestant North remained tense. A boundary commission was set up with the aim of redrawing the border between the sixteen southern counties and the six northern counties in favour of the former, but when this failed to reach a consensus, the Irish Free State signed an agreement with Great Britain, confirming the existing border with only a handful of minor changes. The Catholics of Northern Ireland, who represented a third of the population, first took up their seats in the lower house in Belfast in 1925. Here the pro-British Unionists enjoyed an unassailable majority that merely fuelled the enmity between Protestants and Catholics, a hostility that increased when the advocates of Irish unification gained ground in the south with the rise of Fianna Fáil. The radical Republicans in Ulster refused to work with their parliamentary colleagues. In their rivalry with the paramilitary units of the Protestant Orange Order, the Republicans, through the military wing of the IRA, ensured that for decades Ulster remained Great Britain's principal source of unrest.

The Republic of Ireland's new status as an independent state marked an important turning point in the country's history, bringing to an end four centuries of English rule that had begun with Henry VIII's subjugation of the island. Ever since Gladstone's day the Conservatives had thwarted every Liberal attempt to grant Ireland home rule and even after 1918 had opposed the end of the Union with England. But in the wake of the First World War very few Tories were still willing to become embroiled in a major conflict to prevent Irish secession, with the result that at the urging of Lloyd George they agreed to a solution that allowed the English crown at least to preserve the semblance of British rule over Ireland. Most Tories must have suspected that this was merely a transitional phase on the road to complete independence.

The decision to grant Irish independence was the last major achievement of Lloyd George's cabinet, for by the autumn of 1922 there were increasing signs that the Liberal–Conservative coalition was about to end. On 7 October *The Times* published a letter from Andrew Bonar Law, the Conservative Party leader and lord privy seal, distancing himself from the prime minister's policy towards Turkey, a policy felt to be confrontational and dangerous. And for many in the party it was an open secret that the foreign minister, Lord Curzon, was no longer willing to support Lloyd George. On 19 October 275 Conservative MPs met at the Carlton Club to discuss their party's future. By the end of the meeting there was a clear majority of 185 to eighty-eight in favour of ending the coalition. Within hours Lloyd George had resigned as prime minister and was succeeded on the 24th by Bonar Law. Curzon remained foreign minister, and Stanley Baldwin, until then the trade minister, took over as chancellor of the exchequer. Baldwin was regarded as a rising star in the Tory Party, or the Conservative Party as it became known in the wake of Irish independence.

The new government's first action was to dissolve the lower house. The Conservatives emerged as clear victors from the election in November 1922, winning 347 seats – an eighty-seven-seat majority over the opposition. But the Labour Party, too, enjoyed a major success, increasing the number of its members of parliament from seventy-five to 142. The Liberals of both camps – Asquith and Lloyd George – together won 147 seats, forty-five fewer than in the election in December 1918.

Bonar Law remained in office for only six months, resigning on health grounds in May 1923 and dying in the October of that same year. He was succeeded by Stanley Baldwin, who was maintain a strong grip on the Tory Party until 1937, even though he had previously failed to distinguish himself in British politics. The most urgent problem to be faced by his first cabinet was the high rate of unemployment, which he planned to combat with high protective tariffs of a kind that had been introduced on cars, clocks and musical instruments during the war. In October 1923 he announced a comprehensive protective tariff for the British economy. Since his predecessor, Bonar Law, had promised only a year earlier that no fundamental changes would be made to the tariff system, Baldwin felt that new elections were unavoidable. The general election that was held on 6 December 1923 left his plans in ruins, for although the Conservatives remained the largest party, they had ninety fewer seats. The electoral victors were the Labour Party and the Liberals, both of whom had demanded a return to free trade. Labour increased the number of its representatives from 142 to 192, while the Liberals now had 158 instead of 117 seats.

This meant that, taken together, Labour and the Liberals had more seats than the Conservatives. Baldwin had failed to achieve a majority which meant that George V asked the Labour leader, Ramsay MacDonald, to form a government. MacDonald duly became leader of the first Labour government which, although it lacked a parliamentary majority of its own, was at least tolerated by the Liberals. The new cabinet's policies were liberal rather than socialist. The chancellor, Philip Snowden, abolished the wartime protective tariffs and lowered taxes, but he was unable to reduce unemployment in this way. If the government's policies could be described as 'social', then it was its practice of encouraging the building of council houses for working-class families – a policy pursued with considerable success by the health minister Arthur Greenwood – to which this label would apply.

This first Labour government had been in office for only a week when it took the spectacular step of recognizing the Soviet Union on 1 February 1924, a move followed by lengthy negotiations over a new trade agreement and a treaty designed to deal with the question of Russia's pre-war debts and the rights of British citizens living in the Soviet Union. In turn this treaty was intended to provide the basis on which to offer Russia a British loan. When the relevant agreements were signed on 6 August 1924, there was a storm of protest from the Conservatives and from Lloyd George's Liberals, who accused the Labour government of acting against vital British interests.

It was doubtful if MacDonald would obtain a majority in the lower house in support of these agreements. Against this background, the cabinet can hardly have welcomed a letter, allegedly written by Harry Pollitt, the chairman of the British Communist Party, which appeared in J. R. Campbell's Communist *Workers Weekly*, in which British workers were asked not to take part in wars in which they would have to fight their own comrades. An accusation of incitement to mutiny was quickly withdrawn by the attorney general – in response, the Tories maintained, to pressure from the government. In a debate that was held in the lower house on 30 September, MacDonald denied that he had tried to influence the judiciary but was unable to avoid a censure motion by the Conservative opposition. As a result he tied the vote to a question of confidence. On 9 October, however, MacDonald was forced to concede that he had spoken to the attorney general about the case, with the result that in the ensuing vote on the Conservative motion, the government lost by 368 votes to 128. MacDonald responded by dissolving parliament and calling for new elections, the third within two years.

On 25 October, four days before the election, *The Times* published a letter purporting to have been written by Grigory Zinoviev on 15 September. In it the secretary general of the Executive Committee of the Communist International called on British Communists to bring the Labour Party to heel and prepare for the coming revolution. A copy of the letter was also sent to the *Daily Mail* and, on 10 October, to the Foreign Office, which duly informed *The Times*, adding a note of protest and questioning the document's authenticity. The letter was in fact a forgery drawn up by Russian émigrés in Vienna. To what extent it influenced the course of the election must remain an open question.

Although the Labour Party gained a few votes at the expense of the Liberals, the number of its seats fell from 192 to 151. The Liberals, who had voted against MacDonald's government on 10 October, returned only forty-two MPs, their share of the vote falling from 30 per cent to barely 18 per cent. The Conservatives won 48 per cent of the vote and 414 seats, a gain of 161. One prominent Liberal, Winston Churchill, who had held numerous cabinet posts since 1906, including minister for trade, war and the colonies, was elected as a 'Constitutionalist' with the support of many Conservative voters. He now moved back to the Tories, the party to which he had belonged before joining the Liberals in 1904. In the new government he became chancellor of the exchequer. Baldwin was again the prime minister, a post he retained until the date of the next elections to the lower house, almost five years later, on 30 May 1929.

The elections to the lower house in October 1924 not only spelt the end of the post-war period in Britain but also marked what Baldwin, echoing President Warren Harding, called a 'return to normalcy'. The election victory also heralded the start of the new two-party system: it was no longer the Liberal Party but the Labour Party that was the Tories' principal adversary. The Liberals had decided to work closely with the growing labour movement in the later nineteenth century, but they remained a party of middle-class dignitaries and notables, incapable, therefore, of forming any lasting links with the mass of working people. The Conservatives, conversely, managed to transform themselves into a right-of-centre people's party and to appeal to a considerable section of the workers by their populist rhetoric and social promises. Even in October 1924 they won more working-class votes than the Labour Party, although it was soon to become clear that the latter had by no means grown to its full size. Following the elections of May 1929, Baldwin had to hand over his office of prime minister to the man whom he had replaced in November 1924 – Ramsay MacDonald.

Confrontations and Compromises: France 1919–22

As in Great Britain, so in France, the sense of national unity that had been solemnly and regularly invoked since 1914 had largely disappeared within months of the end of the war. When measured by the number of its inhabitants, France had suffered more war dead than any other country: over 10 per cent of its adult male population had perished. By the end of 1918 the purchasing power of the franc had fallen to 28 per cent of its pre-war value, and by 1919 real wages were between 15 per cent and 20 per cent lower than in 1914. An eight-hour day was introduced in April 1919 in an attempt to placate the workforce, but such concessions proved ineffectual in preventing strikes. In the spring of 1919 the mineworkers went on strike, followed soon afterwards by workers from the metal industry and by the capital's public transport workers, but their protests produced few practical results of any note.

Yet the fact that revolutionary slogans were heard in the course of a number of these strikes, especially in Paris, served to instil a sense of fear in the middle classes, who were convinced that the strikers' actions heralded the spread of Bolshevism. And no politician was keener to combat Communism than the prime minister, Georges Clemenceau. Shortly before the elections to the Chambre des Députés on 19 November 1919 the majority of the parties that supported the government formed an electoral pact, the Bloc National, which succeeded in winning 437 of the 616 seats in the chamber. Their success was also due to the electoral reforms that guaranteed that the joint lists of candidates would receive all the seats that could be allocated if they gained an absolute majority in any one of the eight most heavily populated *départements*. The other parties were left high and dry. The left-wing opposition won 180 seats, including eighty-eight for the middle-class Radical Socialists and sixty-eight for the Socialists of the SFIO. The centre right won 130 seats, the centre left 100. As in the past, only men were entitled to vote for their elected representatives, women's suffrage having been rejected by the French Senate.

Shortly afterwards, in January 1920, elections for the post of president were held. Having emerged victorious from the November elections, Clemenceau hoped to succeed Poincaré but was dismayed to discover that many of the deputies who had supported him in the past now had very different aims and wanted a malleable head of state, with the result that they chose the politically colourless president of the Chambre des Députés, Paul Deschanel. Clemenceau responded by resigning as prime minister and retiring to the provinces, an embittered man. He was succeeded by Alexandre Millerand, a former Socialist who had switched allegiance to the political right. When Deschanel fell seriously ill a few months later and was obliged to step down on health grounds in November 1920, Millerand was voted his successor. By January 1921, after a brief interregnum, Aristide Briand was appointed the new prime minister, he, too, a former Socialist who had moved to the political right.

Millerand's period in office was marked by further industrial action on a grand scale. In February 1920 the railway workers demanded not only higher wages but also the nationalization of the railways. An indefinite general strike was called for 1 May, when the CGT – the umbrella organization of all the socialist trade unions – persuaded workers from other public industries, including mineworkers, metalworkers and construction workers, to join them. Even so, by no means all workers took part, and not even all the railway workers. Millerand accused the CGT of planning a coup. Students and grammar school pupils made themselves available as strike-breakers. The railway companies remained unyielding.

By the end of May the CGT had been forced to abandon its action. Many of the railway workers who had been dismissed were not re-employed. In January 1921 the supreme court of the *département* of the Seine ordered the CGT to be disbanded, and although the sentence was not carried out, the union's political defeat was not in doubt. The experiences of 1920 led to splits first in the SFIO and then in the CGT. (This latter split has already been mentioned in the context of the Second World Congress of the Third International.) It was the Communists who profited most from the disaffection and bitterness among the French proletariat, but others exploited the divisions within the labour movement, principally the employers' confederations who in 1919 had formed an umbrella organization, the Confédération Nationale de la Production Française (CNPF), under the aegis of the minister for trade, Étienne Clémentel.

France's non-Communist left was much further to the political left than the German Social Democrats. At its first post-war conference in Paris in April

1919, the SFIO endorsed the proletarian class struggle, insisting that it demanded 'unyielding opposition to bourgeois power' and condemning 'all involvement in the exercise of this power'.[44] In this way the Socialists drew a line under the 'Union sacrée' of the war years and returned to the 'Kautsky Resolution' agreed to by the Second International at its congress in Paris in September 1900. According to this resolution, any socialist involvement in a bourgeois government was a 'dangerous experiment' permissible only as a temporary expedient if a country was faced by a particular dilemma.

Ever since the party had split into Socialists and Communists at its confer-ence in Tours in December 1920, the SFIO's leading spokesman had been the forty-eight-year-old Léon Blum, who hailed from a family of middle-class Jews in Paris and who had made a name for himself as a man of letters and a theatre critic. He sought to depict the rivalry with the Communists not as irreconcil-able but as a 'family squabble' that could yet be resolved. He was a firm believer in the dictatorship of the proletariat, but, unlike the Communists, who inter-preted this as the dictatorship of a handful of party leaders, he saw it as the dictatorship of an entire class or party. The only form of power that the Socialists regarded as legitimate until such time as the working class seized power was the willingness to tolerate a left-wing middle-class cabinet first seen in the wake of the elections of May 1924 in the form of a 'cartel des gauches'.

The difference between the French 'cartel des gauches' and the German Social Democrats was striking: if, after 1918, the latter had withdrawn to their pre-war position and refused to enter into a coalition with the moderate bour-geois parties, there would have been no Weimar Republic. In France the Socialists relied on the fact that the forces of the republican bourgeoisie to the left of centre were sufficiently powerful to be able to govern with the parlia-mentary connivance of the SFIO, assuming that the electoral results permitted them to do so.

After 1918, practically every aspect of French politics was affected by the arguments that raged between the divided left and the right. Indeed, there was not even a comprehensive national consensus on how to deal with the prov-inces of Alsace and Lorraine following their return to France, the Communists insisting on the region's virtual autonomy and finding themselves completely isolated in consequence. Some 200,000 former Germans who had settled in the area only after the annexation of the region in 1871 and who included teachers at the 'Reich University' of Strasbourg and all higher-ranking civil servants were evicted in 1918/19, a move that gave rise to little public debate in France. (In response to massive American pressure about half of those who were exiled were later granted the right to return to their former homes.)

Even the enforced linguistic and cultural reassimilation of the Alsatians and the German-speaking inhabitants of Lorraine was regarded as largely uncontro-versial. Schools and universities were entrusted with this challenge as their principal task in hand. For committed laicists, conversely, it was a source of annoyance that the separation of Church and state enshrined in a law of 5 December 1905 marking the end of the French struggle between these two institutions was not introduced into Alsace-Lorraine lest it offend the sensibilities of the largely Catholic population. Catholic and Protestant clerics henceforth received their stipends from the secular French state. As a result, Alsace-Lorraine was the only part of France in which Napoleon Bonaparte's Concordat of 1801 continued to apply.

This regional deal with the Catholic Church chimed with the policy towards the Church adopted by all the governments in the Bloc National. In order to offer the conservative right a positive signal, Briand began his term in office by renewing diplomatic relations with the Vatican that had been broken off in 1904, a move ratified by the Senate in May 1921. For his part, Pope Pius XI, who was elected head of the Catholic Church in February 1922, demonstrated his willingness to accept the separation of Church and state, except in Alsace-Lorraine, and in that way achieved tacit toleration of the activities of monastic orders that had been dissolved under the law of 1901. There was also a symbolic act at this time that helped to resolve the tension between Church and state: in 1920, Joan of Arc – the Maid of Orleans – was canonized and declared France's second patron saint alongside the Virgin Mary, a move that was welcomed even among patriotic circles otherwise hostile to the Church.

Any rapprochement between Church and state was as vigorously contested by the secular left as it was by the tradition-conscious sections of the clergy, who were afraid that the clear dividing line between the two would become blurred. But as far as the political middle ground was concerned, this development allowed the formation, in 1924, of a Christian democratic party, the Parti Démocrate Populaire (PDP), which solicited votes within the framework of the Republic as it then existed and would undoubtedly have been even more successful if women had had the vote at this time, a right they did not acquire in France until 1944. One of the PDP's leading parliamentarians was a lawyer from Metz, Robert Schuman, who in the wake of the Second World War was to become one of the pioneers of western European integration. Catholic workers loyal to the Church found their trade-union home in the Confédération Française des Travailleurs Chrétiens (CFTC) that was founded in February 1920 and which rejected the class struggle but not the negotiating lever of strikes, appealing in the process to the manifesto of Catholic social teaching, the encyclical *Rerum Novarum*, promulgated by Pope Leo XIII in 1891. In 1920 it had only 150,000 members and as such was dwarfed by the two million members of the still undivided CGT. In a number of regions, however, it was powerful enough to be regarded as a serious negotiator by employers' confederations.

It was not only in its dealings with the Catholic Church that Briand's government deserved the label 'moderate', for in the most important area of its foreign policy – its relations with a defeated Germany – Briand, who was also France's foreign minister, sought a compromise starting in the summer of 1921.

His first such attempt was the Wiesbaden Agreement that was signed after lengthy negotiations on 6 October 1921. The two signatories were Louis Loucheur, the minister for the liberated territories, and Walther Rathenau, the minister responsible for German post-war reconstruction. The agreement stipulated that German reparations could be paid for the most part not in gold marks but in kind, a move designed to counter any further fall in the value of Germany's currency. But most French industrialists were able to get round this agreement, with the result that a measure vehemently criticized by the political right made little practical difference.

When, only a few months later, Germany demanded a moratorium on the payment of its reparations, Lloyd George responded positively, and when Briand visited London in December 1921 he asked his French colleague to agree to the German request. Briand was ready to do so, but he did not have the backing of President Millerand, who in the absence of his prime minister chaired all the cabinet meetings. The subject was again discussed at an inter-Allied conference in Cannes in early July 1922, when Lloyd George suggested resolving the problem at a world economic conference to which Germany and the Soviet Union would also be invited. He offered to honour French compliance on the matter of reparations by providing a British guarantee on the borders of France and Belgium but not on those of the states of eastern central and south-east Europe that were allies of France.

Briand gave his consent, whereupon the participants agreed to convene a world economic conference in Genoa on 10 April, only for their plans to be thwarted by Millerand and Raymond Poincaré, the president of the Senate's Foreign Committee, who telegraphed their disavowal of Briand's proposal. Briand returned to Paris, where he resigned on 12 January without even waiting for the all too predictable outcome of the vote of no confidence in the Chambre des Députés. Three days later he was replaced by his keenest critic, Poincaré, who, like Briand, also held the office of foreign minister.

The new cabinet was markedly more right-wing than its predecessor. Poincaré insisted that the British offer of a guarantee be linked to conditions that amounted to a rejection, demanding a reciprocal allegiance that also guaranteed the borders of the eastern central and south-east European states and that would additionally apply in the event of Germany's marching into the Rhineland's demilitarized zone. Nor could there be any deal linking reparations with the British guarantee pact.

The world economic conference opened in Genoa on 10 April and ended on 19 May 1922. Most European states were represented, including Germany and the Soviet Union. Also represented were Japan and the British Dominions, but not the United States or Turkey, even though they had been invited. The French delegation was headed by the justice minister, Louis Barthou. Acting on Poincaré's instructions, he demanded that Germany waste no more time but comply with its obligations with regard to reparations. Soviet Russia was also required to acknowledge the pre-war debts incurred by its tsarist predecessor and to compensate the foreign shareholders of nationalized companies. In this way France once again thwarted British willingness to make concessions to the two 'pariah' states that were taking part in an international conference for the first time since the war ended. In turn, Paris unwittingly laid the foundations for the Russo-German Treaty of Rapallo, about which we shall have more to say in due course. That the world economic conference produced no tangible results was in no small measure a consequence of French intransigence.

France's abiding hostility to Germany also influenced debate within the country concerning a new defence act in the spring of 1922. Poincaré's government insisted on a standing army of 400,000 men, but reduced their period of military service by half, from thirty-six to eighteen months. The Socialists who were in opposition had no chance at all of implementing their own policy of a people's militia involving only a brief period of military service.

By the summer of 1922, just as the period of post-war depression was gradually drawing to an end, further major strikes hit the country, albeit no longer on the scale of those witnessed in 1920. The French currency remained weak: between December 1920 and April 1922 the rate of exchange with the pound sank from 59 francs to 48. The French economy recovered only slowly in 1922, whereas the export-orientated German economy seemed to prosper, a state of affairs due to the far greater devaluation of the German mark. Poincaré believed that German inflation was politically intentional and, indeed, a trick designed to allow the Reich to avoid its obligation to pay reparations. As a result, he remained obdurate on the question and emphatically rejected a further German request for a moratorium in July 1922, a request to which Lloyd George had responded with some sympathy and understanding. Four years after the end of the war there was nothing to suggest that Franco-German relations had in any way thawed. Instead, a new period of confrontation seemed to be looming. The 'policy of productive securities' that was used to justify the Franco-Belgian occupation of the Ruhr in January 1923 was already casting its long shadows.

A Democracy Self-destructs: Italy's Road to Fascism

The social struggles of the post-war years assumed far more dramatic proportions in Italy than they did in France or Great Britain. Here the two years 1920 and 1921 have gone down in history as the *biennio rosso*, a time of frequent major strikes and the occupation of country estates and factories. In the summer and autumn of 1919 railway workers, postal workers, the day labourers of the Po Valley, the *mezzadri* (*métayers*, or share-croppers) of central Italy and even ministerial officials came out on strike; in Lazio and other parts of central Italy peasants occupied the estates of the larger landowners; and in many places the protests against rising prices even turned into open revolt. When parliamentary elections were held in November 1919, the system of proportional representation was used for the first time in Italy, enabling the Socialists to emerge as the largest party with 165 seats, followed by the Christian Democratic Popolari with 100. The liberal prime minister, Francesco Nitti, was able to cling to power until June 1920 only with the help of the Catholic People's Party and, in the end, only by dint of a series of emergency measures. He was then replaced by Giovanni Giolitti, the grand old man of the Liberals, who had already held the post in 1892–3 and then again between 1903 and 1914.

The Socialists' principal strongholds were in the industrial north, and nowhere were they as powerful as in the capital of Piedmont, Turin, with its influential circle of political theorists associated with *L'Ordine Nuovo* and including Antonio Gramsci, Angelo Tasca and Palmiro Togliatti. In August 1917 the city had witnessed a workers' rebellion that had been bloodily suppressed but which resonated in Italian minds as a myth worthy of the struggling proletariat. The first Italian soviets had been established here on the Russian model. Following a split in the Socialist party at its rally in Livorno in January 1921, the extreme left had formed the Italian Communist Party and now expected that Turin would be the starting point of the proletarian revolution on the Italian peninsula, turning it into an Italian Petrograd. In April 1920 the city's metalworkers went on strike, a move which, although deliberately provoked by their employers, was at the same time the focus of attention of the radical left, which placed great hopes in this development, and yet the revolt turned into a total failure thanks to the carefully planned and highly effective countermeasures of the newly formed industrial confederation, Confindustria. The employers and the political right could draw only one conclusion from this failure: the left could be defeated and the Red revolution stopped in its tracks.

Social unrest increased in September 1920, when, following the breakdown of tariff negotiations in the northern Italian metal industry, the employers locked out their workers, a move to which the latter replied by occupying some of the largest factories and raising the Red flag. Their actions were not dictated by the Socialists but were spontaneous. Giolitti decided against sending in the police but decided simply to wait, and his assumption that this experiment in self-government by the workers would founder on its own inefficiency proved all too accurate. Even so, large sections of the Italian public felt that the government's passive stance was tantamount to capitulating to a radical minority that had not shied away from openly breaking the law. As a result, the state's authority was much reduced, initiating a process of erosion that continued when new strikes and bloody reprisals affected Turin and Tuscany in the autumn and winter of 1920/21. Once again the government reacted as if it were some neutral observer and did nothing.

This impression of a power vacuum benefited a group of individuals determined to make up for this decline in the authority of the state by systematically deploying physical and psychological force against the left: this group was the

Fascists, or *fasci di combattimento*, that Benito Mussolini had summoned into existence in Milan on 23 March 1919 and that took their name from the fasces, or bundles of rods, carried by the Roman lictors. Mussolini had been born in Predappio in the province of Forlì-Cesena in 1883 and, a failure as a teacher, had moved to Switzerland in 1902, where he eked out a living by doing odd jobs, sleeping in shelters for the homeless or under bridges. Here he came into contact with the Russian revolutionary Angelica Balabanoff, read Georges Sorel's *Réflexions sur la violence*, Gustave Le Bon's *La Psychologie des foules* and the writings of Friedrich Nietzsche, and attended some of the lectures given by the antiparliamentary and antidemocratic theorist Vilfredo Pareto in Lausanne.

On completing his military service in Italy in 1906, Mussolini moved to Trento but the following year was deported by the Austrian authorities and returned to Italy, where he began his career as a radical syndicalist, becoming editor in chief of the party's newspaper *Avanti* in 1912. But he broke away from the Socialists in October 1914, switching his allegiance to the Interventionist camp and shortly afterwards founding his own newspaper, the nationalist *Il Popolo d'Italia*, which he set up with financial help from the armaments industry and French backers. Between 1915 and early 1917 he served as a soldier on the Isonzo front but was discharged from the army after sustaining injuries in an explosion. With that he resumed his journalistic and political struggle on the home front and after the war ended became one of the most eloquent champions of Italian Irredentism, with its talk of a 'mutilated victory'.

In Mussolini's case the radical shift from the political left to the extreme right was not as astonishing as it may seem at first sight, for the later 'Duce' was never a Marxist in the strict sense of that term. Rather, he was an eclectic, an actionist and a voluntarist. Sorel's doctrine of *action directe* impressed him not least because it could be interpreted from both a left-wing and a right-wing standpoint, Sorel himself spending his entire life vacillating between these two extremes. All that mattered for Mussolini was where he could find the greatest opportunity for self-expression and acclamation. After 1914 the cult of nationhood seemed to him to be the most appropriate way of increasing his political influence and ultimately coming to power. And it was this that influenced his choice of followers and allies. Since the political left was internationalist, anti-imperialist and anti-militaristic, these supporters could only be found on the right of the political spectrum – men such as Gabriele D'Annunzio and the Arditi, those former elite troops who in April 1919 set fire to the building in Milan that housed the offices of the newspaper that Mussolini had once edited, *Avanti*, in order to signal the start of a national uprising.

In addition to Milan, Trieste was another city where the activities of the Fascists made themselves felt from an early date. Here they found a national enemy in the Slovenes, who were unwilling to trade Austrian for Italian sovereignty without a fight. The destruction of the Balkan Hotel, the headquarters of the Slovenes' umbrella organization, Narodni Dom, on 14 July 1920 was an early instance of Fascist terror. But it was not until 21 November 1920 that the Fascists' shock troops – the *squadre* – achieved their first significant breakthrough in Bologna, a Socialist stronghold. This was the day on which the newly elected Socialist town council took up office, an opportunity that Mussolini's followers seized to unleash bloody riots and engineer a mood close to that of a civil war. During the weeks and months that followed, the Fascist Blackshirts proceeded on a systematic basis to attack institutions and officials of the political left in the whole of Emilia-Romagna, Tuscany and, eventually, many other parts of Italy, too.

Violent assaults on Socialists and Communists were soon followed by increasingly frequent attacks on the Popolari. Among the methods regularly used to humiliate their political opponents was forcing them to drink retsina. In Emilia it was the local landowners who financed the Blackshirts, using them in their attempts to intimidate and punish recalcitrant peasants whose sympathies were with the political left. The *squadre* described their attacks as *spedizioni punitive* (punitive raids) designed to inflict bloody retribution on Communists or Socialists who they felt had provoked them or when one of their own number had been the victim of left-wing violence. From the beginning of 1921 the *biennio rosso* was replaced by a *biennio nero*, two years of blackshirted terror.

The Fascists suffered a humiliating defeat in the elections of November 1919, managing to put forward a candidate of their own only in Milan, where he polled a mere 4,000 votes. The political situation within the country changed in the spring of 1921 when – at the urging of the Vatican – the Popolari withdrew their parliamentary support for Giolitti's government. The reason for their action was a law that was passed in September 1920 and designed to reduce the country's huge budgetary deficit. Until then church possessions had not been subject to the same fiscal rules as the rest of the country but were now liable to taxation, a move that the Curia opposed with all the vigour it could muster. Giolitti responded by dissolving parliament and calling for new elections in May 1921. In order to ensure that he won a majority he entered into an electoral pact with the Nationalists and Fascists, who formed a National Bloc with Giolitti's Liberals. Mussolini's movement received an emphatic boost from its de facto merger with Giolitti's Liberals and gained a semblance of social respectability that it had previously not commanded.

Throughout the electoral campaign the Fascists' widespread reign of terror effectively prevented the Socialists and Communists from electioneering in many parts of the country, and the actual day of the election, 15 May, was overshadowed by countless bloody incidents triggered by the Fascists and resulting in dozens of deaths. The election result proved a bitter disappointment for Giolitti, his National Bloc winning only 120 out of a total of 535 seats, thirty-six of which went to the Fascists – a spectacular result for a party that had previously not had a single representative in parliament. Among the other winners were the Popolari, with 108 deputies, and the bourgeois Radicals, with sixty-eight. The biggest losers were the Socialists, who won only 123 seats, while the Communists returned fifteen members.

In the circumstances, there could be no talk of a stable coalition. Giolitti fell back on the obvious idea of implementing all the necessary measures by means of emergency legislation, including a reduction in the vast numbers of civil servants, but he was unable to obtain a parliamentary majority and so he resigned on 27 June 1921. His successor was Ivanoe Bonomi, until then the minister of war, a former Socialist who had been excluded from his party for supporting the war against Libya in 1911–12. In order to ensure himself of Mussolini's good will he accepted the Fascists' acts of violence with the same degree of indifference as that previously shown by Giolitti. In this he found himself in the best possible company, for a similar attitude was struck by all his other ministers as well as by the military and by the country's prefects. In many places army officers even worked together with the *squadre* and made weapons and lorries available to them. When Bonomi suspended the tax law that was so unwelcome to the Church following the stock exchange crash in August 1921, he was able to enjoy the support of Mussolini, who shortly afterwards ensured that the Act was permanently repealed.

Mussolini may have headed the Fascist movement in Italy, but he was not its only leader, for considerable influence was wielded not only by the representatives of the 'Agrarian Fascism' of northern and central Italy (the term was coined by contemporaries but fails to do justice to the movement's aims) but also by three radical regional leaders, Roberto Farinacci in Cremona, who was a former Socialist, the left-wing republican Dino Grandi in Bologna and Italo Balbo in Ferrara. These and other regional leaders resisted Mussolini's attempts to run the party along excessively rigid lines, and they rebelled against him in August 1921 when on the insistence of Bonomi he concluded a 'pacification pact' (*patto di pazificazione*) with the Socialists. But the truce had no practical effect as the regional leaders were supported in their resistance to the agreement by the larger landowners and employers, and at the Fascists' congress in Rome in November 1921 Mussolini saw himself obliged to draw a line under this particular chapter in his party's early history.

In spite of this setback, the congress turned out to be a major success for Il Duce, who, in the face of widespread opposition from several different quarters, was able to turn the Fascist movement into a coherent party, the Partito Nazionale Fascista, leading in turn to a formal explosion of Fascist brutality involving attacks not only on left-wing institutions but also on those of the Popolari and Liberals; Socialist deputies were 'expelled' from their constituencies without the police coming to their assistance. By the spring of 1922 increasing numbers of towns and cities were being occupied by *squadristi*, D'Annunzio's actions in Fiume serving as a model. In April and again in May

Ferrara, for example, was overrun by *squadristi*, who for a time cut off the city from all contact with the outside world. The local police forces proved completely powerless in the face of such concentrated brutality on the part of tens of thousands of Blackshirts trained as paramilitaries.

This Fascist terror culminated at the end of July 1922, when Italo Balbo led a large number of *squadristi* in a military campaign against the left-wing city of Ravenna, where he found covert support from certain sections of the state. The newly formed Alleanza del Lavoro (Alliance of Labour) enjoyed the support of the proletariat, Socialists, Communists and even anarchists but in the absence of any state help was unable to offer any effective resistance to the right-wing violence and was quickly defeated by the Fascists. Figures cited by left-wing sources and claiming that between October 1920 and October 1922 300 Fascists and 3,000 anti-Fascists were killed in the unrest, including street fighting and other excesses, may be debatable, but there is no doubt that the *squadristi* adopted a far more systematic approach to their violent activities than the left-wing Arditi del Popolo, who were created in an attempt to defend their members from the brutality of such attacks.

While large parts of Italy descended into chaos and anarchy, governments continued to change in Rome. In early 1922 the Socialists decided to topple Bonomi. At their party conference in October 1921 they had categorically refused to countenance any form of 'collaboration' with the bourgeois parties and since there was no conceivable political alignment that would allow them to gain any political influence, their actions proved to be a dangerous contribution to the country's continuing destabilization. The election of a new pope in February 1922 exacerbated this process when Pius XI lost no time in withdrawing his pontifical support from Don Sturzo's Popolari. Bonomi was replaced on 25 February 1922 by Luigi Facta, a friend of Giolitti from the right wing of the Democratic Party, who for a time was able to rely on the support of the Fascists but who enjoyed no parliamentary majority.

Facta's government fell on 19 July 1922, and King Victor Emanuel III invited all the party leaders, including the Socialists, to take part in talks. At the request of the majority of Socialist parliamentarians, Filippo Turati was also invited to speak to the king, a step that was unprecedented since the Socialists had hitherto refused to kowtow to the court. But the Socialist Party executive responded at once by excluding Turati and his group from the party, forcing Turati to appeal to the party conference in Rome in October 1922. By a small majority the conference confirmed the executive's decision, prompting the outlawed group to form a new party, the Partito Socialista dei Lavoratori Italiani, under the leadership of Turati, Emanuele Modigliani and Claudio Treves, with Giacomo Matteotti as its secretary general. As a result, there were now three socialist parties in Italy: the new grouping, which soon renamed itself the Partito Socialista Unitario, the old Socialist party, which became the Partito Socialista Massimalista, and the Partito Comunista Italiano.

Exploratory talks having foundered on the Socialists' refusal to negotiate, Victor Emanuel III reappointed Facta the prime minister on 1 August, and this time Facta received a broad parliamentary majority. The anti-Fascist Alleanza del Lavoro had called a general strike for that day, resulting in a complete breakdown of the rail network and almost all of the country's economic life. Mussolini reacted by issuing an ultimatum to the government: if Facta did not end the revolt within twenty-four hours, the Fascists' military units would. True to their word, the *squadristi* again set fire to the *Avanti* building in the course of bloody street fighting in Milan. Elsewhere, too, they stormed socialist buildings in Ancona, Livorno and Genoa, occupying the railways and brutally forcing back into the factories those workers who had not already returned to work of their own accord. Socialist workers suffered their most severe defeat to date, while the Fascists had taken an important step on their ruthless road to power.

On 24 October 1922 the Fascists organized a large-scale demonstration in Naples that was attended by many high-ranking public figures. Three days later, on the evening of 27 October, Mussolini ordered his paramilitary cohorts to 'march on Rome', prompting Facta to ask the king to declare a state of emergency. Victor Emanuel initially agreed, but the following morning refused to sign the order even though the proposed measure was already public knowledge. It was now left to Mussolini to take the initiative. Until then his only thought had been to participate in a right-wing government under Salandra, but now he demanded for himself the post of prime minister. Only when the king had bowed to this demand in a telegram did Mussolini make the legendary train journey that took him to Rome during the night of 29/30 October. There he formed a government in which he assumed not only the role of prime minister but also those of foreign minister and interior minister, while the former chief of the general staff, Armando Diaz, became minister of war and the philosopher Giovanni Gentile was appointed the new minister for education.

The 'march on Rome' had been no more than a threat and as such was very different from its classical model, when the consul Lucius Cornelius Sulla had captured the city with the help of Roman legionaries in 88 BC. Victor Emanuel's pusillanimity had saved the Fascists from actually having to confront the forces of the state. When Mussolini arrived in Rome on the morning of 30 October 1922, his 25,000 or so troops, only partially armed, were still encamped some thirty miles from the capital. Had the political will existed, it would have been easy for the military and the police to defeat them, but with the king's gracious permission they were allowed to demonstrate outside his palace on 31 October. They played no active role in the transfer of power. The intimidated chamber of deputies expressed its confidence in the new prime minister by 306 votes to 116. Among those who voted for Mussolini were Giolitti, Bonomi, Orlando, Salandra and the then forty-one-year-old Alcide de Gasperi of the Popolari, who was later to be the country's prime minister and leader of the Democrazia Cristiana after the Second World War.

Mussolini and his Fascists had learnt much from Lenin and the Bolsheviks: what mattered was not the support of a majority of the electorate but the firm resolve to strike fear and terror in their opponents and to seize power as soon as the right moment presented itself. If this will was there, even a resolute minority could gain political control. The Italian Fascists found it far easier to achieve their aims than the Russian Communists since they had allies in the country's civilian and military institutions as well as financial and political backers among the industrial and agricultural elite and were able to convince those bourgeois Liberals who set the tone and even intellectuals of the stature of Benedetto Croce that Fascist rule was the lesser of two evils when compared with the continuing chaos of the post-war period.

The only counterforce that could be taken seriously was the socialist workers' movement, but this had been fatally weakened by the split in its ranks fomented by Lenin's supporters and by the refusal of the non-Bolshevik left to work together with moderate bourgeois forces. The widespread tendency on the part of many workers to pursue their ends by anarchistic means without regard for the law was actively encouraged by the Communists but it played into the hands of the Fascists and gave them a perfect pretext systematically to ignore the law of the land in turn.

The representatives of the state accepted the escalation of violence, first from the left, then, on a far more massive scale, from the right, as if it were some natural force about which they could do nothing. As early as January 1921 the young Socialist deputy Giacomo Matteotti had complained in the chamber about the progressive abandonment of the state's grasp of power:

> The government and local authorities are assisting unmoved at the overthrow of law and order. Private justice is in operation, substituting public justice. [. . .] So the workers are saying that the bureaucratic state is just a joke, and has renounced its duty of guaranteeing the same law for everyone.[45]

Within four years of the end of the war the Fascists had achieved their goal and persuaded the bulk of bourgeois Italy that they alone were in a position to end the state of lawlessness that they themselves had caused by means of excesses far worse than those perpetrated by the extreme left.

The legend of the 'mutilated victory' that they promoted as enthusiastically as the middle-class nationalists of the Associazione Nazionalista Italiana with whom they joined forces in February 1923 provided them with an important psychological tool with which to fashion their success, but it was by no means the only one. Fascism would not have acquired the significance that it did after 1918 if Italian democracy had not already been seriously impaired. Among the other factors that played a part here were illiteracy, which was still rife among large sections of the rural population in southern Italy, the gross material disparity between the developed industrial north and the underdeveloped agricultural south, the Curia's long-standing – and for the most part closely heeded – instruction to devout Catholics not to vote in elections and the refusal of many Socialists to agree to any compromise with bourgeois forces in keeping with the rules of the parliamentary system. As a result, it was impossible to build up trust in the democratic state, and there was nothing that helped the Fascists' cause more than the absence of this necessary basis for the legitimacy of a system that rested on free elections.

That the Fascists would be ruthless in exploiting the power that was handed to them in October 1922 was one of the few certainties of this period in Italian history. It could be assumed that a new type of dictatorship would be established if there was even a grain of truth in all that Mussolini and his regional leaders had declared in previous years. All that remained unclear was how long the Fascists would need to enforce their claim to total control. There was, however, another question that only the future could answer: were the events that unfolded in Italy in the autumn of 1922 a purely national phenomenon or might they turn out to set an example that would be followed in countries that were equally torn by social, political and philosophical conflicts similar to those on the Italian peninsula?

Even at this early date, there was at least one perceptive observer who already suspected what the answer to this question would be. On 29 October 1922 the German journalist Count Harry Kessler wrote in his diary:

> The Fascists have mounted a *coup d'état* in Italy and seized power. If they are able to hold on to it, this will be a historic event that may have incalculable consequences not only for Italy but for the whole of Europe as well. Will it prove to be the first move in the victorious advance of the counterrevolution? Until now the counterrevolutionary governments in France, for example, have at least pretended to be democratic and peace-loving. But here an antidemocratic, imperialistic form of government has quite openly returned to power. In a certain sense Mussolini's coup can be compared with Lenin's in October 1917, albeit as its antithesis. Perhaps it will usher in a period of renewed turmoil and war in Europe.[46]

A Republic Put to the Test: Germany 1919–22

Germany had already put behind it the revolutionary battles of early 1919 and the violent internal political arguments over whether or not to accept the Treaty of Versailles when, in the course of the summer of 1919, public interest began to shift towards fundamental questions concerning the constitution on which the National Assembly had been working since the February of that year. By June many decisions had already been taken. The state of Prussia was preserved but in a way that prevented it from asserting itself at the expense of the other states: whereas it contained three-fifths of the Reich's population, it could take up only two-fifths of the seats in the federal constitutional body, the Reichsrat. Half of these seats were filled by government representatives, the other half by delegates from the provincial administrations. The Reichsrat had far less influence on legislation than its predecessor, the Bundesrat of the old Kaiserreich. And the southern German states no longer enjoyed the discretionary powers that they had had between 1871 and 1918. Constituted as a republic, the new Reich was ultimately more unitarian than the federalist states would have wanted and more federalist than the unitarians would have wished.

For a long time there were arguments over the relative importance of parliament and the head of state. The bourgeois parties wanted a more powerful president as a counterweight to the Reichstag, while the Social Democrats, who had initially been opposed to this idea, became reconciled to it after the conflicts of the early months of 1919, when the country had effectively been torn apart by what amounted to a civil war. They voted for the direct election of the president by the people, for a seven-year term in office, for the possibility of his unlimited re-election and finally also for the definitive form of Emergency Decree 48, according to which the president could, in the event of a substantial disruption or threat to public order, take measures that the Reichstag did not have to sanction but which it could repeal. For his part, the president could insist that an act passed by the Reichstag should be the subject of a plebiscite. A plebiscite could also be ordered if a tenth of the country's population demanded as much in a referendum. As a result the principle of a parliamentary and representative democracy was limited not only by the president as a replacement legislator but also by the possibility that the public at large could also enact legislation.

The chancellor was not elected by the Reichstag but if he was appointed by the president he needed the trust of the Reichstag and would have to step down if the Reichstag no longer had any confidence in him. All of this meant that the president had considerable leeway when choosing his head of government. When we also recall that the president was commander in chief of the country's entire armed forces and had the right to dissolve parliament, it will be clear why contemporaries spoke of a 'substitute Kaiser' or 'Kaiser substitute'. The Reichstag could assume that the head of state would step into the breach if the parties in government were unable or unwilling to agree on a compromise. In this way parliamentary opportunism and presidential 'Bonapartism' could easily lead to a silent change to the constitution, as power shifted from the body elected to represent the people to the head of state, who owed his legitimacy to a plebiscite and who might even head a dictatorship which in a time of crisis might seem to guarantee stability in the eyes of those who championed this particular construction of the situation.

There was an impassioned debate over the colours that would represent the Reich. The political right had the support of the majority of members of the German Democratic Party and a minority of the Catholic Centre Party in its desire to retain the black, white and red of the flag associated with Bismarck and his empire, while the Social Democrats and sections of the bourgeois middle ground were keen to return to the colours of the revolution of 1848–9: black, red and gold. The result was a compromise fraught with conflict: the colours of the Reich were black, red and gold, but a special merchant flag was introduced ostensibly because it was more clearly visible at sea. This was black, white and red with a black, red and gold canton in its upper inner corner. No less controversial was the restructuring of the school system. The Social Democrats insisted on interdenominational schools as the norm, but these could be replaced by faith schools or by non-denominational schools at the request of those who were entitled to be educated in them.

The section of the constitution that dealt with basic rights was an expanded and more up-to-date version of the corresponding provisions of the 1849 constitution. With the necessary two-thirds majority, the Reichstag could depart from the wording of the constitution without the constitution itself being affected. The National Assembly placed no obstacles in the way of changes to the constitution except for that of a qualified majority: two-thirds of its members had to be present, and two-thirds of those present had to agree. As a result, the constitution contained no guarantee that it would not be abolished, assuming that the necessary majority could be found. Constitutional restrictions on the majority will of the assembly would have struck the progenitors of the 1919 constitution as a relapse into the bad old days of the authoritarian state.

In the final vote on 31 July 1919 a broad majority spoke out in favour of the new constitution: of the 420 members, 338 took part in the vote, 262 voting yes, seventy-five no, with one abstention. The yes votes were those of the 'Weimar parties', the Social Democrats, the Centre and the German Democratic Party, while the no votes came from the Independent Social Democrats, the German Nationalists and the German People's Party. The country's president, Friedrich Ebert, who had remained in office for the duration, signed off the constitution on 11 August, and it came into force three days later. Not until 21 August 1919, however, did president, National Assembly and cabinet bid farewell to Weimar. From then on Germany was ruled from Berlin.

Germany was now 'the most democratic democracy in the world'. Nowhere had democracy been as comprehensively and rigorously introduced as in this constitution. When the Social Democrat minister of the interior, Eduard David, hailed the adoption of the Weimar constitution with these words on 31 July 1919, he was thinking above all of those provisions for direct democracy contained in the Republic's basic laws. The public at large reacted by noting the existence of the new constitution rather than by welcoming it with open arms, and it became a symbol of the Republic only in the wake of the campaigns of hatred and violence waged by the extreme right. The gain in political freedom that the Weimar constitution brought the Germans was great, but the constitution contained no guarantee that that freedom would not be taken away again when things became difficult. The 'most democratic democracy in the world' was threatened not only by the forces that rejected and opposed it but also and above all by the fact that it was drafted in such a way that it could effectively abolish itself.

The Weimar constitution was just seven months old when on 12 March 1920 the German defence minister Gustav Noske informed the cabinet of the chancellor, Gustav Bauer, that moves were afoot to topple the government. The driving forces behind the planned putsch were said to be Wolfgang Kapp, the director general of the Agricultural Credit Institute of East Prussia, and Captain Waldemar Pabst. These were the two men who had jointly been responsible for the murders of Rosa Luxemburg and Karl Liebknecht in January 1919. The coup, which has gone down in history as the Kapp–Lüttwitz Putsch or the 'Kapp Putsch', had the backing of considerable sections of the armed forces. Ever since the Treaty of Versailles had come into force on 10 January 1920, prominent members of the military under Walther von Lüttwitz, supreme commander of Group Command 1 in Berlin, had been spoiling for a fight with the government. For many officers, the very idea of caving in to Allied demands and hauling German war criminals before German courts of law seemed impossible to reconcile with the idea of national honour. There was also the still unresolved matter of reducing the strength of the army to 100,000 men, a move that would have affected the Freikorps regiments above all, especially the regiments from the Baltic who after the end of the war had fought the Bolsheviks in Latvia and Estonia with Allied approval. Noske named one of the regiments in particular: the Ehrhardt Marine Brigade.

The civilian wing of the conspiracy was made up of German Nationalist politicians from the extreme right, landowners from the area to the east of the Elbe and officials from the former Prussian provinces who had once supported the monarchy. Its centre of operations was the National Association formed in Berlin in October 1919 under the patronage of Erich Ludendorff, and its short-term aim was the establishment of an authoritarian regime which, initially not monarchical, would pursue an actively revisionist policy on the international stage.

Noske's attempts to counter the planned coup proved ineffectual, and on the morning of 13 March the Ehrhardt Brigade marched on Berlin. By around seven Kapp had already taken the Imperial Chancellery. Since most of the generals, including the head of the Troop Office, Hans von Seeckt, believed that military countermeasures were pointless, the president, Friedrich Ebert, his chancellor, Gustav Bauer, and the majority of his ministers had already left for Dresden, where Noske assumed that the local commanding officer would still be loyal to the government. Meanwhile, back in Berlin, the government's

Social Democratic press officer had called a general strike and invited the proletariat to unite, an appeal said to have been signed by Ebert and the Social Democrat members of his government, all of whom, however, quickly distanced themselves from the move.

A general strike was a risk because it could easily get out of control and turn into open civil war. It was a foregone conclusion, after all, that neither the Communists nor the syndicalists would be satisfied with restoring Bauer's government. On the other hand there were good reasons for banking on a successful general strike in the spring of 1920: in the wake of the economic boom that had resulted from inflation, there was practically full employment in Germany, so that workers who went on strike had no need to fear that the unemployed would be drafted in to replace them. A general strike aimed at resisting a military putsch and restoring the constitutional power of the state had an undeniable democratic legitimacy. And there was much to be said for the view that it needed a powerful signal on the part of the workers and other employees to persuade officials to unite against the putsch and force its leaders to capitulate.

The task of organizing the strike was assumed by the Free Trade Unions, in which the Majority Social Democrats were still working together with the Independent Social Democrats. The Communist Party joined the strike only after its members had ignored their leaders' original instructions and taken part in demonstrations against the putsch, support for which was largely limited to conservative forces to the east of the Elbe. Since most of the ministerial officials boycotted the coup, it was clear by 14 March that it would fail. In the circumstances it was all the more surprising that Gustav Stresemann, the chairman of the right-wing liberal German People's Party, should blame Bauer's government for causing the putsch and that he should then offer to mediate between the enemy camps. Republicans must have been even more puzzled when the vice-chancellor, Eugen Schiffer, of the German Democratic Party, which had again become involved in government in October 1919, together with several Prussian ministers, including a number of Social Democrats, met 'Chancellor Kapp' and 'Commander in Chief Lüttwitz' halfway and, in the event of their withdrawal, promised to form a grand coalition government, to hold new elections to the Reichstag as soon as possible and to move swiftly to the direct election of a new president.

Bauer's government, which had in the meantime decamped to Stuttgart, refused to compromise with the rebels and in doing so did the best that it could. Under pressure from the military, both Kapp and Lüttwitz stepped down on 17 March. The Ehrhardt Marine Brigade withdrew from the government quarter to the strains of the German national anthem, while chanting its usual slogan ('With the swastika on our helmets and a black, white and red armband, we are called the Ehrhardt Brigade'), but it then proceeded to cause a bloodbath among civilian protesters, leaving twelve people dead and a further thirty injured.

The end of the putsch did not mean the end of the general strike, however. On 18 March the umbrella organizations of the Social Democratic unions decided to prolong the strike until a series of demands was met: these included the dismissal of Noske, who had stood idly by while the armed forces fomented sedition against the Republic, the disbandment and disarming of unreliable military units and a republican restructuring of the armed forces. The Free Trade Unions also demanded that all who had been involved in the putsch should be punished, that disloyal units within the security services be disbanded, that the country's administration be fundamentally democratized, that the mining and energy industries be nationalized and that a number of Prussian ministers be dismissed on the grounds that they had been too indulgent towards the perpetrators of the putsch. Among these ministers was Wolfgang Heine, the Social Democrat minister of the interior. Only when there was evidence that the most important of these demands would be met did the three umbrella organizations declare the general strike at an end on 20 March. (In the case of the nationalization of the mining and energy industries, this meant that the commission set up in November 1918 was obliged to reconvene.) The USPD did not follow suit until three days later, by which time the chancellor had made a number of additional concessions.

The government reshuffle was completed on 27 March 1920. Bauer was replaced as chancellor by Hermann Müller, who, well known for his command of multiple foreign languages, had until then been his country's foreign minister. Together with Otto Wels, he was one of the two chairmen of the German Social Democrats. The new defence minister was Otto Geßler, who had previously been responsible for post-war reconstruction and who was on the right wing of the German Democratic Party. Hans von Seeckt, who on 13 March had refused to allow his soldiers to fire on their own comrades, took over the running of the army.

The repercussions of the Kapp–Lüttwitz Putsch proved even more far-reaching in Prussia than in the Reich. Here the politically undistinguished prime minister, Paul Hirsch, was replaced by the far quicker-witted Social Democrat Otto Braun, the country's former minister of agriculture, who hailed from Königsberg and who had trained to become a printer. As his new interior minister Braun appointed the Social Democrat parliamentarian Carl Severing, a trained metalworker from Westphalia who had proved his usefulness as the Reich and Prussian commissar in the troubled Ruhr Valley. In his new post Severing undertook a major reshuffle among the chairmen of the regional councils, the regional councillors and the police chiefs. Officials who had collaborated with the leaders of the putsch were replaced by men who the new minister of the interior trusted would defend the Republic more resolutely than their predecessors had done. With this, there began a new chapter in Prussian history, allowing the former Hohenzollern state to develop within only a few years into a bulwark of the German Republic.

Developments in Bavaria, conversely, took a very different turn. Munich witnessed its own particular kind of coup on 14 March 1920, when Arnold von Möhl, the commanding officer of Group IV of the German armed forces, delivered an ultimatum to the Social Democrat prime minister, Johannes Hoffmann, demanding that in the interests of law and order he should transfer all his executive powers to Möhl, a demand for which he, Möhl, had the backing of royalist politicians and of the paramilitary civil guard. In spite of Hoffmann's opposition, the Bavarian cabinet – a minority government made up of Social Democrats, the Bavarian Farmers' League and independents – complied with Möhl's request, and on 16 March the regional assembly elected a new prime minister in the person of Gustav von Kahr, the president of Upper Bavaria and a committed supporter of the house of Wittelsbach. Among members of his government were parliamentarians from the Bavarian People's Party, the German Democratic Party and the Bavarian Farmers' League. The Social Democrats became the party of opposition, a situation that was to remain unchanged until the end of the Weimar Republic. By the spring of 1920 Bavaria had become a hotbed of right-wing politics and hence the very opposite of republican Prussia, which remained in the hands of the Social Democrats. Bavaria thus became a stronghold for all those forces that sought to bring about a shift to the right in the country as a whole and to replace parliamentary democracy by a more authoritarian regime.

The government reshuffles in Prussia and Bavaria as well as the Reich in general by no means drew a line under the Kapp–Lüttwitz Putsch, and it required the suppression of the Ruhr uprising to put a bloody end to it all. In the industrial region of Rhineland-Westphalia a Red Ruhr Army had been formed in the wake of the coup. This was the armed wing of a mass movement that commanded proletarian support among Communists and non-Communists alike, assuming control of all the larger towns and cities. Its leaders had no intention of abandoning their positions once law and order had been restored in Berlin. In the 'Wild West' of the mining region, where left-wing Communists and syndicalists had the final say, local executive councils were far more radical than in the eastern and southern areas of the Ruhr Valley, where the metal industry was paramount and the Independent Social Democrats set the tone.

The governments in both the Reich and in Prussia exploited this situation to drive a wedge between the different fronts. On 24 March Severing negotiated the 'Bielefeld Agreement' with the more moderate executive councils, but this failed to satisfy the more radical elements. A number of towns and cities in the western part of the area, especially Duisburg, were for a time reduced to a state of chaos and anarchy, bringing a military solution to the conflict ever closer. The army also sent in units that had only recently supported the putsch. The total number of fatalities caused by this civil war within the country's industrial region has never been precisely established, but more than one thousand miners lost their lives, while the army recorded 208 deaths and 123 missing in action. A total of forty-one police offers were also killed.

The uprising in the Ruhr industrial region marked the end of the proletarian movement in Germany that had begun with the wild-cat strikes of 1917. There is much to be said for the argument that the uprising of the spring of 1920 was the third stage of the German revolution that had entered a latent phase in May 1919 following the suppression of the second Munich *Räterepublik*. The radical workers' protests were directed in part at a political and social system that they blamed for the war and at the people who wanted to restore this system after 1918, and in part at outdated workers' organizations that the radical left reproached for having in the meantime become a part of the capitalist system.

The wish to see a radical shift in social conditions survived the end of the revolutionary period, and yet the experiences of these weeks and months in the spring of 1920 had a sobering effect. The general strike had been successful to the extent that it had brought a rapid end to the putschists' aspirations, but it had also developed a momentum of its own, in the face of which the trade unions and Social Democrats were powerless. Riding roughshod over the will of the moderates, the radical left turned the political strike into an armed struggle from which the military, rather than the workers, emerged victorious. The uprising in the Ruhr Valley was followed by several attempted putsches on the part of German Communists, including one fomented by the Comintern in central Germany in March 1921, but like all the others it was quickly put down by the Prussian police and led to no mass uprising by the proletariat. There were no more general strikes in the Weimar Republic after 1920.

The rebels in the Ruhr Valley were punished far more severely than the participants in the previous putsch, most of whom, including Kapp and Lüttwitz, were allowed to settle abroad. Although he had a price on his head, Ehrhardt enjoyed the support of the authorities in Bavaria and was able, therefore, to prepare the next stage in the counterrevolution. Meanwhile, few of the promises made to the trade unions by central government were kept, and the work of the newly established commission on nationalization remained as ineffectual as it had been in 1919. Unreliable police forces were disbanded only where the Social Democrats had the necessary means to do so. Politically speaking, the army kept its distance in order to avoid the suspicion that it was supporting activities hostile to the Republic, but at the same time Freikorps officers who had played an active role in the putsch and who had been amnestied in August 1920 were accepted into both the army and the navy. An outspoken anti-republican attitude was no impediment to a career in the military, a 'state within a state', as it became under Seeckt.

The first elections to the Reichstag to be held after the war took place on 6 June 1920 and turned into a debacle for the forces of the Republic. The parties that made up the Weimar coalition had had a two-thirds majority in the

National Assembly, but they lost that majority in the election. The Majority Social Democrats' share of the vote dropped from 37.9 per cent to 21.6 per cent, while the Independents' share rose from 7.6 per cent to 18.6 per cent. The German Communist Party, which was contesting an election for the first time, won 1.7 per cent. The German Democratic Party's share dropped from 18.5 per cent to 8.4 per cent, whereas that of the German People's Party rose from 4.4 per cent to 13.9 per cent. The German Nationalists also improved their standing from 10.3 per cent to 14.4 per cent. The Centre Party, finally, suffered only modest losses, dropping from 15.1 per cent to 13.6 per cent outside Bavaria.

At its simplest, the elections brought a shift to the right among the bourgeoisie and a move to the left among the workers. Electors rewarded those parties that bore no responsibility for the compromises involved in forming the Republic, while punishing the moderates for what they had done or not done since the beginning of 1919. On the left the previous governments of the Republic were punished for allegedly allowing the forces of reaction to gain in strength, while the right blamed all the Weimar parties for everything they felt impugned national honour and jeopardized the interests of property-owners. Versailles and a tax reform implemented by the former finance minister Matthias Erzberger and involving a graduated income tax and a one-off property levy designed to help the country's ailing finances, the Kapp-Lüttwitz Putsch and the subsequent fighting – all of these factors affected the decision of the electorate, a decision that ultimately amounted to a vote of no confidence in Weimar.

But there was no sight of a majority that was capable of forming a government. Inconceivable from a political point of view, at least for the present, were a 'bourgeois bloc' that would include the German Nationalists and a grand coalition encompassing the MSPD at one end of the political spectrum and the German People's Party at the other. Only two types of minority government remained as viable alternatives: either a Weimar coalition tolerated by the German People's Party and by the USPD or a bourgeois minority cabinet supported in parliament by the Social Democrats. The Social Democrats preferred the second alternative as it seemed to offer them a better chance to demonstrate their Social Democratic credentials. President Ebert named the Baden Centrist politician Konstantin Fehrenbach his country's new chancellor on 25 June. Until then the president of the National Assembly, Fehrenbach formed a cabinet made up of members of the Centre Party, the German Democratic Party and the German People's Party, together with two independent ministers. This was the first time since October 1918 that Germany had had a government without any Social Democrats. But the country could not be governed without the Social Democrats, a point of which the latter were well aware and on which the bourgeois minority cabinet relied.

Fehrenbach's government survived for barely a year, two crises conspiring to topple it in the early months of 1921. The first – the conflict surrounding the future of Upper Silesia – has already engaged our attention in the context of the events in Poland after 1918, while the second concerned the question of the country's wartime reparations, which proved such a burden on the economy that any 'normal' way of dealing with the problem in the form of higher taxes was unthinkable. As a result, inflation grew worse. The peace treaty had not fixed the level of reparations, and this vagueness was to have disastrous consequences, for it robbed potential private investors of any possibility of realistically assessing the country's creditworthiness. In turn this meant that Germany was unable to accept any further long-term foreign loans.

On 5 May 1921, acting on behalf of the Allies, Lloyd George handed the German ambassador in London an ultimatum, demanding the phased repayment of 132,000 million gold marks, together with 6,000 million for Belgium, which Germany had overrun in 1914. These sums did not include any interest that would accrue to them in future. An instalment of 1,000 million gold marks was to be paid within twenty-five days, namely, by 30 May. The Allies also demanded the payment of the balance of 12,000 million gold marks out of the total of 20,000 million due on 1 May 1921 under the terms of the Treaty of Versailles. The country must also disarm in keeping with the Allies' earlier demands. And German war criminals were to be tried and sentenced. If these conditions were not met, the Allies threatened to start occupying the whole of the Ruhr beginning on 12 May. (Düsseldorf, Duisburg and Ruhrort had already been occupied on 8 March 1921 to punish Germany for its failure to comply with the terms of the earlier ultimatum.)

Fehrenbach's government had announced its resignation on the day before the London ultimatum was handed over since it had been unable to persuade the United States to intervene in the matter of reparations. (The United States and Germany signed a separate peace treaty only several months later, on 25 August 1921.) As a result the crisis over reparations coincided with a crisis in government, and the two could only be solved together. The German National People's Party, the Germany People's Party and the German Communist Party demanded that the ultimatum be rejected, whereas the Social Democrats, the Centre Party and the Independent Social Democrats were in favour of accepting it in view of the threatened sanctions. The German Democratic Party was divided on the issue.

If the advocates of a hard-line approach had prevailed, the result would have been Germany's economic collapse. The right-wing parties were fully aware of this fact, but, as had been the case with the vote on the Treaty of Versailles in June 1919, they could assume that even without them there would still be a majority in favour of the lesser of the two evils. And their calculations proved to be correct: the Social Democrats, the Centre Party and the German Democratic Party assumed responsibility for accepting the ultimatum and together formed a government, the first minority cabinet of the Weimar coalition. With effect from 10 May it was headed by the Baden Centrist politician

Joseph Wirth. A former mathematics teacher, he had succeeded Erzberger as finance minister in March 1920. He was a brilliant orator and an ardent nationalist but also an impassioned republican. In terms of the country's internal politics he occupied a position on the left of the Centre Party. Wirth's appointment marked the start of what was to become known as the Weimar Republic's 'policy of fulfilment'.

The 'policy of fulfilment' meant taking the payment of reparations to such absurd lengths that Germany's economy was stretched to breaking point, and the catastrophic consequences were all too predictable. But this predictability at least persuaded the victorious powers to revise the London repayment schedule. Not only did Wirth see the logic of this, so, too, did the majority of members of the Reichstag, which on 10 May 1921 voted for acceptance of the London ultimatum by a majority of 220 votes to 172. The Majority Social Democrats, the Independent Social Democrats and the Centre Party all voted for acceptance, as did a sizeable minority of the German Democratic Party and smaller minorities of the German People's Party and the Bavarian People's Party. Wirth's government had survived its first major test.

Of the political demands of the London ultimatum – political in the narrower sense of the term – one was not really met at all, and this affected the sentencing of German war criminals. Between May and July 1921 twelve defendants had been tried in nine separate trials in Leipzig, but only in half of these cases was a verdict reached. The greatest stir was caused by the sentences handed down to two naval lieutenants, who had taken part in the sinking of the life boats sent out by a torpedoed steamer. Both men were sentenced to four years' imprisonment, a sentence that provoked vehement indignation on the part of the navy. In January 1922 these sentences came to an abrupt end when members of the right-wing Consul Organization led by Hermann Ehrhardt forcibly freed the two officers from their cells. The Allies protested at the small number of convictions and at the lenient sentences handed down but failed to act on their objections. With the exception of these six convictions in 1921, Germany's war crimes went unpunished.

At least in principle the Allied demand that Germany should disarm was met in the early summer of 1921 and affected the Bavarian civil guard above all. The previous year the government in Munich had vigorously resisted its disbandment, but by early June 1921 the Allied pressure on the prime minister had reached the point where he could no longer resist the calls to order his country's disarmament. Three weeks later, on 24 June, the national government declared not only the Bavarian civil guard but also the related organizations in East Prussia and the paramilitary organization run by Georg Escherich in Bavaria to be permanently disbanded.

But this move was far from putting an end to paramilitary activities, for Bavaria remained the home of countless 'patriotic associations' much more radical than the disbanded civil guard. In the Germany of the Weimar Republic the state's monopoly on violence continued to be a far more effective force than was the case in Italy between 1918 and 1922. Even so, paramilitary associations and partisan armies still had their heyday ahead of them. Indeed, the enforced demilitarization of the country was to a certain extent more than compensated for by the paramilitarization of German society. Works of literature glorifying the war also played a part in keeping alive the spirit that was intended to build a new body for itself in the form of a militarily powerful Germany capable of wreaking vengeance on its enemies for the events of 1918.

The hard core of the demands enshrined in the London ultimatum could not be watered down, and in 1921 Germany had to pay 3,300 million gold marks in reparations, 1,000 million by 30 May. In the event the country could pay only 150 million marks in cash and had to finance the rest by means of bills of exchange that could be redeemed only with extreme difficulty when they fell due three months later. The inflationary impact of this operation was clear for all to see and on 19 May 1921 it prompted the Social Democrat minister of trade and industry Robert Schmidt to demand that the country's finances be placed on a new footing by expropriating 20 per cent of the capital assets of agriculture, industry, trade, banking and home ownership.

With his demand that material assets be seized Schmidt proclaimed the end of the tacit 'inflation consensus' that had characterized Germany's economic, financial and social policies since 1919. High wages were one way in which governments and employers had tried to counter social radicalization. The Social Democrats and the trade unions had helped to support this line, but by the early months of 1921 they were starting to see that devaluation was causing a progressive shift in the balance of social power and that it was the workers who were paying the price for this. At the same time they recognized that the country's finances could be turned around only with massive government intervention. Employers and the bourgeois parties, including the SPD's coalition partners, refused to accept this insight. Walther Rathenau, the minister for post-war reconstruction and a member of the German Democratic Party and former president of the supervisory board of AEG, was the first to criticize Schmidt. He was soon followed by the chancellor, Joseph Wirth, who also ran the country's finance ministry. In this way the demarche by the Social Democratic minister of trade and industry was comprehensively thwarted.

From the standpoint of the political right, the 'policy of fulfilment' was reprehensible not least because 'Marxists' in the guise of the Majority and Independent Social Democrats lay behind the acceptance of the London ultimatum. But even the political centre ground came into the right's line of fire as a result of its decision to work with the moderate left. Violent verbal attacks were soon followed by murderous actions, and on 9 June 1921 the chairman of the Independent Social Democrats in the Bavarian regional parliament, Karl Gareis, was shot dead by an unknown gunman in Munich. Ten weeks later, on 26 August, two members of the Consul Organization and of the Munich-based

Germanic Order shot dead the former finance minister Matthias Erzberger near Griesbach in the Black Forest. Erzberger, it will be recalled, was one of the signatories of the armistice on 11 November 1918. The gunmen escaped to Hungary via Munich. The assassination had been ordered by the leader of the Germanic Order, Lieutenant Commander Manfred Killinger, who was acquitted of the charge of being an accessory to the murder when the case was heard before a jury at Offenburg in June 1922.

Most of the country's nationalist newspapers expressly defended Erzberger's murder, the German Nationalist *Kreuz-Zeitung*, for example, comparing the culprits to Brutus, William Tell and Charlotte Corday (who killed the Jacobin leader Jean-Paul Marat in 1793). The political left responded to this glorification of violence on the part of the political right by holding mass demonstrations that were also attended by the German Communist Party. By 29 August a meeting of the national government chaired by President Ebert felt obliged to pass emergency legislation according to Article 48 of the country's constitution, authorizing the minister of the interior to ban publications, assemblies and organizations deemed hostile to the Republic.

The subsequent ban on several radical right-wing newspapers, including the *Völkischer Beobachter*, the official paper of the National Socialist German Workers' Party that had been founded in Munich in 1919, triggered a bitter row with Bavaria, where the regional government refused to implement the order. A second emergency decree followed on 28 September in the wake of negotiations with the Bavarian government under the premiership of the moderate Count Hugo von und zu Lerchenfeld, who belonged to the Bavarian People's Party and who had been elected to the post only a week previously. The new decree no longer protected only 'representatives of the republican and democratic state' but 'all persons in public life'. The regional authorities were responsible for carrying out all injunctions and undertaking all seizures designed to protect the Republic. For its part, the Free State of Bavaria agreed to lift the state of emergency that had been in force since November 1919 and to do so by 6 October 1921 at the latest.

At the end of October Wirth's cabinet became involved in a major crisis that could and should have been avoided. Its origins lay in the decision by the Allies' Supreme Council to partition Upper Silesia. Determined to show the world that they would not tolerate any disregard for the Germans' right of self-determination, the German Democrats and, with less conviction, the Centre Party demanded the immediate resignation of the national government. The Social Democrats regarded such a step as both dangerous and pointless but were unable to persuade the others to back down, and on 22 October Wirth informed the country's president of his cabinet's resignation.

The various parties then began talks with the aim of forming a grand coalition, a solution to the crisis that the Social Democrats were on this occasion willing to accept. The German People's Party, conversely, was not prepared to do so and as the reason for its refusal cited its doubts as to whether the SPD would really be willing to join a 'national united front' on the question of Upper Silesia. When the German Democrats, too, decided to play no part in the new government, the only remaining option was a rump coalition made up of the SPD and the Centre Party. The German Democrats now accepted that one of their members, Otto Geßler, would continue to be responsible for the armed forces, thereby exposing their previous antics as little short of farcical. Wirth returned to the post of chancellor on 26 October 1921. For a time he was also responsible for the Foreign Office but on 31 January 1922 he handed over this post to the former minister for post-war reconstruction, Walther Rathenau. As a result, the German Democratic Party was once again a party of government after a three-month interruption.

Two weeks before Rathenau took up his new appointment, Germany had received an invitation from the Allies' Supreme Council to attend the international conference in Genoa to which reference has already been made. This was the first time that both the victors and the defeated – including Germany and Soviet Russia – were to have a chance to discuss the problems of post-war economic reconstruction. An agreement between Berlin and Moscow, the two 'have nots' in international politics, was close. True, the government of Prince Max of Baden had broken off diplomatic relations with Russia on 5 November 1918 in protest at Russian payments to German revolutionaries, with the result that neither country had any diplomatic representation in the other, but both had exchanged trade missions since May 1921. These had been established shortly after the uprising in central Germany, a sign of the fact that in the eyes of Soviet Russia an attempted coup by the Comintern was by no means the same as Moscow's official policy: while the 'Internationalists' were preparing a world revolution, the representatives of Realpolitik were attempting to consolidate their country's position in capitalist states such as Germany.

This was particularly true of the military situation, for in September 1921 the German armed forces began to work together with the Red Army in a highly secretive and increasingly systematic way, a policy dictated on the one hand by Soviet Russia's interest in profiting from superior German technology and on the other by Germany's wish to use Russian help in ridding itself of the fetters of the Treaty of Versailles, especially in the areas of the air force and poison gas production. And then there was the matter of their joint opposition to Poland, neither Russia nor Germany having taken kindly to its territorial losses to the new Polish state. As early as February 1920, on the eve of the Russo-Polish War, the chief of the army command, General von Seeckt, had expressed the view that only in a strong alliance with a Greater Russia did Germany have any hope of recovering those of its territories that it had lost to Poland and regaining its status as a 'world power'. As finance minister, Wirth had actively encouraged the secret military cooperation between the German armed forces and the Red Army. He shared Seeckt's opinion and in 1922 repeatedly demanded that Poland be destroyed and that Germany and Russia be neighbours once again.

The true architect of Germany's policy towards Russia was the head of the Eastern Section of the Foreign Office, Ago von Maltzan, whose diplomatic background had been shaped by Wilhelmine Germany. In early 1922 he and Karl Radek, the Soviet leadership's expert on all things German, worked together on the draft of an agreement that respected the Russian wish for closer economic cooperation with Germany but without being monitored by an international syndicate of a kind proposed by the Allies for Soviet Russia's post-war reconstruction. Rathenau initially declined to follow this line, for, unlike Wirth, Seeckt and Maltzan, he was emphatically western-orientated, something he shared with Ebert and the Social Democrats. Keen to prevent Germany and Russia from going it alone, he supported the idea of an international economic consortium, with the result that negotiations between the two countries ground to a standstill and were not resumed until early April, when the Russian delegation under the country's foreign minister, Georgy Vasilyevich Chicherin, stopped off in Berlin on its way to Genoa. No agreement was reached at this time, but there was enough common ground on so many points that it seemed likely that a treaty would be signed in the not too distant future.

In Genoa nothing went as Ebert and Rathenau had planned, for although the Allies' experts agreed with the German view that reparations had led to a fall in the value of the German mark and should not be allowed to exceed the country's ability to pay, an unsettling rumour began to circulate to the effect that in separate negotiations between the Allies and the Russians there were signs that an agreement would be reached at Germany's expense. Although this rumour later proved to be unfounded, it persuaded Rathenau to accede to Maltzan's demands and to invite the latter to resume the interrupted negotiations with the Russians.

This decision was reached on the night of 15/16 April 1922 at the legendary 'pyjama party' in Rathenau's hotel room, where the foreign minister allowed the head of the delegation – Chancellor Wirth – and Maltzan to talk him into signing a deal with the Russians the very next day and to do so, moreover, without the explicit instructions of the German president and without informing the British prime minister, Lloyd George. This agreement has become known as the Rapallo Treaty after the Upper Italian resort where it was signed. Under its terms Germany and Soviet Russia jointly agreed to forgo any claims for compensation that might have been caused by the war, to resume diplomatic relations and to accord each other the status of most-favoured nation, granting each other trading advantages that they were later to accord to other states, automatically benefiting the other partner in the treaty.

In Berlin the agreement met with a mixed response that was none the less predominantly positive in tone. Ebert, it is true, was annoyed that his chancellor and foreign minister had ignored his instructions, but he supported the government in public, and the Reichstag adopted the treaty at its third reading on 4 July, with only a handful of votes against it from the German National People's Party. One of those who warned against it was Rudolf Breitscheid from the rump of the Independent Social Democrats, who at the end of April 1922 described the treaty as a serious threat to German interests, arguing that it harmed the country's emerging economic cooperation with the West.

The Western Powers and especially France were profoundly alarmed at the way in which the Germans and Russians had reached their accord. And while the treaty contained none of the secret military clauses that its critics initially feared, the almost conspiratorial manner in which it had been signed was calculated to provoke mistrust, a mistrust that would have been even greater if the Allies had been aware of the secret cooperation between the German and Russian armies. Whether there would have been any substantive progress on the question of reparations in Genoa if there had been no treaty is debatable, given America's refusal to attend the talks. But in the wake of the events in Rapallo, any Allied concessions were remoter than ever. The Genoa conference ended without agreement on 19 May 1922, the Soviets continuing to refuse to accept any responsibility for their country's pre-war debts.

By 24 April – a week after the Treaty of Rapallo had been signed – France's prime minister, Raymond Poincaré, gave a speech in Bar-le-Duc in which he was already indicating the possibility of his country's military intervention. On 2 May, the commander in chief of the allied troops in the Rhineland, Jean Degoutte, wrote to the minister of war, André Maginot, stating that in the light of the rapprochement between Germany and Soviet Russia, France should waste no more time but should occupy the Ruhr Basin without delay. The Treaty of Rapallo marked a return to the risky policies of Wilhelmine Germany and was driven by forces still in thrall to the thinking of that period. When Wirth spoke to Chicherin in Genoa and urged a 'restoration of the borders of 1914', he knew that he had the backing of large sections of Germany's ruling class.

The man who as Germany's representative had reluctantly signed the Treaty of Rapallo with Chicherin did not live to witness its ratification. Late on the morning of 24 June 1922, Walther Rathenau was shot by two men who overtook his car on its way from his villa in Grunewald to the Foreign Office. The perpetrators – a retired navy lieutenant, Erwin Kern, and a reserve lieutenant, Hermann Fischer – were arrested by the police at Saaleck Castle near Kösen on 17 July. Kern died from gunshots sustained while trying to escape and Fischer immediately took his own life. Both men were members of a militantly anti-Semitic nationalist organization that had around 170,000 members and also of the Consul Organization that was behind Erzberger's murder. Other members of the same secret organization that had planned the more recent attack were quickly arrested by the police.

For those who had instigated the attack on Rathenau, the country's foreign minister embodied the policy of fulfilment and, indeed, the Weimar Republic as such: no other public figure was such a potent symbol of all that they hated. He was a critic of the old Germany and as a Jew could not have become his country's foreign minister without the revolution. He upheld the policy of fulfilment towards the West without the ulterior motives towards the East that characterized a man like Joseph Wirth. At the same time, however, Rathenau was a product of Wilhelmine Germany and a patriot who as recently as October 1918 had called upon his fellow countrymen and women to rise up in a 'levée en masse'. Since the summer of 1919 he had also done what he could to circumvent the terms of the Treaty of Versailles. It was not least the contradictions that he represented that made him the target of all who wanted to topple the Weimar Republic by means of a right-wing revolution.

The murder of Walther Rathenau shook the Weimar Republic to its very foundations, leaving almost as great a mark on the country as the Kapp–Lüttwitz Putsch had done, and yet the increase in left-wing violence that the extreme right had hoped would ensue failed to materialize. Major demonstrations were called by the General German Trade Union Association and attended by members of the Majority and Independent Social Democrats and also by the Communists. On 25 June Wirth delivered a tribute to his dead minister in the Reichstag and at the end of it, to tempestuous applause from the majority of members of the house and their guests in the gallery, he accused the political right of complicity in the murder in words that left a deep impression on contemporaries: 'There stands the enemy, dripping poison into a nation's wounds. There stands the enemy – and there is no question about it: the enemy stands on the right.'[47]

Rathenau's murder also forced the government to take a number of administrative and legislative countermeasures, initially in the form of two emergency decrees, then in the guise of a law to protect the Republic, which received the necessary two-thirds majority at its third reading in the Reichstag on 18 July 1922, after Gustav Stresemann's German People's Party had voted for it. All actions hostile to the Republic, from insulting the national flag to murdering the country's official representatives, were now subject to the severest penalties. A special court was established in Leipzig to deal with all such crimes.

As had been the case following Erzberger's murder the previous year, the sanctions imposed by the government triggered a conflict with Bavaria, which repealed the act the following day and replaced it by a decree that took over the act's material regulations but transferred the powers of the Leipzig court to the Bavarian courts. The national government's reaction was weak but ultimately successful, offering to negotiate in talks that led to a compromise on 11 August, the third anniversary of the Weimar constitution: to the new federal court was added a second supreme court with jurisdiction over crimes committed in southern Germany, such cases to be tried by southern German judges. On 25 August 1922 the Bavarian government responded by repealing the decree that it had issued on 24 July. But Lerchenfeld was punished for this tactical retreat by the right-wing majority in the regional parliament and on 2 November he was obliged to resign. He was succeeded a week later by Eugen von Knilling, a man far more sympathetic than Lerchenfeld to the 'Patriotic Associations' and to Hitler's National Socialists.

The new law was designed to protect the Republic, but its impact fell far short of the expectations of its proponents. The judiciary was still in thrall to the mentality associated with the authoritarian state that Germany had been until recently and had no interest in availing itself of the resources enshrined in the act. If it chose to do so at all, then it was by preference against left-wing political criminals rather than against their right-wing counterparts. To take an example: a Communist who referred to the 'robbers' republic' was sentenced to four weeks' imprisonment, whereas a defendant from nationalist circles who had used the phrase 'Jews' republic' as a term of abuse was fined only seventy marks.

All attempts to counter the fanatical anti-Semitism that had found expression in the unprecedented hate campaign against Rathenau and that had finally led to his murder proved ineffectual. In the eyes of the extreme right, the Jews were to blame for Germany's defeat in the war because they had allegedly fed the workforce a divisive diet of pacifist, Marxist and Bolshevik ideas or grown rich at the expense of the German people. They were depicted as fomenting and exploiting revolution, inflation and the policy of fulfilment. In this way they served as scapegoats for everything that Germany had had to endure – or which it thought it had had to endure – since November 1918.

Anti-Semitism was particularly rife among students and academics, many of whom saw the Jews as their rivals in the struggle to climb the social ladder. Many would-be academics and even their established counterparts felt it as a personal affront that the 'Marxist' workers' movement had come to power in 1918: their claim to be their country's true leaders was being called into question by forces which they felt lacked the requisite intellectual and moral fibre. The role played by Jews on the political left was in itself sufficient to lend anti-Semitic weight to the feeling that the Germans had forfeited their status and suffered a loss of prestige. Nationalist students and young academics saw themselves as a part of the tradition of the Wars of Liberation in the early nineteenth century and, above all, as the natural heirs of such nationalist writers as Johann Gottlieb Fichte, Ernst Moritz Arndt and Friedrich Ludwig Jahn, in whose writings they found what they were looking for: a view of a German nation that would last for ever, while the Jews were the representatives of a foreign sense of nationhood and the embodiment of the Weimar Republic, whose very nature they were said to encapsulate.

Rabid anti-Semites were to be found not only in anti-Jewish organizations but also among royalist German Nationalists, especially on their *völkisch* wing. Their official newspaper was the *Konservative Monatsschrift*, which in June 1922 published an article by one of the Reichstag deputies, Wilhelm Henning,

claiming that 'German honour' was 'not a commodity to be bartered by international Jews'[48] and that Rathenau and his henchmen would be held to account
by the German nation. In the wake of Rathenau's murder, the party leaders of
the German Nationalists, including the former Prussian finance minister
Oskar Hergt, felt it appropriate to draw a line under the activities of their
more extreme *völkisch* elements. By stripping Henning of his party membership, the German Nationalist People's Party aimed to demonstrate to other
bourgeois parties that it was capable of governing. But the decision was left
to the party's representatives in the Reichstag, who felt that it was sufficient
to exclude Henning from their own ranks but not from the party. Henning
himself and two of his like-minded associates took this step voluntarily only a
short time later, founding the German People's Workers' Cooperative in
September 1922. Three months later this party became the German Nationalist
Freedom Party.

Munich became one of the new party's strongholds, a development due to
the party's ability to merge with the local German nationalists. Here in the
Bavarian capital there was particularly fertile ground for right-wing German
nationalist ideas but also a rival whose hatred of Jews and 'Marxists' could
simply not be equalled. This rival was Hitler's National Socialist German
Workers' Party (NSDAP), a party whose meetings and methods struck many
contemporary observers as modelled on those of the Italian Fascists. The
NSDAP reacted to the murder of the country's foreign minister by circulating
flyers during a Social Democrat rally in honour of the dead minister: 'Rathenau,
now he's dead!! Ebert and Scheidemann, however, are still alive.'[49] For the
German National People's Party, the loss of its radically right-wing *völkisch*
element had more advantages than disadvantages, for the German Nationalists
were by now coming a little closer to their principal goal, namely, inclusion in
a bourgeois coalition that would govern without the Social Democrats and
drive them into opposition.

The left, too, regrouped following Walther Rathenau's murder: in July 1922
the Reichstag members of the Majority and Independent Social Democrats
joined forces to work together in the Reichstag as a cooperative union, and in
the September they once more came together to form a single party. By 1922,
of course, the Independent Social Democrats were no longer the party that
they had been in 1917. At its conference in Halle in October 1920, the left-wing
members of the party had voted to join the Communist International and
hence the German Communist Party. Those members who in 1922 were
reunited with the Majority Social Democrats belonged to the moderate
minority and included the party's leaders Wilhelm Dittmann and Artur
Crispien and its intellectuals Rudolf Hilferding and Rudolf Breitscheid as well
as former Communists associated with the party's former chairman, Paul Levi,
all of whom had been thrown out of the Communist Party in 1921 and moved
further to the political right. It required the experience of growing right-wing

radicalism and the murder of Walther Rathenau on 24 June 1922 to convince the Majority and Independent Social Democrats that they could no longer afford to maintain their damaging divisions.

The merger of the two parties in September 1922 considerably strengthened the political and, above all, the parliamentary importance of the Social Democrats in Germany, and yet it also had a drawback, for the previous year, at its party conference in Görlitz in September 1921, the Majority Social Democrats had adopted a predominantly reformist programme largely drafted by Eduard Bernstein and designed to promote the party's image as 'the party of all working people in town and country' and as an 'action group for democracy and socialism'. As such, the party was open to all like-minded individuals, regardless of their class. From the standpoint of the rump of the Independent Social Democrats such a watering down of its views on the class struggle could not be reconciled with its continuing tradition as a Marxist party. The wording of the programme of action agreed to at its joint conference in Nuremberg was far more reminiscent of the old Erfurt programme of 1891 than the more recent Görlitz programme, while Rudolf Hilferding's Heidelberg programme of 1925 was likewise couched in much more 'Marxist' terms than its predecessor of 1921 had been.

Another factor that contributed to the changes to the party's ideological outlook was the hardening of its attitude to the role of government. The creation of a cooperative union between the two Social Democrat parties in the Reichstag meant that any attempt on the part of right-wing Social Democrats to form a grand coalition now had to be put on hold, for most members of the Independent Social Democrats and the left wing of the Majority Social Democrats would not have helped to support a coalition with a party as friendly towards the employers as the German People's Party. Even so, Stresemann's party was now a silent member of Wirth's government. On 19 July 1922, five days after the Majority Social Democrats and Independent Social Democrats had merged, the German People's Party, the German Democratic Party and the Centre Party formed a coalition which, loyal to the constitution, occupied the middle ground and was intended to counterbalance the new preponderance of the Social Democrats. The previous day the German People's Party had voted for the law designed to protect the Republic and in doing so signalled its shift to the political centre ground. On 24 October the party was able to ensure that the Reichstag could extend Ebert's term as president until 30 June 1925, the house now having the necessary two-thirds majority required to take this step. This meant that the direct election by the people that had been planned to take place in early December 1922 was now unnecessary, as it was an election that the moderate bourgeois parties preferred to avoid lest it disturb the country's internal peace. (In the case of the German People's Party there was an additional motive in that they were keen as far as possible to avoid voting directly for or against Ebert.)

In the autumn of 1922 there would have been compelling reasons to form a grand coalition. Rathenau's murder had destroyed what little confidence was left in the mark: Germans and foreigners alike were panicked into disposing of their credits in marks, and the flight of capital assumed gigantic proportions. It was also at around this time that the inflationary boom that had protected Germany from the world economic crisis of the early 1920s came to an end. The interest in cheap German imports sank in direct proportion to the ability of local industry to return to its former levels of production. As a result German exports lost the advantage that they had had when global production fell after 1920. Inflation, which turned to hyperinflation in July 1922, was finally robbed of its economic appeal, objectively raising the chances of a currency reform. Politically speaking, however, such a reform was feasible only if employers and trade unions worked closely together with both the moderate bourgeois parties and the Social Democrats.

In the summer of 1922 large sections of the German employers' organizations were still refusing to accept this. They included Hugo Stinnes, who had used inflation to build up a vast industrial empire and who since 1920 had represented the German People's Party in the Reichstag. He expressed his ideas on currency reform in a speech that he gave, significantly, on 9 November, the fourth anniversary of the revolution, to the Provisional Economic Council, a professional body anchored in the constitution but without the power to reach any decisions of its own. In demanding that German workers should work two hours longer each day for no extra income over a period of between ten and fifteen years he unleashed a veritable storm of indignation on the political left. Stinnes's views were shared by the industrial wing of the German People's Party, but not by the rest of the party, including its chairman, Gustav Stresemann, who was now convinced that the more moderate forces in the bourgeoisie needed to work more closely with their moderate counterparts in the country's workforce. On 26 October he therefore voted for the chancellor's proposal to set up a commission made up of the parties in government and the German People's Party in order to create a common platform that would take all necessary politico-economic decisions, including that of the question of reparations.

The German People's Party elected the electrical industrialist Hans von Raumer, an architect of the Central Cooperative Union of November 1918, to sit on the commission, while the SPD sent its leading theorist, Rudolf Hilferding, whose book *Finance Capital* had appeared in 1910. Both men played a decisive part in the decision to draw up a list of measures that the government used in its note on reparations on 13 November 1922. The one real sensation of the commission's proposals was a compromise on the controversial question of the length of the working day. The eight-hour day was to remain the norm, but legally binding exceptions were to be allowed as long as they had the agreement of the workers and the authorities. Although the commission did not entirely call into question one of the most important social gains of November 1918, it none the less recommended that for certain sections of the economy a temporary increase in the number of hours that could be worked in a week should be considered in order to facilitate a reform of the country's finances and, with it, Germany's economic recovery and its peaceful coexistence with its neighbours.

This was the spirit behind Wirth's note on reparations of 13 November 1922. As the Allies had demanded, it proposed that the German Federal Bank should take vigorous steps to support the mark. If an international loan were to raise 500 million marks, then the bank would provide matching funds. This note had the agreement not only of the chairmen of the coalition partners – the SPD, the Centre Party and the German Democratic Party – but also of the representatives of the German People's Party.

In this way it seemed as if the foundations of a grand coalition had been laid, but appearances proved deceptive, and by 14 November the Reichstag members of the United Social Democratic Party of Germany voted by an overwhelming majority to boycott such a coalition. It was above all the Prussian prime minister, Otto Braun, who had advocated such a move, but he was fighting a losing battle: so soon after the two Social Democrat parties had merged, the party's leaders were unwilling to risk a trial of strength with the former Independents, most of whom – unlike Hilferding – remained vehemently opposed to a merger with the German People's Party, which was regarded as the party of big business.

In keeping with an agreement made with the centre-ground parties, Joseph Wirth resigned as chancellor later that same day and was replaced on 22 November by the general manager of the Hamburg-America Line, Wilhelm Cuno, a Catholic who had been born in Suhl in Thuringia in 1876 and, although he had no party affiliations, clearly stood to the right of centre. Ebert will have hoped that with an experienced businessman at the head of his cabinet he would be able to bring German employers closer into line with the Republic and also make a good impression on the international community. In addition to Cuno, four other members of the cabinet belonged to no single party. They included Essen's former mayor Hans Luther as the minister with special responsibility for nutritional and dietary matters and Wilhelm Groener, the country's former quartermaster-general, who had already served under both Fehrenbach and Wirth and who now became minister for transport. The other cabinet posts were held by members of the Centre Party, the Bavarian People's Party, the German Democratic Party and the German People's Party. Cuno's bourgeois minority cabinet was far from enjoying a parliamentary majority and could survive only if it was tolerated by the Social Democrats.

No other ministerial team in any other Weimar government bore such striking similarities to a cabinet of pre-war civil servants as Cuno's, and never had the country's president exerted such influence on the choice of chancellor as was the case in November 1922. It would be no great exaggeration to call Cuno's government a presidential cabinet in disguise. But it was not just a mistake on Ebert's part that allowed the country to relapse into the ways of an authoritarian state. Rather, it was the Social Democrats who had established the Weimar Republic who were largely to blame for this development. Concerned for their survival as a party, they had refused to countenance a parliamentary solution to the crisis that beset the country but had opted instead for what we can only call a presidential solution.

A Year of Decisions: 1923. From the Occupation of the Ruhr to the Dawes Plan

Cuno's government had been in power for less than two months when French and Belgian troops occupied the Ruhr on 11 January 1923, triggering the most serious international confrontation since the Russo-Polish War of 1920, if not since the end of the First World War. The reasons given for the move were little more than a pretext, Germany standing accused of violating its commitment to provide timber, telegraph poles and coal under the terms of the Allies' demands as formulated by its commission on reparations.

This failure was due to the previous cabinet of Joseph Wirth, which since August 1922 had consciously upheld the popular slogan 'First bread, then reparations'. The delay was irresponsible, since France had been waiting for an opportunity to occupy the Ruhr ever since the Treaty of Rapallo. By overrunning the region, France hoped to secure its frontiers against its neighbour to the east, a move that it had been unable to make in Versailles thanks to the opposition of the two Anglo-Saxon countries represented there. But more than just the country's security was at stake, namely, the desire to bolster French claims to be regarded as the dominant power in Continental Europe. France's actions were close to declaring war. In the event, Paris received no support from the Allies: Great Britain lodged a formal protest, while the Vatican condemned it unequivocally.

The German response to this act of aggression was a policy of passive resistance in the form of a refusal to comply with the orders issued by the occupying powers. In this, Cuno's government had the backing of the vast majority of members of the Reichstag and the active support of the trade unions, only the extreme left and the extreme right refusing to join the united front. On 22 January the Communists adopted the slogan 'Defeat Poincaré and Cuno in the Ruhr and on the Spree!' But in the weeks that followed, they stressed their opposition to Poincaré rather than Cuno, an emphasis dictated by the Soviet Union's anti-imperialist policy towards France. A more extreme position was taken by the National Socialists. On 11 January 1923, at a meeting in the Zirkus Krone in Munich, Hitler told his followers that their watchword should be 'Down with the November criminals!' not 'Down with France!'

As a result of the German boycott, neither France nor Belgium was able to obtain any reparations until March 1923, and to that extent the policy of passive resistance achieved its principal aim, at least for the present. But then the occupying forces began to seize the coal mines and coking plants and to take control of the railways. Germany still had to pay the wages of the railway employees who were driven from the occupied areas and also paid millions of marks in credits to the coalmining industry and the iron and steel industry in order to ensure that wages could still be paid after these facilities had all been shut down. From a financial point of view, the policy of passive resistance meant that the Ruhr Valley became a bottomless pit. Hyperinflation spiralled out of control. The mark's foreign value, which the German Federal Bank had stabilized at around 21,000 marks to the dollar between February and April 1923 by selling gold reserves and foreign currency, fell to 48,000 marks in May 1923 and to 110,000 marks in June 1923.

The more it became clear that the policy of passive resistance had failed, the greater became the tendency on the part of the radical right to switch to active resistance in the form of acts of sabotage. In March and April 1923 several railway installations in the occupied region were blown up. One of the perpetrators, the Freikorps officer Albert Leo Schlageter, was arrested by the French police in Essen in April. On 9 May he was found guilty of espionage and sabotage by a French war tribunal in Düsseldorf and sentenced to death by firing squad, a sentence carried out on 26 May.

Schlageter's execution triggered a storm of protest in Germany that was heard as far away as Moscow. In a speech to the Enlarged Executive Committee, Karl Radek – the Communist International's expert on Germany – described him as a 'martyr of German nationalism' and a brave soldier of the counter-revolution who deserved 'to be honoured by us soldiers of the revolution'. But men like Schlageter would become 'travellers into the void' – the expression is borrowed from a contemporary Freikorps novel by Friedrich Freksa – unless they learned to fight for the cause of the great mass of German workers, who were a part of the larger family of nations fighting to gain their freedom.[50]

Radek's speech was an attempt to drive a wedge between the nationalist masses and their leaders and to turn the nationalist revolution into a socialist revolution. From the standpoint of the Soviet Union and the Comintern, the Franco-German confrontation of 1923 offered an unexpected chance to undermine the whole of the post-war order. If Germany were to be supported by Soviet Russia, a national war of liberation could prove to be a decisive battle in the world revolution, always assuming that the national masses currently under 'Fascist' control could be persuaded to unite with the Communists under Communist leadership. To give practical expression to this strategy was the goal of the 'national Bolshevik' agitators among the supporters of the nationalist right, a course of action adopted by the German Communist Party in the summer of 1923, when they made remarkable rhetorical concessions to anti-Semitism but still failed to make a significant breakthrough.

Among the workers, conversely, the Communist Party's slogans found a far more immediate response. The Communists may not have caused the wild-cat strikes that took place in the Ruhr in the middle of May, but they certainly knew how to turn them to their own advantage. In works committee elections, trade union elections, local elections and the elections to the Landtag in the summer of 1923 the Communists recorded substantial gains, and the number of party members rose between September 1922 and September 1923 from 225,000 to 295,000. By August 1923 there were signs of an imminent political explosion as the increase in social deprivation had produced a mood of despair that found expression in what became known as the 'Cuno strikes'. The Free Trade Unions did what they could to prevent the state-owned printing works that were also responsible for printing banknotes from being affected by the walkout, but their efforts proved futile. The presses stopped rolling for only a day – 10 August 1923 – but the resultant shortage of paper money was immediately felt throughout the whole country.

Until then the Social Democrats had at least tolerated Cuno's government. Opposition on the left of the party to cooperation with the German People's Party was so pronounced that the party leadership saw no alternative but to continue to accept the most right-wing of Germany's post-war cabinets. There was also the fear that if at the height of the crisis the Social Democrats were to assume responsibility for governing the country and abandon, what turned out to be, the disastrous policy of passive resistance, the party would again be accused by the nationalists of stabbing their country in the back. It required the 'Cuno strikes' to convince the Social Democrat leaders that continuing to tolerate the Cuno government was no longer the lesser of two evils but, compared with a grand coalition, the greater.

By now dissatisfaction with the government had reached a critical point with the bourgeois parties and the employers, too, leading to a sudden and overdue resolution of the crisis within a matter of days. In their negotiations with the existing governing parties the Social Democrats tabled a whole series of demands, including a rapid containment of inflation, preparations for the introduction of a gold currency, a clear dividing line between the regular army and all illegal military organizations and a change in foreign policy designed to resolve the question of reparations. For some time the chairman of the German People's Party, Gustav Stresemann, had been touted as a new chancellor, a proposal with which the Social Democrats were in agreement because they had their own internal reasons for not wanting to occupy this key position. The most powerful party was content to provide the finance minister, the business secretary, the home secretary and the justice minister. Within twenty-four hours of Cuno's resignation, Ebert had replaced him as chancellor by Gustav Stresemann. A day later – 14 August 1923 – the new chancellor, who also held the post of foreign secretary, won a vote of confidence in the Reichstag. Around a third of the Social Democrat and German People's Party representatives absented themselves from the vote, a clear sign that the grand coalition remained hugely controversial in both of these parties.

The Social Democrats' return to government was greeted with outrage on the political right in Bavaria and in the occupied Ruhr, two of its cabinet members bearing the brunt of the hostility: the finance minister Rudolf Hilferding, who was reviled because he was Jewish, and the justice minister Gustav Radbruch who was loathed because he had filled the same post under Wirth and embodied the hated law passed to protect the Republic. But the workers were reassured by the formation of a grand coalition, and the number of 'Cuno strikes' gradually dropped. There could no longer be any talk of a revolutionary situation in Germany.

Back in Moscow, the Comintern saw things differently. Under the impact of the 'Cuno strikes', the secretary general of the Third International, Grigory Zinoviev, wrote to the German Communist Party in the middle of August and urged it to prepare for the coming revolution. On 23 August the Politburo of the Russian Communist Party met in secret session. In the face of opposition from Stalin in his role as party secretary, Zinoviev, Radek and the people's commissar for defence, Leon Trotsky, pushed through a resolution setting up a committee with the task of systematically preparing for a Communist revolution in Germany.

Trotsky believed that the 'German October', as it was known, should take place on 9 November 1923, the fifth anniversary of the revolution that had brought a republic to Germany in 1918. This decision was taken on 1 October, the same day that Zinoviev instructed the central committee of the German Communist Party to form a pact with the minority government in Saxony that was led by the left-wing Social Democrat Erich Zeigner and that had been supported by the Communists since March. The next step was to be the arming of the Saxon proletariat. Saxony, then, was to be the launch pad for the German revolution, the starting point of a civil war whose end would be marked by the victory of the Communists over not only the Fascists but also the bourgeois Weimar Republic.

While the Communists were preparing the ground for the revolution, the political crisis in Germany continued to worsen. On 26 September, after hesitating for a long time, the president and his government announced the end of the country's policy of passive resistance. The Bavarian government reacted to this development that same day by proclaiming a state of emergency and transferring the state's executive powers to the president of Upper Bavaria, Gustav von Kahr. In turn the federal government responded on the evening of 26 September by declaring a state of emergency in the whole of the Reich and by transferring executive power to the country's defence minister who for his part could delegate that power to regional military commanders. From a purely legal point of view, Bavaria would have had to repeal its emergency measures if the Reich's president or the Reichstag had so demanded, but Stresemann and his ministers assumed that Kahr would refuse to comply with such a request and so they thought it better not to raise the matter at all with Munich.

In the days that followed, the weakness of the Reich's position became clearer. On 27 September the *Völkischer Beobachter* – the National Socialists' official newspaper – attacked 'the dictators Stresemann and Seeckt' with particular viciousness, the former on the grounds that he was married to a 'Jewess', the latter because his wife was 'half Jewish', prompting the Reich's defence minister, Otto Geßler, to order Kahr to ban further publication of the paper. Kahr refused, and in this he had the support of Otto von Lossow, the commander of the federal troops that were stationed in Bavaria. It was a clear case of insubordination but, as had been the case during the Kapp–Lüttwitz Putsch in March 1920, the army's commander in chief, Hans von Seeckt, had no intention of ordering federal troops to fire on their comrades, preferring to play the same sort of role in the Reich as Kahr was doing in Bavaria. In this he found widespread support, prominent industrialists such as Hugo Stinnes and all those who regarded the German Nationalists as their natural political home demanding a 'national dictatorship' under a 'directorate' led by Seeckt.

A different type of dictatorship was proposed by the Centrist labour minister Heinrich Brauns and the finance minister Rudolf Hilferding at the cabinet meeting on 30 September, when they demanded an enabling act that would allow the government to do whatever was needed from a financial and political standpoint. Both believed that it was necessary to extend the working day, a point that had the support of the employers but which placed them on a collision course with the unions. But not even Hilferding's party, the SPD, was willing to agree to their demands for the statutory power to fix the length of the working day. Opposition to the policies of Stresemann's cabinet assumed far more extreme forms on the right wing of the grand coalition: on 2 October, the leader of the German People's Party, Ernst Scholz, having consulted with the right wing of his party and especially with Hugo Stinnes, demanded a comprehensive rejection of the eight-hour day, a 'break with France' and the inclusion of German Nationalists in the grand coalition. Given the situation at that time, this amounted to a declaration of war on the chancellor and a tacit acceptance of the idea of a 'national dictatorship'. Stresemann drew the logical conclusion and handed in his resignation later that same day.

Within four days, however, Stresemann was back in office, again in charge of a grand coalition cabinet. Ebert had been instrumental in renewing the old allegiances, an aim in which he was successful because the moderate forces in the German People's Party were unwilling to bow to the pressure exerted by Stinnes and to topple Stresemann from power. The party leaders achieved their decisive breakthrough during the night of 5/6 October, agreeing to a formulation on the matter of the length of the working day that their experts had already proposed on 13 November 1922, on the eve of the collapse of Wirth's cabinet. The eight-hour day was to be retained in principle but could be extended either by mutual agreement or else by legislation.

The Social Democrat Party, too, was now comfortable with an enabling act that avoided all mention of the length of the working day and that would remain in force only for the duration of the present coalition, and on 13 October the Reichstag passed the new law with the majority needed to alter the constitution. It formed the basis of ordinances on welfare for the unemployed, on staff cutbacks in the public services and on a measure enforcing government mediation in the matter of wage disagreements. In this way the state became the supreme judge in labour disputes. There were clear parallels with the extraordinary powers of Article 48.

While the fate of the grand coalition was being decided in Berlin, right-wing forces and Communists alike were working for regime change. In Bavaria Hitler had himself elected leader of the German Combat League, a new umbrella organization for the patriotic associations. Four days later Kahr repealed the law designed to protect the Republic and, from the middle of October, gave instructions for large numbers of eastern European Jews to be deported from Bavaria, a move designed to ingratiate himself with the National Socialists. On 20 October the country's defence minister, Otto Geßler, ordered the long-overdue dismissal of Otto von Lossow, the Munich district commander, prompting Kahr to launch his most spectacular blow against the Reich, when he appointed Lossow regional commander of the Bavarian armed forces and declared the Seventh Division of the Reichswehr, which was stationed in Bavaria, under the direct control of his own government in Munich.

Neither Kahr nor Lossow nor their ally, the commander in chief of the Bavarian regional police force, Hans von Seißer, wanted to drive a wedge between Bavaria and the Reich. Rather, their aim was to remodel the Reich along Bavarian lines. A 'march on Berlin' modelled on Mussolini's 'march on Rome' was to provide a fitting climax to the establishment of a 'national dictatorship'. The National Socialists were to be allowed to join in, but the role of the 'Duce' was to be taken not by Hitler but by Kahr and later, on a federal level, by a man who shared Kahr's outlook. One possibility was Seeckt, and yet no one knew whether in a crisis a man who was regarded as a stickler for the law would oppose the declared will of the federal president.

The Communists focused their activities on central Germany. On 10 October three Communists, including the party leader Heinrich Brandler as head of the state chancellery, joined the Saxon government led by the left-wing Social Democrat Erich Zeigner. On 16 October a coalition made up of Social Democrats and Communists under the Social Democrat August Frölich was formed in Thuringia, too. The formation of left-wing united front governments in Dresden and Weimar was in keeping with the constitution, and both were based on parliamentary majorities. Nor did the cabinets of Zeigner or

Frölich take any steps that could be described as hostile to the Reich. Even so, there was no doubt in the minds of the ruling Social Democrats in Berlin that the Communists were planning to extend their struggle for power from Saxony and Thuringia to the rest of the country, with the result that on 13 October the Saxon district commander, Alfred Müller, who exercised executive control, banned the Communist Party's paramilitary Proletarian Centuries. Three days later, after consulting with Geßler, he placed the Saxon police under the control of the federal army, thereby depriving the government in Dresden of its only real instrument of power.

On 21 October an attempt to stage a Communist revolution failed even before it had begun. At a labour conference in Chemnitz convened by the German Communist Party the Social Democrats refused to heed the Communists' call for a general strike that was to mark the start of a proletarian uprising. In doing so they thwarted the plans for a 'German October', with the result that the attempt to repeat the events set in train by the Bolsheviks in November 1918 never got off the ground. Only in Hamburg was there a putsch-like uprising by the Communists, but after three days of bloody fighting the police were able to restore order to the city on 25 October.

At the same time the whole of Saxony was placed under the control of the federal army, leading to bloody clashes in a number of towns and cities. On 27 October Stresemann issued an ultimatum demanding that Zeigner should form a government without any Communists, but within twenty-four hours Zeigner had rejected this demand, whereupon Stresemann, without convening his cabinet, appointed Karl Rudolf Heinze of the German People's Party as civilian commissioner for Saxony. By the 30th Heinze had forced Zeigner to resign. At the urging of the Social Democrat leadership a moderate politician, the former business secretary Alfred Fellisch, formed a Social Democrat minority government that was tolerated by the German Democrats. The following day, immediately after the Landtag had confirmed the cabinet, Ebert responded to a request from his chancellor and ended Heinze's mandate as commissioner.

Stresemann's ultimatum of 27 October had had the support of the SPD. Only later did the party start to harbour serious doubts about its response, doubts that it justified by pointing out that the cabinet had had no opportunity to confer on Zeigner's rejection of the ultimatum. Under tremendous pressure from its own left wing and in the face of stern warnings from the Prussian minister of the interior, Carl Severing, the Social Democrat members of the Reichstag drew up an ultimatum of their own on 31 October, demanding that Stresemann's government lift the state of emergency, declare the actions of the Bavarian authorities unconstitutional and take whatever steps were necessary to put Bavaria in its place. The bourgeois members of Stresemann's cabinet were convinced that neither militarily nor politically was a civil war with Bavaria desirable and, as was only to be expected, they rejected the SPD's demands, prompting the Social Democrat ministers to resign their posts on 2 November. Four days after the end of the grand coalition federal troops marched into Thuringia with Ebert's approval and forced the local Proletarian Centuries to disband. New elections were called for February 1924. Until then Frölich remained in office as head of a Social Democrat minority cabinet.

The Bavarian crisis escalated on the evening of 8 November, when Hitler used a meeting of Kahr's supporters in the Bürgerbräukeller to proclaim a 'national revolution'. At gunpoint the National Socialist leader extorted a promise from Kahr, Lossow and Seißer that they too would take part in the action. But Hitler's co-conspirator, Erich Ludendorff, who had been the German military's strong man during the First World War and whom Hitler had only recently appointed commander in chief of his 'national army', quickly restored the triumvirate's freedom to act, allowing the Bavarian authorities to retaliate. Hitler's putsch ended at midday on 9 November when the Bavarian regional police fired on the Munich Feldherrnhalle. Hitler himself was able to escape but was arrested two days later. Sixteen of his followers paid for the 'national revolution' with their lives.

The events in Munich had dramatic consequences in Berlin, where Ebert immediately transferred command of the country's armed forces to Seeckt and, altering the ordinance of 26 September 1923, invested him with executive power. Ebert and Stresemann evidently felt that this transfer of power to Seeckt was the only way to persuade the Bavarian army to oppose the rebels, although there was, of course, no guarantee that Seeckt himself would not support the putsch. Ebert presumably thought that if Seeckt was directly responsible to the head of state, the Republic was less at risk than it had been previously, when it had little or no control over Seeckt.

Hitler's putsch marked a turning point not only for Bavaria but for the country as a whole. The plans for a 'serious' dictatorship on the part of Kahr and his allies were discredited for good by the events of 8 November and Kahr's authority severely undermined. And without solid support from the Bavarian triumvirate there was little prospect of a 'national dictatorship' in Germany. In short, Hitler's putsch achieved the opposite of what he had intended, the leader of the National Socialists contributing substantially to the consolidation of a Republic that had been under extreme threat.

On 15 November, a week after the Munich putsch, Stresemann's rump cabinet succeeded in pulling off what has become known as the 'Rentenmark miracle'. The new currency that was introduced on this day was intended to be a temporary measure designed to last only until the new and definitive gold-backed currency came into force at some future date. Under proposals put forward by the new finance minister, Hans Luther, who had replaced Hilferding on 6 October, debenture bonds and loans taken out on industrial and agricultural land would guarantee the value of the Rentenmark until then. On 20 November, the mark's exchange rate, which had been 1,260 billion to the dollar on 14 November, was stabilized at 4,200 billion, whereupon the Federal Bank set an exchange rate of 1,000 billion paper marks to 1 Rentenmark, re-establishing the pre-war exchange rate between the mark and the dollar.

It was the occupied Rhineland that suffered most from the introduction of the Rentenmark, for until the gold-backed Reichsmark came into force on 30 August 1924 the region was largely abandoned by the Reich and had to contend with communal emergency funding. Cologne's mayor, Konrad Adenauer, who was a member of the Centre Party, protested in vain on 13 November, arguing that 'the Rhineland must be worth more than one or two or even three new currencies'.[51] The federal government evidently felt that the Rhineland's temporary autonomy, whatever form that independence may take, was the lesser of two evils when compared with the economic collapse that would threaten Germany if the new currency was undermined by the continuing subsidization of the occupied territory.

By 25 October 1923 there were signs that another miracle was about to take place, for this was the day on which the French prime minister Raymond Poincaré sent word to his British counterpart, Andrew Bonar Law, that under certain conditions he was prepared to agree to a re-examination of the question of reparations. In announcing this willingness, he was responding to a suggestion that the American secretary of state Charles Hughes had put forward in a speech made to the American Historical Association in New Haven at the end of December 1922, when he proposed that the question of reparations be discussed at a conference of international experts, taking account of Germany's ability to pay. This was an idea that had first been mooted in London. Poincaré's conditions were as follows: a panel of experts was to be appointed by the Allied Reparations Commission; the amount owed by Germany, as set down in the London ultimatum of May 1921, was to be independent of the findings of the inquiry; and a second panel of experts would ascertain the amount and whereabouts of Germany's foreign assets. Once the United States had agreed to this suggestion, Paris formally proposed that the two commissions be set to work at a meeting of the Reparations Commission on 13 November. This move prepared the way for the Dawes Plan, named after the American banker Charles G. Dawes who chaired the Reparations Commission. This plan was to be inseparable from Germany's economic upturn in the mid-1920s.

There were several reasons for Poincaré's change of heart: his country's occupation of the Ruhr had turned into a crippling burden that was jeopardizing the French economy; there was increasing resistance at home, above all from the Socialists and Communists; and in terms of the country's foreign standing, France was becoming increasingly isolated, especially with regard to its worsening relations with Great Britain. But there was another reason that was even more critical, for on 23 October the American secretary of state had made it clear to Poincaré that the United States would allow France to be represented on the international panel of experts and discuss the question of reparations only if France agreed to address the problem of inter-allied debts. In short, France could expect that if it made certain concessions to its own debtor Germany, its own position as one of America's debtors would improve in turn.

Poincaré's concession on the question of reparations did not, however, mean that France had abandoned its goal of cutting the Rhineland off from the rest of Germany, and on the day that he informed the British government of France's new political line, Poincaré also decided to adopt a policy of active and official support for the occupied territory's struggle for independence. Starting on 21 October, there had been a number of attempts to declare a 'Rhenish Republic' in Aachen, Trier, Koblenz, Bonn, Wiesbaden and elsewhere. These subversive activities on the part of local separatists were supported by the French and Belgian troops that were occupying the region, but such activities did not have the backing of the vast majority of the local population. Even as early as November 1923 it was already clear that neither the Prussian Rhineland nor the Bavarian Palatinate would ever voluntarily break free from the Reich. By December Poincaré had instructed Paul Tirard, the head of the Allied High Commission for the Rhineland, to stop supporting the separatists.

There were signs, therefore, that the situation was becoming progressively less tense both inside the country and abroad, only for another government crisis to erupt in Berlin. On 22 November the Social Democrats, ignoring all the president's warnings, brought a motion of no confidence against Stresemann's bourgeois minority cabinet, justifying their action by arguing that the federal government had taken draconian steps to deal with Saxony and Thuringia while doing little about the unconstitutional situation in Bavaria. The motion was worded in such a way that the German Nationalists, on whose attitude everything depended, would be unable to vote for it. In other words, the Social Democrats were not interested in toppling Stresemann but in making a political point designed to placate the left wing of their party. But the chancellor was unwilling to accept a further weakening of his position and responded to the SPD's initiative by calling for a vote of confidence. On 23 November the Reichstag rejected the motion by 231 votes to 156, with seven abstentions. As Stresemann later told foreign correspondents, this was the first time in the history of the German Republic that a government had fallen 'on the open field of battle'.[52]

Attempts to form a new government proved extremely difficult and took an entire week. Not until 30 November 1923 did the leader of the Centre Party, the Cologne lawyer Wilhelm Marx, replace Stresemann as prime minister, while Stresemann himself became foreign minister, a post he already held since August 1923 and which he was to retain until his death on 3 October 1929. Marx's minority cabinet was dependent on the grudging support of the party that had toppled its predecessor, the Social Democrats. But Ebert, acting behind the scenes and threatening the party with Article 48, even managed to persuade them to pass an enabling act on 8 December. Timed to run until

14 February 1924, this gave the government a chance to introduce all the measures it needed by parliamentary means. One such measure affected the length
of the working day, which was in urgent need of regulation since the demobilization ordinances that had been in force since the revolution had expired on
17 November, with the result that pre-war conditions once again applied wherever the working day was not already regulated by formal written agreements.

Major changes were introduced in Germany during the three months that
the enabling act was in force. Although the eight-hour working day continued
as the norm, a ten-hour day was now legally permissible in large areas of the
economy. In January 1924 the Free Trade Unions responded to this defeat by
declaring an end to the Central Cooperative Union that had been established
in November 1918, although the announcement amounted to little more than
a symbolic protest. And in December 1923 the salaries of civil servants were set
at a level far below that of pre-war Germany. On 14 February 1924, the day on
which the enabling act expired, an emergency tax law made it possible to start
reducing the amount of state control that existed in the housing market. This
was an important step in doing away with the 'war socialism' that had survived
the war by more than five years.

This same measure also affected the highly controversial revaluation of
outstanding debts from certain types of capital investment such as savings
accounts, mortgages, bonds and life insurance that had been destroyed by
inflation. The flat revaluation rate of 15 per cent of their value in gold marks
was tantamount to an admission that Hans Luther's long-championed principle of 'mark for mark' was in flagrant disregard of the most elementary sense
of justice. But repayment of the revalued debts was delayed until 1932, that of
the war loans until the burden of reparations had finally been lifted – in other
words, *sine die*. The embittered protests by the millions of Germans affected by
this measure failed to alter its wording. But Marx's government had no alternative if it was not to jeopardize the new currency. In short, it was savers and
those who had underwritten war loans who were the real victims of inflation.

It was not the middle classes as a group who faced financial ruin as a result
of devaluation or who were at least substantially affected by it but large sections
of that group, all of whom had been used to getting by on their savings or by
relying on the interest on stocks and shares. Householders and landowners,
conversely, were the beneficiaries, since they were now debt-free and able to
profit from the privileged status of material assets. But the real winners were
the owners of large industrial fortunes and large landowners, most of whom
had been heavily in debt, only to see those debts evaporate as a result of devaluation. Materially speaking, the state benefited from inflation, but in a non-
material sense it was among the losers. Devaluation helped by freeing it from
its debts but harmed it in the longer term by undermining confidence in it. It
was the Republic that bore the brunt of the Germans' disappointed hopes, not
the monarchy, even though it was the monarchy that started the process of

devaluation. Five years after the end of the war the old empire began to appear to many Germans in a transfigured light.

Inflation had a levelling effect: the difference in the incomes of the highest- and lowest-paid civil servants and between those of civil servants in general and of workers shrank, but it was certainly not the workers who gained from this situation, for in December 1923 real wages were barely 70 per cent of their pre-war level. And unemployment was high. The unions had to pay a high price for the role they had played during the Ruhr conflict, the number of members of the General German Workers' Association falling from 7.7 million in September 1923 to 4.8 million in March 1924. Everything pointed to the fact that the proletariat's potential for protest was far greater by January 1924 than it had been twelve months earlier.

At the same time, however, there were also signs that the political situation was growing calmer. By the end of November 1923 things had returned to normal on the labour front in the Ruhr, and once the economic situation in that region had been stabilized there was no longer the same desire to implement the plan for a loosely structured Rhineland state of the kind advocated by Stinnes and Adenauer at the end of 1923. By January 1924 the country's foreign minister, Gustav Stresemann, was able to turn down Adenauer's proposal in no uncertain terms, prompting the latter to shelve the idea once and for all.

The military state of emergency was lifted on 29 February 1924 at the urging of Hans von Seeckt, who was anxious to ensure that the authority of the armed forces was not undermined in a running battle with civilian agencies, especially in Saxony, Thuringia and, above all, Prussia. More especially he was afraid of the malign influence of radically right-wing defence organizations. In short, the internal consolidation of the army was more important to him than the mere exercise of power with no political benefits.

As head of the executive, Seeckt had banned the Communist Party, the NSDAP and the German Nationalist Freedom Party under the terms of a decree dated 23 November 1923, and there was initially some debate over whether or not this ban should continue in force. Seeckt wanted it to be maintained, whereas Severing was in favour of its being lifted, and it was Severing who as Prussian minister of the interior eventually prevailed, with the result that the bans on all three parties were lifted at the same time as the military state of emergency. For the present, however, open-air public gatherings were as a rule still proscribed. Not until 25 October 1924 was the civilian state of emergency lifted.

By February 1924 the conflict between the Reich and Bavaria had officially been settled. Under the terms of an agreement dated 14 February 1924, the regional commander of the Reichswehr in Bavaria could be recalled only with the agreement of the regional government. The wording of the oath of allegiance to the army and navy was also changed so as to include a pledge of loyalty to the recruit's home state, thereby settling the question of the use of

Reichswehr troops by the government in Munich. Four days later Kahr resigned as general state commissar, Lossow as commander in chief in Bavaria. Their unconstitutional actions in the autumn of 1923 had no legal consequences whatsoever.

The dissidents who had taken part in the putsch on 8/9 November 1923 were sentenced on 1 April 1924, when the People's Court in Munich acquitted Ludendorff of the charge of high treason. Five other leaders of the putsch, including Ernst Röhm, who went on to organize the National Socialists' SA brigades, were sentenced to three months' imprisonment and a fine of 100 marks. Together with three of his co-conspirators, Hitler himself received a five-year sentence and a fine of 200 marks. All the prisoners, however, were eligible for parole after only six months, with the result that Hitler was released from Landsberg Prison at Christmas 1924 after spending his time there writing his programmatic and propagandist autobiography *Mein Kampf* (My Struggle). In the case of all the accused, the court accepted the defence plea that they had 'acted in a purely patriotic spirit and according to the noblest of selfless motives', believing that 'they were compelled to act in order to save their country, merely doing what leading figures in Bavaria had intended to do only a short time earlier'.[53] Morally speaking, the sentence and the justification for it amounted to an acquittal, which is how they were interpreted in Bavaria and, indeed, in the country as a whole.

The furore caused by the sentence passed on Hitler had not yet abated when a further incident hit the headlines on 9 April 1924: the publication of the report by Charles Dawes's commission set up in January to examine the question of Germany's reparations. It was to have a lasting impact on all future developments in the Weimar Republic. Its authors did not indicate the total amount that Germany should pay, but they clearly set out from the assumption that the figure of 132,000 million gold marks stipulated by the London ultimatum of May 1921 was excessive. In order not to endanger the country's currency, the report recommended that a reparations agent be appointed by the creditor nations to arrange for 'transfer protection', a method of payment designed to safeguard the external stability of the mark. The initial repayment, or annuity, of 1,000 million marks would rise to 2,500 million within a timescale of five years. In order to meet French demands for guarantees, the German railways were to become a limited company with certain obligations, its supervisory board to include members of the creditor nations. (The same stipulation applied to the German Federal Bank.) Further guarantees were to be provided in the form of a number of other sources of federal revenue and an interest-bearing mortgage on German industry to the tune of 5,000 million marks.

The restrictions on German sovereignty that were provided for under the terms of the Dawes Plan were far-reaching and yet still far less burdensome than the territorial guarantees demanded by France and Belgium when they occupied the Ruhr in January 1923. And the Dawes Plan was also good news for the German economy in another way inasmuch as a foreign loan of 800 million marks was to provide the basis of a new bank, the proceeds of which were initially intended to finance only domestic payments to the Allies such as material supplies and the costs of the occupation. But behind the provision lay the prospect of future American credits and investments, a prospect that had a stimulating effect on the country's economy. Germany had been one of the leading markets for American exports before 1914 and could now bank on the fact that the United States had recognized the opportunities that lay in dealing with a country which, however much it may have needed capital, had a highly efficient economy.

The Dawes Plan was America's contribution to the stabilization of the German economy. Such an act was designed to demonstrate that the world's most powerful economy was finally acknowledging its sense of responsibility towards the rest of the world, a responsibility so successfully denied by American isolationists when they had voted against the League of Nations in 1919. Another contribution to German stability that was made at this time came from a very different quarter – the Soviet Union. Lenin had died after a long illness on 21 January 1924. (He had played no part in the decisions that led to the 'German October' uprising.) He was replaced as his country's most powerful leader by the party official whom he had most mistrusted on account of his coarseness and capriciousness, so much so, indeed, that in a codicil to his will dated 4 January 1923 he had explicitly instructed his comrades to relieve Stalin of his post as secretary general of the Communist Party of the Soviet Union. As Stalin's position grew stronger, so the desire for world revolution grew markedly less pronounced in Moscow. Instead, Stalin focused on what he termed 'the growth of socialism in *one* country', namely, the Soviet Union. The improvised putsches that the Comintern had tried to stage in Germany, most recently in the autumn of 1923, could not be reconciled with a motto that Stalin officially proclaimed in 1925 but which he had already adopted before this date.

Meanwhile, major political changes were also taking place in London and Paris. In Great Britain the Labour Party and Liberals had triumphed over the Conservatives in the elections to the lower house on 6 December 1923, and in January 1924 the country had its first Labour prime minister in the person of Ramsay MacDonald, who headed a minority cabinet at the mercy of the Liberals. In the event MacDonald remained in office for only nine and a half months, but this period witnessed the London conference of July and August 1924, when the Allies accepted the Dawes Plan and Germany was subsequently invited to attend the proceedings. MacDonald, who was also the foreign secretary, played a conciliatory role and contributed substantially to the successful outcome of the talks and to the London Agreement that was based upon it.

In France Poincaré's Bloc National lost its majority to the Cartel des Gauches – an electoral pact of Socialists and bourgeois Radical Socialists – on

11 May 1924, when a new prime minister and foreign minister were appointed. Tolerated by the Socialists, the Radical Socialist Édouard Herriot was an advocate of German idealist philosophy, with the result that Germany might expect a greater show of understanding from the new government than from its various right-wing predecessors.

By the early months of 1924 it was clear that France's attempt to change the post-war order by force had failed. Germany may have been economically weakened by the Ruhr conflict, but thanks to American intervention it was now politically stronger. Between November 1923 and April 1924 the post-war period in Europe effectively came to an end, and it was impossible not to see that there was now a new, albeit relative, stability not only in Germany but also in the relations between the leading European states.

Right Against Left: Culture and Society in the Weimar Republic

A certain stabilization in economic and political conditions was a necessary precondition for the *Goldene Zwanziger* (Golden Twenties) – the term was not in fact coined until the following decade, when it sprang from a spirit of dewy-eyed nostalgia. In the United States, prosperity returned in 1922. Only later did Europe follow suit, while it was not until the winter of 1923/4 that the Germans again felt anything like firm ground beneath their feet. The period is nowadays associated with the international triumph of American jazz, the Charleston and the shimmy, the dances of Josephine Baker and the films of Charlie Chaplin. We also think of the montages of the Dadaists, art deco, the deliberate breaking of taboos by artists critical of society such as George Grosz and surrealist writers like André Breton and Louis Aragon. Other salient features of the time include mass consumerism, aggressive advertising and functional architecture, the heyday of the culture associated with the labour movement and the breakthrough of a new and more permissive sexual morality.

The term 'Weimar culture' has long been used to describe the German variant of the spirit of the 1920s, and yet the incessant questioning of traditional values, which the political right saw as a sign of cultural decline, had started well before 1918: as Peter Gay has noted,[54] the 'Weimar style' predated Weimar. This is certainly true of the revolutionary Expressionist movement in painting, literature and the theatre, a movement whose origins can be traced back to the first decade of the twentieth century. And it is also true of the no less revolutionary shift to atonality in music as well as the great revolutions in science, in Freudian psychoanalysis, in Einstein's theory of relativity and the sociology of Max Weber. All of the pioneering studies associated with these disciplines date from the years before 1914. Even the 'New Objectivity' that displaced Expressionism in every branch of the arts after 1923 can be traced back to the pre-war period. Walter Gropius, who in 1926 designed the Bauhaus in Dessau and created a model of the new functional aesthetics that was reviled as much as it was admired, had already developed his style before the First World War. In short, all the constituent features of Weimar culture were already in place when the Republic came into being. But the change of political regime had a liberating effect, opening up opportunities to innovative spirits that they had not enjoyed under the old system and permitting them to achieve a more widespread impact that allowed 'Weimar' to be seen retrospectively as a large-scale experiment in classical modernism.

In terms of culture in its widest sense, it was Berlin that was the capital of Europe in the 1920s. Here, after 1918, modernism seemed almost literally to explode into life. Avant-garde artists from Europe and America were repeatedly drawn to either Berlin or Paris, the latter continuing a tradition for cutting-edge experimentation that had been established before 1914. Berlin was the first city to articulate ideas that later became a trend elsewhere. Jews played a leading role in the cultural life of the German capital, whether in journalism, the cinema, the theatre or the cabaret, and it was this aspect in particular that turned the new Berlin into the quintessential embodiment of all that conservative Germany hated about the state of Weimar. Intellectual Jews were mostly liberal in their outlook or were on the left wing of the political spectrum – in many cases on the extreme left wing. The ground to the right of the political centre was in any case closed to them as this was occupied by anti-Semites. Anti-Semitism was almost always synonymous with anti-modernism, anti-urbanism and anti-intellectualism. It was this that made Weimar culture an elite project that was endangered from the outset, a culture that could vanish at a moment's notice.

The fate of the Bauhaus – that stronghold of modern architecture – is a barometer that allows us to measure the pace of cultural and political reaction in Germany. Originally based in Weimar, it had been obliged to move its headquarters in 1925 when the Thuringian parliament halved its grant to the institution, effectively making it impossible for it to continue to operate. (Since the early months of 1924 Thuringia had been ruled by a bourgeois cabinet tolerated by the extreme right in the form of the Nationalist Socialist Bloc.) But even in its new home in Dessau, where a Social Democrat prime minister held office almost continuously from 1918 to May 1932, the Bauhaus remained a thorn in the flesh of right-wing forces. When a housing settlement for workers and employees of the Junkers Works in Dessau-Törten designed by Walter Gropius was officially opened in 1929, the occasion prompted protests from National Socialists and German Nationalists at the 'Moroccan huts' of the 'nigger colony'.[55] The attacks were triggered by the fact that the buildings did not have pitched roofs in the German tradition but flat roofs typical of the architecture of the New Objectivity.

Attempts to combat the spirit of the new age might also assume more high-brow forms. In Germany as elsewhere in Europe, the intellectual right felt that it was threatened by a levelling collectivism that privileged the mass over the individual. In 1927, three years before the Spanish philosopher José Ortega y Gasset described the threat posed to civilization by 'the mass man', by the 'intellectual plebs' and by a new barbarism, Martin Heidegger published his main philosophical study *Being and Time*, in which he spoke of a 'dictatorship of the "they" ':

> The 'they' is there alongside everywhere, but in such a manner that it has always stolen away whenever Dasein presses for a decision. Yet because the 'they' presents every judgment and decision as its own, it deprives the particular Dasein of its answerability. The 'they' can, as it were, manage to have 'them' constantly invoking it. It can be answerable for everything most easily, because it is not someone who needs to vouch for anything. It 'was' always the 'they' who did it, and yet it can be said that it has been 'no one'. In Dasein's everydayness the agency through which most things come about is one of which we must say that 'it was no one'.[56]

No less current than the cliché of oppressive collectivism was the idea of a corrosive pluralism that was destroying the parliamentary system and leading to the disintegration of the state. In his 1926 foreword to the second edition of his book *The Crisis of Parliamentary Democracy*, the lawyer Carl Schmitt claimed that parliament was no longer a forum where arguments could be openly and freely exchanged but only a place where vested interests collided. Rational argument had been replaced by ideological polarization, with the result that the present parliamentary system had lost the ability to produce any sense of political unity:

> In a few states, parliamentarism has already produced a situation in which all public business has become an object of spoils and compromise for the parties and their followers, and politics, far from being the concern of an elite, has become the despised business of a rather dubious class of persons.[57]

In Germany, criticism of parliamentary democracy – the 'rule of the inferior' as invoked by the Young Conservative Edgar Jung in a widely read study in 1927 – was aided and abetted by the frequent crises and changes of government that revealed the abiding legacy of monarchical constitutionalism. Even when they put forward ministers, all parties regarded the government as their enemy, just as the country's leaders had been under the Kaiser, not as the executive committee of the parliamentary majority that needed to be supported and defended in the face of the opposition, an attitude that would have reflected the logic of a parliamentary democracy. But doubts in the efficiency and relevance of the parliamentary system were by no means restricted to Germany and other recent democracies, most of which had been established after 1918. Such doubts were also to be found in older democracies such as England and France, and, as we shall see, they became worse at a later date than in central Europe thanks to the world economic crisis of 1929. In every case the critics of the ostensible decline of the parliamentary system contrasted that system with an ideal picture that had never existed in real life: if ever a regime deserved to be described as 'government by corruption', it was Walpole's regime during the early days of British parliamentary rule in the first half of the eighteenth century.

Specifically German, by contrast, was another way of dealing ideologically with the nation's defeat in the First World War and the post-war crisis that ensued, and this was the renaissance of the myth of the Reich. The first salvo was fired in 1923 by Arthur Moeller van den Bruck in his programmatically titled book *The Third Reich*. The term had been coined by a twelfth-century Italian theologian Gioachino da Fiore but only now was it launched on its questionable political career. The first Reich was the Holy Roman Empire of the German Nation that had ended in 1806, while the second was Bismarck's Reich of 1871, which Moeller van den Bruck dismissed as an imperfect 'intermediary empire'. The third, conversely, was to be a pan-German empire that would also incorporate Austria. The German nationalists were acclaimed as 'the champions of the ultimate empire':

> It is always being prophesied. And yet that promise is never kept. It is perfection, which can be reached only through imperfection. [. . .] There is only One Reich, just as there is only One Church. Everything else that lays claim to this name is a mere state or a community or a sect. There is only The Reich.[58]

The German Empire as the power that would protect Latin Christianity had from time immemorial been associated with the idea of salvation. According to the myth of the German Reich, the Holy Roman Empire was identical to the Roman Empire following its conversion to Christianity and, hence, to the *katechon*, the force which according to St Paul's Second Epistle to the Thessalonians maintained the rule of the Antichrist. Among the writers and scholars who after 1918 contributed to the spread of the myth of the German Reich were many associated with the poet Stefan George, notably George himself, as well as Catholic thinkers, the proponents of the Conservative Revolution who influenced public opinion around 1930 and, last but by no means least, the National Socialists. According to this myth, the Germans had a historical mission, their task being to play a leading role in the European struggle to resist the advance not only of Bolshevism in the east but of democracy in the west.

Like many advocates of the 'ideas of 1914', the adherents of the Conservative Revolution sought to reinterpret the term 'socialism' in an anti-Marxist and anti-western sense. Oswald Spengler is best remembered as the author of the two-volume *Decline of the West*, the two parts of which were published in 1918 and 1922 and immediately translated into several other languages. In 1919 he published a further title, *Prussianism and Socialism*, in which he argued that the great question that exercised the present-day world concerned the choice between Prussian and English ideas, between socialism and capitalism, and between state and parliament:

> Prussiandom and socialism stand *together against the inner England*, against the world-view that infuses our entire life as a people, crippling it and stealing its soul. [...] The working class must liberate itself from the illusions of Marxism. Marx is dead. As a form of existence, socialism is just beginning, but the socialism of the German proletariat is at an end. *For the worker, there is only Prussian socialism or nothing.* [...] For conservatives, there is only conscious socialism or destruction. But we need to liberate ourselves from the form of Anglo-French democracy. We have our own.[59]

As interpreted by Spengler and other Conservative Revolutionaries, socialism had nothing to do with the redistribution of property. Rather, it was a question not so much of financial order as of financial attitudes, and in this regard there were no fundamental differences between the Young Conservatives and the National Socialists. And yet the latter really wanted a revolution, whereas the former were merely playing with the idea of one. Before 1933 the Young Conservative intellectuals were more sympathetic to the Italian Fascists than to the German National Socialists, who struck them as excessively populist, not to say vulgar, in their outlook.

But even describing the Conservative Revolutionaries as 'Fascists' is problematical. Fascists and National Socialists mobilized masses and used organized violence, whereas the agents of the 'right-wing revolution' discussed by the sociologist Hans Freyer in his 1931 study remained within the sphere of influence of the educated public in all that they thought and wrote. This was the audience they addressed with their writings; and this was the circle to which they themselves belonged. Traditional conservatives regarded their natural home as the German National People's Party, differing from most Young Conservatives in that the latter lost interest in restoring the monarchy once the last Kaiser had fled to the Netherlands, preferring a state with a strong leader that was structured according to profession and legitimized by a plebiscite but at the same time under the rule of law.

As a rule, Young Conservatives were anti-Semitic but they regarded the Jewish question as less important than the National Socialists did. Although they were radical nationalists, their nationalism was less extreme than that of the National Socialists, whose nationalism found classic expression in a piece that Hitler wrote in early 1924 in an attempt to justify his failed putsch of 8/9 November 1923. In it the National Socialist leader wrote that

Marxist internationalism can be broken only by means of a fanatically extreme National Socialism of the highest social ethics and morality. We cannot take the false gods of Marxism away from the people without giving them a better god in return. [. . .] It is to the credit of Benito Mussolini that he recognized this as clearly as he did and put that conviction into practice with the greatest logical consistency by deciding that international Marxism needed to be eradicated and by replacing it with fanatical national Fascism, with the result that almost every Marxist organization in Italy has now been disbanded.[60]

At about the same time as Hitler was committing these programmatic lines to paper, a conference convened by the praesidium of the Executive Committee of the Communist International was meeting in Moscow. Its aim was to examine the lessons that could be learned from the failure of the 'German October' uprising. Karl Radek spoke of the 'victory of Fascism over the November Revolution', but his thesis was rejected by Zinoviev, the secretary general of the Communist International, who argued that since 1918 Germany had been dominated by a 'bloc' in which the Social Democrats had assumed the role of co-regents. It was, Zinoviev claimed, a 'Fascist wing', 'a Fascist Social Democratic Party'. A few months later, Stalin, too, described the Social Democrats as 'the moderate wing of Fascism': social democracy and Fascism were 'not antitheses but twins'.[61] This speech marked the birth of the doctrine of 'Socialist Fascism' that was to influence the actions of the Comintern and of the German Communist Party during the final phase of the Weimar Republic.

Unlike the Social Democrats, the German Communists enjoyed a substantial following among artists and intellectuals. George Grosz and the master of the photographic montage, John Heartfield (whose real name was Helmuth Herzfeld), are both said to have been members of the German Communist Party from its very inception on 31 December 1918. Ten years later Communist painters and sculptors founded ASSO, the Association of Revolutionary Artists, while Communist writers formed the Union of Proletarian and Revolutionary Writers, defining 'proletarian and revolutionary literature' as one 'that wins the hearts and minds of the working class and of the broad working masses, helping them to prepare for the proletarian revolution and organizing their development'. A further aim was to 'win over the middle classes, whether they toil with their hands or their brains, and enlist their support for the proletarian revolution or at the very least neutralize them'.[62]

By joining the Union of Proletarian and Revolutionary Writers, a number of prominent contemporary authors proclaimed their allegiance to the aforementioned goals. Bertolt Brecht, Anna Seghers, Arnold Zweig and Ludwig Renn all became members, as did Erich Weinert, Hans Marchwitza, Willi Bredel, Johannes R. Becher and Friedrich Wolf. The Union's journal, *Linkskurve*, attempted on the one hand to reach out to an intellectual readership by publishing theoretical articles by Georg Lukács criticizing the literary Proletkult and by the Sinologist Karl August Wittfogel on Marxist aesthetics, while at the same time holding competitions designed to foster novels and plays aimed at a mass working-class audience.

Indeed, many of the writers and artists who nailed their colours to the Communist Party's mast were notable for their wish to reach as broad an audience as possible: Brecht, for example, helped to write the script for the first German proletarian feature film, *Kuhle Wampe*, of 1931–2, while Hanns Eisler wrote the music for it and Ernst Busch sang the moralizing ballads in it. The 'Agitprop' works of all these writers and artists were by no means limited to targeting the bourgeoisie and the forces of reaction but also pilloried the Social Democrats, the social grouping which, according to the Comintern's prescriptive definition of March 1931, was the 'bourgeoisie's principal support'.[63]

Independent left-wing intellectuals such as Kurt Tucholsky were not as hostile to the Social Democrats as the Communists, but they made no attempt to conceal their contempt. Tucholsky was the best-known contributor to the left-wing periodical *Die Weltbühne*, and when the Social Democrats adopted a new reformist programme in Görlitz in 1921, he dismissed the party delegates as 'a band of skat-playing brothers who have read Marx'. Five years later he portrayed them as 'modest radishes, red on the outside and white on the inside'. For Tucholsky, the Social Democrats' compulsive need to compromise whenever they were in government was 'a matter of parliamentary routine'.[64]

The intellectuals who championed the Weimar Republic were generally fully aware of its lack of internal stability. In October 1922, Thomas Mann, who right up until the end of the war had defended the idea of the authoritarian state, marked the sixtieth birthday of Gerhart Hauptmann by professing his faith in the German Republic in a widely reported speech to a not entirely sympathetic student audience in Berlin. And in late November 1926, by which date he was living in Munich, he expressed his anger and sadness at the way relations between Munich and Berlin had taken a turn for the worse since the pre-war period. The occasion was an event convened by the German Democratic Party. Before the war, he told his audience, Munich had been democratic, Berlin military, but the situation was now the exact opposite:

We have felt shame at the refractory pessimism that the people in Munich have used to offset the political insights of Berlin and the political longings of an entire world. It is with dismay that we have seen its healthy and cheerful blood poisoned by anti-Semitic nationalism and God knows what other kinds of dark folly. We were forced to stand by while Munich was decried not only in Germany itself but also in the wider world as a hotbed of reaction, as the seat of all stubbornness and of the obstinate refusal to accept the will of the age and we were obliged to listen while it was described as a stupid city and, indeed, as the stupidest city of all.[65]

Mann hoped to improve the situation by calling a spade a spade, an attitude he shared with the academic champions of the Republic, for all that the latter were no more than a minority among the upholders of German academe. Within this minority, the largest group was formed by the 'republicans by reason' who had turned their backs on the monarchy and accepted the new situation only after mature consideration. Among their number were scholars such as the Lutheran theologian Adolf von Harnack, the expert on constitutional law Gerhard Anschütz and the historian Friedrich Meinecke. At a meeting of the Association of Democratic Students in Berlin in early 1925 Meinecke recalled the law under which the Weimar Republic had first come into existence:

> The Republic is the great escape valve for the class struggle between workers and bourgeoisie, it is the constitutional form of the social peace that exists between them. [...] Social discord no longer exists between workers and bourgeoisie in general, but the rift has shifted to the right and now passes right through the bourgeoisie itself.[66]

Meinecke could also have argued that the rift had shifted both to the right *and* to the left and that it passed through both the bourgeoisie and the workers, for political divisions were now even less likely to coincide with class divisions. Between the bourgeois 'republicans by reason' and the extreme right there was a yawning gulf, but the same was true of the relationship between the Social Democrats and the Communists. Both workers' parties continued to use the same terminology, but their interpretation of it could not have been more different. For the Communists, the term 'class struggle', for example, implied a deliberate attempt to exacerbate social conflict with the aim of fomenting the proletarian revolution, whereas for the Social Democrats and the Free Trade Unions it meant a pluralist policy dictated by the interests of the workers.

In German society in the Weimar Republic, as in other post-war European societies, the bourgeoisie and nobility no longer set the tone to the extent that they had done before the war. Post-war societies were more 'proletarian' than their pre-war counterparts had been. In Germany there were particularly obvious signs of the material decline of broad sections of the middle classes as a result of inflation. The worsening economic situation went hand in hand with a profound sense of personal shock at the loss of all that had previously provided a sense of security, namely, a modest amount of wealth, the individual's ability to predict his or her future prospects and those of the next generation with some degree of certainty, and trust in the existing order and ultimately in the state. The feeling of a threat 'from below' produced a defensive response in the form of a mentality that merely served to deepen the differences between the social classes. Grammar schools and universities remained class-orientated institutions to which members of the working class struggled hard to gain admittance. A 'class bias to the legal system' was not just a polemical slogan of the left but a social and political reality. A 'bourgeois bloc' directed against the Social Democrats was a goal championed by powerful forces within all the bourgeois parties with the partial exception of the German Democratic Party.

But even after five turbulent years these forces had not yet gained complete control of the field. There were still those who strove to reach an understanding between the bourgeoisie and the workers. If it had not been so, then it would have been impossible for governments of a grand coalition and, from April 1925, a Weimar coalition to maintain a grip on power in the largest German state, Prussia. By the middle of the 1920s there were already signs of a return to the 'class compromise' of 1918/19 and at the same time of developments that tended, rather, to indicate a polarization of the political scene. Only one thing was certain: any stabilization of the Weimar Republic after 1923 was no more than relative when compared with the instability of the previous years. Internal threats to democracy had not gone away completely but had merely faded into the background.

Authoritarian Transformation (I): The New States of Poland, Czechoslovakia and the Baltic Region

Germany was not the only new democracy in Europe. The term 'Zwischen-europa' (literally 'between Europe') was coined by the Young Conservative German journalist Giselher Wirsing in 1932 to describe the new democracies between Germany and Russia that had either come into existence in the wake of the First World War or that owed their independence to that conflict or, as in the case of Poland, had succeeded in re-establishing their independence at that time. All were democracies at least on paper, and yet only two of them – Czechoslovakia and Finland – were able to survive as democracies beyond the crises of the immediate post-war period. Sooner or later all the others were transformed into more or less authoritarian states, although there were many reasons for this change. Most of the new states were agricultural economies with few industrial centres and no powerful urban bourgeoisie; few succeeded in implementing the sort of land reforms that would have made an appreciable difference to the hardships endured by local smallholders; in practically no case was a satisfactory balance achieved in reconciling national differences; and in every case the shift to a more authoritarian form of government repre-sented a reaction to the twofold experience of an economic crisis and of polit-ical instability.

The new states included one that did not even want to claim that status for itself: the Republic of Austria. Here the three largest parties – the Social Democrats, the Christian Socialists and the Pan-Germans – all wanted their country to unite with Germany. Otherwise, there were only deep divisions within the coalition government, which was made up of Social Democrats and Christian Socialists and which came to power in March 1919. The Social

Democrats were centralists who strove for a new type of society based on the notion of common property and were eager to grant the workers' councils that had been set up in 1918/19 a leading role in controlling the people's militia, whereas the Christian Socialists were federalists who wanted to maintain the status quo and reduce the socialist influence on the military. The grand coalition under the Social Democrat Karl Renner finally foundered on the question of the future of the soldiers' councils and ended on 10 June 1920, when it was replaced by a government elected by proportional representation and headed by the Christian Socialist historian Michael Mayr, who had previously been the minister for constitutional and administrative reform. It included members of both parties, together with a number of ministers with no political affiliations chosen by a consensus between the two partners in the coalition.

The new cabinet's most pressing task was the ratification of the federal constitution that had been drafted by Hans Kelsen, a Viennese expert on constitutional law. It established a federal state with a two-chamber system of government consisting of a National Council elected by universal equal suffrage and a Bundesrat, or Federal Council, in which the eight regional governments of Burgenland, Carinthia, Lower Austria, Upper Austria, Salzburg, Styria, Tyrol and Vorarlberg were all represented. Even though it was a part of Lower Austria, the federal capital, Vienna, enjoyed special status, being treated as an autonomous region in the Bundesrat. (A change to the constitution on 30 July 1925 meant that the city acquired the same rights as all the other regions.) The two chambers together elected the head of state – the federal president – at a joint session: not until 7 December 1929, following a further change to the constitution, was the president elected by the people in keeping with the German model. The Constituent National Assembly adopted the law enshrining the new constitution on 1 October 1920. It came into force on 10 November.

Elections to the National Council were held on 17 October 1920, when the Christian Socialists won eighty-five seats, the Social Democrats sixty-nine, the Pan-Germans twenty-one and the German Peasants' Party seven. The former foreign minister Ottokar Czernin was elected as a 'Bourgeois Democrat'. The cabinet, which was made up of Christian Socialists and Independents, was once again headed by Michael Mayr, but he was forced to resign on 1 June 1921, when the Pan-Germans withdrew their support. The reason for this change of heart on the part of the country's third-largest party was an extremely unpopular measure by the government which, responding to intense pressure from the Allies, had banned an unofficial plebiscite in Styria on the question of its annexation by the German Reich, a vote in which an equally high number of yes votes was expected as had been the case in the recent plebiscites in the Tyrol and Salzburg, where around 99 per cent of the local populations had opted to become part of Germany. Mayr was replaced by Johann Schober, an Independent who had been chief of the Viennese police and now headed a cabinet of bourgeois bureaucrats.

But Schober, too, was fated to spend only a few months in office, for the increasing devaluation of the Austrian currency had persuaded the Christian Socialists and Pan-Germans of the need to act quickly and form a stable government sustained by a solid parliamentary majority. The leader of the Christian Socialists, Ignaz Seipel, was elected the new chancellor on 31 May 1922. His cabinet included ministers from both the main parties. In October 1922, under the terms of the Geneva Protocols, he received a guaranteed loan of 650 million gold crowns from Great Britain, France, Italy and Czechoslovakia, the use of which would be monitored by a commissioner general to be appointed by the League of Nations. In return the country agreed not to forfeit its independence for twenty years and to maintain public order by means of extraordinary powers ratified by parliament. The Social Democrat opposition protested with all the vigour it could muster at this abandonment of its pan-German aspirations, while the rigorous economies implemented by Seipel's government failed to achieve their desired result. The Christian Socialists emerged as victors from the elections to the National Council in October 1923, winning eighty-two seats against the sixty-eight of the Social Democratic Party of German Austria.

But if the Social Democrats were powerless on a federal level, they partly made up for this state of affairs by dint of the position that they had in the meantime acquired in the Austrian capital, where the city was known as 'Red Vienna' throughout the 1920s, a centre of the European workers' movement with exemplary welfare organizations and housing developments such as the fortress-like Karl-Marx-Hof in the district of Döbling, the largest single complex of residential buildings in the world. The class conflict between proletarian and bourgeois Austria became dramatically worse in Vienna in the second half of the 1920s. An important stage in the process of political radicalization was the Social Democrats' party conference in Linz in November 1926, when the party adopted a programme that sounded more extreme than it was actually intended to be. In order to meet halfway the demands of its left wing, the party announced that if the working class emerged victorious from the forthcoming elections and if the bourgeoisie opposed the idea of social change, then it was prepared to break down that resistance by all the means available to a dictatorship.

Such radical remarks on the part of the Social Democrats were a boon to the bourgeois parties, allowing them to contest the elections in the spring of 1927 on a single ticket as an anti-Marxist 'bourgeois bloc'. The results of the election on 24 April turned out to be a disappointment for the Christian Socialists, who lost nine seats when compared to 1923, while the Social Democrats won three, giving them a total of seventy-one, only two seats fewer than the Christian Socialists. Even so, Seipel was able to form a 'bourgeois bloc' government with the help of the Pan-Germans and the Rural Federation (the 'Landbund').

By this date both camps had long since had an armed wing: the Social Democrats in the form of the Republican Defence League that had been created in 1923, the bourgeois parties with a whole array of defence leagues equipped with arms from the days of the Austro-Hungarian Empire. The two sides clashed in Schattendorf in the Burgenland at the end of January 1927, a bloody confrontation that was to have serious repercussions for both sides, when members of the right-wing Association of Frontline Soldiers fired on workers from the Republican Defence League. Among their victims were a war veteran and a child. On 14 July 1927 the three men who were accused of the crime were acquitted by a jury in Vienna, triggering mass demonstrations the very next day by socialist workers, all of whom were determined to vent their anger at such a blatant example of class bias within the legal system. After a number of bloody clashes with the police, a handful of protesters set fire to the Palace of Justice in the Ringstraße, whereupon Seipel's government armed the police with army carbines in an attempt to clear the square in front of the building. When the protesting workers began to throw stones, the police responded with gunfire. At the end of the fighting, eighty-five protesters and four policemen lay dead. The number of injured ran into the hundreds.

For the Social Democrats this outbreak of anarchy and violence in the summer of 1927 was a serious setback. A nationwide one-day general strike and a transport strike that ended after three days were symbolic acts designed to demonstrate that party and trade unions were still in control of the work-force. But their chances of power-sharing were permanently reduced after the events of 15 July 1927. In a way the Social Democrats were paying the price for their specifically 'Austro-Marxist' lurch to the left, a move that had enabled them to thwart their Communist rivals and prevent them from growing in size and influence. It was all too clear, after all, that their openness to the sort of left-wing ideas to which the party had paid tribute in the revolutionary-sounding statements in its Linz programme was among the deeper causes of the Viennese debacle. Among the consequences of 15 July was the impetus given to right-wing paramilitary organizations within Austria, all of which enjoyed a considerable boost in their membership at this time, as well as an increase in the number of their donations from employers both at home and abroad, notably from Italy and Hungary.

Three years later, on 9 November 1930, elections were held for the National Council – as it turned out, they were the last to be held during the First Republic, although no one could have known this at the time. The bourgeois camp entered the campaign rent by internal divisions. The former Independent chancellor, Johann Schober, who had once again headed the government between September 1929 and September 1930, had formed around himself a Schober bloc that included the Pan-Germans. Together they won nineteen seats. The Christian Socialists lost ground, returning sixty-six representatives, seven fewer than in 1927, while the 'Homeland Bloc' headed by one of the leaders of one of the defence organizations, Rüdiger von Starhemberg, returned eight deputies. The largest party, with seventy-two rather than seventy-one seats, was the Austrian Social Democrat Party, which was able, therefore, to nominate the first president of the National Council in the person of Karl Renner.

But the Social Democrats were as far away as ever from governing the country. The country's president, Wilhelm Miklas, invited the head of the regional government of Vorarlberg, the Christian Socialist Otto Ender, to form a cabinet. Schober became vice-chancellor and foreign minister, retaining both posts in June 1931 when Ender was replaced by another Christian Socialist, the former head of the regional government of Lower Austria, Karl Buresch. As foreign minister, Schober also bore much of the responsibility for the failure of a project that he finally set in motion in March 1931 with his German counterpart, Julius Curtius, who was the foreign minister in Heinrich Brüning's first cabinet: this was the plan for an Austro-German customs union.

Unsurprisingly, the project foundered on the determined opposition of the Western Powers, especially France. At the request of Great Britain, the Council of the League of Nations asked the International Court in The Hague to assess the legality of the plan on 19 May 1931. The Court delivered its verdict on 5 September 1931, arguing by eight votes to seven that the customs union ran counter to the Geneva Protocol of 1922, which had been drawn up to regulate Austria's economic and financial reconstruction. In short, it was unconstitutional. Two days earlier Curtius and Schober had announced that they would not pursue the plan, a decision that was the price that Austria had to pay for international loans. If it had not received this help, the collapse of the Austrian Credit-Anstalt Bank on 11 May 1931 resulting from the withdrawal of short-term French loans would have triggered a major economic catastrophe and led directly to the bankruptcy of the entire country. Even after it had received these foreign loans, Austria continued to languish in a state of deep economic depression: until 1938 the unemployment rate was invariably above 20 per cent of the working population as a whole.

By late January 1932 Buresch's cabinet had been undermined by the mutual mistrust between the Christian Socialists and the Pan-Germans, who were the most eloquent advocates of the customs union. Buresch remained in office until the end of May as the head of a bourgeois minority government. His second term in office coincided with the elections to the Landtag on 24 April 1931, when the National Socialists recorded a marked increase in their share of the vote and entered parliament for the first time. Local elections that were held on the same day in Carinthia and Styria likewise saw National Socialist gains. Buresch was replaced on 20 May 1932 by the former Christian Socialist agriculture and forestry minister, Engelbert Dollfuß, whose cabinet included members of the Rural Federation and Homeland Bloc, giving his coalition a single-vote majority over the Social Democrat and Pan-German opposition.

On 15 July 1932, under the terms of the Lausanne Protocol, the League of Nations agreed to loan Austria the sum of 300 million schillings on condition that it refrained from entering into any economic or political union with Germany for a period of thirty years. The following month the agreement was debated by the lower house, Dollfuß's government surviving the vote by only the narrowest of margins. In October he used the enabling act of 1917 – passed as a wartime expedient and still in force fifteen years later – in order to avoid the risks involved in the normal legislative process. It was a clear sign of the crisis that now beset the parliamentary system and of the chancellor's determination to place the affairs of state on a new, authoritarian basis.

On 4 March 1933, the presidium of the National Council unwittingly did the government a favour when the Social Democrats forced Karl Renner to resign in order for him to be able to vote with his party, something he was prevented from doing as president. The move came in the wake of an argument over the correct interpretation of a point of order during a vote on a planned amnesty law. Since both of Renner's acting representatives followed their president's lead, the National Council was no longer capable of acting. Dollfuß saw in this his chance to continue to rule without the approval of parliament. He prevented the constitutional court from intervening by forcing the resignation of all those judges who supported the Christian Socialists, thereby paralysing the country's Supreme Court. On 31 March 1933 the government banned the Republican Defence League and transferred the functions of the auxiliary police force to those sections of the Home Guard that were deemed loyal to the government.

The actions of Dollfuß's government amounted to nothing less than a *coup d'état*. Its reliance on the Home Guard units under Starhemberg and his ally Emil Fay that were supported by Fascist Italy implied a rapprochement with Mussolini's state in terms of the country's domestic and foreign policies. By March 1933, only weeks after Hitler had come to power in Germany, Austria began to witness the growth of an authoritarian system decried by its critics as 'Austro-Fascist' but more clearly dependent on the Catholic Church than its Italian model, not least in its appeal to Pope Pius XI's 1931 encyclical *Quadragesimo anno* as the basis of an ideal Christian corporate state. But only certain sections of the Home Guard movement had sided with Dollfuß. Both the emphatically Pan-German Styrian Home Guard and the Pan-German People's Party reacted to events in Germany by forming an alliance with the Austrian National Socialists, who in the local elections in Innsbruck in late April 1933 won 41.2 per cent of the vote, making them the largest party.

The Social Democrats seemed paralysed. Following Renner's resignation they had ensured that the National Council no longer had any part to play in politics and in doing so provided Dollfuß's government with a chance to sideline parliament for the foreseeable future. In the circumstances active resistance would have been an act of democratic self-defence designed to salvage the constitution and, as such, entirely legitimate: if there were ever the prospect of preventing the establishment of a dictatorship, this was it. The fact that the Social Democrats accepted not only the putsch but also its immediate conse- quence – the ban on the Republican Defence League – without lifting a finger to avert it was due no doubt to the lingering trauma of July 1927 and to the continuing fear of a renewed outbreak of undiscriminating mass violence. By the time that the Social Democrats finally announced a policy of armed resist- ance at their party conference in October 1933, their threat sounded distinctly hollow. And by February 1934, when Austria's socialist workers did indeed have recourse to arms, it was too late, for by then the Austro-Fascist regime already had at its disposal all the means of power needed to suppress the insurrection.

Until 1918 Austria and Hungary had been linked together in a personal and real union. The development in the direction of an increasingly authoritarian state began at a much earlier date in Hungary than in the former heartland of the Cisleithanian half of the empire. The course was set on 1 March 1920, when the commander in chief of the Hungarian army, Admiral Miklós Horthy of Nágybánya, was elected imperial regent. The Social Democrats had refused to take part in the elections in January 1920, this being their way of protesting at the 'White' terror that was itself a reaction to Béla Kun's short-lived Communist soviet dictatorship, with the result that all the parties to their right felt at home together in parliament. As early as March Horthy proclaimed Hungary a monarchy with a vacant throne. In 1921 Karl I, the last Habsburg emperor, who had not, however, abdicated as the king of Hungary in November 1918, made two failed attempts to enlist the support of sections of the army in order to win back the crown, but Horthy had no wish to see the monarchy restored in the spirit of the Habsburgs because such a restoration would inevitably have culmi- nated in an Allied intervention. A law passed in October 1921 ended the house of Austria's right to the throne of Hungary once and for all.

The Treaty of Trianon meant that for Hungary there was no longer any question of nationality in the narrower sense of the term, for nine-tenths of the region's inhabitants, including even the Roma, defined themselves as Magyars, while barely 7 per cent gave German as their mother tongue. There remained the problem of the Jews, who made up around 6 per cent of the population but who comprised around half of the country's lawyers and doctors, exerting tremendous influence on trade and banking. The anti-Semitism that had already been widespread in nineteenth-century Hungary was given a decisive boost by the soviet dictatorship – the same was true of Bavaria. The Jews had played a prominent role in the Communist-led government, and so they were comprehensively suspected of plotting to overthrow the status quo and of being the sworn enemies of the Hungarian people. Even under Count Pál Teleki – the first of three counts to run the country between 1920 and 1932 – Hungary began to drive Jews from the apparatus of state and to restrict their access to higher education, leading to a reduction in the number of Jewish students and academics.

There was no land reform worthy of the name. Although the poorest farmers received a little additional land at the insistence of the Smallholders Party, the rural economy, with its tiny farms, was hardly viable, while the larger landowners remained unaffected by any such reforms, their social and political power unbroken.

Count Teleki was succeeded in 1921 by Count István Bethlen, who developed a more tolerant attitude to the Social Democrats after the latter had agreed not to foment dissent among civil servants or farmworkers and to eschew political strikes and republican propaganda, both promises forming part of a secret deal between Bethlen and the Social Democrats' anti-Communist leader, Károlyi Peyer. By 1922 Bethlen had managed to bring together all the larger parties in the National Assembly and to create a united party, but a new electoral law curtailed the right to vote to such a drastic extent that only half the adult population still enjoyed that entitlement. And from then on the principle of a secret ballot applied only to the larger towns, not to the rural constituencies.

The results of the elections in May and June 1922 turned out to be everything that the government could have wished for: although there was a Liberal and Social Democrat opposition and a free press, the position of Bethlen's government, which remained in office until 1931, was now unshakeable. The Western Powers rewarded the country for its new political stability by welcoming Hungary into the League of Nations in September 1922 and by helping it to deal with its rampant inflation by granting it a loan in 1924. During the years that followed, the Hungarian economy recovered, and the country enjoyed a growth in industrialization that lasted until the world economic crisis in 1929.

Hungary's foreign policy was dictated in no small way by its desire to revise the terms of the Treaty of Trianon. Bethlen began by demanding the return of those territories that were home to a more or less purely Hungarian population. Behind his demand lay an ambitious programme that had the support of almost every party and social group: a return to the country's pre-1914 borders. Bethlen saw Fascist Italy as a possible partner in realizing his vision and signed a friendship treaty with Mussolini in April 1927. He also approached Great Britain, but London was unwilling to take a similar step.

Bethlen's government came to an end in 1931, when Hungary came close to going bankrupt in the wake of the world economic crisis. Bethlen's successor, Count Gyula Károlyi, fell from power in September 1932, when he failed to find sufficient parliamentary support for his austerity measures. Horthy replaced him with a former army captain, Gyula Gömbös de Jákfa, who had previously helped him to suppress Karl I's second attempt to reclaim the throne in October 1920 and who remained in office until his death in October 1936, enjoying widespread support among the middle classes. The leader of the Party of National Unity, he was an ardent nationalist and a rabid anti-Semite who made no secret of his sympathy for Italian Fascism and, later, for German National Socialism. In 1932 the battle to alter the terms of the Treaty of Trianon became the ultimate goal of Hungarian politics.

The same policy was pursued by Gőmbős's two successors, Koloman Darányi and, from May 1938, Béla Imrédy. Imrédy was forced to resign in February 1939, when it was rumoured that one of his great-grandmothers had been Jewish. Count Pál Teleki returned as prime minister in May 1939 and introduced strict anti-Semitic legislation, while also acting decisively against the Hungarian followers of the German National Socialists, Ferenc Szálasi's Arrow Cross Party. His attempt to distance himself from the Third Reich was to end tragically early in 1941: when, in the face of the prime minister's determined opposition, Horthy and the country's military leaders became accomplices to Hitler's attack on the Kingdom of Serbs, Croats and Slovenes, Teleki took his own life.

The years between the end of the First World War and the world economic crisis witnessed the development of a yet more critical situation in the Kingdom of Serbs, Croats and Slovenes than had been the case even in Hungary. Internally, by far the most serious problem turned out to be the relations between the Orthodox Serbs and the Catholic Croats, who had been lumped together in the 1921 census as a single Serbo-Croat nation. They made up around four-fifths of the total population, while the Slovenes comprised 8.5 per cent. There were also a handful of smaller German, Magyar and Albanian minorities. (The Montenegrins, Macedonians and Muslim Bosnians were not counted separately but included with the Serbo-Croats.) Under the terms of the electoral law of July 1920, all men over the age of twenty-one were entitled to vote regardless of their level of literacy, which ranged from 91.2 per cent in Slovenia to 16.2 per cent in Macedonia, with a nationwide average of 48.5 per cent. Proportional representation meant that the party system was fragmented, making it difficult to form stable majority governments. Between 1920 and 1928 there were no fewer than twenty-eight cabinets in Belgrade, no parliament succeeding in staying in office for the full four-year term.

It was the centrist parties that emerged as the victors from the elections in November 1920, while the federalists were the losers. The kingdom's constitution was adopted on 28 June 1921 by a narrow Serbian majority. Since the federalist Croat Peasants' Party had refused to take part in the discussions, its wording proved more unitarian than the make-up of the country's parliament, the Skupština, might have led observers to expect. The former, largely historical administrative units of Serbia, Montenegro, Bosnia-Herzegovina, Dalmatia, Croatia-Slavonia, Slovenia and Vojvodina were replaced by administrative regions, or *oblasti*, that were modelled on the French *départements* and had no independent rights. The most militant opposition party was the Communist Party, with fifty-eight seats out of a total of 401. They were the third largest party after the Democrats and Old Radicals. After its followers had made several attempts to assassinate members of the government, all Communist organizations were banned on 3 August 1921 and Communist members of parliament barred from holding office. Shortly afterwards, on 16 August, King Peter died and was succeeded by his son, the prince regent, who became King Alexander I.

By November 1925 it seemed as if an agreement between Serbia and Croatia was within reach, when the leader of the banned Croat Peasants' Party, Stjepan Radić, entered prime minister Nikola Pašić's cabinet as education minister, but the differences between the centrists and the federalists were impossible to reconcile, and in February 1926 Radić fell out with Pašić's successor, Nikola Uzunović. By February 1927 his party was no longer represented in the government. On 20 June 1928 a member of the Serbian Old Radicals shot three deputies from the Croat Peasants' Party and seriously wounded two others inside the parliament building. Among the dead was Stjepan Radić's brother, Pavle, while Radić himself was among the injured. He died of his injuries on 8 August. From then on the Croats no longer attended any parliamentary sessions. On 6 January 1929 – the day of the Orthodox Christmas festivities – King Alexander drew the most radical conclusion from the recurring government crises and dissolved parliament, at the same time suspending the constitution of 1921. An apolitical general, Pera Živković, was appointed prime minister, ushering in an new phase in the history of the Kingdom of Serbs, Croats and Slovenes, namely, a monarchical dictatorship kept in place by military backing.

Relations between the Kingdom of Yugoslavia, as it was officially known after October 1929, and its neighbours continued to be strained. Belgrade and Sofia were at loggerheads over the question of Macedonia, which had been divided up between Serbia, Greece and Bulgaria following the Second Balkan War of 1913. Meanwhile Hungary had laid a historical claim to Vojvodina, which was principally settled by Magyars, while the South Slavs had their eyes on large tracts of Albania along its Mediterranean coast, only for their ambitions to be thwarted by a conference of Allied ambassadors in November 1921, when Albania's borders were settled. Italy had secured areas in Istria and on the Dalmatian coast that were inhabited by powerful Slovene and Croat minorities totalling around half a million in all. The kingdom had agreed to uphold the rights of its own minorities in a treaty drawn up in 1919: the 'Little Entente' masterminded by the French and signed by the Kingdom of Serbs, Croats and Slovenes on the one hand and by Czechoslovakia on the other was intended to provide protection from the aspirations of Hungarian revisionists, and in June 1921 a similar treaty followed with Romania, a country which for its part had formed an alliance with Czechoslovakia two months earlier.

The new kingdom was willing to negotiate with Italy, agreeing under the terms of the Treaty of Rapallo that Rijeka, or Fiume, should become a free state and that Zadar, or Zara, be ceded to the peninsula. It did not insist on a treaty to protect the local minorities similar to the one granted to ethnic Italians living within its territories. In January 1924, by which date Mussolini was already in power, the Treaty of Rome was signed between Belgrade and Rome, agreeing to Fiume's annexation by Italy in return for which Belgrade received a part of the former free state, including the port at Porto Baross. Both states also agreed to work together for a period of five years, to retain the status quo and to maintain their respective neutrality in the event of an unprovoked attack.

The treaty was accepted by the Skupština by only the slenderest of margins – the same was true of a later treaty with Italy on the matters of trade and shipping. Several additional technical agreements known as the Nettuno Conventions encountered such widespread public opposition that the government initially withdrew them. Mussolini reacted by signing a treaty with Albania in November 1926 and a friendship and arbitration treaty with Hungary in April 1927, both treaties being seen in Belgrade as provocative gestures and as a way of isolating the Kingdom of Serbs, Croats and Slovenes. As a result the Treaty of Rome was not renewed when it expired in January 1929, even though the government had in the meantime ratified the Nettuno Conventions. In November 1927 the kingdom had signed a pact of alliance with France, which to a certain extent compensated it for the loss of Italy as a partner.

By the summer of 1926, relations with Bulgaria were similarly being compromised by a series of attacks by a group of Macedonian guerrillas, the Internal Macedonian Revolutionary Organization, that in 1927 led to the complete closure of the border between the two countries, and it was not until 1934 that the situation improved, when a number of army officers mounted a coup in Sofia and the Internal Macedonian Revolutionary Organization was removed from the scene. As for Greece, Belgrade was unable to persuade Athens to agree to its demands for a sovereign territory in Salonika and an agreement to protect ethnic minorities. An arbitration treaty was signed by Belgrade and Athens in March 1929, two months after the monarchy had become a dictatorship, but it contained no mention of these aims. Nor did it list any obligations associated with the alliance. In February 1934 the existing bilateral agreements between Yugoslavia, Romania, Greece and Turkey were renegotiated as the Balkan Pact between all four countries. From then on the signatories were committed to assist one another if one of the Balkan states were to take part in a non-Balkan attack on another Balkan state.

Among the socio-political problems that needed to be addressed, the agrarian question was no less urgent in the Kingdom of Serbs, Croats and Slovenes than it was elsewhere. In May 1922 parliament agreed to compensate the larger landowners for the expropriation of their lands, a move that affected the former Habsburg regions first and foremost. A quarter of the land area acquired in this way was newly settled, a further area of woodland became the property of the state, and the remaining half was transferred to tenant farmers. In this way the problem of agricultural overpopulation and of the fragmentation of the land into farms too small to be financially viable remained as far away from a settlement as in other parts of south-eastern and central eastern Europe.

Alexander I's personal dictatorship began in 1929 with his abolition of press freedom, his ban on all political parties and his attempt to form a single South Slav nation by creating larger administrative regions – *banonina* – and by rigorously centralizing the state. From October 1929 the state's new name was the Kingdom of Yugoslavia, a change designed to further this same goal of greater centralization. But Alexander's plans were far from all being realized: his aim of introducing the Latin script and Gregorian calendar to the whole of his kingdom foundered on opposition from Serbia's Orthodox Church, with the result that the Latin and Cyrillic alphabets continued to exist side by side, as did the Gregorian and Julian calendars, meaning that the major Christian feasts were still celebrated on different days in different parts of the country. The old antagonism between the Eastern and Western Church and between those parts of the new state that reflected Byzantine influence and those still marked by Habsburg history went deeper and continued to leave a more powerful impression than the people responsible for building a single Yugoslav nation were willing to accept.

In September 1931 Alexander announced a new constitution which enshrined some of the older basic rights but perpetuated the ban on political parties and at the same time forbade the formation of religious, national and regional organizations. Secret ballots were abandoned. And elections to the Skupština were henceforth conducted on the basis of a list of national candidates with a unified minimum number of backers in every constituency, a change that lent massive support to the strongest list, which now received two-thirds of the seats. At the same time it gave broad scope to electoral fraud. In addition to the National Assembly the new constitution also provided for a Senate whose members would in part be appointed by the king and in part be elected by the people.

Even under Alexander's personal dictatorship, the greatest challenge remained Croatian nationalism. At the beginning of 1929 the Zagreb lawyer Ante Pavelić founded an underground terrorist organization that was initially called Domabran (Home Guard), then Ustaša (Uprising) and that demanded the complete independence of Croatia and, with it, the break-up of Yugoslavia. In its radicalism and ideology it was no less extreme than the Internal Macedonian Revolutionary Organization. Backed by Fascist Italy and Hungary, the supporters of Ustaša also sought to pursue their goals by means of foreign propaganda, while in Croatia itself they undertook a number of bomb attacks, starting in 1931. One such attack was launched on the Orient Express. An attempt to foment an uprising in the summer of 1932 failed through lack of support among the peasants. The group also planned to assassinate Alexander I during his visit to Zagreb in December 1933, but in the event the assassin ultimately chose not to carry out his attempt on the king's life.

Not until 9 October 1934 did these Croatian extremists achieve their goal when they murdered both Alexander and the French foreign minister Louis Barthou in Marseilles. The assassin was a member of the Internal Macedonian Revolutionary Organization acting on the orders of a group of Ustaša exiles. Alexander was succeeded by his son, the underage Peter II, who was to be the last king of Yugoslavia. The actual task of running the country passed to the government, which after 1935 was led by the businessman and politician Milan Stojadinović. Since France resisted Belgrade's demands that Italy and Hungary be punished for supporting the Ustaša movement and since the Council of the League of Nations was unable to agree on any sanctions against either of these two countries, Yugoslavia began to draw closer to a third country on which it was now increasingly dependent from an economic point of view: National Socialist Germany.

Under Stojadinović, too, Croatian nationalism remained the most difficult problem to solve. In the elections in May 1935 the Maček List named after the leader of the Croat Peasants' Party and Stjepan Radić's successor, Vladko Maček, won 35.4 per cent of the vote, while the government list won 62 per cent. But because the electoral law favoured the ruling party, the latter returned 301 members to parliament, the opposition only sixty-seven. Maček and his supporters responded by boycotting the Skupština. In the elections in July 1938 the Maček List increased its share of the vote to 40.2 per cent but won even fewer seats than three years previously, namely, sixty-one out of a total of 371. Under the terms of the constitution of June 1921 all men and women over the age of twenty-one had the right to vote as long as they enjoyed all civil rights.

But there were also compelling reasons why the makers of Yugoslavia's foreign policy felt a greater need to come to some arrangement with the movement for Croat independence. Chief of these reasons was Austria's annexation by the German Reich in March 1938, which meant that Germany and Yugoslavia now shared a common border. It was Stojadinović's successor, Dragiša Cvetković, who in August 1939 agreed to Maček's demands that Croatia should become a banship with its own regional assembly and its own government and with a ban at its head. The central government in Belgrade lost some of its authority in consequence and was reshaped, Maček taking over as prime minister in Cvetković's government, while four members of his party assumed important ministerial positions. Yugoslavia seemed to be set for a shift in the direction of a multinational federation of independent states, but in the event the country's new identity could not be put to the test as the outbreak of the Second World War prevented the 'Sporazum' – the agreement reached by Cvetković and Maček in August 1939 – from ever being fully implemented.

Unlike Yugoslavia, Poland was not a recent creation. In the wake of the First World War it regained the national independence that it had lost following the third partition of the country in 1795. Poland had always been a part of the old Latin West and, unlike Yugoslavia, it was not burdened by the continuing schism between Rome and Byzantium. But in terms of its internal development, it suffered a series of crises no less serious than those endured by most of the other countries in eastern central and south-east Europe.

Poland's new borders had already been established when the second elections to the Sejm were held on 5 and 12 November 1922. As in the previous elections in January 1919, none of the parties contesting the election could claim a clear parliamentary majority. The political left, which included the Wyzwolenie Polish Peasants' Party as well as the Socialists, lost a considerable number of votes, while the right in the form of the National Democrats and two smaller parties won a much-increased share of the vote. The parties that had previously occupied the middle ground had shrunk to next to nothing. Only if the nationalist minorities, which between them had won around a fifth of all the seats, were to work together could a majority government be formed.

The first task facing the Senate and the Sejm was the election of a president. The country's former president, Józef Piłsudski, declined to put forward his name as a candidate because under the terms of the constitution of 17 March 1921, the head of state had little real authority. Nor did he have any wish to be dependent on his enemies, the National Democrats. Gabriel Narutowicz, a member of the Polish Peasants' Party, was finally elected in the fifth round of voting on 9 December 1922. He owed his election to non-Polish and, above all, Jewish deputies, triggering a violent anti-Semitic hate campaign on the political right that cost him his life: on 16 December, only a week after his election, he was assassinated by a fanatical National Democrat supporter. The two chambers elected Stanisław Wojciechowski his successor on 20 December. An undistinguished politician from the right wing of the Polish Peasants' Party, Wojciechowski remained in office until May 1926 and, as a former Socialist, enjoyed cordial relations with Piłsudski. Conversely, it was impossible to find a parliamentary majority for a prime minister, so that on 17 December the leader of the Sejm finally invited General Władysław Sikorski to form a small cross-party cabinet that was tolerated by the Sejm for only five months.

On 28 May 1923 the leader of the right-wing Piast Peasants' Party, Wincenty Witos, who had already been prime minister in 1921–2, succeeded in forming a centre-right cabinet. Piłsudski took the opportunity to resign his posts as chief of the general staff and president of the Inner War Council and to retire to his estates at Sulejówek. Witos's second cabinet marked the start of a period of parliamentary supremacy that was to last until Piłsudski's military putsch in May 1926. These three years saw three different cabinets, for all that they were invariably made up of bureaucrats. Domestic issues preoccupied public interest in the form of the fight against inflation, the agrarian question and the matter of nationality.

The government led by the financier Władysław Grabski succeeded in stabilizing the country's currency. The złoty was introduced in April 1924 and initially fixed at parity with the Swiss franc. Its purchasing power and exchange rate were to be overseen by the Bank Polski, which in principle was independent. Conversely, agrarian reform remained extremely modest in scope, since Polish landowners had a highly effective advocate in the powerful political right. Once the Land Reform Act came into force in December 1925 it was really only the German landowners in the western parts of the country who had to hand over any land, but this was insufficient to create a broadly based class of medium-sized farmers, so Polish agriculture continued to be marked by the contrast between the larger landowners who owned vast tracts of land and also exported their produce and the subsistence farming of smallholders whose working methods were simply not financially viable. The Poland of the interwar years remained an agrarian country that saw few real signs of industrialization. And it continued to be beset by a problem typical of all societies in eastern central Europe, that of the fragmentation of property caused by the divisions of the country's real estate and rural overpopulation.

Non-Polish minorities were granted the same rights as the rest of the population under the 1921 constitution, but in practice the political right regarded the parliamentary representatives of national minorities as inferior, no matter whether they were Germans, Jews or Lithuanians. In the case of Ukrainians and White Ruthenians, there were signs of an attempt at assimilation, but this was made more difficult by the emergence of a powerful anti-Polish movement in eastern Galicia that boycotted the 1922 elections with some success. The Jews were viewed with extreme distrust by the National Democrats and by other right-wing parties, including the Piast Peasants' Party, and suffered all manner of discrimination, while the Germans living in the areas around Poznań and Pomerania on the lower Vistula were encouraged to move to Germany: more than half the Germans living there, around half a million in all, took this step. Not one of the interwar governments included a minister from a national minority, and the same was true of most of the top administrative posts in the regions, whether *voivodes* ('warlords') or *starostas* ('elders'). Polish politicians sought to establish a homogeneous national state that was western in character, an aim that could never be reconciled with the country's de facto ethnic variety.

Of paramount importance in terms of Poland's foreign policy was its dependence on France, with which Warsaw signed a treaty of alliance and a secret military agreement in February 1921. Poland additionally signed a treaty of alliance with Romania in March 1921 and a friendship treaty with Latvia and Estonia in March 1922. In every case there was an anti-Soviet thrust behind the move. A similar treaty with Finland was not ratified by the parliament in Helsinki. Conversely, an agreement signed by the foreign ministers of Poland and Czechoslovakia in November 1921 and providing for limited cooperation between the two countries failed to achieve the required majority in the Sejm, and although an agreement with Prague dealing with the contested area of Teschen was ratified in April 1925, it still fell far short of the failed agreement of 1921.

Following the annexation of the area around Vilnius in March 1922, relations with Lithuania remained extremely tense, a situation exacerbated by the lack of any diplomatic relations between the two countries. With Germany, by contrast, such relations did exist, and yet even here they were no guarantee of international normality. Germany refused to accept the loss of its former territories to the east, notably West Prussia and the southern part of Upper Silesia, but increasingly questioned the legitimacy of its eastern neighbour and in June 1925 started a trade war with Poland that left the free city of Gdańsk particularly badly affected. Poland responded by systematically expanding the port of Gdynia. By the middle of the 1920s there seemed no prospect of any improvement in German-Polish relations. If Poland, still profoundly Catholic as a country, could draw any consolation from Germany's lack of recognition of its territorial possessions, then this took the form of the concordat of February 1925, when the Vatican reorganized the Polish bishoprics in keeping with the country's post-war national borders.

Given the antagonisms between the parties and the frequent changes of cabinet, there could be no question of any continuity in government after 1918. Generally it was personal intrigues and tactical manoeuvres that led to the fall of one government and its replacement by another. On 13 November 1925 Piłsudski sought out President Wojciechowski in person and tried to persuade him of the need for some control of parliament but was unable to overcome the latter's constitutional scruples. Two days later, in a speech that he delivered at a rally of Legion officers, Piłsudski implied that in future he would use more than mere words against those who, in his view, 'were making the state powerless and holding back the punitive hand of justice'.[67]

Piłsudski found an ally in General Lucjan Zeligowski and was able to engineer his appointment as minister of war in Aleksander Skrzyński's cabinet in November 1925. Zeligowski helped Piłsudski with the military preparations for his planned putsch by gathering together regiments loyal to the marshal. A further government crisis, this time triggered by Skrzyński's resignation and by the formation of a centre-right cabinet under Wincenty Witos on 5 May 1926 that was vigorously opposed by the political left, provided Piłsudski with his chance to take the decisive step. On 12 May he placed himself at the head of a group of fifteen regiments and occupied the Praga part of Warsaw on the right bank of the Vistula. For two days there was fierce fighting with government troops, the decisive factor in Piłsudski's victory proving to be the intervention of the party that he himself had once led but from which he had long since distanced himself: the Polish Socialist Party, which called a general strike and in that way prevented troops loyal to the government from travelling to the capital. Wojciechowski and Witos resigned on the evening of 14/15 May. Piłsudski ended the fighting on 22 May 1926 with an appeal for reconciliation in which he paid tribute to the patriotism of his defeated opponents.

Piłsudski's military putsch of May 1926 marked the first stage of his 'moral dictatorship'. It was to last four years. Initially he did not govern himself but left others to do so for him. At his bidding, Kazimierz Bartel, a teacher of mathematics who led the small Workers' Party, was appointed prime minister, Piłsudski himself becoming minister of war in the new cabinet. On 31 May both the Senate and the Sejm, backed by a two-thirds majority, named him state president, but just as he had done four years previously, he turned down the highest office in the land and ensured that Ignacy Mościcki, a chemistry teacher, was nominated in his place. With right-wing help an amendment was made to the constitution on 2 August 1926, giving the president the right to dissolve parliament and, during parliamentary recesses, to issue decrees with the force of law, such decrees being subject to subsequent ratification by the National Assembly. The government could also spend money on the scale of the previous year's budget if parliament had not ratified the current budget on time.

Piłsudski had assumed power in a revolutionary way reminiscent of a Spanish *pronunciamiento*. The changes to the constitution in August 1926 were not revolutionary as such. The president's emergency powers were no more permissive than those enjoyed by the German president under Article 48 of the Weimar constitution. The clause dealing with the emergency budget was by no means unusual in parliamentary democracies. Parliament was not dissolved, the opposition was not suppressed, and the press was not censored. Although it had been brought about by force, the change of regime produced internal stability that initially bore all the signs of a conservative democracy, certainly not a military dictatorship, still less the sort of 'Fascist' dictatorship that Piłsudski loathed.

Piłsudski took over as prime minister in October 1926 and formed a largely conservative cabinet that led to a cooling of relations between himself and the Polish Socialist Party. The rift deepened when he visited the home of the Radziwiłłs in late October 1926 and, himself a member of the lower aristocracy, demonstratively underlined his closeness to the landed gentry in the east of the country. But it was the National Democrats under Roman Dmowski and Wincenty Witos's Piast Party who proved his most implacable enemies. In order to establish a unifying basis on which to work in parliament, he asked Walery Sławek, a colonel loyal to him, to form an independent bloc that would work closely with the government. This non-party bloc, or BBWR, was formed shortly before the elections to the Sejm and Senate in March 1928, and although it had no clearly outlined programme, it gained considerable support among the peasants and urban middle classes.

The BBWR won a total of 122 out of 444 seats in the 1928 elections and was the biggest party, inflicting dramatic losses on the National Democrats and Piast Party, whereas left-wing parties were able to report major gains, winning a total of some 140 seats. Since the composition of the Sejm was no guarantee of a firm majority for the government, Piłsudski entrusted the post of prime minister to a series of personal and political confidants: first, Kazimierz Bartel, then the former education minister Kazimierz Świtalski, then Bartel again and, finally, in March 1930, Walery Sławek. He himself remained minister of war and, as such, the dominant figure in the regime. One of his keenest critics was the newly elected marshal of the Sejm, the Socialist Ignacy Daszyński. The government's 'strong man' felt that the increasingly close parliamentary cooperation between the left-wing and centrist parties, which entered into a formal partnership, the Centrolew ('Centre Left'), in October 1929, represented a threat that needed to be addressed. Piłsudski reacted by lambasting parliament and the opposition parties, attacks backed up by extreme attempts at intimidation.

Świtalski's government was toppled by a vote of no confidence on 5 December 1929, leading to a worsening of the power struggle between the executive and the legislative. In June 1930 the opposition parties met in Kraków, a meeting that was to be followed in September by nationwide demonstrations on behalf of freedom and against dictatorship. On 25 August Piłsudski himself took over as prime minister, and four days later the country's president, Ignacy Mościcki, dissolved parliament. In early October, Piłsudski ordered the arrest of eighteen of his parliamentary enemies, including Witos, as well as a number of deputies representing the Ukrainian minority and several prominent Socialists. All were subsequently imprisoned in the fortress at Brest-Litovsk, where they were subjected to humiliating ill-treatment.

The parliamentary elections on 17 and 23 September were no longer free but took place in a climate of political intimidation and military tyranny, producing a result that largely reflected the wishes of the government. With 243 out of a total of 444 seats the government bloc was assured of a majority in the Sejm, whereas the Centrolew and the national minorities had to contend with major losses. The government majority was even more pronounced in the Senate, and yet the government failed to achieve the two-thirds majority needed to change the constitution, so that for the present there could be no thought of enacting a new constitution of the kind that Piłsudski was striving to enforce. From December 1930 he contented himself once again with the post of minister of war, while giving the position of prime minister to men whom he could trust, all of them army colonels.

The 'regime of the colonels' attempted to counter the world economic crisis, which by now had engulfed Poland, with emergency laws and deep financial cuts. Massed strikes that the Socialists organized in the country's principal industrial regions, starting in February 1932, led to restrictions on the right of assembly and to a deliberate curtailment of the independence of the judiciary. On 23 March 1933 – the same day as that on which events entirely similar in character unfolded in Hitler's Germany – the Sejm passed an enabling act that gave the government the power to enact ordinances and decrees with the force of law, with the result that parliament was almost completely sidelined.

By the autumn of 1930 Poland was in the second stage of its transformation into an authoritarian state, a transformation described by its perpetrators as a *sanacja* ('cleansing') but the outcome might be more accurately termed a dictatorship. Admittedly, the press was still relatively free, there was still a multiparty system and individual liberties were still protected, but there could be no talk of a government legitimized by free elections. It was the military that effectively wielded power, parliament having been reduced to a shadowy existence at least since the time of the enabling act of March 1933. The new constitution of 23 April 1935 did nothing to alter this state of affairs, for it merely invested the authoritarian presidential state with a new legal basis. Barely three weeks later the man who had done more than any other to re-establish an independent Poland but who had then been uniquely responsible for restricting the country's political liberties was no more: the first marshal of Poland, Józef Piłsudski, died on 12 May at the age of sixty-seven.

Like Poland, Lithuania – its neighbour to the north-east – was an agrarian country with a largely Catholic population. In April 1919 Antanas Smetona, a journalist from the nationalist right, was elected the country's president. A year later elections were held for the Constituent Assembly and resulted in an absolute majority for the country's Christian Democrats, with fifty-nine out of a total of 112 seats. The Popular Socialists won twenty-nine, the Social Democrats fourteen and the national minorities nine. (The Jews made up the largest of these national minorities with 7.5 per cent of the population, while, according to the 1923 national census, the Poles accounted for at least 3.25 per cent, the Germans for 1.5 per cent.) The Tautininkai Nationalist Party won no seats, while the Communist Party was banned.

Government and parliament met in the provisional capital of Kaunas. The constitution of 1 August 1922 provided for a president who was for the most part a figurehead with little real power. He did, however, have the right of veto over laws that did not have a two-thirds majority from the single chamber, or Seimas. And he also had the right to dissolve parliament. Under the terms of the 1922 constitution, the capital was Vilnius, but this had been annexed by Poland following Warsaw's unilateral action in the previous March. The Vilnius question was a permanent obstacle to any normalization of relations between

Lithuania and Poland, exerting a traumatic influence on Lithuanian politics throughout the interwar period.

The desire to obtain some kind of compensation for the loss of the area annexed by Poland also played a role in the occupation of the Memel region by Lithuanian troops on 10 January 1923, the day before the French occupied the Ruhr. Once the Treaty of Versailles had come into force, the Memel region, which had previously belonged to Germany, had been placed under joint Allied control. According to the 1910 census, there were 71,000 German-speaking inhabitants and 67,000 who spoke Lithuanian. In February 1923 a conference of Allied ambassadors transferred sovereignty over the Memel region to Lithuania but attached two conditions to the transfer: the region should be granted independent status, and Poland should have use of the port of Memel (Klaipeda). In the wake of the contested status of Vilnius, Lithuania declined to meet the second of these demands but respected the first by signing the Memel Convention with the Allies on 8 May 1924.

Under the terms of this convention, the Memel region acquired its own regional parliament and, in the form of a five-man directorate, its own government. Although the first elections in October 1925 gave the German parties an overwhelming majority, with twenty-seven out of twenty-nine seats, only Lithuanians from outside the region were placed at the head of the directorate by the governor appointed by the Lithuanian president, a situation that lasted for ten years and that flew in the face of the wishes of the regional assembly. It also meant that in the longer term relations with Germany were adversely affected. And yet there was an important difference from the conflict with Poland, for diplomatic relations existed between Kaunas and Berlin but not between Kaunas and Warsaw.

The occupation of the Memel region coincided with a period of internal political instability. In the elections of October 1922 the Christian Democrats lost their absolute majority, which they regained only in May 1923 after the president, Aleksandras Stulginskis, had dissolved parliament. The main domestic concern at this time was agrarian reform, but this was hardly a contentious issue, such was the predominantly rural character of the region. A law passed in April 1922 provided for compensation for ecclesiastical, aristocratic and private landowners if they lost lands of over eighty hectares. In 1928 the upper limit was raised to 150 hectares. During the early stage of land reform, it was the smallholders who owned little or no land who benefited most from this redistribution process. During the second phase it was also communes and non-profit-making institutions. The landowners most affected by these changes were generally Poles or Russians, with the result that there was not only a social but also an ethnic dimension to this redistribution of the land, which served to confirm the Lithuanians' sense of national identity. Further parliamentary elections were held in May 1926, and on this occasion the Memel region was able to take part for the first time. This time it was the left-wing parties that were the victors: the National Socialists won twenty-two seats, the Social Democrats fifteen, making a total of thirty-seven out of eighty-five. The Christian Democrats won only thirty seats. With the backing of the Jewish and Polish deputies, two National Socialists were elected to high office: Mykolas Sleževičius became the state president, Kazys Grinius the prime minister.

The left-wing government encountered the keenest conceivable opposition from the Christian Democrats and from the nationalist Tautininkai, which entered parliament for the first time with five representatives. But the greatest danger came from the military, their opposition provoked not least by a non-aggression pact signed with the Soviet Union in September 1926. General Povilas Plechavičius mounted a putsch on 17 December 1926, a move clearly inspired by Piłsudski's coup the previous May. The parliament building was occupied, the government deposed and the post of state president given to Antanas Smetona, while that of prime minister passed to Augustinas Voldemaras, the chairman of the radically nationalist organization Geležinis Vilkas (Iron Wolf), who had already been prime minister in 1918. He now proceeded to form a government made up of Christian Democrats and Tautininkai. Four months later, President Smetona dissolved the Seimas on 12 April 1927 but without calling for new elections. This marked the beginning of a nine-year period of authoritarian rule during which Lithuania no longer had an elected parliament.

With the support of the army, Smetona spent this period bolstering his own position of power. A new constitution that was proclaimed on 15 May 1928 concentrated all the state's power on the president. Styling himself the 'nation's leader', Smetona replaced Voldemaras in September 1929 with his own brother-in-law, Juozas Tubelis. Following a failed military coup in June 1934 and a strike by farmers in the summer of 1935, the regime exercised even tighter control of the country. By February 1936 a new law meant that the opposition parties had to suspend operations, and the elections in June 1936 – the first for ten years – were organized in such a way that only Tautininkai could field candidates. On 11 February 1938 the one-party parliament approved a new authoritarian constitution that provided for a presidential regime with parliamentary trimmings and stressed the duties of its citizens rather more than their rights. Although the state committed itself to upholding freedom of conscience and of religion, there was no mention of freedom of speech, freedom of assembly and press freedom.

The new constitution had no practical consequences. A month after it came into force, Poland issued an ultimatum forcing the country to resume diplomatic relations and to recognize the existing border. In short, it had to renounce Vilnius and the surrounding area. Lithuania was not to enjoy the sort of parliamentary elections based on proportional representation for which the constitution provided.

Like the Lithuanians, the Letts were members of the family of Baltic nations, a family that including the Old Baltic Prussians who had either been eradicated or assimilated into the East Prussians. The Republic of Latvia that had been established in 1918/19 included Latgale, Courland and southern Livonia, areas that until the downfall of the tsars had been subjected to Russian rule. Latvia's northern neighbour, the Republic of Estonia, included the former Russian province of the same name and the four northern districts of Livonia. Estonian, like Finnish, belongs to the Finno-Ugric family of languages. Unlike Lithuania, which remained Catholic, Estonia, Livonia and Courland converted to Protestantism at the time of the Reformation, a change that found expression, not least in the fact that practically the entire population was able to read and write. The upper class was made up of German Balts, and almost all the larger estates were owned by members of the German Baltic nobility. By the end of the nineteenth century the term 'Baltic states' was used to describe Estonia, Livonia and Courland. After 1918, it covered Estonia and Latvia. Not until the 1930s was Lithuania included in this group of countries. The 'Baltic Entente' gained acceptance as a linguistic term after 12 September 1934, when Lithuania joined an alliance between Latvia and Estonia dating back to 1923.

The constitutions of Estonia (June 1920) and Latvia (February 1922) gave their respective parliaments more power than their governments. Estonia had no state president, the prime minister acting as head of state. In Latvia the president was elected by the country's parliament, or Saeima. He was also the commander in chief of the army and could issue emergency decrees but was unable to dissolve parliament. In both countries elections were contested according to the rules of proportional representation. And in Lithuania, all men and women had the right to vote. Initial fragmentation of the party system was followed by a concentration on three camps: a peasants' party, a bourgeois centre party and the Social Democrats. As in Latvia, the most powerful parties were the peasants' parties, who produced the two most important leaders of the interwar years: the Estonian prime minister and later president Konstantin Päts and the Latvian president and prime minister Kārlis Ulmanis. In Latvia the Communist Party was banned by way of a reaction to the civil war of 1920, while a similar ban was imposed in Estonia at the end of 1924 following the suppression of an attempted Communist putsch by Johan Laidoner, the hero of the struggle for liberation and the commander in chief of the Estonian troops.

Neither country was a pure nation state. The second-largest ethnic group was made up of Russians, with 10.6 per cent of the population in Latvia in 1935 and 8.2 per cent in Estonia in 1934. At this same period Germans made up 3.2 per cent of the population in Latvia and 1.5 per cent in Estonia. As we have already observed in the context of the treaties designed to protect national minorities, it was only in Estonia that the question of nationalities was solved in a way that was widely regarded as a model of its kind: this was the settlement of 1925, which gave non-Estonians complete cultural autonomy, assuming that they wanted to claim this right for themselves. Both the German and the Jewish minorities made use of it. Latvia, by contrast, pursued a policy of Latvianization, a policy that after 1930 led to increasing tensions with the region's German minority.

Estonia and Latvia were the only states in eastern central Europe that adopted a policy of radical agrarian reform. In both countries the major estates, which were mostly owned by German Balts, were expropriated, and some two-thirds of the arable land was distributed among new settlers from the peasant class, while forests and woodlands passed into state ownership. In Estonia the major landowners who took part in the scheme were given back around 3.6 per cent of their lands. In 1926 they received compensation amounting to around 3 per cent of its actual value. Later they were also allocated any remaining lands up to an area of fifty hectares. In Latvia there was no such compensation, although former landowners could retain up to fifty hectares of the lands that they had previously owned. Both states remained largely agrarian in character: in Estonia only around 17.4 per cent of the working population was employed in industry in 1930, while the equivalent figure for Latvia was 13.5 per cent.

Like most eastern central European states, Estonia and Latvia were affected by the world economic crisis, leading them to turn their backs on parliamentary democracy and establish authoritarian regimes. It was a process that took a far more radical turn in Latvia than in Estonia. In May 1934 Ulmanis mounted a coup that excluded the extreme right and the extreme left from politics. The constitution was rescinded, the activities of parliament and parliamentary parties suspended, a government formed that was made up of representatives of the more moderate parties and legislative authority was transferred to the executive. In April 1936 Ulmanis assumed the role of state president in addition to that of prime minister.

In Estonia the government sought to escape from the pressure exerted by a radical right-wing antiparliamentary movement called 'Vapsen', a band of freedom fighters inspired by Fascist models, especially that of the Finnish Lapua movement, about which we shall have more to say in due course. A plebiscite on the question of constitutional reform was initiated by Vapsen, 73 per cent of the population voting for a presidential regime in place of the existing parliamentary system, but it was the prime minister, Konstantin Päts, who most benefited from the constitutional changes that were introduced in 1933. He took over the new powers of head of state, ordered a state of emergency designed to prevent the appointment of a radical right-wing president, transferred the supreme command of the armed forces to Laidoner, who had stepped down as commander in chief in 1925, ordered the arrest of the leaders of Vapsen and postponed *sine die* both parliamentary elections and the appointment of a new president. The representative body agreed to the state of emergency, even the Social Democrats regarding a dictatorship under Päts as the lesser of two evils when compared to a Vapsen-led dictatorship. Parliament did not meet again after October 1934, and the parliamentary parties ceased their activities. From then on Päts ruled by means of decrees. Vapsen was banned in 1935 after the discovery of plans to mount a putsch.

Päts organized a referendum in February 1936 that confirmed him in his existing course of action. A new constitution was passed by a Constituent National Assembly in August 1937 and ushered in a system with a powerful president and a two-chamber national assembly: a chamber of deputies elected according to the first-past-the-post system and a national council made up of elected and appointed members. In April 1938 Päts was elected president of the republic. The 'controlled dictatorship' that he practised differed on the one hand from the unstable parliamentary system that had prevailed between 1919 and 1933, when governments had remained in office for an average of less than nine months, and the authoritarian dictatorship of 1934–5. By the eve of the outbreak of the Second World War, Estonia was, therefore, by far the most liberal of the three Baltic republics of Latvia, Lithuania and Estonia.

On the other side of the Gulf of Finland, too, the fate of parliamentary democracy hung in the balance more than once during the interwar years. Until well into the 1930s Finland had to contend on more than one occasion with the threat of a violent overthrow of the government by the radical right, while the Finnish Communist Party that had been established in Russia in August 1918 but which was banned from the very outset repeatedly tried to enlist the help of the masses in fomenting a second Red revolution, an aim it sought to achieve by means of cover organizations and by deliberately targeting the country's trade unions. Under the leadership of Väinö Tanner, conversely, the Social Democrats turned their backs on the radicalism of the civil war and espoused a reformist agenda typical of the other Scandinavian workers' parties. It was a move that was a necessary precondition of their parliamentary cooperation with the moderate bourgeois and peasants' parties to which the country owed a whole series of laws designed to protect workers' rights, as well as a law requiring pupils to attend school for six years and the land reforms of 1922, carried out at the expense of the larger Finnish and Swedish landowners. In 1926–7 Tanner was appointed the country's prime minister, heading a Social Democrat minority government that was at the mercy of the Swedish People's Party and that survived for barely a year.

The governments of the liberal prime minister Kaarlo Ståhlberg, who remained in office from 1919 to 1925, and his successor Lauri Kristian Relander of the Agrarian Union, who was prime minister from 1925 to 1931, were almost all minority governments, and all were subjected to tremendous pressure by the state-supported, largely right-wing and virulently anti-Communist Civil Guard, an organization set up during the civil war with the aim of defending the country and claiming almost 100,000 members in 1919. It was at the bidding of this organization that Kyösti Kallio's government took particularly harsh reprisals against the Communist-backed Finnish Workers' Party in

August 1923, when the party's twenty-seven parliamentarians and several party officials were arrested and sentenced to lengthy terms of imprisonment for planning acts of high treason. The party itself was disbanded.

The ban caused the Communists no more than a temporary setback, for a new cover organization, the Socialist Electoral Organization of Workers and Smallholders, first entered parliament in 1927 and again, this time with a marked increase in its representation, in 1929. Within the trade unions, the Communists had already gained a majority by 1920. An eight-month dock strike in 1927–8 led to new and even more draconian measures on the part of the state: most of the leaders of the banned Communist Party were arrested in April 1928 and, accused of fomenting treason, sentenced to forced labour in the Tammisaari Prison Camp. A year later, in May 1929, the Social Democrats walked out of the management committees of the Finnish trade unions and founded the new Central Association of Finnish Trade Unions. The left-wing association that had in the meantime severed its links with the Communist Party was banned by a court order in July 1930. The Communists regrouped as part of the banned Red Trade Union that had been founded in 1929, but in spite of this, they were unable to persuade the masses to join them in their public demonstrations.

During the first ten years of Finnish independence the right-wing threat was embodied by the Civil Guard whose members were for the most part made up of peasants but which also recruited civil servants and white-collar workers. The Civil Guard was particularly vocal in its criticism of the policies of the country's foreign minister, Rudolf Holsti, who was keen to promote closer cooperation not only with the Baltic States but also with Poland and the Western Powers. Ståhlberg responded by dismissing the Civil Guard's commander in chief, Colonel Georg Didrik von Essen, in the summer of 1921, but when the Civil Guard proposed General Carl Gustav Mannerheim as Essen's successor, the minister of war, Bruno Jalander, emphatically rejected the idea. In order to pre-empt a possible coup by the political right, Per Evind Svinhufvud, the country's former regent, sought to mediate, and his compromise solution was finally accepted in September 1921: Jalander resigned, the Civil Guard was given greater powers of self-administration, and Lauri Malmberg, a colonel in the country's air force, was appointed its commander in chief, a post he held until the Civil Guard was disbanded in 1944.

On 14 February 1922, the country's minister of the interior, Heikki Ritavuori, was assassinated by right-wing radicals after he had become the target of Finnish nationalists critical of what they saw as his unduly lenient attitude to Soviet Russia. Behind his murder lay the crisis in Eastern Karelia, where an uprising against Soviet encroachment on this largely Finnish-speaking region had begun in 1921, encountering widespread support in Finland and leading to a movement advocating the annexation of Eastern Karelia and even the deployment of Finnish volunteers across the border with

Soviet Russia. The conflict was settled, but only superficially, when a peace treaty was signed with Russia in the summer of 1922.

The Eastern Karelia question also played a part in the power struggle within the Civil Guard that flared up in 1924 between the former tsarist officers who were regarded as conservative in their political outlook and the younger airforce officers who had been trained in Germany. The latter group enjoyed the support of Malmberg, who in 1924 also assumed the defence minister's portfolio. The armed forces' commander in chief, Major General Karl Fredrik Wilkman, was initially required to spend a lengthy period of study abroad before being dismissed by Relander in May 1926. He was replaced by the thirty-six-year-old air force major Aarne Sihvo, whose appointment represented a clear victory of the younger and more radical camp over its more moderate elders.

Founded in 1922, the Academic Karelia Society ensured that the question of Eastern Karelia and the idea of a Finnish linguistic community were not forgotten. Indeed, it was not long before the society had enlisted the support of the vast majority of Finnish-speaking students. The champions of such a union also included Russian-owned Ingria, the Norwegian Finnmark and the Swedish Västerbotten in their new pan-Finnish culture group. After 1924 the group's efforts were concentrated entirely on eradicating the Swedish language from Finnish culture. (Around 11 per cent of the Finnish population spoke Swedish, a figure that rose to 25 per cent among students at the University of Helsinki and 50 per cent among its teaching staff.) A new law was passed in 1922 that aimed to respect the demands of the moderate representatives of the linguistic minority and which specified the extent to which Swedish could be used in dealing with the authorities and the courts as well as on a communal level. At the insistence of the Academic Karelia Society, a draft law relating to the formal organization of the University of Helsinki was changed so that in future only a small percentage of its teachers could conduct their courses in Swedish. The ultimate aim of the 'authentic Finnish' movement, with the Academic Karelia Society as its hard core, was a monolingual Finland, but at this date in its history it was an aim that was still far from having been achieved.

In terms of its economy, the Finland of the interwar period was still largely an agrarian country: in 1920 75 per cent of the working population was employed in agriculture, and even as late as 1940 that figure still stood at 63 per cent, with the result that the agricultural crisis that affected the whole world in the late 1920s had a particularly devastating impact on Finland, temporarily eclipsing the language question, especially in the countryside, and resulting in a series of political and social conflicts between 'White' and 'Red' Finns. In November 1929, at a commemorative event held by the Communist Youth Association in the Ostrobothnian town of Lapua, the red shirts worn by the participants were torn from their backs by enraged nationalists, marking the start of the Lapua Movement which, largely supported by the peasant population, was very soon radicalized. By December 1929 it was already demanding that Kyösti Kallio's government take legal steps to combat the Communists and all other organizations that they felt had violated the law and offended against common decency.

Parliament met most of these demands in January 1930, although the limits on press freedom that the Lapua Movement had demanded were rejected, prompting radical right-wing activists to respond by destroying the printing presses of a left-wing socialist newspaper in Vaasa. The next step was the abduction of hundreds of politicians, officials and supporters of the radical left, who were taken to the border with the Soviet Union and told to cross over it in order to return to their ostensible political homeland. Three of these abductions during the summer of 1930 ended with the victim's death. The trials of the perpetrators were taken to the most absurd lengths when hundreds of Lapua members pleaded guilty.

Kallio's cabinet shied away from any vigorous intervention as it feared that the Civil Guard would close ranks with the supporters of the Lapua Movement. The government was able to avoid a threatened putsch by the extreme right only by means of a concession negotiated by Svinhufvud, a concession amounting to a promise to ban all Communist organizations once and for all. After passing a new law designed to protect the Republic, Kallio's third cabinet resigned on 2 July 1930, when Relander appointed Svinhufvud his new prime minister. No sooner had the new cabinet been formed when two deputies from the Socialist Workers' and Smallholders' Party were abducted at a meeting of the constitutional committee. The government was able to obtain their release only by agreeing to arrest all the Communist deputies.

But parliament was unwilling to follow the government down its confrontational road, and so Relander dissolved the house and ordered new elections for 1 and 2 October 1930. The real winners proved to be the right-wing coalition party. The Social Democrats were able to win a few more seats, but they could not prevent the government camp from obtaining the two-thirds majority needed to change the constitution. Once the anti-Communist laws had been passed, the Lapua Movement abandoned its plans to stage a putsch, which it had intended to set in motion if the laws were not approved.

The autumn of 1930 marked the culmination of the threats posed to Finland's democratic institutions by the Lapua Movement. When its supporters abducted the country's former president, Kaarlo Ståhlberg, and his wife in October 1930, thereby violating a directive issued by the movement's leaders, public opinion turned decisively against these representatives of Finnish Fascism. The narrow victory that Svinhufvud won in the presidential election on 1 March 1931 – 151 votes for him and 149 for Ståhlberg – robbed the Lapua Movement of many of its targets. Svinhufvud entrusted Mannerheim with the task of chairing the reorganized defence council. And in September 1931 a new attempt to overthrow the government by the Lapua Movement was crushed by legal means, means that parliament had been obliged to agree to under pressure from the extreme right. Since most members of the Civil Guard remained loyal to the government, the minister of the interior was finally able to disband the Lapua Movement in March 1932.

The Lapua Movement was succeeded by the Patriotic People's Movement, which promised to operate within the framework of the law. It adopted the forms of combat and symbols associated with the Italian Fascists and German National Socialists, including black shirts and blue ties. Its Youth Movement even took over the typical 'Hitler greeting'. The Patriotic People's Movement won fourteen seats in the elections in July 1933, while the coalition slumped from forty-two seats to eighteen. It was the Social Democrats, however, who proved most successful, returning seventy-eight members to parliament, an increase of twelve over their previous total. In April 1934 parliament banned the wearing of all uniforms. Shortly afterwards, the language question flared up once again. A draft bill designed to reorganize the University of Helsinki was obstructed by supporters of the movement for an 'authentic Finland'. In 1937 a federal law finally made Finnish the official language for teaching at the University of Helsinki, although Swedish continued to remain the language spoken by most of the country's educated upper-middle classes.

In February 1936, the prime minister, Toivo Kivimäki, who had been in power since 1932, lost the support of the Swedish People's Party and with it his parliamentary majority. The victors in the elections in July 1936 were once again the Social Democrats, who now had eighty-three seats in parliament. Väinö Tanner's party declared its willingness to return to government for the first time since 1927, but Svinhufvud turned down its approach and appointed Kyösti Kallio of the Agrarian Union to the post of prime minister, the fourth time that he had held the appointment. On 1 March 1937, with the backing of the Social Democrats, Kallio was elected the country's new president, thereby overcoming the one remaining obstacle that lay in the way of a coalition government made up of Social Democrats, Agrarian Unionists and the Progressive Party. It was the small National Progressive Party that provided the prime minister for this broadest alliance since the country's independence in the person of Aimo Cajander; the Social Democrat Väinö Tanner became finance minister, and Rudolf Holsti of the Progressive Party again became foreign minister. With the agreement of the cabinet, the minister of the interior, Urho Kekkonen of the Agrarian Union, banned the Patriotic People's Movement's youth brigade in May 1938, whereas an attempt to ban the radically right-wing parent organization the following November was frustrated by the Helsinki District Court.

The agreement between the Social Democrats and the Agrarian Union was the most important factor in the stabilization of the democratic system, while the country's gradual economic recovery also played its part in preventing the Patriotic People's Movement from making any further electoral gains and in avoiding the danger of a right-wing coup. By the middle of the 1930s Finland was drawing visibly closer to the level of development found in the other Nordic democracies, with which it shared not only linguistic ties but also denominational links in the form of its Protestant faith and, finally, its high level of literacy. Changes which, thanks in no small part to the Social Democrats, had already been implemented in Denmark, Sweden and Norway were now introduced on an even greater scale in Finland, laying the foundations for a welfare state that was emphatically northern European in character.

In terms of their foreign policies, too, the Nordic democracies drew closer together. Finland and Sweden had long argued not only over the language question but also over the sovereignty of the Åland Islands, whose Swedish population wanted to be Swedish. But they remained Finnish with the agreement of the League of Nations, which imposed certain conditions on its consent, including a ban on the building of fortifications. In the autumn of 1933 Finland, Sweden, Denmark, Norway, Belgium and Luxembourg formed the Oslo States, which agreed to work together closely in matters of customs and trade. Finland first attended a ministerial meeting of the Scandinavian states in 1934, and the following year Kivimäki's government agreed to closer cooperation with the Scandinavian states in the interests of security and joint neutrality, a move that was a reaction to the threat of a major new war in Europe.

Relations with the Soviet Union remained complex. In January 1932 Finland signed a non-aggression pact with Moscow – Estonia and Latvia followed suit later that same year – but in the summer of 1935 a campaign aimed at Finnish nationalists began in Soviet Karelia, finally involving most of the leaders of the illegal Finnish Communist Party who were living in the Soviet Union. The few Finnish Communists to survive Stalin's terror were those locked up in Finnish prisons. According to later estimates, 20,000 Finns died in Stalinist labour camps in the infamous Gulag Archipelago. Pan-Finnish propaganda played into the hands of Moscow, allowing it to accuse Finland of wanting to annex Eastern Karelia and Ingria. Conversely, Finland felt threatened by the construction of strategically important railway lines in Eastern Karelia. As long as the conservative forces under Svinhufvud remained in control in Finland, Hitler's Germany was regarded as by far the lesser of two evils when compared with Stalin's Russia. And yet even after the Social Democrats had returned to government, fear of Moscow and international Communism was still powerful enough to discourage Finland from adopting any kind of anti-German stance.

Unlike Finland, Czechoslovakia suffered no internal crises in the twenty years between 1918 and 1938, certainly none that posed a serious risk to the country's parliamentary system. The Republic of Czechoslovakia was the most heavily industrialized, most middle-class, most politically stable and, in this sense, the most 'western' of the new states of eastern central Europe. And, like France, it was also the most secularized of those European states that had previously been staunchly Catholic. The constitution of 29 February 1920 described the country in words that echoed the famous French formula of a 'nation une et indivisible', only the former Hungarian territory of Podkarpatská Rus enjoying a special status with at least a nominal degree of self-rule and its own governor. The country's legislative power lay with its House of Representatives, which was elected by all adult men and women for a period of six years on the basis of proportional representation, and also with its Senate, whose members were likewise elected by the population at large, although in this case they remained in office for eight years. The president was elected by both houses for a seven-year period and enjoyed a right of veto over laws adopted by both chambers. The government was answerable to the House of Representatives and could be forced to resign by a vote of no confidence.

Under the terms of a law enacted at the same time as the constitution, the official language was Czechoslovak, which in fact was made up of two closely related languages, Czech and Slovak. Other linguistic groupings were allowed to use their own languages in dealing with the authorities, including the courts, and to establish their own schools if their language was spoken by at least 20 per cent of the population in a particular juridical district when measured by the latest census. In 1921 the Czechs and Slovaks together numbered 8.8 million and made up 64.35 per cent of the country's population, followed by the Germans with 22.94 per cent (3.1 million), the Hungarians with 3.38 per cent (745,000), the Carpathian Ukrainians with 3.4 per cent (461,000), the Jews with 1.32 per cent (180,000) and 'Poles and others' with 0.75 per cent (102,000).

Proportional representation favoured a large number of different parties. On the Czechoslovak side there were two right-of-centre parties, the National Democrats and the Agrarians; two socialist parties, namely, the Social Democrats and the largely petty-bourgeois National Socialists; and the Catholic People's Party as the classic centre party. It was these five parties – known as the *pětka* – that helped to found the new state and, more often than not, provided the government of the day. In Slovakia there were two additional parties: the Catholic Slovak People's Party and the Slovak National Party which, its extreme right-wing views notwithstanding, remained insignificant as a political force. The main parties in the Sudetenland were the Social Democrats, the Farmers' Union and the Christian Socialists. Ideologically speaking, all were far too divided to be able to form a unified bloc. The Hungarians who were living in Slovakia formed a Social Democrat Party and a Christian Socialist Party. The only party whose interests remained consistently supranational was the Communist Party that had been founded in Russia in 1918: its most active members were Czechs and Germans. In the country's first elections in 1920, it fielded no candidates but was represented in parliament by members who defected from the left wing of the Social Democrats. Its first representatives were returned in the country's second elections, which were held in 1925.

The two leading Czechoslovak politicians of the interwar years were Tomáš Masaryk, who was president from 1918 to 1935, and Edvard Beneš, who held the post of foreign minister continuously during the same period, succeeding Masaryk as president in 1935. Prague's cabinets were at no time either purely bourgeois or purely Social Democrat but coalition governments that transcended class distinctions. In the six years that followed the adoption of the constitution in 1920, there were several minority cabinets and others made up of civil servants, each of which remained in office for only a short period of time. In October 1926 Antonín Švehla of the Agrarian Party managed for the first time to persuade two bourgeois German parties, the Christian Socialists and the Farmers' Union, to join his cabinet. Four months later, concessions on the subject of greater autonomy allowed him to bring in the Slovak People's Party, too.

As early as 1920 – far sooner than was to be the case with the German bourgeois parties – the German Social Democrats had declared their willingness to work more closely with the government of the day, but it was not until the end of 1929 that they first had a place at the cabinet table, when their chairman Ludwig Czech was appointed minister for welfare in František Udržal's second term of office. Udržal was a member of the Peasants' Party. Land reform had been agreed in 1921 without the participation of the German parties but, in contrast to what happened in Poland, it did not place an unduly heavy and one-sided burden on the major landowners of a national minority – in this case the Germans and the Hungarians. Administrative reforms undertaken in 1927–8, conversely, proved something of a disappointment for the Germans living in the Sudetenland, for the amalgamation of Moravia with what had been the Austrian half of Silesia meant that it was no longer possible to create a Silesia in whose national assembly Germans and Poles would presumably have had a majority. In general the Sudeten Germans were far better integrated into the Czechoslovak state in the late 1920s than either the Hungarians or the Poles.

The greatest danger to national cohesion was posed by the proponents of Slovak autonomy in the form of the Slovak People's Party centred on a Catholic priest by the name of Andrej Hlinka. The party won twelve seats in the new republic's first parliamentary elections in April 1920, doubling that number five years later and becoming de facto leader of all the Slovak parties. Relations with the government in Prague broke down over the trial of Vojtěch Tuka, a Slovak member of parliament who founded the Rodobrana, a Slovak defence league that called into question the whole idea of a common state embracing Czechs and Slovaks. In October 1929 he was accused of treason and sentenced to fifteen years' imprisonment, a sentence that triggered violent protests in Slovakia and prompted the Slovak People's Party to resign from the government and pursue an aggressive policy of opposition. Hlinka now demanded cultural and political autonomy and as a result came to be seen as a separatist.

The Sudetenland was particularly dependent on processing industries and was severely affected by the world economic crisis, leading in turn to a radicalization of political views in the region. The most right-wing group was the German National Socialist Workers' Party, or DNSAP. Originally founded in 1904 as the German Workers' Party, it won eight out of sixty-six seats in the Prague House of Representatives in the 1929 elections and soon gained increasing support from voters disenchanted with the other German parties that were in principle willing to work with the government of the day. When they began to build up a paramilitary organization modelled on Hitler's Storm Troopers, they were taken to court. A ban on the party seemed inevitable, but the DNSAP pre-empted the ban by disbanding in the autumn of 1933 and regrouping on 1 October 1933 as the Sudeten German Home Front under the gymnastics teacher and leader of the Sudeten German Gymnasts' Organization, Konrad Henlein.

Nothing gave such a boost to the new organization as the Third Reich's alleged or real successes in its attempts to combat mass unemployment, successes that were abundantly exploited for the purposes of propaganda. In the parliamentary elections in May 1935, Henlein's Sudeten German Party, as it came to be officially known in late April 1935, won forty-four seats: two-thirds of all the German seats. For the present, it proposed regional autonomy for the Sudetenland, rather than devolution and annexation by Germany. In total, the groups that for various reasons rejected the whole idea of the Czechoslovak state or sought to reorganize it in a spirit of national autonomy made up more than a third of all the members of parliament in Prague: in addition to the forty-four campaigning for German autonomy, there were twenty-two in favour of Slovak independence, nine Hungarian nationalists, six who belonged to the Czech Fascist Party led by the former chief of the general staff Radola Gajda, and thirty Communists, who since 1929 were led by a self-declared Stalinist, Klement Gottwald, who was to become prime minister from 1946 to 1948 and state president from 1948 to 1953. When threatened by arrest in 1938, he fled to the Soviet Union. The growth of left- and right-wing opposition groups may have been the sign of an impending crisis, but it did not prevent the formation of a majority government. Even after 1935 the 'activist' German parties had at least two ministers with cabinet portfolios.

In respect of its foreign policy, Czechoslovakia enjoyed particularly close ties with France, forming a regular alliance with the country in January 1924. Within the 'Little Entente' – the system of treaties linking Czechoslovakia, Yugoslavia and Romania and signed in 1920–21 – Prague enjoyed the role of first among equals, a privileged status that became even more important in the context of the greater political, military and economic cooperation that began in 1929 and culminated in February 1933 with an organizational pact under a permanent council made up of the region's foreign ministers, with a permanent secretariat and a joint economic council. Relations with revisionist Hungary remained tense, and much the same was true of Poland, albeit on a smaller scale, the two countries remaining at loggerheads over Teschen. A bilateral agreement in April 1925 provided only a superficial solution to the conflict.

Under the terms of the Treaty of Versailles Germany had had to cede the tiny region of Hultschin (Hlučín) to Czechoslovakia. In spite of this, relations between the two countries improved to such an extent during the years of the Weimar Republic that they could almost be described as good, but following the National Socialists' seizure of power in January 1933, the situation inevitably took a turn for the worse, the feeling that Germany posed a threat leading to a rapprochement with Soviet Russia: the two countries established diplomatic relations in June 1934 and signed a mutual assistance pact in May 1935 that was, however, tied to the condition that France, too, would provide simultaneous military support.

When the eighty-five-year-old Tomáš Masaryk stepped down as president in December 1935 and was replaced by Edvard Beneš, Czechoslovakia's position both internally and on the world stage was far less secure than it had been even five years previously. And yet, when compared with the other new states in eastern central and south-eastern Europe, Czechoslovakia still seemed to be a paragon of democratic stability. The wave of authoritarian transformations that swept across the region, affecting countries even as far away as Finland, was prevented from doing any real damage in the most highly developed of these new states by the well-established political practice of pragmatic cooperation between the Social Democrats on the one hand and the bourgeois and agrarian forces on the other, a situation that sheds important light on the close connection between social backwardness and an authoritarian solution to the crises that beset the countries in question.

Authoritarian Transformation (II): From the Balkans to the Iberian Peninsula

It was not only most of the new states of *Zwischeneuropa* that underwent an authoritarian transformation during the interwar years but also many that had existed before 1914, including the Balkan states that had achieved independence in the nineteenth or, in the case of Albania in the early twentieth, century, and the two countries that made up the Iberian peninsula, both of which were among the older states of the Catholic West. (The Balkan states, conversely, were either Orthodox in their denominational orientation or, in the case of Albania, Muslim.)

Romania, Czechoslovakia's partner in the 'Little Entente' and, from a strictly geographical point of view, not a part of the Balkans, came to play an increasingly prominent role in the interwar years in spite of its defeat in the struggle with the Central Powers. In April 1918, shortly before the humiliating Treaty of Bucharest, it had annexed Bessarabia. Thanks to the victory of the Western Powers, it soon acquired extensive territories in what had been Hungary, including Transylvania and, following a violent struggle with Serbia, two-thirds of the Banat. With a population of almost sixteen million, the new Romania was a multiracial state. According to pre-war census returns, only two-thirds of the population were ethnic Romanians. The largest minority was the Magyars, who made up 12 per cent of the population. Between 1914 and 1930 the emigration of non-ethnic Romanians helped to tip the balance further in favour of the titular nation, ethnic Romanians now making up some 72 per cent of the population, while the Magyar minority was reduced to 8 per cent, the German minority to a little over 4 per cent. It was the Magyars who called into question the very foundations of the new state by demanding annexation by Hungary, while the Bulgars of Dobrudja sought unification with Bulgaria. Only the Germans living in Transylvania regarded themselves as loyal citizens of Romania.

The constitution of 1866 provided the basis of the country's whole legal system until 1923, defining Romania as a constitutional monarchy. The new constitution came into force on 29 March 1923 and left things as they were. Under both constitutions, elections almost always led to the victory of the party whose prime minister was appointed by the king. After 1923, only men over the age of twenty-one were entitled and, indeed, obliged to vote in spite of the continuing high level of illiteracy. The electoral law of 27 March 1925 ensured that the party that received at least 40 per cent of the votes cast was automatically given at least 70 per cent of the seats in parliament. As a rule the influence exerted by the government of the day on the outcome of the elections was practically unchecked, so that the term 'parliamentary democracy' cannot really be applied to the Romania of the interwar years.

King Ferdinand I of Hohenzollern-Sigmaringen died on 20 July 1927 after a reign of thirteen years. Crown Prince Carol had already renounced his claim to the throne following an extramarital affair with Magda Lupescu, the Jewish wife of a Romanian army officer, with the result that it was Carol's younger brother, the fifteen-year-old Prince Michael, who succeeded Ferdinand, his powers initially assumed by a regency council. In June 1920 Carol temporarily renounced his affair with Magda Lupescu and was declared king by the National Assembly.

One of the most pressing domestic problems that required a solution was the agrarian question, and nowhere more so than in the Regat, the old kingdom where 5 per cent of landowners owned more than 60 per cent of the land. Several laws containing different regulations for different regions led to a redistribution of the land, resulting in the loss of most of the larger estates, which were divided up and apportioned to farmers and smallholders. Even so, the result was unsatisfactory, for the overwhelming majority of farmers – almost 85 per cent – each had less than five hectares of agricultural land to cultivate.

Most farms were reduced to subsistence level, with only a small minority capable of producing enough produce for export. Following the introduction of the relevant acts in 1918 and 1921, agricultural exports declined dramatically in quantity.

In the elections of December 1928, which, exceptionally, were free from official interference, the National Peasants' Party under Iuliu Maniu emerged as the front runner, but Maniu's failure to deal with the repercussions of the serious agrarian crisis meant that he forfeited the sympathies of the farming community and he was stripped of his powers as prime minster following Carol II's accession. He resigned in October 1930. The elections of June 1931 were rigged from above like most of those that had been held before 1928. The National Peasants' Party suffered a serious defeat.

Maniu returned briefly to power as prime minister in October 1932. During 1933 several governments succeeded one another in quick succession, but none was able to provide a lasting solution to the country's deepening economic crisis. In November 1933 the king appointed the leader of the National Liberals, Ion Duca, as the new prime minister. Duca was murdered six weeks later, on 29 December, by members of the Iron Guard, an extreme right-wing, virulently anti-Semitic militant organization. He was by no means the first victim of this Romanian Fascist organization, whose insignia included a blue, yellow and red ribbon with a swastika: in October 1924, the organization's founder and leader, Corneliu Zelea Codreanu, had shot the chief of police, Constantin Manciu. Codreanu was the son of a Polish father called Zelinski and a German mother. His crime went unpunished, his judges evincing a show of blatant solidarity and acquitting him of all charges.

Duca was succeeded by Gheorgiu Tătărescu, who remained in office until 1937, bringing a degree of financial and economic stability to the country. The Iron Guard, which had originally been called the Legion of St Michael, was banned, only for it to reconstitute itself as All for the Country, which won 16 per cent of the votes cast in the elections in December 1937. No party won more than 40 per cent of the vote in this election and so none was able to form a majority government, prompting Carol to appoint a prime minister of his own choosing. He chose the poet and rabid anti-Semite Octavian Goga, the leader of the Christian Nationalists, which had won 9 per cent of the votes. But Goga was unable to form a parliamentary majority, and so the king dissolved parliament and, emulating the actions of Alexander I in Yugoslavia in 1929, established a monarchical dictatorship. He convened a cabinet of resolutely nationalist hue under the patriarch Myron Cristea, suspended the constitution and banned all political parties. A rigged plebiscite gave the king's putsch a semblance of legitimacy, and a new constitution dated 27 February 1938 allowed the authoritarian regime to wear a fig leaf of legality. The illegal Iron Guard that had perpetrated numerous acts of terror was once again persecuted, its leader, Codreanu, arrested and, on the king's instructions, 'shot while trying to escape' in late November 1938. In other words, he was murdered. The following year the minister of the interior, Armand Calinescu, who had been one of the implacable enemies of the Iron Guard, was assassinated by Codreanu's followers.

As we have already noted, Romania, Czechoslovakia and Yugoslavia had formed the Little Entente in 1921, the same year as Romania concluded an alliance with Poland. Five years later alliances and friendship treaties were signed with France, Italy and, again, Poland. Relations with Germany improved once the National Socialists had come to power, the Third Reich being particularly interested in importing agricultural produce and petroleum from Romania, while at the same time making south-eastern Europe in general, including Romania, dependent on German exports.

Carol II also sought to consolidate his political alliance with France by way of countering the increased economic cooperation between his country and Germany. Related to this policy was the Balkan pact that Tătărescu's government signed with Turkey, Greece and Yugoslavia in February 1934. Later that same year – after Moscow had recognized Bucharest's sovereignty over Bessarabia – Romania also established diplomatic relations with the Soviet Union, but it could not bring itself to sign a mutual assistance pact with Russia similar to the one that it had concluded with Czechoslovakia in May 1935: such a pact would have been regarded as too much of a challenge by National Socialist Germany and flown in the face of the anti-Communist sentiments harboured by large sections of the population. The radical anti-Semitic right may have been plunged into retreat by the royal dictatorship, but it remained a powerful social and political force that enjoyed considerable support among students, farmers and members of the petty bourgeoisie.

Romania's southern neighbour, Bulgaria, was the quintessential Balkan country: geographically, it belongs to the Balkan peninsula, while culturally it was marked by its Orthodox faith and by centuries of Ottoman rule. Unlike Greece, Albania and parts of Yugoslavia, it had not turned to embrace the Mediterranean world. An agricultural country, it suffered like all the Balkan states from its economic backwardness and from widespread illiteracy. Of the various problems raised by the question of nationality, that of Macedonia was the most serious. As we have already observed, the subversive activities of the terrorist Internal Macedonian Revolutionary Organization placed a severe strain on relations with Yugoslavia. In 1920 83.4 per cent of a population of 4.8 million were ethnic Bulgarians. The largest national minority – 11 per cent – was made up of Turks. An exchange of population was agreed with Greece in the context of the Treaty of Neuilly of November 1919, an exchange implemented in the course of the years that followed. Bulgaria was particularly pained by the loss of southern Dobrudja to Romania, a region largely settled by Bulgarians: ratified by the Treaty of Neuilly, this was one of the outcomes of the Second Balkan War of 1913.

Even after 1918 Bulgaria remained a constitutional monarchy under the terms of its constitution of 1879. From 1918 to 1943 the head of state was King Boris III of the house of Saxe-Coburg-Gotha. All men over the age of twenty-one were entitled to vote. In the years around 1920 four-fifths of the population still lived in the countryside, with the result that the peasants' movement played a significant role in the political life of Bulgaria, but here – unlike in Romania – the Communists were successful in winning the support of a considerable proportion of the rural population. Following the elections in August 1919 Boris appointed the leader of the regional Peasants' Party, Alexander Stamboliyski, to head a coalition government that also had the backing of the Social Democrats. The main opposition party was the Communist Party, which recorded extensive gains in the local elections in December 1919. Shortly afterwards they called a transport strike that lasted until February 1920, inflicting serious damage on the country's economy.

Made up entirely of members of the Peasants' Party, Stamboliyski's second cabinet took office in May 1920. One of its first legislative acts was the introduction of universal labour service in June 1920: men were required to work for twelve months, women for six. It was a move that the National Socialists were to introduce to Germany thirteen years later. Even more controversial were the agrarian reforms undertaken in May 1921, when all privately owned lands measuring more than thirty hectares were expropriated. Since Stamboliyski's policies were emphatically anti-urban, they met with increasing opposition in the towns and cities. But his enemies also included large sections of the officer corps, and from their ranks came the leaders of the putsch who in June 1923 toppled Stamboliyski's government with the king's approval. A proponent of greater ties with the Kingdom of Serbs, Croats and Slovenes, Stamboliyski himself was assassinated on 14 June by fanatical supporters of the Internal Macedonian Revolutionary Organization. His successor was Alexander Zankov, who taught economics at the University of Sofia and had no political affiliations.

The officers' putsch of June 1923 was followed in September 1923 by a Communist uprising led by the party's chairman, Georgi Dimitrov, and by the Secretary of the Bulgarian Communist Party's Central Committee, Vasil Kolarov, whom the Comintern had sent back to his Bulgarian homeland. The uprising was bloodily suppressed after only a few days, although Dimitrov, Kolarov and a number of leaders of the Peasants' Party who had taken part in the fighting were able to escape abroad. The elections of November 1923 resulted in a victory for the official government party, the Democratic Union, which enjoyed the support of the Social Democrats. The Democratic Union remained in power until 1931, allowing Bulgaria to enjoy a degree of internal stability that was little short of astonishing by Balkan standards.

And yet not even Bulgaria was spared a number of major upheavals, most of which were caused by the Communist Party. After fomenting further unrest, the party was banned in 1924 but remained active as an underground organization. A series of political assassinations was followed on 16 April 1925 by the bombing of St Sophia's Cathedral, an atrocity aimed at the ministers and officers assembled there, together with the king. Although Boris and the members of his government all escaped, there were more than 100 fatalities, including several generals and the mayor of Sofia, and over 300 injured. A state of emergency was declared and remained in force for the next six months. Following their act of terror, the Communists forfeited much of their previous popularity; the Peasants' Party distanced itself from the extreme left, and it took two years for a new Communist organization to replace its predecessor: the Independent Workers' Party was even able to take part in parliamentary elections.

In the elections in 1931, the opposition parties that had formed a National Bloc under the leadership of the Peasants' Party emerged as the victors in spite of the government's sustained and determined attempt to influence the electorate. But the internal divisions within the National Bloc were so deep that by May 1934 the government of the prime minister, Nikola Mushanov, had already lost its parliamentary majority. The dissolution of parliament was seized on by an anti-parliamentary alliance of army officers, intellectuals and politicians from the Peasants' Party that was known as 'Zveno' to mount a putsch on 19 May 1934. The new government under Colonel Kimon Georgiev proclaimed a state of emergency, declared sections of the 1879 constitution null and void and introduced a number of draconian measures designed to make financial savings. Its greatest efforts were directed at defeating the Internal Macedonian Revolutionary Organization, whose leader, Ivan Mihaylov, and a number of his comrades in arms managed to flee abroad, where they sought to revive the movement. Militant left-wing opposition was systematically suppressed by means of an emergency measure dated 31 August 1934.

Georgiev's government was no less internally divided than its predecessor, the National Bloc, had been, with committed monarchists and convinced republicans squaring up to each other. In January 1935, King Boris, who had merely tolerated the putsch of May 1934 rather than actually supporting it, actively interfered in events by removing Georgiev from his post as prime minister. His replacements changed frequently, on each occasion having to reshuffle their cabinets. In October 1937 Boris passed a new electoral law that reduced the size of parliament, introduced women's suffrage and allowed only individuals, not parties and other political organizations, to submit candidates. Voting in the elections of March 1938 was relatively free and fair and gave a safe majority to those candidates who were closest to the government and who won 104 seats as against the opposition's fifty-six. The authoritarian regime of Boris III that was established in 1935 undoubtedly amounted to a dictatorship, and yet it was the most liberal of the region's interwar regimes, at least when measured against Yugoslavia under Alexander I and Romania under Carol II.

In justifying their coup in May 1934, the officers who staged it argued that the country's political situation was so serious that they had been left with no alternative. They were referring to Bulgaria's political isolation as a result of the Balkan Pact signed by Turkey, Greece, Yugoslavia and Romania in February 1934, the anti-Bulgarian thrust of which was unmistakable. King Boris was particularly keen to reach an agreement with Yugoslavia, and in January 1937, after negotiations that had often proved extremely difficult, he signed a friendship treaty and a non-aggression pact with his neighbour, a goal that he had been pursuing for some considerable time. When coupled with the Balkan Pact that was concluded in Salonika in July 1938, a non-aggression treaty freed Bulgaria from the terms of the Treaty of Neuilly that had placed restrictions on its rearmament programme and enabled the country to station troops in the demilitarized zone on the border with Greece.

Like Romania, Bulgaria spent the 1930s building up its trade links with Germany, which had traditionally been the leading market for agricultural produce from the country. In turn, Bulgaria imported most of its industrial products from Germany. But Boris avoided any closer political ties with the Third Reich, a policy he was able to maintain even after the outbreak of the Second World War.

No Balkan country suffered as many violent upheavals and attempted coups during the interwar years as Greece. Turkish victories in the Graeco-Turkish War were followed by a period of revolutionary unrest in the early autumn of 1922 that swept the supporters of the former prime minister, Eleftherios Venizelos, back into power – Venizelos had already held the post from 1910 to 1915 and again from 1917 to 1920. King Constantine I was forced to abdicate on 27 September 1922 in favour of his son, George II. The new junta has gone down in the annals of Greek history thanks to a show trial that it held against five leading politicians from the toppled government and the last commander in chief of the Greek armed forces in Asia Minor: although there was no evidence to condemn them, all the accused were sentenced to death and executed in November 1922 in the face of international protests. The death of the country's legal system exacerbated the disastrous polarization between supporters and detractors of Venizelos, establishing a dichotomy that was to leave its mark on Greek politics for the next two decades.

In October 1923 sections of the military, angered by an electoral law that placed Venizelos's enemies at a disadvantage, mounted a putsch, but it was suppressed after only a few days. The anti-Venizelists did not take part in the elections to the Constituent National Assembly in December 1923. The Liberals and Republicans formed an electoral pact and following their victory they effectively forced George II to abdicate. In March 1924 the Constituent Assembly proclaimed a republic, a decision ratified by a plebiscite the following month. But in spite of a certain economic upturn between 1924 and 1926,

Greece failed to become the stable parliamentary democracy that it had aspired to be ever since its liberal constitution was enacted in 1863. General Theodoras Pangalos mounted a putsch in late June 1925 and, in spite of the promises that he had made to the government of Alexandros Papanastasiou of the Social Democrat Republican Union, he dissolved the National Assembly in September without calling new elections. Instead, he had himself elected the country's president in April 1926.

The period of Pangalos's dictatorship coincided with a serious political crisis on the international stage, when a border incident led Greece to occupy the demilitarized zone that lay close to the border with Bulgaria. The League of Nations forced Greece to withdraw at the end of October 1925 and to pay reparations. Greece's economic and financial problems grew dramatically worse under Pangalos, prompting General Georgios Kondylis to topple the regime in August 1926. Elections were held the following November and resulted in a victory for the republican parties. A new constitution – the third since 1925 – came into force on 2 July 1927, creating a two-chamber system comprising a legislative Chamber of Deputies (Boulé) and a Senate (Gerousía) whose members were made up for the most part of elected representatives, the rest consisting of members chosen jointly by the Chamber and by the Senate.

Venizelos returned to power in May 1928 after a grand coalition government made up of republican and moderate royalist parties foundered on economic and financial arguments. With this there began a four-year period of relative stability, when legal certainty grew not least as a result of the creation of a Supreme Administrative Court and Greece signed friendship treaties with Italy, Yugoslavia and Turkey. But internal tensions remained, and under the impact of the world economic crisis the Greek currency, the drachma, lost around three-quarters of its value. Venizelos considered strengthening the country's executive along the lines of the German presidential cabinets since 1930 but in the event he did nothing to get in the way of a democratic change of government in the parliamentary elections that were held in September 1932.

The winner in these elections was Panagis Tsaldaris's royalist People's Party, which formed a government with the help of the smaller republican parties, but his majority proved extremely precarious, persuading President Pavlos Kountouriotis to dissolve parliament five months later and call for new elections, which were now conducted according to the recently introduced system of proportional representation. The new elections were held on 5 March 1933 and saw the People's Party and two smaller right-wing parties win an outright majority, prompting the Venizelist general, Nikolaos Plastiras, to mount a coup the very next day. With little support from the officer corps, it was quickly suppressed. Under Tsaldaris's new government, tensions between the Venizelists and the anti-Venizelists continued to mount, and in March 1935 the supporters of Venizelos made one further attempt to stage a coup, only to fail as a result of lack of mass support and inadequate military preparations. Venizelos fled abroad and died in Paris in March 1936.

The Venizelists' failed putsch gave the anti-parliamentary and anti-republican forces in the government camp the incentive that they were waiting for. Although the moderate royalists won the parliamentary elections in June 1935, Tsaldaris was forced to step down by radical monarchist officers in the October of that year. He was replaced by General Georgios Kondylis, who also assumed the role of regent. Once the moderate majority of members representing the royalist People's Party had walked out of the Chamber, the latter proclaimed the restoration of the monarchy and a return to the constitution of 1911. A rigged plebiscite that was held in November 1935 produced a majority of almost 98 per cent in favour of a restoration of the monarchy and, hence, for a return to power of King George II.

On the other hand, the elections that were held in January 1936 were generally considered to be fair and free. The result was an approximate parity between Venizelists and anti-Venizelists, while the Communists, with their fifteen seats, held the balance of power. Since the military was unwilling to tolerate any government dependent on the Communists, George II, who returned to Greece from exile on 25 November 1935, took steps to restore discipline in the army by appointing Ionnis Metaxas minister for the army in March 1936. Metaxas, who was the leader of the Freethinkers' Party, succeeded the moderate Independent prime minister Konstantinos Demertzis on the latter's death in April 1936.

From the outset, Metaxas was determined to break completely with the parliamentary system. Strikes were put down by the police with extreme brutality, and in August 1936 he mounted a coup with the aim of introducing an authoritarian dictatorship modelled in many ways on that of Fascist Italy. Political parties were banned, newspapers and magazines subjected to censorship, and trade unions, associations and universities were purged of opposition forces. The newly established security services persecuted political opponents with unprecedented ruthlessness, relying in the process on an extensive network of spies. Paramilitary organizations, including a national youth brigade, and a radical and ideological nationalism completed the picture of a right-wing dictatorship whose hard core comprised the indoctrinated military. But, however much Metaxas may have drawn closer to the power structures and means of control of a Fascist regime, he took care not to become dependent on either Rome or Berlin, preferring, rather, to maintain good relations with the Western Powers.

The frequency with which putsches were mounted in Greece between 1922 and 1936 recalls the republics of Latin America. A deeper reason for the country's peculiar blend of parliamentary instability and authoritarian stability lay in the fundamentally reactionary attitude of the Orthodox Church, whose privileged status was demonstratively highlighted in the very first article of the

1927 constitution. Related to the influence of the Orthodox clergy was the low level of education: even as late as 1928, 23 per cent of the male population and 58 per cent of the female population were unable to read or write. Between 1920 and 1928 the proportion of the population working in agriculture, forestry and fishing rose from 58 per cent to 61 per cent. Many of the tiny farms were unprofitable and prevented the economy from growing. A handful of families set the tone, in every case tending to serve the interests of their own particular clientele.

Although Metaxas's regime brought the country a handful of social improvements such minimum wages, a shorter working week and national insurance, it is impossible to describe it as a modernizing dictatorship: even after 1936, Greece not only remained socially backward but was still dominated by profoundly hostile camps, by a politicized military and by widespread corruption.

The foregoing comments apply even more to Albania than to Greece. Here political developments during the interwar years were a permanent reflection of a backward society. Even as recently as 1945 80 per cent of the population was illiterate. In the years around 1918 the country had been almost exclusively agricultural in character as well as being the only predominantly Islamic state in Europe. Around 70 per cent of the population was Muslim, 20 per cent was Greek Orthodox and 10 per cent was Catholic Christians. The higher echelons of Albanian society were made up of Muslim landowners, or beys, from whom the leading families recruited their members; the vast bulk of the population was made up of farmers and shepherds who were nominally free but economically dependent on the families of the leading landowners. Tirana was declared the country's capital in 1920, when it had a population of 15,000, compared with under a million Albanians in the country as a whole. Albania had gained its independence in 1912 in the wake of the First Balkan War. During the First World War the south of the country was occupied by Greek, Italian and French troops, the north by Serbs and, later, Austro-Hungarian forces. After the departure of the latter, units of the South Slav army repossessed the region.

After 1918, Albania's borders and, indeed, its whole survival as a country were jeopardized by claims raised by two neighbouring states, Greece and the newly formed Kingdom of Serbs, Croats and Slovenes, as well as by Italy, which regarded Albania as a future protectorate and occupied Valona (Vlorë) as a security, only to have to abandon this bastion in the wake of fierce fighting in the summer of 1920. Rome recognized the integrity and independence of Albania on 2 August 1920 and agreed to withdraw all its troops from the region. As a result, Albania was now free, the only exceptions being a small number of border areas occupied by Greek and South Slav units. It became a member of the League of Nations in December 1920.

During the months leading up to this moment, the governments of Suleiman Bey Delvina and, after November, of Elias Bey Vrioni had extended their authority over the whole of Albania from their centre of operations in Tirana. The parliament that was elected in April 1921 on the basis of equal, but indirect, male suffrage was made up of two parties, the Progressive Party dominated by the country's major landowners and the slightly more left-wing People's Party. In October a new government under Pandel Evangheli was installed in an attempt to avert an uprising by the Catholic Mirdites. Its dominant figure was the minister of war, Ahmed Bey Zog, who put down the uprising both promptly and energetically. By December 1921 he was the minister for the interior in the new cabinet of Xhafer Ypi, in which capacity he overthrew a further uprising in the spring of 1922, this one directed at him personally. In December he became Albania's prime minister. Thanks to the decision taken at a conference of Allied ambassadors in September 1922, the country's borders were now clearly demarcated: essentially they were the ones that had existed in 1913; the Kingdom of the South Slavs and Greece both had to withdraw their troops from Albanian soil.

Inseparable from Albania's political climate were the political murders which, in keeping with the tradition of blood vengeance, were perpetrated by members of the rival clans. An attempt on the life of Ahmed Bey Zog in February 1924 in which he was merely wounded was followed in April by a fatal attack on a member of parliament, Avni Rustem, which was ordered by Zog himself. It triggered a further uprising that on this occasion affected the whole country and ended with the rebels marching into the capital, forcing Zog, who had already stepped down as prime minister, to flee to the neighbouring Kingdom of Serbs, Croats and Slovenes.

From there Zog headed a force which, armed by Yugoslavia, regained power in Tirana in December 1924. In the middle of January 1925 he persuaded the rump parliament to appoint him prime minister and commander in chief of the Albanian armed forces, and on 22 January parliament proclaimed the new republic, thereby clarifying the as yet unresolved question of the type of state that Albania was to become. On 31 January Zog had himself appointed president for a seven-year period and passed a constitution that granted the head of state extraordinarily wide-ranging powers.

This marked the beginning of a fourteen-year dictatorship whose hallmarks were not only an outspoken nationalism but also political assassinations that Zog personally ordered. Economically speaking, he sought to strengthen his country's standing by granting concessions to Italian and Anglo-Persian oil companies; and in terms of his foreign policy he relied increasingly on Italy in an attempt to avoid undue dependence on his South Slav neighbour. In 1926 and 1927 he concluded two Tirana Pacts, the second of which committed both signatories to defend one another in the event of an invasion by a third party, although the military weakness of Zog's Albanian militia meant that the treaty amounted to little more than an Italian obligation to protect the country on the eastern side of the Adriatic.

Zog dissolved both chambers of parliament in the summer of 1928 and replaced them with a Constituent Assembly that altered the 1925 constitution in such a way as to allow him to be elected king of Albania on 1 September 1928. The new constitution of 1 December 1928 defined Albania as a 'democratic, parliamentary and hereditary monarchy' which, like the Turkey of Mustafa Kemal Atatürk, adopted the statute books of other countries, including France's Code Civil and the penal code of Fascist Italy. The administration was reorganized along the lines of the centralized French state. The agrarian reforms of 1930 looked more radical on paper than they did in practice: individuals were not allowed to own more than forty hectares of private land, with a further fifteen hectares for the owner's wife and for each of his children. But landowners had to sell a third of their lands to the state-owned Agrarian Bank. If they agreed to modernization, they could retain the remaining land for a period of fifteen years.

Albania became increasingly dependent on Italian loans during the world economic crisis. Mussolini wanted a customs union in order to guarantee further loans, but Italy was unable to force through this measure in spite of a demonstration of its naval might off the coast at Durazzo – Albanian Durrës – in June 1934. On the other hand, it was able to impose conditions that represented a severe incursion on Albania's sovereignty. From 1935 the country was an economic protectorate of Fascist Italy, but other international factors were needed to ensure Albania's political subjugation, and these conditions were not to be created until the crisis that engulfed the whole Continent of Europe on the eve of the Second World War.

If there was any Western country which in the first quarter of the twentieth century repeatedly invited comparisons with a Balkan state, then it was Portugal. The revolution of 1910 may have turned the monarchy into a republic but it certainly did not lead to greater stability, and governments changed with a frequency seen nowhere else in Europe. Uprisings dignified with the name of 'revolutions', *coups d'état* and bombings were so frequent that they largely went unnoticed outside Portugal. In January 1915 the country experienced its first dictatorship under General Joaquim Pereira Pimento de Castro, but it lasted only until April, when it was toppled by a 'revolution' mounted by sections of the army and navy.

During the First World War Portugal initially remained neutral in spite of its traditionally close ties with Great Britain, not joining in the hostilities until 1916, when it sided with the Entente and sent some 100,000 soldiers to Flanders and the African colonies. The country's decision to go to war proved costly, with a total of 35,000 dead and injured combatants. Coupled with increasing food shortages, this led to violent unrest and, from the summer of 1917, to strikes backed by the anarcho-syndicalists. The Democratic Party government responded by declaring a state of emergency but failed to restore order. The general discontent persuaded a group of officers and civilians to mount a coup in December 1917. The leader of the conspirators was Sidónio Paes, a mathematics professor at the University of Coimbra and a former ambassador in Berlin. It was he who became the country's new prime minister.

Paes introduced universal suffrage for men, had himself elected president, founded his own National Republican Party and established a kind of presidential dictatorship sanctioned by a plebiscite. By suppressing rival parties and the trade unions, he won the backing not only of the Catholic Church but also of employers, landowners and the army. In December 1918 two attempts were made on his life. The first misfired, but in the second he was fatally shot.

However brief Paes's dictatorship may have been, it continued to reverberate for a long time afterwards as an early form of an interwar Fascist regime. Among the precursors of such a regime was the Portuguese Integralismo Lusitano, whose principal ideologue, António Sardinha, modelled his thinking on that of Charles Maurras and Action Française. Following the return to the constitution of 1911, similar views were promoted by the radically right-wing National Crusade that sought the abolition of parliamentary democracy and its replacement by an authoritarian regime. The existing order was opposed not only by integralists and nationalists but also by monarchists, who made several attempts to topple the regime. The republicans responded by calling for a people's militia. This internal unrest reached a bloody climax on the night of 19/20 October 1921.

In the eyes of many members of the property-owning classes, especially the major landowners and Catholic Church, the military seemed the most reliable antidote to the political chaos that was sweeping across the country. In April 1925 sections of the army that shared this view attempted a coup, but it was thwarted by a number of regiments and by the Republican National Guard. The military mounted a further putsch in May 1926, and this time it was successful: the government of the Democratic Party was toppled from power. The uprising had been led by General Gomes da Costa, a relatively unpolitical figure, who was replaced by General Antonio Carmona in July 1926. Carmona established a military dictatorship and in April 1928 had himself elected president, a post he retained until his death in 1951.

The biggest challenge facing the new regime was the task of restoring the country's finances, a task which in April 1928 was entrusted to Antonio de Oliveira Salazar, who taught economics at the University of Coimbra and whose policies proved so successful that he quickly came to be seen as the government's strong man, becoming prime minister in July 1932 and retaining the post for thirty-six years, until September 1968.

The new constitution of 19 March 1933 formally turned Portugal into a presidential regime in which the prime minister was responsible solely to the state president. In fact it was Salazar who as prime minister was the dominant figure. The country's elected representatives in the National Assembly owed their seats to a graduated and, therefore, unequal right to vote on the part of the electorate. The upper house was divided according to professional class, employers and employees being separately represented. A labour law of September 1933 banned strikes and lockouts. Other laws enacted in 1933 covered press censorship and placed limits on the freedom of assembly. Both laws contributed significantly to the fact that the elections always favoured the government. Like Austro-Fascism, Salazar's Estado Novo borrowed many of its concepts from the ideal of a Christian corporate state as promoted by Pius XI's encyclical *Quadragesimo anno* of 1931. The term 'clerical Fascism' came close to summing up the situation, while failing to take account of the fact that state and Church remained separate. Since the Church was not recognized as a person in law, there were repeated conflicts that were not resolved until the concordat of 1940.

If the government enjoyed the support of the masses, this was due above all to the official party, the União Nacional, which was founded in 1930, and to two organizations established six years later, the paramilitary Legião Portuguesa and the Mocidade Portuguesa, a national youth movement. But the official party served only to bolster the government and, unlike the situation in fully developed Fascist – and Communist – regimes, it was not an independent factor in the balance of power. The chief instrument in intimidating and repressing the opposition was the secret police, the Policia de Vigilância e de Defesa do Estado that was established in 1933 and that changed its name in 1945 to the Policia Internacional e de Defesa do Estado. Its resources included special courts, its own prisons and an extensive network of spies. The national ideology revolved around a mystic nationalism centred in turn on a cultic belief in the Catholic mission of Portugal and of its colonial empire.

Portugal remained an agrarian country under the Estado Novo: even as late as 1950 only a fifth of the working population was employed in industry. The country's economic policies were aimed as far as possible at self-sufficiency but unwittingly encouraged stagnation. In 1911 70 per cent of the population had been illiterate, and this figure fell only slowly. In short, the 'new state' was far from being a dictatorship bent on modernization, but nor did it possess the ideological dynamism typical of totalitarian systems. Salazarism adopted a defensive attitude towards the outside world. The support that the authoritarian system enjoyed both at home and abroad was not just a consequence of repression and propaganda but was also a reaction to the lasting experience of instability and chaos in the years before 1926. Both, moreover, were a result of the social backwardness of the country, a legacy for which reactionary Iberian Catholicism was in no small measure to blame.

Unlike Portugal, Spain retained its neutrality throughout the First World War – even after German submarines torpedoed Spanish merchant vessels in 1917 as part of their all-out war. That same year the kingdom's oligarchical system of government was repeatedly placed under pressure. Ever since the constitution of 1812 had opened up the army to every social class, it had been the bourgeois officers who had set the tone. In 1916 they had closed ranks as *juntas de defensa* and attacked the major aristocratic landowners, together with the government and the parliamentary system, in no uncertain terms. In August 1917 they demanded that King Alfonso XIII should conspire with them and all forces bent on reform in order to topple the regime, which they blamed for their low pay and for the chaos and corruption at home. The king refused to put his name to a putsch, but the juntas insisted, continuing in consequence to pose an abiding threat to the constitutional order.

A further challenge came from a parliamentary faction led by the Catalan Lliga Regionalista under Francesc Cambó, the Republicans of Alejandro Lerroux and the Socialists associated with Pablo Iglesias. The opposition MPs would almost certainly have achieved at least some of their aims if they had formed an alliance with the juntas, but the latter were too cautious to agree to any kind of a merger with Catalan regionalists, Republicans and Socialists.

The situation grew markedly worse in the summer of 1917, when social protests at the economic beneficiaries of the wartime economy – the exporters of raw materials, together with agricultural and industrial produce – took a more radical turn. In August a strike by railway workers and dockworkers that enjoyed widespread support from Socialists such as Francisco Largo Caballero and Julián Besteiro was turned into an indefinite general strike. The government of the conservative prime minister, Eduardo Dato e Iradier, responded by declaring a state of siege and within only a few days had overthrown the militant workers with the help of the army. The actions of the police and military were particularly bloody in Barcelona and the Asturias mining region, where the young Major Francisco Franco attracted attention with his firm actions directed against the striking workers. The proletarian uprising also failed because it received no support from the forces of reform in parliament and in the army, neither group being willing to make common cause with Socialists who were bent on class warfare.

New elections to the Cortes were held in February 1918. As usual, they were rigged by the local caciques. The following month a grand coalition was formed from conservatives and liberals under Antonio Maura y Montana, but irreconcilable differences between the two camps meant that it was able to hold on to power for barely eight months. There followed a series of short-lived cabinets that felt threatened by strikes by the Andalusian agricultural workers who for the first time in their country's history were heard to shout Bolshevik slogans, hailing Lenin and the soviets and demanding the collectivization of the land. The unrest continued during the period of Dato's last cabinet, which took office in May 1920 and sought to deal with the state of anarchy not only by calling in the Civil Guard but also by means of a socio-political offensive that included establishing a ministry of labour and introducing national insurance. But Dato failed to convince the radical left, and on 8 March 1921 he was assassinated by Catalan anarchists in Madrid.

Between 1919 and 1921 Spain seemed more than once to be on the brink of civil war. In Barcelona, *pistoleros* hired by the employers clashed with militant anarcho-syndicalists, while in Andalusia there were countless instances of land being occupied. At the same time there were increasing signs of the influence of the Russian Bolsheviks. The socialist umbrella trade union, the Unión General de Trabajadores, and the Partido Socialista Obrero Español refused to join the Third International but were unable to avert a split within the Marxist workers' movement. Spain's first Communist Party was formed in April 1920, with a second one following in 1921. Both merged in March 1922 as the Partido Comunista de España. The anarcho-syndicalist Confederación Nacional de Trabajo adopted a policy of agrarian communism but did not regard the Russian October Revolution as a model and declined to join the Third International and the Red Trade Union International.

The year 1921 also witnessed an annihilating defeat for the country's troops in its colonial war with Spanish Morocco, a war that had begun in 1909 only to be interrupted by the First World War. The uprising of the Rif tribes under Muhammad Ibn Abd al-Karim came to a bloody climax in July 1921 with the Desastre de Annual that cost the lives of more than 12,000 Spanish soldiers. The sense of international shock caused by this incident contributed in no small way to the ever more positive response to the call for a dictatorship that would restore order to the country, ideally under the military.

Two years later, on 13 September 1923, the captain general of Barcelona, Miguel Primo de Rivera, mounted a coup against the government of Prime Minister Manuel García Prieto. In this, he had the backing of a group of high-ranking officers in Madrid and, above all, leading members of the Catalan upper middle classes. Since the government could not count on the support of the military, it resigned, prompting Alfonso XIII to ask Primo de Rivera to form a new government. Alfonso decided against civil war and in favour of a military dictatorship, thereby giving the putsch a formal legality and investing the new regime with a validity that was initially entirely negative: the parliamentary system was no longer capable of maintaining a monopoly of state power and of safeguarding law and order, making its failure complete. The fact that the *pronunciamiento* – the Spanish term for a military revolt – had sidelined a system that had for a long time no longer been capable of functioning meant that the coup received a largely positive response in the press and in public opinion, and this was also true of the first official action of Primo de Rivera's government: the suspension of some of the most important articles pertaining to basic rights in the 1876 constitution, including those guaranteeing the freedom of the press, the right of assembly and the freedom of association.

Within Spanish society, the principal pillars of the military dictatorship were the major landowners, the Catalan industrial bourgeoisie and the Catholic Church, which enjoyed far-reaching privileges in the field of education. The vast majority of the military initially maintained its distance, and it was only Primo de Rivera's military successes in a coordinated Franco-Spanish offensive in North Africa following Abd al-Karim's attack on French Morocco that led them to change their allegiance: by 1927 the colonial war could for the most part be regarded as over.

Remarkably, the Socialist Party and the Unión General de Trabajadores were willing to work together in government, a state of affairs due not least to the broadly based social appeal of Primo de Rivera, who maintained good personal relations with Largo Caballero, the Unión's secretary and subsequently the leader of the Socialists, and who was able to impress the moderate left by encouraging the building of cheap council flats and by settling wage disputes by means of committees made up equally of employers and employees. Conversely, those sections of the proletariat that were deemed incapable of integration were actively opposed, starting with a ban on the anarcho-syndicalist Confederación Nacional de Trabajo, while the Communist leaders were arrested following a series of general strikes in Biscay and Asturias in 1927. The ban also affected the Catalan Lliga Regionalista. The royalist parties disbanded soon after the putsch, and many of their members joined the government Unity Party, the Unión Patriotica, which had been formed in 1924.

By December 1925 Primo de Rivera had established a military directorate that included civilian ministers who were responsible to it. Among the government's most important tasks were a protectionist economic policy that helped with Spain's industrialization process, and a modernization of the country's infrastructure achieved by building modern motorways, channelling the course of rivers, building dams and bringing artificial irrigation to some of Spain's more arid regions. Attempts were also made to reafforest regions eroded by centuries of deforestation; even today this remains one of Spain's most serious environmental problems. But the government failed to tackle the problem of agrarian reform, which was no less pressing than that of deforestation. In this case, any attempt to intervene would have resulted in a conflict with the country's major landowners, a powerful elite whose support Primo de Rivera believed was essential to his own continuing rule.

The wishes of another important group were not treated as seriously by the prime minister: that of the Catalan bourgeoisie, whose members had sided with the general in 1923 because they saw in him a champion of regional autonomy. But he began to move away from this policy in 1925, leading to an increasing sense of alienation between him and one of his most important support groups. He set even less store by the approval of the country's intellectuals, many of whom, including the philosopher José Ortega y Gasset, had expressed support for the military putsch in 1923. But this initial enthusiasm soon faded when the entirely non-intellectual Primo de Rivera expressed his public opposition to the university teachers and students who were against him. In 1928 he even shut down the University of Madrid in the wake of anti-government protests. Several professors, including Ortega, resigned their chairs, while the philosopher Miguel Unamuno y Jugo and the historian Gregorio Marañon y Posadillo opted for temporary exile.

With the beginning of the world economic crisis in the autumn of 1929, Spain's economy suffered a dramatic decline. In January 1930 the country's finance minister, José Calvo Sotelo, resigned in the face of the mounting national debt, rising prices and the devaluation of the peseta. A further sign of the crisis that beset the country at this time was the evident helplessness of the government in the matter of the constitution. At the insistence of Alfonso III, Primo de Rivera had convened an assembly of predominantly conservative dignitaries in September 1927. A little under two years later, in July 1929, they submitted a draft constitution, a document that departed in important ways from the unpopular constitution of 1876 but which was rejected almost unanimously by liberals, monarchists and Republicans since it included no provisions for a government responsible to parliament. For his part, Alfonso had his own reasons for rejecting the draft for its authors were keen to withdraw certain prerogatives from him. The fate of the draft was sealed, and so the government withdrew it.

A constitution that took account of the weaknesses and failure of the former parliamentary system and laid the foundations for a fully functional representative democracy, together with an electoral law that prevented ballot-rigging on both a local and national level and counteracted the fragmentation of the different political parties, would have spelt the end of the military dictatorship, while at the same time lending it a kind of belated justification. Primo de Rivera was unwilling to take this historic step and was probably incapable of doing so. Ultimately, his position was fatally compromised by the loss of the support that he had received from the military, a situation caused by reforms to the army designed drastically to reduce the number of officers both commissioned and non-commissioned. On 26 January 1930 Primo de Rivera saw himself obliged to ask the country's ten regional captains general whether they still had confidence in him. They responded in the negative, with the result that on 28 January Alfonso forced his dictatorial prime minister to resign. Primo de Rivera went into voluntary exile in Paris, where he died of diabetes barely seven weeks later.

Primo de Rivera was succeeded by General Dámasco Berenguer, a political opponent of his predecessor and until then the head of the Royal Military Cabinet. He reversed the army reforms and dismissed many of the civil servants whom Primo de Rivera had appointed. He also announced a return to the 1876 constitution, but this failed to provide a solution to the crisis. In August 1930 Republican and Socialist politicians led by the Catalan left formed the

Pact of San Sebastián whose aim was sweeping reform and the establishment of a republic. Leading intellectuals such as Ortega and Marañon, who had in the meantime returned to Spain, spoke openly in favour of a republic, and in the army, too, officers who held republican views began to organize support for such an idea.

Berenguer was replaced by Admiral Juan Bautista Aznar on 18 February 1931. Aznar included in his cabinet the former Liberal prime minister Count Alvaro de Romanones and retained Berenguer as his minister of war. On 12 April 1931 the government organized local elections in order to delay having to hold national elections for as long as possible. The Republicans and Socialists gained sizeable majorities in the larger towns and cities, whereas the monarchists won the upper hand in the country – and, hence, in Spain in general. Aznar's government was panicked into regarding the outcome of the election as a plebiscite in favour of a republic, and a republic was indeed proclaimed in a number of cities, including Madrid. It was the country's second republic after the short-lived first republic of 1873–4. On 14 April Alfonso III bowed to an ultimatum from a revolutionary committee under Niceto Alcalá Zamora, and he left Spain, travelling by sea from Cartagena to Marseilles, but without renouncing his right to the throne.

The fall of the monarchy was the direct result of the inability of the military dictatorship to solve the problems that had brought about the end of the parliamentary system in 1923, namely, the agrarian question, the relations between central government and the regions, the position of the Church and the military and the implementation of the state's monopoly on power in the face of the forces of anarchy. Shortly after the change of regime, these forces demonstrated that they had learnt nothing from history: responding to rumours that the monarchists were planning to attack the Republic, they burned down countless monasteries and churches on the night of 11/12 May 1931 in Madrid and subsequently in other parts of Spain, especially Andalusia.

It was the Socialists who, with 117 votes, emerged as the largest party from the elections for the constituent Cortes on 28 June 1931. Together with the left-wing Republican parties, which together won eighty seats, and with a number of regional groups, they had a majority that allowed them to form a government. The opposition was made up of 100 anti-socialist and anti-clerical radicals and eighty Liberals, right-wing Republicans, Agrarians and Carlist traditionalists. The monarchists had demanded a boycott of the polls and as a result were not represented in the Cortes.

The Constituent Assembly adopted the Spanish Republic's new constitution on 9 December 1931 by 175 votes to fifty-nine. It was liberal and strictly secular, explicitly stating that the Spanish state had no official religion, granting denominational groups the status of associations, abolishing the previous budget for the clergy, giving all men and women over the age of twenty-three the same active and passive voting rights, protecting private property, while allowing for the possibility of expropriation, usually in return for compensation and for purposes of the social good, and providing for the formation of autonomous regions within the united Spanish state. The president of the Republic was elected for a six-year term by the members of the Cortes and by a similar numbers of electors, male and female. He had the right to dissolve parliament, but otherwise he was a figurehead with no real powers of his own. His ministers were dependent on the trust of the Cortes. In the interests of state security the government could overrule certain basic rights by means of a decree as long as it gained the subsequent approval of the Cortes.

It seemed that Spain had completed its transition from an authoritarian state and could look forward to a democratic future. But although the anti-Republican right had refused to be represented in parliament, it still commanded considerable support in Spanish society – and not just within its upper echelons. For their part, the Republican forces were deeply divided, a point that emerges with particular clarity from the agrarian reforms of 1932. Bourgeois Republicans wanted to redistribute the land stripped from the major landowners and give it to peasants who owned no land at all, whereas their Socialist partners in the coalition government preferred to nationalize the land, which they wanted to be collectively farmed. The law of September 1932 was a compromise, giving the government wide-ranging powers of acquisition, while leaving the question as to the private or collective cultivation of the expropriated lands to the discretion of rural communities, leading to substantial delays in implementing the reforms and resulting in growing discontent among the rural population.

But the Socialists, too, were split: the party chairman and leader of the Cortes, Julián Besteiro, preferred to leave the realization of a socialist order to the democratic process, which effectively meant abandoning it to the distant future. The minister for labour, Francisco Largo Caballero, conversely, who headed the Partido Socialista Obrero Español from 1932, shifted his position to the left under the influence of the growth of the anarcho-syndicalist Confederación Nacional de Trabajo and came increasingly to champion an uncompromising class struggle and even the dictatorship of the proletariat. Only on the question of Catalonia were the Socialists and left-wing Republicans in agreement. (It was the last-named party that from October 1931 provided the coalition government's prime minister in the person of the keenly anti-clergy Manuel Azaña y Diaz.) On 9 December 1932 the Catalan Institute declared Catalan, as well as Spanish, the region's official language; and Catalonia was granted its own parliament, its own government made up of generals, and far-reaching administrative autonomy.

In February 1933 a moderate right-wing party emerged under the leadership of the lawyer José Maria Gil Robles y Quiñones: the Confederación Española de Derechas Autónomas, or CEDA, was a Christian Conservative party that left open the question of a republic or a monarchy, taking its cue from papal doctrine on social matters and advocating a reform of society based on professional principles. The CEDA was a part of the Acción Popular, a conservative umbrella organization in which Gil Robles likewise played a leading role. To the right of the CEDA were the royalists, some of whom formed the Renovación Española that was loyal to Alfonso XIII, while others – the Carlists – advocated the principle of an absolute monarchy.

Far more radical were the militia-like Juntas de Ofensiva Nacional-Sindicalista that were summoned into existence in October 1931 and that demanded the comprehensive re-Catholicization of Spain. Even so, it was not they that formed the most extreme right-wing party but the Falange Española founded in October 1933 by José Antonio Primo de Rivera, the son of the country's former dictator. This was a combat organization modelled on those of the Italian Fascists. In February 1934 the Juntas de Ofensiva and the Falange Española merged under the leadership of José Antonio Primo de Rivera and formed a single organization, the Falange Española de la Juntas de Ofensiva Nacional-Sindicalista. Among its outward hallmarks were the blue shirts worn by its members. There was also a right-wing faction within the military, the Unión Militar Española, which was keen above all to challenge the reforms undertaken by Azaña, especially his reduction in the size of the officer corps and the subordination of the military to the control of the government, which in turn was controlled by parliament.

The coalition of Socialists and Republicans imploded in September 1933, and it was the political right that emerged victorious from the new elections, winning a total of 217 seats, while the centre parties won 163, the left only ninety-three. Even so, the right did not have a sustainable majority, and it was only after a series of difficult negotiations that a minority government was formed. Made up of Radicals and Independents, it was led by the bourgeois Radical Alejandro Lerroux but remained at the mercy of the CEDA. Lerroux's first government marked the end of the Spanish Republic's two years of reform – the *bienio de reformas* – and the start of its *bienio negro*, when many of the earlier reforms were rescinded. The principal beneficiaries of this period of reaction were the Church and the major landowners: anti-clerical laws were repealed, and expropriated land was returned to its former owners.

The growth in power of the right was also a reaction to the increasing militancy of the anarcho-syndicalists of the Confederación Nacional de Trabajo, which gained in support in the course of 1933 and in December attempted a regular putsch. The reversal of the country's agrarian reforms increased the radicalism of the political left. In May 1934 the trade unions called a strike among agricultural workers. It was joined by Largo Caballero's Unión General de Trabajadores and by the hitherto moderate socialist Agricultural Workers' Trade Union, which now adopted a policy of social revolution. The government declared the uprising illegal and organized emergency measures to deal with the harvest. The strike movement spilled over for a time to Madrid and other cities but achieved none of its goals, contributing, rather, to the continuing social and political polarization of Spain.

In early October the Radicals entered into a regular coalition with the CEDA. Lerroux was once again appointed Spain's prime minister. Since Gil Robles had moved increasingly to the right during the previous months, Largo Caballero declared the Confederación's entry into government to be the first stage in Fascism's rise to power along Italian and German lines, at the same time calling on the masses to begin a general strike. In the majority of towns and cities the proletarian demonstrations that did not have anarchist backing ended after only a few days, but the situation was different in Catalonia and Asturias. On 6 October the generals under Lluis Companys, the leader of the Esquierra Republicana de Catalunya, declared Catalonia an independent state within a Spanish federal republic. The government responded by suppressing the uprising with the help of the military, and Catalonia's bid for independence was over.

In Asturias the general strike escalated into insurrection among the mining community, even descending to the level of a local civil war in the course of which the cities of Oviedo and Gigon fell into the hands of the proletarian revolutionaries, who proclaimed a soviet republic. Here, too, the government sent in troops, including – on the advice of the two commanding generals, Manuel Goded Llopis and Francisco Franco – the Foreign Legion, which had already played a major role in the victory over the Rif tribes in Spanish Morocco. Up to 30,000 mineworkers took part in the uprising, which was put down after two weeks. The numerous atrocities committed by the 'Reds' were followed by even worse excesses by the 'Whites'. There were 1,300 reported deaths and 3,000 injuries. Tens of thousands of arrests were made in the wake of the failed 'October Revolution'. Twenty leaders of the uprising were sentenced to death, and two of them were executed. The others, including Companys, were pardoned by President Alcalá Zamora, prompting a protest on the part of the CEDA, which temporarily left the government. Caballero and several of his comrades in arms were sentenced to thirty years' imprisonment, although few believed that they would serve out their sentences to the full.

There followed heated and embittered parliamentary debates between the left and the right over the suppression of the October uprisings, leading in turn to the revocation of further reforms, to the appointment of Gil Robles as minister of war in May 1935 and to the latter's naming of General Franco as his chief of the general staff. Then, at the end of 1935, a number of scandals were exposed involving corruption among leading radical politicians. The resultant instability left President Zamora with no alternative but to dissolve parliament on 7 January 1936. Just over a week later, on 15 January, left-wing Republicans, Socialists and Communists formed a Popular Front with a list of joint candidates. At Caballero's urging, the Socialists took the disastrous decision not to accept any ministerial portfolios in the event that the left-wing parties won the election. The anarchists, who had previously boycotted the elections, took part in the electoral process for the first time on 16 February 1936.

The Popular Front was the clear winner, polling 4.7 million votes, while the right-wing National Front won barely four million, the centre parties only 449,000. The electoral law favoured the largest list and helped the left-wing parties to return 277 members to the Cortes, giving them an absolute majority. Of these, the Socialists made up ninety seats, the Izquierda Republicana eighty-six, the Catalan left thirty-six and the Communists seventeen. The opposition parties had 132 representatives, the centre parties fifty-two. Since the largest party, the Partido Socialista Obrero Español, stuck to its electoral promise and refused to put forward any names for ministerial appointments, the parties of the Popular Front agreed that the bourgeois Republican Manuel Azaña y Diaz, who had been prime minister from 1931 to 1933, should again be invited to become the country's prime minister. One of the new government's first official acts was to relocate Generals Franco and Goded and place them in command posts as far removed as possible from the centre of political power: Franco was sent to the Canary Islands, Goded to the Balearics.

Nothing in the spring of 1936 suggested that Spain's domestic situation was becoming any more stable. Many left-wing victory parades descended into riots, with churches, newspaper offices and prisons all being attacked. Among the prisoners freed in this way were Companys and Caballero. In the countryside farmworkers turned to looting, leading to violent clashes with the Civil Guard; and *pistoleros* of the Falange Española and Federación Anarquista Iberica made attempts on the lives of their political opponents. Led by Franco's brother-in-law, Ramón Serrano Suñer, large numbers of younger members of the CEDA joined the Falange Española. And Largo Caballero, who had been chairman of the Partido Socialista Obrero Español since 1932, gave speeches all over the country, proclaiming the imminent proletarian revolution and garnering applause from Socialists and Communists alike. At around this time conspirators in the military acting under the aegis of General Emilio Mola Vidal were planning to topple the Popular Front government. Among the conspirators' other leaders were Franco, Goded and General José Sanjurjo, who had already attempted to overthrow the government in August 1932, when his putsch was quickly put down. The Falange Española of the imprisoned José Antonio Primo de Rivera and the two monarchist groupings – the Carlists and the supporters of Alfonso XIII – were also implicated in the planning. Gil Robles knew about Mola's intentions but played no active part in preparations for the coup.

Azaña stepped down as prime minister in May 1936 and became the country's president. His replacement as prime minister was the left-wing Republican Santiago Casares Quiroga, whose thinking was markedly more left-wing than that of his predecessor. The new government forced through the agrarian reforms that had either stalled or been reversed but was still unable to prevent continuing strikes among farmworkers and the illegal occupation of farmland. During the first half of July barely a day passed without a political assassination being committed. On 12 July José Castillo, a lieutenant in the Republican Guardia de Asalto, was murdered by members of the Falange Española in a revenge attack after Castillo had killed a prominent Falangist in a gun battle the previous April. The Guardia de Asalto responded by killing one of the best-known right-wing politicians, the monarchist deputy and former finance minister, Calvo Sotelo, who was dragged from his Madrid apartment by uniformed members of the Guardia on the night of 12/13 July 1936, forced into a car and shot in the back of the neck.

The murder of Calvo Sotelo shocked bourgeois Spain to the core and added urgency to the military's plans for a coup. At the same time, the Carlists were persuaded to overlook their remaining differences with the conspirators. Mola set a time and a date for the attack: five o'clock in the afternoon of 17 July. The signal for the national insurrection against the Spain of the Popular Front was to come from the garrison at Melilla in Spanish Morocco. Plans were therefore in place for an action that was to turn the Spanish crisis overnight into one of European dimensions: that action was the start of the Spanish Civil War.

To quote the German historian Walther L. Bernecker, it was between 1931 and 1936 that

> the basic problem of Spanish society became apparent, a problem that prevented Spain from being modernized and made it impossible for a 'bourgeois' revolution to take place in the country: this was the clash between, on the one hand, the landowning oligarchy that was still rooted in archaic structures and those of its allies who were unwilling to brook any changes to their nineteenth-century attitudes, and, on the other hand, those sections of the farmworkers and industrial workers who saw in the Republic a means by which to overcome their traditional disadvantages and who, having been disappointed in their hopes of a swift change to their situation, had turned their backs on the bourgeois and democratic Republic with the same resolve that their 'class enemies' had already shown. The Civil War was the result of these irreconcilable antagonisms and of the desperate attempt of the right and then, by way of a reaction, of the left to put in place their social, economic and national model by violent means once they had failed to achieve their ends by dint of more peaceful reforms.[68]

But it was not only social structures and collective mentalities that clashed with each other at the time of the Second Republic. It was also men of flesh and blood who bore the responsibility for the country's increasing polarization: they included politicians such as Manuel Azaña who, with the support of the whole of the political left, declared war on Catholic Spain and in doing so intimidated men and women who may have been won over to the cause of the

Republic by a rather more sensitive policy; Gil Robles, who was willing to realize his vision of a professionally organized society with the help of the military if he was unable to obtain a parliamentary majority; and Largo Caballero, who regarded himself increasingly as a 'Spanish Lenin', encouraging others to acclaim him as such and, following his shift to the left, occupying a position that was Communist rather than Social Democrat. As a result of this radicalization of forces that had once been relatively moderate, there could no longer be any question of a compromise, whether in the form of an alliance between the centre ground and the political right or between the centre ground and the left. Left- and right-wing extremists took advantage of this situation: the anarchists and anarcho-syndicalists on the one hand and the united Fascists and National Syndicalists on the other. The nationalist wing of the officer corps could also be included under the heading of the extreme right. And it was they who in the summer of 1936 provided the decisive impetus for the bloody civil war that was to last for the next three years and bring to the surface internal conflicts that had been building up in Spain over a period of many years.

Democracy Evolves: From Sweden to Switzerland

When compared with the Mediterranean and Balkan states that we examined in our previous section, the three Scandinavian kingdoms presented the world with an almost idyllic picture of domestic stability throughout the interwar period. Sweden, Norway and Denmark had all remained neutral during the First World War, initially profiting from the dramatic increase in their exports to the countries that were waging the war, but then suffering badly as a result of the German submarine attacks that began in 1917. The years between the end of the post-war slump and the world economic crisis of 1929 were marked by high rates of growth, and in spite of mass unemployment after 1929, none of their democratic systems was ever at serious risk. After 1918 the Social Democrats were able more or less continuously to extend their influence in Denmark, Sweden and Norway. During the 1930s they were the most powerful political force in northern Europe, allowing far-reaching social reforms to be introduced in all those countries in which they held sway.

In the immediate post-war period there had in fact been little initially to indicate such a development, for in Scandinavia, as elsewhere, the workers' movement was split. Sweden was the first country to witness this phenomenon: here, in 1917, the left wing of the Social Democratic Workers' Party left the main party in protest at the formation of a coalition of Liberals and Social Democrats and assumed an autonomous identity as the Independent Socialist Party. Four years later, this party, too, split, the majority of its members joining the Third International as the Swedish Communist Party. And yet not even this marked the end of the process of fragmentation, for in 1923 the party's leadership under Carl Höglund and some 3,000 of his supporters were excluded from the Communist International after they had expressed dissent at the line taken by the Comintern. They founded the Independent Communist Party, which was initially loyal to Moscow, but in 1929 this Independent Communist Party, now led by Karl Kilbom, suffered exactly the same fate as its predecessor and was excluded from the Comintern on account of its shift to the right. From then on it was known as the Swedish National Communist Party. The rump of its members remained no more than a splinter group. The left-wing Socialists had already rejoined the Social Democratic Workers' Party in 1923.

In Norway, conversely, radicals took over the running of the Norwegian Workers' Party in the spring of 1918. This party helped to found the Communist International in March 1919, while its moderate wing reconstituted itself as the Norwegian Social Democratic Workers' Party in 1921, though representing only a minority of the country's workers. The Workers' Party itself underwent a shift to the left. Like his Swedish counterpart, its chairman, Martin Tranmael, was no Bolshevik but a champion of internal party democracy. The definitive break with Moscow came in September 1923, when a Workers' Party congress decided to leave the Comintern, while their remaining colleagues formed the Norwegian Communist Party, which, like its Swedish equivalent, remained a tiny splinter group. In 1927 the Workers' Party and the Social Democratic Party merged to form a single party, in that way laying the foundations for the party's growth until it became the country's largest party. Denmark's Communist Party was not founded until 1922, far later than its counterparts in Sweden and Norway, and it never rose beyond subsistence level: in the 1924 elections, it polled only 6,000 votes, compared with 470,000 for the Social Democrats.

Sweden entered the post-war period with two important constitutional innovations: in 1919 universal equal male suffrage was introduced for the first chamber, women's suffrage for the second chamber. The following year the Swedish Social Democratic Workers' Party adopted a new, reformist programme whose demands included a more progressive form of income tax, a higher level of inheritance tax and national insurance, the nationalization of major industries and state control over private enterprise. In March 1920 King Gustaf V invited the leader of the Social Democrats, Hjalmar Branting, to form a government. It was the world's first Social Democratic government to come to power without a *coup d'état*. Its minister of war was Per Albin Hansson, a newspaper editor who was one of the authors of the party's new programme.

Branting's first cabinet survived in office for only a few months, its programme of local taxes proving its undoing. The Social Democrats emerged as the largest party from the elections in 1920, and Branting again formed a government, resigning in April 1923, when he failed to push through his plan for national insurance. He was succeeded by the Conservative Ernst Trygger, who was likewise forced to step down when the elections in the autumn of

1924 left substantially unchanged the balance of power in the second chamber. There followed a series of minority cabinets led in turn by Social Democrats, by the Freeminded People's Party from 1926 to 1928, by the Conservatives from 1928 to 1930 and again by the Freeminded People's Party from 1930 to 1932. The first pure Social Democratic government was formed in 1932 by Per Albin Hansson, who had become leader of the Social Democratic Workers' Party on Branting's death in 1925.

Throughout these years one of the country's most pressing domestic concerns was prohibition. Among the proponents of a complete ban on the production and sale of alcoholic drinks was the leader of the Freeminded People's Party, Gustaf Ekman, who held the post of prime minister from 1926 to 1928 and again from 1930 to 1932. In August 1922 a consultative referendum made possible by a change to the constitution undertaken at the time of Branting's second government had merely produced a state monopoly and a strict ban on the sale of alcoholic beverages. (Prohibition laws had already been passed by Norway and Finland in 1919 but the ban was lifted in 1926 in the case of Norway and in 1932 in that of Finland. In Norway public opinion polls had on each occasion determined the government's actions.)

After 1929 Sweden, too, was drawn into the eddying vortex of the world economic crisis and two years later was obliged to follow Great Britain's lead in abandoning the gold standard. In the autumn of 1932 Sweden's biggest employer, Ivar Kreuger, who was the head of the world's largest dealer in matches, Svenska Tändsticks AB, and, unknown to most of his contemporaries, a fraudulent speculator on a massive scale, committed suicide in Paris, his death triggering a stock market crash that spelt the end of his financial empire.

Following the elections of September 1932 the Social Democrats were returned to power, albeit without an overall majority. With the exception of a brief spell in 1936, they continued to provide the country's prime ministers until 1976. Until his death in October 1945, it was Per Albin Hansson who held the post. Under him, the country moved increasingly quickly away from an agrarian society and towards its industrial counterpart: in 1920 44 per cent of the working population had been employed in farming, forestry and fishing, whereas that figure had fallen to 29 per cent by 1940, while the number of those employed in industry rose from 35 per cent to 36 per cent. Unemployment, which peaked in March 1933, was brought down by the ruling coalition of Social Democrats and Agrarians by means of emergency measures, including financial support for agriculture and restrictions on imports. Hansson's social vision of a *folkhem*, or people's home, was set forth in a speech that he delivered to the second chamber in 1928 and revolved around the idea of a society based on reconciliation between the social classes and of patriotism tinged by specifically Social Democratic convictions. 'In a good home', Hansson explained, the basic rules are those of equality, consideration, cooperation and the willingness to help others. If this concept is transferred to the home of a nation and to each and every one of its citizens, then this will mean the disappearance of those social barriers that nowadays keep our citizens apart.[69]

The concept of the *folkhem* can be traced back to the world of ideas of peasants and conservatives in the early twentieth century and was in part a response to the traumatic experience when a quarter of the country's population emigrated in the second half of the nineteenth century in order to escape from poverty at home. By the 1930s the term had become, in the words of the German writer on Scandinavia Bernd Henningsen, 'the topos of a secular theology based on the idea of a welfare state' and, as such, a feature not only of the Scandinavian Social Democrats but also of 'Scandinavian consensual democracy'.[70] The central idea was that of *trygghet*, a sense of security that it was the state's duty to safeguard and that demanded the redistribution of the country's resources and an emphasis on social equality. Against this background social expenditure was no longer viewed as a financial burden on the state but as an investment designed to boost the economy and to ensure a peaceful society and a stronger democracy.

In 1934 Hansson's government was able to introduce a voluntary form of national insurance that was supported by the state; it was followed in 1935 by a pension law that replaced the universal but wholly inadequate state pension of 1913. These were two pillars of the Swedish welfare state that was being created at this time. Further laws were enacted in 1937, covering antenatal help, child welfare and the limited legalization of abortion. In 1938 all workers were guaranteed two weeks' annual paid leave. No less fundamental to the Swedish model was the cooperation between labour and capital as agreed by trade unions and employers' organizations at the resort of Saltsjöbaden near Stockholm in 1938: contentious questions were to be settled on a voluntary basis by agreement, if possible without recourse to strikes and lockouts. The state was not directly involved in such talks, but it encouraged the two parties involved in any wage agreements to work more closely together by facilitating the creation of a denser network of organizations based on the idea of *trygghet*.

And yet the concept of a *folkhem* had its drawbacks in terms of the pressure to conform that is an integral part of even the mildest form of collectivism. And there was one respect in which the Swedish type of collectivism was far from being mild, namely, the social Darwinism that excluded and even eradicated all individuals regarded as socially inferior. The world's first state institute for racial biology was established in Uppsala with broad cross-party support in 1922: behind it lay the widespread conviction on the part of right- and left-wing eugenicists that it was the responsibility of all to ensure that the next generation was based on a process of healthy selection. Left and right also agreed that the declining birth rate needed to be counteracted by means of a pro-natal policy that included measures designed to help those parents who were regarded as making a valuable genetic contribution to society.

Eugenicists regarded the feeble-minded as inferior, such a definition increasingly coming to include asocial types and women who were markedly promiscuous. The first sterilization law was passed by Hansson's government in 1935 and was followed by a second and even stricter law in 1941. Meanwhile it became increasingly unimportant for the individuals affected in this way to give their consent. Those who were deemed incapable of making up their own minds did not have to give their consent at all. But even in the case of those who *were* fit to decide, there could be no question of a voluntary choice, for the indirect pressure on them to opt for sterilization was far too great to resist.

Conservative eugenicists tended to view the higher echelons of society as the most genetically valuable and to deny this label to the lower orders. Right-wing racial biologists drew a distinction between superior and inferior races. Among the Social Democratic proponents of social engineering were Alva and Gunnar Myrdal, both of whom were later awarded the Nobel Prize, Gunnar for economics in 1974, his wife Alva for world peace in 1982. Under the influence of American Taylorism, they too thought in terms of the categories of 'superior' and 'inferior' parents but rejected the idea of a racial hierarchy and also the equation of higher social status with higher genetic value. Instead, they advocated improvements to living conditions, public health and education.

At the same time, there was a considerable degree of agreement between left- and right-wing eugenicists inasmuch as both groups believed in the idea of biological selection, both wanting to reduce the number of 'inferior types' and subject the personal will of the individual to the ostensible interests of the collective. In the words of the German historian Ann-Judith Rabenschlag: 'For racial biologists this collective was race, whereas for social engineers it was the *folkhem*.'[71]

There was, however, one conclusion that Swedish eugenicists failed to draw from the belief in selection that underpins social Darwinism: they did not support the sort of euthanasia that was advocated at this time by two German scientists, the expert in criminal law Karl Binding and the psychiatrist Alfred Hoche, whose book, *Die Freigabe der Vernichtung lebensunwerten Lebens*, appeared in 1920, long before the National Socialists came to power. (An English translation was published in 2012 under the title *Allowing the Destruction of Life Unworthy of Life*.) In writing it, Binding and Hoche were also belatedly justifying a practice that had been common in Germany and elsewhere since 1914: during the years of famine between 1914 and 1918 the mentally ill were deliberately left undernourished, leading to a marked rise in the number of reported deaths in mental institutions.

In Norway, which had become an independent state only when its union with Sweden was severed in 1905, the country's bourgeois parties were able to maintain their predominance for longer than in Sweden. Until the middle of the 1930s the dominant figure was the leader of the bourgeois Venstre Party, Johan Ludwig Mowinckel, who headed the government from 1924 to 1926, from 1928 to 1931 and, finally, from 1933 to 1935. Not until January 1928, when they became the largest party in the Storting, was a Social Democrat able to fill the post of prime minister, and yet the party was unable to win a parliamentary majority for its socialist programme, Christopher Hornsrud's government being toppled by a vote of no confidence after only two weeks in office, at which point Mowinckel returned briefly to the post of prime minister.

As a maritime nation, Norway was more seriously affected than Sweden by the world economic crisis: during the winter of 1932/3, 42 per cent of the organized workforce was for a time unemployed. The elections in 1930 had led to a shift to the right, and the country's political leadership passed into the hands of the Bondeparti, or Peasants' Party. Under its prime minister, Peter Kolstad, the extreme right-wing major in his general staff, Vidkun Quisling, was appointed defence minister. Quisling left the cabinet in 1933 and formed his own party, the Nasjonal Samling, which was modelled on both the Italian Fascists and German National Socialists but failed to gain a single seat in parliament in either 1933 or 1936.

It was the Workers' Party that emerged victorious from the 1933 elections, with around 40 per cent of the vote. Even so, it was not until March 1935 that it was able to supplant Mowinckel, when it formed a coalition with the Peasants' Party. The new prime minister was Johan Nygaardsvold, who had previously been employed in a brickworks and who headed the government until Norway was invaded by Germany in March 1940. The post of foreign minister was given to the historian Halvdan Koht, that of justice minister to the lawyer Trygve Lie, who won universal acclaim between 1946 and 1952 as the first secretary general of the newly established United Nations.

It was under Nygaardsvold, who was a committed reformer, that Norway began its journey down the road to a welfare state characterized by Social Democratic ideas. The introduction of a state pension for all Norwegians over the age of seventy met with widespread support, as did the national insurance provisions that came into force in 1938. For the most part the new social policies were financed by higher taxes. Even so, unemployment fell only slowly: as late as 1939 it was still 18 per cent of the working population. In the meantime Norway's social fabric had undergone a fundamental change, as the country moved away from a rural economy to a society dominated by urban industry and the service sector. In 1920 36 per cent of the working population was employed in agriculture, 27 per cent in trade and industry. The equivalent figures for 1950 were 26 per cent and 35 per cent respectively.

Denmark witnessed a similar shift in the interwar period. Here 33 per cent of the working population had been employed in agriculture in 1920, 29 per cent in the secondary sector. Two decades later the secondary sector was responsible for employing 33 per cent of the working population, agriculture for only 29 per cent. Since 1924 it was generally Social Democrats who ran the country, and it was they who provided the prime minister in the person of Thorvald Stauning, who held the post from 1924 to 1926 and again from 1929 to 1942. Even as a member of the coalition government made up of the bourgeois Radical Venstre and Social Democrats, Stauning, the first Nordic labour minister, had persuaded his colleagues to accept an eight-hour day, initially in state industries, then, from 1920, in private concerns. In general, Danish social policy had made significant progress even before 1924 in terms of disability insurance, unemployment benefit and old age pensions. The cabinet that Stauning formed in April 1924 was a coalition government made up of Social Democrats and politicians from the Radical Venstre. For the first time, it included a woman, the historian Nina Bang, as minister for education. After 1918 the main problem facing Denmark's politicians was the high rate of unemployment: by the winter of 1925/6 around 30 per cent of the organized workforce was without work. Stauning's long-term attempt to deal with the crisis was deemed too 'socialist' by his coalition partner, with the result that the Social Democrats walked away from government in December 1926 but returned to power under Stauning's leadership in April 1929 following major election successes. Unemployment peaked four years later at 40 per cent, largely thanks to the import restrictions imposed first by Germany and then by Great Britain, Denmark itself having already made these restrictions. The coalition of Social Democrats and the Radical Venstre financed the growing need for social benefits by reducing the defence budget.

On 30 January 1933 – the day on which Hitler came to power in Germany – the Kanslergade Agreement was signed in Stauning's Copenhagen apartment. The signatories were the government and opposition parties. It was a reformist document enshrining many of the features of a planned economy and entrusting the state-run Central Exchange with the task of steering the country's finances. The 1933 programme included a new law relating to national insurance, another raising contributions for old age pensions and disability insurance and a reform of the old age pension that had been introduced in 1922 and that applied to all Danes over the age of sixty-five: from then on it was the state that decided on the level of contributions. Throughout the 1930s the Social Democrats were the victors in every one of the country's national elections. But neither they nor the Radical Venstre could reform the constitution in such a way as to abolish the first chamber, or Landsting: a referendum in May 1939 failed to produce the necessary agreement of 45 per cent of the electorate.

Denmark was the only Nordic country able to expand its territories in the wake of the First World War: following a plebiscite organized in February and

March 1920 under the terms of the Treaty of Versailles, the kingdom reac-
quired the largely Danish-speaking region of North Schleswig – Südjütland in
Danish – that it had lost in the German-Danish War of 1864 and which,
psychologically speaking, represented a degree of compensation for the loss of
the Virgin Islands to the United States, a decision confirmed by the left-wing
Liberal government of the prime minister, Carl Theodor Zahle, in 1917. On 1
December 1918 Iceland became an independent state, while retaining its links
with Denmark. The North Atlantic island, which could boast having the oldest
parliament in the world (the Althing dates back to 930), had become a Danish
dependency in 1541 but had been granted the right of self-administration in
1904. Its newly won sovereignty was confirmed by a plebiscite. Its independence became complete in June 1944, when a further plebiscite ended the union
with the Danish crown, and Iceland became a republic.

The question of Greenland proved contentious. Following the dissolution
of the union of Denmark and Norway in 1815, Greenland – the largest island
in the world – had remained a part of Denmark and in 1917 was recognized as
a Danish colony by the United States in the context of the latter's purchase of
the Danish part of the Virgin Islands. But Norway laid claim to Greenland's
eastern coast, its claims dictated in no small measure by its whaling interests. A
treaty signed by Oslo and Copenhagen in 1924 went some way to meeting the
demands of Norway's whalers but failed to satisfy them in the longer term. The
conflict grew markedly more serious in 1931 when the Peasants' Party government in Oslo gave its official recognition to the occupation of Myggbukta
(Mosquito Bay) by a group of Norwegians. Denmark appealed to the
International Court in The Hague, which in April 1933 declared that both this
occupation and a second one in 1932 were illegal. The majority of members of
the Norwegian Storting aligned themselves with international law and thus
found themselves at odds with their own government, but the disagreement
between the two Scandinavian states was at last finally resolved.

Twelve years earlier, in June 1921, a further dispute between two Nordic
lands had again been resolved by international intervention, when Sweden
accepted a decision on the part of the League of Nations and agreed that the
Åland Islands that were inhabited by ethnic Swedes should remain with
Finland. Taken in Geneva, the decision was complemented later that year by a
treaty signed by ten states insisting on the islands' military neutrality. Less
controversial, conversely, was the recognition of the status of Spitsbergen, a
whole series of countries, including the United States, Great Britain, France
and Denmark, all agreeing that Norway should own this group of coal-rich
islands situated in the Arctic Ocean. The Soviet Union added its name to the
agreement only after Norway recognized its existence four years later. Norway
officially took possession of Spitsbergen in 1925.

The 1930s were notable for increasing cooperation between these Nordic
democracies. In 1930 Norway, Sweden and Denmark agreed to work more

closely with the Netherlands, Belgium and Luxembourg on questions of trade and customs tariffs: Finland joined this Oslo Convention in 1933. On the other hand, the countries in question were unable to agree on a common defence alliance, which Denmark, alarmed by developments in National Socialist Germany, was particularly keen to see implemented but which Sweden, determined to maintain its neutrality, refused to support.

All the Nordic countries continued to be closely linked not just by the foregoing treaties but by their shared political beliefs. Among their most basic principles were a free, self-confident peasant population, a pragmatic workers' movement insistent upon concrete improvements and, last but not least, an educational system marked by the spirit of Lutheranism. It was the confluence of all these factors that ensured that after 1918 Scandinavia was a safe haven for democracy and, indeed, for the growth of a new, specifically Nordic type of modern democracy, namely, a form of representative government based on social partnership rights and the peaceful settlement of competing interests.

In the light of developments in Scandinavia in the years before 1918, it is no surprise that democracy was able to thrive there during the interwar period. More astonishing is the fact that the parliamentary system was able to survive in a country that did not become independent until 1921 and that was shaken to its very foundations by a violent civil war that lasted from 1921 to 1923: the country in question was the Free State of Ireland. Not until 1927 did it acquire a degree of political stability, when Eamon de Valera's Fianna Fáil party accepted the terms of the Anglo-Irish Agreement of 1921 and took over the role of parliamentary opposition following its growing success in the elections that were held in June and September 1927.

The ruling conservative party, Cumann na nGaedheal, under its leader William T. Cosgrove had signed an agreement with Great Britain in 1925 that laid down the existing border with Ulster, which remained British. During the years that followed, the Dublin government focused in particular on the use of the Irish language, which became compulsory in schools and which would-be civil servants had to have mastered before they could begin their careers. And yet in spite of this measure English remained the dominant language in large sections of the country. On the international stage, Ireland worked closely with Canada and South Africa to ensure that the independence of the British Dominions was recognized by Britain, a goal gradually achieved, first at the Imperial Conference of 1926 and later by the Statute of Westminster of 1931. In terms of Ireland's economic policies, Cosgrove tended in the direction of free trade, which helped in exporting Irish agricultural produce to Great Britain but not with the country's industry, which continued to remain very weak.

The world economic crisis led to increasing criticism of Cosgrove's liberal trade policy and to a change of attitude on the part of the electorate that was exploited by the openly protectionist Fianna Fáil, which emerged as the largest party from the elections in January 1932 and which, together with the Labour Party, formed the new government under Eamon de Valera, who was repeatedly confirmed as the Irish prime minister between then and 1948.

Relations with Great Britain worsened dramatically following the election victory of the Republicans. One of de Valera's very first acts was to abolish the oath of allegiance to the British throne that until then had been sworn by Irish members of parliament. An even more momentous decision was that of halting the annual payments to the United Kingdom that were used by the latter to compensate the Irish landowners who in the wake of the land reforms at the end of the nineteenth century had had to abandon their estates in Ireland. London responded by imposing higher import duties on Irish agricultural produce, leading de Valera in turn to raise the level of duties on industrial goods imported from Great Britain, a move fully consonant with the policy of industrial protectionism that was one of Fianna Fáil's chief articles of faith.

This trade war damaged Ireland's agrarian economy far more seriously than it harmed an industrial power like Great Britain, with the result that the Irish gross national product fell by 3 per cent between 1931 and 1938, while Great Britain's rose by 27 per cent. In February 1937 Dublin was forced to sign a trade deal with Great Britain that was designed to remove some of the measures that were so harmful to both their economies. Not until April 1938 was the trade war finally resolved, when de Valera's government declared its willingness to make one final payment to Great Britain to compensate Irish landowners. In return London handed back its naval bases in Ireland. A new trade treaty opened up not only the British market to Irish agriculture but also the Commonwealth countries that were dependent on Great Britain. The closure of the remaining military installations allowed Ireland to remain neutral in the Second World War, the only Commonwealth nation to do so.

Not even Ireland was spared a process of political radicalization at the time of the world economic crisis. In February 1933, the former head of the Irish police, Eoin O'Duffy, formed the Army Comrades Association, a paramilitary organization whose members wore blue shirts similar to those of the Spanish Falangists. It was initially made up for the most part of army veterans and served to protect the halls used by Cosgrove's party, regarding its principal enemy as the Irish Republican Army, or IRA, which found itself increasingly at odds with de Valera's government, and committed a series of atrocities during the election campaign in the winter of 1932/3.

In September 1933, by which time it had rebranded itself as the National Guard, the Army Comrades Association joined forces with Cosgrove's Cumann na nGaedheal and other smaller parties to form Fine Gael under O'Duffy's leadership. In spite of a number of superficial influences, the right wing of Irish politics could not be accused of the sort of Fascist mentality that characterized its Continental models. Fine Gael remained a conservative party that for the most part operated within the ambit of parliament, especially after Cosgrove became party leader in 1935. In the absence of a Marxist or Communist movement in Ireland, it was the IRA that made up the extreme left of Irish politics. Following a new wave of political assassinations, it was banned by de Valera's government in 1936 but continued to lead an underground existence on both sides of the border with Ulster.

Ireland acquired a new constitution on 1 July 1937. From now on the name of the country was Eire. The constitution was intended to apply to the whole of Ireland, including Ulster. There was no reference to the British crown. The head of state was a president, or Uachtarán na hÉireann, who was elected for a seven-year term of office, while the government was headed by the prime minister, or Taoiseach. Irish was the first official language, English the second one. Parliament consisted of two chambers, a lower house – the Dáil Éireann –and a Senate – the Seanad Éireann. As had already been the case with the 1922 constitution, all men and women over the age of twenty-one were entitled to vote in the elections for the lower house. The constitution defined Ireland as a sovereign, independent and democratic state. The preamble appealed to the Holy Trinity as the source of all authority, the Catholic Church being accorded a special position within the country in spite of the claim expressed elsewhere in the constitution that the Irish were free to practise whatever religion they wanted. On the other hand, neither the Catholic Church nor any other recognized religion received any financial support from the state. In keeping with Catholic teaching, the family was regarded as the natural and original basic unit of society, marriage as indissoluble. Divorce was consequently ruled out.

No other twentieth-century European constitution was as Church-orientated as the Irish one. From the standpoint of Ireland's politicians, the Catholic Church was an indispensable part of the national identity and, indeed, its principal spiritual support. In the words of the German historian Michael Maurer, this spirit helps to explain

a particular feature of Ireland in the twentieth century, a feature that largely sets it apart from European and American modernism, namely, restrictive censorship and a curtailment of the freedom of the political press. The list of writings banned in Ireland amounts to a catalogue of the modern world; sexuality and birth control were forbidden subjects, but even topics felt to be politically or scientifically offensive were withheld from Irish readers for decades.[72]

It is no accident that one of the greatest Irish writers of the twentieth century, Samuel Beckett, left his native country in 1937, the year in which the country's new constitution came into force, and, following the example of Bernard Shaw and James Joyce, wrote his later works abroad, mostly in Paris.

The counterpart to the Catholic variant of the backward-looking mentality found in Eire was the Protestant fanaticism of the Unionists and their paramilitary arm, the Orange Order. Even though more than a third of the population of Ulster was Catholic, there could be no question of the two denominations enjoying equal rights. The parliament in Belfast was elected on the first-past-the-post system, even though this system ignored the will of London and flew in the face of the terms of the Anglo-Irish agreement of 1921, which had demanded that elections be held on the basis of proportional representation. The first-past-the-post system clearly favoured the Protestants, producing an effect similar to that of the infamous gerrymandering that was used to manipulate the boundaries of electoral constituencies. In terms of their employment in the public sector, Catholics were far worse off than Protestants. In the years before 1925, Catholics boycotted the elections, increasing the predominance of the Protestant majority.

Fianna Fáil's rise to a position of political power in the south led to a further worsening of the denominational conflict in the north. A special law granting the police far-reaching powers, albeit for a limited period, was extended in 1933: now no time limit was attached to it. The economy of Ulster – a region that was industrialized from a relatively early date – had for a long time been in decline; Belfast's slums were among the worst in Europe; and without subsidies from London, the partially autonomous province would not have survived at all. The boost given to the armaments industry by the Second World War helped the north to recover economically, with the result that by 1950 the standard of living in the north was some 75 per cent higher than in the south.

When compared with the rest of north-west Europe, both halves of Ireland during the interwar years gave the impression of being economically, socially and intellectually backward. In Ulster the denominational divide ran so deep that the conflict between Protestants and Catholics overshadowed all others, including the one between capital and labour. More than nine-tenths of the population of the south was Catholic, so that the election of a Protestant – the founder of the Gaelic League, Douglas Hyde – as the country's first president in 1937 seems a distinctly demonstrative act, serving as a counterweight to the 'ultramontane' elements in Eire's new constitution.

In independent Eire, it was not the clash between two different religions but arguments over the right way to assert itself as a nation that eclipsed the modern class conflict. Presumably a radical left wing bent on fomenting class warfare would have led anxious voters from the middle classes to seek refuge in a Fascist right in Ireland, too, but there was in fact a further reason why the Free State of Eire clung to the parliamentary system, and this was the country's debt to the political culture of Great Britain, whose influence was so powerful that it survived the long and ultimately successful struggle for independence and the division of the island into a predominantly Catholic south and a largely Protestant north.

Unlike Ireland, the Kingdom of the Netherlands was one of the few countries in Europe whose development was remarkable for its unbroken continuity between the pre-war years and the post-war period. Unlike its southern neighbour Belgium, the Netherlands had been able to maintain its neutrality throughout the First World War. In terms of the country's domestic politics, the most important year was 1917, when universal male suffrage was introduced. Women were granted the same right five years later, when the first-past-the-post system was replaced by proportional representation.

Every Dutch government of the interwar period was 'bourgeois', a state of affairs due not least to the fact that the Social Democratic Workers' Party, which became the second-largest party after the electoral reforms of 1922, steadfastly refused to take part in any of the coalition cabinets until August 1939. Throughout this time, moreover, the Communist Party never rose above the status of a splinter group, polling 36,000 votes in the parliamentary elections in 1925, when the Social Democrats won 706,000. The bourgeois parties were generally denominational in character: on the Protestant side there were the Christian Historical Union and the Anti-Revolutionary Party, on the Catholic side – from 1926 – the Roman Catholic State Party.

By the early 1930s not even the Netherlands could avoid the impact of the world economic crisis. In the face of a dramatic fall in stock market prices and wholesale prices combined with rising unemployment figures, the leader of the Anti-Revolutionary Party, Hendrikus Colijn, formed a crisis cabinet in May 1933 that quickly agreed on a series of measures designed to deal with the financial crisis. These measures included new rules on production and sales as well as protective tariffs for agriculture. On the other hand, there were no job creation schemes. The government refused to devalue the gulden, but by September 1936 Colijn's third government was forced to abandon the link between the gulden and the price of gold, leading to a devaluation of the Dutch currency of 20 per cent, a correction that allowed the country's economy to compete internationally again within a very short period of time. On the other hand, unemployment sank only slowly, remaining above that of every other European country for which statistics are available between 1935 and 1939.

Colijn remained his country's prime minister until July 1939. From the very outset he saw it as one of the central tasks of his cabinet to resist the radicalism of the political right with all the energy he could muster. Head of this faction was the National Socialist Movement founded in Utrecht at the end of 1931 by the engineer Anton Adriaan Mussert. His was an organization that saw the German National Socialists as its model, one it imitated in many respects, including in the wearing of uniforms. By the autumn of 1933 they had around 20,000 members, polling 8 per cent of the votes in the 1935 elections for the first chamber of the federal assembly and a further 4.2 per cent in the elections for the second chamber two years later. The government's ban on the wearing of uniforms was specifically aimed at Mussert and was backed up by a further ban prohibiting civil servants from joining his movement. Catholic bishops in the Netherlands repeatedly warned against the movement in their pastoral letters. But if Mussert never achieved mass support, this was due above all to the common stance adopted by the major bourgeois parties and the Social Democrats, together with the newspapers that were close to them.

In the Netherlands, too, fear of the extreme left played a role in mobilizing the supporters of the radical right. In January 1933 a mutiny on the warship *Zeven Provincien* provoked widespread disquiet and was much exploited for propagandist purposes by the National Socialist Movement, not only Mussert and his supporters but whole sections of the population seeing in the incident an attack on the fleet by the Third International and hence an assault on the Netherlands as a colonial power.

Communist uprisings in Java and Sumatra, two of the largest islands in the Dutch East Indies, were suppressed in 1926–7 only after heavy fighting, leading to a period during which leadership of the independence movement in the region fell increasingly into the hands of the radical nationalists associated with Ahmed Sukarno. The 1930s witnessed a second threat in the form of Japan's increasing aggression. But the Netherlands were as yet far from grasping the unsustainability of colonial rule and accepting the legitimacy of the anti-colonial struggle for independence, preferring instead to see in their colonial possessions in south-east Asia a token of their national greatness. By the 1930s the fear of losing possessions that they had owned since the early seventeenth century was no less great than the entirely justified fear that if Mussert was not opposed, the Netherlands could all too easily fall victim to National Socialist Germany's expansionist ambitions.

While the Netherlands was struggling to hold on to its colonial possessions, Belgium was able to expand its own colonies in the wake of the First World War. In 1916 the Force Publique of the Belgian Congo – a group of mercenaries led by white officers – had succeeded in capturing a part of German East Africa in the context of a British offensive in the region. The area in question, Ruanda-Urundi (now the states of Rwanda and Burundi), passed into Belgian hands in May 1919 following an agreement with Great Britain. Six years later Ruanda-Urundi became an administrative part of the Belgian Congo.

Under King Leopold II, the local population of the Belgian Congo was exploited and oppressed in such barbaric ways that there were international protests. In 1908 Leopold II had finally been obliged to relinquish his personal control over the 'free state', but this move did little to reduce the colonial exploitation of this vast region with its plentiful natural resources. A leading role within this system fell to the Union Minière du Haut Katanga which in 1906 had started to mine Katanga's vast copper reserves. In turn, the Union Minière was controlled by the Belgian Société Générale, half of whose shares were state-owned. Following its merger with the Banque d'Outre-Mer in 1928, the Société Générale owned 70 per cent of all the capital invested in the Belgian Congo.

The result of this confluence of state and private enterprise was the emergence of the largest industrial region in Africa, a place where black workers on starvation wages boosted the profits of white owners.

The Union Minière began its self-styled policy of creating a 'stabilized workforce' in the mid-1920s: black workers and their families were housed in the most primitive conditions close to the mines, where they were subjected to far stricter controls than when they had been migrant workers. There was no lack of attempts to oppose this development, prophetic movements such as Kimbanguism and the Kitwala Cult appealing to the Bible to justify the downtrodden population's right to resist. Belgium's Catholic Church, which enjoyed a privileged position in its missionary work in the Belgian Congo as a result of the Concordat of 1906, was emphatically opposed to this kind of Biblical exegesis. But its contribution to the region's education at its missionary centres was limited to training support teachers for the simplest tasks in all types of production and the service industries. Even after the First World War the Belgian Congo remained a byword in the imperialist exploitation of a colonial region in which the interests of the black workers were completely overshadowed by those of the capitalists who controlled them.

Belgium itself moved closer to greater democratization with universal male suffrage in 1919. (Women, though they were now eligible for political office right to the vote, did not receive equal suffrage with men until 1949.) Most of the short-lived cabinets of the interwar period were either made up of the three main parties, namely, the Catholics, Socialists and Liberals, or were Catholic-Liberal coalitions. The three parties were jointly in power from 1918 to 1921, in 1926 to 1927 and from 1936 to 1939, while Catholic-Liberal coalitions ran the country from 1921 to 1925, from 1927 to 1935 and again from April to September 1939. Only in 1925 and 1926, and in February 1939 were there Catholic-Socialist cabinets. The Communists first entered parliament in 1925 but never played more than a marginal role.

The dominant theme of Belgium's domestic politics was the cohesion of the country as a binational state. (For the purposes of the present discussion we shall ignore the tiny German minority in Eupen-Malmedy.) During the First World War, the occupying German troops had encouraged the separatist aspirations of Flanders and found in a minority of Flemish activists a group of individuals willing to collaborate with them. After 1918 the moderate wing of the movement for Flemish autonomy, which supported a federalist restructuring of the country and especially the use of Dutch in preference to French, gained the upper hand, reporting a number of successes, including the metamorphosis of the University of Ghent into a purely Flemish institution in 1930. (The German occupiers had already issued a decree in this regard in March 1916.) Between 1932 and 1938 a series of laws was passed determining the official language to be used in Flanders, Wallonia and Brussels and in that way reflecting the wishes of the more moderate activists.

But this was by no means enough for the radical wing of the Flemish move-ment associated with the Vlaamsch Nationaal Verbond, which increased its number of representatives from eight to sixteen in the 1935 elections. Instead, the group demanded independence for Flanders. An even more extreme line was adopted by the Verbond van Dietsche Nationaalsolidaristen founded in 1931 by Joris Van Severen, a former member of the Flemish Front Party. He supported the idea of a greater Dutch national state that would also include the French-speaking part of Flanders and, together with the Dutch and Belgian colonies, have more than fifty million inhabitants. (Wallonia and Luxembourg were later added to this list under the banner of the 'Grand Burgundian' idea.) Van Severen's organization also maintained its own militia, the Dinasco (short for Dietsche Nationaalsolidaristen), whose members wore dark green uniforms and greeted each other with the words 'Heil t'Dinasco', while raising their right arms by way of a salute. But this Belgian brand of Fascism never managed to enlist more than a few thousand members in western Flanders.

More of a threat to the Belgian state was the Rexist movement named after the right-wing Catholic publishing house of Rex in Leuven. Its leader was Léon Dégrelle, a demagogic orator who was a follower of Charles Maurras's Action Française and who from 1935 onwards attacked with unprecedented fury the politicians of all parties and their allegedly corrupt system, holding up his own organization as the only effective alternative to Marxism and Bolshevism: 'Rex or Moscow!' was one of the movement's catchphrases that appeared in large letters on hoardings and posters throughout the country. The group waged an aggressive campaign in the 1935 elections and was rewarded with twenty-one seats out of a total of 200 in the new parliament.

Two years later Dégrelle represented the Rexists in a by-election in Brussels in April 1937, when the tables were turned. On this occasion the prime minister, Paul Van Zeeland, of the Catholic Bloc, who until then had not had a mandate of his own, put his name forward as the candidate for all the main political parties, winning 275,000 votes against Dégrelle's 70,000. An important factor in Van Zeeland's victory was the intervention of Cardinal Josef Ernst Van Roy, who, invited by the challenger to give him his vote of approval, spoke out against Dégrelle. After that, the Rexist movement quickly fell apart. Middle-class and rural voters who had supported the movement returned to the bour-geois fold. It is debatable whether the Rexist movement of the years between 1935 and 1937 can really be described as 'Fascist', for however militant and demagogic Dégrelle may have been, his movement had none of the other characteristics traditionally associated with Fascism including, first and fore-most, a paramilitary uniformed guard and the use of force against its political opponents.

The fleeting successes of these radical right-wing organizations were in part a reflection of Belgium's severe economic crisis and its consequences: high unemployment, lower wages for miners, major strikes and the repeated devaluation of the Belgian franc. A slow economic recovery began under Paul Van Zeeland, who was in charge of the Catholic-Liberal-Socialist coalition cabinets between March 1935 and October 1937, helping him to push Dégrelle into second place in the 1937 by-election. Even more important, however, was the solidarity of the three main parties, a feature that demonstrated that for the majority of Flemings and Walloons there was something more important than the cultivation of their own linguistic and cultural identity, namely, their shared interest in preserving freedom and democracy and, hence, the constitution of the Belgian state that safeguarded both of these ideals.

Like Belgium, Luxembourg had discovered in August 1914 that its neutrality, although guaranteed by international law, was no bar to a German invasion. In Belgium King Albert I and his government fled to the small area in western Flanders that had not fallen into German hands, while in Luxembourg, Grand Duchess Marie Adelheid and her government continued their work at least to the extent that this was possible in the prevailing conditions. (Unlike Belgium, Luxembourg had not declared war on Germany but merely insisted on maintaining its neutrality.) The arrival of the Allies in November 1918 plunged the country into a major crisis. On 10 November the Socialists formed a workers' and peasants' soviet inspired by events in Russia and Germany and demanded the abdication of the grand duchess, the nationalization of heavy industry and the introduction of an eight-hour day. At the same time a pro-French movement began to agitate for the country's annexation by France. On 13 November, the majority of members of the Luxembourg chamber of deputies voted in favour of a referendum to decide on the form of the future state and agreed to establish a parliamentary commission to examine the question of the neutrality of the crown and government since 1914.

In January 1919 an attempt by the radical left to establish a provisional republican government failed to produce the desired result, but on 14 January Grand Duchess Marie Adelheid abdicated in favour of her sister Charlotte and took the veil. By September 1919 Allied agreement meant that it was finally possible to hold a referendum on the future form of the state. The result was a narrow four-fifths' majority in favour of independence and the retention of the royal family as the head of state.

The customs union with France that Luxembourg had wanted failed to materialize. For its part, Belgium sought a customs union with Luxembourg for which it was willing to pay a high price in the form of a secret military alliance with France dated 7 September 1920. Belgium's agreement to act in the event of an unprovoked attack by Germany meant that it had to abandon the neutrality that had been one of the conditions of its foundation in 1831. A customs union between Belgium and Luxembourg was signed in July 1921, marking the first stage in the creation of the union between Belgium, the Netherlands and Luxembourg that came into force as the 'Benelux' treaty on 1 January 1948. The referendum of September 1919 marked the start of a period of internal calm that was further helped by the introduction of universal suffrage for men and women at the end of the year. In the ensuing elections the Catholic Party won an outright majority. From 1925 the duchy was ruled by a coalition of Catholics, Liberals and Conservatives. Until May 1940, when it was again overrun by German troops, Luxembourg was spared any further serious upheavals.

Unlike Belgium and Luxembourg, Switzerland had been able to maintain its neutrality unchallenged throughout the First World War, only to succumb to a serious internal crisis in the autumn of 1918, when plans by the federal parliament to introduce compulsory community service triggered violent protests among the workforce. When troops were mobilized in Zurich in early November with the aim of preventing a planned demonstration from taking place to mark the first anniversary of the October Revolution in Russia, the recently founded Olten Action Committee under the leadership of the left-wing member of the National Council, Robert Grimm, called on all workers to mount a general strike. (The Olten Action Committee had been established as a rival to the committee set up by the Social Democratic party leaders.)

The walkout began on 12 November and prompted the upper and lower houses to deploy army units under the command of Colonel Emil Sonderegger and to issue an ultimatum to the Olten Action Committee that was timed to expire on 14 November. Not every section of the workforce had taken part in the strike, and so the Committee bowed to the pressure placed on it by the state, and by 15 November the strike was over.

There was, however, one demand that the strikers made that was met in 1919, and this was the introduction of the forty-eight-hour week. By contrast, the call for immediate new elections and for women to be given equal voting rights went unheard. On 10 April 1919 three of the strike's organizers, including two members of the National Council, Robert Grimm and Fritz Platten, were sentenced to six months' imprisonment for mutiny. A further consequence of the strike was the end of diplomatic relations with Soviet Russia, which the government in Berne accused of being actively involved in the events in Switzerland in November 1918.

The elections for the National Council in October 1919 were the first to be held according to the principle of proportional representation, which had been introduced a year earlier following a referendum on the subject. The losers were the Liberal Freethinkers who had dominated Swiss politics until then and who had won 105 seats in the 1916 elections, a figure that fell to sixty in 1919. The other losers, albeit on a smaller scale, were the Catholic Conservatives. The winners, conversely, were the new Peasants' Party and the Social Democrats. The former won twenty-nine seats at its first attempt to enter parliament, while the latter increased the number of its seats from twenty-two to forty-one. For the present, however, the victorious parties were not allowed to take up their mandates. The Peasants' Party representatives had to wait until 1929, the Social Democrats until 1943, a punishment meted out to them for their participation in the nationwide strike in 1918. In 1920 the Social Democrats had declined to join the Third International, leading to the formation of a Swiss Communist Party in March of the following year, although it never acquired any great political significance. The year 1921 also saw the end of the powers introduced in 1914 that were designed to extend the authority of the Federal Council at the expense of the National Council and Upper Chamber.

Internationally, the most important question to exercise the Swiss during the interwar period was their relationship with the League of Nations. In view of the 'perpetual neutrality' that Switzerland had espoused since the early sixteenth century, it was by no means a matter of course that the country would join the League of Nations, and this remained the case even after it had become known that Geneva would be the seat of its principal institutions. In November 1919 the newly elected National Council recommended joining on condition that the country retained its neutrality and that the Council's decision was ratified by a referendum. The London Declaration of the Council of the League of Nations on 13 February 1920, which limited the imposition of sanctions to non-military areas, helped persuade the Swiss to vote yes in the referendum.

In spite of this, the question of Switzerland's entry into the League of Nations continued to stir up controversy. The leaders of the bourgeois parties adopted a positive attitude but in doing so they were speaking for only a section of their members, while the left wing of the Social Democrats was emphatically opposed to membership. The referendum on 16 May 1920 resulted in a clear majority in favour of entry, by 415,000 votes to 323,000. The victory of the yes campaign was due above all to the positive vote of the Francophone cantons in the west of the country, whereas the German-speaking cantons were opposed to such a move. As a result, the proponents of entry won by only a slender majority in the upper house.

The official interpretation of Switzerland's neutrality changed after the country had become a member of the League of Nations: its neutrality was no longer 'integral' but 'differential', limited, as it was, by its obligation to impose economic sanctions to protect the peace of nations. In part as a way of compensating for the weakening of the principle of neutrality, the country's foreign policy, which between 1920 and 1940 was dictated by the foreign minister Giuseppe Motta, stressed good relations with those of its neighbours that were most expected to break international law: Fascist Italy and, after 1933, National Socialist Germany.

Switzerland's dependence on exports and foreign labour left the country badly hit by the world economic crisis, leading to the formation of a militant opposition hostile not only to the parliamentary system but to all that was left wing and liberal. Although its membership included a number of workers, it was above all middle-class industrial workers who set the tone in the National

Front movement of the early 1930s. Two of its slogans were 'Middle class, wake up!' and 'Switzerland for the Swiss!' The largest of the country's radical right-wing organizations, it took its cue from Italian and German models in terms of its cult of its leader, its uniforms, its forms of greeting and its symbols. Its leader in Switzerland was Rolf Henne, a vocal opponent of 'Jewish cultural Bolshevism' who demanded that restrictions be placed on the number of Jewish students at the country's universities. When, for tactical reasons, the National Front adopted a less anti-Semitic tone and in general began to moderate its behaviour, Emil Sonderegger, the 'hero' who had suppressed the nationwide strike in November 1918, founded the Volksbund, or National League, in 1933. Its anti-Semitism and anti-parliamentarianism were much more openly expressed. On Sonderegger's death in 1934 the National League was subsumed into the Federal Front. Even more radical were the National Socialist Confederates who demanded annexation by Germany, while the Swiss Fascists were notable for their cult of Mussolini and for organizing an international congress of Fascists at Montreux in December 1934.

Only one of these radical right-wing organizations – the National Front – enjoyed any success in local elections in 1933, notably in Schaffhausen, where it won more than 26 per cent of the votes cast. Within three years hardly any of these groups still existed. Their greatest defeat was their failure to bring about a root-and-branch revision of the federal constitution in a referendum in September 1935, when their supporters won only 194,000 votes in favour of a more authoritarian, corporate state as against 510,000 votes against such a change.

The Social Democrats emerged as the largest party from the elections to the National Council in 1935. They now advocated a national defence policy, which they had not done since 1914, leading to a gradual easing of tension in their relations with the bourgeois parties. Two years later, the trade unions, starting with the metalworkers and watchmakers, began to sign peace agreements with the employers' organizations, and the country's economic recovery likewise played its part in calming the political situation, with the result that by the second half of the 1930s there was no longer any danger from the right. The parties of moderation, including the Social Democrats, had asserted their sway, and the National Ring of Independents founded in 1936 by the businessman Gottlieb Duttweiler, who advocated complete economic freedom, was far more successful politically than the National Front and similar organizations had ever been. Swiss democracy emerged a more potent force from the years of crisis, and the country was able to maintain its independence throughout the Second World War.

Fascism in Power: Italy under Mussolini

By the 1930s the term 'Fascist' had long since broken free from its Italian origins and was being used by many observers to describe the Swiss National

Front and numerous other right-wing organizations of the interwar years. Whenever Marxist or liberal critics spoke of 'Fascism', they were referring to right-wing movements and regimes distinguished from traditional conservatism by the extreme militancy with which they countered their left-wing enemies and by their ability to win over the masses by means of demagogic and, above all, nationalist slogans. Most contemporary authors regarded the urban and rural middle classes as the Fascists' principal source of support, that social group between the bourgeoisie and the working class that felt threatened by big business on the one hand and by the industrial proletariat on the other and which had not yet managed to create an independent political organization of its own.

In Italy, the left-wing reformist writer Giovanni Zibordi was one of the first to attempt a detailed examination of the social basis of Fascism, describing Italy in 1922 as a country in which the petit bourgeois was 'superfluous'. In Fascism Zibordi saw, first, a 'counter-revolution of the bourgeoisie proper in response to a *red* revolution which only threatened but never took place (as an insurrectionary act)'; second, 'a revolution, or rather an upheaval, of the middle classes, of the disoriented, the deprived and the discontented'; and, third, a 'military revolution'. This last-named term was used by Zibordi to refer to those sections of the officer corps, together with the *carabinieri* and the police, who, like many former soldiers, were sympathetic to Fascism because for them it signified 'a prolongation of the state of war internally, and a possibility of war externally'. The great strength of Fascism lay in the fact that

> it brought into combination against the socialist proletariat both the cold, calculating hostility of the authentic bourgeoisie, and the fanatical hatred of these middle classes who were overwhelmed in the post-war crisis, and who directed all the ferment and rancour of their distress on to the proletariat rather than on to the class, or rather regime, that was socially dominant.[73]

By drawing attention to the bourgeois, middle-class and militant elements of Fascism, Zibordi was seeking to avoid a one-sided sociological interpretation of the term. In his view, Fascism was also, but not exclusively, a movement on the part of the *ceti medi*, or middle classes. This is an assessment that is confirmed by professional statistics for the Partito Nazionale Fascista (PNF) in 1921, when 24.3 per cent of its members were farmworkers and 15.4 per cent were employed in industry. Students and schoolchildren accounted for 13 per cent of the total, peasants and smallholders for 11.9 per cent, the privately employed 9.9 per cent, businessmen, craftsmen and dealers 9.2 per cent, the self-employed 6.6 per cent and public employees 4.7 per cent.

These figures for 1921 indicate the way in which Fascism had made broad inroads into society, while failing to explode the theory that the movement had a particular appeal for the middle classes. When measured against the makeup of the population in general, farmworkers and industrial workers were under-represented in the PNF, while the middle class and, in particular, the 'new middle class' of white-collar workers was overrepresented. This was especially true of schoolchildren, students and teachers, three groups in which the lack of available jobs had led to a widespread fear that, far from climbing the social ladder, they were condemned, instead, to descend it.

The German historian Jens Petersen has described the PNF as 'the first bour-geois mass party in Italy'.[74] But the fact that almost 40 per cent of its membership was made up of workers suggests that it might be better described as a people's party or even as a nationalist party. The Fascists differed from other parties by dint of the fact that their ranks included many young people: in 1921 around a quarter of their members were under the age of twenty-one. In October 1922 the average age of members in the province of Reggio Emilia was twenty-five. By the date of the 'March on Rome' in October 1922, the PNF had more members than any other party in Italy, and during Mussolini's first year in power its numbers increased dramatically: by December 1923 it had 783,000 members.

But Mussolini's government included more than just Fascists, for the Duce, who held the posts of prime minister, foreign secretary and home secretary, also gave cabinet appointments to independent experts such as the former chief of the general staff, Armando Diaz, whom he appointed minister of war, and Admiral Paolo Thaon di Revel, who became minister for the navy. Other cabinet ministers were members of the Christian Democrat Popolari, the Democratic Party and the Liberal Party. The most prominent Liberal was the philosopher Giovanni Gentile, although even by this date Gentile was already moving away from his Liberal convictions in the direction of Fascism.

One Fascist member of Mussolini's cabinet was the finance minister from 1922 to 1925, Alberto De Stefani, who taught economics and also ran the Italian Exchequer from 1923 to 1925. His laissez-faire economic policy was supportive of business leaders and meant that industry closed ranks behind the new government. He was particularly admired for sorting out the country's finances with the help of the special powers that the Chamber of Deputies and Senate granted the government for a twelve-month period. But the Liberals' hope that Mussolini would keep his promise of *normalizzazione* in general and disband his storm troops in particular proved to be misplaced, and in January 1923 his *squadre* were incorporated into the Milizia Volontaria per la Sicurezza Nazionale, a new and voluntary reserve army that was initially not based in barracks or required to swear an oath of allegiance to the king. Financed by the state, it lent its support to Mussolini as 'il Duce del Fascismo'. The PNF's Supreme Advisory and Executive Council, the Gran Consiglio del Fascismo, had been created the previous month, in December 1922, a development that marked the start of a process typical of Fascism, with the Supreme Council in competition with parliament, while the Fascist militia provided a pillar of support alongside the Italian army.

In March 1923 the Associazione Nazionalista Italiana that Enrico Corradini had founded in 1910 as a radically nationalist defence league merged with the Fascist party. Two of its leaders, Luigi Federzoni and Alberto Rocco, later assumed key roles in the government, Federzoni becoming minister of the interior in June 1924, Rocco taking over the Ministry of Justice in January 1925. The ministers from the Popolari Party were dismissed from the cabinet at the end of April 1923 after a Catholic Party congress in Turin had criticized the Fascists' continuing acts of violence and questioned their ideology, as well as opposing the electoral reforms introduced by Mussolini. The new electoral law – the *Legge Acerbo* – was passed in July 1923, its sole function being to provide a solid majority for the joint list of Fascists and their bourgeois allies, or *Fianchegiattori*. If it received at least a quarter of the votes cast, then the most successful list was allotted two-thirds of the seats. In the Chamber of Deputies 235 members voted for the measure, 140 against it. In the Senate the votes were 165 in favour, forty-one against.

Among those who voted against the new bill were the Communists and the Socialists, the Reform Social Democrats associated with Ivanoe Bonomi and the members of Giovanni Amendola's Democratic Party. Most of the Popolari members abstained, while the thirty-nine who voted for or against the bill were excluded from the party. A number of members of the Senate who were particularly close to the Vatican then proceeded to leave the party of their own volition, a move interpreted as the Curia's rejection of the party. The Liberals, including three former prime ministers, Giolitti, Salandra and Orlando, voted for the *Legge Acerbo* and were guilty, therefore, of rejecting the parliamentary system. They continued to regard Mussolini's government as the lesser of two evils when compared with the chaos of the early post-war period. They accepted the reign of terror on the part of local Fascist leaders because it was directed not against them but against the political left.

The 'March on Rome' brought no respite from the Fascists' reign of terror in the streets, and long after Mussolini had come to power his party members continued to commit countless acts of violence against their political enemies. Between 18 and 20 December 1922, for example, between eleven and twenty-two Communists, anarchists and Socialists were murdered in Turin by way of reprisal for the death of two Fascists. (Sources cannot agree on the exact figure.) Few members of the *squadre* were ever arrested and sentenced, whereas large numbers of Communist officials were rounded up: between December 1922 and February 1923, 2,235 such officials were taken into custody, 252 of them in connection with the arrest of Amadeo Bordiga, the ultra-left-wing leader of the Communist Party and a man vehemently opposed to all forms of cooperation between Communists and Socialists. He was relieved of his position in April 1923 by the Executive Committee of the Communist International, which had adopted the tactics of the left-wing United Front in the wake of the Fascists' seizure of power. Bordiga's group no longer had a majority in the new party leadership that was put in place by the Comintern.

The first elections to be held after the new electoral law had come into force took place on 6 April 1924. The election campaign was marked by acts of violence committed by the *squadre* and visited on the left-wing opposition. But in spite of vote-rigging and sustained attempts to intimidate their opponents, the Fascists and their allies still won only 65 per cent of the votes cast, returning 374 members to parliament as against the opposition's 140, a total that included thirty-nine Popolari, twenty-four Reformists from the Partito Socialista Unitario, twenty-two Socialist Maximalists and nineteen Communists. In the northern regions of Piedmont, Liguria, Lombardy and Venetia the opposition parties were actually in the majority, only elsewhere did the government *listone* prevail.

On 30 May 1924, barely two months after the elections, Giacomo Matteotti, the secretary of the Partito Socialista Unitario, delivered a speech in the Chamber of Deputies in which he inveighed against the Fascist terror during the election campaign and demanded that the election be declared invalid, a call repeatedly interrupted by shouts from the Fascists and their allies. Nor did the Fascists limit their response to verbal attacks, for on 10 June Matteotti was attacked by five *squadristi* under Amerigo Dumini while on his way to the parliament building on the Lungotevere Arnaldo di Brescia, dragged into a car and stabbed through the heart. His body was not recovered until 16 August, when it was found in the Macchia della Quartarella, a forested area in the parish of Riano outside Rome.

Matteotti's disappearance plunged Italy into a state of extreme disquiet and presented the ruling Fascists with their most serious crisis to date. With the exception of the Communists and a few independent Liberals, including Giolitti, the opposition members of the second chamber under Amendola, walked out of the building and in doing so followed the legendary classical example of the *secessio plebis* at the beginning of the fifth century BC, repairing to the Aventine in order to constitute a body truly representative of the common people. On 13 June Mussolini told the chamber that only one of his enemies could have thought up and perpetrated a deed as dastardly as the one committed on 10 June, and the following day he dismissed a number of his discredited officials, including his chief press officer, Cesare Rossi, and the undersecretary of state at the Ministry of the Interior, Aldo Finci. On 16 June Mussolini stepped down as minister of the interior and transferred his powers to the former Nationalist politician, Luigi Federzoni. In the course of the weeks that followed, the chief of police, Emilio de Bono, ensured that the *squadristi* who had committed the murder and who in the meantime had been arrested were able to flee and avoid punishment. De Bono was then relieved of his duties and placed in charge of the militia.

No matter how many denials the Fascists may have issued, few Italians were in any doubt as to who was ultimately responsible for Matteotti's murder, and by the middle of August it was clear beyond peradventure that the guilty party was Mussolini. And yet his enemies failed to act. The Aventine opposition may have established a precarious unity, but it remained ineffectual. A general strike demanded by the Communists did not take place because the majority of anti-Fascist representatives in the lower house felt that this would be playing with fire and risked causing a civil war. Instead, many Italians, including Amendola, placed their hopes in the intervention of King Umberto II, but the latter merely shifted the burden of responsibility to the Chamber of Deputies, which had been a rump parliament since the withdrawal of the opposition, and to the Senate, which expressed its confidence in Mussolini's government on 26 June and again on 5 December.

On 27 December, Amendola's newspaper, *Il Mondo*, published a 'Memoriale' by the dismissed Rossi that incriminated Mussolini, claiming that shortly after Matteotti's speech on 30 May, the Duce had asked Rossi: 'Cosa fa questa Ceka?' (What is this Cheka doing?) Mussolini had allegedly gone on: 'What is Dumini doing? After a speech like that, this man should be taken out of circulation.'[75] Amerigo Dumini was in charge of an organization similar to the Bolsheviks' secret police force, or Cheka. If this is what Mussolini really said, then his comment could be interpreted only as an invitation to silence an opposition member of the lower house. Rossi's article, accusing the head of government of commissioning a murder, seemed to lend credence to the anti-Fascists' suspicions and turn it into a certainty.

Mussolini had spent much of the late summer and autumn of 1924 hesitating over whether he should pay greater heed to radical Fascists such as Roberto Farinacci, who were urging him to deal more decisively with the opposition, or whether it would be better to continue to work closely with his Liberal supporters, which would mean adopting a more moderate policy. At a Liberal Party conference in Livorno in early October, the government position was in a minority. In November, Giolitti and Orlando turned against the government and were joined by Salandra at the end of December, following the publication of Rossi's piece in *Il Mondo*. In the wake of the defection of his former partners, Mussolini was left with only the hard core of the Fascist movement to support him. His position was now compromised, and his only way of remaining in power was to end the crisis by what effectively amounted to a *coup d'état* – his second, if we also count his 'March on Rome'.

On 2 January 1925 Mussolini discussed his intentions with the king, and on the 3rd he appeared before the Chamber of Deputies, delivering what was his most important speech to date and taking complete 'political, moral, and historical responsibility for all that had happened':

> If Fascism has been nothing more than castor oil and the rubber truncheon, instead of being a proud passion of the best part of Italian youth, then I am to blame! If Fascism has been a criminal association, then I am the chief of

this criminal association! [. . .] When two irreducible elements are locked in a struggle, the solution is force. [. . .] Italy wants peace, tranquillity, calm in which to work. We shall give her this tranquillity and calm, by means of love if possible but by force if necessary. You may be sure that within the next forty-eight hours after this speech, the situation will be clarified in every field.[76]

In order to provoke his listeners even further, Mussolini directed their attention to the potential use of Article 47 of the constitution of March 1848, which gave them the right to indict ministers of the king and hale them before the country's Supreme Court.

The events of 3 January 1925 marked a turning point in the history of Italian Fascism. The regime was now established as the open dictatorship that had been the aim of every move since the 'March on Rome' in October 1922. Within the forty-eight hours that Mussolini referred to in his speech, the last remaining Liberal ministers were dismissed. The former Nationalist Alfredo Rossi was placed in charge of the Ministry of Justice. Countless opposition newspapers were impounded and afterwards placed under strict censorship. The country's most important newspaper, *Il Corriere della Sera*, had already adopted the government line in November 1924, when the Crespi family which owned the paper, responding to intense pressure, sacked its liberal editor in chief, Luigi Albertini. Shortly afterwards the Fascists also took control of the Turin-based *La Stampa*.

On 7 January 1925 the minister of the interior, Luigi Federzoni, reported on the steps that he had taken: numerous political clubs had been closed down, allegedly seditious organizations had been disbanded, many suspicious premises had been searched and dangerous troublemakers had been arrested. The Aventine opposition protested in a manifesto dated 9 January, complaining at the infringement of civil liberties and describing events as the final stage of the conflict between Fascism and the people. When a number of opposition members of the Chamber of Deputies tried to enter the building, their passage was barred. On 18 February, Roberto Farinacci, the driving force behind attempts to suppress the independent press, was elected secretary general of the Fascist Party by the Gran Consiglio. Appealing to Mussolini, he declared that hitherto Fascism had won only a single victory and still had to win the war.

The opposition could not have been crushed so comprehensively if it had realized in good time that it could be politically effective only if it agreed on a common policy and stuck to that plan. The belated critique of Mussolini's policies that was voiced by Giolitti, Orlando and Salandra was unconvincing not least because they had already forfeited their moral credibility by collaborating with the Fascists. The bourgeois Liberals were additionally weakened by the fact that their main supporters in society – industrialists and major landowners – had no intention of crossing swords with a system that protected their interests far more effectively than any previous government had done. Those of Italy's previous representatives who eschewed all further political involvement were generally left in peace by the new dictatorship. Prominent figures in the country's intellectual life such as the philosopher Benedetto Croce, who did not turn unequivocally against the Fascist regime until the beginning of 1924, were treated with relative forbearance, and his journal, *La Critica*, was able to continue publication without being subjected to Fascist control.

The measures undertaken in the early months of 1925 were merely the first step on the road to a Fascist dictatorship. It was a development that was driven in no small part by the Fascist trade unions, or Sindacati Nazionali, which merged as the Confederazione Nazionale delle Corporazioni Sindacali in early 1922 under the leadership of Edmondo Rossoni. While arguing for an end to the class struggle and for cooperation between capital and labour, the Sindacati also maintained the right to strike, in which respect they differed from the 'yellow' trade unions that were friendly to employers and that existed in other countries. Within the PNF they were always on the side of the extremists associated with Roberto Farinacci and Italo Balbo.

The insistence on the right to strike was not merely theoretical, for in the early months of 1925 the Sindacati Nazionali unleashed an anti-capitalist campaign that culminated in a strike by Fascist metalworkers in February and March. Six months later, on 2 October 1925, the Fascist trade unions signed a deal with the employers' umbrella organization, or Confindustria: under the terms of the Patto di Palazzo Vidoni, they agreed not to strike as long as the employers' organization refrained from locking them out. Both parties also agreed on the need to sideline the Commissioni Interne that the Fascists had never managed to bring under their control. The Sindacati Nazionali ensured that they enjoyed the sole right to negotiate collective wage agreements and in doing so robbed the other trade unions of their entire raison d'être. The socialist Confederazione Generale del Lavoro duly disbanded itself. In April 1926 the agreements signed in October 1925 were given legal form by the minister of justice, and the specialist organizations of employers and employees were accorded state recognition as long as at least one-tenth of their members were professional members of those organizations.

On 4 November 1925, a month after the Patto di Palazzo Vidoni was signed, Tito Zaniboni, a former member of the Chamber of Deputies who had represented the Partito Socialista Unitario, made an attempt on Mussolini's life. Although the attempt was thwarted at the last minute, it had major repercussions when the government banned the PSU (one of Zaniboni's fellow conspirators, General Luigi Capello, was a Freemason) and Rocco rushed the *Leggi fascistissime* through parliament. The most important of these laws concerned the Capo del Governo and his new and comprehensive extraordinary powers, while at the same time depriving parliament of its right to initiate laws. A law dated 31 January 1926 gave the executive the right to pass ordinances with the force of law whenever it felt that it was appropriate to do so, a move that effectively abolished the previous division of power. A series of laws was then enacted that consolidated the position of the prefects, abolished local government (elected mayors were replaced by a *podestà* appointed by the state), forced all journalists to join a regulatory organization and allowed politically unreliable civil servants to be dismissed from their posts without further ado.

The *Leggi fascistissime* were nothing if not statist: in other words, it was not the Fascist movement that set the tone, but the state. And yet it was not the existing state that used the Fascist Party as its instrument of power but the Fascist state led by the Capo del Governo e Duce del Fascismo, namely, Benito Mussolini. In 1926 the movement's mouthpiece, Roberto Farinacci, was forced to step down as its secretary general, and many of his followers lost their positions within the party. At the same time, many regional party leaders were stripped of their powers. Only those who adopted the new party line were allowed to remain in their posts. Farinacci was replaced by Augusto Turati, who retained his position until 1930, gradually turning the Partito Nazionale Fascista into an instrument of government.

In 1927 membership of the Fascist Party passed the one million mark. On 5 January Mussolini placed the regional party secretaries under the direct control of a prefect, a development that Wolfgang Schieder has described as

> a turning point in the history of the PNF from a united party that governed the country to one that was directed in turn, a bureaucratic mass organization of careerists and conformist fellow travellers whose motivation was not primarily political. In the process it lost the aggressive thrust that extremists had brought to the party. At the same time, however, it turned out that Mussolini's plans for integration could only partially be realized. The traditional elites remained largely remote from the Fascist Party and as a result were not under the Fascist dictator's direct political control.[77]

A further attempt on Mussolini's life in the autumn of 1926 resulted in yet more repressive measures. It took place in Bologna on 31 October and was carried out by the fifteen-year-old Anteo Zamboni, who immediately afterwards was lynched by a Fascist mob. By 5 November the regime had disbanded all political parties, banned opposition newspapers, created not only a special political police force – the Divisione Polizia Politica, known as 'POLPOL' for short – but also an actual secret police, the Organizzazione di Vigilanza e Repressione dell'Antifascismo (OVRA), and cancelled all travel permits. Opposition groups were banned, their members arrested and often tortured on one of the so-called *isole maledette* that included Ustica and Lipari. One of the eminent individuals sent into internal exile in this way was the writer and general practitioner Carlo Levi, who in 1945 described his experiences in his novel *Cristo si è fermato a Eboli* (Christ Stopped at Eboli).

On 9 November the Fascist majority in the Chamber of Deputies declared that all the members on the opposition benches had forfeited their seats. On the strength of a law designed to protect the state and rushed through parliament on 25 November, a special court was set up to deal with political offences: new and retroactive punishments, including the death sentence, were introduced for crimes that were regarded as anti-Fascist; and individuals could be detained by the police without recourse to the courts. On the basis of the new law, the de facto leader of the country's Communists, Antonio Gramsci, who had already been arrested on 8 November 1926, was haled before the special court in July 1928 and sentenced to twenty years' imprisonment. All left-wing politicians and dignitaries who had not yet emigrated or been imprisoned now tried to leave the country. By November 1926 Italy was officially a one-party state and more than ever a police state.

The politics of repression could work only because it was accompanied by a politics of integration. Created in 1925, the leisure organization Opera Nazionale Dopolavoro set out to win over the workers, its manifold lures in the field of sports, culture and tourism seeking to compensate the masses for their loss of political freedom and for their lower wages. To a certain extent it did indeed achieve this aim, its membership rising from 280,000 in 1926 to 1.6 million in 1929 and finally to 4.6 million in 1940.

Far less effective were attempts to overcome class differences and deal with the class struggle in the new *stato corporativo*. On 21 April 1927, the anniversary of the legendary foundation of Rome, the Grand Fascist Council passed the *Carta del Lavoro*, which provided for the incorporation of all the state-recognized professional associations of employers and employees – the *confederazioni* – within a series of *corporazioni*. The aim was for representatives of capital and labour to work together under the guidance of state and party in the national interest in order to regulate and plan industrial production. In May 1928 a new electoral law gave the *confederazioni* the right to propose candidates for the Fascist list in parliamentary elections, a right which, given the crucial influence of the PNF, existed only on paper.

The first election to take place on the basis of the new law was held in March 1929 and produced the expected result, 8.5 million voters supporting the Fascist list, with only 136,000 against it. Five years were then to pass before another law was passed on 5 February 1934, defining the formation and tasks of the *corporazioni* and creating a national assembly for the total of twenty-two such bodies. Within the *stato corporativo* it was no longer possible for autonomous interests to be represented. Throughout this period it was the Fascist centre of power around Mussolini that proved decisive: with their ponderous apparatus, the *confederazioni* and *corporazioni*, together with the one-party parliament, served only as a legitimizing façade. It was a situation that remained unchanged even after parliament and the corporations merged in January 1939 as the Camera dei Fasci e delle Corporazioni.

The Lateran Pacts of 11 February 1929 were also intended to promote the regime's policy of integration. The first of them restored the Church state that had ceased to exist in October 1870, when Rome had been annexed by the kingdom of Italy. The recognition of the pope's sovereignty and rule over the Città del Vaticano allowed the See of Rome to declare that the 'Roman Question' – the status of the pope – was now finally settled. The second treaty was a financial agreement that offered the Vatican generous compensation for the loss of its temporal power in 1870. The third treaty, or Concordat, granted the Catholic Church privileges that it would never have enjoyed under a liberal government and included the acknowledgement of Catholicism as the country's official religion; a guarantee that the Church could teach religion and assume responsibility for the spiritual welfare of the nation's schools; and the recognition that marriages concluded in church were also valid under civil law.

One obstacle that lay in the way of any agreement was the monopoly enjoyed by the Fascist Youth Organization, or Opera Nazionale Ballila, a movement established in 1926 and named after a fifteen-year-old boy who in 1790 had thrown a stone that marked the start of the uprising against the Austrians in Genoa. All boys between the age of seven and fourteen could be members of the Opera Nazionale Ballila, during which time they were to receive physical and military training and a political education. Membership was not compulsory. Parallel organizations were the Piccole Italiane for girls of between eight and fourteen and the Avanguardisti and the Giovani Italiane for girls and boys between fourteen and eighteen. The Church was able to ensure that its own youth movement, the Associazione di Azione Cattolica, was granted special status and was allowed to continue on condition that its members refrained from engaging in any of the activities that were the legal preserve of the Opera Nazionale Ballila. At universities, conversely, Catholic and all other non-Fascist societies were banned. Practically all male students were members of the Gruppi Universitari Fascisti.

The Lateran Pacts drew a line under a long-standing conflict that had soured relations between Church and state for almost six decades. With the restoration of the pope's secular rule and the new privileges accorded to the Catholic Church in Italy, one of the fundamental decisions of the Risorgimento – its support for a secular nation state – was reversed. Of course, Fascism had no intention of declaring itself 'Catholic' or even 'Christian'. But the Pacts of 1929 allowed it to consolidate its position not only internally by binding the country's Catholics even more firmly to the new order but also abroad, where the prestige of Fascist Italy and its leader was substantially enhanced: throughout the rest of the world Catholics now had a reason to feel a certain fondness for Mussolini and his regime.

If Mussolini's government acquired any real legitimacy in the years after the 'March on Rome', then this was due above all to the economic upturn that the country enjoyed after December 1922. Although this development reflected events taking place in the international economy, it was helped in no small way by the liberal economic policies and rigorous budgetary planning of the finance minister, Alberto De Stefani. (Italy did not yet have its own Finance Ministry.) Between 1922 and 1929 industrial production increased by 50 per cent, and agriculture, too, recorded impressive growth rates thanks, not least, to the government's *battaglia di grano*, which boosted cereal production. For ideological reasons, too, agriculture enjoyed the regime's attention, for the Fascists were so convinced that industrialization had inflicted untold social and mental harm on the country that they encouraged a policy of *ruralizzazione*, or ruralization. The growth of the cities was felt to be unhealthy and had to be stopped, while rural areas needed to be developed. In this way the government also hoped to stem the tide of Italians leaving the country to work abroad.

The sort of agrarian reforms that would have damaged the interests of the major landowners and that might have included a redistribution of wealth or the abolition of the metayage system in Tuscany were ruled out from the very beginning: the owners of the latifundia were the Fascists' principal allies and so they could not be antagonized, for without their help Mussolini's party would not have come to power. In turn this meant that the process of ruralization could assume the form only of internal colonization, and here the only areas that came into question were the Maremma in Tuscany, the Maccarese to the north of Rome and the Pontine Marshes to the south of the capital.

The task of draining the Pontine Marshes began in 1930. It was a project that had long been planned but which at the time of the world economic crisis additionally became a state-funded job-creation scheme designed to boost the economy. Five new towns were created here in the course of the 1930s: Littoria, present-day Sabaudia, Pomezia, Aprilia and Pontina. All were conceived as communal rural centres and were modelled on the ideal Fascist city: at the centre of each of them stood the town hall facing the Catholic church, both of which were dwarfed by the local party headquarters, or Casa del Fascio, with its lictors' tower. As a rule, the heart of the new town also featured a barracks for the local militia and a leisure centre for the Opera Nazionale Dopolavoro.

Like the *battaglia di grano*, the country's ruralization programme benefited from a vast amount of political propaganda, and yet it still failed to achieve the desired results. Between 1921 and 1930 the number of people in work rose by 1.1 million, whereas in the agricultural sector it fell by 530,000. By 1940 only 100,000 people had been resettled in newly cultivated areas. Since Fascism had no wish to present itself as a backward-looking movement, it could not systematically privilege the countryside over the towns, and in order to counter the crisis of 1929 and later, it was required to boost industrial production which, adopting the practices of previous governments, it achieved by means of protectionist measures that were now dictated by the utopian goal of economic self-sufficiency: the country's steel industry produced goods worth between 50 per cent and 100 per cent more than those on the international market.

The principal instrument of the Fascists' industrial policies was the Istituto per la Ricostruzione Industriale (IRI) that was established in 1933 and that for a time controlled 42 per cent of the capital of all public limited companies and all the industries that would be important in wartime. With a management that was part private, part nationalized, the IRI presumably helped to ensure that in the 1930s the growth rates of Italy's gross domestic product exceeded those of the European average for the first time, which meant that in 1938 Italy's share of world industrial production reached 2.8 per cent, slightly higher than the 1928 figure of 2.7 per cent.

Fascism sought to impose its imprint not only on the newer towns but also on the older ones. Under the watchword *sventramento*, historic city centres were torn down wherever possible in order to make room for monumental Fascist buildings and new axial roads. But it was Rome that bore the brunt of the regime's policy of urbanization. Here the entire road network in the inner city was redesigned in the shape of a star by Mussolini's chief architect, Marcello Piacentini. At the centre of the star was the Palazzo Venezia, Mussolini's head-quarters since 1929. The wide new streets were not only suitable for parades but also allowed crowds to converge on the Palazzo Venezia, from whose balcony the charismatic Duce harangued his audiences.

Of the older buildings in Rome, only those from the city's imperial past struck Mussolini as worth preserving. Buildings were demolished in order to grant an unimpeded view of the remains of imperial Rome: the Capitol, the Forum Romanum, the Palatine, the Colosseum and the Circus Maximus. All of these were to be transformed into a single vast memorial. This was also the aim of the project that revolved around the Via dell'Impero, now the Via dei Fori Imperiali: the old centre of Rome's imperial rule was in this way surrounded by a broad ring road that Mussolini was equally keen should be used for parades.

Under Mussolini, the ancient city of Rome was radically redesigned, as Wolfgang Schieder has noted:

> Topographically speaking, the Rome of classical antiquity, above all impe-rial Rome, was henceforth present only in a Fascistically alienated form. In order for visitors to get to know the ancient monuments in their authentic guise, they must first remove the Fascist layers that have been superim-posed on them. Or at the very least they need to know what these layers are. As long as this is not the case, then Roman antiquity will continue to be represented only by Fascism.[78]

The Fascists' cult of Rome – *romanità fascista* – was a reflection of the regime's desire to enhance its reputation by appealing to a historic model both unparalleled and peerless. The Roman Empire was regarded as the prototype of the new *impero fascista* that was still to be created. Most of Fascism's symbols and concepts derived from ancient Rome, from the *fasci* and lictors' towers to the hierarchical structure of the militia in the form of *manipoli, centurie, coorti* and *legioni* and including the right arm raised in salutation. In 1926 Mussolini visited Libya, where Italy was involved in a series of struggles with the local independence movement and where he had himself acclaimed as a latter-day Scipio Africanus. Following the Abyssinian War of 1935–6 he modelled himself on the Emperor Augustus and proclaimed himself a peacemaker. To mark the two-thousandth anniversary of the birth of the first Roman emperor, he reconstructed the Ara Pacis of AD 9 as part of a modern pavilion between the completely rebuilt Mausoleum of Augustus and the Tiber. Italy and the world were to be left in no doubt as to the identity of Augustus's legitimate heir, a man uniquely qualified to preserve his forebear's spirit: il Duce del Fascismo.

Unlike Communism, Fascism did not have a detailed ideology that could lay claim to scholarly validity, its propagandists' pronouncements being based for the most part on an irrational philosophy dating back to the late nineteenth and early twentieth centuries, notably Henri Bergson's theory of the existence of an *élan vital* and Georges Sorel's plea for 'direct action' and for the courage to embrace myth. In March 1925 a conference of Fascist intellectuals in Bologna agreed on a manifesto written by Giovanni Gentile and addressed to the 'intellectuals of all nations':

> Like all great individual movements, fascism is becoming stronger all the time, more able to attract and to absorb, more effective and integrated in the complex of souls, ideas, interests, and institutions that compose it (the vital merger of the Italian folk). For this reason, it is now beside the point to count and measure mere individuals. The time has come to look at the idea itself and to evaluate it. Like all true ideas, this one is alive and powerfully vibrant. It is not made up *by* man but made *for* man.[79]

In a response published shortly afterwards, Benedetto Croce dismissed the manifesto as 'brimming over with half-baked notions worthy of a schoolchild. At every turn one encounters philosophical confusions and faulty reasoning.'[80]

Not until 1932 did Mussolini think that the time had come to comment on the 'doctrine of Fascism', which he did in an article he contributed to the *Enciclopedia Italiana*. In his view, 'the man of Fascism' led 'a life in which the individual, through the denial of himself, through the sacrifice of his own private interests, through death itself, realizes that completely spiritual existence in which his value as a man lies'. Fascism was

> a religious conception in which man is seen in his immanent relationship with a superior law and with an objective will that transcends the particular

individual and raises him to conscious membership in a spiritual society. Whoever has seen in the religious politics of the Fascist regime nothing but mere opportunism has not understood that Fascism besides being a system of government is also, and above all, a system of thought. [. . .] In this sense Fascism is totalitarian, and the Fascist State, the synthesis and unity of all values, interprets, develops and gives strength to the whole life of the people.

The concept of Fascist authority had nothing to do with a police state: 'A party that governs a nation in a totalitarian way is a new fact in history.'[81]

According to this horse's mouth definition proffered by Mussolini, Fascism amounted to a repudiation of enlightened reason and set store instead by the power of the instinctual will. Fascism was anti-individualistic, anti-liberal and anti-materialist. It opposed the whole idea of a democracy that equated the people with the majority and claimed to embody a purer form of democracy because it had a qualitative understanding of the people. Fascism saw in the state an absolute, whereas individuals and groups were relative. It was nationalist, bellicose and expansionist and rejected the whole idea of the international brotherhood of man:

War alone brings up to their highest tension all human energies and puts the stamp of nobility upon the peoples who have the courage to meet it. [. . .] For Fascism the tendency to Empire, that is to say, to the expansion of nations is a manifestation of vitality. [. . .] Peoples who rise or re-rise are imperialist, people who die are renunciatory.

Mussolini had no hesitation in calling Fascism 'the doctrine of the present age', a claim he justified by arguing that the nations of his own day wanted authority, guidance and order. Indeed, he even insisted that Fascism now had a universality that was shared by all doctrines that 'have significance in the history of the human spirit'. In short, Mussolini seemed to believe in 1932 that Fascism was no purely Italian phenomenon but a particular type of regime that could be adopted by other nations prepared to accept a radical break with the illusions of the age of liberalism and the promises held out by Marxism.[82]

But whenever he struck a more concrete note, Mussolini invariably emphasized the uniqueness of Italy and its historic mission. It was, rather, the anti-Fascists on the political left who stripped the term 'Fascism' of its Italian connotations in order to characterize a particular type of violent, right-wing movement, with the result that the term no longer had the same meaning as it had in the case of Italy, for whatever lessons might be learnt from Italian experiences beyond the confines of the Italian peninsula could be effective only when wedded to an equally powerful nationalism that stressed that particular country's uniqueness. 'Fascist' regimes might form alliances of convenience to resist third parties and strive to enlist sympathizers outside their own countries, but a 'Fascist International' would have been a contradiction in terms.

When Mussolini used the word 'totalitarian' in his 1932 article for the *Enciclopedia Italiana*, this was not the first time he had done so, for he had referred to the *'feroce volontà totalitaria'* of Fascism seven years earlier. Nor was the word a neologism on his part, for liberal critics such as Giovanni Amendola and Socialists such as Lelio Basso had been describing the Fascist regime as totalitarian since 1923. But what Mussolini had in mind was a state created by a unified will and unthreatened by any opposition in keeping with his motto: 'Tutto nello Stato, niente al di fuori dello Stato, nulla contra lo Stato' (Everything in the State, nothing outside the State, no one against the State).[83]

From the 1930s onwards, those regimes were regarded as totalitarian for which politics was essentially a struggle between friend and foe, where all forms of opposition were violently suppressed and all who held divergent views were intimidated by an omnipresent secret police, and where a single party maintained a monopoly of power, using ideology, propaganda and terror to gain the acclamatory approval of the masses it needed to achieve legitimacy both at home and abroad. Fascist Italy had evolved in this direction by stages: ever since the establishment of a one-party state at the end of 1926, Mussolini's Italy had been drawing ever closer to a totalitarian regime, the only comparable country being the Soviet Union, where Stalin was currently in the process of eradicating all his remaining rivals.

And yet Mussolini's rule was by no means absolute, for alongside the Duce there was also the king who, if lacking in any personal charisma, enjoyed the status of his office and remained the commander in chief of his country's armed forces. There was also the military, which was never under the complete control of the Fascist Party. And there was the civilian apparatus of the state and the Catholic Church, which commanded considerable respect among large sections of Italian society. Nor was this society 'aligned' in the spirit of Germany's *Gleichschaltung*. Although the regime had succeeded in neutralizing the workforce, it was never really able to integrate it. And if we may draw general conclusions from the behaviour of Liberal politicians and from Benedetto Croce's change of attitude, then objections to the regime were even more pronounced after 1924 than they had been before the Matteotti crisis.

The Fascist state's supporters continued to include major landowners and industrialists, whose help had been decisive in ensuring Mussolini's election as prime minister in October 1922. But far from determining the regime's policies, they found themselves increasingly put on the defensive by the growing influence of the Fascist apparatus. At no point did the famous definition of Fascism proposed by Georgi Dimitrov at the Thirteenth Plenary Session of the Executive Committee of the Communist International in December 1933 apply to Italy: 'In power, Fascism is the open, terroristic dictatorship of the most reactionary, generally chauvinist and generally imperialist elements of financial capital.'[84]

A far better account of the reality of Fascist Italy was proposed in 1930 by a right-wing Communist deviant from Germany, August Thalheimer, whose starting point was Karl Marx's analysis of the Bonapartist regime in France as expounded in his 1852 article 'The Eighteenth Brumaire of Louis Bonaparte', according to which the political system of Louis Bonaparte – later the Emperor Napoleon III – was 'the executive authority which has made itself independent'. Total control of the state had fallen into Louis Napoleon's lap because the bourgeoisie and the proletariat were by then so battle-weary that neither class was strong enough to fight a new battle. The bourgeoisie had come to realize that if it was to salvage its social power, it would have to forgo any further attempt to exert its political influence over parliament and must seek refuge, rather, behind a powerful executive authority.

As a result, Thalheimer was able to observe a number of parallels with the present age. Like Bonapartism in France, the Fascist dictatorship in Italy was an example of an

'executive authority which has made itself independent' and of the political subjugation of the masses, including the bourgeoisie, to the authority of the Fascist state, for all that the upper middle classes and major landowners have retained their social dominance. At the same time, Fascism, like Bonapartism, claims to be the universal benefactor of every social class, hence the way in which one class is constantly played off against the next, and hence, finally, the endless internal contradictions.[85]

Can Mussolini really be seen as a reincarnation of the second emperor from the house of Bonaparte? In spite of all the differences between Bonapartism and Fascism, none of which Thalheimer denied, there were undoubtedly a number of striking parallels between the two systems. Neither in France in the 1860s nor in Italy seventy years later was the proletariat successful in its attempts to come to power. In both cases broad sections of the bourgeoisie were weary of an unstable parliamentary system and correspondingly receptive to the promise of a powerful state. In both cases the usurper had at his command a private army that was willing to use force: Louis Napoleon's army was his 'Society of 10 December', Mussolini's his *squadre*. Mussolini was far more charismatic a leader than Louis Napoleon and capable of mobilizing the masses. He knew that he needed to manipulate his audiences in order to appear in the eyes of the masses as the man he wanted to seem: a strong-willed and dynamic leader whom nothing and no one could unsettle. As long as he remained in control of his apparatus of state, with the Gran Consiglio del Fascismo at its head, and as long as he remained successful, he could be certain of the Italians' acclamation, not least because terror and vote-rigging were even more widespread in Fascist Italy than they had been in Second Empire France.

It was initially in its dealings with the outside world that Mussolini's Italy differed most markedly from the France of Louis Napoleon, who repeatedly tried to stabilize his rule by pursuing foreign policies that were aimed at enhancing his prestige, often by means of wars, but which involved a high degree of risk. Mussolini, conversely, had recourse to military action only once during his early period in office, and that was in the summer of 1923, following the murder of General Enrico Tellini, the Italian delegate at an international conference set up to rule on the Graeco-Albanian border. Tellini and his companions were killed on Greek soil. In order to ensure that Italy had a security in case of claims for compensation and also to enhance his country's international standing, Mussolini sent Italian troops to occupy the Greek island of Corfu but quickly withdrew them in response to pressure from the League of Nations and especially Great Britain after a conference of Allied ambassadors, meeting in Paris, had fined Greece fifty million lire.

During the years that followed, foreign acts of violence were confined to Italy's colonies in Africa, namely, Eritrea, Somalia, Tripoli and, above all, Cyrenaica. Here the chief of the general staff, Pietro Badoglio, who had been governor general of Tripoli and Cyrenaica since 1929, and his deputy, Rodolfo Graziani, both of whom were veterans of the Libyan War of 1911–12, spent much of 1930–31 waging a ruthless war against insurrectionists in the north of the country and ultimately against the local nomadic population in general. Poison gas was used, tens of thousands of North Africans died in concentration camps, and the rebel leader, Omar Al-Mukhtar, was publicly executed in September 1931 following a show trial. Shortly afterwards Badoglio was able to inform Rome of the successful outcome of his campaign.

In Europe, conversely, Italy's foreign policy was much more measured and in some cases even decidedly cooperative in character. In January 1924 the country reached an agreement over Fiume with the Kingdom of Serbs, Croats and Slovenes. (It had annexed the region in September 1923, during the Corfu crisis.) Friendship treaties were signed with Romania in 1926 and with Hungary in 1927. As we have already observed, Albania, by contrast, received rather shorter shrift, the two Treaties of Tirana of 1926 and 1927 serving only to make the country more dependent on Italy both politically and militarily. And Mussolini paid no heed to Austrian sensitivities when in the summer of 1923 he began his scheme rigorously to Italianize the South Tyrol and to make Italian the official language in administration and schools. By 1925 Italian had also been declared the official language in the region's courts, and in early 1926 the inhabitants of the South Tyrol were legally required to Italianize their names. By 1927 German political parties and other associations had all been banned. Italy's actions provoked impassioned cross-party protests not only in Austria but in Germany, too, and yet German policy remained essentially unaffected by these developments, Germany arguing that Rome's actions in Alto Adige were an internal matter for the Italians themselves to decide. Only once, in February 1926, did Germany's foreign minister, Gustav Stresemann, object with some force in the Reichstag to one of Mussolini's anti-German outbursts.

In the mid-1920s attitudes to Fascist Italy within the rest of Europe were divided. The Social Democrats and Communists saw Mussolini as a tyrant who in the interests of the capitalists was bloodily suppressing the working class. On the extreme right, conversely, there was enthusiastic approval for his overthrow of the 'Marxists' and his removal of a weak parliamentary system. Even among conservative politicians, however, Mussolini was widely admired. During the winter of 1926/7, for example, Winston Churchill, at that date the chancellor of the exchequer in Stanley Baldwin's second cabinet, visited Italy and reported that 'this country gives the impression of discipline, order, good-will, smiling faces'.[86] Following an audience with Mussolini in January 1927, he told a press conference that in view of a system that had been so willingly adopted, it would be absurd to claim that the Italian government was not broadly based or that it was unable to rely on the active support of the masses. 'If I had been an Italian I am sure I should have been wholeheartedly from start to finish with Fascism's triumphant struggle against the bestial appetites and passions of Leninism.'[87]

Liberals, too, admired the Fascist system of Italy and its leader. On 11 May 1930, Theodor Wolff, the editor in chief of the *Berliner Tageblatt*, described Mussolini as a moderate exponent of Realpolitik with no 'nationalistic vanity'. When, in the course of an extended interview that he conducted with the Duce, Wolff ventured to criticize the repression and imprisonment of people who disagreed with him, Mussolini had merely replied that he needed to establish an 'authoritarian democracy'.[88]

In the early months of 1932, another German liberal, the writer Emil Ludwig, conducted a series of interviews with Mussolini which he went on to publish in book form. In it he hailed the Italian leader as a 'great statesman' and 'genuine dictator' who was 'polite to a fault' and 'the most natural man in the world'. Questioned as to the dangers of his dictatorship, Mussolini had offered an explicit assurance that Fascism was 'not an article for export'.[89] Both Ludwig and Wolff were Jewish, and both were reassured by Mussolini's insistence that Fascism was not anti-Semitic, a claim that stemmed from the Italian leader's unspoken wish that he should not be lumped together with his most passionate German admirer, Adolf Hitler.

From Poincaré to Poincaré: France between 1923 and 1929

A year after the Fascists came to power in Italy, France, too, seemed to be on the verge of a crisis that threatened the country's entire political system. On 14 October 1923, the president of the Republic, Alexandre Millerand, gave a speech in Évreux near Paris in which he unambiguously demanded an increase in his presidential powers and aligned himself so clearly with the ruling Bloc

National under the prime minister, Raymond Poincaré, that the left-wing opposition interpreted his address as a thinly veiled attack on the existing parliamentary system. The gulf between Millerand – a former Socialist – and the opposition parties could no longer be bridged. Criticism of Millerand was underpinned by a large-scale campaign by the bourgeois Radical Socialists directed against the government's foreign, domestic and, above all, economic policies. During the winter of 1923/4, the leader of the Radicals, Édouard Herriot, even went so far as to demand an end to the Franco-Belgian occupation of the Ruhr Valley. The bourgeois left wanted to replace the confrontational approach of the Bloc National by closer cooperation with Great Britain and greater understanding with Germany.

In this regard there was widespread agreement between the Radicals and the Socialists, with the result that in January and February 1924 the Radical Socialists and the SFIO signed an electoral pact in the form of the Cartel des Gauches that proved extremely successful in the elections for the Chamber of Deputies in the May of that same year. Although the Bloc National polled more votes than the political left – 4.5 million as compared with 4.4 million – the electoral law that was then in force and the left wing's electoral agreements meant that the latter won a safe parliamentary majority: the parties of the Cartel returned 287 deputies, including 139 Radicals and 104 Socialists, whereas the right could muster only 228. The Communists had twenty-six deputies, a figure due in no small measure to such traditional strongholds as Paris. The radical right, in the form of Action Française, remained an altogether insignificant force.

The Cartel's victory made Millerand's position untenable. He had ignored the non-party stance required of the president and had to pay a correspondingly high price, bowing to pressure from the left and resigning on 11 June. Two days later he was replaced by Gaston Doumergue, a right-wing Radical who was leader of the Senate and who enjoyed Poincaré's support. Immediately after becoming president, Doumergue invited Herriot to form a government.

Herriot, who had taught literature at the lycée in Lyons and for many years been the city's mayor, wanted to include Socialists in his cabinet, but as long ago as April 1919, at their first post-war party conference in Paris, they had refused to be a part of any coalition government on the grounds that they supported the proletarian class struggle. The SFIO maintained this stance under Léon Blum, arguing that any deviation from the party line would risk splitting the party: its left wing could no longer be prevented from founding a left-wing socialist party or even from joining the Communists. The most that the SFIO would agree to countenance was cooperation with the progressive bourgeois parties in the form of support for a Radical government, which is what the SFIO announced it would do in June 1924.

The transfer of power in 1924 meant a radical break in France's foreign policy. Herriot, who was foreign minister as well as prime minister, could count on the Socialists' support when, at the London Reparations Conference in July and August 1924, he agreed to accept the Dawes Plan and vacate the Ruhr within a year, promises he had already given to Ramsay MacDonald in preliminary talks at Chequers at the end of June 1924. France received no guarantees from Britain or America, nor even any recognition of the link between German reparations and the debts run up by the Allies during the war. But in view of the weakness of the franc and France's resultant dependence on British and American goodwill, not even a more 'nationalist' government than Herriot's could have afforded to become embroiled in a conflict with either London or Washington. The occupation of the Ruhr had proved to be a blatant miscalculation, and by the summer of 1924 there could no longer be any doubt on that particular score.

To the east, France established diplomatic relations with the Soviet Union at the end of October 1924, a move announced by Herriot in his government's first official pronouncement and one that had the support of the ruling Radicals and the Socialists who kept them in power. France had been the main creditor of tsarist Russia and had been opposed to the Bolshevik regime not least because the latter had refused to repay the country's pre-war debts. But in 1924 Moscow signalled its willingness to enter into negotiations over compensation for French investors and to renounce any further interference in France's internal politics. (In the event, neither promise was kept.) For France's emphatically anti-Communist employers the question of reparations had in the meantime lost its significance, their main concern now being to improve economic ties with the Soviet Union, with the result that this change of political direction in October 1924 triggered no storm of protest in middle-class France.

In terms of the country's financial policies, conversely, there were fundamental differences of opinion between the Radicals and the Socialists. The former were keen to protect savers, who had been hit by the fall in the value of the franc, a fall due at least in part to international speculators, whereas the latter wanted to restore the value of the country's currency by means of a capital gains tax of 10 per cent. France's minister of finance, Étienne Clémentel, rejected this demand and resigned on 2 April 1925. He was succeeded by Anatole de Monzie, a Radical member of the Senate, who announced that he would agree to the SFIO's demands, precipitating a flight of capital to Switzerland. On 10 April the Senate voted down a finance bill and in doing so brought down Herriot's government.

Herriot's resignation marked the start of a period of political instability in French politics, six different governments holding office between April 1925 and July 1926. Only the Quai d'Orsay remained calm throughout this period, the former Socialist Aristide Briand retaining the office of foreign minister practically uninterruptedly from 17 April 1925 to 12 January 1932. Among the most notable achievements of his first year in office were the Locarno Treaties of 10 October 1925, which finally acknowledged Germany's western border. The treaties, about which we shall have more to say in due course, marked the beginning of a new chapter in Franco-German relations that was dominated by Briand and his German counterpart, Gustav Stresemann, and that was hailed by many contemporaries – but certainly not by all – as a new dawn in the Continent's history.

None of the governments of this period was able to stabilize the currency. Indeed, the franc's exchange rate sank dramatically in the summer of 1926: in the middle of 1925 the rate had been £1 to 91 francs (in 1914 it had been only 25), whereas it reached 200 in July 1926, plummeting within days to 240. On 17 July France's minister of finance, Joseph Caillaux, proposed that the government – Briand's ninth cabinet – be granted special powers, but his request was turned down by the Chamber of Deputies thanks in no small part to a speech by Herriot, who was, however, unable to achieve a parliamentary majority for a new government under his own leadership. With that, the Cartel des Gauches was over after twenty-five months in office. Its inability to prevent the fall of the franc struck most French people as an admission of defeat on the part of the political left, while at the same time appearing to supporters of the radical right as proof of the inadequacies of the parliamentary system in general.

In France the extreme right was traditionally spearheaded by the monarchist and radically nationalist Action Française and for the most part owed its political significance to the support that it received from the French clergy, including a number of prominent bishops and cardinals. In the mid-1920s the ultra-right-wing thrust of French Catholicism gained further, if temporary, impetus from the Cartel des Gauches' plans to do away with the special position of the Church in Alsace-Lorraine, where the Concordat of 1801 remained in force even after the region had been reintegrated into France in 1918. A meeting of French cardinals and archbishops in March 1925 responded to Herriot's move by condemning the country's progressive secularization and, with it, all of the country's secular laws. In turn the government withdrew its proposal in the face of opposition in the Chamber of Deputies, with the result that the Church's own opposition to Herriot's policies quickly evaporated.

In the autumn of 1926 Action Française, which had stood on the side of the Church in the struggle against secularization at the time of the Third Republic, suddenly found itself the object of a bull of excommunication, Pope Pius XI having finally seen in the 'integral nationalism' preached by Maurras and his supporters a substitute religion of a militantly secular kind. Maurras's writings were added to the Index of banned publications and Catholics risked excommunication if they read the group's daily newspaper. There followed a purge of the clergy and, above all, of the episcopacy: bishops who continued to support Action Française were replaced, and a cardinal who sympathized with Maurras was defrocked.

The break with Action Française left the nationalist movement permanently weakened. The principal beneficiaries of the Church's change of direction were those Catholics who since the *ralliement* of the 1890s had supported the Republic as a state and pursued a Christian Democratic Realpolitik. For its part the Vatican had no scruples in giving its public backing to Briand's foreign policy of peaceful understanding with Germany, which it did in a particularly demonstrative manner in the early part of 1927, only months after the fall of the Cartel des Gauches, when the papal nuncio in Paris declared the Vatican's support for the French foreign minister's approach.

In the mid-1920s Action Française was, of course, only one expression among many of right-wing radicalism in France. Among the other organizations that sprang up in the wake of the struggle to deal with the Cartel des Gauches were the Ligue Républicaine Nationale associated with the former president Alexandre Millerand; Faisceau founded in 1925 by the journalist and former committee member of Action Française, Georges Valois, the very name of whose organization reflected its debt to Italian Fascism; and Jeunesses Patriotes, set up in 1924 by the extreme right-wing member of the Chamber of Deputies, Pierre Taittinger, and an offshoot of the much older Ligue des Patriotes. Millerand's Ligue had around 300,000 members in 1926, Valois's Faisceau 60,000 and Taittinger's Jeunesses Patriotes 65,000. Many of Taittinger's members were still at school and university. Like the Camelots du Roi, the shock troops of Action Française, they engaged in running street battles with the left-wing Ligue d'Action Universitaire Républicaine et Socialiste in Paris's Latin Quarter. Action Française, Faisceau and Jeunesses Patriotes were united in their desire to bring down the Third Republic. When the Cartel des Gauches collapsed in the summer of 1926 and France entered a period of domestic stability under Poincaré, there was a temporary drop in the number of new members joining these radical organizations, and Faisceau was even disbanded in 1928. But the danger from right-wing extremism was far from over, as was to become clear during the world economic crisis after 1930.

At the other end of the political spectrum, the Communists at this period were seeking to displace the Socialists as the major party of the proletarian masses. Although the Communist Party's membership had fallen from 130,000 to 30,00 between its formation in Tours in December 1920 and 1931, the hard core of militant members still consisted of determined fighters who followed their leaders' orders with iron discipline, toeing the Comintern line and refusing to be intimidated by the repressive measures of the French state. Indeed, the Communists went out of their way to be confrontational but paid the price for their countless clashes with the police and their party leaders, including Marcel Cachin, Maurice Thorez and Jacques Duclos, spending frequent periods behind bars. On 30 April 1929 – the eve of May Day – 4,000 members of the Communist Party were taken into preventive custody; and in the October of that year the whole of the Central Committee and board of editors of the party's principal newspaper, *L'Humanité*, were haled before the country's courts.

The Communists categorically refused to countenance electoral pacts with the Socialists or bourgeois left, with the result that they were unable to turn their growing support in elections into electoral gains: in the elections for the Chamber of Deputies in 1924 the party received 875,000 votes; by 1928 that figure had risen to 1.06 million, but the introduction of the first-past-the-post system and the party's self-ordained isolation meant that the number of seats that it held in the Chamber dropped from twenty-six to twelve.

The active members of the Communist Party were for the most part recruited from the ranks of mineworkers, metalworkers and railway workers. They were also members of the Communist trade union, the CGTU. The strongholds of Communism were to be found in the heavily industrialized regions of Seine and Seine-et-Oise, as well as the suburbs of Paris, which soon became known as the *banlieue rouge*. Here the Communists won control of several town halls in the local elections in 1925, including St-Denis, where Jacques Duclos became mayor. At the same time the party was able to win over many farmers and peasants in rural areas with a long-standing anti-feudal tradition, notably in the Massif Central and the surrounding area. Here the Communists were particularly successful in the *départements* of Corrèze, Dordogne, Haute-Vienne, Allier, Cher and Lot-et-Garonne. Unlike the radical right, the Communists gained increasingly broad support among the masses through the second half of the 1920s, a situation that was noted with mounting concern by large sections of the middle classes.

For three years, starting on 23 July 1926, French politics bore the imprint of a single man: the Conservative Republican Raymond Poincaré. Once Herriot had failed to find a parliamentary majority for his cabinet, Poincaré formed a 'grand ministry' that included no fewer than six former prime ministers: among them were Briand as foreign minister and Herriot as minister of education. Poincaré himself combined the roles of prime minister and minister of finance. Also included in his government were left-wing Radicals and members of the right-wing Fédération Républicaine under Louis Marin. Among the Radicals, only a left-wing minority under Édouard Daladier refused to support Poincaré. Thanks to his expertise and reliability, the prime minister also enjoyed strong support from industry and the banking sector. A mere change of government was enough to help the franc gain in value against the pound, and within a week the exchange rate of the latter had fallen from 245 to 184 francs.

In his attempt to stabilize the economy, Poincaré began by raising taxes to a level above that recommended by a commission of experts, by making comprehensive savings to the national budget and by drastically reducing the number of civil servants. In this way he reduced first the deficit in the budget, then the deficit in the balance of payments. The Banque de France raised the basic interest rate from 6 per cent to 7.5 per cent. The special powers that Poincaré needed to implement the new rate were granted him by a large majority, a situation that differed markedly from that of the previous government. On 16 August 1926 he called a joint session of the Chamber of Deputies and Senate designed to reassure not only the signatories of war loans but also small savers: its ultimate aim was to establish a Caisse d'Amortisation that would deal with public debt.

Poincaré initially hoped to restore the franc to its pre-war rate of £1 = 25 francs but such was his fear of social unrest that he quickly abandoned this plan. On 20 December 1926 the Banque de France was authorized to buy as much foreign currency as was necessary to hold the franc at a rate of 122 francs to £1. The period of prosperity in which the western world found itself in the winter of 1926/7 also played a substantial part in ensuring that the French economy could be stabilized without any major upheavals. Only a minority of its members took part in strikes organized by the Communist CGTU.

The next elections to the Chamber of Deputies were due to take place in 1928. Poincaré used his remaining time in office to undertake a number of far-reaching reforms, including the gradual introduction of free lessons for ten- to thirteen-year-olds in grammar schools and obligatory national insurance for illness, pregnancy, old age and death, although these latter reforms, which came into force on 1 July 1930, were largely ineffectual thanks to the procrastinatory resistance on the part of most businesses. In 1927 the Chamber of Deputies restored the first-past-the-post system that had been in operation until 1919 and that involved two rounds of elections. At the urging of Léon Blum, the Socialists, who tended to support proportional representation, agreed to accept the change. At the elections in April 1928, the centre and right-wing parties formed a single bloc under the slogan 'Unité Nationale', while the Radicals and Socialists formed electoral pacts in a sizeable number of constituencies.

The first round of elections took place on 22 April 1928, when the Socialists emerged for the first time as the largest party, with 1.69 million votes. The Radicals polled 1.66 million, the right-wing parties 2.4 million and those on the centre right 2.1 million. In the second round a week later many Radical voters switched to the Unité Nationale parties, giving them a clear advantage in the form of 325 out of a total of 610 seats. If the Communists had supported the Socialist or Radical candidates in the second round of voting, rather than leaving their own candidates in the running, the result would presumably have been very different.

Poincaré used the result to stabilize the franc, which on 24 June 1928 was set at an exchange rate of 124 francs to the pound and 25.5 francs to the American dollar, once again making it a gold-based currency. This amounted to a devaluation of 80 per cent when compared with the pre-war exchange rate. It was the signatories of war loans and small savers who were the real victims of France's currency reform, but few of them complained at the inevitability of their fate. The Banque de France spent the following period hoarding gold reserves on such a scale as to invite British and American disquiet. For a time it seemed as if Poincaré had turned France into an island of stability.

But the government of national unity fell apart within months of the devaluation of the franc. The left wing of the Radical Party associated with Daladier and Caillaux insisted that it cut its ties with Poincaré, arguing that the right wing's support for the Church made it impossible for the party to remain in government any longer. Herriot was unable to prevent the party from adopting a motion at its conference in early November 1928 that demanded the resignation of its ministers. The Radical ministers duly resigned, whereupon Poincaré formed his fifth and final cabinet, this time without any Radical members and much further to the right than its predecessor had been. Two of its members were particularly notable for their right-wing views: the minister of the interior, André Tardieu, and the minister for the colonies, André Maginot.

This shift to the right had no impact on France's foreign policy. Poincaré had placed no obstacles in the way of Briand's attempts to reach a peaceful settlement with Germany, and he maintained this stance in the new government too. A new reparations agreement in the form of the Young Plan committing France to withdrawing prematurely from the Rhineland was accepted by a narrow majority on 12 July 1929. Two weeks later, on 26 July, Poincaré announced his resignation on health grounds in order to undergo an urgent operation. Since 1926 he had shifted from being a determined nationalist to being a proponent of Realpolitik willing to reach an understanding with his enemies. Throughout this period the parliamentary system had functioned better than ever in France, where the country's ability to restore order to its finances had enhanced its reputation in the eyes of the world at large. Whether or not this development would continue after Poincaré's resignation depended on more than merely political factors at home.

France's political stabilization since 1926 coincided with a marked upturn in the country's economy. Between 1924 and 1929 the gross national product had grown by around 3 per cent a year, productivity by around 2.4 per cent. The driving force behind the country's newfound prosperity was industry, whose production had grown by an average of 9.5 per cent a year between 1921 and 1929. If we take 1913 as the base year, then the index of industrial production was 140 by 1929. During the second half of the 1920s there was a comprehensive rationalization of French industry inspired by the Taylorism that had been taken over from America. Particularly remarkable was the growth in mechanical engineering, aircraft construction, car manufacture and the chemical industry. Production methods developed in the armaments industry during the war were now applied to the production of top-of-the-market consumer goods such as private cars.

In spite of the widely held view that French society remained static throughout the interwar period, there was in fact a continuous, if slow, change from an agrarian society to one dominated by industry and the service sector. In 1906 43 per cent of all the country's workers were employed in the primary sector, agriculture, whereas that figure had fallen to 30 per cent by 1932. During the same period the numbers of those employed in the secondary sector – industry and trade – rose from 30 per cent to 34 per cent, while the corresponding figures for the service sector were 27 per cent and 30 per cent. Agriculture played little part in the process of modernization but remained in a state of decline throughout the 1920s: only in four years – 1924, 1925, 1927 and 1929 – did the level of agricultural production surpass that of 1914. Between 1913 and 1929 wages of workers in Paris rose by 12 per cent, those in the provinces by 21 per cent. During the same period employers' profits went up by 50 per cent. And whereas the workforce was divided both politically and in terms of its trade union affiliations, their industrial bosses had the advantage of a unified organization to represent their interests: the Confédération Nationale de la Production Française was formed in 1919 at the suggestion of the then minister of trade, Étienne Clémentel.

Protectionist customs policies meant that the French colonies, too, played a part in the economic growth of the mother country during the interwar period. The colonies' exports doubled between 1913 and 1933. In 1929 they imported goods to the value of 19,000 million francs, 3,000 million of which came from France. Their exports were valued at 14,000 million francs. Of these, almost half were exported to France. That year France's total imports amounted to 53,000 million francs, its exports to 51,000 million. The most important export market was Algeria, which, legally speaking, consisted of three French *départements*. All three were represented in both the upper and the lower house of the French parliament, and the same was true of Cochin-China, the old colonies of Martinique, Guadeloupe, Réunion, four towns in Senegal and the French possessions in India, including Pondicherry, Chandernagore and Mahé. Apart from Senegal and the French possessions in the Caribbean, none of the native populations had the right to vote.

With the exception of the mandated territories of Syria and the Lebanon, France more or less consistently withheld the right of self-determination from all of its colonies, banking on the cultural assimilation of the elite and in this regard enjoying greater success in its black African colonies than in North Africa. France did more for colonial schooling than any other colonial power.

In the course of the 1920s and 1930s French colonial rule was questioned and challenged in south-east Asia, the Middle East, North Africa and the French Congo. In Indochina, the bourgeois revolutionary Vietnamese Nationalist Party that had been founded in Tonkin in 1927 attempted an insurrection in February 1930, the Yen Bay Mutiny, which was bloodily suppressed. Leadership of the independence movement passed increasingly into the hands of the Communists. In 1930 Nguyên Ái Quôc – later to become known as Ho Chi Minh – founded the Communist Party of Indochina in Hong Kong, having been converted to Marxism–Leninism during his years in France. In May 1930 the killing of several demonstrators in the northern city of Annam triggered a Communist uprising that quickly spread and that was not put down until 1931. Countless independence fighters were killed, and tens of thousands were deported to the plantations of Cochin-China. But the Communist Party regrouped as an underground organization and laid the foundations for the partisan struggle that was to prove such a challenge to the region's Japanese occupiers during the Second World War and, later, to France and finally to the United States of America.

In the Middle East France had to confront the problem of increasing Arab nationalism soon after the end of the First World War. In the mandated territories of Syria and the Lebanon, Paris initially banked on the Christian minority, thereby incurring the wrath of the Muslim majority. The Lebanon was occupied immediately after the end of the war, whereas it was not until the summer of 1920 that French troops drove King Faisal from Syria following his recent election by a gathering of notables in Damascus. An independent state was created in the Lebanon. Here a Christian majority faced a powerful Muslim minority. In Syria the French initially created two states, one in Damascus, the other in Aleppo, before establishing two autonomous administrative regions for two Islamic sects, the Druze and the Alawi, or Shiites.

In 1923 the Druze mounted a revolt that by 1925/6 had grown into a full-scale Syrian uprising. At its height the French bombarded Damascus, provoking outrage even in France itself: as in other questions of colonial policy, it was the Communists who were the government's sternest critics. The high commissioner who was responsible for this decision, Maurice Sarrail, was replaced by a Liberal member of the Senate, Henri de Jouvenel. The Druze uprising was over by 1927, and the following year Jouvenel's successor, the diplomat Henri Ponsot, convened a constitutional assembly, only for France to reject its conclusions, which included a joint Syrian and Lebanese state, with no mention of the rights of the mandatory power. In 1930 France imposed a constitution on Syria that reflected its own wishes. It was on the basis of this constitution that the first Syrian parliament was elected in 1932.

The mandatory power also convened a constituent assembly in the Lebanon, which in May 1926 proclaimed a constitutional Lebanese Republic. Its constitution guaranteed the rights of the mandatory power but did nothing to regulate the division of power between the various faiths, whose differences made it almost impossible for parliament to function, with the result that the constitution was repeatedly repealed and rewritten. The creation of a republic in 1926 brought the Lebanon a major step closer to independence, while additionally fuelling Syrian nationalism. Its principal organization was the National Bloc, whose president, Hashim el-Atassi, was a proponent of pan-Arabism. Another group within the National Bloc strove principally for a Greater Syria that would include not only the Lebanon but also Palestine and Transjordan, two British mandated territories. A treaty signed by France and the Syrian government in November 1933 provided for Syrian independence within the framework of an alliance with France. Due to come into effect in 1937, the plan was thwarted in 1934 by nationalists in the Syrian parliament, which was immediately dissolved by France, delaying Syria's independence for the foreseeable future.

Throughout the interwar year, pan-Arabism found a certain degree of support not only in the Middle East but also in North Africa. The movement's intellectual spokesman was the writer and historian Shakib Arslan, a Druze who had been born in the Lebanon and who settled in Geneva after the First World War. Writing in the newspaper *La Nation Arabe*, he advocated the union of all Arabs of all nations. For the Maghreb he demanded a unified state independent of France and based on Islamic orthodoxy, a demand that echoed the even more far-reaching ambitions of the pan-Islamic movement. Considerable influence was also exerted by the Egyptian Wafd Party, which had been the main force in the country's domestic politics since 1924. In the spring of 1919 the party had issued a manifesto addressed to Woodrow Wilson, inviting him to speak out in favour of the Arab people's right of self-determination.

The same demand was made by Sheikh Abdelaziz Tàalbi of Tunisia, who founded the Constitutional Liberal Party, or Destour Party, in June 1920. The party repeatedly called on the Tunisian people to demonstrate against the French authorities. Soon afterwards it adopted a more pragmatic stance and recognized the French protectorate, whereupon the country's nominal head, the Bey of Tunis, aligned himself with the party, leading to a series of heated confrontations with the French resident-general, Lucien Saint. In 1922 the protectorate power allowed the Tunisians to form local committees made up of Europeans and Tunisians and invested with certain powers in terms of their trade policies. In 1928 there was a reorganization of the Grand Council that had emerged from the Advisory Conference of 1896 and that consisted of a section directly elected by the French and another, Tunisian, section whose members were appointed by local councils and chambers.

For the younger generation of Tunisian nationalists such a symbolic division of power was far too little. The Destour Party split in 1934, when the New Constitutional Liberal Party, or Neo Destour Party, led by the then twenty-one-year-old Habib Bourguiba, demanded Tunisian sovereignty and a parliament based on universal suffrage in which Europeans and Jews would be represented in accordance with their own particular percentage share of the population. The Neo Destour Party was culturally closer to France and was also more secular – in other words, less Islamic – than the old Destour Party, with the result that it quickly gained the support not only of intellectuals but also of broad sections of the Tunisian middle classes.

The reaction of the far right resident-general, Marcel Peyrouton, was a series of repressive measures that included a ban on meetings and newspapers and the removal of Bourguiba and other party officials to the south of the country. By March 1936, the government in Paris had replaced Peyrouton by the Liberal Armand Guillon, and Bourguiba and his followers were released, but the clashes between the Tunisian nationalists and the French protectorate forces continued, escalating to bloody confrontations on 9 April 1938 between the police and demonstrators from the Neo Destour Party and to the declaration of a state of emergency. Even before the outbreak of the Second World War, French rule in Tunisia had already been rocked to its very foundations.

After 1918 the most violent struggles with an indigenous population were the ones that France had to face in Morocco, the more recent of the country's two protectorates in North Africa. The region was rich in raw materials and had already been partially industrialized. The number of Europeans in the region was relatively small when compared with the local population: some 300,000 out of a total of more than eight million. (In Tunisia there were around 200,000 Europeans out of a total of some three million, the majority of the Europeans being Italian rather than French.) The Rif rebellion against Spanish rule in north-eastern Morocco began in 1920 under the leadership of Muhammad Ibn Abd al-Karim. Three years later the Spanish abandoned their opposition and handed over much of their former protectorate to the rebels, whereupon Abd al-Karim turned his attentions to French Morocco. French and Spanish troops under Philippe Pétain launched a series of attacks on the Rif tribes, starting in 1925, forcing Abd al-Karim to capitulate in March 1926. His rebellion was too clearly modelled on older 'tribal' patterns of Berber insurrection for us to be able to label it an example of a modern anti-colonial movement, but there is little doubt that it inspired anti-colonial forces not only in Morocco but further afield as well.

Following the death of Sultan Yusef in 1927, the French resident-general Théodore Steeg persuaded the Ulema – the sultanate's supreme council of scholars and lawyers – to appoint the eighteen-year-old Mohammed as the new sultan, rather than any of his father's older sons. It was hoped that as Mohammed V he would follow the protectorate power's orders unquestioningly, and for the most part the young sultan met these expectations.

In 1930 Mohammed V triggered a major crisis when, at the urging of the new resident-general, Lucien Saint, he granted the Berber tribes autonomous jurisdiction on the basis of their own common law but limited this independence to the field of civil law, while the French judiciary continued to be liable for the region's penal legal system. This meant that the Berbers were no longer subject to sharia or Islamic law, causing violent protests on the part of Moroccan Arabs. It was not long before secular nationalists joined the protests, the privileged status accorded to the Berbers striking them as a deliberate attempt to prevent the emergence of a unified Moroccan nation. The countermovement was partially successful and in April 1934 the sultan and pasha were once again given jurisdiction over penal law.

The nationalist movement remained unimpressed by this concession, a ban on its newspaper likewise failing to deter it from continuing its protests. At the end of 1934 a Moroccan Action Committee that had been established earlier that year demanded that the protectorate's powers be curtailed, that the educational system be improved and that representative institutions be introduced. But the nationalist movement now found a new leader in Allal al-Fassi, a man with close links to the pan-Arabist Shakib Arslan and a proponent of a strictly Islamic state. After 1935 he enjoyed the sympathy of the masses to a far greater extent than the champions of secular nationalism.

Unlike Morocco and Tunisia, Algeria was officially a part of France, having been divided into three *départements* since 1848 and in 1936 numbering 950,000 French settlers, most of whom lived in major cities such as Algiers and Oran. Algeria was also the home of six million Arabs and Berbers. Some 175,000 Muslim Algerians had fought in the First World War, and 25,000 of them had fallen in battle, representing the highest loss among all the non-European nations that had fought alongside the French between 1914 and 1918. In recognition of their contribution to the Allies' victory over the Central Powers, a law was passed in February 1919 guaranteeing that French and Muslims were treated as equals for tax purposes. The same act gave Arabs and Berbers the right to elect representatives on local councils, but the French continued to be in the majority here. Only in the Financial Agencies was there parity between the two groups.

Discontent with the discrimination practised against Arabs and Berbers found expression in an initiative backed by the French Communist Party, namely, the Étoile Nord-Africaine that was formed in 1926 with demands that focused from the outset on Algerian independence. Under the influence of the charismatic Ahmed Messali Hadj the group gradually broke free from Communist influence, while remaining a revolutionary organization that drew most of its support from the working class. Messali Hadj was repeatedly arrested and his organization banned, but such official acts failed to weaken his influence. In the mid-1930s he joined the pan-Arab movement under Shakib Arslan and began to forge links with the extreme right in France. Following the definitive ban on the Étoile Nord-Africaine by Léon Blum's government in January 1937, Messali Hadj founded the Parti Populaire Algérien, only for this party, too, to be proscribed shortly after the start of the Second World War.

Unlike the Étoile Nord-Africaine, the Association des Oulémas Musulmans Algériens that was founded in 1935 by Abdelhamid Ben Badis and supported in the main by scholars and lawyers was an emphatically Islamist independence movement. Central to its activities was the building of Koranic schools and the attempt to revive traditional Islamic values. With a programme like this, the organization could no more hope to win over the masses than its diametrical opposite, the Fédération des Élus Algériens formed in 1930 by a general practitioner, Mohammed Saleh Bendjelloul, and a dispensing chemist, Ferhat Abbas. Its members were mostly Algerians with an academic training and a French education, their aim being equal rights for Arabs, Berbers and

French within a French framework and, especially, the cultural assimilation of Algerian Muslims.

This line chimed with the ideas held by the French Socialists but met with violent opposition on the part of the Étoile Nord-Africaine and the Association des Oulémas Musulmans. The plan to grant French civil rights to Arabs and Berbers that was proposed by the French government, starting in 1936, when the move was intended to cover between 20,000 and 30,000 Algerians, was thwarted by the determined opposition of the country's French settlers, resulting in a radicalization of the movement for Algerian independence: more and more members joined Messali Hadj's Parti Populaire Algérien; the assimilatory forces that were supportive of France felt rejected; and Ferhat Abbas became an advocate of complete Algerian autonomy within the framework of a federation with France. There were already early signs of the Algerian War of Independence that was to break out in 1954.

Unlike the Maghreb, French colonial possessions in black Africa were largely unaffected by any serious upheavals during the interwar years, the main exception being the French Congo. The French writer André Gide paid an extended visit to the colony between July 1925 and February 1926 and on his return to France drew public attention to the brutality with which the local population was treated by colonial officers as well as by white traders and plantation owners. His report, which was published in 1927, caused something of a sensation. By this date the religiously coloured, anticolonial protest movement of Kimbanguism that had started in the Belgian Congo had already spread to the neighbouring colony and in June 1928 took the form of violence against colonial officers and European travellers in the area around Gbaya in the Haute Sangha district. The charismatic leader of the movement was a man known only as Karnu, who together with his brother was murdered by colonial troops from Senegal in December 1928. In 1930 the authorities arrested André Matswa, the founder of the anticolonial Société Amicale des Originaires de l'Afrique Équatoriale Française, who was held responsible for fomenting unrest among the black population. His arrest was followed by strikes and further protests that were put down in the usual manner. Superficially, order had been restored, but the black population retained its sense of anger at the continuing discrimination. Although French colonial rule may have been more securely grounded in black Africa than in other parts of the world, there was no doubt that even here the first cracks were already appearing.

From Empire to Commonwealth: Britain under Baldwin

Like their French counterparts, the three British mandated territories in the Middle East – Iraq, Transjordan and Palestine – belonged to Category A among the League of Nations' mandates: they were all regarded as sufficiently well developed to be granted their independence within a relatively short space of time. Since 1921 Iraq had been ruled by King Faisal of the Hashemite dynasty that had briefly ruled over Syria, and by 1924 it was a constitutional monarchy, the first mandated territory to be granted independence. The treaty of 30 June 1930 that made this possible imposed close military and political ties with the United Kingdom that included leaving two air force bases in British hands. In Transjordan, the eastern part of the former Turkish province of Palestine, a new emirate was established in 1921 under Faisal's brother, Abdullah. Transjordan remained dependent on Great Britain to a far greater extent and for a much longer period than Iraq, not achieving its nominal independence until 1946, when it became the kingdom of Jordan.

Developments in Palestine proved far more fraught with conflict. The Balfour Declaration of November 1917 had promised the Jews a national homeland in this region, leading to increasing numbers of Jews migrating to the country. London backed such immigration, but obstacles were placed in its way by civil servants in the mandated territory, who were concerned at a possible backlash on the part of the majority Arab population. (By the early 1920s the 84,000 Jews made up just over a tenth of the total population.) The first Arab protests against Jewish immigration took place in 1920 and 1921. The treaty under whose terms the League of Nations entrusted Palestine to Great Britain in 1922 granted the Jews the right to play a part in founding a national homeland, which was to be achieved through the Jewish Agency. That same year a Supreme Muslim Council was established under the mufti of Jerusalem, Mohammed Amin el-Husseini. In 1931, by which time he was already grand mufti of Jerusalem, el-Husseini convened a General Islamic Congress in Jerusalem, turning the conflict between Jews and Palestinian Arabs into a matter of concern for the whole of the Arab and Islamic world.

Meanwhile tensions between the two sections of the population had grown markedly worse. In May 1924 the United States had introduced strict quotas on immigration, leading to a sudden and dramatic rise in the number of Polish Jews arriving in Palestine. The first bloody uprising by the Arabs took place in 1929 and ended with the deaths of 133 Jews and eighty-seven Arabs. Four years later a flood of Jewish refugees began to arrive from Germany. In 1936 the Arabs organized a general strike with the aim of putting an end to immigration, banning the sale of land to Jews and electing a Palestine parliament, demands that led to further violent clashes. In view of the persecution of Jews in National Socialist Germany, the mandated power was neither able nor willing to prevent more Jews from migrating to Palestine. By the eve of the Second World War, Jews comprised some 30 per cent of the population of Palestine. The British dream of establishing a joint state for Jews and Arabs had proved an unrealizable utopian vision, leaving the Palestinian problem unresolved.

Unlike Palestine, Egypt was not a mandated territory but a British protectorate, a status that it had enjoyed since 1914. In 1922 Great Britain, reacting to pressure from the nationalist Wafd Party under its charismatic leader Saad Zaghloul, unilaterally declared Egypt independent, but retained the right to guarantee the safety of the Suez Canal, to defend Egypt as a whole and to protect foreign interests in the country. The following year Egypt became a constitutional monarchy under King Fouad I. In the elections that were held that same year the Wafd Party emerged as the most powerful political force. In November 1924 the governor general of the Sudan and commander in chief of the Egyptian army, Sir Lee Stack, was murdered by Egyptian nationalists, prompting London to exclude Cairo from the administrative process, while continuing to charge it for the cost of jointly running the country. In 1936 violent nationalist unrest forced the British to give way and restore joint control over the Sudan and end the military occupation of Egypt. But the United Kingdom retained the right to station troops along the Suez Canal for a period of twenty years. In the event of war, Great Britain committed itself to helping the country. In return, Egypt had to make its territories available to the British. Egypt joined the League of Nations in March 1937.

Egypt was the only African country that largely broke free from British rule during the interwar years. Tanganyika consisted of the bulk of the former German colony of East Africa and was a Category B mandated territory. Here the United Kingdom attempted to maintain control through a policy of indirect rule, which involved transferring powers to traditional authorities. The first move in the direction of independence came in 1929 with the formation of the Tanganyika African Association that was not to come of age until after the Second World War. In neighbouring Kenya an independent mouthpiece for the indigenous population had been established four years earlier in the form of the Kikuyu Central Association under Jomo Kenyatta. That same year also marked the foundation of the West African Students Union in London, a breeding ground for the independence movement in Nigeria. In Southern Rhodesia, which had been a British crown colony since 1923, a small white minority used the land distribution act of 1930 to secure 52 per cent of the territory, as well as all the towns and cities, including the black townships, and all of the country's natural resources. Racial segregation along the lines practised in South Africa helped to maintain discrimination, a fate also suffered by the black population in the former German South-West Africa, a Category C territory that had been governed by the Union of South Africa – a member of the British Empire – since 1920. Uprisings by the Bondelswarts and Rehoboths were bloodily suppressed between 1922 and 1924.

It was in India, however, that the British Empire was most severely shaken during the interwar period. Since December 1919 the Government of India Act had provided a constitution for the subcontinent. It drew a distinction between central government, which was responsible for foreign policy, defence and penal law and answerable only to London, and the country's provincial governments. It was here that the principle of diarchy, or double rule, was to apply in the future. The 'reserved subjects', including police and finance, were administered by a British governor general and an executive committee made up of two Britons and two Indians, whereas 'transferred subjects', chief of which was education, were entrusted to Indian ministers who in turn were answerable to elected legislative councils in the Indian provinces. The new corpus of laws came into force in June 1921.

The practical effects of these reforms were modest in scope. The refusal of a British commission to condemn the bloodbath at Amritsar in April 1919, to which we have already referred in another context, prompted the Indian National Congress to set up its own commission of inquiry and to boycott the new constitution. In 1920 Mahatma Gandhi led the National Congress in its campaign of non-cooperation – *asahayoga* – with the new institutions, including civil disobedience and the demand for home rule, or *Swaraj*. The campaign was called off in February 1922 following the murder of twenty-two policemen in Uttar Pradesh. Gandhi, a Hindu from the merchant class, had studied law in London but had moved to South Africa in the 1890s and organized resistance to the discriminatory laws against Indian immigrants. Arrested in March 1922, he was sentenced to six years' imprisonment but pardoned on health grounds at the end of 1924.

The rejection of the 1919 constitution by the vast majority of Indians persuaded the British government of the need to propose further reforms. But the second commission set up to deal with this question was made up exclusively of Britons, prompting the Congress Party to protest in the strongest possible terms and in August 1928 to demand that India be granted the status of a dominion within a year. A counterproposal for an Indian constitution drawn up at a conference of all the Indian parties in Calcutta in December 1928 was vetoed by Mohammad Ali Jinnah's Muslim League. Since the government in London was unwilling to meet the Congress Party's demands, the latter called for complete independence – *purnasvara* – in December 1929.

In March 1930 Gandhi began a new campaign of civil disobedience aimed at lifting the British monopoly on salt production that had existed since 1836. After leading a 240-mile march to the coast at Dandi, he symbolically picked up a few grains of salt on 6 April 1930, whereupon he and his closest supporters were arrested. There followed the mass arrest of thousands of other Indians who, inspired by his actions, boiled salt in the country's marketplaces. By March 1931 all political prisoners had been released following an agreement between Gandhi and the British viceroy, Lord Irwin, later Lord Halifax. From then on, Indians were allowed to boil salt for their own domestic use.

A round-table conference in London in the autumn of 1931 was attended by Gandhi in person but brought no solution to the conflict since it proved impossible to help those minorities who were entitled to vote and who included Muslims and casteless Hindus to be shielded from the electoral preponderance of the Hindu majority. An attempt by Ramsay MacDonald to solve the problem by dividing the Hindus into caste members and those outside the caste system was vehemently opposed by Gandhi, who went on hunger strike, threatening to starve himself to death. The British octroi was finally revoked on 24 September 1924 in what became known as the Poona Pact.

The beginning of the end of the conflict came on 4 August 1935 in the form of a constitution forced on India and providing for a federation made up of the provinces of British India and the Indian principalities which were contractually bound to the British crown. But most princes refused to join the federation, with the result that only the non-federal part of the constitution could come into force in 1937, marking the end of diarchy on a provincial level and meaning that the provinces were now ruled by ministers responsible to elected parliaments. At the same time Burma ceased to be a part of the Indian empire and was granted partial autonomy, a success due to the nationalist student movement associated with Aung San. With the approval of Gandhi, who had in the meantime withdrawn from active politics in order to devote himself to social questions, the Congress Party took part in the elections to the provincial parliaments. But India seemed as far away as ever from the goal of national sovereignty – certainly further away than the island of Ceylon off the southern coast of India, which in 1931 had been granted a constitution of its own on the basis of universal suffrage for men and women and a two-chamber system, laying the foundations for its eventual independence.

The six Dominions of the Empire where English was the principal language and which were all marked by European influence had long since achieved their independence: Canada, Australia, New Zealand, Newfoundland and the Union of South Africa had all become independent between 1867 and 1910, with Ireland following suit in 1921. During the Chanak Crisis of September 1922, Lloyd George had been forced to accept the fact that neither Canada nor the Union of South Africa was willing any longer blindly to follow Great Britain into its war with Turkey. An Imperial Conference in 1923 failed to provide an answer to the question of the Dominions' claims on sovereignty, but at a follow-up conference in London in October and November 1926 the delegates agreed on a formula proposed by the former prime minister Arthur Balfour, according to which the Dominions were 'autonomous Communities within the British Empire, equal in status, in no way subordinate to one another in any aspect of their domestic or external affairs, though united by a common allegiance to the Crown, and freely associated as members of the British Commonwealth of Nations'. This last-mentioned term had been coined not by Balfour but by Jan Smuts, the South African general and air force minister in Lloyd George's war cabinet, at a banquet of members of the upper and lower houses in May 1917.

The Balfour Declaration laid the foundations for the Statute of Westminster that was drawn up at a further Imperial Conference in December 1931. It served as a joint constitution for all the Dominions and granted exclusive legislative authority to the parliaments of all of these members of the

Commonwealth. The Colonial Laws Validity Act of 1865, which had prevented the colonies from passing laws that departed from those of Great Britain, was repealed. By 1931 at the latest the Dominions were sovereign states, even if they had no elected heads of state but were governed by governors general who represented the British crown. Whatever agreements they reached with Great Britain or between themselves were voluntary, notably when, at an Imperial Economic Conference in Ottawa in 1932, they agreed to favour mutual trade and to use the pound as the principal currency in the sterling zone. There were also ideological links between the former colonies in terms of their common values, to which Britain could appeal in 1939, when it was more seriously challenged by Germany than at any point since the Napoleonic Wars at the start of the nineteenth century.

By transforming the Empire into the Commonwealth, the United Kingdom managed to achieve the unique feat of retaining its international standing while eschewing the outdated formal dependence of those parts of its Empire that were the most advanced in terms of their development. Not since the 'Augustan threshold' of the Roman Empire – the term was coined by the American political scientist Michael W. Doyle to describe the far-reaching imperial reforms of the emperor Augustus in the decades before and after the birth of Christ – had an empire demonstrated such an ability to learn from its mistakes as the British Empire did in the early twentieth century. It was a remarkable achievement, given the actual decline in the economic potential of the mother country, whose share of world trade had fallen from 25 per cent in 1860 to 14 per cent in 1938. No less remarkable was the fact that this period also witnessed the gradual shift of financial, military and political power in the Anglo-Saxon world from London to Washington.

The 1926 Imperial Conference took place during Stanley Baldwin's second cabinet. Baldwin had been born in the Midlands in 1867 and worked in the iron industry before entering politics, leading the British government from November 1924 to June 1929 and embodying the desire to return to what was thought of as pre-war normality. The dominant figure in his cabinet was his chancellor Winston Churchill, who had returned to the Conservative fold as recently as 1924, having abandoned it for the Liberal Party twenty years earlier. Churchill's chief contribution to the normalization process was his return to the gold standard that had been abandoned in 1914. He announced its return in his budget speech to the lower house on 28 April 1925. But the move had the opposite effect of creating economic stability: the pound was overvalued, the British export industry had serious difficulties finding markets for its goods, and social unrest increased.

It was the mineworkers who were the most radicalized. In June 1925 their employers announced massive cuts to their wages. Baldwin tried to gain time by setting up a Royal Commission to examine the economic situation in the coal-mining sector, and he also gave the mines' owners temporary subsidies.

The Commission submitted its report in March 1926, rejecting the nationaliza-tion of the mines demanded by the miners and confirming the need for lower wages, but not for longer working hours. The miners responded by calling a strike on 1 May 1926. Two days later the leaders of the Trades Union Congress (TUC) declared a general strike, which began at midnight on 3/4 May 1926.

The TUC had moved much further to the left in the preceding period. More than the trade union movements in other countries, it had sought to reach an agreement between the 'Amsterdam' – reformist – trade union move-ment on the one hand and its Communist counterpart on the other. In April 1925 it had helped to create a Permanent Anglo-Russian Trade Union Committee that was hailed in Moscow as an important staging post on the road to world revolution. The general strike in Great Britain had the support not only of these two rival international trade union movements but also of the Socialist Workers' International that had been established in Hamburg in May 1923 following a merger between the Second International and the more left-wing Vienna International, also known as the International 2½. Finally, it had the backing of the Communist International. Dockworkers in France, Germany, the Netherlands, Belgium and Scandinavia refused to load coal on to British vessels, while railway workers and sailors declined to transport coal to Great Britain. In his history of the International, Julius Braunthal described the European coal blockade against Britain as 'almost total'.[90]

In Britain itself the call for a general strike received widespread support among the organized trade unions. On 5 May 1926 the writer Virginia Woolf noted in her diary: 'Everyone is bicycling; motor cars are huddled up with extra people. There are no buses. No placards, no newspapers. [. . .] Gas & electricity are allowed, but at 11 the light was turned off.'[91] Two days earlier Churchill had told the lower house that either parliamentary institutions and, with them, the nation would emerge victorious from this encounter, or the existing constitu-tion would be 'fatally injured' and 'some Soviet of trade unions' would be estab-lished and gain control of the economic and political life of the country.[92] The Times spoke of 'the gravest threat that has hung over the country since the fall of the Stuarts', while the Daily Mail inveighed against a 'revolutionary move-ment' that sought to subject the nation to its violent thrall at the cost of the population as a whole.[93]

Baldwin's government was determined to end the general strike as quickly as possible by means of emergency measures that it had already passed on 1 May. Hyde Park became a distribution centre for milk and other foodstuffs; in the East End soldiers were deployed to resume operations in the docks; the police patrolled the streets and station forecourts, where they were supported by volunteers from the semi-private Organization for the Maintenance of Supplies that had been formed in September 1925 and by special constables in khaki uniforms and armoured cars; and Buckingham Palace and other royal buildings were protected by additional guards. After nine days the general strike came to an end on 12 May with the TUC's unconditional surrender. The government and public opinion had proved more powerful than the organized workforce.

The success that was enjoyed by the Conservative cabinet allowed it to abolish the eight-hour day and on 23 June 1927 to pass the Trades Disputes and Trade Unions Act that declared general strikes and sympathy strikes illegal: to call such a strike was punishable by two years in prison. Civil servants and local government employees were banned from joining a union that was affiliated to the TUC. The intimidation of workers by their striking colleagues was also declared illegal. From then on, trade union contributions to the Labour Party required the consent of members. In the wake of the act, the number of working days lost to strikes fell dramatically as did the number of trade union members, which dropped from 5.2 million in 1926 to 4.8 million in 1928. But it was the mineworkers who suffered the greatest defeat. Not until December 1926 did they finally end their strike, having attained none of their intended goals. Instead they had to work longer hours for lower wages.

For the British workers' movement, the events of May 1926 marked an important turning point. The general strike brought to an end the mass strikes of the post-war period, and never again did the country suffer another general strike. The TUC drew from its defeat at the hands of the government the conclusion that in future the trade unions must not allow observers to doubt their loyalty to parliamentary democracy. The Communist Party of Great Britain, which had supported the strike but exerted no influence upon it, was briefly able to report an increase in membership from 6,000 in May to 10,730 in October, but by the end of 1928 this figure had fallen to 3,500. In 1927 the Labour Party closed twenty-three of its local party offices, including fifteen in London and the surrounding area, all of which had been infiltrated by Communists. In the elections to the lower house in May 1929 the Communists received 50,000 votes, 5,000 fewer than five years previously, and as a result they lost the only seat that they had won in 1924. Following the failure of the general strike, the Comintern and the Russian Trade Union Federation branded the British trade unions 'downright traitors', prompting the TUC to return a donation to the striking miners from the Russian trade unions and to disband the Anglo-Russian Trade Union Committee. This period also marked the start of talks between the trade unions and employers that culminated in a joint conference in July 1928 and in mutual agreement on the need to rationalize British industry and preserve peace in the workplace.

If the Communists played only a small part in the general strike, the extreme right did even less to suppress it. In March 1923, six months after Mussolini's March on Rome, a militantly anti-Communist and anti-Semitic organization calling itself the British Fascisti had been formed, renaming itself the British Fascists in 1924. In the early months of 1926 its members flocked in large numbers to the aforementioned Organization for the Maintenance of Supplies and to the special constables but in general they were kept at arm's length by the authorities. A far greater influence on public opinion was exerted by ultra-Conservative press barons such as Lord Beaverbrook and Lord Rothermere, the owners of the *Daily Express* and *Daily Mail* respectively, together with the Duke of Northumberland, who financed the *Morning Post* and *The Patriot* as well as the relatively highbrow *English Review* that became more and more of a mouthpiece of the extreme right wing of the Tory Party after 1925. But the way in which Baldwin's government had dealt with the general strike also commanded the respect of even the most radical Conservatives. In the opinion of the *English Review*, the strike proved that England still had men who knew how to govern, and even the Duke of Northumberland felt obliged to praise the 'vigour and resourcefulness' of the government.[94]

Whereas the anti-trade unions act of June 1927 was entirely to the liking of Conservative diehards, another law that Baldwin's government passed triggered widespread disquiet: this was the law of July 1928 that gave equal rights to men and women and at the same time removed the discriminatory provision of the electoral act of 1918 that allowed women to vote only after they had turned thirty, whereas men were entitled to vote from the age of twenty-one. According to William Sanderson, who went on to found the esoteric and influential English Mistery [sic], women were guided purely by their instincts, instincts that were sexually conditioned. 'She has a total ineptitude for politics, for she lacks political virtue.' And since women allegedly had no social instincts, they were incapable of developing their intellectual abilities and applying them to creativity or organization.[95] Like Sanderson, other leading right-wing intellectuals such as Douglas Jerrold, who from 1931 edited the *English Review*, and Anthony Ludovici, who was a prominent contributor to the journal and an admirer of Nietzsche, saw in feminism and in the alleged feminization of society a danger threatening all that had made Britain great. Above all, it was, in Ludovici's view, a danger for women themselves since their only purpose in life was to foster life and propagate the species.

The first elections to take place under the new electoral law were held in May 1929. With their 8.25 million votes, the Conservatives won marginally more votes than the Labour Party's 8.04 million. The Liberals won 5.1 million. But the Labour Party won more seats – 287 – than the Conservatives' 260 and the Liberals' 59. The Labour Party's success was due in no small part to the fact that Baldwin's government was regarded as hostile to the workers – and this in spite of a handful of socially progressive measures such as the Widows, Orphans, and Old Age Contributory Pensions Act of 1925, which provided for equal contributions for employers and employees alike, and the reform of the poor laws by means of the Local Government Act of 1929. At the same time, the Labour Party was helped by the fact that under Ramsay MacDonald's leadership it had held back during the general strike in 1926. In its new programme, 'Labour and the Nation', that was drawn up by the historian R. H. Tawney and adopted after lengthy discussion at the party's annual conference in Birmingham in October 1928, the party declared its desire to see an evolutionary change from a capitalist to a socialist society. Urban and rural lands were to pass into state ownership by a slow and steady process, while mining, electricity works, the railways and the transport system were to be nationalized and the Bank of England placed under state control.

The election results could hardly be interpreted as a mandate to put this programme into action. If it was to govern at all, the party was dependent on the goodwill of the Liberals, just as it had been when forming its first cabinet in January 1924. As on that occasion, so in 1929 King George V invited Ramsay MacDonald to form a cabinet. MacDonald's foreign secretary was Arthur Henderson, who had already served as home secretary in MacDonald's first cabinet. His chancellor was Philip Snowden, a committed advocate of the gold standard, free trade and a balanced budget, while the minister for the colonies was the Fabian, Sidney Webb. The minister for education was Sir Charles Philip Trevelyan, a notable member of the party's left wing. The cabinet also included its first woman, the minister for labour, Margaret Grace Bondfield. The government's most pressing problem was the high level of unemployment, which the lord privy seal, James Henry Thomas, was asked to reduce. In this he was helped by the chancellor of the Duchy of Lancaster, the then thirty-two-year-old Sir Oswald Mosley, who at that date belonged to the left wing of the party and who sought to revive the stagnating economy by raising consumer spending, awarding contracts for public works and ensuring customs protection for the Empire. (The Liberals had entered the election campaign with a very similar programme drawn up by their former prime minister, Lloyd George.)

By the spring of 1929 unemployment had already passed the one million mark. Reducing that number had been the Labour Party's key promise in the election campaign. The new cabinet began work with a series of social reform laws, including a public works programme totalling £2,500 million. Not only did Mosley and Lloyd George demand that more should be done, so, too, did the economist John Maynard Keynes and the Fabian historian G. D. H. Cole, two members of the government's economic council. But MacDonald, Snowden and Thomas refused to act even after the New York stock exchange crash of October 1929, which caused unemployment to climb even higher. Within months of Ramsay MacDonald's second cabinet starting work, the first cracks had already appeared in his minority government. They were the harbingers of a deeper crisis into which the Labour Party was to be plunged in 1930 and 1931.

From Dawes to Young: Germany under Stresemann

Unlike Great Britain, Germany enjoyed something of a golden age between 1924 and 1929. There was again a stable currency; production, consumption and national income continued to grow; and the federal budget showed a sizeable surplus in 1924 and only a small deficit in the years between 1925 and 1928. And yet, as the economic historian Wolfram Fischer has pointed out, Germany's economic recovery remained at risk:

> The investments on which the growth and contraction of a country's economy largely depend reveal no consistent upward trend between 1924 and 1929, for although fixed asset investments continued to rise every year until 1928, the volume of goods that was being stored during this period fluctuated to such an extent that the total internal gross investments – fixed asset investments and the value of goods in storage – actually sank in 1926, 1928 and 1929 when compared with the figures for the previous year. Only in one year, 1927, was there an 'investment boom'. The trade balance, which had been almost entirely passive before the war, likewise showed a surplus only in 1926. And although the balance in the service sector invariably showed a surplus, helped in particular by the merchant fleet, this was too small to offset the balance of payments deficit, still less to produce a surplus to pay for reparations.[96]

If Germany was still able to meet its obligations to pay reparations under the terms of the Dawes Plan, then this was due to the surplus on movements in capital in the form of foreign and, more especially, American loans. After 1924 Germany was a country hungry for capital: its high interest rates and the credit restrictions imposed by the Reichsbank made the country attractive to foreign investors, and to that extent the economic upturn in the second half of the 1920s was not just an illusory boom for the dollar. But the use to which foreign investments were put was problematical in the extreme, for most of them were handed out as short-term loans – in 1927–8 this was true of around half the total – but then passed on by German banks as investment loans and used by the German regions and by local government for long-term purposes on which there was no immediate return. Local government, which not unfairly felt itself to be the victim of Matthias Erzberger's economic reforms of 1919, used such loans to finance the building of schools, town halls, hospitals and sports centres or, as in Konrad Adenauer's Cologne, the city's famous 'green belt'. As long as the economy grew, these short-term loans were generally extended without difficulty. But even in the 'good' years of the Weimar Republic, experts such as the president of the Reichsbank, Hjalmar Schacht, and the American financial expert, Parker Gilbert, who was the agent-general for reparations, were already warning against the unsound financial practices of local government: if the economy were to slip into the red, then a serious financial crisis was inevitable.

It was not only the regional and local authorities who drew down on themselves the criticism of the agent-general for reparations and of the president of the Reichsbank but also the Reich itself. In December 1927 a salary reform raised the salaries of civil servants by 16–17 per cent on average, effectively making up for the losses that they had incurred as a result of inflation and acknowledging the fact that since 1924 the salaries of civil servants had gone up much less than the wages of the rest of the workforce. By 1927 German industry was making bigger profits than it had done at any other time during the Weimar Republic. Gilbert was not alone in pointing out that if tax revenues were to fall, the state would not be able to continue to pay such high salaries; so, too, did Heinrich Brüning, the Centre Party's budgetary expert in the Reichstag. He abstained from voting in the debate on the budget on 15 December 1927.

But it was not on account of the level of civil servants' salaries that the year 1927 has gone down in the annals of German history. More important was the greatest increase in social security ever enjoyed by workers and employees in the Weimar Republic, which they owed to the introduction of statutory national insurance. The relevant law was passed by an overwhelming majority in the Reichstag on 7 July and transformed the existing system of state welfare for the unemployed into a form of insurance that required both employers and employees to contribute equally – at the time in question, this amounted to 3 per cent of the employee's gross salary. But it was not only capital and labour that had to bear the cost of insurance but also – and entirely in the spirit of Bismarck – the state: the Reich was obliged to agree to a loan to the newly created body responsible for running the country's labour exchanges and benefit offices if their financial needs could not be met from their own emergency reserves. In 1927, few observers seem to have realized that a situation might arise in which the Reich would be plunged into serious financial difficulties.

Throughout the Weimar Republic the state was an extremely active participant in the economic life of the nation. A decree passed on 13 October 1923 under the terms of the enabling act had introduced compulsory arbitration for wage disagreements, thereby making the state the supreme arbiter in labour disputes. As the Social Democratic theorist Rudolf Hilferding noted in 1927 when discussing the term 'political salary', this decree was the expression of a highly developed 'organized capitalism' and a step in the direction of socialism, largely invalidating the right to free collective bargaining and riding rough-shod over market forces.[97]

The theory of the economic historian Knut Borchardt that compulsory state arbitration contributed to higher wages and hence to the 'sickness' of the Weimar economy[98] has led to a lively and continuing debate among scholars, but what remains undeniable is that the role of the state as supreme arbiter was at least one of the factors that weakened Germany's market economy. Other factors involving the state include the subsidies paid to farmers to the east of the Elbe in the form of protective tariffs on cereals and other agricultural produce, which the Reichstag reintroduced in August 1925 in response to pressure from the German National Party, and direct payments – 'help for the east' – that were a major bone of contention during the latter part of the Weimar Republic.

But market laws were also undermined by industrial employers who formed a comprehensive cartel that they claimed was justified by the need for rationalization and, hence, to help Germany to compete in international markets but which in fact reduced domestic competition. The end result of this enforced rationalization was considerable overcapacity and high levels of unemployment even before the great crisis in the autumn of 1929: during the third quarter of that year the number of job-seekers registered at the country's labour exchanges was 1.53 million. Hilferding's phrase, 'organized capitalism', proved to be a euphemism: in the circumstances, it would be more accurate to speak of badly organized capitalism.

Politically speaking, the relative stabilization of the Weimar Republic began with an occurrence that pointed, rather, in the direction of instability: the Reichstag elections of 4 May 1924, when right- and left-wing radicals reported large gains, while most of the moderate parties recorded substantial losses. The royalist German Nationalists, who during the election campaign had appealed above all to those sections of the middle classes who were the hardest hit by inflation, increased their share of the vote from 15.1 per cent in June 1920 to 19.5 per cent, making them the largest of the bourgeois parties and the second-largest party in all. The German Nationalist Freedom Party that had joined forces with the leaderless National Socialists won 6.5 per cent of the vote at their first attempt to enter parliament. In short, more than a quarter of German voters had opted to support the anti-Republican right.

To the left of centre, there were two points worth noting. First, there was a remarkable shift from the Social Democrats to the Communists and a sizeable drop in 'Marxist' votes overall. In 1920 the workers' parties had received 41.7 per cent of the total vote, whereas now it was 34 per cent. The SPD's share fell from 21.7 per cent to 20.5 per cent, which may seem to represent only a small loss, but it was in fact catastrophic, for the reunited Social Democrats received fewer votes in 1924 than the Majority Social Democrats had done in 1920. Of the 17.9 per cent who had voted for the Independent Social Democrats on the earlier occasion, most had presumably transferred their allegiance to the Communist Party, which was now able to assert itself for the first time on a national level as the proletarian party of the masses. The liberal parties, namely, the German People's Party and the German Democratic Party, suffered serious losses, whereas those sustained by the Catholic Centre Party and the Bavarian People's Party were relatively small in comparison. With 8.5 per cent of the vote, the bourgeois splinter groups all did remarkably well.

Following their devastating defeat, the Social Democrats could not seriously consider a role in government in the form of a grand coalition, for all that they were still the largest party. If the party leadership had agreed to such a deal, the SPD would have been destroyed by its left wing, which was made up of former Independent Social Democrats. On the other hand, the moderate bourgeois parties had no inclination to enter into a coalition with the radical nationalist German National People's Party and to leave the latter to fill the post of chancellor, a post for which the German Nationalists proposed Alfred von Tirpitz, who had singlehandedly created the German fleet. The result of all this was the formation of another bourgeois minority government under the centrist politician Wilhelm Marx, with Gustav Stresemann – the leader of the German People's Party – again as his foreign minister. The government could count on the support of the Social Democrats at least on important questions of foreign policy such as ratification of the Dawes Plan.

But the votes of the Social Democrats were not sufficient to pass all the legislation needed to deal with the question of reparations. One of these laws concerned turning the state railways into a company saddled with certain obligations and overseen by a supervisory board whose members would include representatives of the countries to which Germany owed money. The Railways Act was a serious encroachment on German sovereignty and had implications that affected the constitution, hence the need for a two-thirds majority.

To achieve this majority required the support of at least a number of German Nationalists. In order to overcome opposition from the German National People's Party, the government offered a markedly 'nationalist' explanation of the question of its alleged guilt in causing the war, an explanation proffered on 29 August 1924, the day before the signing of the London Agreement. There was also pressure exerted by two powerful interest groups, the Confederation of German Industry, which, formed in 1919, was the main body representing German employers, and the Agricultural League, the powerful successor of the Agrarian League. For its part, the bourgeois camp weighed in with a mixture of threats and promises. If the bill was rejected, then the government threatened to prorogue parliament, whereas if it was passed, the German People's Party would invite the German Nationalists to join them in government. On 29 August, fifty-two members of the German National People's Party voted to reject the bill, while forty-eight voted in favour of it. This was enough to give the Railways Bill a two-thirds majority and enough for the government to accept the terms of the London Agreement.

But this was far from ensuring a working majority for the government's day-to-day business, with the result that on 20 October Marx's government decided to ask the president to dissolve parliament. Ebert responded immediately, setting the date for new elections as 7 December 1924. These second elections to the Reichstag within a matter of months took place against a background of economic recovery. The temporary Rentenmark had been abandoned on 30 August and replaced by the new Reichsmark, 40 per cent of which was covered by gold and currency. Once the London Agreement had been implemented, foreign loans flowed into Germany and unemployment numbers fell sharply, as did the length of the average working day, while contractually agreed hourly wages rose considerably.

These improvements to the country's economy were reflected in the politically deradicalized election results. The extreme wings of the various parties – on the one hand, the German People's Party, which had campaigned as the National Socialist Freedom Party, and, on the other, the Communists – were both weakened by the results, while the Social Democrats reported gains. The SPD's share of the vote rose from 20.5 per cent to 26.5 per cent, that of the German National People's Party from 19.5 per cent to 20.5 per cent, whereas the Communists' share fell from 12.6 per cent to 9 per cent, that of the combined National Socialists and German People's Party from 6.5 per cent to 3 per cent. The centre parties and the moderate right more or less retained their existing share of the vote.

The election results allowed one of only two kinds of government to be formed: either a grand coalition or a bourgeois right-of-centre cabinet. The German People's Party refused to govern with the Social Democrats, while the German Democrats were unwilling to enter into a coalition that included the German Nationalists, although this did not necessarily preclude a bourgeois bloc, which would have a majority even without the left-wing Liberal Party. Following lengthy negotiations, the first national government to include German Nationalists was formed on 15 January 1925. At its head was the former finance minister, Hans Luther. Stresemann stayed on as foreign minister, while Otto Geßler became minister of defence, even though his party, the German Democrats, was not a part of the government. The German National People's Party provided the ministers of the interior, finance and business, while the minister of agriculture, Count Gerhard von Kanitz, was at least close to this last-named party.

Soon after the cabinet had been formed, the German Nationalist business secretary, Karl Neuhaus, found himself forced to disappoint large numbers of his party's supporters: at the end of January, with the support of a unanimous vote on the part of the leading organizations in agriculture, industry, trade and banking, he explained in a memorandum that a revaluation of the savings accounts and war loans at more than 15 per cent above their former value in gold marks that had been settled in February 1924 but violently resisted by the German National People's Party could not be expected of the asset holders in question and was therefore impossible to implement.

Friedrich Ebert died on 28 February 1925, only six weeks after the formation of the first bourgeois bloc cabinet. He was fifty-four. The immediate cause of his death was appendicitis and peritonitis. But during the final months of his life the one and only Social Democrat to hold the highest post in the Republic had had to contend with the charge of treason levelled against him by a nationalist journalist by the name of Erwin Rothardt on account of his role in the

Berlin munition workers' strike in January 1918. (At that date Ebert had been leader of the Socialist Party and had joined the strike leaders simply in order to end the unrest as quickly as possible.) In turn, Ebert sued the journalist for libel. The sentence handed down by the Magdeburg District Court on 23 December 1924 was a blatant example of judiciary anti-Republicanism, for although Rothardt was sentenced to three months' imprisonment for insulting Ebert, the court, in justifying its verdict, noted that Rothardt's claim that Ebert had been guilty of treason by participating in the strike was in a legal sense valid so that it was impossible to convict the journalist of defamation.

Wilhelm Marx's cabinet immediately declared its support for Ebert, and leading voices in German society quickly followed suit, including the theologian Adolf von Harnack, the historians Friedrich Meinecke and Hans Delbrück and the jurists Gerhard Anschütz and Wilhelm Kahl. But in spite of their attempts to rescue Ebert's reputation, the judgment had a pernicious effect and contributed to the president's illness by undermining his mental and physical health. Only after his death did his political opponents, foremost among whom were the German Nationalist members of the new government, concede that he had administered the office of president conscientiously in difficult times, demonstrating an exemplary lack of partisanship. The extreme right, conversely, remained silent on the issue, while the Communist member of the Reichstag, Hermann Remmele, had no hesitation in recalling the president in a speech on 1 March 1925 in which he declared that Ebert had 'gone to his grave with the curse of the German proletariat ringing in his ears'.[99]

The first direct election of a national president by the German people took place on 29 March 1925. The candidate for the government right was Karl Jarres, formerly the minister of the interior and currently mayor of Duisburg. He had the backing of the German People's Party, the German National People's Party and the small Economic Party that had been formed in 1920 and was made up of members of the German middle classes. The Social Democrat candidate was Otto Braun, who had recently resigned as prime minister of Prussia in the wake of a government crisis in the region. The Centre Party was represented by the former chancellor Wilhelm Marx, the German Democratic Party by the state president of Baden, Willy Hellpach, and the Bavarian People's Party by Heinrich Held, who had been prime minister of the Free State of Bavaria since 1924. The Communists put forward the name of their party leader, Ernst Thälmann, a former dockworker from Hamburg, while the National Socialist candidate was Erich Ludendorff. In the first round of voting none of the candidates received the required absolute majority. Jarres polled the best result, with 38.8 per cent of the vote, with Braun in second place on 29 per cent and Marx in third place with 14.5 per cent.

For the second round, the 'Weimar' parties – the Social Democrats, Centre Party and German Democrats – all agreed to endorse Marx, in return for which the Centre Party committed itself to re-electing Braun as prime minister of

Prussia. Jarres stood no chance against Marx, with the result that the political right set out to find a more popular candidate. Under the law of 4 May 1920, which laid down the terms for the election of a new president, this candidate could also be someone who had not taken part in the first round of elections. The choice fell on the former field marshal Paul von Hindenburg, who had been born in Posen on 2 October 1847 and, now seventy-seven years old, was living in retirement in Hanover following his resignation from the army supreme command in the summer of 1919.

It was above all the German Nationalists and the Agricultural League who championed Hindenburg, a legend in his own lifetime who as the 'victor of Tannenberg' had been viewed as a substitute Kaiser during the First World War. Leading industrialists and the German People's Party headed by Gustav Stresemann initially had serious misgivings, Stresemann fearing particularly adverse criticism abroad. But once Jarres had withdrawn his candidacy, the German People's Party, too, accepted Hindenburg, not least because there was a good chance that he would emerge as victor from the second round of voting. He could count on the votes of committed royalists and most Evangelical Christians. The Bavarian People's Party also agreed to back the Prussian Protestant Hindenburg, an agreement due in no small part to their dislike of the Catholic Marx, who was supported by the Social Democrats. It also helped Hindenburg that the Communists continued to pin their hopes on Thälmann, who had won only 7 per cent of the vote in the first round and stood no chance whatsoever of being elected.

The second round of voting took place on 26 April 1925, when Hindenburg won 900,000 more votes than Marx: his total share of the vote was 48.3 per cent, that of Marx 45.3 per cent, while Thälmann managed only 6.4 per cent. Although Hindenburg had narrowly failed to win an outright majority, this was not necessary in the second round of voting.

Hindenburg's election was tantamount to a conservative realignment of the Weimar Republic. His victory was not a plebiscite in favour of a restoration of the monarchy but nor was it a vote against the only form of parliamentary democracy that Germany had known since 1919. Disenchantment with the Republic's uninspiring daily round went hand in hand with a nostalgic trans-figuration of the past. The liberal *Frankfurter Zeitung* regretted 'the romantic yearning for the glory and greatness of the past', while the equally liberal *Berliner Tageblatt* spoke of a 'surprise victory of reactionary forces achieved by the Communist betrayal of the Republic'.[100] Like the two bourgeois papers, the Social Democratic *Vorwärts* also likened Hindenburg's election to the victory of a clerical monarchist, Patrice de MacMahon, as president of the French Republic in 1871, implying the expectation that Germany would survive the present danger just as surely as France had done half a century earlier.

Such hopes were by no means groundless. Hindenburg's promise to respect the Republic's constitution made it hard for those who had previously despised the Republic to maintain their hostility towards the new state. The Evangelical Church's Realpolitik was significant in this regard: only now did it accept the Republic as a fact, albeit one that it disliked. But it was above all the milieu from which Hindenburg himself hailed and to which he continued to feel very close that had the greatest cause for satisfaction: this was the world of the military and of the Prussian aristocracy. For the army and the country's major landowners, it was of some significance that they would once again have immediate access to the head of state, for in times of crisis the only real power was wielded by the president. The social and political balance of power did not shift suddenly after 26 April 1925, but from that day onwards the old Prussian elite from pre-Republican Germany once more had a hand on the reins of power, which they could seize whenever the Reichstag refused to see what the country needed. From the standpoint of the political right, this represented a major step forward.

For the Weimar Republic, Hindenburg's election was one of two striking events in 1925. The other was the signing of the Locarno Treaties on 26 October 1925, thereby sealing Germany's return to the fold of the major European powers. The Locarno Treaties were intended to consolidate the status quo of the post-war order but, in keeping with Germany's express wishes, they did so in what may be termed an asymmetrical fashion. Only the country's western borders were secured under international law, Germany, France and Belgium agreeing not to use force to alter the existing frontier, which was guaranteed by both Britain and Italy. But with its eastern neighbours Poland and Czechoslovakia, Germany signed only arbitration treaties. France, conversely, committed itself to assisting Poland and Czechoslovakia militarily in the event of a German invasion.

In short, the Locarno Treaties certainly did not rule out a peaceful solution to the question of Germany's eastern border, and in his capacity as foreign minister, Stresemann left observers in no doubt that he was working towards this goal and doing so, moreover, in complete agreement with public opinion in Germany. On 19 April 1925 he told the German Embassy in London that a peaceful solution to the question of Germany's border with Poland could be achieved 'only if the economic and financial predicament in which Poland finds itself at present degenerates to the point where Poland as a whole is reduced to a state of impotence'. It was necessary, therefore, to 'delay Poland's definitive and lasting recovery until the country is ready for a border agreement that respects our wishes and our own position of power is sufficiently consolidated. [...] Only the unqualified restitution of sovereignty over the territories in question can satisfy us.'[101]

In the Reichstag the Locarno Treaties were ratified on 27 November 1925 only because the Social Democrats voted with the majority of other deputies. The German Nationalist ministers had walked out of Hans Luther's cabinet on 26 October because the concessions regarding the western border had not gone far enough in the eyes of the German National People's Party, with the result that the German Nationalists voted against the treaties. If the Social Democrats had attached a condition to their approval and demanded a place in government, it is unlikely that Luther and Stresemann would have been in a position to turn them down. But the Social Democrats were internally divided not only in the latter half of 1925 but on two further occasions in 1926 and in consequence they refrained from making any demands with regard to power-sharing.

Luther's bourgeois minority cabinet had to resign on 12 May 1926 in the wake of an argument over the flying of flags, an argument that stemmed from a cabinet decision taken on 1 May, according to which ambassadorial and consular agencies had the right to fly the navy's black, white and red ensign alongside the Republic's black, red and gold flag. Luther's bourgeois minority cabinet was replaced by one under Marx that was definitely interested in sharing power with the SPD, but the Social Democrats now paid the price for their active support of a Communist Party-backed nationwide plebiscite demanding that the former German princes be stripped of their property with no recourse to compensation. Although the referendum on 20 June 1926 failed to achieve its goal, since only 36.4 per cent, rather than the required majority, voted for the draft bill, the SPD felt that in the wake of its extra-parliamentary dalliance with the Communists, it could not without further ado return to the politics of class compromise with the bourgeois centre ground. As a result, the grand coalition that Stresemann, too, had championed did not come about.

In mid-December 1926 there might have been a further opportunity to move from a bourgeois minority government to a parliamentary majority government, if the centre and the left could have come to some agreement. At Stresemann's urging, Marx's government offered the SPD a grand coalition in order to avoid a defence debate tabled by the Social Democrats, but the SPD was unwilling to agree to such a deal. On 16 December 1926 Philipp Scheidemann delivered himself of a spectacular speech in the Reichstag, instilling a sense of outrage in all the bourgeois parties by talking about a clandestine armaments programme, the financing of which had been cloaked in a veil of secrecy. He described how the army was working closely with radical right-wing organizations and mentioned the 'Black Reichswehr' in the form of the small-calibre rifle clubs that the army used to circumvent the limit of 100,000 men. In particular, Scheidemann alarmed the Communists by claiming that their cell at the port of Stettin was fully aware of the arms and munitions shipments that Soviet vessels had unloaded there in September and October 1926.

The very next day – 17 December 1926 – the Reichstag brought down Marx's government by 249 votes to 171. The vote of no confidence was tabled by the SPD and received the support of the two People's Parties, the German Nationalists and the Communists. The question of a grand coalition had been settled by the former prime minister's speech. There was no one else in any of the bourgeois parties who would have advocated such a solution to the crisis or even seriously considered it. The outcome of the government crisis of the winter of 1926/7 was a centre-right government under Wilhelm Marx that began work on 29 January 1927. The German Nationalists provided the ministers of the interior, justice, agriculture and transport. The Ministry of the Interior was now run by Walter von Keudell, who as a regional councillor in Königsberg had worked with the Kapp–Lüttwitz government in March 1920. Thanks to its tactics, the SPD had involuntarily brought to power the most right-wing cabinet of any that served under the Weimar Republic.

Stresemann remained the foreign minister in this second bourgeois bloc cabinet and as a result was closely associated with two events that took place in 1926 in the wake of the Treaties of Locarno, namely, the Berlin Treaty with the Soviet Union and Germany's membership of the League of Nations. The German-Soviet treaty was accepted almost unanimously by the Reichstag on 10 June 1926 and was designed in part to dispel Moscow's mistrust of Germany's actions at Locarno, but the agreement was also intended to increase pressure on Warsaw. The partners to the treaty committed themselves to remaining neutral in the event that one or other of them was attacked by a third party. They also agreed not to enter into any coalition with a country that planned to impose an economic or financial boycott on another power. Germany promised not to take part in any sanctions that the League of Nations might impose on the Soviet Union, a promise already exacted from the Western Powers the previous year. In all other respects the Rapallo Treaty of 1922 was to remain the basis of German-Soviet relations for the foreseeable future.

The second major event in terms of Germany's foreign policy took place in Geneva on 10 September 1926, when Germany joined the League of Nations, also becoming a member of its most important body, the Council of the League of Nations, whereas Poland, its principal rival in the struggle to gain this status, had to settle for a non-permanent seat and the promise that it would be re-elected to this committee. The Social Democrats, who had advocated this move sooner and more consistently than any other German party, celebrated their achievement as an important moment in the country's history, *Vorwärts* even speaking of a 'giant leap forward in the history of the world'.[102]

On 17 September 1926, a week after the official ceremony at the Palace of the League of Nations in Geneva, the foreign ministers of France and Germany, Aristide Briand and Gustav Stresemann, met at a restaurant in the nearby village of Thoiry for a general discussion. The good food and abundant flow of fine wines put both men in a euphoric mood, and they agreed that in return for material help in stabilizing the franc – specifically, the early repayment of a further tranche of German reparations – France would make a number of political concessions, chief of which were the early return of the Saarland, the withdrawal of troops from the Rhineland by September 1927 and France's consent to the German-Belgian agreement concerning the return of Eupen-Malmedy to Germany.

The mood of elation was followed by one of sobering disenchantment, for Raymond Poincaré, who until then had loyally supported Briand's policy of rapprochement, failed to back him on this occasion. Legally speaking, Briand had acted without his authority in Thoiry. In Germany, too, there were serious misgivings concerning the high price that Stresemann was willing to pay the Western Powers for any political concessions. In the end the meeting on 17 September 1926 produced little more than an agreement that the International Military Commission overseeing the implementation of the military provisions of the Treaty of Versailles would leave Germany on 31 January 1927. Thoiry had raised expectations that on closer examination were simply unrealistic.

Germany's joining the League of Nations was the high point of the Stresemann era. At the time of the First World War, Stresemann had been an ardent supporter of annexation, and even as recently as the Kapp–Lüttwitz Putsch he had been seen as an opportunistic tactician, but now he had matured into a 'republican of reason' and become a statesman. As chancellor during the crisis of 1923, he did more than anyone else to maintain the unity of the Reich and the survival of the country as a democratic republic. As foreign minister he was an early champion of the idea of peaceful coexistence with the West. Towards Poland, it is true, Stresemann was just as nationalistic as most other German politicians, whether from the right or the left. From 1923 to 1929 he was an enlightened advocate of a policy designed to show Germany as a great power, while also championing closer ties between the states of Europe. He could reconcile these aspirations because from his point of view they were not mutually exclusive. No other German politician of the post-war period enjoyed such a high level of international respect: on 10 December 1926 he and his French colleague Aristide Briand were awarded the Nobel Peace Prize in Oslo.

Marx's centre-right government was the eighth that Stresemann served in as foreign minister. All in all, this second bourgeois bloc government was less reactionary than left-wing politicians had feared. In May 1927, under the aegis of the German Nationalist minister of the interior, Walter von Keudell, and with the backing of the German National People's Party, the *Republikschutzgesetz* that was designed to protect the Republic was extended for a further two years. And in December 1927 the aforementioned law relating to national insurance was steered through parliament by the Centre Party minister of labour, Heinrich Brauns, who had held this post continuously since August 1923.

By now there were clear signs that the centre-right government was falling apart. Since July the coalition partners had been arguing over a bill drafted by Keudell and designed to place Christian interdenominational schools and faith schools on the same legal footing. The bill had the support of the Centre Party, the Bavarian People's Party and the German National People's Party but was opposed by the German People's Party, which had inherited the mantle of the

National Liberals who had played a major role in the *Kulturkampf* at the end of the nineteenth century. They justified their stance by pointing out that according to the country's constitution interdenominational schools must be given priority over all others. By 15 February 1928 the leader of the German National People's Party and chairman of the coalition committee's meetings, Count Kuno von Westarp, was forced to announce that no agreement on the question was possible and that the coalition was therefore over.

Throughout the Weimar Republic, all forms of minority government clearly contained within them the seeds of their own destruction. In any grand coalition, it was socio-political questions that were the areas of disagreement, while centre-right coalitions foundered on matters of foreign policy and education. Parties that dated back to the days of the constitutional monarchy had never been used to compromise and tended, therefore, to regard individual goals as non-negotiable. Even established parties that represented the interests of the state continued to behave as if the battle lines were between the government and the Reichstag, as they had been before October 1918, rather than between the government majority and the opposition, as the logic of the parliamentary system demanded. The government was often felt to be hostile even by those whose own party was involved in government. The legacy of the Kaiserreich helps to explain the instability that remained a feature of the German parliamentary system even during the few relatively calm years of the first German Republic. But the 'false consciousness' of parliamentarians was also encouraged by the constitution of the Weimar Republic, for if a coalition government foundered on a failure to compromise on the part of the parties in power, they could still fall back on the president's 'reserve constitution' in the form of the emergency decrees enshrined in Article 48.

Hindenburg dissolved parliament on 31 March 1928 and set 20 May as the date for new elections. Also on 31 March the Reichsrat took a decision that was to plunge the next government into a major crisis. The German navy was planning to build Battleship A as the first of a series of replacement vessels, which meant committing the legislature to a long-term programme that would extend over several parliamentary terms. Led by Prussia, the Reichsrat had opposed any spending on the project the previous December, but by the end of March a majority of the bourgeois bloc in the Reichstag had approved the first budgetary instalment. The Reichsrat responded on 31 March by asking Marx's cabinet to delay work on the battleship until the financial situation had been re-examined and to do nothing before 1 September 1928. The new defence minister, Wilhelm Groener, who had replaced the battle-weary Otto Geßler on 19 January 1928, agreed to this condition.

For the left-wing parties in the Reichstag, Battleship A was a rallying call. Ernst Thälmann had earlier become an increasingly pliant puppet of Stalin, and he now demanded free school meals for primary schoolchildren instead of the construction of an armoured cruiser. (The bourgeois majority in the

Reichstag had already turned down a request for the five million marks needed for such a subvention.) It was a popular demand, and the Social Democrats, too, took up the catchphrase of 'School meals instead of battleships', in the process appearing to be more radical than they actually were. At its conference in Kiel in May 1927 the SPD had left observers in no doubt as to its wish to prevent the formation of a new right-wing cabinet and, if it was to do well in the elections, to assume responsibility for governing the country.

On the extreme right wing of the political spectrum, it was a newly consolidated NSDAP that entered the election campaign in the spring of 1928. The National Socialists' undisputed leader was Adolf Hitler, the left wing of the party, which been stronger in northern Germany and centred on the brothers Otto and Gregor Straßer, having ceased to provide a counterweight to the 'Brown House' in Munich since the Bamberg Party Conference in February 1926. Although the NSDAP continued to affect support for the labour movement and to parade its 'socialist' credentials, it was clear even before the Reichstag elections that its greatest support was to be found not in the larger towns and cities but in those rural areas that had been particularly badly hit by the sudden drop in the price of pigs in 1927, a fall that marked the start of a global crisis in agriculture. It was the rural population that Hitler had in his sights when on 13 April 1928 he offered a new and binding interpretation of point 17 in his party's programme: the expropriation of land for community purposes was now said to apply only to those lands that had been acquired illegally, chief of which were 'Jewish land speculation companies'.[103] No compensation was to be paid for such expropriations.

Within German society at large, however, there was no sense of a looming crisis on the eve of the elections. The economy was continuing to grow, and unemployment was lower than in 1927. In the run-up to no other Reichstag election under the Weimar Republic did democratic forces have such grounds for optimism as they did before 20 May 1928.

It was the Social Democrats who emerged as clear victors from this fourth set of elections to the Reichstag since the creation of the Weimar Republic, winning 29.8 per cent of the vote – 3.8 per cent higher than their share of the vote in the previous election on 7 December 1924. The main losers were the German Nationalists, whose share of the vote fell from 20.5 per cent to 14.3 per cent. Of the moderate bourgeois parties, the Centre Party suffered the greatest losses: 1.5 per cent. The two liberal parties each lost 1.4 per cent. If, under the terms of the Weimar constitution, there had been a clause requiring parties to poll at least 5 per cent of the votes in a particular area to have a stake in the allocation of seats, then the German Democratic Party would have failed to qualify, for it won only 4.9 per cent – 0.3 per cent more than the Economic Party. The NSDAP won on average only 2.6 per cent in the country as a whole, although it chalked up sensational gains in a number of regions hit by the agricultural crisis. These regions included the western coast of

Schleswig-Holstein, North Dithmarschen, where they won 28.9 per cent of the vote, and South Dithmarschen, where the figure was 36.8 per cent.

The election result effectively ruled out any form of majority government with the exception of a grand coalition, which finally came together after lengthy negotiations on 28 June 1928. For the present, it was not, however, a formal coalition but was what was described as a 'cabinet of individual personalities', and yet the political independence implied by this name is misleading: misgivings among members of the German People's Party, who objected to an alliance under the leader of the SPD, Hermann Müller, were so pronounced that Stresemann had to exert extreme pressure to persuade his party to accept two members of the German People's Party into his cabinet: Stresemann himself as foreign minister and Julius Curtius as business secretary.

Müller's government had been in power for only a few weeks when it was plunged into a major crisis: on 10 August 1928, the cabinet approved the construction of Battleship A, which the Social Democrats had vigorously opposed in the election campaign of only a short time earlier. The Social Democrat finance minister, Rudolf Hilferding, was unable to raise any fiscal objections to the project since the costs were covered by cuts made in other areas of the defence budget, so that confirmation of the decision taken by the previous government was a correct one. Moreover, a veto by Social Democrat ministers would have spelt the immediate end of Müller's government. Many members and supporters of Germany's largest political party took a different view. Foremost among them was Otto Wels, who, as long as his co-chairman was chancellor, was effectively running the SPD on his own. On 31 October, after parliament had returned from its summer break, Wels, acting on behalf of all the Social Democrat members of the Reichstag, proposed a motion demanding that work on the battleship be suspended and that the money released in this way be spent on free school meals.

But worse was in store for the Social Democrats, for on 16 November 1928 Wels forced them to toe the party line and vote against the cabinet decision of 10 August. The chancellor, Hermann Müller, together with his minister of the interior, Carl Severing, his finance minister, Rudolf Hilferding, and his labour minister Rudolf Wissell, were in this way obliged, as it were, to declare their lack of trust in themselves. In the event, the government was not defeated in the vote, since all the bourgeois parties and National Socialists voted against the SPD's motion, but the impression left on the public at large was little short of devastating. Echoing the whole of the liberal press, the Berlin-based *Vossische Zeitung* accused the SPD of a lack of credibility: 'It wishes to continue in power simply to save face. [...] Shall we be content to allow the Social Democrats to pound the table in the house, while hoping that others will prevent things from being smashed to pieces?'[104]

In April 1929 the government parties finally confounded expectations and formed a grand coalition. This was preceded by agreement on the federal budget for 1929, an agreement facilitated by the fact that first Hilferding and then the various experts from the other parties had adjusted upwards the preliminary estimates for tax revenues. But the main reason for this sudden rapprochement between the parties was related to the country's foreign policy, for talks on Germany's wartime reparations had opened in Paris in early February. The Dawes Plan of 1924 was only a temporary ruling, leaving open the actual amount that Germany would have to pay. In 1928/9 the annual payments due under the plan first reached their full amount: 2,500 million marks.

Given the country's worsening financial situation, all the government parties were keen to reduce this burden. The agent-general for reparations, Parker Gilbert, was also seeking to revise the plan. As long as it remained his remit to decide whether or not the German balance of payments and the stability of the mark could justify a transfer of funds by way of reparations, the Germans could, as it were, hide behind his decisions. Gilbert himself felt that this situation was harmful and wanted a new agreement that would force Germany to become economically and financially independent.

The result of the Paris talks was the Young Plan, so called after the American banker Owen D. Young who chaired the conference of financial experts that ended on 7 June 1929. They all agreed that Germany would have to continue to pay reparations until 1988: that is, for nearly sixty years. During the first ten years the annual payments would remain below the average of 2,000 million marks, but would then rise, before falling again after thirty-seven years. No further foreign monitoring of Germany's finances was planned, nor were mortgages on industry and federal revenues.

Moreover, the agent-general for reparations would no longer be responsible for the transfer. His place would be taken by the federal government, which would be able to choose between the 'protected' and 'unprotected' part of the reparations: 'unprotected' payments had to be made on time, whereas 'protected' ones could be delayed for up to two years. The payments would also be received by a new body, the Bank for International Settlements in Basel. If Germany had difficulty meeting its obligations, it could appeal to a committee of international experts, which would have to suggest ways of revising the Young Plan to deal with Germany's economic situation. Provisions were also made for a further eventuality: if the United States were to reduce the amount of money owed to it by its inter-Allied debtors, two-thirds of this sum was to be offset against Germany's reparations bill.

For Germany the Young Plan had one major advantage over the Dawes Plan in that it restored the country's sovereignty in the field of political economics. But it also had a disadvantage in that the removal of transfer protection meant that it would still have to pay reparations even during a period of economic depression. The prospect of having to make payments to the country's former wartime enemies for the next fifty-eight years was a depressing one, and yet there was political compensation for this: the German government's accept-ance of the Young Plan persuaded France to meet Germany halfway on the question of the Rhineland. On 30 August 1929, at the end of a conference in The Hague attended by Britain, France, Italy, Belgium, Japan and Germany, an agreement was signed providing for the early withdrawal of Allied troops from the Rhineland. Allied troops had already withdrawn from the first zone during the winter of 1925/6: the second zone was to be returned by 30 November 1929, the third by 30 June 1930, five years earlier than the date stipulated by the Treaty of Versailles.

Germany's right-wing extremists did not even wait for the talks in The Hague to be concluded but convened a National Committee for a German Referendum in Berlin on 9 July 1929. Its members included Heinrich Claß of the Pan-German League; Franz Seldte of the Stahlhelm, a paramilitary League of Frontline Soldiers founded at the end of 1918; the film and press magnate Alfred Hugenberg, who had become leader of the German National People's Party in October 1928; and Adolf Hitler of the NSDAP. Together they signed a declaration calling on the German people to rise up against the Young Plan and the 'lie concerning Germany's war guilt' and announcing plans for a refer-endum on the subject.

While the right wing was mustering its forces, the gulf between the moderate and radical left was widening. Ever since the Sixth World Congress of the Communist International in the summer of 1928, about which we shall have more to say in due course, the most pressing task of every Communist party was the need to combat the Social Democrats who had ostensibly become more bourgeois and were growing ever closer to Fascism. It is entirely possible that this slogan would have remained an abstract formula for the German Communist Party if, in the spring of 1929, the Social Democrat chief of police in Berlin, Karl Friedrich Zörgiebel, had not used measures against the extreme left that gave a semblance of justification to the new 'ultra-left' line adopted by the Comintern. Zörgiebel had banned all open-air demonstrations and meet-ings in the wake of a wave of violent clashes in December 1928 but had then upheld the ban the following May Day, which was the workers' traditional 'day of action'. The Communists ignored the ruling and erected a number of barri-cades, thereby giving the police an excuse to move against the extreme left, which they did with the utmost brutality, using armoured cars and firearms. Thirty-two civilians were killed in addition to almost 200 injuries and well over 1,000 arrests.

The intervention of the police in Berlin was followed by an administrative measure which, starting out from Prussia, soon engulfed the country as a whole and took the form of a ban on the Red Frontline Fighters' League, a Communist defence organization founded in 1924. The Communist Party reserved its most violent response for Wedding, the quarter of Berlin where the bloodiest clashes had taken place in May and where it convened a party

conference the following month, relocating it from Dresden, where it was originally scheduled to be held. The bloody events of early May and the ban on the
Red Frontline Fighters' League were taken by the party leaders as proof that the
Social Democrats were turning into 'Social Fascists'. Thälmann, who was
acclaimed at the rally as the leader of the revolutionary German proletariat,
went even further, describing the 'Social Fascism' of the Social Democrats as a
particularly dangerous form of Fascism.

The radicalization of the political left was closely connected to the increasing
rate of unemployment, the worsening economy causing the number of unemployed to rise above three million for the first time in February 1929, while the
usual recovery in the spring proved only weak: by March there were still 2.7
million men and women out of work. The federal agency for unemployment
had enough funds to pay only 800,000 of those entitled to primary support and
was forced to take out a loan. Since the exchequer itself had insufficient funds,
it was obliged in turn to ask for help from a consortium of banks. Only in this
way was it possible to avoid a total collapse of the Federal Unemployment
Agency in March 1929.

By now it was clear that unless the national insurance system was reformed,
the country's finances in general could not be restored to an even keel, but
nowhere were the standpoints of the coalition partners as far apart as in the
field of social security: after conferring with the Free Trade Unions, the SPD
advocated an increase in the contributions from employers and employees
alike, but the German People's Party, out of respect for the employers, rejected
this and instead demanded a lower rate of contributions.

Despite numerous discussions among experts there was still no sign of any
agreement by the end of September 1929, prompting the chancellor to
announce on 1 October that if the government failed to find a solution to the
problem, he would resign from office. The German People's Party fell into line
that very same day, declaring that if the SPD and the Centre Party were willing
to delay the implementation of their demand for an increase of 0.5 per cent
until December, the German People's Party would abstain from voting on a bill
lowering the rates of support and correcting anomalies in the system, thereby
helping the bill to complete its passage through parliament. The Social
Democrats and the Centre Party agreed to this compromise, with the result
that the bill was passed on 3 October. The grand coalition had survived its
most difficult test to date.

By now the politician who had done the most to keep Müller and his
government in office was dead: Gustav Stresemann had succumbed to a stroke
in the early morning of 3 October 1929 at the age of fifty-one. He had been in
failing health for some time and had exhausted his last reserves of strength
preventing a change of government that would have undermined his policy of
rapprochement with France. In order to protect his foreign policy from right-
wing interference, he had occasionally struck a more nationalist note than his

opinions actually merited. But he remained firmly convinced that renegotiation of the Treaty of Versailles did not justify another war. The prerequisite for a foreign policy based on this belief was closer cooperation with the more moderate forces within the bourgeoisie and working class. Stresemann knew this, which made him his party's most committed advocate of a grand coalition. His death considerably weakened this alliance. The only true statesman to be produced by the Weimar Republic was soon to prove irreplaceable in terms of his country's domestic and foreign policy.

By 2 November 1929 – four and a half weeks after Stresemann's death – it was clear that the attempt by the extreme right to engineer the rejection of the Young Plan by means of a referendum had cleared its first hurdle, albeit narrowly, when 4.1 million Germans, or 10.02 per cent of those entitled to vote, had demanded a referendum: this was 0.02 per cent more than was required by the country's constitution. The draft bill drawn up by the Federal Committee for the German Referendum threatened the 'chancellor, his ministers and those of their authorized representatives' who had signed the Young treaty with the charge of treason, the punishment for which was a prison term of no less than two years. It was clear, of course, that the Reichstag would reject this move by an overwhelming majority, the only uncertainty being the way that the German National People's Party would vote. After a debate lasting several days, the vote was taken on 30 November. Of the seventy-two German Nationalist members who attended, only fifty-three voted to send the chancellor and his associates to prison. The countermeasures that Hugenberg took in an attempt to punish those deputies who had deviated from the party line served only to divide the party. Twelve of them, including the former minister Walter von Keudell, the landowner Hans von Schlange-Schöningen, the chairman of the Association of German Nationalist Shop Assistants,[105] Walter Lambach, and the former lieutenant commander Gottfried Treviranus, all announced that they were leaving the party and founding the German Nationalist Cooperative Union. The party leader in the chamber, Kuno von Westarp, resigned in protest at Hugenberg's policies.

It was only after the Reichstag had rejected the bill that the unavoidable referendum was held on 22 December, when 5.8 million – 13.8 per cent of those entitled to vote – signalled they were in favour of it. In order for it to be accepted, it would have required twenty-one million yes votes, making the National Committee's failure all too apparent. But in nine of the thirty-five electoral districts more than one-fifth of voters had supported the proposal. Even more important was that, through his work on the committee, Hitler had made himself socially acceptable. In turn, his party profited from the support that heavy industry and farming had given the referendum.

And there were other signs in the late autumn of 1929 that the National Socialists were in the ascendant. In the regional and local elections in November and December they recorded substantial gains. In Thuringia, they even filled a cabinet post in a government that also included the German National People's

Party and the German People's Party: Wilhelm Frick was the minister for the interior and education. During this time Hitler's National Socialists also began to win over the universities. The National Socialist German Students' Association was the big winner in the elections for the General Student Committees during the winter of 1929/30. In Würzburg it won 30 per cent of the vote, at the Technical University in Berlin 38 per cent and in Greifswald as much as 53 per cent.

This lurch to the right on the part of the country's students was a form of social protest: here was a young generation of academics rebelling against attempts to turn it into a proletarian mass and declaring war on a system they blamed for their material hardship and uncertain career prospects. Hatred of the state of Weimar went hand in hand with anti-Semitism, for although Jews made up only 1 per cent of the country's population, they accounted for between 4 per cent and 5 per cent of students, with even higher percentages in disciplines such as medicine and law, especially in cities like Frankfurt and Berlin. In the eyes of many of their non-Jewish colleagues, this simply meant that the Jews enjoyed an unjustifiably privileged position in German society. The advances made by the National Socialist student organization rested not least on the mass mobilization of feelings of social envy.

By the end of 1929 the economic reasons for the increasing support for the extreme right were clear. The agricultural crisis had worsened and in northern Germany at least had led to a radicalization of the farming community: starting in the spring of 1929, bomb attacks on tax offices and local government buildings, especially in Schleswig-Holstein, repeatedly made the headlines. The number of job-seekers in Germany as a whole rose from 1.5 million in September to 2.9 million in December, around 350,000 higher than in the same month in 1928. If we take 1924–6 as the starting point, then share prices rose by 58 per cent during the boom year of 1927, falling by 10 per cent in 1928 and by a further 14 per cent in 1929. But it was from America that the most strident alarm signals could be heard: on 24 October 1929 prices on the New York Stock Exchange crashed, triggering a seismic reaction. American banks immediately limited the export of capital to Europe and especially to Germany.

It became increasingly difficult not only for local and regional government but for the country as a whole to obtain credit. For the president of the Reichsbank, Hjalmar Schacht, who had helped to found the German Democratic Party at the end of 1918 only to gravitate to the political right, the country's financial problems were a godsend, and he used the looming deficit to issue an ultimatum and demand that the grand coalition sort out the country's finances in the longer term. With the support of Parker Gilbert, he forced the government and the Reichstag to set aside the sum of 450 million marks for debt repayment in 1930.

Only after the Reichstag had agreed to this demand on 22 December did the government receive a bridging loan from a consortium of German banks headed by the Reichsbank that saved the country from bankruptcy. The programme of financial measures agreed to by the grand coalition and passed by the Reichstag only with considerable reservations could finally come into force. It included an increase in national insurance contributions from 3 per cent to 3.5 per cent, an increase in the duty on tobacco and a reduction in direct taxes designed to help in creating capital. By now Rudolf Hilferding was no longer the country's finance minister: he had resigned on 21 December in protest at Schacht's intervention and was replaced by the economist Paul Moldenhauer of the German People's Party, who had become a government minister only a few weeks earlier, on 11 November, after the previous incumbent, Julius Curtius, had succeeded Stresemann as foreign minister.

By the winter of 1929/30 there was no longer any doubt that parliamentary democracy was in crisis in the Weimar Republic, a crisis illustrated by more than simply the conflict between the president of the Reichsbank and the government, for there were also signs that large sections of the country's most powerful elite were beginning to turn their backs on the government and even on parliamentary rule as such. From the outset large-scale agricultural interests, aided and abetted by the Agricultural League, had been opposed to the grand coalition. In December 1929 the Confederation of German Industry sent Müller's government a memorandum headed 'Rise or Fall?' and making demands that amounted to an ultimatum: social policies should be adapted to economic production and the government should have the right to veto spending increases authorized by parliament. Since the end of 1929, the defence minister, Wilhelm Groener, and his closest adviser, the head of the newly created Ministerial Office, Kurt von Schleicher, had been working closely with Otto Meissner, the secretary of state in the president's office, to establish a government that did not include the Social Democrats. In the circumstances, such a government could be only a presidential cabinet.

Hindenburg had already expressed his support for such a change of direction in the spring of 1929. Westarp, at that date still leader of the German National People's Party in the Reichstag, was one of the first to learn of the president's aims. Hindenburg expressed himself more clearly at the beginning of 1930, enquiring of Hugenberg on 6 January and of Westarp on the 15th whether – in the event of a government crisis triggered by the financial reforms – the German Nationalists would support a cabinet that did not include the Social Democrats and that he himself, Hindenburg, would form. Hugenberg said that his party would not do so, whereas Westarp was in favour of such a move.

The government camp was still held together at this date by their mutual interest in passing the Young laws. The plan was passed in The Hague on 20 January 1930 following months of detailed discussions on the experts' various subcommittees. For Germany it was supremely important that the payment schedule and the amount to be paid were the same as those proposed by the panel of experts in June 1929. The final chapter in the story of the grand coalition began on 28 January. At the suggestion of Heinrich Brüning, who had been elected leader of the Centre Party in the Reichstag the previous month, the Centre Party decided to make its backing for the Young Plan dependent on agreement on the country's financial reforms. Brüning's proposed deal was a rejection of neither the grand coalition nor the new reparations agreement but represented an attempt to use the coalition's shared goal on foreign policy as a means of placing the country's finances on a much firmer footing.

There were a number of SPD deputies who demanded an alternative deal: if they were to agree to the Young laws, then the financial reforms should bear a Social Democratic stamp. But the vast majority rejected such linkage between domestic and foreign policy and in doing so involuntarily weakened the negotiating position of the largest government party. On the right wing of the coalition the German People's Party refused to make any further concessions on the question of national insurance and to raise direct taxes. They also declined to introduce an emergency levy on civil servants and others on fixed salaries, a proposal that had the support of Hindenburg himself. But on 5 March, much to the surprise of the parties in question, agreement was reached in cabinet on ways of covering the federal budget for 1930: Moldenhauer agreed to a proposal put forward by the SPD for a direct property tax in the form of an increase to the levy on industry from 300 to 350 million marks, a levy that was to be abandoned once the Young Plan had come into force. At the same time the Federal Unemployment Agency was able to raise national insurance contributions from 3.5 per cent to 4 per cent. In return the SPD ministers agreed that there would be no income tax refund in 1931.

The agreement in cabinet was a triumph for the moderates in every political camp, and yet it was built on sand, for on 6 March the German People's Party deputies in the Reichstag, encouraged by the Employers' Association and the Confederation of German Industry, rejected the government compromise on all its essential points. The Bavarian People's Party, which was represented in Müller's cabinet by the postmaster general, announced that it would not accept the planned increase on beer duty. Hindenburg again played a part in the discussions on 10 and 11 March, informing Brüning and Müller of his willingness to grant the government the powers contained in Article 48 of the federal constitution. This seemed to meet Brüning's demand that the question of reparations be linked to financial reform, and the Young laws were passed at their third reading on 12 March by 256 votes to 192. Almost all the Centre Party members voted in favour of the bill.

But whatever Hindenburg may have had in mind in his discussions with Brüning and Müller, his closest circle of advisers – his notorious Camarilla – was resolved to use the new situation to engineer a change of direction to the right, taking it away from a parliamentary system and closer to a presidential one. By 18 March the country's heavy industrialists who were members of the

German People's Party had been informed that Hindenburg, no doubt at the insistence of Groener and Schleicher, had decided not to allow Müller's government to use the emergency laws enshrined in Article 48. The following day Hindenburg peremptorily demanded measures to help agriculture in the east of the country. His secretary of state, Otto Meissner, commented on this change of heart in a message to Kurt von Schleicher: 'This is the first stage of *your* solution! It also lays the foundation for the best thing we can have, namely, Hindenburg's leadership.'[106]

Now that the German People's Party knew the president's aims, it could afford to adopt a more moderate tone towards the Social Democrats at its conference in Mannheim on 21 and 22 March. On the 26th and 27th Brüning again sought a compromise aimed at postponing the arguments over the national insurance reforms: the Federal Unemployment Agency was to introduce savings, whereas the government would decide only at a later date whether it would raise contributions, reduce benefits or raise indirect taxes in order to finance government loans.

This proposal, which weakened the cabinet decision of 5 March at the expense of the unemployed, was accepted by the majority of German People's Party deputies on 27 March, but when the Social Democrat deputies met, most of them, including those who represented the trade unions and the labour minister, Rudolf Wissell, spoke out against what they called the 'Brüning compromise'. The chancellor and the other SPD ministers were among a small minority that backed the Centre Party proposal. The cabinet was left with no alternative but to minute its failure and tender its resignation to the president.

The events of 27 March 1930 mark one of the major turning points in the history of the Weimar Republic. In retrospect we can see very clearly that it was on this day that the period of relative stability in Germany came to a definitive end and the first German Republic began to fall apart. But even contemporaries were aware of the changes that were taking place. On 28 March the *Frankfurter Zeitung* spoke of a 'black day, doubly disastrous because the trivial cause of the argument is so grotesquely disproportionate to the fatal consequences that may arise from it'.[107] Even members of the Social Democrat Party whose decision had sealed the fate of Müller's government were not slow to voice their criticism: in the May issue of his own theoretical journal *Die Gesellschaft*, Rudolf Hilferding explained why he could not agree with the argument that if Brüning's proposal had been accepted, it would no longer have been possible to avoid a reduction in benefits in the autumn of 1930:

> In terms of ring-fencing national insurance, resigning from the government represents no perceptible gain. The fear that the situation would have deteriorated in the autumn does not seem sufficient to justify such a momentous step; it makes no sense to commit suicide because of one's fear of death.[108]

The shift in power from parliament to the president could already be foreseen on 27 March. The political right both inside and outside parliament had wanted this development, because to them there seemed no other way of destroying the Weimar welfare state. This was the short-term goal of the proponents of presidential government – their aim was not just to prevent a trivial increase in national insurance contributions. As a result, the political right bore most of the responsibility for all that was to follow on from the fall of Müller's government.

The moderate left accepted this rejection of parliamentary democracy as a price worth paying and cannot therefore be acquitted of the charge of complicity in the shift to a presidential system. The Social Democrats could have prevented the disintegration of the grand coalition at the end of March 1930, albeit at the price of party unity. And their actions would in any case have been effective only in the shorter term, for the government alliance would almost certainly not have survived once its principal goal – the ratification of the Young laws – had been achieved. Even so, it would have been only right and proper for them to accept the solution held out to them by Brüning, for now the Social Democrats could only reproach themselves in the bitterest of terms: at the decisive moment they had not done everything in their power to preserve parliamentary democracy and prevent Germany's relapse into an authoritarian state.

Socialism in One Country: The Soviet Union under Stalin 1924–33

While the capitalist countries of the West were being sucked into the maelstrom of a world economic crisis in 1929, the Soviet Union was devoting itself to what Joseph Stalin called 'building socialism in one country'. 'Undoubtedly, things would be vastly easier if the victory of socialism in the West came to our aid,' the secretary general of the Russian Communist Party explained to an audience of students at Moscow's Sverdlov University on 9 June 1925. 'But, firstly, the victory of socialism in the West is not "happening" as quickly as we would like; and, secondly, those difficulties can be surmounted and we are already surmounting them, as you know.'

Misguidedly appealing to Lenin, Stalin claimed that in 1915 the latter had already given a basically affirmative answer to the 'question of the possibility of building socialism in one country' at the time of the 'imperialist war'.[109] In his article 'On the Slogan for a United States of Europe', Lenin had declared that 'the victory of socialism is possible first in several or even in one capitalist country alone' if the 'victorious proletariat of that country' were to succeed in 'attracting to its cause the oppressed classes of other countries, stirring uprisings in those countries against the capitalists, and in case of need using even armed force against the exploiting classes and their states'.[110]

Lenin had fallen out with Stalin in 1922, accusing him of being 'too rude' and in a codicil to his will of 4 January 1923 asking the Communist Party to strip Stalin of his position as its secretary general. The man without whom there would have been no October Revolution in Russia and no Soviet Union had certainly not become a liberal when he invited his comrades to replace Stalin after his – Lenin's – death with someone who would be 'more patient, more loyal, more polite, and more attentive to comrades, [and] less capricious'.[111] Even during his own lifetime, it was thanks chiefly to Lenin that the Bolshevik state had become a party dictatorship in which internal party opposition to the majority view of the Politburo was possible to only the most limited degree. But the Communist Party had not yet become the organization that Lenin was most anxious to avoid when issuing his warning about Stalin: it was not yet dominated by a single man exercising his tyrannical rule by means of an apparatus of party officials blindly devoted to him, with a secret police bent on persecuting all who held divergent views and even where the evidence was dubious in the extreme pursuing those people with the most deadly rigour.

Iosif Vissarionovich Dzhugashvili was born in Gori in Georgia in 1879, the son of a shoemaker who had once been a serf. He joined the Social Democrat Workers Party in 1898 and the following year was expelled from the seminary where he was studying for the priesthood on account of his political activities, which included organizing strikes. It was around this time that he took the name of Stalin, which is derived from the Russian word for 'steel'. By 1904 he had escaped from exile to Siberia and was working for the Bolsheviks as part of the revolutionary underground movement in the Caucasus, a task that included political murders, abductions, the springing of prisoners from gaols, extortion, stealing weapons, robbing banks and attacking people transporting money, all for the financial good of the party. Following the Bolshevik victory, he became the people's commissar for workers' and peasants' inspection and during the civil war was appointed political commissar with the Red Army. In terms of his later power base, it helped that from 1919 he belonged to both the Politburo and the Organizational Bureau of the Russian Communist Party and became the party's secretary general in 1922. With regard to Marxist theory, the other leading Bolsheviks – Lenin, Trotsky, Zinoviev, Kamenev and Bukharin – were all his superiors. Stalin's strength lay not only in his organizational gifts but also in his instinctive ability to identify his rivals' weaknesses and to forge alliances that consolidated his position of power.

Even before Lenin died on 21 January 1924 one such alliance had already been forged in the triumvirate of Stalin, Zinoviev and Kamenev that was directed at Trotsky, the only one of the leading Bolsheviks who could compete with Lenin intellectually. The creator of the Red Army and from March 1918 the commissar for war, Trotsky was accused of 'Bonapartist leanings' by all three men: in other words, they were convinced that he was seeking to establish a personal dictatorship based on the military. Moreover, the first generation of Bolsheviks held it against him that he had waited until July 1917 to join the party and align himself with Lenin's cause. In May 1924 – four months after Lenin's death – the former leader's will was read out at a plenary session of the Central Committee. Also read out was the later codicil relating to Stalin. On this occasion it was Zinoviev who saved Stalin, claiming that Lenin's fears about the party's secretary general had proved unfounded, and at the urging of Zinoviev and Kamenev Stalin remained in office, while Lenin's will was withheld from the general public and consigned to the party's secret archive.

With his confirmation as secretary general, Stalin had already achieved his principal goal, a goal he had been pursuing with Zinoviev and Kamenev. When, in the autumn of 1924, he began to steer the party in the direction of 'building socialism in one country', the thrust of his new policy was directed not only against Trotsky, the principal proponent of 'permanent revolution', but also, indirectly, against Zinoviev, the secretary general of the Communist International and party secretary in Leningrad, and against Kamenev, the party's leading figure in Moscow. Like Trotsky, all three men had actively promoted the 'German October', and its total failure left them politically weakened, albeit not to the same extent as Karl Radek, the Comintern's expert on Germany, who was one of Trotsky's supporters. In January 1925 Trotsky had to stand by while the Central Committee dismissed his theory of 'permanent revolution' and give up his post as commissar for war, although he remained a member of the Politburo after Stalin turned down Zinoviev's request to have him excluded from the party.

Zinoviev and Kamenev were regarded as two of those left-wing members of the party who were urging world revolution, whereas the right wing included Nikolai Bukharin, the editor in chief of *Pravda* and principal advocate of the New Economic Policy that Lenin had introduced in 1921, Alexei Rykov, the chairman of the Council of People's Deputies, and Mikhail Tomsky, the leader of the trade unions. These three right-wing members of the seven-man Politburo demanded a policy that was supportive of the country's peasants following a peasant uprising in Georgia in the summer of 1924. Shortly before the Fourteenth Party Conference in late April 1925 Bukharin even went so far as to echo a slogan ascribed to the French liberal François Guizot and to demand: 'Enrich yourselves, develop your farms, do not fear that you will be subjected to restrictions.'[112] Stalin disapproved of this appeal but at the party conference he voted for a lowering of taxes on agriculture and for other measures demanded by right-wing party members and designed to help the country's peasants.

Not until the second half of 1925 did Zinoviev and Kamenev begin to appreciate the danger inherent in Stalin's strategic volte-face and openly to resist the right wing's attempt to change Soviet agricultural policy. In doing so they cast themselves in the role of opponents of the new and informal alliance between Stalin on the one hand and Bukharin, Rykov and Tomsky on the other. At the Fourteenth Party Conference in December 1925, when the Communist Party of Russia renamed itself the Communist Party of the Soviet Union, the delegates approved the doctrine of 'building socialism in one country' as well as the new agricultural policy. Immediately afterwards the party's leaders began to purge the party organization in Leningrad of all of Zinoviev's supporters. A leading role in this process was played by the thirty-nine-year-old Sergei Kirov, who was soon to replace Zinoviev as party secretary in Leningrad. Stalin brought out his book *Problems of Leninism* in January 1926, using the occasion to launch a violent attack on Zinoviev and Kamenev, while avoiding all mention of Trotsky.

The catchphrase about 'building socialism in one country' was a popular one inside the Soviet Union since it appealed to a feeling later described as 'Soviet patriotism' involving a sense of pride at the fact that the Soviet Union was the only country where the 'Red' revolution had triumphed and asserted itself in the face of an entire world of enemies. In terms of the country's foreign policy, the new right-wing line led to a whole series of tactical alliances with reformist trade unions and workers' parties. The earliest example of this development was the formation of the Anglo-Russian Trade Union Committee in April 1925. Others include the cooperation between the German Communist Party and Social Democrat Party at the time of the 1926 referendum calling for the princes of the realm to be dispossessed. Neither kind of proletarian joint action achieved what it set out to do, but this did not help the left-wing element in the Soviet Communist Party in its struggle with the political right.

In the spring of 1926 Zinoviev and Kamenev made the serious mistake of allying themselves with Trotsky, a move that merely served to precipitate their own downfall. Trotsky was removed from the Politburo in October 1926, and at the same time Zinoviev was replaced by Bukharin as secretary general of the Comintern. By November 1927 both men had been expelled from the party, with Kamenev following suit at the Fifteenth Party Conference of the Soviet Communist Party a month later. The opposition was now split. Zinoviev and Kamenev recanted, allowing them to be readmitted to the party in 1928, whereas Trotsky refused to defend himself and in December 1927 was exiled to Alma Ata in Kazakhstan before being deported from the Soviet Union in January 1929, marking the start of an eleven-year exile that ended with his murder by an agent of the Soviet secret police in Mexico on 21 August 1940.

Stalin's foreign policy suffered two serious setbacks in 1927. In May Great Britain broke off diplomatic relations with the Soviet Union after a search of the Soviet Trade Mission revealed incriminating evidence relating to propaganda and other subversive activities. (Relations were resumed in 1929 under the new Labour administration.) And Soviet Russia's policy towards China, for which Stalin had been mainly responsible since 1924, took a catastrophic turn. Since 1923 the Bolsheviks had been urging the Chinese Communist Party to involve itself in the civil war that had been going on since 1916, but only in close cooperation with the nationalist Kuomintang under Sun Yat-sen. Following Sun Yat-sen's death in March 1925, Chiang Kai-shek began his inexorable rise to power and in 1926 embarked on a campaign of systematically excluding and persecuting the Communists in his country.

The bloody climax of this development came in April 1927 with the Shanghai Massacre. The city had been taken by Kuomintang troops only the previous month after a Communist uprising against the local military commander. Immediately after his entry into the city, Chiang Kai-shek ordered all the Communists in Shanghai and Nanking who had not fled to be executed. A further workers' uprising was bloodily suppressed, an alternative government to the left-wing Kuomintang government in Wuhan was set up in Nanking, and relations with the Soviet Union were broken off.

At the behest of both the Comintern and Stalin, the Chinese Communists responded with a series of putsch-like demonstrations, the last of which was a workers' uprising in Canton that was suppressed in December 1927 with the same brutality as that already witnessed in Shanghai. The failure of the Chinese Communist Party was also a personal failure for Stalin. It was from this debacle that the young Mao Zedong – a peasant's son who had trained as a librarian and who, like all early Chinese Communists, was influenced by the anti-imperialist movement of 4 May 1919 – drew lessons of his own. As early as 1925 he had already come to believe that the Communists would come to power in China only if they revolutionized the peasants. Two years later he urged the Communist Party to create its own fighting force and began to establish a Communist order, first in the Jinggang Mountains and then, after he was driven back there, on the border between the provinces of Jiangxi and Fujian in south-west China. China's first Communist state was created here in November 1931, the Soviet Republic of Jiangxi, with Mao as its head of state.

Once the left wing of the party had been destroyed, Stalin's alliance with the right had served its purpose, and by the end of 1927 there were signs that the Communist Party's secretary general was moving to the left. One of the factors that triggered this shift was the poor harvest of 1927, when yields fell far short of the overoptimistic expectations: cereal sales on the Soviet domestic market, for example, were a quarter lower than the previous year. In any case, most of the smaller farmers were producing only enough for their own use, while the kulaks, exploiting their market power to the full, demanded prices beyond the reach of the bulk of the population, and so the Central Committee of the Soviet Communist Party decided in December 1927 to take exceptional, if temporary, steps to deal with the kulaks in an attempt to improve supply.

In the middle of February 1928 Stalin wrote to the Communist Party to explain that the kulaks would now be placed under greater pressure to ship more wheat to the towns and cities. Moreover, Stalin's claim that the peasants were hoarding agricultural produce was undoubtedly true. In short, his letter marked a radical rejection of Bukharin's policy of adding to the wealth of the villages, a policy vehemently criticized by the left. Clearly Stalin was determined to break with Bukharin, Rykov and Tomsky. His personal desire to increase his own power and his fear of a nationwide famine were inextricably intertwined in his change of political direction at the beginning of 1928.

Practical measures designed to stop the peasants from hoarding kulak food supplies and sell them on the open market were agreed to at the plenary session of the Central Committee and Central Control Committee of the Soviet Communist Party in early April 1928. Shortly afterwards Stalin informed the Central Committee that he was striving to achieve far more than an end to the present crisis and wanted a rapid collectivization of agriculture. A further announcement followed in May: Stalin wanted the rate of industrialization to be speeded up, especially in heavy industry. In the absence of any other sources, the money needed for such investment could come only from the kulaks. For right-wing Bolsheviks there was no longer any doubt that if Stalin got his way, then the days of Lenin's New Economic Policy, with its calculated protection of private property, were numbered, which in turn meant that they too would soon be ousted from power.

This move against right-wing elements in the Soviet Communist Party demanded a parallel action on an international scale. At the ninth plenary session of ECCI in February 1928 the relevant guidelines were put in place with the announcement that the Social Democrats and reformist trade unions were henceforth to be regarded as the Communists' principal enemies. The Sixth World Congress of the Comintern, which was held in Moscow between 17 July and 1 September 1928, was given over in its entirety to the implementation of the new left-wing course of action, a course soon described by its critics as 'ultra-left'.

There is a certain irony in the fact that it was the right-wing secretary general of the Communist International, Nikolai Bukharin, who was obliged to shore up the radical shift to the left by means of a series of theoretical pronouncements. According to Bukharin, a new historical period had begun in international post-war developments. The period of an acute revolutionary crisis that had lasted from the spring of 1917 to the autumn of 1923 had been followed by one when the capitalist system was partially stabilized, but that period was now over. The third period was that of capitalist reconstruction, when production forces outstripped their pre-war values, but when forces hostile to capitalism also began to grow in strength.

In this context Bukharin drew attention to the great economic progress that had been made in the Soviet Union as well as to the Chinese revolution and the unrest in India. The contradictions inherent in capitalism were said to be growing more and more acute and at the same time the danger of war was allegedly increasing. The Comintern must take a stand here:

> And when the hour approaches in which the flags of imperialism are raised in war, our Communist International, together with all our parties and the countless masses of workers throughout the world, will speak their weighty

word. This word will be our cue for civil war, for our life-and-death battle with imperialism, a cry of victory on the part of the Communist International.[113]

The resolutions passed by the Sixth World Congress were fully in keeping with Stalin's wishes. In one resolution on the international situation and the challenges facing the Communist International, it was said that the leaders of the state and of the employers' organizations were 'in a process of growing closer together' with the heads of the workers' organizations under Social Democrat control:

> This process whereby the heads of the workers' bureaucracy are becoming increasingly bourgeois is being consciously supported and encouraged by the Social Democrats. [. . .] Throughout the whole of the recent period the Social Democrats have, as the bourgeois workers' party, played the role of the bourgeoisie's final reserve. [. . .] The ideology of class collaboration, which is the official ideology of Social Democracy, has many points in common with the ideology of Fascism. Embryonic forms of the sort of Fascist methods that are employed against the revolutionary workers' movement may be found in the practices of many Social Democrat parties as well as in the bureaucratic practices of reformist trade unions.[114]

The suggestion that Fascism and Social Democracy were ideologically closely related was not new, for as early as January 1924 Zinoviev had called Social Democracy a 'wing of Fascism', and in the September of that year Stalin had insisted that Social Democracy and Fascism were 'not opposites but twins'. In the summer of 1928 Stalin had a second reason for declaring war on the reformists: not only did he have to contend with the battle between the opposing wings of the Soviet Communist Party, but the formation of a grand coalition under Hermann Müller in Berlin meant that the most western and most Francophile German party had come to power in the form of the Social Democrats. Stalin felt that any rapprochement between France and Germany was dangerous because in his eyes France was still the most anti-Bolshevik country in the world. Nor could Moscow pin its hopes on Great Britain now that the trade unions and the Labour Party had clearly shifted to the right in the wake of the failure of the general strike in May 1926. If the Sixth World Congress of the Communist International invoked the danger of an 'imperialist war' with the Soviet Union, this was not, however, the result of a serious analysis of the international situation but the product of a strategic calculation: the Communist parties of the entire world were obliged to have recourse to a bogeyman that reflected the struggle with the right within the Comintern's party leadership.

It was above all the German Communist Party that was the target of these criticisms: it had the largest membership and the greatest following among the electorate of any Communist party outside the Soviet Union. After 1924 all Communist parties had had to toe a more Bolshevik line and model themselves ideologically, politically and organizationally on the Soviet Communist Party, including the formation of subversive, military underground organizations that were centrally controlled from Moscow. But ECCI was rarely satisfied with the practical results of this process, and this was true even in the case of the German Communist Party. First 'right-wing' deviations from the official line had to be combated, but then, following the rift between Stalin and the Zinoviev–Kamenev faction, it was 'left-wing' aberrations that needed to be dealt with, before the shift in the Soviet Union in the direction of the ultra-left meant that it was again the 'right wing' that had to be resisted. In October 1928 Stalin took steps to ensure that Ernst Thälmann was reinstated as party chairman, a post he had forfeited following his involvement in an embezzlement affair within the party. Under Thälmann, the party continued on its journey down the road of greater Stalinization, and from 1929 onwards no party was as dogged and as spiteful in combating 'social Fascism' as the German Communist Party.

Toeing the new ultra-left party line did little to help Bukharin, who committed the twofold failing of siding with the left-wing Kamenev in his battle with Stalin and of publicly criticizing the secretary general of the Soviet Communist Party, thereby unwittingly precipitating his own downfall. In July 1929 he was replaced as secretary general of ECCI by Dmitry Manuilsky, a party official who was blindly devoted to Stalin. Shortly beforehand, one of Bukharin's two most important comrades-in-arms had lost his position, when Nikolai Mikhailovich Shvernik replaced Tomsky as leader of the Soviet trade unions in early June. The last member of the right-wing troika to be ousted was Rykov, who in January 1930 was replaced as chairman of the Council of People's Commissars by Vyacheslav Molotov. Bukharin and Tomsky were expelled from the Politburo in November 1929, Rykov at the end of 1930. Rykov and Tomsky confessed their 'mistakes' at the Sixteenth Party Conference in the summer of 1930, while Bukharin expressed his remorse at the Seventeenth Party Conference in February 1932. At least for the present, they had ceased to represent a threat to Stalin.

By the end of 1929 Stalin's position seemed unassailable now that he had successively stripped each of his rivals of power, and on 21 December he celebrated his fiftieth birthday with a degree of pomp and circumstance that turned this day into an early example of the cult of his personality. Throughout the Soviet Union he was hailed as *vozhd*, or 'leader', and as the 'Lenin of our day'. Statues of him were erected in public places, while busts appeared inside town halls; his image was displayed in every town and city and even in many villages, invariably alongside that of Lenin, who in the wake of his death had become the leading cult figure in the country. His breach with the right had consolidated his position in the Politburo, allowing him to devote himself with increased vigour to his great goal, which was to destroy the New Economic Policy by means of a second revolution even more radical than Lenin's.

The preconditions for this large-scale transformation were already encapsulated in the First Five-Year Plan. According to its draft, which had been submitted by the State Planning Commission in March 1929 on the basis of the relevant resolution from the Fifteenth Party Conference in December 1927, gross industrial production was to rise by at least 135 per cent within a five-year period. If conditions were favourable and there was a good harvest in each of the five years covered by the plan, this figure might even rise to 180 per cent. But the country's political leaders decided to commit themselves to the optimistic higher alternative as the aim of their programme of industrialization, and it was this figure that was enshrined in the First Five-Year Plan that was ratified by the Fifth Soviet Congress in May 1929. During the summer it was announced that the whole project should be completed within four, not five, years. At the same time the target figures were raised still further in certain areas of heavy industry, shifting industrial policy even further away from consumer goods and towards investment. When the favourable conditions in the agricultural market failed to materialize, the plan was not revised. Instead, pressure on producers was increased in an attempt to oblige them to meet the requirements of the plan.

At the plenary session of the Central Committee in July 1928 Stalin had not yet been able to force through his new plans for agriculture and industry in the face of opposition from Bukharin, Tomsky and Rykov. But by the winter of 1928/9 his battle with the kulaks and his struggle to bring about the collectivization of agriculture had assumed a new quality as resistance from the kulaks in the form of local uprisings, violations of the law and even the murder of government officials was greeted by extreme reprisals by the state, including the security services and the Communist Party. The authorities seized crops, prompting the farmers to respond by destroying wheat and feeding meal to their pigs. On the middle section of the Volga the peasants rose up in huge numbers.

Even before the Soviet Union had begun its policy of buying up grain supplies in the summer of 1929, large areas of the country were already in the grip of a crisis tantamount to a civil war and recalling the 'War Communism' of the years before 1921. Stalin signalled the start of his offensive against the kulaks on 27 December 1929. His aim, he declared, was 'to smash the kulaks, eliminate them as a class. [. . .] To launch an offensive against the kulaks means that we must prepare for it and then strike at the kulaks, strike so hard as to prevent them from rising to their feet again. That is what we Bolsheviks call a real offensive.'[115]

It is reckoned that there were between 1.5 and two million kulaks in 1929, while the farmers operating medium-sized farms numbered between fifteen and eighteen million. The number of smallholders, or *muzhiks*, working with wooden ploughs, was between five and eight million. The total of Russian peasants was therefore between twenty-five and twenty-eight million. Statistically speaking, collectivization was a complete success. Between October 1929 and the end of January 1930, the number of collective farms rose from 4.1 per cent of all farms to 21 per cent, and by 10 March 1930 that figure had risen to 58 per cent. But the methods used to nationalize agricultural concerns were brutal. 'Kulak families were dispossessed and resettled,' writes the German historian Helmut Altrichter:

> The farmers killed off their own cattle before joining the newly founded collective farms, or *kolkhozy*. Wave after wave of party and soviet officials, militia, brigades of urban industrial workers and groups of the Communist Youth Movement, Komsomol, swept through the villages in their attempt to accelerate the process of collectivization. Village assemblies had to pass the relevant resolutions and anyone who spoke out against them was regarded as a kulak or kulak labourer. The activists became intoxicated by their own success, and the government did nothing to restrain them.[116]

In early March 1930 the unexpectedly vociferous protests by the farmers forced Stalin to condemn a number of illegal excesses on the part of his agents and to order a halt to the violence against the *muzhiks*. In the wake of this announcement, many of the new *kolkhozy* were disbanded, and the collectives' share of the market fell from 58 per cent to 21 per cent between March and September 1930. Mass demonstrations followed in the western half of the Ukraine, the Central Black Earth Region, the northern Caucasus and Kazakhstan, leading in turn to a return to the policy of collectivization and to a rise in the number of *kolkhozy*: by 1931 they made up more than half of all the farms in the country and by 1934 they accounted for around three-quarters of all farms.

Stalin had evidently never asked himself the question of what he should do with the dispossessed kulaks who, together with their families, numbered between eight and ten million. During the winter of 1929/30 the Secret Police, or GPU, divided the kulaks into three categories: those who had been involved in counterrevolutionary activities were arrested and deported to labour camps or, if they resisted, were liquidated on the spot; a second group consisted of farmers who, although opposed to the regime, had not been engaged in any overtly counterrevolutionary activities but who were arrested and together with their families deported to remote parts of Siberia; and, thirdly, there were kulaks loyal to the government who were resettled away from the collective farms and set to work on improvement schemes.

By the summer of 1930 the GPU had built up an extensive network of camps, chiefly on the Solovetsky Islands off the Karelian coast and stretching as far north as Archangelsk. More than 80,000 prisoners were forced to work on the Stalin Canal linking the White Sea and the Baltic as well as on roads and railways. Other tasks included peat-digging and wood-cutting, while 15,000 prisoners from the Far Eastern camps built the railway line to Boguchachinsk. The 25,000 prisoners in the Vishera group of camps had the task of constructing the large chemical works at Berezniki in the Urals. The system of penal colonies described by Alexander Solzhenitsyn as the 'Gulag Archipelago' was already taking shape at this time. Kulaks in the second category had to settle in uninhabited areas of Siberia, where the land needed to be improved but where the deported farmers were generally sent without provisions or tools. The homes intended for them had been built in only the rarest cases, although farmers forced to resettle in the vicinity of major building sites had at least a chance of finding accommodation in primitive barracks.

By the start of 1934 at least half a million men, women and children were imprisoned in Soviet concentration camps and by 1935 that figure had risen to almost 790,000. Not included in these figures are the 280,000 prisoners in labour camps for criminals serving sentences of up to three years and a further 160,000 prison inmates, most of whom were farmers. The number of people who between 1930 and 1932 lost their lives as a result of being deported as part of the programme to eliminate kulaks as a class is reckoned by the French historian Nicolas Werth to have been around 300,000.[117]

The total number of kulaks who were executed is unknown. According to the records of the GPU, in 1930 alone 20,200 people were sentenced to death by the secret police's special courts. A secret report dated 15 February 1930 recorded 65,000 deaths. Not all the victims were kulaks, of course, but included other 'alien elements' such as police officers from the old regime, 'White officers', priests, nuns, peasants who also worked as craftsmen, former traders and members of the 'village intelligentsia'. Along the central section of the Volga and also in the Ukraine and Caucasus, rebellious peasants were dealt with by units of the Red Army using artillery and poison gas. Tens of thousands of men, women and children were killed in this way in the Caucasus in 1930.

A direct consequence of the collectivization of agriculture was the great famine of 1932/3. Harvest yields had fallen dramatically since 1928, not least as a result of the brutal intervention of the regime and of resistance to it, and the lack of food was made worse by the export of grain to the 'capitalist' West. (In 1933, 1,800 million kilos of wheat were lost in this way.) Even when the famine was at its worst, the Soviet leaders continued their policy of exporting grain to the West, partly in order to obtain the foreign currency needed to mechanize agriculture and especially to buy tractors.

The principal victims of the famine were the dispossessed peasants in the richer agricultural regions such as the Ukraine and northern Caucasus. In a number of these areas both the GPU and foreign diplomats reported cases of cannibalism in 1933. As far as possible, the proletarian population of the cities who continued to be the Bolsheviks' main support still received food supplies, but peasants who sought refuge there were left empty-handed, and in December 1932 the government reintroduced the internal passes that had last existed under Pyotr Arkadevich Stolypin in the decade before the First World War. The peasants from the *kolkhozy* were not granted such permits but remained tied to their farms. Anyone in the towns and cities who was found not to have an internal pass was deported. In Moscow alone 300,000 individuals were affected by such measures in 1933.

Western and, since 1991, Ukrainian historians have occasionally claimed that the famine was a means that Stalin deliberately used to break the resistance of the peasants and destroy Ukrainian nationalism, but this is untrue. Rather, it was a consequence of the collectivization of agriculture and of enforced industrialization for which he was willing to pay the price: his plans could simply not have been realized without the forced labour of former peasants. Werth believes that more than six million men, women and children died during the great famine of 1932/3. Of these, four million came from the Ukraine, the region with the highest density of kulaks. There were also a million deaths in Kazakhstan, most of them nomads who were forced to lead sedentary lives when their cattle were seized. A further million deaths occurred in the northern Caucasus and Central Black Earth Region.

The way in which collectivization was implemented caused lasting damage to Soviet agriculture. In 1933 the grain harvest fell 5 million tonnes short of its 1928 figure, and a quarter of a century was to pass before the keeping of livestock returned to the level seen in 1928. Not until the 1950s did the figures for per capita agricultural production reach the level found before collectivization. If agriculture began to recover after 1933, this was due to far-reaching concessions to the farmers. Stalin broke up most of the state-owned *sovkhozy* and transferred their land to the *kolkhozy*. It was entirely Stalin's intention that there should be rich and poor *kolkhozy* and rich and poor peasants. The *kolzhozy* did not become Communist communities but cooperatives in which the peasants were able to farm a small scrap of land covering perhaps 5 per cent of the arable area, and they could also keep a few head of cattle. Until well into the 1950s these *priusadebnyj učastok* provided more than 70 per cent of potatoes, around 70 per cent of milk and 90 per cent of eggs. If the farmers had been dependent exclusively on the money they received from the *kolkhozy*, they would never have survived. It was the *priusadebnyj učastok* that ensured their survival.

The regime also had to lower its expectations in the field of industrialization when the overambitious aims of the First Five-Year Plan proved unachievable. In 1930 Stalin had demanded that coal and steel production be increased by around a half within the space of a year, but, as the secretary general of the Soviet Communist Party was obliged to concede in 1931, the increase had been in the order of between 6 per cent and 10 per cent. Nor was the process of industrialization in any way helped by the fact that in 1928 the regime began to wage war on 'bourgeois specialists', or *spetzys*. This was a development that was triggered by the discovery of a case of alleged 'industrial sabotage' in a concern belonging to the Donugul Trust in the Shakhty region, a coalmining area in the Donets Basin. A show trial resulted in death sentences being handed down to eleven of the fifty-three accused, who were mostly engineers and company directors. Five of them were executed.

There followed further arrests of the leaders of industry, chiefly in the metal industry, all of whom had to serve out their sentences on building sites and in businesses that were a part of the First Five-Year Plan. In August and September 1930 the campaign against 'bourgeois specialists' also impinged on prominent university teachers who were working in ministries, the state bank and Gosplan. One of them was Nikolai Dmitriyevich Kondratiev, the internationally respected discoverer of 'long waves' – 'Kondratiev waves' – in economic cycles and until 1928 head of the Economic Institute of the People's Commissariat. The fact that he credited capitalism with the ability to recover from a cyclical crisis similar to the one that occurred in 1929 made him a dangerous deviant in the eyes of orthodox Bolsheviks. After eight years in solitary confinement he was sentenced to death by a military tribunal on 17 September 1938 and executed later that same day.

Although the results of the First Five-Year Plan fell far short of the goals that Stalin had set, a Second Five-Year Plan was agreed in 1933. In 1938 its rather more modest goals were declared to have been met and a Third Five-Year Plan was announced. The reliability of Soviet data relating to the success of industrialization is contested. It is claimed, for example, that between 1928 and 1940 industrial production rose from 100 per cent to 587 per cent, whereas western estimates place the second figure at between 250 per cent and 450 per cent. Purely quantitatively, the Soviet Union overtook Germany, Great Britain and France in terms of its volume of industrial production and was second only to the United States. But the increase relates only to a growth in volume: as for productivity, the Soviet Union continued to lag far behind western industrialized nations, a situation that could never be changed by the combination of terror, force and proletarian enthusiasm that were typical of the Soviet Union under Stalin.

Stalin explained his reasons for undertaking a second revolution designed to transform a backward agrarian country into a developed industrialized nation within a matter of only a few years in a remarkable speech that he delivered to an audience of business executives in Moscow on 4 February 1931:

It is sometimes asked whether it is not possible to slow down the tempo somewhat, to put a check on the movement. No, comrades, it is not possible! The tempo must not be reduced! On the contrary, we must increase it as much as it is within our powers and possibilities. This is dictated to us by our obligations to the workers and peasants of the U.S.S.R. This is dictated to us by our obligations to the working class of the whole world.

To slacken the tempo would mean falling behind. And those who fall behind get beaten. We do not want to be beaten. [...] One feature of the history of old Russia was the continual beatings she suffered because of her backwardness. [...] All beat her – because of her backwardness, because of her military backwardness, political backwardness, industrial backwardness, agricultural backwardness. They beat her because it was profitable and could be done with impunity. [...]

We are fifty or a hundred years behind the advanced countries. We must make good this distance in ten years. Either we do it, or we shall go under.[118]

The political voluntarism that marked the decision to collectivize Soviet agriculture and embark on the First Five-Year Plan was based on a correct diagnosis: Russia was every bit as backward as Stalin said it was. His reference to an external threat was an effective argument designed to win over those who were urging a slower rate of industrialization. None of the capitalist powers had any intention any longer of engaging in military action against the Soviet Union or of reversing the effects of the October Revolution, but the country *was* threatened by the most radical of all the Fascist movements, namely, German National Socialism, and it was precisely this movement that Stalin encouraged by urging the Communist parties of foreign countries – especially the one in Germany – to redouble their attacks on the Social Democrats in the wake of the shift to the ultra-left in Soviet politics.

And there were other ways, too, in which Stalin was undermining his own aims: his campaign against 'bourgeois experts', for example, meant that his plan for industrial growth lacked any rational, scientific basis. All that remained was pure will and brute force, resulting in the loss of countless human lives and the squandering of material resources on the grandest scale. When, in June 1931, Stalin declared that his war on 'bourgeois experts' was over, the key economic posts were already in the hands of Bolsheviks whom he felt he could trust.

At the beginning of 1926, two years before the lurch to the left, Stalin had argued that 'the main task of the bourgeois revolution consists in seizing power and making it conform to the already existing bourgeois economy, whereas the main task of the proletarian revolution consists, after seizing power, in building a new, socialist economy'.[119] This amounted to a complete reversal of Marx's theory of the relationship between base and superstructure, but it also implied something else, namely, a further increase in the dialectics of backwardness and radicality, a debate to which the young Marx had already contributed in his 1843 introduction to his *Critique of Hegel's Philosophy of Right*, in which he had invited Germany to face up to the challenge of carrying out the most radical of all revolutions: the proletarian revolution.

Lenin had ascribed this very task to backward Russia but had also argued that the proletarian revolution would be completed only in the wake of successful revolutions in developed capitalist countries. Although Stalin did not abandon the idea of world revolution when proclaiming his doctrine of 'building socialism in one country', he did not think that the working class and Communist parties in the West were capable on their own of helping the proletariat to triumph, nor did he regard such revolutions as the necessary precondition for building socialism in the Soviet Union. The more powerful the Soviet Union became, the more it could bend other, non-Russian Communist parties to its will and in that way influence the policies of other countries where those parties were active. The world revolution could wait because it was worth striving for only if it bore the hallmarks of the Soviet Union. As Stalin put it in 1926, the aim was now

> the utilisation of the rule of the proletariat for the suppression of the exploiters, for the defence of the country, for the consolidation of the ties with the proletarians of other lands, and for the development and victory of the revolution in all countries.[120]

As for the matter of political voluntarism, Stalin and Lenin were kindred spirits, both men believing that socialism could and, indeed, must address the whole person if it was to produce a new, socialist man or woman. This totalitarian claim demanded a totalitarian system. Lenin had laid the foundations for this development, and Stalin proceeded to build on them. His regime amounted to a permanent state of civil war, a dictatorship based on the mobilization of the masses carried out by a class of professional revolutionaries for whom terror was second nature. Under Lenin, it had still been possible to voice dissent within the collective leadership of the Communist Party, but this possibility was much reduced under Stalin. If need be, it was he who embodied the collective will of the party. What he had achieved in this respect during the decade after Lenin's death was impressive but by no means everything that it was possible to accomplish from such a position of power.

To create the new Soviet man and woman required a cultural revolution which in the words of the historian Jörg Baberowski was no mere episode in Soviet history but the 'very hallmark of Stalinism'. The agents of the socialist counterrevolution were above all men and, to a lesser extent, women eager to climb the social ladder, people who had entered their professions through 'workers' faculties' that had previously been the preserve of 'bourgeois' academics. All who were reckoned to be 'socially alien elements' no longer had any access to higher forms of education. The 'new man' had to keep proving his credentials by denouncing the alleged enemies of socialism, including bourgeois teachers. He needed an enemy to understand what exactly constituted him as the new socialist man. He had to satisfy a new, socialist morality in order to evolve into an intellectually and physically perfect human being of a kind that had never existed in any class-based society.[121]

The struggle to create the new Soviet man implied the defeat of the older type of Russian who indulged his immoderate love of vodka and the opium of traditional religion. Hand in hand with the collectivization of agriculture went the closure of countless churches, leading in turn to resistance within the villages affected. Church bells were melted down and used in industry. Nowhere was the clash between the new quasi-religion of a socialist utopia and recalcitrant reality as blatant as in the Islamic societies in the central Asian republics on the periphery of the Soviet Union. Sharia law was abandoned here in 1927. Gangs of Komsomol youths stripped women of their veils, while women who had voluntarily cast aside the veil and joined the Communist Party had to contend with the embittered opposition of devout Muslims. In Uzbekistan some 400 women were killed between the spring of 1929 and the spring of 1930. A far greater number of these women were mutilated and raped by traditionalists or subjected to collective punishments or banished from their village communities.

The Bolsheviks responded to violent resistance with increasingly repressive measures, as Baberowski explains:

> They sent mobile courts to the regions in questions, executed men who had killed or raped women and staged show trials to demonstrate to the population how the regime dealt with counterrevolutionaries and class enemies. For the Bolsheviks, these women had not been murdered but had fallen in battle with the counterrevolution.[122]

While the regime was inflicting a reign of terror on kulaks and other counter-revolutionaries, the Soviet Communist Party was waging an internal war against unreliable elements within its own ranks. In April 1929 the Central Committee ordered a purge of the party with the aim of ridding the socialist offensive of 'capitalist' and 'petit bourgeois' acts of sabotage. Around 11 per cent of members and candidates were expelled from the party, most of them on account of minor infringements of party discipline, 'un-socialist behaviour' and the careless execution of directives. At the end of 1930 Stalin once again found himself facing a challenge from a right-wing group within the party leadership. At its head were two officials who had previously supported the secretary general in his battle with the right: they were the chairman of the Council of People's Commissars of the Russian Federated Soviet Republic, Sergei Ivanovich Syrtsov, who had the temerity to mock a showcase tractor factory near Stalingrad as a 'Potemkin village' and to describe the alleged breakthrough in the field of industrialization as 'eyewash'; and the secretary of the Transcaucasian Communist Party, Vissarion Vissarionovich Laminadze, who criticized the regime for its 'seigneurial and feudal' treatment of the peasants.[123]

Even worse was the criticism levelled at the regime by the district secretary of the Moscow party, Martemyan Nikitich Ryutin, in 1932. Together with other like-minded individuals, he drew up a programme in which he described Stalin as 'the evil spirit of the Russian revolution', a man whose thirst for revenge and desire for power had driven the regime to the edge of the abyss.[124] Stalin was beside himself with fury and in the autumn of 1932 demanded that Ryutin be executed but was unable to persuade the Politburo to heed his request. The majority of its members, including the Leningrad party secretary, Sergei Kirov, were willing only to expel Ryutin from the party and banish him from the capital. Clearly criticism of Stalin's policies and leadership style was far more widespread within the Communist Party than even well-informed observers were aware. A second purge was agreed to in early January 1933 and led to the expulsion of a further 17 per cent of party members and candidates, and yet not even this was capable of satisfying Stalin's need to exercise total control. The fact that he could rely on only a minority of Politburo members associated with Vyacheslav Molotov and Lazar Kaganovich served merely to spur him on yet further: his power was still not absolute.

The parties that made up the Comintern knew next to nothing about the differences of opinion within the Soviet Communist Party's leadership. Nowhere did Stalin's Soviet Union have such ardent defenders as in the Communist parties in the West. The more that social hardship grew in capitalist countries after 1929, the brighter was the light put forth by the country that had cast aside capitalism in revolutionary fashion. All that the Soviet Union did seemed exemplary not only in the eyes of the leaders of the world's Communist parties but even in those of the broad mass of their proletarian supporters. This was true of the books, plays and films that emanated from the home of socialism, and it was also true of the methods used to defeat the class enemy. 'Shoot! Shoot! Shoot!' was the banner headline of *Die rote Fahne* in Berlin on 25 November 1930. Although not an invitation to German Communists, it *was* said to be 'the voice of the people in the factories' of Berlin responding to the show trial in Moscow against the 'party of industry', an alleged group of saboteurs who according to the prosecution were acting on behalf of the French chief of the general staff and of the French government and preparing for a war of intervention against the Soviet Union. Yet it was German voices that the official newspaper of the German Communist Party invoked in the form of a questionnaire that left its readers in no doubt that in the event of a Communist overthrow in Germany the German counterrevolutionaries would 'hear Russian spoken'.[125]

But there was also sympathy for the Soviet Union outside the confines of the international Communist parties. At the Congress of the International Federation for Human Rights in Paris in 1927 the movement's president, Victor Basch, who had once defended Alfred Dreyfus, invited all those who were present not to fear the word 'revolution', adding, to sustained applause, 'And let us be clear in our own minds that every revolution must necessarily involve a temporary interruption of legality.'[126] According to Basch, the October Revolution in Russia was a revolution mounted by those classes that had not profited from the bourgeois revolution. From this point of view, events that were currently unfolding in the Soviet Union were comparable to the Reign of Terror of the French Revolution and, as such, a transitional stage on the road to a new legality. Many on the French left seemed unconcerned by the fact that the Russian '1793' was lasting far longer than its French counterpart.

Not even visits to Russia could be counted upon to inspire a more sober insight into the reality of the situation. When, in September 1933, Édouard Herriot, the leader of the French Radicals, returned from a tour of the Ukraine that had been carefully planned and stage-managed by the local authorities, he noted how impressed he had been at all that his hosts had permitted him to see:

> I crossed the Ukraine. So! I assure you that it looked like a garden in full yield. You tell me that this land is reputed to be going through a depression right now? I cannot speak of what I have not seen. And heaven knows, I made them take me to afflicted areas. All I witnessed, however, was prosperity.[127]

A number of British Fabians who visited Soviet Russia during the early 1930s returned home with even more favourable impressions than those reported by Herriot. Two of them, Bernard Shaw in 1932 and H. G. Wells in 1934, even had the opportunity to speak at length with Stalin and were impressed by his candour and shrewdness. Shaw reported afterwards that he had not seen a single malnourished person in the Soviet Union. Sidney and Beatrice Webb, both of them already in their seventies, visited the country in 1932 and wrote of their experiences in *Soviet Communism: A New Civilisation?*, published in 1935, insisting that the Soviet Communist Party was a democratic mouthpiece of the Russian people and that Stalin had 'not even the extensive power which the Congress of the United States has temporarily conferred upon President Roosevelt. He is only the General Secretary of the Party.'[128] The picture of the Soviet Union promoted by the Webbs was that of a democracy of cooperative producers who had rid themselves of large-scale landownership and capitalism and were creating a new society and a new type of human being in the name of science. In later editions of their book, the authors even removed the question mark after their subtitle: *A New Civilisation*.

The conservatives and liberals from Churchill to Emil Ludwig who had been impressed by Fascist Italy and its leader had fallen victim to the same deceit as the British and French left following brief visits to the Soviet Union, where they found confirmation of what they wanted to believe, cutting themselves off from all that might have shaken their preconceived ideas.

Boom, Crisis and Depression: The United States 1928–33

Nowhere in the Western world was there so little enthusiasm for 'building socialism in one country' as in the United States of America, a country described by the German economist Werner Sombart in 1906 as 'the Canaan of capitalism, the land of promise'.[129] And yet even here there were a number of intellectuals in the 'progressive' tradition who gazed at the Soviet Union's achievements with respect and admiration. (Such sentiments were shared, of course, by the registered members of the Communist Party, who in 1929 numbered under 10,000.)

The most prominent of these American intellectuals was the philosopher John Dewey, who visited the Soviet Union in 1928 and took a particular interest in the country's schools. Writing in *New Republic* in November 1928 he described a land 'freed from the load of subjection to the past' and seemingly 'charged with the ardor of creating a new world'.[130] In May 1930 the political scientist Frederick L. Schuman argued in the pages of the same periodical that the Soviet Union would achieve not Marxist but 'progressive' ideals and insisted that Stalin's regime was an administrative agency through which economic chaos and exploitation would be replaced by 'intelligently directed planning and cooperation'.[131] Well-known writers like John Dos Passos, Theodore Dreiser and Upton Sinclair went even further. All three had been involved in founding the Workers' Cultural Federation in May 1931, a crypto-Communist Party initiative; and all three served as honorary presidents of what in the event was to prove a short-lived organization.

Fascist Italy had far more sympathizers in the United States than Soviet Russia. The Fascist League of North America drew its members from the most radical followers of Mussolini in 'Little Italy' – those districts in the major towns and cities where Italian immigrants lived. Admittedly, it attracted only a tiny minority – at its inaugural rally on Staten Island on Independence Day in 1928, 350 Fascists faced a crowd of some 1,000 anti-Fascists, and the organization was disbanded at the end of 1929 in the wake of internal wrangling – but in the higher echelons of American society and even among intellectuals, Mussolini was the man who had rescued Italy from chaos and Communism and who was held in correspondingly high regard. In 1924, Irving Babbitt, a leading representative of the 'New Humanists' who were critical of democracy and of competition, wrote that 'we may esteem ourselves fortunate if we get the American equivalent of a Mussolini; he may be needed to save us from the equivalent of a Lenin'.[132]

Like the majority of right-wing intellectuals, the American administrations of Harding and Coolidge turned a blind eye to the terror of the Italian Fascists, and at no point were relations between Italy and the United States as cordial as they were under Hoover between 1929 and 1933. Hoover's secretary of state, Henry L. Stimson, later recalled that in Mussolini he and his president had found a 'sound and useful leader, no more aggressive in his nationalism than many a democratic statesman'.[133]

Herbert Hoover had been secretary of commerce since 1921. In 1928, when Coolidge decided not to stand for re-election, Hoover was selected as the Republican presidential candidate. His Democrat rival was the governor of

New York, Alfred ('Al') E. Smith, a Catholic and an emphatic opponent of prohibition. The turnout in the election was barely 57 per cent. Hoover won a resounding victory with 58.2 per cent of the vote, as compared to Smith's 40.7 per cent. Hoover had 444 delegates, Smith eighty-seven. Among the other candidates, the Socialist Norman Thomas was the most successful, with 268,000 votes, or 0.7 per cent of the total. The Communist candidate, William Z. Foster, had to make do with 49,000 votes (0.1 per cent). The vast majority of Americans were happy with the existing social order and with the way in which their country had been governed during the last eight years: no other interpretation can be placed on such unambiguous election results. And another finding, too, was incontestable: Protestant America still had no desire to be run by a Catholic president.

Coolidge delivered his final State of the Union address to both houses of Congress on 4 December 1928:

> No Congress of the United States [. . .] has met with a more pleasing pros-
> pect than that which appears at the present time. In the domestic field there
> is tranquility and contentment, harmonious relations between management
> and wage earner, freedom from industrial strife, and the highest record of
> years of prosperity. In the foreign field there is peace, the good will which
> comes from mutual understanding, and the knowledge that the problems
> which a short time ago appeared so ominous are yielding to the touch of
> manifest friendship.

The country could regard the present with satisfaction and anticipate the future with optimism: 'The main source of these unexampled blessings lies in the integrity and character of the American people.'[134]

In terms of American foreign policy, the Kellogg–Briand Pact initiated by the secretary of state Frank B. Kellogg and his French counterpart, Aristide Briand, is a good example of the sort of policy of détente advocated by Coolidge: an American note dated 23 June 1928 summed up the pact's essential point, condemning 'recourse to war for the solution of international controversies' and denouncing it 'as an instrument of national policy'.[135] The right of self-defence remained unaffected by this, and there was no attempt to define the concept of the aggressor or to regulate sanctions. None the less, the agreement, which had been signed by fifteen states, including Germany, by the end of August 1928 and by a further forty-eight by 1939, provided indirect legitimacy for a war involving sanctions against an aggressor and against anyone who disturbed the existing world order.

Within the western hemisphere, in its Central American backyard, the United States had again been active as an interventionist force since the summer of 1926: with the help of US marines, the country was currently supporting the conservative president of Nicaragua, Adolfo Diaz, against an uprising by the

Partido Liberal and its ally, the Grupo Armado Liberal, under Augusto César Sandino, who was later to be dubbed the 'General de Hombres Libres'. The fighting in Nicaragua was still continuing when the Pan-American Conference convened in Havana in January 1928 and the United States made an important concession to the states of Latin America, renouncing the 'Roosevelt Corollary' to the Monroe Doctrine of 1904, namely, the right that the United States claimed to intervene in Latin America as a police force if the countries there were unable to maintain law and order and national sovereignty by themselves. This concession laid the foundations for Hoover's 'good neighbor policy', a policy of maintaining peaceful relations with Latin America to which Franklin D. Roosevelt, too, felt committed after 1933.

The optimism that Coolidge felt as he prepared to leave office seemed to be additionally justified by the economic figures from the boom years. Between 1925 and 1929 the number of industrial concerns rose from 184,000 to 207,000 and the value of their output from $60.8 million to $68 million. The production index of the Federal Reserve Board rose from 100 in the years between 1923 and 1925 to 110 in July 1928 and to 126 in June 1929. Car production went up from 4.3 million in 1926 to 5.4 million three years later. Between 12 March and 16 June 1928 the volume of trading rose from 3,875,910 to 5,052,790 shares.

Herbert Hoover was born in Iowa in 1874 and had trained as an engineer. He was an eloquent advocate of what, in a campaign speech in New York on 22 October 1928, he described as 'rugged individualism'. By this he meant the essential character of the American system when compared to the European doctrines of paternalism and state socialism. It was not in Europe but in America, he insisted, that liberalism had demonstrated its true spirit:

> We are nearer today to the ideal of the abolition of poverty and fear from the lives of men and women than ever before in any land. And I again repeat that the departure from our American system by injecting principles destructive to it which our opponents propose, will jeopardize the very liberty and freedom of our people, and will destroy equality of opportunity not only to ourselves but to our children.[136]

As secretary of commerce, Hoover had promoted the concept of 'associationalism' – the voluntary national amalgamation of individual branches of industry – since he believed that this provided the means by which to increase efficiency in both production and sales. As president, he drew on these experiences to address the problem of agricultural overproduction by means of the Agricultural Marketing Act of June 1929. This problem was a result of the rapid mechanization of the agricultural sector during the 1920s. Hoover's aim of stabilizing agricultural production by means of state-funded but voluntary farming cooperatives was far less protectionist than the idea of the state buying agricultural produce, a policy twice proposed by Congress in 1926 and 1928 in the form of the McNary-Haugen Bill but twice successfully vetoed by Coolidge. And yet not even Hoover's initiative in the summer of 1929 produced any real results, and American farmers remained the biggest problem for the country's national economy.

By the early part of 1929 fluctuating stock market prices were a favourite topic of conversation not only in the newspapers but also among people whose professional jobs were not primarily concerned with the economy. As John Kenneth Galbraith observed, it was then the 'stock market' that 'dominated culture'.[137] There was no shortage of signs that the economy was overheating: on 14 February, for example, the Federal Reserve Bank in New York asked for the discount rate to be raised from 5 per cent to 6 per cent in order to rein in speculation but was unable to persuade the Federal Reserve Board in Washington to agree. In June the industrial share index of the *New York Times* rose by fifty-two points, by a further twenty-five in July and by thirty-three in August, making a total of 110 points in three months, going up from 339 to 449. In the whole of 1928 the increase had been only 86.5 points. Even the Federal Reserve Board now felt that the time had come for it to take the steps that it had refused to contemplate the previous February, and on 9 August the discount rate was raised by one percentage point.

It was above all investment trusts that encouraged speculation on the stock market, a form of amassing capital that had been introduced in England and Scotland in the 1880s and in the United States only at a much later date. By early 1927 there were around 160 such trusts in America, with a further 140 being added in the course of that year. In 1928 186 more investment funds were established, and in 1929 a further 265. The volume of shares that they sold amounted to $400 million in 1927, a figure which by the autumn of 1929 is reckoned to have reached $800,000 million. In December 1928 Goldman, Sachs and Company created the Goldman Sachs Trading Corporation to specialize in the investment business. On 26 July 1929 this last-named corporation founded its own trust, the Shenandoah Corporation, with a capital of more than $102 million, followed on 20 August by the even bigger Blue Ridge Corporation with $142 million. Both trusts shared a common board of directors under John Foster Dulles, who was later the American secretary of state. Within only a few months, therefore, Goldman Sachs had risen to the top of the American investment business.

By this date there were already serious signs that the economy was in crisis. For years the profits of the construction industry had been falling, followed in June by the steel industry and in October by freight-car production. The industrial production index of the Federal Reserve Board fell from 126 in July to 117 in October 1929. A sober analysis indicates that a stock market crash was only a question of time. Share prices began to fall on 21 October. By the 24th – Black Thursday – they were plummeting at such a rate that there was already a state of panic in New York; some speculators took their own lives. A joint declaration by the biggest banks served to calm the market at least for a time.

But on 29 October, Black Tuesday, the market could no longer be shored up, and sixteen million shares were sold on the New York Stock Exchange, the index of industrial shares falling by forty-three points, or almost 10 per cent, thereby wiping out all the gains of the previous twelve months. Worst affected were the investment trusts, with shares in Goldman Sachs falling from sixty to thirty-five points. In early September Blue Ridge had stood at twenty-four points, but on 24 October it fell to twelve and by 29 October it was trading at only three, before recovering a little. Other trusts were completely wiped out. In October 1929 the world entered a period of sustained and serious depression, although it was really only very much later that contemporaries became aware of this fact – and this in spite of the global shockwaves emanating from the crash on the New York Stock Exchange.

Many reasons have been adduced for the crisis that broke out in the autumn of 1929 in the world's largest economy. The historian Alan Brinkley has adduced five reasons that strike him as particularly important. First, there was only a weak diversification in the American economy in the 1920s, meaning that prosperity depended on the well-being of only a handful of sectors, notably the construction and car-making industries. The second factor in Brinkley's view was the way in which mass consumption lagged behind production as a result of the extremely unequal distribution of income. Thirdly, there was the credit structure, by which Brinkley means the fraudulent behaviour of many who owed money to small banks as well as the irresponsibility of large banks when lending money to their customers. Fourthly, there was the worsening situation of the United States in international trade, which Brinkley believed was due above all to the rationalization of industry and agriculture in Europe and the resultant drop in imports from America. And, fifthly, there was the international debt structure: in other words, the double problem of British, French and Italian war debts that were owed to the United States and of the German reparations which for their part could be paid only by means of American loans. Brinkley also drew attention to the high American tariffs that made it difficult for Europeans to sell their goods on the American market.[138]

Brinkley's list is instructive, but we may add to it by including a number of other factors: the investment trusts' tendency to encourage literally bottomless speculation; the failure of the Federal Reserve Board, which raised the discount rate too little and too late, while at the same time not having sufficient assets to pursue a genuine open-market policy and in that way to be able to influence the scope for credit on the part of the credit banks; and 'blind' rationalization and mechanization of industry and agriculture that failed to see market conditions and as a result created overcapacity; and the lack of distance between Republican governments and the wishes of big business in the 1920s.

Failings in America before and after the events of the autumn of 1929 are not in themselves sufficient to explain the world economic crisis but at best help to account for why it lasted so long. And the same is true of some of the long-term effects of the First World War, which had severed old trade links and created new ones, while causing some branches of industry to wither and others to grow. Overproduction in the textile industry was largely a consequence of the war, and at least in part much the same may be said of overproduction in agriculture. Not only in the United States but in Canada, Argentina and Australia, the rapid mechanization of farming – a purely technological development – made this development come about. Agricultural prices began to fall throughout the world in 1925 and by 1927 had caused an international crisis in agriculture.

Like the world economic crisis that began in 1929, the agricultural crisis was cyclical in nature. The most plausible explanation for the Great Depression is the one proposed by the Austrian (and from 1939 American) economist Joseph Schumpeter, who was briefly his country's finance minister in 1919. According to Schumpeter, it was in the autumn of 1929 that three periods of recession of varying length coincided, namely, a Kitchin cycle, a Juglar cycle and a Kondratiev cycle. Named after its inventor, a Kitchin cycle is a forty-month cycle that describes the time that employers need to build up and run down their stock or, to put it another way, it is a kind of buffer between pre-production and processing. The Juglar cycle is an eight- to ten-year wave triggered by technological innovations in the field of consumer goods. The Juglar upturn had started in 1925 and came to an end in 1929. According to Schumpeter, its origins were to be found in the opening up to new classes of customers of electrical and chemical goods and of the products of the motor industry, most notably the motor car.[139]

A Kondratiev cycle describes a long wave of around sixty years, the first half of which is given over to the upturn, the second half to the ensuing downturn, in the economy. If we combine Kondratiev's theory of long waves with Schumpeter's analysis of fluctuating lead sectors, we shall arrive at the following sequence of cycles: the first Kondratiev cycle from 1782 to 1842 was that of the Industrial Revolution in which the cotton industry was the lead sector, and the second long wave from 1843 to 1897 was the cycle of iron and steel, with railway construction as the economic motor behind the development.

The third Kondratiev cycle began around 1898 and was determined by the new growth industries of electricity, chemistry and car manufacture. The upturn in this cycle ended in the years before the First World War, the period between 1914 and 1929 representing the downward turn in Kondratiev's third cycle, a period characterized by numerous innovations, not least those of Juglar's cycle. They were no longer 'basic' in nature, however, but constituted merely a refinement and perfection of existing innovations. The crisis of the early 1920s, the rapid rationalization programme and the resultant high levels of unemployment: these were all typical manifestations of a long upturn wave that had already passed its peak, as was the speculative overproduction that ultimately led the New York Stock Exchange to crash in October 1929, ushering in the downturn phase in Kondratiev's third cycle. If we accept the theories of Kondratiev and Schumpeter, then this account may sum up the long prehistory of the greatest economic crisis in the history of the world.

The Great Depression affected the United States particularly badly. Between 1929 and 1932 America's foreign trade fell from $10,000 million to $3,000 million, its gross national product from $104,000 million to $76,400 million, dropping by a quarter in the space of only four years. Between 1930 and 1933 more than 9,000 banks ceased trading. The income of the country's farmers dropped by 60 per cent between 1929 and 1932. A third of all farmers lost their land, a situation also caused by an extreme drought that lasted throughout the 1930s and turned the Great Plains between Texas and the two Dakotas into a vast dust bowl described by John Steinbeck in his 1939 novel *The Grapes of Wrath*. By 1932 at least a quarter of the workforce was unemployed, and even by the end of the decade the number of those out of work remained above 15 per cent. The black population of the southern states was particularly badly hit, more than half being without work in 1932. That year there were 250,000 fewer weddings than in 1929, and the birth rate fell from 18.8 to 17.4 per thousand. With no prospect of earning a living, many Americans were in no position to start and feed a family.

According to the American historian William E. Leuchtenburg, the country's first reaction to the Great Depression was a sense of fatalism: inflationary cycles were inevitable, the fatalists argued, and all that Americans could do was wait for this latest disaster to end.[140] But the government could not afford to adopt such a simplistic view of the situation, and Hoover began by trying to persuade the representatives of industry and agriculture as well as the trade unions to agree to work together on a voluntary basis in the interests of the country's economic recovery. He appealed to the employers to maintain existing production levels and not lay off any workers, while warning the trade unions not to demand higher wages and shorter working hours. But such appeals had no practical effect to speak of.

Hoover's first major economic decision in the wake of the great crash was to sign a bill introducing the highest tariffs in American history. Enacted on 17 June 1930, the Smoot–Hawley Tariffs were named after their two proponents, the Republican senator Reed Smoot from Utah and the Republican congressman Willis C. Hawley from Oregon. Both men were committed protectionists whose aim was a largely autonomous national economy, an aim that they hoped would be served by raising customs duties on seventy-five agricultural products and on a whole series of industrial goods. The Republican majority leader in the Senate, Jim Watson from Indiana, even claimed that once this bill had become law, the American economy would recover within a month and that the country would again be uniquely prosperous within a year.

Around 1,000 economists warned the president in vain that if he did not use his veto to prevent this bill from passing into law, the countries affected by it would retaliate by raising taxes on American exports, which in turn risked jeopardizing the repayment of inter-Allied debts. There is no doubt that the Smoot–Hawley Tariffs played an important role in increasing worldwide protectionism and hence in exacerbating the world economic crisis. As early as 1931 the twin problem of inter-Allied debts and German reparations proved so burdensome that Hoover was forced to perform a volte-face in order to safeguard American credits in Germany. This took the form of the Hoover Moratorium of 20 June 1931 which proposed a twelve-month moratorium on payments of fixed-term state debts.

There were a number of other occasions when Hoover did indeed make use of his presidential veto. In March 1931, for example, he blocked a public job-creation programme submitted by the Democratic senator Robert F. Wagner of New York that would have cost $2,000 million, not including national insurance. A similar fate befell two other senators in February 1932: the Republican Robert M. La Follette, Jr, from Wisconsin and the Democrat Edward P. Costigan from Colorado had wanted the government to grant an extra $375 million to individual states to be used in public services.

But in the wake of the elections in November 1930 the Republican Hoover was no longer able to respond with a categorical no to publicly financed programmes, for the Democrats now had a majority in the House of Representatives in addition to gaining a number of extra seats in the Senate. In January 1932 he created a new authority, the Reconstruction Finance Corporation that could give federal loans to endangered banks, railway companies and other businesses. In 1932 it had $1,500 million at its disposal for public works. Hoover wanted only those schemes to be supported that ultimately promised to be self-financing: toll roads and council housing, for example. But there was too little money to have any major effect on the American economy. For Hoover, it was a golden rule to stick to the gold standard, and anyone who demanded otherwise was, in his view, risking inflation.

In the course of 1932 public protests at Hoover's policies assumed an increasingly strident quality. From its base in Iowa, the Farmers' Holiday Association called for a boycott of the markets, amounting to a strike on the part of the nation's farmers. War veterans demanded an immediate start to the bonus payments of $1,000 agreed to by Congress but not due to come into force until after 1945. In June 1932 20,000 members of their Bonus Expeditionary Force took part in a march on Washington, where they built a series of camps and announced that they would not leave until their demands had been met. A group of Communists struck a more radical note but were ignored by the leaders of the Bonus Expeditionary Force.

The House of Representatives sided with the veterans, whereas the Senate rejected their demands. Hoover replied at the end of July by sending in the district police. On 28 July some of the demonstrators threw stones at the police who were trying to clear the government buildings occupied by the veterans; the police responded by firing on the demonstrators, two of whom were killed.

But Hoover had no intention of giving in and later that same day was persuaded by his secretary of war, Patrick J. Hurley, to deploy army units under General Douglas MacArthur in order to clear the largest of the camps at Historic Anacostia some two miles from the Capitol. Among MacArthur's officers were his adjutant Dwight D. Eisenhower and a man who was to earn military fame during the Second World War, George S. Patton. MacArthur's forces included a cavalry regiment, two infantry regiments, a machine-gun unit and six tanks. His actions on the evening of 28 July went far beyond anything envisaged by Hoover, including, as they did, the use of tear gas and bayonets. The veterans set fire to their own temporary shelters; panic spread; a small child was killed; and hundreds of members of the Bonus Army were injured.

The events of 28 July 1932 did much to destroy Hoover's remaining standing. In the eyes of those who suffered most from the crisis, the erstwhile organizer of humanitarian aid for famine victims in Europe had become a cold-hearted cynic. During the winter of 1931/2 there were many 'Hoovervilles' – shanty towns for the homeless unemployed – on the edges of numerous larger towns and cities; men with no roof over their heads slept on park benches, covering themselves with newspapers that became known as 'Hoover blankets'; and empty pockets turned inside out were called 'Hoover flags'. Few initiates knew that MacArthur's troops had dealt with the bonus marchers far more ruthlessly than the president had ever intended. All that mattered for the broad mass of the population was that he had ordered the military to be deployed, with the result that he now had to bear the political responsibility for his actions.

Presidential elections were due to be held in November 1932. Hoover wanted to put his name forward, and so the Republicans adopted him as their candidate at their convention in Chicago in the middle of June. Two weeks later, the Democrats held their own convention, again in Chicago. The outcome of their deliberations remained undecided until the very last moment, but on 2 July they selected the governor of New York, Franklin Delano Roosevelt, FDR, a cousin, five times removed, of the former president, Theodore Roosevelt. He had been born in New York on 30 January 1882 as the son of an old and well-respected family that owed its considerable wealth to trade with China. Admitted to the New York Bar in 1907, he turned to politics soon afterwards and served as a state senator from 1910 to 1913, then as assistant secretary of the navy from 1913 to 1920. In 1921 he was stricken by polio and paralysed, leaving him with a permanent disability. But in 1928 he succeeded 'Al' Smith, the Democrats' presidential candidate, as governor of New York and was confirmed in the post in 1930, this time by election.

When accepting the presidential nomination, Roosevelt demanded that the Democratic Party must be 'a party of liberal thought, of planned action, of enlightened international outlook, and of the greatest good to the greatest number of our citizens'. He promised to ease the burden on all sections of society, whether at the top or the bottom of the social pyramid. He advocated 'retrenchment and economy' and announced an end to prohibition, stricter banking laws, public works, a shorter working week, reforestation, planned agricultural production and a lowering of tariffs. The American people, he went on, wanted nothing more than work and security. Unless they turned away from the 'era of selfishness', there was no saving them. But the sentence that left the deepest impression on delegates and on the public at large was this: 'I pledge you, I pledge myself to a new deal for the American people.'[141]

The term 'new deal' was not Roosevelt's but had been coined by the journalist Stuart Chase, who began a series of articles in the left-wing liberal *New Republic* on 28 June with a piece headed 'A New Deal for America'. Chase wanted to break with capitalism, to reflate the economy by means of public investment even if this increased inflationary pressures, to plan production and to introduce universally binding minimum wages and maximum working times. In the case of FDR, conversely, it remained open what exactly the 'new deal' offered. He gave only a vague indication of his desire for social equality, merely pointing in the same general direction as his reference to the 'forgotten man' whom he had frequently invoked in his election speeches, a man he claimed should be the increasing concern of all American politicians.

During the election campaign Roosevelt had clearly made promises that were mutually irreconcilable: generous work creation schemes on the one hand and public economies and a balanced budget on the other. His two principal advisers on economic matters were Rexford G. Tugwell and Adolf A. Berle of New York's Columbia University, but neither of them was an outspoken advocate of an anti-cyclical 'deficit spending' programme requiring the state to spring into the breach as an investor in times of stagnation in order to bring the economy closer to full employment, an idea that the British economist John Maynard Keynes was to promote in 1936 in his book *The General Theory of Employment, Interest and Money*, in which he elaborated concepts already put forward in his earlier writings. It was impossible to tell from Roosevelt's election speeches how he planned to finance the public works that he had already announced.

For some observers on the intellectual left, the differences between Hoover and Roosevelt seemed negligible. In their eyes the Democrat candidate merely embodied a variant of the existing system, not an alternative to it. Indeed, he was not even the lesser of two evils when compared with the previous incumbent. To claim the opposite was 'suicidal', according to John Dewey, the chairman of the League for Independent Political Action that had been founded in 1929.[142] Among Dewey's colleagues were Stuart Chase and the Evangelical theologian Reinhold Niebuhr. All three supported their fellow League member, the chairman of the Socialist Party, Norman Thomas, in the 1932 election campaign. More radical intellectuals such as Theodore Dreiser, John Dos Passos, the political scientist Frederick L. Schuman and the former 'muckraker' Lincoln Steffens advocated the revolutionary overthrow of the capitalist economic and social order and championed the Communist candidate William Z. Foster. For Steffens this appeal cannot have been entirely unproblematic, for he had previously expressed his very public admiration not only for Lenin but also for Mussolini.

Roosevelt emerged as the clear winner from the presidential election on 8 November 1932, polling 57.4 per cent of the votes, representing 472 delegates, while Hoover's 39.7 per cent share was reflected in fifty-nine delegates. Existing incumbents were returned in only Delaware, Pennsylvania, Connecticut, Vermont, New Hampshire and Maine. In every other state it was the challenger who made the running. Thomas won 2.2 per cent of the vote, Foster 0.3 per cent. Only 56.9 per cent of the electorate voted, the same as in 1928. If the 1928 elections had been a plebiscite for the status quo, the country showed equal determination four years later in voting for the reform of existing social conditions within the framework, and on the basis, of the American constitution. An end to prohibition was an important aspect of the changes promised by Roosevelt.

As was traditional, four months elapsed between the election and the new president's inauguration, which took place on 4 March 1933. This intervening period witnessed the withdrawal of American forces from Nicaragua in early January 1933. Barely four years earlier, in May 1929, the country's rebellious liberals had signed an agreement with Washington ensuring that they would take over the presidency of Nicaragua. The Grupo Armado Liberal under Augusto César Sandino continued its armed struggle against the American marines in the north of Nicaragua, ending the conflict only after the American forces had withdrawn, as agreed, in January 1933. Sandino was murdered in February 1934 by members of the National Guard under Anastasio Somoza García. Three years later the dictatorship of the Somoza family began with the presidency of Somoza García and lasted until 1979.

Foreign policy was the only area of agreement between the old US government, represented by its secretary of state, Henry L. Stimson, and the president elect. Conversely, Roosevelt rejected all attempts by Hoover to make him commit to the principles of the country's previous economic and financial policy. The crisis in the American banking system came to a sudden head on the day before Roosevelt's inauguration and, early in the morning of 4 March 1933, only hours before the new president was due to be sworn into office, the governor of the state of New York, Herbert H. Lehman, ordered the closure of all the banks in his state. Illinois followed shortly afterwards.

Roosevelt's inauguration address was delivered in keeping with tradition on the steps of the Capitol building and was a classic example of grand political rhetoric. Within minutes he had uttered a sentence that was to ingrain itself on the hearts and minds of contemporaries and acquire the status of a catchphrase:

'The only thing we have to fear is fear itself.' The nation was calling for immediate action. Specifically, Roosevelt referred to the need for a national transport
and communications system and a national energy supply. Americans must
stop speculating with other people's money and ensure the stability of the dollar.
Restoring the country's economy was more important than cultivating international trade relations. The maxim underpinning his practical politics was 'the
putting of first things first'. Only in time of war had there been the sort of
national discipline that was needed now. If necessary, he would ask Congress to
grant him the 'broad executive power to wage a war against emergency' – the
kind of power that would be granted the president in the event of an attack by a
foreign power.

Roosevelt spoke only briefly about international politics, merely committing the United States to a 'policy of the good neighbor': such a neighbour
demonstrated a high degree of self-esteem and respected the rights of others by
fulfilling his obligations and by upholding the sanctity of contractual agreements within a world of neighbours. The phrase had already been used by
Roosevelt's predecessor to describe his country's relations with Latin America,
but by extending its application to the rest of the world, he was indirectly giving
a signal to Europe, a part of the world nowhere explicitly mentioned in his
speech.

Roosevelt ended his inaugural address by invoking the legacy and ethos of
American democracy:

> We face the arduous days that lie before us in the warm courage of the
> national unity; with the clear consciousness of seeking old and precious
> moral values, with the clean satisfaction that comes from the stern perform-
> ance of duty by old and young alike. [...] We do not distrust the future of
> essential democracy. The people of the United States have not failed. In
> their need they have registered a mandate that they want direct, vigorous
> action. They have asked for discipline and direction under leadership. They
> have made me the present instrument of their wishes. In the spirit of the gift
> I take it.[143]

The solemn tone was appropriate to the occasion. The speech raised hopes,
and there was nothing that America needed more than this in March 1933. The
new president had survived his first challenge.

The Logic of the Lesser Evil: Germany under Brüning

No country in Europe was as badly affected by the world economic crisis as
Germany, which was one of the most highly industrialized nations in Europe.
Its economy was already in recession when the crisis erupted in America.
National income fell slightly in 1929, and, if we take 1924–6 as the base, then

share prices fell from 158 in 1927 to 148 in 1928 and to 134 in 1929. By the summer of 1929 there were some 250,000 more workers registered as unemployed than in the previous year. In September 1928 there had been 1.16 million Germans out of work. By September 1929 that figure had risen to 1.52 million. When the world economic crisis struck, the basic rate of unemployment was therefore far higher in Germany than in the United States, where there had been almost full employment on the eve of the Great Depression. In 1929 the average unemployment rate for the whole year was 9.3 per cent, whereas in the United States it was only 3.2 per cent.

We have already examined the problems affecting the German economy in the 1920s, problems that included the restrictions on a market economy caused by the creation of an industrial cartel, protective tariffs in agriculture, compulsory arbitration by the state, 'political wages', the reparations that could be paid for only by means of foreign loans and the tendency of the banks to pass on short-term, foreign – mostly American – loans as investment loans to Germany's regions and local authorities as well as to industry.

German banks had lost more of their investments as a result of inflation and had therefore needed to draw on foreign capital, mostly in the form of foreign loans, in order to be able to offer loans of their own. In 1929 the relation between a bank's own resources and foreign resources was 1:10.4, rather than the 1:3 predicated by the classic rule. And in the case of the major banks in Berlin it was 1:15.5. In consequence the German banking system could quickly be shaken to its very foundations by the withdrawal of foreign investments, a situation that arose soon after the great crash. Moreover, German credit abroad was heavily dependent on estimates of the political situation in Germany, with the result that the extreme right wing's opposition to the Young Plan in the autumn of 1929 led swiftly to a perceptible reluctance on the part of foreign banks to meet Germany's requests for credit.

Unemployment rose as quickly in Germany as it did in the United States: during the first quarter of 1930, 3.47 million were registered as unemployed at the country's labour exchanges, a figure that rose to 4.97 million in the first quarter of 1931 and to 6.13 million in the same period in 1932. If we include 'invisible' unemployment in the form of those Germans too embarrassed to admit that they were out of work, the figure for February 1933 was, in the estimation of contemporary experts, 7.78 million, an all-time high that takes no account of the widespread practice of short-time contracts. In September 1932 22.7 per cent of the members of 100 trade unions were on short-time contracts, while 43.6 per cent were unemployed. In a word, only a third of the population, 33.7 per cent, was in full-time employment. A census in June 1933 revealed that 32.2 per cent of workers were in industry and business, 15.5 per cent in trade and transport, 14.4 per cent in domestic services and 3.3 per cent in agriculture and forestry. It is understandable, therefore, that in agriculture Germany was less badly affected than the United States: in Germany agricultural production fell by 36.7 per cent between 1929 and 1932, whereas the equivalent figure for the United States was 53.6 per cent. Conversely, industrial production during the same period fell by 55 per cent in Germany – rather more than the 46 per cent in the United States. In terms of national income in general, American losses were far greater than those in Germany: 54 per cent as compared with 40 per cent.

In many respects, the social repercussions of the Great Depression were similar in Germany and the United States. Germany, too had its 'Hoovervilles' in the form of shanty towns inhabited by the homeless and the unemployed who lived in primitive wooden shacks on land leased for the purpose on the edge of the larger towns and cities; there were the same streams of homeless workers drifting from one part of Germany to another in search of employment and a roof over their heads; many of these men and women were seasonal workers in agriculture who worked on the estates to the east of the Elbe during the summer months; there were also municipal soup kitchens and worsening dietary conditions that in 1931 persuaded the physician and nutritionist Helmut Lehmann to speak of 'a concealed famine of the greatest imaginable extent with the danger of the most serious consequences for body and soul alike'.[144]

Unlike their counterparts in America, most German workers were insured against unemployment after 1927, even if only for a limited period. As a result, they were not dependent on voluntary charitable support or on alms payments from individual states and local authorities, as was the case in the United States. After October 1929, unemployed men and women who were willing and able to work and who had spent at least fifty-two weeks of the last two years in a form of employment that was subject to compulsory insurance could also claim support from national insurance. Such support was initially available for twenty-six weeks, although this period was reduced to twenty weeks in October 1931, and from June 1932 it was dependent on a means test after six weeks. The payments were made up of primary support for the insured and, where necessary, additional support for family members who were entitled to such assistance.

For those times when the situation in the labour market was particularly bad, the country's labour minister also allowed crisis payments to be made, although whether people received such payments depended on a means test undertaken by the employment exchange. Workers who were unable to claim emergency welfare payments or who had already exhausted that possibility could in certain circumstances receive welfare support, which was intended to cover 'vital needs'. Among such needs were shelter, food, clothing, medical care and, where applicable, funeral costs. Welfare support might consist of monetary payments or benefits in kind that the recipients were required to pay back as quickly as possible. After the spring of 1931 the number of recipients receiving primary support fell, while that of the men and women in receipt of emergency welfare payments rose. During the economic crisis, not only was the length of time during which the unemployed were entitled to support repeatedly reduced, but the level of support was also lowered. And those who had lost their jobs had to contend with longer and longer waiting times, resulting in progressive impoverishment on the lowest levels of the social pyramid.

From the very outset, protests at worsening conditions in Germany during the great crisis were not purely social, as they were in the United States, but had a radical political dimension to them, with the Communists, above all, turning themselves into the mouthpiece of the unemployed, while those groups that were afraid of sliding down the social ladder were championed by the National Socialists. After 1929, bloody street battles between the extreme forces on the left and right of the political spectrum became increasingly frequent, as did clashes between Hitler's 'brown battalions' – his Storm Troopers – and the republican, predominantly Social Democrat Reichsbanner that had been founded in 1924. Other clashes took place between Communists and the Reichsbanner and between Communists and the Stahlhelm.

Unlike Hitler's Storm Troopers, the Communists were also involved in direct confrontations with the police, with the result that from the standpoint of the authorities and the bourgeois parties, it was the Communists who, compared with the National Socialists, were seen as the greater danger in terms of law and order. Following the ban on the Red Frontline Fighters' League in May 1929, the Communists no longer had a formal paramilitary wing at their disposal. After March 1931 only the party's secret protection unit was still armed, whereas the members of the Battle League against Fascism that was formed in 1930 were not allowed to bear arms. The state's monopoly on violence was challenged by these violent paramilitary groups, but, unlike the situation in Italy between 1920 and 1922, it was not rendered increasingly ineffectual: in general, federal and local government could still rely on the loyalty of the police during the dying years of the Weimar Republic.

Following the collapse of Germany's grand coalition in late March 1930, the country's fate had been in the hands of a bourgeois minority cabinet rather than a parliamentary majority government. It was headed by the former leader of the Centre Party in the Reichstag, Heinrich Brüning, an ascetic forty-four-year-old bachelor from Münster in Westphalia who had studied history and the social sciences before taking his doctorate with a study on the national economy and serving as a front-line soldier in the First World War, when he had been wounded and decorated. His work as general secretary of the Christian National Trade Unions, which he started in 1920, meant that, unlike Ludwig Kaas, who took over as party leader at the end of 1928, he avoided being branded 'right-wing' by his party. At the other end of the political spectrum, Brüning's work in the Reichstag as its budgetary expert from 1924 ensured that he was also held in high regard in conservative circles. The fact that he was a Catholic may have harmed him in the eyes of those liberals who espoused the ideas of the *Kulturkampf*, but from the standpoint of Hindenburg and his circle, the new chancellor's denomination was an advantage, because it meant that politically engaged Catholics were willing to support a silent change to the constitution that the country's president and his entourage were hoping to effect.

Brüning's government was initially only covertly a presidential cabinet. In addition to the independent defence minister Wilhelm Groener, it also included representatives of the bourgeois parties that had previously held cabinet posts, together with individual ministers from the German National People's Party, the Economic Party and the new People's Conservative Association that was made up of former German Nationalists and deputies from the Peasants' and Farmers' Party. The German Nationalist minister for dietetics, Martin Schiele, resigned his seat in the Reichstag on entering government, so that it remained unclear, at least for a time, how the party of the press baron Alfred Hugenberg would react to Brüning's cabinet. In fact the German Nationalists repeatedly voted inconsistently in April 1930, so that the government, much against Hugenberg's wishes, had a narrow majority in several votes in the Reichstag.

Some three months after Brüning's appointment a situation finally arose that Hindenburg had envisaged when he had entrusted him with the post of chancellor: a government bill designed to deal with the budget was rejected by the Reichstag's taxation committee, whereupon the president let it be known that his chancellor had his full authority to pass the budgetary programme under Article 48 of the constitution if the Reichstag failed to enact it. He also announced that he would dissolve the Reichstag if it voted to suspend the emergency measures or passed a vote of no confidence in his chancellor.

Protests by the Social Democrats could not prevent the government from mutating into a regime that ruled by emergency decree. After the budget bill was rejected at a plenary session of the Reichstag on 16 July, Brüning announced that his government saw no point in continuing the debate, and the first two emergency measures came into force later that same day, although in the event they lasted only two days, for on the 18th the Reichstag accepted the Social Democrat motion to lift them. Hindenburg immediately dissolved parliament, setting 14 September 1930 as the date of the new elections. On 26 July Hindenburg issued a new emergency measure designed to deal with all financial, economic and social problems and introducing a civic tax graduated according to social class, in which respect it differed from previous emergency measures. The new emergency decree also formed the legal basis for enforced protection for heavily mortgaged agricultural estates in the east of the country, federal help for those on fixed incomes, an income tax increase, a tax on unmarried people and – unavoidable in view of the higher level of unemployment – an increase in unemployment contributions from 3.5 per cent to 4 per cent.

There was a certain inevitability to the change from a covert to an open form of presidential government in 1930. After Hindenburg had rejected the concept of government by parliamentary majority in March 1930, the July crisis merely witnessed the implementation of the law that had brought Brüning to power in the first place. He could not accommodate the Social Democrats without alienating the president and the right wing of the government camp, and he was unable to do this because it would have contravened the very logic of his appointment. For their part, the Social Democrats could not accept the non-graduated civic tax on which the government had been insisting right up to the time when the Reichstag was dissolved without violating their own supporters' sense of justice and handing the Communists a cheap victory. In short, the main protagonists in the July crisis had so little room for manoeuvre that a simple solution to the conflict was now all but impossible.

The new elections to the Reichstag were preceded by attempts to focus the forces of the bourgeois parties, but these had modest success. The German Democratic Party merged with the People's National Reich Association, which was the political arm of the conservative and, by contemporary standards, only moderately anti-Semitic Young German Order as the German State Party, a move that upset not only many of their Jewish supporters but others, too. By the beginning of October the Young Germans had abandoned the party, citing irreconcilable ideological differences, but its new name was retained. The Conservative People's Party was formed at the end of July by a merger between the People's Conservative Party under Gottfried Treviranus and the anti-Hugenberg faction under Kuno von Westarp and had the backing of industry.

On the political left, nothing changed organizationally, the only novel feature being the aggressive nationalism displayed by the German Communist Party. In its 'Declaration on the National and Social Liberation of the German People' of 24 August 1930 it had described the leaders of the Social Democrats

> not only as the henchmen of the German bourgeoisie but at the same time the willing agents of French and Polish imperialism. All the actions of the treacherous and corrupt Social Democrats are tantamount to a continuous act of high treason against the vital interests of the working masses of Germany.[145]

The elections on 14 September 1930 witnessed a turnout of 82 per cent, more than in any other Reichstag election since 1920. But the real sensation was the showing of the National Socialists, who polled 6.4 million votes compared with just over 800,000 in May 1928, a rise from 2.6 per cent to 18.3 per cent and from twelve to 107 seats in parliament. Communist gains were also sizeable, if less dramatic: their share of the vote increased from 10.6 per cent to 13.1 per cent, their number of seats from fifty-four to seventy-seven.

The other parties were all among the losers. The German Nationalists were reduced by half, falling from 14.3 per cent to 7 per cent of the vote, while the German People's Party dropped from 8.7 per cent to 4.5 per cent, the German State Party – formerly the German Democratic Party – from 4.9 per cent to 3.8 per cent. Conversely, the losses suffered by the Catholic parties were relatively insignificant: the Centre Party, which had polled 12.1 per cent of the vote in 1928, won 11.8 per cent in 1930, while the Bavarian People's Party polled 3 per cent as compared with 3.1 per cent two years earlier. Rather greater were the losses sustained by the Social Democrat Party, which was still Germany's largest party and which saw its share of the vote fall from 29.6 per cent to 24.5 per cent. Even after its electoral pact with the regional German Hanover Party, the newly formed Conservative People's Party could manage no more than 1.1 per cent.

But it was the National Socialists who were the principal beneficiaries of the increased turnout, and yet those voters who had not exercised their franchise in previous elections were by no means the main reason for the party's success. Most of the NSDAP's supporters had previously voted for other parties, generally the German Nationalists and Liberal parties. Protestants were twice as likely to vote for the NSDAP as Catholics, while their supporters included more farmers, government employees, pensioners, self-employed workers and men and women of independent means than might have been assumed from their percentage share in the population at large, whereas the opposite was true of workers and white-collar employees. The unemployed, who in September 1930 numbered around three million, played only a relatively minor role in the rise of the National Socialists, unemployed workers tending to vote for Ernst Thälmann's Communist Party rather than for Hitler's National Socialists.

The National Socialists' powerful appeal to the middle classes persuaded a number of contemporary observers to suggest that National Socialism was a middle-class movement. In fact, the catchment area of Hitler's party extended so far beyond this social class that it would be more accurate from a sociological standpoint to describe the NSDAP as a 'people's party'. By 1930 the fault lines between the old social and denominational classes in Germany were starting to become obscured as the gramophone, cinema and radio had begun to prepare the ground for a new mass culture that transcended the boundaries between these different groups. And yet the 'old' parties scarcely acknowledged the challenge that lay within this development, whereas the National Socialists consistently exploited the resources of modern mass communications and took account of the widespread need for a sense of community that extended beyond the confines of class and denomination, a need that was especially pronounced in the younger generation but which had lain dormant until then. Although much that the NSDAP promised its voters was backward-looking, its success was due in no small part to its ability to adapt to the conditions of the era of mass culture and in that sense to demonstrate its 'modernity'.

The National Socialists' answer to this national need for a sense of community was the same in 1930 as it had been previously: an extreme nationalism that was directed above all at a home-grown enemy in the guise of Marxism in all its manifestations, pillorying those parties that supported the Young Plan and, with them, the hated Weimar Republic. Nationalism was intended to provide an overarching structure bridging the divisions between the different groups of Germans. Anti-Semitic slogans that included attacks on the alleged 'yoke of international finance' often went hand in hand with an appeal to nationalist instincts but were less prominent during the 1930 election campaign than they had been previously, not least because the NSDAP was keen to win over working-class voters who, to the extent that they tended to support the Social Democrats and Communists, were largely impervious to anti-Semitic propaganda. The word 'socialism', which risked frightening off many bourgeois electors, especially the older ones among them, was consistently reinterpreted by the NSDAP: as understood by Hitler, socialism meant not the abolition of private property but equality of social opportunity and an economic policy based on the party's 1920 manifesto: 'the common good before private interest'.

The distribution of seats in the new Reichstag forced Brüning's cabinet to cast round for allies. In the eyes of the bourgeois centre-ground parties, it was inconceivable that the government would move further to the right by inviting the National Socialists to join the cabinet, while the armed forces and German industry likewise regarded the NSDAP as unfit for government. This attitude remained unaffected by Hitler's spectacular intervention in the trial of three army officers from Ulm who were National Socialist sympathizers accused of high treason. Appearing before the federal court in Leipzig on 25 September 1930, Hitler declared under oath that his party would take power only by legal means, although when asked by the presiding judge to explain what he meant by this, he admitted that on coming to power he would establish a court through the normal legislative process with the aim of trying all those who were guilty of the events of November 1918: in other words, they would be executed by legal means.

But if a National Socialist role in government was ruled out, so too was a return to a grand coalition, for both the country's president and the right wing of the government camp were vehemently opposed to such a solution. Even the Social Democrats were unwilling to consider any kind of collaboration with Brüning and the forces behind him. On the left wing of the Social Democrat Party, the Centre Party chancellor was regarded as a man whose policies were no less 'Fascist' than those of the National Socialists. Since neither the NSDAP nor the Social Democrats could be considered a party of government, the bourgeois minority cabinet could form a majority only by enlisting the support of one or more of the other parties. Here, too, the Nationalist Socialists were ruled out from the standpoint of foreign policy, quite apart from the fact that even Hitler himself would have refused to countenance such a situation. In short, there was no realistic alternative to an agreement with the Social Democrats.

The leaders of the Social Democrat Party shared this view. From a Social Democrat point of view, there were three reasons above all why, in the wake of the September elections, they should tolerate Brüning. First, this was the only way to avoid a more right-wing government dependent on the National

Socialists. Second, the Weimar coalition in Prussia under the Social Democrat Otto Braun would be put at extreme risk if the Social Democrats in the country as a whole were to bring down the Centre Party chancellor. But the loss of government officers in the largest German state would also have meant losing control of the Prussian police, the state's most important resource in its clashes with National Socialists and Communists alike. And, third, there was a broad field of agreement between the Social Democrats and the government camp based on the realization that the consequences of an unstable 'credit economy' after 1924 had been overcome only by means of a policy of rigorous cost-cutting. This consensus on the best way to turn round the economy did not exclude the possibility of disagreement on the best way to share the social cost of such savings, but at least the consensus itself was not called into question.

The foundations of the new policy of toleration were laid in the course of talks between Brüning and the Social Democrats in the Reichstag that were held at the end of September. On 3 October the Social Democrats passed a resolution declaring their intention of supporting Brüning's minority cabinet on the grounds that in the wake of the Reichstag elections their prime concern was to uphold democracy, safeguard the constitution and protect the parliamentary system. Social Democrats were fighting for democracy in order to protect social policies and raise the living standards of working people: 'While safeguarding the vital interests of the working masses, the Social Democrat faction in the Reichstag will continue to ensure that the parliamentary basis of our society is assured and that the most pressing fiscal concerns are addressed.'[146]

The debates that took place in the Reichstag on 17 and 18 October 1930 were among the stormiest that the Weimar Republic had witnessed until then. But there was no doubt about their outcome, for in the vote on 18 October the government had the backing of the Social Democrats, voting first on a government bill concerning debt repayment, then on the transfer of proposals to suspend the emergency decree of 26 July to the budgetary committee and, finally, on a government motion to pass over all the proposed votes of no confidence and proceed to the business of the day. To furious protests from the National Socialists and Communists, the Reichstag was then adjourned until 3 December. The government had not only won a battle but, equally importantly, it had gained time.

With the help of the Social Democrats, Brüning's cabinet also survived the equally tempestuous December session of parliament. The price that the government had to pay for this was a number of concessions in the field of social welfare: the civic tax was more sharply graduated and the unemployed were granted free health insurance. In return the Social Democrats assumed partial responsibility for raising unemployment contributions from 4.5 per cent to 6.5 per cent, a 6 per cent cut in the salaries of government employees and new measures to protect agriculture, including higher duties on wheat and barley. On 7 December the Reichstag was again adjourned, this time until 3 February 1931.

The Social Democrats' official newspaper welcomed the move, noting in its edition of 13 December that three months after the elections everyone must have felt 'that this Reichstag is a failure and that we can be glad to see and hear nothing more of it'.[147] The party's leader in the Prussian Landtag, Ernst Heilmann, who also had a seat in the Reichstag, argued that a house with 107 National Socialists and seventy-seven Communists could not function effectively: 'A nation that elects such a Reichstag effectively renounces all claim to self-governance, and its legislative right is automatically replaced by Article 48.'[148] In a radio broadcast on 17 December, Otto Braun expressed the view that if the Reichstag, partly as a result of its infiltration by antiparliamentary groups, was unwilling and unable to perform the tasks conferred on it by the constitution, 'then, but only then, a political SOS must be sounded and the safety valve of the constitution must be opened long enough to deal with the acute emergency that parliament is unable or unwilling to confront'. *Vorwärts* published Braun's speech under the headline 'An Education in Democracy'.[149]

When the Social Democrats met in Leipzig at the end of May 1931 for their first party conference after their departure from power, there was much criticism from their left wing of their policy of cooperation, but such criticism was outweighed by delegates' approval for the main argument of its proponents: 'We have kept the National Socialists from gaining power,' declared Wilhelm Sollmann, the party's deputy leader in the Reichstag,

> and if, in October 1930, the National Socialists were prevented from taking over the army and the police, then I believe that no criticism on points of detail should attach to us and discourage us from saying that this was not just a major success, but a European success, for Germany's Social Democrats.[150]

Given the balance of power in the Reichstag in the wake of the elections in September 1930, there was really no responsible alternative for the Social Democrats but to give their backing to Brüning's government. But their policy had a disadvantage that by the spring of 1931 could no longer be ignored. The fact that the Reichstag now met only infrequently – on 26 March it had adjourned until 13 October – played into the hands of the anti-parliamentary forces on the extreme right and the extreme left, and no one was more adept at exploiting this chance than Hitler, who could now appeal both to the widespread resentment at the western and, hence, 'un-German' parliamentary democracy of the years after 1919, which by the autumn of 1930 had become a mere sham, and to the people's right to have a say in politics in the form of universal equal suffrage, a right codified under Bismarck but rendered largely ineffectual by Brüning's presidential cabinet. In this way Hitler benefited from Germany's lopsided process of democratization: on the one hand, the early introduction of a democratic right to vote and, on the other, the late transition to a type of government that was responsible to parliament. And not only that: since the Social Democrats tolerated Brüning's unpopular austerity measures, the leader of the National Socialists could present his party as the only popular opposition movement to the right of the Communists and at the same time as an alternative to 'Marxism' in both its Bolshevik and reformist manifestations.

On 5 June 1931 – the day on which the Social Democrats ended their party conference in Leipzig – Hindenburg announced a new emergency decree that had long been expected but whose social impact was far worse than had been feared: unemployment benefit was reduced by on average between 10 per cent and 12 per cent; the salaries of government employees were cut by between 4 per cent and 8 per cent; and payments to invalids and disabled veterans were reduced. The Social Democrats joined in the universal outcry of indignation, but Brüning turned down their request that the Reichstag or at least its budgetary committee be reconvened, not least because he could see that the country was on the verge of bankruptcy, if not of civil war. All that he could offer the Social Democrats was a promise to mitigate the negative impact of some of the emergency measure's social consequences. In an attempt to force the Social Democrats to back down, Hindenburg threatened to end the Prussian coalition. His threat worked, and on 16 June the representatives of the Social Democrat group in the Reichstag withdrew their motion to convene the budgetary committee.

The left wing of the party revolted and on 1 July published an open letter inveighing against any further continuation of the party's policy of cooperation. This was to become the starting point for a new political grouping, the Socialist Workers' Party that was founded in early October. But the majority of Social Democrats were not prepared to break with Brüning or to give up power in Prussia. In the July issue of *Die Gesellschaft* Rudolf Hilferding referred to the 'tragic situation' in which his party now found itself, arguing that this tragedy stemmed from a combination of the country's grave economic crisis and the exceptional political state caused by the elections on 14 September:

> The Reichstag is a parliament at odds with the parliamentary principle, its very existence a threat not only to democracy but also to the working class and to our country's foreign policy. [. . .] To defend democracy against a majority that rejects democracy, and to do so by recourse to the political resources of a democratic constitution that presupposes a fully functioning parliamentary system, is tantamount to squaring the circle, a task that the Social Democrats have been asked to solve – this is truly an unprecedented situation.[151]

Only in the course of 1931 did Germans begin to see that the low point of the economic crisis was still to come and that the world was in the middle of a great depression. On 20 June there was what appeared to be a ray of hope, when

Herbert Hoover proposed a year-long international 'holiday from debt', during which governments would have a respite from the repayment of their international debts, including German reparations. Pending ratification by the American Senate, the Hoover Moratorium to which we have already referred came into provisional force on 6 July after the United States had overcome French resistance to the proposal, but within days Germany had been shaken by a severe banking crisis whose immediate cause was the collapse of the Darmstadt and National Bank ('Danatbank') on 13 July, resulting in turn in a serious loss of confidence in capitalism and in a market economy. Two days later foreign exchange transactions were rigorously curtailed by the government and by the federal bank, which effectively meant abandoning the gold standard for private industry. The drastic increase in the discount rate and in the Lombard rate had disastrous repercussions for an already stagnant economy. Public taxes were used to restore the banks to an even keel, which effectively amounted to a partial nationalization.

In September 1931 Brüning's government suffered a humiliating defeat in terms of its foreign policy, when the customs union planned jointly by Stresemann's successor as foreign minister, Julius Curtius, and by Austria's chancellor and foreign minister Johann Schober was declared illegal by the International Court at The Hague. In full agreement with Brüning, Curtius and his secretary of state, Bernhard von Bülow, had seen in the customs union a way of consolidating German influence in central and south-east Europe and of laying the foundations for a later union between the two German-speaking states, which is why the plan ran into such massive opposition from the French.

The embarrassing failure of his policy towards Austria meant that Curtius's position as foreign minister was no longer tenable, and on 3 October he asked the chancellor to accept his resignation. By now, however, more was at stake than a mere change at the top of the Foreign Office. The previous month, first Kurt von Schleicher, chief of the ministerial office at the Defence Ministry and Wilhelm Groener's political adviser, and then Hindenburg had demanded from the chancellor an emphatic shift to the right, a demand that Brüning sought to meet by reshuffling his cabinet on 9 October. He himself took over as foreign secretary, while Groener assumed the dual responsibility of defence minister and home secretary, the latter post as the successor to the left-wing Centre Party politician and former chancellor Joseph Wirth. The ultra-Conservative secretary of state Curt Joël became justice minister.

The German People's Party – Curtius's party – was no longer represented in Brüning's second cabinet. On 3 October, its industrial wing had demanded that the party join the opposition and table a motion of no confidence in the government. A week later the party executive and its members in the Reichstag agreed to do precisely that, with the result that a year after the policy of toleration had been implemented the chancellor had to pay the price for the occasional concessions that he had made the Social Democrats on whose mercy he depended: the right wing of the employers' camp broke with Brüning because his policies were insufficiently right-wing for the industrial right.

On 11 October 1931 the conservative industrialists in the Ruhr had the chance to go one step further and publicly align themselves with the 'national opposition'. This was the day on which the various political parties and other associations that were emphatically right-wing in their outlook organized a military parade in Bad Harzburg, although no well-known industrialists attended the event, which had been planned by Hugenberg; the only exception being Ernst Brandi, one of the directors of the United Steel Works. Evidently even Brüning's sternest critics among German employers were still reluctant to join the radical right.

The Harzburg Front was made up of the NSDAP, the German National People's Party, the Stahlhelm, the National Land League and the Pan-German League as well as countless members of former ruling houses, the former head of the army, Hans von Seeckt, who had represented the Germany People's Party in the Reichstag since 1930, and the former president of the Reichsbank, Hjalmar Schacht, who had resigned his post in March 1930 in protest at the Young Plan. With his attacks on the Reichsbank, Schacht succeeded in triggering a heated debate that went on for days. Hitler, who had been received for the first time by Hindenburg only the previous day, caused a stir during the march-past by reviewing his own Storm Troopers, then demonstratively leaving the platform before the Stahlhelm units could follow: it was his deliberately provocative way of proving his independence from the 'old' right wing.

The Harzburg conference made it easier for the Social Democrats to work with Brüning's second cabinet, which was clearly to the political right of its predecessor. The violent attacks on the government by the 'reactionary forces of Fascism' were in themselves enough to make the government seem tolerable in the eyes of the Social Democrats. Schacht's comments on the government's monetary policy inspired *Vorwärts* to publish a piece on 12 October under the headline 'The Harzburg Inflation Front'. On this point *Vorwärts* was in full agreement with Brüning, who was equally critical of all experiments with the country's currency, and in the brief session of parliament that took place two days after the Harzburg conference he was again able to rely on the Social Democrats, helping him to reject all the motions of no confidence tabled against his government on 16 October.

Brüning's position was much strengthened by this development, allowing him to issue a new emergency measure on 9 December that linked wage and price reductions in such a way as to ensure that the purchasing power of the masses was not significantly impaired, while increasing the attractiveness of German exports. Its negative effect, however, was to curtail the freedom of employers and reduce the scope for free collective bargaining. The move was also a reaction to Great Britain's abandonment of the gold standard on 21 September 1931, which had led to a devaluation of the pound vis-à-vis the mark by around 20 per cent and a corresponding advantage for British exports. In Brüning's eyes, it was not possible to respond to London's move by devaluing the mark not only because to have done so would have played on Germany's traumatic fear of inflation but also on account of Germany's dependence on American loans, together with its obligations with regard to reparations and, not least, questions of national prestige.

Brüning continued to reject out of hand a loan-financed job creation programme of the kind demanded by sections of industry from the summer of 1931 and, from December, by experts from the General German Trade Union Association, for such a programme would have flown in the face of his fundamental belief in the need for a balanced budget and at the same time contradicted his priorities in terms of Germany's foreign policy: Germany could not give the impression that it still had financial resources at its disposal, for this would have undermined its argument that the burden of reparations was crippling the German economy. But the end of reparations was the short-term goal that Germany had to achieve if it was to rid itself of all the other shackles associated with the Treaty of Versailles, not least the military constraints, and win back its old status as a major power.

When, at the end of 1931, it seemed as if there was a chance to reach a compromise on the question of reparations, it was only logical, therefore, that Brüning did not seize it. On 22 December the American Senate voted for the Hoover Moratorium after a lengthy debate. The following day the Special Advisory Committee of the Bank of International Settlements in Basel submitted a report that the German government had asked it to draw up the previous month in keeping with the procedures laid down in the Young Plan. The committee came to the conclusion that, in order to avoid any further financial problems, all of the existing debts between states, including the German reparations, would have to be adjusted without further delay so as to take account of the present parlous state of the international economy.

This was tantamount to a plea that the Young Plan be renegotiated from start to finish. But Brüning was not interested in attending the conference on reparations that was due to discuss this report in Lausanne in January 1932, since he believed that it would lead only to a new moratorium and to a reduction in the burden of reparations – a half-hearted, temporary solution that fell far short of the definitive end of all reparation payments that he was striving to achieve. As a result his government banked on delaying the conference, which was due to start on 25 January and which was finally postponed sine die on the 20th. The price that Brüning had to pay at home for this foreign-policy decision was huge: the rigorous deflationary course continued unabated, and the country's decline in living standards grew progressively worse, as did the degree of political radicalization.

By the early months of 1932 the main topic of political conversation within the country was the presidential election that was due to take place in the spring. For Brüning, it was clear from the outset that Hindenburg, now eighty-four years of age, would have to contest the post again in order to prevent an extreme nationalist and possibly even a National Socialist from winning, whereas Hindenburg himself was naturally willing to stand only if he could be certain of gaining sufficient support on the political right.

It was by no means certain that this condition would be met. The 'Hindenburg Committee' that met on 1 February 1932 to call for the re-election of the elderly field marshal comprised, among others, the writer Gerhart Hauptmann, the painter Max Liebermann, the chairman of the Confederation of German Industry, Carl Duisberg, and two former defence ministers, Otto Geßler and Gustav Noske. But the appeal was signed by none of the leaders of national organizations or major agricultural interests. Since the Stahlhelm, of which Hindenburg was an honorary member, was reluctant to vote for the incumbent, another veterans' association, the Kyffhäuser League, likewise hesitated to back its honorary president. Not until 14 February did the full committee of the Kyffhäuser League declare its loyalty to Hindenburg, with the result that the very next day the president let it be known that, conscious of his 'responsibility for the fate of our fatherland', he was available for re-election.[152]

Hindenburg's announcement persuaded the parties of the moderate right and centre ground to declare their public support for him, whereas the Harzburg Front fell apart: the Stahlhelm and German Nationalists were unwilling to accept the National Socialists' claims to leadership and on 22 February proposed their own alternative candidate: the deputy leader of the Stahlhelm, Theodor Duesterberg. That same day Joseph Goebbels, the NSDAP's Gauleiter in Berlin, declared in the city's Sportpalast: 'Hitler will be our country's president.'[153] Four days later Hitler had himself named government councillor at the Brunswick legation in Berlin, a legation which represented a region that since October 1930 had been ruled by a coalition cabinet of German Nationalists and National Socialists. In this way, Hitler, who had been born in Austria but who since April 1925 had been stateless, obtained the last thing that stood in the way of his candidacy as German president: German citizenship.

On the extreme left there had already been a presidential candidate since 12 January: Ernst Thälmann. Both the Comintern and the leaders of Thälmann's own German Communist Party expected that if the Social Democrats were to back Hindenburg, Thälmann might be able to win over a sizeable number of Social Democrat workers. Nor were their calculations entirely unfounded, for even if members and supporters of the Social Democrats had had to bear responsibility for much that ran counter to the party's traditional ideas since it had first backed the government in October 1930, many Social Democrats will have felt that they could hardly be expected to accept a recommendation that they throw their weight behind as committed a monarchist as Hindenburg.

The Social Democrats finally announced their official support for Hindenburg on 26 February 1932, the final day of another brief and tempestuous session of parliament. In its appeal to voters in the election on 13 March 1932, the party's executive committee declared that the German people faced a stark choice: Hindenburg or Hitler.

> Hitler instead of Hindenburg means chaos and panic in Germany and, indeed, in the whole of Europe, a radical worsening of the economic crisis and of the plight of the unemployed, and the utmost threat of bloody clashes both among our own people and also with other nations. Hitler instead of Hindenburg means the victory of the most reactionary forces over the most progressive elements within the bourgeoisie and the working class, the destruction of all civil liberties as well as of the press and of political, trade union and cultural organizations, increased exploitation and slave wages. [. . .] Defeat Hitler! Vote for Hindenburg![154]

Hindenburg's most impassioned advocate within the government camp was the chancellor, Heinrich Brüning. On 11 March, at Hindenburg's last major election rally in the Berlin Sportpalast, Brüning drew a picture of the president that was positively hagiographic. He would, he claimed, like to see the man who was Hindenburg's equal in 'assessing a situation as keenly and as quickly as the president and in summing it up in only a few sentences'. Brüning reckoned that Hindenburg was a 'true leader', a 'man sent by God' and a 'symbol of German power and unity in the whole world'. He ended by declaring that 'Hindenburg must win because Germany must live'.[155]

By the evening of 13 March it was clear that a second round of voting would be necessary, for Hindenburg had narrowly failed to win the necessary outright majority, having polled 49.6 per cent of the vote. Hitler was second with 30.1 per cent, followed some distance behind by Thälmann on 13.2 per cent and by Duesterberg on 6.8 per cent. A mere 173,000 extra votes would have been sufficient to ensure the incumbent's victory. Unlike the situation in 1925, he fared well in all the Social Democrat strongholds and in all those parts of the country where the Catholic share of the population was disproportionately high. In Protestant areas and rural communities, conversely, where he had been the clear victor seven years earlier, Hindenburg's results were far below the national average. If we exclude Bavaria, then Hindenburg had lost out with his traditional voters, while increasing his support among his former enemies.

Although Hitler had polled five million more votes than his party had managed in the Reichstag elections in September 1930, he stood little chance of defeating Hindenburg in the second round of voting. The Communists decided to send Thälmann back into the ring and, in keeping with a directive from Stalin, who had argued in November 1931 that 'the main thrust of the working class' should be directed against the Social Democrats, the Communist

Party insisted that the principal aim of Thälmann's campaign was 'to make voters clearly aware of the character of the Social Democrats as the moderate wing of Fascism and as the twin brother of Hitler's own particular brand of Fascism.'[156] Duesterberg did not take part in the second round of voting. The Stahlhelm advised its members to abstain. And the German Nationalists decided not to play an active role in the second ballot.

The second round of voting took place on 10 April 1932. By the evening it was apparent that Hindenburg had a clear mandate for a second term as president: he had received 53 per cent of the vote, Hitler 36.8 per cent, Thälmann 10.2 per cent. Above all, Hindenburg's victory was a direct result of the Social Democrats' policy of supporting Brüning's government, for if the party's supporters had not had an opportunity since the autumn of 1930 to grow used to a 'policy of accepting the lesser of two evils', they could hardly have allowed themselves to be convinced in the spring of 1932 that they had to elect a dyed-in-the-wool monarchist as their country's president in order to prevent a National Socialist dictatorship from materializing, for this was the only choice available to voters: apart from Hindenburg, there was no one else in a position to enlist the support of the traditional right and in that way to relegate Hitler to second place. The Social Democrats knew better than anyone that Hindenburg was no democrat, but until then the second president of the Weimar Republic had at least shown himself to be a champion of law and order and a man who respected the unloved constitution. In the circumstances, this was the most that could be hoped for, but when compared with what was avoided on 10 April – the proclamation of a 'Third Reich' – this was already a great deal.

Hindenburg himself felt no real joy at the outcome of the election, for it pained him deeply to think that he owed his victory not to the right but to the Social Democrats and Catholics. He took out his resentment on the one man who had been his most active campaigner, Heinrich Brüning. The 'emergency decree to safeguard the authority of the state' that was passed on 13 April and that banned Hitler's two private armies, his Storm Troopers (SA) and Protection Squadrons (SS), was Hindenburg's excuse to berate his chancellor in no uncertain terms. The ban had been urged on him by the most important German regional governments, Prussia, Bavaria, Württemberg, Baden, Hessen and Saxony, and was based on material concerning the National Socialists' secret military plans seized by the Prussian police during house searches conducted in the middle of March.

This material had initially persuaded the head of the ministerial office in the Defence Ministry, Kurt von Schleicher, to support the ban on the SA and SS, but he changed his mind before the second round of voting for the presidency, and he managed to persuade his former regimental comrade, Oskar von Hindenburg, to convince the latter's father, Paul von Hindenburg, that a ban on the SA and SS was politically inadvisable since it was bound to lead to a conflict between the president and the political right. Hindenburg reluctantly signed the emergency decree, but two days later he went behind the back of his defence minister, Wilhelm von Groener, and asked the head of the army command, Kurt von Hammerstein-Equord, to obtain compromising material about the Reichsbanner that would incriminate this republican defence organization and justify a ban.

Nothing came of this. Groener, who was acting minister of the interior as well as minister of defence, felt that the material from the Ministry of Defence was worthless and agreed to a tactical measure with the Reichsbanner's leader, Karl Höltermann, whereby the organization's elite units were sent away on leave. The emergency decree of 13 April remained in force, but as a result of these disagreements, Groener now had three influential enemies: his former political adviser, Kurt von Schleicher, and the Hindenburgs, father and son.

On 24 April 1932, two weeks after the second round of presidential elections, the majority of Germans once again went to the polls in the regional government elections in Prussia, Bavaria, Württemberg, Anhalt and the Free City of Hamburg. In all five regions, the National Socialists recorded substantial gains and became the largest party, the only exception being Bavaria, where the Bavarian People's Party maintained a two-seat lead. In Prussia, the Weimar coalition lost its majority, although none of the right-wing parties – the NSDAP, the German National People's Party or the German People's Party – was able to win a majority of its own.

The old Landtag had pre-empted this possibility at its final meeting before the elections on 12 April, altering its election procedures with the help of the three parties in government: the Social Democrats, the Centre Party and the German State Party. Until then the election of the prime minister had been a runoff between the two candidates with the best chances of success and had been held during the second round of elections, when a relative majority was all that the successful candidate needed to win. Following the change, an absolute majority was needed in the second and every subsequent ballot. The impact was that of a constructive vote of no confidence, for the Landtag could remove the incumbent from office only by voting for his successor by a majority of the votes cast. The newly elected Landtag met for its first session on 24 May. That same day the coalition government of the Social Democrat Otto Braun announced its resignation but remained in office as a caretaker cabinet as no majority could be found willing to restore the old procedure.

A four-day session of the Reichstag began on 9 May 1932 and was to prove the immediate prelude to Brüning's dismissal. It was Groener who on 10 May set events in motion when he delivered an unfortunate speech that was drowned out by scornful heckling from the ranks of the National Socialists. The following day Brüning himself gave a speech in which he drew attention to the forthcoming reparations conference in Lausanne and warned parliament and the general public alike not to lose their composure 'during the last one hundred metres before the finishing line'.[157] But as a damage limitation exercise, it was only partially successful.

On 12 May the government again won every vote thanks to the help of the Social Democrats, but by now the leaders of the army, with Schleicher at their head, were determined not only to break with Groener but also to bring down Brüning. Groener himself announced on 12 May that he wanted to step down as minister of defence and concentrate on the Ministry of the Interior, which until then he had overseen in only a temporary capacity. This would have required Hindenburg's agreement, but under Schleicher's influence, the president insisted on Schleicher leaving the government completely. When he set off for his Whitsun break on 12 May, Hindenburg made it a condition that Brüning would not undertake any changes to his government while he, Hindenburg, was away.

Schleicher's change of attitude towards Brüning was due only in part to the ban on the SA, for by April 1932 he had come to believe that the national crisis that was affecting Germany could be solved only with the help of the National Socialists. He held secret talks with Hitler on 28 April and 7 May, and at least in the second of these discussions the question was raised as to the conditions under which the NSDAP would be willing to accept a more right-wing cabinet. By 7 May Schleicher knew the price that Hitler was asking: the dissolution of the Reichstag, new elections and the lifting of the ban on the SA and SS. Hindenburg knew about these talks. Brüning's position was further undermined in the eyes of both Hindenburg and Schleicher by the fact that he had returned practically empty-handed from the disarmament talks in Geneva on 30 April. The press had good reason to assume that Brüning would not be able to hang on to power for much longer now that Groener had announced his resignation as minister of defence.

While Hindenburg was vacationing on his estates at Neudeck in East Prussia, another elite group long eager to see Brüning's fall from power was at work: the landowners to the east of the Elbe. The National Land League, which had been controlled by the 'national opposition' in the form of the German Nationalists and National Socialists since the autumn of 1930, was the only economic interest group of any significance to have come out in support of Hitler before the second round of presidential elections. On 21 May it was the government itself that provided the leading agricultural umbrella organization with its cue to start a large-scale campaign against Brüning, when Hans Schlange-Schöningen, the national commissioner with special responsibility for assisting the eastern part of Germany, submitted a cabinet-approved draft of a settlement decree providing for the possibility of acquiring lands that were no longer redeemable either privately or by means of a compulsory auction and of using the lands so acquired for the purposes of creating farming settlements.

Immediately after the contents of the draft became known, the presidents of the National Land League and German Agriculture Day, together with several regional offices of the Land League, lodged complaints with Hindenburg. Each of their submissions made the same point: in the words of the director of the

East Prussian Land Society, Baron Wilhelm von Gayl, the right to hold compulsory auctions represented a further 'descent into state socialism' and weakened the 'resistance of those groups which until now have embodied the national will to defend Germany against the Poles'.[158]

The pressure soon had the desired effect, and on 25 May Hindenburg informed Schlange-Schöningen that he could not agree to the decree in its present form. Two days later, the German Nationalists in the Reichstag described the measure as 'unqualified Bolshevism'. By 27 May Hindenburg could no longer go back on his word, and in the face of opposition from the German Nationalists the shift to the right that he had wanted to see was no longer possible.

On his return to Berlin, Hindenburg received Brüning on the evening of Sunday 29 May in order to tell him that he expected the government to resign. The following morning Brüning informed his cabinet of his conversation with the president, and shortly before noon Brüning submitted his government's resignation to the head of state. The exchange lasted only a few minutes. At midday Hindenburg had to appear on the steps of his presidential palace for a march-past by the Skagerrak Guard, a guard of honour in the navy.

Of all the chancellors who served under the Weimar Republic, none is as controversial as Heinrich Brüning, none whose image has been so distorted by partisan praise and hostility. By some he is seen as a man who systematically undermined democracy in Germany and in that way unwittingly prepared the ground for Hitler, while others see in him a conservative alternative both to a failed parliamentary system and to a National Socialist dictatorship. According to this second reading, Brüning's policies were for long periods historically necessary: only with his fall from power did the country begin its downward spiral into disaster.

It is certainly true that parliamentary democracy had already failed in the Weimar Republic by the time that Brüning became chancellor on 30 March 1930. Once the grand coalition had broken down, it was only a question of time before an openly presidential system took over. Brüning became, as it were, the executor of policies whose basic thrust was ultimately determined by the president and his entourage. Until well into 1931, Brüning represented a consensus which, transcending party and factional lines, was aimed at reforming the country's finances but which led in the final analysis to deflation. Moreover, there was until the winter of 1931/2 an objective obstacle in the way of an alternative, anti-cyclical economic policy, and this was the unresolved problem of German reparations. Only when it became clear that there was no possibility of returning to the Young Plan could Brüning have changed his economic course. But he had no wish to do so since he rejected any kind of compromise on the question of reparations for reasons of national prestige and of his more far-reaching foreign policy objectives. But he would presumably have been prevented from pursuing a less revisionist foreign policy during the winter of 1931/2 as he would almost certainly have met with Hindenburg's veto.

Hindenburg's position was so unassailable that the question of Brüning's own long-term goals is of only limited interest. Both in exile and in his memoirs, which appeared in 1970 shortly after his death, Germany's chancellor from 1930 to 1932 claimed that he had worked consistently for the restoration of the monarchy in an attempt to erect a barrier that would have prevented the National Socialists from establishing a dictatorship. There is no doubt about Brüning's sympathy for the old German Empire that had vanished in 1918. But if as chancellor he had really wanted to restore the Hohenzollerns to the throne, we would need evidence in support of this claim, and no such evidence exists. Brüning's belated attempt to justify himself was manifestly designed to enhance his own reputation and to raise a monument to what he believed were his achievements as a conservative statesman with a far-reaching vision.

The truth of the matter is that Brüning was the half-willing, half-unwilling executor of policies that cannot be adequately described as 'conservative'. The true centre of power during the latter part of the Weimar Republic consisted of Hindenburg and his camarilla, their joint aim being to create an authoritarian state in which the will of the people would find only muted expression. Brüning, conversely, was willing to accept a restriction on the rights of parliament, especially with regard to national expenditure, an aim he was indeed able to implement through appropriate reform measures in February 1931. He believed that the National Socialists could be tamed but attached conditions to their participation in government, conditions that the party was unable to accept without radically altering its very identity. Like the leader of the Centre Party, Ludwig Kaas, he endorsed a shift to the right in German politics, while wanting to adhere strictly to the country's constitution. When, in the early months of 1932, Hindenburg and his circle decided to ignore the Social Democrats' policy of cooperation and to make more concessions to the National Socialists than Brüning felt were advisable, Brüning was forced to go.

Brüning's fall from power marked a turning point in German history: the first and more moderate phase of the presidential system came to an end on 30 May 1932, a phase that had still been tolerated by parliament. The second phase was authoritarian and openly hostile to parliamentary values. The army leadership and the major landowners who had helped to bring about the change of regime wanted to enlist the National Socialists as their junior partners – not to be dominated by them but to turn them into a prop that would support their own regime. Meeting Hitler's conditions for the acceptance of a right-wing cabinet presupposed the dissolution of the Reichstag, whose legislative period was not due to end until September 1934. If new elections had taken place at that time, then Germany would have looked very different from how it did in the summer of 1932. In the wake of the economic recovery that we may assume would have taken place by September 1934, unemployment would have fallen and the popularity of the extremist parties would have waned. With their shift from a moderate to an anti-parliamentary presidential system, Hindenburg and the old Prussian elite destroyed that opportunity, bringing the crisis affecting Germany to a head and in that way placing the country in a situation that was practically impossible to deal with any longer by purely constitutional means.

Stagnation and Criticism of the System: France's Third Republic 1929–33

While the United States, Germany and Great Britain were badly hit by the world economic crisis, France was able to bask in a state of relative prosperity in 1930. The country's leading industrial sectors reported even better results than in 1929: with 254,000 cars rolling off the production lines each year, car production, for example, was second only to the United States. Not until 1931 did the crisis make itself felt in France. Prices fell, and output dropped: in 1931 the production index in the iron industry was seventeen points lower than it had been in 1929, and by 1932 it was forty-eight points lower. In 1934 wholesale prices were only 46 per cent of what they had been in 1929. In 1931 the Banque Oustric collapsed amid scandal. In 1934 Citroën went into receivership and following state intervention was taken over by the tyre manufacturer Michelin. Unemployment rose, but at no point did it reach the levels seen in Great Britain, Germany and the United States. In 1935, 12.5 million French men and women were in work, while the number of unemployed is reckoned to have been around half a million.

If France was less badly affected by the Great Depression than more highly developed industrialized countries, then this was due to its relative backwardness when compared with Germany, Great Britain and the United States. Up to the time of the 1931 census the majority of the population lived in municipalities numbering fewer than 2,000 inhabitants. Agriculture and small and medium-sized businesses in trade and crafts suffered from the worldwide depression more than large-scale industry that was well supplied with capital. But if the crisis started at a later date in France than it did in Germany, then it also lasted longer here than to the east of the Rhine. The early 1930s witnessed the start of a period of industrial stagnation that lasted until the early 1950s. The French historians Serge Berstein and Pierre Milza have spoken in this context of a twenty-year obstacle, or barrier, to modernization that had its counterpart in the archaic economic thinking of the country's rulers and of public opinion in general, reflecting attitudes that were fundamentally protectionist in character.[159]

Up until the time of the elections to the Chamber of Deputies in May 1932, governments in Paris relied on the support of the centre right. In the three years between Poincaré's resignation in July 1929 and the elections in May 1932, France had no fewer than eight cabinets, three of which were led by André Tardieu. Born in Paris in 1876 and long regarded as Clemenceau's heir apparent, Tardieu was an astute advocate of the upper middle classes in France. He was fully conscious of the country's economic backwardness and banked, therefore, on increasing industrial capacity but also on extending social legislation, including the gradual introduction of free grammar school education in 1930 and of universal child benefit in 1932. Two cabinets were headed by Pierre Laval who was born in Châteldon in the *département* of Puy-de-Dôme and began his political career with the Socialists, but, like Tardieu, he moved progressively further to the right during the country's economic crisis.

Until January 1932 the foreign minister was Aristide Briand, whose principal goal throughout this period was Franco-German accord as the guarantor of a peaceful Europe, an aim that earned him the continuous parliamentary support of the Socialists who until 1910 had been his own political party and who were now the party of opposition. In Germany, conversely, the death of Gustav Stresemann meant that after 1929 Briand no longer commanded the degree of support that he needed to pursue his foreign policy with any degree of success. After 1930 the tone in Berlin was set by two politicians and a diplomat keen above all to change the post-war world order: the chancellor Heinrich Brüning, his foreign minister Julius Curtius and the secretary of state at the Foreign Office, Bernhard von Bülow.

In May 1930 Briand wrote to every European government with his 'Memorandum on the Organization of a System of Federal European Union', refining ideas that he had developed in a speech to the League of Nations on 5 September 1929, while Stresemann was still alive. His memorandum sketched out his vision of a union of sovereign states closely working together and agreeing on their common economic and political interests by regularly consulting with one another in the hope that they could speak with a single voice when representing those interests at the League of Nations. But in Germany and Great Britain, Briand's ideas were greeted with reserve, at least as far as their specifically political component was concerned: in Berlin the government was unwilling to abandon its determination to revise the conditions of the Treaty of Versailles, while in London the Commonwealth represented a far more obvious form of international community than a 'federal' Europe. Even so, it would be wrong to describe French foreign policy during this period as naive. In late 1929 the country began work on the Maginot Line, named after the country's minister of war at this time. It was a system of fortifications along its north-east border and also on its frontier with Italy and was designed to protect the country in the event of an attack from the east or south-east.

In France as elsewhere, the world economic crisis led to a radicalization of the political scene. On the right, the earliest unequivocally pro-Fascist organization, Georges Valois's Faisceau, was disbanded in 1928. Other right-wing groups that survived were Action Française, whose shock troops, the Camelots du Roi, had a reputation for naked brutality, and the Jeunesses Patriotes associated with the parliamentarian Pierre Taittinger. All these right-wing organizations lost members and forfeited public support in the wake of the country's economic and financial stabilization, but this picture began to change in the early 1930s. The Croix de Feu, a frontline fighters' league founded in 1927 and led since 1929 by Colonel Casimir de La Rocque, became the most powerful of these radical right-wing organizations after 1931. Its members were not Fascists, however, but radical nationalists who enjoyed the financial support of right-wing industrialists such as François Coty and Ernest Mercier, while also having the backing of politicians like André Tardieu, who from March to December 1930 was not only France's prime minister but also its minister of the interior.

By 1933 the Croix de Feu had some 80,000 members, almost all of whom were ex-soldiers, with a further 40,000 youths who made up its Volontaires Nationaux. According to the organization's own estimates its membership rose to between two and three million in 1936. A paramilitary organization, they claimed to be French nationalists and sought to establish a regime in which power lay not with parliament but with the president of the Republic. On the other hand, its members were not interested in the violent overthrow of the existing government. Founded in September 1933 and funded by François Coty and by Mussolini's Italy, Francisme, conversely, was a self-declared Fascist organization, as was Solidarité Française, a paramilitary grouping that likewise received support from Coty and was formed in 1933. Neither of these last two organizations managed to muster more than a few thousand followers.

As in the mid-1920s, so in the early 1930s a favourite place for violent clashes between the right and the left was the Sorbonne and, indeed, French universities in general. Jeunesses Patriotes and the Camelots du Roi vied with each other in their campaigns against left-wing and pacifist teachers and students known to support the Radicals and Socialists. These militant leagues also received 'intellectual' support from non-conformist organizations such as Jeune Droite and L'Ordre Nouveau, the first of which had emerged from Action Française, while the spokesmen of the second sympathized with socialist ideas. Among the party newspapers of these various groups were *Cahiers, Réaction, La Revue Française, L'Ordre Nouveau* and *Plans*. In December 1932 Robert Aron sought to encapsulate the views of L'Ordre Nouveau:

> We are neither on the right nor on the left, but if we are to be pigeonholed according to a traditional parliamentary taxonomy, then we would stress that we occupy the middle ground between the extreme right and the extreme left, behind the president and with our backs to the National Assembly.[160]

That L'Ordre Nouveau was in fact a right-wing party and not one associated with the political centre ground is clear from two books that Aron and his comrade-in-arms, Arnaud Dandieu, published in 1931 under the titles *Décadence de la Nation Française* and *Le Cancer Américain*. Both writers felt that Europe was under threat not only from Russian Bolshevism but also from American capitalism. In their eyes, the Hoover Moratorium was an attempt to subject the old Continent of Europe to the hegemonic control of the New World. It was France's mission to save the West, but to do so, it needed a rapid internal change involving a rejection of the parliamentary system and an increase in the power of the president. The followers of the Jeune Droite movement were agreed in opposing Briand's policies, and in 1931 202 intellectuals signed a 'Manifeste des jeunes intellectuels mobilisables contre la démission de la France', rejecting any further attempts to undermine the peace established in 1919 and warning of the risk of yet another partition of Poland.

In spite of this, a number of right-wing French groups with predominantly young members, including L'Ordre Nouveau, maintained close links with right-wing intellectuals in Germany, including young National Socialists like Otto Abetz, who was to be the German ambassador in occupied France during the Second World War. A leading spokesman of this pro-German school was Alexandre Marc, whose real name was Aleksander Markovich Lipiansky and who had been born into a Jewish family in Odessa in 1904. He and his family fled to France in the wake of the October Revolution. He studied philosophy in Germany, where he was particularly influenced by Max Scheler's 'ethical personalism' and by *The European Revolutions and the Character of Nations* that was published in 1931 by the Breslau historian Eugen Rosenstock-Huessy and that accorded the French Revolution of 1789 a far less significant role in world history than other writers were inclined to ascribe to it. Hand in hand with a critique of the French Revolution went an advocacy of regional autonomy, a view that Marc shared with Aron and Dandieu and that has points in common with the Neo-Thomism of Jacques Maritain and especially with the subsidiarity principle of Catholic social teachings as developed by Pope Pius XI in his 1931 encyclical *Quadragesimo anno*.

L'Ordre Nouveau and Jeune Droite had much in common with the proponents of the Conservative Revolution in Germany, even if Rosenstock-Huessy had little to do with this particular school of thought. Suffice it to mention its anti-parliamentary thrust, its positive interest in the Italian *stato corporativo*, its outspoken anti-liberalism and anti-Marxism and its critique of the rationalism of the Enlightenment and of eastern materialism and western utilitarianism. And yet there was one important point on which the younger members of the French and German far right held widely divergent views, for in France there was none of the glorification of the war that was to be found to the east of the Rhine.

The trauma of the First World War continued to be felt in France, while at the same time acting as a warning: this was a war that in no circumstances could be allowed to repeat itself. The French of all political persuasions were unsettled by the demographic stagnation that left their country at a disadvantage when compared with Germany, which had a larger population and a higher birth rate than theirs. In the years around 1930 only 35 per cent of French families had three or more children. The percentage of men and women over sixty – 13.5 per cent – was far higher than in Germany, Great Britain and Italy, where it was around 9 per cent. There was still a widespread fear of over-population ('Malthusianism'). If France's population increased from 39.2 million in 1919 to forty-two million in 1939, then this was due exclusively to immigration from other European countries and North Africa. A war, it was feared, would cause further blood-letting. As one of the victorious powers, France was almost entirely lacking in the sort of bellicism that was currently being promoted by right-wing groups in Germany.

On the extreme left of the political spectrum, the French Communist Party and, indeed, all the parties that belonged to the Third International were forced to undergo a strict process of Bolshevization after 1924, leading to the resignation of many of their members. In the wake of the shift to the ultra-left decreed by the Sixth World Congress of the Comintern in the summer of 1928, the French Communist Party distanced itself increasingly from the reformists in the SFIO and in the French Trades Union Congress and was obliged to pay the price for this with its political isolation and parliamentary marginalization. In the elections to the Chamber of Deputies in April 1928, there were only twelve Communists, fourteen fewer than during the previous legislative period.

The clashes with the police that were deliberately orchestrated by the French Communist Party resulted in repeated court appearances and prison sentences for its leading officials. Maurice Thorez, a former coalminer, took over as the party's leader in the spring of 1930, immediately after his release from prison, becoming its general secretary the following year. All of his political decisions were taken only in close consultation with the Comintern's official representative, the Czech Communist Eugen Fried. Thorez was an eloquent orator and as popular with French militants and with many of the country's workers as Ernst Thälmann was in Germany. Neither man gave Stalin any reason to doubt his willingness to toe the party line.

In those areas where the Communists enjoyed their greatest support – the *banlieue rouge* in Paris and the rural communities of south-west France, including those in the *département* of Corrèze – a vote for the French Communist Party was above all a form of social protest at French society, which was still dominated by class divisions. Political extremism was less pronounced among French Communists than among their German counterparts, largely because there was less mass poverty in France, and although there were radical right-wing tendencies, there was no mass following for Fascism: the bourgeois republican Radicals were still sufficiently powerful in the 1930s to prove effective as a barrier to any major right-wing radicalization process.

Like all Communist parties, the French Communist Party numbered several intellectuals among its members, including the co-founder of the Surrealist movement, Louis Aragon. But it also had many intellectual sympathizers, most of whom were more committed to the Soviet Union than to the French Communist Party. The most outspoken of these sympathizers was Henri Barbusse, the author of the anti-war novel *Le Feu* (1916), but other writers who belong in this group, albeit with reservations, were Romain Rolland, André Gide and André Malraux, all of whom were members of the pro-Communist Association des Écrivains et Artistes Révolutionnaires and contributors to its journal, *Commune*. The majority of these intellectuals owed their conversion to Communism to the rise of National Socialism in Germany: in their view, the best way to combat National Socialism was by joining forces with the Communists. Only after Hitler had come to power were they confronted with the reality of Soviet Communism.

The rise of National Socialism and the growth of right-wing movements in France was a challenge for the Socialists, who had polled more votes than any other party in the 1928 elections, while failing to win the most seats. At a party conference in Paris in January 1926, Léon Blum, the leader of the Socialists in the Chamber of Deputies and also the party's de facto leader, had expressed the SFIO's motto: within the parliamentary system the exercise of power must be carefully distinguished from the revolutionary seizure of power. In keeping with the 'Kautsky resolution' agreed to at the International Socialist Congress in September 1900, the exercise of power in the form of a coalition with bourgeois parties was something that the Socialists could countenance only in exceptional circumstances such as wartime or the need to avert a danger like Fascism or counterrevolution. In Blum's view the exercise of power was dangerous because it could lead workers into thinking that it might produce results that were in fact only achievable through the violent seizure of power.

In Blum's view, the German Social Democrats could be excused for behaving differently and for forming alliances with the country's bourgeois parties. Indeed, such alliances were even to be welcomed for reasons of Germany's foreign policy. The danger of what he termed 'confusion' was less pronounced in Germany than in France for the Social Democrats' partners were Catholics and Liberals who were clearly distinguished from the Socialists, not bourgeois, progressive, republican and secular radical Socialists, who in many areas held views relatively close to those of the Socialists proper. In France, conversely, the only form of support that as a rule came into question was that of a government explicitly opposed to the forces of reaction. For the French Socialists, the law of self-preservation dictated that they should not cross the line that would lead to power-sharing. During the later period, Blum argued that this position might change only if the SFIO, like the German Social Democrats, were to become the largest party in parliament.

Within the SFIO, Blum's doctrine was by no means uncontroversial, and in October 1929 the party's deputies voted by a large majority to accept ministerial posts, a vote taken in the face of bitter opposition from their leader. Only his veto was able to prevent a coalition of Radicals and Socialists from being formed, leading directly to Tardieu's first cabinet. The spokesman of those members of the party who were in favour of power-sharing was the right-wing thinker Pierre Renaudel, who refused to be discouraged by this setback. He invited Kautsky himself to write a brilliant article championing a coalition that appeared in *Vorwärts* in January 1930 and in Renaudel's own *La Vie Socialiste*, the official paper of the reformists, in February 1930. 'There are situations', wrote Kautsky, justifying his stance by reference to the foreign policy of both countries, 'when the evil of a coalition government is the lesser or two such evils when compared to the greater one that threatens us whenever we entrust control of the state's immense power to our worst enemies, even though we could reduce this danger by entering into a coalition.'[161]

At the Socialists' party conference in late January 1930 those who advocated power-sharing were once again defeated. When the right-wing delegate Marcel Déat announced that the minority would continue to advocate their own position, the secretary general of the SFIO, Paul Faure, threw down the gauntlet, declaring war on his opponents in such strident terms that many feared for party unity. Much to the dismay of those who wanted power-sharing, the internally divided SFIO had demonstrated to the world that it was incapable of ruling the country. At their party conference in Tours in May 1931, a group of reformists under the deputy Joseph Paul-Boncour seized upon another conflict – the question of the country's defence – as an opportunity to draw a line under the matter, when he and his followers left the SFIO and founded a new party, the Républicains Socialistes, who, unlike the Socialists, advocated a policy of maintaining a level of military strength adequate to the country's defence needs.

The first round of elections to the Chamber of Deputies took place on 1 May 1932. In advance of the vote the ruling parties had ignored the protests of the political left and changed the rules on voting, with the result that a candidate could now be elected if he won at least 40 per cent of the votes in the first round of voting, making a second round unnecessary. Even so, the left-wing parties won around one million votes more than the right, the SFIO polling 1.96 million compared to the Radicals' 1.84 million. The Communists dropped from 1.06 million to 797,000 votes. The radical right did not take part in the election. On 7 May – the day before the second round of the ballot – the country's president, Paul Doumer, who had been elected only the previous year, was assassinated by an anti-Communist Russian émigré at a book fair in protest at France's failure to bring down the Soviet regime. On 10 May the Senate and Chamber of Deputies jointly elected the conservative president of the Senate, Albert Lebrun, as the new French president.

Thanks to regional pacts between the Socialists and Radicals, the second round of elections on 8 May produced a centre-left majority. Together, the Radicals and Socialists won 157 seats, pushing the SFIO into second place with 129. On the political right there were three relatively large parties: the Union Républicaine Démocratique with seventy-six seats, the Républicains de Gauche with seventy-two and the Radicaux-Indépendants with sixty-two. The Communists won only twelve seats, the Socialistes-Communistes who occupied the political ground between the SFIO and the French Communist Party, eleven. Paul-Boncour's Républicains-Socialistes returned thirty-seven deputies to the lower house.

The bourgeois Radicaux-Socialistes were far from united as a party. The party's leader, Édouard Herriot, who had been invited to form a government, had in the meantime gravitated from the left to the centre. The left wing of the party now included the 'Young Turks' Pierre Cot, Pierre Mendès-France and Jean Zay, and formed a minority within the party. It augured badly for the coalition that in the presidential election most of the Radicals voted against the Socialist candidate Paul Faure, preferring to back Albert Lebrun instead.

Herriot offered the Socialists an equal share in government, and at a party conference that they convened in Paris the latter declared their fundamental willingness to accept this offer, only to attach strict conditions to their agreement, conditions which, drawn up in consultation with the Reformist Marcel Déat, became known as the 'Cahiers d'Huyghens' and included nationalization of the country's rail network and of all other transport companies and insurance firms, stricter banking controls, the introduction of a forty-hour week and a reduction in military spending. Since Herriot was unable to accept this catalogue of demands, he formed a cabinet made up for the most part of Radicals and a handful of representatives of the centre ground. Herriot himself assumed the role of foreign minister in addition to that of prime minister, while the former Socialist Paul-Boncour became minister of war. Herriot's cabinet won a vote of no confidence thanks to the support of the Socialists.

Herriot's brief period in office witnessed the Lausanne conference on reparations, about which we shall have more to say in due course. On 9 July he made the costly mistake of agreeing to a treaty effectively ending German reparation payments without first having obtained American agreement for an end to the repayment of inter-Allied debts. Unlike most of the members of the Chamber of Deputies as well as those in his own party, Herriot was willing to transfer to the United States all instalments for 1932 that were still due following the end of the Hoover Moratorium in the December of that year. Having suffered a parliamentary defeat on this point on 14 December 1932, he was left with no alternative but to resign.

Following Herriot's fall from power, France endured four short-lived governments under Joseph Paul-Boncour, Édouard Daladier, Albert Sarraut and Camille Chautemps, a period of political instability that ended only in late January 1934 and that was due, above all, to the profound differences of opinion between Radicals and Socialists on the economy. The left-wing bourgeois cabinets pursued a policy of deflationary cost-cutting and, in spite of its drawbacks for exports and its high social costs, they insisted on maintaining the gold standard that Great Britain had abandoned in September 1931, the

United States in April 1933. The Socialists thought differently, the party's leaders taking an even more anti-governmental view than its members in the Chamber of Deputies.

In May 1933 a serious disagreement broke out between the SFIO's party executive and its members in the Chamber of Deputies after the latter had wilfully ignored the party whip and voted for the budgetary measures contained in a government bill. The reformist group associated with Pierre Renaudel and Paul Ramadier and three of the younger members of the chamber, Marcel Déat, Adrien Marquet and Barthélemy Montagnon, justified their position in a statement in which they declared their willingness to work more closely with the bourgeois left, advocating a greater sense of 'social patriotism' and a readiness to be more receptive to the middle classes. Déat in particular felt that courting the middle classes was the principal lesson that could be learnt from the failure of the German Social Democrats and ultimately from the downfall of the Weimar Republic: if the Socialists wanted to block the progress of the Fascists, they needed to win the support of those classes that were the basis of the Fascists' mass following not only in Germany but in every part of Europe.

The 'Neo-Socialism' of Déat and his followers was a reaction to the ideological sterility and political stagnation of the party's official line, a line embodied in its purest form by Léon Blum. Ever since it had been reconstituted in 1920/21 Blum had sought to preserve party unity by bringing together its two opposing and increasingly fractious wings. The academic distinctions that he drew were an expression of this attempt to achieve a balance. But to the extent that the majority of the 'militants' were on the left of the party, Blum felt that he needed to take greater account of the traditional left than of the reformist ideas of the right-wing minority. The worse the economic crisis grew in France in the course of 1931, the more it became clear that the SFIO was politically out of its depth, giving old answers to the new challenges and reacting to the demands of the right-wing activists by adopting a largely administrative response. By early 1933 the Neo-Socialists had abandoned all hope of reforming the party from within. Like their opponents, they regarded a split in the party as inevitable.

It was predictable, therefore, that the party conference in Paris in July 1933 would prove to be a crucial test of its unity. The leaders of the Neo-Socialists made it completely impossible for the majority to reach any kind of agreement with them, so determined were they to learn from their Fascist enemy that they gave the impression that they themselves were on the way to becoming Fascists. And when Marquet, in a conference speech, acknowledged the values of 'ordre, autorité, nation', Blum expressed his outrage by heckling him. His feeling that a number of Neo-Socialists were indeed proto-Fascists was by no means misplaced, for both Déat and Marquet later joined a movement that they were still opposing in 1933. Other Neo-Socialists, conversely, returned to the party fold many years after the split.

The party conference in Paris condemned the behaviour of its parliamentarians by a large majority, encouraging Renaudel to protest at their verdict on behalf of the Neo-Socialists, while Blum wrote a series of articles for the party newspaper in which he sought to underscore his charge of Fascism, in the process perpetuating the ideological divide. The definitive breach came in the autumn of 1933: in a vote on Daladier's proposed budget on 24 October, ninety-one Socialist deputies voted against the government, twenty-eight for it, with eleven abstentions. On 4 and 5 November the SFIO's National Council voted to exclude the leading Neo-Socialists from the party. Among them were Renaudel, Déat, Marquet and Montagnon.

Twenty-seven members of the Chamber of Deputies and seven members of the Senate joined the Parti Socialiste de France that was founded by the Neo-Socialists in early December 1933, but the new right-wing Socialist party failed to win mass support. Even so, the break with the Neo-Socialists harmed the SFIO far more than the German Social Democrats had been damaged by the split in the Socialist Workers' Party only two years earlier. It was clear that each and every Socialist party could be beset by crisis not only if it adopted a reformist stance but also if it maintained an orthodox anti-reformist line.

The Power of Continuity: Britain in the Early 1930s

The world economic crisis hit Great Britain sooner and more deeply than France. The United Kingdom had had a high level of unemployment throughout the 1920s: the proportion of men and women out of work rose above 10 per cent for the first time in 1921 and sank below that level only once, in 1927. By 1929 it was 10.4 per cent and by 1932 it had reached an all-time high of 22.7 per cent. Thereafter it continued to drop, but not until 1940 had it again fallen beneath 10 per cent. In absolute terms, unemployment – at three million – was at its worst between August 1931 and January 1933. In the summer of 1931 it had stood at 2.5 million, falling again to a little over two million by June 1932.

The older industrial regions in central and northern England, south Wales, Scotland and Northern Ireland were particularly badly affected by the crisis. In the coal-mining districts, the number of people out of work was as high as 70 per cent of the workforce. The decline of mining, steel-making, shipbuilding and cotton manufacture had already begun long before 1929, of course: the cotton mills of Lancashire were the main victims of the loss of overseas markets, especially India, during the First World War. In 1913 one million miners had produced 787 million tons of coal, but by 1933 the number of miners had fallen to half a million and the amount of coal produced to 207 million tons. Between 1929 and 1932 steel production fell from 9.6 to 5.2 million tons. After 1925 the United Kingdom's export industry was hit by a return to the gold standard, which led to a 10 per cent overvaluation of the pound. The gradual economic recovery after 1933 was part of a more general trend, the depression having reached its low point in the summer of 1932.

The economic policies pursued by Ramsay MacDonald's second Labour cabinet were not substantially different from those adopted by Heinrich Brüning's government in Germany. It took office in June 1929 and, like its predecessor in 1924, it remained at the mercy of the Liberals. The chancellor, Philip Snowden, was a convinced advocate of a balanced budget and of free trade, with the result that he emphatically rejected all calls for a generous state-funded job-creation programme, for protective tariffs and for a transition to flexible exchange rates. In February 1930 the minister without portfolio, Sir Oswald Mosley, and the minister for public works, George Lansbury, submitted a memorandum seeking to increase mass consumerism by means of public works such as road-building schemes, but the idea encountered almost universal opposition on the part of their cabinet colleagues.

Mosley had begun his political career as a Conservative, entering the lower house at the end of 1918 at the age of only twenty-one. His first wife, Cynthia ('Cimmie'), was the daughter of Lord Curzon, the former viceroy of India and later foreign secretary. Mosley soon fell out with the Tories over the Irish question, and in the elections of 1922 and 1923 he stood as an Independent, in both cases successfully. In March 1924 he joined the Labour Party, playing an active role on its left wing, the Independent Labour Party. When his memorandum was rejected, he resigned his ministerial post but in October 1930 tried to persuade the party conference to adopt his line, failing by only the narrowest of margins. Within the parliamentary party he enjoyed the support of a number of leading MPs at this time, not least of whom were Aneurin Bevan and John Strachey.

Mosley left the Labour Party on 28 February 1931 and the very next day founded the New Party, with a programme designed to deal with the economic crisis. In it he demanded state control of the country's banks, a publicly funded work creation programme and a plan to develop agriculture. A reduced cabinet was to be given extraordinary powers similar to those held by the War Cabinet from 1914 to 1918. He attracted the support of four Labour MPs, including Lady Cynthia Mosley and John Strachey, while he was also able to enlist the services of the writer Harold Nicolson to edit his party's official newspaper, *Action*. In the by-election in Ashton-under-Lyne, which had previously been held by the Labour Party and where 46 per cent of the workforce was unemployed, his New Party won 16 per cent of the vote. The by-election was won by the Tories.

Even if the Labour government's attempts to deal with the problem of unemployment were far too little in the eyes of Mosley and other critics, MacDonald's government could not be accused of inactivity in this regard. The Unemployment Insurance Act of December 1930 increased national insurance benefits and made it easier for the unemployed to claim them, with the result that state support for unemployment insurance continued to rise inexorably: in 1929 it amounted to £51 million but had risen to £125 million within only two years. By the beginning of 1931 Snowden had come to the conclusion that national expenditure needed to be drastically cut. In response to Conservative and Liberal motions, he established an independent committee in February 1931 under the chairmanship of the departing president of the Prudential Insurance Company, Sir George May. Its task was to suggest savings.

The committee had yet to complete its work when a Royal Commission that had been set up to examine the problem of unemployment insurance submitted an interim report in June, recommending a rise in contributions and a reduction in benefits. In July the May Committee, in the face of opposition from its two Labour Party members, submitted a report that was deliberately couched in dramatic terms. The deficits incurred by national insurance and by the budget in general persuaded the panel of experts that the United Kingdom was on the brink of financial disaster. It recommended a reduction in state expenditure by around £96 million and in national insurance by no less than £66.5 million. Unemployment benefits would have had to be cut by 20 per cent to take account of this second recommendation. The committee also recommended a cut in teachers' salaries and in the expenditure on public works.

The government immediately set up a finance committee that was to convene under the chairmanship of the prime minister and examine ways of implementing the May Committee's recommendations. Among the consequences of the report was a flight away from the pound to gold, exacerbating a development that had already begun in May with the collapse of the Austrian Credit Bank. When the Bank of England tried to obtain further foreign loans from New York and Paris to the tune of £80 million, it was faced by the condition that the British government must accept the recommendations of the May Committee and in any event agree to rigorous savings and to the retention of the gold standard.

MacDonald and Snowden informed the leaders of the Labour Party and TUC of the planned changes to national insurance on 20 August 1931. The TUC's reaction was negative, its chairman, Walter Citrine, and the leader of the transport workers' union, Ernest Bevin, both announcing that they were unable to agree to the cuts. Three days later the cabinet met to discuss the programme and voted by a narrow majority of eleven to nine to accept the changes proposed by the prime minister and his chancellor. MacDonald felt that he needed more support for his plans and on the morning of 24 August drove to Buckingham Palace to inform George V of his resignation. The king responded by inviting him to form a cabinet made up of Labour, Conservative and Liberal ministers, an invitation that MacDonald accepted without hesitation.

The new National Government took up office on 25 August. It comprised four ministers from the previous Labour cabinet, including MacDonald himself and Snowden, both of whom retained their existing portfolios, four Tories, including Stanley Baldwin as lord president of the council and effectively deputy prime minister, and two Liberals, one of whom, Sir Herbert Samuel, was the new home secretary. Presented with these changes as a fait accompli, the Labour Party rebelled, and by the end of the day the trade unions and the party organizers outside parliament had effectively assumed control. Only four members of MacDonald's old cabinet attended the meeting of Labour MPs on 25 August, when the former foreign secretary, Arthur Henderson, was elected the new chairman. On 28 August the party excluded MacDonald, Snowden and the two other Labour members of the National Government, the minister for the colonies, James Henry Thomas, and the lord chancellor, John Sankey. From then on MacDonald, Snowden and their followers were regarded as traitors by supporters of the Labour Party.

The way in which Labour MPs and trade unions behaved in late August 1931 was in many respects reminiscent of the revolt staged by the Social Democrats in the Reichstag and the Free Trade Unions against the chancellor, Hermann Brüning, and against two of the three other Social Democrat members of the German government on 27 March 1930 after the latter had voted for Brüning's compromise on the question of reforms to national insurance in Germany. In both cases party and trade unions opposed changes to social welfare that the governing minority felt were necessary. In Germany, the confrontation between the two groups led to the downfall of the last parliamentary majority government and the transition to a presidential regime, while in Britain the trade union veto and the split within the Labour Party resulted in the formation of an alternative majority government. At a time when the small right-wing minority of the workers' party in Britain was reconstituting itself as the National Labour Organization, the Socialist Workers' Party in Germany was splitting away from the left wing of the Social Democrat Party in protest at the main party's policy of keeping the government in power. The new party was to find even less support among voters than the National Labour Organization. In both countries the crisis within the party and within government meant that social democracy lost some of its power, leading to a shift to the right. In Germany parliamentary democracy was immediately placed at risk, whereas in Britain the parliamentary system was able to weather the crisis.

Events suddenly gathered pace in the United Kingdom in 1931. New loans were taken out in an attempt to support the pound. Snowden announced an emergency budget that reduced the salaries of government employees by 10 per cent and of teachers by as much as 15 per cent. In the case of police officers, the reduction was limited to 5 per cent out of fear for public safety. On 15 September the navy mutinied off the coast at Invergordon. On the 21st, on the advice of the Bank of England, the government was forced to abandon the link between the pound and the gold standard, resulting in a devaluation of the former, which immediately fell from $4.86 to $3.80 and then to $3.40. The government could hardly have devised a more effective means of dealing with the crisis, and if the British economy began to recover after the summer of

1932, then this was due entirely to the increased competitiveness of the country's export industry, especially car manufacture.

For the outside world, conversely, the decision taken by the government in London had disastrous consequences, as the British economic historian Adam Tooze explains:

> The anchor of the global financial system had torn loose. Britain's abandonment of gold turned a severe recession into a profound crisis of the international economy. By the end of September, twelve countries had followed Britain in allowing their currencies to float freely. Eleven more currencies had devalued their exchange rates while retaining a gold peg; whilst those that stayed on gold at their old parities, like Germany, France and the Netherlands, had no option but to defend their balance of payments by adopting draconian restrictions on currency convertibility and trade.[162]

Tooze believes that it was essentially as a result of the devaluation of the British pound that the volume of German exports fell by a further 30 per cent in 1931–2.

It was a reflection of the British understanding of democracy that in spite of its parliamentary majority the National Government wanted an electoral mandate at the earliest available opportunity. Elections were set for 27 October 1931. The government parties pooled their resources and agreed on a single candidate in each constituency. In the course of the election campaign no one attacked the Labour Party as stridently as Philip Snowden, who insisted that electors had a choice 'between prosperity and ruin' and accused his former friends in the party of 'bolshevism run mad'.[163] The Conservatives openly advocated protective tariffs, while twenty-nine out of Sir John Simon's fifty-nine Liberals added their voices to this demand as an emergency measure, campaigning as the National Liberal Party. Conversely, thirty Liberal parliamentarians, under the leadership of Sir Herbert Samuel, continued to champion free trade. The National Government parties jointly asked electors for a 'doctor's mandate' in the form of powers to do whatever they thought was necessary.

The outcome of the elections was a triumph for the ruling parties, who won 67 per cent of the votes cast, returning 554 MPs to the lower house. The Conservatives won a 55 per cent share of the vote, with 473 MPs, while the National Liberal Party returned thirty-five MPs, the Liberal Party thirty-three and the National Labour Organization thirteen. The three smaller government parties won 3.7 per cent, 6.5 per cent and 1.5 per cent of the total votes cast. The Labour Party, which had had 288 seats in May 1929, now had only fifty-two, although its share of the vote – 30.8 per cent in 1931 compared with 37.1 per cent two and a half years earlier – fell rather less dramatically than these figures might suggest. The Independent Liberals in opposition won four seats, other parties five. The Communist Party and the New Party returned no MPs at all, the former polling 70,000 votes, or 0.3 per cent of the total, the latter around 40,000, or 0.2 per cent. It is possible that more voters would have supported the radical parties on the extreme right and extreme left if the electoral system had been based on proportional representation, but the traditional first-past-the-post system meant that every vote for an extreme party seemed to the voter to be wasted, encouraging a trend to support the centre-ground parties that voters trusted to form the next government or at least to play a part in government.

In spite of the Conservatives' success, Ramsay MacDonald remained the country's prime minister with the agreement of the parties in government. Sir John Simon, who was the leader of the National Liberals, became foreign secretary, while the Tory Neville Chamberlain took over as chancellor of the exchequer. The protective tariffs promised in the election campaign were introduced in February 1932 in the form of a 10 per cent surcharge on imported goods, a move that marked Great Britain's rejection of its Victorian legacy of free trade. As for the Commonwealth nations, a system of preferential tariffs was established at the Empire Conference in Ottawa in August 1932, and the pound was elevated to the status of the leading currency within the sterling zone. In the wake of the Ottawa resolutions, the share of British exports to the nations and colonies of the Empire rose between 1934 and 1938 from 35 per cent to 41.3 per cent of the pre-war figures, while the share of imports from the Empire went up from 29.6 per cent to 41.2 per cent, an important factor in overcoming the depression not only in Great Britain but also in the Commonwealth, but not in the rest of the world.

The National Government turned its back on economic liberalism in the domestic market, too. Two acts passed in 1931 and 1933 established supervisory bodies to oversee the marketing of potatoes, milk, pork and other types of agricultural produce. In 1932 a Wheat Act established a nationally guaranteed standard price for this particular cereal crop, while the next three years witnessed the enactment of laws designed to encourage the economic reconstruction of those regions particularly badly hit by the crisis and to improve production and market conditions in the cotton industry and the country's shipyards. But at the height of the depression the unemployed did not have the impression that the government in London was doing enough to mitigate their plight. In 1931 hunger marches in around thirty British towns and cities, including Rochdale, Belfast and Liverpool, were marred by clashes with the police and army units deployed to control the unemployed demonstrators. In comparison with Germany, these clashes were, admittedly, generally harmless.

A national hunger march in October 1932 was particularly widely reported. Like many other similar marches, it was organized by the National Unemployed Workers Movement (NUWM), an organization founded in 1921 and led initially by Wal Hannington and later by Sid Elias, two members of the Communist Party. In other such groups, too, Communists set the tone. In the course of the demonstrations in October 1932, public buildings and welfare offices in many towns and cities were besieged, and in London, Manchester, Glasgow and south Wales there were clashes with the police. By December 1932 some 1,300 members of the NUWM had been arrested, and 421 of them, including Hannington and Elias, were imprisoned for affray. In January 1933 the TUC made a half-hearted attempt to form an unemployed association of its own, but without any real success.

The Labour Party drew a clear distinction between itself and the Communists when in 1930 it declared that membership of pro-Communist organizations such as the League against Imperialism, the Left Wing Movement, the Friends of Soviet Russia and the NUWM was incompatible with holding elected office within the Labour Party. The left wing of the party felt that such measures were far too defensive. Starting in the summer of 1930, the Independent Labour Party, which hoped to give the party as a whole a clear-cut socialist profile, began to distance itself increasingly from the Labour Party and at the elections for the lower house in October 1931 it put forward its own candidates, who were independent of those of the Labour Party itself, although following their election, all five of the ILP MPs joined the Labour benches. The definitive break came in 1932, when the majority of members of the ILP decided to part company with the Labour Party, leading to a rapid fall in ILP membership from 17,000 in 1932 to 4,400 in 1935.

Shortly before the Labour Party conference in Leicester in October 1932, when George Lansbury took over the running of the party following Henderson's resignation, several ILP activists under their chairman Frank Wise joined forces with Ernest Bevin's Society for Socialist Inquiry and Propaganda that had been formed the previous year and founded the Socialist League that was led initially by Wise, then, following his death in 1933, by the left-wing Labour MP Sir Stafford Cripps. In spite of this, the Labour Party did not move to the left as the Socialist League had hoped. In opposition, too, the Labour Party pursued a policy of moderation, advocating social reform within the framework of the existing political system.

In 1931–2, the changes that took place on the right of the political spectrum were more far-reaching than those on the left. Little remained of Mosley's New Party following the debacle of the elections to the lower house, and in January 1932, Mosley visited Italy in the company of Harold Nicolson and other comrades-in-arms. Here he had a chance to get to know Mussolini's Fascist regime at first hand and to meet the Duce in person. He was deeply impressed by all that he saw and heard. In April he broke with Nicolson, whose response to Fascism was as cool as that of Lady Cynthia Mosley. In the summer of 1932 Mosley drafted a programme with the title 'The Greater Britain', a title first used in 1868 by Sir Charles Dilke in his bestselling book. In it Mosley attacked Britain's technological backwardness, demanded a consistently protectionist economic policy and criticized the present parliamentary system for its failure to adapt to the needs of the twentieth century. The alternative could be only an authoritarian state, a modern dictatorship in which a corporative parliament would from time to time receive reports from the government and if necessary respond to them with a vote of no confidence, in which case the king, not parliament, would have the power to appoint a new government.

Mosley founded the British Union of Fascists, or BUF, on 1 October 1932. According to its own estimates, it had built up a membership of between 40,000 and 50,000 within a matter of only two years, but it never achieved a higher figure than this. With their black party uniforms, Mosley's followers attracted as much attention as they did with their violence towards their political opponents, chief of whom were the Communists, to say nothing of their attacks on Jews. Until 1935 Fascist Italy and Mussolini's regime remained Mosley's ideal but, following his meeting with Hitler in April of that year, he looked increasingly to National Socialist Germany.

Mosley was encouraged in his sympathy for National Socialism by Diana Mitford, the daughter of Lord Redesdale, who became his mistress in early 1933 and his wife in 1936, three years after Lady Cynthia's death. For a time the right-wing broadsheets gave the British Union of Fascists their unstinting support: 'Hurrah for the Blackshirts!' ran the headline of the first of a series of articles about Mosley that appeared in Lord Rothermere's *Daily Mail* on 15 January 1934. On 7 June, during a speech that Mosley delivered at a major rally organized by the BUF at Olympia in London, his supporters launched a well-organized attack on left-wing hecklers. The general public reacted with considerable shock to this demonstration of violence, which was in stark contrast to the traditional style of political debate in Britain. Public support for the BUF began to ebb away, and within a short space of time the organization had lost the majority of its members.

Apart from the British Union of Fascists, there were two other organizations in Great Britain that flaunted their Fascist credentials: the British Fascists were formed in 1923–4 and supported Mosley's movement, while the Imperial Fascist League of 1928 claimed to feel repulsed by the plebeian appearance of his Blackshirts. But sympathy for Italian Fascism went beyond the confines of those organizations that called themselves Fascist, applying in particular to the 'Neo-Tories' associated with the journalist Douglas Jerrold, who edited *The English Review* from 1931 to 1935, historians Charles Petrie and Arthur Bryant, the Nietzschean Anthony Mario Ludovici, the acting editor in chief of the crypto-Fascist journal *Everyman*, Francis Yeats-Brown, and Conservative MP Viscount Lymington. This group of individuals influenced the intellectual life of the country from the late 1920s, not least through their contributions to the aforementioned journals. (The term 'Neo-Tories' was in fact coined by George Orwell in 1945.)

The position adopted by these Neo-Tories was in many respects similar to that taken by the advocators of the Conservative Revolution in Germany. Both groups were in regular contact with one another and both shared a characteristic wholly lacking from groups such as Jeune Droite and L'Ordre Nouveau in France, namely, the tendency to glorify the experience of war. The Neo-Tories' critique of liberalism and democracy was no less radical than that of the Young Conservatives in Germany. Both groups regarded parliamentarianism as an outmoded political system that needed to be replaced by a well-organized authoritarian state. But unlike most German Young Conservatives, the Neo-Tories had no desire to see this state backed by a mass plebiscite: rather, the monarchy was to be strengthened at the expense of the existing representation of the people. Their ideal was not a charismatic leader but a king of the kind that England had known before the Glorious Revolution of 1688. And eugenics played a more significant role with the Neo-Tories than it did with the authors of the Conservative Revolution inasmuch as they were afraid of the progressive biological degeneration of British society. Both groups were anti-Semitic, but both shied away from physical violence against Jews.

Fascist Italy fascinated the Neo-Tories above all on account of the resolve with which it curtailed the activities of the political left. Like many of the Young Conservatives in Germany, the Neo-Tories saw in the *stato corporativo* an alternative to a parliamentary system that they felt had outlived its usefulness. Their expert on Fascism was Charles Petrie, whom Jerrold appointed the foreign affairs editor of *The English Review* in 1931. In November 1932 Petrie and Lymington attended an international conference on Fascism organized by the Fondazione Volta. Among other conference visitors were the two economists Werner Sombart and Erwin von Beckerath, the former president of the Reichsbank, Hjalmar Schacht, and two prominent National Socialists, Hermann Göring, who at that date was the leader of the Reichstag, and Alfred Rosenberg, the editor in chief of the *Völkischer Beobachter*. Petrie gave a speech on 'The Fundamental Unity of European Civilisation' that amounted to a sustained attack on the spirit of the French Revolution and that met with Mussolini's explicit approval. Petrie called Fascist Italy, with its combination of tradition and modernity, a 'microcosm of the continent', describing his homecoming to Great Britain as 'returning to nonsense from sense'.[164]

For all their admiration of Mussolini (and, in the case of other Neo-Tories such as Bryant and Yeats-Brown, of Hitler, too), the Neo-Tories kept their distance from the Fascist and, more especially, the National Socialist tendency to mobilize street protests, don paramilitary uniforms and glorify violence. They were not interested in introducing the Fascist system to their own country or in any form of violent overthrow of the existing system. Central to their arguments was a critique of the status quo at home as embodied, in their view, by the Conservative leader, Stanley Baldwin, who was perpetually at pains to reconcile opposing factions.

Baldwin's willingness to allow India to slide gradually into independence met with indignant opposition not only from the Neo-Tories but also from Tory diehards such as Churchill and Lord Lloyd, the former governor of

Bombay and later the high commissioner in Egypt and the Sudan. In January 1931 Churchill resigned from Baldwin's shadow cabinet in protest at its policy towards the subcontinent, and in November 1933 Lord Lloyd caused a stir with his radically Conservative catalogue of demands including autarchy for the Empire and national labour service. But he was unwilling to mount a putsch to oust Baldwin from power, as the Neo-Tories hoped he would.

Baldwin's Conservative critics enjoyed journalistic support from both Beaverbrook and Rothermere, who used their newspapers and their United Empire Party, which they founded in 1931, to demand the transformation of the Empire into a free trade zone, while at the same time resisting the idea of any further weakening of the British Empire. Their mass-circulation newspapers – principally Beaverbrook's *Daily Express* and Rothermere's *Daily Mail* – reached an audience of millions. By 1933/4 they had abandoned all pretence of defending parliamentary democracy and turned, instead, to lauding the advantages of right-wing dictatorships such as those in Italy and Germany, prompting the *New York Times* to draw the conclusion in October 1933 that they were hoping to introduce a similar system into Great Britain. But if this were to come to pass, the paper went on, the change would find symbolic expression not in 'the black shirt of Italy' or 'the brown of Germany' but in 'a dash of scarlet to suggest the ceremonial robes which Viscount Rothermere and Baron Beaverbrook wear in the House of Lords on spectacular occasions'.[165]

The Neo-Tories were no mere marginal phenomenon in British politics but commanded firm support among Conservative grandees and, like them, had no hesitation in maintaining links, however infrequent, with Mosley's Fascists, which they did through elitist circles such as the January Club that was formed in early 1934. Like many Conservative diehards they were encouraged by Herbert Butterfield's *The Whig Interpretation of History*, which first appeared in 1931, to reject what they regarded as the Liberal falsification of English history since Magna Carta and to propose in its place a transfiguring image of a medieval and chivalric 'Merry England'. With their bellicose cult of manhood, they consorted with the chauvinist gutter press to oppose the widespread pacifism that found expression not only in the lively public interest in the American film version of Erich Maria Remarque's German anti-war novel, *All Quiet on the Western Front*, but also in the legendary resolution of the Oxford Union in February 1933, 'This House will not fight for King or country'.

In no other area did the differences between the political climate in Great Britain and that in Germany find such stark expression in the early 1930s as in the arguments between pacifists and bellicists. In Germany, all public screenings of *All Quiet on the Western Front* were banned at the end of 1930 following violent protests by the National Socialists, the government arguing that any further showings risked 'jeopardizing Germany's standing'. Books that glorified the war found a mass readership in Germany, but not in Britain. (From a purely literary point of view, most of these novels were on a substantially lower

level than Ernst Jünger's *Storm of Steel* of 1920.) At more or less the same time
as Oxford's students were declaring their unconditional desire for peace, the
Student Committees of the German Universities had long since been taken
over by the National Socialist German Students' Union.

In Germany it was Young Conservative writers who represented the dominant intellectual trend in the early 1930s, whereas the British Neo-Tories'
appeal remained restricted to the upper classes and, within those classes, to the
generation of military officers who had fought on the front line in the First
World War. It was beyond their means to acquire any kind of cultural hegemony
in Britain. Bloomsbury was the stronghold and epitome of left-wing intellectual England and continued to be even more influential than the circle of
writers associated with *The English Review*. The Left Book Club of the publisher
Victor Gollancz had 50,000 subscribers, substantially more than the Right
Book Club, which, formed in 1937, never had more than 20,000.

The differences between Great Britain and Germany in the early 1930s can
be traced back to different political traditions in general and to the fact that
political liberalism proved more resilient in Britain than in Germany, where,
almost without exception, liberal voters switched to the National Socialists
between 1930 and 1933. In Britain, conversely, liberalism had, as it were, long
since subverted both the Conservatives and the Labour Party. In short, the
decline of the Liberal Party was by no means synonymous with the decline of
English liberalism, which continued to thrive in both of the major political
parties and remained the dominant political force even during the crisis of
1929 and later, guaranteeing the continuity of the country's institutions.

Weimar's Downfall: Hitler's Road to Power

On 1 June 1932 the evening edition of the Social Democrats' party newspaper
Vorwärts carried a banner headline that has entered the history books: 'The
Cabinet of the Barons'. The cabinet that took over from Heinrich Brüning after
the latter had been toppled from power comprised a count, four barons, two
other aristocrats and only three bourgeois ministers. At its head was a politician who had been specially chosen by the new defence minister Kurt
Schleicher: Franz von Papen, a former officer in the general staff, who had
been born in 1879 and who later served as military attaché at the German
Embassy in Washington. He owned lands in Westphalia, was a keen horseman,
a major shareholder and chairman of the supervisory board of the Centre
Party's official newspaper *Germania* and a board member of several agricultural organizations. Through his wife he was also closely associated with heavy
industry in the Saarland.

Right up until the elections of 24 April 1932, Papen had been a member of
the Prussian Landtag, a Centre Party backbencher who was on the extreme
right of the party. Schleicher reckoned that Papen would bind the Centre Party

to the new government just as effectively as Brüning had done before him. But on 31 May, immediately after Hindenburg had invited Papen to form a new government, the leader of the Centre Party, Ludwig Kaas, made it clear to Papen that his party would regard him as a traitor if he attempted to succeed Brüning. Hindenburg responded by appealing to Papen's sense of honour, whereupon the latter accepted the post of chancellor and resigned from the Centre Party. In order to invest the new government with a sense of cross-party unity, three German Nationalist members of the cabinet resigned from their party: the minister of the interior, Baron Wilhelm von Gayl; the minister for nutrition, Baron Magnus von Braun; and the justice minister, Franz Gürtner. Two other ministers who were close to the German Nationalists were the foreign minister, Baron Konstantin von Neurath, who had previously been the German ambassador in London, and the finance minister, Count Lutz Schwerin von Krosigk. The defence minister, Kurt von Schleicher, was generally regarded as the most powerful figure in the government.

On 4 June, two days after Papen had named his cabinet, Hindenburg met one of the conditions laid down by Hitler in return for his support for the new government: he dissolved the Reichstag and set a date for new elections on 31 July. And on 14 June he signed Papen's first emergency decree: based on preliminary work by Brüning's government, it reduced unemployment benefits by an average of 23 per cent and shortened from twenty to six weeks the period for which such support was payable, effectively removing any claim to welfare and replacing it with a system that came nowhere near providing a subsistence level of income. Two days later the government made good on a second promise that Schleicher had given Hitler on 4 June, lifting the ban on the SA and SS that Brüning's government had imposed on 13 April 1932. The ban on the wearing of uniforms, which had been in place since December 1931, was likewise lifted.

That same day, 16 June 1932, the reparations conference that should have begun in January but which had been postponed at Brüning's request finally opened in Lausanne. Papen was now able to reap the rewards of his predecessor's policy of holding out, and the agreement that the new chancellor signed on 9 July provided for a final German payment of a maximum of 3,000 million Reichsmarks only after three years at the earliest or over a longer period of time in the form of national debenture bonds – always assuming that the country's finances had in the meantime been restored to an even keel. Ratification of the agreement by the parliaments in Paris, London and Rome still depended on the United States' willingness to accept a satisfactory settlement of inter-Allied debts, with the result that the Lausanne agreement never actually came into force. In practice, however, it spelt the end of both German reparations and inter-Allied war debts.

The outcome of the Lausanne conference was a triumph for Papen's foreign policy, and yet it was acknowledged as such only by the liberal press and by the Social Democrats, with the result that it did little to calm the situation at home.

The Reichstag elections of July 1932 were the bloodiest ever seen in Germany, most of the acts of violence being committed by Communists and National Socialists. The lifting of the ban on the SA was followed in many parts of the country by bloody clashes that were particularly violent in the industrial regions of the Rhine and the Ruhr. During the first half of June there were three fatalities in political rioting in Prussia: two National Socialists and one Communist. During the second half of the month – following the lifting of the ban on the SA and on the wearing of uniforms – the number of politically motivated deaths rose to seventeen: twelve National Socialists and five Communists. Sundays were particularly bloody, and on 10 July, for example, there were seventeen fatalities throughout the country, not including ten individuals who later died of their injuries and 181 who were seriously injured.

There was a clear connection between the end of the ban on the SA and the escalation of violence, and yet Papen's cabinet consistently blamed the Prussian police and, with it, the Prussian government for the reign of terror that threatened to engulf the nation's streets. At the cabinet meeting on 11 July, the minister of the interior, Wilhelm von Gayl, demanded the appointment of a federal commissioner for Prussia, recommending Papen for the post and suggesting that he then appoint a series of assistant commissioners. The federal government agreed to the proposal and the very next day set a deadline of 20 July, only for Prussia's minister of the interior, the Social Democrat Carl Severing, to counter this plan by issuing a decree on the 12th that made it easier to ban open-air meetings and processions and requiring the police to proceed with the utmost rigour against the illegal bearing of weapons. For the present, the blow that was aimed at Prussia seemed to have been averted.

In the event, however, the government was able to stick to its original timetable thanks to the events of Bloody Sunday in Altona on 17 July. An unusual combination of poor decisions by politicians, bureaucrats and the police meant that a march by the SA through Communist strongholds in Altona – at that date still a part of Prussia – ended in nineteen civilian deaths, most of them caused by police bullets. Severing's failure to impose a state of emergency and to demonstrate his strength of purpose allowed the federal government to step in, and on 18 July, without consulting any of the regional assemblies, it issued a total ban on outdoor meetings and invited three members of the Prussian cabinet – the welfare minister, Heinrich Hirtsiefer of the Centre Party replacing the prime minister Otto Braun, who was on sick leave; the minister of the interior, Carl Severing; and the independent finance minister, Otto Klepper – to attend a meeting at the federal chancellery at ten o'clock in the morning of 20 July.

Papen greeted the three ministers with what amounted to the announcement of a coup against Prussia: appealing to Article 48 of the federal constitution, Hindenburg appointed Papen the commissioner for Prussia, empowering him to dismiss the members of the Prussia state ministry, to take over the duties of the prime minister and to appoint other commissioners to run the various Prussian ministries. Papen then announced that on the basis of the decree he was relieving Braun and Severing of their posts and appointing the mayor of Essen, Franz Bracht, as the Prussian minister of the interior.

The Prussian government responded by lodging an appeal with the Federal Court in Leipzig, arguing that the measures violated both the national and the Prussian constitution. On the other hand there was no attempt on the part of the Prussian government to appeal to the nation as a whole or to the working masses. Nor did the Social Democrats, the Free Trade Unions or the Reichsbanner issue any such call to arms, the Social Democrats merely announcing that the 'Cabinet of Barons' would receive its just deserts in the Reichstag elections on 31 July. Young Reichsbanner activists in particular were appalled at the lack of any real resistance, seeing in it a capitulation to violence, a judgement subsequently repeated by history.

And yet there were compelling reasons for the Social Democrats' actions. The majority of Germans were no longer behind the Prussian government, having demonstrated their lack of trust in it in the elections on 24 April, in the process dealing a fatal blow to the Social Democrats' sense of democratic legitimacy. A general strike was unthinkable in the light of mass unemployment: in June 1932 it stood officially at 5.5 million but in reality was rather higher. To that extent the situation in July 1932 was completely different from the one in March 1920 when a general strike had been organized against the Kapp–Lüttwitz Putsch, at a time of almost full employment in Germany. On that occasion, moreover, the striking workers had known that they had the backing of the state's legitimate authority. But the Prussian coup had been ordered by a president whom the nation had elected only a short time previously, making it unlikely that government employers or police officers would rebel in any appreciable numbers.

Meanwhile, the workforce was more divided than ever. In the summer of 1931 the Communists had tried to bring down the coalition in Prussia by supporting a call for a referendum demanding the dissolution of the Landtag and initiated by the nationalist right. Although it was ultimately unsuccessful, it was simply inconceivable that the Social Democrats and Communists would join forces to reinstate Braun's government, making the Communists' question as to whether the Social Democrats and Free Trade Unions were willing to take part in a general strike with them a mere exercise in empty rhetoric. Moreover, the Reichsbanner was unprepared both militarily and psychologically for an armed struggle against the country's armed forces. In this regard the Republican Reichsbanner lacked the muscle of right-wing paramilitary organizations such as the SA, SS and Stahlhelm, all of which would undoubtedly have played an active role in any confrontation with the 'Marxists'. In the summer of 1932 a civil war would inevitably end badly for the democratic left and involve the most terrible sacrifices.

The reasons for this dilemma can be traced back to much earlier events. The Social Democrats' supine acceptance of the Prussian coup was also a consequence of their having spent the previous twenty months propping up the Prussian government and, indeed, of having played a leading role in government over a much longer period. Objectively speaking, it was impossible for the Social Democrats to be both a party of government – formally in Prussia and informally in the country as a whole – and at the same time a party preparing for civil war. On 20 July 1932 the Social Democrats forfeited all their remaining power, which they had been able to maintain for so long only because they had staked everything on a single card since the autumn of 1930, namely, their ability to defeat the National Socialists on the basis of the constitution and in league with the moderate forces of the bourgeoisie. When the SPD decided to adopt this policy, it remained true to its underlying principles, its vote for a legally binding course of action deriving from its view that a civil war, which it saw as the greatest of all evils, had to be avoided at all costs. It had followed this belief on the outbreak of the First World War in the summer of 1914 and again during the revolution of 1918/19. And it clung to this creed even when there was practically no one left, apart from the Centre Party and its own members, willing to defend the Weimar constitution any longer and when the democratic parties knew that they still had only a minority of the German people behind them.

The removal from office of Braun's government brought to an end an exceptional chapter in Prussian history. After 1918 the Hohenzollern state had turned into the Republic's most reliable prop. The old state of Prussia had not disappeared completely from the map but until the spring of 1932 it remained dominated by the three Weimar coalition parties. The great purge began immediately after the Prussian coup. Secretaries of state and ministerial heads were pensioned off, as were all the heads of regional councils and police chiefs who had belonged to the previous coalition parties. All of them were replaced by Conservative officials, most of whom were German Nationalists. Of the four Social Democratic regional presidents, only one remained: Gustav Noske, who headed the provincial administration in Hanover. In the view of the federal government, the former Social Democratic defence minister occupied a position so far to the right of his party that he was allowed to retain the post that he had held since July 1920.

The Social Democrats hoped that in the Reichstag elections on 31 July 1932 they would be able to give Papen's government the reply that they felt it deserved in the wake of the Prussian coup, but in the event their hopes remained unfulfilled. At first sight, at least, the result was a triumph for Hitler. Some 84.1 per cent of the electorate took part, the highest turnout since 1920, with the NSDAP polling 37.4 per cent of the total, an increase of 19.1 percentage points when compared with the previous elections to the Reichstag on 14 September 1930. The number of National Socialist seats went up from 107 to 230. The Communists recorded far more modest gains, climbing from 13.1 per cent to 14.3 per cent. The two Catholic parties also improved their showing: the Centre

Party's share of the vote rose from 11.8 per cent to 12.5 per cent, that of the Bavarian People's Party from 3 per cent to 3.2 per cent. The other parties all lost votes. The Social Democrats dropped from 24.5 per cent to 21.6 per cent, the German National People's Party from 7 per cent to 5.9 per cent, the German People's Party from 4.5 per cent to 1.2 per cent and the German State Party from 3.8 per cent to 1 per cent. Between them, the other parties polled 2.5 per cent of the total votes cast.

The National Socialists had succeeded in taking votes from the Liberal centre ground and the moderate right as well as from the various splinter parties, while also attracting the votes of numerous first-time voters and of Germans who had never voted before. The north and east of the country showed a far greater swing to the National Socialists than the south or the west, but even in Hessen, Franconia, the Palatinate and northern Württemberg, the NSDAP had outstripped all the other parties. Among all the thirty-five constituencies the National Socialists' front runner was Schleswig-Holstein, where the NSDAP received 51 per cent of the votes.

As had been the case in 1930, Catholics and, to a lesser extent, the internally divided 'Marxist' camp remained relatively untouched by the slogans of the National Socialists. Among middle-class Protestants, only conservative voters had maintained a modicum of independence from the NSDAP. Liberalism had been practically wiped out and could no longer rely on any fixed group of voters but was so marked by nationalism as to be susceptible to the promises of the National Socialists. The NSDAP was now the biggest protest party opposed to the Weimar Republic and derived support from all who did not hold strong convictions to the contrary. Few noticed that Hitler and his party were making such contradictory promises. All that mattered for them was the hope that in the wake of a 'national revolution' Germany and the Germans would fare better than they felt was the case at present.

But the elections failed to produce a parliamentary majority. There was a negative majority for the two totalitarian parties, the National Socialists and the Communists, who together polled 51.7 per cent of the votes, winning 319 out of a total of 608 seats in the Reichstag. If we add together the seats of all the right-wing parties, namely, the NSDAP, the German National People's Party, the German People's Party and a number of smaller groups, they still did not have a majority. A coalition between the NSDAP and the two Catholic parties was ruled out when the latter insisted on constitutional guarantees that Hitler was unwilling to provide.

In spite of their electoral successes, the National Socialists were bitterly disappointed at the fact that they were manifestly no closer to political power than they had been before the election. Their anger found expression in a wave of bloody confrontations with their political opponents in early August, the SA orchestrating a series of particularly violent attacks in the area of Germany where it was strongest: the east of the country. By 9 August the government had accepted the need for a new emergency decree aimed at combating political terror, extending the death penalty to counts of political murder and setting up special courts in the areas that were especially at risk.

Three days earlier Hitler had met the country's defence minister for secret talks near Berlin. In the course of their meeting, he was able to persuade Schleicher to let him run the government and to entrust the NSDAP with a whole series of posts ranging from prime minister of Prussia to joint appointments of the posts of minister of the interior, education and agriculture in both Prussia and the country as a whole. The National Socialists, Hitler insisted, must also be allowed to run the federal ministry of justice and a new ministry of aviation. In agreeing to Hitler's demands, Schleicher was guilty of a dramatic volte-face, for as recently as the beginning of August 1932 he had felt that it was sufficient for him to ensure that the armed forces did not fall into National Socialist hands.

Hindenburg, who was currently on holiday on his estates at Neudeck in East Prussia, took a very different view of the situation and rejected Schleicher's proposal in no uncertain terms, maintaining his position on his return to Berlin, when Papen suggested appointing Hitler chancellor at the head of a majority government that also included the Centre Party. This was the occasion when Hindenburg made his oft-cited remark that people were deluding themselves if they thought that he was going to make a 'Bohemian private' the chancellor of Germany.

In government circles, too, there was widespread disagreement on the best way to deal with Hitler. The minister of justice, Franz Gürtner, and the finance minister, Lutz Schwerin von Krosigk, both supported the idea of the National Socialists' playing a part in government, whereas the minister of the interior, Wilhelm von Gayl, was emphatically opposed to it. He was even ready to fight a life and death battle with the NSDAP, preferring to advocate a 'revolution from above' involving the dissolution of the Reichstag, a delay to new elections beyond the sixty days demanded by the constitution and the imposition of a new law affecting franchise.

The following day, 11 August, the government's traditional constitutional celebrations were held in the presence of the president. This was the first time in this history of the Weimar Republic that a speaker inveighed against the 1919 constitution, the minister of the interior, Wilhelm von Gayl, beginning his address by observing that the Weimar constitution, far from uniting his fellow countrymen and women, was driving them apart. He advocated changes to the constitution in the direction of greater authoritarianism, such changes to include raising the voting age, additional votes for breadwinners and mothers, greater independence for government authorities and the creation of a new first chamber made up of professionals as a counterweight to the Reichstag. Gayl's proposals looked forward to the 'new state' that was described at greater length by the journalist Walther Schotte in an official pamphlet with the same title and with an introduction signed by the chancellor. They also encapsulated the internal reforms long envisaged by the proponents of the Conservative Revolution and discussed in particular by the Ring Movement associated with Heinrich von Gleichen-Russwurm, the founder of the Gentlemen's Club, and with the group of contributors to the journal *Die Tat* (Action) and its editor, Hans Zehrer.

Hitler planned to hold talks with the chancellor on 12 August and with Hindenburg on the 13th. In order to underline his claim to power he had summoned several units of his SA to Berlin and deployed them around the capital. But on the morning of the 13th he learnt from Schleicher and Papen that Hindenburg was unwilling to offer him the post of chancellor. Acting without authority, Papen offered him the post of deputy chancellor and even promised to step down in favour of Hitler after a suitable period of time had elapsed. But Hitler turned down the offer and continued to insist on the post of chancellor.

The meeting with Hindenburg on the afternoon of 13 August was also attended by Papen and the president's secretary of state, Otto Meissner, together with two representatives of the National Socialists, the chief of staff of the SA, Ernst Röhm, and the leader of the NSDAP in the Reichstag, Wilhelm Frick. It proved to be Hitler's worst political defeat since his failed putsch of 8/9 November 1923. According to Meissner's minutes of the meeting, Hindenburg rejected Hitler's demand to be appointed chancellor with a 'clear and emphatic no': 'He could not answer to God, to his conscience or to his country for granting complete control of the government to a single party, especially a party unilaterally opposed to all who thought differently.'[166]

The official account of the meeting was so brief that Hitler felt publicly humiliated, too. Even before he saw a copy of the communiqué, he was already reproaching Papen for his alleged failure to make it clear that Hindenburg had already reached a decision. And he threatened Papen and Meissner, claiming that subsequent developments would lead inexorably to the solution that he himself had proposed or, alternatively, to Hindenburg's fall from power. The government, he went on, would be placed in a serious predicament, with increasingly outspoken opposition. He refused to accept responsibility for the consequences. It was a clear case of blackmail: if Hitler's claim to power was not met, he threatened to abandon his former promise to rely on the legal process and to resort instead to revolutionary violence and civil war.

On 30 August, Papen, Gayl and Schleicher descended on Neudeck to discuss the situation with Hindenburg. Papen spoke of the need to dissolve the Reichstag and recommended delaying the new elections beyond the sixty-day deadline demanded by the constitution. Although such a delay violated Article 25 of the constitution, there was a 'national emergency' that justified such a course of action: 'In his oath the president has taken it upon himself to defend the German people from harm, and new elections in these politically charged times, with all their acts of terror and murder, would undoubtedly cause great harm to the German people.'[167] A similar view was expressed by Gayl, who at the cabinet meeting on 10 August had been one of the first to propose a delay in holding the new elections.

Hindenburg had no hesitation in agreeing to Papen's and Gayl's recommendation, declaring that 'in the state of national emergency following the dissolution of the Reichstag', his aim was to avoid making things worse for the German people and that he could square it with his conscience 'that the provisions of Article 25 be interpreted in such a way that in the current situation new elections be postponed to a later date'.[168] For Papen, Gayl and Schleicher, Hindenburg's agreement was no less important than the authorization to dissolve the Reichstag, which the president granted unconditionally and signed at once.

The emergency meeting at Neudeck took place on the same day – 30 August 1932 – as the constituent session of the newly elected Reichstag. In keeping with an unwritten ruling, the candidate from the largest party was elected its leader: the National Socialist Hermann Göring. The second session took place on 12 September 1932, when the only item on the agenda was the acceptance of a government statement, but the Communists opened the session by asking for a change to the agenda, proposing that the house begin by dealing with their party's motions to revoke two new decrees – the emergency decree of 4 September designed to stimulate the economy, the other a related decree dated 5 September and intended to increase and preserve job opportunities – and then to proceed to a series of votes of no confidence in Papen's cabinet. It would have been enough for a single member of the Reichstag to object to this proposal for it to be rejected in its entirety, but not a single voice was raised in opposition. The NSDAP asked for a half-hour delay in order to consult with Hitler. A majority of members agreed to this request.

Papen was taken by complete surprise by this move on the part of the Communist Party and spent the half-hour break getting hold of Hindenburg's order dissolving the Reichstag, which he then placed in front of the leader of the house after Göring had twice deliberately ignored his, Papen's, attempts to take the floor. Göring also proceeded to ignore the file from Hindenburg and instead asked the house to vote on the two Communist Party motions together, announcing the outcome of the vote long after the members of the government had left the chamber: of the 560 votes cast, one was invalid; 512 delegates had voted yes, forty-two no and five had abstained. The no votes were those of the German National People's Party and the German People's Party; the representatives of a handful of smaller parties had absented themselves from the vote. All other parties, from the National Socialists to the Communists, had voted in favour of the Communist Party's motions.

The vote was invalid because the Reichstag had been dissolved the moment the chancellor placed the order for its dissolution on Göring's desk, but the political impact of the vote could not be ignored, more than four-fifths of all delegates having expressed their lack of confidence in Papen's government. Indeed, it was Papen's negligence that had led to this debacle.

By the time the cabinet met two days later to decide on its next move, Papen no longer felt equal to the trial of strength for which he had gained Hindenburg's support in Neudeck on 30 August. Only Gayl and Schleicher now supported an indefinite delay to the new elections. Schleicher pointed out that three experts on constitutional law, Carl Schmitt, Erwin Jacoby and Carl Bilfinger, all of whom had defended the government in the case of Prussia vs the Reich, agreed that in the present case there was indeed a 'true state of emergency', but Papen and his other ministers were not convinced that the time had come to depart from the constitution. On 17 September the cabinet decided to propose 6 November as the date of the new elections. This was the last possible date that they could offer the president, who signed the relevant decree on 20 September.

In spite of his defeat in the Reichstag, Papen was still keen to make sweeping changes to the constitution, and on the evening of 12 September he used a radio address to announce that he was working on a revised constitution in keeping with the proposals put forward by Gayl on 11 August. A referendum would be held to decide the matter. A month later, Papen used a conference of the Association of Bavarian Industrialists in Munich on 12 October 1932 to present his ideas on conservative reform within a wider historical and, indeed, theological framework. In this he was almost certainly inspired by the Young Conservative writer Edgar Jung, a High-Church Protestant whose anti-parliamentary, anti-democratic book, *The Rule of the Inferior*, had appeared in 1927. In particular, Papen appealed to the 'invisible floodwaters of the sacrum imperium, the indestructible idea of the Holy German Empire'.

Throughout this crisis, the myth of the German Empire continued to increase in potency, while at the same time support for the Republic increasingly ebbed away. But the idea of the Reich also served to justify Germany's claim to be seen as more than just a national state in the western, post-1789 sense. In 1932, the editor of the Young Conservatives' *Deutsches Volkstum*, Wilhelm Stapel, announced that 'Only a Germany led by Germans can be a Europe at peace'. For his part, the Catholic journalist Waldemar Gurian, a critic of the new political romanticism, proclaimed that

> The Reich is becoming a watchword both at home and abroad, a watchword for the Reich and against Versailles and parliamentary democracy. [. . .] The Reich may be described as the German image of humanity, an image contrasted with western humanitarianism but different from eastern apocalypticism by dint of its close links with European history.[169]

In the course of the early 1930s the idea of the Reich underwent a renaissance that extended well beyond its traditional denominational confines and was regularly accompanied by pan-German aspirations and by a belief in the German nation – the *Volk* – that transcended all national boundaries. Now that the Habsburg Empire no longer existed, Protestant and Catholic ideologues were in any case not interested in drawing a distinction between *kleindeutsch* and *großdeutsch*, a distinction they regarded as superannuated, and in this they were in agreement with contemporary German historians. In proposing a 'positive' answer to the West and to the state of Weimar, it was possible to appeal either to the idea of a supranational German Reich as a force for order in central Europe or to the Prussia of Frederick the Great. But it was also possible to appeal to both of these myths at once, which is what most of the authors of the Conservative Revolution did. So, too, did a number of eminent German historians. And yet the mystical glorification of the sacrum imperium was above all a hallmark of those right-wing Catholics whose number included Papen. It was a quasi-religious belief that gave many Germans, not least the chancellor's political enemies, good reason to harbour doubts about his grasp on reality.

Political reality caught up with Papen on 25 October 1932, the day on which the Federal Court in Leipzig delivered its verdict on the 'Prussian coup' of 20 July. The presidential decree was constitutional, it was decided, to the extent that Papen had appointed his chancellor commissioner for Prussia and authorized him temporarily to strip Prussian ministers of their powers and assume those powers himself. But, to quote the court's ruling, this did not mean that the commissioner had the right 'to prevent the Prussian State Ministry and its members from representing the state of Prussia in the Reichsrat or vis-à-vis the Landrat, the State Council and other countries'.[170]

The Leipzig verdict did not end the dualism between Prussia and the Reich that had been the source of so many complaints but declared that both the plaintiff and the defendant were in the right. This meant that the authority of the Prussian state was divided between Braun's caretaker government and the temporary government installed by the Reich. The latter enjoyed the real executive authority, while the former's principal right was to represent Prussia in the Reichsrat. Although Braun's cabinet regained no real power in consequence, it could at least feel vindicated that it had not been found guilty of any violation of its duties. The federal government continued to retain control over the authorities of Germany's largest individual state, including its police, but had to accept that it had acted unconstitutionally when it dismissed the Prussian government on 20 July. This verdict also applied to the federal president in whose name the measure had been taken. However one looked at it, the verdict announced on 25 October 1932 represented a setback for all of those who advocated an authoritarian reform of the German constitution.

The Leipzig verdict had little impact on the outcome of the second elections to the Reichstag in 1932, but the same cannot be said of a second event that took place that year and that hit the national headlines only days before the country went to the polls. The event in question was a public transport strike in Berlin that began on 3 November and was notable for the fact that Communists and National Socialists were united in their opposition to both the state and the trade unions. Three people were killed by police bullets in rioting on 4 November, and eight were seriously injured. Not until 7 November, the day after the elections, did public transport return to normal in the capital.

The most notable aspect of the elections on 6 November was the poor showing of the NSDAP not only in Berlin but in the country as a whole. They lost a total of more than two million votes when compared with the results on 31 July, while their share of the vote fell from 37.3 per cent to 33.1 per cent. Among the other losers were the Social Democrats, who polled 700,000 fewer votes than in July and fell from 21.6 per cent to 20.4 per cent. The winners were the German Nationalists and the Communists, Hugenberg's party adding more than 900,000 votes to its tally, a rise from 5.9 per cent to 8.9 per cent, while the Communist Party rose from 14.5 per cent to 16.9 per cent, its 600,000 extra votes allowing it to return the magical figure of 100 members of parliament, an increase of eleven on its previous tally of eighty-nine. There were few changes among the other parties, although it is noteworthy that only 80.6 per cent of the electorate turned out to vote, compared with 84.1 per cent in July.

The result was a reflection of the sense of political frustration that was felt by the country as a whole. If we include the two rounds of presidential elections and the five regional assembly elections on 24 April, the elections on 6 November were the fifth time that most Germans had gone to the polls in 1932. The NSDAP had previously been the greatest beneficiary of the politicization of non-voters and was now the most affected by the lower turnout, for 'non-political' voters must have felt particularly disillusioned to discover that their vote had had almost no influence to speak of on practical politics.

Nor could it be overlooked that Papen's cabinet had marginally improved its rating, a point evident from the relatively good showing of the German National People's Party and the German People's Party, whose share of the vote rose from 1.2 per cent to 1.9 per cent. The government and the parties that supported it benefited from the early signs of an economic recovery, which could be seen as a result of the active stabilization policy that Papen had introduced in September 1932. There was also a sense of disillusionment at the political and social radicalism of the National Socialists, their cooperation with the Communists in the Berlin transport strike not only proving a shock in the capital's leafy suburbs but also acting as a deterrent to many middle-class voters in the country as a whole. Even so, the government had no cause to feel triumphant, for almost nine-tenths of all Germans had voted for parties opposed to the 'cabinet of barons'.

The drop in the National Socialists' share of the vote was a source of some satisfaction for their political opponents, especially the Social Democrats, who thought that Hitler was now beaten. But the increase in the Communist vote was bound to be unsettling, for the gap between the Social Democrats and the Communists had shrunk from 7.1 percentage points in July to a mere 3.5 in November. Leading officials in the party expressed their fears that if more elections were held in early 1933, when unemployment reached its peak, the Social

Democrats might be overtaken by the Communists. And once the Communists were the largest working-class party, the Social Democrats were afraid that the situation might take a dramatic turn for the worse and end in revolution, which is precisely what the Communists were hoping for.

Astute observers were aware, of course, that the confluence of Communist gains and National Socialist losses meant that Hitler was better placed than Thälmann to take advantage of the new situation. On 8 November, Julius Elbau noted in the liberal *Vossische Zeitung*:

> One hundred Communists in the Reichstag! Transports of joy on the fifteenth anniversary of the October Revolution in Moscow! Eighty-nine made no difference, either in parliament or in the country, but one hundred! That is something else, at the very least a nice round number! And for Hitler a veritable Godsend!

Elbau was convinced that Germans would be 'frightened out of their wits' and 'seek refuge in the arms of the one true patent saviour'.[171] Fear of civil war was now Hitler's most powerful ally. Elbau's analysis was accurate to a fault, and it reflected the calculations of the leading National Socialists in the weeks after the elections on 6 November.

In October 1932, the constitutional lawyer Johannes Heckel had spoken of 'constitutional paralysis', and the November elections did nothing to change this situation, for there continued to be a negative majority of National Socialists and Communists, with the result that not even a coalition of the NSDAP, Centre Party and Bavarian People's Party would have produced a parliamentary majority. As things stood, the Reichstag was not fit for purpose. At the cabinet meeting on 10 November, Gayl proposed a return to the national emergency plan of 30 August, which would have meant dissolving parliament without setting a date for new elections within the sixty-day period required under the constitution, but he failed to find any support among his fellow ministers.

As in August 1932, so in November Papen pursued a twin-track policy, on the one hand informing Hindenburg of his willingness to continue with a presidential cabinet under his own – Papen's – leadership, while at the same time working behind the scenes and throwing his weight behind a submission signed by National Socialist supporters, prominent among whom were middle-class industrialists, bankers and landowners, demanding that Hitler be appointed chancellor. The letter in question was handed to Hindenburg on 19 November. Among its signatories were the president of the National Land League, Count Eberhard von Kalkreuth, the former president of the Reichsbank, Hjalmar Schacht, the Cologne banker Kurt von Schröder and two major industrialists, Fritz Thyssen and August Rosterg. Two other industrialists, Paul Reusch, the chairman of the board of the Good Hope Iron and Steel Works, and Fritz Springorum, who was the director general of Hoesch, sympathized with the contents of the letter, but declined to add their signatures because they had no desire to open up divisions in the industrial concerns of the Ruhr Valley. In short, the submission was not a vote on the part of all the country's employers.

On 17 November the government announced its resignation, attempts by the chancellor to enter into negotiations with all the different parties having failed to produce a positive outcome. At Hindenburg's request the government remained in office in a caretaker capacity. The next day Hindenburg himself began talks with a number of selected party leaders. The most important of these discussions were with Hitler and took place on 19 and 21 November, but the outcome was negative. Hugenberg was vehemently opposed to Hitler's chancellorship, and so there was no prospect of the NSDAP obtaining a parliamentary majority. Nor was Hindenburg prepared to ask Hitler to head a presidential cabinet. Hitler was not even able to persuade Hindenburg to change his mind by threatening that if the present system of government were allowed to go on, it would lead within a matter of only a few months to a new revolution and a descent into Bolshevik chaos.

On 24 November Hindenburg sent a written message to Hitler via his secretary of state, Otto Meissner, the contents of which were also made public. In essence, it repeated the terms of his earlier declaration of 13 August: in the present circumstances, the writer was bound to fear that

> a presidential cabinet under your [Hitler's] leadership is bound to turn into a party dictatorship, with all the attendant consequences for an exceptional worsening of the antagonisms within the German people, a situation which, if he [Hindenburg] were to bring it about, he could not reconcile with his oath and with his conscience.[172]

Hindenburg drew the only possible conclusion from his talks with Hitler: it was no longer possible to avoid proclaiming a state of national emergency. But Papen and his cabinet were by no means as resolute as Hindenburg, and on 26 November Schleicher sought and obtained permission to undertake a further round of exploratory talks, which on this occasion included the Free Trade Unions and the Social Democrats. Encouraged by the journalist Hans Zehrer, Schleicher was keen to find cross-party agreement extending from the reformist left to the National Socialists, or at least the latter's Realpolitik wing as represented by the leader of the NSDAP's national organization, Gregor Straßer.

The talks with the leader of the General German Trade Union Association, Theodor Leipart, were held on 28 November and proved useful, since Schleicher was willing to promise to lift the contentious decree of 5 September, which allowed employers to pay less than the contractually agreed wages to new workers. Conversely, the leader of the Social Democrats in the Reichstag, Rudolf Breitscheid, reacted very differently to a similar approach from Schleicher later that same day. The critical point was reached when Schleicher asked how the

Social Democrats would react to a possible delay to new elections until the spring of 1933. Schleicher demanded to know 'whether the Social Democrats would immediately mount the barricades'. Breitscheid later recalled the ensuing exchange:

> I said that I wouldn't commit myself to the barricades but that I was compelled to inform him that the Social Democrats would resist such a violation of the constitution and that they would do so with all their might. In the circumstances, Schleicher replied, the future looked very bleak.[173]

On the right of the political spectrum, Schleicher's efforts to broker a deal were even less successful than those on the left. Hitler cancelled a meeting with the defence minister at the last minute, and not even Straßer was able to persuade his leader to change his mind. On 30 November Hitler also turned down an offer of the post of vice-chancellor in a Schleicher cabinet, although even if he had accepted the post, this would not, of course, have ensured that the danger from the political left had been averted, for the appointment of National Socialist ministers would inevitably have encountered emphatic opposition from the Social Democrats and, regardless of the differences between the Trade Union Association and the Social Democrats, it would also have been resisted by the Free Trade Unions. In short, the polarization that Schleicher was trying to avoid would simply have become much worse: his policy of trying to reconcile left and right was tantamount to attempting to square the circle.

Even so, Schleicher enjoyed broader political and social support than Papen, for he enjoyed good relations with the parties of the centre ground and with the Christian-Nationalist and liberal trade unions and, more recently, with those trade unions that had links to the Social Democrats. Much the same was true of his relations with the Reichsbanner. Even with Gregor Straßer he had forged a working relationship, though it remained unclear if this would be of any real value in an emergency. In general, Schleicher was regarded as far less reactionary than the current chancellor, and he had made it clear that he had no time for authoritarian experiments with the constitution. All of this could be important if the Reichstag were to remain dissolved and a military state of emergency continued for any length of time. In November 1932 neither Schleicher nor Papen ruled out the expedient of declaring a national state of emergency, but Schleicher had a more realistic view of the risks of a military dictatorship, however veiled that dictatorship might be, which is why he was anxious to do everything that seemed to him necessary to avert a civil war.

In acting in this way, Schleicher set himself on a collision course with Hindenburg, who by the end of November 1932 was determined to cut the Gordian knot by once again dissolving the Reichstag and delaying new elections, which effectively meant proclaiming a state of emergency that would be above the law. Papen was willing, albeit reluctantly, to go down this particular road but failed to win support for it when the cabinet met on 2 December and Schleicher invited Lieutenant Colonel Eugen Ott to spell out to his ministerial colleagues the lessons to be drawn from a 'war games' exercise that the Reichswehr had conducted only a short time earlier. According to this report, the country's armed forces could not win a war fought on two different fronts against the Communists and the National Socialists, especially if it simultaneously had to resist a Polish attack on Germany's eastern border, as the study presupposed. The cabinet was deeply impressed by this, and when Papen reported on the meeting to Hindenburg, the latter abandoned his opposition to Schleicher's chancellorship, saying: 'I'm too old to assume responsibility for a civil war at the end of my life.'[174] According to Papen's report of their meeting, it was with these words that Hindenburg justified his decision to turn his back on a standpoint that he had been advocating only twenty-four hours earlier.

Schleicher was appointed chancellor on 3 December 1932, at the same time retaining his old post of defence minister in the new government. With Schleicher's agreement, his predecessor, Papen, who still enjoyed Hindenburg's confidence, was allowed to retain his official residence in the Wilhelmstraße, allowing him to continue to enjoy the privilege of direct access to the president, a privilege that might prove to be more important than any official government position. Papen's ministers retained their old cabinet posts, the only exception being the Ministry of the Interior, where Wilhelm von Gayl was replaced by the deputy commissioner for Prussia, Franz Bracht.

Schleicher had little difficulty clearing his first official hurdle, for no vote of no confidence was tabled at the brief session of the Reichstag that began on 6 December. With the chancellor's agreement, the Reichstag lifted some of the emergency laws that had been in place since 4 September, when the government had been granted the power to suspend the right to free collective bargaining. The house also passed an amnesty law, again with the agreement of the government. And in response to a motion from the NSDAP, it altered the wording of Article 51 of the constitution, which appointed the chancellor the president's replacement in the event of the latter's being prevented from exercising his office in person. Hindenburg had celebrated his eighty-fifth birthday on 2 October 1932. If he were to fall seriously ill or die during Schleicher's chancellorship, then the powers of the president, chancellor and defence minister would all devolve on a single person, General Kurt von Schleicher. In order to prevent this from happening, the National Socialists proposed that the president of the Federal Court replace the president and in this they won the backing of most of the bourgeois parties as well as the Social Democrats, who viewed with dismay a further increase in Schleicher's power. With the necessary two-thirds majority, the motion was passed on 9 December, the last day of the current parliamentary session.

Schleicher used a radio address on 15 December 1932 to announce his government's platform, giving priority to work creation programmes, stressing his antipathy to both capitalism and socialism and labelling himself a 'social general', while calling his predecessor a 'fearless and blameless knight' but at the same time distancing himself from him: 'It is uncomfortable to sit on the point of a bayonet, which is to say that in the longer term it is impossible to govern without broad popular backing.'[175] As a result, he concluded, the new government would adopt as its guideline the motto of the former chief of the general staff, Count Helmuth von Moltke the Elder: 'Look before you leap.'

Papen – the 'fearless and blameless knight' – was far from sharing Schleicher's view that his successor was a better chancellor than he was, and in an attempt to lever himself back into a position of power he joined forces with another of Schleicher's enemies, meeting Hitler at the Cologne home of the banker Kurt von Schröder on 4 January 1933. The participants had intended their deliberations to remain secret, but within days their contents were making headlines in the national and international press. Their aim was to bridge the gap between the leader of the National Socialists and the country's president and prepare the way for Schleicher's downfall, a further point on which Hitler and Papen were in agreement. But before Papen could mediate between Hitler and Hindenburg, he first had to clear up his personal relationship with Hitler, which had been strained since 13 August. Once this had been achieved, the two men were able to agree on a 'duumvirate', although it was still unclear exactly who would head the new government.

It seems likely that Hitler repeated his claims to the chancellorship at his meeting with Papen in Cologne. In the light of all that we know about Papen's attitude in August and November, we may assume that he will not have insisted on heading a 'cabinet of national unity'. But at his meeting on 4 January he will not have failed to mention Hindenburg's continuing misgivings at the idea of Hitler's chancellorship. In the course of their discussions, Hitler clearly did not rule out a temporary alternative to his own chancellorship involving National Socialists taking over both the defence ministry and the home office. This conclusion receives some support from an entry in Goebbels's diary dated 10 January 1933 and is also confirmed by Papen's remarks to four leading industrialists in Dortmund on 7 January, namely, Krupp, Reusch, Springorum and Vögler. When Papen reported to Hindenburg on 9 January, the president gained the impression that Hitler was no longer insisting on the transfer of all the government's powers to the NSDAP but would be content to play a part in a right-wing coalition government. Hindenburg accordingly authorized Papen to remain in contact with Hitler on a strictly confidential basis.

On 11 January 1933, two days after the talks between Hindenburg and Papen, the National Land League, which eight months earlier had played an active role in toppling Brüning from power, returned to the fray. Immediately before a meeting with the president that was also attended by the chancellor, the economics minister, Hermann Warmbold, and the minister of nutrition and agriculture, Magnus von Braun, the League informed the press of a decision that amounted to a declaration of war. In it the signatories maintained that with the connivance of the government German agriculture, especially animal husbandry, had suffered a catastrophic decline of a kind that would scarcely have been thought possible under a Marxist regime. After that the government broke off all contact with the National Land League. Only Hindenburg, who had always felt personally close to the landowners to the east of the Elbe, refused to join the boycott, and on 17 January he wrote to the prae-sidium of Germany's largest agricultural pressure group to say that he hoped that the measure he had just signed for improvements in enforcement protec-tion would help to reassure the agricultural community.

The spectacular breakdown of relations between the government and the National Land League was followed within days by a further headline-grabbing event in the form of the regional elections in the second-smallest German state of Lippe-Detmold, where the National Socialists had mounted an unprece-dented wave of demonstrations, all of them under Hitler's personal supervision and all of them designed to make amends for the party's loss of votes in the Reichstag elections on 6 November. Their efforts were rewarded by an addi-tional 6,000 votes and a rise in the share of the vote from 34.7 per cent to 39.6 per cent. The victory was much exploited for propagandist ends. And from now on it was unthinkable that Hitler would refuse to accept the post of chancellor in a 'national government'. On 16 January he had a serious falling-out with his former national organizer, with the result that Gregor Straßer no longer had any supporters left and Hitler's position within the party was now so strong as to be practically unassailable.

That same day the government agreed that in the event of a vote of no confidence it would dissolve the Reichstag and delay new elections till October or November 1933. An alternative to this violation of the constitution, which demanded new elections within sixty days, would have meant ignoring the vote of no confidence on the part of a negative majority that was incapable of forming a government and leave the toppled government in office in a caretaker capacity. During the winter of 1932/3 several political practitioners, including eminent constitutional lawyers such as Heinrich Herrfahrdt and Carl Schmitt, had advised the chancellor to adopt this policy, which they argued to be fully justi-fied, and a report to this effect was added to the minutes of the ministerial meeting on 16 January. But Schleicher clearly felt that a vote of no confidence represented such a serious loss of prestige for his government that he never really considered this option as a solution to his difficulties. It was extremely unlikely that the president would have agreed to the incomparably more risky solution to the crisis that the cabinet proposed and delayed the new elections until the end of the year: with his 'Ott plan' Schleicher had unwittingly given Hindenburg grounds to oppose the government on this very question.

Within days of the cabinet meeting, the press had begun to speculate that a state of emergency was about to be declared, and on 19 January the leader of the Social Democrats in the Reichstag, Rudolf Breitscheid, told a meeting of party officials in Friedrichshain in Berlin that as early as 28 November Schleicher had mentioned that new elections might be delayed. He also quoted his own response on that occasion: 'Such a provocation will undoubtedly cause the greatest conceivable convulsions.'[176]

An even greater stir was caused by another revelation later that same day at a meeting of the Reichstag's budgetary committee, when the Centre Party member of parliament, Joseph Ersing who was one of the secretaries of the Christian-Nationalist trade unions, reported the misuse of public funds that had been intended to help heavily indebted manorial estates, especially in East Prussia. If the groups behind the National Land League, which had received huge sums of money from the German nation as a whole, adopted the kind of language that they had recently used in their dealings with the government, then the Reichstag would have to look into the matter. And, Ersing went on, if the federal funds had been used not to cover debts but to buy luxury cars and race horses and to fund trips to the Riviera, the government must demand the repayment of such sums. The major landowners, Ersing concluded, were attempting to prevent any further parliamentary deliberations on the question of help for eastern Germany, hence the intense efforts that were being made behind the scenes to dissolve the Reichstag as quickly as possible.

The very next day, the Reichstag's Council of Elders agreed to postpone the full session of parliament planned for 24 to 31 January, the delay being demanded by the National Socialists, who had every reason to avoid a plenary session at least for the present: nothing was to get in the way of the political negotiations that Hitler had resumed shortly after the regional elections in Lippe-Detmold. He met Hugenberg on 17 January and Papen on the 18th, but neither meeting produced any concrete results. On 21 January the German Nationalists in the Reichstag declared their formal opposition to Schleicher's cabinet, citing as their reason the argument that the country's economic policies were increasingly straying into the field of 'socialist-internationalist ideas', in the process adding to the 'threat of Bolshevism in the countryside'.[177] It was a charge that the German Nationalists had already levelled at Brüning in May 1932.

On 22 January Papen and Hugenberg met for the third time in as many weeks. As on 18 January, the meeting took place in the Dahlem villa of Joachim von Ribbentrop, a champagne dealer who additionally dabbled in politics. The meeting was given added weight by the fact that it was also attended by the secretary of state, Otto Meissner, and by Hindenburg's son, Oskar, while the National Socialists were represented by Göring and Frick. Crucially, Hitler had sent word to the meeting, seeking to reassure the participants that he was willing to include a sizeable number of bourgeois ministers in a presidential cabinet under his own leadership, even if those ministers would not be answerable to their own individual parties.

By the time that Hindenburg received Schleicher on 23 January, he already knew about the Dahlem meeting. Schleicher reported on the cabinet's plans for a state of emergency but met with a rebuff. Hindenburg insisted that he was still deliberating on the question of the dissolution of the Reichstag, but for the present he was unwilling to agree to a delay in holding new elections:

> Such a step would be interpreted on all sides as a violation of the constitution. Before deciding on such a step, the party leaders would have to be consulted in order to ascertain if they would recognize the state of national emergency and not complain that it represented a violation of the constitution.[178]

By 27 January Berlin was buzzing with rumours that a dictatorship was to be established, not under Schleicher, but under Papen. It was certainly true that Hindenburg still wanted Papen rather than Hitler to succeed Schleicher, but he was counting on the support of the National Socialists and on sufficient backing in the Reichstag. The German Nationalists, conversely, were proposing the idea of an anti-parliamentary emergency cabinet. On 27 January Hugenberg and Hitler came to blows over the contentious question of which party would run the Prussian ministry of the interior, with the result that Hitler, in a fit of pique, cancelled a meeting with Papen arranged for later that day. A public declaration by the NSDAP that it would resist a dictatorship under the former chancellor with all the resolve that it could muster left such a profound impression on Papen that on the evening of the 27th he told Ribbentrop that he was now more firmly in favour of a Hitler-led cabinet than he had been until then.

Schleicher resigned the very next day, 28 January 1933. The most obvious reason for his resignation was Hindenburg's refusal to ask him to dissolve the Reichstag. (By now there was no longer any question of postponing the new elections.) The general public, however, was less exercised by the news of Schleicher's dismissal than by the announcement that Hindenburg had invited Papen to talk to the various parties, clarify the political situation and establish the possibilities that were open. The two leaders of the Confederation of German Industry and the Association of German Chambers of Industry and Commerce, Ludwig Kastl and Eduard Hamm, as well as Otto Meissner, were all profoundly alarmed at this development and warned of the dangers threatening the German economy as a result of the political crisis engulfing the country, while trade unionists of every shade of political opinion expressed their fear that the appointment of a 'socially reactionary government hostile to the working class' would be seen as a provocation by workers up and down the country.[179]

For the present the general public remained in the dark about Papen's true intentions, namely, a cabinet headed by Hitler with Papen himself as his vice-chancellor enjoying special privileges. Several former ministers, including the foreign minister, Konstantin von Neurath, and the finance minister, Lutz

Schwerin von Krosigk, declared their willingness to serve in such a cabinet, and when Papen informed Hindenburg of this new development on the evening of 28 January, he was suitably impressed and for the first time seemed prepared to overcome his doubts about Hitler's appointment as chancellor. Papen encountered substantially more difficulty with the German Nationalists, many of whom were still resolutely opposed to such a move. Hugenberg continued to have profound misgivings about the National Socialists' demand for new elections but was irresistibly tempted by the fact that Hindenburg was ready to offer him the posts of minister of economics and of nutrition both in the country as a whole and, on a regional level, in the state of Prussia.

In the National Socialist camp, Hitler had to come to terms with the fact that it was Papen, not he, who would become commissioner for Prussia, but by way of compensation Göring was appointed assistant commissioner with special responsibility for the Prussian Ministry of the Interior and, hence, for the Prussian police. On a national level Göring became minister without portfolio and commissioner for aviation, while Wilhelm Frick became minister of the interior. In short, the cabinet contained only three National Socialists. The conservatives, including the Stahlhelm leader Franz Seldte as labour minister, had a clear numerical advantage.

Hindenburg himself chose one cabinet member, General Werner von Blomberg, the military commander for East Prussia, who on 29 January was still in Geneva as technical adviser to the German delegation at the disarmament conference that was being held there. At Hindenburg's behest, Blomberg was appointed Schleicher's successor as defence minister. Rumours to the effect that the Potsdam garrison was planning a putsch persuaded the president to summon Blomberg to his presidential palace as soon as he arrived back in Berlin on the morning of 30 January and to appoint him defence minister without further delay, although in the event the rumours proved to be unfounded. Since the president was able to appoint ministers only on the chancellor's recommendation and since the chancellor himself had not yet been appointed, Hindenburg was guilty of violating the constitution.

For a long time it remained unclear whether Hindenburg would accede to National Socialist demands and dissolve parliament and call for new elections. Hitler justified his demand by pointing out that he had no majority in the Reichstag and that he needed such a majority for the enabling law that he believed was vital. On 29 January Papen seems to have persuaded Hindenburg to agree to this move in the event that it proved impossible to gain the support of the Centre Party and the Bavarian People's Party for the new government. It was not hard for Hitler to announce talks with the two Catholic parties. Once Hugenberg had capitulated on the question of new elections, Hitler and the members of his cabinet could be sworn in by the president during the late morning of 30 January 1933. Hindenburg ended the brief ceremony with the words: 'And now, gentlemen, onward with God!'[180]

There was no resistance whatsoever to the appointment of the new government. During the days leading up to the events of 30 January rumours of a 'putsch cabinet' run by Papen and Hugenberg had caused more disquiet among the general public, as well as among employers' organizations, trade unions, centre-ground parties and even the Social Democrats, than the possibility of a government led by Hitler. The dangers of the Papen–Hugenberg alternative were equated – not without good reason – with those of a civil war, for a presidential cabinet dominated by German Nationalists would have been opposed by nine-tenths of the population and violently resisted by Communists, Social Democrats, trade unions and National Socialists. If a 'national government' under Hitler were to gain the parliamentary support of the Catholic parties, then most observers, including the out-of-office Schleicher, would have regarded this as the lesser of two evils. Even the Social Democrat *Vorwärts* had expressed this view in its evening edition on 28 January.

On the morning of 30 January 1933, while Germany's fate was being decided in the presidential palace in the Wilhelmstraße, the party leaders of the Social Democrats were meeting their members of parliament and representatives of the Free Trade Unions in the nearby Reichstag building. The Social Democrats present reacted to the news of the appointment of Hitler's cabinet with an appeal warning against 'undisciplined and independent actions on the part of individual organizations and groups' and insisting that the situation called for 'cool heads and determination'.[181] The following day, Rudolf Breitscheid, standing in for his ailing leader Otto Wels, emphatically rejected non-parliamentary action, arguing that if Hitler remained within the framework of the constitution, it would be wrong to give him an opportunity to violate the terms of that constitution.

The Communists, conversely, believed that the time had come for direct action. For the first time since the Prussian coup of 20 July 1932, the Central Committee of the German Communist Party spoke directly to the leaders of the Social Democrats and trade unions. The Social Democrats, the German Trade Union Association, the Cooperative Union of Free Employees' Federations and the Christian trade unions were all urged to 'join forces with the Communists in holding a general strike in protest not only at the Fascist dictatorship of Hitler, Hugenberg and Papen but also at the destruction of workers' organizations and in that way demonstrate their support for the freedom of the working class'.[182]

But a united front among the proletariat was an even more hopeless prospect on 30 January 1933 than it had been on 20 July 1932. At a time when more than six million Germans were officially registered as unemployed, a protracted general strike was clearly out of the question, while a general strike of limited duration would be seen by the new government as a sign of weakness rather than a demonstration of strength. It was also extremely unlikely that the Communists would have heeded a call to end the walkout. The Communist

Party had for years been attacking the Social Democrats, reviling them as the 'principal social buttress of the bourgeoisie' and as 'social Fascists', while *Die Rote Fahne* had as recently as 26 January 1933 dismissed the suggestion put forward by *Vorwärts* that the Social Democrats and Communists should agree on a 'non-aggression pact', labelling the idea an 'infamous insult aimed at anti-Fascist Berlin'.[183] In short, the Communist slogan about working-class solidarity was fundamentally lacking in credibility. The Social Democrats and Free Trade Unions had to assume that the Communists would resort to the kind of revolutionary force that the National Socialists were waiting for in order for them to invest their reign of terror with a semblance of legitimacy. And a civil war could end only with the bloody suppression of all workers' organizations: the divided left stood no chance in the face of the combined forces of right-wing paramilitary associations, the police and the army.

By the evening of 30 January, the streets in Berlin and many other German towns and cities belonged to Hitler's 'brown battalions'. The following day Hitler held talks with the Centre Party, as he had promised Papen he would do. But the exercise was merely for show and designed simply to demonstrate that it was impossible to govern the country with the parliament that had been elected on 6 November 1932. The Centre Party, by contrast, was interested in a genuine coalition with the NSDAP and far less concerned at Hitler's appointment as chancellor than at the 'reactionary' makeup of his cabinet. But the leader of the Centre Party, Ludwig Kaas, had no choice but to turn down Hitler's demand that the Reichstag be adjourned for a whole year, and in doing so he gave Hitler an excuse to declare the talks on 31 January a failure and to trigger his cabinet's first important decision, which was to ask Hindenburg to dissolve the Reichstag. The relevant decree was issued on 1 February, together with a second one, setting 5 March 1933 as the date of the new elections. Until then Hitler's cabinet had to rely on the emergency powers that it enjoyed under Article 48 of the constitution.

Hitler's appointment as chancellor was not the only possible solution to the crisis that beset Germany at this time, a crisis that had begun with the breakdown of the grand coalition on 27 March 1930 and become dramatically worse following Brüning's dismissal on 30 May 1932. Hindenburg was no more obliged to break with Schleicher than he was forced to replace Brüning with Papen, for even after a vote of no confidence in the Reichstag, he could still have invited Schleicher to stay on as the head of a caretaker government or else he could have replaced him with a chancellor who, enjoying cross-party support, would not have polarized opinion. He was not barred from dissolving the Reichstag again within the constitutional limit of sixty days, while a delay in holding new elections until the autumn of 1933 was scarcely less risky than it had been a year earlier, especially when we take account of the relevant declarations from the centre-ground parties and the Social Democrats. There was nothing that forced Hindenburg to appoint Hitler the new German chancellor.

True, Hitler was still the leader of the largest party, even after his defeat in the Reichstag elections on 6 November 1932. But he did not have a majority in the Reichstag.

Until January 1933 Hindenburg had opposed the whole idea of Hitler's chancellorship, so keen was he to avoid a National Socialist dictatorship. If Hindenburg changed his mind on this point, it was because his closest advisers urged him to do so and because he believed that the risk of a dictatorship was reduced, if not entirely removed, by the preponderance of conservative ministers in Hitler's cabinet. Presumably his personal disappointment at Schleicher also played a role here, for Schleicher had never explicitly countered the charges levelled at the president and his entourage in connection with the scandal surrounding the subsidies to help the eastern parts of Germany. Influential elements among landowners to the east of the Elbe, who had been receiving state support since Bismarck's day, had been advocating Schleicher's dismissal and Hitler's appointment for some time, as had right-wing industrialists in the Rhineland and Westphalia. Almost everyone with access to the president exerted pressure on him to act, and the eighty-five-year-old Hindenburg was simply not strong enough to resist. By January 1933 the centre of power around the president had thrown its weight behind Hitler, and Hindenburg was merely one part of this centre of power, albeit its most important element.

In short, the events that unfolded on 30 January 1933 were neither the inevitable outcome of earlier political developments nor the result of mere chance. The mass support that Hitler enjoyed made his appointment a possibility, but if he became chancellor, it was thanks to Hindenburg and the political milieu that the president embodied. Like the increase in NSDAP support, the political strength of the ancient elite that was urging a government of national unity under Hitler had a long prehistory that included, first and foremost, the erosion of trust in the democratic state. If a 'belief in legality' – in Max Weber's eyes the most important abstract resource of any system of rule[184] – had always been relatively weak in the Weimar Republic, then the reasons for this can be traced back to the birth of the Republic from the ashes of the First World War and even to events that preceded the outbreak of the war by many years. If there is a single root cause for the collapse of Germany's first democracy, then it must be sought in the nineteenth century's repeated refusal to deal with the question of freedom or, to put it another way, the fact that the modernization process in Germany had never been properly synchronized, the democratization of suffrage coming at a much earlier date than the democratization of a parliamentary system of government. In this contradiction lay the deeper reason for the success that Hitler enjoyed after 1930 with his pseudo-democratic political agitation designed to overthrow a semi-authoritarian presidential system.

In his attempt to destroy the Weimar Republic, Hitler exhausted all the possibilities that the Weimar constitution had to offer him. His tactical insistence on legality was incomparably more successful than any advocacy of revolutionary force of the kind that he had espoused ten years earlier at the time of his Beer Hall Putsch on the night of 8/9 November 1923 and that the other totalitarian party – the Communists – continued to champion. Since the Communists were openly propagating the idea of civil war, they allowed the National Socialists, who maintained the largest army capable of being deployed in a civil war, to portray themselves as the defenders of the constitution and as the agents of law and order ready to call in the army in order to put down any left-wing attempt to overthrow the government. At the same time, of course, Hitler could himself threaten the country's rulers with revolutionary violence and civil war if they broke the law or changed it to the disadvantage of the National Socialists, as had been the case with the emergency legislation designed to combat political terror that had been enacted on 9 August 1932.

Ever since the Thirty Years War in the seventeenth century there was nothing that the Germans feared more than civil war. Hitler's tactical appeal to legality was a skilful way of taking account of that fear, and his conditional promise to respect the due process of law served its purpose, while also containing an implied threat of blackmail. The fear of the National Socialists' revolutionary character that was felt by the right-wing establishment gradually gave way to the belief that the leader of the 'nationalist' masses would create the necessary popular basis for his authoritarian policies. The illusions felt by the authoritarians were aided and abetted by the illusions felt by the democrats. In order to ensure that the state remained under the rule of law, its advocates would have had to violate the letter of a constitution that was ultimately neutral with regard to its own validity, even if that violation had taken the form of a tactical disregard of a negative vote of no confidence. But such a course of action was at odds with a 'functionalist' view of legality, a view that Carl Schmitt pilloried in the summer of 1932 in his book *Legality and Legitimacy*, where he argued that it 'insisted on its own neutrality even to the point of suicide'.[185] This view was shared by the Social Democrat lawyer Ernst Fraenkel, who in an article published in *Die Gesellschaft* in December 1932 criticized the widespread 'fetishization of the constitution'.[186] Weimar had fallen into the trap of legality that the authors of its constitution had unwittingly set.

Hitler launched the Reichstag election campaign with a speech in the Berlin Sportpalast on 10 February 1933 and began by attacking 'the parties of decline, of November and of revolution', parties which for fourteen years were said to have destroyed, fragmented and torn apart the German people, after which he appealed to his audience to give his new government four years before judging him. His final words were inspired by the Bible and, more especially, by the Protestant version of the Lord's Prayer. In this way Hitler sought to equate his own will to power with service to his country and with the fulfilment of a divinely appointed task:

For I cannot rid myself of the conviction that this nation will one day rise up again, I cannot put aside my love for this people of mine, and I am utterly convinced that the hour will come when the millions who hate us today will stand behind us and, together with us, will welcome the new and hard-won German Reich that we have created together and that has been so painfully achieved, a kingdom of greatness and honour and strength and glory and justice. Amen![187]

Exactly what he planned to do if the Germans were to heed his appeal Hitler had already explained in some detail a week earlier in a secret speech that he delivered in the presence of army and navy commanders in the official residence of the army chief, General Kurt von Hammerstein-Equord, and that covered most, if not all, of his plans for the future of Germany:

> The root-and-branch eradication of Marxism. [. . .] The strictest authoritarian leadership. The removal of the cancer of democracy! [. . .] The building up of the army as the most important precondition for achieving the goal of regaining political power. Universal compulsory military service must be reintroduced. [. . .] How should political power be used once it has been achieved? Cannot yet say. Perhaps by winning new export opportunities, perhaps – and arguably even better – by conquering a new Lebensraum in the east and ruthlessly Germanicizing it.[188]

Storm Clouds in the Far East: Japan Invades Manchuria

Another war over Lebensraum had already begun at around this time in a different part of the world, a conflict that was likewise to culminate in the Second World War. This was the war with which Japan had been seeking to extend its sphere of influence into mainland Asia since 1931. Many of the political developments that took place in the far eastern empire after 1918 bore striking parallels with events that were unfolding in Europe at this time. Japan was one of the victorious powers in the First World War, but, like Italy, it felt that it had been robbed of its deserts. At the insistence of its western allies it had handed back the former German colony of Kiaochow to China in 1921, committing itself to an 'open-door policy' towards China, and under the terms of the Washington Naval Treaty of February 1922 it agreed to limit the size of its fleet. For the nationalist right these various treaties were an important reason for public hostility to the West, which was accused of pursuing a policy of racial prejudice.

There is no doubt that during the interwar years the United States in particular treated Japan in a way that fully supports this assessment. At the Paris Peace Conference in 1919 the United States and Great Britain prevented the League of Nations from including in its statutes a ban on racial discrimination, as demanded by Japan. In 1921 California introduced segregated schools for whites and Asians. In 1922 the Supreme Court made it illegal to confer American citizenship on Japanese nationals. And in 1924 a federal law placed a total ban on Japanese immigration, which was already severely restricted at this date. America's undisguised racism was grist to the mill of Japanese nationalists. The 'West' became a propagandist bogeyman for the radical Japanese right, just as it was for right-wing Germans at the time of the Weimar Republic.

Ever since the Meiji Restoration of 1868, Japan had pursued a policy of modernization unique in Asia. Technologically and industrially, its models were Great Britain and the United States, whereas its political and constitutional template was Prussia. Like the German Empire, Japan was a constitutional monarchy. In 1919 the right to vote in elections to the lower house was extended to include all male taxpayers, and in March 1925 universal equal franchise for men over the age of twenty-five was introduced. A week later the lower house passed a bill designed to maintain public order and directed at Communist, anarchist and internationalist tendencies, throwing the gates wide open for police brutality against anyone deemed guilty of left-wing activities. Throughout the 1920s socialist and Communist parties had practically ceased to play any role at all in the political life of Japan. The 'rice riots' that shook the country in 1918 were not politically motivated but were the direct result of famine and led to no lasting mobilization of workers, peasants or smallholders.

The two leading parties were the older Seiyukai party and the more recent Minseito party. Both described themselves as liberal but both were right-wing groups. They maintained close links with the major industrial concerns, the *zaibatsu*, but enjoyed no organized mass support. The end of the First World War marked the start of a de facto process of parliamentary democratization in Japan, even if many governments were effectively run by cabinets of civil servants. By the end of the 1920s the upturn in the Japanese economy had led to a period of relative political stability: the production index rose – if we take the years between 1920 and 1924 as the base, then the average had reached 313 by 1925–9. The value of imports rose by 199 per cent between 1913 and 1929, while exports during the same period increased by 205 per cent.

The parliamentary system that was in operation at least for a time was never fully accepted by Japanese society. The British historian W. G. Beasley saw the reasons for the widespread hostility to this western practice

> in those ideas and institutions which had turned the Japanese people away from the pursuit of individual freedoms and towards the attainment of collective goals: the formative pressures of the education system; an emperor-centred state religion; conscription, with its accompanying indoctrination; and the persistence of traditional authoritarian attitudes in important areas of bureaucratic and family behaviour.[189]

Parliament was regarded as un-Japanese because it encouraged a call for civil rights and individual freedoms. During the Meiji era, everything that was taken over from the West was seen as the price of affluence and strength. Moreover, Japan had been successful in defending essential elements of its native traditions, including the imperial system, Confucian ethics and the Samurai tradition in public service. But during the 1920s it seemed increasingly as if these traditions, too, were at risk and that the very essence of all that was Japanese was threatening to become a victim of modernization.

As early as 1919 Kita Ikki, a writer whom Germans would have numbered among the supporters of the Conservative Revolution, had demanded far-reaching social changes, including the nationalization of major industries, the confiscation of personal fortunes greater than one million yen and land reform, while at the same time expressing his backing for a military coup designed to promote an expansionist foreign policy on the Asian continent and provide an effective defence of Asian interests vis-à-vis the West. In spite of a police ban on its distribution, *An Outline Plan for the Reconstruction of Japan* found a widespread following. Like the founder of the Associazione Nazionalista Italiana, Enrico Corradini, Kita Ikki based his imperialist claims on the argument that Japan was a proletarian nation and must continue the class struggle on an international level.

In 1921 Kita Ikki joined forces with Okawa Shumei to found the Society for the Preservation of the National Essence (Yuzonsha), an organization that influenced the thinking of leading military figures and of clubs friendly to the military. Two slogans played a particularly important role in this Japanese manifestation of the Conservative Revolution: the 'imperial way', or *kodo*; and the 'Showa Restoration', or Showa Ishiu. (Showa Tenno was the title of the young Emperor Hirohito, who ascended the Japanese throne in 1926.) A group of officers inspired by Kita Ikki's ideas took the name of Kodo, while another organization called itself the Tosei (Control) Faction and was distinguished from its rival organization by its less socialist, more employer-friendly attitudes. Its aim was to prepare Japan for total war by means of a dense network of state controls. But on the question of territorial expansionism, Kodo and Tosei were in total agreement.

The first elections to the lower house based on the new rules for universal male suffrage took place in January 1928 and produced a narrow majority for the Seiyukai party under General Tanaka Giichi. In June 1928 Japanese officers in Manchuria, the southern half of which had been under Japanese influence since 1905, murdered a local Chinese warlord, Zhang Zuolin. Although Tanaka generally took a hard line towards China, he insisted in the present case on a thorough investigation of the affair and in doing so put himself on a collision course with his general staff, with the result that in July 1929 he was obliged to resign under pressure from the army. His successor was Hamaguchi Osachi, the leader of the Minseito party.

Under Hamaguchi Japan agreed to the London Naval Treaty of April 1930, which imposed further restrictions on the country in terms of its ability to rearm. The ratio agreed to in Washington in 1921, which provided for a relationship of 5:5:3 for the larger warships of the United States, Great Britain and Japan, was now extended to smaller vessels, while the ratio between American and Japanese naval vessels in general was raised to 5:3.5, a ratio more favourable to Japan. At their cabinet meeting, every minister, including the navy minister, voted to accept this ruling, but the supreme commander of the navy, backed by ultra-nationalist organizations, vetoed it, arguing that by signing the treaty the government had ignored the will of the emperor as enshrined in the 1889 constitution. In the event Emperor Hirohito sided with the government and signed the agreement in October 1930. The following month a young nationalist made an attempt on Hamaguchi's life. He died of his wounds in August 1931 and was succeeded by Wakatsuki Reijiro, a Minseito politician who the military expected to be less confrontational than his murdered predecessor.

In the meantime the world economic crisis had hit Japan. The price of its principal export, raw silk, which had stood at 100 points in 1914, fell from 225 in 1925 to 151 in 1929 and to sixty-seven in 1931. At the same time demand for Japanese cotton goods fell, leading to increasing unemployment in the textile industry and widespread poverty in rural areas, especially the north and northeast of the country, which were the army's favourite recruiting grounds.

In Japan as elsewhere, the depression led to a mounting radicalization of the political climate. In May 1931, Ishiwara Kanji, who since 1928 had been responsible for the strategic planning of the Kwantung Army that was deployed in southern Manchuria to protect the local railways, wrote an *Outline on the Question of Manchuria and Mongolia* in which he expressed the view that Manchuria and Mongolia were of signal importance not only for the defence of Japan but also for the control of Korea, the influencing of China and the revival of the Japanese economy, concluding that in view of the international situation Japan's very survival depended on the annexation of both of these regions:

> The world, which in the wake of the Great War in Europe, is in the process of forming five superpowers, will undoubtedly continue with this development and in the end form a single system. Where there is control over the centre of this system, there will be a struggle for supremacy between the representative of the West, the United States of America, and the master of the East, Japan. That is why our country must lose no time in developing the basics of a national policy that allows it to acquire the status of master of the East. In order to deal with the present situation and achieve mastery in the East, we must extend our sphere of influence as far as is necessary and do so without delay.[190]

Ishiwara's demand for action did not go unheeded, and after detailed preparations the Kwantung Army staged a bomb attack on the South Manchurian

Railway on 18 September, blaming it on Chinese bandits and using the incident as a pretext to attack strongholds of the regional warlord Zhang Xueliang, an ally of the Chinese president Chiang Kai-shek and son of the murdered Zhang Zuolin. They also overran several Manchurian towns and cities, including Mukden (now Shenyang). Wakatsuki's government was not informed of these plans. A putsch financed by the Kwantung Army and involving Hashimoto Kingoro, a Japanese army officer, and the ultra-nationalist Okawa Shumei, was discovered and thwarted at the last minute by the military police. Against the wishes of Emperor Hirohito, the Kwantung Army brought the last Chinese emperor, Puyi, who had been deposed in 1912, to Manchuria and established a puppet government under his nominal rule. Wakatsuki's government resigned in December, and Inukai Tsuyoshi of the Seiyukai party was appointed the new prime minister. Throughout this period the Kwantung Army continued to occupy Manchuria.

On the other side of the Pacific Ocean, in the United States of America, there were differing attitudes to the question of the best way to deal with Japanese aggression. The secretary of state, Henry L. Stimson, saw in Japan's actions a 'deadly threat to the authority of the great peace treaties' of 1919–20,[191] while Hoover argued that they 'do not imperil the freedom of the American people, the economic or moral future of our people'.[192] Even so Hoover agreed to work with the League of Nations, which for its part set up a commission of inquiry in December 1931 under the chairmanship of the British diplomat Victor Lytton. On 7 January 1932 Stimson announced the doctrine that bears his name, declaring that the United States refused to acknowledge any change to the status quo that Japan had undertaken in violating the open-door principle in China. The League of Nations unanimously adopted the Stimson Doctrine on 11 March 1932.

In China itself there was massive unofficial opposition to Japan's occupation of a region that under international law was still a part of China, and in several Chinese towns and cities Japanese businesses were attacked and a boycott on Japanese goods was imposed. After a particularly serious incident in Shanghai, the Japanese navy, with support from the marines, bombarded the city from sea and air. In February Inukai's government sent additional troops to the region. After fierce fighting involving considerable loss of life, the military intervention was brought to an end on 2 March 1932, when an agreement was signed with Chiang Kai-shek. But it was no more than a temporary truce, for it was clear that in occupying Manchuria Japan had achieved only a small part of its expansionist aspirations at the expense of mainland China.

Two weeks earlier, on 18 February 1932, the new 'state' of Manzhuguo that had been created by the Kwantung Army declared its independence from China, and in March Puyi was named head of state. Inukai's government refused to recognize the new state. A particularly implacable opponent of the Kwantung Army's actions, the country's finance minister, Inoue Junnosuke, was assassinated on 9 February by members of a band of conspirators associated with the radical nationalist Inoue Nissho. A similar fate overtook the prime minister on 15 May 1932. His assassination was part of a planned coup mounted by another radical right-wing group that also involved Okawa Shumei, the co-founder of Yuzonsha. The new prime minister, Admiral Saito Makoto, was sworn in that same month and remained in office until July 1934, when he was replaced by another general, Okada Keisuka, marking the end of a series of governments led by party politicians. In none of the following cabinets was there any civilian resistance to the army's expansionist plans. In September 1932 the lower house unanimously recognized the de facto protectorate of Manzhuguo as an independent state.

The Lytton Commission set up by the League of Nations submitted its report in October 1932. It could detect no signs of a struggle for national autonomy in the region occupied by Japan and recommended that Manzhuguo be granted autonomous status within China, with the Japanese police given the right to patrol the region. The League of Nations voted to accept these recommendations on 24 February 1933. Japan, which had been a permanent member of the Council of the League of Nations since its establishment in 1919, was the only country to vote against acceptance, while only Siam abstained. Japan responded by resigning from the League of Nations on 27 March 1933: it was not the last resignation that year, for on 14 October National Socialist Germany followed Japan's example.

By 1932–3 Japan had become an authoritarian, militaristic and radically nationalist state bearing many similarities to Mussolini's Italy, while stubbornly defying the label 'Fascist', for it lacked most of the essential qualities typical of a Fascist regime, namely, a single party run along rigorous lines, the constant mobilization of the masses, a systematic reign of terror exercised by an omnipresent secret police and a single leader at the centre of power and the object of a cult of personality pursued with propagandist zeal. In Japan, the political participation of the people was far less advanced than in Italy, to say nothing of Fascist Germany. And there were none of the militant proletarian mass movements that the upper and middle classes might have regarded as a threat to their social status. As a result the military elites in Japan were able to place their stamp on a regime that was growing increasingly authoritarian without having to depend on any pseudo-plebiscitary acclamation to legitimize their rule.

Like many European states of the interwar years, Japan turned its back on parliamentary democracy during this time. Almost everywhere that this system had not been firmly rooted in society in the years leading up to the First World War, parliamentary democracy was replaced by authoritarian or totalitarian regimes in the course of the 1920s and 1930s. Of the new states that came into existence in Europe after 1918, only three – Czechoslovakia, Finland and Eire – were still parliamentary democracies by the end of the 1930s. With a single exception the countries ruled by right-wing dictatorships were predominantly agricultural in character, the one exception being Germany, a highly industrialized country which with the transfer of power to the leader of the National Socialists drew a radical line under the fourteen years of the country's first democracy and under a much older tradition of a constitutional state governed by the rule of law. What kind of a future western democracy and, with it, the entire normative process of the West could look forward to in 1933, the fourth year of the Great Depression, when Hitler came to power in Germany at almost the same time as Franklin Delano Roosevelt in America, was still an open question.

3

Democracies and Dictatorships: 1933–9

A New Deal for America: Roosevelt's Presidency 1933–6

ACCORDING TO A GREEK proverb quoted by Aristotle in his *Politics*, 'Well begun is half done.' If ever a government abided by this insight, then it was Roosevelt's first administration, beginning in 1933. During his famous first hundred days in office, he addressed Congress no fewer than fifteen times and introduced fifteen major reform bills. The day of his inauguration, 4 March, was a Saturday. The government agreed that banks in the capital would be closed for a long weekend, thereby following the example of New York and Illinois, which had already closed their banks on the morning of 4 March.

The Emergency Banking Act was rushed through Congress on 9 March, giving the government comprehensive powers to deal with any private bank at risk of collapse and allowing it to monitor all gold movements and to issue new banknotes through the Federal Reserve. The government's resolute actions prevented panic from affecting the markets and avoided a complete collapse of the American banking system. They were followed by the Glass–Steagall Act, named after its sponsors, Senator Carter Glass from Virginia and Congressman Henry B. Steagall from Alabama, and designed to separate business banks from investment banks with the aim of curbing speculation, at the same time creating the Federal Deposit Insurance Corporation guaranteeing savings up to $2,500.

Roosevelt's government had been in office for barely seven weeks when on 19 April 1933 it was forced to take a decision that had worldwide repercussions and that involved abandoning the gold standard. Roosevelt hoped that in this way he would be able to counter his government's unpopular price rises and avoid the dangers of further deflationary pressures. Agriculture and the export industry did indeed profit from the fall in the rate of the dollar, but imports fell. And Roosevelt paid no attention to the impact of his measures on any of the world's other economies. On 3 July he informed the World Economic Conference that had been meeting in London since 12 June that the value of the dollar would henceforth be measured by its domestic purchasing power.

The aim of this 'bombshell message' was clear: the United States had no intention of allowing other nations to shackle its movements in terms of its currency.

The large number of socio-political innovations associated with the concept of the 'New Deal' began on 31 March 1933 with the creation of the Civilian Conservation Corps, which was designed to help unemployed young men between the ages of eighteen and twenty-five to work for the common good at a symbolic wage of one dollar a day. Central to the scheme's activities was environmental protection in the form of farming and reforestation. Its camps were set up by the Department of War. By September 1935 the number of young people living in these camps was over half a million, and by 1941 a total of 2.5 million youths and young men had spent time with the CCC.

The country's trade unions viewed the experiment as dangerous, claiming that it threatened to exacerbate the tendency to reduce wages and to disempower the labour force. William Green, the president of the American Federation of Labor, complained that it 'smacked of Fascism, Hitlerism and a form of Sovietism' when he appeared before a joint session of the House and the Senate in 1933.[1] There had indeed been a similar scheme in Germany since 1931, the Volunteer Labour Service, which in June 1935 gave way to the National Labour Service in which all Germans between the ages of eighteen and twenty-five had to do six months' voluntary service. The Civilian Conservation Corps, on the other hand, was a voluntary organization, adding substantially to its popularity, although both organizations had a paramilitary aspect to them. In the United States this aspect seemed distinctly out of place, whereas in National Socialist Germany it fitted seamlessly into the general scheme of things.

On 12 May the Civilian Conservation Corps was followed by the Federal Emergency Relief Administration and the Agricultural Adjustment Administration, or 'Triple A'. The former was run by Roosevelt's long-term colleague, Harry Hopkins, and had the task of coordinating social assistance measures for the unemployed. Under Hopkins, the Civil Works Administration was set up with the aim of creating public work schemes paying minimum wages. By mid-January 1934 it was employing more than four million workers building roads, schools, children's playgrounds, sports facilities and airports.

'Triple A' aimed to raise the prices of agricultural produce from wheat and maize to cotton, dairy produce and pig farming by working together with farming organizations and limiting the amount of produce that reached the market, leaving fields fallow and in some cases even destroying produce, including the mass slaughter of pigs. These measures increased farmers' income, but the principal beneficiaries were not those who worked the land but the major landowners. A related scheme was the Emergency Farm Mortgage Act that was passed on 12 March 1933 at the same time as the Agricultural Adjustment Act and designed to place rural mortgages on a new financial footing. Agricultural credits were reformed under the terms of the Farm Credit Act of 16 June 1933.

The most spectacular project undertaken by Roosevelt during his first hundred days in office was the creation of the Tennessee Valley Authority, or TVA, on 18 May 1933. With this gigantic scheme for creating energy, the Roosevelt administration was responding to a demand by progressive reformers to use the country's vast reserves of water to generate cheap electricity. The TVA was authorized to revive a project that had been initiated during the First World War but never completed, namely, the building of a dam at Muscle Shoals in Alabama, in addition to building other dams and power stations in the Tennessee Valley and in that way helping the economy of one of the country's largest underdeveloped regions. This last-mentioned aim was only partially achieved, but the TVA was none the less able to bring electricity to parts of the state where it had not previously been available and at the same time to force energy suppliers throughout the country as a whole to reduce their prices.

Roosevelt's first hundred days were barely over when the National Industrial Recovery Act came into force on 16 June 1933. In turn, the National Recovery Administration was established on its basis under General Hugh Johnson. The NRA was an umbrella organization for self-governing bodies in individual branches of the economy, where employers and employees enjoyed equal representation. Its 'codes' were specific to individual branches of the economy and governed minimum wages (between 30 and 40 cents an hour), the length of the working week (no more than forty hours), a ban on child labour and general regulations covering employment and production. Under Paragraph 7(a) employees had the right to organize themselves in trade unions and to agree on wages through a process of free collective bargaining. On the other hand, the relevant section of the act included no provision for measures to enforce wage negotiations. The NRA received $3,300 million to finance public works that were offered out for tender under the highly effective symbol of the Blue Eagle. Less apparent were the shortcomings inherent in the system from the outset, including the tendency to favour large firms at the expense of smaller ones and the arbitrary way in which wages and prices were frequently fixed.

There was no unifying philosophy underpinning the New Deal. Most of the ideas that it enshrined sprang from the 'progressive movement' of the early twentieth century. The intellectuals who advised Roosevelt all shared a common conviction, which was the belief that market mechanisms were not enough to help America out of its present crisis, meaning that the state had to intervene. Neither the president nor the economists to whom he listened were Keynesians. Rather, Roosevelt's overriding aim was to balance the books. At least one of the early New Deal laws had a markedly 'pro-cyclical' quality: the Economy Act of 20 March 1933 reduced war veterans' pensions and the salaries of federal employees by 15 per cent and in that way reduced the spending power of the masses. Roosevelt ended the Civil Works Program abruptly in 1934, when he found that it was too expensive to maintain. In

1933–4 he certainly did not accord public work creation schemes the same degree of importance that Keynes and his colleagues felt that such programmes should enjoy.

On 31 December 1933 the *New York Times* published an open letter from Keynes in which the economist invited the president to offset the lack of consumer demand by introducing a generous policy of 'deficit spending' in order to reflate the economy. Five months later, on 28 May 1934, Keynes was received at the White House, but he was unable to persuade his host to revise his economic policies. Shortly afterwards Roosevelt told his labour minister Frances Perkins, the first female cabinet minister in American history, that Keynes had bombarded him with numbers and was a mathematician rather than an economist. For his part, Keynes was left with the impression that Roosevelt understood nothing about economics.

The vast majority of the American people were impressed by the way in which the new government tackled the problems that it faced. Roosevelt, his ministers and administrative chiefs exuded dynamism and vigour, setting them gratifyingly apart from the fatalism that seemed retrospectively to be the salient feature of Hoover's regime. Roosevelt had a gift for using his regular radio broadcasts from the Oval Office – his legendary 'fireside chats' – to address Americans directly and to turn the new mass medium into an effective means of government. He was a gifted, charismatic orator who time and again succeeded in putting his political enemies and hostile journalists on the defensive and in turning himself into a direct mouthpiece of the people. The fact that he had few unassailable convictions and preferred to avoid clear statements but opted for the line of least resistance was well known to all who had access to him, but these qualities did nothing to detract from his standing among the wider public.

In every country the world financial crisis encouraged isolationism, and the United States was keener than most to espouse this tendency, concentrating on domestic policies even more than it had done under Hoover and playing into the hands of the isolationists. In order not to be drawn into further dealings with Europe, Washington was content to leave the dictators in Rome and Berlin to pursue their policies unchecked, and although the anti-Jewish riots in Germany in April 1933 were noted with some concern, they elicited no major protests. During the early years of his rule, Hitler was seen for the most part as a relatively moderate representative of the National Socialist movement. In November 1933 the United States was the last major power in the West to resume diplomatic relations with the Soviet Union, a step that earned Roosevelt the lively approval of those economic circles that were interested in foreign trade.

Under Roosevelt, the United States continued its good-neighbour policy towards Latin America, a policy already inaugurated by Hoover. In December 1933, in the course of a visit to Montevideo, the secretary of state Cordell Hull expressly declared that no state had the right to meddle in the affairs of another.

To the delight of the peoples of Latin America, Roosevelt underlined this assertion only a few days later, when he issued an emphatic rejection of a policy of
armed intervention. Of course, this line also applied to brutal dictatorships like
that of Rafael Trujillo in the Dominican Republic, a country entirely dependent
on the United States. The United States had only one overseas colony, the
Philippines, which it had acquired from Spain in 1898. In March 1934 it passed
the Tydings–McDuffie Act, granting the country the status of an autonomous
commonwealth, with full independence after ten years. It was above all financial reasons that prompted this step. In Japan, of course, Congress's decision
was interpreted to mean that America had decided to withdraw from Asia.

Within a year of the first New Deal laws coming into force, the initial wave
of euphoria had vanished. It was the National Recovery Administration that
received the most criticism: the trade unions were unhappy that most of its
provisions affecting free collective bargaining remained ineffectual, while
employers complained at the fact that the government was constantly interfering in their affairs. For their part, consumers took exception to rising prices.
Progressives among the Republicans such as senators William Borah of Idaho
and Gerald Nye of North Dakota regarded the codes as a way of suppressing
small businesses and encouraging the growth of monopolies, and even
Roosevelt himself increasingly came to believe that the NRA was a step too far
in the direction of overregulation, with the result that in September 1934 he
forced General Johnson to step down and replaced him with one of his closest
confidants, Donald Richberg. From then on Roosevelt sought only solutions
that he was sure would win the support of big business. By then, the Public
Works Administration under the direction of the secretary of the interior,
Harold Ickes, had been re-established as a separate organization from the NRA.

In the first year of the New Deal there was widespread support for the
government's measures, but this support began to wane in 1934. Roosevelt's
'broker state' – an American variant of corporatism – was opposed not only by
the major industries and banks but also by Conservative Democrats, including
even the 1928 presidential candidate, 'Al' Smith. Their protests found articulate
expression in August 1934 in the foundation of the American Liberty League, in
which companies such as Du Pont and General Motors were hugely influential.
The Democrats who joined the League included many who held it against
Roosevelt that his government, in fulfilling one of its election promises, had
passed the Twenty-First Amendment in 1933, ending prohibition.

The American Liberty League invoked the spirit of the American constitution, arguing that that spirit was far superior to all foreign systems of government, be they Communist, National Socialist or Fascist. In November 1934 its
leader Jouett Shouse declared that its aim was to uphold 'fundamental
Americanism' in the face of all subversive theories and foreign doctrines. By
'fundamental Americanism' he meant a free entrepreneurial economy in the
spirit of Manchester capitalism that was not regulated by state bureaucracy: a

liberal idyll that necessarily assumed reactionary qualities in the wake of the world economic crisis, when the League in all seriousness proposed that all cases of direct welfare be transferred to the Red Cross, while 'self-help' was prescribed as the panacea in every other instance.

The reactionary activities of the Liberty League were eclipsed, however, by the politicking of the press baron William Randolph Hearst, who in 1933 abruptly switched from Roosevelt's ally to one of his fiercest critics. The mere fact that the government 'interfered' in private business opened it up to the suspicion that it had been infiltrated by Communists, and Communism needed to be resisted in every possible way. It was to the credit of Hitler and Mussolini that they had done precisely that in Europe. As Hearst explained in November 1934 to the editors in chief of the thirty or so newspapers and magazines that he owned, there was 'as yet' no genuinely Fascist movement active in the United States, but he was by no means willing to exclude the possibility of the need for such an organization in the future. The clear aim of Fascism, he explained, was to defeat Communism and render it harmless and in that way to prevent the least capable and least credible class from gaining control of the country: 'Fascism will only come into existence in the United States when such a move-ment becomes really necessary for the prevention of communism.'[2]

Hearst did not regard this development as desirable. As long as the existing social order could be maintained by traditional means, Hearst was inclined to prefer the American system of government to all 'crazy isms', but in order to preserve this system it was necessary, he argued, to reduce the number of what he deemed to be un-American activities. Academic freedom, for example, was 'a phrase taken over by the radical groups as a new camouflage for the teaching of alien doctrines'.[3] In the autumn of 1934, immediately after his return from a visit to Hitler, Hearst organized a press campaign in support of the violent suppression of a general strike in San Francisco. Admiration for the Fascist regimes in Europe turned increasingly into the promotion of a policy designed to bring America into line with those systems.

Opposition to Roosevelt outside government circles began to form in 1934 not only among the upper classes but also in much broader swathes of the population. The earliest signs of this development appeared in Louisiana, a stronghold of the southern Democrats that was effectively a one-party state governed by Huey P. Long, a Ciceronian lawyer who at the time of his election in 1928 was only thirty-five and who owed his electoral success to the popula-tion in rural areas where the 'populists' had been powerful before the turn of the century. His image was that of an advocate of the white lower orders, and there is no doubt that he had little time or patience for the existing system whereby the state was dominated by plantation owners and by the Standard Oil Company. His political achievements at home included taxation legislation that benefited the poor, an extensive road-building programme and the intro-duction of free learning aids at state-run schools; these ensured that he commanded widespread support not only among whites but among the black population too. He brought the administration under his control by means of a system of improved patronage, quickly taking charge of the legislative and judiciary and acquiring such exhaustive opportunities for vote-rigging that it would be no exaggeration to speak of a personal dictatorship. None of this changed when he stepped down as governor in 1932 and represented Louisiana in the Senate.

Huey P. Long became a factor in national politics only when he stopped supporting Roosevelt and became his political enemy in the summer of 1933. In Long's view, the president's policies were insufficiently radical, prompting Roosevelt to regard the senator from Louisiana as a political demagogue and a dangerous rival. His decision to exclude Long's supporters from the autocratic distribution of official posts merely intensified the breach between the two men. From then on Long lost no opportunity to criticize Roosevelt for reducing war veterans' pensions, for a lack of willingness to redistribute the nation's wealth and for a growing dependence on banks and business concerns.

From January 1934 onwards Long's national platform was built upon his Share Our Wealth programme, a random collection of eye-catching principles often lacking in any real grasp of economics. He believed that every family should be guaranteed a debt-free minimum income of $5,000. In order to achieve this goal, no single individual should be allowed to possess a fortune worth more than $5 million. All persons over sixty should receive a monthly pension and all should be guaranteed an annual income of at least $2,000. The working week should be cut, agricultural production offset by government purchases, and gifted children should receive a free college education. Share Our Wealth clubs quickly spread across the whole country, with the result that by February 1935 there were 27,000 of them. In addition, Long's successful advertising campaigns attracted such strong support among farmers in the Midwest that the White House was obliged to take seriously the senator's obvious ambitions in terms of the highest office in the land. In the event, however, Long was never to be a presidential candidate, for on 8 September 1935 he was shot in Baton Rouge by a young left-wing doctor. He died of his injuries two days later.

Many of Long's contemporaries saw him as a potential American Hitler, though the most frequent reproach that was levelled against him was his alleged desire to establish a Fascist regime à la Mussolini in the United States. And yet the large-scale removal of all those elements that guaranteed a democratic representative constitution in the state of Louisiana is scarcely enough to describe his regime as Fascist. His governorship was distinguished from Fascist dictatorships not least by the fact that it was not directed at the organized workforce. In his wish to remove the traditional upper echelons of society from their role as political leaders he was in fact faithful to a far more populist tradition. Indeed, his regime bore a number of the features typical of a Latin American dictatorship and could have come into existence only because of the special conditions that existed in Louisiana. Any attempt to extend that regime to the rest of the United States would almost certainly have failed.

Long was not the only figure who sought to mobilize the masses against the policies of the Roosevelt administration in the course of 1934, for a similar aim was pursued with considerable success by Father Charles Coughlin, a Catholic priest from Holy Oak in Michigan, whose nationwide radio broadcasts, starting in 1930, reached an audience of up to forty million Americans. Like Long, Coughlin had initially been a supporter of Roosevelt and his New Deal but by 1934 his language was growing increasingly critical. Annoyed at the lack of appreciation that he had received for lending his backing to Roosevelt, he henceforth concentrated his attacks on what he regarded as the unduly slow rate of progress in the president's struggle to deal with the Great Depression and also on the inadequacy of Roosevelt's measures to protect farmers and the continuing power of finance capital. In consequence he targeted his campaign on rural America, which was constitutionally hostile to modern capitalism, and also on the urban lower classes who felt neglected by the New Deal. It was here that Coughlin found most of his supporters after he had created a political platform for himself in November 1934 with his National Union for Social Justice. Central to his support group were farmers in the Midwest and badly paid workers and the unemployed in the north-east, whereas small businesses were relatively poorly represented.

The new organization's programme demanded, among other things, a fair minimum wage for every type of work, fair prices for farmers, the acceptance that Congress alone should be able to decide on questions of monetary policy and, finally, guaranteed rights for workers combined with a duty on the part of the state to protect workers' organizations from the 'vested interests of wealth and intellect'. The most radical point in the organization's programme was the demand for the nationalization of those branches of the economy that were by nature too important to be controlled by private individuals. In particular Coughlin meant energy suppliers and mineral resources. In every other area private property was to remain inviolate.[4]

Among the National Union for Social Justice's regional strongholds were Catholic districts in towns and cities in the states of Massachusetts and New York, where in 1935 there were four times more local subgroups than in the agricultural and Protestant states of Minnesota and Wisconsin. In this way Coughlin was able to go far beyond the catchment area of the agrarian populism of the years before 1900. In his speeches and writings he played off the unspoilt folk against the corrupt ruling classes, while his call for a silver-backed currency – in effect a policy of creating easy money – and his direct appeal to the spokesmen of the agricultural protest movement of the late nineteenth century made it clear in which tradition Coughlin saw himself. No one could have called him a 'Fascist' in 1934 or 1935. And if he sympathized with the Fascist regimes in Europe at this time, he never revealed this in his speeches and public statements.

In the extreme west of the country, too, there were protests at the rule of government during Roosevelt's second year in office. In January 1934 Francis Townsend, a sixty-seven-year-old physician, and an estate agent by the name of Robert Clements established an organization calling itself Old-Age Revolving Pensions, Ltd. Its central demand was an old age pension of $200 a month for everyone over the age of sixty as long as they had retired from gainful employment and agreed to spend the sum in question within a month on American soil. The pension was to be financed by a 2 per cent tax on all business transactions, the money in question to be paid into a national pension pot described as a 'revolving fund'. Townsend and his colleagues believed that in this way they could overcome mass unemployment. Young unemployed people would take over their elders' jobs once the latter had become vacant and stimulate the economy through increased demand. Although experts soon raised their voices in protest at the idea, many Americans of the older generation clearly felt that the Townsend Plan offered a solution to their material hardship, and by the end of 1934 there were already 1,200 clubs promoting the idea of the revolving fund, most of them in the west of the United States.

The major strikes that swept the country in 1934 and that often involved violence were directed less at the government than at individual businesses. In Milwaukee, for example, a walkout by tram workers descended into rioting. In Philadelphia and New York the taxi drivers went on strike, in Des Moines power station employees stopped working, and in California and southern New Jersey it was the farmers who went on strike. In May a lorry drivers' strike in Minneapolis ended in bloodshed when two of the strike-breakers paid for by the employers were killed, while two more striking workers were killed in the general strike in San Francisco in July. Labor Day – the first Monday in September, which had been a public holiday since 1894 – marked the start of a walkout by textile workers that turned into the biggest strike in American history. In Rhode Island, fifty workers were injured in violent clashes between strikers and the police, and in Honea Path in southern California six workers were killed by paid blacklegs. Almost every labour dispute ended in defeat for the workers. In many cases the driving forces were socialists, Communists or Trotskyists. But there can be no question of a revolutionary movement designed to do away with the capitalist economic system: in 1934 the mass of workers were interested solely in higher wages and better working conditions.

From an economic point of view, the year 1934 was still overshadowed by the Great Depression. At 11.3 million, the number of unemployed workers was around 1.5 million fewer than it had been in 1933, when unemployment had reached its all-time high. As a proportion of the workforce, the percentage of unemployed fell from 24.9 per cent to 21.7 per cent between 1933 and 1934. In 1934 national income was some 25 per cent higher than in 1933 but was still only a little over half of what it had been in 1929. Roosevelt's government could not interpret these data as signs of a successful economic policy, but nor could they be used by his enemies as arguments against the New Deal.

The year 1934 also witnessed the country's mid-term elections. The government was under no threat from any forces outside parliament, since such forces were nowhere organized as effective parties. The Republicans had still found no convincing alternative to the New Deal. Traditionally, opposition parties did well in mid-term elections, but not on this occasion, when the Republicans won thirteen fewer seats in the House of Representatives and recorded their worst ever results. A third of the seats in the Senate were due for re-election, and here the Republicans' losses were even more dramatic, the Democrats winning a comfortable two-thirds majority – the best result that any party ever achieved. One of the new Democrat senators was Harry S. Truman from Missouri, who was to be his country's president from 1945 to 1953.

The Democrats' election victory was a personal triumph for Roosevelt, which not even his enemies could dispute. And yet his great success had a negative aspect to it, for there was now a tendency on the part of the Democrats to urge FDR to adopt more radical policies than he had pursued until then. His party was more interested in maintaining its mass support than in enlisting the sympathies of the elite. Roosevelt, conversely, refused to accept that big business had more or less closed ranks in its opposition to him, and so he continued his attempts to reach an agreement with the banks and major industries. But he was no doubt aware that he could not avoid a modest shift to the left and even a Second New Deal.

Among the laws enacted under the terms of the Second New Deal in the early months of 1935 was one that was indeed aimed at corporate interests, namely, the Public Utility Holding Company Act, the aim of which was to break up those holding companies in the field of energy supply that were unable to demonstrate their social necessity to the Securities and Exchange Commission by 1 January 1940. In response to pressure from the affected concerns, the House of Representatives ended up leaving the SEC to take whatever decisions it deemed appropriate.

The Social Security Act overseen by Frances Perkins's Department of Labor was even more interventionist in its impact inasmuch as it prescribed federal aid for the elderly of $15 a month and created a retirement insurance scheme financed by additional taxes paid by employers and employees alike. The payments were to start in 1942 and provide anyone over sixty-five with between $10 and $85 a month. Agricultural workers and domestic servants were excluded from these provisions. All those who did not have insurance were to be assisted by welfare payments from the federal government and from the individual states. The act also included provisions for a rudimentary national insurance scheme to be set up by the federal government and by the individual states, the costs of which were to be borne by employers alone, together with regulations covering federal aid for single mothers and the disabled and, finally, public work in the health service. When judged by European standards, these measures were extremely modest and even meagre, but for the United States the introduction of obligatory national insurance represented a breakthrough in the direction of a welfare state.

The continuing high level of unemployment meant that the government felt obliged to continue its ambitious efforts in the field of work relief, evincing a more Keynesian approach to politics than had been the case until then. Responsibility for implementing this new policy devolved on the Works Progress Administration, or WPA, that was run by Harry Hopkins. Under its aegis more than 600,000 miles of new roads were built, including multi-lane national park-ways through areas of great natural beauty, as well as almost 125,000 bridges, more than 125,000 public buildings, over 800 parks and 850 airports. The WPA was able to draw on funding of $5,000 million and on average employed more than two million people at any one time. A sub-department at the WPA, the Emergency Housing Division, was entrusted with the task of encouraging the building of council houses using federal funds, while the Rural Electrification Administration took on the challenge of bringing electricity to rural America: in 1935 nine out of ten farms had no electricity, a figure that had fallen to six out of ten by 1941 and to one in ten by 1950.

The WPA also provided aid for individual organizations that helped not only young people but also artists and writers. The National Youth Administration provided charity work for unemployed young people, including part-time work, and also awarded college grants, while the Federal Writers Project helped unemployed writers. A similar service was provided for unemployed musicians and theatre workers by the Federal Music Project and the Federal Theater Project. Among the government commissions awarded to unemployed painters and sculptors by the Federal Art Project were many murals that still adorn the walls of public buildings such as libraries and post offices, all of them built by the WPA. A favourite motif was that of workers in heroic poses vaguely reminiscent of the Proletkult of the Soviet Union and of contemporary 'works of art' in Germany and Italy at this period.

By the end of May 1935 only one of the laws associated with the Second New Deal had been passed by Congress: the Relief Bill. All the other acts were delayed in the main because of resistance from 'progressive' senators and representatives who felt that the president's policies were too employer-friendly. In this context Roosevelt's government suffered its worst defeat to date on 27 May 1935, when the Supreme Court declared in a unanimous decision that the National Industrial Recovery Act was unconstitutional. The case had been brought by Schechter Poultry Corp. of Brooklyn, which supplied live poultry to kosher slaughterhouses and which had been sentenced under Paragraph 7(a) of the act of 16 June 1933 to a substantial fine for violating codes relating to minimum wages and the length of the working week. The Supreme Court declared the economic activities of Schechter Poultry to be 'intrastate commerce' rather than 'interstate commerce' and argued, accordingly, that the state had no right to legislate in the matter. By placing this restrictive interpretation on the definition of commerce in Article 1 of the American constitution, the court called into question most of the laws passed under the New Deal. The headline in the *Daily Express* hit the nail on the head: 'America Stunned: Roosevelt's Two Years' Work Killed in Twenty Minutes.'

Behind the judgment of 27 May 1935 were not only the conservative judges who, together with the middle-of-the-roaders, were in a small majority, but also self-appointed progressives such as Louis D. Brandeis and Benjamin N. Cardozo. For them, the provisions of the National Industrial Recovery Act weakened competition by encouraging monopolies, inviting the Supreme Court's intervention. In subsequent rulings on New Deal legislation the conservative judges stuck together, the court's decisions commanding a majority of five to four or six to three. Public opinion was almost entirely against the Supreme Court's decisions, but there was also hostility to the president's plans to raise the number of judges by appointing a further judge for each of them who had reached the age of seventy, and in March 1937 Congress rejected a draft bill to this effect. Shortly afterwards the conflict between the Supreme Court and the government came to a sudden and surprising end when one moderately conservative judge, Owen J. Roberts, switched sides and joined his liberal colleagues. Soon afterwards several of the judges who had been in the majority retired and were replaced by liberals, with the result that the Supreme Court ceased to be a bulwark of opposition to the New Deal.

Shortly before the Supreme Court announced its decision on 27 May 1935, Roosevelt had realized that he could no longer avoid an open confrontation with big business, a realization prompted by a clear declaration of war by the United States Chamber of Commerce at the beginning of that month. The quashing of the National Industrial Recovery Act by the Supreme Court was merely the last straw, prompting a new political offensive often described by historians as Roosevelt's 'second hundred days'. In early June he informed Congress that he was keen for several important new laws to be passed with immediate effect, laws that included the Social Security Bill, the Public Utility Holding Company Bill and the draft of a new banking bill. The Senate and House of Representatives responded positively to his appeal, with the result that all of these laws had been enacted by the end of 1935.

Surprisingly Roosevelt now committed himself to a project that he and Frances Perkins had initially viewed with scepticism. The draft of a National Labor Relations Act had been submitted by the Democrat senator Robert Wagner, who had been born in Germany in 1877 and whose bill was the most radical of any during the New Deal era, raising the principle of collective bargaining to the level of a legally binding provision and obliging employers not to place any obstacles in the way of workers wanting to form trade unions. The draft did not make any provisions for comparable conditions for trade unions, thereby incurring the wrath of conservative critics. The Senate had already approved the bill on 2 May, and it was passed by a large majority in the House of Representatives on 27 June. Roosevelt signed the new legislation on 5 July.

The Wagner Act increased the power of the unions, which at this date in their history were suffering from a serious organizational crisis. The unions' largest umbrella organization, the AFL, had always looked after the needs of skilled workers, while neglecting the untrained workers in those branches of industry that relied on mass production. In 1934 a minority of supporters of the president of the United Mine Workers of America, John L. Lewis, with the backing of barely 30 per cent of all members of the AFL, openly opposed the one-sided emphasis on support for the craft unions and proposed instead the more modern principle of an industrial union that was not limited to a particular profession.

The AFL's congress in Atlantic City in October 1935 turned into a trial of strength, with the majority of delegates emphatically rejecting the principle of an industrial union, prompting those unions that had been in the minority, namely, the mineworkers and workers in the clothing and textile industries, to form an organization of their own, the Committee for Industrial Organization, or CIO. When the majority refused to accept this, the conflict escalated, and in 1936 membership of the rival unions was suspended. Attempts to reverse this measure by legal means proved unsuccessful, and in October 1938 the Committee for Industrial Organization declared its independence and changed its name to the Congress of Industrial Organizations, allowing it to retain the abbreviation CIO.

The CIO reached far more female and black workers than the AFL and in general adopted a more militant stance than the older umbrella organization. But it never developed into an anti-capitalist force even though its ranks included many socialists and Communists. The opportunities for development contained in the Wagner Act meant that both the CIO and the AFL helped in fact to bring stability to the system. In time the differences between the two unions were eroded, opening up the way for their reunification as the AFL-CIO in 1955.

Among the left-wing signals emanating from the president in the early summer of 1935 was the announcement of a tax bill on 19 June. In his message to Congress Roosevelt proposed a national inheritance tax, levies on particularly high net incomes, a gift tax and a tax on joint-stock companies graduated according to the size of the businesses in question. Roosevelt left his adviser Raymond Moley in no doubt about the motive behind his demarche: he wanted to 'steal Long's thunder'.[5] William Randolph Hearst lost no time in suggesting that his editors launch a campaign and ascribe the 'bastard' plan to a 'composite personality which might be labeled Stalin Delano Roosevelt' and that they speak not of a 'New Deal' but of a 'Raw Deal' by accusing the president of pursuing a policy of 'soaking the successful'.[6]

In the House of Representatives the president's message found widespread support among the Democrats, whereas the Senate reacted with a demonstrative show of silence. By the end of the legislative process all that the president still had to show was a weakened bill with no inheritance tax and a far lower rate of taxes on joint-stock companies. In the view of the historian William E. Leuchtenburg, the Wealth Tax Act did little to help the tax affairs of smaller businesses or to redistribute affluence on a more equitable basis, still less to increase federal income:

> Yet since the act stepped up estate, gift, and capital stock taxes, levied an excess profits tax, which Roosevelt had not asked, and increased the surtax to the highest rates in history, it created deeper business resentment than any other New Deal measure.[7]

All the laws that Roosevelt personally championed in 1935 were simultaneously designed to improve his chances of being re-elected the following year. Following his break with big business, the outlines of the Roosevelt coalition became far clearer, embracing, as they did, workers, Catholics, women, ethnic minorities and black Americans. Organized workers were the target group that the Wagner Act was intended to help, while unemployed workers were the intended beneficiaries of a whole series of other aid programmes. The president's wife, Eleanor Roosevelt, took a particular interest in women's issues. Catholics and those ethnic minorities that had not yet been fully assimilated into American society were generally among those social groups that were less well-off and as a result more remote from the Republicans, who were famously well disposed to employers. The Democrats, after all, had always been keen to present themselves as the party of the 'little people'.

The black population benefited from the New Deal at least to the extent that these policies helped the lower strata in society in general, but Roosevelt's policies did not extend to granting civil rights to blacks. He turned a blind eye to the fact that the Civilian Conservation Corps established separate camps for black Americans, that the National Recovery Administration put its name to wage agreements that gave lower wages to black workers for doing the same as their white colleagues and that the Works Progress Administration regularly gave the worst-paid jobs to blacks. He did not even champion an anti-lynching bill proposed by the Democrat senators Robert F. Wagner from New York and Edward P. Costigan from Colorado. (In 1935 alone there were no fewer than eighteen lynch-mob murders in the southern states.) He was afraid that by committing himself to such legislation he would forfeit the support of southern Democrats and in that way jeopardize the New Deal in general. If he succeeded none the less in including blacks in his Roosevelt coalition, it was simply because from their point of view the Democrats were now the lesser of two evils when compared with the party once led by Abraham Lincoln.

The Republican candidate in the 1936 race for the presidency was the governor of Kansas, Alfred M. Landon. As a Canadian, Coughlin was prevented from entering the race, while Francis Townsend and Gerald L. K. Smith – the latter having replaced the murdered Huey Long as the head of the Share Our Wealth movement – formed a new party, the Union Party, in June 1936. Their candidate was the nominally Republican congressman from North Dakota, William Lemke, but there could be no talk of a united campaign, for Coughlin and Smith both frightened away moderate voters with their anti-Semitic outbursts, and – Smith even more than Coughlin – with their manifest sympathy for Fascism, prompting Lemke and Townsend to distance themselves from Long's successor. The Socialist candidate was again Norman Thomas, while the Communists fielded their party leader, Earl Browder.

The Republican campaign suffered from the fact that it lacked both a charismatic candidate and any rousing slogans. Lemke appealed above all to workers' fears that wages would fall as a result of the deductions for old-age insurance that were due to come into force on 1 January 1937. In his acceptance speech at the Democrat Convention in Philadelphia on 27 June, Roosevelt – or at least his speech writer and chief press officer, Thomas Corcoran – coined a phrase that has gone down in the history books: 'This generation of Americans has a rendezvous with destiny.' As he went on to explain, 'We are fighting to save a great and precious form of government for ourselves and for the world.'[8]

The elections were held on 3 November 1936, when Roosevelt's share of the vote – 60.8 per cent – was the highest ever won by a presidential candidate and was reflected in the Democrats' record results in the Senate and House of Representatives. The Republican Landon won 36.5 per cent, polling more votes than the incumbent in only two states, Maine and Vermont. The Unionist William Lemke won 2 per cent of the votes, the Socialist Norman Thomas 0.4 per cent and the Communist Earl Browder 0.2 per cent.

During the election campaign Coughlin had announced that he would make no more radio broadcasts if he failed to persuade nine million Americans to vote for Lemke, but in the event the Unionist candidate had to settle for fewer than 900,000 votes. Coughlin briefly kept his promise but it was not long before he was promoting even more extreme messages than before both through his speeches and through his writings. By 1938 he was openly describing himself as an anti-Semite and dismissing Communism and international finance capital as different manifestations of the same Jewish conspiracy. In his own journal *Social Justice* he published an anti-Semitic forgery under the title 'Protocols of the Elders of Zion'. He founded a new right-wing radical militant organization, the Christian Front, which held anti-Semitic demonstrations, hid caches of arms and celebrated Hitler, Mussolini and Franco as the saviours of western culture. The organization was banned in 1940, but it was not until 1942 that Coughlin ended his radio broadcasts in response to public pressure and a church ban, bringing to a close the political career of the parish priest from Holy Oak.

Roosevelt's re-election coincided with a period in American history when it seemed as if the country had weathered the economic storm. When compared with 1933, the national income had risen by around 50 per cent, while the number of people out of work fell for the first time since 1932, dropping to under the ten million mark, and although it still represented 16.9 per cent of the working population, this was 8 percentage points lower than its peak in 1933. By 1936 the Dow Jones Industrial Index was 80 per cent higher than it had been three years earlier. For the automobile industry 1936 was the most successful year since 1929. The upturn was so remarkable that Winthrop Aldrich, who was in charge of the Chase Manhattan Bank, was already warning of the dangers of inflation.

The economic recovery was only relative and, as Americans were soon to discover, it was premature to talk of a definitive end to the years of depression. It is impossible to say exactly how effective were the government's laws and other measures in boosting the economy. Conversely, we can say with some certainty what the New Deal failed to achieve: there had been no redistribution of income and no real measures to ensure equality between men and women; racial discrimination continued unabated; the lowest echelons in society such as slum dwellers, unemployed blacks, seasonal workers in agriculture and smallholders had few, if any, organizations to champion their cause, with the result that they played no part in shaping public opinion; and although Native Americans had been granted the right to own communal lands and elect their own tribal assemblies under the terms of the Indian Reorganization Act of 1934, the land that they owned was generally of such poor quality that white Americans had no interest in acquiring it.

In part it was political resistance that prevented the proponents of the New Deal from achieving more than they did, and in part it was their continuing attachment to the American way of life that deterred them from striving to implement more radical changes. Even so, they could pride themselves on the fact that the risk of starving to death was now much reduced. In short, they had brought America a little closer to a welfare state of the kind that existed in Europe. And they had helped to modernize America by bringing electricity to large areas of the countryside. But their greatest success was in overcoming the psychological depression that had plagued the United States since 1929. And because America began to believe in itself again soon after Roosevelt became president, the country's democratic system was never at serious risk during the world economic crisis. Herein lies the fundamental difference between the United States and those European nations that were transmogrified into dictatorships in the course of the 1920s and 1930s.

Of course, many contemporaries believed that under Roosevelt, America was developing in a direction that invited comparisons with the Fascist Italy of Mussolini and the National Socialist Germany of Hitler. Even as early as 1933 a left-wing liberal journalist like I. F. Stone – the pen-name of Isidor Feinstein

– was already claiming that Roosevelt's policies were understandable only if one assumed that the president was moving ever more clearly in the direction of Fascism, while the leader of the Socialists, Norman Thomas, argued in 1934 that the economic policies of the New Deal were indistinguishable from Mussolini's corporatism and Hitler's totalitarianism. That same year the leader of the American Communist Party, Earl Browder, wrote that Roosevelt's policies were 'a program of hunger, fascization and imperialist war. [. . .] In political essence and direction it is the same as Hitler's program.'[9]

But it was not only left-wing observers who equated the New Deal with Fascism and National Socialism. In 1933 the Democrat senator Carter Glass from Virginia complained in the context of the National Recovery Administration's codes of the 'utterly dangerous effort of the federal government at Washington to transplant Hitlerism to every corner of this nation.'[10] And in 1934 an isolationist Republican like Senator Arthur Vandenberg of Michigan had no hesitation in describing Roosevelt's decision to lower customs tariffs according to the principle of reciprocity as 'Fascist in its philosophy, Fascist in its objective.'[11] Congressman James Willis Taylor, a party friend of Vandenberg's, declared in a speech that he gave in the House of Representatives on 18 June 1934, marking Lincoln's birthday, that 'I have seen a dictatorship spring up which must have made the noses of Herr Hitler, Stalin, Mussolini, and Mustapha Kemal of Turkey turn green with envy. Independence in private business is a thing of the past, and individual liberty is only a memory.'[12]

Roosevelt's American opponents were not the only ones to see close links between the New Deal on the one hand and Fascism and National Socialism on the other. Mussolini himself read a review of the Italian edition of Roosevelt's *Looking Forward* in *Il Popolo d'Italia* of 7 July 1933 and discovered striking similarities between Italian Fascism and the America of the New Deal:

> The appeal to young people and the resolve and manly sobriety with which the struggle has been taken up here recall the manner in which Fascism awoke the Italian people. [. . .] No less reminiscent of Fascism is the fact that the state no longer abandons the economy to its own devices since its well-being is now identical to that of the people. The mood of this change is undoubtedly similar to that of Fascism. But it is impossible to say any more than this at present.[13]

The official newspaper of the German National Socialists, the *Völkischer Beobachter*, expressed itself in equally positive terms in its edition of 17 January 1934: 'We German National Socialists likewise turn to America and see Roosevelt undertaking experiments that are bold indeed. We too fear the possibility that they may fail.' And on 21 June 1934 the same paper reported that 'on a narrow and inadequate basis Roosevelt has done everything humanly possible.'[14]

There is no doubt that there are a number of similarities between the America of Franklin D. Roosevelt and the dictatorships of Hitler and Mussolini. The increase in the power of the executive, the state control of the economy, the cult of labour and the bellicose rhetoric used in the attempt to deal with the economic crisis, and the emotionally charged appeal to the historic mission of the nation in question: all of these factors existed not only in Italy and Germany but also in the United States after 1933. Anyone visiting the National Mall in the centre of the American capital will still find it dominated by neoclassical monuments dating for the most part from the period between 1933 and 1939 and bearing a marked likeness to the state architecture of Fascist Italy and National Socialist Germany. These buildings include the Federal Triangle with the National Gallery, the National Archives, the Supreme Court, the complex of buildings associated with the Smithsonian Institution, the Jefferson Memorial and many ministries and administrative offices.

But the architects of the New Deal did not need to mimic their colleagues working under European dictatorships to design monumental buildings, for they were developing plans first mooted in the early years of the twentieth century and in some cases at the end of the eighteenth century, plans that reflected the neoclassical tradition in autochthonous American architecture. In many countries, not just the United States, the world economic crisis encouraged a propensity for monumental architecture intended to underscore the increased importance of state control and to that extent created a 'post-liberal' impression. In the words of the cultural historian Wolfgang Schivelbusch,

> It makes no difference whether we are dealing with societies shaken by Bolsheviks and Fascists or with others restored to an even keel by capitalism and democracy, they all needed a kind of architecture that conveyed a sense of confidence, respect and even quasi-religious meaning and cohesion to the community over which that architecture raised its temple-like structures, while at the same time making it clear to the rest of the world exactly who those societies were.[15]

The similarities between these different kinds of architecture, all of which were intended to discourage thoughts of economic depression, are a reflection of the challenges that all these countries faced during these years of crisis. But the answers given in Rome, Berlin and Washington could hardly have been more different, at least where the political foundations of the community in question were concerned. There was no regime change in the United States but, instead, a series of reforms designed to strengthen the country's democracy. America retained its constitution, which by 1933 was 146 years old, and it abandoned none of the principles that had seemed so important to its founding fathers. Few European countries had experienced such an unbroken democratic tradition and a political culture marked by such a tradition. Italy and Germany were certainly not among them. Had the situation been different, they would presumably have been more effective in resisting the establishment of a dictatorship.

The Process of Seizing Power: The Establishment of the National Socialist Dictatorship 1933–4

With effect from 30 January 1933 the German government was headed by a man who saw himself as the saviour of the German people and, with them, the entire Germanic race. Believing himself appointed by divine providence, he hoped to free the Germans not only from the shame of the Treaty of Versailles but also from Marxism, liberalism and parliamentarianism and, indeed, from evil in all its manifestations, evil which sought to disguise itself behind manifold masks in an attempt to conceal its corrosive work but which may be summed up in two words: international Jewry. In Hitler's eyes, Marxism was only one of the Jews' disguises, albeit the most successful, since it had helped the Jews to dominate the workforce. Rescuing workers from the influence of international Marxism and winning them over to the cause of the nation's best interests could succeed only with the help of a movement and of a leader that were resolved to combat the Jews in the most ruthless ways imaginable.

Hitler believed that he himself was that leader. During his months of imprisonment in Landsberg in 1924 he had summed up his belief in his mission in words that were intended to be every bit as apocalyptic as they sounded:

> If, with the help of his Marxist creed, the Jew is victorious over the other peoples of the world, his crown will be the funeral wreath of humanity and this planet will, as it did millions of years ago, move through the ether devoid of men.
>
> Eternal Nature inexorably avenges the infringement of her commands.
>
> Hence today I believe that I am acting in accordance with the will of the Almighty Creator: *by defending myself against the Jew, I am fighting for the work of the Lord.*[16]

The religious phraseology makes it clear what its leader intended National Socialism to be: a worldly *ecclesia militans* that had a monopoly on salvation, a totalitarian religion comparable in its all-embracing claims only to Italian Fascism on the one hand and to Soviet Communism on the other. As a totalitarian regime, National Socialist Germany was a new kind of dictatorship that clearly differed from all other authoritarian systems such as the military dictatorships of Europe and Latin America. Among its innovatory features was its mobilization of the masses and its claims to address each and every citizen in his or her entirety, its aim being to create a 'new man'. Such a system did not yet exist in Germany on 30 January 1933 or even in the weeks immediately afterwards. But anyone familiar with Hitler's public pronouncements from his 'time of struggle' knew that he was eager to establish a system that would be at least as totalitarian as the Fascist system of Benito Mussolini.

German National Socialism had much in common with Italian Fascism: radical nationalism, anti-Marxism and anti-liberalism, the militarization of the political struggle at home, the cult of youth, manhood and violence and the central role of the charismatic leader. Both movements can trace back their origins to the traumatic experience of the outcome of the First World War: just as the National Socialists blamed their country's military defeat on the 'stab in the back' by the 'November criminals', so the Italian Fascists blamed the weakness of the liberals and the internationalism of the left for the country's 'mutilated victory' and for the Western Allies' abilities to thwart its ambitious plans for annexation. Both parties were adept at exploiting the widespread fear of a 'Red revolution' like the one mounted by the Russian Bolsheviks, and both took advantage of the split in the Marxist workers' movement in the wake of the First World War and the October Revolution.

The similarities between Mussolini's Fascists and Hitler's National Socialists were so pronounced that many contemporaries, especially on the political left, regarded National Socialism as no more than a German manifestation of Fascism, and there is no doubt that this was true to the extent that the term 'Fascism' is used to describe a new kind of militant mass movement on the part of the extreme right and, therefore, a type of movement that had not existed anywhere in Europe in the years before the war. But National Socialism was not just 'German Fascism': far more than Italian Fascism, it was a political religion that sought to appeal to the whole man, in which regard it was in fact closer to its antithesis, Soviet Bolshevism. It was in every regard more extreme and more totalitarian than its Italian model, and it was able to draw on a mythological scapegoat unavailable to Mussolini or to his movement and his regime: Italian Fascism was largely innocent of the all-consuming hatred of the Jews that was central to Hitler's view of the world.

A counterpart to the war on the Jews was the fight for the racially pure pan-German Reich of the future behind which Germany's two previous empires – the Holy Roman Empire and Bismarck's Reich – paled into insignificance. 'The boundaries of the year 1914 mean nothing at all for the German future,' wrote Hitler in *Mein Kampf*:

> Neither did they provide a defence of the past, nor would they contain any strength for the future. [. . .] *Germany will either be a world power or there will be no Germany.* And for world power she needs that magnitude which will give her the position she needs in the present period, and life to her citizens.
>
> *And so we National Socialists consciously draw a line beneath the foreign policy tendency of our pre-War period. We take up where we broke off six hundred years ago. We stop the endless German movement to the south and*

west, and turn our gaze towards the land of the east. At long last we break off the colonial and commercial policy of the pre-War period and shift to the soil policy of the future.[17]

For Hitler, the 'east' meant Russia and 'her vassal border states'. Hitler was convinced that fate itself had sought to give a sign to Germany by abandoning Russia to Bolshevism. From his point of view, the Bolsheviks' seizure of power had resulted in the replacement of the country's previous rulers, who were quintessentially Germanic in origin, with Jews incapable in the longer term of holding together so vast an empire:

> The giant empire in the east is ripe for collapse. And the end of Jewish rule in Russia will also be the end of Russia as a state. We have been chosen by Fate as witness of a catastrophe which will be the mightiest confirmation of the soundness of the folkish theory.[18]

Hitler regarded the largest major power in the west, the United States of America, with a mixture of admiration and concern. In his 'Second Book', which he wrote in 1928 but which was not published during his lifetime, he had described the United States as 'a new power of such dimensions [...] as threatens to upset the whole former power and orders of rank of the States'.[19] In America he saw a 'young, racially select Folk' and argued that only 'a conscious Folkish race policy would be able to save European nations from losing the law of action to America, in consequence of the inferior value of European Folks vis-à-vis the American Folk'.[20] Elsewhere in the same text he writes that

> in the far future it may be possible to think of a new association of nations, consisting of individual States with a high national value, which could then stand up to the threatening overwhelming of the world by the American Union. For it seems to me that the existence of English world rule inflicts less hardships on presentday nations than the emergence of an American world rule.[21]

In the same context Hitler refers to Great Britain – the other major Anglo-Saxon power – with nothing but respect:

> If today the globe has an English world empire, then for the time being there is also no Folk which, on the grounds of its general civil political characteristics as well as its average political sagacity, would be more fitted for it.[22]

Hitler felt that an alliance between Germany as a land power and Great Britain as a maritime power was not only conceivable but also so desirable that he was willing to forgo any German colonial aspirations in the future. France, conversely, remained Germany's ancestral enemy inasmuch as it had spent the last 300 years actively seeking the breakup of Germany. Its antithesis was Fascist Italy, which was the natural choice for an alliance with National Socialist Germany, with the result that it went without saying that Hitler would not venture to criticize Italy's policy towards the South Tyrol, still less to question that region's status. On this point the National Socialists held very different views from all the other German parties, be they right- or left-wing.

Hitler's public pronouncements between 1930 and 1933 revealed little about his core convictions, which is also one of the reasons for the mass appeal of the National Socialists. It was its combination of nationalism and socialism that set Hitler's movement apart from all the right-wing movements in pre-war Germany. The NSDAP was not a party of dignitaries but owed its electoral successes to the demagogic abilities of its leader and to the commitment of its supporters rather than to financial assistance from right-wing industrialists and bankers. The 'socialism' of the National Socialists deterred many bourgeois voters, especially those members of the middle classes with independent means. As late as December 1932 the newly formed Battle League for middle-class tradesmen and women felt that it was necessary to assure smaller businesses that the aim of the National Socialists' economic and social policy was to 'deproletarianize' the German workers: 'The whole meaning behind the Socialist idea is to make owners out of those who own nothing. Adolf Hitler's Socialism is thus in the sharpest possible contrast to the sham Socialism of the Marxists whose goal is expropriation.'[23] But for 'nationalist' blue- and white-collar workers, for students and younger academics, 'National Socialism' was attractive, for by rallying under its banner they could distance themselves from both international Marxism and the nationalist forces of reaction and in that way occupy a third position that seemed to point the way forward beyond the proletarian class struggle and the protection of middle-class vested interests.

It was the nationalism of the NSDAP that provided a link between the party and bourgeois Germany, or least seemed to provide such a link. There was no party that defended the Treaty of Versailles or rejected the notion of a Greater Germany. The National Socialists demanded equal rights for Germany and unification with Austria, adopting a more radical tone than any other party. But as far as reforming the post-war order was concerned, there seemed on the surface to be a broad national consensus. It certainly helped Hitler that as a Pan-German from Austria he had no difficulty in demanding that his country be annexed by the German Reich or in combining that demand with his profession of faith in the Prussian tradition of Frederick the Great and Bismarck. Nor did it harm him that he had been brought up a Catholic. At least to the extent that they were not Marxists or religious, younger Germans felt that the denominational divide was no more relevant than the class struggle. Hitler's chance lay in the fact that many trusted him to reconcile existing antinomies that had until then seemed irreconcilable: not just nationalism and socialism but also Lutheran and Catholic Germany.

The mantras of this major synthesis were 'folk community' and 'Reich'. The first writer to use the term *Volksgemeinschaft* was probably Friedrich Schleiermacher in a manuscript dating from 1809. Within decades it had found its way into jurisprudence and sociology, and by the end of the First World War all political parties, with the exception of avowed Marxists, were using the term, conservatives and liberals availing themselves of it with the same enthusiasm as trade union leaders and Social Democrat reformers.

The term could acquire the most disparate meanings depending on who was using it: a profession of faith in the peaceful resolution of social differences in a free people's state or the call for an authoritarian order, whereby decisions affecting the common good were imposed on the nation from above. But the National Socialists were the most radical proponents of this slogan, demanding that Marxism be crushed because the call for a class struggle was tantamount to a denial of the 'community of the folk'. And, unlike all the other parties during the Weimar Republic, the National Socialists also interpreted the term in keeping with their ideas on race: in the National Socialist community of the folk there was room only for 'Aryan' Germans, not for Jews, Roma and the members of other races deemed to be inferior.

In the years before 1933 the 'Reich' had increasingly become a right-wing slogan directed against the Weimar Republic, while at the same time acquiring associations that pointed both back into the past and forward into the future. As a term, it had always had soteriological connotations, which emerged with particular force whenever the Germans referred to the 'Third Reich', a phrase to which we have already drawn attention in the context of the 1923 book *The Third Reich* by the Young Conservative journalist Arthur Moeller van den Bruck.

It was not long after Moeller van den Bruck's book had appeared in print that the National Socialists adopted the term in the belief that it encapsulated their own aspirations to particularly memorable effect. Gregor Straßer's brother Otto is believed to have passed on the phrase to Hitler. Otto broke with Hitler in July 1930, alleging that the latter had abandoned the 'socialism' enshrined in the party's 1920 programme. Only much later did Hitler begin to entertain doubts about the term and to argue that it could lead observers to speculate about a 'fourth Reich' and to question the continuity of the German Reich. In June 1939 the Chancellery informed the world of the Führer's desire that the term 'Third Reich' not be used any longer. By then, of course, its impact could no longer be denied, many Germans having come to see Hitler as their saviour.

Even after 1939, Hitler himself continued to speak of the 'Reich'. On the night of 17/18 December 1941 – almost nine years after he had come to power – he tried to see the events of 1933 as part of a wider historical context. He was staying at the time at his headquarters, the Wolfsschanze near Rastenburg in East Prussia.

I was faced with the question when we first took power. Should we preserve the Christian chronology, or should we inaugurate a new era? I reasoned that the year 1933 merely renewed our link with a military tradition. At that time the notion of the Reich had been, so to speak, lost, but it has again imposed itself on us and on the world. When one speaks of Germany, wherever one may be, one no longer says anything but 'the Reich'.[24]

Hitler was guilty of overestimating the importance of his own contribution to this development, because for most educated Germans in the years leading up to 1933, the 'Reich' had already acquired a new, as yet merely conceptual, grandeur, allowing Hitler to reap the benefits of what others had already sown.

Like the notion of a 'folk community' and the myth of the 'Reich', the 'idea of the Führer' was not a National Socialist invention, for terms such as 'Führer' and 'Führerschaft' (leadership) had enjoyed a boom not only on the nationalist right but also in the bourgeois centre during the final phase of the Weimar Republic. On the right the idea of a strong leader was contrasted with the anonymity of bureaucrats, the fragmentation of political parties and the fractiousness of the parliamentary system. Many Young Conservative writers even regarded a prospective Führer as a national Messiah, an agent of history and the proponent of a national dictatorship. When Hitler had himself hailed as the country's 'Führer', he was merely banking on a widespread discontent with the Weimar Republic and counting on a longing for release for which others had already prepared the ground. But only a man as charismatic as Hitler could produce the impression that he alone was destined to assume the role of the country's saviour in its hour of need. Without that quality he would never have been in a position to become chancellor and remain in office for twelve years.

The Reichstag election campaign that was conducted against the background of a 'national revolt' was the first in which the NSDAP was generously supported by the whole of German industry and all the major banks, rather than just by a handful of business leaders like Fritz Thyssen, Friedrich Flick and the directors of IG Farben, as had been the case in the past. Another novel element was the party's ability to use the public airwaves for its propaganda. The campaign was overshadowed by countless acts of terror committed by the SA, most of them ending with the death or injury of Communists and Social Democrats. On 17 February, Hermann Göring, the acting Prussian minister of the interior, instructed the police to use their firearms ruthlessly in case of doubt. Five days later he appointed the SA, SS and Stahlhelm as volunteer police officers, the more effectively to combat the alleged increase in left-wing violence. On 27 February the Reichstag building went up in flames.

Without being able to offer any proof in support of their claim, Hitler, Göring and Goebbels immediately declared that the crime was the work of Communists seeking to give 'the signal for bloody rebellion and civil war'.[25] On the other hand, there is no evidence to support the view taken by many contemporaries and later commentators that it was the National Socialists themselves who set fire to the building. The overwhelming majority of writers now tend to the opinion that the fire was the work of one man, the Dutch anarchist Marinus van der Lubbe, who was seeking to express his hatred of National Socialism and Fascism and who was taken into custody at the scene of the crime.

That same night, 27/8 February 1933, the cabinet passed an emergency decree designed to protect the people and the state and removing the most important basic rights until further notice, granting the government new powers to deal with the individual regions and introducing the death penalty for acts of terror such as arson. This new measure under Article 48 of the constitution spelt the end of Germany as a state governed by the rule of law. Among the earliest victims of this arbitrary act were Communist officials and well-known intellectuals. On 28 February the editor in chief of *Die Weltbühne*, Carl von Ossietzky, the writers Erich Mühsam and Ludwig Renn, the 'raging reporter' Egon Erwin Kisch, the sexologist Max Hodann and the eminent defence lawyer Hans Litten were taken into 'protective custody'. By 3 March the leader of the Communist Party, Ernst Thälmann, had been arrested at a secret hideout in Charlottenburg, as also were a number of his closest colleagues.

Acts of terror and propaganda proved effective, and Hitler's government emerged as the victor from the Reichstag elections that were held on 5 March 1933, the two groups that made up the cabinet between them polling 51.9 per cent of all the votes cast: the NSDAP won 43.9 per cent, while the union of German Nationalists, Stahlhelm and non-aligned conservative politicians, including Papen, that campaigned as the Black, White and Red Battle Front won 8 per cent. Persecuted with particular brutality by the National Socialists, the Communists fared badly, their share of the vote falling by 4.6 per cent, while that of the Social Democrats dropped by 2.1 per cent. The two Catholic parties, conversely, did relatively well, the Centre Party winning 11.2 per cent of the vote, the Bavarian People's Party 2.7 per cent. The two liberal parties remained no more than splinter groups, the German People's Party winning 1.1 per cent, the German State Party 0.9 per cent of the vote. Not only did the NSDAP enjoy a dramatically increased share of the vote – up by 10.8 per cent – but the turnout, too, rose from 80.6 per cent of the electorate on 6 November 1932 to 88.8 per cent.

Hitler's electoral victory was followed by what the National Socialists termed a 'national revolution'. One of its principal results was the alignment, or coordination – *Gleichschaltung* – of the individual regions, where governments that had been either purely bourgeois or kept in power by the Social Democrats were replaced by cabinets led by National Socialists. This process was the result of combined pressure exerted from above by the minister of the interior, Wilhelm Frick, and from below by the columns of SA and SS. The transfer of power took longest in the stronghold of German federalism, Bavaria, but by 16 March the National Socialists were the ruling party in Munich, too.

At the same time as the regional governments were being brought into line, the National Socialists were also seizing power in towns and local communities. The SA and SS occupied town halls and in many places arrested 'Marxist' – that is, Social Democrat – councillors, while forcing mayors whom they disliked to step down. Labour exchanges and local health insurance offices were subjected to similar interference.

Many, but by no means all, of the National Socialists' political enemies who were arrested in this way were handed over to the police, but the SA and SS often meted out their own forms of punishment. In Berlin and the surrounding area the first unofficial concentration camps sprang up soon after the Reichstag elections. In these camps old scores were settled with 'Bolsheviks' in particularly brutal ways. The first official concentration camps followed in March 1933, beginning with Dachau in Bavaria. Run by the SA and SS, they quickly became detention centres not only for Communists but also, and increasingly, for Social Democrats and other opponents of the regime. By the end of July 1933, by which time the SA's reign of terror was already beginning to abate, there were, according to official estimates, 27,000 individuals in 'protective custody' within the country as a whole. No figures are available for the number of those who died in the torture chambers of the SA and SS during the early months of the Third Reich.

The 'national revolution' also involved countless pogroms. In Breslau, for example, the SA mounted a putsch against Jewish lawyers and judges. Elsewhere, too, Jewish doctors were told that they were no longer able to practise, and Jewish theatres, cabarets, jewellers, clothing outlets, banks and department stores were stormed. Protests from German nationalists forced Hitler to ask his supporters on 10 March to desist from any further acts 'likely to inconvenience individuals, to impede the passage of private cars or to disrupt the business life of the nation'.[26] Two days later he delighted conservative Germany by using a radio broadcast to announce an unconstitutional presidential decree: until the colours of the Reich had been definitively decided, the black, white and red flag of the Kaiserreich could be flown alongside the flag bearing the National Socialist swastika.

This announcement was a prelude to 'Potsdam Day'. The official ceremony marking the opening of the newly elected Reichstag was held in the Garrison Church in Prussia's unofficial capital on 21 March. 'Marxists' did not attend, those Communist members of the chamber who had not already been arrested having gone to ground, while the Social Democrat members had met the previous day and decided in the absence of nine of their colleagues who were in 'protective custody' that they would absent themselves from the event, which was designed to underscore Hitler's profession of faith in the link between 'ancient greatness' and 'youthful strength'. Weimar was finally laid to rest with the active participation of the country's two leading Christian churches. When Hindenburg descended on his own into the crypt containing the tomb of Frederick the Great in order to commune in silence with the monarch, many

Germans felt the same degree of patriotic emotion that had been evoked for many years by the *Fridericus* films made by Hugenberg's UFA company.

The Reichstag met in its new home at the Kroll Opera on the Platz der Republik on 23 March to discuss the draft of a bill nominally presented by the NSDAP and German National People's Party and designed to 'alleviate the sufferings of the people and country': this Enabling Act gave the government unrestricted powers to pass whatever unconstitutional laws it wanted in the course of the next four years, the only proviso being that such laws were not to impinge on the institutions of the Reichstag and Reichsrat as such or to affect the rights of the president. In short, neither the Reichstag nor the Reichsrat could lay claim any longer to a share in the legislative process, and this was also the case with treaties with foreign countries. All that was now needed for the government's laws to come into force was the signature of the chancellor and an announcement in the *National Law Bulletin*.

In order to achieve the majority needed to change the constitution, the government had violated the said constitution even before the law had passed through parliament. It treated the Communist members as non-existent, thereby reducing the legal number of members by eighty-one. The Reichstag then proceeded to change its order of business on 23 March: delegates absent without permission could be excluded from debates for up to sixty daily sessions, but delegates excluded in this way were still counted as if they were present. Even if the Social Democrats had boycotted the session en bloc, they could still not have prevented the remaining deputies from meeting the conditions necessary to change the constitution, when two-thirds of those present were required to vote for the change.

Hitler gained the support of the Centre Party and the Bavarian People's Party by working into his inaugural speech a number of unctuous phrases on the relationship between Church and state associated with the leader of the Centre Party, Ludwig Kaas, and by making a handful of additional promises to the Catholic party's negotiators. (The Centre Party waited in vain for these promises to be confirmed in writing.) It had been calculated in advance of the vote that the ninety-three Social Democrats present in the chamber would vote against the bill, a veto justified by the party leader, Otto Wels, in a speech that went some way to salvaging the honour not only of his own party but of German democracy in general: 'You can take away our freedom and our lives, but not our honour,' he declared in a famous sentence that has since become part of the Germans' collective consciousness.[27] The representatives of the smaller bourgeois parties, including the German State Party, all voted for the bill, with the result that the necessary two-thirds majority was comfortably achieved, with 444 votes for the measure, only ninety-four against it. In short, this hurdle would have been overcome even without the unconstitutional manipulation of the legal number of members required to take part in the vote.

The yes vote of the bourgeois parties was the result of deception, self-deception and blackmail. From their point of view the 'legal' dictatorship desired by the majority was still the lesser of two evils when compared with an illegal dictatorship, a very real possibility if the draft bill had been thrown out. The semblance of legality promoted a semblance of legitimacy and ensured that the regime had the loyal support of the majority, which crucially included the country's government employees. This tactic of gaining their loyalty had been an important precondition for Hitler's seizure of power and had not yet fully served its purpose on 30 January 1933 but proved its worth once again on 23 March, when it was effectively used to do away with the Weimar constitution. From then on Hitler could sideline the Reichstag and make his actions seem as if he were following the Reichstag's own instructions.

The regime's first major action after the Enabling Act had come into force was its boycott of Jewish businesses on 1 April 1933. In organizing this boycott, the National Socialist leadership hoped that in this way it would not only provide an outlet for the pressure from within its own ranks but at the same time offer a response to the criticisms levelled at the March pogroms by Jewish organizations as well as by liberal and socialist newspapers all over the world. Julius Streicher, the NSDAP's Gauleiter in Franconia and editor of the anti-Semitic *Der Stürmer*, was given the task of spearheading the campaign against what Goebbels called the 'abominable global persecution' of the 'new Germany' mounted by the Jews. It was Goebbels himself who masterminded the campaign following his appointment as minister of public enlightenment and propaganda on 14 March. He was more than happy with the outcome of the one-day nationwide boycott. 'The outside world is slowly coming to its senses,' he wrote in his diary on 2 April. 'The world will realize that it isn't a good idea to let Jewish émigrés enlighten it about Germany.'[28] There was no mistaking his implied threat to Germany's Jews, and from then on the possibility of their exclusion from the business life of the country hung like a sword of Damocles over the whole of the Jewish community. The regime retained the right to decide on the time and the extent of the steps that it would take against the economic influence of the Jews: this was the message of 1 April 1933.

Even before they were excluded from business and commerce, the country's Jews had already been driven from public office. On 7 April 1933 the government passed a law reintroducing a professional civil service that was aimed at all government employees who were regarded as unreliable in the eyes of the ruling National Socialists: employees who owed their appointments to acts of political patronage at the time of the Weimar Republic, especially those who were members of left-wing parties, who had links with such parties or who were 'non-Aryans'. They were all pensioned off, the only exceptions being frontline fighters, the fathers or sons of soldiers killed in the war and employees who had been civil servants prior to 1 August 1914. These exceptions were made at the request of Hindenburg, who had been asked by the Federal League of Frontline Jewish Soldiers to intercede on their behalf.

The act of 7 April 1933 brought an end to the unofficial pogroms and ushered in a period of comprehensive purges organized by the state. Among those affected were hundreds of university teachers. The universities of Berlin and Frankfurt lost almost a third of their teaching staff, Heidelberg a quarter and Breslau more than one-fifth. Among those driven from their posts were several Nobel Prize winners, including the physicists Albert Einstein and Gustav Hertz and the chemist Fritz Haber. Others who were dismissed for racist or political reasons – or both – included the philosophers Theodor Wiesengrund Adorno, Max Horkheimer and Helmuth Plessner, the lawyers Hermann Heller, Hans Kelsen and Hugo Sinzheimer, the sociologists Karl Mannheim and Emil Lederer, the economists Moritz Julius Bonn and Wilhelm Röpke, the psychologist Erich Fromm, the Evangelical theologian Paul Tillich and many others. Most of them emigrated, with the result that entire research centres such as the Frankfurt Institute for Social Research were lost, as were whole areas of expertise that included Freudian psychoanalysis.

Not only the teaching staff was purged, so too was the student body at universities up and down the country. On 28 April the number of 'non-Aryan' students was reduced to 1.5 per cent of the total in order to bring it into line with the percentage of Jews in the population as a whole. Students who had belonged to, or sympathized with, the German Communist Party were obliged to abandon their studies. University deans who had fallen out of favour with the government were replaced by others more acceptable to the regime. Martin Heidegger was elected dean of Freiburg University on 20 April 1933, Hitler's forty-fourth birthday. He joined the NSDAP on 1 May – the same day that the constitutional lawyer Carl Schmitt took the identical step. On 27 May, in his inaugural speech as dean, Heidegger invited teachers and students alike to uphold the three virtues of labour service, military service and hard work in the pursuit of knowledge.

The fight against everything that the National Socialists deemed 'un-German', 'decadent' and 'corrosive' was directed not only at the living but also at the dead. Public book burnings were held in German cities and university towns on 10 May 1933, when members of the National Socialist German Student Association set fire to writings by left-wing, pacifist, liberal and Jewish authors, including works by Heinrich Heine, Karl Marx, Karl Kautsky, Sigmund Freud, Alfred Kerr, Heinrich Mann, Erich Kästner, Lion Feuchtwanger, Erich Maria Remarque, Arnold Zweig, Theodor Wolff, Bertolt Brecht, Kurt Tucholsky and Carl von Ossietzky. Most of those victims of the campaign who were still alive had already left Germany. One of them, Carl von Ossietzky, had been arrested on 28 February, while another, Erich Kästner, attended the nocturnal ceremony outside Berlin's Friedrich Wilhelm University incognito.

This literary auto-da-fé was followed by other campaigns directed at all forms of 'degenerate art' in literature, music, painting and architecture. Within months, radio, the cinema, the theatre and the press had all been purged and brought into line, although the government revealed a certain degree of nuance in its attitude towards the newspapers. It was, after all, in the interests of the Third Reich that an internationally respected paper like the *Frankfurter Zeitung* should adopt a more factual style than the *Völkischer Beobachter* and might even venture limited criticisms. A façade of professional probity and calculated diversity was expedient not only for reasons of the country's foreign policy but for domestic reasons too. What mattered was that in the case of matters of any real importance, the linguistic rules of the Ministry of Propaganda were respected and applied in keeping with Goebbels's diktat.

In addition to restoring a professional civil service on 7 April 1933, the government also placed the relationship between Reich and regions on a new legal footing. An initial law passed on 31 March had altered the composition of the regional parliaments in order to reflect the outcome of the Reichstag elections on 5 March – the Communist votes were, of course, ignored – and the regional governments were empowered to pass laws and make constitutional amendments without regard for their regional assembly. On 7 April the institution of Reich governor was created, a figure that henceforth represented the highest authority in each individual region. In most regions it was the local Gauleiter whom Hitler invited to fill the post, Hitler himself becoming the governor in Prussia, where a new regional assembly had been elected on 5 March. On 11 April he appointed a new prime minister for Prussia, Hermann Göring, who added the premiership to his existing posts of leader of the Reichstag and minister without portfolio in the federal government.

The National Socialists' main political enemy was 'Marxism', which, although substantially weakened by the Enabling Act, was not yet completely destroyed. Only the Communists may be said to have been definitively excluded from power. Their parliamentary mandates were revoked on 31 March, although by then this had little more than symbolic significance. The Social Democrats, conversely, survived as an organization. Some of their leaders who were at particular risk of arrest had already left the country, including Otto Braun, Rudolf Hilferding and Philipp Scheidemann, and others had been arrested. A number of the party's senior officials played for time, while refusing to align themselves with the new regime in the way that the General German Trade Union Association was currently doing. On 15 April the Association's national leader expressly welcomed the government's decision to declare 1 May 'National Labour Day' and to make it a public holiday.

Black and white flags were flown from trade union buildings on 1 May 1933. At the central demonstration organized by the regime at Tempelhof in Berlin the Textile Workers' Union even marched beneath a swastika flag. Hitler used the occasion to deliver a major speech that was broadcast by all the country's radio stations. Referring to the 'gigantic task' of road building, he insisted that manual work and mental work formed an indivisible unity, while at the same time emphasizing his desire for peace. But the opportunism of the trade union leaders did not pay off, and the very next day the regime struck a blow against the Free Trade Unions that had long been planned by the general staff. Throughout the country union buildings were occupied by the SA and SS, as were the unions' newspaper offices and the Bank of Manual Workers, White-Collar Workers and Civil Servants, together with all its branches. Theodor Leipart and other union leaders were taken into 'protective custody', which in most cases lasted two weeks, although Leipart and his deputy, Peter Grassmann, were not released until June. Less prominent officials were told to continue their work under the leadership of the National Socialist Factory Cell Organization.

Intimidated by the fate of the Free Trade Unions, who were closest to the Social Democrats, the other two unions – the Christian-Nationalist Unions and the Liberal Hirsch-Duncker Unions – unconditionally accepted Hitler's leadership on 4 May. Two days later, Robert Ley, who had replaced Gregor Straßer as the NSDAP's national organizer, announced the formation of the German Workers' Front, whose inaugural congress was held in Berlin on 10 May under the aegis of Hitler himself. He used the occasion to describe himself as an 'honest broker' mediating between the different strata of German society. Ley was appointed the Front's chairman, while leadership of the Workers' Associations was entrusted to Walter Schumann, the leader of the National Socialist Factory Cell Organization. The Third Reich was now in control of the labour market. By 4 May 1933 there were no longer any independent workers' organizations. Wage agreements, too, were a thing of the past. Under a law passed on 19 May 1933 trustees appointed by the chancellor were henceforth to set all legally binding conditions governing contracts.

Unlike the trade unions, the employers' organizations were able to maintain their organizational independence. Admittedly, they had to dismiss their leading officials, be they Jewish or otherwise politically compromised in the eyes of the National Socialists, but they were at least able to retain a high degree of corporate continuity. In June 1933 the Confederation of German Industry and the Association of German Employers' Organizations merged to form the Reich Estate for German Industry. The word 'estate' was a nod in the direction of National Socialist middle-class ideologues, although the concession did little to compensate them for the defeat that they suffered in the summer of 1933, when they failed to reduce big business to their overall control after they were forced to abandon their campaign against 'Jewish' department stores and 'Marxist' cooperative societies, a move dictated by Hitler's deputy, Rudolf Heß. Crushing these organizations would have resulted in the dismissal of countless manual and white-collar workers and was no longer a viable option. It made no difference for middle-class officials in the NSDAP to draw attention to contradictory statements in the 1920 party programme: now that the party was in power, it had other priorities.

The country's agricultural organizations suffered a rather different fate. The National Land League, which had contributed substantially to Hitler's appointment as chancellor in January 1933, was amalgamated with the newly formed Reich Food Estate in the July of that year. This was headed by Richard Walther Darré, the NSDAP's head of agrarian policy, who had succeeded Hugenberg as minister of economics and agriculture the previous month. Darré increased his power at the expense of the major landowners to the east of the Elbe, a pressure group that for years had left its mark on the policies of the National Land League and the German National People's Party. This shift in power from the larger landowners to peasant farmers was a part of Hitler's strategy to create as much economic independence as possible as the precursor of a war over Lebensraum designed to make Germany self-sufficient in every area of the economy. From this point of view, the restructuring of those organizations that represented agricultural interests was as logical as the decision not to implement radical changes in industrial organizations.

The crushing of the Free Trade Unions was bound to affect the country's Social Democrats, and on 4 May the party's executive committee decided that three of its full-time members, led by Otto Wels, should leave Germany in order to continue their fight against Hitler from abroad. The committee in exile initially established itself in Saarbrücken, at that date the capital of the French-run Saar territory established under the terms of the Treaty of Versailles. The move marked the fragmentation of the German Social Democrats, with Wels leading the party in exile, while the party at home found an unofficial spokesman in the former leader of the Reichstag, Paul Löbe.

It was not long before the two camps were in open conflict. The Reichstag met on 17 May, its first session after the adoption of the Enabling Act. Hitler intended to use the occasion to state his government's position on the Geneva Disarmament Conference and hoped that a show of national unity would help to counteract the country's diplomatic isolation, but the Social Democrat leaders in Saarbrücken planned a rather different kind of demonstration and advised their deputies not to attend the session of the Reichstag. In the event, only a minority of members under Kurt Schumacher did as they were asked, whereas the majority succumbed to the blackmail exerted by the minister of the interior, Wilhelm Frick, who threatened that Social Democrats currently interned would be murdered if their colleagues refused to back the joint declaration and approve the government statement.

Hitler's speech on 17 May 1933 was the most moderate and placatory that he ever delivered. He expressed his understanding of his neighbours' security needs, mentioning in particular the French and the Poles, and professed his desire for peace in terms more insistent than those used by any of his predecessors. For Germany he demanded only the same right. Even a veiled threat sounded defensive: 'As a nation for ever being defamed, we should find it difficult to remain a member of the League of Nations.'[29] The government statement was cheered to the rafters, after which Göring, as leader of the house, read out the resolution submitted by the NSDAP, German National People's

Party, Centre Party and Bavarian People's Party. Those members in favour of the resolution were asked to stand. Everyone did so, including the Social Democrats. All then joined in the German national anthem, which was afterwards sung by the upper house, too. Conversely, only the National Socialists joined in the subsequent rendition of the Horst Wessel Lied, which famously begins with the line 'Flag high, ranks closed'.

The vote for Hitler resulted in a breakdown of relations between the Social Democrats still in Germany and the Socialist Workers' International, which disapproved of the way the Social Democrat deputies had voted. By 17 May the party's leader, Otto Wels, was convinced that the Reichstag sitting marked the start of a life-and-death struggle that the party's committee could win only with the help of the International. On 21 May it decided to move its headquarters from Saarbrücken to Prague, a move dictated by strategic considerations: it was easy to slip across the densely wooded mountains in the west and north of the country that marked the border with Bavaria, Saxony and Silesia, an important precondition for the illegal activities that the party's exiled leaders now saw themselves obliged to undertake. The first issue of *Neuer Vorwärts* was published in Karlsbad (Karlovy Vary) on 18 June and included an appeal from the party's leadership under the heading 'Break your chains!' It was the most outspoken declaration of war on Hitler's regime that the Social Democrats had uttered until then.

The following day Löbe's Social Democrats in the Prussian Landtag met to discuss the situation, prompting their leader, Ernst Heilmann, to spell out the majority line by declaring that 'We must continue to spin the thread of legality for as long as it can be spun.'[30] A six-man directorate, entirely 'Aryan' in its makeup, was entrusted with the task of conducting party business and immediately sought to distance itself from the old committee, arguing that party members who had gone abroad could not issue statements on the party's behalf: 'The party expressly disclaims responsibility for all of their declarations.'[31]

As minister of the interior, Frick was left distinctly unimpressed by this declaration and on 21 June he ordered a comprehensive ban on all of the Social Democrats' political activities, citing in his defence the 'treasonable actions' undertaken against Germany by the exiled committee. The decree came into force on 22 June. That same day four members of the new directorate, including Löbe, were arrested as part of a large-scale wave of arrests that extended to party officials and even to members of the Reichstag and Prussian Landtag. One member, the former prime minister of Mecklenburg-Schwerin, Johannes Stelling, was brutally murdered by the SA in the wake of the Köpenick Week of Blood, and on 6 July the Gestapo arrested the Reichstag deputy Kurt Schumacher, who had been the keenest critic of Löbe's whole approach. In August he was sent to the Gestapo's first concentration camp at Heuberg near Stuttgart and was not released until ten years later.

The elimination of the Social Democratic Party was the prelude to the dismantling of the party system in general. On 21 June Frick not only banned the Social Democrats from undertaking any further political activities, he also proscribed the paramilitary arm of the German National Front, which was known as the German National Battle Rings. (The German National Front was the name adopted by the German National People's Party after the middle of May.) His scarcely credible rationale was that the organization had been infiltrated by Communist elements and by other individuals hostile to the state. Hugenberg, who only a few days earlier had incited Hitler's anger by demanding a German colonial empire in Africa at the world economic conference in London, announced on 27 June that he was resigning all his ministerial posts not only in Prussia but in the national government, too. The German National Front was disbanded that same day, when it signed a 'friendship agreement' with the NSDAP, ensuring that its members of parliament were able to sit on the National Socialist benches. In this way German conservatism lost its political arm by capitulating to the revolutionary movement that it had set out to tame.

Over the next few days, the country's two liberal parties – the German State Party and the German People's Party – were likewise disbanded. The fate of political Catholicism was sealed in Rome during negotiations conducted by Papen since April 1933. An important role in these negotiations for a Reich Concordat with the Holy See was played by Ludwig Kaas in his capacity as papal house prelate. In return for the assurance that the Church would have scope to develop in Germany, the Curia abandoned the political, social and professional organizations of German Catholicism. On 5 July, three days before the Concordat was initialled, the Centre Party disbanded itself. The Bavarian People's Party had taken the same step the previous day.

On 14 July 1933 – the 144th anniversary of the Storming of the Bastille – Hitler's government passed a law that meant that from then on there was only a single political party in Germany, namely, the NSDAP. Anyone who tried 'to maintain the organizational support of another political party or to form a new political party' was threatened with imprisonment.[32] It had taken the National Socialists less than half a year to establish their monopoly of power. Of course, they still shared that power with the armed forces, with senior civil servants and with the major industries, but the elimination of all competition from other political parties was an important milestone in Hitler's seizure of power, a process that had begun on the day that he was appointed chancellor.

If the new government was to prove at all popular, it needed to be able to report a number of palpable successes in its struggle to deal with mass unemployment. The National Socialists were fortunate in that they did not need to formulate any new job creation schemes, for previous cabinets, most notably Schleicher's, had already planned most of the projects that the NSDAP was now able to implement. One such project was an emergency programme backed by a federal guarantee of 500 million marks and designed to create new jobs financed in advance by extendable bills of exchange that were guaranteed by the government and covered by a rediscount agreement from the Reichsbank. As had been the case with Schleicher, so the present administration's initial concern was to encourage the population to settle in rural areas once the land there had been improved. Another project that dated back to the days of the Weimar Republic was a road-building programme that was used by the National Socialists for propagandist purposes and designed from the outset to serve a military end by allowing rapid troop movements. But road-building played only a small part in reducing unemployment: by the end of June 1934 no more than 38,000 labourers were working in this area of the economy in the entire country. In general, the job creation schemes undertaken by Hitler's government meant that unemployment did not rise substantially above the four million mark during the winter of 1933/4, having peaked at this figure in September 1933.

Germany's economic recovery was made more difficult by the devaluation of the American dollar that had resulted from Roosevelt's abandonment of the gold standard in April 1933. The German trade balance immediately fell into the red and the Reichsbank's foreign exchange reserve rapidly drained away. On 8 June 1933 the government agreed to a unilateral moratorium on all long-term foreign debts at least to the extent that those debts were not subject to earlier moratoria. Ostensibly as a sign of 'good faith', German debtors would go on making payments in Reichsmarks into accounts administered by the Reichsbank, but the Reichsmarks accumulated in the creditors' accounts would no longer be transferred into foreign currency. Adam Tooze has rightly described this suspension of debt repayments as 'the first overtly aggressive foreign policy move by Hitler's government'.[33]

This period also witnessed the decision to adopt an extremely risky means of financing Germany's rearmament programme in the form of a scheme devised by Hjalmar Schacht, who in March 1933 had returned to his former position as president of the Reichsbank: special bills of exchange with the Metallurgical Research Company (Mefo) were to be used to pay all armaments contractors from April 1934 onwards. These IOUs were a central element in Schacht's 'New Plan' to boost the economy and could be redeemed at a small discount by any company that had a defence contract but they generally remained in circulation for a considerable period of time because of the high rate of interest that they paid. The first of these Mefo bills was issued in the autumn of 1933, but it was not until April 1934 that the payments started to be made on any appreciable scale – conveniently timed to coincide with the renewed propaganda surrounding the second wave of work creation schemes. The bills of exchange were also backed up by a rigorous policy of foreign exchange controls and by a state-subsidized export offensive.

The moratorium on debt repayments and the new policy of forcing the pace of rearmament were followed on 14 October 1933 by the Third Reich's most spectacular move to date: its withdrawal from both the Geneva Disarmament Conference and the League of Nations. In taking this step, Hitler was reacting to the western proposal for a system of controls that would have prevented Germany from rearming for an eight-year period. His demonstrative declaration of war on the Versailles system was popular at home, helping him to turn a foreign policy defeat into a domestic victory. On 12 November 1933 the Germans had an opportunity to vote on their country's withdrawal from the League of Nations and at the same time to elect a new Reichstag. Of the votes cast in the referendum on the matter, 95.1 per cent were in favour of withdrawal, meaning that 89.9 per cent of the electorate agreed with the move. In the Reichstag election the NSDAP candidates won 92.1 per cent of the votes cast, representing a share of 87.8 per cent of all those who were entitled to vote.

Two months after the referendum and Reichstag election, Germany was able to offset its political isolation by forming a surprise alliance with Poland. During the years of the Weimar Republic, the country's eastern neighbour had been seen almost exclusively as a threat, its borders and even its very existence being regarded as irreconcilable with Germany's interests. When Hitler became chancellor, Poland's 'strong man', Józef Piłsudski, had taken soundings via strictly confidential channels that were almost certainly opened up in April 1933 and possibly even the previous month, his aim being to establish whether France would join in a preventive plan similar to the one used when the Ruhr was occupied in 1923 and to take temporary control of Danzig, East Prussia and German Upper Silesia in order to force Germany to abide by the terms of the Treaty of Versailles at least to the extent that those terms applied to rearmament and the position of Poland's borders. But the reply he had received had not been encouraging. On 2 May 1933 Piłsudski sent Hitler an ultimatum, asking him what plans the chancellor might have for revising the terms of the treaty. In his reply, Hitler sought to reassure Warsaw and stated that Germany intended to respect its existing borders with Poland.

In December 1933 Piłsudski took further soundings in Paris but again to no avail, and it was then that he decided to come to an agreement with Germany. The result of the ensuing negotiations was the German-Polish Non-Aggression Pact signed on 26 January 1934. For a native Austrian like Hitler, this sensational volte-face in terms of Germany's foreign policy was easier to stomach than it was for the traditionally anti-Polish Foreign Office, which was essentially Prussian in outlook. Hitler was in fact more exercised by another enemy: the Soviet Union. From his point of view the anti-Communist, anti-Russian Poland was most certainly capable of taking on the role of junior partner in Germany's anti-Russian foreign policy, a perspective that would have been completely unthinkable before 1933.

Four days after the German-Polish Non-Aggression Pact was signed, Germany marked the first anniversary of Hitler's seizure of power with much pomp and ceremony, and the government used the occasion to force through the Reichstag a new law which, changing the constitution, was designed to restructure the Reich by abolishing the representative assemblies in the different regions and transferring their sovereign jurisdiction to the Reich itself. From then on the regional governments came under the jurisdiction of the federal government, while the regional governors were placed under the supervision of the minister of the interior. The result was a far-reaching change that marked the definitive victory of unitarian forces over their particularist counterpart.

The more powerful governors had little or no inclination to submit unconditionally to ministries in Berlin, and since they were repeatedly able to win over Hitler to their point of view, their opposition was by no means ineffectual. Hitler was in any case fixated on his ultimate goals and had no clear ideas on questions of internal government, with the result that he preferred to avoid having to take any decisions at all. In consequence he repeatedly frustrated tendencies that a National Socialist regime would logically have followed, notably the systematic centralization demanded by Wilhelm Frick at the Ministry of the Interior. But in a certain sense there was a method even to this lack of coherence, Hitler's policies being directed more at 'movement' than at 'order', perpetual dynamics being impossible to reconcile with the formation of stable structures. Rivalries between his followers also had the advantage that he himself would have to be called on to arbitrate, and even if he took no decision, this still meant that he remained in charge of the game.

In his relations with the country's Christian Churches, Hitler likewise tried to present himself as the ultimate authority in the event of conflict. Papen, as his vice-chancellor, had largely been left to deal with relations between the Reich and the Catholic Church. The result was the Concordat which, signed in the Vatican on 20 July 1933, came into force on 10 September 1933. The Catholic Church was allowed to continue to regulate its own internal affairs and received an assurance from the state that it would be able to go on running faith schools, to teach religion and to organize Church societies, including youth groups. In return the Curia agreed that the Catholic clergy should no longer undertake any political activities. In this way the government had won a partial victory, for the political neutralization of the Catholic Church was necessary if the National Socialists were to reduce its ideological influence.

In Evangelical Germany, the National Socialists had already taken control of a number of powerful bastions even before 30 January 1933, although their influence was more widespread among local parishioners than among Church leaders, who were predominantly German Nationalist in their outlook. In the Prussian Church elections in November 1932 the National Socialist German Christian Faith Movement, which occasionally styled itself the 'SA of Jesus Christ' and the 'Church SA', had already won one-third of the seats. In advance of the Evangelical Church elections in July 1933 Hitler – nominally still a Catholic – broadcast an appeal from Bayreuth, where he was attending that summer's Wagner Festival, inviting his radio audience to vote for the Christian Faith Movement. His appeal produced the desired result, the movement winning a two-thirds majority in the elections on 23 July. Hitler then turned his attention to the Evangelical Church, which initially seemed to offer little resistance, with the result that at the end of September the head of the German Christians in East Prussia and Hitler's personal adviser on all matters relating to the Church, Ludwig Müller, was elected Reich Bishop of the newly established German Evangelical Church at the German National Synod in Wittenberg.

But the Wittenberg synod also witnessed the first signs of a countermovement in the form of the Pastors' Emergency League established by three prominent figures in the religious life of the nation: Martin Niemöller, a former submarine commander and Freikorps member who was now the local pastor in the Berlin suburb of Dahlem; Dietrich Bonhoeffer, an outside lecturer at the University of Berlin; and Otto Dibelius, who in June 1933 had been removed from his post as superintendent-general of the Kurmark. Within months the Pastors' Emergency League had spawned the 'Confessing Church', which by the end of 1933 numbered around a third of all Evangelical pastors among its ranks.

The Confessing Church did not see itself as the voice of political opposition, and this remained the case even after May 1934, when it broke with the German Christians at the Barmen Synod. Rather, it merely opposed the politicization of the Gospel, which also meant resisting political pressure within the Church and opposing the 'Aryan paragraph' demanded by the German Christians and aimed at removing all Jewish Christians from ecclesiastical appointments. But this was far from being synonymous with a declaration of war on the general policies of the National Socialist leadership or with a declaration of solidarity with those Jews who had not converted to Christianity.

From the standpoint of the German Christians, however, even this limited level of resistance was seen as political in character since it flew in the face of the National Socialists' claim to address the individual in his or her entirety. Hitler, too, saw the situation in this light, but he was a realist and as a result felt that other goals were more pressing than the subversion of the Evangelical Church from within. In the autumn of 1934 the unexpected strength of the forces lined up against him persuaded him to reassess the situation. Bishops who had been removed from their positions by the German Christians were able to return to their bishoprics, and the Reich Bishop retained his title, even though he no longer exerted any actual influence upon the Church.

Although the battle over the Church may have suffered a setback, the struggle to win the hearts and minds of Protestants and Catholics alike went on and was coordinated by Alfred Rosenberg, the editor of the *Völkischer Beobachter*, who since January 1934 had been the commissar for supervision of intellectual and ideological education of the NSDAP. God-fearing Lutherans and Catholic believers alike regarded Rosenberg as the quintessential embodiment of the National Socialists' 'neo-paganism'. His book *The Myth of the Twentieth Century* was placed on the papal see's index of banned books in

February 1934. Hitler himself was particularly keen to ensure that young people were not exposed to the influence of the Church itself or of parental homes with strong ties to the Church. In this respect the battle with the Church was by no means a failure, for by the end of 1933 the 1.2 million members of Evangelical youth groups had been absorbed into the Hitler Youth movement and could now begin their education and be inducted into the tenets of National Socialism.

Hitler's decision to withdraw from the battle over the Church enhanced his reputation in the eyes of the Church and especially of the conservative educated middle classes whose most important standard-bearers continued to be university teachers. Following the removal of their Jewish and left-wing colleagues they had no need to make any fundamental changes to their teaching or to their research: all who had been nationalists before 1933 were left alone as long as they did not criticize National Socialism or the way the country was being run. Nor were they required to proclaim their support for anti-Semitism, although many did so voluntarily, no longer making any secret of their anti-Jewish sentiments.

As in the country's two main Churches, so it was the younger generation of academics who made up the bulk of committed National Socialists. Many of the younger lecturers had been influenced by the Bündische Jugend – the youth movement established in the wake of the First World War by those of its leaders who were disillusioned by their recent experiences – and by the ideas of the Conservative Revolution. Their espousal of National Socialism was by no means a foregone conclusion, but once the National Socialists had seized power, they needed to be powerfully convinced not to join the movement. By 1933 few young academics had the intellectual and moral fibre to resist such a move.

The whole of German culture was affected in this way, the removal of Jews and left-wing thinkers of every hue going hand in hand with an increasingly universal tendency to fall into line with the regime. Goebbels was able to set up the Reich Culture Chamber in September 1933, a vast umbrella organization for all who were involved in cultural activities in every shape and form and subdivided into numerous specialist chambers responsible for the political and ideological indoctrination of the individuals concerned. They were required to become members of a particular chamber – whether for writers, journalists, broadcasters or artists working in the theatre, music or visual arts – if they wished to continue to contribute to the cultural life of the nation. By including the desirables, the regime was also able to exclude the undesirables, who were driven from the country's academies and in the case of those who fled abroad and continued to criticize Germany in exile stripped of their German citizenship under a law passed on 23 August 1933, when their property was also impounded. Among those affected by this move were not only many left-wing politicians but also the theatre critic Alfred Kerr, the writer Lion Feuchtwanger and the journalists Kurt Tucholsky and Leopold Schwarzschild.

By the autumn of 1933 most of the urban intelligentsia had already been driven from Germany. Their complete opposite, at least according to National Socialist ideologues, were the farmers, who were regarded as the sons of the earth, and it was the aim of the Reich Farm Law of 29 September 1933 to preserve and support this group. The bill bore the signature of Richard Walther Darré, the minister of food, head of the Reich Food Estate and a prominent representative of the myth of 'blood and soil'. It applied to around a third of agricultural concerns – neither the largest farms nor the very smallest, but medium-sized family-run farms. The heir, who in most cases was the youngest son, had no choice but to become a farmer. His property could be mortgaged only within certain limits and could no longer be divided up among other members of the family, as tended to be the case in south-west Germany.

The inevitable consequence of this new law was an increase in the numbers of agricultural workers leaving the countryside and moving into the towns. Although this move flew in the face of the NSDAP's slogans, with their romantically coloured view of the countryside, it served a higher goal, for the new industrial 'reserve army' provided the labour needed for the armaments industry, where the wages were much higher than in agriculture. The resultant shortage of farm labourers was met by the 1931 Volunteer Labour Service, a precursor of the paramilitary Reich Labour Service in which all Germans between eighteen and twenty-five were intended in principle to work for six months. The scheme came into force in June 1935. In turn the Labour Service offered the government an opportunity to keep a promise that Hitler had made in a speech on 1 May 1933, according to which 'brainworkers' too had to undertake some form of physical labour at least once in their lives.

This attempt to enhance the value of work from a psychological point of view went hand in hand with a de facto erosion of workers' rights. On 20 January 1934 the government passed a new law governing labour relations in the country as a whole. As such, it may be described as the Magna Carta of industrial relations in the Third Reich. Under its terms a 'company leader' was responsible for the welfare of his workforce, now known as the *Gefolgschaft* (literally, followers) and charged with the task of taking all the decisions relating to running the company. In this he was assisted by a committee whose role was purely advisory and whose members were chosen from a list made up of candidates selected in advance by the company leader and a representative of the German Labour Front. These committees had nothing in common with the works committees of the Weimar Republic. The principal beneficiaries of this new arrangement were the employers who could once again feel that they were masters in their own homes – assuming, at least, that they did not fall foul of the German Labour Front. There was little sign of any opposition to the new system on the part of the country's workforce for the decline in unemployment, which fell from 4.1 million to 2.3 million between December 1933 and November 1934, was generally credited to the Third Reich and its leader.

Workers were no longer afraid of losing their jobs, which more than made up for the loss of political and trade union freedoms.

This was also true of most female workers. Admittedly, the National Socialists had declared war on double incomes even before 30 January 1933, but after this date they continued to do so in words alone. Their rhetoric about a woman's place being in the home taking care of her husband and children had few practical implications. Under the Third Reich more married women were in work than ever before, and only in the academic field were women in general systematically excluded from important positions. The government was also able to call on a federal law passed on 25 April 1933 and designed to reduce class sizes in German schools and universities in order to reduce the number of female students to its historically lowest rate of 11.2 per cent in the summer of 1939. Most of what Germany had achieved before 1933 in terms of women's legal and actual equality was reversed. In short, National Socialism was radically anti-emancipatory: the theory proposed by a number of historians and sociologists that willingly or otherwise the Third Reich contributed to a comprehensive modernization of German society is simply untenable.

Within a year of the National Socialists' seizure of power, their interpretation of a 'folk community' had begun to take on clearer outlines. In essence the 'folk community' was intended to remove the differences in Germans' minds between Protestants and Catholics, between the urban and the rural populations and between those who worked with their brains and those who toiled with their hands. It was dominated by men, divided into estates, chambers and the German Labour Front and subjected to the Führer principle. Employers had become company leaders, while workers had been turned into 'followers'. At the same time, the elected representatives of agricultural organizations made way for local farmers' leaders appointed by the Reich Food Estate; the country's universities were now run by their dean, who was appointed by the Ministry of Education; and under the terms of a law of 4 October 1933 the editors of all newspapers and magazines assumed responsibility for everything that their colleagues wrote or said. There were also a huge number of minor and middle-ranking leaders of the NSDAP from the block leader and cell leader to the local group leader, the district leader and the Gauleiter, to say nothing of the officials in charge of the party's organizations and affiliated societies such as the National Socialist Women's Association, the National Socialist People's Welfare Association and the National Socialist Motor Corps. All were dependent on the will of a single leader, while at the same time they were able to feel that they somehow had a proprietorial share in that leadership.

Anyone who was critical of Hitler and of his leadership could expect to be denounced to the authorities and, depending on the severity of the criticism, might be sent to one of the country's concentration camps. In order to keep the population under a tight rein, the regime was not only reliant on paid spies and the relatively few officials of the Gestapo but could also depend on the countless 'national comrades' who believed that they were helping their Führer whenever they reported alleged 'enemies of the people' to the authorities.

Within twelve months of the National Socialists' coming to power, faith in Hitler and in his historical mission had become the most important element holding together the 'folk community'. The myth of the Führer could not be permitted to lose its potency since the Third Reich was simply unthinkable without it. It was on this entirely appropriate insight that Goebbels based his propaganda, propaganda that no German citizen was ultimately able to avoid.

If Hitler's rule was threatened a year after he had seized power, the threat came not from any subversive activities on the part of a banned party like the Communists or the Social Democrats, but from within the National Socialist movement itself: from the SA. As early as June 1933 the SA's chief of staff, Ernst Röhm, had published an article in the National Socialists' monthly journal, demanding an end to the 'national' revolution and the launch of a 'National Socialist revolution'. The SA had at least 1.5 million members after it merged with the Stahlhelm in July 1933. But Röhm continued to regard himself as the spokesman of the 'old warriors' who in turn felt that it was they who had brought Hitler to power on 30 January 1933. They were unhappy with the changes that had taken place in Germany since then and demanded a second revolution that would give Hitler's 'brown battalions' control over state and society.

But Hitler knew that he could not achieve his long-term goals without the help of the army, the civil service and the business community. On 6 July 1933 he responded to Röhm's challenge by telling a meeting of regional governors in Berlin that the revolution was not a permanent state but must be channelled into the secure bed of evolution. 'The party has now become the state. All power lies in the hands of the Reich authority. The focus of German life must not be allowed to shift back into separate areas, much less into separate organizations.'[34]

This public reprimand had as little effect on Röhm as his appointment to the post of minister without portfolio on 4 December 1933, a move that Hitler hoped would help to curb the SA. Röhm now demanded that the SA should also play a key role in building up the country's offensive and defensive capabilities and form the nucleus of a future militia. On 1 February 1934 he sent a memorandum to the defence minister, Werner von Blomberg, relegating the army to the level of a mere training organization. Röhm's aim was clear: the army and the SA were to exchange roles.

Blomberg had no difficulty persuading Hitler to take the side of the military, and on 28 February the chancellor emphatically rejected Röhm's plans for a militia at a meeting of the heads of the army, SA and SS. He was resolved, he announced, to 'set up a people's army based on the Reichswehr, thoroughly trained and armed with the most modern weapons'.[35] This new army, he went on, must be ready to defend the country within five years and to assume an offensive role within eight. The SA must obey Hitler's orders. For the present its task would be to defend the country's borders and to undertake pre-military training. For the rest, only the Wehrmacht must be allowed to bear arms. The army responded to Hitler's concession by issuing a decree dated 28 February 1934 in which Blomberg committed the army to adopt the 'Aryan paragraph' in the Law for the Restoration of the Professional Civil Service.

During the next few weeks Röhm made no attempt – at least in public – to question his Führer's new guidelines. But in conversation and especially in the presence of the Diplomatic Corps on 18 April his remarks remained as revolutionary as ever, while incidents involving the SA and the army continued to increase. Among the population at large these were the first signs of weak leadership, creating a mood of discontent that Goebbels sought to counter in May 1934 with his campaign against 'killjoys and criticasters'. The continuing disquiet caused conservative circles associated with the vice-chancellor, Franz von Papen, to demand clarification on the question of power. A suitable means to this end seemed to them to be the restoration of the monarchy following the death of Hindenburg, an eventuality that appeared to be increasingly likely, given the elderly president's worsening health in the early months of 1934.

On 17 June 1934 Papen gave a speech at the University of Marburg that was designed as a rallying cry calling for the formation of a conservative front against the radical forces within the National Socialist movement. The speech had been written by one of the vice-chancellor's closest allies, the Young Conservative journalist Edgar Jung, who placed in Papen's mouth a profession of faith in the values of humanity, freedom and equality before the law, values said to be Germanic and Christian rather than liberal. It was impossible not to interpret his remarks as a declaration of war on those who were advocating a second revolution:

> No nation can tolerate a perpetual revolution from below if it wishes to assert itself in the face of history. At some point the movement must come to an end, and at some point a firm social structure must come into being, held together by an incorruptible system of justice and by the uncontested authority of the state. Germany must not become a train steaming off into the unknown, with nobody knowing when it may stop.[36]

Papen's speech was well received by the overwhelming majority of his audience in Marburg and would no doubt have met with an equally positive response in the country as a whole if Goebbels had not taken immediate steps to ban its broadcast and publication. Edgar Jung was arrested by the Gestapo on 25 June. By then Hitler had realized that he was fighting a domestic battle on two political fronts and that his only chance of success lay in defeating both of his opponents – Röhm's 'revolutionary' SA and the monarchist forces of reaction – with a single blow. If he turned on only Papen and his circle, then this would have represented a triumph for the SA that would have placed Hitler in grave danger, whereas a move against the SA would have strengthened the hand of his own bourgeois confederates, a development that he cannot have wanted either. Papen's speech in Marburg gave him the opportunity to launch a two-pronged surprise attack and resolve the internal crisis in a radical way.

The events of late June and early July 1934 were described by contemporaries as the 'Röhm revolt' – this was the National Socialists' term – and by posterity as the 'Röhm putsch', although the truth of the matter is that the chief of staff of the SA was guilty of neither. Following a lengthy conversation with Hitler, Röhm had taken sick leave in early June and ordered the SA to go on leave of absence in July, making it much easier for Hitler to side with the Reichswehr and SS – formally still linked to the SA – and launch an attack on his comrade-in-arms, who had been his friend for many years. On 30 June, with Hitler's personal involvement, Röhm and other SA leaders were arrested at Bad Wiessee in Bavaria and taken to Stadelheim Prison in Munich, where all of them, with the exception of Röhm, were summarily executed that same day. Röhm himself was shot on Hitler's order on 1 July.

The leaders of the SA were not the only victims of the alleged 'Röhm putsch', for Hitler, Göring and Heinrich Himmler, the leader of the SS, seized the opportunity to liquidate political enemies from the most disparate camps. The former Bavarian general state commissioner Gustav von Kahr was murdered on 30 June, as were the chairman of the Catholic Action Group, Erich Klausener, who had close links with Papen, Papen's two colleagues Herbert von Bose and Edgar Jung, the former national organizer of the NSDAP, Gregor Straßer, and the former chancellor Kurt von Schleicher and his colleague General Ferdinand von Bredow. Hitler accused Schleicher of high treason for helping Röhm, while Bredow was said to have helped Schleicher in matters of foreign policy – both charges were completely groundless. Fully authenticated, conversely, is the number of individuals known to have been murdered as part of this clean-up operation: eighty-five, some fifty of whom were members of the SA.

On 30 June, in addition to SA leaders, Hitler also managed to get rid of a number of conservatives to whom he had taken a personal dislike. Papen, who had been a temporary, if largely passive, figurehead of the resistance, escaped relatively lightly. Göring had him placed under house arrest, but after two days Hitler responded to his request for a personal declaration vindicating his honour. He resigned as vice-chancellor on 7 August and at Hitler's request became special ambassador in Vienna, where, with the Führer's approval, the Austrian National Socialists had already mounted a coup on 25 July and shot dead the country's chancellor, Engelbert Dollfuß – which had not been a part of the plan. Although the coup was quickly put down, it triggered an international crisis, when Mussolini, whom Hitler had met for the first time in Venice only a short time earlier, deployed troops to the Brenner Pass in order to warn Germany against annexing Austria. Papen's mission was to restore Germany's credibility in Vienna. In this way Hitler hoped that there would be no repetition of an incident like his speech in Marburg.

On 3 July 1934 the German government passed a law retroactively declaring its actions on 30 June, 1 and 2 July to be legally justified inasmuch as they were ostensibly required to suppress acts of high treason as part of a national emergency. Hitler justified his actions to the Reichstag on 13 July:

> If anyone were to reproach me for not using the regular courts to pass sentence on the perpetrators, I can say only that at that moment I was responsible for the fate of the German nation and hence the supreme judge of the German people![37]

It was left to the constitutional lawyer Carl Schmitt, who since November 1933 had been the head of the section for university teachers in the League of National Socialist German Jurists, to provide a semblance of legitimacy for a series of murders said to have been sanctioned by 'the healthy instincts of the folk' and effectively to undermine the independence of the country's judiciary. Under the heading 'The Führer Protects the Law', Schmitt helped himself to Hitler's phrase about the 'supreme judge' and used it as the starting point for his own line of argument, such as it was:

> The true leader is always a judge, too. From the office of leader stems that of the judge. Anyone who tries to separate the two or, worse, to set one against the other turns the judge into a counter-leader or into the tool of a counter-leader and seeks to use the state to overturn the state. [. . .] The truth of the matter is that the Führer's action was a genuine judicial act. Not subject to justice, it was itself the highest form of justice. [. . .] The Führer's legal authority issues from the same source of the law as that from which every law of every nation issues. It is in our greatest emergency that the supreme law proves its true worth, and the highest degree of the law's avenging justice is realized. All laws stem from the people's right to exist.[38]

Apart from Hitler himself, the principal beneficiaries of the crisis in the SA were the army and the SS. The leaders of the army had made themselves complicit in a crime designed to ensure that they alone had the right to bear arms for their country. In order to achieve that goal they were even willing to countenance the murders of two of their generals. From that moment on they were susceptible to moral blackmail. On 20 July 1934 Hitler acknowledged the SS's help in eliminating the SA leadership by making it an independent organization within the NSDAP. As a result, Heinrich Himmler, who had been head of the Political Police in Germany since April 1934, moved up a rung on the ladder of the Third Reich's hierarchy, and his SS was able to embark on the process of becoming a state within a state.

Since early June Hindenburg had been staying at his country house at Neudeck in East Prussia, and it was there that the eighty-six-year-old president died on 2 August 1934. The Weimar Republic's second head of state had treated Hitler with deep mistrust right up until the end of January 1933, but once Hitler had become chancellor, all his objections had evaporated. Only twice between 30 January 1933 and 2 August 1934 did Hindenburg exert a moderating influence on the events unfolding in Germany: first, when the anti-Jewish provisions of the Law for the Restoration of the Professional Civil Service were toned down in April 1933 and, second, in the struggle with the Church in the summer of 1933. Under Hitler's chancellorship, the elderly president finally felt that the country had found the inner peace that it so fervently desired. Hindenburg had always felt a profound personal loathing of the SA's homosexual chief of staff and greeted the suppression of the ostensible 'Röhm putsch' by sending congratulatory telegrams to both Hitler and Göring. All that he learnt about the events in question was calculated to increase his estimation of his chancellor.

At the time of his death, Hindenburg had yet to achieve his own personal political ambitions. As a young Prussian officer he had been present when Wilhelm was proclaimed Kaiser at Versailles on 18 January 1871. In May 1934 he had signed a document headed 'Last Wish', professing his desire to see the Hohenzollerns restored to the throne. It was addressed to his country's new chancellor with instructions that it be handed to Hitler on the president's death. Hitler had long been familiar with the letter's contents when Papen, acting on behalf of Oskar von Hindenburg, handed it to him in Berchtesgaden on 14 August 1934. But it was only Hindenburg's last will and testament that he released to the press the following day. It too had been passed on to him by the country's former vice-chancellor and referred in the most glowing terms to 'my chancellor Adolf Hitler and his movement', but said nothing that hinted at the late president's 'Last Wish'.

As always, Hitler acted according to his own best interests. He refused to contemplate a restoration of the monarchy because it was incompatible with his interpretation of his own leadership. Hindenburg's death gave him the chance to cement that position still further. On 1 August – even before Hindenburg was dead – the government had already decided to combine the posts of president and chancellor, in the process proposing a solution diametrically opposed to Hindenburg's 'Last Wish' and also flying in the face of the Enabling Act, which had explicitly left the president's authority inviolate. At the same cabinet meeting, moreover, Blomberg had announced that on Hindenburg's death the armed forces would immediately swear an oath of allegiance to their 'Führer and Chancellor'.

On 2 August 1934 the country's soldiers were required to repeat the new oath, which had no legal backing and contained no commitment to defend country, fatherland or constitution but merely bound them to a single man:

I swear this sacred oath by God, that I shall unconditionally obey the leader of the German Reich and nation, Adolf Hitler, the supreme commander of the armed forces and that as a brave soldier I shall risk my life in fulfilment of this oath.[39]

By 2 August 1934 Hitler wielded a degree of personal power greater than anything seen in Germany since the age of absolutism. Institutionally speaking, the process of seizing power was now at an end. All that remained was for Hitler to receive the acclamation of the people. On 19 August 1934, four days after the publication of Hindenburg's last will and testament, the Germans had an opportunity to express their views on the Law Concerning the Head of State of the German Reich that had been passed on 1 August. As was to be expected, the vast majority – 89.9 per cent – voted for the law, representing acceptance of the legislation by 84.3 per cent of the electorate.

At first sight, the result represented a resounding victory for Hitler, but a comparison with the referendum of 12 November 1933 invited a rather more sober assessment, for the number of those who had registered their discontent by not voting had increased, while the number of those who agreed had fallen from 89.9 per cent to 84.3 per cent of all those who were entitled to vote. The number of no votes was particularly high in urban centres such as Hamburg (20.4 per cent), Aachen (18.6 per cent) and Berlin (18.5 per cent). In the capital, the no vote was in double figures in every district, the former Communist stronghold of Wedding topping the poll with 19.7 per cent.

Clearly Germany's withdrawal from the League of Nations was a far more popular move than the merger of its two most important offices of state. Hitler's prestige was not seriously impaired by the announcement that he was mistrusted by a minority of the population, but when measured by his own expectations, the outcome of this second plebiscite still represented a failure which Goebbels recorded as such in a diary entry of 22 August.[40]

This temporary setback in the regime's popularity was also a reflection of economic factors, for in spite of massive export grants Germany felt the effects of the decline in the country's exports in 1934, a decline due in part to international protectionism but also to German measures designed to protect its trade with the rest of the world. The attempt to make up for the collapse of trade with the United States and Great Britain was only gradually rewarded by a realignment of trade with south-eastern Europe and Latin America. On 14 June 1934 the president of the Reichsbank, Hjalmar Schacht, announced a complete moratorium on foreign debt repayments and the introduction of foreign currency allocations on a daily basis. According to surviving Gestapo reports, the Germans were more unsettled by the economic problems stemming from the foreign exchange crisis than by the so-called 'Röhm revolt'.

By 1934 it was above all the armaments industry that profited from state commissions: during the second year of the Third Reich military expenditure made up more than half of all state expenditure on goods and services, with the result that between 1933 and 1934 the part played by military expenditure in the growth of the gross domestic product rose more than tenfold from 4.2 per cent to 47 per cent. If unemployment fell during 1934, this was due for the most part to the expansion of the military sector, not to any job creation schemes among the civilian population. And if wages rose a little above their all-time low in 1929, then this was simply because Germans were working longer hours. It was no accident, therefore, that there was such a large percentage of no votes in working-class districts of the larger cities in the plebiscite on 19 August.

In spite of this, there could be no question of any widespread proletarian opposition to National Socialism in the summer of 1934. The leisure organization Kraft durch Freude (Strength Through Joy) that was established under the aegis of the German Workers' Front by analogy with the Italian Opera Nazionale Dopolavoro offered a wide range of holiday trips, sports, concerts, theatre visits and social events and played a large part in helping to make the Third Reich popular with workers. Soon after the 'Röhm putsch' a Berlin confidant of the exiled leader of the Social Democrats reported that 'The attitude of the workforce to the regime must continue to be described as benevolently neutral – even in the wake of recent events there has been no perceptible change to this situation.'[41]

Rome's Second Empire: Fascist Italy and the War in Abyssinia

There was no other country in Europe to which Hitler felt as ideologically close as he did to Fascist Italy and no other political leader whom he respected and even admired as much as Benito Mussolini. When Hitler became German chancellor on 30 January 1933, Italy was the only country whose newspapers reacted positively to the change at the top. In its edition of 31 January, *Il Popolo d'Italia* headed its report: 'The collapse of the world's old democratic and liberal systems. Adolf Hitler takes over the government in Germany in coalition with nationalist forces and defence leagues.' *Il Resto del Carlino* appeared later that same day with the headline, 'On the trail of Fascism. Chancellor Hitler brings the young forces of renewal to power in Germany.'[42]

In the wake of the Reichstag elections on 5 March 1933, when Hitler's position was confirmed, Mussolini attempted to impress the world by mediating between Germany and the Western Powers, playing an active role in plans for a consultative pact between Britain, France, Germany and Italy that Ramsay MacDonald had already put forward in the summer and autumn of 1932 and that was finally initialled in Rome on 7 July 1933. In the event, of course, the treaty was ratified only by Italy and Great Britain in August and September 1933, its failure largely due to the aggressive policies that Germany had adopted towards Austria: Mussolini was keen for Austria to retain its independence as he had no wish to see the German Reich as his immediate neighbour to the north.

The conflict between the Austrian National Socialists and the authoritarian regime of the Christian Socialist chancellor Engelbert Dollfuß grew dramatically worse in May and June 1933, when assassinations, bombings and the blowing up of bridges brought the republic to the brink of civil war. The government responded with arrests, house-to-house searches and a ban on public assemblies. After several incendiary speeches in Vienna and Graz, Bavaria's National Socialist justice minister Hans Frank was expelled from the country at the end of May. On 27 May the German government introduced a measure requiring all German tourists entering Austria to pay 1,000 marks – around £4,000 at today's prices. In this way Berlin hoped that Vienna would be forced to capitulate within a very short period of time.

At the end of July, in its attempts to cling to power and prevent Germany from annexing the country, the Austrian government appealed to London and Rome to urge Berlin to abandon a policy that violated international law. Until then Mussolini had sought to avoid taking sides and even now he preferred to attempt to influence the German government unilaterally, but he had no more success than London and Paris with his demarche of 4 August. Drawing the lessons from his failure, Mussolini adopted a policy that was aimed at a fascisization of Austria and its reduction to an Italian satellite state. On 19/20 August 1933, in the course of his third visit to Italy within four months, Dollfuß met Mussolini in Riccione and was left with no choice but to commit himself to giving his government an emphatically dictatorial character, leading to increased attacks on his country's Social Democrats.

The Austrian government had already disbanded the Social Democrats' Republican Protection League the previous March, driving it underground. In October the Social Democrats convened a special party conference at which they resolved to adopt a policy of armed resistance if any of four different contingencies arose: if the party was banned; if the trade unions were proscribed; if there was an attack on 'Red Vienna'; or if a Fascist constitution were to be introduced. On 18 January 1934, the Italian undersecretary of state at the Foreign Ministry, Fulvio Suvich, travelled to Vienna as Mussolini's representative to demand that Dollfuß implement the terms of the agreement that he had signed at Riccione and adopt a course that was both rigorously anti-parliamentary and strenuously anti-Marxist. The paramilitary militia groups adopted a similar line in late January and early February.

On 12 February the police moved against the Linz Workers' Home, prompting the banned defence league to resort to desperate measures and fire at the forces of law and order from the besieged building. When news of these events reached Vienna, the Social Democrat party executive proclaimed a general strike, leading to an armed uprising in the capital. It took the police, army and militia groups three days to break down the resistance of the workers who had barricaded themselves in large tower blocks such as the Karl-Marx-Hof in Döbling, from where they had fired on the forces of law and order. The latter sustained heavy casualties: more than 100 were killed and almost 500 injured, while the defence league and civilian population incurred equally substantial losses: 200 dead and more than 300 injured. The rebels were rounded up and summarily executed, all Social Democratic organizations were banned, and the mandates of the party's parliamentarians were revoked. The victors were Dollfuß's Austro-Fascist regime and the two powers that had lent it their substantial support: Fascist Italy and authoritarian Hungary under its governor Miklós Horthy and the country's radically right-wing, anti-Semitic prime minister, Gyula Gömbös.

A month later, on 17 March 1934, all three states agreed to work together politically and economically under the terms of the Rome Protocols. Dollfuß's regime passed a new constitution in May, and this was ratified by the rump parliament, appealing to Almighty God and declaring Austria a 'Christian, German, federal state on a corporative basis'. Insisting on the authoritarian nature of the Austrian state was scarcely calculated to pacify the population, and on 25 July 1934 the Austrian National Socialists mounted a putsch. They were responding to instructions from Theo Habicht, who had been sent to Austria in 1931 to oversee the reorganization of the Austrian National Socialists. Following his deportation in 1933, he established his headquarters in Munich, where he worked in close consultation with Hitler himself. Dollfuß was killed when the National Socialists stormed the chancellor's office. In total the attempted putsch resulted in 269 deaths and between 430 and 660 injured.

Dollfuß's violent death had not been a part of the plan, and it caused the putsch to fail. On 25 July Mussolini sent four divisions to the Brenner Pass and to Tarvisio, while Hitler disavowed his amateurish followers and that very night demonstratively dismissed Habicht and disbanded the Austrian leadership of the NSDAP. Dollfuß was succeeded by the minister of education, Kurt von Schuschnigg, who continued to pursue his predecessor's authoritarian, pro-Fascist policies. As a result of the National Socialists' failed putsch, relations between Germany and Italy reached a new historical low.

Austria was not the only bone of contention between the German National Socialists and the Italian Fascists. Another area where the interests of the two regimes clashed was the neighbouring Danube region, the Third Reich regarding the agrarian lands in the southern part of east central and south-east Europe as ripe for the picking, an area of economic importance worth incorporating into Germany and subjecting to its political control. In particular, Berlin sets its sights on Hungary and Yugoslavia, signing a trade deal with Budapest in July 1933 that was clearly aimed at making Hungary part of a large-scale economic region under German hegemony. By the beginning of 1934 Germany was making a sustained attempt to woo Belgrade and to redirect Hungary's revisionist aspirations away from Yugoslavia and towards Czechoslovakia. The Rome Protocols of March 1934 led Berlin to fear that its own strategy in south-east Europe was about to be thwarted and, indeed, there is no doubt that for some time Rome had been trying to ensure that Hungary and Yugoslavia were increasingly dependent on Mussolini's Italy.

As Yugoslavia had been a member of the Little Entente since 1920–1 and a direct ally of France since 1927, Paris viewed with suspicion Italian and, in particular, German policy towards Belgrade. By the autumn of 1934 the National Socialist putsch in Austria and Germany's increasing influence in Yugoslavia had persuaded Rome to seek a rapprochement with Paris, a move not anticipated by Berlin but one which in the French camp was encouraged by the sympathy for Mussolini and the Italian Fascists felt by France's foreign minister, Pierre Laval, while Mussolini's desire for colonial expansion in Africa played a significant role in his attempt to win over France as an ally. Mussolini and Laval signed a series of protocols in Rome in January 1935, marking what the historian Jens Petersen has called 'Italy's definitive defection to the camp of anti-revisionist forces'.[43] If Germany were to violate the terms of the Treaty of Versailles, then France and Italy would confer on whatever countermeasures they deemed should be taken. The same was true of the threat posed by Austrian independence.

Central to the agreements, however, was a secret arrangement regarding North Africa, France giving Italy a free hand in Abyssinia, including the right to use military force. This offered Rome the chance finally to deal with 'the shame of Adua', namely, the defeat inflicted on Italy by Abyssinian troops in 1896. This was a goal to which Mussolini had been systematically working since the early summer of 1932. His imperialist designs were intended to turn Italy into one of the leading colonial powers and help the country achieve the status of an *impero*, or empire, something that Italy had long aspired to become. From the standpoint of Italy's Fascists, this was the most effective answer to the 'mutilated victory' of 1918 and the crippling experience of economic depression.

This was not the only time that Hitler contributed to Italy's rapprochement with the Western Powers, for in March 1935 he twice violated the terms of the Treaty of Versailles: on 1 March he declared his intention of rebuilding his country's air force and on the 16th he reintroduced general military conscription. The Italian press reacted to this second provocation with an outcry of indignation, and Mussolini agreed to French demands for a summit conference that would condemn Hitler's actions. The summit was held on Italian soil – at Stresa on Lago Maggiore – between 11 and 14 April. The prime ministers of Britain, France and Italy – Ramsay MacDonald, Pierre-Étienne Flandin and Benito Mussolini – agreed 'to use all appropriate means to counter all unilateral revocations of treaties that could jeopardize peace in Europe' and 'to work together to that end in a spirit of friendly cooperation'.[44]

Among the few practical consequences of the Stresa conference were military agreements between France and Italy designed to resist any German moves against Austria and a German invasion of France. The subject of Abyssinia was not mentioned at Stresa. Soon afterwards London made it clear that it had serious misgivings about Italy's aims in north-east Africa, prompting Mussolini to change his foreign policy and move closer to Hitler. By now the Reich was by far Italy's most important trading partner in terms of both imports and exports. There was also the ideological affinity between Italian Fascism and German National Socialism. Mussolini's aggressive expansionist policy was likely to encounter far greater understanding north of the Alps than in either of the two western democracies that had sat round the same table in Stresa.

For Mussolini, there was no question of forgoing a war with Abyssinia. As the historian Hans Woller has noted, there were expansionist forces at work not only within the Fascist party, but also in the wider population, which was emphatically imperialist in its outlook:

> Mussolini had a national mission to fulfil, but he was unwilling to leave it merely at that. Rather, his aim was to combine that mission with another large-scale national concern: the creation of a new man, whom he wanted to mould entirely in his own Fascist image. Mussolini wanted to make his nation harsher and more implacable towards itself and other nations, nations that the Italians were ostensibly called upon to rule. Unless it expanded and proved itself in war, his regime would sink into a state of stagnation and its destiny would remain incomplete, his anthropological revolution no more than a dream.[45]

On 21 May 1935 Hitler, too, took a major step closer to Mussolini, declaring in a speech to the Reichstag that Germany had no intention of interfering in Austria's domestic concerns, still less of annexing the country. He explicitly regretted that the conflict with Austria had soured relations with Italy, especially because there were no other areas of disagreement between the two countries. Five days later Mussolini told a German diplomat that the Franco-Soviet Assistance Pact signed on 2 May had introduced an entirely new factor to international politics, necessitating a fundamental reappraisal of his country's stance. At the end of May Germany and Italy agreed that their respective presses would stop sniping at one another, and soon afterwards Mussolini recalled his German ambassador, Vittorio Cerruti, from Berlin, where he had proved an unpopular figure, and appointed him to the Italian Embassy in Paris.

But Hitler had no intention of helping Italy to gain a quick victory in Abyssinia. Although he had no wish to see Mussolini defeated, he was keen that the war should be sufficiently protracted to divert the Western Powers' attention from Germany and central Europe. In July 1935, after consulting with his foreign minister, Konstantin von Neurath, he responded positively to an appeal from the emperor Haile Selassie for military help. Under the terms of a highly secretive agreement, Ethiopia received 10,000 rifles, ten million rounds of ammunition, machine guns, hand grenades and around seventy artillery pieces, for which the country paid some three million marks in credit. Throughout the months that followed, Berlin sought to give the impression that it was a wholly impartial observer in the matter of Abyssinia.

In preparing the ground for war, Mussolini and Fascist propagandists fell back on the old argument, once advanced by pre-war nationalists, that there was a fundamental antagonism between capitalist and proletarian nations, and on 2 October 1935 – the day before Italy launched its assault on Ethiopia – Mussolini used the phrase 'Italia proletaria e fascista' to justify Italy's claim to colonial expansion. The war against the Empire of Abyssinia – a member of the League of Nations – began without any declaration of hostilities. The League of Nations condemned Italy as the aggressor but at the insistence of the French imposed only moderate economic sanctions on the country, rather than any military sanctions. There was no ban on the supply of petrol, steel and all the most important metals. And few countries heeded the embargo on weapons and raw materials or respected the credit restrictions. Germany declared its neutrality on 7 November and at the same time announced a ban on the export of armaments to the countries involved in the war, but provided Italy with huge amounts of raw materials, albeit at a very high price.

The Conquest of Abyssinia was a racist war of extermination bordering on genocide, the first such war to fall into this category in the twentieth century and at the same time the greatest colonial war until then. Between 350,000 and 760,000 Ethiopians out of a total population of some ten million fell victim to the war itself and the ensuing occupation, which lasted until 1941. As the Swiss historian Aram Mattioli has observed, the war against Haile Selassie's hopelessly inferior forces witnessed

> the most massive and most brutal use of air power that the world had seen until this point in its history. With the authority of the highest powers in the land, squadrons of the Regia Aeronautica undertook thousands of missions, dropping fragmentation bombs, incendiary bombs and gas bombs on human targets. Before Italy, only Spain had dropped poison gas from aeroplanes on its protectorate in northern Morocco. Italy was thus only the second country to use this weapon of mass destruction from the air.

In Mattioli's view, the Abyssinian campaign was 'a "bridge" between the colonial wars of the imperialist age and Hitler's war over Lebensraum'.[46]

In June 1925 Italy had ratified the Geneva Protocol for the Prohibition of the Use in War of Asphyxiating, Poisonous or Other Gases and of Bacteriological Methods of Warfare, but by December 1935 Marshal Pietro Badoglio was systematically deploying poison gas in the Abyssinian uplands not only against soldiers but increasingly against the civilian population, including spraying rivers, waterholes and pastureland. Not even the field hospitals of the Red Cross were safe from air attacks. Fleeing soldiers and civilians were mown down from the air by machine gun fire. The Ethiopians – the oldest nation in

Africa – were regarded as uncivilized savages and as such could be attacked using resources that would never have been deployed against European nations. The Italian military also used Muslim mercenaries from Eritrea and Libya against Christian Abyssinians, who were the victims of particularly cruel and barbarous treatment at their enemies' hands.

The use of poison gas was ordered by Mussolini and the Italian supreme command as a reaction to the unexpectedly stiff resistance from the Ethiopians. Italian war correspondents were banned from reporting on its use. The protests on the part of Haile Selassie and the imperial government in Addis Ababa against the systematic violation of international law went unheard. If sanctions were to have worked, they would have had to have been applied to fuel, above all oil, and the Suez Canal, which was under British control, should have been closed to Italian troops and military transports. Neither step was taken. Although the British foreign minister, Samuel Hoare, was forced to resign on 18 December 1935 after an offer to mediate that had been worked out between him and his French counterpart, Pierre Laval, and that made extensive concessions to Mussolini was deliberately leaked, causing a violent storm of protest in the British press, Great Britain failed to act decisively even under Hoare's successor, Anthony Eden. Italian troops entered Addis Ababa on 5 May 1936, formally marking the end of the war but by no means signalling the end of Ethiopian resistance to Italy's occupation.

Within weeks of the fall of his capital, Haile Selassie travelled to Geneva from his exile in the south of England and on 30 June 1936 was the first head of state to address a plenary session of the League of Nations:

> There is no precedent for a Head of State himself speaking in this assembly. But there is also no precedent for a people being a victim of such injustice and being at present threatened by abandonment to its aggressor. Also, there has never before been an example of any Government proceeding to the systematic extermination of a nation by barbarous means, in violation of the most solemn promises made by the nations of the earth that there should not be used against innocent human beings the terrible poison of harmful gases.[47]

Haile Selassie appealed in vain to the world's conscience. The League of Nations had lost its remaining moral authority during the Abyssinian conflict, so that it was only logical when on 4 July 1936 it lifted all the sanctions that had been imposed on Italy. Most nations quickly followed suit and recognized the conquest and annexation of Abyssinia by Fascist Italy. The few exceptions were the United States of America, the Soviet Union, Mexico, New Zealand and Haiti. Aram Mattioli's verdict hits the nail on the head: 'For the sake of peace in Europe, Abyssinia was sacrificed to a dictator's expansionist aspirations. In this way the Western Powers sent a signal encouraging copy-cat murderers.'[48]

As a result of government restrictions, the war in Ethiopia was covered by the Italian media to only a limited extent and as a result enjoyed the support not only of dyed-in-the-wool Fascists but of all Italian nationalists. It was seen as revenge for the defeat that the country had suffered four decades previously in Adua and enhanced Mussolini in the eyes of his people, proving a personal triumph for the Duce and making Fascism more popular than ever. Within hours of the fall of Addis Ababa, Mussolini had appeared on the balcony of the Palazzo Venezia and told a jubilant crowd that their country was again at peace:

> Ethiopia is Italian! It is Italian in practical terms because it has been occupied by our own victorious army, it is Italian in legal terms because with the sword of Rome ours is the civilization that has triumphed over barbarism, ours is the justice that has triumphed over cruel tyranny, it is we who have liberated the downtrodden masses and triumphed over thousands of years of slavery.[49]

Four days later, on 9 May 1936, Mussolini delivered himself of another speech which, frenetically acclaimed by the masses, proclaimed the new Roman Empire, the *Impero*:

> The Italian people has created the *Impero* with its blood. It will make that empire fertile with its labours and defend it against its enemies with its arms. In this supreme certainty, O legionaries, raise your insignia, your swords and your hearts in order to welcome the *Impero* to the destined hills of Rome after fifteen centuries.[50]

From 9 May 1936 King Victor Emanuel III bore the title of 'Emperor of Ethiopia'. Italy was now the third largest colonial power after Britain and France. The increase in prestige that accrued from the war went hand in hand with the growth of racism in Italy, starting with the feeling of superiority over the dark-skinned Africans with whom there could never be any question of racial interbreeding. In turn this feeling gave rise to a cult of racial purity that led to the exclusion of the Italian Jews as well, producing a rabid sentiment close to the anti-Semitism of the National Socialists in Germany.

The Africa Italiana Orientale was created by the Legge Organica of 1 June 1936 and comprised Ethiopia, Eritrea and Somalia, a single vast colony ruled by a viceroy. In reality, it was in marked contrast to the lofty tone struck by the Fascist propaganda of the period. Between 1935 and 1940 the region devoured more than 20 per cent of the total Italian budget. Only around 300,000 Italian settlers found a home here, eking out pitiful existences that were repeatedly placed under threat as the continuing resistance of the Ethiopians soon assumed the form of a guerrilla war, in turn provoking increasingly violent waves of brutal repression on the part of the colonial power. Mussolini himself set the tone of the reprisals in a telegram to the viceroy, General Rodolfo Graziani, dated 8 July 1936: Italy's foremost representative in Ethiopia was authorized 'to initiate and systematically conduct policy of terror and extermination against rebels and population in complicity with them. Without the law of ten eyes for one we cannot heal this wound in good time.'[51]

The viceroy did as was expected of him. When two intellectuals from Eritrea tried to assassinate him on 19 February 1937, killing seven bystanders and leaving Graziani himself with shrapnel wounds, the latter unleashed an orgy of violence of positively pogrom-like proportions in which he was aided and abetted by Fascist militiamen and many members of the Italian colony: within three days some 3,000 innocent men, women and children had been butchered. Further reprisals were undertaken in May, when the medieval monastery town of Debre Libanòs was attacked on the grounds that members of its religious community were suspected of complicity in the assassination attempt. Between 1,000 and 2,000 monks, deacons and visitors to the monastery lost their lives in the massacre.

The chauvinism that was encouraged by the Conquest of Abyssinia was shared by bishops, cardinals and intellectuals, including the writer Luigi Pirandello, as well as by a number of liberal and left-wing anti-Fascists such as the philosopher Benedetto Croce, the journalist Luigi Albertini and the former Socialist Arturo Labriola. Only exiled Italian leaders, whether Communist, Socialist or left-wing Liberal, remained unwavering in their opposition to Fascism and the war. The most influential mouthpiece of the émigrés was the journal *Giustizia e Libertà* that was established by Carlo Rosselli following his escape from the island of Lipari, where he had been held since 1927. Set up with the help of like-minded intellectuals such as Gaetano Salvemini and Emilio Lussu, it enjoyed a reputation that extended beyond its émigré readership and impacted on domestic Italian politics. 'Everything about Fascism is war,' wrote Rosselli in 1936,

> its origins, its mentality, its view of the world. [...] Since 1925 Fascism has been nothing more than preparation for war. [...] Fascism is a class war that begins at home and then turns on the outside world, a development that is by no means fortuitous because this is the only way in which it can survive.[52]

Together with his brother Nello, Carlo Rosselli was murdered by members of a radical right-wing secret organization in Bagnoles-de-l'Orne on 11 June 1937. Their assassins were presumably acting on the orders of the Italian foreign minister, Count Galeazzo Ciano, who was Mussolini's son-in-law. Their double murder was the regime's most brutal blow against Italian anti-Fascists since the murder of Giacomo Matteotti on 10 June 1924.

The Great Terror: Stalin Builds Up his
Dominion over the Soviet Union

Throughout the 1930s no country was more politically at odds with Fascist Italy than the Soviet Union – not that their ideological differences prevented Stalin from responding positively to an offer from Mussolini and signing a non-aggression pact with him in September 1932. Between 1925 and 1927 the Soviet Union had already signed similar treaties with Turkey, Afghanistan, Lithuania and Persia, followed in 1932 by a veritable avalanche of non-aggression pacts, including contractual agreements not only with Italy but with Finland, Poland, Latvia, Estonia and finally, on 29 November, with France.

In May 1933 – three months after Hitler seized power in Germany – the German-Soviet Neutrality and Non-Aggression Pact of April 1926 was renewed for a further three years, bringing to an end a ratification process that Brüning's government had begun but never pursued with any real seriousness of purpose. On the other hand, Hitler demonstratively ended the secret cooperation between the Reichswehr and the Red Army in July 1933. In 1934 the Soviet Union's non-aggression treaties with the Baltic States and also with Poland and Finland were extended, in part as a reaction to the German-Polish Non-Aggression Treaty of January 1934. The following September the Soviet Union became a member of the League of Nations, transforming the erstwhile pariah state of 1917 into a member of an international group of countries that at least in theory claimed to exist for reasons of collective security.

The Western Powers reacted positively to the Soviet Union's new official foreign policy, which was deliberately designed to appear more moderate. In 1929 Great Britain resumed diplomatic relations, which it had broken off two years earlier, and in November 1933 the United States accorded the Soviet Union its diplomatic recognition. The following year Moscow renounced its claims to Bessarabia and recognized its existing borders with Romania, thereby normalizing its relations with Bucharest. But it was his mutual assistance treaties with France and Czechoslovakia in 1935 that marked the greatest triumphs of Russia's foreign minister, Maxim Litvinov, who was regarded as particularly pro-western. Both treaties were clearly designed to send a clear signal to National Socialist Germany and its non-aggression pact with Poland in January 1934.

Initially at least the policies of the Communist International were unaffected by the Soviet Union's attempts to draw closer to the West and even after the National Socialists' seizure of power it continued to insist that its 'general line', including its struggle with 'bourgeois' democracy and with the 'social Fascists' of the Second International, remained the only proper one, even denying that the German Communists and working class had suffered a defeat. Not until 26 January 1934 – a year after Hitler had become chancellor – did Stalin first comment on 'the victory of Fascism in Germany', insisting that it must be regarded not only as a symptom of the weakness of the working class and a result of the betrayals of the working class by Social-Democracy [. . .]; it must also be regarded as a sign of the weakness of the bourgeoisie, a sign that the bourgeoisie is no longer able to rule by the old methods of parliamentarism and bourgeois democracy, and, as a consequence, is compelled in its home policy to resort to terrorist methods of rule – as a sign that it is no longer able to find a way out of the present situation on the basis of a peaceful foreign policy, and, as a consequence, is compelled to resort to a policy of war. Such is the situation. As you see, things are heading towards a new imperialist war as a way out of the present situation.[53]

The various non-aggression and mutual assistance pacts that the Soviet Union signed after 1933 with a select number of European nations, including Fascist Italy, were an attempt to drive a wedge between the 'imperialist' powers and to divide the less aggressive among them from the most aggressive one, namely, National Socialist Germany, thereby providing Moscow with what might be called reinsurance cover. The Soviet Union's official foreign policy was a classic case of Realpolitik, whereas on the level of the Communist International the ideological and political struggle with the bourgeoisie could – and must – be continued at least in the shorter term. Not until eighteen months after Hitler had come to power did Moscow realize that this act of calculated schizophrenia was weakening the anti-Fascist forces in the West, while proving highly beneficial to the most extreme form of Fascism, National Socialism.

France's was the first Communist Party to enter into a pact with the Socialists that was designed to defeat Fascism. The pact dates from July 1934. By February 1935 the exiled German Communist Party was demanding the formation of a 'united anti-Fascist people's front' that would provide a rallying point for all 'who are willing to work towards the overthrow of the Hitler government and the Fascist barbaric regime'. The Communists' ultimate goals were not laid out at this time:

> The united proletarian front is the lever for the popular front and for the people's revolution. The Communist and Social Democrat workers and officials hold this lever in their hands, they can turn the united front into a people's front and hence into a massed struggle, the struggle of the broad masses of the working people that will lead to the overthrow of the Fascist dictatorship.[54]

In August 1935, the secretary general of the Comintern, Georgi Dimitrov, speaking at the Seventh World Congress of the Third International, repeated a phrase first used at the Thirteenth Plenary Session in December 1933, when Fascism had been described as 'the open terrorist dictatorship of the most reactionary chauvinist and imperialist elements of finance capital'.[55] New, by contrast, was Dimitrov's appeal to the followers of the Second International to merge with the Third International to create an 'anti-Fascist popular front':

> We need to create a united front made up of all sections of the working class, no matter which party or organization they belong to, even *before* the majority of members of the working class have united in the struggle to overthrow capitalism and to achieve the victory of the proletarian revolution.[56]

With Dimitrov there was no hint of any Communist self-criticism. The reformers were to forget that for years they had been dismissed by the Comintern and their affiliated parties as 'the main social support of the bourgeoisie' and as 'social Fascists'. If they failed to forget this, then from the standpoint of the Communists they would be guilty of sabotaging their principal aim, which was to ensure a comprehensive merger of all anti-Fascists under the leadership of the working class.

The Comintern's new general line did not imply the abandonment of the goal of the Communist revolution but merely indicated a new way of approaching that goal. More than ever, since 1935 the Third International had been a tool of Soviet foreign policy. Its leading officials were soon to become the latest victims of Stalinist terror and, whenever it seemed appropriate, liquidated in the same way that leading Bolsheviks had been disposed of in the past. From this point of view the Seventh World Congress was the beginning of the end for the Comintern, which was finally disbanded in May 1943.

For a time it seemed as if the Soviet Union had entered a phase of moderation and consolidation that could be described as a Russian Thermidor. In March 1933 the right to vote was restored to the children of kulaks, and in May 1934 it was agreed to grant civil rights to those farmers who had been resettled, at least to the extent that they had in the meantime given credible proof of their loyalty to the Soviet state. In July, the Secret Police – OGPU – was formally disbanded and merged with the Ministry of the Interior. In February 1935 the Central Committee of the Soviet Communist Party and the Soviet Congress proposed changing the 1934 constitution with the aim of introducing 'further democratization' in the form of universal, equal and direct suffrage by secret ballot. A commission set up to examine the question reported in July 1936 with a draft proposal that was discussed in countless assemblies in the course of the following months, the discussions proving broadly based, open and remarkably outspoken, clearly revealing the level of mistrust and hostility felt towards the Soviet regime by large sections of the rural population.

The draft bill had been slightly emended by the time that it was adopted by the Soviet Congress on 5 December 1936. The new constitution provided the Union of Soviet Socialist Republics with a joint parliament elected by direct, secret ballot: the Supreme Soviet, which was divided into the Soviet of the Union and the Soviet of Nationalities, thereby abolishing the All-Russian Soviet Congress and the Central Executive Committee. The Soviet Union was defined as a 'socialist state of workers and peasants' whose political basis was the Soviets of Working People's Deputies, which 'grew and attained strength as a result of the overthrow of the landlords and capitalists and the achievement of the dictatorship of the proletariat'. In the section on social order, work was described as a duty and a question of honour for every citizen capable of working in keeping with the principle: 'He who does not work shall not eat.' Under the heading 'Fundamental Rights and Duties of Citizens', the constitution guaranteed the right to work, to recreation, to material provision in old age and in the case of illness, to education, to freedom of conscience, to freedom of religious worship and to freedom from anti-religious propaganda. Also guaranteed were freedom of speech, freedom of the press and the right of assembly, sexual equality, the equality of all nationalities and races, the inviolability of the person and residence and the independence of judges and state lawyers.

However liberal many of these articles may have seemed, the constitution also contained provisions that made it clear that the existing balance of power was by no means open to renegotiation. The Communist Party's claim to leadership was enshrined in Article 126, which described the party as 'the vanguard of the working people in their struggle to strengthen and develop the socialist system' and 'the leading core of all organizations of the working people, both public and state'. Articles 130 and 131 stated that it was the duty of every Soviet citizen to maintain discipline in the workplace, to perform all public duties and 'to respect the rules of socialist intercourse'. Citizens were also enjoined to 'safeguard and strengthen public, socialist property'. All who failed to do so were declared 'enemies of the people'. According to Article 141, the right to nominate candidates for public office was reserved for 'public organizations and societies of the working people: Communist Party organizations, trade unions, cooperatives, youth organizations and cultural societies'. There was no recourse to the law in the case of any violation of an individual's fundamental rights by party or state organs, while the courts were independent on paper only, allowing the powers that be to interpret the constitution in whatever ways they thought fit.

The 1936 constitution was undoubtedly also intended to lend credence to the country's attempts to improve its relations with western democracies. But for Stalin something else was presumably more important: a lasting and outwardly legal institutional validation of all the social and political changes that he and the Soviet regime had undertaken in the barely two decades since the October Revolution. For a time Stalin seems to have hoped to achieve the same effect by proposing several candidates for the elections to the soviets, but warnings from local party organizations that this might result in hostile elements growing more influential were sufficient to persuade him to abandon the experiment in the autumn of 1937 and to revert to the former system, with its sham election of only a single candidate. As for the reality of the party's dictatorial rule, the 1936 constitution produced nothing that could be interpreted as a historic change to the status quo.

Nothing reveals the specious character of the constitution as clearly as the fact that a new wave of terror had begun even while the bill was being discussed and passed. On 1 December 1934 Sergei Mironovich Kirov, the Communist Party's popular secretary in Leningrad and a man widely regarded as a 'liberal', was gunned down by a young unemployed Communist. The local branch of the People's Commissariat for Internal Affairs, the minister of the interior, Genrikh Grigoryevich Yagoda, and Stalin himself immediately alleged an anti-Soviet conspiracy, while Kirov's enemies quickly suspected that it was Stalin who had ordered the assassination, a suspicion that increased when the members of the Cheka who were involved in the investigation were themselves killed off in often mysterious ways. On the other hand, there is no evidence to link Stalin directly to the crime.

Kirov's murder was the signal for a large-scale persecution of real or imagined enemies of the regime both inside and outside the party apparatus. By 1 December 1934 Stalin had already issued orders allowing the People's Commissariat for Internal Affairs to deport and kill suspects without trial. And if 'terrorism' cases did come to court, then Stalin specifically ruled out the possibility of the accused's defence and appeal against his or her sentence. Cases brought before the Military Tribunal of the Supreme Court had to be completed on the day of the arraignment and death sentences carried out without delay. By a decree of April 1935 the death sentence was extended to adolescents who had reached their twelfth birthday.

Immediately after Kirov's assassination in Leningrad, Stalin's former adversaries, Zinoviev and Kamenev, were arrested, tried in secret and sentenced to ten years' imprisonment. Both were accused by the People's Commissariat for Internal Affairs of complicity in Kirov's murder. Their trial was followed by a purge initiated by Nikolai Ezhov, a native Lithuanian who had succeeded Yagoda as commissar for the interior and who was now secretary of the Central Committee. In the course of his initiative supporters of both Zinoviev and Kamenev as well as Trotskyites and other dissidents were tracked down, expelled from the party and arrested. In the summer of 1935 110 employees of the Kremlin were arrested after being accused of responding to orders from Trotsky and Zinoviev and of detaining and murdering the party leaders.

By the summer of 1936 a whole series of show trials had been initiated against well-known former party leaders, beginning with Zinoviev and Kamenev, then, in 1937, moving on to Bukharin, Rykov, Yagoda and many others. The accused stood no chance in court, where Stalin's chief prosecutor, Andrey Januarevich Vyshinsky, systematically intimidated his victims. Vyshinsky had made a name for himself in the early 1930s as the advocate of a relatively independent judiciary, but from 1936 he put his name to Stalin's show trials, confronting defendants with absurd accusations and persuading them to admit to the charges brought against them, perhaps in the hope that in doing so they might escape with their lives. Bukharin, for example, confessed to being responsible for political crimes but denied any personal responsibility. Many, including Bukharin himself, wrote to Stalin to plead for clemency, while assuring him of their unfailing loyalty and affection. All their appeals were in vain. In his final letter of 10 December 1937 Bukharin even begged to be allowed to take his own life with morphine rather than face a firing squad.

Most of these show trials ended with death sentences and the execution of the accused, only very few of whom received prison sentences instead. One such prisoner was the Comintern's former German specialist, Karl Radek, who died in prison in 1939. Many leading Bolsheviks were also panicked into taking their own lives, such was their fear of a show trial or of being denounced by innocent third parties who were blackmailed into incriminating them. The most prominent of these figures was the people's commissar for heavy industry, Grigory ('Sergo') Ordzhonikidze, who shot himself on 18 February 1937. The doctors who, acting on orders from on high, diagnosed 'paralysis of the heart' as the cause of death were later haled before the courts and executed in turn.

These show trials went hand in hand with a radical purge of the party apparatus directed at spies, saboteurs, members of the White Guard, Trotskyites, alcoholics and corrupt elements in general. According to Ezhov, a third of all banned members of the party were categorized as spies, as members of the White Guard and as Trotskyites in the second half of 1935: this represented a total of 43,000 members of the Soviet Communist Party. The party's first secretary in 1956, Nikita Sergeyevich Khrushchev, admitted that ninety-eight of the 139 members of the Central Committee who had been elected in 1934 were liquidated in 1937–8: more than 70 per cent of the total. Others affected by the great purge were Communist parties in exile, especially those members who had fled to the Soviet Union from Germany. In 1937 619 members of the German Communist Party were arrested. Most of them died, presumably in custody. Eighty-two are known to have been executed, while 132 were handed over to the German authorities in 1939–40.

By the spring of 1937 the army high command, too, was suspected of being in league with spies and saboteurs. The first to be arraigned was one of the heroes of the civil war, the deputy defence minister, Marshal Mikhail Nikolayevich Tukhachevsky, who was accused of being a German agent. The incriminating material consisted for the most part of forgeries provided by the German secret service, which passed the documents to the Soviet side via the unsuspecting Czech president Edvard Beneš. The popular marshal would probably have been stripped of his powers and liquidated even without the complicity of the German secret service, for both Stalin and Ezhov had long regarded Tukhachevsky as responsible for the many shortcomings of the Red Army. He was tortured while in prison, condemned to death by a military tribunal and executed on 12 June 1937 by being shot in the neck. Six other high-ranking generals suffered the same fate as his alleged co-conspirators.

In the wake of the purported 'military conspiracy' at least 33,400 officers were drummed out of the army in 1937–8. At least 7,280 were arrested, including three out of five Soviet marshals, fifteen out of sixteen army commanders and sixty out of seventy corps commanders. Some 5,000 officers were executed. By the end, the Red Army's officer corps had been almost entirely wiped out, the victim of a party leadership that believed the armed forces had been infiltrated by their enemies and that was determined to ensure unconditional loyalty by means of a systematic show of terror.

While suppressing the alleged 'military conspiracy', the party leaders waged a simultaneous and equally murderous campaign against party and state officials whom they suspected of subversive activities. Under Nikolai Ezhov, the People's Commissariat for Internal Affairs provided Stalin with almost daily lists of candidates for execution, starting in June 1937. In most cases the party's general secretary complied with his ministry's suggestions. In the course of 1937 and 1938 Stalin received 383 such lists, and around 39,000 of the suspected officials, including numerous members of the Cheka, were summarily executed on Stalin's instructions. In this the Russian dictator was acting according to the motto that he had passed on to his security organizations in June 1937: every Communist, no matter how well he may disguise himself, was potentially a 'covert enemy'. And because enemies were not always instantly identifiable, as many people as possible had to be killed. The aim of the exercise would be achieved even if only 5 per cent of all the murdered individuals had in fact been actual enemies.[57]

In the case of the terror inflicted on business leaders, activists of the 'Stakhanovite campaign' played a significant role. The mineworker Alexey Stakhanov from Irmino in Kadievka had become a celebrity in 1935 when, as part of the 'socialist competition', he had mined a record 102 tonnes of coal in a single shift, fourteen times his quota. The 'Stakhanovite movement' recruited its members from unskilled workers willing to emulate his example, workers who were used by the Communist regime to break down the resistance of factory managers to the raised production targets. Hated by the other workers, these Stakhanovites applied themselves to their task with such enthusiasm that the number of officials denounced by them and called to account by the country's security organizations suddenly shot up exponentially. By April 1938 a quarter of all engineers and managers in Kadievka had been arrested and liquidated.

The Stakhanov movement had an additional raison d'être in that the rate of Soviet industrial production had slowed down between 1933 and 1936. This was due in part to the fact that the production figures envisaged under the second Five-Year Plan of 1933 had been lowered when compared with the figures for 1929, but it was the result, above all, of the vast influx of unskilled workers from the outlying villages, who flooded into the towns and factories but were unused to industrial factory discipline. The regime responded with draconian punishments for idling in the workplace and also for bungled work and alcoholism. In the countryside the reign of terror was directed in the main at *kolkhoz* managers and agricultural technicians, who at show trials were held to account for poor harvests and for discontent among the peasant population.

By the second half of the 1930s the regime again had to confront the problem of the kulaks. From 1935 onwards, many former kulaks returned to their villages following an amnesty in August 1935 that applied to 78,000 kulaks and members of the clergy. In most cases the villagers accepted these kulaks into their *kolkhozy*. A far greater problem was posed by the almost 400,000 former kulaks who between 1931 and 1937 had fled from the special settlements allocated to them in Siberia. To the east of the Urals in particular, refugee kulaks, escaped prisoners, vagrants and common criminals banded together to attack *kolkhozy*, trains and police stations, frequently not recoiling from rape and murder. In the northern Caucasus such violence was generally perpetrated by armed bands of Chechens and Ingushetians.

In June 1937 the Politburo of the Siberian Communist Party gave orders for all members of 'counterrevolutionary rebel organizations of exiled kulaks' to be registered and for all activists to be shot. Stalin fine-tuned these orders in a telegram of 3 July 1937, specifying that the most hostile of the kulaks, priests, criminals, former officers and members of the pre-revolutionary parties were all to be liquidated. The Central Committee was to be informed within five days who was to be deported and who was to be shot. The leaders of the Western Siberian People's Commissariat for Internal Affairs recommended that 11,000 individuals be shot and 15,000 sent to labour camps. In Moscow, the party's leader, Nikita Khrushchev, advised the Politburo that 8,500 individuals be shot and 32,000 sent to concentration camps. On the basis of these figures the Politburo issued its secret 'Order 00447' on 31 July 1937, coincidentally the same day that Stalin ordered free elections by secret ballot. Under the terms of this order kulaks who had returned from exile or who were living in hiding, as well as members of former anti-Soviet parties, members of the clergy, sectarians, members of the White Guard and former officials of tsarist Russia, bandits, criminals and imprisoned recidivists were all to be taken into custody. Of these 75,950 were to be executed and 193,000 sent to one of the Gulag camps.

Regional leaders of the People's Commissariat for Internal Affairs subsequently sought to increase their quotas for killing their real or perceived enemies, encouraging the Politburo in turn to revise its figures upwards. At the end of January 1938 Stalin gave instructions for a further 57,200 enemies of the people to be arrested by the middle of March and for 48,000 of them to be shot in an effort to reduce the number of prisoners in the country's labour camps. The order resulted in around 30,000 executions, mostly of men and women who had been convicted of political crimes or who had violated one or other of the camp rules. In Moscow the mass killings were extended to include invalids and amputees, people who were blind and others who were suffering from tuberculosis, while in Leningrad deaf mutes were also rounded up and shot. All were expendable on the grounds that they were unable to work in the camps.

From 1936 ethnic minorities suspected of anti-Soviet activities were also included in this campaign of collective persecution. Among such groups were Germans, Poles, Letts, Armenians, Koreans and Chinese. In July 1937 all Germans working in the Soviet armaments industry, including members of the German Communist Party, were arrested and deported. These measures led directly to the deaths of 42,000 men, women and children. At the end of December 1937 a Leningrad court sentenced 992 Letts to death. In the summer of 1938 35,000 Poles were deported from the border region between Poland and the Ukraine. In 1937 and 1938 143,810 individuals – mostly Poles – were accused of spying for Poland and arrested. Of these, 111,091 were executed. By the end of 1938 almost a quarter of a million members of persecuted ethnic minorities had been shot. According to the People's Commissariat's own figures, well over 1.5 million people were arrested and 668,305 of them were shot between 1 October 1936 and 1 November 1938, when the mass terror was finally brought to an end on Stalin's instructions.

The reasons for Stalin's sudden decision to end this orgy of mass executions are unclear. He had first criticized the use of excessive force in the struggle against party members at a plenary session of the Central Committee in January 1938. In the November of that year Ezhov was replaced by Stalin's loyal henchman Lavrentiy Pavlovich Beria. Perhaps it was the growing threat of war that persuaded Stalin to end the mass terror, but it is also possible that as general secretary of the Soviet Communist Party he was afraid that the country's security services were growing increasingly autonomous and that their power was increasing at the expense of his own position. In February 1940 Ezhov was accused at a secret trial of leading a foreign conspiracy within the People's Commissariat and was condemned to death and shot, as were his closest colleagues and their families, including women and children. In total 346 went to their deaths in this way.

The German historian Jörg Baberowski has made a compelling attempt to explain Stalin's reign of terror in structural and socio-psychological terms, describing the Soviet Union at this time as a 'medieval feudal state ruled by powerful cliques and their followers', a state in which the provincial potentates were Stalin's vassals 'who, if they obeyed their leader, were allowed to maintain their own feudal networks'. According to Baberowski, Stalin's social model took the form of the bands of robbers whose members survived in brutal reality only if they remained loyal to each other through thick and thin. [. . .] The Stalinist official came from the villages and was a product of that culture, which he pursued with fire and sword. [. . .] Stalinism was a violent process designed to establish unambiguous conditions, an attempt to create the new man through the physical annihilation of the old one. But Stalinism triumphed through the ceaseless exercise of excessive violence, a violence that stemmed from the very traditions that it was seeking to combat. [. . .] It was the alliance of Manichaean delusions and archaic traditions of brutality that made it possible for Stalinism to indulge its worst excesses, which is why the idea of cultural homogeneity led to mass terror when subjected to Bolshevist conditions.[58]

Stalin was no lone culprit but needed like-minded individuals at every level of his hierarchical power structure, from the very top right down to the many who saw it as their civic duty to denounce ostensible enemies of the socialist order. And he also needed the masses who, responding to orders, demanded the severest punishment – death by firing squad – for traitors and saboteurs. The fact that the secretary general of the Soviet Communist Party enjoyed such widespread support among his comrades-in-arms was due in no small measure to the extremely backward nature of a political culture that had itself produced both Stalin and the Bolsheviks. Stalin exploited the category of class warfare, as developed by Marx and adapted by Lenin to the conditions in Russia, in order to settle internal party rivalries to his own advantage: anyone who opposed him or whom he suspected might oppose him in the future was 'objectively' in league with Russia's class enemies and needed, therefore, to be eliminated. Whereas Lenin had still been able to invoke the distant goal of freedom from domination by rendering the state superfluous, Stalin could not envisage a world beyond mass terror. Terror had become the raison d'être of his regime, time and again justifying its existence by exposing enemies who had to be liquidated. As a result, periods of moderation were not destined to last. For Stalinism, a Soviet Union without external and internal enemies represented the most dangerous of all threats, for such a situation would have robbed the regime of its meaning.

Later apologists have repeatedly claimed that unlike Italian Fascism and, more especially, German National Socialism, Stalinism was a dictatorship notable for its programme of modernization, and there is no doubt that it was an enormous achievement on the Soviet Union's part to move from being an agrarian society to an industrialized society within a little over a decade. In terms of its volume of industrial production, the Soviet Union was second only to the United States on the eve of the Second World War, outstripping Germany, Great Britain and France. Such a rapid increase in growth would have been inconceivable without forced labour on the most massive scale.

The institutional embodiment of this forced labour was what Alexander Solzhenitsyn called the 'Gulag Archipelago', in which 821,000 prisoners worked in 1938 – by 1940 that figure had risen to 1.5 million. Without their slave labour, the Soviet Union would not have been able to complete such major construction projects as the White Sea–Baltic Canal and the Moscow–Volga Canal within the space of only a few years. Shortly after the first of these had been opened in August 1933 as the Stalin Canal, 120 Soviet writers headed by Maxim Gorky undertook a cruise along the new artificial waterway, and in a volume titled *The White Sea–Baltic Canal Known as the Stalin Canal* they praised the organization of 'human raw materials' in the form of forced labour and described the system of concentration camps that provided the workforce for this and similar projects as 'beacons of progress'.[59] When the Moscow–Volga Canal – one of the largest projects to be undertaken as part of the second Five-Year Plan – was formally handed over to general freight and passenger traffic in July 1937, state propaganda fell over itself in its praise. The thousands of workers who had perished during its construction were nowhere mentioned. On its completion 55,000 convicts who had worked on the canal were released from the Gulag and others received official recognition. Conversely, many of the technicians and engineers who had overseen the project were charged with sabotage and political agitation before being arrested and shot.

Most employers were fully aware of the fact that theoretical attempts to increase production did not automatically lead to an actual increase. The Stakhanovite movement meant not only the excessive use of forced labour, it also led to the disruption of the production process, to the overloading of machines and to countless industrial accidents. There is much to be said for the argument that less brutal methods would have resulted in a higher rate of sustained growth. Less amenable to rational criteria is the wholesale annihilation of large sections of the Red Army's officer corps. If – as many of Stalin's later advocates have maintained – the Soviet dictator had really been interested in arming his country against the threat of an attack from National Socialist Germany, such a weakening of his own armed forces would have ruled itself out. But the need to identify enemies wherever problems arose and the desire to find scapegoats were both more powerful than any sober calculation.

In 1936 a failed harvest provided the authorities with an excuse to blame saboteurs for the resultant food shortages. By the second half of the 1930s black market trade and queues outside shops were a regular feature of Soviet life, while housing shortages continued to be crippling. On the other hand, those who were spared Stalin's terror must have found their lives relatively 'normal'. Rationing had ended in 1935, and peasant uprisings were now a thing of the past. There was no shortage of work. 'Normality' included the all-pervasive cult of the great leader, Stalin, the emotionally charged glorification of workers and peasants by the painters, sculptors and writers of 'Socialist Realism', a state-run movement promoting the cult of the body, apparently apolitical films such as *Jolly Fellows, Volga-Volga* and *Circus*, music, dance and sporting activities in Moscow's Gorky Cultural and Recreational Park, which opened in 1937, architecture both heroically monumental and kitschily ornamental, the 1935 ban on the writings of Boris Pasternak and the first performance of Shostakovich's Fifth Symphony in Leningrad's Philharmonic Hall on 21 November 1937.

By contrast, many aspects of Soviet life in the mid- to late 1930s were reactionary. Here one thinks of period films such as Vladimir Petrov's *Peter the Great* and Eisenstein's *Alexander Nevsky*; the new 'Soviet patriotism' that complemented and relativized 'proletarian internationalism'; the popularization of some of the classics of Russian literature, including, first and foremost, Alexander Pushkin; the reintroduction of army ranks that had been abolished at the time of the Revolution; and the new emphasis placed on family values. According to the census of 1937, there were still more believers than non-believers in the Soviet Union: 56.7 per cent against 43.3 per cent of the population aged over sixteen. Atheism assumed less militant forms than in the previous decade, but the Church remained the victim of persecution. Older estimates drawn up by dissidents claimed that between 1936 and 1938 800,000 members of the clergy were arrested and that 670 bishops were murdered, but more recent figures suggest that in 1937 alone 150,000 believers were arrested and 80,000 murdered. Of 80,000 Orthodox churches only 20,000 still served their original purpose as places of worship. Many, such as the Cathedral of Christ the Saviour in Moscow, were blown up or destroyed in other ways.

Soviet citizens remained in the dark about the spread of religious beliefs within their own country since the results of the 1937 census were never made public, no doubt because to have released them would have meant allowing Russians to draw conclusions about losses due to collectivization, famine, executions and deportations. In 1934 the country's population officially stood at 168 million, whereas it 1937 it was only 162 million. But the authorities were not content merely to suppress and sometimes destroy statistical information, for many of the statisticians employed by the Central Archives of the National Economy and involved in gathering material for the census were rounded up and shot as 'Trotskyite-Bukharinist spies' and 'enemies of the people'.

Stalin's reign of terror evoked disparate responses in western democracies. The show trials were condemned by conservative, liberal and Social-Democrat newspapers, while reports of forced labour in Soviet camps led to calls for Russian goods to be boycotted in the United States. But even in the mid-1930s left-wing intellectuals generally continued to regard the Soviet Union as a bulwark of progress and anti-Fascism. According to François Furet, the French writer Romain Rolland's visit to Moscow in 1935 'bestowed on the Soviet Union the blessing of democratic universalism'.[60] A committed pacifist and the winner of the Nobel Prize for literature in 1915, Rolland was granted the honour of a two-hour interview with Stalin and returned to France under the impression that thanks to the leadership of an enlightened ruler, the Soviet Union had answered the clarion call of the French Revolution and overseen the rebirth of humankind. Another French writer who had sympathized with the October Revolution, André Gide, arrived in Moscow in June 1936 but it was in a state of total disillusionment that he left Stalin's empire on 23 August 1936 – the day on which the sentences were handed down on Zinoviev, Kamenev and other alleged enemies of the party. His book *Return from the USSR* appeared in October 1936. In it he summed up his reaction to his visit: 'I doubt', he wrote, 'whether the spirit of any other country today, except for Hitler's Germany, is less free, more curbed, more fearful (terrorized), more reduced to vassalage.'[61]

Gide's book triggered an outcry of indignation among French Communists, and the party's intellectual leaders accused the eminent author of a frivolousness that stemmed from his evident debt to Trotskyism. Raymond Rosenmark, the reporter and legal expert for the Ligue pour les Droits de l'Homme, did not have to contend with reproaches of this kind, for in his account of the first of the Moscow show trials against Zinoviev, Kamenev and other old Bolsheviks, he declared in October 1936 that it was out of the question that the confessions extorted from the sixteen defendants could possibly have stemmed from torture or the threat of torture. He regarded the existence of a National Socialist plot as proven beyond doubt and came to the remarkable conclusion that

> It would be a negation of the French Revolution, which, according to a famous saying [by Georges Clemenceau], was a 'bloc', if we were to deny a nation's right to take strong measures against agitators for civil war, against conspirators with foreign connections.[62]

An equally pro-Soviet response was that of the writer Lion Feuchtwanger, who left National Socialist Germany in 1933 and settled in the French resort of Sanary-sur-Mer. He visited the Soviet Union during the winter of 1936/7 and, like Gide, was invited to spend several hours talking to Stalin. He too wrote up his experiences and impressions in a book. Although he was critical of the excesses of the cult of Stalin and reported on various problems in Soviet society, he saw nothing frightening about the show trial of the assistant people's commissar for heavy industry, Georgy Piatakov, Karl Radek and other alleged members of an anti-Soviet Trotskyite circle:

> The whole thing was less like a criminal trial than a debate carried on in a conversational tone by educated men who were trying to get at the truth. Indeed, the impression one received was that the accused, prosecution, and judges had the same, I might almost say sporting, interest in arriving at a satisfactory explanation of what had happened, without omitting anything.[63]

Since the accused, almost all of whom were condemned to death, admitted to having committed the crimes of which they were indicted and which included sabotage and the preparation of acts of terror, Feuchtwanger saw no reason to doubt the validity of their admissions.

Feuchtwanger's book was published in the summer of 1937 under the title *Moscow 1937: My Visit Described for My Friends*. It appeared in German and English, the German edition issued by the Amsterdam firm of Querido, the English edition by Victor Gollancz's Left Book Club in London. Among left-wing intellectuals positive accounts of conditions in the Soviet Union found a far greater response than critical testimony of the kind submitted by Gide. And this was true not only in Paris and London but also in New York, where Viking Press brought out an American edition of *Moscow 1937*. When compared with the Fascist dictatorships in Rome and Berlin, the Soviet Union appeared to be the lesser of two evils, even at the time of the Great Terror, and in some cases was even seen as the repository of all the hopes of those who wanted to save Europe and the world from Fascism.

Setting the Course for War: National Socialist Germany 1934–8

National Socialist Germany was able to celebrate something of a triumph on 13 January 1935, when the referendum provided for under the terms of the Treaty of Versailles finally took place in the Saarland, resulting in an overwhelming majority – 90.8 per cent – voting for a return to Germany. Only 0.4 per cent wanted to form a union with France, while 9.8 per cent responded to the slogans of the Social Democrats and German Communist Party and voted for the continuation of the status quo, whereby the region continued to be administered by the League of Nations. Both parties hoped that in this way the Saarland, at least, would be protected from National Socialist rule. The regime was able to interpret the result as proof of its powerful support among the workers, while the workers' parties, conversely, had to admit that they had suffered a major defeat.

By this date only a minority of Germans were still opposed to National Socialism. Even smaller was the number of those who actively resisted the regime by issuing illegal appeals or painting anti-government slogans on houses and bridges. The Communist opposition groups that were particularly active in this regard were among the first to be infiltrated by the Gestapo, with the result that other oppositional forces kept their distance. By the end of 1934 around 2,000 Communists had been killed. In 1933–4 the number of Communists under arrest was around 60,000, with a further 15,000 joining them in 1935.

The Social Democrats adopted a more cautious approach than the Communists, remaining a cohesive force by meeting at gatherings of consumer groups or – as in the days of Bismarck's Socialist Law – at the funerals of colleagues. Bolder members maintained links with the 'Sopade', the party's leaders in exile in Prague, and helped to distribute their writings, which were generally disseminated under fake titles, including those of classical plays and cookery books.

By 1935 the number of arrests of 'Marxist' opponents of the regime had shown a marked increase, as did the successful strikes against illegal groups of Social Democrats and trade unions. Those arrested were sentenced at mass trials: on one occasion 400 Social Democrats, on another 628 trade union members and yet again, in Cologne, 232 Social Democrats. As before, the regime continued to set its sights on organized Christianity, at least to the extent that its representatives sought to circumvent its policy of coordination. In 1936–7 Catholic priests and members of religious orders were subjected to a wave of trials on the grounds of immorality, a move backed up by press campaigns against the Catholic Church. At around the same time, schools were ordered to remove crucifixes, although this requirement triggered so many protests from the faithful that the National Socialists were forced to back down and repeal the decree in question.

There was similar resistance from the Protestants who belonged to the Confessing Church. On 1 July 1937, Martin Niemöller, who had repeatedly used his sermons at St Anne's Church in Dahlem to chastise Hitler for breaking his promises to the Evangelical Church, was arrested by the Gestapo. The sentence handed down by a special court in Berlin on 2 March 1938 – a fine of 2,000 marks and a prison sentence of seven months that was deemed to have been served by the time spent by Niemöller in custody – and, more especially, the reasons given by the court for its judgment were tantamount to an acquittal, but Hitler refused to accept the judges' decision, and as a 'prisoner of the Führer' Niemöller was taken straight from the court house in Moabit to the concentration camp at Sachsenhausen near Oranienburg. In July 1941 he was transferred to the camp at Dachau, where he remained until the end of the war.

The Evangelical pastor was a privileged prisoner – up to a point he was protected by his standing within the Church and by the international protests that his two arrests had caused. But the vast majority of concentration camp prisoners had to endure far worse conditions. In particular Communists and Social Democrats were made to suffer for their opposition to National Socialism both before and after 1933. Humiliating treatment, beatings, torture and the risk of being shot 'while fleeing' were all part of the daily routine for them. A former Social Democrat member of the Reichstag, Kurt Schumacher, who had lost an arm in the First World War, was forced to haul heavy rocks in Dachau. Only after a four-week hunger strike did the camp leaders abandon their attempt to destroy Schumacher by work. He was finally released in March 1943. Two of his party colleagues, Julius Leber and Carlo Mierendorff, were released in 1937 and 1938 respectively. As a Jew, Ernst Heilmann, who had been the leader of the Social Democrats in the Prussian Landtag and a member of the Reichstag during the Weimar Republic, was subjected to particularly sadistic forms of torture. He was murdered in Buchenwald in early April 1940 on the orders of Heinrich Himmler, who since 1936 had been the chief of the German police. Another Buchenwald victim was Ernst Thälmann, the long-standing chairman of the German Communist Party, who was arrested in March 1933 and murdered on Hitler's orders on 18 August 1944.

At the end of July 1933 there had been around 27,000 political prisoners in the whole of Germany. By June 1935 the number of prisoners in concentration camps was fewer than 40,000, a figure that might be interpreted to suggest that the National Socialists' rule had acquired a certain degree of stability. In 1937 there were still four concentration camps in the country as a whole: Dachau, Sachsenhausen, Buchenwald and Lichtenburg. They were run by the SS, which stationed a Death's Head Unit of between 1,000 and 1,500 men at each camp. After 1934 'political' prisoners were joined by a number of other categories: 'elements injurious to the folk' included those defined as 'asocial', 'work-shy', homosexual, Jehovah's Witnesses, émigrés who had returned temporarily or permanently to Germany and Jews, who were numbered among one or more of these groups. Under the laws as they existed at this time in Germany, there was no place for these 'elements', still less was there any place for them in the 'folk community' of National Socialism. The National Socialist answer to the dilemma was to ship them off to a concentration camp.

In 1941 the Social Democrat jurist Ernst Fraenkel, who had managed to flee to the United States three years earlier, published a study under the title *The Dual State*, in which he drew a distinction between the 'Normative State' that continued to exist at this time and the constantly expanding 'Prerogative State' that found its most striking expression in the country's concentration camps. At the same time these camps were increasingly becoming the backbone of the SS's economic empire. The work done by the prisoners was so lucrative that the need for prisoners continued to grow. The quarries worked by concentration camp prisoners provided much of the building material for the National Socialist monumental buildings designed by Hitler's chief architect Albert Speer and erected in Nuremberg, Munich and Berlin. New camps were set up for reasons of convenience in the vicinity of granite quarries, notably at Flossenburg in the Upper Palatinate and, following the annexation of Austria, at Mauthausen near Linz. As in Germany, the prisoners at Mauthausen were made up of such disparate groups as criminals, the 'asocial', homosexuals, Roma, Jews and opponents of the regime whose hostility to National Socialism was motivated by their religious and political beliefs.

A wide range of attitudes existed between, at the one extreme, resistance to Hitler's regime aimed at bringing it down and, at the other end of the spectrum, unconditional support for National Socialism. Often enough, admiration for the 'Führer' went hand in hand with contempt for the 'little Hitlers' who surrounded him, a gulf that affected broad sections of the NSDAP, which many Germans joined for reasons of professional expediency. (By the end of the war

the party had 8.5 million members.) Many 'national comrades' gave their
backing on the whole to National Socialist policies but had misgivings about
measures in individual areas such as the National Socialists' policies towards
the Church and schools. In some cases these reservations were taken to the
point where, as far as possible, the individuals in question avoided giving the
Hitler salute, refused to fly the swastika flag and either declined to join National
Socialist organizations or, where it was unavoidable, became members of relatively harmless groups such as the National Socialist People's Welfare organization. Although this was not in itself a form of resistance, it did represent a sense
of distance, a refusal to go along with the regime. Privately, Germans could
express doubts in, and criticism of, Hitler, at least when they were certain that
no one was listening who was not supposed to be, but for the vast majority of
their fellow countrymen and women, the Führer was sacrosanct: Hitler's
triumphs and his popularity largely made up for all the objections that Germans
may have entertained about daily life under the Third Reich.

Hitler's popularity with most Germans increased, the longer the country
remained at peace, but the same was not true of many right-wing intellectuals.
Those who in 1933 had welcomed Hitler's seizure of power were subsequently
so appalled at the plebeian tenor of the movement and so disillusioned at the
mediocrity of its 'intellectual' representatives that they abandoned their public
support for National Socialism. This was certainly true of the writer Gottfried
Benn, for example, and of the sociologist Hans Freyer, whose *Right-Wing
Revolution* of 1931 is one of the few intellectually remarkable books by a Young
Conservative writer, as well as the philosopher Arnold Gehlen and, with reservations, Martin Heidegger, who was subjected to repeated attacks on the part
of radical National Socialists declaring him philosophically unreliable.

In the case of the constitutional lawyer Carl Schmitt, it was less a question
of his losing faith in National Socialism than of National Socialism losing faith
in him. In October 1936, in his capacity as head of the organization of university teachers within the National Socialist Jurists' Association, Schmitt organized a conference on 'Jewry in the Legal Profession' and in his concluding
remarks appealed directly to Hitler's tenet: 'In resisting the Jew, I am upholding
the work of the Lord.' Schmitt also demanded that if the works of a Jewish
writer were cited, then their author's Jewish background should be explicitly
mentioned. And he expressed the hope that 'the mere mention of the word
"Jewish" ' would 'serve as a salutary exorcism'.[64]

Schmitt's speech combined a deep-seated loathing of Jewry with a syco-
phantic and opportunistic appeal to the regime. But his submissive gesture
proved useless, and in early December 1936, in response to criticism from
German émigrés, he was attacked by *Das Schwarze Korps*, the SS's official
publication, for his earlier links with Jews and Catholic politicians and for his
opposition to National Socialism before 1933. Schmitt was stripped of all his
political appointments with the exception of his membership of the Prussian

State Council, which he owed to Göring, and his professorship in Berlin. But he continued to be associated with the Third Reich through his publications.

The intellectuals who had remained in Germany in 1933 but had not embraced National Socialism withdrew into themselves, a state generally described by writers on the subject as an 'inner emigration'. They included some of the country's best-known writers such as Ernst Jünger, Ricarda Huch, Reinhold Schneider, Ernst Wiechert and Werner Bergengruen. As long as they kept their political views to themselves, they were allowed to continue to publish. Even veiled criticism of National Socialism sometimes slipped past the censor, notably in the case of Bergengruen's *The Great Tyrant and the Court* (1935) and Jünger's *On the Marble Cliffs* (1939). The works of these writers were ignored by the party-controlled press but were still read by the public at large. Officially, however, it was other writers who set the tone: Hans Friedrich Blunck, for example, the author of prose works on north German myths and for a time president of the Reich Writers' Chamber; Hans Grimm, who wrote a colonial novel, *A Nation Without Space*; and Werner Beumelburg, whose novels on the experience of war viewed the events of 1914–18 in a transfigured light.

'Inner emigration' remained a phenomenon confined to the middle and older generation: younger intellectuals tended, rather, to see in National Socialism a force that would lead to a comprehensive rejuvenation of Germany. By the mid-1930s key positions in the SS, in its security service and in the Gestapo were held by young academics who had completed their studies under the Weimar Republic. The lawyer Werner Best, for example, a civil servant's son who had been born in Mainz in 1903, worked for the Gestapo as organizer, head of personnel, legal adviser and ideologue.

The 'experience of war' of the young National Socialist technocrats was limited to the internal conflicts in Germany in 1919–20 and between 1930 and 1933, but above all to the conflict in Upper Silesia and the occupation of the Ruhr Valley in 1923. Young National Socialist intellectuals were marked by *völkisch* nationalism and determined to create a racially homogeneous community using the resources of a totalitarian state. The exclusion of 'Bolsheviks', 'Marxists' and other ostensible enemies of the state was their area of responsibility, and after 1933 they felt that they were making good progress in this field. But the removal of Jews was a challenge that remained unresolved. The young academics in the SS, the secret service and the Gestapo, whom the German historian Michael Wildt has described as the 'uncompromising generation',[65] knew this, and so they set about trying to resolve the matter.

In theory the 'Jewish question' could have been resolved in the spirit of National Socialism if the country's Jewish population had been forced to emigrate, and an attempt to bring about this solution was indeed made in 1933: in the August of that year the Reich Ministry of Finance signed the Haavarah Agreement with Zionist representatives from Germany and Palestine, making it easier for

Jewish émigrés to transfer at least a part of their wealth to Palestine. (The rest was appropriated by the Reich, which was additionally able to export more goods to Palestine in consequence.) For most of the 60,000 Jews who emigrated to Palestine between 1933 and 1939, the agreement provided a degree of material assistance. But anyone wanting to take advantage of this option needed to have considerable financial resources, and few German Jews had access to such means. And even in the case of wealthy Jews, only a small minority regarded their situation in Germany as so dangerous at this time that they thought of emigrating at all. Between 1933 and 1937 some 129,000 out of a total of 525,000 Jews left Germany, most of them heading for western Europe.

Anti-Semitic pressures increased in the early months of 1935, when National Socialist members of the middle class took part in spontaneous demonstrations, seeking to rid themselves of unwelcome competitors by attacking Jewish shops, for example. The economic damage was considerable and the negative reaction abroad so great that in August 1935 the regime decided to channel these protests along legalistic lines, a decision prompted above all by Hjalmar Schacht, who since August 1934 had been Germany's finance minister in addition to president of the country's federal bank.

The result of this move was the Nuremberg Laws that the Reichstag enacted on 15 September 1935 during the NSDAP's party conference in Nuremberg. The Reich Flag Act repealed the earlier act of March 1933, whereby the swastika flag and the black, white and red flag of the old Reich were flown alongside each other. In their place the symbol of National Socialism was declared the country's only national flag. The Law for the Protection of German Blood and German Honour banned marriages between Jews and citizens of German or 'kindred' blood. It also banned Jews from employing 'Aryan' female domestic servants under the age of forty-five and from flying the swastika flag. The Reich Citizenship Act defined the concept of citizenship and created the legal category of 'Reich citizen' for all 'Aryan' Germans. Only 'Reich citizens' had full political rights, including the right to vote. All other citizens were reduced to the status of guests whose presence in Germany was merely tolerated.

Hitler was shown four drafts of the Citizenship Bill, and of these he chose the 'mildest', while striking out the clause that limited the law to 'full Jews'. As a result it was left to the courts to decide who was a 'full Jew', who was a 'half-breed of the first and second degree', who was 'considered a Jew' and who was 'of German blood'. The courts also had to decide the consequences for those who were not purely 'German'. Hitler himself reserved the right to decide the matter in those cases where there was still any doubt.

The Nuremberg Laws brought an end to Jewish emancipation and reduced the question of German identity to one of biology. It was a clear declaration of war on culture in general and it not infrequently encountered support in Germany. Limiting Jewish influence by legal means found greater acceptance among Germans than unofficial demonstrations and acts of violence. An official report from Berlin stated that after years of conflict between Germans and Jews, 'clarity' had 'finally prevailed', resulting everywhere in 'great contentment and enthusiasm among the people'. In Koblenz there was 'satisfaction' because the new law would 'lead to the desired isolation of Jews more than the unedifying actions of individuals'. Those close to the Social Democrats, conversely, claimed that these laws had been rejected by the workers and bourgeoisie and 'even in National Socialist circles'. According to this source, of course, there was at least as much criticism of the replacement of the imperial flag by the swastika as there was of the fact that the Jews had been stripped of their rights. In official reports, too, it was this regulation concerning the flying of flags that was the most unpopular of the Nuremberg Laws.[66]

Outwardly, the Nuremberg Laws brought a period of calm. The Olympic Games were held in Garmisch-Partenkirchen and Berlin in 1936 and the National Socialist leadership was keen to present to the world a welcoming picture of Germany. When the Jewish medical student David Frankfurter shot the leading representative of the NSDAP in Switzerland, Wilhelm Gustloff, on 5 February, the regime banned all anti-Semitic demonstrations: the Winter Olympics were due to start the very next day in Garmisch-Partenkirchen.

Two months after the Saar referendum Hitler took a step that was to prove one of the most significant stages on his road to the Second World War, when on 16 March 1935 he reintroduced general military conscription. The move was in open violation of the terms of the Treaty of Versailles, which had limited Germany to a professional army of 100,000 men. The new army was to have a peacetime strength of thirty-six divisions and 550,000 men.

The victorious powers in Europe, including – initially – Italy, were content to protest in writing. Great Britain had no qualms about signing a naval agreement with Germany only three months later, on 18 June 1935, whereby Germany undertook that its navy would not exceed a third of the tonnage of the Royal Navy. Hitler now felt confident in striking a further and, in this case, fatal blow against the Treaties of Versailles and Locarno, and on 7 March 1936 he declared the Locarno Treaties null and void and, in a move designed to restore his country's military sovereignty, occupied the demilitarized zone of the Rhineland. If France had resorted to arms in order to resist the invading German troops, the Wehrmacht would have had to retreat, an unimaginable humiliation for Hitler. But France was not ready for war, Great Britain even less so. Moreover, France had refused only a short time earlier to impose harsh sanctions on Italy after it launched its campaign in Abyssinia, thereby undermining the credibility of the West in general. It was very much to Hitler's advantage that in the early months of 1936 international public opinion was more exercised by Italy than by Germany, giving him a chance that he had no intention of ignoring.

The occupation of the Rhineland was backed up by propaganda: in a radio address and a memorandum Hitler invited the signatories of the Locarno

Treaties to undertake a comprehensive renegotiation of its terms. His aim was to sign non-aggression pacts with France and Belgium that would last for twenty-five years and be guaranteed by Great Britain and Italy. He also tried to entice London with an air treaty, and if the West were to agree to his offer, he even held out the possibility of Germany's return to the League of Nations. The Rhineland crisis ended just as Hitler had hoped: the League of Nations merely condemned Germany for violating the Treaty of Versailles but imposed no sanctions on the country; and France, Belgium and Great Britain guaranteed to defend each other's territories in the event of one or other of them being attacked by Germany.

In Germany this surprise move gave a tremendous boost to Hitler's popularity, and the increase in his prestige offered him a welcome opportunity to confirm his position by means of a plebiscite. In the hastily arranged elections to the Reichstag on 29 March 1936, when Jews were not allowed to vote and, where necessary, local election officials revised the results upwards, 98.9 per cent of those who voted supported Hitler's list, appearing to confirm the Führer in his belief in his own infallibility, so much so, indeed, that as Ian Kershaw has observed, he was now a 'believer in his own cult'.[67] In the most dangerous crisis in the Third Reich's foreign policy to date – the occupation of the Rhineland – he had succeeded with his tactic of presenting the world with a fait accompli and shown that western democracies and the League of Nations were incapable of acting resolutely. Against this background, what could possibly go wrong for him in the future? At the Party Rally of Honour in September 1936 he adopted the role of a national redeemer and spoke of the mystic union between himself and his nation: 'That you have found me [. . .] among so many millions is the miracle of our time! And that I have found you, that is Germany's fortune!'[68]

The fall in German unemployment also contributed substantially to Hitler's popularity: between 1935 and 1936 the figure dropped from 2.1 million to 1.6 million, from 11.6 per cent to 8.3 per cent of the working population. (In the United States the figure still stood at 16.9 per cent in 1936.) When the British economist John Maynard Keynes put forward his *General Theory of Employment, Interest and Money* in 1936 and the book was translated into German later that same year, he added a preface to the German edition, noting that on the whole his general theory of production could be applied far more readily to the conditions that existed in a totalitarian state than the classic theory that was geared to a free market. In National Socialist Germany the state had invested far more in the economy during the world economic crisis than any other capitalist country, pursuing a policy of a 'somewhat comprehensive socialization of investment' that Keynes recommended as a means of stimulating the economy.[69]

But almost half – 47 per cent – of national economic growth between 1936 and 1938 was directly due to the increase in military spending. As Adam Tooze has noted in this context:

If we add investment, of which a very large part was dictated either by the priorities of autarchy or rearmament, the share rises to two-thirds (67 per cent). Private consumption, by contrast, was responsible for only 25 per cent of the growth over this same period, even though in 1935 it had accounted for 70 per cent of total economic activity. If we consider only that part of economic activity that was directly under the control of the state, the dominance of military spending is even more dramatic. Of the goods and services purchased by the Reich, the Wehrmacht accounted for 70 per cent in 1935 and 80 per cent three years later.[70]

Keynes, who saw in his anti-cyclical economic policy a stratagem for peace, justified his optimistic assumption by arguing that increased military expansionism would not be necessary if full employment could be achieved by means of domestic policies. To describe the economic policies of National Socialist Germany as 'Keynesian', as has frequently been done, is to ignore the economist's political message.

By September 1936 – the date of the Party Rally of Honour – Hitler had already drawn up a secret timetable for preparations for war. Dating from August 1936, his memorandum on a four-year plan was based on the same geostrategic maxims as those that he had laid out in *Mein Kampf*:

Ever since the outbreak of the French Revolution, the world has been drifting with increasing speed towards a new confrontation whose most extreme solution is known as Bolshevism but whose ideas and goal amount to no more than the removal and replacement by international Jewry of what have until now been the leading social strata of humanity. No state will be able to escape this historical confrontation or even to remain aloof from it. *Now that Marxism, with its victory in Russia, has created one of the largest empires in the world as the starting point for its further operations, this question has become one that represents a threat to us all. An ideologically divided democratic world is now being brought face to face with a self-contained, authoritarian and ideologically well-founded desire to attack.* The military means that underpin this desire to attack are growing from year to year.[71]

Germany remained the 'focus of the western world against Bolshevik attacks':

If Bolshevism were to triumph in Germany, such a victory would lead not to another Treaty of Versailles but to the definitive annihilation, nay extirpation, of the German people. [. . .] In view of the need to resist this danger, all other considerations must necessarily pale into insignificance. [. . .] The scale and speed of the military enhancement of our powers cannot be undertaken quickly enough or on a large enough scale. [. . .] Unless we succeed in building up the German Wehrmacht in the shortest possible time and unless we are able to set up the formations, rearm and, above all, develop into the foremost army in the world in terms of our intellectual education, then Germany will be lost![72]

Turning to the economic situation, Hitler concluded that Germany was overpopulated and not in a position to feed itself on the basis of its own resources. The same was true of its need for raw materials. Although it was conceivable in theory that the country could export more, this was unlikely in practical terms. The main conclusion to be drawn from all this was that Germany should try, as far as possible, to become self-sufficient. Petrol and rubber should be produced synthetically without regard for the cost, while German steel and coal production needed to be greatly increased. Industrial sabotage must be punishable by death, and Jews in general must be held accountable for all the harm caused to the German economy. But the ultimate solution could be only to 'extend our Lebensraum or, to put it another way, to increase our nation's base of raw materials and food', which meant war in the shorter, rather than the longer, term. The two principal conclusions with which Hitler ended his memorandum were as clear as they were succinct: 'I. The German army must be ready for deployment within four years. II. The German economy must be capable of sustaining a war within four years.'[73]

In order to meet the ambitious goal of achieving the greatest possible independence within the shortest possible time, the regime created a large-scale state-run economic sector under the leadership of Hermann Göring, who added the present post to his existing portfolio of appointments that included leader of the Reichstag, prime minister of Prussia, minister for aviation, commander in chief of the air force, Reich forestry commissioner and Reich master of the hunt. His agency thus came into direct opposition to the country's Finance Ministry, with Göring himself on a collision course with Hjalmar Schacht, who held the posts of president of the Reichsbank, minister for economic affairs and, from May 1935, plenipotentiary-general for the wartime economy.

The Four-Year Plan – the term itself was borrowed from the Soviet Union – ushered in the transition to National Socialist state capitalism, whereby the regime's influence on the country's economy acquired a whole new quality. In July 1937 the Hermann Göring Public Limited Company for Ore Mining and Ironworks was founded in Salzgitter as the nucleus of the Hermann Göring Reichswerke that was summoned into life a year later and that by 1940 was employing almost 600,000 people at every stage of the production process. Schacht drew the obvious conclusion from his gradual loss of power and in August 1937 asked Hitler to accept his resignation as minister for economic affairs and plenipotentiary-general for the wartime economy. Hitler accepted his request on 26 November 1937. Schacht retained the post of president of the Reichsbank until January 1939.

The decision to give absolute priority to the armaments industry inevitably drove up the national debt to dizzying heights, especially when the government decided against increasing taxes and, by extension, reducing mass consumption. At no point did Hitler consider this alternative, for there was nothing that frightened him more than discontent among the workforce. In a study published in German in 1975 under the title *Arbeiterklasse und Volksgemeinschaft* (Working Class and Folk Community), the British Marxist historian Timothy W. Mason discussed the altogether traumatic memory of November 1918 on the part of Hitler and other leading National Socialists, an event which, like the later legend of the 'stab in the back', was interpreted as one that had prevented Germany from achieving ultimate victory by means of a revolution at home.[74]

The economic upturn since 1933 had improved the material conditions of the majority of Germans: by 1937 average weekly wages were some 20.6 per cent higher than at the height of the depression in 1932, although they were still 28.8 per cent lower than in 1929. The cost of living index, conversely, had risen by only 3.7 per cent between 1932 and 1937. Only now could many Germans afford to buy a radio ('folk receiver'), which was the most important means for spreading National Socialist propaganda. Some 650,000 sets were sold between August 1933 and August 1934, a further 854,000 by the end of 1935. By 1938 80 per cent of all German households in the country's major towns and cities had a radio. Only in the countryside was the ownership of a set still relatively uncommon.

In 1933 only one household in thirty-seven owned a car. In 1934 Hitler promised to build a popular model that would cost no more than 1,000 Reichsmarks, and in July 1936 he chose the Volkswagen, which was built by a state-owned company run by the Strength Through Joy leisure organization, a subdivision of the German Labour Front. Work began on the new car at the purpose-built Volkswagen Works in the recently founded city of Wolfsburg on the Mittellandkanal in May 1938. It was run by Ferdinand Porsche. By 1939 270,000 Germans had opened a savings account that would allow them to buy a Volkswagen car once they had paid 750 Reichsmarks into the scheme. By the end of the war the number of subscribers had risen to 340,000. Although not a single civilian customer had received a Volkswagen by 1945 and the 275 million marks netted by the German Labour Front were wiped out by post-war inflation (the interest had been pocketed by the Reich), even the expectation that Germans would be able to drive along the nation's new motorways – the 'Führer's roads' – in their own cars in the not-too-distant future was sufficient to increase the popularity of the regime and also of Hitler personally.

In 1937 unemployment sank to 912,000, representing 4.6 per cent of the working population, and by 1938 it had again been halved, dropping to 430,000, or 2.1 per cent of the workforce. Germany was thus the first of the industrialized nations to have been hit by the world economic crisis to return to full employment. For the most part the boom was based on 'creative' accounting in the form of Mefo IOUs, a federal debt that could have been settled only by the invasion of foreign territories and by the exploitation of their resources and labour markets. Even if Hitler had not already long since planned the next war, he would have had to have drawn up plans to that end by 1936 at the latest. Otherwise it would not have been possible to avoid the consequences of huge investment in unproductive projects and, with it, the collapse of the country's finances. In order not to have to defer the start of the war to some distant date in the future, Hitler turned down the request for a comprehensive rearmament programme demanded by Georg Thomas, the Wehrmacht's chief economic expert at the Ministry of War, as it became known in May 1935. Instead, he insisted on a more broadly based rearmament programme that would not have permitted a lengthy war but only a blitzkrieg. The spoils of these wars would finance the next blitzkriegs. In this way Hitler planned to defray the incalculable cost of realizing his plan for a new Lebensraum for the Germans.

The more the unemployment figures fell, the more the market value of labour rose. As Timothy W. Mason succinctly observed:

> After 1936, the situation in the labour market made it possible for workers to lay down certain conditions for their own political subjection. Since the German Labour Front was responsible for stabilizing this subjugation, it largely made its own the conditions of the working class, aiming at the very least at a share in the country's rising prosperity and necessarily leading to a worsening of the conflict between the German Labour Front and those authorities and interests that were bound to oppose all wage increases, holiday pay and an extension to existing company-based welfare schemes.[75]

If the German Labour Front had supported the country's employers, the civil service and the military in limiting consumption, it would – as Mason aptly notes – very quickly have become unusable as a mass organization:

> Because of the continuing concern on the part of the powers that be that they were not a legitimate form of government, the negative force of the working class proved strong enough to make this road impracticable from the outset. The regime had to sue for its favours through le plébiscite de tous les jours.[76]

Between December 1935 and June 1939 the average hourly wage in industry rose by 10.9 per cent – in the goods-producing sector, which included most of the armaments industries, the figure was even higher at 11.3 per cent. As a result of the longer working week, weekly wages went up even more, namely, by 20.7 per cent. Here those areas of the economy dealing with consumer goods fared better than the goods-producing industries. In 1939 a male worker earned on average 5.80 Reichsmarks a week more than in 1936. (For women, the increase was 2.50 Reichsmarks a week.) The purchasing power of the working population rose in consequence by 85 million Reichsmarks. As a result of the rising employment figures it rose by a further 115–120 million Reichsmarks a week.

According to contemporary sources, the increase in income that was recorded every year after 1935 was due in no small part to pressure exerted by the workers. This pressure found expression in various ways whereby workers simply withheld their labour – sick leave, careless work, absenteeism and sheer unhelpfulness. In the summer of 1939, the owner of a tannery in Dresden spoke – presumably without exaggeration – of a 'strike in disguise'. Mason described the increasing numbers of acts of insubordination as 'a kind of passive political opposition' and a 'primitive form of class warfare'.[77] The second phrase is presumably accurate, whereas the former may be an overinterpretation. In only the rarest cases does the reluctance to work appear to have been politically motivated. Even so, it invariably resulted in the intervention of the Gestapo: the regime's routine response to every threat consisted in the use of applied terror.

By the summer of 1939 it seemed impossible to increase armaments production any further. By then the policies of the Third Reich had resulted in a paradox: the gradual and continuing fall in unemployment and the rise in incomes – both of these developments primarily a consequence of rearmament – had led to an expansion of private consumerism that ultimately affected the armaments industry, for any attempt to limit consumption now struck the regime as politically dangerous, producing a dilemma for which the only long-term solution seemed to be military expansionism. As we shall see, the war was triggered on 1 September 1939 not by economic factors, and yet without recourse to military force Germany would not have been able to pursue its wartime economic policies for very much longer.

When, in August 1936, Hitler instructed the German armed forces to be ready to be deployed within four years, he cited as his justification only the danger from the east in the guise of Bolshevism. He may have struck a dismissive note when referring to western democracies, but he did not describe them as future enemies on the battlefield, and he did not express his desire to go to war with them. In February 1935, at a time when in France arguments were raging over the ratification of the mutual assistance pact with the Soviet Union, Hitler assured the French journalist Bertrand de Jouvenel that it was 'nonsense' to speak of a traditional enmity between Germany and France. If he had expressed a contradictory view in *Mein Kampf*, then such an opinion belonged to the past. And he promised to correct it in 'the great book of history'.[78]

And Hitler continued to court Great Britain as a future ally following the naval treaty that he had signed with London on 18 June 1935. If at the same time he struck a more belligerent note in his propaganda on colonial policy, it was not because he regarded colonial expansionism as a significant goal in German politics or even as an alternative to increasing Germany's Lebensraum by seizing lands to the east. Rather, the colonial question was for Hitler a means by which to place pressure on London: Great Britain was to enter into an alliance with him that would allow him a free hand in eastern Europe, while he promised to recognize the Empire as a sphere of exclusively British interests.

With regard to western Europe and America, Hitler attached the greatest importance to his country's militant anti-Bolshevism. If western democracies were finally to learn to regard Germany as the decisive bulwark against the threat posed by the Soviet Union, they would – he believed – be reconciled to his increasing violation of the terms of the Treaty of Versailles. The signing of the Franco-Soviet mutual assistance pact in May 1935 and the formation of popular front governments, first in Madrid in February 1936 and then in Paris in June 1936, were setbacks in terms of Hitler's foreign policy, while at the same time containing within them an opportunity for propaganda, for Hitler had every reason to hope that his anti-Communist slogans would find a greater response with right-wing elements in France, Spain and even Great Britain than had been the case until then.

On 13 September 1936, two months after the outbreak of the Spanish Civil War, Hitler addressed the Party Rally of Honour and presented himself to Germany and to the world as the man who would save them from Bolshevism. Striking a distinctly apocalyptic note, he claimed that the fighting in Spain was 'symptomatic of an age that was descending into evil':

> For years we have been preaching about the great threat that the world faces as it draws towards the end of the second millennium of Christian history, and this is now becoming a terrible reality. Everywhere the Bolsheviks who are pulling the strings are achieving increasing success with their subversive activities. At a time when bourgeois statesmen speak only of non-intervention, the international Jewish revolutionary central command in Moscow is seeking to bring revolution to this continent of ours by means of every radio station, by channelling money along a thousand different conduits and by dint of a thousand different forms of political agitation.

The conclusion that Hitler drew from this state of affairs seemed compelling: just as National Socialism had dealt with this 'international persecution' internally, so he would 'ward off all external attacks with the most brutal resolve'. Hence Germany's determination to rearm.[79]

Rome proved more amenable than London when it came to winning allies for an anti-Communist International. The war in Abyssinia had deepened the divide between Fascist Italy and western democracies and inevitably led to a rapprochement with Germany, on which Italy was in any case economically dependent in no small way. Hitler had helped Mussolini with substantial supplies of raw materials and in that way rendered largely ineffectual the sanctions imposed by the League of Nations, prompting Mussolini to show his gratitude by de-escalating the tensions over Austria and forcing the Austrian chancellor to reach an agreement with Germany. The keenest critic of this policy was the Austrian vice-chancellor and leader of the Fatherland Front, Rüdiger Starhemberg, who had been removed from the government by Schuschnigg following an unauthorized and highly undiplomatic telegram that he had sent to Mussolini, congratulating him on the capture of Addis Ababa. Schuschnigg himself took over the leadership of the Fatherland Front, an umbrella organization for forces close to the government. As a result, Vienna was now able to adopt a more pro-German line without any serious opposition, a policy which, with Hitler's backing, Franz von Papen had done much to promote since his appointment as German ambassador in August 1934.

A treaty between Germany and Austria was signed on 11 July 1936. In the section of it that was made public, Germany acknowledged 'the full sovereignty of the federal state of Austria' and abandoned the financial controls placed on Germans travelling to Austria since May 1934. In return Austria professed itself to be a 'German state'. In the section of the treaty that remained secret, Vienna committed itself to conduct its foreign policy 'with regard for the peaceful aspirations of the German government' and in the case of questions that affected both governments to engage in an exchange of views with Berlin. Austria also promised to implement a wide-ranging political amnesty and to allow 'the so-called national opposition in Austria' to share a role in government. By 11 July two new members of the government had been appointed with close links to nationalist circles: Guido Schmidt as secretary of state at the Federal Chancellery and Edmund Glaise-Horstenau as minister without portfolio. (The following November Schmidt moved to Schuschnigg's Foreign Office, while Glaise-Horstenau took over the Home Office.) The various defence leagues were disbanded in October 1936, and in June 1937 the National Socialist jurist Arthur Seyß-Inquart was appointed to the State Council. From then on he served as an intermediary both between Schuschnigg and Hitler and between the chancellor and the 'national opposition'. The Austrian NSDAP remained a banned organization. After July 1936 Austria was a state with drastically reduced sovereignty and, as such, little more than a satellite of the German Reich.

This consensual, but specious, solution to the Austrian question prepared the way for a sustained and serious attempt to resolve relations between Germany and Italy. On 23 October 1936 the two foreign ministers, Baron Konstantin von Neurath and Count Galeazzo Ciano, Mussolini's son-in-law, signed a secret cooperation and consultation agreement, laying the foundations for the Berlin–Rome Axis that Mussolini announced on 1 November. Henceforth this axis could provide a focus for all those European states that were 'inspired by the will to work together and by the desire for peace'.[80] In fact, this declaration amounted to no more than a wilful justification of the cooperation between Germany and Italy in the Spanish Civil War, when both powers had lent their assistance to Franco's nationalists, officially recognizing the dictator's putsch-based regime on 18 November 1936.

A week later, on 25 November, Germany and Japan signed an anti-Comintern pact. This agreement was drawn up by the German ambassador in London and Hitler's foreign policy adviser, Joachim von Ribbentrop, without consulting the Foreign Office, which was on friendly terms with China. The agreement provided for a joint propaganda campaign against the subversive activities of the Third International and in the secret section of its provisions expressly forbade the signatory states to undertake measures that might exculpate the Soviet Union in the event of its attacking one or other of the signatories. Neither of the signatories, moreover, was permitted to conclude any treaties with the Soviet Union that contravened the anti-Comintern pact.

In Japan the army had established itself as a force for order following the suppression of a bloody military putsch that was undertaken by radical right-wing officers in February 1936. Within the army, it was the employer-friendly Tosei (Control Party) that set the tone. By August 1936 Tokyo had adopted the 'Fundamental Principles of National Policy', a compromise between the army, which was seeking to expand Japanese rule into Eastern Asia, and the navy, which sought, rather, to extend the country's maritime might into the Pacific. As a result, Japan needed to arm itself for confrontation with both the Soviet Union and the Western Powers, especially the United States.

On 7 July 1937, only weeks after Prince Fumimaro Konoe, the head of a well-respected family of aristocrats, had assumed control of the government, shots were exchanged between members of the Chinese armed forces and Japanese soldiers at the Marco Polo Bridge in Beijing. Japan had had the right to station soldiers in the city since the Peace of Beijing that had ended the Boxer Rising in September 1901. The incident marked the start of the Sino-Japanese War that was to culminate in the Second World War four years later. Shortly afterwards the Chinese leadership under Chiang Kai-shek signed a non-aggression pact with the Soviet Union. In November 1937 the Japanese government proposed peace terms aimed at turning China into a Japanese satrapy. Germany, which since the time of the Weimar Republic had supported the Chinese army through unofficial military advisers and which maintained extensive trade links with Beijing, sought to mediate, but to no avail.

The Japanese took Nanking on 13 December 1937, leading to a bloodbath among the local Chinese soldiers and civilian population that ended in the deaths of up to 300,000 men, women and children and also involved mass rapes and looting. By the end of 1938 the Japanese army had overrun large areas of northern and central China, including the principal transport routes and coastal regions, but it did not undertake any further major offensives. On 3 November 1938 Konoe's government proclaimed a 'New Order in East Asia', a peace zone that was to include Japan, China and Manchukuo. By this date

Germany had already withdrawn its military advisers and agreed to stop supplying arms to Chiang Kai-shek and to curtail its trade with China. But Tokyo's hopes of forming an alliance with the Axis Powers remained unfulfilled. Berlin and Rome insisted on an alliance directed not only against the Soviet Union but also against Great Britain and France, a desire rejected above all by the Japanese navy, which did not yet feel strong enough to wage a major naval war.

In the course of 1937 National Socialist Germany and Fascist Italy moved even closer together, and at the end of September Mussolini undertook a triumphal tour of Germany, the high point of which was an elaborately staged visit to Berlin. On 28 September the Italian leader addressed a jubilant crowd on the city's Maifeld, explaining in German what he meant by the 'ethics of Fascism' and also by his 'personal morality': 'to speak openly and candidly and if one has a friend, to march together with him to the very end'.[81] Barely six weeks later, Italy joined the anti-Comintern pact on 6 November 1937. On 11 December Mussolini took the same step that Hitler had taken four years earlier and announced that his country was leaving the League of Nations.

By this date Hitler had already drawn up a detailed timetable for war, which he expounded on 5 November 1937 at a secret meeting attended by the minister for war, Werner von Blomberg, the foreign minister, Konstantin von Neurath, the commanders in chief of the three branches of the armed forces – Werner von Fritsch for the army, Erich Raeder for the navy and Göring for the air force – and, finally, Hitler's military adjutant, Friedrich Hoßbach. According to a record of the meeting drawn up by Hoßbach five days later, Germany's land shortage could be resolved only by force. The raw materials that Germany needed for an empire which, encompassing the world, would be ruled by a fixed racial nucleus, should be sought not overseas but in areas adjacent to the Reich. It was Hitler's 'unshakeable resolve to solve the question of German space by 1943–45 at the latest'.[82] But, Hitler went on, it might be necessary to act before this, if France were to degenerate into civil war or be drawn into a war with a third party. If Germany's military and political situation were to be improved, its primary aim must be to defeat Czechoslovakia and Austria in order to eliminate any threat to its flanks by any possible action in the west.

The military and strategic plans that Hitler presented to his assembled ministers and representatives of the country's armed forces were essentially a summary of the programme already set forth in *Mein Kampf*. Indeed, he had made it clear to Germany's military leaders as long ago as 3 February 1933 that as Germany's chancellor he was determined to stick to these goals, and to that extent his comments on 5 November 1937 can hardly have come as a surprise to his audience. If Neurath, Blomberg and Fritsch were persuaded to oppose his plans, then it was because of Hitler's assumption not only that Great Britain and France would stand idly by while Germany attacked Czechoslovakia but that in the wake of the Spanish Civil War France and Great Britain would declare war on Fascist Italy. Neurath's misgivings seem to have been particularly serious and indistinguishable from criticism of Hitler himself, so that there is much to be said for the supposition that this was the occasion when Neurath set in train the events that were to lead to his dismissal in early February 1938.

On the other hand, there is no evidence that on 5 November 1937 Hitler was already thinking of cutting himself adrift from either Blomberg or Fritsch. If neither of them was still in office three months later, then this was the result, rather, of two unrelated and unforeseen circumstances that gave Hitler an opportunity to undertake a major reshuffle designed in the first instance to cover up events that were deeply embarrassing to him. The first affair concerned the second marriage of his minister of war. On 12 January Hitler and Göring had been witnesses at the wedding of Blomberg and Margarete Gruhns. Nine days later Hitler learnt that Gruhns had once modelled for pornographic photographs and worked as a prostitute.

Possible successors to the compromised Blomberg included the commander in chief of the army, Werner von Fritsch, but he was the subject of a police file that Hitler had tried in vain to have destroyed in 1936. According to a statement given by a professional criminal, Fritsch had been blackmailed for committing an act of indecency with another man. In March 1938 a court established that there were no grounds to the accusation, which was based on a case of mistaken identity. For the present, however, the charge against Fritsch, which had been unearthed by the Gestapo on Himmler's instructions, seemed to incriminate the commander in chief of the army, with the result that, like Blomberg, he lost his post. In both cases the official reason given for their dismissal was failing health.

The post of minister of war was abolished on 4 February 1938, when the duties of the minister in question were taken over by the newly created Wehrmacht Supreme Command headed by Hitler himself. His immediate subordinate was Wilhelm Keitel, an artillery general who was equal in rank to a federal minister. Walther von Brauschitsch replaced Fritsch. And Göring, the commander in chief of the air force, was appointed general field marshal, making him the highest-ranking German soldier. In addition to numerous other changes within the military that were officially designed to create a more youthful image, there were also two new ministerial appointments, Joachim von Ribbentrop replacing Neurath at the Foreign Office and Walther Fink, hitherto secretary of state at the Ministry for Propaganda, replacing Hjalmar Schacht at the Ministry of Economics. Both appointments were announced on 4 February 1938.

The Blomberg and Fritsch affairs had repercussions that proved extremely welcome to Hitler. The Wehrmacht finally had a unified leadership. The 'Prussian' army lost its special status. And Hitler's power increased. The influence of the old elite faded elsewhere as well, notably in the diplomatic service and in business, thanks to changes at the head of the Foreign Office and the

Ministry of Economics. The shift in the balance of power that took place on 4 February 1938 produced an overall picture that persuaded contemporaries and historians that this was all the result of long-term planning, whereas the events of early February 1938 merely proved that Hitler was a genius at improvisation with a masterly ability to take advantage of a situation that was as much a surprise for him as it was for the rest of the world.

Early Signs of Appeasement: Britain 1933–8

Hitler's partner of choice was Great Britain, which had viewed the change of leadership in Germany on 30 January 1933 with remarkable sangfroid. The conservative and liberal press interpreted the high level of continuity between the cabinets of Schleicher and Hitler as a sign that for the present at least there was no need to fear a dramatic change in German policy. In general, those sections of the press that were close to the Labour Party expected the new government to remain in office for only a brief space of time. The boycott of Jewish businesses on 1 April 1933 triggered a more general outcry of indignation, but once the boycott had ended, the outrage quickly evaporated. The British public remained divided. Right-wing tabloids such as the *Daily Mail* and *Daily Express* found words of praise for the National Socialists' militant anti-Bolshevist stance, while conservative papers like *The Times* and the *Daily Telegraph* adopted a similar, if more moderate, line. Liberal papers led by the *News Chronicle* and *Manchester Guardian* took an increasingly critical view. Only the Labour Party's official newspaper, the *Daily Herald*, was emphatically anti-Fascist and anti-National Socialist in its outlook.

By 1934 prominent journalists and politicians were keen to form a personal impression of Hitler and of other well-known representatives of his regime. In December of that year the Führer received a visit from the publisher of the *Daily Mail*, Lord Rothermere, who was well disposed towards him. Rothermere was followed in January 1935 by Lord Lothian, a leading member of the Liberal Party. In the course of 1936 – the year of the Berlin Olympics – a whole series of English visitors paid their respects to Hitler: the former Liberal prime minister Lloyd George, who made no secret of his admiration for the German leader; the press baron Lord Beaverbrook; Lord Rothermere again; and the pacifist Labour politicians Lord Allen of Hurtwood and George Lansbury. Hitler, Göring and Ribbentrop held several meetings with the Marquess of Londonderry, the former secretary of state for air, who had stepped down in May 1935, while Ribbentrop was twice the guest of Lord Londonderry on the latter's estates in Ulster, first in May 1936, then in November 1936. Hitler's first official visitors from Great Britain were the foreign secretary Sir John Simon and his parliamentary secretary of state, Anthony Eden, who travelled to Berlin in late March 1935 in order to take soundings about a possible agreement between the two countries but returned to London empty-handed.

Practically all of Hitler's visitors took away the same message: his warnings about the threat posed by Bolshevism, his insistence that Germany had the same military rights as other countries and his interest in an Anglo-German arrangement that would give the Reich a free hand in central and eastern Europe and allow Germany to recognize the Empire as a British sphere of interest. He also demanded the return of Germany's colonies in Africa, a demand that was tactical and therefore negotiable. Hitler had a chance of being heard not only by his unofficial visitors from London but also by various upper-class circles such as the Cliveden Set, a group of largely Conservative figures who met at Cliveden, the home of Lord and Lady Astor, and who strove for closer Anglo-German cooperation in their combined opposition to Bolshevism. A similar goal was pursued by the Anglo-German Fellowship that was formed in 1935 with backing from the German Embassy in London under the chairmanship of a former army general, Ian Hamilton, who was also the head of the Scottish branch of the British Legion. A predecessor of the Anglo-German Fellowship, the Anglo-German Association had been founded in 1928 but was disbanded in April 1935 in order to avoid a discussion of the exclusion of its Jewish members.

After 1933, for the majority of Neo-Tories – younger intellectuals on the right wing of the Conservative Party – Mussolini enjoyed a far higher standing than the 'vulgar' Hitler. Within their ranks, the most prominent supporters of National Socialism were the historian Arthur Bryant and the journalist Francis Yeats-Brown, while the Nationalist Socialists' most radical followers were Sir Oswald Mosley's British Union of Fascists, which he established in October 1932. But any sympathy that the BUF may have enjoyed among British Conservatives was forfeited, as we have already noted, in June 1934, when left-wing hecklers were brutally attacked at a BUF rally at Olympia in London.

In the eyes of Ramsay MacDonald's National Government a greater threat was posed at this time by the seditious propaganda of the Communist-led National Unemployed Workers' Movement, whose subversive activities were meant to be curtailed by the hugely controversial Incitement to Disaffection Act that came into force in November 1934. Parallel measures against the extreme right were implemented only much later at the insistence of the Labour Party and trade unions and in response to the increasingly militant anti-Semitism of the BUF.

On 4 October 1936 a march by 1,900 uniformed Blackshirts led to violent scuffles in Royal Mint Street in London's East End between a far greater number of anti-Fascist demonstrators and the police who were hoping to avoid a confrontation between the left and the right. The home secretary then banned a planned march through the rest of the working-class area and forced Mosley to move his parade to the other side of the river. The legislative response to these events was the Public Order Act of 1 January 1937 banning uniforms and paramilitary associations and granting the government powers to deal more effectively with public marches and demonstrations. The Act played a by no means insignificant part in the country's return to political normality.

Official relations between Great Britain and Germany entered a new phase in 1935. Although the government in London was surprised when on 9 March Göring officially admitted that Germany once again had an air force whose existence had, of course, been an open secret in Britain for some considerable time, and although the reintroduction of general conscription a week later caused understandable disquiet, London contented itself with expressing polite reproaches for this twofold violation of the terms of the Treaty of Versailles, reproaches that Simon and Eden delivered in person during their visit to Berlin on 25 and 26 March. Only three months later Britain agreed to Germany's proposal for a bilateral naval agreement that had been drawn up in November 1934. Signed on 18 June 1935, it allowed Germany to increase the size of its navy up to a third of the tonnage of the British Royal Navy.

At this point, Japan seemed to pose a rather greater danger to Britain than Germany. If London had not accepted Berlin's offer, Germany might have rearmed to a far greater extent. At the same time, the worsening of the situation in Abyssinia demonstrated that the British-French-Italian Stresa Front of April 1935 was not worth the paper it was written on. France was furious at London's high-handed actions. But the British government had not been asked for its agreement when France signed its mutual assistance pact with the Soviet Union in May, a pact that provoked serious misgivings in anti-Bolshevik Britain.

If the Marquess of Londonderry had had his way, there would not only have been a naval treaty but also an agreement covering the relative sizes of the British and German air forces. In his capacity as secretary of state for air, Londonderry wanted to increase the strength of the Royal Air Force, which he was able to do to only a limited extent in 1934, and at the same time come to some arrangement with Germany in this regard. Unlike his cousin, Winston Churchill, who even before 1933 had been warning of the danger of an increase in Germany's air power, Londonderry did not believe that Britain faced a serious threat from Germany at least for the next few years. When at the end of March 1935 Hitler informed Simon and Eden that the Luftwaffe had already achieved parity with the Royal Air Force, Londonderry found himself under massive pressure, and even the prime minister, who was temperamentally a pacifist, expressed the belief in private that the Air Ministry had 'slept through' Germany's rearmament programme.

Londonderry was obliged to defend his position in the upper house on 22 May 1935, when he spoke admiringly of Hitler's ostensible willingness to limit his country's armaments programme and gave his backing to the possibility of deploying bombs in areas bordering on the Empire even without concrete justification for doing so. In making this claim, he incurred the wrath not only of the political left but, worse, of many of his own Conservative Party friends.

An ailing MacDonald, who had previously supported him in public and parliament, was by now becoming increasingly weary of government and less and less capable of carrying out his duties, with the result that he resigned on 27 June 1935 in favour of the leader of the Conservative Party, Stanley Baldwin, who had previously been prime minister in 1923–4 and from 1924 to 1929. Baldwin made Londonderry the lord privy seal and, hence, a minister without portfolio. The new secretary of state for air was another Tory, the former colonies' minister, Philip Cunliffe-Lister. The National Liberal foreign secretary Sir John Simon moved to the Home Office and was succeeded by Sir Samuel Hoare, an old friend of Baldwin. Neville Chamberlain remained the chancellor of the exchequer.

On 18 October 1935, two weeks after the start of the war in Abyssinia, Baldwin asked King George V to dissolve parliament in the light of the worsening international situation and to hold new elections, which would otherwise have fallen due by October 1936 at the latest. The Labour Party accused the prime minister of fomenting the fear of war in the British people, while pinning its own colours to the mast of international disarmament and collective security within the framework of the League of Nations, emphatically rejecting the idea of an increase in British military spending. The Tories, for their part, described rearmament as a condition for peace, in which context Baldwin gave his solemn word that there would be 'no great armaments'.[83]

The anti-war rhetoric of the Labour Party proved effective, and in the elections to the lower house on 14 November 1935 it increased its share of the vote by 7.4 per cent when compared with the results in 1931, polling 38 per cent of the total and returning 154 MPs to parliament, an increase of fifty-two. The Conservatives' share of the vote fell by 7.2 per cent, resulting in a total of 386 seats, eighty-three fewer than before. The Liberal Party won 6.7 per cent of the vote, losing eleven of its thirty-two MPs, while the National Liberal Party that had held power with the Tories won 3.7 per cent of the vote, returning thirty-three MPs, two fewer than in 1931. MacDonald's National Labour Party won 1.5 per cent of the vote, representing eight seats, five fewer than in 1931. Of the remaining parties, none polled more than 0.7 per cent of the total. In the spirit of the new united front, the Communists had withdrawn their candidates in all but two constituencies, winning one of them at the expense of the incumbent Labour candidate. Although the Tories had a comfortable majority in the lower house, Baldwin again invited members of the National Liberal Party and National Labour Party to help him form a cabinet that was still able to describe itself as a National Government.

Within weeks of coming to power, Baldwin's government was plunged into its first serious crisis. On 7 and 8 December, his foreign secretary, Samuel Hoare, stopped off in Paris on his way to Switzerland and met Pierre Laval, France's prime minister and foreign secretary, and discussed ways to settle the conflict in Abyssinia, whereby large tracts of north-eastern and southern

Abyssinia would be handed over to Fascist Italy, while the rest of the country would remain independent and be given access to the sea. Thanks to an indiscretion on the part of the Quai d'Orsay, details of the Hoare–Laval Pact became public knowledge, leading to a storm of protest in the press. Baldwin tried to defend his foreign secretary in the lower house but was unable even to win the support of his own cabinet.

On 18 December the government decided to abandon the Anglo-French proposal and Hoare was forced to resign. Anthony Eden, hitherto minister without portfolio with special responsibility for the affairs of the League of Nations, was named his successor on 22 December. Eden spent the following weeks and months trying to persuade France and the United States to accept the one sanction that Mussolini feared the most and over which he was threatening to go to war: a ban on petroleum imports. But Eden failed to get his way.

In February 1936 Baldwin's government fulfilled one of the promises on which it had fought its election campaign and asked the lower house to agree to spend £394 million over the next five years on increasing Britain's defence budget. A new minister for defence coordination was to oversee the United Kingdom's defence needs. A number of Conservative politicians wanted to see a forceful figure like Churchill in this post. Baldwin thought initially of appointing Hoare but then adopted a proposal from within his own party and appointed the attorney general, Sir Thomas Inskip.

In terms of British foreign policy, the outstanding event of the spring of 1936 was Hitler's most provocative action to date: his occupation of the demilitarized Rhineland. Both Paris and London had reckoned on such a turn of events but had failed to agree on any joint measures to prevent it. In the wake of Hitler's coup the Belgian prime minister, Paul Van Zeeland, and the French foreign minister, Pierre-Étienne Flandin, urged Brussels, Paris and London to act in a coordinated manner and invite the League of Nations to impose sanctions on Germany for its treaty violation. The British response was negative. The major newspapers had not regarded these recent events as a threat. The occupation of the Rhineland was seen for the most part as an internal affair: according to Lord Lothian, the Germans were 'only going into their own back garden'.[84] When Flandin hurried to London to discuss the situation, Baldwin informed him that sanctions required military backing, which Britain was unable to provide. In cabinet he claimed that the Soviet Union would inevitably become embroiled in any war and that Germany would end up becoming Communist.

As a result, Hitler's treaty violation went unpunished, which in the circumstances could hardly be otherwise. But it was bound to encourage the Führer to commit similar acts of provocation. Baldwin hoped that Hitler's aggression would be directed not against the West but – in the spirit of *Mein Kampf* – against the East. In July 1936, the month in which the Spanish Civil War began, the prime minister informed Churchill, 'If there is any fighting in Europe to be done, I should like to see the Bolshies and the Nazis doing it.'[85]

The year 1936 has gone down in British history as the year of the abdication crisis. George V died on 20 January at the age of seventy, having only recently celebrated the twenty-fifth anniversary of his accession in 1910. He was succeeded by his son, the forty-one-year-old Edward VIII, who was still unmarried but notorious for his numerous affairs with married women and for his open sympathies with Germany. His undoing proved to be his relationship with an American divorcee, Wallis Simpson, with whom he took a Mediterranean cruise on a hired yacht in the summer of 1936, a cruise widely reported by the American, Canadian and Continental European press but comprehensively ignored by British newspapers. By the autumn concerned voices were growing increasingly strident at court, forcing Baldwin to intervene, but his conversation with the king on 14 October produced no results. The following day Edward's private secretary informed the prime minister that Wallis Simpson was planning a divorce – her second. On 16 October, Edward summoned Lords Beaverbrook and Rothermere to his summer residence at Balmoral and persuaded them to say nothing about the affair for the time being.

While Edward continued to insist on his determination to marry Wallis Simpson, the chancellor of the exchequer, Neville Chamberlain, was equally adamant that he would resign if the king went ahead with his plan. The Anglican Church likewise opposed the idea, and the governor general of Canada, Lord Tweedsmuir, warned of the devastating consequences of such a move in a puritanical country like Canada and also of the monarchy's loss of prestige as the centre of the whole Empire. Australia's prime minister, Joseph Lyons, announced that if Edward were to marry Wallis Simpson, the king would have to abdicate. Baldwin felt obliged to increase the pressure on the king and inform him that if he persisted in his plans, he would have no alternative but to abdicate. Churchill was one of the few public figures to support the king. The vast majority of the 'political class' regarded the king's marriage as incompatible with the dignity of the monarch and, hence, of the United Kingdom. Most of the country's MPs believed that the majority of the British population thought the same. On 10 December 1936, a week after Wallis Simpson had left for Paris, Edward finally gave in to his prime minister's entreaties and announced his abdication. He was succeeded by his younger brother, George VI, Britain's third king in under a year.

Baldwin's prestige had been badly affected by the brouhaha surrounding the Hoare–Laval Pact, but his resolution of the abdication crisis helped him to restore and enhance his standing, so that whenever he appeared in public from then on he was greeted with loud applause. But Baldwin had turned sixty-nine in August 1936 and was exhausted and weary of his work in office. He planned to wait until the coronation on 12 May 1937 and then stand down. The king accepted his offer and on 28 May appointed Neville Chamberlain the country's new prime minister. The son of Joseph Chamberlain, Neville was himself sixty-eight, a businessman from Birmingham, where he had been lord mayor in

1915–16. Since 1922 he had headed several ministries, first as postmaster general, then as minister for health and, since 1931, as chancellor of the exchequer. In 1937 Chamberlain was replaced as chancellor by the home secretary, Sir John Simon, who in return was replaced by Sir Samuel Hoare. For the present no one expected any significant changes in government policy under Chamberlain.

From an economic standpoint, the year 1937 was a relatively good one. Unemployment fell to 10.8 per cent of the working population, its lowest since 1929, when it had stood at 10.4 per cent. As chancellor, Chamberlain had been an orthodox champion of a sound economic policy, and under his successor the Treasury adopted a middle course between taxation and borrowing as a way of financing national expenditure. By 1938, unemployment was beginning to rise again in the wake of a recession, peaking at 13.5 per cent and leading to increased dependence on government borrowing. But even as late as 1938 the Treasury was still resisting the idea of boosting the economy by increasing defence spending.

As far as the armaments industry was concerned, Chamberlain consistently maintained a policy of defence. Increased spending on the military was accompanied by the National Fitness Campaign of 1937–8 which, triggered by German successes at the Berlin Olympic Games, took Germany as its model and, as the left wing immediately pointed out, was demonstrably part of the country's defence policy. But whereas the Hitler Youth movement, the League of German Girls and German national service all relied on force and coercion, the National Fitness Council and the Board of Education were intended to encourage young people's physical fitness by appealing to reason. The individuals responsible for implementing these policies felt that it made sense to adopt a number of German measures, but only a tiny minority on the political right demanded that the British system pursue an authoritarian line.

In terms of British foreign policy, Chamberlain's cabinet spent its first few months in office wrestling with the same problem, continuing to adopt the line first taken by Baldwin and refusing to intervene in the Spanish Civil War. By the autumn of 1937, however, divisions were beginning to appear in the political outlook of Chamberlain and his foreign secretary. Neither wanted a confrontation with the dictatorships in Germany, Italy and Japan; and both were keen to reach a peaceful settlement with their three international political rivals, but whereas Chamberlain was inclined to adopt a more conciliatory approach, Eden insisted on making clear what was non-negotiable, believing that military strength was necessary to discourage Hitler and Mussolini from going to war in pursuit of their expansionist goals. Chamberlain assumed that Hitler wanted to establish a racially pure pan-Germany but that he was unwilling to unleash a major war in order to achieve that aim.

In November 1937 a favourable opportunity seemed to present itself to open high-level talks between the British government and the National Socialist leadership when Lord Halifax, the former viceroy of India and briefly the minister for war, who was now chairman of the Privy Council, a close adviser to the prime minister and Master of the Middleton Hounds, received an invitation to attend an international hunting exhibition in Berlin. He arrived in the German capital on 17 November and held talks with Neurath, Göring, Goebbels, Blomberg and Schacht, but his most important meeting was with Hitler at Berchtesgaden on the 19th. Halifax praised the Führer for his attempts to eradicate Communism, hailed the Reich as a western bulwark against Bolshevism and informed Hitler that Britain had no qualms about a peaceful resolution of the contentious issues of Danzig, Austria and Czechoslovakia, at least to the extent that such a solution gave rise to no further problems. Hitler spoke of his determination to destroy Bolshevism and asked Britain to give him a free hand in central and eastern Europe. On reading Halifax's report of the meeting, Chamberlain felt that his own view of the situation was vindicated and asked his cabinet to make concessions to Germany with regard to its colonial policy in Africa, not least at the expense of Portugal, in order to achieve a settlement with the Reich. Eden, on the other hand, remained sceptical.

In January 1938 a letter from Franklin D. Roosevelt to Chamberlain led to an open disagreement between the latter and his foreign secretary: Roosevelt had suggested an international conference to decide on basic rules for all dealings between the different states, which Eden felt was a useful move that could be used to test the credibility of both Hitler and Mussolini, whereas Chamberlain found little of merit in the proposal, which he was convinced would provoke only a negative reaction in Berlin and Rome. Without consulting Eden, he wrote to Roosevelt, turning down the president's proposal.

But it was Hitler who was the immediate cause of the rift between Chamberlain and Eden. The Führer received the Austrian chancellor, Kurt von Schuschnigg, at his Alpine residence at Berchtesgaden on 12 February 1938, a meeting also attended by a number of high-ranking generals, including Wilhelm Keitel, whose presence was designed to be a deliberate demonstration of strength. In the course of the meeting, Hitler demanded an amnesty for all Austrian National Socialists who were currently in custody, freedom to operate for the NSDAP, the appointment of the National Socialist Arthur Seyß-Inquart as foreign secretary and minister for homeland security and the first of a series of steps designed to incorporate Austria into Germany's economic system. Hitler expected his terms to be implemented by 15 February, on which day he was informed by Vienna that all his conditions had indeed been met.

Three days later the Italian ambassador in London, Count Dino Grandi, witnessed an embarrassing confrontation between Chamberlain and Eden. Grandi had refused to explain Italy's stance on the Austrian question but announced that Mussolini was willing to enter into new negotiations with London. Chamberlain was keen to accept, but Eden, who was profoundly mistrustful of the Duce, believed that the offer was not serious and suspected that Mussolini had already agreed to Austria's annexation by Germany. In order to sort out their differences, both men briefly withdrew from the room but not before Grandi had seen Chamberlain criticize his foreign secretary for repeatedly missing opportunities: the situation could not be allowed to continue. In cabinet all but two ministers backed Chamberlain, and on 20 February Eden resigned. Five days later his portfolio was taken over by Lord Halifax.

It would be wrong to see Eden's replacement by Halifax as marking the start of Great Britain's policy of appeasement. Rather, the change of leadership at the Foreign Office reflected a shift from a more cautious and balanced form of appeasement to one that was more thoughtless and all-embracing. By the early months of 1938 appeasement was far from being a new line in British politics. Strictly speaking, the country's failure to respond to the reintroduction of general conscription in Germany or to the occupation of the Rhineland as well as its acceptance of the movement of Italian troops and weapons through the Suez Canal during the Conquest of Abyssinia were also examples of appeasement. In Britain's relations with Germany there had long been a critical attitude to the terms of the Treaty of Versailles, an attitude triggered in part by Keynes's 1920 study on the economic consequences of that treaty. As a result, Germany struck many Britons as a country that had been treated with undue harshness and that it was in Britain's best interests to approach with greater understanding, not least in order to prevent France from growing immoderately powerful.

For the most part, this essentially benevolent attitude continued to dominate Conservative circles after 1933. Indeed, a number of politicians and economists even pointed out that Germany's economic and financial problems were in part a result of the protectionist stance that Britain had adopted in 1931. It made sense, therefore, to expect a more liberal approach to foreign trade to have a positive impact on Britain's political relations with Germany. In short, the country should pursue a policy of political *and* economic appeasement.

All the 'appeasers' were motivated by the thought of the British Empire: if Britain were to be drawn into a conflict in Continental Europe, this would strengthen the resolve of foreign groups eager to free themselves from every kind of colonial rule and economic dependence. This in itself was enough to persuade Britons to do everything in their power to avoid a confrontation with the dictatorships in Italy and Germany. Moreover, these regimes were emphatically anti-Communist and therefore possible allies in any attempt to resist the spread of Bolshevism. The appeasers were not so naive as to believe that either Hitler or Mussolini was unconditionally committed to peace. From their point of view a certain degree of rearmament was necessary in order to discourage both Italy and Germany from fomenting armed conflict in Europe or, at least, in western Europe. Britain had started to rearm in 1936 but was still far from having reached the point where we could speak of a deterrent. There was also fundamental agreement among the appeasers that Great Britain had to work more closely with the other great Anglo-Saxon power, the United States of

America. To them, dependence on America seemed to pose fewer risks than dependence on an over-powerful Germany.

The only bone of contention among the appeasers was the extent to which an attempt should be made to meet Hitler and Mussolini halfway. In this regard pessimists like Eden were reluctant to go as far as optimists like Chamberlain and Halifax. By the end of 1937 a sceptical Eden was drawing closer to an anti-appeaser like Churchill, who had no illusions about Hitler's desire for war and who had long been demanding that far greater efforts be made to rearm the country. But the biggest obstacle on the road to military parity with Germany – a goal that even Baldwin had believed was no longer achievable – was not the lack of insight on the part of Conservative politicians but the unwillingness on the part of the great mass of the population to countenance another war. During the winter of 1934/5 the League of Nations Union – the association of friends of the League of Nations – had conducted a 'peace ballot', inviting 11.5 million Britons to express their views on collective security. Ten million supported economic sanctions against an aggressor, while only 6.8 million were in favour of military sanctions.

Traditionally, it was the Labour Party and the trade unions that were the most outspoken champions of international disarmament and collective security. Within the Labour Party the most radical pacifists, such as the party leader from 1932 to 1935, George Lansbury, who rejected even the League of Nations and the whole idea of national defence, represented only a tiny minority. Even as late as 1937 Lansbury's successor, Clement Attlee, was still refusing to give his party's backing to rearmament, although he had been in favour of supplying arms to the Spanish Republic during the Spanish Civil War and had supported the idea of sending in volunteers from other countries. In 1937, at its annual conference, the party agreed to abstain in the event of a vote on raising the defence budget but not to vote against such a move. By 1938 Hitler's aggressive policies and the compliance of the British government persuaded the Labour Party to review its policy and in September it spoke out forcefully against any further appeasement, prompting Churchill to telephone Attlee and inform him that the declaration of the workers' party was a credit to the British nation.

The Labour Party remained consistently opposed to right- and left-wing dictatorships, every party conference turning down Communist attempts to form a united front. The Independent Labour Party, which had broken away from the main party in 1932 and which by now was no more than a splinter group, the Socialist League, Victor Gollancz's Left Book Club of 1935 and London's left-wing Bloomsbury Group continued to champion the idea of an anti-Fascist bloc made up of all the left-wing parties, but from the standpoint of the Labour Party leadership this amounted to a Communist attempt to subvert the party and to rob it of any chance of ever again becoming the most powerful political party in the country.

At the 1937 party conference the Socialist League's organizational 'affiliation' with the Labour Party was formally suspended and any thought of a united front was rejected once and for all. Shortly afterwards Sir Stafford Cripps disbanded the Socialist League that he had helped to form but continued to advocate a left-wing united front and to speak out against all military expenditure by the government until he was finally excluded from the party in May 1939, when a number of his closest allies, including Sir Charles Trevelyan and Aneurin Bevan, suffered a similar fate. The Labour Party was resolved not to allow observers to entertain even the slightest doubts in its profession of faith in a *democratic* form of socialism, with the result that it was as vehemently opposed to Stalin as it was to Hitler.

Mobilization of the Right, Popular Front on the Left: France 1933–8

As in Great Britain, so in France very few observers regarded Hitler's seizure of power as marking a profound break in German politics. True, the socialists and Communists were rather more alarmed at this development than the bourgeois parties, but they still did not believe that European peace or French security were in any immediate danger. On the parliamentary right, the allegedly weak foreign policy of Aristide Briand was blamed for the rise of National Socialism, while the moderate left in the guise of the socialists may have been appalled at the domestic policies of Germany's new rulers, but they continued to place their hopes in international disarmament and in collective security within the framework of the League of Nations. France's Radical Socialist prime minister, Édouard Daladier, who had come to power on 31 January 1933, only the day after Hitler had seized power, told a Senate army commission on 13 February that he did not see any worsening of his country's international situation as Hitler's foreign policy was barely distinguishable from Schleicher's, just as Schleicher's had been practically indistinguishable from Brüning's. France's foreign minister, Joseph Paul-Boncour, who had been an outspoken critic of the SFIO's pacifist illusions, felt that the League of Nations Disarmament Conference in Geneva was the best chance of preventing Hitler from rearming.

The first unofficial contact between the heads of government in Paris and Berlin was established by a personal friend of Daladier, Fernand de Brinon, who was in touch with Ribbentrop, but a meeting with Hitler on 9 September 1933 produced no concrete results beyond the chancellor's assurance that he was bent only on peace. By the time that Brinon met Hitler again on 16 November, Germany had already announced that it was leaving the League of Nations and would take no further part in the Disarmament Conference in Geneva, while Daladier had taken over the War Office and been replaced as prime minister by the Radical Socialist Albert Sarraut. With Hitler's approval, the outcome of the meeting was published in the form of an interview in *Le Matin* on 22 November. Once again Hitler sought to allay French fears that he was still trying to carry out his threat in *Mein Kampf* and settle old scores with his country's ancestral enemy. If the interview failed to achieve its intended effect, this was due, not least, to the fact that only a few days earlier, Paul-Boncour had sanctioned the publication of documents from Latin America allegedly proving that Germany had far-reaching expansionist aspirations in Europe and beyond.

At the end of December 1933 France had been buffeted by an incident that shook the political system of the Third Republic to its very foundations, when the Crédit Municipal in Bayonne collapsed in the wake of the fraudulent activities of the financier Alexandre Stavisky, who had had close links with journalists and with Radical Socialist politicians. On 8 January 1934 he was discovered, fatally injured, at his chalet near Chamonix – whether it was suicide or murder remains unclear. Shortly afterwards two members of the cabinet of the Radical Socialist Camille Chautemps, the colonial minister Albert Dalimier and the justice minister Eugène Raynaldi, were forced to resign, the former for his involvement in the Stavisky Affair, the latter for different reasons altogether. In the eyes of the nationalist right and especially Action Française, these events brought not only the Radical Socialists but the parliamentary system in general into disrepute. Such was the vehemence of their campaign that Chautemps's government – France's fourth cabinet since January 1933 – was forced to resign.

Chautemps was replaced by Daladier but the latter was fated to remain in office for only a week: in order to win the support of the SFIO, he dismissed the chief of police in Paris, Jean Chiappe, a self-declared enemy of the left and a right-wing sympathizer, a move that was immediately met by the resignation of the only two moderate right-wing ministers to have seats in his cabinet. Daladier's second cabinet was presented to the Chamber of Deputies on 6 February, when thousands of demonstrators gathered in the Place de la Concorde not far from the Palais Bourbon, where the Chamber of Deputies met. Summoned to take part in this show of solidarity, they were made up of various right-wing groups, including Action Française, the Croix de Feu, Jeunesses Patriotes and Solidarité Française. A second demonstration aimed both at the government and at 'Fascists' was organized by the Communists. In the course of the evening serious clashes broke out between demonstrators and the police, resulting in fifteen fatalities, mostly among the demonstrators, and over 1,500 injuries. Paris had not witnessed such bloody street battles since the Commune in 1871.

The political right was presumably too fragmented and too disunited to be able to aspire to more than merely toppling Daladier's government on 6 February 1934. More ambitious goals such as abolishing the parliamentary system and, with it, the Third Republic appear to have been beyond its reach. But it achieved at least its immediate goal, even though the Chamber of Deputies went ahead with its session and expressed its confidence in Daladier's government by 343 votes to 237. The very next day, however, the country's largest trade union, the CGT, called a general strike in an attempt to force the government to act more decisively against the right-wing militias. Daladier believed that it was crucial to form a more broadly based coalition and so, ignoring the advice of the SFIO's leader in parliament, Léon Blum, he resigned on 7 February, marking an unprecedented triumph for the political right, which through extreme extra-parliamentary pressure had brought down a government that had just succeeded in gaining the backing of a majority of deputies.

Appointed by the president of the Republic, Albert Lebrun, on 9 February, the government of Gaston Doumergue, a centre-right Radical Socialist who had been president from 1924 to 1931, was markedly more right-wing than any of the six cabinets that had ruled France since the elections of May 1932. Apart from himself, his cabinet included no fewer than five other former prime ministers: Louis Barthou as foreign secretary, Albert Sarraut as home secretary, Pierre Laval as minister for the colonies and Édouard Herriot and André Tardieu as ministers without portfolio. The new minister of war was Marshal Philippe Pétain, the army's commander in chief in 1917–18, while the Ministry of Public Works was taken over by a Neo-Socialist, Adrien Marquet. Louis Marin, the leader of the conservative Union Républicaine Démocratique, took over as minister of health. Apart from the Socialists and Communists, all the parties – 402 deputies in all – expressed their confidence in Doumergue's government. Only 125 voted against it. Thanks to its large majority, the cabinet was able to persuade the Chamber to grant it powers to deal with the economic and financial crisis by means of emergency decrees, a procedure that reminded the Socialists and others, too, of the politics pursued by Heinrich Brüning during the final years of the Weimar Republic.

Even after 6 February it was a while before calm returned to the streets of the capital. A Communist demonstration on 9 February led to further bloody clashes with the police, resulting in several deaths. Three days later a general strike began. Initially called by the SFIO, by the socialist CGT and by the Ligue pour les Droits de l'Homme, it also received the backing of the Communists and their own union, the CGTU, and had widespread support among the workers. The Socialist Party and the Communist Party had originally organized separate demonstrations, but in response to pressure from the masses, they pooled their resources. During the weeks that followed, it was above all left-wing intellectuals who, having come together in early March under the leadership of the Socialist anthropologist Paul Rivet to form a Comité de Vigilance des Intellectuels Antifascistes, urged the Socialists and Communists to bridge the wide gulf between them.

At their party conference at Ivry in June 1934 the Communists finally agreed to end their bitter rivalry with the Socialists and support an anti-Fascist alliance, initially with the Socialists and then, from the autumn of 1934, with a broad-based popular front that also included progressive Radicals. (The term 'Front Populaire' was first used on 9 October 1934 by the secretary general of the Communist Party, Maurice Thorez.) The alliance was due less to the political involvement of the left-wing intelligentsia than to a change of direction by the Communist International that stemmed in turn from a change in French foreign policy in the form of the persistent efforts by the French foreign minister, Louis Barthou, to work together with the Soviet Union in order to create a bulwark against National Socialist Germany. The party secretary of the SFIO, Paul Faure, and the party leader, Léon Blum, were initially mistrustful of the Communists' sudden volte-face but then, in mid-July, decided to seize their chance and form an alliance against Fascism. The two parties reached an agreement on 27 July 1934, committing themselves to putting an end to their mutual sniping in order to oppose the nationalist right and all manifestations of Fascism, in addition to countering the threatening danger of war.

By 6 February 1934 there was no longer any doubting the danger that the political right posed for the Third Republic. This was the day on which all those organizations that harboured right-wing elements demonstrated in favour of a powerful state dominated not by the legislative but by the executive. Even so, the term 'Fascist' can be applied to only a handful of defence leagues and other right-wing associations. Although some of them may have fought their political battles by violent means, nothing could have been more alien to their thinking than a revolutionary 'appel au peuple' of a kind that was typical of Italian Fascism and German National Socialism. The monarchist Action Française and the Jeunesses Patriotes were elitist organizations in terms of their social profile and makeup, while the followers of Casimir de La Roque's Croix de Feu turned out to be legalists when the situation took a more serious turn. They were part of the older tradition of the counterrevolution or of Bonapartism and were unwilling, therefore, to take their cue from non-French models.

According to the strikingly succinct definition offered by René Rémond, Fascism is a 'degenerate form of democracy' that 'derives its legitimacy from its appeal to the sovereignty of the very people who transfer this sovereignty to others'.[86] By this definition, Marcel Bucard's Francisme league, with its 10,000 members at most, was a Fascist grouping, and much the same could be said for the even smaller Solidarité Française, which, like Francisme, was financed by the industrialist François Coty. We could also apply the term to the far more successful Parti Populaire Français, or PPF, which was formed in 1936 by the former Communist Party official Jacques Doriot, who had been expelled from his party in June 1934 when, as mayor of St-Denis, he had formed an anti-Fascist popular front some months ahead of his party's change of heart. But not even the PPF was a major player in terms of mass demonstrations. The democratic traditions in the political culture of France were simply too powerful to allow a 'degenerate form of democracy' to assert itself here along the same sort of broad front as those found in both Italy and Germany.

Much against its will, it was the Doumergue government's economic policy that encouraged voters to migrate to the radical right and even, to a certain extent, to the radical left. Previous cabinets had sought to implement deflationary measures, but under Doumergue, whose government might best be described as right- rather than left-wing, civil servants' salaries and pensions were slashed ever further, war widows lost their pensions if they remarried, and the purchasing power of the masses was so drastically reduced that numerous businesses were forced to close down. The number of registered unemployed, which had stood at 243,000 in 1926, rose to over 453,000 in 1935 and to 864,000 in 1936, representing 8 per cent of the workforce. It was above all small traders who turned to the anti-parliamentary right, while discontented civil servants tended to drift to the left.

The only groups to benefit from the government's higher defence spending were a minority of employers and workers, but the additional costs exceeded any savings to such an extent that the budget deficit, which the cabinet had been trying to reduce, continued to increase. The government refused to consider devaluing the franc, even though this would have helped exports and raised tax revenues: the powers that be believed that retaining the gold standard was a question of national honour.

Attempts to reform the constitution proved futile. Among Doumergue's advisers were André Tardieu and a commission whose members included the conservative politician Paul Reynaud and René Coty, who was to be his country's president from 1954 to 1959. Encouraged by their counsel, Doumergue sought to strengthen the position of the prime minister, to limit parliament's right to approve expenditure, to grant the president the right to dissolve the Chamber of Deputies without the approval of the Senate, to increase the powers of the National Economic Council and to give greater independence to the judiciary. His aims were by no means anti-parliamentary but were inspired by the British model of a working, representative democracy. In spite of this, his reforms were vigorously contested by the Socialists and Communists in opposition as well as by the majority of bourgeois Radical Socialists. All shades of left-wing opinion regarded Doumergue's reforms as no more than an attempt to solve the country's problems by authoritarian means.

Of all the cabinet members, it was the foreign minister, Louis Barthou, whose achievement was the most impressive. Born in 1862, he was a member of the conservative Alliance Démocratique and spoke fluent German, being fond of German culture in general and of Wagner's music dramas in particular. But in the spirit of the old French tradition of drawing a distinction between Germany's intellectual and literary achievements on the one hand and its propensity for power politics on the other, he was critical of Germany's foreign policy and in the wake of the First World War advocated the country's breakup. He was probably the only French politician to have read *Mein Kampf* in the original German, with the result that he was correspondingly reluctant to believe Hitler when the latter repeatedly insisted that his only goal was peace.

Barthou's own overriding aim was to ensure Germany's political isolation, hence his attempts to achieve an 'eastern pact' with the Soviet Union that would protect Poland and the states of the Little Entente – Czechoslovakia, Yugoslavia and Romania – from Germany's expansionist aspirations. Germany, too, was invited to join this new security arrangement, even though Barthou rightly suspected that Berlin would reject the proposal out of hand. He also sought to forge closer links with Fascist Italy and in that way to ensure that a power that Hitler was currently courting could be aligned against the Reich.

Barthou's attempts to bring his great plan to fruition involved a great deal of travel: in April 1934 he visited Poland, where he encountered considerable resistance on Piłsudski's part to an alliance with the Soviet Union, and in June he travelled to Romania and Yugoslavia. In May, meanwhile, he had conferred with the Soviet foreign minister, Maxim Litvinov, in Geneva, where he had laid the foundations for the later Franco-Soviet mutual assistance treaty. In the event he was not to witness the signing of the treaty on 2 May 1935, for he and King Alexander I of Yugoslavia were assassinated by a Croat nationalist in Marseilles on 9 October 1934. France's most significant foreign minister of the interwar years after Aristide Briand had been in office for only seven months.

If the French security services had been more effective, the assassination of both the king and the foreign minister could have been averted, a situation for which the minister of the interior, Albert Sarraut, paid with his job on 11 October. Two days later the justice minister, Henri Chéron, was forced to resign on account of his involvement in the Stavisky scandal. Barthou was replaced as foreign minister on 13 October by Pierre Laval, one of the finest political minds that France has ever known. Unlike Barthou, he was from the outset willing to make compromises with Germany, an attitude clear from his refusal to indulge in any pro-French propaganda before the Saarland referendum in January 1935. On 8 November, only a few weeks after Laval's appointment, Édouard Herriot and the other Radical ministers resigned their cabinet posts in protest at the constitutional plans of Doumergue and Tardieu, with the result that Doumergue lost his parliamentary majority and was left with no alternative but to resign.

Doumergue was succeeded on 9 November 1934 by Pierre-Étienne Flandin, a politician from the ranks of the Alliance Démocratique, while Laval remained foreign secretary. The new government attempted to deal with the country's economic crisis with the same deflationary measures as those adopted by previous cabinets, and with the same lack of success. The drop in the birth rate during the First World War had led to a fall in the number of recruits, with the result that in the face of vehement protests from Socialists and Communists alike the government decided on 15 March 1935 to extend military service from one to two years. In turn Hitler used this as an excuse to reintroduce general military conscription in Germany the very next day. A number of politicians such as Paul Reynaud had been impressed by the writings of the young

Charles de Gaulle, a military expert who also turned his hand to journalism and whose highly regarded *Vers l'armée de métier* of 1934 advocated the formation of a professional army supported by major tank divisions and capable of offensive warfare, but their demands foundered on the obdurate opposition of the army generals under their new commander, Maurice Gamelin, and his predecessor, Maxime Weygand, both of whom continued to pin their hopes on a successful defence of the Maginot Line.

As far as France's defence policy was concerned, a remarkable change took place on the extreme political left in May 1935. Whereas the Socialists continued to insist on international disarmament and collective security within the framework of the League of Nations, the Communists now gave their clear approval to national defence by way of their reaction to the Franco-Soviet mutual assistance pact signed in Paris on 2 May 1935 by Laval and the Soviet ambassador, Vladimir Petrovich Potemkin, and to a sensational communiqué issued in the wake of Laval's return visit to Moscow on 13 May. In this Stalin, speaking on behalf of the Soviet Union as a whole, had declared his total approval of the policy of national defence that France was pursuing with the aim of keeping its armed forces at the level needed for the country's security.

It was not long afterwards that Flandin's seven-month period in office came to a sudden end: on 30 May 1935 the Chamber of Deputies refused to grant the cabinet the emergency powers that it had asked for. When Flandin resigned, Lebrun replaced him with Laval, the latter's third term as prime minister. Laval, who retained the post of foreign secretary, was granted the powers that the Chamber of Deputies had refused to give Flandin, and he used them without delay to implement a number of decisive measures: the salaries and pensions of civil servants were reduced by 10 per cent, while the tariffs for gas and electricity as well as rents were likewise cut by 10 per cent.

As the foreign secretary in Flandin's government, Laval had travelled to Rome in January 1935 in order to meet Mussolini, a man whom he much admired and with whom he reached agreement on various matters relating to their two nations' foreign policy. Mussolini accepted a gradual reduction in the privileges that Italians had enjoyed in Tunisia, while Laval offered the Italian leader a number of territorial concessions in North Africa and in secret talks guaranteed Mussolini a free hand in Abyssinia, a guarantee that he later claimed was restricted to Italy's economic impact on the Ethiopian Empire. Once the war in Abyssinia had broken out in October 1935, Laval was prepared to go so far towards siding with Mussolini that London suspected that he had been bribed by the Italian leader. The pro-Italian agreement that Laval concluded with the British foreign secretary, Samuel Hoare, in London on 8 December foundered – as we have already observed – on the outraged reaction of the British public.

In the Chamber of Deputies, too, Laval was sharply criticized at the end of December, when his response to the war in Abyssinia was censured not only by

Léon Blum but also by the Radical deputy Yvon Delbos and the conservative Paul Reynaud. On 10 January 1936, the Chamber passed a law with the backing of the right-wing parties that allowed the government the right to ban all armed organizations of every political hue, while also increasing the severity of the penalties for libel. When Laval hesitated to implement the relevant measures, the Radicals withdrew their support and nailed their colours to the mast of the Popular Front that was founded on 14 July 1935 by left-wing parties, trade unions and other left-wing organizations as well as by artists and intellectuals such as Gide, Picasso, Irène Joliot-Curie and Julien Benda. On 22 January 1936, acting on the instructions of their party leadership, Herriot – an outspoken critic of Laval's pro-Italian and pro-German foreign policy – and other Radical ministers announced their departure from the cabinet, which lost its parliamentary majority and as a result was obliged to resign.

The new cabinet under the Radical Socialist Albert Saurrat was intended from the outset as a caretaker government until the elections in May 1936. The former prime minister, Pierre-Étienne Flandin, became foreign minister. Ludovic-Oscar Frossard, the first secretary general of the Communist Party, who had returned to the SFIO in 1924 only to part company with it again on account of his increasingly right-wing views, was appointed labour minister, while the aviation minister was the Neo-Socialist Marcel Déat. The resultant shift to the left may have been slight, but it was sufficient to ensure the support of the Socialists in the confidence vote, when the Communists abstained. It was the first time that they had done so in a vote of this kind.

The Chamber of Deputies ratified the Franco-Soviet mutual assistance pact on 27 February 1936, with the Senate following suit on 4 March. The pact remained a contentious issue among right-wing groups and was used by Hitler very soon afterwards to justify his occupation of the Rhineland. Unlike Laval, Sarraut was vehement in his opposition to the extreme right and in February ordered the disbandment of the Camelots du Roi, the paramilitary wing of Action Française, a move he was able to justify following an attack on Léon Blum by followers of Action Française on 13 February. The group's founder and principal ideologue, Charles Maurras, was accused of incitement to murder after he had publicly demanded in April 1935 that Blum be 'shot in the back' as a 'naturalized German Jew'. He was sentenced to four months' imprisonment, which he served in 1937 – not that this prevented the Académie Française from electing him one of its members in 1938.

The hate campaigns and violent attacks by the nationalist right played a considerable role in strengthening opposition to them on the political left. By January 1936 the Popular Front was being run by the Rassemblement Populaire. The Front's programme proposed the defence of civil liberties and peace, while remaining content to promise to improve the conditions of the working classes, to reduce the length of the working week, to provide public welfare for the unemployed and to set up a state-run wheat board. Although the SFIO also

wanted the banking industry and a number of other industries to be nationalized, this proposal was rejected by the Communists on tactical grounds and by
the Radicals for reasons of inner conviction. Only the idea of nationalizing the
armaments industry was supported by all the partners in the Popular Front.

The largest umbrella organizations of the French trade unions – the socialist
CGT and the Communist CGTU – met in Toulouse at the beginning of March
1936, when the CGT immediately made demands that the Popular Front was
unable to make on its own: public works to deal with unemployment, a forty-
hour week and a comprehensive programme of nationalization. If the
Communists had had their way, not only would the trade unions have united in
common cause, so too would the PCF and SFIO, but the socialists were
mistrustful of this sudden desire for peace and harmony and settled instead for
an electoral pact between all the parties that made up the Popular Front.

The Communists' political volte-face included an ostentatious show of
support for the tricolour flag, for the Marseillaise and for the Jacobin tradition
of the French Revolution. Their electoral rhetoric, which was aimed at all social
groups and designed to achieve a state of national and social reconciliation,
culminated in a radio address by the party's general secretary, Maurice Thorez,
on 17 April 1936 in which he declared that his party – a party of laymen – was
willing to hold out its hand to Catholics, blue- and white-collar workers and
farmers because they were their friends and beset by the same cares as they
themselves were. But Thorez went even further in soliciting the support of the
right: 'We hold out our hand to you, the man who serves voluntarily, and to the
veteran who has become a member of the Croix de Feu, because you are a son
of our people and, like us, you suffer from disorder and corruption and, like us,
you want to prevent our country from descending into ruin and catastrophe.'[87]

The forthcoming elections for the Chamber of Deputies were one of the
reasons why France did not react more robustly to Germany's occupation of
the demilitarized Rhineland on 7 March 1936. Although Sarraut had the
backing of the minister without portfolio, Joseph Paul-Boncour, in wanting to
take immediate military action to punish Berlin for its renewed breach of the
terms of the Treaty of Versailles, they were vigorously opposed by the minister
for war, Louis Maurin, by the chief of the general staff, Maurice Gamelin, and
by the minister for aviation, Marcel Déat. Not a single member of the government was willing to support the idea of calling up all of the country's reservists,
a move that even they themselves believed was necessary if France was to
provide a show of military strength. Such a step might well have sparked serious
riots and seemed to represent an incalculable risk only weeks before the
planned elections. As a result, a broad consensus that stretched from the
extreme right to the extreme left was quickly reached: France must do all in its
power to avoid the dangers of a European war.

The political left presented a far more united front than the centre ground
and the political right, and this was reflected in the election results, the Popular

Front emerging as the clear winner from the two rounds of elections on 26 April and 3 May 1936. In the final runoff, the most successful candidate from the left-wing parties – the SFIO, the PCF and the small Union Socialiste Républicaine – was consistently supported by the followers of the other partners in the electoral pact, so that the Front gained 369 seats compared with the 236 of the centre and right-wing parties. In all, 5.13 million voters backed the left, while 4.3 million voted for the right in the widest sense of the term. But it was the Communists who recorded the biggest gains, their new line in patriotism allowing them to break new ground and appeal to new groups of voters: in comparison to 1932, they won almost 700,000 additional votes, polling almost 1.5 million votes in all. The Socialists, conversely, lost ground, polling 37,000 fewer votes, while the Radicals suffered considerably more substantial losses – 360,000 fewer votes than in 1932. The right-wing parties polled 84,000 fewer votes. For the first time in its history, the SFIO, with 146 seats, was the biggest party, followed by the Radical Socialists with 115 and by the Communists with seventy-two.

In the wake of the election results, only one party – the Socialists – could be asked to lead the government, and only one politician – the leader of the SFIO, Léon Blum – could be invited to become prime minister. From his point of view, the victory of the Popular Front did not mean that the proletariat was anywhere close to its goal of acquiring power, but it did at least provide the conditions necessary for the proletariat's exercise of power within the framework of the capitalist system, an *exercise du pouvoir* that went beyond any mere participation in a bourgeois-led coalition. Ever since the party conference in Tours in December 1920, when he had effectively become the leader of the SFIO in the Chamber of Deputies, Blum had repeatedly rejected the idea of such a coalition, believing that it would lead to ideological 'confusion'. An electoral pact with the Radicals and parliamentary support for a left-wing bourgeois government were a different matter, since they were not bound up with the danger of any such 'confusion', which explains why the SFIO had reached such agreements whenever it was possible to do so. But now that the SFIO was the biggest party and the Socialists and Communists were together far stronger than the Radicals, it seemed not only tenable to assume responsibility for government, but politically expedient as well.

In keeping with the constitution, a new government could be formed only after the new Chamber of Deputies had met for its constituent session, which traditionally took place some four weeks after the elections. This period between the elections and the formation of its first Popular Front government was filled with the worst wave of strikes and unrest in France's history. Within a week of the elections the first riots broke out in Le Havre and Toulouse. Three days later the strikes spread to Paris as well. Here it was the metal industry that suffered the most. Walkouts were by no means the only problem, for factories were occupied all over France, with the striking workers demanding higher wages, shorter working hours and better conditions in the workplace, especially in the areas of hygiene and safety. René Rémond has compared the 'cahiers de revendications' in which the striking workers listed their grievances with the 'cahiers de doléances' of 1789.[88] But these grievances were not revolutionary in character, for what the workers were demanding were the sort of social reforms that had long been achieved in other countries, most notably Scandinavia.

The demonstrations were for the most part spontaneous, having been organized by neither the CGT nor the PCF. The only active role was played by the few surviving anarchist-syndicalist trade unionists, Trotskyites and members of the extreme left wing of the SFIO associated with Marceau Pivert, the head of the Fédération de la Seine, who on 27 May announced 'Tout est possible' in the pages of the Socialists' official daily newspaper, Le Populaire de Paris. Two days later L'Humanité felt it necessary to counter such revolutionary exuberance: 'Tout n'est pas possible' ran the headline of the Communist Party newspaper. In early June a second wave of strikes began, reaching their climax later that month with 12,000 strikes involving some 1.8 million workers.

Large sections of the middle classes reacted to the events of May and June 1936 by fearing a Communist revolution and a repeat of the Paris Commune of 1871, resulting in a massive flight of capital out of the country: within a month the Banque de France had lost 1,500 million francs. The historian Charles Bloch has described as follows the mood among the bourgeoisie during these weeks:

Parallels were drawn between the strike movement in France and the events in Russia in 1917 and in Italy in 1919–20, when the revolutionary workers and peasants had likewise occupied the factories and landed estates, or latifundia, but the people who drew these parallels overlooked the fundamental difference between the real revolutionary masses in Russia who were striving to dispossess the major landowners and industrialists and the French workers, whose peaceful occupation of factories was designed to provide them with a lever guaranteeing the introduction of the reforms that they were demanding, without – at least for the present – calling into question the principle underpinning the capitalist economic system.

Bloch saw a link between the early summer of 1936 and the events of 1940: in their search for a 'saviour from the Communist danger', sections of the French bourgeoisie even turned to the Third Reich for help. 'More than anything else, the events of May and June 1936 created the mentality that was to lead in 1940 to the acceptance of the German occupation and of Marshal Pétain's authoritarian regime.'[89]

The government which until 4 June 1936 was responsible for maintaining law and order in the country was headed by Albert Sarraut. At the insistence of the Communists, it did everything in its power to avoid exacerbating an already tense situation, with the result that the police made no attempt to interfere in the strike action or to clear the occupied factories. But the Communists turned down Blum's invitation to join his cabinet, and on 14 May the PCF declared that if they were loyally and unreservedly to support a Socialist-run government, they could in that way serve the people better than by joining the cabinet and 'providing a pretext for campaigns by the enemies of the people designed to induce panic and confusion among the population at large'.[90]

The Communists' reasons for refusing to play an active part in government were presumably no mere excuse. Rather, their decision was justified on the grounds of the country's current foreign policy, for Communist ministers would inevitably have alarmed the bourgeoisie and thus made it more difficult for France and the Soviet Union to work together more closely, as Moscow was hoping would be the case. But another consideration would also have played a role here: the Popular Front government could pursue a reformist agenda but revolution was out of the question, with the result that not only was there no need for the PCF to enter the cabinet, but such involvement would have been counterproductive. As a party that merely kept the Popular Front in office, the Communists found it easier not to have to accept direct responsibility for decisions that they knew were bound to fall far short of the expectations of many, if not most, of their supporters. The fact that the PCF's tactics were respected by large sections of the population is clear from its growth in membership, which rose from 50,000 in 1933 to 280,000 by the end of 1936.

Not until the evening of 4 June 1936, only hours before the constituent assembly of the Chamber of Deputies, was Blum finally able to present his cabinet to the president of the Republic, Albert Lebrun. The foreign secretary was the Radical Socialist Yvon Delbos, the home secretary the Socialist Roger Salengro, who committed suicide only a few months later when falsely accused by the far right of having been a deserter in 1915 and having defected to the enemy. He was replaced in November 1936 by the Socialist Marx Dormoy. The Radical Socialist Édouard Daladier took over at defence, while the Socialist Vincent Auriol, who was to be the president of the French Republic from 1947 to 1954, became minister of finance. Another member of the SFIO, Charles Spinasse, became the first Socialist minister of commerce in the Third Republic. Since women did not have the vote in France, there was something distinctly sensational about the appointment of three female undersecretaries of state: the feminist Cécile Brunschvicg for education, the Socialist teacher Suzanne Lacorre for the protection of children and adolescents, and the physicist Irène Joliot-Curie for scientific research. Blum's cabinet was also the first to include undersecretaries of state for leisure and physical education as well as for sport.

The first great challenge facing the Popular Front government was the need to end the strikes and factory occupations that were paralysing the country. On

7 June Blum convened a meeting of the main bodies representing employers and employees, the Confédération Nationale de la Production Française and the Confédération Générale du Travail. It met at the Hôtel Matignon, which since 1935 had been the prime minister's seat of office. By that same night the partners to the negotiations had signed the 'Accord Matignon', the contents of which were not dissimilar to those agreed to in Germany in November 1918 in the context of the Central Cooperative Union of Employers' and Employees' Organizations in Trade and Industry. Its key points were the immediate introduction of free collective bargaining (this had existed in theory since 1919, but few employees had benefited from it), the freedom to organize and join trade unions, the election of workers' delegates in factories and other places of employment and a general increase in wages of between 7 per cent and 15 per cent, the average being 12 per cent. Parliament was left to settle the questions of the forty-hour week and paid leave. The workers were required to leave the occupied factories and resume work, but there would be no sanctions against them.

The Accord Matignon did not end the strikes and factory sit-ins, for in spite of all the appeals by Blum and the leader of the CGT, Léon Jouhaux, many workers refused to abandon the sites that they had occupied as a way of ensuring better conditions for themselves. The strikes began to crumble only when Thorez, acting in the name of the Communists, called on the strikers to suspend their actions on 11 June, although even by July there were still 1,688 strikes in progress, involving 176,947 striking workers.

The meeting at the Hôtel Matignon had restricted itself to points on which employers and workers could agree, and it was left to parliament to enact the socio-political changes that the Third Republic needed to implement if it was to catch up with the rest of Europe. By June Blum had already proposed the first basic laws, guaranteeing workers the right to two weeks' paid leave, a reduction of the working week from forty-eight to forty hours made up, as far as possible, of five days of eight hours each, a legal basis to free collective bargaining and an increase in the salaries and pensions of civil servants.

Later that summer further laws were passed banning child labour (except for agricultural work), raising the school-leaving age to fourteen, nationalizing the armaments industry, implementing a large-scale programme of job creation schemes in the public sector, extending the provision of family welfare and disability pensions, and radically reorganizing the Banque de France, which was now more closely tied to the executive and legislative power of the state and renamed the Banque de la France in order to underline its character as France's national bank. In addition, a state-run wheat board was set up, the Office National Interprofessional du Blé, to regulate the production, distribution and price of grain, with a monopoly on exports and imports. A further law was passed in December 1936, providing for obligatory arbitration in wage disputes. The main areas of social policy that still needed to be addressed were unemployment benefit and retirement insurance.

It was not long before the country began to feel the economic consequences of the reduction in the working week, including the new provisions for two weeks' paid leave and an increase in the level of wages and salaries. Employers now had to pay their staff on average 25 per cent to 35 per cent more than previously; production fell, while prices rose; France's international competitiveness fell; the gold reserves of the Banque de la France sank to the legal minimum of 30,000 million marks since the government needed advance funds; and the flight of capital continued. The free convertibility of the franc into gold was suspended on 26 September 1936. The franc lost between 25 per cent and 35 per cent of its value in the wake of the transition to a flexible rate of exchange.

Since the franc had long been overvalued, a number of politicians, including Paul Reynaud, had repeatedly demanded its devaluation, but hitherto without success. The reforms that were undertaken during the summer of 1936 meant that the devaluation of the franc turned out to be greater than would have been the case in previous years. Production rose somewhat in the wake of the actions of 26 September, but French industry remained uncompetitive on the international market. Unemployment figures fell by only 20 per cent to 25 per cent, far below the expectations of the Popular Front's experts, who were influenced by Roosevelt's New Deal and by the doctrines of John Maynard Keynes. Wholesale prices continued to rise, and since Blum's government was reluctant to introduce currency controls, capital continued to flow out of the country.

Blum's government had been in office for only six weeks when Nationalist officers staged a putsch in Spain on 17/18 July and triggered the Spanish Civil War. The Popular Front was sympathetic to the Frente Popular that had ruled in Madrid since 16 February 1936, and when the Spanish government secretly asked Paris to help it with weapons, Blum's first impulse was to comply, not least on account of the existing trade agreement between the two countries. But both the president of the Republic and the leaders of the Chamber of Deputies and of the Senate warned him in no uncertain terms not to become involved in the Spanish conflict, arguing that it could easily spill over into France and perhaps even lead to war in Europe as a whole.

The leader of the Chamber of Deputies was Édouard Herriot, and he spoke for most of the members of his party. Within the cabinet, too, the majority of Radicals, including the foreign secretary Yvon Delbos, and the defence minister, Édouard Daladier, were opposed to any such intervention. Only the aviation minister, Pierre Cot, and the minister for national education, Jean Zay, supported the idea. There was also opposition from leading officials at the foreign ministry. The nationalist right fought a vigorous campaign against French intervention, and their campaign presumably influenced many officers. The British refusal to become involved also played a major role here: when Blum and Delbos visited London in late July, Baldwin and his foreign secretary, Anthony Eden, made it clear that if France became embroiled in the Spanish Civil War, it could not count on the support of the United Kingdom.

Blum was convinced that any responsible French foreign policy must be based on close cooperation with London. As a result, he had no choice but to adopt the line taken by Britain and all the major European powers and not become involved in the conflict. By the end of August 1936 twenty-seven European states, including Italy and Germany, had signed the declaration of non-intervention drawn up by Britain and France. In London, a non-intervention committee was set up in the second week of September: its members included representatives not only of France and Britain but also of Germany, Italy and the Soviet Union. Since neither Berlin nor Rome had any intention of abiding by the principle of non-interference and since Moscow had soon begun to play an active role in the conflict, Britain and France were in the end the only major European powers to adopt the motto enshrined in the treaty. And even here, Great Britain was far more consistent in its approach than Paris.

Since his policy of non-intervention was evidently not working, Blum for a time considered resigning as prime minister but was eventually persuaded to stay by the president of the Second International, the Belgian socialist leader Louis de Brouckère, and also by the Spanish ambassador. During the months that followed – and in spite of the official ban on arms exports in place since 8 August 1936 – the Spanish Republic received aeroplanes from France, some of which arrived via Mexico, while the writer André Malraux assumed command of a French air force squadron called España, even though he himself was unable to fly. The government in Paris also turned a blind eye to the recruitment of volunteers for the International Brigades that fought on the side of the Spanish Republic and that were made up for the most part of French recruits. It also operated a very open policy towards its border with Spain. But the Popular Front was too internally divided to be able to do any more than this. The Communists, meanwhile, demanded far greater commitment from France and finally distanced themselves from Blum's government on 6 December 1936 by abstaining during a confidence vote following a major debate on foreign policy in the Chamber of Deputies.

The French right saw in the Spanish Civil War a welcome opportunity to increase its attacks on the Popular Front, complaining that Blum's government was pursuing an ideological policy that was threatening to plunge the country into a European war. Domestically, too, the opposition found plenty of reasons to lambast the political left. On 18 June, Blum was able to use the law of 10 January 1936 to disband the anti-parliamentarian right-wing leagues, including de La Roque's Croix de Feu, which had in the meantime spawned the Syndicats Professionnels Français, associations organized along the lines of trade unions, soon afterwards forming a political party, the Parti Social Français, or PSF, which had members all over France, more than half of whom, however, lived in the Paris region. By the beginning of 1937 it had more than one million members. Although it was emphatically right-wing, anti-Marxist and anti-parliamentary in its rhetoric, it remained to all intents and purposes within the framework of the parliamentary system and existing legal provision.

In that respect it differed from another party that had been summoned into existence in the summer of 1936, the aforementioned Parti Populaire Français, or PPF, of Jacques Doriot, the mayor of St-Denis and former leader of the Communists. With its demand for a corporative state, the PPF could be likened to the Italian Fascist party, and the same was true of its deliberate targeting of workers, its radical nationalism and its use of physical violence against its sworn enemies. At no point, however, does it appear to have had more than 100,000 members, the vast majority of whom were workers and farmers.

No other right-wing party was as openly Fascist as Doriot's, no other was as massively supported by industry and finance, no other enjoyed such widespread journalistic backing, including even the respected dailies *Le Figaro* and *Le Temps*, and no other attracted so many prominent intellectuals such as the writers Pierre Drieu La Rochelle, Alfred Fabre-Luce and Bertrand de Jouvenel, all of whom left the party in the autumn of 1938 after the Munich agreement to reduce the size of Czechoslovakia. Contributors to *Le Combat*, the official newspaper of the Jeune Droite, including Robert Brasillach, Georges Blond and Thierry Maulnier, also wrote for Doriot's paper, *L'Émancipation Nationale*, while La Rochelle and de Jouvenel – both of them members of the Central Committee of the PPF – also published in *Le Combat*. Among the party's younger activists were two who were later to become better known, the political scientist Maurice Duverger and the bourgeois rebel Pierre Poujade.

Various right-wing journals such as *Candide* and, above all, *Gringoire* conducted a vicious campaign against the Popular Front, *Gringoire* in particular unleashing a ferocious attack on the home secretary, Roger Salengro, and reaching a wide readership with its print-run of 600,000 copies. Blum was the preferred target of the anti-Semites in Action Française, who claimed that his real name was Karfunkelstein, that he had been born in Bessarabia and that he was following orders from Moscow. Writing in his own journal, *Je Suis Partout*, on 13 June 1936, the historian Pierre Gaxotte felt that France was faced with two alternatives: Bolshevism or national revolution. A year later an even more radical anti-Semite, Robert Brasillach, took over as the paper's senior editor, while its prominent authors included the fanatical anti-Jewish writer Louis-Ferdinand Céline, whose virulently anti-Semitic pamphlet *Bagatelles pour un massacre* was published at the end of 1937.

In the autumn of 1936 the right wing of the leading industrial organization, which had always been opposed to the Accord Matignon, staged a revolt against the organization's leadership and in an act of defiance changed its name from the Confédération Nationale de la Production Française to the Confédération Générale du Patronat Français (General Confederation of French Employers). A new leader was appointed in October 1936 in the person of the spokesman of the younger employers, Claude Grignoux, who taught jurisprudence and admired all Fascist regimes, believing that liberalism was outdated. Specifically he championed a corporative state based on the Italian model. Under his leadership the CGPF adopted an outspokenly anti-Communist line directed against the Popular Front.

On 31 October 1936 five French cardinals called on the country's Catholics to reject what they termed its 'practical atheism' and combat the 'virus of revolution'. Meanwhile, the military spawned La Cagoule, a group of conspirators hostile to the Republic and responsible for the murders of the two Italian anti-Fascists Carlo and Nello Rosselli in Bagnoles-de-l'Orne in July 1937. The strategic goal of La Cagoule was the violent overthrow of the present regime and the establishment of a military dictatorship. The conspiracy was uncovered in November 1937 and its leaders were arrested on the orders of the home secretary, Marx Dormoy. At the end of 1936 the actions of the extreme right were not yet a serious threat to the Republic, but within months of its coming to power the Popular Front found itself dealing with a countermovement that showed every sign of increasing in strength.

For all its ideological antagonism to National Socialism, the Popular Front tried to maintain diplomatic relations with Germany, much as Germany sought to remain on good terms with France. On 28 August 1936, four days after Germany had introduced a compulsory two-year period of military service, Blum received a visit from Hjalmar Schacht, the president of the Reichsbank and finance minister, who was acting as Hitler's envoy. Blum introduced himself as 'a Marxist and a Jew' but stressed that in spite of German anti-Communism and French anti-Fascism, the two countries could still come to some 'general agreement'. Schacht demanded the return of the German colonies and the annulment of the Treaty of Versailles. If these conditions were met, Germany would return to the League of Nations and would consider new disarmament talks. Blum passed on Schacht's colonial demands to the Foreign Office in London, but the meeting had no practical consequences.

Nor was there any rapprochement with Fascist Italy. When Mussolini made a conciliatory move in that direction in January 1937, he tied it to the condition that France should leave Spain to Franco, prompting Blum to reject his demand out of hand. Blum also declined to form a Franco-Soviet military alliance proposed by the Russian defence commissar, Marshal Kliment Yefremovich Voroshilov, during a visit to Moscow by the chief of the general staff, General Victor-Henri Schweisguth. If Blum had responded positively to Russia's initiative – and Schweisguth's reaction to it was entirely negative – relations with Great Britain would have been compromised, a risk that Blum was unwilling to contemplate.

Most of France's allies reacted negatively to the change of government in Paris in June 1936. Even before this date, Romania and Yugoslavia had already begun to draw closer to Germany, and the formation of a Popular Front government merely served to confirm their growing alienation from France. In the case of Poland, which under Piłsudski's authoritarian rule was progressively forming closer ties with Germany, there were also ideological reasons for the country's change of direction under its pro-German foreign minister, Józef Beck. Belgium, which in October 1920 had formed a military alliance with France, stressed its independence in the wake of Germany's unopposed violation of the terms of the Treaties of Locarno, but opposition to the Popular Front also persuaded King Leopold III of the Belgians to end the military alliance with France on 14 October 1936, effectively signalling a return to his country's former neutrality. On 30 January 1937 Hitler declared Germany's intention of guaranteeing Belgian independence, and a treaty to that effect was signed on 13 October 1937. Six months earlier, on 24 April, the Western Powers had already declared that they would support Belgium in the event of an attack.

If French politics lurched to the left at this time, there was still no need to fear that fewer efforts would be made in the field of defence, a fear fomented by the earlier anti-military rhetoric of the Socialists and Communists. Blum supported Daladier's call for an increase in military expenditure to 14,000 million francs for four years and in March 1937, with the broad agreement of the Chamber of Deputies, he arranged for a large defence loan. On 14 October 1936 he received a visit from de Gaulle and was informed of the latter's ideas for a professional body of armoured troops and a French offensive strategy in the event of Germany's attacking Poland or Czechoslovakia. Blum was impressed, but the same was not true of the chief of the general staff, Maurice Gamelin, or of his still influential predecessor, Maxime Weygand, or, finally, of Philippe Pétain. As a result, France's armaments policy remained defensive in character, while the army continued to be convinced that Germany was incapable of breaching the Maginot Line.

By the beginning of 1937 Blum believed that France's economy was so precarious that on 13 February he ordered a suspension of all socio-political reforms and an end to all further wage increases. There followed measures designed to reassure private business, including a return to the free trade in gold. The left wing of the SFIO was outraged, Marceau Pivert speaking of a capitulation to militarism and to the world of banking and resigning in protest from his various posts in the prime minister's general secretariat. Anger among the workers increased when the police, attempting to prevent a clash between the left and de La Roque's PSF at Clichy on 16 March, fired into the crowd, killing five protesters and injuring around 200. Meanwhile, wild-cat strikes were increasing in number, threatening to disrupt the 1937 Paris World Fair. By the time the fair finally opened, more than three weeks late, on 24 May 1937, the site was still covered in building rubble. Although the German and Soviet pavilions were complete, those of France and many other nations were not. Foreign visitors included Hjalmar Schacht, who used the occasion to confer with Blum again, but the meeting was just as unproductive as their first encounter in August 1936.

By the middle of 1937, Blum and his government could no longer avoid the conclusion that their attempts to combat the country's worsening economic situation had failed to produce any tangible results, and on 15 June Blum asked parliament to grant him emergency powers intended to allow the government to introduce a new tax on property and counter the flight of capital. The Chamber of Deputies voted to accept this proposal by 346 votes to 247, but it was thrown out by the Senate on 21 June by 168 votes to ninety-six. Most of the Radical senators voted against the measure. The following day Blum announced his resignation.

Blum's departure threw a spotlight on the collapse of the Popular Front but did not yet spell its definitive end. On 22 June the country's president, Albert Lebrun, invited the Radical politician Camille Chautemps to form a government and to return to a post he had already held in 1930 and again in 1933–4. Blum became deputy prime minister, while most of the ministers from his first cabinet retained their posts. The Socialist minister of commerce was replaced by Fernand Chapsal of the Radicals, while the Socialist finance minister, Vincent Auriol, moved to the Ministry of Justice. The finance department was taken over by Georges Bonnet from the right wing of the Radical Party, whose members also included the minister for public works, Henri Queuille, and the minister without portfolio, Albert Sarraut. The three female undersecretaries of state were replaced. Whereas the Socialists had had a slight numerical advantage in Blum's cabinet, it was now the Radicals who held the upper hand. The new government was clearly to the right of its predecessor.

Among the cabinet's first measures was the definitive abandonment of the gold standard on 1 July 1937, resulting in a further devaluation of the franc amounting to around 25 per cent. With the agreement of the Communists, new taxes were levied, and the French railways were placed under the state control of the newly created Société Nationale des Chemins de Fer (SNCF). French foreign policy also underwent a shift to the right, when Delbos urged the Czech government to be more accommodating towards Germany on the question of the Sudetenland. When Schacht paid a further visit to Paris in November 1937, the foreign secretary, Georges Bonnet, spoke in support of closer cooperation between Germany and Austria and of far-reaching autonomy for the Sudeten region. Chautemps made no secret of his anti-Communism, a view shared by large sections of the French public in the wake of the Moscow show trials. At the same time the prime minister stressed his willingness to work with Berlin.

By the latter part of 1937 the country's worsening economic situation resulted in increasingly vocal calls for an abandonment of the forty-hour week. At the same time, there was a new wave of strikes. In January, when the government asked the Chamber of Deputies to grant it extraordinary powers to stabilize the currency, the Communists made it known that they would no longer abstain in any future votes, whereupon Chautemps declared his party's pact with the PCF at an end. The SFIO interpreted this to mean the end of the

Popular Front alliance and withdrew its ministers from the cabinet. Chautemps resigned on 15 June 1938.

Four days later he formed a new government that excluded Socialists and included only Radicals and two members of the independent Union Socialiste Républicaine. But on 21 January both the SFIO and PCF voted for the new cabinet in order to avoid an even greater shift to the right. In the event, however, Chautemps's new government remained in office for only two months. By 10 March, when a vote of no confidence took place in the Chamber, the Austrian crisis was coming to a head – Hitler marched into Austria two days later – and Chautemps was replaced by his predecessor. Blum failed to form a government of national unity embracing both Thorez and Reynaud and instead formed a cabinet that resembled his first one in terms of its political makeup. Blum himself took over the Finance Ministry in addition to the premiership, and Paul-Boncour of the Union Socialiste Républicaine became foreign secretary. A young left-wing Radical politician, Pierre Mendès-France, who was to be prime minister in 1954–5, became undersecretary at the Treasury.

Although Blum's second cabinet remained in office for only a short period of time, it witnessed an important event in terms of France's foreign policy. On 15 March, immediately after German troops had marched into Austria, Paul-Boncour assured Prague that if Germany were to attack Czechoslovakia, France would meet its obligations under the Franco-Czech Treaty of January 1924 and come to its assistance. In early April Blum asked for extra powers to deal with his country's economic crisis, including the introduction of a capital gains tax and foreign exchange controls, and won a majority in the Chamber of Deputies, but at the insistence of the conservative Joseph Caillaux the Senate voted against him on 7 April, prompting Blum to resign the very next day. If the left wing of the SFIO associated with Pivert and the Fédération de la Seine had had its way, then the prime minister would have opposed the decision of the first chamber and appealed to the masses to resist the obstructive policies of the Senate, by force if necessary. Although this would have involved no violation of the constitution, it would in Blum's view have amounted to a declaration of war. He did not think that the conditions were yet ready for such a confrontation in the spring of 1938 and as a result he sought to avoid a trial of strength with the upper house.

The collapse of Blum's second cabinet marked the end of the Popular Front, a development that was the result not only of the massive pressure from the right that all left-wing governments had had to confront since June 1936 but also of the inexperience of the Socialists in dealing with questions of government and administration. With the exception of the war years from 1914 to 1917, the SFIO had not been represented in cabinet, and so their ideas on the exercise of power were correspondingly abstract, a shortcoming that found expression in many laws, several of which were enacted with precipitate haste. The doctrinaire 'no' to the mere idea of a ministerial role in government propounded by Blum as a theoretical Marxist and a practising anti-revolutionary demanded its price when he finally abandoned it in the early summer of 1936.

Even so, the work of the various Popular Front governments was by no means futile, for they helped France to advance along the road to a modern social state, while also aiding the extreme left in the form of the Communists in their attempts to become more fully integrated into the political system of the Third Republic and in that way keeping the extreme right in check. If France avoided sliding into revolution and civil war in the wake of the serious economic crisis of 1936, then this was thanks to those elements in the workers' movement and on the left wing of the bourgeoisie that were able to learn from the past. In a sense France spent the years between 1936 and 1938 catching up with the 'class compromise' that had been brought to Germany by the revolution of 1918–19. Of course, this compromise was no more permanent in France than it was in Germany, for in both cases the coalition that had been based on social understanding soon foundered on inner contradictions and on the loss of a parliamentary majority. In Germany this stage had already been reached by June 1920, whereas in France it was not until the spring of 1938 that cracks began to appear. Even so, the decisions that were taken at a time of increasingly reformist politics continued to resonate on both sides of the Rhine, in many cases retaining their impact right down to the present day.

Blum was succeeded on 10 April 1938 by the Radical Socialist Édouard Daladier, who became head of the government for the third time in his career, remaining in office until 20 March 1940 – an unusually long period by the standards of the Third Republic. His cabinet was made up of Radical Socialists, mostly from the right of the party, and of members of the Union Socialiste Républicaine. The new foreign minister was the right-wing Georges Bonnet, who was widely regarded as an advocate of appeasement towards Germany. Both chambers granted Daladier the sort of sweeping powers that the Senate had denied Blum. In order to avoid destabilizing the country any further, both the SFIO and the PCF voted for Daladier in the confidence vote. The extreme left wing of the Socialists – those associated with Pivert and his Fédération de la Seine – objected to their party's parliamentary support of the government and were expelled from the SFIO at its annual conference in Rouen in June 1938, a reminder to the remaining left-wing members to keep in line.

As the summer ran its course, it became increasingly clear that Daladier intended to use his powers not to further the reforms of the Popular Front but in some cases to reverse them. When he announced on the radio on 21 August that France needed to get back to work and that the length of the working week in the armaments industry was to be increased, the Union Socialiste Républicaine's two cabinet ministers, Paul Ramadier at the Ministry of Labour, and Ludovic-Oscar Frossard at the Ministry of Public Works, resigned, and although their replacements came from the same party, they held rather more moderate views than Ramadier and Frossard had done. From now on wild-cat strikes were met with police brutality and factory sit-ins no longer tolerated. The CGT protested and the SFIO and PCF demanded Daladier's resignation, but the government was able to continue to function thanks to the support of the centre and right-wing parties.

Faced with the gravity of the international situation, the Socialists and Communists were reluctant to mobilize the masses in an anti-parliamentary revolt, with the result that France enjoyed a period of domestic stability, making it easier for Daladier's government to pursue policies towards Germany that were aimed at peaceful understanding at practically any price.

Battlefield of Extremes: The Spanish Civil War 1936–9

On the afternoon of 17 July 1936 a military putsch in Melilla – an enclave belonging to the Spanish protectorate of Morocco – marked the start of the Spanish Civil War, which began a few hours earlier than planned. The action was triggered unintentionally by security forces loyal to the Republic, when their attempt to arrest the conspirators was thwarted by the defection of a unit of the Spanish Foreign Legion which, called upon to help, decided to support the putsch instead. Within hours the rebel officers had taken control of the coastal fortress of Melilla. The Nationalist centre of the *pronunciamiento* associated with General Emilio Mola thereupon gave the signal for other mutinies in mainland Spain. After Melilla, the next town to fall into Nationalist hands was Tetuán, the headquarters of the high commissioner for Spanish Morocco, followed in turn by Ceuta. The British Neo-Tory Douglas Jerrold had earlier sent a light aircraft to Las Palmas in the Canary Islands, ensuring that one of the conspirators who had been exiled to Tenerife, General Francisco Franco y Bahamonde, who was to assume command of the African army, was able to reach Tetuán on 18 July. While still in Las Palmas, Franco had issued a radio appeal calling on divisional commanders and navy chiefs to support the uprising.

On the Spanish mainland many garrisons joined the insurrectionists after 18 July. General Gonzalo Queipo de Llano y de Serra was entrusted with the task of reducing Andalusia to Nationalist control, an aim he achieved in Seville, Córdoba and Cádiz after often violent fighting with troops loyal to the Republic as well as with striking workers. In Granada, where the commanding general, Miguel Campins, hesitated for two days before submitting to Queipo, artillery was used against the working-class quarter of Albaicín. Among the victims on the Republican side was the poet Federico García Lorca, the author of *Blood Wedding*, who was shot on the morning of 18 August. Campins paid for his vacillation with his death: on Queipo's orders he was court-martialled, sentenced to death and executed in the face of Franco's wishes.

The uprising on the part of Nationalist elements in the armed forces was successful not only in Morocco and parts of Andalusia but also in Galicia,

Navarra, León, the island of Majorca, the predominantly agricultural areas of what had once been the kingdom of Castile around Burgos and Valladolid and also in Oviedo and Saragossa. The whole of eastern Spain, including Catalonia, Valencia and Murcia, remained republican, as did much of the north of the country, including the Basque region, Santander and Asturias, and, in the south of the country, Extremadura and parts of Andalusia. In short, the Republic retained control of the larger towns and cities and of those regions that were economically the most developed, namely, Catalonia and the Basque region, together with Madrid, totalling around two-thirds of the country's territory. Of the seventeen highest-ranking generals only four took part in the mutiny, while only a single head of a military region – Saragossa – was involved. On the other hand, only 3,500 out of 15,000 officers remained loyal to the Republic. In the navy, it was the officer class that tended to side with the rebels, while ordinary seamen and NCOs supported the Republic. In total the Republicans had 112,000 troops at their disposal, the Nationalists 98,500. Among the population at large it was initially only in Navarra and in the conservative parts of Castile that the rebels enjoyed their most powerful support.

Apart from the members of the military who had staged the putsch, the rebel camp also included the Carlist or monarchist traditionalists who were on good terms with General Mola, and the supporters of José Antonio Primo de Rivera, the charismatic leader of the Falange Española de las JONS (Juntas de Ofensiva Nacional-Sindicalista), which of all the political organizations in Spain was the one that was closest to the Italian Fascists and to the German National Socialists. With the exception of the Basque region, the Catholic Church every-where sided with the rebels. The only bishop who refused to do so was the bishop of Vitoria, whose diocese included the Basque country. But even in 'Nationalist' Spain there were members of the clergy and monastic orders who objected to the arbitrary executions of the military's real or imagined enemies. Following the murder of the monarchist politician José Calvo Sotelo on the night of 12/13 July, the leader of the Catholic-conservative opposition party, the Confederación Española des Derechos Autónomas (CEDA), José Maria Gil-Robles y Quiñones, had fled to northern Spain, thence to France and, in the wake of his deportation by Blum's government, to Portugal, from where he supported the Nationalists and transferred his party's funds to General Mola.

Following the elections on 16 February 1936, the Republic's government was made up of members of the Popular Front headed by the left-wing Republican Santiago Casares Quiroga, who succeeded Manuel Azaña after the latter was named president on 16 May. Even during the election campaign, the largest party, the Partido Socialista Obrero Español (PSOE), under its leader Francisco Largo Caballero, had already announced that it would not put forward the names of any ministers and it duly kept its word. On the evening of 18 July, following the military putsch, José Giral of the Izquierda Republicana formed a new cabinet. It too was purely bourgeois in its makeup and immediately decided to arm the people. Early the next morning the two biggest trade unions, the Socialist Unión General de Trabajadores (UGT) and the anarchist or, rather, anarchist-syndicalist Confederación Nacional de Trabajadores (CNT), were provided with weapons by the Ministry of War. Immediately the cry went up in the working-class districts of Madrid and many other towns and cities 'No pasarán!', a call broadcast late the previous evening on Spanish radio by the best-known female Communist politician, Dolores Ibárruri ('La Pasionaria'). By 19 July power no longer lay with the government in Madrid but with the trade unions and ultimately with the people in the streets.

On the night of 19/20 July some fifty churches were torched in Madrid. On the 20th fierce fighting broke out around the Real Alcázar and on the Punta del Sol, ending in victory for the champions of the Republic. Following the capture of the fortress, numerous rebels were killed. Of the officers who had fought on the Punta del Sol, many escaped to Toledo and Guadalajara, where the rebellion had been successful. In Barcelona, Lluis Companys, the president of the regional government – the Generalitat – of Catalonia, had refused to arm the people, whereupon the CNT stormed several arsenals and assumed command of the Republican forces. Exceptionally, the Guardia Civil sided with them. By the evening of 20 July the insurrection had been put down in Barcelona as well as in Madrid.

It is unclear how many men and women lost their lives in mass executions and massacres during this early phase of the rebellion. On principle, Franco granted pardons only after the individual in question had been executed, the only exceptions being left-wing foreign journalists who sympathized with the Republican cause: Arthur Koestler, for example, witnessed at first hand the capture of Malaga in early February 1937 and reported on it to the liberal *News Chronicle*. He was sentenced to death without a proper trial and spent three months in a Nationalist prison. The total number of victims of politically motivated murders in Nationalist Spain between 1936 and 1939 is unknown, although recent research puts the figure at 90,194.

In Republican Spain recent estimates put the number of people executed or massacred between 1936 and 1939 at around 50,000. This left-wing reign of terror included the precautionary shooting of 2,000 prisoners near Madrid in November and December 1936, allegedly on the orders of Santiago Carillo Solares, who was responsible for public safety on the Madrid Defence Junta and who later became secretary general of the Spanish Communists. The Catholic clergy suffered particularly harshly at the hands of Republican extremists, who murdered thirteen bishops and more than 6,800 priests, monks, nuns and novices, most of them during the first six weeks of the Civil War and mostly in Catalonia, which was a stronghold of anarchism and anarcho-syndicalism. Here hatred of the Catholic Church was particularly deeply rooted.

In those parts of Spain like Andalusia that were largely made up of vast landed estates, militant anti-clericalism was part and parcel of a radical agrarian revolution: in the wake of the putsch and the arming of the people, day labourers and farmworkers felt that the time had come to wreak vengeance on the landowners who they felt were exploiting them, together with the bourgeoisie and the Church which they regarded as the landowners' closest allies. And they proceeded to exact vengeance in the most primitive and brutal manner by burning down monasteries and churches and by abducting and murdering particularly hated representatives of the old regime. The American writer Ernest Hemingway, who was working in Spain as a reporter, noted in his novel *For Whom the Bell Tolls* how in a small Andalusian pueblo all the middle-class men were driven together with flails and then thrown over a cliff. His account was modelled on events in the town of Ronda, where 512 men and women were killed during the first four weeks of the Civil War.

The CNT and the socialist agricultural workers' trade union, the Federación Nacional de Trabajadores de la Tierra (FNTT), set themselves the task of organizing the revolutionary movement from below, occupying warehouses and silos, distributing food supplies and cereals to the rural population, dispossessing the majority of the larger landowners, including those who had not supported the putsch, and introducing a process of collectivization. During the winter of 1936/7 there were 1,500 legalized agricultural collectives in Republican Spain. By August 1938 this number had risen to over 2,200.

In Catalonia it was the anarchist-syndicalist CNT that was the driving force behind the collectivization programme and for a time the only ruling body. In the matter of Catalonian autonomy it was in agreement with the regional government, which remained in office and which was left increasingly to run the region's finances. By the end of September the CNT was even being represented on the regional council.

In the Basque region, too, regionalism was the common denominator among the most varied social and political forces. Once the Cortes in Madrid had granted the region autonomous status in October 1936 and the leader of the conservative Partido Nacional Vasco (PNV), José Antonio Aguirre, had been elected the first president of the region, his party declared its unequivocal support for the Republic, and although Aguirre's attempts to force through the region's independence led repeatedly to conflict with central government, it also contributed to the fact that the Basque clergy tended on the whole to remain loyal to the Republic.

It was Burgos that became the political centre of the Nationalists and here that a Junta de Defensa Nacional was established under General Miguel Cabanellas on 24 July 1936. And it was in Burgos that General Franco, who on 30 September had had himself proclaimed 'Generalissimo' and commander in chief of all the Nationalist troops, was named head of state on 1 October. On the Republican side, the Socialist Party leader and trade union leader Francisco Largo Caballero replaced the former prime minister, José Giral Pereira, on 4 September. The new Popular Front cabinet was made up of

Liberals, Republicans, Socialists and Communists, who on 4 November, following the Nationalists' march on Madrid, were joined by the anarchists of the CNT under the central control of the Federación Anarquista Iberica (FAI). A former terrorist, Juan García Oliver, became justice minister: only shortly before his appointment he had been defending the murder of clerics and other class enemies as examples of the justice of the people.

Surprising though it may seem at first sight, it was the Communists who together with the bourgeois parties formed the conservative wing of the government. It was entirely in the spirit of Stalin and the Comintern that as far as the Partido Comunista de España, or PCE, was concerned, defence of the Republic against a Fascist attack was infinitely more important than any proletarian revolution and, indeed, more important than any redistribution of wealth. In a letter that they addressed to Largo Caballero on 21 December, Stalin, Voroshilov and Molotov advised the Spanish government to implement measures that would help the peasants, win over the petty bourgeoisie and the bourgeoisie in the towns and cities, guarantee free trade and proscribe all forms of confiscation and dispossession. The Soviet leaders even stressed that for Spain the parliamentary route could be a more effective way of bringing revolution to the country than had been the case in Russia.

The Socialist prime minister replied on 12 January 1937, thanking Moscow for its advice, but adding that not even among simple Republicans was it possible to find any 'enthusiastic champions of parliamentary institutions'.[91] Within the cabinet, Largo Caballero was one of the most outspoken advocates of far-reaching social change, and much the same was true of the anarchist ministers. But the CNT and FAI found themselves in a dilemma from which there seemed to be no way out. By playing a role in government and by helping to disband the soviet-like committees and local militias of rival workers' organizations that had sprung up everywhere in the summer of 1936, they had become complicit in a process aimed at the centralization and militarization of power, making their goal of a society free from domination seem even more remote a prospect and alienating large sections of their supporters to whom this particular brand of Realpolitik had nothing whatever to offer.

By the time that the new government was installed in Madrid, it was clear that neither Britain nor France would side with the Republic in the Spanish Civil War, whereas Franco's Nationalists already enjoyed the support of two other major powers, Italy and Germany. Unlike Berlin, Rome was largely conversant with Franco's plans for revolution, although Mussolini initially hesitated before agreeing to help the rebels on 30 July 1936 by sending twelve aeroplanes from Sardinia to Tetuán. His aim was clear: a Spain ruled by Fascist sympathizers and owing a debt of gratitude to Italy would be a valuable ally in his battle to win strategic control over the Mediterranean and its transformation into a 'mare nostro'. Particularly important in this context was the establishment of an Italian base on the Balearics and perhaps even the islands' annexation.

Franco made contact with Hitler through two members of the NSDAP's overseas organization, who had a chance to meet the Führer on the evening of 25 July in Bayreuth, where he was attending that summer's festival. That very night Hitler agreed to send twenty unarmed Junkers Ju 52 transport machines, with six fighter planes, to Tetuán, an offer that he made without consulting the Foreign Office but after taking soundings with Göring and Blomberg, who were also in Bayreuth. It was these aircraft that helped Franco to transport his army of 35,000 men – mostly Moroccan Muslims – from Spanish Morocco to Spain.

There has been much speculation over Hitler's reasons for helping Franco in late July 1936. One thing is certain: with the establishment of a Popular Front government not only in Paris but in Madrid as well, the Führer felt that his endless warnings about the spread of Communism had been confirmed. If Germany supported Nationalist Spain and if the Nationalists defeated the country's Communists, then Germany had a good chance of gaining an ally in its planned restructuring of Europe. At least as important in Hitler's view was the opportunity to work with Italy in Spain and in that way to drive a wedge between Rome and London. Economic and military considerations were evidently secondary. For Göring as the head of the Luftwaffe, it was important to provide German airmen with an ideal training ground in Spain in case the situation grew more critical in Europe as a whole. Since Göring was also responsible for the current four-year plan, he was bound to be keen to ensure that raw materials such as iron ore and iron pyrites that were crucial to the war effort could be imported from Spain. But on 25 July 1936 these considerations appear not to have played a major role. In order to avoid foreign policy complications, Hitler sought throughout the Spanish Civil War to maintain the appearance of non-intervention and certainly had no wish to compete with Mussolini over which of them would offer Nationalist Spain the greater support.

Starting at the end of 1936, Italy sent between 70,000 and 80,000 soldiers to Spain, while Germany sent around 10,000 pilots, technicians and instructors. It also seems likely that the number of tanks supplied by Italy exceeded the 200 provided by Germany. It was the German Luftwaffe unit of the Condor Legion that launched the three-hour attack on the town of Guernica on 26 April 1937, a town that had quasi-religious associations for the Basque population. The attack resulted in 1,654 deaths, all of them civilians, and 889 injuries. Germany immediately denied any involvement in the atrocity. The Nationalists' military command in Salamanca, which had played a part in planning the attack, claimed that the Basques themselves had set fire to the town in order to blame the Nationalists, but the general public in western democracies refused to be taken in: shrapnel from German bombs revealed the true perpetrators. Posterity has come to associate Guernica with Picasso's famous painting which was exhibited only a few weeks later in the Spanish Republic's pavilion at the Paris World Fair.

Stalin took longer than Mussolini and Hitler to decide to support what was effectively his own side in the Spanish Civil War. In the shorter term he was not interested in seeing the Communists come to power in Madrid but was concerned, rather, to turn Spain into part of an anti-Fascist front that would also include France and, following what he hoped would be the victory of the Labour Party, Great Britain, too. In the longer term, however, Stalin was evidently following a rather different plan: the better the Spanish Communist Party played the part that was allotted to it, the better the prospects for the sort of Communist revolution that had initially not been on the Soviet leader's agenda.

While it is unclear at what point Moscow decided on covert intervention in Spain, it was at the end of September 1936 that a ship laden with weapons left the Crimea for that country. The Soviet Union demanded a high price for its help, for Largo Caballero's government moved much of Spain's remaining gold reserves to Moscow. (The other part of the reserves had already been used to buy weapons from France.) Some 510 tons of gold valued at 1,500 million gold pesetas were handed over to Soviet officials at Cartagena in the second half of October 1936 and turned into hard currency during the fourteen months from early February 1937 to late March 1938, allowing the Spanish government to buy the weapons that it urgently needed.

At least as important as the supply of weapons from the Soviet Union were the International Brigades provided by the Communist International: units of volunteers from Europe and America who were willing to fight on the side of the Spanish Republic. The first units arrived in Spain in early November 1936: some came by sea, others by crossing the Pyrenees. Although Communists ran these units, it was by no means only members of Communist parties who flocked to join these units but left-wing fighters in the broadest sense, ranging from Social Democrats to bourgeois liberals wanting to contribute to the fight against international Fascism. Some independent left-wing writers such as George Orwell and W. H. Auden from Britain and Simone Weil from France preferred to have nothing to do with the International Brigades: Orwell joined a left-wing Communist militia group in Catalonia, while Auden drove ambulances for a Republican unit and Weil fought with an anarchist militia group.

According to one anti-Fascist source, the International Brigades active in Spain in June 1937 included 25,000 fighters from France, 5,000 from Poland, 5,000 from Great Britain and the United States, 5,000 from Germany and Italy, 3,000 from Belgium, 2,000 from the Balkans and 1,000 from Latin America, making 46,000 in total. More cautious estimates speak of 25,000 brigade members. It was almost exclusively Communists who held the leading political and military positions in the International Brigades. They included the French Communist André Marty, who was a member of the Comintern's executive committee and who assumed the role of supreme political controller and instructor; the Italian Luigi Longo; the Hungarian László Rajk; and the Germans Franz Dahlem, Wilhelm Zaisser and Hans Beimler, who was killed in action in

December 1936 while fighting close to Madrid. Among other Communists were the German writers Ludwig Renn, a former frontline officer whose real name was Arnold Vieth von Golssenau, and Gustav Regler, whose experiences in the Spanish Civil War persuaded him to break with Communism. For a short time their number also included the English writer Stephen Spender. Among leading socialists in the International Brigades were Pietro Nenni from Italy and Julius Deutsch, a former leader of the Austrian defence association. Another Austrian was General Emilio Kléber, a man who was already a legend in his own lifetime and whose real name was Lazarus Stern. During the First World War he had been a prisoner in Russia and had converted to Bolshevism, later working in the German Communist Party's illegal military apparatus and, later still, taking on the role of military adviser to the Comintern in China, where he commanded troops in the fighting against the Japanese, before winning military glory in Spain while defending Madrid.

By the time that the first International Brigades arrived in Spain in early November 1936, the Republic's position had deteriorated markedly. The Burgos Junta was formally recognized by Germany and Italy on 7 November. By the end of the year the Spanish Nationalist forces included not only the Spanish Foreign Legion, or Tercio, but also almost 50,000 Moroccans. The officers who had been marked by their experiences in the colonial war with the Rif and who shared the Church's view that the Civil War was a crusade against Communism and a new Reconquista tried to convince the North African mercenaries that they were fighting atheists – the enemies of every religion, including Islam. The Moroccans were also joined by the German pilots of the Condor Legion, by soldiers from Antonio Salazar's authoritarian Portugal, and, increasingly from early 1937 onwards, by soldiers from Mussolini's Italy and by volunteers from the ranks of Eoin O'Duffy's Irish Blueshirts.

The Nationalist troops were by now far more numerous than the *ejército popular* and were certainly better equipped and better disciplined: by November 1936 they had overrun almost half of the country. On 27 September, a symbol of Nationalist resistance, the Alcázar of Toledo, which had been under siege since July, was liberated by Franco's troops. By now large areas of central Spain and Andalusia were under Nationalist control. By the middle of October the front had moved so close to Madrid that the capital seemed about to fall. When Mola gave a press conference in Avila, where he had established his headquarters, and was asked by foreign journalists which of his four columns would overrun the capital, his reply, which was later to become proverbial, was 'The fifth column', by which he meant the Nationalist sympathizers in the city. On 6 November, Largo Caballero's government, expecting the worst, moved its seat of operations to Valencia.

Immediately afterwards the Communists and their Soviet military advisers seized control of the capital. It was the old Bolshevist Jan Karlovich Berzin who was given the task of defending the city. He had advised on preparations for the

'German October' in 1923 and became known in Spain as 'General Grishin'. The Communists worked closely with General José Miajá Menant, the regional commander and the government representative on the Junta for the Organization and Supervision of the Defence of the Capital that had been in place since 6 November. They mobilized most of the proletarian population, including the women, who formed a battalion of their own and who soon saw action on the Segovia Bridge.

The battle for Madrid began on 7 November. The Nationalists fired artillery rounds on the city, while planes dropped incendiary bombs almost without interruption in a deliberate attempt to spread panic among the civilian population. Firefighters were gunned down by machine-gun fire from fighter planes. On the Republican side, the well-disciplined Fifth Regiment distinguished itself in combat: trained by Soviet military instructors and dominated by Communists, it was commanded by the Communist Enrique Líster, a former quarry worker who had been trained in Moscow and who figures as 'Manuel' in André Malraux's novel *L'Espoir*. The first International Brigades joined the fighting on 8 November. Emilio Kléber assumed command of all the Republican troops in the Ciudad Universitaria and the Casa de Campo.

On 12 November, 3,000 armed anarchists under Buonaventura Durruti arrived in Madrid. Durruti was a 'social bandit' with a turbulent terrorist past. He was killed on 21 November, allegedly by a stray bullet fired from the Ciudad Universitaria that was by then under Nationalist control, though it is also possible that he was shot by an anarchist disgruntled at his commanding officer who expected his troops to display an unusual degree of discipline and an exceptional willingness to take risks. By early January 1937 the front had stalled around Madrid – a major triumph for the defenders who thanks to their courage had succeeded in preventing the Nationalists from taking the capital.

The next great success for the Republican forces came in March 1937, when they reported a significant victory over Italian forces who on Mussolini's orders had marched on Sigüenza to the north-east of Madrid, from where they pushed forward to Guadalajara and the capital. They were met by units of the International Brigades, including the Italian Garibaldi Battalion under the Republican Randolfo Pacciardi, and by Spanish militiamen under Enrique Líster and Valentín González, also known as 'El Campesino'. The soldiers defending the Spanish Republic fought Franco's allies not only with weapons but also with extremely cleverly and effectively worded leaflets appealing to their comrades' proletarian sympathies and to feelings of international solidarity. By 18 March the International Brigades had achieved their objective: out of a total of 50,000 men, around 2,000 Italians had been killed and 4,000 wounded. Most of their surviving compatriots turned tail and ran, abandoning war material, weapons and munitions. Several hundred – according to some estimates, more than 1,000 – were taken prisoner and politically 're-educated'.

The French historians Pierre Broué and Émile Témime have described the Battle of Guadalajara in March 1937 not only as a military victory but also as a political triumph that allowed the victors to win over a number of enemy soldiers:

> The victory appeared to be a triumph of international 'anti-Fascism' and was hailed as such by Mikhail Koltsov in his reports for *Pravda*. But 'anti-Fascism' celebrated its final victory here, for the war devoured not only the revolution but also one particular manifestation of it: revolutionary war. War had become an end in itself and now turned on the revolutionary instincts that had lent it the lambent flame of intellectual significance and humanity.[92]

Militarily speaking, the fighting around Guadalajara, although seen by Hemingway – a Republican sympathizer – as among the most decisive battles in world history, did not mark a turning point in the Spanish Civil War. The Nationalists, who had overrun Malaga on 8 February, followed up their setback at Guadalajara by advancing along several fronts. In the north Franco's troops took Bilbao in June 1937 and, in the months that followed, Santander and finally Asturias, with the result that the whole of northern Spain and, with it, several of the country's most important industrial regions, were now under the control of the rebels. Teruel, which the Republicans had won back in December 1937, fell to the Nationalists in February 1938. They launched their offensive in Aragon in March and by August had advanced as far as Vinaroz on the Mediterranean coast, in that way cutting off Catalonia from the rest of Republican Spain. The Battle of the Ebro began in July 1938 and lasted until the end of October, bringing the Republicans their last major territorial gain, and even then it was only of short duration, for by November 1938 their units had been forced to withdraw from the Ebro. A month later the Nationalists took up the fight for Catalonia. From the autumn of 1938 the Republicans were reduced to a defensive position from which they were never able to recover.

Politically speaking, the left began to fall apart in the spring of 1937, while the right grew increasingly unified. In April the Falangists, who had lost their charismatic leader through the execution of José Antonio Primo de Rivera in prison in Alicante on 20 November 1936, joined forces with the Carlists, a union which, far from being voluntary, was foisted upon them by force of circumstances. The combined party was known as the Falange Española Tradicionalista y de las JONS and was led by Franco, its programme dominated by traditionalist and clericalist features, making it authoritarian but not totalitarian. The Falange had never really been a mass movement. The head of the new party, the Caudillo or Generalissimo, was a man from the military and from the old power elites, not a Fascist Führer. Under Franco the reformed Falange undertook important social and propagandist tasks but it had no influence on the country's politics either during the Civil War or afterwards.

When the Civil War began in summer 1936, it was not Fascists and Communists who were the driving forces but anarchists and members of the military. On the political right nothing subsequently changed in this regard, whereas the changes on the left were far-reaching. The political influence of the Partido Comunista de España became much stronger after it joined Largo Caballero's government in September 1936, and the same was true in Catalonia of the newly formed left-wing unity party, the Communist-dominated Partit Socialista Unificat de Catalunya (PSUC), which soon afterwards was invited to join the Council of the Generalitat. The line taken by the PCE and PSUC was mutually agreed with Moscow and aimed entirely at the defence of the Republic, making both parties important factors in guaranteeing law and order in the country and, as such, attractive to the petty bourgeoisie. Within central government the Communists presented themselves as the champions of total freedom of religion and of the restoration of the right to attend church services, a right that had been abolished only in practice, not by law. In this, however, they encountered stiff and successful resistance from the prime minister and the minister of justice, the anarchist Juan García Oliver.

For Largo Caballero the support of the Communists and of their Soviet military advisers was a source of considerable concern, and on 23 April 1937 he dissolved the Madrid Junta, which had been a bastion of authority in the PCE. Soon afterwards he limited the powers of the political army commissioners, all of whom were Communists and whose number included several who were to achieve prominence in the party: Josip Broz Tito, Klement Gottwald, Palmiro Togliatti and, for a time, Walter Ulbricht. In some cases he simply dismissed them from office. The Communists regarded this as a deliberate provocation and responded with a violent campaign against the head of government. One development that made this situation additionally dangerous for the prime minister was the rapprochement between the reformist right wing of his own party, the PSOE, under the navy and aviation minister Indalecio Prieto and the finance minister Juan Negrín, and the PCE. Both of them shared the Communists' view that serious steps in the direction of a socialist society would have to wait until the Fascists were defeated. Largo Caballero and the anarchists, by contrast, wanted to achieve both of these goals simultaneously.

The major clash between the Communists and the forces of social revolution came in May 1937 – not, however, in Madrid, but in Barcelona. In September 1936 the Council of the Generalitat had been joined not only by the PSUC and CNT but also by the Partido Obrero de Unificación Marxista (POUM), whose secretary general, Andrés Nin, became the justice minister. The POUM was a small left-wing Communist party that had emerged from the Izquierda Comunista, whose keen criticisms of Stalinism had initially been inspired by Trotsky only for it to break with him in 1934, after he demanded that it join the Socialist Party and form its left wing. Instead, the Izquierda Comunista joined forces in 1935 with the Catalonian Marxist Workers' and Peasants' Bloc to form the POUM. In Stalin's eyes the POUM remained a Trotskyite party and, in keeping with the latest Soviet linguistic usage, a melting pot for the agents of Fascism. On 16 December 1936, Nin, responding to intense pressure from the Communists, left the Catalonian regional government, prompting *Pravda* to refer the next day to a 'purge of Trotskyites and anarchists' that had been implemented just as energetically in Spain as in the Soviet Union.[93]

On 3 May 1937, members of the Civil Guard acting on the orders of a PSUC politician who was in charge of law and order in the region entered the Barcelona Telephone Exchange that had been occupied by the CNT since July of the previous year. The occupiers fired on them with machine guns from the upper floors. Immediately afterwards workers in the Catalan capital began a general strike not sanctioned by the CNT, surrounding strategically important sites, building barricades and in that way reducing large sections of the city to their control. While the CNT tried to reach an agreement with the Generalitat, the members of a new organization of extreme anarchists, the Amigos de Durruti, called on the anarchist youth movement Juventud Libertaria and the POUM to take up arms against the enemy within. It is unclear if agents provocateurs from the Franco regime had a hand in this development, although such claims were being voiced even at the time.

The fighting in Barcelona lasted for five days: members of the Civil Guard and Communists fired at the anarchists, and the anarchists fired back. Contemporary estimates speak of between 400 and 500 fatalities and 1,000 injuries. The central government in Valencia sent police reinforcements and three warships to Barcelona on 6 May, and their presence helped to encourage both sides to respond to the CNT's urgent appeals to end the fighting, with the result that something approaching a state of order was restored on 8 May.

As far as the armed workers were concerned, this regional civil war within the wider context of the Spanish Civil War was the expression of a spontaneous protest on the part of the anarchist masses at the national policies of the workers' organizations, including – up to a point – the CNT. The POUM did what it could to avoid an open break with the CNT and after 6 May sought to adopt a conciliatory stance by limiting itself to calling on the workers not to leave the barricades. But the PSUC, which was no longer represented in the reconstituted Generalitat, and the PCE finally felt that the time had come to deal with the 'Trotskyites'. The Communist press spoke of the members of the POUM as 'crypto-Fascists' and as 'Franco's fifth column'.

On 15 May two Communist members of the central government, the education minister Jesús Hernández and the agriculture minister Uribe Galdeano, demanded a ban on the POUM. Although Largo Caballero refused to meet their demands, only the anarchists backed him up. Most of the Socialists, including Indalecio Prieto and Juan Negrín Lopez, and the bourgeois Republicans sided with the Communists and then flounced out of the debate, precipitating a government crisis that ended with Largo Caballero's resignation on 17 May and with the appointment of the finance minister, Juan Negrín Lopez, as his replacement. A pragmatist who held a chair in physiology, Negrín was a Socialist who was also the Communists' preferred candidate: they all felt that victory over the 'Fascists' should be given absolute priority over all other objectives. The anarchists refused to join the new cabinet. Since a right-wing Socialist took over as minister of war – a post formerly held by Largo Caballero in addition to the premiership – and since Negrín had no intention of allowing himself to be used by the Communists and the Soviet Union, it is difficult to describe the PCE as the winner in this crisis.

But Negrín was either unable or unwilling to prevent the suppression of the POUM. The party newspaper, La Batalla, was banned at the end of May, and in the middle of June the members of the party's executive committee, including Nin, were arrested. The indictment of 11 June referred specifically to the party's attempt to engineer the violent overthrow of the Republic and its democratic government and to establish a dictatorship of the proletariat in its place. The influence of the Spanish Communists' Soviet contacts was particularly evident in the claim that in the context of the Moscow show trials, the POUM had attacked the Soviet justice system and maintained links with international Trotskyite organizations whose actions 'on the soil of a friendly power' proved beyond doubt that they were in the pay of the Fascists.[94]

The police were now largely under the control of the PCE and in the course of their enquiries produced counterfeit documents to show that Nin was a Fascist agent, although by the time that the case came to court in October 1938, these charges had already been dropped. But he remained accused of attempting to overthrow the existing order. Five leading officials of the POUM were sentenced to terms of imprisonment ranging from eleven to fifteen years, and the POUM and its youth organization, the Juventud Comunista Ibérica, were banned. Although the case did not produce the sort of Muscovite show trial that the Communists had hoped for, it none the less allowed the PCE to achieve its principal aim.

Nin did not live to see the trial. His name was no longer included in the list of the POUM's indicted officials drawn up by the Ministry of Justice on 29 June 1937. Immediately after his arrest he had been taken to a 'private' prison run by the Communist Cheka, a branch of the Soviet NKVD. On 4 August the government was forced to admit that he had been taken to a special prison from where he had 'disappeared'. The episode caused a furore that extended far beyond Spain's borders and triggered international protests. By early August the New York Times was reporting that Nin's body had been found on the outskirts of the capital. He had been abducted by agents of the Soviet NKVD, who were a ubiquitous presence in Republican Spain, after which he was interrogated and tortured, but he had steadfastly refused to confess to his alleged crimes. He had to pay a high price for maintaining his position. German members of the International Brigades claimed it was the Gestapo that had sprung him from prison at Alcalá, whereupon he was thrown into a locked car and murdered. He was only one of the NKVD's many victims, albeit the most famous.

Nothing undermined the sympathy of left-wing and liberal Europeans for the Spanish Republic as much as the countless murders committed by agents of the Soviet secret services against alleged Trotskyites in the POUM. (It was only later that it became clear that Communist leaders such as Emilio Kléber, who had been ordered back to the Soviet Union in 1937, were also victims of Stalin's reign of terror.) The POUM maintained close links with a number of left-wing socialist parties in Europe, including the Independent Labour Party in Great Britain and the German Socialist Workers' Party, which was formed in early October following a rift with the German Social Democrats. Among the former's sympathizers was George Orwell, who has left a vivid account of the bloody fighting in Barcelona in May 1937 in his book *Homage to Catalonia*, which was first published in London the following April.

At the beginning of March 1937 the German Socialist Workers' Party sent Willy Brandt to Barcelona. Brandt had been born Herbert Frahm in Lübeck in 1913 and since April 1933 had been working for his party in Norway. In his reports he criticized the POUM's policies as ultra-left and sectarian, hence largely flawed, but he reproached the Spanish Communist Party for undermining morale in the war on Fascism by slandering its proletarian opponents:

> The Communist Party is currently the most decisive political force in anti-Fascist Spain. It may not run the government, but it still controls most of the state apparatus. The country's army officers are for the most part organized within it, and the police are largely in its hands. Spain is in the process of turning into a Communist Party dictatorship. We are on the way, if not to a Communist Spain, then at least to a Communist Party Spain.[95]

This weakening of the position of the political left was exploited by the right. When, in May 1937, the British foreign secretary, Anthony Eden, adopted an initiative put forward by the Spanish president, Manuel Azaña y Diaz, and proposed a truce between the various parties involved in the Civil War, allowing first all foreign 'volunteers' to withdraw and then for negotiations for a peace treaty to take place, he received the support of the Vatican but was flatly turned down by Franco, who insisted on the unconditional surrender of all the Republican forces. By the summer of 1937 Franco's position in the Nationalist camp was stronger than ever. A possible rival, General Mola, had been killed in a plane crash on 3 June, while the Generalissimo's regime was strengthened nationally and internationally by the fact that on 31 July 1937 the country's Catholic bishops, writing to bishops all around the world, described as just and necessary the struggle to topple the Republican government. On 28 August the Vatican recognized the authorities in Burgos as Spain's official government.

Beginning in August 1937, Germany and Italy increased their naval patrols in an attempt to prevent the Soviet Union from helping the Republic, but their efforts were undermined by the French, who from October 1937 turned a blind eye to arms smuggling across the Pyrenees, which had been closed as a border since August 1936. In March 1938 Léon Blum's second cabinet even opened up the border to arms traffic, only for Daladier's government to bow to pressure from London and reverse this measure in July 1938. Since Germany and Italy continued to increase their aid, the Nationalists' military advantage went on growing in consequence. Franco formed his first government on 1 February 1938 and included in it five military figures as well as civilian ministers. His brother-in-law, Ramón Serrano Suñer, who had united the Falangists and the traditionalists on the Caudillo's instructions and created a new party of unity, took over the portfolios of minister of the interior and minister for propaganda and the press. The government's main challenge was to lay the foundations for the authoritarian system that was to characterize the whole of Spain following the right-wing victory in the country's civil war.

The Republican government had moved its seat of power from Valencia to Barcelona on 31 October 1937, believing that it was safer there. On 5 April 1938, ten days before Franco's troops reached the Mediterranean at Vinaroz, the minister of war, Indalecio Prieto, who regarded victory as an increasingly unlikely prospect, was dismissed from the cabinet at the urging of the Communists. Negrín, who refused to share his pessimism, took over his former colleague's portfolio. Since the central government was cut off from the bulk of Republican Spain in the centre and south-east of the country, it became more dependent than ever on the military, and in the southern zone had no choice but to abandon its political and military powers to General José Miajá Menant. Even so, Negrín banked on the survival of the Republic, believing that Germany's aggression towards Czechoslovakia would lead to a full-scale European war and ultimately save the Spanish Republic.

The Anglo-French policy of appeasement that culminated in the Munich Agreement of 30 September 1938 destroyed these calculations, but it also had repercussions for the Republic's principal ally, the Soviet Union: from that point onwards, Stalin felt that an alliance with Great Britain and France against Hitler was scarcely achievable any longer, although it is unclear whether he had already decided at this stage that he would try to work together with his arch-enemy in Berlin. Whatever the answer, there is no doubt that he was keen to reduce as far as possible his increasingly risky commitment to Spain. From his point of view, the International Brigades had completed their task, for in most of them Spaniards far outnumbered foreigners; there were now sufficient well-trained airmen; and the withdrawal of foreign volunteers would be relatively easy to accept, a position shared by Negrín. On 1 October, at the suggestion of the Spanish Republic, the League of Nations assumed the task of overseeing the withdrawal of all volunteers from Spain. The International Brigades held a final march-past in Barcelona on 15 November, and the following day the Battle of the Ebro came to an end with the retreat of the Republicans to the left bank of the river.

The final phase of the Spanish Civil War began in December 1938, when the Nationalists invaded Catalonia. By 26 January 1939 Barcelona had fallen, practically without a struggle. On 7 February President Azaña fled to France, together with Negrín's government. Within two days all resistance had ended in Catalonia. Negrín returned to Spain on 10 February and on the 24th travelled to Madrid. Four days later Azaña announced that he was standing down as president after Britain and France had recognized Franco's government on the 27th.

Negrín's insistence on continuing a war that was now completely hopeless triggered a putsch, and on 5 March a junta headed by General Sigismondo Casado, who had previously been loyal to the Republic, and by the moderate Socialist Julián Besteiro, the country's former ambassador in London, assumed the business of government and extended an offer of peace to Franco's government in Burgos. A Communist divisional commander began to march on Madrid, but the other army commanders refused to lend him their support. The very next day Negrín again fled the country, this time for good. He was accompanied by leading Communists and by members of his own government. A four-day civil war – a war within a war – began in Madrid on 7 March, when a Communist army commander turned on Casado and called for resistance to the junta. Casado was able to maintain his position, but the negotiations with Franco's government that were conducted by representatives of the Caudillo's 'Fifth Column' in Madrid produced no results acceptable to the junta. Meanwhile the Nationalist troops had continued to advance, and on 28 March, the day after the government in Burgos had announced that it was joining the anti-Comintern pact, they occupied Madrid. Alicante, which had previously transferred its allegiance to Casado, fell on 31 March. The Spanish Civil War was over by 1 April 1939.

Writers cannot agree on the number of people killed during the fighting as a result of the atrocities committed by both sides in the conflict, estimates ranging from 270,000 to 500,000, while the number of soldiers who fell in battle is put at between 100,000 and 300,000. Nor was the end of the Civil War the end of the reign of terror. In 1939 Gonzalo de Aguilera, Franco's press officer, told Charles Foltz, the correspondent of the Associated Press, that 'it's our program, you understand, to exterminate a third of the male population of Spain. That will clean up the country.'[96]

Aguilera's remark had deep historical roots in the ideal of the *limpieza de sangre*, the purity of blood, which had motivated the persecutors of the Jews who had converted to Christianity in the late fifteenth and sixteenth centuries. Men like Aguilera believed that it was their historical task to purge Spanish society of those whose thinking was 'wrong', by which they invariably meant left-wing.

The project was never fully realized, but the mass executions that took place wherever the Nationalists drove out the Republicans were almost unprecedented in scale. According to British estimates, there were at least 10,000 executions in the first five months after the end of the war. Mere membership of a left-wing organization was often enough for the individual in question to be denounced, charged, sentenced and executed. Recent research suggests that the total number of victims of Nationalist terror between 1936 and 1950 is in the order of 150,000, a number that would undoubtedly have been much higher if 441,000 Spaniards had not succeeded in crossing the Spanish border by April 1939 and escaping to France across the Pyrenees. Since many of them returned to Spain as a result of the catastrophic conditions in the first improvised reception centres, the number of those who emigrated for good was much lower and is believed to have been between 160,000 and 300,000.

Of the refugees who settled abroad – mostly in France but also in Mexico – many fought for the Allies during the Second World War or were active in the French Resistance. Some 15,000 were taken to German concentration camps following the occupation of France, and only half of them survived. Largo Caballero was one of them. He died in Paris in 1946, a year after he was liberated. Other Spanish politicians who had once been prominent and who included Lluis Companys, the former president of the Catalan Generalitat and Julián Zugazagoitia, the Socialist minister of the interior, were extradited to Spain, where they were executed. Negrín was granted asylum in Great Britain.

Of the Communist fighters from eastern central Europe and the Soviet Union, many were victims of Stalin's purges. Kléber probably died in 1939, whereas others were killed in the wake of the Budapest show trial of László Rajk in 1949, a trial that ended with his execution. Others who were liquidated include Marcel Rosenberg, the Soviet ambassador during Largo Caballero's years in power, General Jan Bersin, who coordinated the defence of Madrid, and Mikhail Koltsov, *Pravda*'s Spanish correspondent, who was also active as a political adviser and military organizer. The leader of the Spanish militia, Valentín González ('El Campesino'), was twice able to escape from the Soviet Union, on the second occasion from the Gulag camp at Vorkuta. Among those who survived their years in exile were La Pasionaria, Enrique Líster and Santiago Carillo, who played an important role as secretary general of the Spanish Communists after Franco's death in 1975 and was one of the founders of Eurocommunism.

Many of the leading Spanish artists and intellectuals remained in exile: they include the painter Pablo Picasso, who had of course been living in Paris since 1906; the film director Luis Buñuel; and the historian Salvador de Madariaga. The philosopher José Ortega y Gasset left Spain in 1936 and did not return until 1946. The poet Antonio Machado died shortly after emigrating in July 1939 to the French commune of Collioure close to the border with Spain.

Of the supporters of the Republic who were unable or unwilling to leave Spain, around 270,000 were sentenced to varying terms of imprisonment, while well over 100,000 were sent to labour camps or 'labour battalions', ostensibly with the aim of re-educating them. They were forced to work on reconstruction projects, including road-building, or else they were sent to work in the mercury mines at Almadín, where the conditions were particularly inhuman and unhealthy. Their release from custody or from labour camps did not mean a return to normality, however, but usually ended in exile or in their having to report to the police on a daily basis. Republicans were effectively excluded from public office. According to a decree of August 1939, 80 per cent of all vacant positions had to be offered to those who had fought on the side of the Nationalists or who had been persecuted by Popular Front governments. Many Republican supporters were fined or dispossessed; and 'Red' parents were often denied the right to raise their own children: in 1942, for example, some 9,000 children were being raised by the state.

The social changes introduced by the Republicans failed to survive the Nationalists' victory, and this was as true of agricultural and industrial collectives as it was of the secularization of schools, the full legal equality of women, the provisions granting greater autonomy to Catalonia and the Basque region and, of course, the changes in the political complexion of those working in administration and in the judiciary, the police and the military. The Fuero del Trabajo (Basic Labour Law) that was enacted by the Burgos government in March 1938 and that came into force throughout Spain in April 1939 went well beyond its model, the Italian Carta del Lavoro of 1927, and created state-controlled, uniform, hierarchical syndicates of employers and employees. The main positions within these national syndicates had been taken by Falangists – members of the only party that was acknowledged to exist.

Not until July 1942, three years after the end of the Civil War, was a law enacted that dealt with the formation of the Cortes, which was to be made up of elected members and professional deputies, including ministers, high-ranking officials from the Falange's national councils and from the national syndicate and individuals deemed particularly worthy by the head of state. For the present the question as to the form of state that Spain would be was left unresolved. Not even the charter of July 1945 shed any light on the matter, for all that it resembled a constitution of sorts. In July 1947, following a referendum, Spain was declared a monarchy, although this was to have practical consequences only once the head of state had completed his term of office. It was the prerogative of the Caudillo of Spain and of the Crusade, and of the Generalissimo of the Spanish Armed Forces, Don Francisco Franco Bahamonde, to propose to the Cortes the name of the person he wanted to succeed him, a suggestion he could put forward at whatever point he liked.

By the end of the Civil War, Spain lay in economic ruin. Most of the production plants had been destroyed, and by 1940 the national income had fallen to its 1914 level. Between 1935 and 1939 industrial production fell by 31 per cent, agricultural production by around 21 per cent, and the average per capita income by 28.3 per cent. Since the victors were determined to savour their triumph to the full, the country remained deeply divided. The regime that had total control of the country after April 1939 was authoritarian, reactionary and tainted by clericalism, a military dictatorship and a police state. But it was neither totalitarian nor Fascist. For that, it lacked the ideological and social dynamism that characterized the regimes of both Hitler and Mussolini.

No other contemporary observer has left such a succinct and compelling analysis of the specific features of Spain in the 1930s as Franz Borkenau, who was born in Vienna in 1900 and left Germany in 1933. A former Communist, he visited Spain in the summer of 1936 and again in the spring of 1937 and published an account of his experiences in his book *The Spanish Cockpit*, which was published in London in 1937. According to Borkenau, the Spanish right was far too dependent on the Church and army to be able to achieve the sort of modernization that the Fascist dictatorships of the time had done in terms of greater coordination and efficiency. But nor was the Spanish left a force for modernization:

> The history of the Spanish civil war, as far as the Left camp is concerned, is the history of the spontaneous resistance of the masses against two things: on the one hand against the revolt of clergy and army, and on the other hand against the necessity to beat down this revolt with modern means of warfare and organization. The masses wanted to fight and did fight heroi-cally, but they wanted it to be a fight in the old guerilla [*sic*] manner of 1707 and 1808, a rising from village to village, from town to town, against the threat of tyranny. That it could not be.[97]

In Borkenau's view both the Spanish workers' movement and the Spanish left in general 'had been able to *fight*' but were 'not able to organize an *efficient* fight'.[98] By analogy, this also applied to the right-wing camp.

> Had the Spanish revolution met Franco only, it would probably have evolved a superiority over him of the same type as that evolved by the revolution-aries in France and Britain. But here the revolution met, not its own reac-tionary adversaries, but the strongest military powers in the world.[99]

As a result, the Republic was left at the mercy of the very power that had offered to help it: the Soviet Union. But the Soviet Union was no revolutionary force in Spain, for it was convinced that a revolution could not be allowed to take place in the Iberian peninsula. 'On the battle-field of central Spain, to-day, the Comintern and the Faschintern are meeting in their first military battle; the course of history has involved the Spaniards, but the Spaniards are only auxiliaries.'[100]

Two years before the end of the Spanish Civil War, Borkenau came to the conclusion that

> whatever the final result of the armed fight may be, Spain will not emerge out of it as a genuinely Europeanized country, be it in the fascist, the liberal-democratic or the communist sense. It will remain what it was, a country whose evolution has been arrested at the end of the seventeenth century, which has since displayed an enormous amount of resistance to foreign intrusion, but no capacity for rejuvenation. There may be, in the end, a régime claiming to be liberal-democratic or claiming to be fascist; in reality, it will be something profoundly different from what these names designate in Europe.[101]

It is a judgement that pointedly sums up the Spanish dilemma.

A Model for Germany: The Anti-Semitic Policies of Fascist Italy

For one country, active involvement in the Spanish Civil War resulted in an economic and financial burden that was to prove almost intolerable: Italy. In 1936–7 public spending was nearly twice as high as it had been in 1934–5: 40.9 million lire compared with 20.9 million. Over the same period the national budgetary deficit had risen almost eightfold, from 2.1 million lire to 16.2 million. The cost of living rose by 20 per cent in 1937 in the wake of a marked devaluation of the lira the previous year.

Mussolini's support for Franco led to his increasing dependence on Hitler. Germany had long been Italy's principal trading partner, while trade with Britain and France continued to fall. By the end of the 1930s even the United States had to settle for second place after Germany as the main recipient of Italian exports, and the same was true of Italian imports. By 1935 Italy was already importing more than half its coal from Germany, and by 1940 Germany had a virtual monopoly in this field.

Economic dependence went hand in hand with an ideological rapprochement, a rapprochement that was only to be expected, given the many points of contact between Italian Fascism and German National Socialism. Only the countries' differences in the area of foreign policy had made such a development difficult at least up to the outbreak of the war in Abyssinia. The Spanish Civil War brought Berlin and Rome closer together than ever. This was the period when the two countries gradually came to hold very similar views in a field in which Italian Fascists and German National Socialists had previously been clearly differentiated, namely, racist ideology and especially anti-Semitism. It was not that Germany needed to force Italy to emulate it, for all of Fascist Italy's anti-Jewish measures were undertaken on its own initiative.

Within the Fascist Party there was a radically anti-Semitic faction associated with Roberto Farinacci, who was the party's secretary general in 1925–6. Even at this time the party was already stirring up hatred of the Jews. The fact that Jews were active in anti-Fascist organizations abroad and in the anti-Fascist Resistance – they included the brothers Nello and Carlo Rosselli, who were murdered in France in 1937 – led to the first official anti-Semitic campaign in 1934. Mussolini was never entirely free from anti-Jewish prejudices but nor did he have any misgivings about promoting Jews in the Fascist movement and entrusting them with government appointments. Not until the end of the 1920s did his attitude start to harden. Thereafter he suspected Jews of being behind every setback to his regime, especially when those setbacks came from western democracies and from the League of Nations.

It was hard to whip up mass hysteria against the Jews in Italy not least because in the 1920s there were no more than 48,000 Jews in the country as a whole, a number that included 8,500 Jews who were not from Italy at all. By 1931 the total number was around 50,000. In short, Jews made up only 1.1 per cent of the Italian population. The largest Jewish communities were in Rome, Milan and Trieste. Their situation deteriorated in the wake of the Lateran Treaties of 1920, for although they remained Italian citizens, the promotion of Catholicism as the state religion meant that from then on Jews were seen as members of those religious communities that were merely tolerated by the state, adding to the pressure on Jewish students to attend classes in Roman Catholicism.

But it was the war in Abyssinia that caused the country to lurch much further in the direction of open racism. The tendency to think in terms of a racial *superiorità* was traditionally directed in the main at Slavs and Africans and received much support from the colonial war in North Africa, involving, as it did, discrimination not only against individuals with a darker skin colour but, more generally, against those who were Italian only in a legal sense but who did not belong to the *razza italiana*. First and foremost, these people were Jewish. As the historian Hans Woller has written,

> The rabid racism that had its most powerful roots in the colonies was combined with a declaration of war on the lurking bourgeois spirit that everywhere had an inhibiting influence, with the Jews inevitably coming to the centre of attention here: they were regarded as the embodiment of the complacently bourgeois mentality that was now under permanent attack and were said to destroy the picture of national and racial homogeneity that was so dear to Mussolini's heart. If the Jews were bullied and deprived of their rights, it was reckoned that the bourgeoisie, the monarchy and the Vatican could all be threatened with a similar fate if they opposed the Fascists' plans for the country's reorganization.

The progressive exclusion of the Jews was part of an ongoing process of radicalization that Woller rightly sees as one of the basic tenets of Fascism:

> Every form of moderation meant a threat, and every period of stasis could
> lead to the loss of popular support in society, support that could be guaran-
> teed only by constant mobilization and agitation and by a kind of permanent
> state of emergency. The fact that Mussolini had to obey this fundamental law
> just as surely as did Hitler and the leaders of smaller Fascist movements that
> would never have come to power on their own merits alone will not have
> troubled him any further. Nothing was further from his purpose than to
> stand still and rest on the laurels of his Fascist revolution, for that revolution
> was, much to his own dismay, far from having been completed.[102]

It was no accident, therefore, that the systematic discrimination against the
Jews that began in the autumn of 1938 on the model of Germany's Nuremberg
Laws coincided with a violent campaign against the bourgeoisie that was
organized by the party secretary Achille Starace. From now on the bourgeoisie
stood accused of placing private profit above the national cause. Mussolini's
first call for greater vigilance vis-à-vis the Jews dates from February 1938 and
demanded that at universities, in administration, in the free economy and in
the cultural life of the nation the part played by Jews should be reduced to the
point where it reflected their actual percentage within the population as a
whole. A *Manifesto degli scienziati razzisti* published in July and signed by the
Duce categorically excluded Jews from the *razza italiana*.

There followed a whole series of measures that had a radical impact on the
daily lives of Italian Jews. Jewish pupils and teachers had to leave Italian schools.
Foreign Jews living in Italy were no longer recognized as Italian citizens and
had to leave the country within six months. In October 1938 the Gran Consiglio
del Fascismo issued a Declaration on Race in which Jews were defined as
persons who had a Jewish father and a Jewish mother: religion played no part
in this, becoming important only in the case of the children of a mixed
marriage. If the child was baptized, he or she was deemed Italian but was otherwise classified as Jewish. Unlike in Germany, there were no half-, quarter- and
eighth-Jews according to this taxonomy.

Provisions designed to protect the Italian race – Provvedimenti per la
Difesa della Razza Italiana – were passed on 17 November 1938, a week after
the great Crystal Night pogrom in Germany. They brought together all existing
anti-Jewish legislation and added a number of new discriminatory measures of
their own. From now on Jews were allowed to marry only Jews; existing mixed
marriages had to be annulled; Jews were prevented from working in the armed
forces or for the civil service; and they could not be members of the Partito
Nazionale Fascista. There were also drastic limits placed on their economic

activities: Jews were no longer allowed to run larger firms and could no longer own estates covering an area of more than fifty hectares.

There were exceptions for those Jews who had served Italy and Fascism, and yet even these 'privileged' individuals were barred from holding public office, from becoming members of the armed forces and from joining the Fascist Party. Many Jews left the country. One of the most famous of them was the physicist Enrico Fermi, who settled in the United States and played a significant role in the research that led to the production of the first atom bomb. The anti-Jewish measures undertaken by the state were far from popular, but nor was there a broadly based protest movement. The Catholic Church merely signalled its solidarity with those Jews who had converted to Catholicism.

In the matter of racism, Fascist Italy had drawn closer to National Socialist Germany entirely on its own initiative and in certain respects, including the question of the annulment of mixed marriages, it had even outdone the Germans. It seemed as if Hitler could be satisfied with his tractable Axis partner who had once been his inspiration. On 9 May 1938 he paid a state visit to Rome and was acclaimed alongside Mussolini. Both men seized the opportunity to announce their desire to continue aligning their countries' domestic and foreign policies.

In April 1939, barely a year later, Italian troops overran Albania, an attempt on Mussolini's part to emulate Hitler, who the previous month had invaded *Resttschechei* – literally, the 'remainder of Czechia', namely, those parts of Czechoslovakia annexed on 15/16 March as the Protectorate of Bohemia and Moravia. In both cases, the other partner in the Axis learnt of the operations only once they were already under way. By the spring of 1939 the Berlin–Rome Axis was best described as a 'brutal friendship' – the term was first used by the British historian F. W. Deakin in his book about the wartime alliance between National Socialist Germany and Fascist Italy, *Brutal Friendship* (1962).

Neighbours at Risk: Czechoslovakia, Poland and the Third Reich 1935–8

Relations between Germany and Czechoslovakia had been tense since 1935, and by the spring of 1938 they were also casting a shadow over Spain. In May 1935 Prague signed a mutual assistance pact with the Soviet Union that was intended to complement the treaties it had already signed with Romania and Yugoslavia in 1920–21 within the framework of the Little Entente and the friendship and alliance treaty with France in 1924. The pact also tied Soviet help to simultaneous support from France. Although it was directed against Germany, it did not stop Hitler from putting out feelers in November 1936 to see if Edvard Beneš, who had replaced Tomáš Masaryk on 18 December 1935 as the Czech president, might be interested in signing a non-aggression pact with Germany. In the event, this initiative was not pursued by Berlin, in spite of Beneš's positive reaction to it.

In a secret discussion on 5 November 1937 that was minuted by Friedrich Hoßbach, Hitler was already talking about 'acting against Czechoslovakia': the time for such action would come when the internal weakness of France and of the French army made this move possible or France became involved in a war with some other power. Hitler calculated that by incorporating Czechoslovakia and Austria into the German Reich, he would be able to provide food for an additional five or six million people and ease the burden on Germany both militarily and politically. On 5 November 1937 there was no more than a passing reference to 'German values in Czechoslovakia', Hitler being concerned not with the Sudeten Germans' right of self-determination but with expanding the Lebensraum of the Germans.[103]

In the elections to the Czech parliament in May 1935 Konrad Henlein's Sudeten German Party, or SdP, received two-thirds of all the German votes, winning 15.2 per cent of the total and becoming the biggest party in the country, bigger even than the Agrarians on 14.3 per cent, followed by the Social Democrats on 12.6 per cent and the Communists on 10.3 per cent. At this date in its history the SdP was still a moderate party. Henlein had distanced himself from the National Socialists in the autumn of 1934 and refused to redraw the country's borders. Only after its election successes did the SdP forge any closer links with Berlin. Both before and after the elections the party's public demands were aimed at greater autonomy, not the secession of the region. In a lecture that he delivered at Chatham House in London in December 1935, Henlein attacked both pan-Slavism and pan-Germanism, declaring the formation of national states in the eastern corner of central Europe to be impossible.

By 19 November 1937 Henlein had changed his tack completely, arguing in his *Report to the Führer and Reich Chancellor on Current Questions of German Policy in the Czechoslovak Republic* that the SdP must 'disguise its profession of faith in National Socialism and present it as a philosophy and as a political principle'. As a political party operating within the democratic and parliamentary system that was currently in force in Czechoslovakia, it must use democratic language and democratic and parliamentary methods. But it had now become 'senseless in terms of Realpolitik to support the idea of autonomy in the Sudeten region because this region has been turned into a concrete wall and enceinte of the Czechoslovak state'.[104] In the course of further lecture tours of England that Henlein undertook in July 1936, October 1937 and May 1938, his hosts, including Winston Churchill, were assured that the exact opposite was the case. On each occasion he gave his word as a gentleman that he had received no instructions from Berlin and that he was striving to achieve a solution in Czechoslovakia that would give the Sudeten Germans greater autonomy. His assurance was welcomed by the majority of British Conservatives, but not by Churchill himself.

The government in Prague, which had been led by the Slovak Agrarian politician Milan Hodža since November 1935, included members of the German 'activist' parties, namely, the Social Democrats and the Agrarian

League. In July 1936 they were joined by the Christian Socialists. On 18 February 1937 Hodža signed an agreement with all three parties in which he held out the promise of decentralization in the sense of economic and administrative regionalism but explicitly ruled out the whole notion of political autonomy. He also promised the activist parties – who represented only a third of Sudeten Germans – more government jobs for Germans and higher state subsidies for crisis-hit areas of the country. In reality little changed in Czechoslovak politics. For Beneš and most leading politicians in Prague the Czechoslovak Republic remained the 'National State of the Czechoslovak Nation' that had been created at the end of 1918. Ethnic minorities enjoyed greater political freedom and political influence in Czechoslovakia than in any of the other states in eastern central and south-east Europe that had been formed or reconstituted in 1918. But in the country's own view of itself, there was no room for nationalists other than those of the 'Czechoslovak nation'.

Among the active opponents of this state ideology were not only the Sudeten German Party but also the Slovak People's Party associated with Father Andrej Hlinka, with whom Henlein developed a closer working relationship in February 1938. A conversation between Henlein and Hodža in September 1937, at which the former had demanded the immediate introduction of self-rule for the German-speaking areas, produced no results. On 14 November 1937 serious clashes broke out in Teplitz (Teplice) between Henlein's supporters and the police, leading to the arrest of an SdP deputy who had delivered a particularly incendiary speech and resulting in a further worsening of relations between the government in Prague and the majority of Sudeten Germans, a development observed with marked satisfaction in Berlin.

The Czechoslovak Republic's fourth-largest party, the Czech Communist Party, had always been bitterly opposed to the government. Insofar as every cabinet since 1929 had included the emphatically reformist Social Democrats, there was never any likelihood that a popular front would be formed in Czechoslovakia. But the Czech-Soviet mutual assistance pact of 1935 and the Comintern's new general policy forced Stalin's followers in Prague to undertake certain tactical manoeuvres of their own under their leader Klement Gottwald and to support the government's official foreign policy at least to the extent that this policy affected the terms of the pact with the Soviet Union.

There was a further need for this policy shift in that Stalin was by the mid-1930s attaching extraordinarily high importance to Czechoslovakia's strategic significance in view of its geographical position and its alliance with France. But the Czech Communist Party's new line could also accommodate the most violent threats to the government. Speaking in the lower house on 22 April 1936, the Communist deputy Bohumír Šmeral declared that if the bourgeoisie was incapable of retaining the present conception of an alliance with the Soviet Union, then it was in the interest of all nationalities within the state 'to bring about a change in the political balance within this country of ours'.[105]

Czechoslovakia was not only the one state in east central Europe whose democratic system survived the world economic crisis; it was also the most highly developed industrial state in this part of the Continent. With the exception of 1932, its trade balance was invariably in the black, as was its balance of payments, the only exceptions here being the three years 1932, 1933 and 1936. The consumer goods industries that for the most part produced for the export market suffered badly as a result of the depression in the agricultural countries in east central and south-east Europe. (This had a particularly serious impact on the German-speaking regions, where unemployment was substantially higher than the national average.) The economic historian Alice Teichova has described as follows the repercussions of the great crisis for Czechoslovakia:

In comparison to 1929 the Czechoslovak economy had a distinctly more autarkic character. Its foreign trade remained below the level reached in 1929, whereas its industrial production came close to returning to its earlier level. At a time when it was facing a great military threat, this necessarily exacerbated the country's situation in terms of the world economy and contributed to its political weakness.[106]

Poland was even more badly hit by the world economic crisis than Czechoslovakia. There had been a brief period of economic growth in the late 1920s, which the colonels' regime interpreted as the successful outcome of the policy of *sanacja* (cleansing) introduced in the wake of Piłsudski's military putsch in May 1926, but this came to an end in 1930. If we take 1929 as the base year, then the index of industrial production fell, dropping from 100 to 69 in 1931 and to 54 in 1932. By 1932 shares on the Warsaw stock exchange were trading at only 20 per cent of their 1928 value. During the same period agricultural prices fell by around two-thirds. Even as late as 1935 a farmer was receiving on average only a third of what he had earned in 1928. According to the historian Włodzimierz Borodziej, 'Whereas the great crisis in the towns and cities recalled conditions in Germany and America, in the country it assumed the proportions of a catastrophe affecting every aspect of civilization.'[107]

Politically, too, the years of the world economic crisis were a turbulent time for Poland. In 1929 a group of radical Ukrainian nationalists formed the Organizacija Ukrajinskih Nacjonalista (OUN) that had no scruples about resorting to armed terror. On 15 June 1934 they murdered the minister of the interior, Bronisław Pieracki, in the very heart of Warsaw. That same year a concentration camp was built at Bareza Kartuska on the orders of the country's president, Ignacy Mościcki. Anyone suspected of criminal activities by the local authorities could be sent there without trial for up to six months. The first prisoners were right-wing extremists from the Obóz Naradowo-Radikalny (ONR) who were falsely accused of murdering Pieracki. On 14 September 1934 the country's foreign minister, Józef Beck, informed the League of Nations that he was terminating the treaty protecting minorities on the grounds that there was no equivalent law that applied to Europe as a whole.

Ever since Piłsudski's military putsch of 1926, Poland's government had been a provisional one. Legally speaking, the parliamentary and democratic constitution of March 1921 which had been modelled on that of the Third French Republic remained in force, but it had in fact been largely overtaken by events. After Piłsudski resigned as prime minister for a second time at the end of November 1930, the government was run almost entirely by army officers: seven of the country's eight prime ministers between 1931 and 1939, together with fifteen ministers and fifteen regional voivodes, hailed from the army, many of them holding the rank of colonel. Piłsudski, the regime's 'strong man', remained the minister of war and the general inspector of the armed forces.

Starting in March 1931, a special committee of the Sejm worked on drawing up a new authoritarian constitution intended to provide the dictatorship with a solid legal framework. The result was the 'April Constitution' of 1935, which was geared entirely to installing Piłsudski as the future head of state, on whom would devolve the task of assuming 'responsibility for the fate of the state in the face of God and history'. Embodying within his own person the 'unified and indivisible power of the state', he could choose his country's prime minister as he deemed fit and could also designate his own successor as president, in addition to being the 'supreme commander of the armed forces' and empowered to appoint one-third of the members of the Senate. The other organs of state were all under his control: the government, the Sejm, the Senate, the armed forces, the courts and a Court of Auditors. The president was elected by an electoral body whose members were for the most part made up of the 'worthiest citizens' who in turn were elected by the Sejm and the Senate in the ratio of two to one. Under the terms of a specially enacted decree, candidates for the Sejm were chosen not by the political parties but by local electoral bodies, ensuring that the state apparatus had extensive influence over their appointment. The voting age was raised from twenty-one to twenty-four.

The 'April Constitution' would have guaranteed Piłsudski almost unlimited powers, but he did not live to see his election as state president, for he died after a long illness on 12 May 1935. The office of head of state remained in the hands of his loyal supporter, the professor of chemistry, Ignacy Mościcki, who had held the position since May 1926. Piłsudski was buried amid great pomp at the Royal Castle in Wawel in a ceremony attended by Hermann Göring and Pierre Laval, who used the occasion to discuss Franco-German relations in some depth. Even more than during his lifetime, the dead Piłsudski became a mythical figure in Polish history, memories of the authoritarian ruler of the later years gradually being supplanted in the collective consciousness by his merits as an army commander and statesman who in 1926 had saved his country from economic, financial and political ruin.

The first elections to take place under the new constitution were held in September 1935 but resulted in a low turnout of only 46.5 per cent, a figure influenced in no small part by left-wing calls for a boycott. The government bloc known as the BBWR – a non-party alliance that had been formed in 1928 and was prepared to work closely with the government of Marshal Piłsudski – received a three-quarters majority, only for it to disband itself a short time afterwards. It was replaced in March 1937 by a more rigorously organized Camp of National Union, or OZN, led by Colonel Adam Koc and bearing a certain similarity to the official party of Fascist Italy, while never achieving the latter's dynamism. As inspector general of the armed forces Piłsudski was replaced by Edward Rydz-Śmigły, who was acclaimed as 'leader of the nation' but never came close to achieving his predecessor's authority or popularity. In May 1938 the OZN demanded that the country's Jews be driven from public life, but the hope of triggering a popular movement in favour of the government failed to materialize, and the OZN remained an association of worthy notables.

The shift to the right on the part of the colonels inevitably provoked a response from the political left. Poland's Socialist Party, the PPS, had become increasingly radicalized in the years since 1929 and in 1935 it demanded land reform without compensation and a dictatorship of the proletariat rather than a restoration of parliamentary democracy, but with the exception of a brief episode in 1935/6 it refused to countenance a popular front alliance with the country's illegal Communist Party. Far more damaging to the Polish Communist Party were Stalin's purges. Those of its leaders who were living in the Soviet Union and who were suspected of Trotskyism were almost all deported or liquidated between 1933 and 1937. Of its 3,800 officials, only 100 survived the Stalinist Terror. The 'Polish operation' aimed collectively at all Poles living in the Soviet Union began in 1937. The Polish Communist Party was officially disbanded in May 1938, a move justified the following year by the claim that the party had been infiltrated by the agents of Polish Fascism.

In the spring of 1936 major strikes broke out in the country's industrial regions, followed by violent clashes that ended in eight deaths in Kraków and fourteen in L'viv. A year later, in April 1937, the country was shaken by bloody strikes among the peasants, strikes that had been called by the Peasant Party demanding not only economic and political reforms but also a return to a parliamentary democracy. The clashes resulted in forty demonstrators being shot by the police and around 100 policemen being injured. Five thousand farmers were arrested and around 1,000 brought before the courts. By now, control over the state's apparatus of power was working so well that the colonels' regime was able to survive even this crisis, its worst to date.

But there was also powerful opposition on the political right. Roman Dmowski's National Democrats had grown more radical under Piłsudski and become more virulently anti-Semitic. By January 1937 the National Democrats were even demanding the deportation of all Jews, a demand taken up in May and June 1937 by the OZN. An extreme right-wing rival of the National Democrats was the aforementioned ONR, which had been formed in 1934 and whose political programme centred on Poland for Poles alone and on a totalitarian Fascist 'Catholic state of the Polish nation'. Among the population at large there was much support for its anti-Semitic rhetoric. In the mid-1930s there were repeated pogrom-like excesses, generally at weekly street markets, that resulted in the deaths of twenty individuals, fourteen of whom were Jews.

The Catholic clergy played a key role in fomenting anti-Jewish sentiment. In March 1936 the Synod of Catholic Bishops demanded that non-Jewish children be segregated from their Jewish classmates at school. On 29 February 1936 the primate of the Catholic Church, Cardinal August Hlond, had written a pastoral letter arguing that the Jewish problem would last as long as the Jews remained Jews. Although universal hatred of the Jews was to be rejected,

> it is a fact that Jews are waging war against the Catholic church, that they are steeped in free-thinking, and constitute the vanguard of atheism, the Bolshevik movement, and revolutionary activity. It is a fact that Jews have a corruptive influence on morals and that their publishing houses are spreading pornography. It is true that Jews are perpetrating fraud, practicing usury, and dealing in prostitution. [. . .] One should stay away from the harmful moral influence of Jews, keep away from their anti-Christian culture, and especially boycott the Jewish press and demoralizing Jewish publications.[108]

The prime minister from 1936 to 1939, Felizian Sławoj-Składkowski, rejected the use of physical force against the Jews but declared that an economic boycott was legitimate. During this period there were internationally coordinated plans in government circles to force the country's Jews to resettle in Madagascar. This was an alternative to the idea of resettlement in Palestine that was demanded by Polish Zionists but on which Great Britain was currently placing ever greater restrictions. For a time this alternative project was pursued with Léon Blum's Popular Front government in Paris, for all that it ultimately came to nothing. The enforced expulsion of Polish Jews to Madagascar was primarily intended to solve a socio-political problem: that of rural overpopulation. The vast numbers of Polish peasants could move to the towns and cities only once the middle classes who were already living there and who were made up of Jewish tradesmen, merchants and other artisans had been forcibly removed.

Easier to implement were internal political measures such as the introduction of a limit on the number of Jewish students at colleges and universities. In this way the government was able to reduce the number of Jewish students from over 20 per cent of the total in 1928/9 to 10 per cent in 1937/8, a reduction that represented the percentage of Jews in the population as a whole. This official anti-Jewish policy was backed up by a demand made by anti-Semitic students and implemented by university vice-chancellors, whereby Jews had to sit in special rows of seats when attending lectures at Polish universities. An 'Aryan paragraph' was also introduced by many professional organizations with the aim of driving Jews from all freelance professions.

In terms of its political economy, Poland had subscribed to orthodox maxims until 1935, maintaining the stability of the zloty and ensuring a balanced budget and a positive trade balance. By the mid-1930s the government was beginning to change tack and adopt an anti-cyclical economic policy in the spirit of Keynes, with state investment being used above all for the armaments industry. In the wake of a four-year programme agreed in 1936, some 100,000 new jobs were to be created, chiefly in southern central Poland, and the yawning gulf between the industrialized and the agricultural regions was to be reduced.

Poland's economic development profited from the new policy, even if the benefits were modest. Not until 1938 were Polish factories producing more than they had done in 1913. If we take the year 1913 as the base, then production output rose to 86 per cent of its pre-war level in 1929, dropping to 52 per cent in 1932 and rising to 105 per cent only in 1938. On the other hand, the social structure of the country changed little during the interwar period. If we take 1921 as the index year, the proportion of peasants in gainful employment had dropped only slightly to 94 per cent, while the proportion of workers rose to 106 per cent, that of the petite bourgeoisie to 107 per cent and that of the intelligentsia to 112 per cent. On the strength of these statistics, Włodzimierz Borodziej has drawn the sobering conclusion that Poland was one of those states that 'could in general report no economic growth during the whole of the interwar period'.[109]

In terms of its foreign policy, Poland could feel satisfied with its signing non-aggression treaties with two of its potentially most dangerous neighbours: with the Soviet Union in July 1932 and with Germany in January 1934. In March 1934 Piłsudski spoke privately of an unprecedented situation in Polish history. But he was clear-sighted enough to predict that his country's improved relations with Berlin would last no more than four years, in spite of the fact that the treaty with Germany was due to run for a ten-year period.

The foreign minister Józef Beck, who had been a member of every Polish cabinet since November 1932 and was felt to represent a markedly pro-German outlook, honoured the treaty with Berlin by issuing only the mildest of rebukes for Germany's occupation of the Rhineland in March 1936 while approving of it in practice. He refused, however, to join the anti-Comintern pact, as Hitler had wanted, since he did not want to be forced into a position where Poland was directly opposed to the Soviet Union (and indirectly opposed to the Popular Front in France), a position that in turn would have made Poland dependent on Germany. In November 1937 Beck signed a bilateral treaty with Germany designed to safeguard their countries' minorities, and this led to a further thawing of relations between Berlin and Warsaw, while the worsening of relations between Germany and Czechoslovakia was welcomed by Beck with unalloyed enthusiasm. Poland and Czechoslovakia were still arguing over Teschen (Cieszyn), which had been divided up by a conference of Allied ambassadors in July 1920 in a way that Poland felt was unacceptable. If Czechoslovakia were to crumble beneath German pressure, Poland might have a chance of resolving the Teschen question in its favour.

Beck pulled off a spectacular coup on 17 March 1938, when, in the wake of Germany's annexation of Austria, he delivered an ultimatum to Lithuania, demanding that his eastern neighbour finally establish diplomatic and economic relations with Poland and recognize the existing border, including the loss of the area around Vilnius. Given Poland's military superiority, the government in Kaunas felt that it had no choice but to comply with these demands.

Beck seemed to have come much closer to achieving his goal of a 'Third Europe' in the form of a bloc of eastern central European states under Polish leadership, but he would be able to realize his ambitions only if relations between Germany and Poland remained as good as they seemed to be in the spring and summer of 1938. Whether Hitler was interested in such an aim was unclear, but the autumn of 1938 was to bring clarity to the situation, albeit not in the way that Warsaw wanted.

Roosevelt's Realpolitik: The United States from 1936 to 1938

Attempts to appease the dictators in Berlin and Rome were by no means limited to Europe, for the United States of America was also a party to this process. When the Abyssinian conflict came to a head in the summer of 1935, Roosevelt asked for special powers that would allow him to impose sanctions on the aggressor, but the largely isolationist Congress declined to grant his request. A Neutrality Act passed by the secretary of state Cordell Hull in August 1935 against Roosevelt's wishes merely banned American ships from supplying war materials to countries involved in the war. Neither oil nor steel was covered by the American embargo or by the sanctions of the League of Nations, a loophole exploited not only by Fascist Italy but also by the relevant branches of industry within the United States itself.

In the wake of the outbreak of the Spanish Civil War in July 1936 the government in Washington supported the British line of non-intervention. Roosevelt asked Congress for a law banning the supply of war materials to countries involved in the Civil War, and the Senate and House of Representatives agreed to his request in January 1937. The embargo hit the Spanish Republic far harder than the rebels, who were well supplied with arms from Germany and Italy, but for domestic reasons Roosevelt was by no means displeased with this outcome. In conversation with his secretary of the interior, Harold Ickes, the president observed that lifting the embargo would cost the Democrats many Catholic votes in the mid-term elections in 1938. The White House never lost sight of the fact that the majority of American Catholics were on Franco's side. Equally important were the interests of major industries such as Texaco and General Motors, which supplied the Spanish Nationalists with huge quantities of oil and trucks throughout the Civil War.

Public opinion in America was divided over the events in Spain. A powerful minority supported Franco, while a much smaller minority backed the Republic. From the ranks of the latter, between 2,000 and 3,000 volunteers were recruited who fought in the Abraham Lincoln and George Washington Battalions as part of the International Brigades that were on the side of the Republic. But the vast majority of Americans were neutral and would undoubtedly have backed a law passed by Congress in May 1937 which, entirely in the isolationist spirit, imposed a universal weapons embargo, thereby coming close to the goal of all the isolationists: permanent neutrality. But here too the interests of big business were taken into account, a 'cash-and-carry' clause allowing states engaged in the war to buy American goods for cash and export them on their own ships, the only exception being war materials. An avowed isolationist like Senator William Borah from Idaho denounced this compromise, dismissing it with the phrase 'the whole sordid cowardly cash and carry proposition',[110] but convinced internationalists such as Cordell Hull regarded the act as a blatant attempt to gag American foreign policy.

The president was more of an internationalist by nature, but as a proponent of Realpolitik he shied away from open conflict with the isolationists as he needed their votes for his internal policies. On 5 October 1937, less than a year after his triumphant re-election, he gave a speech in Chicago – a traditional stronghold of the isolationists – and, responding to Japan's recent invasion of China, appeared to signal a change in American policy in favour of greater interventionism. The address has become known as his 'Quarantine Speech':

> The peace-loving nations must make a concerted effort in opposition to those violations of treaties and those ignorings of human instincts which today are creating a state of international anarchy and instability from which there is no escape through mere isolation or neutrality. [...] When an epidemic of physical disease starts to spread, the community approves and joins in a quarantine of the patients in order to protect the health of the community against the spread of the disease. [...] War is a contagion, whether it be declared or undeclared. [...] The will for peace on the part of peace-loving nations must express itself to the end that nations that may be tempted to violate their agreements and the rights of others will desist from such a course. There must be positive endeavors to preserve peace.[111]

In fact Roosevelt's speech did not mark a turning point in American foreign policy, for 'quarantine', the president believed, was a milder expression than 'sanctions'. He had wanted to make his country's moral position clear to his audiences at home and abroad, but he was unwilling to make any commitments. On 12 December 1937, when Japanese aircraft dropped bombs on a flagged American gunboat, the *Panay*, that was lying at anchor in the Yangtze River outside Nanking, and fired on it with machine guns, killing two crew members and an Italian journalist, the USA declined to retaliate after Tokyo issued an apology. Not for a moment did Washington consider declaring war on Japan.

Conversely, the United States did feel that the realignment in Germany's trade policies implied by Schacht's 'New Plan' posed a serious threat to the western world in general. This realignment involved the opening up of Latin America to German exports and increasing the amount of raw materials imported to Germany from that corner of the world, without Germany demanding any foreign currency in return. Whereas German exports fell in total by 2.73 per cent between the first quarter of 1934 and the equivalent period in 1935, German imports from Latin America rose by 17.5 per cent. Total exports dropped by 11.62 per cent, while exports to Latin America rose by 18.32 per cent. Between 1932 and 1936 Germany's share of all the imports to Latin America almost doubled, rising from 7.3 per cent to 14 per cent. During this same period the United States was able to increase its share by only 0.6 per cent from 28.8 per cent to 29.4 per cent.

The United States did what it could to oppose this development and succeeded in maintaining its lead as Latin America's largest trading partner, the only exceptions being Argentina, Brazil and Chile, the subcontinent's three biggest economies. Washington exerted particular pressure on Brazil, which Getúlio Vargas had been running as an authoritarian regime since 1930 and, since his *coup d'état* in November 1937, as a dictatorship modelled on Antonio de Oliveira Salazar's Estado Novo in Portugal, finally persuading Vargas to decline to sign a new trade agreement with Germany – the earlier contract had been signed in 1931 and had ended in July 1936. But Washington's success was merely apparent, for Brazil continued to exchange goods with Germany on a currency-free basis until the start of the Second World War.

Under Roosevelt there were no more violent incursions in Latin America, for these no longer harmonized with the 'good neighborhood' policy that he had announced in his inaugural address in March 1933. But the new policy of non-intervention also meant accepting and supporting dictatorships like those of Fulgencio Batista, the American-backed victor in the 1933 civil war in Cuba, and Rafael Trujillo in the Dominican Republic. Yet America also tolerated not only the left-wing nationalist regime of Lázaro Cárdenas in Mexico, a regime which, bent on social reform, was profoundly anti-clergy, but also the popular front coalition of Radicals, Socialists and Communists that came to power in Chile in 1938 and remained in office until 1946.

Three Pan-American conferences were held between 1933 and 1938: in Montevideo in December 1933, in Buenos Aires in November 1936 and in

Lima in December 1938. At each of them Roosevelt attempted to persuade the states of Latin America to adopt the foreign policy maxims of the United States. But Argentina, which had been a covert military regime since 1930, succeeded in resisting American attempts to force the subcontinent's republics to commit themselves to resisting any external threat. The result was a promise of mutual consultation tied to a ban on intervention that effectively amounted to a formal obligation to act on the part of the United States. Not until July 1940, almost a year after the outbreak of war in Europe, did an inter-American conference in Havana comply with Washington's wishes and regard any foreign attack on a signatory state as an attack on all of the treaty's signatories.

On the domestic front, the first twelve months of Roosevelt's second term in office were overshadowed by three major crises. The first resulted from his aforementioned plan to break the conservative majority of the Supreme Court by insisting on the appointment of an additional judge for each one who had reached the age of seventy. Not only the Republicans but many liberal Democrats regarded this 'court-packing' as an attack on the American constitution. In the event the problem that important New Deal laws might be obstructed by the Supreme Court resolved itself when a relatively conservative judge moved over to the liberal camp at the end of March 1937, helping the advocates of reform to gain a majority. Shortly afterwards several conservative judges stepped down and were replaced by progressive judges, encouraging commentators to refer to a 'Roosevelt Court'. But the sense of bitterness generated by the president's attempt to manipulate the balance of power within the Supreme Court lasted beyond the actual struggle, which ended officially in August 1937. Even after that date Roosevelt could no longer rely on the loyal support of his own party in Congress to the extent that he had done previously.

A second crisis was social in character. At the end of December 1936 the workforce at General Motors in Flint, Michigan, had begun a series of sit-ins that for many observers recalled the early years of the Popular Front in France. The company leaders capitulated in February 1937 and met all the demands of the United Automobile Workers, the UAW, a union whose key positions were held by socialists, Communists and Trotskyites. The fact that the old umbrella organization, the American Federation of Labor, or AFL, excluded the UAW in 1937 did not harm the latter in the slightest. Quite the opposite: its membership shot up from 35,000 to 400,000 and it quickly became one of the most powerful pillars in a new and more radical umbrella organization, the Congress of Industrial Organizations (CIO). There were further sit-ins in other large industries in the course of 1937, including United Steel, Firestone Tire and Rubber, and American Woolen. The employers and the conservatives were particularly incensed at the attitude of the Democratic governors and of the president, for the former refused to end the occupations by sending in the

National Guard, while the president thwarted an attempt by the Democrat senator James F. Byrnes to persuade the Senate to condemn the sit-ins.

The third crisis was one that affected the American economy in general. In June 1937 Roosevelt had reacted to positive economic figures by drastically reducing public expenditure. His cuts were aimed in the main at the Works Progress Administration, or WPA, while the activities of the Public Works Administration, or PWA, were completely stopped. Two months later industrial production recorded its biggest drop in American history. Within three months the full capacity of the steel industry had fallen from 80 per cent to 19 per cent, and in the second half of the year the stock market index of the *New York Times*, which in the spring of that year had for the first time returned to its pre-1929 level (= 100), fell to 85 points, wiping out all the gains that had been made since 1935. Between August and October the Dow Jones Index fell from 190 to 115 points. Additional difficulties were caused by falling agricultural prices, forcing Congress to take extensive measures in February 1938, including quotas on wheat, cotton and tobacco production.

Within the cabinet it was the secretary of the Treasury, Henry Morgenthau, Jr, who was the most outspoken advocate of a balanced budget and a reduction in the national debt. He ascribed the drop in production solely to lack of investment. In his view, higher state expenditure would lead only to inflation and higher taxes. His two most determined opponents were Harold Ickes and the governor of the Federal Reserve Board, Marriner Eccles, whose arguments were Keynesian, even though he had never read any of the British economist's writings: during a period of deflation the government needed to offset the lack of investment by higher expenditure financed by loans, whereas at times of economic growth the government should build up its reserves. During the early months of what was to become known as the 'Roosevelt Depression', the president adopted the position of Morgenthau and his orthodox advisers.

But Roosevelt could not ignore the worsening plight of the men and women on welfare and the first deaths from starvation. Nor could he turn his back on the growing number of unemployed. Between 1937 and 1938 the number of unemployed grew from 14.3 per cent of the workforce to 19 per cent, which in absolute figures meant a rise from 7.7 million to 10.4 million. In 1939, ten years after the great stock exchange crash of 1929, the number of unemployed again rose above ten million. Another sharp fall in prices on the New York Stock Exchange on 25 March 1938 played a major part in persuading Roosevelt to align himself with the supporters of deficit spending, and on 14 April he asked Congress to help finance a major aid programme funded by loans: the PWA was to receive almost 100,000 million dollars, the resurrected WPA more than 140,000 million. Further funds were channelled into building cheap housing, into agricultural credits and into work schemes for unemployed young people.

At the end of April 1938 Roosevelt asked Congress to set up a commission of inquiry to address the problem of the way in which power was concentrated in the American economy, but it produced few concrete results. In June Congress passed the Fair Labor Standards Act that Roosevelt had asked for, but in a form that admitted of so many exceptions that it was barely possible to speak of any improvement to the situation of wage earners. It was the last of the New Deal reform laws and came at a time when there were already signs of an economic recovery.

Mid-term elections were held in 1938, when the whole of the House of Representatives and one-third of all senators came up for re-election. The Democrats were able to hold on to their majority in the House of Representatives, albeit with the slenderest of leads: 48.6 per cent for the Democrats and 47 per cent for the Republicans, reflecting an increase of 7.4 percentage points for the 'Grand Old Party' when compared with 1936. In the Senate the Republicans won an additional six seats, but the Democrats maintained their two-thirds' majority with sixty-nine seats against twenty-three. The elections of November 1938 were not a plebiscite on the New Deal, although they left the New Dealers weakened. They had already suffered a serious defeat in April 1938 when the Reorganization Bill that was intended to grant the president powers to restructure government agencies in order to improve efficiency was thrown out by the House of Representatives by 204 votes to 196. After 1939 the funds available for the New Deal were reduced, and some of them, including the popular Federal Theatre Project, were abandoned altogether in June 1939.

Unlike the crisis of the early 1930s, the 'Roosevelt Depression' did not give rise to a new wave of radicalization. On the political right there were extreme anti-Semites who denounced the New Deal as a 'Jew Deal' and who included groups such as William Dudley Pelley's Silver Shirts, Father Coughlin's Christian Front, the German-American Bund that was funded by the NSDAP and the Black Legion, a terrorist organization active in the Midwest. All of them remained splinter groups. On the political left, the Communists gained new supporters by forming a broad anti-Fascist alliance and passing themselves off as the true heirs of the American Revolution. They were especially successful with the CIO, which welcomed their organizational skills. And yet the Communists were never a mass movement even during the second half of the 1930s.

The House Committee on Un-American Activities that was established by the House of Representatives in May 1938 under the chairmanship of the Democrat Martin Dies from Texas devoted itself almost without exception to the alleged machinations of the Communists, largely ignoring the American supporters of Fascism and National Socialism and turning a blind eye to the activities of the Ku Klux Klan. It believed that Communists had infiltrated the Public Works Administration, especially the Federal Theatre Project and the Federal Writers' Project, and identified 640 organizations, 483 newspapers and 280 trade unions as Communist-infiltrated or Communist-led. During the election campaign of the autumn of 1938, liberal candidates were denounced as Communist pawns. They included the governor of Michigan, Frank Murphy, who owed his stigmatization to the good relations that he maintained with Communist officials in the CIO but whose denunciation earned him the demonstrative backing of the president, Roosevelt reproaching Dies's committee for allowing itself to be used for the un-American aim of influencing the election. When Murphy lost the election, Roosevelt appointed him attorney general in February 1939.

The setbacks that Roosevelt suffered at home after 1937 raised doubt all over the world about whether the western democracies would be able to assert themselves in the face of right- and left-wing dictatorships. The malicious comments made by National Socialist Germany and highlighting the contrast between Germany's successes in its attempts to deal with its own economic crisis and the failures of the Roosevelt administration were noted on the other side of the Atlantic. But Roosevelt refused to be discouraged by his opponents at home and abroad and, as we have already observed, he proposed to the British prime minister Neville Chamberlain in January 1938 that they should convene an international conference to consider the question of fundamental norms in international relations, only for his proposal to fall on deaf ears in London. In September 1938 the crisis in the Sudetenland prompted him to appeal twice to Hitler, Chamberlain, Daladier and Beneš to do everything in their power to maintain peace. In his second message on 28 September he proposed an international conference on neutral soil and invited Mussolini to work towards this end.

Roosevelt initially regarded the Munich Agreement of 30 September as a step in the direction of international détente and even as a successful outcome of his own endeavours, but it was not long before he realized his error, and on 11 October, responding to Hitler's new armaments programme, he announced that America would spend $300 million on arms. On 2 November 1938 he signed an Anglo-American trade agreement whose anti-German thrust was plain for all to see. The pogroms of 9 and 10 November were a point of no return in the president's dealings with Germany. At the end of the year he threw his weight behind France's attempts to sell up to 1,000 fighter planes to the United States, by which date there was no longer any doubt that Washington had abandoned its former policy of strict neutrality.

Even now, however, the American public was far from prepared to counter National Socialist aggression in Europe with military force. A Gallup poll in mid-September 1938 in which Americans were asked if their country could avoid being dragged into the conflict if Britain and France declared war on Germany revealed that 57 per cent of those questioned believed that it could; 68 per cent demanded that a national referendum be held before America declared war, the only exception being if the country was invaded directly. If the day was to come when Roosevelt would conclude that the United States could no longer avoid providing military support for western European democracies, then he still had a lot to do to persuade Americans that this was the case.

Reaching Out Across Borders: From the Austrian Anschluss to the Munich Agreement

On 9 March 1938, three weeks after he had accepted Hitler's ultimatum and complied with the Führer's humiliating demands, the Austrian chancellor Kurt von Schuschnigg ordered a referendum, hoping in the process to secure his country's last remaining vestiges of independence. In a radio address he invited his fellow Austrians to vote on 13 March for a 'free and German, independent and social, Christian and united Austria'.[112] Hitler saw in this a violation of the agreements that he had reached with Schuschnigg at Berchtesgaden on 12 February, and on 11 March he demanded that the referendum be abandoned. When Vienna agreed to do so, he pressed home his advantage and insisted on Schuschnigg's resignation and on the appointment of the National Socialist Arthur Seyß-Inquart as his successor. By the time that the country's president, Wilhelm Miklas, reluctantly agreed to these demands, Austria's National Socialists were already in positions of power in many areas of the country's public life. At dawn the next day the Wehrmacht marched into Austria. By now it was clear to Hitler that Mussolini would on this occasion do nothing to oppose him, in marked contrast to what had happened in July 1934.

Hitler accompanied the German troops as far as Linz. The acclaim with which he was everywhere greeted played a significant role in his decision to sign the law decreeing the reunification of Austria and the German Reich, to which he put his name in Linz on 13 March. Two days later he addressed a vast cheering crowd in Vienna, informing his audience that 'as Führer and chancellor of the German Nation and Reich, I report before history the entry of my homeland into the German Reich'.[113]

In his first cross-border offensive, Hitler once again rode roughshod over international law – in this case the Treaties of Versailles and St-Germain – but he had no need to worry about serious opposition from western democracies: in neither France nor Great Britain was the population ready to go to war for a victor's right that until then had prevented the Germans and Austrians from practising their right of self-determination. Moreover, France was in a political vacuum at the time that Germany marched into Austria, Camille Chautemps having resigned on 10 March. Not until three days later was he replaced by Léon Blum. And although Chamberlain condemned Germany's actions, he accepted events as a fait accompli.

In Germany itself there was an overwhelmingly positive response to the Anschluss and to the announcement of a plebiscite on 10 April. Even the exiled leaders of the Social Democrats in Prague concluded on the basis of reports that they received from their followers in Germany that 'the national euphoria [. . .] is genuine and that only a more far-seeing minority remains staunch in its criticism and refuses to have anything to do with it'.[114] In Austria the Catholic bishops and even a prominent Social Democrat, the former chancellor Karl Renner, campaigned for a yes vote in the referendum, and on 10 April over 99 per cent of those Austrians who voted supported 'reunification' and 'the list of our Führer Adolf Hitler' – the only list in the election for the new pan-German Reichstag. The figures were identical to those in Germany.

There could no longer be any talk of a 'secret ballot' in April 1938. In many places spoilt ballot papers were counted as yes votes, while no votes were declared invalid. And yet there could be no doubt about the popularity of the Anschluss or of the man who had brought it about. In the eyes of many who had hitherto mistrusted him, Hitler was now regarded as a statesman who had completed Bismarck's task by overcoming the gulf that had opened up in 1866 and creating a bridge between modern Germany and the old Holy Roman Empire that had ceased to exist in 1806. By 1938 there were few Germans or Austrians who believed in a 'lesser' Germany: the age of the Protestant National Liberals had ended long ago, and the view – first proposed in Frankfurt in 1848–9 – that a German national state could not be formed with Austria had become outdated following the dissolution of the Habsburg monarchy.

It was really only the experts who spoke of the economic and strategic advantages of the pan-German solution that had now been achieved. The fact that as the man responsible for the Four-Year Plan Göring had been particularly insistent in urging the Anschluss was only logical since Austria enlarged the German volume of industry by some 8 per cent. Most valuable of all were the rich iron ore deposits in the Erzberg in Styria, which until then had been mined by the Austro-Alpine Coal and Steel Company but which now passed into the hands of Göring's Reich Works. The 400,000 or so Austrians who were unemployed – more than a fifth of all employees – formed an additional workforce that the German armaments industry could certainly use. The gold and foreign currency reserves amounting to at least 782 million Reichsmarks allowed the Reich to avoid any reductions in imports, reductions that would otherwise have been necessary now that the world economy was again showing signs of collapsing in the wake of the problems in America. Materially speaking, however, the most important aspect of the Anschluss was the consolidation of Germany's position vis-à-vis those countries in eastern central and south-eastern Europe that were Germany's preferred foreign trading partners following the implementation of the New Plan.

There was, of course, one of Austria's neighbours that had every reason to be worried by the events of March 1938: Czechoslovakia, which was now hemmed in on three sides – north, west and south – by the pan-German Reich. Politicians in Prague were in no doubt that Hitler's expansionist ambitions had not been satisfied by the annexation of Austria. On 20 February, in a speech to the Reichstag, the Führer had referred to the Reich's obligation to protect those 'ten million Germans' living in 'two of the states lying on our borders', nations which 'until 1866 had been united with the whole of the German people in a constitutional bond'.[115] One of those states, Austria, was now a part of Germany. The other, Czechoslovakia, had formed alliances with two major powers, France and the Soviet Union. As a result, any threats issued against Prague would have serious international ramifications.

Hitler's 'fifth column' in Czechoslovakia was Konrad Henlein's Sudeten German Party, which had polled two-thirds of all the German votes in the elections to the Czech parliament in May 1935. (In the local elections in May and June it even managed to increase its share of the vote to 85 per cent.) For the present, Henlein was prevented from demanding the annexation of the Sudetenland into the German Reich, for to have done so would have spelt his party's immediate demise. But he could do what Hitler asked of him at a meeting on 28 March 1938 and make impossible demands of the government in Prague. From then on this was the official line of the Sudeten German Party.

By now the threat to Czechoslovakia was so obvious that the Soviet foreign minister, Maxim Litvinov, addressing foreign correspondents in Moscow on 17 March, spoke of the need for collective action to safeguard peace and shortly afterwards suggested that the governments in Prague, Paris, London and Washington should convene an international conference to this end. The British government's attitude to the Soviet Union had been adversely affected by its experience during the Spanish Civil War and so London turned down the request. Chamberlain even informed the lower house on 24 March that such a conference would merely exacerbate international tensions. Equally negative was the response from Washington, while the French government – Blum's second cabinet – found that its own hands were tied after London had signalled its disapproval. Litvinov continued to insist that the Soviet Union would meet its obligations towards Czechoslovakia if France were to do the same and if Poland and Romania allowed the Red Army to pass through their territories.

On 28 and 29 April, during an official visit to London, Blum's successor, Édouard Daladier, and his foreign minister, Georges Bonnet, were informed by Chamberlain and Lord Halifax that if Germany attacked Czechoslovakia, the United Kingdom would not feel under any obligation to side with France. The news can hardly have come as a surprise as Chamberlain had already made a similar point in a note dated 22 March. If the Sudetenland problem was to be solved, then Chamberlain advised the Czech government to make far-reaching concessions and to negotiate directly with Berlin. Daladier and Bonnet, too, felt that such an attitude was both appropriate and necessary.

Tensions between Berlin and Prague grew dramatically worse in the second half of May. On 20 May, reacting to false reports of an imminent German attack (the reports were almost certainly inspired by the Russian secret service), Czechoslovakia mobilized part of its armed forces. The British government informed Hitler that if France went to the assistance of its Czech ally, London would have no choice but to stand by France, while at the same time informing the Quai d'Orsay that the British would not resort to armed conflict. On 30 May Hitler told the Wehrmacht of his 'unshakeable resolve to crush Czechoslovakia by military force in the near future'.[116] He set 1 October 1938 as the date by which the Wehrmacht was to be ready to march into Czechoslovakia and take possession of Bohemia and Moravia.

Faced with the danger of a major European war that might even spill over into the rest of the world, in the summer of 1938 leading military figures, diplomats and well-known conservatives spoke out for the first time against Hitler. Relying on his own memoranda relating to the current military situation, the army's chief of the general staff, Ludwig Beck, asked the army's commander in chief, Walther von Brauchitsch, to signal the army's collective refusal to obey orders. When Brauchitsch declined to do so, Beck resigned on 18 August. His successor, Franz Halder, for a time supported plans for a coup that would have involved the Berlin regional commander, General Erwin von Witzleben; the chief of the defence staff, Admiral Wilhelm Canaris, and Theodor Kordt, a member of the embassy staff in London. Among the other conspirators was Leipzig's former mayor, Carl Goerdeler, who no doubt to avoid police prosecution spent the months between August and mid-October in Switzerland.

Brauchitsch was not initiated into the plan. If he refused to do as he was asked, the conspiracy could not succeed. Another precondition for striking while the iron was hot was the unyielding attitude of the British: only if London stood up to Hitler did the conservative resistance movement believe that it had a chance of toppling him and reinstating the monarchy under one of Crown Prince Wilhelm's sons, a solution that struck many of the conspirators as the most popular alternative.

Beck and the other conservatives did not rule out war as a way of extending German influence in central Europe. And they too felt that Czechoslovakia posed an intolerable threat to Germany. But they were convinced that Germany must have a realistic chance of winning the war, which meant limiting its aims, keeping the number of the country's enemies to an absolute minimum and finding the right time to start hostilities. Above all, they were keen to avoid a military conflict with Great Britain and France. On this point they were in total agreement not only with Ernst von Weizsäcker, the secretary of state at the Foreign Office, and with the president of the Reichsbank, Hjalmar Schacht, but also with Göring. The conservative faction wanted to pursue an expansionist policy in the spirit of Wilhelmine Germany, but without resorting to its anti-English excesses. They refused to jeopardize Germany's future by adopting Hitler's dangerous all-or-nothing policies.

In August 1938 the former conservative politician Ewald von Kleist-Schmenzin visited London on Beck's behalf but was able to see only Conservative critics of Chamberlain's policy of appeasement, among them Churchill and the undersecretary of state at the Foreign Office, Lord Vansittart, who had been chief adviser to the former foreign secretary, Anthony Eden. Although Chamberlain was aware that the Conservative faction was urging a resolute response, he regarded Kleist-Schmenzin's warnings about Hitler's belligerent intentions as exaggerated. The conservative politicians in Berlin reminded the prime minister of the 'Jacobins at the French court at the time of King William', in other words, the exiled supporters of James II, who in the wake of the Glorious Revolution of 1688–9 had worked to restore the Stuarts to the throne.

Kordt's experience was much the same. He was received by Lord Halifax in his capacity as foreign secretary on 7 September and with Weizsäcker's approval asked his host to make it plain to Hitler that Great Britain was ready to go to war. Like Chamberlain, however, Halifax saw no advantage in a pact with Prussian politicians and military figures whose foreign policy aims, including their demand for more German colonies, struck them as potentially even more dangerous than the aims of Hitler himself. The ruling Tories were grateful to Hitler for turning Germany into a bulwark of anti-Bolshevism, an achievement which from their point of view lay in the best interests of both Britain and Europe and which should not be jeopardized by an openly reactionary regime.

By the time Kordt met Halifax on 7 September, Britain had already opened a new chapter in the tale of its policy of appeasement. Acting on Chamberlain's behalf, the former trade minister Lord Runciman – a National Liberal politician and shipping magnate – had arrived in Prague on 4 August 1938 with the aim of mediating between the Czechoslovak government and the Sudeten Germans. He was sympathetic to the cause of the German minority. Although the Czech government was now willing to grant a considerable degree of autonomy to the Sudeten Germans, thereby meeting practically all of the demands of the Sudeten German Party and belatedly distancing itself from the idea of a national state of the entire Czechoslovak nation on which the country had based its own existence, this was no longer enough for Henlein and his party, who at Hitler's bidding now demanded the right of self-determination, including the right to secede from Czechoslovakia and join the German Reich.

As a result, Runciman's mission failed. On his return to London, he laid the blame firmly at the door of the government in Prague and insisted on the right of the Sudeten Germans to secede. *The Times* expressed a similar sentiment in its editorial on 7 September – the day on which Halifax and Kordt met in London. This was immediately interpreted all round the world as the 'official' British view, an interpretation that the Foreign Office was immediately obliged to deny.

The Greater Germany party conference began in Nuremberg on 6 September. In his closing speech on the 12th Hitler attacked Czechoslovakia in no uncertain terms, chastising the leadership in Prague for 'terrorist black-mail' and for pursuing 'criminal ends', while stressing Germany's tremendous military efforts, assuring his listeners that his sole concern was the right of self-determination of four and a half million Germans in Czechoslovakia and threatening that

> If the democracies were to convince themselves that they must do every-thing in their power to ensure the repression of the Germans, then there will be serious consequences! [. . .] The Germans in Czechoslovakia are neither defenceless nor have they been abandoned. Let this be taken into account.[117]

Towards the end of his speech, Hitler sought to invest his policy with a greater historical dimension by drawing a parallel between Germany under his own leadership and Italy under Mussolini, while appealing to the special status of the 'old German Reich' to which Bohemia and Moravia had once belonged. Within this context the return of the imperial insignia, including the crown, orb, sceptre and sword that Hitler had arranged to be transferred from Vienna – the city of the Habsburg emperors – to the scene of the Nuremberg party rallies, acquired a topical significance:

> When we consider the incredible provocation that even a small state has seen fit to offer Germany in recent months, then we may find an explana-tion for this in the unwillingness to regard the German Reich as a state that is more than a peace-loving parvenu. [. . .] The Roman empire is beginning to breathe again. But Germany, although historically infinitely younger, is no new-born infant on the international stage. I have had the insignia of the old German Reich brought to Nuremberg in order to remind not only our own German people but the whole world that more than five hundred years before the discovery of the New World, there was already a mighty Germanic-German Reich. [. . .] The German people has now been wakened and has presented itself as the wearer of its thousand-year-old crown. [. . .] The new Italian-Roman empire and the Germanic-German Reich are, in truth, ancient phenomena. One does not have to love them. But no power in the world will ever be able to remove them.[118]

The party rally was barely finished when German newspapers fell over one another reporting alleged atrocities committed by Czechoslovaks in the areas inhabited by Germans. After several incidents the government in Prague imposed military law on thirteen districts on 13 September. Editions of the *Völkischer Beobachter* on 18 and 20 September included banner headlines such as 'Terrible Atrocities by Czech Thugs', 'Murderers Without Masks', 'Witnesses of the Czech Bloody Terror', '23,000 Refugees', 'Commune and Hussites Hand in Hand', 'German Blood Demands Atonement' and 'Murder By Every Means'.[119] The reports were fabricated at the Ministry of Public Enlightenment and Propaganda and were based on facts and figures made up by the 'experts' seconded to the task.

While the crisis in the Sudetenland was coming to a head, the British prime minister took the sensational step on 14 September of announcing that he was visiting Hitler. Chamberlain knew that he had the backing not only of his own government but also of most of the Dominions: the prime ministers of Canada and Australia, William Mackenzie King and Joseph Lyons, had both encouraged him in recent weeks to continue his efforts to ensure European and, hence, international peace, while the prime minister of the Union of South Africa, James Hertzog, a staunch advocate of racial segregation, was all in favour of a pro-German policy, a position shared by Ireland's Eamon de Valera. Only the New Zealand prime minister, Michael Joseph Savage, who had headed his country's Labour government since 1935, was an outspoken enemy of appeasement. Conversely, France was unequivocal in its support for Chamberlain: reacting to a pessimistic assessment of the situation on the part of his own military, especially the head of the French air force, Joseph Vuillemin, Daladier urged his British counterpart to find an honourable way out of the Sudetenland crisis.

Within hours of the announcement of Chamberlain's visit, the British prime minister met Hitler at the latter's mountain retreat on the Obersalzberg near Berchtesgaden on 15 September. Hitler tried to intimidate Chamberlain in the same way that he had done in his negotiations with Schuschnigg seven months previously. But the head of a power that Hitler had always wanted to see as his maritime partner reacted differently and responded to Hitler's threats of war by asking why he had invited him, Chamberlain, to visit him if he was already resolved on a show of strength. In the circumstances, Chamberlain concluded, it was probably best if he returned home.

Hitler relented. If Chamberlain would accept the basic principle of the Sudeten Germans' right of self-determination, the two men could then discuss the implementation of that agreement. Chamberlain agreed to confer with his cabinet colleagues on the right of self-determination and even the secession of those areas where the population was more than 50 per cent German. In return he made Hitler promise that in the meantime he would not use force against Czechoslovakia.

Chamberlain had the backing of his own cabinet, just as Daladier had the support of *his* government, which at that date was still being kept in power by the French Socialists. In response to massive pressure and an ultimatum from London and Paris, the Prague leadership under President Beneš and Prime Minister Hodža bowed to the inevitable and on 21 September agreed to the British proposal to cede their country's purely German territories to Germany and to hold referendums under international supervision in the contested areas.

Chamberlain and Hitler met for a second time on 22 September, this time at Bad Godesberg. But their talks were less productive than the prime minister had hoped. Hitler insisted that his Wehrmacht be allowed to march into Czechoslovakia immediately and that the territorial claims of Hungary and Poland that he himself had encouraged be met. Chamberlain could not agree to Hitler's demands without exposing himself to the reproach that he had surrendered to blackmail. The two men were still locked in negotiations when, late in the evening of 23 September, news came that Czechoslovakia had mobilized its armed forces. Despite the dramatic worsening of the situation, Chamberlain declared his willingness to communicate the German ultimatum – euphemistically described as a 'memorandum' – to the government in Prague. Hitler set the time and date of 14:00 on 28 September for the unconditional acceptance of his demands.

When Hitler received news on 26 September that the Czechoslovak government had rejected his demands, the world seemed to be on the brink of another major war. The previous day Great Britain had mobilized its fleet and France had called up its reservists. And on the 26th Chamberlain announced that in the event of military action against Czechoslovakia, Britain would support France. That same evening Hitler delivered a speech in the Sportpalast in Berlin that was broadcast by every German radio station, inviting Beneš to choose between war and peace and assuring the world that the Sudetenland would be his final territorial demand in Europe: 'We don't want any Czechs.'[120] His fanatical speech was greeted by frenzied applause. But the mood in the Sportpalast was not shared by the Germans in general, for according to official reports there was practically no stomach for war in the country. Peace was uppermost in the thoughts of all Germans at this time.

The very next day, 27 September, Hitler ordered forces to be prepared for an initial assault and for nineteen divisions to be mobilized. Hitler's enemies at home were bound to assume that the order for attack would come the very next day, but no such order was given. On 28 September, before Hitler's ultimatum to Czechoslovakia expired, Mussolini responded to a request from Chamberlain and Roosevelt and offered to mediate, even if only by asking Hitler to delay mobilization by twenty-four hours.

Hitler had agreed to the Berlin–Rome Axis in October 1936 and could not turn down Mussolini's request without appearing to be warmongering in the eyes of the world, including his own people in Germany, and within hours he had given orders to delay mobilization and agreed to Chamberlain's suggestion of an international conference to settle the argument over the Sudetenland, albeit with one important change: he invited Chamberlain, Daladier and Mussolini to meet him the next morning in Munich but refused to include Beneš, who Chamberlain had wanted to be present as well.

The four leaders met in the Bavarian capital on 29 September, and the result of their talks came close to meeting the demands that Hitler had made at Bad Godesberg: Czechoslovakia was to begin clearing its purely German territories on 1 October, a move that had to be completed by the 10th. During this ten-day period the Wehrmacht could progressively occupy the area that had been cleared. A referendum was agreed for the ethnically mixed regions, although this was later abandoned, while Germans and Czechs living outside the new border should be given the right to choose. Great Britain and France guaranteed the safety of the remainder of Czechoslovakia in the event of an unprovoked attack. Germany and Italy were willing to provide this guarantee only once the question of the Polish and Hungarian minorities had been settled, but in the event they did not keep their word.

Hitler was both the winner and the loser of the Munich conference. Germany had been enlarged by the addition of a further region settled by Germans and once again he had achieved this aim without a single blow having been struck – further grist to the propaganda mills as proof of his genius as a statesman. But he had wanted far more than the annexation of the Sudetenland: according to his original plan, the Wehrmacht would have advanced as far as Prague, Czechoslovakia would have been destroyed as a state and Bohemia and Moravia would have been overrun. Thanks to Mussolini's mediation, he had failed to achieve these objectives. Indeed, he would have been unable to do so without declaring war and presumably becoming embroiled in a war of European, if not global, dimensions. But the Germans were not ready for such a development in the autumn of 1938. 'I cannot yet wage a war with the help of this people,' he was forced to admit to himself when, on the afternoon of 26 September, he stood at the window of the Reich Chancellery in Berlin and saw how indifferent and dejected the Berliners looked as they watched a march-past that he himself had ordered.[121] Conversely, the applause that Chamberlain and Daladier received from the people of Munich was a potent reminder of the German population's love of peace. In the circumstances the Munich Agreement was a highly respectable interim result for Hitler.

On their return from Munich the leaders of the western democracies were showered with flowers and cheered. Most British and French newspapers reported on the outcome of the meeting with Hitler in positively euphoric terms. Chamberlain famously declared that the document he and Hitler had signed, announcing their countries' determination never to go to war with each other again but to resolve all contentious issues by means of negotiations, as a guarantee of 'peace for our time'.[122]

In the lower house, conversely, Chamberlain was criticized not only by the Labour Party but also by his Conservative Party colleagues, Anthony Eden, Alfred Duff Cooper and Winston Churchill. Cooper even resigned as first lord of the Admiralty in protest at the Munich Agreement, while Churchill, speaking in the house on 5 October, declared the outcome of the conference to be the result of an act of unprecedented blackmail on Hitler's part. The British people must know that

we have passed an awful milestone in our history, when the whole equilibrium of Europe has been deranged, and [. . .] the terrible words have for the time being been pronounced against the Western democracies: 'Thou art weighed in the balance and found wanting.' And do not suppose that this is the end. This is only the beginning of the reckoning. This is only the first sip, the first foretaste of a bitter cup which will be proffered to us year by year until by a supreme recovery of moral health and martial vigour, we arise again and take our stand for freedom as in the olden time.[123]

After a debate lasting four days, the house voted on 6 October, when 366 MPs voted for the position that the prime minister had adopted in Munich, with 144 rejecting it. The latter group included the Labour Party and the Liberals. Some eighty Tories, among them Churchill, Eden, Cooper and Harold Macmillan, who was to be his country's prime minister from 1957 to 1963, abstained. For Chamberlain the Munich conference had an agreeable side-effect, for on 16 April Britain and Italy signed a treaty in which the two powers agreed to maintain the status quo in the Mediterranean, although the treaty was due to come into effect only after Italy had withdrawn its troops from Spain. In Munich Mussolini assured Chamberlain that he would withdraw 10,000 soldiers from Spain, an offer designed to create a favourable atmosphere for the eventual implementation of the Anglo-Italian pact. Chamberlain shared this view, not least because Italian attacks on British ships in Republican ports were to cease on Franco's instructions. At this date some 12,000 hand-picked Italian soldiers were still fighting on the Nationalist side in Spain, but by the time the treaty finally came into force on 16 November 1938 the Republicans were fighting their final rear-guard action on the Ebro.

In France it was really only the Communists who objected in the press and in parliament to the terms of the Munich Agreement and to the abandonment of a country that had been a loyal ally of France, whereas the extreme right applauded the move. In a vote on Daladier's foreign policy on 4 October 1938, 535 deputies, including – with a single exception – all of Blum's Socialists, voted for the government, only seventy-five against it. Three parliamentarians abstained. The no votes were those of the seventy-three Communists, the Socialist Jean Bouhey and the right-wing deputy Henri de Kerillis. The foreign minister, Georges Bonnet, who even more than Daladier was an advocate of appeasement, felt it appropriate to write to his Czech counterpart Kamil Krofta on 2 October and assure him of the 'profound sympathy' with which 'hour by hour' he had 'followed your noble and courageous personal activities at a time when your nation is being so painfully tested'.[124] A poll revealed that not all Frenchmen and women approved of the attitude taken by the government and by the majority of members of the Chamber of Deputies. Only 57 per cent supported it, while 37 per cent disapproved. When asked whether France and Great Britain should in future oppose Hitler's demands, 70 per cent said yes, only 17 per cent disagreed.

One immediate consequence of the Munich Agreement was the definitive breakup of the Popular Front. At Daladier's urging, the Radicals refused to work with the Communists after the latter had voted no in the Chamber of Deputies. Shortly afterwards the Socialists, too, joined the opposition, in their case by way of a reaction to the rigorous financial policies of the new finance minister, Paul Reynaud, who was appointed on 1 November and who was an outspoken critic of the forty-hour week. (On 4 October, in the vote on the enabling act on which Reynaud's measures were based, the SFIO had abstained.) A general strike called by the CGT for 30 November 1938 was by no means a failure, but nor could it be declared an outright success, for less than half of all workers took part in it.

By the end of the year arguments over the Munich Agreement had driven a wedge between the secretary general of the SFIO, Paul Faure, and the party leader, Léon Blum: Faure was in favour of continuing the policy of appeasement towards Germany, whereas Blum, regardless of his commitment to international disarmament, demanded resistance to aggression, bringing him closer to the bellicose attitude of the left wing of his party and the figure of Jean Zyromski. Blum's position gained a small majority at a special conference of the Socialists in the Paris suburb of Montrouge in December 1938. The CGT, too, was divided, critics of the Munich Agreement, including the organization's leader Léon Jouhaux, winning a two-thirds majority at the union's congress in Nantes in the middle of November. Daladier's government was strengthened by the failure of the general strike and by the divided opposition, allowing it to continue unhindered its policy of appeasement towards Germany. On 6 December the French and German foreign ministers – Bonnet and Ribbentrop – signed a non-aggression pact in Paris, with Germany expressly agreeing to respect France's existing borders. The agreement was, of course, just as worthless as the written protestation of a mutual desire for peace that Chamberlain had persuaded Hitler to sign in Munich on 1 October 1938.

For Czechoslovakia – the country most affected by the Munich Agreement – the treaty was a disaster. It had been forced to capitulate to Hitler by the Western Powers. Only after the negotiations had been concluded were the Czech representatives who had travelled to Munich officially informed of the decisions that had been taken. Nor was the loss of the areas of their country largely settled by Germans the only loss that the Czechs had to endure, for shortly before midnight on 30 September a Polish ultimatum arrived in Prague demanding the secession of the region around Cieszyn by noon the next day. The Czech government agreed to the demand, and on 2 October the disputed region was occupied by Polish troops. The coup, which had been coordinated with Germany, proved so popular in Poland that in the elections in November the OZN won practically all the seats in the Senate that were being contested in addition to 161 of the 208 seats in the Sejm. The turnout was 67.4 per cent.

President Beneš resigned on 5 October, three days after Polish troops had marched into Cieszyn. On 2 November the country was forced to accept the first judgment handed down by the court that had been convened in Vienna by Germany and Italy and cede to Hungary a large part of southern Slovakia, with its predominantly Hungarian population. On 19 November Prague created the legal framework for the autonomy of the rest of Slovakia and Carpatho-Ukraine, an autonomy that had already existed de facto for some time previously.

The Soviet Union, which was the most important ally of Czechoslovakia after France, was not invited to the Munich conference. It drew its own conclusions from the crisis that beset Europe in the autumn of 1938 and decided that the capitalist powers could all too easily overcome the political differences between democracy and Fascism in order to make common cause against Communist Russia, which felt, therefore, that it had no choice but to come to some arrangement with Germany, a point underscored by the deputy Soviet foreign minister, Vladimir Potemkin, at his meeting with the French ambassador, Robert Coulondre, on 4 October. Opposition to the revolutionary power in the east was certainly a factor that united the nations that took part in the Munich conference, but the anti-Bolshevism of London and Paris was in fact defensive rather than offensive, in which respect it differed from the policies pursued by three other major powers: National Socialist Germany, Japan, which had signed the anti-Comintern pact in November 1936, and Italy, which joined the pact the following year.

Stalin had every reason, therefore, to feel threatened. But the Soviet Union, too, was not above issuing threats. If Germany were to attack Czechoslovakia, then it would respond by attacking Poland, since it was assumed in Moscow that Poland would not allow the Red Army to march through its territories. Operating through the Comintern, Moscow supported the aim of the Czech Communists, which was to turn a national defensive war into a central European civil war that would eventually lead to the victory of the proletarian masses. Hitler's ability to generate sympathy for his anti-Bolshevik policies among the western democracies was also a response to Stalin's policies at home: to the great purges in the Soviet Union, to the civil war propaganda and to the revolutionary activities of the Communist International in the West.

The western democracies, including the government in Prague, never lost sight of the fact that the Soviet Union might emerge even stronger from a European war, whereas most British Conservatives and the bourgeois parties that once again were setting the tone in France preferred to close their eyes to the danger posed by National Socialist Germany. Worse, the vast majority of people in both Britain and France simply refused to take the threat seriously.

And yet it must remain an open question whether in the autumn of 1938 even confrontational realists like Churchill could have commanded enough of a majority to persuade their fellow Britons to adopt a policy that must necessarily have led to military confrontation with Hitler. It is equally unclear whether a government bent on war would have had the support of the Dominions. It is conceivable that the increasingly illusionary policy of appeasement needed to be seen to have failed before contemporaries were convinced that the democracies of western Europe must do more than merely arm themselves but must make the most extreme efforts to assert themselves in the face of the most dangerous of all aggressors. The fact that even as late as September 1938 only a minority of individuals had come to this conclusion resulted in a policy that led inexorably to the Munich debacle, whereby the only state in eastern central Europe that had remained a democracy was sacrificed by the western democracies, in the name of Realpolitik.

The ninth of November 1938: The History and Consequences of the Jewish Pogroms in Germany

No group of people was as adversely affected by Germany's cross-border invasions as the Jews. The annexation of Austria alone delivered 190,000 Jews into the hands of the National Socialists. As Saul Friedländer has noted, the persecution of the Jews in Austria and especially in Vienna, a stronghold of Austrian anti-Semitism, went beyond anything previously known in Germany:

> Public humiliation was more blatant and sadistic; expropriation better organized; forced emigration more rapid. The Austrians [. . .] seemed more avid for anti-Jewish action than the citizens of what now became the Old Reich (Altreich). Violence had already started before the Wehrmacht crossed the border; despite official efforts to curb its most chaotic and moblike aspects, it lasted for several weeks. The populace relished the public shows of degradation; countless crooks from all walks of life, either wearing party uniforms or merely displaying improvised swastika armbands, applied threats and extortion on the grandest scale: Money, jewelry, furniture, cars, apartments, and businesses were grabbed from their terrified Jewish owners.[125]

Officially, around 5,000 Jews were deported to Czechoslovakia, Hungary and Switzerland between March and November 1938. Meanwhile, other Jews left legally, the emigration of poorer Jews being financed by compulsory levies on Jewish communities. Among those allowed to leave the country was the eighty-two-year-old Sigmund Freud, who travelled to England in June 1938, having previously been forced to sign a declaration that he had not been mistreated – he added a sarcastic comment to the document: 'I, Prof. Freud, hereby confirm that after the Anschluss of Austria to the German Reich I have been treated by the German authorities and particularly by the Gestapo with all the respect and consideration due to my scientific reputation.'[126] By May 1939 some 100,000 Jews had fled Austria – more than half of all the Jews who had been living in Austria at the time of the Anschluss. Forced emigration went hand in hand with the 'Aryanization' of Jewish property, a process that was more systematically and promptly expedited in Austria than had been the case in Germany, although here, too, the pace quickened after 1936.

The deportation and emigration of Jews added an international dimension to the problem of Jewish refugees. On Roosevelt's initiative a conference was convened at Evian on the French side of Lake Geneva in July 1938 to deal with the question of Jewish refugees. It was attended by representatives from thirty-two different countries. But, as Saul Friedländer has observed, its objective was made clear from the outset in the wording of the invitation: no country was expected to accept more émigrés than its laws would allow. This also applied to the United States and its restrictive immigration laws that had been in place since 1924. In spite of many humanitarian appeals from outside, the conference produced no concrete results, the only exception being the appointment of an international committee for refugees under the American lawyer George Rublee. The National Socialists were able to capitalize on the failure of the conference. Since no country was willing to alter its immigration policy in favour of the Jews, the *Völkischer Beobachter* was able to strike a triumphalist note: 'No One Wants Them.' On 12 September Hitler informed the Nuremberg party rally that the large and thinly populated western democracies were willing to offer the Jews 'only moral support', but no real help.

Even before the Anschluss, there were already signs of more radical anti-Semitism in Germany. At the beginning of 1938 all Jews were required to hand in their passports, and new passports were issued only to those planning to leave the country. In April Jews were ordered to report their wealth. In June a decree under the Reich Citizen Act of 1935 defined the circumstances in which a business was to be regarded as 'Jewish'. Another law of 6 June 1938 listed commercial services that Jews were in future banned from providing, including the job of estate agent. A decree drawn up on 17 August 1938 by Hans Globke at the Ministry of the Interior – he later ran Konrad Adenauer's Federal Chancellery – ordered Jews who did not have a specifically Jewish first name to add 'Israel' or 'Sara' to their list of first names. The decree came into force on 1 January 1939. After 30 September Jewish doctors could no longer be registered. Meanwhile Goebbels in his capacity as Gauleiter of Berlin implemented various measures designed to drive the Jews from the capital: party members dressed in civilian clothes painted the word 'Jew' and a Star of David on the shop windows of Jewish businesses. By the autumn of 1938 the number of anti-Semitic disturbances was increasing in many parts of the country: in Munich and Nuremberg synagogues were set on fire.

Other countries, too, adopted discriminatory policies towards Jews. After Poland but before Fascist Italy, Hungary passed its first anti-Semitic law in May 1938. Nor was it only authoritarian or totalitarian regimes that introduced anti-Jewish measures. Germany's policy of forcing Jews to emigrate meant that Switzerland felt particularly threatened and on 28 May 1938, two weeks after the Anschluss, the Bundesrat in Berne decided to demand that all holders of Austrian passports be in possession of a Swiss visa when entering Switzerland. Once Austrian passports had been replaced by German passports, the measure was extended to the holders of all German travel documents. The inevitable consequence was that Swiss citizens now needed a German visa when entering

Germany. In order to offset the problems raised by this requirement, Switzerland proposed that the security police in Berlin who were responsible for issuing travel documents and who were the forerunners of the later Reich Main Security Office should mark Jewish passports in some distinctive way. The result was the large 'J' with which the German authorities stamped all Jewish passports from then on. According to an official Berne report, the new ruling, which came into force on 4 October 1938, made it possible to check on the border to see 'if the owner of a German passport is an Aryan or a non-Aryan'.[127]

When German troops marched into the Sudetenland, the Jews who were living there were ordered to move to the remaining part of Czechoslovakia, prompting the authorities in Prague to deport the individuals in question. Since Hungary refused to take them, several thousand Jews ended up in a no-man's-land along the Danube between Czechoslovakia and Hungary, where they were forced to live in intolerable conditions in insanitary makeshift camps.

The fate of the Jews driven from the Sudetenland was a prelude to the one later faced by a much larger group of Jews: the 56,000 or so Polish Jews who were living in Germany at the time of the 1933 census. Warsaw banned their deportation to Poland by passing a law on 31 January 1938 that allowed the authorities to deny Polish citizenship to citizens living abroad. Generally the law was applied only to Jews. In October the regulations were made stricter when the passports of Poles living abroad were declared invalid unless their holders were able to produce a special entry permit by the end of the month. Those who did not receive such a permit became stateless with effect from 1 November 1938.

The Germans decided to react to this move without delay, and on the orders of Heinrich Himmler, the head of the SS and of the German Police, all male Polish Jews living in Germany were given until 29 October to leave for Poland. (It was assumed that their wives and children would follow them.) Since the Polish border police refused entry to the deported Jews, the latter were left wandering around in no-man's-land for several days without food. Most of them were finally sent to the Polish concentration camp at Zbaszyn, although the remainder were allowed to return to Germany.

Among the 16,000 Polish Jews who were deported from Germany and who ended up at Zbaszyn was the Grynszpan family from Hanover. One member of the family, the seventeen-year-old Herschel Grynszpan, was currently staying illegally in Paris. Alerted by his sister to his family's fate, he decided to protest in a way that ensured the attention of the entire world: he bought a gun and on 7 November went to the German Embassy in Paris, where he shot the first secretary, Ernst vom Rath, who was so seriously wounded that he died of his injuries on the afternoon of 9 November.

The assassination in Paris was used by the National Socialists as the pretext for the biggest wave of pogroms that Germany had witnessed since the Jewish massacres of 1348 to 1350, when Jews had been held responsible for the Black Death. Within hours of Ernst vom Rath's death being made public, synagogues all over Germany were torched: 267 were burnt down, and some 7,500 Jewish businesses were destroyed. At least ninety-one Jews were killed, while hundreds committed suicide or died in concentration camps as a result of the ill-treatment that they received there. Tens of thousands of wealthy Jews were taken to these camps in order to force them to emigrate.

The signal for the pogroms – popularly known as 'Reich Crystal Night' – was given by Goebbels after consulting with Hitler, who was staying in Munich as part of the events surrounding the annual celebration of his Feldherrnhalle March in 1923. The atrocities were carried out by the SA, SS and countless party members as the organized advance guard of German anti-Semitism. The population at large was barely involved and evinced little sympathy for the acts of vandalism ostensibly perpetrated in its name. 'Rarely did their faces betray what their owners were thinking,' a report from Munich read. 'Here and there, there was gloating but occasionally also expressions of revulsion.' In the town of Hellbrunn near Bad Tölz some observers 'expressed their approval of the actions against the Jews, others looked on passively, and still others showed sympathy even if they haven't expressed it publicly.' The exiled leaders of the Social Democrats, who had in the meantime moved their headquarters to Prague, were informed by their colleagues in Germany that 'the excesses' were 'much criticized by the vast majority of the German people'.[128]

The democratic press, notably British and American newspapers, reported in detail on the events that took place in Germany on 9/10 November 1938, generally expressing a note of revulsion, but only one country reacted with more than words, when Roosevelt ordered the American ambassador to Germany, Hugh R. Wilson, to report on the situation, shortly afterwards recalling him to Washington and leaving his post unfilled, a situation that remained unchanged until the embassy was closed following Germany's declaration of war on the United States in December 1941. At a press conference that he gave on 15 November – the day on which Wilson paid his final visit to Ribbentrop – Roosevelt expressed his incredulity 'that such things could occur in a twentieth-century civilization'.[129] In a nationwide radio broadcast, former President Herbert Hoover, the secretary of the interior, Harold Ickes, and spokesmen of various religious groups all expressed their outrage at the new wave of Jewish persecution in Germany. From then on Berlin regarded the United States as the main centre of international Jewry.

Goebbels ordered the pogrom to end on 10 November. According to an announcement by the Ministry for Public Enlightenment and Propaganda, Germany's Jews would be given their final answer by legislative means. The first decrees were issued two days later. German Jews had to pay an 'atonement fee' of 1,000 million marks and must foot the bill for reopening their businesses. They were also banned from making any legal claims against the Reich. The order prohibiting Jews from playing any part in the economic life of the nation prevented them from running individual retail outlets, mail-order firms and freelance trades. Jews had until 1 January 1939 to sell their property, their businesses, their stocks and shares, their jewels and their works of art. The money that they received in return was so little that this process of Aryanization amounted to an act of expropriation. In practice it resulted in a vast redistribution of Jewish property in favour of non-Jewish rivals, a redistribution that continues to be felt to this day.

This Aryanization process was accompanied by measures designed to bully the Jews. They were no longer able to visit swimming baths, cinemas, theatres, concert halls and museums, and they were prevented from travelling in train compartments already occupied by 'Aryans'. They were no longer allowed to own gold, silver, precious stones and radio sets, their telephones were cut off and their driver's licences were withdrawn. New laws allowed Jews to be herded together in 'Jewish houses' and to be made to do forced labour. German schools were henceforth closed to Jews, as was the universal welfare system.

By the winter of 1938/9 the social isolation of the Jews was practically complete, but as yet no decision had been taken as to what to do with the 214,000 Jews who according to the census of May 1939 were still living in 'Greater Germany'. The Reich Central Office for Jewish Emigration established in February 1939 under Reinhard Heydrich succeeded in reducing the number by 30,000, but since no other country was willing to take in a large number of poor German Jews and since Great Britain had effectively blocked all further Jewish emigration to Palestine as a result of the increasingly pro-Axis mood in the Arab world, forced immigration could not be expected to provide a quick and comprehensive solution to the German 'Jewish question'.

Even so, there was no doubt that the National Socialist leadership was determined to get rid of the Jews. At Berchtesgaden on 5 January 1939 Hitler himself informed the Polish foreign minister, Józef Beck, that he was resolved 'to get the Jews out of Germany. They will still be allowed to take part of their possessions with them, [. . .] but the more they hesitate, the less they will be able to take with them.'[130] On 30 January 1939 – the sixth anniversary of the day on which he had seized power – Hitler informed the Reichstag that as so often in his life he was once again speaking as a prophet:

> If international finance Jewry inside and outside Europe were to succeed in plunging the nations of the world into another world war, then the result will not be the Bolshevization of the earth and, with it, the victory of Jewry, but the destruction of the Jewish race in Europe.[131]

An Alliance of Opposites: The Second World War is Unleashed

The future course of German politics was outlined in two secret speeches at the end of 1938. On 8 November Himmler informed the leaders of the SS that their Führer would 'create a Greater German Reich, [. . .] the greatest empire ever established by humanity and ever seen on earth'. For Himmler the choice was between 'the great Germanic Reich or nothing'. Two days later Hitler confided in a number of handpicked representatives of the German press that the regime's 'peace propaganda' that it had been forced to promote for reasons of foreign policy but which had its 'questionable side' was no longer relevant. It was now necessary to 'change the German people's whole psychological outlook and gradually make it clear that there are things which, if they cannot be brought about by peaceful means, must be achieved by force'.[132]

It was not only Hitler's 'peace propaganda' that later proved, in part, to have been 'questionable'. Re-educating the Germans and preparing them for war also had to take account of the fact that, in spite of the Hitler Youth, labour service and general conscription, everyday life in Germany in the later 1930s was dominated by the regime's civilian achievements, including increased security in the workplace, a whole series of social improvements, primarily for women and families, and the leisure activities of the Strength Through Joy movement, which was the most popular of the German Labour Front's programmes. The expectations of countless millions of Germans had nothing to do with wartime conquests but with Strength Through Joy cruises to Norway and the Mediterranean or even the acquisition of a new Volkswagen.

By 1938 the number of unemployed men and women in Germany was 0.4 million or 1.9 per cent of the workforce. We can only speculate on the extent to which falling unemployment could be credited to the armaments industry, how much higher personal income would have been without the vast sums of money being spent on rearming Germany and what the Reichsmark was actually worth – always assuming that it could have been converted to other currencies and that prices, wages and rents had obeyed the law of supply and demand rather than state controls. What mattered was that the country's achievements should not be put at risk. At the end of 1938, of course, few Germans believed that their Führer was bent on war. According to official reports on the mood in the country, the overwhelming majority of party comrades regarded the Munich Agreement as yet further proof of Hitler's ability to deal with even the most serious international crisis in a statesmanlike manner without recourse to war.

By the time that Himmler and Hitler gave their secret speeches in November 1938, the next stages of Germany's massive expansion programme had already been set out. Hitler gave orders on 21 October to 'deal with the remainder of Czechia' and to occupy the Memel Territory (Klaipeda region), which had been annexed by Lithuania in 1923 and had been an autonomous region since 1924. On 24 November he gave additional instructions to prepare to overrun the Free City of Danzig (Gdańsk), which in accordance with the Treaty of Versailles had been under the protection of the League of Nations since 1920.

The question of Gdańsk brought Poland into the sights of Germany's expansionist policies, and on 24 October Germany's foreign secretary, Joachim von Ribbentrop, proposed an arrangement with the Polish ambassador, Józef Lipski, under which Gdańsk would be returned to Germany, there would be transport links between East Prussia and the rest of the Reich, Poland would have a free trade port in the Gdańsk region with transport links to Germany, the non-aggression pact between the two countries would be extended by twenty-five years and Poland would join the anti-Comintern pact. If Poland had agreed to Germany's proposals, it would at best have been the junior party in any future war with the Soviet Union, a prospect indistinguishable from total loss of the country's identity.

When Hitler tried to interest the Polish foreign minister, Józef Beck, in a slightly modified version of these ideas at their meeting in Berchtesgaden on 5 January 1939, Beck did not turn them down outright but he made it clear that the Polish people could not be expected to accept the disappearance of the Free State of Gdańsk without demur. The proposals were finally rejected three weeks later during a visit that Ribbentrop made to Warsaw between 25 and 27 January. The compensation that the German foreign minister proposed to pay in the form of Soviet Ukraine, which the two countries were to overrun together, was not sufficient to persuade the Polish leadership under Mościcki, Rydz-Śmigly and Beck to change their position. 'We're not Czechs,' Beck informed his German colleague.[133]

On 10 February 1939 Hitler explained to a group of senior commanders what had persuaded him to bank on war and war alone. The successes of 1938, he explained, were merely way-stations on the road to a much more ambitious goal:

> When the collapse came in 1918, the numerically strongest people in Europe lost its position of political influence and, with it, the means by which to assert its most important and most natural interests in life with all the resources at its command and in all conceivable circumstances. We are talking about the most powerful nation not just in Europe but effectively in the world. [. . .] [We must] represent the interests of our people as if the fate of our race in the coming centuries had been placed exclusively in our hands today. [. . .] We can acquit ourselves of the obligation to act as if our actions today will shape the entire future of Germany. [. . .] We must make good the omissions of the last three centuries. [. . .] Ever since the Peace of Westphalia our people has been travelling a path that has led us increasingly away from the position of a world power into a state of destitution and political impotence.

Germany's rebirth, which had begun in 1933, did not represent the end of its journey, but only the beginning. And Hitler was convinced that 'The next war will be an ideological war, that is, a consciously ethnic and racial war.'[134]

Hitler's speech of 10 February 1939 made it clear what separated his own agenda from that of the old Wilhelmine elite: whereas they wanted to return to a Germany that had flourished before the First World War, he wanted to return to the period before the Thirty Years War. They thought that they were representing German interests, whereas he knew that he was fired by a uniquely true, National Socialist ideology. When Hitler spoke of a 'world power', he used an expression familiar to his listeners. But for a man at the head of ostensibly the greatest nation in the world, it was not enough to lead one world power among many. The German Reich had to become the most powerful empire in the world, and that in turn meant world dominion, hence Hitler's orders at the end of January 1939 to build a vast underwater fleet and his decision in March to begin preparatory work on a new Colonial Office.

On 12 February 1939, two days after the speech in which he laid out his basic principles, Hitler received the Slovak politician Vojtěch Tuka, who in 1929 had been sentenced to a lengthy term of imprisonment for high treason. Hitler told him of his sympathy for the Slovak independence movement. He had evidently decided to settle the problem of 'the remainder of Czechia' as soon as he possibly could. With the help of Slovak separatists, he was able to ensure that by 14 March Slovakia had declared its independence.

By the evening of 14 March Hitler had already summoned Emil Hácha, Edvard Beneš's successor as president of the Czechoslovak Republic, to Berlin and forced him to agree to the unconditional surrender of his country. Early the next morning Hácha and his foreign minister, František Chvalkovský, signed an 'agreement' declaring that 'in order to achieve lasting peace' the Czech president was 'confidently placing the fate of the Czech nation and country in the hands of the leader of the German Reich'.[135] Immediately afterwards the German Wehrmacht marched into the 'remainder of Czechia', and by 16 March Hitler was able to proclaim the creation of the Protectorate of Bohemia and Moravia from Prague's Hradčany Castle. On the 18th Germany's former foreign minister, Konstantin von Neurath, was appointed the Reich protector with effectively unlimited powers, while Hácha henceforth required the trust of the Führer and German chancellor. Germany and Slovakia signed a defensive alliance treaty on 18 March, imposing tight controls on the new state, notably in terms of its foreign policy but also militarily, economically and financially.

Given its industrial capacity, the Protectorate of Bohemia and Moravia represented a considerable gain for Germany's arms-based economy. The National Socialists showed considerable skill in involving sections of the Czech bourgeoisie in the Aryanization of Jewish property, a process which here too was carried out with systematic rigour. In this way the bourgeoisie was made compliant with National Socialist demands. The immediate military advantage of destroying 'the remainder of Czechia' lay in the fact that what German propaganda called the 'mother airship' of the Soviet Union in central Europe was now sidelined. Since the start of 1939 Germany had a wholly oppressive strategic weight that seemed to guarantee it permanent hegemony in eastern central and south-east Europe.

Prague was a watershed in more than one respect. In his third foray into a foreign country, Hitler had crossed a border that was bound up with the whole concept of a German national state and, with it, the idea of belonging to the German nation. By annexing the Czech part of Czechoslovakia as the Protectorate of Bohemia and Moravia, Germany had ceased to be a national state like any other, for the term 'Reich' now acquired a new dimension that at the same time implied a much older quality. According to the Austrian legal historian Karl Gottfried Hugelmann, an outspoken pan-German who from 1935 taught at the University of Münster in Westphalia, 'the essential hallmarks' of the Reich in the Middle Ages had been 'greatness, power and dignity', whereas by 1940 this dignity was based 'on the consciousness of a mission'. The 'incorporation' of the Czech people into the German Reich was justified and meaningful in terms of the concept of the Reich, and people must see that 'with the incorporation of the Protectorate of Bohemia and Moravia into the Greater German Reich, the latter's character as an empire emerges even more clearly'.[136]

On 1 April 1939 the German constitutional lawyer Carl Schmitt delivered a lecture at the University of Kiel that was published later that same year in expanded form. Here he drew attention to German linguistic usage whereby 'the great historically important polities – the empires of the Persians, the Macedonians and the Romans, the empires of the Germanic peoples as well as those of their adversaries – were always called *Reich* in a very specific sense'. Located at the heart of Europe, the German Reich lay 'between the universalism of the powers of the liberal-democratic West, with their tendency to assimilate nations, and the universalism of the Bolshevist, world-revolutionary East', and was 'forced to defend on both fronts the sanctity of a non-universalist, Volk-orientated way of life that respects the concept of nationhood'. According to international law, the concept of 'empire' was one of

> a large-scale territorial order dominated by specific ideological beliefs and principles, precluding the intervention of foreign powers and having as its guarantor and guardian a people that has proved itself equal to that task. [...] It is our concept of the Reich as an ethnically orientated, large-scale territorial order sustained by a single Volk that is the new concept of order under a new kind of international law.[137]

National Socialist jurists in Himmler's inner circle lost no time in criticizing Schmitt for attempting to propose a German counterpart to the Monroe Doctrine of 1823, an attempt they dismissed as both half-hearted and ideologically unsound. Werner Best, who was the security services' head of personnel, argued in August 1939 that according to the popular understanding of the term, international law could not even be considered a proper form of law:

The only purpose of every nation is self-preservation and self-development, and the standards according to which it acts are entirely conditioned by this aim. In its dealings with other nations, no nation can allow itself to be bound by rules that claim to be valid but which disregard its own existential aims.[138]

In short, Hitler's Reich could not only lay claim to a higher law than other states and nations within its own territories, but it was the quintessential Reich, and there was no law that any other states or nations could assert in the face of it.

For western Europe's two biggest democracies, the ideas of March 1939 marked a turning point. In France indignation at the brutal violation of the Munich Agreement was arguably even greater than in Britain, almost the whole of the press and most politicians, including Daladier, demanding a stricter line against Hitler. France's foreign minister, Georges Bonnet, continued to shy away from direct confrontation with Germany but in this he found himself isolated within Daladier's cabinet. Speaking to Conservative Party supporters in Birmingham on 17 March – the eve of his seventieth birthday – Neville Chamberlain described the breakup of Czechoslovakia as an instance of total disregard for the obligations that the German government had agreed to in Munich and asked a series of rhetorical questions that left his listeners in no doubt about his fears for the future:

> Is this the end of an old adventure, or is it the beginning of a new? Is this the last attack upon a small State, or is it to be followed by others? Is this, in fact, a step in the direction of an attempt to dominate the world by force?[139]

Britain drew its first practical consequence from Hitler's act of aggression on 21 March, when it proposed a consultation pact with Poland, a pact that France and the Soviet Union were also to join. That same day Ribbentrop issued an ultimatum to Poland, demanding that it return Gdańsk to the Reich and agree to a transport link between East Prussia and the rest of Germany. Two days later German troops marched into the Memel Territory with the coerced consent of Lithuania, annexing Klaipeda too. That same day – 23 March 1939 – Germany signed an extraordinarily advantageous trade agreement with Romania, which had been exposed to tremendous pressure by Berlin from the start of their negotiations a month earlier.

Also on 23 March 1939 Poland began to react to the extortionate demands that Germans had been making of Slovakia, Lithuania and Poland itself in the course of recent days. Warsaw introduced partial mobilization and moved three divisions and a cavalry brigade to a position close to the country's western border. Two days later Poland comprehensively rejected Germany's demands of 21 March. On 31 March Chamberlain told the lower house that Britain guaranteed the national independence of Poland, if not its borders and its integrity, a declaration repeated almost immediately by France. The Polish foreign minister, Józef Beck, visited London on 6 April and succeeded in turning Britain's unilateral guarantee into a provisional Anglo-Polish mutual assistance pact. But Beck refused to contemplate a similar agreement with Soviet Russia. Nor did he consider it opportune to enter into a three-way pact with France, a country with which Poland had been allied since 1924. Beck gave a famous speech in the Sejm on 5 May, setting forth his country's priorities in a programmatical way:

> Peace is a precious and desirable commodity. Our own generation, which has been baptised by the blood of war, undoubtedly deserves a period of peace. But, like almost everything in this world, peace has a high and yet calculable price. We Poles do not acknowledge the concept of peace at any price. In the lives of the nations and states of this world there is only one commodity that has no price: honour.[140]

Italian troops marched into Albania on Good Friday, 7 April 1939, the day after the provisional Anglo-Polish pact was signed. King Zog fled to Greece, and on 12 April an ad hoc 'national assembly' offered the Albanian crown to King Victor Emanuel III, who gratefully accepted it four days later. A viceroy was then installed and a new constitution announced, followed by the formation of a Fascist Party and of a Supreme Fascist Council modelled on its Italian counterpart. Mussolini clearly wanted to show the whole world that Hitler was not the only leader capable of imposing his will on another country with the help of the military. A few days earlier, on 3 April, Hitler had given instructions for Germany to make military preparations for an attack on Poland and for the armed forces to be ready to act at any given moment after 1 September 1939.

On 13 April Great Britain and France countered the aggressive actions of the Axis Powers by declaring their readiness to come to the assistance of Romania, Greece and Turkey. The Netherlands, Switzerland and Denmark were offered similar guarantees, but in every case they declined to accept them lest they provoke Germany. The following day Chamberlain asked the Soviet Union to assist its western neighbour in the event of an unprovoked attack, but Moscow turned down the invitation and instead proposed a triple alliance involving Britain, France and the Soviet Union. Five weeks earlier, in his famous speech to the Eighteenth Party Conference of the Soviet Communist Party on 10 March, Stalin had declared that it was his party's task 'to be cautious and not allow our country to be drawn into conflicts by warmongers who are accustomed to have others pull the chestnuts out of the fire for them'.[141] This could only be interpreted to mean that Great Britain and France, which six months earlier had signed the Munich Agreement with Hitler without first consulting the Soviet Union, could not count on Soviet help in any confrontation with National Socialist Germany.

On 17 April, the Soviet ambassador in Berlin, Alexei Fyodorovich Merekalov, informed the secretary of state at the Foreign Office, Ernst von Weizsäcker, that his government was interested in improving relations with Germany. On 4 May an even clearer signal came from Moscow, when Stalin replaced his foreign minister, Maxim Litvinov, who had always been regarded as western-orientated and a supporter of the League of Nations but who was always ridiculed in the National Socialist press as 'the Jew Finkelstein', with the chairman of the Council of People's Commissars, Vyacheslav Molotov. This was the first time that a member of the Politburo had run the Foreign Ministry. Stalin now had more effective control of Soviet foreign policy and could keep open his conflicting options – namely, an arrangement with the West or, alternatively, an agreement with his Fascist archenemy in Berlin.

Hitler addressed the Reichstag on 28 April, spelling out his reaction to the diplomatic activities of the Western Powers and Poland by announcing the end of both the Anglo-German naval agreement of 1935 and the German-Polish non-aggression pact of 1934. For long stretches, the speech was a rhetorically skilful rebuttal of a move by Franklin D. Roosevelt, who on 14 April had sought assurances from Hitler and Mussolini that they would not attack thirty-one named countries in the course of the next twenty-five years. If Germany and Hitler were to demand something similar of the United States, Hitler retorted, then Roosevelt would undoubtedly appeal to the Monroe Doctrine, according to which the European powers were not allowed to interfere in the affairs of North, Central and Latin America. 'This is exactly the kind of doctrine we Germans are now claiming for Europe, certainly for the territory and the affairs of the Greater German Reich.'[142] Hitler had already postulated the idea of a 'German Monroe Doctrine' in the sense of a 'Germany for the Germans' in an interview with an American news agency in October 1930. It was presumably Carl Schmitt who encouraged him to expand this postulate and apply it to the whole of Europe after he, Schmitt, had referred to the American model in his speech in Kiel. The concept had no doubt come to Hitler's attention via high-ranking National Socialist jurists. From then on he regarded it as his own.

On 22 May 1939, three and a half weeks after his Reichstag speech, Hitler concluded the so-called 'Steel Pact' with Mussolini, committing each country to come to the other's assistance if it were to wage war with a third party. It mattered not a whit if it was an offensive or a defensive war. Both powers were interested only in *Lebensraum*. In a diary entry, Italy's foreign minister, Gian Galeazzo Ciano, Mussolini's son-in-law, commented wryly: 'I've never read a treaty like it – it's pure dynamite.'[143]

Mussolini had agreed to Hitler's proposal because he accepted the Führer's assurance that the forthcoming great war would not take place for several years. In 1939 Italy was far from being in a position to play the role that Hitler had planned for it. Meanwhile the camp of Germany's 'allies' in the wider sense had continued to grow. After Japan and Italy, the Japanese satellite state of

Manchukuo and Hungary both joined the anti-Comintern pact on 24 February 1939, with Franco's Spain following suit on 27 March. It remained completely unclear what these countries would do for the Reich if the situation were ever to become serious – especially if Hitler were to take the unprecedented step of forming an alliance with Stalin.

Until August 1939 it was possible only to speculate on the direction that the Soviet Union's foreign policy might take. On 24 May the British cabinet had agreed to enter into negotiations with Moscow on a military alliance, a move accepted by Chamberlain only with reluctance but actively encouraged by Daladier. Public opinion in Great Britain favoured such a pact: in a poll taken in June 1939, 84 per cent of those asked said that they supported the idea of a military alliance between Britain, France and the Soviet Union. But it was only on 24 July that an agreement was reached that would come into force after a military convention. Under its terms the signatories would come to each other's assistance in the event of a direct or indirect attack not only on one of them but also on Finland, the Baltic States, Poland, Belgium, Romania, Greece and Turkey. Stalin himself had insisted on extending the terms to cover indirect aggression, however difficult it was to define such attacks. He also demanded the inclusion of the Baltic States and Finland, even though the countries in question had no wish to receive Soviet assistance.

The military negotiations began on 12 August, a delay caused by the fact that the western experts had to travel to Leningrad by sea. The sticking point turned out to be a Soviet demand that the government in Warsaw was not prepared to consider, namely, the right of the Red Army to march through Polish territory on its way to the West. The French representative was instructed by his superiors in Paris to agree to the terms of the treaty in the form desired by the Soviet delegation. The British representative was merely empowered to state that in the event of war Poland should accept Soviet support, an outcome with which the Soviet negotiators could declare themselves satisfied.

By the summer of 1939 Chamberlain's mistrust of Stalin was at least as profound as Stalin's mistrust of the Western Powers and especially of the Tory government in London. In spite of his outrage at Hitler's treaty violation of 15 March 1939, Chamberlain had not yet abandoned his belief in appeasement. And he was not alone in this. The Federation of British Industry, which had long been an advocate of economic appeasement, began negotiations with its German counterpart on the very day that the Wehrmacht marched into the 'remainder of Czechia'. Two days later, on 17 March 1939, both organizations signed an agreement expressing a desire for Anglo-German negotiations that would put an end to the destructive rivalry between their two countries and allow the maximum cooperation. In June and July 1939 several face-to-face discussions were held between Chamberlain's principal diplomatic adviser, Sir Horace Wilson, and Helmuth Wohlthat of Göring's Four-Year-Plan Authority, during which Wilson stressed Britain's desire for economic cooperation, for greater access to British markets for German producers and for concessions on the matter of Germany's colonial policy – on condition, of course, that the Reich took steps to restore international stability.

Even at the height of appeasement, Great Britain had not lost sight of the need to rearm. In October 1938, shortly after the Munich conference, the lower house raised the military budget from £1.5 million to £2.1 million, much of the increase earmarked for the Royal Air Force. On 29 May 1939 the lower house voted to reintroduce general conscription in the face of opposition from the Labour Party. (The policy had been abandoned in 1920.) France, which economically speaking had been recovering swiftly thanks to its use of special powers, likewise began to force the pace of rearmament under the impression left by Germany's aggressive actions in March 1939. When Marcel Déat, a former Socialist and now the leader of the radical right-wing Rassemblement National Populaire, famously answered the question 'Mourir pour Dantzig?' with a resolute 'no' in the newspaper L'Œuvre on 4 May 1939, he was not speaking for the majority of his fellow countrymen and women. In a poll asking if France should respond to Hitler with force in the event of his trying to take the Free City of Gdańsk, 76 per cent said yes, 17 per cent said no and 7 per cent had no opinion at all.

The military efforts of the two biggest democracies in western Europe suffered a setback on 11 July 1939, when, by twelve votes to eleven, the Foreign Policy Committee of the American Senate frustrated Roosevelt's attempts to loosen the 1937 Neutrality Act so that in the event of war Great Britain and France could buy military material from the United States and transport it back home on their own ships using the cash-and-carry policy to which we have already referred. The House of Representatives had already agreed to this motion on 30 June by a narrow majority of 200 votes to 188. But the isolationists had the upper hand in the Senate. In the summer and autumn of 1939 there was no question of any active American support for Great Britain and France in the event of a war with Germany. With Japan, conversely, America chose to be openly confrontational, and on 26 July 1939, acting at the bidding of the Senate, the secretary of state, Cordell Hull, announced that the United States would not be renewing the trade treaty of 1911.

During the period between the political and, in the narrower sense, military negotiations that Great Britain and France conducted with the Soviet Union in the summer of 1939, a meeting took place in a Berlin wine bar on 26 July between two Soviet diplomats, the Berlin chargé d'affaires, Georgi Astakhov, and the deputy head of the Soviet Trade Mission in Berlin, Yevgeny Babarin, and Julius Schnurre, an adviser at the Foreign Office, in the course of which Schnurre openly asked for greater German-Soviet understanding and, more specifically, for a non-aggression pact and an agreement on their mutual interests in eastern central Europe. His main argument was that Great Britain could offer the Soviet Union only involvement in a European war and enmity with Germany, whereas an agreement with Germany would mean neutrality and, hence, non-involvement in any European conflict.

This meeting marked the start of more intensive contacts between Germany and Soviet Russia. In early August Ribbentrop told the Soviet chargé d'affaires directly that there was no problem that Germany and the Soviet Union could not agree upon, whether it affected the Baltic or the Black Sea. On 14 August Ribbentrop pointed out that both Germany and the Soviet Union shared a common foe in 'capitalist Western democracies' and once again offered Moscow the opportunity to define its sphere of interest between the Baltic and the Black Sea. Two days later Molotov hinted that a visit from the German foreign minister would not be unwelcome in Moscow, and on the 19th Berlin and Moscow agreed to the framework for a credit and trade treaty. On the 20th Hitler sent a telegram to Stalin, inviting him to receive Ribbentrop in Moscow, the German foreign minister being equipped with comprehensive authority to sign a non-aggression treaty. On the 21st Berlin received word that Ribbentrop was expected in the Soviet capital on 23 August.

Shortly before midnight on 24 August 1939 a bemused and in many cases shocked world learnt that after three hours of talks Ribbentrop and Molotov had signed a German-Soviet non-aggression pact. It was dated the previous day. Both states would refrain from undertaking any aggressive acts for a ten-year period. They would not assist a third party in the event of a war with their co-signatory. Nor would they play any part in coalitions aimed directly or indirectly against the other party.

What the rest of the world did not know was that the two countries had also signed a secret addendum to the treaty, which provided for the partition of Poland and the Baltic States, including Finland, into German and Soviet spheres of influence separated by the northern border of Lithuania and by a line marked by the courses of the Narew, Vistula and San rivers. As for south-east Europe, Germany recognized the Soviet interest in Bessarabia, which belonged to Romania. Unresolved was the question of 'whether the interests of both sides make the preservation of an independent Polish state seem desirable, and how this state should be demarcated'.[144] As the treaty pointedly stated, this question could be resolved only in the course of subsequent political developments.

The pact positively invited Hitler to attack Poland, a prospect that Stalin did not find in the least intimidating. Not only did the Soviet leader gain a large area of land that the Western Powers had been unable to offer him, he also gained the time that he needed to continue arming his country and preparing for the eventuality that Hitler might at some point revert to his earlier plan of extending Germany's Lebensraum at the expense of Soviet Russia. In the meantime he could see the extent to which the capitalist powers were tearing each other apart. Speaking to a small group of party members that included Georgi Dimitrov, the secretary general of the Communist International, Stalin admitted on 7 September 1939 that it would 'not be bad' if Germany and the capitalist countries were weakened. 'Hitler, without understanding it or desiring it, is shaking and undermining the capitalist system.'[145] It was he, Stalin, who was playing off the capitalist powers against one another, the Soviet leader concluded.

Ideologically speaking, the pact between the Soviet Union and Hitler's Germany was an alliance of opposites and hard to fathom. In December 1933 Dimitrov had defined 'Fascism in power' as 'the open terrorist dictatorship of the most reactionary, chauvinistic, and imperial elements of finance capital',[146] a definition officially adopted at the Seventh World Congress of the Comintern in August 1935. To form any kind of an alliance with such a system presupposed the abandonment of principles that had been held in high esteem until then, and this was certainly the criticism that – initially at least – was levelled at the Hitler–Stalin Pact by many western Communists. But observers who set out from the premise that there could not possibly be a contradiction between the international working class and the Soviet Union would certainly be able to justify the German-Soviet agreements of 23 August and see them as benefiting the world's proletariat and furthering world revolution. All that was needed was the right way of seeing things, namely, a dialectical perspective.

After a brief period of uncertainty, this was the interpretation placed on the situation by the Communist parties of western Europe, foremost among them the French Communist Party, which insisted that the 'land of socialism' had broken through the 'front of the imperialist states' and secured not only its own future but also peace in Europe. In short, it was entirely the 'imperialist' Western Powers that were to blame for the failure of the Soviet Union, Great Britain and France to reach an agreement. They had supported Germany's 'eastern thrust' in Munich and refused to sign up to a policy of collective security. At the same time the French and British Communists and the German Communists in exile in Moscow asserted their determination to continue their struggle to defeat the warmongering Fascists.

The most remarkable assessment of the Hitler–Stalin Pact came from Mao Zedong, the secretary general of the Chinese Communist Party, who following the outbreak of the Sino-Japanese War in 1937 had formed a new, albeit precarious, united front alliance with the nationalist Kuomintang of Chiang Kai-shek. In an interview with the *New China Daily*, Mao claimed that the Moscow agreement had thwarted the attempt on the part of 'the reactionary international bourgeoisie represented by Chamberlain and Daladier' to provoke a war between the Union of Soviet Socialist Republics and Germany and

> broken the encirclement of the Soviet Union by the German-Italian-Japanese anti-Communist bloc. In the East it deals a blow to Japan and helps China; it strengthens the position of China's forces of resistance to Japan and deals a blow to the capitulators. [. . .] Badly hit by the Soviet-German treaty, Japanese imperialism is facing a future beset with still greater difficulties.[147]

The treaty of 23 August 1939 certainly came as an unpleasant surprise to Tokyo. On 11 May 1939, in the course of the Sino-Japanese War, there had been serious clashes with the Soviet Union on the border with Manchukuo and the Mongolian People's Republic, which had been founded in 1924 and was completely independent of Moscow. The episode was known as the Nomonhan Incident and lasted from May to September 1939. The German–Soviet agreement not only violated the anti-Comintern pact but also gave the impression in Japan that the country had been abandoned by National Socialist Germany. Hiranuma's compromised cabinet was toppled. When war broke out in Europe on 1 September, Japan remained neutral but was also isolated in the Far East. The Nomonhan Incident ended on 15 September with a truce that was tantamount to a complete defeat for the Japanese Empire, triggering a sense of profound demoralization within the Japanese army.

With his dramatic volte-face Hitler managed not only to wrong-foot his Far Eastern partner in the anti-Comintern pact, he also confused many of his loyal supporters at home. It was no easier for him to justify the treaty of 23 August 1939 than it was for Stalin, for the Führer had repeatedly portrayed National Socialist Germany as the power that was destined to act as a bulwark against evil in the form of Bolshevism. At the Nuremberg party rally in September 1934 he had delved far into the past in order to back up his belief in Germany's mission, claiming that

Just as the waves of peoples and races from the east were once fragmented by their impact on Germany, so our people have once again become the breakwater in a flood that would have buried Europe, together with its welfare and its culture.[148]

The following year he told the American journalist Hugh Baillie, who was head of United Press, that 'Germany is the bulwark of the West against Bolshevism and will fight propaganda with propaganda, terror with terror, and force with force in order to fend it off'.[149] And at the 1937 Party Day of Labour he described 'international Jewish Bolshevism' as 'an absolutely foreign body in the community of European cultural nations', while 'the claim of an uncivilized, Jewish-Bolshevist international guild of criminals to rule over the old European cultural country of Germany from Moscow' was no more than a 'shameless provocation'.[150]

Now, barely two years later, Hitler was signing a pact with 'Satan' in order to drive out the 'devil', as he described the new situation on 28 August 1939. Litvinov's dismissal (and, retrospectively, the fall of Trotsky and other Jewish Bolsheviks) struck Hitler as proof that under Stalin the Soviet Union was willing to break with its former policy of internationalism and interventionism and to evolve in the direction of a kind of National Socialism. It was no longer permissible to speak of 'Jewish Bolshevism' and of the struggle to combat it.

Countless propaganda texts promoting the old message were consigned to the waste-paper basket overnight, and anti-Bolshevik propaganda films were taken out of circulation.

Once the German-Soviet non-aggression pact had been signed, Hitler felt that Germany's position was so strong that he seriously considered accepting the offer that he received on 25 August from the British ambassador Sir Nevile Henderson: Germany would use its influence to secure the continuing existence of the British Empire if London did nothing to prevent Germany from solving its problem with Poland. He then decided to begin hostilities at 4:30 the following day. But on 25 August he was informed that Mussolini, who had not discovered that Hitler was planning to invade Poland until 12 August, was unable to fight alongside Germany because of resistance to the idea on the part of King Victor Emanuel III, the Italian foreign minister, Gian Galeazzo Ciano, and leading members of the country's military. He also learnt that the Anglo-Polish mutual assistance pact was on the point of being signed. The result was the threat of a situation that he was still unwilling to contemplate: a war on two fronts, as in 1914. On the evening of 25 August, acting on advice received from Walther von Brauchitsch, Hitler countermanded his orders to the army.

The secretary of state at the Foreign Office, Ernst von Weizsäcker, and the career diplomat at the German Embassy in London, Theodor Kordt, used the breathing space to make frantic attempts to avert war, as did Hermann Göring, who sought the help of a Swedish mediator, the businessman Birger Dahlerus. But neither Brauchitsch nor the army's chief of the general staff, Franz Halder, had any intention of opposing war with Poland. Hitler himself was resolved on going to war. He still hoped that he could prevent Great Britain and France from becoming involved, although it was no longer anything more than a hope.

Britain could not accept Hitler's proposals without violating its commitments to Poland, while the proposals that Hitler put to Warsaw in the form of an ultimatum on 29 August were designed only to serve as an alibi in the face of the tribunal of history. There was also something unreal about Mussolini's idea, put forward on 31 August, that the British government might agree to the return of Gdańsk to Germany and in that way prepare the ground for a conference involving all the major powers. At 12:40 that same day Hitler gave orders for hostilities to begin against Poland: they would start at 04:45 on 1 September 1939. In order to provide some semblance of legitimacy the SS had to ensure that there were suitable 'incidents' on the border between Germany and Poland, one of which was a feigned attack on the German radio station at Gleiwitz in Upper Silesia by SS men wearing Polish uniforms late on the evening of 31 August.

Hitler was under no economic constraints when he unleashed the Second World War on 1 September 1939. True, he could not have continued his war economy policies for much longer without the need to encroach on foreign territory, but the annexation of Austria and of the Sudetenland and the establishment of a Protectorate of Bohemia and Moravia had lifted some of the economic burden from Germany's shoulders. He was determined that war would begin at the earliest available opportunity. To have waited would have meant allowing Great Britain and France more time to rearm, threatening Germany's lead in this area. The non-aggression pact with the Soviet Union freed Hitler from the danger of a major war on two different fronts. In the summer of 1939 American isolationism was still powerful enough to make it unlikely that the United States would enter the war alongside Britain and France at least in the foreseeable future. In the circumstances it made sense to attack Poland as soon as possible, especially since Hitler was not yet convinced that London and Paris would honour their commitment to come to Warsaw's assistance.

In marked contrast to the situation a quarter of a century earlier, there was no enthusiasm for war in Germany in September 1939. At the end of June, the regional council of Ebermannstadt in Upper Franconia had noted that

> the desire for peace is greater than the desire for war. As a result, the vast majority of the population would be willing to support a solution to the Danzig question only if it were to be as swift and as bloodless as other annexations in the east. [. . .] We cannot reckon on the same degree of enthusiasm today as there was in 1914.

A month later the same civil servant summed up the mood among the population as follows: 'Among the public at large the answer to the question as to how to solve the problem of Danzig and the corridor remains the same as before. Annexation to the Reich? Yes. By war? No.' On 31 August – the last day of peace – the writer echoed the reports from other parts of the Reich: 'It is likely that public confidence in the Führer will now be subjected to its sternest test to date. The overwhelming majority of party comrades expect him to prevent war from breaking out, even if this means abandoning Danzig and the corridor.'[151]

In the speech that he delivered to the Reichstag on 1 September 1939, only hours after the start of the war, Hitler appealed to Frederick the Great, the historical figure whom he admired the most and whom he invoked as a witness to the fact that, if necessary, Germany could defy even a major coalition:

> There is one word that I have never learnt, and that word is 'capitulation'. But if anyone thinks that we may be facing a difficult time ahead, I would ask them to remember that a king of Prussia once stood up to one of the greatest coalitions in history with a ridiculously small army and that he emerged successful after three battles because he had a faithful and a strong heart of a kind that we too need at a time like this. But I should like to assure the rest of the world that there will never be another November 1918 in the history of the German Reich.[152]

The German invasion of Poland was followed within hours by British and French demands to cease all hostilities forthwith and to withdraw German troops from Polish territory. On 2 September London followed up its note from the previous day by issuing an ultimatum and insisting on compliance by 11:00 the following day. Since no German answer was forthcoming, Britain was now at war with Germany. The French ultimatum was handed to Ribbentrop at 12:20 on the 2nd and expired at 17:00 that same day, after which France, too, was on a war footing with the Reich. Two other members of the Commonwealth, Australia and New Zealand, together with British India, also declared war that day, followed on the 6th by the Union of South Africa, whose prime minister, James Hertzog, had championed his country's neutrality, only to be overruled by the majority of members of his government and of parliament, all of whom favoured intervention. Canada followed suit on the 10th. In short, Hitler's war had from the outset not merely a European but a global dimension.

In Britain the lower house gave Chamberlain its full support on 3 September. Two days earlier the Labour Party had published its own war manifesto with an appeal to Britons to resist Hitler's latest act of aggression by force of arms. In spite of the failure of his earlier policy towards Germany, Chamberlain declined to resign but consolidated his position within his party by giving three Conservative 'anti-appeasers' cabinet seats on 3 and 4 September: Winston Churchill as first lord of the Admiralty, Anthony Eden as minister for the Dominions and Harold Macmillan as head of the newly established Ministry of Information.

The French government, too, could count on parliament's backing when it declared war: on 2 September both the Chamber of Deputies and the Senate by a show of hands unanimously empowered Daladier's government to raise new loans which, even if the prime minister avoided the term, were war loans. In both chambers the Communists, too, voted for the government bill. Three and a half weeks later, on 26 September, the Communist Party was declared an illegal organization after it had begun to turn the army against the 'imperialist war' and to describe the invasion of eastern Poland by the Red Army as an act of liberation. In both cases it was responding to a directive from the Comintern.

Hitler was surprised by the speed with which western democracies reacted to his invasion of Poland and decided that attack was the best form of defence. By 3 September he once again had a clear bogeyman in his sights: Jewry. Now, however, it was no longer Jewry in its 'Bolshevik' manifestation, but its 'democratic', 'plutocratic' and 'capitalist' form. As a dialectician, Hitler was now second only to Stalin, and in this capacity he blamed the Jews for the war that he himself had just unleashed. According to an appeal that he made to the German people on 3 September and which he had written before France had entered the war, it was not Great Britain that should be held responsible for hostilities but that Jewish-plutocratic and democratic ruling class that wishes to see only subservient slaves in all the nations of the world and which hates our new Reich because it sees in it a model for the sort of social enterprise that it fears will infect its own country, too.[153]

Addressing the 'men and women of the NSDAP' on 3 September, Hitler insisted that it was 'our Jewish-democratic international enemy' that had 'succeeded in harrying the English people into war with Germany. The reasons are just as mendacious and threadbare like [sic] they were in 1914.' And all members of the party were exhorted to prepare for a fight to the death:

Within a matter of weeks the National Socialist readiness for war must be transformed into a spirit of unity ready to stick together through thick or thin. Then the capitalist warmongers in England and its satellites will very soon discover what it means to attack the largest people's state in Europe without good reason.[154]

Hitler's language on 3 September 1939 was powerfully reminiscent of a particular variant of his rhetoric associated with the 'ideas of 1914' in which he had drawn a distinction between social and, indeed, socialist Germany and capitalist, not to say plutocratic, England. The 'international Jewish conspiracy' seemed to have moved its headquarters overnight from the Kremlin in Moscow to the City of London. Hitler's anti-capitalist rhetoric presumably found an echo in the workforce because Germany was currently enjoying full employment, with an extensively developed welfare state and a range of popular leisure activities offered by the German Labour Front. And Hitler needed to be able to rely on the backing of the workforce if he wanted to avoid a new 'November 1918'. One novel aspect of the present situation, when compared with the one that had obtained in Wilhelmine Germany, was the fact that the appeal to anti-Jewish sentiment came not from any particular social or political groups but from 'above', lending it an official character. But whatever the response to these slogans, anti-Semitism had been the dominant force in Germany since 1933, which was one of the principal differences between the events of 1914 and those of 1939 and also between the wars that began to unfold at that time.

Another difference was signalled by Hitler with a decree that he signed in October 1939, backdating it to 1 September, the day the war had begun. It read:

Reichsleiter Philipp Bouhler and Dr Karl Brandt MD are hereby given responsibility for extending the authority of specified doctors so that, after a critical assessment of their condition, mercy killing may be used on those patients who, at least as far as is humanly possible, have been deemed to be incurably ill. Adolf Hitler.[155]

In this way the Führer was now master of life and death. His war was to give him the opportunity of taking to its ultimate conclusion his social Darwinian view of the world and helping a new, racially pure and healthy Aryan type of human being to gain ascendancy. While the attention of the German people was focused on the war on its various fronts, it was easier than it had been previously to take the necessary step from 'preventing the birth of children suffering from hereditary diseases', which was allowed under a law passed on 14 July 1933, to the 'destruction of life that is unworthy of living', and to do so, moreover, without attracting attention. It was a move from eugenics to the euthanasia championed by Karl Binding, an expert in criminal law, and by the psychiatrist Alfred Hoche, who, as we have already observed, had demanded the 'destruction of life unworthy of life' – thus the title of the book they had co-authored in 1920. But in large sections of society and especially among members of the Christian Churches, 'mercy killing' for the mentally ill was still regarded as murder. Once the war was under way, Hitler hoped to be able to put his world-changing plan into practice. It was entirely within the logic of the totalitarian state that he himself had created that it would be possible to ignore and invalidate, where necessary, any inconvenient norms associated with the bourgeois tradition of the rule of law. In National Socialist Germany this logic could find consummate expression only once the country was at war.

Fault Lines in Western Civilization:
The Second World War and the Holocaust

War as Annihilation: The Fifth Partition of Poland

ONLY ONE COUNTY had deliberately set out to unleash a war in 1939 while knowing that it was not in its power to ensure that it remained a localized conflict. That country was National Socialist Germany. It must remain an open question whether Hitler would have invaded Poland in the autumn of that year if Stalin had not come to his assistance with the Moscow non-aggression pact of 23 August 1939, but it is scarcely conceivable that Germany would have turned down the chance to go to war, given the extent to which it had rearmed itself and the level of rearmament that could be found among the other powers at that time. The German-Soviet non-aggression pact, which was in fact an invitation to attack, reduced the risks associated with Hitler's dangerous game inasmuch as it made the Soviet Union the co-aggressor and, as such, dependent on the policies of the principal aggressor for the foreseeable future.

Addressing a group of high-ranking generals on the Obersalzberg on 22 August, Hitler gave as his reason for declaring war on his eastern neighbour the 'annihilation of Poland, the aim being to remove living forces, not to attain a particular line'. According to another version of his remarks which, although contested, is entirely credible, Hitler added that 'for the present' he had deployed his 'Death's Head Divisions only in the east' with orders 'to send all Polish-speaking men, women and children ruthlessly and mercilessly to their deaths, because only in this way can we acquire the Lebensraum that we need. Who nowadays still speaks of the extermination of the Armenians?'[1]

Hitler was able to rely on the broad support of the army leadership in his decision to turn on Poland. During the Sudeten crisis of the spring and summer of the previous year, there had been military opposition to his plans. Among those opposed to his plans had been Franz Halder, who later became chief of the general staff. By the time that Hitler had changed the direction of his attack and set his sights on Poland in the spring of 1939, there was no longer any trace of opposition in his country's army. The Sudetenland had not been a part of the

German Reich in 1871, but this was not true of large sections of Poland, and for that very reason it was regarded by the political right in Germany as a 'robber state' and a 'seasonal state' – both terms were expressions of contempt for those countries that had been created in 1918 only to vanish again in the wake of Germany's expansionist ambitions. Halder described the termination of the German-Polish non-aggression pact on 28 April 1939 as 'a weight off his mind'. The Wehrmacht would be able to deal with Poland within a matter of two to three weeks, Halder announced in a confidential speech in late April or early May. Following the Polish 'Cannae', he concluded, it would, if necessary, be possible for the Wehrmacht to strike a blow against the Western Powers.[2]

From the very outset the war with Poland was a racist war of extermination, no longer a European war in the 'normal' sense of the term but the first *völkisch* conflict in Europe and, like the ensuing occupation, a foretaste of what lay in store for the Slav countries to the east. Even during the First World War, the Slav nations – unlike their Germanic and Latin counterparts – had not been numbered among the leading civilized nations by the German elite but had been the target of ethnic resentment and negative clichés such as 'filthy' and 'backward'. This was even truer of the Jews who made up some 10 per cent of the Polish population. Ideas on what needed to be done in Poland were correspondingly radical. Writing in 2006, the German historian Jochen Böhler noted that

> even in the summer of 1939 German plans to expand eastwards already included the extermination of large sections of the population that was living there and the oppression of the survivors. The Wehrmacht was fully informed about this programme at the start of the war and it played an active role in its implementation.[3]

Poland knew about the German plans to invade its territory thanks to the news service of its general staff, with the result that it had been progressively mobilizing its armed forces since the middle of August, ordering a general mobilization on the 30th. In turn this meant that the units close to the border when war broke out early on 1 September with airborne attacks and shots fired from the *Schleswig-Holstein* battleship on the Westerplatte near Gdańsk were already on high alert. Within hours the Polish air force had been completely destroyed even before it had taken to the air. For its part, the army fought doggedly and tenaciously but had no real chance of defeating the vastly superior forces of the Wehrmacht. By 11 September the Third German Army was able to cross the Bug River to the east of Wyszków.

From the outset the German troops were fed reports that had no basis in fact, namely, that they had to deal with attacks by Polish guerrillas. The only truth was that the Polish troops who had withdrawn into the country's interior preferred to avoid open conflict but to fight, instead, from the cover of woods, hedges, farmsteads and hamlets, which the invading army interpreted as a sign of Slav treachery. They reacted by setting fire to villages and small towns and by shooting captured Polish soldiers and civilians, including old men, women and children. The total number of Polish soldiers killed while not fighting was more than 3,000. Between early September and late October there were 714 mass executions resulting in the deaths of 16,000 civilians. Jews in particular were suspected of being responsible for ambushing German soldiers. It is unclear how many of them were killed, although there were numerous instances of German soldiers cutting off or singeing the beards of Jewish men in public places or of their beating them. Looting of Jewish properties was often accompanied by the rape of Jewish women.

Throughout the Polish campaign, the distinction between the Wehrmacht and the SS was not always clear. In August 1939 the SS Dispositional Troops and the SS Death's Head Units had been granted the status of a 'standing armed force'. The Fourteenth Army consisted of the SS's Germania Combat Regiment, while the SS Death's Head Brandenburg Combat Regiment was another separate unit that was responsible for the burning down of several synagogues. Hitler's Personal Body Guard fought with the Eighth Army, while the SS Deutschland Artillery Regiment saw active service as a subdivision of the Kempf Panzer Division. Like the SS Reconnaissance Detachment, it took part in the defeat and subjugation of Poland. Members of the Kempf Panzer Division carried out a pogrom at Goworowo near Różan on 6 September, when the town's Jews were herded together into the synagogue, where the bodies of murdered Jews already lay. The building was then set on fire. Only the last-minute intervention of a Wehrmacht officer prevented a mass murder from taking place.

In addition to the 1.5 million Wehrmacht and SS soldiers, five units of the Reich Main Security Office that had been created in 1939 were also active in Poland, with initially some 2,000 men. According to the minutes of a discussion of the Office's heads, its task was 'to render as harmless as possible the leading stratum of the Polish population'. Or, as the Office's director, Reinhard Heydrich, put it the following day: 'We plan to spare ordinary people, but we have to kill the aristocracy, the priests and the Jews.'[4] It is not known how many Jews were killed by the units deployed in Poland in September and early October 1939, although we do know that between 500 and 600 Jews were murdered in the biggest massacre, which took place between 16 and 19 September in Przemyśl and the surrounding area under Udo von Woyrsch. In total it is thought that 7,000 Jews were killed in Poland between September and the end of the year. The activities of the Wehrmacht, SS and special units were aided and abetted by death squadrons of the paramilitary German Ethnic Self-Defence Force, which during the initial months of the occupation killed between 20,000 and 30,000 Polish citizens.

On the Polish side there were also a number of excesses committed against the German minority during the month of September, resulting in the deaths of around 2,000 Germans, some 400 of whom perished on 3 September in Bromberg (Bydgoszcz), where paramilitary organizations from both sides were active. A tipping point in Polish history came on 17 September, when the country's president, Ignacy Mościcki, and the army's commander in chief, Edward Rydz-Śmigły, fled to Romania, taking Felizian Sławoj-Składkowski's government with them, leaving the Red Army to march into eastern Poland along a broad front – officially to protect the Ukrainians and the White Russians who were living there. Three days later the Poznan and Pomerelia armies capitulated on the Bzura, and Warsaw fell on 27 September 1939.

The following day Ribbentrop and Molotov signed a German-Soviet border and friendship treaty in Moscow. In a secret addendum to it, the border was moved from the Vistula to the Bug further east, while by way of compensation the whole of Lithuania, with the exception of a tip of land in the country's south-west corner, became a part of the Soviet sphere of influence. As a result of this agreement, Germany now occupied 48 per cent of Polish territory, or 63 per cent of its population, with the Soviet Union occupying 51 per cent, or 37 per cent of the population. Eastern Poland, under the control of the Red Army, was the part of the country where Poles and Jews were in a minority compared with the Ukrainians and White Russians.

The final Polish units capitulated on 5 October. In the course of the fighting, the Polish army lost 66,300 men, the German army 10,572, the Red Army 737. Almost 700,000 Polish soldiers were taken prisoner by the Germans, more than 200,000 by the Soviet army. Some 110,000 officers and soldiers were able to leave Poland via Lithuania, Latvia, Hungary and Romania. By the time the cannons fell silent, there was already a Polish government in exile under General Władysław Sikorski, which was formed in Paris on 30 September after Ignacy Mościcki, by that date living in exile in Romania, had stepped down as president two days earlier. Its strongest support came from the Polish army in exile, which recruited its members from those officers and soldiers who had left Poland in 1939 and travelled to France and Great Britain via Hungary and Romania. In total, it numbered around 84,000 men. Additionally, there were experienced secret service officers who were to provide valuable service to the Allies during the war.

The German population had been markedly unenthusiastic about the war when it broke out on 1 September, but the rapid victory of the country's troops in Poland was greeted with relief and even enthusiasm. Public opinion in the Reich was not concerned with the fate and welfare of the Polish people. Germany's victory was followed by the fifth partition of Poland, after those that had taken place in 1772, 1793, 1795 and 1815. Germany now annexed a large part of the country in the west and north, while the Soviet Union did the same in the east. The rest of the country – the 'General Government' that also included Warsaw – now formed a kind of annexe to the Reich.

On Hitler's instructions, the military administration of Poland ended on 25 October 1939. But the conditions did not exist for a civilian administration to take its place, with the result that until the spring of 1940 – to quote the German historian Martin Broszat – the Führer's decision left 'an often completely unresolved situation in which the state, the police and the NSDAP were all jointly responsible for running the country, opening up an anarchical legal vacuum and almost certainly not unintentionally providing the basis for large-scale retaliatory measures against both Poles and Jews that were more or less entirely lacking in the due process of law and that lasted for several weeks'.[5]

On 6 October Hitler informed the Reichstag that the most important challenge facing Germany's future policy towards Poland was 'achieving a new ethnographic order, in other words, resettling nationalities in such a way that once this development is over there will be clearer lines of demarcation than is the case today'.[6] The implementation of this programme devolved for the most part on the NSDAP, the SS, the SD and the special units, which initially devoted themselves to the mass execution of Jews and members of the Polish intelligentsia, including university teachers, clergymen, schoolteachers, lawyers, doctors and landowners. The usual form of execution was by firing squad. Among the worst of these atrocities was the 'Extraordinary Pacification Action' in the spring of 1940, when several thousand intellectuals, artists and politicians, including the former leader of the Sejm, Maciej Rataj, were shot. Some 88,000 Poles, Jews and Roma were deported to the General Government between September and December 1939 in order to resettle ethnic Germans – mainly Balts from Estonia and Courland, Volhynian Germans from the Ukraine and Bessarabian Germans from Romania – in the new regions of the Reich, namely, the Wartheland Reichsgau (Okręg Warcki), the Danzig-West Prussian Reichsgau (Gdańsk-Prusy Zachodnie), the new administrative district of Zichenau (Ciechanów) in East Prussia, the area around Suwalki that was annexed to East Prussia and the enlarged region of Upper Silesia. Hitler was resolved that in future only Germans would live on German soil, an aim whose implementation was entrusted to the head of the SS, Heinrich Himmler, who on 7 October 1939 was appointed Reich Commissar for the Strengthening of German Ethnic Stock.

In May 1940 Himmler drafted a memorandum spelling out the consequences of this policy for Poles living in the General Government. The memorandum, headed 'Treatment of Ethnic Aliens in the East', had Hitler's explicit approval. All Poles who were not 'of good blood' and, hence, capable of being 'Germanized' would never rise above the status of serfs. For the non-German peoples of the east, no education would be permitted beyond that provided for in a four-year elementary school: 'The aim of this elementary schooling will be limited to simple sums up to 500, writing one's name and the lesson that obeying the Germans, together with honesty, hard work and decency, are divine commandments. I do not consider reading to be necessary.' The parents of children 'of good blood' should either go to Germany and become loyal citizens there or hand over their children. 'They will then probably have no more children, thus removing the danger that this subhuman race in the east could ever be ruled by these people of good blood, who might form a dangerous ruling elite that would be our equals.' The great majority of Poles could not be 'turned into Germans', and for them there was only one prospect: they were to 'become available as a leaderless nation of labourers, providing Germany with migrant labour every year and constituting a workforce that can be used for special assignments such as roads, quarries and construction work'.[7]

This policy was duly implemented. All those men and women who were German or who were regarded as capable of being turned into Germans were placed in one of four different groups in the German People's List extending from self-professed members of what had until then been the German minority to men and women of German stock who had not behaved as ethnic Germans (*Volksdeutsch*), and from those men and women of German stock who had become assimilated into the Polish way of life but who could still be turned into Germans to *Volksdeutsch* 'renegades' who could none the less be saved. But the vast majority of Poles had no prospect of becoming members of the master race. German rule in Poland was that of a colonial power that regarded the subjugated nation as its racial inferior. Unlike colonial rule during the Wilhelmine era, however, the real power was placed not in the hands of officers and civil servants but of two irregular bodies: the NSDAP, which appointed Hans Frank as governor general with his headquarters at Wawel Castle in Kraków, and the SS, which executed Hitler's racist policies. This disempowerment of the traditional bureaucracy was deliberate. The kind of thinking that operated in the tried and tested categories of norms, regulations and accepted areas of competence and that characterized the higher bureaucracy was not to be given the opportunity to impede the dynamics of the NSDAP's racist revolution.

The Sovietization of eastern Poland may have assumed different forms but it proceeded along lines similar to those adopted by the Germans in subjugating 'their' part of the country. In order to give their domination at least the semblance of democratic legitimacy, the Soviet authorities ordered the 'election' of popular assemblies in October 1939, assemblies that immediately asked to be accepted into the Ukrainian and Belorussian Soviet Republics, leading to the systematic loss of Polish identity in the annexed territories, to the nationalization of industry and, soon afterwards, to the collectivization of agriculture. The social changes were accompanied by shootings, arrests, prison sentences and, from February 1940, deportations to the east and south of Russia. By June 1941 between 760,000 and 1.25 million individuals had been forcibly removed from eastern Poland. Many, especially small children, died of the cold on the journey. Initially at least, those who were deported were members of the upper classes and the previous state apparatus or members of the intelligentsia. In June 1940 Jews – generally refugees from the German-administered part of the country – made up the bulk of those who were driven out of the country. In June 1941 it was Ukrainian and White Russian 'nationalists'.

Of all the atrocities committed by the Soviet regime in eastern Poland between 1939 and 1941 it is the murder of thousands of Polish officers in the spring of 1940 that has seared itself most deeply in the collective consciousness. On 5 March 1940 the Politburo of the Soviet Communist Party under the chairmanship of Stalin himself decided to shoot 25,700 'officers, civil servants, landowners, police officers, gendarmes and prison guards' who were currently in Soviet prisoner-of-war camps and in Ukrainian and White Russian prisons. In total, 21,300 individuals were executed. Of the officers, 4,000 were killed at Kharkiv, 6,300 at Mednoye in the Kalininsky District of Tver Oblast and 4,000 at Katyn. There were other mass shootings of Poles, notably at Bykivnia near Kiev, where the bodies of the Poles were buried alongside the victims of the great terror of 1937–8, but it is impossible to put a number on them.

The bodies buried at Katyn were discovered in the spring of 1943 by retreating German troops and presented to the world as a blatant example of the criminal character of Bolshevism, a claim – ironically enough – made in the very same year as that in which the systematic murder of European Jews at the hands of National Socialist Germany had sunk to new and terrible depths. The world was denied all knowledge of this particular genocide, just as it failed to hear about the extent to which the Polish upper classes had been liquidated in those parts of Poland that were subject to Germany's tyrannical rule.

From 'Drôle de guerre' to the Battle for Norway

Of the Western Powers, France and Britain gave Poland practically no military assistance. Although Paris had promised that it would launch a large-scale offensive fifteen days after the start of the war with the aim of relieving the pressure on the Polish forces, it merely sent a handful of units to the territory in front of the Siegfried Line, the German equivalent of the Maginot Line that had been built in 1938. There were a few skirmishes, which according to figures released by the Wehrmacht resulted in 196 German deaths up to and including 19 October. The first two British divisions did not land in France until early October, followed by two more divisions during the third week of October.

A more effective measure was Britain's naval blockade, which was imposed at once and which – as in the First World War – was designed to cut Germany off from international trade. In the ensuing naval warfare, both the Germans and the British chalked up victories: in September German submarines destroyed the aircraft carrier *Courageous* in the Bristol Channel and in October they sank the battleship *Royal Oak* in Scapa Flow, while in December British warships damaged the German armoured ship *Admiral Graf Spee* so badly that the commander saw himself obliged to scuttle his vessel off the estuary of the River Plate. The most important gesture of solidarity with Poland consisted in the two western democracies rejecting the 'peace offer' that Hitler proposed in his Reichstag speech on 6 October. In general the first seven months of the war in the west became known as 'the phoney war' in the Anglo-Saxon world and 'drôle de guerre' in France.

In the autumn of 1939 Hitler was minded to force a decisive battle by launching an offensive in the west but finally abandoned the plan because of the weather, postponing it until the following spring. In this way he robbed his conservative opponents, who for a time included the fickle chief of the general staff, Franz Halder, of the whole raison d'être for their plot to overthrow Hitler. One plot that did come to fruition was an attack by the Württemberg carpenter Georg Elser on the Bürgerbräukeller in Munich on the evening of 8 November. But by the time that Elser launched his assault, Hitler had already left the scene of his annual speech marking the anniversary of his 1923 putsch. The Führer immediately suspected that the British secret service lay behind the attempt on his life, but Elser was acting on his own. London was aware of the conservative conspirators' plans to topple Hitler, but Chamberlain's government had no intention of offering a truce or a strategic cessation of hostilities to the Prussian factionists even in the event of a change of regime in Berlin.

Conversely, there was political and military activity in the east. At the end of September the Soviet Union forced Estonia to sign mutual assistance and trade agreements, imposing similar treaties on Latvia and Lithuania in early October. In every case the counties in question were required to provide Russia with military bases. In return Lithuania was granted the area around Vilnius that had fallen into Soviet hands as a result of the fifth partition of Poland only a short time earlier. Only Finland refused to bow to Soviet pressure. On 10 October reservists were called up, which effectively amounted to mobilization. On 13 November the negotiations between the Finnish and Soviet governments were broken off, and on 30 November the Winter War began with an attack by the Red Army. The following day Moscow established a 'People's Government of the Democratic Republic of Finland' in the border town of Terijoki under the Finnish-born old Bolshevik Otto Wilhelm Kuusinen, signing a friendship and mutual assistance treaty with the puppet government on 2 December. In Helsinki Risto Ryti of the Progressive Party became prime minister, while the Social Democrat Väinö Tanner was appointed foreign secretary. Field Marshal Carl Gustav Mannerheim remained chairman of the Defence Council and assumed overall command of the country's armed forces.

In those parts of Europe that had retained their democratic governments, the Finnish struggle against Soviet aggression found many sympathizers. A Swedish solidarity committee provided the watchword 'Finland's cause is our own' and some 8,000 Swedes signed up as volunteers, although only two enlarged battalions were actually deployed on the front. Otherwise Per Albin Hansson's Social Democrat government in Stockholm remained strictly neutral, so much so that Rickard Sandler, an advocate of intervention, was obliged to resign in the middle of December, when he was replaced as foreign secretary by Christian Günther, who shared his prime minister's views on

Swedish foreign policy. Support from the League of Nations remained purely symbolic, although Helsinki appealed to the organization for help in early December, and on 14 December the Soviet Union was excluded from its list of members as the aggressor in the conflict. The Scandinavian and Baltic members of the Council of the League of Nations did not take part in the vote, which was to be the League's final sign of life.

The neutrality of the Scandinavian states proved to be a decisive obstacle in providing the French and British help that Paris and London had promised Helsinki at the start of the war. In both countries the public mood was unequivocally pro-Finnish. But, as the Finnish historian Seppo Hentilä has observed, the real reason for agreeing to provide help was rather different:

> The Western Powers were chiefly interested in the ore deposits in northern Sweden and were afraid that these might fall into the hands of Germany or, following the conquest of Finland, of the Soviet Union. It was therefore in France's and Britain's best interests to draw out the Winter War. Sweden's situation was complicated as it was threatened by occupation on three sides. Even though the Western Powers were a more tolerable alternative to Sweden than Germany or the Soviet Union, it remained steadfast in its opposition to the transit of aid across its territory throughout this period.[8]

The Finnish armed forces initially put up stiff resistance and withstood the vastly superior forces of the Red Army, even succeeding in preventing the aggressor from breaking through their lines at Summa (now Soldatskoye) on the Karelian Isthmus, but an attempt to surround the enemy forces there cost so many Finnish lives that it had to be abandoned on 23 December. After that the fighting on the Karelian Isthmus descended into positional warfare. To the north of Lake Ladoga, conversely, the Finnish strategy was successful, and here two Soviet divisions were encircled. In early January 1940 Finnish troops destroyed the Red Army's motorized Forty-Fourth Division and encircled other divisions.

Not until early February were Soviet units under the defence commissar Marshal Kliment Voroshilov able to achieve a breakthrough on the Karelian Isthmus. On 23 February the Soviet leadership sent word via Stockholm, informing the Finnish government of its peace terms. Finland was to lease the Hanko Peninsula to Russia for thirty years and cede the whole of the Karelian Isthmus to the Soviet Union, including the town of Vyborg and the western and northern shores of Lake Ladoga. The Finnish government was reluctant to agree to these terms and again asked the Western Powers for their help, which on this occasion consisted of the promise to send an expeditionary force of over 10,000 men by April. Once again, however, Stockholm refused to allow British and French troops to march through Sweden. Since Mannerheim believed that it was pointless to continue fighting, the government decided to begin peace talks on 29 February. Paris and London reacted with a renewed offer of help, which the Finns examined only to dismiss it as inadequate. After a series of further successes by the Red Army, the Finns were finally prepared to agree to additional demands by Soviet Russia to annex parts of Kuusamo and Salla. The peace treaty was signed in Moscow on 13 March and came into force the next day. The Finnish casualties were numbered at around 24,000, while those of the Red Army – by its own estimates – amounted to 49,000.

Finland had suffered serious territorial losses, but it had at least achieved its principal aim of maintaining its independence. The experience served to forge a closer bond among Finns, and the result was tantamount to a rebirth of the Finnish nation. But the Winter War had far-reaching consequences not only in Finland itself. The Soviet Union drew the lesson that its aim of conquering Finland and turning it into a Soviet republic was for the present beyond its means, while Hitler's Germany concluded from the events of 1939–40 that, if the situation were ever to arise, it would be relatively easy for the Wehrmacht to inflict a comprehensive military defeat on the Red Army.

In France, Finland's ultimate capitulation triggered a major government crisis, when, at a secret session of both chambers of the National Assembly, Daladier's government was reproached for not providing Finland with effective support. In a vote of no confidence in the Chamber of Deputies on 20 March, 239 deputies voted for the government and one against, but 300 abstained. Daladier drew the obvious conclusion from his political defeat and resigned after almost two years in the post. The following day, 21 May, his finance minister, Paul Reynaud, took over as both prime minister and foreign secretary. Reynaud had always been an outspoken critic of the policy of appeasement towards National Socialist Germany. Daladier remained the defence minister and in that way was able to prevent Charles de Gaulle – a military reformer who had played a major role in formulating Reynaud's declaration of his government's belligerent aims – from being appointed secretary to the Military Cabinet. In the confidence vote in the Chamber of Deputies on 22 March Reynaud received only one more vote than an absolute majority: 268 yes votes, 156 no votes and 111 abstentions. The vote was an accurate reflection of the inner divisions and tensions that existed in France in the spring of 1940.

On London, too, the Winter War left its mark. As first lord of the Admiralty, Winston Churchill had repeatedly urged his cabinet colleagues to ignore Norway's neutrality and mine its coastal waters – not just to pre-empt a German attack and cause lasting harm to the Reich by cutting off its supply of ore from northern Sweden but also to draw Norway and, if possible, the whole of Scandinavia into the British sphere of interest. This violation of international law seemed to Churchill to be justified by the higher good, namely, securing the freedom of the free peoples of Europe, first and foremost the British. The Soviet attack on Finland in late November 1939 confirmed the Admiralty and its first lord in their conviction that Scandinavia was strategically important. From now on there were demands not only that Norway's coastal waters be mined but that Bergen and above all Narvik, where Swedish ore was loaded on to German ships, be occupied.

Churchill had already convinced his prime minister, Neville Chamberlain, of the strategic necessity of an offensive in the North Sea, when France's new prime minister arrived in London on 28 March 1940 for the fourth meeting of the Anglo-French Supreme War Council. Both countries agreed not to conclude a separate peace and, once the war was over, to work together to secure peace. But the main item on the agenda was Swedish ore exports to Germany. At Reynaud's urging, Sweden was asked to suspend these supplies. The two allies also agreed to mine Norway's coastal waters and to send an expeditionary force to Scandinavia, where it would occupy first Narvik, Trondheim, Bergen and Stavanger and then the area where Swedish ore deposits were to be found, including the port at Luleå on the Bay of Bothnia. The details were settled during Churchill's visit to Paris on 5 April.

Early on 8 April – even before the government in Oslo had been informed – Norway's coastal waters were mined. An Anglo-French expeditionary force was due to occupy Narvik on 10 April and advance as far as the border with Sweden, but on 9 April, before the plan could be put into action, the Wehrmacht invaded Denmark. After offering only brief resistance, Denmark bowed to the inevitable, leaving the Wehrmacht to march into Norway. The commander in chief of the German navy, Admiral Erich Raeder, had already proposed this idea in October 1939, and at his suggestion, Hitler received Vidkun Quisling on 14 December. Quisling, who was the former minister of war and the leader of the radical right-wing Nasjonal Samling, alerted Hitler to the fact that Norway's neutrality was being threatened by Britain. That same day Hitler gave orders to prepare a study on military action in Scandinavia, resulting in the 'Weser Exercise', the precise timetable for which was set by Hitler on 2 April.

In Norway the German occupation encountered far greater resistance than in Denmark. Although German troops were able to occupy the country's leading ports on 9 April, the battleship *Blücher* that was due to land the occupying forces' general staff and Gestapo officials was sunk by the Norwegian military as it passed through the narrows near Oscarsborg, giving the royal family, together with the government and countless civil servants and members of parliament, time to flee the capital and escape to Elverum. The state bank's gold reserves were also salvaged at this time. On 9 April King Haakon VII turned down a German demand that his country capitulate with a single 'Nei', a refusal to surrender in which he was supported by the government of the Social Democrat prime minister Johan Nygaardsvold. They also rejected the German request that they recognize the legitimacy of the 'government' formed by Quisling. That same day the Storting granted Nygaardsvold's government the extraordinary powers that it needed to continue the military struggle.

British, French and exiled Polish units landed on the Norwegian coast between 14 and 18 April, but in most places the German advance meant that they had little choice but to put to sea again. Only in the vicinity of Narvik was there fierce and protracted fighting, which ended when the city fell into Allied hands on 28 May. By 8 June, however, the troops were ordered to withdraw, the king and his government having left Tromsö and fled to England the previous day. The Norwegian units that had inflicted heavy losses on the German navy, especially in the Oslofjord and in the north of the country, laid down their arms on 10 June.

Hitler's puppet, Vidkun Quisling, had appointed himself 'minister of state' on 9 April and was placed at the head of an Administrative Council by the occupying power. The council owed its existence to an initiative on the part of judges from the Supreme Court but failed to gain any legitimacy and was disbanded at the end of September. The actual business of government was conducted by Josef Terboven, the former Gauleiter in Essen, who was named Reich commissar for Norway on 24 May 1940. He was assisted by a twelve-man state council that he himself appointed. With the exception of Quisling's Nasjonal Samling, all political parties were banned. In February 1942 Terboven appointed Quisling prime minister, even though he enjoyed practically no support among the wider population.

In Denmark, conversely, King Christian X remained on the throne and the government continued in office. Supreme power lay in the hands of Hitler's plenipotentiary – until October 1942 the diplomat Cécil von Renthe-Fink, thereafter SS group leader Werner Best. The Social Democrat prime minister Thorvald Stauning, who headed the government until his death in May 1942, enlarged his cabinet by including liberal and conservative politicians as well as non-party civil servants in order to form a government of national unity. Denmark also aligned itself with Germany by joining the anti-Comintern pact in November 1940 and by taking steps to deal with Communists at home. By making concessions of this kind the Danish government was able to retain a considerable degree of autonomy until the summer of 1943, enjoying a greater level of independence than any other country occupied by German troops.

The loser in the race to control Scandinavia was Great Britain, at least in the shorter term. As Ian Kershaw has pointed out, the main responsibility lay with Churchill,

> but it was Chamberlain who paid the political price. The knives were now sharpened for the Prime Minister who had tried to appease Hitler. Churchill, whose warnings from the wilderness now appeared so prophetic, had gained in stature. By early May much of Chamberlain's own party had lost confidence in him as the leader Britain needed in war. The opposition parties were adamant that they would not work with him in a war cabinet. On 10 May, after faring badly in a vote of confidence in the House of Commons, he resigned.[9]

The foreign secretary, Lord Halifax, was regarded by many as Chamberlain's most likely successor, but in order to take up a seat in the Commons, he would first have had to resign his seat in the Lords, which in turn would have triggered a by-election, quite apart from the fact that he doubted his ability to lead the country in time of war, and so he decided that same day to renounce an appointment that would have marked the high point of his political career.

The way thus lay open for the then sixty-five-year-old Churchill in spite of his reputation for political inconstancy – he had twice switched his allegiance in the past, from the Conservatives to the Liberals in 1904 and from the Liberals back to the Tories in 1924. As chancellor of the Exchequer from 1924 to 1928 he had been a minister without a fortune. And as an imperialist diehard, he had doggedly resisted every step on the road to Indian independence, incurring the wrath of the moderate Conservatives, the Liberals and the Labour Party. But his determined opposition to the policy of appeasement, together with his dynamism and energy and his brilliance both as a public speaker and as a writer, ensured that he was at least well respected by his numerous enemies. When, on 10 May, he offered the Labour Party a share in government in order to place his war cabinet on a broad political basis, Clement Attlee accepted his invitation. Attlee became Churchill's deputy as lord privy seal, and the Labour politician Hugh Dalton took over as minister for economic warfare. Dalton's party colleague Herbert Morrison became minister of supply at least until October 1940, when he was promoted to home secretary. Halifax remained foreign secretary until December 1940, while his predecessor in the post, Anthony Eden, became war minister. The press baron Lord Beaverbrook became minister of aircraft production. Churchill himself retained overall control of defence.

When George VI appointed Churchill his new prime minister on the evening of 10 May 1940, the Wehrmacht's expected western offensive had just begun, ushering in a new phase in the Second World War. Hitler sought a resolution in his war with the Western Powers at the very moment that an adversary emerged who was determined to resist him at all costs and force Germany to its knees. In his first speech to the lower house on 13 May, Churchill told MPs and the British people that he had nothing to offer them but 'blood, toil, tears and sweat' and that war must be waged by land, sea and air against the most monstrous tyranny in history: 'for without victory, there is no survival [. . .] for the British Empire, no survival for all that the British Empire has stood for'.[10] The challenge facing Great Britain eight months after the war had been unleashed could hardly have been couched in more dramatic or more apposite terms.

France's Collapse: The Campaign in the West

The German attack in the west began early on 10 May, when the Wehrmacht, ignoring the neutrality of the Netherlands, Belgium and Luxembourg, thrust westwards along a front stretching from the North Sea coast to Luxembourg in the south. The first country to abandon any pretence of resistance was the Netherlands. Even while the negotiations for the country's capitulation were still in progress, Rotterdam was being bombarded, resulting in the loss of some 900 lives. On 13 May Queen Wilhelmina and her government went into exile in London. Two days later the military capitulation was complete, and by the 18th the former leader of the Austrian National Socialists, Arthur Seyß-Inquart, had been installed as Reich commissar for the occupied territories and had begun to put in place a German civilian administration.

Belgium took a little longer to subdue, but by 16 May the fortresses at Liège and Namur and on the Dyle Line had all been taken. By the 17th Brussels had been occupied, Antwerp by the 18th, allowing the Wehrmacht to cut off the Belgian troops to the north of this line from the British and French units that had in the meantime advanced from France into Belgium. The Belgian government fled first to France and then to England. King Leopold III remained in the country, where he officially surrendered on 28 May, after which he returned to his royal palace at Laeken, effectively a German prisoner of war. General Alexander von Falkenhausen assumed the role of military governor of Belgium, while Eggert Reeder, an SS group leader who was regional president of Cologne and Düsseldorf, became head of the governor's administrative staff.

Once Grand-Duchess Charlotte of Luxembourg and her government had gone into exile in London, the country was to all intents and purposes annexed, thereafter becoming a part of the Gau of Mosel-Trier, which was renamed the Moselland Gau in early 1941. The entire population was subjected to a radical programme designed to impose German culture and the German language on it, while all men old enough to do military service were drafted into the Wehrmacht. Around 100,000 Francophile men, women and children from Alsace-Lorraine were forced to leave the region, which had likewise been effectively annexed. They were all sent to Vichy France. A general strike intended to protest at this last-named measure at the end of August 1942 had no effect but served, rather, to encourage the principality's new masters to adopt even harsher measures against 'national comrades' who had no desire to be any such thing.

The German army marched into France not along the Maginot Line, which had been massively fortified during the interwar period, but further north, across the Ardennes, a natural barrier that the French military had considered impregnable. In the space of just three days seven German Panzer divisions from Army Group A under General Gert von Rundstedt were able to deal an annihilating blow to the Ninth French Army under General André Georges Corap. Sedan fell into German hands on 15 May, a bridgehead that allowed General Heinz Guderian and his armoured division to advance towards the coast on his own initiative, prompting the French commander in chief, Maurice Gamelin, to report to the prime minister that the army could no longer guarantee the safety of the capital. In northern and eastern France the civilian population began to flee in vast numbers, with the result that many roads became gridlocked. By June some eight million French men, women and children were fleeing from the invading Germans.

Informed by Reynaud as to the gravity of the situation, Churchill travelled to Paris on 16 May, where he found a state of near panic. In the event the expected fall of Paris was delayed because the Germans first wanted to advance to the Channel coast. Reynaud restructured his government on the 19th, taking over the Ministry of Defence while retaining the premiership. Daladier, who had previously been the minister of the interior, became foreign secretary, while the energetic minister for the colonies, Georges Mandel, assumed Daladier's old post. The 'victor of Verdun', the eighty-four-year-old war hero Philippe Pétain, became deputy prime minister, while Gamelin, whom Reynaud held responsible for the present military debacle, was replaced as commander in chief by the former chief of the general staff, Maxime Weygand, a supporter of the extreme right and, like Pétain, constitutionally opposed to the parliamentary democracy of the Third Republic.

On the same day that this major reshuffle took place in Paris, German Panzer units under Ewald von Kleist reached Abbeville on the Somme estuary, completing the 'sickle cut' – as Churchill was later to describe it – and isolating the British and French troops that were north of the Somme and preventing them from rejoining the rest of the Allied forces. Five days later, on 24 May, when the German troops were only ten to fifteen miles from Dunkirk, the German advance was suddenly interrupted, when Hitler, in agreement with Rundstedt but in disagreement with his other generals, including Brauchitsch and Halder, decided to spare the Panzer corps and to leave Göring's air force to complete the encirclement of Dunkirk from the sea.

This unexpected break in the Panzer war was used by the British general, Lord Gort, to evacuate the British Expeditionary Force and withdraw to Dunkirk in order to form a bridgehead there, a move undertaken on his own initiative and in defiance of all the promises given to the French, for all that it gained the later approval of Eden in his capacity as minister of war. The troops began to set sail for Great Britain on 27 May. The German Luftwaffe disrupted Operation Dynamo – as the British called it – by pounding the beaches and port but was unable to prevent the evacuation and suffered serious losses itself at the hands of the Royal Air Force. By 4 June some 224,301 British soldiers and 111,172 French and Belgian troops had been evacuated across the Channel, although they had to leave their weapons and other military equipment on the Continent, in which regard they differed from the Canadian troops who had landed in France and sailed from there to Britain. The 'Dunkirk miracle' meant nothing less than the temporary salvation of Great Britain, for without the evacuation of the bulk of the Expeditionary Force, the United Kingdom would almost certainly have been unable to continue its war with Germany.

During the second half of May the British and French governments both pinned their hopes on Roosevelt. Churchill wrote to the American president on 15 and 18 May, urging him to support Great Britain by arguing that his country would be placed in the direst of predicaments if France was defeated. Roosevelt replied on the 24th, a letter which, however friendly in tone, struck an evasive note dictated by the powerful isolationist lobby in the United States. All that the president was prepared to promise was to attempt to influence Mussolini and persuade the latter to keep Italy out of the war.

When Paul Reynaud arrived in London on 26 May for talks with the British government, he too urged Roosevelt to offer his diplomatic assistance, resulting in an Anglo-French request that Roosevelt received the next day and to which he reacted at once by informing Mussolini that he – Roosevelt – was willing to assume the role of a mediator and, if necessary, to pass on to the Allies any claims that Italy might care to entertain in the Mediterranean. He also assured Mussolini that when the war was over, Italy would be allowed to take part in any peace conference as an equal partner. The approach proved unsuccessful, Mussolini turning down the offer on 28 May.

If Reynaud and Lord Halifax had had their way, Britain and France would then have appealed to Italy directly, but on 27 May, after a certain amount of vacillation, Churchill finally decided against such a step. The concessions approved by the French prime minister included not only a generous compromise on colonial policy in Africa but also the demilitarization of Malta and the neutrality of the Suez Canal and Gibraltar, concessions that struck Churchill as incompatible with the vital interests of the British Empire. While a number of British and French politicians could envisage the idea of Mussolini as a mediator in any dealings with Hitler, this seemed to Churchill to amount to a request for a ceasefire, which the British prime minister was bound to oppose. Great Britain's position was clear: it would remain unyielding.

By the time that Operation Dynamo was completed on 4 June and Dunkirk had fallen into German hands, 1.2 million soldiers from France, Britain, Belgium and the Netherlands were German prisoners of war. The real battle for France began the following morning, ushering in the second phase in Germany's campaign in the west. More than one hundred German divisions faced fewer than fifty French divisions, while Germany's superiority in the air was overwhelming. The same was true of the German Panzer corps. The result was that there were no longer any major battles. The Wehrmacht moved south behind the rear of the Maginot Line, overrunning Alsace and Normandy and taking Rouen on 9 June. The following day Italy, determined not to lose out on the expected spoils, declared war on France and Britain, although the country was in no position to claim military glory for itself as it was simply unprepared to conduct an operational conflict.

On 5 June, the final day of the latest German offensive, Reynaud again reshuffled his cabinet, taking over the Foreign Office from his old adversary

Édouard Daladier and, in his capacity as defence minister, appointing an advocate of unconditional resistance, Brigadier General Charles de Gaulle, as his undersecretary of state. De Gaulle's counterpart at the Foreign Office was Paul Baudouin, who sought to influence Reynaud by pulling him in the opposite – defeatist – direction, an influence that was soon to prove more effective than de Gaulle's.

On 10 June, the day on which Italy entered the war, Reynaud and his government decided to leave Paris. In the course of the next three days, two meetings of the Allies' Supreme War Council met, first near Orléans, then near Tours. In both cases the meetings were attended by Churchill, who was obliged to turn down the French request for the deployment of the Royal Air Force as he needed the planes to defend Great Britain. On 13 June Churchill and Reynaud addressed a joint appeal to Roosevelt. The very next day German troops occupied Paris, which immediately beforehand had been declared an 'Open City'. Reynaud's government moved to Bordeaux, coincidentally the very city where another French government had established its temporary headquarters in the face of the country's imminent defeat in the Franco-Prussian War of 1870–71.

The fall of Paris proved hugely demoralizing not only for the population at large but also for its political and military leaders. Pétain and Weygand had only recently declared that further resistance was futile, whereupon Weygand had insisted that not the army but the state as a whole should capitulate, a move intended to point the finger of blame at the country's politicians. Roosevelt's answer was debated in the Council of Ministers on 16 June and did nothing to improve the atmosphere, for although the president promised to supply more arms, he was unable to hold out the prospect of the United States entering the war at least in the foreseeable future.

Reynaud's cabinet saw only two alternatives: it could either continue the struggle from a base in North Africa or it could invite the Germans to state the conditions for a ceasefire. A British offer to create a 'union' of the two states with shared nationality, a common government and a common army, found favour with Reynaud but encountered only incredulity and rejection elsewhere. Reynaud was inclined to continue fighting alongside Britain but had the impression that he no longer enjoyed the support of the majority of his ministers and in response to a request from the president of the Republic, Albert Lebrun, he announced his resignation. On 16 June Lebrun named as his successor the most popular Frenchman of the time, Philippe Pétain, who formed a cabinet in which the defeatists held sway: Weygand became defence minister, Baudouin foreign minister and Admiral François Darlan, who had switched his allegiance to the peace camp, was appointed the minister for the navy. The deputy prime minister Camille Chautemps, who had played a major role in Reynaud's resignation, retained his post.

The Council of Ministers' request that Germany should state its conditions for a ceasefire was agreed towards midnight and handed to the Spanish ambassador in France to be conveyed to Hitler. In a radio address the following day Pétain informed his fellow countrymen and women that France must suspend hostilities. The speech was effectively an order to the French not to offer any more resistance to the Germans, and most of the country's troops immediately laid down their weapons, leaving the Wehrmacht to take cities such as Cherbourg, St-Étienne and Lyons without a struggle. Coming from Verdun, Guderian's Panzer corps advanced as far as the Swiss border. On 18 June Hitler met Mussolini in Munich to agree on the terms for the ceasefire with France. Mussolini's far-reaching demands for Nice, Corsica, large parts of North Africa, including Tunisia and French Somaliland, and the surrender of the French fleet and air force to Italy, were rejected by Hitler, who was determined to prevent the French fleet from continuing to fight the war not only in Europe but also in the colonies and who was no less resolved to turn Pétain's France into a puppet state loyal to the German Reich.

When the octogenarian marshal asked Germany to discuss the terms for a ceasefire and consciously refused to make his acceptance of Germany's terms dependent on Britain's approval, as he had been asked to do by the Allies' Supreme War Council on 28 March 1940, he presumably had the majority of his compatriots behind him. The country's defeat was a given with a long prehistory that could not be corrected overnight. France had relied on the protection that the fortifications along the Maginot Line appeared to provide. In spite of de Gaulle's repeated warnings, the country had not built up an effective armoured division capable of fighting an offensive war, while its air force, too, had suffered from years of neglect. For far too long the nation had deluded itself into thinking only of peace, a shortcoming shared by the political right and left. Socially and politically, the country was deeply divided.

Although only a small minority had applauded the extreme right-wing slogan 'Rather Hitler than Blum' at the time of the Popular Front, the spirit of defeatist conformity to the demands of the Third Reich continued to thrive under Daladier and Reynaud. Among its most prominent representatives were the neo-socialist mayor of Bordeaux, Adrien Marquet, who became minister of the interior in Pétain's government on 29 June, and two leaders of radical right-wing parties, the ex-Socialist Marcel Déat and the former Communist Jacques Doriot. None of the defeatist politicians was as consistently and ruthlessly opportunistic, however, as the former prime minister, Pierre Laval. On 2 September 1939 he had tried in vain to speak in the Senate against the government's decision to go to war with Germany. By the summer of 1940 he was unconditional in his support for Pétain, and on 22 June he was appointed deputy prime minister.

But the universally revered Pétain did not speak for the whole of France when he addressed the nation on 17 June 1940. By the following day he had received a response from Charles de Gaulle, who as undersecretary at the Defence Ministry had travelled to London four days earlier at Reynaud's request to help coordinate the Allies' war effort. De Gaulle used the British airwaves to appeal to all French officers, soldiers, engineers and specialized workers in the armaments industry who were then living in exile in Great Britain or who were planning to move there to get in touch with him. France's defeat, he told them, was not definitive and their country was not lost for they had a great Empire behind them – the British Empire – and could make use of the vast industrial resources of the United States: 'This war is not over as a result of the Battle of France. This war is a worldwide war. [. . .] Whatever happens, the flame of the French resistance must not be extinguished and will not be extinguished.' The sentence from the speech that was most widely quoted – 'France has lost a battle but France has not lost the war' – was added only later to the published version of the text.[11]

The speech had a tremendous impact and became the basic manifesto of French resistance to the German occupation. Ten days after making the speech de Gaulle founded France Libre in London, the command centre of the French Resistance. The British government recognized the general as leader of a free France on 28 June, and in the French colonies several other generals and governors, including the governors of Chad, Cameroon, French Equatorial Africa and the French Congo, came over to his side. In France itself Pétain's government sought to prevent the dissemination of de Gaulle's speech, in which it was helped by strict censorship laws introduced in the autumn of 1939, but it was unable to suppress it completely. The dissident general was stripped of his French citizenship, and a war tribunal sentenced him to a term of four years in prison on 4 July 1940 and then, on 2 August, to death. The French men and women who agreed with de Gaulle were not impressed by these measures.

On 21 June the French ceasefire delegation under General Charles Huntziger was taken to Compiègne and to the same railway carriage as that in which Marshal Foch had spelt out the Allies' conditions for an armistice to the German negotiators on 11 November 1918. Here, in the presence of Hitler and a number of high-ranking generals, General Field Marshal Wilhelm Keitel, the head of the Wehrmacht's Supreme Command, informed the French delegation of Germany's terms for surrender. Most of northern France, including Paris and the area as far south as the Loire, together with the whole of the Atlantic coast, was to be occupied by German troops, while the German military commander in Brussels was to administer the belt along the border with Belgium consisting of the *départements* of Nord and Pas-de-Calais. All sovereign authority lay in the hands of the occupying power, and only local government remained in local hands, albeit under the supervision of the occupying authority, with which they were obliged to 'collaborate'.

The French army was reduced in strength to 100,000 men at home – the figure was the same as that imposed on the German army in 1919 under the terms of the Treaty of Versailles – while in Algeria and the French colonies the number was set at 279,000. Artillery, tanks, aircraft and heavy military equipment were to be handed over to Germany, and the French fleet was to be decommissioned and confined to port under German supervision in order to prevent the vessels from falling into British hands, a stipulation that did not apply, however, to those ships that were needed to defend the country's overseas territories. In response to a request from Weygand and Darlan, Germany promised not to appropriate the French fleet either during the war or afterwards. For its part France agreed to prevent all its citizens from resuming the fight against Germany, or in other words, from joining de Gaulle. France also released all its German prisoners of war but had to accept that 1.95 million French soldiers remained in German prisoner-of-war camps. German citizens – that is, émigrés – had to be returned to the Reich if so requested. Germany would be compensated for the cost of the country's occupation, which was initially calculated at 400 million francs or 20 million marks, a day and was also entitled to make continuing demands on France's economic resources.

The terms of the armistice contained no specific mention of Alsace and that part of Lorraine that had belonged to Germany between 1871 and 1918. The regions in question – the *départements* of Moselle, Haut-Rhin and Bas-Rhin – were de facto incorporated into Germany, although their legal annexation had to wait. Alsace henceforth formed a part of the Gau of Baden that in future was to be known as the Gau of the Upper Rhine, while Lorraine became a part of the Gau of Saarpfalz that was renamed the Westmark. Both regions were placed under the civilian control of their respective Gauleiters. French place names were replaced by German ones. Steps were taken to prevent the use of the French language, and all men eligible for military service were drafted into the Wehrmacht.

The French delegation signed the armistice agreement on 22 June after the German side had rejected almost all of its counterproposals and issued an ultimatum. It would come into force after a similar agreement had been reached with Italy. Although Pétain had asked Italy for a ceasefire on 20 June, Mussolini launched an offensive in the Alps on the 21st, albeit one that resulted in few territorial gains. In the course of their negotiations with the French delegation in Rome, the Duce's representatives demanded that the newly conquered areas be ceded to Italy, that all of the French Alpine army's military equipment be handed over, that the Franco-Italian border in Europe and Africa be demilitarized and that Italy be allowed to use a whole series of military ports and certain French ports and railways in Africa for military purposes. The agreement was signed on 24 June, and the ceasefire came into force at 1:35 the next morning. By the end of the western campaign France could mourn 85,000 war dead and 15,000 soldiers missing in action, while the equivalent figures for Germany were 27,000 dead and 18,000 missing.

It was not long before Britain protested at the breach of the agreement of 28 March 1940, when both countries had committed themselves not to sign a separate peace treaty. After de Gaulle was acknowledged as leader of the Free French on 28 June, most of the French fleet was destroyed by the Royal Navy on 3 July as it lay at anchor in the harbour at Mers el-Kébir in what was then

French Algeria. Around 1,300 French officers and sailors lost their lives in the attack. Churchill had been keen to prevent the ships from falling into enemy hands and at the same time wanted to show the United States that he was determined to continue to resist Germany even without his Continental allies. Pétain responded to this unprecedented challenge by breaking off diplomatic relations with Britain on 5 July and by bombing Gibraltar, while Germany reacted by suspending its operation to decommission the French fleet.

Since 1 July Pétain's government had been meeting at Vichy on the northern edge of the Massif Central. Unlike Paris and Bordeaux, the once-fashionable and popular spa town lay in unoccupied France. Here, on 10 July, the National Assembly – a joint session of the Senate and Chamber of Deputies convened at the request of the deputy prime minister, Pierre Laval – granted Pétain the special powers needed to draw up a new constitution. The move was approved by 569 parliamentarians from every party, while eighty, including thirty-seven of Léon Blum's Socialists, opposed it. The only preconditions for the new constitution were that it must guarantee the rights of labour, the family and the country, that it be ratified by the people and that it be enforced by the relevant legislative bodies.

By the end of July Pétain had issued five constitutional decrees that largely invalidated the constitutional laws of 1875. Under the decree dated 11 July, the new head of state was Philippe Pétain, marshal of France, in whom were invested far-reaching dictatorial powers, including the whole of the legislative power until such time as new chambers were in place. He was the commander in chief of all the armed forces; the ministers whom he appointed were responsible to him alone; and it was he who negotiated and ratified all international treaties. Only when declaring war did he need the agreement of parliament. The Senate and Chamber of Deputies that had been elected in 1936 were prorogued until further notice.

The Third Republic was over. In its place was an authoritarian presidential dictatorship that marked the start of what Vichy's propagandists called the *révolution nationale*. Laval and other opponents of parliamentary democracy had won an important victory, for France now had the framework of an order that in the longer term was intended to help the country mitigate the severity of the terms of the armistice, to keep out of the Second World War, to restore its sovereignty through a peace treaty and to assume a suitable position in Hitler's new vision of Europe.

The rapid defeat of France was immediately hailed as proof of the Führer's inspired strategy of a blitzkrieg, and yet it had been planned as no such thing. Rather, two factors had turned the campaign into a blitzkrieg: on the one hand, there were the failings of the French and British military, on the other the improvised breakthrough of Guderian's German Panzer corps from Sedan to the Atlantic coast in the middle of May 1940. According to the German military historian and retired colonel Karl-Heinz Frieser, 'the blitzkrieg mentality evolved only *after* the campaign in the west'. In short, the *Blitzkrieg* was 'not the cause but the consequence of victory. What had been achieved to universal surprise in May 1940 was to serve from now on as the "secret of victory" in realizing Hitler's desire for conquest'. Only then could the 'folly of the "world blitzkrieg"' arise that was to have such catastrophic consequences for world history. In Frieser's pointed phrase, 'The campaign in the west was not planned as a blitzkrieg, successful though it proved, whereas the 1941 campaign in the east was planned as a blitzkrieg, but it was one that proved unsuccessful.'[12]

Although Hitler had not been responsible for the rapid victory in the west and had in fact placed that victory at risk by vacillating while his forces were advancing on Dunkirk, the subjugation of France led to a massive increase in his popularity at home. Two decades after the Treaty of Versailles had come into force, the German Reich seemed finally to have won the First World War. 'The superhuman greatness of the Führer and of his work is recognized today by all right-thinking national comrades and recognized, moreover, unconditionally, joyfully and gratefully', reported the chairman of the Regional Council of Swabia on 9 July, while the district leader of the NSDAP in the city of Augsburg noted the following day that 'it can be said in all confidence that the entire nation is now filled with such trust in the Führer as has arguably never been the case before'. German academia was just as enthusiastic as the many nameless 'national comrades': in a letter that he wrote to another German historian, Siegfried A. Kaehler, on 4 July 1940, the liberal conservative historian Friedrich Meinecke, who otherwise had grave misgivings about Hitler and National Socialism, admitted that

> for me, too, joy, enthusiasm and pride in this army must be the dominant emotions, at least for the present. And to have regained Strasbourg! How could a man's heart not beat a little faster at this? After all, building up an army of millions in the space of only four years and rendering it capable of such achievements has been an astonishing and arguably the greatest and the most positive accomplishment of the Third Reich.[13]

When, in the spring of 1940, the National Socialist regime launched its campaign to win European support for a leading role for the Reich and for Italy, it could rely on the backing of many and, indeed, most German historians. Writing in Goebbels's weekly *Das Reich*, which first appeared at the end of May 1940, Peter Richard Rohden contributed an article that was published on 21 July 1940 and declared that the two countries shared a special mission:

> Within the Germanic and Romance world, only Germany and Italy represent a genuine imperial idea of order that aims not at suppression and exploitation but at justice and peace – Italy as the heir of the *pax Romana*, Germany as that of the Sacrum Imperium.

The following year Karl Richard Ganzer published *The Reich as a Force for European Order*, the principal message of which was contained in the following highlighted passage:

> Thanks to its higher political potency, the German nucleus organizes around itself as its determinative centre a group of spaces which, different in kind, may be racially autonomous but which form a political community, within which German leadership and the autonomy of these other races are balanced in an organic hierarchy.[14]

In 1941 Ganzer became the temporary director of the Reich Institute for the History of the New Germany.

For Hitler, of course, 'the autonomy of other races' was not something that would ever dictate his actions even in western Europe. As early as May 1937 he had dreamt of the 'future annulment of the Peace of Westphalia'. And on 7 November 1939, following a conversation with Hitler, Goebbels noted in his diary: 'It will not be long now before we aim a blow at the Western Powers. Perhaps the Führer will succeed in annulling the Peace of Westphalia sooner than we all think. This would be his life's crowning achievement.' Ten days later Hitler returned to the subject: 'The Führer talks about our war aims,' Goebbels noted on 17 November.

> Once started, we need to settle the outstanding questions. He's thinking of the total liquidation of the Peace of Westphalia, which was concluded in Münster and which he wants to do away with in Münster. That's our great goal. Once it has been achieved, we can calmly close our eyes and rest.[15]

To pretend that the Peace of Münster and Osnabrück had never happened was tantamount to wanting to redraw the map of Europe and ensure that Germany gained permanent supremacy over the rest of the Continent. Within this context, the restoration of the Holy Roman Empire's old western border, as it had existed before the Thirty Years War, would probably have been only the first step in a far more ambitious project, and even by the autumn of 1939 Hitler was already going much further than this: according to Goebbels, when he began to divide up the French provinces on 3 November, he considered setting aside Burgundy as a resettlement area for the South Tyroleans who, in keeping with an agreement made between Germany and Italy on 23 June 1939, had until the end of the year to decide whether they wanted to emigrate to Germany or remain in Italy as Italian citizens enjoying no special rights.

Following Hitler's victory over France, Germany took its first steps in the direction of implementing this plan. Himmler left for a tour of inspection of Burgundy on 10 July 1940, the aim of his visit being to test whether the region could be Germanized by the resettlement of German peasant families. By the end of December 1940 a report had been drawn up: one million Germans would be required to resettle nine French *départements*.

The Germanization of Burgundy was a part of the Greater German policy announced by Hitler in the spring of 1940. On 9 April – the day on which Germany invaded Denmark and Norway – he explained to its closest associates: 'Just as Bismarck's empire came into being in 1866 [i.e. in the wake of Prussia's victory over Austria], so the Greater German Reich will come into being today.'[16] Before the war, Hitler had used the word 'Germanization' to describe the conquest of Lebensraum to the east, in the rolling expanses of Russia, but ever since the signing of the German-Soviet non-aggression pact on 23 August 1939, Russia had ceased to play a part in his vision of Germany's future. The Greater German Reich was now to include Germanic nationalities such as the Danes, the Norwegians, the Dutch and the Flemish, who would be united under German leadership and form an entity distinguished by its racial purity but no longer a nation state.

In this way Hitler was resurrecting the old pre-nationalist idea of *Germania magna* that had been invoked by the German Humanists around 1500 and again in the early nineteenth century by Ernst Moritz Arndt. By 1940, however, it had come to seem 'post-nationalist' in character. Apart from the Greater Germanic Reich, only Italy and – had it been able to reach an agreement with Germany – Great Britain could have asserted their right to be regarded as European powers of any stature at this time. These, then, were the outlines of Hitler's new European order to the west of the Russian border at the point of his greatest military triumphs to date.

Tokyo, Washington, Berlin: A Change in International Politics 1940–41

Germany's triumph in its campaign in the west had implications for the Far East as well. Japan had remained neutral when war had been unleashed in Europe in September 1939 but it changed its policy in response to the defeat of the Netherlands and then of France: the chance to conquer the Dutch East Indies and French Indochina suddenly seemed tantalizingly close. Even British Malaysia and Singapore seemed to lie within Tokyo's grasp. In 1940 the army forced the resignation of Admiral Mitsumasa Yonai's government after he had seemed to them to be unduly cautious, allowing the return to power of the prime minister from 1937–8, Prince Konoe Fumimaro. Apart from Konoe, the army's other political favourites were the army minister Tojo Hideki and the foreign minister Matsuoka Yosuke.

The new government was keener than its predecessor to renew the country's ties with Germany, ties that Japan had severed by signing its non-aggression pact with the Soviet Union. Under the propagandist slogan of a 'Greater East Asia Co-Prosperity Sphere' Japan now sought to dominate the whole of East and south-east Asia. The Japanese navy had long been urging expansion in a southerly direction, and by the summer of 1940 the army, too, had adopted a similar line, even though it had traditionally set its sights on Russia. From now on the country's motto was 'Northern Defence and Southern Advance'.

Hitler initially remained cautious in the face of signals from Tokyo, and it was not until August 1940, when he realized that massive American support meant that a quick victory over Britain could no longer be expected, that he agreed to take soundings, the aim of which was a military alliance against the United States as the price for Germany's willingness to recognize that east and south-east Asia belonged to Japan's sphere of interests. The Japanese navy was reluctant to agree to this new policy as it did not feel that it was sufficiently prepared for a war with the United States, but it finally bowed to pressure from the army when the latter demanded that a treaty be concluded with the Axis Powers of Germany and Italy. Japan's foreign minister signed a Tripartite Pact in Berlin on 27 September 1940: it was a defence alliance that would come into effect in the event of an American attack during the next ten years. Germany promised to help Japan in its attempts to reach a settlement with the Soviet Union and was even willing to leave Iran and India to Moscow in the event of the latter's joining the Tripartite Pact.

This renewed rapprochement between Japan and the Axis Powers was accompanied by a realignment in terms of Japan's domestic policies. Shortly after the Tripartite Pact had been signed, all the political parties in Japan were disbanded and replaced by the Taisei yokusankei, or Imperial Rule Assistance Association, which was founded on 12 October 1940, its aim being to fulfil the functions of a single party and form an umbrella organization for all the country's professional and cultural organizations. Its chairman was the country's prime minister. But its political and military leaders held such divergent views on its aims that the Association never achieved the dynamism of Hitler's NSDAP or Mussolini's Partito Nazionale Fascista. Parliament continued to be made up as before, and although the regime grew markedly more authoritarian, the Japanese Empire never became a totalitarian dictatorship of the German or Italian kind.

It was highly questionable whether in signing the Tripartite Pact Tokyo would be able to intimidate the United States – potentially its most dangerous adversary. On 26 September 1940, a day before the pact was signed, the United States had placed a total embargo on steel and scrap metal that caused Japan considerable harm. This was America's answer to an aggressive act by Tokyo that was approved by Berlin and – against its will – by Vichy, namely, the occupation of French Indochina, which allowed Japan to cut off important supplies from the China of Chiang Kai-shek. Regardless of the new alignment of forces between Berlin, Rome and Tokyo, the American embargo was rigorously maintained throughout the subsequent period, while Washington provided China with an increased amount of help.

The Soviet Union, too, reacted to the Tripartite Pact in ways that Tokyo had not anticipated and made no attempt to join the treaty. All that Matsuoka was able to achieve in Moscow in April 1941 at the end of an extended tour of Europe was a neutrality treaty, not the non-aggression pact that he had been hoping for. The Japanese government had no idea that Germany had in the meantime radically revised its attitude to the Soviet Union. At the same time the United States successfully increased its pressure on Japan. While the country's outspokenly anti-American foreign minister was travelling in Europe, Konoe's cabinet went behind his back and took soundings with Washington in order to explore the possibility of a settlement between the two powers.

The United States had declared its neutrality at the start of the war in Europe, but by 4 November 1939 Washington had changed its position in favour of the Allies, when a new Neutrality Act allowed countries involved in the hostilities to buy goods of every kind, including weapons and munitions, from the United States under the terms of the cash-and-carry clause of 1937 and to export them on their own vessels.

On 16 May 1940, six days after Germany launched its campaign in the west, Roosevelt asked Congress to agree to authorize $1,000 million to mechanize and motorize the army and build 50,000 military and naval planes. Both the Senate and the House of Representatives agreed to his request. At the same time Congress raised the upper limit of the national debt to $4,900 million. Three months later, on 19 July 1940, Roosevelt signed the Two-Ocean Navy Act providing for the construction of a much-enlarged fleet that could operate in both the Atlantic and the Pacific and that would be ready by 1945.

At this date in the country's history public opinion as to how to react to the aggressive policies of the totalitarian and authoritarian regimes in Berlin, Rome and Tokyo was still deeply divided. In May 1940 committed internationalists associated with the journalist William Allen White responded to Germany's campaign in the west by forming a Committee to Defend America by Aiding the Allies. As its name implied, it sought to offer massive support to European democracies, especially Great Britain, in order to make it unnecessary for the United States to enter the war. Among its supporters were first and foremost east coast intellectuals, including 'Yankees' who felt committed to England, and Americans of Jewish extraction.

An isolationist countermovement that was formed in July created far more of a stir. This was the America First Committee summoned into existence by the industrialist Robert Wood. Among its star speakers was Charles A. Lindbergh, the internationally celebrated aviator who had been the first man to make a nonstop solo transatlantic flight from New York to Paris. Most of its sponsors and supporters were businessmen from the Midwest, especially from Chicago and the surrounding area, and Americans of Irish and German extraction. All were for the most part Republicans. But the Grand Old Party, too, included internationalists and even interventionists, to two of whom Roosevelt gave cabinet posts in June 1940 in a demonstrative show of support for their cause: Henry L. Stimson, who had been the secretary of war under Taft and Hoover and who now returned to his former post, and William Franklin ('Frank') Knox as secretary of the navy.

During the summer of 1940 the American people became increasingly aware of the dangers threatening their country from abroad. In May 40 per cent of a representative cross-section of Americans emphatically rejected any military involvement, but by July 66 per cent believed that Germany represented a direct threat to their country. That same month, at a conference of Pan-American foreign ministers in Havana, the administration was confronted by the fact that Hitler's attempt to intimidate the countries of Latin America was beginning to pay off: out of regard for their trade with Germany, Argentina, Brazil and Chile were only three of the countries in the region that refused to send their ministers to Cuba. In spite of this, the State Department had succeeded by the end of the year in signing defence agreements with every Latin American republic with the exception of Argentina.

In September 1940, supported by an ambitious campaign by the Committee to Defend America spearheaded by the First World War hero General John Joseph Pershing, Roosevelt took a decisive step that went some way beyond his previous offers of help for Great Britain. Circumventing the 'cash-and-carry' provision of the 1937 treaty and in response to an urgent appeal from Churchill, he handed over to Britain fifty older destroyers, mostly from the First World War, and sent a number of planes back to their factories, so that Britain could buy them from there. In return London gave Washington permission to establish military bases on Newfoundland, Bermuda and the British islands in the Caribbean. The deal was an early expression of what was later to become known as the 'special relationship' between the United States and Great Britain. Of scarcely less value to Britain than ships and aircraft was a law that came into force on 16 September: the Selective Service Act ordered the registration of all men aged between twenty-one and thirty-five, allowing recruits to be called up in peacetime for the first time in American history.

Presidential elections were due to take place in November 1940. Even as late as the summer of that year it had still been uncertain whether Roosevelt would allow his name to be put forward as the Democratic Party candidate. Although the constitution did not rule out a third term in office, there was an unwritten law that an incumbent who had already been re-elected once would not contest the presidency again. It was probably in late May 1940 that in view of the extremely tense international situation Roosevelt decided that he would be the first president to break with tradition and stand for re-election, but not until immediately before the Democratic Convention in Chicago in July did he reveal that he would accept his party's nomination. As was expected, he was nominated by a huge majority. Roosevelt was also able to persuade the delegates to accept his secretary of agriculture, Henry A. Wallace, an avowed internationalist, as his vice-presidential running mate. The Republicans' candidate was a dark horse, Wendell Willkie, a former Democrat and a largely unknown industrial manager from New York. A liberal internationalist whose slogan was 'One World', he used his gifts as an orator and his influential positions to win the support of large and well-respected newspapers like the *New York Times* and the Cleveland *Plain Dealer*, giving him a good chance of winning over voters from the political middle ground.

In the course of the election campaign, both candidates assured potential voters that they would keep America out of any war, with Willkie finally going so far as to question Roosevelt's desire for peace and persuading the president to promise all American fathers and mothers that their sons would never be sent to any foreign wars. Three days before the elections, he even assured voters that 'Your President says this country is not going to war'.[17] Roosevelt's attempt to defeat his political challenger was helped not only by his political experience but also by the clear upturn in the country's economic fortunes, an upturn due above all to the forced pace of rearming America and to the exports to Britain that were a direct result of the war in Europe. What the New Deal had failed to achieve was now accomplished by the war even before the United States had officially entered the conflict: a new economic boom was in the offing.

Although Roosevelt's victory was not as emphatic as it had been in 1932 and 1936, he still won far more votes than Willkie: 27 million against 22 million, resulting in 449 votes for the incumbent and eighty-two for his Republican challenger in the Electoral College. Roosevelt proved most popular with working-class and lower middle-class voters as well as with those of Jewish and Polish extraction and, finally, with black Americans. It was the isolationists who were most disappointed by the outcome of the election since their choice had been between two internationalists. On 19 January 1941 one of the most influential speakers of isolationist America, the Republican senator Gerald P. Nye from North Dakota, told a meeting of the America First Committee in Kansas City that 'I shall be surprised if history does not show that beginning at the Republican convention in Philadelphia a conspiracy was carried to deny the American people a chance to express themselves'.[18]

One of the first foreign policy decisions that Roosevelt took after he had been re-elected was to provide weapons and military equipment to Great Britain, which by now was on the verge of bankruptcy and which was not required to pay for the help offered. Roosevelt explained his actions at a press conference on 17 December 1940, offering a vivid analogy:

> Suppose my neighbor's home catches fire, and I have a length of garden hose four or five hundred feet away. If he can take my garden hose and connect it up with his hydrant, I may help him to put out his fire. Now, what do I do? I don't say to him before that operation, 'Neighbor, my garden hose cost me $15; you have to pay me $15 for it.' What is the transaction that goes on? I don't want $15 – I want my garden hose back after the fire is over.[19]

Two days later, in one of his widely acclaimed 'fireside chats' on the radio, Roosevelt justified the principle of the intended 'lend-lease' by arguing that America must be the 'arsenal of democracy'. On 11 March 1941 Congress passed the Lend-Lease Act that merely required foreign governments to return to the United States any American ships, tanks and aircraft that they had been 'lent' in the course of the war. By now there could no longer be any question of America's 'neutrality'. Economically speaking, the United States was already at war with the Axis Powers by the spring of 1940, and an important element of American politics was economic in nature: it was keen to secure the long-term future of Europe as a market for American goods and as a place to invest American capital.

Roosevelt offered a principled explanation of his country's new and openly interventionist policy in his State of the Union Address to Congress on 6 January 1941. In view of the offensive on the part of the 'aggressor nations' the future of all American republics was under serious threat, the president explained. He promised to provide all democracies with economic and military help to defend their freedom. The world that America wanted to secure must be based on four freedoms: the freedom of speech and expression, 'the freedom of every person to worship God in his own way', the freedom from want and the freedom from fear:

> That is no vision of a distant millennium. It is a definite basis for a kind of world attainable in our own time and generation. That kind of world is the very antithesis of the so-called new order of tyranny which the dictators seek to create with the crash of a bomb. [. . .] Freedom means the supremacy of human rights everywhere. [. . .] To that high concept there can be no end save victory.[20]

With regard to Japan, the secretary of state, Cordell Hull, propounded four principles in April 1941 that Tokyo was required to acknowledge before the United States could begin the negotiations desired by Konoe's government: Japan must safeguard the sovereignty and territorial integrity of every state; it must not interfere in the affairs of other states; it must acknowledge the equality of all nations, especially in respect of their trade opportunities; and it must not use force to alter the status quo in the Pacific. In June a fifth demand was added, albeit in the form of a qualifying clause, whereby the Tripartite Pact must be regarded as dead. It scarcely needs adding that Japan was unwilling to agree to such a radical rejection of its expansionist ambitions. As a result, the United States moved perceptibly closer to the possibility of a war on two fronts – in Europe and in the Pacific – in the first half of 1941.

The European power that Roosevelt was determined to support with every means 'short of war' certainly felt encouraged by America's help, and as long as Churchill remained at the head of the British government, Hitler was unable to count on London's willingness to sue for peace, as he had briefly hoped in the wake of his victorious 'blitzkrieg' against France.

On 19 July 1940, barely two weeks after he had returned in triumph to Berlin from his temporary headquarters at Freudenstadt in the northern part of the Black Forest, Hitler addressed the Reichstag at the Kroll Opera House and again appealed to Britain to 'show reason':

> Mr. Churchill ought, perhaps, for once, to believe me when I prophesy that a great Empire will be destroyed – an Empire which it was never my intention to destroy or even to harm. I do, however, realize that this struggle, if it continues, can end only with the complete annihilation of one or the other of the two adversaries. Mr. Churchill may believe that this will be Germany. I know that it will be England.[21]

Hitler was alluding here to a prophecy by the Oracle at Delphi transmitted by Herodotus, according to which King Croesus of Lydia would destroy a great empire if he waged war on the Persians. The war ended with his defeat by King Cyrus the Great of Persia in 546 BC, when Croesus lost his entire empire.

The truth of the matter is that by this date Hitler no longer believed in a peaceful resolution to his conflict with Great Britain. On 16 July 1940, three days before he addressed the Reichstag, he had given instructions for Operation Sealion, a land invasion of England that was to be launched after the Royal Air Force had as far as possible been rendered ineffectual. Air attacks on Great Britain – the Battle of Britain – increased in intensity on 13 August: among the targets were radar stations, airports, aircraft factories, ports and railway lines in southern England. After the first British bombing raids on Berlin the Luftwaffe systematically extended its attacks to London and other large cities in early September. Many German pilots also deliberately targeted groups of civilians. The Battle of Britain reached its climax on 15 September, when fifty-six German and twenty-six British aircraft were shot down. During the aerial battle for England 43,000 civilians were killed between the start of the war and June 1941. On one night alone, 14/15 November 1940, 600 civilians were killed in Coventry during a raid by the Luftwaffe designed to spread terror.

This was the largest deployment of Göring's Luftwaffe to date, and it proved to be a debacle. The planned destruction of radar stations and anti-aircraft defence installations had failed to produce the desired results, removing an important precondition for a successful land invasion. Even the most modern German aircraft could not linger in British air space for more than half an hour if they were to have enough fuel to return home, whereas the pilots of the Royal Air Force and of the Commonwealth and Polish-exile armed forces did not have this problem. And they had an important ally in the bad weather, which also played a part in thwarting Germany's subsequent planning, when on

17 September autumn storms forced Hitler to postpone indefinitely Operation Sealion, which was due to begin only four days later.

Even before the start of the Battle of Britain, Hitler had already expressed doubts as to whether it would really be possible to defeat Great Britain within the foreseeable future, and on 21 July, addressing the commanders in chief of the three branches of the Wehrmacht, he broached the possibility of turning his attention to the Soviet Union, the first time he had done so since the German-Soviet non-aggression pact of 1939. He explained his decision by insisting that Britain was still pinning its hopes on America and Russia. Ten days later, on 31 July, Hitler expressed himself more clearly in a discussion on the Obersalzberg, pointing out that 'England's hope' was 'Russia and America', but that if Russia was removed from the equation, America, too, would cease to be a problem, which in turn would mean that Japan would gain in importance. Russia, he declared, was 'England's and America's Far Eastern rapier against Japan':

> With Russia smashed, England's last hope would be shattered. Germany then will be the master of Europe and the Balkans. *Decision: Russia's destruction must therefore be made a part of this struggle. Spring 1941. The sooner Russia is crushed the better.* Attack achieves its purpose only if Russian state can be shattered to its roots with one blow. Holding part of the country alone will not do. Standing still for the following winter would be perilous. [. . .] If we start in May, we would have five months to finish the job.[22]

Clearly, Hitler could think only in terms of a blitzkrieg from the summer of 1940 onwards.

According to the German historian Andreas Hillgruber, it was Britain's resistance, in which it received substantial support from the United States, which was responsible for Hitler's change of heart:

> It was the defeat of France and the hoped-for 'settlement' with Great Britain that had been intended to free up Hitler's back and create a strategic basis on which to launch an attack on the east when he deemed that the moment was right. Now, what until then had been his main goal – the conquest of the east – became the means by which to deal with the Anglo-Saxon maritime powers, which, far from accepting his rule over central and western parts of Continental Europe, were determined to challenge that hegemony.[23]

This is the point that Hitler's plans had reached by the end of July 1940, but, as was to become clear, his timetable was by no means set in stone.

The Soviet Union had been able to put to good use the time during which Germany was completing its triumphant campaign in the west. On 15 June, following an ultimatum, the Red Army marched into Lithuania, including the south-western tip of land that had been claimed by Germany on 28 September

1939. Two days later, it occupied Latvia and Estonia. All three countries were declared Soviet republics and hence a part of the Soviet Union on 6 August. By June 1941 almost 170,000 real or alleged anti-Communists had been deported from the Baltic States to the Russian interior, mostly to Siberia: 34,250 from Latvia, 60,000 from Estonia and 75,000 from Lithuania. Stalin's next blow fell on Romania, which on 26 June was instructed to cede Bessarabia and North Bukovina to the Soviet Union. Two days later both regions were overrun by the Red Army.

In the case of Bessarabia, Soviet intervention was limited to dividing the region into south-east and eastern central European spheres of interest as enshrined in the German-Soviet non-aggression pact of 23 August 1939. When King Carol II of Romania asked Germany on 2 July 1940 to guarantee its borders and to send a military mission, the request was more than welcome to Hitler. Under the terms of the Second Vienna Award of 30 August Germany and Italy forced Romania to cede Northern Transylvania and the Székely Land to Hungary. On 4 September Carol II appointed the pro-German general Ion Antonescu prime minster and the country's leader. Two days later, under pressure from Antonescu, Carol abdicated in favour of his son, Michael. On the 7th Romania was obliged to cede southern Dobrudja to Bulgaria. The remaining borders were recognized by the Axis Powers without any attempt on Germany's part to consult with the Soviet Union, which had vital interests in Romania. On 2 September Hitler decided to send a military mission to Romania in response to Carol's request. Germany was now a step closer to one of its strategic goals: control over Romania's oilfields.

Germany's policy towards Romania represented a challenge to the Soviet Union but by no means spelt an end to relations between Berlin and Moscow. The supplies of petroleum, earth metals and grain from the Soviet Union that formed part of the German-Soviet trade agreement of 11 February 1940 and of an earlier agreement of 19 August 1939 continued as before, largely making up for those lost as a result of the British naval blockade. In the middle of September Hitler briefly toyed with the idea of pursuing Ribbentrop's contentious alternative to war with Russia, an anti-British 'Continental Bloc' from 'Yokohama to Spain' that would also include the Soviet Union. Hitler met Mussolini on the Brenner on 4 October to discuss ways in which their interests in Franco's Spain and Vichy France might be reconciled. In Berlin's view both of these countries should also be included in the proposed Continental Bloc.

On 23 October – barely three weeks later – Hitler and Franco met at the railway station at Hendaye on the border between France and Spain. It turned out to be a disappointing encounter for both parties. Although Hitler was willing to agree to Franco's conquest of Gibraltar, the Generalissimo remained reserved, Hitler's desire that Spain enter the war foundering above all on Madrid's demand that Germany relinquish areas of land in North Africa, a demand that Hitler refused to consider at Hendaye. By the time that Hitler had expressed his willingness to agree to it in November, Spain's economic situation was so dire that the country's divided political leaders could not agree to his demand. Later, depending on the military situation, Franco declared that Spain was either not one of the belligerents or that it was neutral. In December 1940 Spain decided to form a group of volunteers that was largely made up of Falangists, the 'Blue Division' that was later deployed on the German side on the eastern front, until Franco ordered its withdrawal in December 1943.

Hitler's meetings with Laval and Pétain in Montoire-sur-le-Loir near Tours likewise produced few concrete results, for although Pétain persuaded Hitler to declare France the protecting power in the case of French prisoners of war in Germany, he received no assurance that Berlin was ready to negotiate a peace treaty in the foreseeable future. Conversely, Pétain refused to enter the war and fight alongside Germany against Britain. The policy of collaboration to which the French chef d'état publicly agreed only on 30 October ran into an almost immediate problem when Pétain, without consulting Germany, dismissed Laval – hitherto the policy's principal advocate – on 13 December 1940 and replaced him as foreign secretary with the Anglophile Pierre-Étienne Flandin. In turn, Flandin left the government in February 1941 in response to pressure from Germany. His successor, Admiral François Darlan, who took over the portfolios of foreign minister, home secretary, minister of information and minister of the navy in addition to the deputy chairmanship of the Council of Ministers, staked everything on forging closer ties with Germany and making France an active member of any future Continental Bloc.

But the most momentous event of October 1940 was not Hitler's discussions in Hendaye and Montoire but the start of the Italian assault on Greece on the early morning of 28 October – the eighteenth anniversary of Mussolini's March on Rome. The driving force behind this move was Italy's foreign secretary, Count Ciano, who thought that it was time for his country to emerge from the shadow of the ever-expanding German Reich. Mussolini was annoyed with Hitler for repeatedly acting on his own, and he deliberately failed to consult with Berlin, so that when Hitler arrived at the Palazzo Vecchio in Florence for a meeting with the Duce later that same day, he found himself facing a fait accompli. For the Italian troops, the undertaking turned out to be a debacle, and in early November Greek units launched a counteroffensive and conquered around a third of Albania, which Italy had occupied in April 1939. British troops landed on the island of Crete on 29 October and reached Athens by early November. Hitler was afraid that the Royal Air Force would bomb the Romanian oilfields at Ploiesti and by the end of 1940 he was planning a German relief operation in Greece.

The Greek adventure proved to have unfortunate consequences for the Axis Powers in Africa. In mid-September 1940 Italy had used its base in Libya to launch an offensive against Egypt only to find itself stalled shortly behind the border. In December the British Nile Army began a counteroffensive that proved hugely successful: the Italian forces were thrown out of Egypt and 38,000 men taken prisoner. A further British offensive began in Eritrea in the second half of January, and by the 21st they had captured Tobruk in the eastern part of Italian Libya, followed by Benghazi, the capital of Cyrenaica, in early February, when they took some 140,000 prisoners. Shortly afterwards, British troops in Kenya launched an attack on Italian Somaliland in the course of which Mogadishu was captured. If Italy had concentrated its troops on the various theatres of war in Africa and especially on the strategically important kingdom of Egypt, instead of sending most of its soldiers to Greece, the British would never have achieved such rapid successes in North Africa.

When the German and Italian leaders met at the Berghof near Berchtesgaden in January 1941, Hitler was left with no choice but to force Mussolini to abandon his 'parallel war' and place himself at the service of Germany's strategic goals. In February the first units of Rommel's German Afrika Korps arrived in Tripoli, where they quickly launched a counteroffensive. By March practically the whole of Cyrenaica had fallen into German hands and the fortress at Tobruk was surrounded. In Greece, meanwhile, the British were continuing to advance and by the end of April they had already landed more than 58,000 men.

As yet, it was still unclear what effect the Italian campaign in the south of the Balkan peninsula might have on Hitler's strategic planning with regard to Russia. Although Ribbentrop's idea of turning the Tripartite Pact into the nucleus of a major Continental Bloc had not been completely unsuccessful (Hungary, Romania and Slovakia joined the alliance in November 1940, Bulgaria and Yugoslavia in March 1941), the Soviet Union made no attempt to join the anti-British grouping. Stalin had rejected Churchill's invitation to break with Germany on 1 August, but the Soviet leader had no intention of seeing his country as a partner in a European alliance headed by Germany.

On 12 November the Soviet foreign minister Vyacheslav Molotov arrived in Berlin for two days of talks with Hitler and Ribbentrop. As the result of a British air raid on the capital, part of the talks had to be held in a government bunker and proved difficult, with no tangible outcome. Hitler tried to persuade the Soviet Union to accept German rule in Europe and German claims to a colonial empire in Africa in return for Soviet expansion in the direction of the Indian Ocean that would have harmed British interests in the region. For his part, Molotov was more interested in Finland and south-east Europe: Germany was to end its use of Finnish territory for the transport of German troops to Norway, which the two countries had agreed to in September. It was also to withdraw the military mission that it had sent to Finland at that time and it was to acknowledge the Soviet Union's right to annex Finland. Moreover, Germany was to agree to the border guarantee given to Romania in return for a Soviet guarantee for Bulgaria. And it was to grant Moscow the right to free use of the Baltic ports and the construction of military bases in the Bosporus and the Dardanelles. Molotov also asked for a note to be taken of Soviet Russia's interest in the future fate of Poland, Hungary, Yugoslavia and Greece.

The deliberations with the Soviet foreign minister did not mean an unequivocal end to the idea of a Continental Bloc. Indeed, Molotov even wrote a letter on 26 November expressing his willingness to turn the Tripartite Pact into a Four-Power Pact at least as long as the governments in Berlin, Rome and Tokyo were willing to agree to Moscow's conditions, which he once again put forward in detail, even adding to his earlier demands. But Hitler had no intention of meeting the Soviet Union halfway. For him, it had been clear since the Berlin talks on 12 and 13 November that there could never be any question of an agreement with Stalin and that war was therefore inevitable. Hitler regarded Molotov's letter as an attempt at blackmail and did not deem it worthy of a reply. On 18 December he issued instructions for Operation Barbarossa: 'Even before the end of the war with England, the German Wehrmacht must be prepared *to crush Soviet Russia in a rapid campaign*.'[24] Preparations had to begin at once and must be completed by 15 May 1941 at the latest.

Hitler's timetable for his war with the Soviet Union could easily have been disrupted by two events in the Balkans: Italy's impending defeat in Greece and the *coup d'état* in Yugoslavia on 27 March 1941. The coup in Belgrade was instigated by the commander in chief of the Yugoslav air force, General Dušan Simović, and by the air force general Borivoje Marković, both of whom opposed their country's membership of the Tripartite Pact, a contentious decision that the prime minister, Dragiša Cvetković, sealed with his signature on 25 March, two days before his overthrow. The organizers of the putsch declared the seven-year-old King Peter II to be of age and made him head of state. In turn, Peter appointed Simović his new prime minister. While Prince Regent Paul went to Greece, violent demonstrations against the Axis Powers broke out in Belgrade.

Although the new government did not formally terminate the agreement of 25 March and although it assured Germany of its good intentions, Hitler regarded the coup as directed against the Reich, which was true to the extent that the British secret services had had a hand in the putsch. By 27 March Hitler had given orders for Yugoslavia to be invaded and persuaded the Bulgarian and Hungarian leadership to join forces with him with the aim of crushing the country. The Hungarian prime minister, Count Pál Teleki, who was at pains to maintain good relations with both Berlin and London and who had signed a friendship treaty with Belgrade in December 1940, declined to violate the treaty but was unable to assert himself in the face of opposition from the Reich governor, Miklós Horthy, and the army leaders. He took his own life on 7 April.

On 6 April, a day after the new Yugoslav government had signed a friendship and non-aggression treaty with the Soviet Union, Hitler launched his Balkan campaign without prior warning. Yugoslavia and Greece were attacked, Belgrade suffering a particularly heavy aerial bombardment, while the German tank units that entered the country from Austria and Bulgaria encountered only token resistance. By 12 April German troops had taken Belgrade. Five days later the Yugoslav supreme command capitulated. King Peter and his government were able to escape to Greece in British planes and shortly afterwards formed a government in exile in London.

Troops from Hungary, Bulgaria, Italy and the Italian satellite state of Albania were all involved in the occupation of the country. Germany and Italy jointly announced the end of the Kingdom of Yugoslavia on 8 July. Germany annexed a major part of Slovenia, together with Lower Styria and parts of Carniola, while Italy took control of the remainder of Slovenia, including its capital Ljubljana, as well as most of Dalmatia and the majority of the islands in the Adriatic. Hungary annexed the former Hungarian parts of Serbia, while Bulgaria annexed the bulk of Macedonia. Albania, which was dependent on Italy, incorporated Kosovo and neighbouring parts of Macedonia.

Croatia, which was occupied in part by German troops and in part by Italian forces, acquired the whole of Bosnia and Herzegovina. It was ruled by Ante Pavelić, a member of the fiercely Catholic Fascist Ustaša movement who had been responsible for the assassination of King Alexander I in Marseilles in October 1934 and who returned from exile in Italy to head a nominally independent state. As its *Poglavnik* ('leader'), he enjoyed the backing of only a small minority of his compatriots, and even *this* support he soon forfeited as a result of extensive corruption, arbitrary decisions and extreme forms of terror. Montenegro was declared an Italian protectorate, while in Serbia power was vested in the hands of a German military administration assisted by a Serbian regional authority that it itself installed and that was run by the former defence minister and Catholic conservative, Milan Nedić. Behind him were more than 500 dignitaries, including Orthodox bishops, teachers at the University of Belgrade, industrialists and former ministers. His government's authority was called into question by the nationalist Četnici associated with Colonel Draža Mihajlović and, after July 1941, by the rapidly growing partisan movement of Josip Broz Tito, the secretary general of the Yugoslav Communist Party.

In Greece, too, German troops made rapid advances after invading the country from Bulgaria on 6 April 1941. By the 9th Salonica had fallen, and by the 21st the Epirus Army had capitulated. Six days later Athens was occupied. The British forces withdrew from the mainland and sought refuge on the island of Crete, which was taken by German parachute troops on 1 June after twelve days of heavy fighting involving considerable loss of life. In Athens a Greek government under General Georgios Tsolakoglou had in the meantime been formed under the watchful eye of the occupying power. At the end of May King George II went into exile in Egypt, taking his government and sections of the military with him. Since Hitler needed the German troops for his campaign in the east, he left most of the country to the Italians as the occupying power, though units of the Wehrmacht remained in Athens, Salonica, on Crete and elsewhere. Bulgarian troops moved into eastern Macedonia and western Thrace.

While the Wehrmacht was enjoying its military triumphs in the Balkans, the war with Britain had ground to a standstill in the west. The last major air raid on London took place on 10 and 11 May 1941, in the course of which more than 1,200 Londoners were killed. At the end of May, the German battleship *Bismarck*, which had destroyed the largest British battlecruiser, HMS *Hood*, three days earlier, was sunk by the British, largely ending the submarine warfare in the Atlantic. The submarine war continued elsewhere but in spite of substantial British losses it failed to bring about the change in Germany's fortunes hoped for by the country's naval command. In North Africa there were no significant battles between the middle of June and the middle of November 1941, whereas in East Africa the British inflicted heavy losses on the Italians, taking Addis Ababa in April. The bulk of the Italian forces deployed in Ethiopia capitulated in May on Amba Alagi. In Iraq the British succeeded in overthrowing the pro-Axis regime of Rashid Ali al-Gaylani that had been brought to power by a putsch on 1 April: units of the British army captured Baghdad on 30 May, whereupon the anti-British rulers went into exile.

A week later British and Gaullist forces invaded Syria from Palestine and Iraq. In July the troops under General Henri-Fernand Dentz that had been stationed there by the Vichy regime were forced to abandon their resistance and agree to a ceasefire. In short, Britain had now asserted itself along a broad front in the Middle East. Hitler could, however, draw some comfort from the fact that Turkey, which had responded to Italy's invasion of Albania by exchanging mutual assistance declarations with Britain and France and agreed to mutual neutrality with the Soviet Union in the event of a war, signed a friendship treaty with Germany on 18 June 1941. The country's president, Mustafa Ismet Inönö, who had succeeded the state's founder, Mustafa Kemal Atatürk, on the latter's death in November 1938, saw no conflict of interest here since he believed that these agreements merely reflected Turkey's determination to maintain its neutrality, no matter what the circumstances might be.

For Turkey's treaty partner, Hitler, the rapid victories in the two blitzkriegs in the Balkans meant that he had no need to alter his timetable for attacking the Soviet Union. Operation Barbarossa could go ahead as planned. But the middle of May 1941 – the earliest date at which Hitler felt able to launch his invasion – proved to be impossible on account of the late thaw, the floodwaters in the major Russian rivers that his forces would have to cross and organizational problems with the army, all of which persuaded him to delay the invasion until 22 June 1941, a date that must have given Hitler – a man with a profound awareness of European history – pause for thought, since this was the day on which another conqueror, Napoleon I, had begun his invasion of Russia in 1812, a war that famously ended in military disaster for him and his forces.

On 3 March 1941, just sixteen weeks before the war actually began, Hitler directed the head of the SS, Heinrich Himmler, to undertake 'special assignments preparatory to the political administration' of the regions in question, assignments 'that stem from the final confrontation between two diametrically opposed political systems'. Speaking to some 200 high-ranking officers on 30 March, Hitler went on to explain – according to notes made by Franz Halder, the chief of his general staff – that Bolshevism was 'asocial and criminal' and that Communism posed an 'enormous threat':

> We must move away from the idea of soldierly camaraderie. Communism is no comrade of ours: it never was and it never will be. We are talking about a war of extermination [. . .], war on Russia: the destruction of the Bolshevik commissars and of the Communist intelligentsia. We must wage war on the poison of decay. This is not a matter for military tribunals. [. . .] This battle will differ greatly from the one in the west. In the east harshness means mildness in the future.

The following day, 31 March 1941, the notorious 'Commissar Order' was first drafted, receiving its final form on 12 May. Its key sentence reads, 'Political functionaries and commissars are to be removed.'[25]

Hitler's language in the spring of 1941 recalled that of the 'years of struggle' before 1933. For him, the war on the Soviet Union was from the outset an ideological, all-or-nothing 'civil war'. The time when he could have fought only the democratic or plutocratic version of 'international Jewry' was fast disappearing. With the start of his offensive against the Soviet Union, the struggle to combat 'Jewish Bolshevism' was once again paramount, a struggle that he seemed to have pushed to the back of his mind when signing the German-Soviet non-aggression pact, just as he appeared to have forgotten his belief that German Lebensraum could be acquired in the east only by destroying the Soviet Union. He could surely feel that he was understood by the majority of the officers whom he addressed on 30 March 1941 and whom he informed of the new situation and of the methods appropriate to that situation. At all events, there was no vocal dissent. And although Halder's account of the occasion suggests that Hitler did not expressly attack the Jews, all of those present must have known who and what was intended.

General Erich Hoepner – an officer who belonged to the military opposition and who was expelled from the army in January 1942 for disobeying orders – drew the conclusions that Hitler wished to be drawn: 'The war with Russia is the inevitable consequence of the struggle for existence that has been forced upon us and in particular of the struggle for the economic self-sufficiency of Greater Germany and of the European territory that it controls,' reads Hoepner's deployment order of 2 May 1941:

> It is the old struggle of the Germanic peoples against the Slav world, the desire to prevent European culture from being swamped by ideas from Moscow and Asia, and the rejection of Jewish Bolshevism. This struggle must have as its goal the destruction of present-day Russia, which is why it must be waged with unprecedented rigour. In its conception and execution,

every military action must be guided by the iron will to wipe out the enemy ruthlessly and completely. In particular, this means no quarter should be given to the representatives of the present Russian Bolshevik system.[26]

It was not only Hitler's war that began at four in the morning on 22 June 1941 with Germany's invasion of the Soviet Union. It was also the war of the Wehrmacht that unquestioningly accepted the Führer's orders.

From 'Barbarossa' to Pearl Harbor: The Globalization of the War

Neither Stalin nor Hitler had ever believed that the German-Soviet non-aggression pact of 1939 meant more than a temporary breathing space in the ongoing struggle between their two powers. A confrontation with the Soviet leader's ideological opposite in Berlin was inevitable because Hitler had never renounced the programme set forth in *Mein Kampf*, where he had announced his intention of conquering Lebensraum in the east and destroying 'Jewish Bolshevism'. The Soviet dictator was in no doubt on this point. On the other hand, Stalin was also convinced that Hitler would never attack the Soviet Union before he had completed his victory over Great Britain. This period was to be devoted to pushing ahead with his country's rearmament programme and avoiding anything that might provoke Germany into launching a premature attack. This explains why Russia, unlike Germany, respected the economic obligations to which it had committed itself in 1939–40. Between January and June 1941 Moscow supplied the Reich with 1.5 million tonnes of grain, 100,000 tonnes of cotton, 2 million tonnes of petroleum products, 1.5 million tonnes of wood, 140,000 tonnes of manganese and 20,000 tonnes of chromium.

As far as the country's armaments were concerned, the Soviet Union had more planes, more tanks and far more pieces of artillery than the German Reich in 1941: in the case of the latter, the respective figures were 42,300 and 7,000. The Red Army maintained an army of 2.5 million men in the west of the Soviet Union and 2.2 million in the Far East. The Wehrmacht, conversely, had at its disposal 152 divisions made up of three million men, in total around three-quarters of the army in the field.

But whatever advantages the Soviet army may seem to have had in the summer of 1941, these had to be offset by serious shortcomings in terms of its technical equipment and operational training but above all by the fatal consequences of the great purge that had taken place in the Red Army. Stalin had effectively removed its head when in 1937–8 he had dismissed more than 34,000 officers from their posts. Of these, some 22,000 were murdered, among them eighty of the country's top military leaders. Of the survivors, some 10,000 of the arrested officers were welcomed back into the army's ranks in 1940. But the Red Army certainly did not feel that it was ready for action in 1941. Stalin reckoned that it would not reach its full fighting strength until the end of 1942.

Strategically speaking, the Soviet Union had banked on being able to move swiftly from defence to attack since the days of Mikhail Tukhachevsky. Underlying the army's strategy was the assumption that any war would begin with a declaration of hostilities and a general mobilization. This assessment did not change when the defence commissar, Kliment Voroshilov, was dismissed in May 1940 following the failure of the Finno-Soviet Winter War and was replaced by Marshal Semyon Timoshenko. If Germany were to attack, then such an assault, they believed, would come from south of Brest-Litovsk and from the Balkans and be directed at the Ukraine.

There was certainly no lack of warnings of an imminent German attack in the first five months of 1941. On 21 April, for example, Churchill sent word to Stalin via the British ambassador in Moscow, Sir Stafford Cripps, a left-wing independent socialist, that the British secret service was expecting such a move, but the Soviet leader suspected that this was a trap – an attempt on London's part to drive Moscow into a war with Berlin. Not even the Soviet secret service's own views on the matter were taken seriously by Stalin, and this remained the case even when trustworthy German informants such as Harro Schulze-Boysen and Arvid Harnack, two members of the legendary 'Red Orchestra', and the Tokyo master spy Richard Sorge reported on Hitler's plans.

On 5 May Stalin took a step that he intended to be interpreted as a powerful demonstration of his wish to raise morale: he took over Molotov's seat on the Council of People's Commissars so that the party and the government were now being run by one and the same person. That same day he addressed graduates from the Military Academy as well as army leaders and the leading members of his government, describing the Red Army as an assault army equipped with modern weapons, but he continued to resist the idea of a preventive war against Germany, which both Timoshenko and the chief of the general staff, Georgi Zhukov, were advising him to consider in a revised plan of operation that they suggested he should adopt at a later stage. His suspicions towards democratic Britain continued to be no less real than those that he entertained towards National Socialist Germany, and when Hitler's deputy, Rudolf Heß, on his own initiative flew to Britain on 10 May, where he was immediately arrested after landing by parachute, Stalin's first response was to see in Heß's action an attempt on Hitler's part to reach an agreement with Britain on an end to the war in the west before unleashing an attack on Russia. But neither in Berlin nor in London was there any support for this amateurish demarche by the Führer's deputy.

By the beginning of June news agencies were reporting in increasing numbers on an imminent German attack, and so Stalin was unable to avoid ordering troop reinforcements on Russia's western border and the forward placement of the army's command centres. On 19 June the Red Army began to camouflage aerodromes and send aircraft to airports closer to the border. But it was necessary to do everything possible to avoid anything that might have provoked the German side, a directive that continued to apply even when, in the middle of June, it became increasingly clear in Moscow that the date for the attack was set for 22 June. The people's commissar for internal security, Lavrentiy Beria, wrote to Stalin on the 21st and demanded the recall of the Soviet ambassador in Berlin, Vladimir Dekanozov, who he alleged was providing Moscow with false information and had just announced that Germany would attack the Soviet Union the very next day. Beria was determined not to be misled. Like all other Soviet leaders he trusted Stalin's superior judgement, and Stalin continued to be convinced that Hitler would not risk waging a war on two different fronts simultaneously.

Once the unthinkable had happened, orders were sent to the Red Army early on the morning of 22 June 1941 to repel and destroy the enemy wherever he had violated the Soviet border. But the Wehrmacht seemed unstoppable. By 28 June Minsk had fallen into German hands, and within a week German troops were already 350 miles inside Russia. On 29 June the Central Committee of the Soviet Communist Party declared the war with the Fascist aggressor the 'Great Patriotic War of the Soviet Union'. Stalin, who since 1 July was also the chairman of the Defence Committee of the Soviet Union, appealed to the population on the 3rd to wage a partisan war behind the front line. This was the day on which the German chief of the general staff, Franz Halder, predicted that Germany could win the war with Soviet Russia within two weeks at the most.

In a radio address on 22 June 1941 Hitler sought to present the attack on the Soviet Union as an act of self-defence. Among the extortionist and aggressive actions on the part of the Soviet Union that had forced him to take this step he mentioned not only the Belgrade putsch of 27 March but also the attempted overthrow of the Romanian *Conducator*, Ion Antonescu, by the Fascist 'Iron Guard', which until then had been actively encouraged by Germany, at the end of January 1941. But the main reason for his intervention, Hitler explained, was the coalition between London and Moscow that the two countries had recently agreed to. After repeated border violations by the Soviet Union, 'the time has now come when it is necessary to counter this plot by Jewish-Anglo-Saxon warmongers and by the no less Jewish powers that be in the Bolsheviks' headquarters in Moscow'.[27]

To the extent that they were not dyed-in-the-wool National Socialists, most Germans reacted with dismay to this new development but quickly allowed themselves to be won over by the Wehrmacht's military successes. Among the first to applaud the invasion of the Soviet Union were Evangelical and Catholic churchmen. The Spiritual Liaison Council of the German Evangelical Church whose chairman was the bishop of Hanover, August Marahrens, wrote to Hitler on 30 June to thank him for having called on 'our people and on the peoples of Europe to take up arms so decisively against the mortal enemy of all order and of all western Christian culture'. The Catholic bishops merely invited their flock to 'perform their duties faithfully, to endure bravely and to show self-sacrifice in working and fighting in the service of our people', but a number of princes of the Church went even further during the months that followed, the bishop of Eichstätt, Michael Rackl, for example, hailing the Russian campaign as a 'crusade, a holy war for home and nation, for faith and Church, for Christ and His most holy Cross'. The bishop of Münster, Count Clemens August von Galen, likewise proclaimed the campaign a just war against the godless Bolsheviks, announcing in a pastoral letter of 14 September 1941 that 'the declaration on the part of our Führer and Reich chancellor' that the 'Russian pact' had run its course had 'liberated us from a serious concern and provided a release from extreme pressure'. It was with approval that he cited Hitler's reference to the 'Jewish-Bolshevik powers that be in Moscow'. In the same letter, however, the bishop was severely critical of National Socialism – and not for the first time. Galen described as 'horrendous'

> adherence to a teaching that claims that it is permissible to take the lives of 'unproductive people', of those poor, innocent people who are mentally ill. It is a doctrine that essentially opens the door to the violent killing of all people who are declared to be 'unproductive', of those who are incurably sick, war invalids and the disabled and those who are old and weak.[28]

Galen's personal standing and the furore caused by his public protests at the euthanasia programme – euphemistically called the 'euthanasia action' – ensured that he was not immediately arrested and sent to a concentration camp. Hitler's decree of 1 September 1939 had resulted in the deaths of more than 70,000 men, women and children by the summer of 1941. They were initially killed by lethal injection, then, from January 1940, by being gassed by carbon monoxide. The programme was interrupted on 24 August 1941, disquiet among the population at large having reached the point where Hitler felt that it was politically dangerous to ignore the outcry, but the interruption did not mean an end to the 'destruction of life not worth living', for Hitler's instructions applied only to those centres of mass killings in the old Reich that had come to public attention, namely, Grafeneck in Württemberg, Hadamar near Limburg and Brandenburg an der Havel. The murders continued in a decentralized form and using other means, including deliberate starvation (a method already employed during the First World War), mass shootings by the SS in the new Gau of Danzig-West Prussia and even the use of dynamite. One group of patients who were invariably killed without even an examination of the individual case were Jews who were mentally ill.

Meanwhile Germany was continuing to conduct its campaign in the east with the help of other European nations. Romania and Italy signed up to the action on 22 June, the former by offering the bulk of its armed forces, the latter with only an expeditionary force, followed by Slovakia on the 23rd. When Finland took a similar step on the 25th, it stressed the fact that it was supporting the Reich not as a federal ally but as 'co-belligerent'. From a Finnish standpoint this was merely a question of pursuing a war that had been in progress for some time and of regaining land that the country had had to cede to the Soviet Union under the terms of the Peace of Moscow of 12 March 1940. On 27 June, a day after Finland declared war on the Soviet Union, Hungary did the same, citing alleged Soviet air raids as its reason for doing so. Three Hungarian divisions were involved in the occupation of the Ukraine, but the country's military engagement remained largely symbolic, at least until the spring of 1942.

Even before the war with the Soviet Union had actually started, the German leadership had decided that from 1942 the Wehrmacht should satisfy its need for food within Russia itself. According to the minutes of a meeting of secretaries of state on 2 May 1941, this meant accepting as many as forty million deaths from starvation inside the Soviet Union. The comprehensive directives for the Germanization of the new Lebensraum in the east were contained in the General Plan for the East, the initial version of which was submitted by Himmler on 15 July 1941. It had been drawn up with the help of agricultural scientists from the Friedrich Wilhelm University in Berlin and proposed that within thirty years eastern Poland, the Baltic States, Belorussia and parts of the Ukraine would all be settled by Germans, which presupposed that thirty-one million local inhabitants would be moved to western Siberia, while fourteen million 'of good race' could remain where they were. Included in this mass deportation project were not only Russians, White Russians and Ukrainians but also Poles and Czechs. Between 80 per cent and 85 per cent of all Poles would be deported, the highest quotient of all the nationalities in question, followed by White Russians, or 'White Ruthenians' (75 per cent), and Ukrainians (65 per cent).

The following day, 16 July 1941, Hitler laid out his plans for the occupied areas in the east. Among those present on this occasion were Hermann Göring and Alfred Rosenberg, who was to be appointed Reich minister for the occupied regions on the 17th. The European part of the Soviet Union was to be divided into four commissariats, namely, the Ukraine, the Eastern Region (Ostland) with the Baltic States and Belorussia, Muscovy and the Caucasus. This 'enormous cake' had to be 'sliced up in a handy way so that we can, first, control it, second, administer it and, third, exploit it'. But the world must not find out that this was a long-term plan:

> All necessary measures – shooting, resettlement and so on – we shall undertake in spite of this, and we *can* undertake them in spite of this. [. . .] The formation of a military power to the west of the Urals must never again be raised even if we have to wage war for a hundred years. [. . .] It must always be our inviolable principle that no one else must be allowed to bear arms except Germans. [. . .] The soldier must always ensure that the regime is secure.[29]

In the course of a conversation in his headquarters three months later, on 17 October 1941, Hitler summed up his ambitions for the east in a single sentence: 'There's only one duty: to Germanise this country by the immigration of Germans, and to look upon the natives as Redskins.'[30]

The campaign in the east was planned by Hitler and his army leaders as a blitzkrieg. But military developments on the eastern front during the summer of 1941 did not always live up to the expectations of the more optimistic of the generals. The German troops continued their advance in the Baltic States and in the Ukraine, but after the fall of Smolensk they were brought to a standstill further south. The military wanted to press ahead to Moscow, but Hitler refused, not least for economic reasons, the capture of Kiev and of the Donets Basin striking him as far more important than the fall of the capital. At the end of August the Soviet Union was able to profit for the first time from the agreement on mutual assistance – and against a separate peace – that it had signed with the United Kingdom on 12 July: Soviet and British troops marched into neutral Iran, defeating its forces and obliging the Axis-friendly shah, Reza Shah Pahlavi, to abdicate. The country was divided into three zones, a Soviet zone in the north, a British zone in the south and a neutral zone in the middle. From then on Great Britain and, at a later date, the United States were able to provide the Soviet Union with military equipment, which reached Russia via Iran.

Along the northern section of the eastern front the Wehrmacht, working together with Finnish units, was able to complete the almost total encirclement of Leningrad by early September 1941. Hitler was resolved to subjugate the city by starving its million or so inhabitants, although Lake Ladoga allowed minimal supplies to get through to them. Kiev fell on 17 September, when 665,000 members of the Red Army were taken prisoner. In early October the Army Group Centre began to advance on Moscow between Smolensk and Orel. Stalin proclaimed a state of siege in the capital on 19 October after the government apparatus and diplomatic corps had already fled from the city.

In the extreme south-east, Rostov, which had only recently been taken, was lost on 21 November. By now Moscow was almost within sight of the German troops but was saved by a period of muddy weather and then by the early onset of a particularly harsh Russian winter. Leningrad, too, remained undefeated. Already exhausted, the Wehrmacht was ill-equipped to face a winter war. Although 3.3 million Russian soldiers had been taken prisoner, the Soviet Union was nowhere near the point of collapse, and by early December it had begun a counteroffensive along several sections of the front. The strategic objective of Operation Barbarossa – the defeat of the Soviet Union by means of a blitzkrieg – had failed. Several generals were relieved of their posts, and the commander in chief of the army, Walther von Brauchitsch, was likewise dismissed. On 19 December 1941 Hitler himself assumed control of the army.

Hitler had not consulted with his Far Eastern partner in the Tripartite Pact when launching Operation Barbarossa. Tokyo's hope that a coalition with Berlin, Rome and Moscow would deter the Anglo-Saxon powers from seeking to counter Japanese expansion in the Pacific had therefore proved misplaced. When the Japanese foreign minister, Matsuoka Yosuke, who in April 1941 had signed the neutrality treaty with Moscow, tried to persuade his government to enter the war, he encountered considerable opposition on the part of both his navy and, to a lesser extent, his army. Both of them rejected the 'northern option' and insisted on the superiority of its 'southern' alternative. Matsuoka was forced to resign on 15 July in the wake of a cabinet reshuffle. He was replaced as foreign minister by Admiral Teijiro Toyoda, one of whose tasks was to explore the possibility of peace talks with the United States.

In practice, however, Tokyo's policies ran counter to this aim. On 24 July a 40,000-strong Japanese army marched into the southern part of French Indochina, an action undertaken in the face of American warnings but with the reluctant backing of the Vichy government, its aim being to cut off the Burma Road, which was the most important of Chiang Kai-shek's supply routes, and provide free access to the oil wells in the Dutch East Indies. The United States reacted on 26 July by freezing all of the Japanese assets that it controlled and extending the existing economic embargo to crude oil. Three days later Great Britain, Canada, New Zealand and the Dutch East Indies followed suit, the last-named country through the Dutch government in exile in London. Japanese oil reserves were enough for three years at the most, and so it became a matter of urgency to seize the resources of the Dutch East Indies. On 3 September a liaison conference including representatives of the government and the military resolved to prepare for war against the United States, Great Britain and the Netherlands but at the same time to continue informal talks with America on condition that a decision was reached by 10 October at the latest. The army and navy were to be ready for action five days after that. On 6 September an imperial conference attended by the vacillating Emperor Hirohito, who was generally reluctant to go to war, confirmed the Principles for the Implementation of Imperial Policies that had been passed three days earlier.

For a time it seemed as if it might still be possible to avoid a conflict with the United States. Roosevelt was not averse to agreeing to a meeting proposed by Konoe, but he insisted on the stringent conditions that his secretary of state, Cordell Hull, had laid down in his Four Points in April 1941, including the withdrawal of Japanese troops from China. He also demanded preparatory talks. On 13 September a liaison conference in Tokyo agreed the basic conditions for peace between Japan and China, under which the Japanese military would withdraw from China only after the government of Chiang Kai-shek in Chungking had merged with the Japanese puppet regime under Wang Jingwei in Nanking, which in the circumstances was never likely to happen. China was also expected to recognize the Japanese satellite state of Manchukuo. On 2 October Hull informed the Japanese ambassador, Kichisaburo Nomura, that America rejected these proposals.

Konoe himself was willing to ignore the 'China incident' – as the Sino-Japanese War that had started in 1937 was routinely described in Tokyo – and in that way to meet America's demands more than halfway, but he was unable to obtain a majority in cabinet. His most outspoken opponent was General Tojo Hideki, the minister of the army, who considered any retreat in the face of American demands to be incompatible with Japanese honour. On 16 October the prime minister bowed to the inevitable and asked the emperor to dismiss him. Konoe took the opportunity to repeat remarks that he had already made to Tojo: he could take responsibility for a major war only if the conflict with China had first been resolved. Tojo succeeded him on 18 October, retaining the post of army minister and also taking over the Home Office. Hirohito rescinded the decree of the imperial conference on 6 September and asked his government to continue its secret talks with the United States, a task that fell to the foreign minister, Togo Shigenori, who had previously been his country's ambassador in Berlin and Moscow.

The die was cast at a liaison conference between the government and the military on 1 November. The 'hawks' finally got their way after a seven-hour debate, arguing that it was better to wage war now rather than later, when America would be even stronger. At 01:30 on the morning of 2 November the assembled members voted to go to war with the United States, Great Britain and the Netherlands in early December if by midnight on the 1st the talks with Washington had failed to reach a satisfactory outcome. An imperial conference confirmed this decision on 5 November. The decisive factor was the conviction that only in this way could Japan prevent itself from running out of fuel for military purposes within the next two years. In November 1941 the country's leaders did indeed believe that they had their backs to the wall. But it was their own policies that had driven them into this impasse, policies which had begun in September 1931, when the country had marched into Manchuria and which it had continued in July 1937 when it had embarked on its war with China.

When Hitler attacked the Soviet Union, the dyed-in-the-wool anti-Communist Winston Churchill lost no time in greeting the Soviet Union as a companion in misfortune and fellow combatant. By the evening of 22 June 1941 he had announced in a radio address heard by millions of Americans in addition to his listeners at home that 'the Russian danger is our danger, and the danger of the United States, just as the cause of any Russian fighting for his hearth and home is the cause of free men and free peoples in every quarter of the globe'.[31]

Two days later Roosevelt, addressing a group of journalists, declared that it went without saying that the United States would offer Russia all the help that it could. In a subsequent declaration on 26 June he made it clear that he would not place the Soviet Union at a disadvantage by appealing to the Neutrality Act.

Ever since the German victory over France in June 1940 Roosevelt had been clear about three things: first, the United States would have to enter the war sooner rather than later (he had first referred to it as the 'Second World War' in March 1941); second, the greatest threat to his country was the one posed by the most aggressive dictator, Adolf Hitler; and, third, there remained practically no prospect of his gaining a majority in Congress for any declaration of war.

Knowing this, Roosevelt proceeded to create what as far as possible was a fait accompli. He had declared a state of national emergency as early as May 1941, a declaration that allowed him to take exceptional measures. In early July, with the agreement of the government in Reykjavík, he sent 4,400 marines to Iceland to replace the British and Canadian troops that had occupied the North Atlantic island in May 1940 but which Churchill felt were needed in the theatres of war in Europe and North Africa. Iceland had tremendous strategic significance for any naval war and could not be allowed to fall into German hands, a point on which Roosevelt was in full agreement with leading military figures in the United States.

In the case of an amendment to the Selective Service Act of September 1940, conversely, Roosevelt needed the approval of Congress, which had not been the case with his occupation of Iceland. The aim of the measure was to extend the period of military service for all conscripts for the duration of the national emergency, to make it possible to deploy them outside the western hemisphere and to raise the upper limit of 900,000 army personnel. In the Senate the draft amendment received a clear majority of forty-five votes to thirty, albeit after a heated debate, while in the House of Representatives, the majority was a single vote: 203 in favour of the motion, 202 against it. If the isolationists had had their way, the United States would have forfeited its military defences at the very time that it was facing its severest threat to date.

At the end of July, even before Roosevelt had won this trial of strength in Congress, his closest adviser, Harry Hopkins, who was also head of the country's Lend-Lease Program, travelled to Moscow from Great Britain via the polar route. With the support of the president and the State Department, he wanted to establish what exactly Stalin envisaged by way of American help. For the Soviet leader, the country's most pressing needs were anti-aircraft guns, machine guns and rifles, but Stalin also took up Hopkins's suggestion of an American-British-Soviet conference in Moscow. Roosevelt was urged to enter the war at the first available opportunity: without American help the Soviet Union and Great Britain would hardly be able to destroy Germany's military might. That Roosevelt shared this assessment was clear from a message he sent and that Hopkins passed on to Stalin.

It was not until 9 August that Hopkins saw Roosevelt again, when, together with Churchill, he arrived at Placentia Bay off the coast of Newfoundland on board the *Prince of Wales*. This was the first time that Roosevelt, who travelled to the meeting on the cruiser *Augusta*, had met the British prime minister in person. They discussed the international situation, including not only what the two Anglo-Saxon powers might do to deal with the aggressors in Berlin, Rome and Tokyo but also the outlines of a post-war order. Their support of the Soviet Union was one of the subjects to be discussed, as was the military protection of British ships in the Atlantic and, one of their most pressing concerns, the threat posed by Japan in the Pacific. For Churchill, the most important outcome of the meeting was Roosevelt's belated promise to provide a military escort not just for American and Icelandic ships but for those from other nations on their voyage between the United States and Iceland. On the other hand, Roosevelt was unable to hold out the promise of America's entry into the war as desired by the British prime minister, who had to make do with the president's announcement that he would keep his eyes open for a suitable 'incident' that might be used to justify the declaration of hostilities. For the present he would continue to fight the war without officially declaring that that was what he was already doing.

The Atlantic Charter on which Roosevelt and Churchill agreed on 12 August and which they made known two days later was intended for public consumption, not least the general public in America. In it, its two signatories assured the world that they were seeking 'no aggrandizement, territorial or other' and would make no territorial changes that did not accord with the freely expressed wishes of the peoples concerned. They went on to insist that they respected the right of all peoples to choose the form of government under which they wanted to live and proclaimed their desire to restore the sovereign rights and self-government of all those peoples who had been forcibly deprived of them. They would endeavour, 'with due respect for their existing obligations', to 'further the enjoyment by all States [. . .] of access, on equal terms, to the trade and to the raw materials of the world which are needed for their economic prosperity'. They went on to assert their desire to bring about the fullest collaboration between all nations in the economic field with the object of securing improved labour standards, economic advancement and social security. After the 'final destruction of the Nazi tyranny' they hoped to establish a peace that would 'afford to all nations the means of dwelling in safety' so that 'men in all lands may live out their lives in freedom from fear and want'. Such a peace, they went on, should 'enable all men to traverse the high seas and oceans without hindrance'. Finally, all nations should 'abandon the use of force', so that all nations that threatened others must be disarmed. And they vowed to undertake 'all practicable measures which will lighten for peace-loving peoples the crushing burden of armaments'.[32]

In its tone and content the Atlantic Charter recalled Woodrow Wilson's Fourteen Points of January 1918. Both documents sought to present themselves as blueprints for a better world order, although the text of the later charter necessarily represented a balancing act, contradictions between theory and practice being obscured as far as possible. Independence fighters in India,

Burma and Ceylon immediately appealed to the right of national sovereignty and self-government enshrined in the Atlantic Charter, forcing Churchill to explain to the lower house that such 'sovereign rights' applied only to the downtrodden nations of Europe. This, he went on, was a problem that had to be separated from the development of organs of self-government within the British Empire. Britain's determination to abide by the 'imperial preference' enjoyed by members of the Commonwealth – the reciprocally enacted tariffs and free trade agreements between the Dominions and colonies of the British Empire – was amply covered by the reference to 'existing obligations'.

The third member of the triumvirate, Stalin, was absent from the meetings off the coast of Newfoundland, but Roosevelt and Churchill sent him their cordial greetings on 12 August. Whatever the two western leaders may have thought of the Soviet dictator's love of peace, their immediate concern was to appeal to the idealism of all Americans and to force the isolationists on to the moral defensive. In the longer term, however, the Atlantic Charter was nothing less than a new, if abbreviated, version of the normative project of the West, a project by which the nations of the West, foremost among which were the United States and the United Kingdom, must be judged if they wanted to retain their credibility in the post-war world. By 1945 a further forty-three nations that had declared war on Germany had signed up to the principles of the charter, at least on paper. They included the Soviet Union and China. It was these forty-three nations that Roosevelt presciently called the 'United Nations' at the Anglo-American Arcadia Conference in Washington on 1 January 1942.

There was no lack of 'incidents' in the autumn of 1941 that were well calculated to lead to a worsening in German-American relations. On 5 September Roosevelt announced that the previous day an American destroyer, the *Greer*, had been attacked by a German submarine. U 652 had in fact been pursued for several hours by the *Greer* with the support of British war planes and a British destroyer in the seas to the south of Iceland before firing torpedoes at the American vessel, none of which hit its target. Even so, Roosevelt used the encounter as the excuse for a shoot-on-sight order on 11 September: from then on the fleet should fire on submarines belonging to the Axis Powers as soon as they appeared in waters important for the defence of the United States.

A second incident on 16 October proved more serious: an American destroyer, the *Kearney*, was attacked by a German U-boat in waters near Iceland, resulting in the deaths of eleven sailors. The following day the House of Representatives agreed to a government request to arm American freighters on their way to Great Britain, thereby weakening the Neutrality Act of November 1939. A further amendment to the act, ending the exclusion of American vessels from declared battle zones, was adopted by a narrow majority in early November. This vote had been preceded on 31 October by the most serious incident to date between the United States and Germany, when the destroyer *Reuben James* was sunk by a German submarine 600 nautical miles to the west of Ireland, with the loss of 115 lives.

By now the press and public opinion in America were markedly less isolationist than they had been at the start of the war in Europe. According to an opinion poll in early October 50 per cent of those questioned felt that the defeat of National Socialist Germany was more important than American neutrality and, regardless of the anti-Communist mood in the country, there was growing sympathy for lending support to the Soviet Union, under the terms of the Lend-Lease Act of March 1941, by sending in supplies, not least because many Americans believed that this way it would be possible to prevent their own country being drawn into a war, or anyway delay such a development. The principal threat was deemed to be Hitler's Germany, not the Japanese Empire. After American experts had succeeded in decoding the encrypted radio traffic between Tokyo and the Japanese Embassy in Washington (the name of the machine used was 'Magic'), the American military felt that the country was relatively safe from surprise Japanese attacks.

America's secretary of state, Cordell Hull, informed the Japanese ambassador of his country's terms for a peaceful settlement of the conflict between their two countries. Central to the conditions were the withdrawal of Japanese troops from China and Indochina, the renunciation of all of Japan's exterritorial rights in China, recognition of the government of Chiang Kai-shek as China's only legitimate representative and the repeal of the Tripartite Pact. Tokyo regarded this catalogue of demands not only as a rejection of its own proposals for a modus vivendi but also as an American ultimatum, and on 1 December an imperial conference decided that the only response was war.

Washington, too, was anticipating a Japanese attack by this time, but the American military assumed that it would be directed at Malaya, Thailand or the Philippines, which since 1935 had been a Commonwealth enjoying internal political autonomy but under American control in terms of its defence and foreign policy. United States territory was not considered a possibility. There were certainly pointers to an imminent attack on Pearl Harbor in Hawaii, where most of the Pacific fleet lay at anchor. These pointers included a report from the American Embassy in Peru, but all of them were either lost in the vast numbers of other reports that were received or they were simply not taken seriously. In fact Pearl Harbor had for some time been at the top of Japan's list of targets. An expeditionary fleet left the Kuril Islands on 26 November, heading for Hawaii. It included six aircraft carriers.

The first Japanese bombers attacked Pearl Harbor at 07:55 local time – 14:25 in Washington, DC – on 7 December 1941, with a second wave of attacks following an hour later. Three cruisers, eight battleships and four other vessels were sunk or badly damaged, 188 aircraft were destroyed and a further 159 were rendered unfit for service. More than 2,400 members of the American armed forces lost their lives and almost 1,200 were wounded. Aircraft carriers were not hit since they were at sea. Also spared were the bunkers sheltering the American submarines. At the same time Japan launched a coordinated attack on the Malayan Peninsula, Singapore and, shortly afterwards, the Philippines and Hong Kong. The American island of Guam was captured on 10 December.

Pearl Harbor was the 'incident' that sparked America's entry into the Second World War, even if Roosevelt had expected that such an occurrence would take place in the Atlantic, rather than the Pacific. The suggestion that he knew about the time and place of the attack but deliberately did nothing to prevent it belongs in the realm of conspiracy theories for which there is not a shred of evidence. The bodies responsible for military security had lamentably failed in their duty, but once the Japanese attack had taken place, Roosevelt no longer ran the risk of rejection when he asked Congress on 8 December to agree to his declaring war on Japan. The Senate gave its unanimous backing, while there was only a single dissenting voice in the House of Representatives.

It was by no means inevitable that the United States would declare war on Germany, but Hitler was keen on such an outcome since only in this way could he bind Japan firmly to him and conflate the Anglo-Saxon war with the Asiatic war, thereby turning two separate conflicts into a world war. On 11 December Hitler informed the Greater German Reichstag that an agreement had just been reached between Germany, Italy and Japan and that all three powers would wage 'the war that has just been forced on them by the United States of America and England' with all the means at their disposal, ensuring a victorious outcome and vowing not to agree to an armistice or to peace with either the United States or Great Britain without the full consent of all the other parties.[33]

In fact it may not have been merely military and strategic considerations that persuaded Hitler to declare war on America and turn the war into a global conflict. Ever since 1 September he had repeatedly threatened to destroy European Jewry in the event of 'international finance Jewry' succeeding in plunging the nations of the globe into another world war. Now a world war was a fact, and Hitler could start to do what he had long been wanting to do but had not yet ordered: the systematic extermination of Jewry throughout Europe.

Genesis of Genocide: The 'Final Solution' (I)

Until the summer of 1941 the National Socialist leadership in Germany had been unclear as to what it should do with those Jews who were living in the regions that had been overrun by the Wehrmacht. Following the occupation and partition of Poland, Berlin was initially inclined to consider a 'territorial' solution within the country itself, especially in Lublin, in the eastern part of the General Government. Here Hitler and Himmler envisaged the creation of a special Jewish ghetto, but the first deportations between October and December 1939, involving almost 90,000 men, women and children, proved so chaotic that the governor, Hans Frank, protested vehemently against the plan to establish a kind of Jewish reservation to the east of the Vistula, with the river providing a natural barrier. His protests initially proved successful.

Frank was helped by the fact that in the early summer of 1940 an alternative solution to the 'Jewish question' found Himmler's approval, this time abroad. In early June 1940, shortly before Germany's victory over France, the head of the Foreign Office's 'Jewish Desk', Franz Rademacher, took up an idea which, first proposed in 1885 by the German anti-Semite Paul de Lagarde, had been revived in the second half of the 1930s by the Polish colonels' regime. All Jews – or, in Rademacher's taxonomy, all 'Western Jews' – were to be deported to Madagascar, which at this date was still part of France's colonial empire. Once Hitler had approved this idea, the Reich Main Security Office submitted a plan in August 1940 under which the East African island would be turned into a monumental ghetto under Germany's overall control.

Of course, the climatic conditions and the lack of any infrastructure on the island meant that the 'Jewish question' would have been solved in a very phys-ical way within a short space of time in the form of mass deaths. But this was not the only reason why the Madagascar plan was no real alternative to killing the Jews, millions of whom were to have been transported to the island on French and British ships. Without a peace treaty with Great Britain, this plan could never have been realized. And since this basic precondition could not be achieved, the plan played practically no further part in German deliberations after the end of 1940.

While the National Socialist leadership was considering first the Lublin solution, then the Madagascar alternative, the Jews were herded together in ghettos in the Warthegau and in the General Government and in that way kept apart from the rest of the population. The conditions in these ghettos were so intolerable that the people living there soon began to die in large numbers – according to the calculations of the Austrian-born American historian Raul Hilberg, more than half a million Jews perished in this manner. The ghettos had been planned as temporary arrangements – as transit camps where Jews would be housed on their way to more permanent settlements, whether in the east of the General Government or on the island of Madagascar, but when the Lublin and Madagascar projects turned out to be chimerical, the German authorities in a number of places, including Lodz, tried to ensure that the Jews who were living in their ghettos could at least survive by giving them work in the armaments industry. But other German authorities, including those in the Warsaw ghetto, preferred to leave the Jews who were under their supervision simply to starve to death. In April 1941 the advocates of 'productivity' prevailed over those who supported starvation, albeit only briefly, for with the invasion of the Soviet Union on 22 June 1941 a new chapter began in National Socialism's policy towards the Jews. With hindsight we can probably say that the fate of the Jews in those parts of Europe under German control was sealed the moment that Hitler decided to destroy 'Jewish Bolshevism' in Russia.

Hitler decided to invade the Soviet Union in December 1940. It was about this time that he announced his desire to 'find a definitive solution to the Jewish question in those parts of Europe dominated or controlled by Germany', a solution that would be taken in hand 'after the war'.[34] According to a report filed by Theodor Dannecker, the Gestapo's 'Jewish Expert' in Paris, it was Himmler and Göring who passed on the Führer's request to come up with the blueprint for a 'final solution' to Reinhard Heydrich in his capacity as head of the Reich Main Security Office. When Dannecker drew up his report on 21 January 1941, the project already lay before Hitler and Göring 'in all its essential outlines'. Subsequent planning was to 'extend both to the work needed to ensure the deportation of every single Jew and the detailed planning of a resettlement campaign in territory that is yet to be determined'.[35]

By March 1941 at the latest Heydrich's thoughts had been focused on the Soviet Union, especially on a remote and particularly inhospitable region: the coast of the Arctic Ocean. On 23 September 1941 he told Goebbels that the Jews should be taken to the camps that had been built there by the Bolsheviks and where they had no chance of surviving. That many Jews would die on their way there was also a part of Heydrich and his associates' calculations. It seems likely that by the spring of 1941 the Reich Main Security Office was also working on plans to exterminate most of the Jews who were capable of working by forcing them to build roads and drain areas of marshland.

Most of the murders of Soviet Jews were carried out from the very first day of the campaign in the east by the four newly formed special units of the SS. Each was assigned an area corresponding to one of the three main army divisions, Army Group North, Centre and South. (Special Units C and D shared the area covered by Army Group South.) Hitler's conflation of Jews with Bolshevik party members and partisans initially meant the death of most of the adult male Jews within the special units' areas of operation, but by the end of July the SS and special units were increasingly bent on shooting women and children as well, an extension of their remit that stemmed from a new regulation: on 16/17 July Hitler had conferred on Himmler in his capacity as the Reichsführer of the SS and chief of the German police responsibility for 'the security of the newly occupied eastern areas', in that way leaving the police to solve the 'Jewish question'. On 14/15 August 1941 Himmler met Otto Bradfisch, the leader of Special Unit 8, in Minsk and informed him of 'the Führer's orders relating to the shooting of all Jews'.[36] And Hitler's orders were duly implemented: in one region alone – the area covered by Special Unit A, namely, the Baltic States and parts of northern Russia – some 125,000 Jews and 5,000 non-Jews were killed between 22 June and 15 October 1941. In one of the worst massacres of the war, 33,700 Jews were shot in the gorge at Babi Yar near Kiev on 29 September 1941. The total number of Jews killed during the first five months of the eastern campaign was around half a million. The genocide had begun.

Not only did the Wehrmacht place no obstacles in the way of the special units but in many places helped with the executions. No doubt the discovery of the bodies of tens of thousands of murdered prisoners held by the NKVD in the areas that had been overrun in eastern Poland and western Ukraine helped the soldiers in question to overcome any moral scruples they may have had. Two German field marshals explicitly told their troops in the autumn of 1941 to regard the war with the Soviet Union not as a traditional conflict but as an ideological and racial war. On 10 October, Walther von Reichenau spoke for Hitler when he declared that the 'soldiers in the east' were the 'agents of an implacable ethnic idea' who needed to have '*complete* understanding of the necessity of harsh but just retribution against Jewish sub-humanity'. Erich von Manstein used almost identical language when he declared in November 1941 that

> the Jewish-Bolshevik system must be eradicated once and for all. Never again should this system be allowed to interfere in our European Lebensraum. Every soldier must understand the need to exact harsh retribution on Jewry, the spiritual agents of the Bolshevik terror.[37]

Even officers like Henning von Tresckow, the chief operations officer of Army Group Centre, and Colonel Rudolf-Christoph von Gersdorff of the general staff, both of whom were to play prominent roles in German opposition to Hitler, initially agreed with the way in which east European Jews were equated with Bolshevik partisans, initialling reports on completed executions and passing on orders to others in keeping with the instructions that they received. It was only after the murder of the Jews – including women and children – in Borisov (Barysaw) on 20 and 21 October 1941, by which date there was no longer any doubt about the genocidal nature of the National Socialists' hostility towards the Jews, that Tresckow and his friends decided to draw the ultimate conclusion from their opposition and murder the tyrant responsible for the genocide.

Local forces were also involved in the mass shootings of Jews in the Baltic States, eastern Galicia and the Ukraine, their hatred being directed not just at the Jews who had sided with the Soviet Union in 1939–40 but at Jews in general, a state of affairs for which a mixture of religious, economic and political motives was to blame. In the small Polish town of Jedwabne in the district of Bialystok, the Jews were murdered by Poles from their own community by being either beaten to death or burnt alive in local barns. The Catholic clergy made no attempt to condemn these and other atrocities. The authors of a report which, originating within the Polish Church itself and covering the period from 1 June to 15 July 1941, was submitted to the government in exile in London argued that

> as far as the Jewish Question is concerned, it must be seen as a singular dispensation of Divine Providence that the Germans have already made a good start, quite irrespective of all the wrongs they have done and continue to do to our country. They have shown that the liberation of Polish society

from the Jewish plague is possible. [. . .] Clearly, one can see the hand of God in the contribution to the solution of this urgent question being made by the occupiers.[38]

The example set by the Germans encouraged likeminded regimes in south-east and eastern central Europe to emulate them. On Ion Antonescu's orders, the Romanian army and gendarmerie murdered between 280,000 and 380,000 Jews in Romania itself and on Russian soil in 1941–2, while the Croatian Ustaše, acting on orders from Ante Pavelić, conducted a crusade against the country's 2.2 million Orthodox Serbs and around 45,000 Jews during which unspeakable atrocities were committed against Serbian women in particular. By the spring of 1942 between 300,000 and 400,000 Serbs and most of the region's Jews had been killed without any attempt on the part of Pope Pius XII or the Catholic clergy to put a stop to the Catholic Ustaše. In August 1941 the Hungarian police handed over around 18,000 foreign Jews to the SS, all of whom were killed in western Ukraine, together with some 5,600 Ukrainian Jews. In the autumn of 1941 Catholic Slovenia took over a large number of anti-Jewish measures from National Socialist Germany, including the yellow star that all Jews had to wear in public and that was introduced into the Reich on 1 September 1941. Excluded from the Slovak Jewish Statute of 1 November 1941 were those Jews who had converted to Catholicism. Slovakia was the first European country to begin deporting its Jews to the east – to the Auschwitz concentration camp – in March 1942.

It was Alfred Rosenberg who, as head of the Reich Ministry for the Occupied Eastern Territories from 17 July 1941, was nominally responsible for the implementation of German rule over those parts of the Soviet Union that had been overrun by the Reich. In fact, the task devolved on two high-ranking officials of the NSDAP: Hinrich Lohse, who was the Gauleiter of Schleswig-Holstein and Reich commissar for the 'Ostland', which was made up of the three Baltic States and Belorussia; and Erich Koch, the Gauleiter of East Prussia and Reich commissar for a reduced Ukraine, who was also placed in charge of the eastern Polish district of Bialystok. Koch regarded the Ukraine as an area ripe for exploitation and saw the Ukrainians as a nation of slaves who were required to work for their German masters. Rosenberg himself thought that this policy was flawed since it made it impossible for him to work with anti-Bolshevik forces in the Ukraine, but his objections were futile since Martin Bormann, the powerful head of the party's Chancellery, invariably sided with Koch, in which regard he could, where necessary, rely on Hitler's support.

But Rosenberg, too, thought merely in terms of expediency where the Jews were concerned. When, in October 1941, the general commissar for White Ruthenia, the former Brandenburg Gauleiter Wilhelm Kube, protested at the mass killing of Jews, including many skilled manual workers, and wrote to Rosenberg to ask if all Jews were to be liquidated 'without regard for age and sex and economic interests (for instance, the Wehrmacht's need of specialists in armament plants)?', Rosenberg assured him that 'in principle economic considerations must be overlooked in the solution of the problem. In general, any question which may arise is to be solved on the spot, together with the Higher SS and Police Leader.'[39]

The extermination of the Jews had begun in the summer of 1941, but there was much that still remained unresolved. For now, the mass killings were confined to sections of the Jewish population in eastern Europe, where the preferred form of killing was shooting. But it was impossible, of course, to kill many millions in this way in a short space of time, quite apart from the 'moral' cost to those actively involved and the impossibility of concealing such killings from the German public and from the world at large. What was still required, therefore, was the 'Comprehensive Plan for Implementing the Proposed Final Solution to the Jewish Question' that Göring, as coordinator for all non-military activities in the eastern campaign, demanded from Heydrich on 31 July 1941.

With regard to his thoughts on a definitive solution to the Jewish question, Hitler continued to divide Jews into eastern European and western European Jews at least until the autumn of 1941. On 30 January 1941 he had reminded the Reichstag of his 'instructions' of 30 January 1939, which he had in fact backdated to 1 September 1939, the day when war broke out, and insisted that 'if the other world is plunged into a general war by Jewry, then the whole of European Jewry will have finished playing its role.'[40] Hitler evidently regarded German and western European Jews as hostages that the United States had to take into consideration in all its dealings with Germany. In his eyes America was the protecting power and the political arm of international 'finance Jewry'. If the United States were to side with Germany's enemies, foremost among which was the Soviet Union, then the 'Jewish-capitalist-Bolshevik world conspiracy' to which he referred in his New Year's Day address on 1 January 1942 was an inescapable reality.[41] Hitler would no longer need to pay any heed to the Jews living in the Reich and in western Europe – and this would be even truer once he had won the war. Whatever the outcome, the Jews had no chance of surviving in a world that was ruled by Germany.

On 14 August 1941, however, Hitler's strategic and political planning was thrown into disarray by the official announcement of Roosevelt's and Churchill's Atlantic Charter. Hitler could no longer assume that Great Britain would capitulate and reach a settlement with him in the wake of a German victory in the east. One consequence of this new situation was his decision to turn his back on the strategy of a blitzkrieg that would have involved taking Moscow as quickly as possible. Instead, he now decided that his plan must be to capture material resources in the south of the Soviet Union and in that way provide Germany with the means to conduct a much longer war.

The other consequence concerned the Jews, for Hitler now expected the United States to enter the war sooner rather than later and to spearhead an Allied invasion along the Atlantic coast, and so he began to plan to destroy all European Jews while the war was still in progress. The eradication of European Jewry was a response to the way in which a war in Europe had been turned into a global conflict: Hitler operated in terms of the categories in which he thought.

On 18 August 1941 Hitler agreed to a proposal put forward by his minister of propaganda whereby every Jew in Germany was required to wear 'a large, visible Jewish symbol', namely, the aforementioned yellow star, the wearing of which was imposed by the courts on 1 September 1941. In the course of the same conversation with Goebbels, Hitler addressed the 'Jewish problem' in more general terms, making it clear that he was now thinking of dealing with the 'Jewish question' by physical liquidation on a European scale while the war was still in progress:

> The Führer is convinced that his earlier prophecy in the Reichstag – namely, if Jewry succeeded in provoking another world war, it would end with the destruction of the Jews – is now being borne out. It has proved to be true in recent weeks and months with an almost uncanny certainty. In the east the Jews must pay the price; in Germany they have already paid the price, at least in part, and they will have to pay even more in the future. North America remains their final refuge; and even there they will one day have to pay the price, be it sooner or later.[42]

Writing in the weekly *Das Reich* on 16 November 1941, the minister of public enlightenment and propaganda informed the German public that Hitler's prophecy of 30 January 1939 had been deadly serious:

> We are currently witnessing the fulfilment of this prophecy, and although the fate that Jewry is now undergoing may be harsh, it is more than deserved. Pity is completely inappropriate, regret even more so. In fomenting this war, world Jewry has completely misjudged the resources available to it and it is now experiencing a gradual process of annihilation that it had previously planned for us and that it would have carried out without a second thought if it had had the power to do so. It is now being destroyed according to its own law of 'an eye for an eye, and a tooth for a tooth'.

Goebbels's message – that Hitler's prophecy concerning the destruction of the Jewish race in Europe was already coming true – could not have been clearer, not least because the print run of *Das Reich* in the autumn of 1941 was over a million. Anyone reading or hearing about the minister of propaganda's article, with its screaming headline, 'The Jews Are To Blame!', will have discovered in this way that the Jews in eastern Europe were being murdered in their thousands and that the regime was resolved to complete this process by taking it to its bitter end. 'In this historical confrontation', Goebbels explained to his readers on 16 November 1941, 'every Jew is our enemy, no matter whether he is vegetating in a Polish ghetto or eking out his parasitic existence in Berlin or Hamburg or blowing the trumpet of war in New York or Washington. [. . .] The Jews are our enemy's emissaries among us. Whoever sides with them is joining the enemy in time of war.'

Goebbels's article was first and foremost a warning to all those Germans who sympathized with the Jews that they were threatened with the harshest reprisals: 'Anyone wearing a Jewish Star is marked out as an enemy of the people. Anyone who continues to have private dealings with him belongs to him and must be evaluated and treated like a Jew.'[43] It is unclear whether Goebbels also intended his article to be read as a kind of final warning to those American Jews whom he accused of attempting to drive the United States into war with Germany. But this seems possible. After all, there was as yet no 'world war' in November 1941, even though Hitler had assumed in the middle of August that such a global conflict was imminent.

Reports in the *New York Times* meant that American readers were fully informed about events in Germany and knew that by the middle of October 1941 Jews were being deported to regions to the east of the Reich. These deportations were Hitler's response to Roosevelt's orders to the American fleet to fire 'on sight' on German and Italian submarines in American waters, an order that he had issued on 11 September 1941 in the wake of the *Greer* incident. But Hitler was unwilling to liquidate German Jews as long as Germany and the United States were still at peace. On 30 November, when around 5,000 Jews had been shot near Kaunas without his authorization, Hitler used the occasion to send a message via Himmler to Heydrich: 'Transport of Jews from Berlin! No liquidation.'[44] The orders were delayed and reached Riga only after 1,000 German Jews had been shot there, but they were implemented in the case of other deportations from the Reich. While Goebbels spoke of 'world Jewry's' responsibility for the war in his article on 16 November and threatened all Jews with liquidation, Hitler seemed willing to wait before issuing orders to annihilate German and western European Jews until the war in Europe acquired an obvious and unambiguous global dimension.

The Japanese attack on the American fleet at Pearl Harbor on 7 December 1941 brought to an end the phase in the war where Hitler had observed a tactical restraint in terms of the 'Jewish question'. It must have been immediately after Pearl Harbor that Hitler decided to kill all Jews within the German sphere of influence even while the war was still being fought. 'We know the power that stands behind Roosevelt,' Hitler told the Reichstag on 11 December. 'It is the Wandering Jew, who thinks that the time has come for him to do to us what we were all forced to observe in horror in Soviet Russia.' The following day he addressed a meeting of national and local leaders, prompting Goebbels to note in his diary:

As for the Jewish question the Führer is resolved to settle the matter once and for all. He has predicted that if the Jews were to cause another world war, they would witness their own destruction. This is no empty phrase. The world war is now upon us, and the destruction of the Jews must be the necessary consequence of this.[45]

One of the regional leaders who attended the meeting on 12 December 1941 was Hans Frank, who four days later told a session of the General Government administration that the Jews would no longer be deported to the 'Ostland' or to the Ukraine but would be killed in the General Government itself:

> We were told in Berlin: why are you making all this trouble? We can't do anything with them in the Ostland or in the Reich. Liquidate them your-selves! [. . .] For us, too, the Jews are exceptionally harmful, devouring all our food like animals. [. . .] We can't shoot these 3.5 million Jews, we can't poison them, but we can take steps that one way or another will lead to their successful eradication, which will be done in the context of measures that must be discussed by the Reich as a whole.[46]

Two days later, on 18 December, Himmler spoke to Hitler and later noted: 'Jewish question. / to be exterminated as partisans.'[47] The meaning of this laconic remark is not hard to decipher: now that the Reich was at war with the United States, all the Jews that Germany could round up were to be liquidated, just as hundreds of thousands of Jews had already been killed in the Soviet Union.

The discussions mentioned by Hans Frank took place in the villa at 56–58 Am Großen Wannsee on 20 January 1942 under the chairmanship of Reinhard Heydrich. The meeting had initially been planned for 9 December 1941 but was then postponed on account of the new international situation. Among those who attended what has become known as the 'Wannsee Conference' were representatives of the SS, the Foreign Office, the Ministry of Justice, the Ministry for the Eastern Territories, the Office for the Four-Year Plan, the General Government and the Reich Chancellery, including four secretaries of state, one undersecretary of state and one permanent secretary. Its aim was to discuss the 'final solution of the Jewish question'. The minutes were kept by Adolf Eichmann, who was the head of the Jewish Desk at the Reich Main Security Office and who recorded Heydrich's coded explanation of what he understood by the 'evacuation of the Jews to the east':

> In the course of the final solution and under the appropriate leadership, the Jews are to be put to work in a suitable way in the east. Jews capable of working will be dispatched to these region in large columns and segregated by sex, building roads as they go, during which process a large number will

undoubtedly be lost to natural attrition. Any that are left over will have to be dealt with appropriately since they will undoubtedly represent the most resistant strain and form a natural elite which, if allowed to go free, would constitute the nucleus of a new Jewish stock. (Witness the experience of history.) In the course of the practical implementation of the final solution, Europe will be thoroughly combed from west to east.[48]

The Wannsee Conference marked the start of a large-scale operation designed to make those parts of Europe that were occupied or controlled by Germans 'free from Jews'. In practice, road building no longer played a significant role in liquidating Jews since the military situation in the east precluded this kind of colonization. The 'final solution' in the sense of mass killings on an industrial scale was to take place for the most part on Polish territory. From the autumn of 1941 experts from Operation T-4 – named after 4 Tiergartenstraße in Berlin, the main centre for murdering the mentally ill – helped with the technical preparations for the mass murders that were being planned. They already had experience in the use of poison gas for killing the mentally ill using mobile 'gas vans'.

By October 1941 the SS had begun building the first camp to be used purely for the purposes of extermination at Belzec near Lublin. Permanent gas chambers were installed there the following month, a clear sign that the decision to begin the systematic liquidation of at least all eastern European Jews had already been taken by this date. Belzec was followed by Sobibór and Treblinka. The existing camps at Auschwitz and Majdanek, conversely, were not pure extermination camps but concentration camps that were a part of larger economic organizations. Polish Jews and gypsies unable to work were gassed at Chelmno for the first time on 8 December 1941. As the Dutch historian L. J. Hartog has noted, Chelmno – also known under its German name of Kulmhof im Warthegau – was 'the first murder factory in the history of humankind'.[49]

At the time of the Wannsee Conference, the machinery of mass murder was still in its infancy, but it grew in efficiency in the course of 1942. The gas vans were replaced by gas chambers in Auschwitz, Belzec, Sobibór, Treblinka and Majdanek. Zyklon B, a hydrocyanic acid gas, replaced the carbon monoxide that had been used previously. At Auschwitz-Birkenau the inmates continued to be worked to death right up to the end, not least at the hands of a subsidiary of IG Farben, although many Jews, together with gypsies and Soviet prisoners of war, were gassed as soon as they arrived at the camp.

Hitler never issued any written instructions for the liquidation of the Jews, reactions to his instructions to kill the mentally ill effectively precluding this kind of order. But he expressed his wishes concerning the 'solution to the Jewish question' in such a way that his underlings, from the head of the SS to the Higher SS and police leaders right down to the heads of the special action groups and special action commandos, were left in no doubt that the most radical interpretation of his instructions was the one that corresponded most closely to his wishes. This is one of the reasons for the increasing radicalization of the process in question.

Another reason may be sought in the results of previous measures that had been taken without regard for their consequences. The resettlement of ethnic Germans in the Warthegau as well as the deportation of Jews from the Reich and from the Protectorate of Bohemia and Moravia to the General Government created a problem that could not be solved by deporting Jews to what had formerly been Soviet territory. The neighbouring territories were already covered by the 'General Plan East', and the Arctic coast that had been earmarked for camps was inaccessible to Germany. As a result, there could no longer be any possibility of a 'territorial solution to the Jewish question' to the east of Poland. Although such a solution would ultimately have led to the physical annihilation of the Jews, this would have taken a relatively long time. Once this option had been ruled out, the only alternative was the 'final solution'. The practical constraints that made mass murder seem inevitable – above all the food situation, which became increasingly critical from the end of 1941 – were the result of decisions for which Hitler was ultimately responsible. The long-debated question as to whether the extermination of the Jews was 'intentional' or 'functional' – in other words, whether it reflected Hitler's intentions or whether it stemmed from the inner logic of the National Socialists' policies on war and race – cannot be answered as a simple either/or, for both aspects came together here.

On 30 January 1942 – ten days after the Wannsee Conference and nine years to the day since he had seized power in 1933 – Hitler gave a speech in the Sportpalast in Berlin in which he again reminded his listeners of his prophecy concerning the eradication of the Jews:

> We are clear in our own minds that the war can end in only one of two ways. Either the Aryan peoples will be exterminated, or Jewry will vanish from Europe. [. . .] For the first time the authentically ancient Jewish law will be applied: 'An eye for an eye, and a tooth for a tooth.' And the more wide-spread these struggles become, the more widespread anti-Semitism will be – and world Jewry should take this to heart. This anti-Semitism will find nourishment in every prison camp and in every family that understands why it ultimately had to make this sacrifice. And the time will come when the most evil enemy ever to have been seen in the world will be played out for at least a millennium.[50]

In the thousand years between victory over the Antichrist and the Last Judgement, the devil would have no more power over human beings. Without actually mentioning his Biblical source, Hitler was referring to Chapter Twenty of the Book of Revelation in his attempt to convince his German audience of the importance of their historical, not to say soteriological, mission. And not just the Germans: no less than Goebbels, Hitler was convinced that Europe and, indeed, the 'Aryan' race in general had every reason to be grateful to Germany for saving the world from the international threat posed by Jewry.

Although the idea that anti-Jewish sentiment could be used as a means of enlisting European support for National Socialist Germany may seem absurd, this development could have been predicted, for the National Socialists' anti-Semitic slogans had found a positive response in all those parts of Europe that were under German influence. After Italy and Hungary, the Vichy government in France enacted its own anti-Jewish laws, which it did soon after the armistice and without any prompting by Germany. At the end of July a law was passed requiring all naturalization papers that had been issued since 1927 to be checked, with the result that some 8,000 Jews lost their French citizenship. The month of August saw the repeal of a law passed only the previous April and intended to forbid incitement on racial or religious grounds. And on 3 October 1940, just a week after the first anti-Jewish decree had been passed by the German military commander, the Pétain regime issued a *Statut des Juifs* that defined a Jew as any person descending from at least three grandparents of the 'Jewish race' or if the person in question was married to a Jew, two such grandparents. It also banned Jews from holding public office and all positions of ownership or responsibility in the press, theatre and film industries. As a result of the *Statut des Juifs*, 140 lecturers and four professors were dismissed from their posts at the Collège de France.

A further law of 4 October 1940 allowed individual *départements* to intern Jews from abroad, although it was not until the May of the following year that the first mass arrests were made. In June, following the introduction of a new and harsher *Statut des Juifs*, a limit was placed on the number of Jews who could work in several freelance professions, including medicine and the law. Measures were also undertaken to 'Aryanize' the French economy. Some 47,000 Jewish businesses – largely branches of the textile industry as well as department stores and banks – were wound up or taken over by non-Jewish concerns. This blow hit Paris's Jewish population particularly badly.

Among early victims of the État français's policy on Jews and émigrés were two German Social Democrats: the leading Marxist theorist and former German finance minister Rudolf Hilferding, who was Jewish, and the former leader of the Social Democrats in the Reichstag, Rudolf Breitscheid, who was not a Jew. The Vichy police arrested them both at the Hôtel du Forum in Arles in southern France on 9 February 1941 and handed them over to the secret services in Vichy, which in turn sent them to the Gestapo's prison in Paris, La Santé, where Hilferding took his own life on 12 February 1941. Breitscheid was deported to the concentration camp at Buchenwald, where he was murdered in August 1944, ostensibly in an air raid. The most prominent Jewish Socialist in France to be handed over to the Germans by the Vichy regime was Léon Blum, who survived his years in the concentration camps at Buchenwald and Dachau and returned to head the French government in 1946–7.

Only in one western European country then under German influence were there protests at the increasing disfranchisement and persecution of the Jews, and that was in the Netherlands. In November 1940 teachers and students at the Universities of Leiden and Delft objected to the dismissal of a number of Jewish members of staff, and on 25 February 1941 the Communists in Amsterdam successfully called a general strike designed first and foremost as a protest at a particularly brutal police operation in the Jewish quarter of the city. But in all the other countries occupied by German troops the National Socialists' anti-Semitic policies encountered a mixture of apathy and muted approval summed up by Saul Friedländer: 'The anti-Jewish measures were accepted, even approved, by the populations and the spiritual and intellectual elites, most blatantly so by the Christian churches.'[51]

In Germany it became clear in the course of the war that the regime's unre-lenting anti-Semitic propaganda had had an effect – this is the only possible explanation for the extraordinarily deep contempt for the Jews that found expression in countless letters written not only by officers but also by ordinary soldiers, especially those deployed to Poland. In spite of this, the National Socialist leadership knew that the aim of murdering European Jews would never have been accepted by the population at large. Notwithstanding pointed references to the 'disappearance', 'annihilation' and 'extermination' of the Jewish race, it was necessary, therefore, to conceal the process as such and, hence, the manner in which the murders were carried out.

It must remain an open question whether Hitler's closest associates shared his apocalyptic vision of a final struggle between the Aryan and the Jewish races. Indeed, it was unnecessary for them to do so to be fanatical anti-Semites. And it was probably not even necessary to hate the Jews to carry out Hitler's orders to eradicate them. It was enough to regard the charismatic Führer as politically infallible in order to rule out the possibility that what Hitler was demanding in the name of Germany could ever be wrong. Certainly, it does not seem to have been necessary to obey orders concerning the extermination of the Jews: nothing that we know about the German policemen in the east who refused to shoot unarmed Jewish men, women and children suggests that any were punished for declining to do so. For the majority – and regardless of what they personally may have felt about the Jews – it seems to have been a case of 'orders are orders'. The social pressure of camaraderie was as a rule more powerful than the individual conscience.

But a dislike of the Jews was by no means negligible, for both in Germany and elsewhere it had long been a part of conservative thinking and, for an even longer period, of the Christian tradition in general. Even if hatred of the Jews grew into a murderous delight in only a minority of cases, this made it easier to look away when Hitler set about carrying out his profession of faith. Both of the country's Christian Churches had protested at the killing of the mentally ill, but few members of the clergy objected to the murder of Jews, about which far more was known than Germany's leaders wanted. One of the protesters was the Catholic dean Bernhard Lichtenberg, who paid for his courage with his arrest and his life. The regime adopted a rather more lenient approach to the Lutheran bishop of Württemberg, Theophil Wurm, who, although an avowed anti-Semite in the tradition of the nineteenth-century Berlin court chaplain Adolf Stoecker, repeatedly used his sermons and letters to inveigh against the treatment of Jews. He even wrote to Hitler and Goebbels on the subject, until he was banned from speaking and writing in March 1944.

Murdering millions of Jews required not only an army of helpers willing to carry out orders, it also presupposed the complicity of the country's various elites: the military, whose successes on the battlefield had made it possible to build the extermination camps in the first place; the industrialists who profited from the policy of working their employees to death; the banks who turned the wedding rings and gold fillings of murdered Jews into currency for the Reich and provided loans to build the camps; the scientists and technicians who set up the machinery for mass murder; the doctors who undertook inhuman experiments on Jewish and other prisoners; the lawyers who gave a semblance of legitimacy to the disfranchisement and persecution of the Jews; and the historians and economists who laid the foundations for the 'solution of the Jewish question' by placing their knowledge at the service of the regime. The murder of the Jews was not a secret project that German history was designed from the outset to complete, but German history can explain why there was so little resistance to it when the man in whom the majority of Germans still believed set about the realization of a project involving the most extreme form of anti-Semitism that the world has ever witnessed.

A Change of Direction: The Axis Powers go on the Defensive

For Germany, the year 1942 began with bad news from the eastern front: the Red Army had succeeded in advancing from the Valdai Heights to an area north of Smolensk, in that way driving a wedge between the Army Group Centre and the Army Group North. And by 18 January Soviet troops had broken through the positions of Army Group South to the south of Kharkiv. It was here, in May, that the German counterattack began on Hitler's orders. In the course of the operation almost 239,000 Red Army soldiers fell into German hands. The German summer offensive brought the Wehrmacht substantial gains in the south-east: by July Voronezh and Rostov had been taken and shortly afterwards the army reached the Don. The Red Army retreated to the Stalingrad front, which was then systematically fortified. Units of the NKVD used extreme brutality to prevent the Soviet troops from retreating any further.

By this date the Wehrmacht was running perilously short of fuel, so that Hitler's principal strategic goal, at least in the shorter term, was to capture the oil wells in the Caucasus, especially at Baku. On 21 August mountain troops hoisted the German flag on Mount Elbrus, the highest peak in the Caucasus, but the assault on the naval port at Sukhumi proved a disaster. Although the Germans managed to persuade sections of the non-Russian population to collaborate with them and formed battalions of Cossacks, Georgians and Kalmucks, the regrouped Army Group A lacked the ability to capture Grozny and Baku. The result was a violent argument between Hitler and the army's chief of the general staff, leading to Halder's resignation on 24 September and to his replacement by General Kurt Zeitzler of the infantry. Seven weeks earlier, on 19 August 1942, the Sixth Army under General Friedrich Paulus had begun its assault on Stalingrad, encircling the city within a matter of days. On 25 August Stalin declared a state of siege in the industrial capital that bore his name. For Hitler, the capture of Stalingrad had more than merely strategic importance for, like Leningrad and Moscow, the city on the Volga was the embodiment of 'Jewish Bolshevism', which was the archenemy that he needed to destroy.

In its war on Great Britain, Germany was able to exploit the fact that in early 1942 much of the British Mediterranean fleet had been moved to the Indian Ocean to discourage Japanese aggression. In early February the German Afrika Korps under Rommel marched on Tobruk, capturing the town on 21 June. Rommel was promoted to field marshal the following day. Both Hitler and Mussolini had wanted Malta to be captured next, but instead Rommel turned his attention on Egypt, reaching El Alamein, around sixty miles west of Alexandria, on 30 June. But the Afrika Korps did not have the reserves to continue its advance on Cairo, and at the end of October Montgomery began a large-scale offensive aimed at recapturing El Alamein, which was held by German and Italian troops. Exiled Polish units fought alongside the British. From that point onwards, the Axis Powers remained almost permanently on the defensive in North Africa, and at the end of November, Rommel's troops withdrew to Marsa al-Brega, explicitly flouting Hitler's orders.

The legendary 'Torch Landings' had taken place two weeks earlier, on 8/9 November 1942, when American and British troops under Dwight D. Eisenhower had landed in Morocco and Algeria. The French navy initially fought back in Casablanca, Oran and Algiers, but on 10 November Admiral François Darlan, who had been replaced as prime minister by Pierre Laval in April 1942 and who, now in charge of the Vichy government's armed forces, happened to be in Algiers in early November, agreed to a truce in north-west Africa and was immediately recognized by the Allies as the head of the French civilian authorities in North Africa. Darlan's actions were presumably taken on his own initiative, rather than in secret agreement with Pétain. The leader of France Libre, Charles de Gaulle, who had not been informed about the Allied invasion of Morocco and Algeria, lodged a formal protest with Churchill. Darlan ignored his dismissal by Pétain on 16 November. On 24 December he was murdered in Algiers by one of de Gaulle's supporters and was replaced as the Allies' partner in the region by the commander of the French troops in North Africa, General Henri Giraud, who had escaped from a German prisoner-of-war camp in April 1942 and was regarded as empathically anti-German.

In Tunisia, conversely, an invasion by German and Italian troops that began by air on 12 November initially encountered no resistance from the French. In February 1943 Rommel inflicted a severe defeat on the Americans at the Kasserine Pass in the south of Tunisia, although this failed to prevent the Allies from advancing further inland. On 9 March Rommel was replaced as commander in chief of the German-Italian Afrika Korps by General Hans-Jürgen von Arnim, who capitulated on 13 April 1943, when 175,000 German and Italian soldiers were taken prisoner, bringing an end to the war in North Africa.

In Europe, too, the first American troops landed in Northern Ireland on 21 January 1942. Between March and May the first carpet bombing of German towns and cities was carried out by the Royal Air Force, resulting in hundreds of deaths during each sortie. Lübeck, Rostock and Cologne were the places targeted. For its part, the Luftwaffe attacked Bath, Exeter and Canterbury but failed to achieve its objective of ending British air raids on Germany. The first – experimental – attempt to land Canadian and British troops in Continental Europe was undertaken at Dieppe on 19 August but ended in heavy casualties. The German submarine war in the North Atlantic climaxed in the summer of 1942 with coordinated attacks on American convoys on their way to Great Britain, but the 'pack tactics' employed by the German U-boats ceased to be effective when the British built a replica of the German Enigma machine and were able to decode the radio traffic between German vessels. In this the British experts were helped by information gleaned by the Polish secret service.

The landing of British and American troops in North Africa on 8/9 November 1942 prompted Hitler to launch an operation that he had long been planning for this precise eventuality: the occupation of those parts of France that had not yet been overrun by German troops. The move began on 11 November, the same day that Italy, after consulting with Germany, began to occupy Provence as far as the Rhône. The following day Italian forces invaded Corsica. When Hitler informed Pétain on 11 November that the operation was already under way, the marshal protested at Germany's violation of the ceasefire agreement of 22 June 1940 but did not call on his fellow countrymen and women to resist. When the Germans occupied Toulon on 27 November with the aim of preventing the French home fleet that lay at anchor there from defecting to the Allies, the commander ordered that the ships be scuttled. Only three submarines were able to escape to Algeria.

The fact that the Western Allies launched their large-scale invasion in November 1942 not in Europe – as the Soviet Union and, initially, the United States had hoped – but in North Africa was due to British insistence: the United

Kingdom felt that it was in a relatively strong position in the southern Mediterranean – a region that had always been strategically important for the Empire – whereas the Axis Powers were comparatively weak in that area. The failure of the attempt to land troops at Dieppe in August 1942 confirmed the government in London in its decision to adopt this set of priorities. An Allied landing on the French Atlantic coast would have required far more preparation and presumably have cost more lives than an invasion of North Africa. Roosevelt and Churchill did, however, agree that victory over Germany should take precedence over the defeat of Japan, a sequence of events that in Washington's eyes also made economic sense. In the Pacific, conversely, the United States and Great Britain were for the present inclined to remain on the defensive in keeping with an agreement that the two leaders had reached at the Arcadia Conference in Washington during the winter of 1941/2.

Japan adopted the opposite expedient. On 22 December 1941 its troops landed on Mindanao, the most southerly of the Philippines. Five days later they took Hong Kong and marched into Manila on 2 January 1942. That same month Japanese troops invaded islands that belonged to the Dutch East Indies, including the oil-rich Tarakan and Celebes. From Thailand they also launched an offensive against British Burma and landed on New Guinea, leading to a full-scale mobilization in Australia. After an eight-day siege, the British crown colony of Singapore capitulated on 17 February, when 70,000 British soldiers under General Arthur Percival were taken prisoner by the Japanese – from a British standpoint one of the worst disasters in the history of the Empire. Three weeks later the Burmese capital Rangoon was taken. On 8 March the Dutch forces on Java surrendered. By now the whole of the Dutch East Indies was in Japanese hands. The conquest of the Philippines was completed by 6 May.

Four weeks later, on 3 June, the battle began for the American Midway Islands, which the Japanese were keen to capture above all because they promised to provide effective protection from American air raids such as those that had been launched against Tokyo and other cities in April 1942. But the Japanese aggressors suffered such serious losses, including four of their finest aircraft carriers, that after four days of fighting they were obliged to call off the operation. Their defeat proved to be a turning point in the war in the Pacific, and the planned assault on Hawaii was called off. For Japan, the period of major military successes and territorial gains came to an end in June 1942.

Japan had also wanted to use the increasingly militant Indian independence movement for its own ends, but for the present this aim, too, proved unrealizable, and in the early autumn of 1942 the British colonial power succeeded in restoring order after rioting had broken out following the arrest of the entire leadership of the Indian National Congress in August. Among those arrested were Jawaharlal Nehru and Mahatma Gandhi, who had tabled the Quit India Resolution at the All India Congress, calling on the British to leave India at once. In the shorter term the Indian nationalists could no longer expect any support from Japan. Nor could they prevent India from continuing to export foodstuffs, textiles and other goods to Great Britain and its Allies and from sending 2.5 million soldiers to fight on the various fronts where the Allies were engaged in hostilities with the Axis Powers. In the wake of its Midway Islands defeat, Japan concentrated its efforts on consolidating its rule in the areas that it had already captured and on fending off American and British attacks.

Just as Japan was suffering its first serious defeat, Germany was making unprecedented territorial gains, its sphere of influence extending from the North Cape to El Alamein and from the Channel Islands to the Caucasus. But within months a dramatic change had taken place not only in North Africa but also in eastern Europe. On 19 November 1942 the Red Army, currently to the west of Stalingrad, set out on a major offensive from its bridgeheads on the Don. Acting on the orders of Stalin himself and of Marshals Zhukov and Vasilevsky, the army first broke through the positions of the Third and Fourth Romanian Army and then encircled the German Sixth Army under Friedrich Paulus.

Hitler categorically refused to allow Paulus to break free from his position near Stalingrad but promised to provide an effective airlift, only for this to prove just as much a failure as a relief attack by the newly formed Army Group Don. Between the middle of December 1942 and the middle of January 1943 the Soviet troops succeeded in crushing the Italian and Hungarian troops who were fighting alongside the Germans on the Don. Shortly afterwards the Red Army pushed forward along the south of the eastern front, driving Army Group A from the Caucasus and also from the bridgehead on the Kuban Peninsula that had been receiving supplies from the Crimea. A few days later, on 18 January 1943, Soviet troops in the north captured Schlüsselburg on Lake Ladoga, in that way creating a land link to Leningrad, which had been besieged and starved since September 1941. The supplies provided by the United States under the terms of the land-lease agreement and including ships, bombers, aircraft, tanks, jeeps, lorries, locomotives and freight cars had clearly had an impact. Equally clear was the fighting spirit of the Red Army as the Soviet Union displayed a military might that taught the Germans the meaning of fear.

Hitler had given strict orders on 23 January 1943 that the Sixth Army was not to capitulate even though its situation was now completely hopeless. On 31 January Paulus – now general field marshal – surrendered, together with the southern half of his Sixth Army. The northern half raised the white flag two days later. Of the original 250,000 men, between 30,000 and 40,000, generally the wounded, had in the meantime managed to break out. At least 120,000 men had fallen, while a further 90,000 ended up as Russian prisoners of war. Stalingrad was the worst defeat that Germany had suffered since 1939, a defeat from which the country would never recover and that dealt an initial blow – not yet fatal – to the myth of the invincible Führer.

In the course of the weeks that followed, the Red Army took Rostov, Kharkiv and Kursk, while the Wehrmacht was driven back across the Don. For a time the front was mired in mud, but in early July Hitler launched one final large-scale offensive, Operation Citadel, a major tank battle that began at Orel and the recently recaptured Kharkiv and inflicted serious losses on the Red Army but which was then called off on Hitler's instructions in the middle of July after a Soviet breakthrough in the central section of the front and the fall of Orel. This was followed by further Soviet offensives, forcing the German army to retreat ever further westwards. Kiev fell in early November, and by the middle of January 1944 the front extended from Leningrad across the Pinsk Marshes to the Crimea. It was no longer possible for Germany to reinforce the eastern front since a second front had opened up in Sicily, where American and British troops under Eisenhower's overall command had landed on 10 July.

Ever since the Japanese defeat on the Midway Islands and the German defeats at El Alamein and Stalingrad Hitler's prospects of successfully engaging with the British Empire on a global scale had progressively diminished. On 28 November 1941 he had received a visit from the Grand Mufti of Jerusalem, Haj Mohammed Amin el-Husseini, and promised to support him in the Arabs' struggle with the Jews in Palestine and with the latter's British protectors. But following British military successes in the Middle East and North Africa el-Husseini could no longer be of any use to the Reich. And much the same was true of the former Iraqi prime minister, Rashid Ali al-Gaylani, who, a declared friend of the Axis Powers, had likewise fled to Germany and who met Hitler on 15 July 1942.

Hitler had slightly more success with another political refugee, the former president of the Indian National Congress, Subhas Chandra Bose, with whom he held discussions on 28 May 1942. In June 1943 Bose was able to escape to Japan on board a German U-boat. Once in Japan, he convened and headed a provisional Indian national government, while also forming an Indian national army numbering between 40,000 and 45,000 Indian prisoners of war in Malaya and Singapore that fought alongside Japanese troops under Japanese command. In February 1944 this joint task force attacked the East Indies from Burma only to be driven back by the British in the April of that year.

Even before the German Sixth Army had capitulated at Stalingrad, Roosevelt, Churchill and their chiefs of staff had met at Casablanca between 14 and 26 January 1943 in order to agree on their subsequent course of action. The meeting's most important outcome was Roosevelt's insistence on the Axis Powers' 'unconditional surrender', a phrase that the president recalled had been used by the commander of the Union forces, General Ulysses Grant, at the end of the American Civil War in April 1865.

It was a demand intended to counter Stalin's fear that the Western Powers might come to some arrangement with Hitler: a special peace with Germany was now out of the question even if there were a change of government in Berlin. Germany, Italy and Japan had to capitulate not only militarily but also on a governmental level. The next stage in the campaign was to be the conquest of Tunisia and a landing on the island of Sicily. Churchill was particularly keen to implement this plan because he felt that in 1943 it was still too soon to attempt an invasion of France, as Stalin was insisting: British losses along Germany's Atlantic Wall would be reduced if the Allies had already inflicted heavy defeats on the Wehrmacht elsewhere. The Western Allies accepted that the demand for 'unconditional surrender' would strengthen resistance in Germany and Japan, their principal concern being to ensure that both states should be deprived of their ability to launch any further attacks in the future.

Home Fronts: Nations at War

On 1 September 1939 – the first day of the war – Hitler had assured the Reichstag that there would never be a repeat of November 1918, and there is no doubt that on this point, at least, he proved to have prophetic powers. The Second World War witnessed no strikes in Germany, no mutinies and certainly no revolution. This was by no means the result of the omnipresence of terror but was due above all to the ruthless exploitation of the occupied areas that protected Germany from the sort of famine that it had known during the First World War. And it was also due to the equally ruthless exploitation of millions of foreign civilian workers, prisoners of war and concentration camp inmates who constituted a new sub-proletariat subjected to a racist hierarchy: 'workers from the east' were treated far less well than those from the west, the latter group containing far more 'volunteers' than the former. The most inhuman treatment of all was that meted out to Jewish slave labourers, for whom forced labour was intended as no more than a staging post on their journey to death.

Forced labour and slave labour by foreigners also ensured that for the Germans war was not as 'total' as might have been supposed on the evidence of Goebbels's notorious Sportpalast speech on 18 February 1943. Speaking only weeks after the catastrophe of Stalingrad, the minister for public enlightenment and propaganda had asked the rhetorical question: 'Do you want total war?' and elicited a frenetic 'Yes' from his fanatical crowd of listeners. Universal conscription for women was never introduced because it would have flown in the face of Hitler's petty-bourgeois image of the middle-class German housewife. The German people was to remain loyal to its Führer, a goal that imposed limits on the extent to which the German workforce and especially working women could be exploited, limits that Hitler personally ensured were never violated.

Even so, the growth in the armaments industry meant that the proportion of women who were economically active in the German civilian workforce was very high at 37.3 per cent – 10.9 per cent higher than in Great Britain. By 1943 women accounted for 48.8 per cent of the workforce in Germany, compared with 36.4 per cent in Great Britain. As in all wartime economies, far more women were occupied in professions in Germany that had largely been the preserve of men in the years leading up to the war: they were now found as postal workers, railway employees and bus and tram drivers. And as in all other countries involved in the war, the German armaments industry was favoured at the expense of all other branches of industry. In the course of several systematic purges, skilled manual workers, tradesmen and women and all those workers active in areas of the economy that had been producing goods for civilian needs were forced to take jobs in the armaments industry, a situation that led to the closure of countless firms, just as was the case with conscription. Between 1939 and 1944, 48.3 per cent of skilled manual workers were lost to their industry, while comparable figures for trade and agriculture were 42.7 per cent and 22.6 per cent respectively.

There was no question of the Germans leading 'affluent' lives during the Second World War, least of all in the final years when air raids were a constant threat. Even before 1939 the standard of living of the civilian population had been kept artificially low as a result of the primacy accorded to the need to rearm the country. The British historian Richard J. Overy has pointed out that after the war began, German policy consisted

> not in maintaining a high standard of living or preserving peacetime conditions but in maintaining a basic minimum beneath which living standards were not allowed to fall. Whatever happened, there could be no repeat of the 'turnip winter' of the First World War. Hitler's true priority was equal distribution not higher consumption. It was a question of ensuring that no section of the German population had to suffer more than any other and that the sacrifices that had to be made were equally distributed.[52]

The exploitation of foreign regions and of foreign labour was by no means the only resource on which the German economy drew in financing the war. The principal material burden was borne by the Germans – not so much through higher taxes and contributions as in a way that they initially did not even notice: through their savings. The vast increase in the national debt between 1939 and 1945 was possible only because all the institutions where Germans kept their savings, from post offices to building societies and from banks to insurance companies, were forced to place their investments at the government's disposal by buying the Reich's long-term debenture bonds and Treasury bills. This debt could have been passed on to others only if Germany had won the war.

The country's defeat meant that after the war the Germans were presented with a huge bill in the form of the disappearance of almost all their savings and the radical loss of the Reichsmark's purchasing power, a loss that only now became fully apparent. Savings had continued to grow during the war since strict economic controls on all goods intended for daily use resulted in a huge surplus of consumer spending power. Each time that food shortages led to discontent in the population, the regime sought to react in as flexible a way as possible: when the workers' displeasure at small meat rations found expression in the summer of 1942, for example, the rations were immediately made bigger, only to be reduced again in May 1943 in the face of renewed shortages.

The more the Wehrmacht had to retreat from east to west during 1943 and later, the worse the food supplies became, especially after the winter of 1943/4. Few foodstuffs were available, and the emphasis shifted away from meat to vegetable products. In this way an average urban working-class family was more or less able to meet its need for calories, but even in those families of labourers who enjoyed larger rations, the reduction in the consumption of animal protein and edible fat led to a fall in the usual dietary standards. As the German economic historian Christoph Buchheim has noted, the mass of consumers had to cut back, childless households being required to make far greater sacrifices than families with small children.[53] Food parcels sent by soldiers on the eastern and western fronts may occasionally have helped their families to deal with the consequences of a failing economy, but the only people to profit from this traffic on a grand scale were those in political, military or economic power, who received these 'care packages' from neutral countries like Switzerland, usually in return for a generous payment. Behind the façade of the 'national community' there still lay social differences between the upper and lower classes, differences that grew more extreme in the course of the war.

The Third Reich's own ambitious plans were also undermined by the haphazard way in which the German economy was refocused after 1939 to meet the needs of the war. Not until March 1940 was a Ministry for Ammunitions and Weapons established under the general inspector for roads, Fritz Todt, who was given the task of planning and guiding the arms industry. Following his death in a plane crash on 8 February 1942, Todt was replaced by Albert Speer, Hitler's favourite architect, who had organized the Nuremberg Party Rallies and designed the New Chancellery in Berlin. Under his guidance, German industry was more rigorously geared to the demands of a wartime economy. Speer also supervised the army of foreign labourers made up of civilians, concentration camp prisoners, Soviet and other prisoners of war and 'working Jews' who were ruthlessly deployed in boosting German armaments production, often being exploited to the point where they were physically destroyed by the work. In this Speer had the not always trouble-free support of the Thuringian Gauleiter Fritz Sauckel, the general plenipotentiary for labour mobilization.

By the end of November 1942 some 4.67 million foreign workers were employed in industry, skilled manual work, agriculture and private households in Germany, the majority of them Soviet prisoners of war and civilian labourers, who made up 1.6 million of the total, followed by 1.3 million Poles and 931,000 French prisoners of war. By the end of 1944 the number of foreign civilian workers and prisoners of war had risen to at least 8.2 million, a number that does not include 700,000 concentration camp prisoners. The total number of German workers in the summer of 1944 was 23.3 million. Civilian workers had the greatest chance of surviving (94 per cent), followed by prisoners of war (70 per cent), 'working Jews' (53 per cent) and, finally, concentration camp prisoners (31 per cent).

If German workers continued to enjoy the social benefits of the pre-war period, including health and safety standards and especially legal protection for expectant and nursing mothers, then this was because it was in the regime's best interests to ensure the loyalty of the workforce. In the autumn of 1940 the German Labour Front announced plans for a large-scale programme of 'Social Services for the German People' for the post-war period, a programme designed to provide a positive picture of the future and in that way to make the present privations appear more palatable. It included comprehensive provisions for old age, health care with provisions for leisure and recreation, a national wage, professional training and social housing. The right to work was also to be enshrined in law alongside the obligation to work. In a memorandum of September 1940 the German Labour Front described the provisions for social housing as 'a bulwark against old age, against subversion by foreigners and against social misery'.[54] Hitler underscored the political significance of this programme by appointing the leader of the German Labour Front, Robert Ley, to the post of commissar for social housing on 15 November 1940.

The repressive counterpart to these social benefits, whether already granted or merely promised, was the increased terror inflicted on all those whose comments or actions were deemed to undermine the Führer and his 'final victory'. As the German historian Rolf-Dieter Müller has observed, the means used to impose internal discipline on the 'national community' extended 'from warnings to deportation to a concentration camp and, finally, to execution'.[55] The People's Court that was established as a temporary expedient in April 1934 before being made permanent on the basis of a law passed in April 1936 assumed the functions of the Supreme Court in all matters relating to treason and other political crimes. Under the chairmanship of Roland Freisler, it evolved after 1942 into a forum for show trials, dispensing a form of justice that pursued with particular rigour every violation of newly created and ever stricter criminal laws. The number of death sentences rose dramatically after the Germans had begun to lose faith in a 'final victory' in 1943. On 26 April 1943, at its final session, the Reichstag conferred comprehensive powers on Hitler as 'supreme court judge', an action that amounted to the removal of the last remaining vestiges of legality and judicial independence in Germany.

According to the reports of official observers, Hitler's address to the Reichstag on 26 April 1942 encountered a largely critical response among the population at large, a reaction due not only to his attacks on the courts but also to his hints that the war would not be over even by the coming winter. Since the last blitzkrieg victories in the summer of 1940, the myth of the Führer had lost at least a little of its glamour, a process accelerated by the army's capitulation at Stalingrad. As Ian Kershaw has noted in The 'Hitler Myth',

It was not the catastrophic defeat at Stalingrad, as often presumed, which saw the turning-point in Hitler's popularity. [. . .] The contribution of the massive shock unleashed by 'Stalingrad', and the enormous loss of prestige accruing to Hitler as a result, was to open the flood gates to the criticism which was already present just below the surface and which – despite the obvious risks involved – now openly allotted blame to the Führer himself.[56]

Reports of the loss of the Sixth Army triggered shock, dismay and despondency, but in spite of increasing criticism of him personally, Hitler continued to be viewed with substantially greater benevolence than his henchmen Goebbels and Göring, to say nothing of the NSDAP's regional and local officials. If any representative of the Third Reich still hoped to command the support of the broad mass of the population, then it was the man at the top. The pact that they had signed with him in 1933 and that they had later renewed at times of national triumph was still upheld by the majority of Germans even at a time of serious defeats and setbacks. Indeed, they were positively afraid of ending it even when the fear of air raid sirens and bombing raids became a nightly reality.

In 1942, just as Hitler's 'European fortress' was reaching its greatest size, so the Führer's adversary in London was undergoing the most difficult period of his wartime premiership: among broad swaths of the population, Churchill was seen as unlucky, both politically and militarily, while the brilliant left-wing independent socialist Sir Richard Stafford Cripps, who had been ejected from the Labour Party in May 1943 and who was currently the lord privy seal, was deemed a suitable successor. It was not until Montgomery's successful breakthrough at El Alamein in late October 1942 that Churchill's position was once more consolidated, whereas his rival's prestige was damaged by his failure during an official visit to India in the spring to persuade the National Congress to come to the Allies' defence in return for the promise of future independence. By the end of November Churchill felt strong enough to remove Cripps from his war cabinet and demote him to the post of minister of aircraft production.

On 1 December 1942, a month after the victory at El Alamein, Sir William Beveridge, an eminent economist and liberal social reformer, submitted a report to the lower house headed 'Social Insurance and Allied Services', a report that he had drawn up at the request of Ernest Bevin, the labour minister and a prominent Labour Party politician. It was a forward-looking manifesto for social change that in many respects resembled the German Labour Front's programme of September 1940.

Beveridge proposed a picture of post-war society in Britain in which there would no longer be any material need, no unemployment, no illness without appropriate medical care and no ignorance caused by a lack of education. Central to his report was the idea of national standard insurance based on weekly contributions from all workers with a regular income and designed to provide a basic existence for the sick, for widows, for the unemployed and for pensioners, while medical care would be provided by state-run public health departments similar to those introduced by the Labour government in New Zealand in 1938. What made the Beveridge Report a bestseller was not the original nature of its proposals, but the plausible focus of many different plans all aimed at overcoming the class-based character of British society.

The British press greeted the recommendations of the Beveridge Report as revolutionary in the extreme, *The Times* insisting that its proposals must be made the basis of government action: 'The Government has been presented with an opportunity for marking this decisive epoch with a great social measure which will go far towards restoring the faith of ordinary men and women throughout the world in the power of democracy.' *The Economist* called the report 'one of the most remarkable state documents ever drafted':

> The true test of the Beveridge Plan is whether or not it will inspire, regardless of vested interests, a nation-wide determination to set right what is so plainly wrong and a series of prompt decisions by the Government to ensure that whatever else this war may bring, social security and economic progress shall march together.[57]

The different political parties were by no means single-minded in their response to Beveridge's proposals, Churchill and most Tories fearing that his demands for reform would distract from the country's primary concern, the war effort, while the Labour Party, conversely, felt reinforced in its political aims but was immediately riven by internal dissent: on the one hand there were those members of the government who viewed the plan as the basis for domestic policies once the war was over but as impracticable in the shorter term, and the majority of members of the lower house, who wanted the cabinet to agree to Beveridge's recommendations and to begin to implement them without delay. A bill to this effect was moved in the House of Commons in February 1943 but was rejected by 335 votes to 119, with ninety-seven Labour MPs voting against the government and only twenty-three for it. Among the latter were all the MPs who belonged to Churchill's cabinet in one function or another, with only a single exception.

Since 1940 Churchill had repeatedly described the conflict as the 'people's war', and there was certainly no lack of impressive examples of national solidarity and of practical support for the weakest members of society. In the case of air raids, for example, better-off families living in the countryside took in children from poorer families from London's East End and from the slum districts of other British cities. But there were also crass examples of Britons clinging to their privileges and of snobbery and egoism: golf clubs, for instance, refused to turn their greens and fairways into farmland, while hotels declined to accommodate impoverished victims of the air raids. Members of the lower classes used the opportunities afforded by the air raids to loot shops: in 1941, 4,585 such cases were reported.

The rhetoric of a 'people's war' was also impossible to reconcile with the racial prejudice to which blacks were still subjected in Great Britain at this time. In spite of the lack of soldiers and especially pilots, they were initially unable to serve in the Royal Air Force, and even the Home Guard, which was made up of civilians intended to be activated in the event of a German invasion, was for a time barred to them. White soldiers from the United States who were stationed in Great Britain managed to have blacks banned from dance halls and restaurants at least until such time as the Colonial Office successfully intervened and reversed the ban. White soldiers continued to have their own hospitals, cinemas and officers' messes.

As we have already observed, the number of women in gainful employment rose markedly during the war. But women who had to look after children under the age of fourteen or to perform domestic tasks such as preparing midday meals for their menfolk were excluded from the universal conscription that was introduced in 1941. For those married women employed in industry and responsible for looking after small children, the government set up kindergartens. The extension of women's work met with sustained resistance on the part of trade unions afraid that their members would be disadvantaged. The officially acknowledged principle of 'Equal pay for equal work' was largely ignored by employers, with the result that even if women did the same, often highly qualified work as men, they generally earned only half as much.

In general, economic mobilization in Great Britain was less 'total' than in Germany, a point well illustrated by the fact that the average level of consumption was cut less radically in the United Kingdom than in Germany: the index of real per capita consumption fell from 100 in 1938 to seventy in 1944, whereas the equivalent figure for Great Britain was a drop of only 12 per cent. In both countries state planning gained in importance during the war. Keynes, who in July 1940 was appointed special adviser to the Treasury, introduced a new kind of budgetary plan that included not only the state's income and expenditure but also national accounts data – periodic accounting using macroeconomic flows ascertained from national product statistics with an account for each aggregate relating to society as a whole, in other words, businesses, private households, the state, foreign countries and changes in assets on which all transactions appeared with the usual aggregates as in any double-entry bookkeeping system. The welfare state that was being planned for the post-war period was already taking shape in the form of Keynes's budgetary reform and the report of the Beveridge Commission.

The repressive side of British wartime politics was felt by foreigners who were members of the Axis Powers. All Germans and Austrians living in Great Britain were divided into three categories in September 1939, although only those placed in the first category – manifest sympathizers of the Third

Reich – were interned at this stage. In May 1940, following the evacuation of British troops from France and Belgium, most of the refugees who had left Germany on racial or political grounds were also interned – by preference, on the Isle of Man, at least as long as the island could accommodate them all. In addition to the 25,000 émigrés who were forced to find temporary refuge in the United Kingdom, there were also around 9,000 who were deported to Canada and Australia. The manifest injustice caused in this way to Hitler's opponents, many of whom were Jewish, helped to convince Churchill to end the 'general roundup' of German and, following Mussolini's entry into the war, Italian émigrés in the summer of 1940 and to release the first group of internees. It was not until two years later, however, that the final internees were released. By then, many younger Jewish volunteers from Germany and Austria were already fighting alongside British volunteers in the war on German National Socialism and Italian Fascism.

The British Dominions went their own way where 'enemy aliens' were concerned, with New Zealand – ruled by the Labour Party since 1935 – adopting the most liberal approach. Here only those Germans were interned who were known to be supporters of National Socialism. Australia was harsher in its treatment of all émigrés from the countries that made up the Axis Powers. Here all 'enemy aliens' had restrictions placed on their movements and were monitored by the police. But even here internment was used only as a last resort against declared followers of Hitler and Mussolini. After 1940 interned Europeans were able to object to these measures, although the same was not true of Japanese internees. Under its Liberal prime minister William Lyon Mackenzie King, Canada, too, pursued a policy of discrimination towards potential 'enemy aliens'. Whereas German and Italian immigrants were interned in only the rarest cases, Canadians of Japanese extraction were indiscriminately interned following the start of the war in the Pacific, a case of applied racist prejudice that Canada shared with its larger neighbour to the south.

In 1940 127,000 men, women and children of Japanese stock were living in the United States. Of these, one-third were first-generation immigrants, while two-thirds had been born in the United States or were naturalized Americans. Following the attack on Pearl Harbor, both groups were without exception suspected of being spies and agents working for their country of origin. At the urging of politicians and of members of the military on America's West Coast where most Japanese Americans lived, but also at the bidding of the Department of War, Roosevelt ordered the internment of all ethnic Japanese on 9 February 1942. Some 110,000 were locked up in isolation in prison-like camps, often in desert-like conditions. Not until 1944 did internees have a chance to leave the camps by declaring their loyalty to the government and either joining the army or taking a job in the country's interior. The racist character of their collective loss of freedom was underlined by the fact that there were no similarly summary measures against Americans of German or Italian stock. Even so, the Supreme Court declared the president's order to be constitutional in a judgment handed down in December 1944.

'Japanese Americans' were not the only Americans who experienced racial prejudice in the war, for American blacks suffered a similar fate. The wartime economy led many of them to leave the rural south and move to the industrial centres in the north-east and Midwest, especially Detroit, where race riots in June 1943 resulted in thirty-four deaths, including twenty-five blacks. The previous year black trade union leaders and civil rights activists had formed the Congress of Racial Equality, or CORE, which opposed all forms of racial discrimination, especially in theatres and restaurants, devising new forms of protest such as sit-ins.

It was thanks to the insistence of one particular black trade union leader, A. Philip Randolph, who was the leader of the Brotherhood of Sleeping Car Porters, that Roosevelt signed Executive Order 8802 on 25 June 1941 banning discrimination in the defence industry and federal administration on the basis of race, religion, skin colour and nationality, but his Fair Employment Practices did not have the force of law, and post-war attempts to give the order legal status foundered on the opposition of conservative Democrats from the southern states.

In the military, too, the 700,000 African Americans who served as soldiers continued to be discriminated against in many ways. The marine corps and the army's flying corps were completely barred to them. In the training camps blacks and whites were segregated, and although more advanced training was sometimes integrated, few blacks went on to this stage of the programme, while even in the integrated camps blacks could not be certain that their white instructors would not subject them to racial discrimination. Some of these incidents triggered protests and even unrest.

Women, too, were disadvantaged. In the course of the war they were intended to fill gaps in factories and more especially in the service industries that had opened up when their menfolk enlisted. Others filled newly created posts in the government apparatus, which grew considerably in size after 1942. Professional women were invariably paid less well than men. Working mothers whose husbands were on active military service had to leave their children unattended at home or in parked cars since there were no kindergartens to speak of. In this regard the New Deal had produced few benefits, and the war meant that building on its achievements was no longer a priority. Instead, the focus was on doing away with institutions that seemed no longer to be needed in the face of imminent full employment. Two of the organizations disbanded at this time were the Civilian Conservation Corps and the Works Progress Administration.

Even before the United States had entered the war, the hostilities had already led to a substantial increase in state spending and in the national debt. On the

West Coast, which was nearest to Japan, government contracts in the aircraft industry and, in their wake, technological research and many highly specialized supply industries gave a boost to the whole of the regional economy, as did investment in infrastructure. The ever-increasing need for workers brought numerous Mexicans to the south-west, especially to California and Los Angeles, where violent clashes lasting several days broke out between local and immigrant workers in June 1943.

It was the trade unions who benefited most from the boom, their membership rising from 10.5 million in 1941 to thirteen million four years later. Of course, not all workers and not even individual trade unions felt bound by the promise given by the country's two biggest unions, the AFL and the CIO, not to strike for the duration of the war: between the end of 1941 and 1945 there were 15,000 work stoppages. A strike by the United Mine Workers persuaded Congress to pass the War Labor Disputes Act (also known as the Smith–Connally Act) in May 1943, when the Senate and House of Representatives gained the required two-thirds majority needed to ignore the president's veto. From then on the unions had to observe a cooling-off period of thirty days before holding a strike in any branch of industry that was vital to the war effort. The same law empowered the president to send in troops to occupy companies involved in the armaments industry. Calls for a strike in any such industry were banned.

At no point in its history did the United States benefit so much from the emigration of highly qualified Jewish scholars from Germany as in the years between 1939 and 1945. Academics driven from Germany by Hitler advised the American government on questions of psychological warfare and post-war planning. Their colleagues from the natural sciences helped to ensure that the United States won the race with Germany to build the first atomic bomb. American and British experts succeeded in developing rocket technology to the point where the Allies had a decisive advantage in defending themselves from enemy submarines, aircraft and missiles. Added to this was the increasingly rapid decryption of German and Japanese codes, the Poles and the British proving themselves to be pioneers in the case of German codes. America's resources seemed limitless, but none was more important than the country's mental resilience. After Pearl Harbor, Americans were unanimously behind whatever their president demanded to ensure that their country and its ideals triumphed over the dictators in Berlin, Rome and Tokyo.

In the wake of Germany's invasion of his country on 22 June 1941, the dictator in Moscow required several days to recover his composure. Among the first measures that he then took were the evacuation of all industrial plants that were important for the war effort and, as far as possible, the relocation of the workforce in all those regions that were close to the front. All were moved to areas that were believed to be safe from the German army and Luftwaffe, namely, the Volga, the Urals, western Siberia and central Asia. Weapons factories, motor and tractor factories, all branches of the aeronautics industry and steel and automobile works were relocated from Leningrad, Moscow, the Ukraine and, shortly afterwards, from the Donets Basin: between July and November 1941 a total of 1,523 industrial concerns were moved. In his book *Russia at War*, Alexander Werth, the Moscow correspondent of the *Sunday Times* throughout the Second World War and later, describes this 'transplantation of industry' as 'among the most stupendous organisational and human achievements of the Soviet Union during the war', while stressing that by no means all industrial sites were evacuated in time. Nor could they be destroyed in keeping with Stalin's 'scorched-earth' policy of 3 July 1941.[58]

From the start of the war between Germany and the Soviet Union, the Russian workforce was placed under immense pressure. A seven-day week and a longer working day were introduced on 22 June, and at the end of 1941 all employees in the weapons industry were declared 'mobilized' persons, meaning that they could no longer change their place of work. Compulsory service was introduced for the entire urban population in February 1942: this applied to men aged between sixteen and fifty-five and to women between sixteen and forty. The rural population was subjected to this same ruling shortly afterwards.

The further east the Wehrmacht advanced, the worse the supply of food became, until it finally reached catastrophic proportions: the areas occupied by the German troops by November 1941 were responsible for 38 per cent of cereal production and for 84 per cent of sugar production in the Soviet Union as well as producing 38 per cent of the country's cattle and 60 per cent of its pigs. As a result, new areas had to be found for farming in the Volga region, the Urals, western Siberia and Kazakhstan and new crops sown. During the war agricultural work was carried out almost exclusively by women and children, who were helped during the harvest by any members of the urban population who were available.

The psychological mobilization undertaken in the name of the 'Great Patriotic War of the Soviet Union' included targeted appeals to Russian national pride, with Stalin promoting the cult of leading poets and composers such as Tolstoy and Chekhov, Glinka and Tchaikovsky, as well as war heroes from the days of Tsarist Russia such as Field Marshals Suvorov and Kutuzov and even Ivan the Terrible, the subject of Sergei Eisenstein's famous epic film of 1944. Also related to the new spirit of Soviet patriotism was the disbandment of the Communist International in May 1943, a move motivated exclusively by foreign policy considerations. And much the same was true of the regime's no less demonstrative rapprochement with the Orthodox Church, with which Stalin signed a kind of concordat in September 1943, allowing the Church to elect its own patriarchs, to re-establish the Holy Synod as its governing council, to resurrect Moscow's patriarchal newspaper which had been banned in 1936, and to reopen a number of theological seminaries and academies. The Church enjoyed a resurgence of its popularity, with growing numbers of worshippers, especially soldiers, and responded to the Communists' concessions by proclaiming its loyalty and patriotism in cloyingly bombastic terms.

While recalling pre-revolutionary traditions and institutions, the regime also sought to foment hatred of the country's German invaders. Among Soviet soldiers, no writer was as widely read as Ilya Ehrenburg, whose articles were regularly published in the army newspaper *Krasnaya Zvezda* (Red Star). On 23 August 1942, as the Germans were already advancing on Stalingrad, he wrote that the Russians could endure privation, famine and death but not the Germans: 'Today there is only one thought: Kill the Germans. Kill them all and dig them into the earth. [. . .] We shall kill them all. But we must do it quickly; or they will desecrate the whole of Russia and torture to death millions more people.' And on another occasion: 'If you have killed one German, kill another. There is nothing jollier than German corpses.'[59]

Hatred of the Germans was fuelled by more than merely the acts of barbarism inflicted on peoples whom they regarded as their racial inferiors. Particularly galling to many Soviets was the way in which the Germans were initially greeted as liberators in the Baltic States, the Ukraine and the Caucasus. In this way entire nationalities were collectively suspected of sympathizing with the enemy. The first to be affected by this hostility were Soviet citizens of German extraction, foremost among whom were the Volga Germans. As early as August 1941, the government in Moscow ordered half a million Volga Germans to be uprooted from their traditional homeland, where many of them had been living since the days of Catherine the Great, and deported to Siberia and Kazakhstan. The Volga German Autonomous Republic was formally abolished. In total, 80 per cent of all ethnic Germans were affected by these measures. A similar fate befell all those nationalities that were accused of collaborating with the aggressors, including Chechens, Ingush, Karachays, Balkars, Meskhetians and Crimean Tartars. Around 45 per cent of Crimean Tartars died as a result of deportation and resettlement. In the areas that they had once inhabited, all memory of them and of their culture was systematically destroyed.

Wherever it was directly involved in the fighting, the Soviet civilian population suffered appallingly, but nowhere more so than in Leningrad. In the course of the siege, which lasted almost 900 days, from September 1941 to January 1944, between 600,000 and 800,000 men, women and children died out of a total population of three million. The Germans' systematic attempt to starve the inhabitants into submission led to many cases of stealing, looting and even cannibalism. Even when the culprits were guilty of stealing only bread, the NKVD frequently reacted by shooting them. No breaks were allowed during the working week, and those workers who left their posts during that time were dragged before the courts and accused of desertion. Imprisonment was the punishment for 'idling'. If the Red Army had not succeeded in providing minimal supplies for the encircled city during the winter months, Russia's 'Gateway to the West' would have become a ghost town by 1944.

The terror suffered by Leningrad at the hands of the NKVD was by no means exceptional, for wherever the Wehrmacht made advances, the troops of the Soviet Ministry of the Interior liquidated or deported anyone who was guilty – or thought to be guilty – of opposing the regime. The bloodiest operations took place in eastern Poland, the western Ukraine, the former Polish part of Belorussia and in the Baltic States. In L'viv on 24 June 1941, members of the Cheka killed around 3,500 of their prisoners on the express orders of the head of the NKVD, Lavrentiy Beria, having previously tortured them in particularly barbaric ways. According to reliable estimates, between 20,000 and 30,000 men, women and children were killed by the Cheka in eastern Poland alone. They died as a result of mass shootings, beatings, torture and rape or else they were forced to march until they literally dropped dead from exhaustion. In October 1941, when panic among Communist Party officials was at its height, Stalin ordered the NKVD to deport to Kuibyshev all remaining relatives of 'enemies of the people' who were still in Moscow and execute them there. In Stalino, shortly before the city was taken by the Germans, the Cheka forced all their prisoners to dig their own graves before shooting them. In the Donets Basin workers were shot for simply criticizing the regime or the supply situation.

But the terror meted out to the civilian population pales into insignificance when compared to that inflicted on a daily basis on the members of the Red Army. Among its earliest victims were the supreme commander on the western front, General Dimitri Pavlov, and three of the generals under him. All were arrested following the fall of Minsk on 4 July 1941, accused of an 'anti-Soviet military conspiracy', sentenced to death and shot on 22 July. On 16 August 1941 Stalin issued Order 00270, according to which troops who had been surrounded were to continue fighting until the last possible moment or regain their own regiment. Those who 'allowed' themselves to be taken prisoner were to be destroyed by whatever means were necessary. The families of members of the Red Army who surrendered were to receive no state support or financial assistance.

By this date 1.5 million members of the Red Army were already prisoners of war in Germany, and that number continued to rise, reaching 3.8 million by the end of 1941. According to later figures, 994,000 men and women were sentenced by military courts and 157,000 of them were shot for desertion or other alleged crimes. A further 400,000 soldiers were sent to punishment battalions for having broken out of an encircled area or having escaped from a prisoner-of-war camp. These battalions also included many prisoners of war who had been liberated by the Red Army. The 1.5 million members of these punishment battalions were sent to the most dangerous sections of the front, where most of them were soon killed by enemy fire.

Stalin's own son, Yakov, also fell victim to the dictator's implacable rigour, when the boy was captured by the Germans in July 1941 and Stalin repudiated him as a coward and a traitor, refusing a German offer to exchange him for a number of German generals. Yakov Dzhugashvili died in the concentration camp at Sachsenhausen in April 1943, probably by his own hand. 'The Red Army had no means of retreating,' writes Jörg Baberowski. 'Its soldiers had the choice of being shot or taken prisoner by the Germans or being killed by NKVD commandos. As a result they generally decided to continue their attack, which gave them a greater chance of surviving than a retreat.'[60]

Occupation, Collaboration, Resistance (I): Eastern Central Europe, South-east and North-west Europe

Opponents of Communism who were willing to work with the Germans could certainly be found in those parts of the western Soviet Union that had been overrun by the Wehrmacht, especially among non-Russian nationalities. But it was hard for these groups to collaborate with their ostensible 'liberators' not only because of the National Socialists' belief in their own racial superiority but also because the German leadership was determined to use the war in the east to further its territorial ambitions and win more Lebensraum for the Germans.

This quest for Lebensraum meant that the Slav population had to make way for the German peasants and artisans who, protected by German weaponry, were to colonize the conquered regions in order for those areas to be used by the Reich. The peoples of the east could hope to survive only if they submitted unconditionally to their new masters and agreed to work for them as their slaves. 'Extra mouths', as they were called, were left to starve to death, a fate also suffered by many of the five million Soviet prisoners of war, only around a million of whom survived the war. The land that had previously been farmed by the native population was now intended to feed the German invaders, while its mineral resources now belonged to the Germans and to no one else. Himmler summed up the 'philosophy' underpinning the quest for Lebensraum when he spoke in Kiev in August 1942 and argued that 'the social question can be solved only by killing others so that you can get their fields'.[61]

The practical implementation of these plans was the responsibility of the two Reich commissars whom Hitler had entrusted with the task of administering the newly conquered areas to the east: the Gauleiter of Schleswig-Holstein, Hinrich Lohse, who was placed in charge of the Baltic States and White Russia ('White Ruthenia') that were lumped together as the Reich Commissariat of the Ostland; and the Gauleiter of East Prussia, Erich Koch, who was responsible for the Reich Commissariat of the Ukraine. The Ukraine was particularly rich in grain and raw materials, persuading Koch to see it as a region that could meet 80 per cent of the Greater German Reich's needs and also provide a workforce. The leading Ukrainian nationalists in the OUN, associated with the name of Stepan Bandera, proclaimed a sovereign state on 30 June 1941 but were arrested only a few days later and sent to the concentration camp at Sachsenhausen. Alfred Rosenberg, who came from a German Baltic family and who from June 1941 headed the

Reich Commissariat for the occupied countries to the east, felt that Koch was committing a serious mistake in so brusquely rejecting the demands of the nationalist and anti-Bolshevik forces, which had many supporters especially in the Ukraine, but, as we have already noted, he was powerless to persuade Hitler to accept his counterproposals. As a result, Rosenberg was unable to hold out the promise of national independence for those Baltic peoples who were a part of the western culture group.

Hitler was equally dismissive when the Soviet general Andrei Vlasov, who had been taken prisoner by the Germans in July 1942, declared his willingness to form an army of Russian prisoners of war and deserters that would fight alongside the Wehrmacht and free Russia from Stalin's tyrannical rule. But in December 1942 Vlasov was able to convene the Smolensk Committee that gathered the names of volunteers prepared to oppose the Soviet armed forces from within German military units. At least half a million former members of the Red Army heeded this appeal – many of them were no doubt motivated less by anti-Bolshevik sentiment than by the fear that they would otherwise starve to death in German prisoner-of-war camps or be shot by the NKVD.

Not until September 1944, when the Red Army was already perilously close to the German border, did Hitler agree to the formation of a 'Russian Liberation Army', known for short as the 'Vlasov Army'. It was made up of prisoners of war, forced labourers and émigrés and for a time numbered 100,000 men. Towards the end of the war it saw active service on the eastern front in Bohemia and Moravia. (The Americans to whom Vlasov surrendered handed him over to the Soviet Union together with his army. He and nine of his generals were executed in August 1946, while his soldiers were sent to labour camps or, where there were deemed to be extenuating circumstances, they were sentenced to six years' exile.)

Among Vlasov's German supporters after early 1944 was Heinrich Himmler, who was always happy to set aside his ideas on racial purity when the 'final victory' made it expedient for him to do so. The Waffen-SS, which in the end comprised thirty-eight divisions, included not only Danish, Norwegian, Dutch and Flemish soldiers – in other words, 'Germanic' units – but also, towards the end of the war, Latvian, Estonian, White Russian, Russian, Polish, Bosnian, Cossack, Uzbek, Indian and Arab units. The Russian units formed in the early months of 1944 also included the Fifteenth Cossack Cavalry Corps, which was assimilated into the Russian Liberation Army in early 1945. It had proved impossible to establish the Greater Germanic Reich of the German Nation using Germanic forces alone, but by 1943 the Germanic slogans had in any case outlived their usefulness. By then Germany's leaders hoped to enlist support for their cause only by promising to save the whole of Europe and, hence, the world from the threat of Bolshevism.

What was true of the Ukrainians was even truer of the Poles, who could not hope to be treated more leniently by the Germans even if they offered to help the Reich in its war with the Soviet Union. Although there were a few supporters of the Russian Communists in Poland, there were even fewer who championed the cause of the German National Socialists. Very soon after Poland's defeat at the hands of the Wehrmacht, the first pockets of resistance had been formed in the General Government, including the Związek Walki Zbrojnej, or ZWZ, which was formed during the winter of 1939/40 and which had the support of General Sikorski's exiled government in London. Renamed the Armia Krajowa (Home Army) in 1942, it was guilty of summarily executing many deserters and informers, while also attacking particularly hated representatives of the occupying regime and destroying rail links, prisons, police stations and prisoner transports. By the winter of 1943/4 the Home Army is said to have had between 300,000 and 350,000 members, although only around 20,000 of them fought as armed partisans. In comparison, the much smaller Communist People's Army, or Armia Ludowa, that was formed in January 1944 as the military arm of the Polish Workers' Party created by representatives of the Comintern in early 1942, was never much more than a marginalized faction.

But armed Poles fought against Germans not only in their native Poland, they were also active on several fronts elsewhere. In 1944 80,000 Polish soldiers were fighting with the Western Allies and a similar number with the Red Army. Between March and August 1942 a small army of 70,000 former prisoners of war and interned Poles under General Władysław Anders – the 'Anders Army' – had been 'evacuated' on Stalin's orders via central Asia to Iran, from where it was deployed under British command in Iraq and Palestine, then in North Africa and Italy, a move made at Churchill's behest. But this did little to improve the tense relations between the Soviet Union and the Polish government in exile as Moscow refused to divulge any details concerning the whereabouts of more than 10,000 missing Polish officers. When the Wehrmacht discovered the buried bodies of the victims of the Katyn Massacre in the spring of 1943, the government in exile asked the International Red Cross to investigate the matter, a step to which Molotov reacted by breaking off diplomatic relations with Sikorski's government on 25 April.

The armed struggle was only one part of the Polish resistance movement. In spite of the occupying power's omnipresent reign of terror, Polish intellectuals, harking back to a tradition that had grown up in Russian Congress Poland in the nineteenth century, established an underground university and underground grammar schools as part of an 'underground state' supported by civilian society and financed by money smuggled in from Great Britain. All were coordinated by a Delegatura structured into twelve departments. If the resistance movement had not been planned in advance and if it had not been well organized practically throughout the General Government, an elite section of its activists would never have been able to strike the blow that we shall discuss in greater detail in due course: the Warsaw Uprising that began on

1 August 1944 and lasted nine weeks – longer than even its organizers had initially believed to be possible.

A sizeable proportion of Poland's 1.3 million civilian population experienced German occupation not in Poland itself but in the Old Reich. As early as October 1939 the governor general, Hans Frank, had introduced the requirement to work for all Poles living in his area of jurisdiction and aged between fourteen and sixty. In 1940 Poles started to be employed in Germany, and it was not long before the number of workers recruited by force had outnumbered those who applied through the usual channels. There was a particular need for workers in the agricultural sector, where, in spite of all official orders and prohibitions, Polish and other foreign workers were generally better treated than in industry. On the strength of special 'Polish decrees', Poles working in the Reich were not only prevented from using public transport but were even banned from keeping bicycles and from attending German church services and going to the cinema or the theatre. They also received substantially smaller food rations than workers from the west. And if they engaged in sexual relations with Germans, they were punished by being publicly hanged in the presence of their assembled compatriots, although after the middle of 1943 this punishment was generally commuted to deportation to a concentration camp, a penalty also meted out to German women who 'gave themselves' to Poles. There were no similar provisions for German men who had sexual relations with Polish women.

In comparison to the Poles, the Czech inhabitants of the Protectorate of Bohemia and Moravia were treated relatively leniently. Politically speaking, the native population was stripped of all its rights, and a unity party, the Národní shromáždění, replaced all the previous political parties. The occupying power was responsible for deciding all questions of foreign policy and defence, and all the authorities that were responsible for implementing the country's domestic policies were overseen by the German administration. Communists, 'left-wing' bourgeois intellectuals and German émigrés who had fled to Czechoslovakia and been unable to escape before the German occupation began were deported to concentration camps. After the autumn of 1941 the country's Jews were sent either straight to the camps in the east or to Theresienstadt (Terezín), which was opened in the Protectorate in June 1940. After 1942 they were sent from Theresienstadt to the extermination camps in Poland.

Strikes and demonstrations held to mark Independence Day on 28 October 1943 were brutally suppressed by the occupying power: one worker was shot and a student so badly injured that he died soon afterwards. Hitler used the demonstrations as an excuse to close all Czech colleges and universities for a three-year period. With the exception of medics, all the country's teachers were left in limbo, while students were set to work. In September 1941 the Czech prime minister, Alois Eliáš, was accused of holding secret negotiations with Edvard Beneš's government in exile in London, a charge that led to his arrest. A show trial ended in a death sentence, and he was shot in June 1942.

In general, those who worked with the Germans had nothing to fear. Czech industry was incorporated into Germany's wartime economy and to all intents and purposes run by German businesses. Numerous smaller, medium-sized and larger employers profited from the 'Aryanization' of Jewish property, and the workforce took advantage of the full employment brought about by the war. The first protector of the Reich, Germany's former foreign secretary, Konstantin von Neurath, was given leave of absence in September, ostensibly for health reasons, but he was effectively stripped of his powers and replaced by his newly appointed deputy, the head of the Reich Main Security Office, Reinhard Heydrich, whose treatment of the local population was marked by incomparably greater brutality.

A turning point in the history of the Protectorate came on 27 May 1942, when volunteer parachutists, acting on behalf of the Czech government in exile, attempted to assassinate Heydrich, who died of his injuries on 4 June 1942. In the course of the reign of terror that his death provoked, some 10,000 Czechs were arrested and over 1,000 shot without trial. The massacres at Lidice and Ležáky on 10 and 24 June 1942 were intended above all to intimidate the local population: the villages were destroyed, all the adult males were shot, and the women and children were sent to concentration camps. Heydrich's place was taken by the colonel-general of the Order Police, Kurt Daluege. In August 1943 the role of protector was assumed by Wilhelm Frick, the German home secretary, who was replaced in that capacity by Himmler. Between then and 1945 there were few major acts of sabotage or other attacks, the reign of terror exercised by the SS and the police ensuring that the Protectorate of Bohemia and Moravia henceforth operated along strictly National Socialist lines.

Collaboration and resistance were also features of occupied Serbia. At least on the surface, one of the collaborators was the head of the Belgrade government installed by the occupying power, General Milan Nedić. At the same time, however, Nedić worked undercover with the Chetniks, the nationalist wing of the Serbian resistance movement, which, motivated by its militant Pan-Slav ideals, evinced the utmost brutality in its dealings with the Croatian Ustaše, as well as with the separatists of Montenegro and Albania and with the Bosnian Muslims, while adopting a defensive stance towards the German occupying power and even receiving occasional support from the Italians. In his dealings with King Peter II and the Yugoslav government in exile in London, Nedić even stressed that he saw himself only as their custodian. Also secretly allied to the conservative resistance movement associated with Colonel Draža Mihajlović was the 18,000-strong armed gendarmerie – the Serbian State Guard – that had been created by Nedić and which was tolerated by the Germans, whereas the smaller 3,600-strong Serbian Volunteer Corps under Dimitrije Ljotić, the founder of the Christian nationalist Zbor movement, manifestly belonged in the camp of the collaborators.

The Communist partisans under Josip Broz Tito, who was a native Croat, gained much support throughout Yugoslavia after the Comintern issued an appeal in July 1941, asking for help with freeing the country from its German oppressors. By the early autumn they already had 15,000 followers, and the number of acts of sabotage and attacks on members of the Wehrmacht and its installations as well as on the Serbian gendarmerie grew from ninety-seven in July to 892 in September 1941. The Germans reacted with extreme reprisals in keeping with the motto of the commanding general Franz Böhme, according to which 100 Serbian hostages were to be shot for every German soldier who was killed. Between April 1941 and February 1942 more than 20,000 civilians, including thousands of Jews, were rounded up and executed. Among them were 2,300 inhabitants of the town of Kragujevac, including pupils and teachers from the local grammar school and Jews, all of whom were executed by the Wehrmacht – rather than by the SS – on 21 October 1941.

The reign of terror inflicted by the Germans and by the Croat Ustaša helped to boost the membership of the Communist partisan movement, encouraging even non-Communists disillusioned by the Chetniks' wait-and-see policy to join the movement. Tito's fighting units were obliged to withdraw from Serbia in November 1941, when their stronghold – the western Serbian town of Užice that they had declared an independent republic – was captured by the Germans. As a result they were forced to concentrate their activities on the Italian protectorate of Montenegro, on western Bosnia and on Herzegovina, all of which regions belonged to the 'Independent State of Croatia' under Italian occupation and influence. Attempts on the part of Tito and Mihajlović to reach an agreement foundered on the irreconcilability of their respective positions, and by November 1941 there had been the first bloody clashes between the Chetniks and the Communist partisans, with the two sides rivalling one another in terms of the horror of the atrocities that they committed.

From Hitler's standpoint, both of these partisan camps posed a threat, more especially since the fall of El Alamein in October 1942, which increased the risk of an Allied invasion of the Balkans. In January 1943 German, Italian and Croat units succeeded in destroying most of Tito's National Liberation Army in south Croatia and western Bosnia, but the Communist forces were still powerful enough to inflict a serious defeat on the Chetniks in the Battle of Neretva in February 1943. Three months later they suffered heavy losses when surrounded by German and Italian troops at the Battle of Sutjeska, but shortly afterwards enjoyed the spectacle of seeing most of the Chetniks units disarmed by the Axis Powers.

In November 1943 Tito convened the Second Congress of the Anti-Fascist Council for the National Liberation of Yugoslavia in the Bosnian town of Jajce.

It resolved that in future Yugoslavia would be a federation, installed a provisional government under Tito's presidency, banned King Peter II from returning to the country and contested the right of the government in exile in London to speak for Yugoslavia. Stalin, who until then had been Tito's only supporter in the Allies' camp, regarded the installation of a provisional government as a threat to the broad-based east–west anti-Hitler alliance and reacted with commensurate indignation, whereas Churchill, who until that point had supported Mihajlović, was enough of a realist to realign his position, from then on banking on Tito and supplying the latter's partisan movement with large quantities of munitions and weapons.

Tito was also helped by Italy's capitulation in September 1943, an event that we shall be examining in greater detail in due course. It was an unexpected turn of events that allowed the Communist partisan movement to consolidate its position in Bosnia and Herzegovina and to regain a foothold in Montenegro, from where it had had to withdraw following the Battle of Sutjeska. In turn this allowed the movement to emerge as victor from the Yugoslav civil war and war of liberation and to take its place in history as the most successful resistance movement of the Second World War. Meanwhile the Chetniks' star sank even lower, a situation not even helped when their leader was appointed minister of war, commander in chief of the Yugoslav Army at home and divisional general by the exiled monarch. When, at Churchill's instigation, Peter II issued an appeal on 12 September 1944, urging all Serbs, Croats and Slovenes to join Tito's National Liberation Army, the die was cast: if Yugoslavia were to be reborn following the expulsion of the Germans, the country would be led by Communists and in that way would be radically different from the former Kingdom of Serbs, Croats and Slovenes.

As in the former Yugoslavia, so in Greece, resistance to the Italian and German occupying forces was divided into a Communist-led and an anti-Communist camp. The National Liberation Front, or EAM, was a popular front with a military arm, the National Liberation Army, or ELAS. Ranged against them was the much smaller National Republican Greek League, or EDES, a more middle-class, democratic organization. Only in response to massive pressure from the British did the rival movements join forces in November 1941 and blow up the railway viaduct over the Gorgopotamos, an important supply route for the German Afrika Korps. After that, further large sums of British money were necessary to persuade the ELAS to cooperate on a regular basis with the EDES, an association that began in July 1943 but which proved extremely short-lived: following the capitulation of Italy two months later, the ELAS disarmed the Italian Pinerolo Division and, using the weapons that it had seized, immediately began an armed struggle against the EDES units that were operating in Epirus. The clashes between the two groups were nothing less than a prelude to the Greek Civil War that broke out in 1946 and lasted until October 1949.

From the autumn of 1943, the struggle to liberate Greece was directed at one occupying power alone, Germany, and at the Greek government that it had installed in Athens. The Germans focused their efforts increasingly on defending the major cities and principal transport links. Among the hallmarks of their rule were the brutal reprisals against the civilian population each time that the partisans' activities offered them an excuse to act. Between December 1943 and July 1944 the inhabitants of entire villages were executed, notably in Kalavrita on 13 October 1943, in Distono on 16 July 1944 and in Klissura on 29 July 1944. Between March 1943 and October 1944 some 21,255 Greek men and women were killed by the occupying powers and a further 20,000 thrown into prison.

It was with brutal resolve and total consistency that the Germans set about removing all Jewish elements from the occupied country: in the face of ineffectual protests from the prime minister, Konstantinos Logothetopoulos, between 45,000 and 50,000 Jews were deported from Thessaloniki to Auschwitz and Treblinka in the early months of 1943. Most were gassed on arrival. There followed the arrest and deportation of Jews from Athens and the Aegean. Of the 70,000 or so Jews who had been living in Greece in 1940, only a little over 10,000 remained in the country after the Germans withdrew in August 1944. Only a handful managed to escape to the countries of the Middle East. Of those who had been deported, around 2,000 survived the Shoah.

In February 1944 the EAM and ELAS on the one hand and the EDES on the other agreed to a ceasefire on the basis of the status quo. By now the Communist-led partisan movement was so powerful that the left-wing liberal, Georgios Papandreou, who had headed the Cairo-based government in exile since April 1944, offered the EAM six ministerial posts in his coalition cabinet. Only at the urging of a Soviet military mission and after King George II had promised to accept the findings of a plebiscite did the Communist leadership agree to enter government in August 1944. On 24 September all the partisan groups, headed by the ELAS and EDES, signed the Caserta Agreement and in doing so accepted the government in exile, which in turn transferred command of the combat units in Greece to the commander in chief of the British armed forces in the country. At about this time the Germans began to withdraw their troops from the Aegean and from Greece, allowing the ELAS to extend its rule over large sections of the country. British and Greek troops then marched into Athens and a number of other large cities. On 27 October, five days after the withdrawal of the Wehrmacht, Papandreou's government moved its headquarters to Athens.

Five weeks later, on 1 December 1944, the EAM announced that it was leaving the government. Shortly afterwards a Communist uprising broke out in Athens, triggered by shots fired by the police at largely unarmed demonstrators. It did not end until the middle of January 1945, when the EAM agreed to a ceasefire with the British, subsequently signing a form of peace treaty with the government on 12 February. Although this development seemed for a time to avert the possibility of a civil war, it merely represented a lull in the fighting.

As in Greece, so in Belgium, Germany's presence in the country until 1944 was predominantly military. The German military commander was General Alexander von Falkenhausen, who received administrative support from Eggert Reeder, whose entire period in office was marked by his attempts to prevent the SS from gaining control of the military apparatus. Falkenhausen, who was closely associated with the military and conservative opposition to Hitler, was relieved of his post on 13 July 1944 and arrested on the 29th, nine days after the failed attack on the Führer. The military administration was replaced by a civilian one under the Cologne Gauleiter Josef Grohé. Since Grohé not only retained Reeder as his administrative head but also appointed him his deputy and since Reeder opposed Himmler's attempts to impose German values on Flanders, relations with the SS remained fraught.

Both the radical right-wing Flemish nationalists of the Vlaamsch Nationaal Verbond that absorbed the Verbond van Dietsche Nationaal-Solidaristen in 1941 and the Walloon Rexists associated with Léon Dégrelle had some sympathy for the idea of working more closely with the Germans – both groups provided volunteers for the Flemish and Walloon legions of the Waffen-SS. And, much to the surprise of the Germans, there was also a willingness to collaborate on the part of the Belgian Socialists associated with the internationally renowned social psychologist Hendrik de Man, who had headed the Parti Ouvrier Belge since 1939. A self-confessed advocate of a planned economy, de Man regarded Belgium's capitulation as a defeat for parliamentary democracy and plutocratic capitalism, which he believed should be exploited for his own Socialist ends. He disbanded the Socialist Party in the summer of 1940 and founded an umbrella trade union modelled on the German Labour Front, the Unie van Hand- en Geestesarbeiders (also known as the Union des Travailleurs Manuels et Intellectuels) that worked closely with the Germans but gained few supporters, with the result that the German side soon lost interest in the new organization.

Among the collaborators in the wider sense was King Leopold III, who unlike the government of Hubert Pierlot did not go into exile but remained in Belgium, where he was held under house arrest at Laeken after having signed the capitulation agreement with Germany. His fondness for an authoritarian form of government cost him the sympathies of many Belgians, as did his attempt to form a government of his own and his willingness to meet Hitler in November 1940. In the end he was obliged to abdicate in favour of his son, Baudouin, in 1950.

After the war some half a million Belgians were accused of collaborating with the Germans. Their number included many civil servants who had continued to hold their posts under the direct supervision of the Germans, as well as a number of employers who profited from Germany's wartime rule. Some 345,000 individuals were placed on trial and 60,000 of them were sentenced. The tally of Belgians engaged in active resistance has been reckoned to be around 70,000. Among their acts of resistance was the help that they offered Jews by offering them a place to hide and thereby preventing them from being deported to extermination camps. Others helped in this way were Allied airmen shot down over Belgium. There were also numerous acts of sabotage, more especially after 1943, including the spectacular blowing up of a bridge in the Ardennes in December 1944, when hundreds of German soldiers lost their lives. But the vast majority of Belgians tolerated foreign rule without collaborating with the Germans or actively resisting them.

Unlike Belgium, there was a German civilian administration in the Netherlands, with the Austrian National Socialist Arthur Seyß-Inquart as commissar. As a result, the NSDAP had far more influence on German policies in the occupied Netherlands than was the case with its southern neighbour. Since the Dutch are a Germanic nation and were regarded by the National Socialists as racially related to them, Germany's long-term policy towards the Netherlands was aimed at integrating the country into the planned Greater Germanic Reich. In the business community and among civil servants there was a widespread willingness to work closely with the occupying power but no desire to see their country swallowed up by Germany either then or in the future.

With its 80,000 or so members, the Nationaal-Socialistische Beweging associated with Anton Adriaan Mussert never commanded much support among the population at large and initially received little encouragement from the occupying authorities, who were more interested in working as smoothly as possible with the established elites in both the state and in industry. In 1941 Mussert founded the Netherlands SS Volunteers Legion, which fought alongside German troops in the war on Russia. A unity party that was formed by conservative elements in July 1940 and that was willing to work with the Germans was the Nederlandsche Unie which won around ten times as many members as Mussert's party but proved insufficiently tractable, with the result that it was banned by the German civilian administration in December 1941, a fate that it shared with other parties like it. Parliament was prevented from meeting after June 1940, and the country was 'ruled' by Dutch general secretaries in the ministries, all of them directly supervised by Germans. Together with Queen Wilhelmina, the country's ministers had gone into exile in London on 13 May 1940, three days after the German invasion. The conservative prime minister, Dirk Jan de Geer, returned to the Netherlands on his own initiative in February 1941 and, encouraged by the Germans, sought a compromise peace that acknowledged the new realities. But he remained little more than a curiosity.

As we have already noted, the Netherlands was the only country occupied by German troops where there were public protests against the persecution of the Jews. Such protests began at the Universities of Leiden and Delft in November 1940, before assuming the form of a general strike in Amsterdam in February 1941. This was not the last strike in the occupied Netherlands, for in 1942 the country's doctors refused to work. And in late April 1943, when Dutch soldiers released from German prisoner-of-war camps were obliged to undertake work in Germany, workers throughout the Netherlands downed tools in protest. In September 1944, as the Allies drew closer, bringing with them the promise of liberation, it was the turn of the railway workers to go on strike.

But such actions were unable to prevent Dutch workers from being forcibly recruited. Under the terms of the laws enacted by the occupying power, all Dutch males between the ages of eighteen and forty-five were obliged to respond to calls to work in Germany. In 1944 passenger trains were rerouted to Germany in order for suitable passengers to be chosen to work in the Reich. By November 1942 the number of Dutch men and women employed in Germany was 153,000, while the equivalent number for Belgian citizens was 130,000.

The occupying power reacted to every strike with the utmost severity: when the railway workers went on strike in September 1944, for example, the authorities responded with a blockade of the country's inland waterways that lasted several weeks, preventing foodstuffs from reaching the major towns and cities. Violence committed by the Dutch resistance and including acts of sabotage and attacks on well-known collaborators, on members of the civilian administration and on soldiers and institutions associated with the Wehrmacht met with wildly excessive reprisals on the part of the German authorities: in February 1943, fifty hostages were shot in reprisal for the murder of a former Dutch general who was known to be working for the Germans. And during the final months of the war hundreds of hostages were executed in response to each attack by resistance groups.

The authorities could do relatively little in the face of less spectacular forms of resistance. When employment offices and public health offices thwarted attempts to send workers to Germany, their actions could often not be proven, and, unless the population at large denounced them, Jews who had gone to ground, those who refused to work in Germany and members of the resistance movement who were concealed by their compatriots were hard to track down. During the war more than 50,000 Dutch citizens were sent to concentration camps. After the war 150,000 collaborators spent longer or shorter periods of time in concentration camps built by the Germans on Dutch soil, atoning for the crimes committed during the years of occupation. A total of 66,000 were sentenced in this way to lengthy terms of imprisonment, including life sentences, while 900 of them received the death penalty. Among those who were sentenced to death was Anton Mussert, who was executed in The Hague on 7 May 1946.

Like the Netherlands, occupied Norway was also governed by a civilian German administration. The only local forces on which Hitler's commissar, the Essen

Gauleiter Josef Terboven, could rely were the 50,000 or so members of the only authorized party, Vidkun Quisling's Nasjonal Samling, together with the 4,000 Norwegian volunteers of the Waffen-SS whom Quisling helped to recruit. Since Terboven doubted Quisling's political abilities, the latter was obliged to appeal to his two patrons in Berlin – the head of the NSDAP's Foreign Policy Office, Alfred Rosenberg, and the supreme commander of the navy, Erich Raeder – to support him. Quisling enjoyed a partial success when the 'temporary state councillors' appointed by Terboven from the ranks of the Nasjonal Samling were allowed to bear the title 'minister' from the end of September 1941. Quisling himself was finally appointed prime minister on 1 February 1942, but this too was no more than an honorary title. Hitler had no intention of meeting Quisling's desire to turn Norway into a 'free, indivisible and independent Reich' that was a part of the Greater German Reich. For the present at least all the real power in Norway continued to be vested in Terboven.

Nor did Quisling's appointment help to win more support for German rule among the Norwegian population. Indeed, he launched his period in office in February 1942 with a series of measures designed to bring the Church and the educational system into line with NSDAP policies, inevitably triggering a conflict that left Norway more deeply divided than before. Some 60 per cent of all schoolteachers signed a declaration stating their inability to contribute to the education of the young people of Norway according to the guidelines of the Nasjonal Samling's 'youth programme'. They refused, therefore, to join the newly founded Norwegian Teaching Union. The government responded by arresting around 1,000 teachers and deporting them to the north of the country, where they were subjected to a harsh regimen of forced labour.

Equally uncooperative were the bishops and other members of the clergy who were faced with the demand that they should publicly proclaim their allegiance to the 'new state'. On 24 February 1942 Norway's bishops resigned from all their positions within the country's Lutheran Church, while declaring their readiness to go on performing their pastoral duties. Quisling responded by suspending the bishops and replacing them with others loyal to his discredited regime. When the clergy declared their solidarity with the bishops and likewise resigned all their official functions, five leading members of the Christian Council for Joint Deliberation, including the bishop of Oslo and primate of the Norwegian Church, Eivind Berggraf, were arrested. Those members of the clergy who even after an ultimatum from the Ministry for the Church and Education still refused to return to their former positions no longer received a stipend, but they were able to continue with their pastoral work and were paid out of sizeable donations collected by the newly created Church leadership.

Quisling's plan in September 1942 to create an umbrella organization – the Riksting – similar to the German Labour Front also proved to be a fiasco, when the trade unions and other associations reacted by asking their members to resign from all their existing organizations. Terboven was able to stem the tide of resignations only by forcing Quisling to abandon his plan for a Riksting: it was a triumph of civil disobedience.

By this time the actual running of Norway lay in the hands of the resistance working closely with the government in exile in London. For a while the occupying power was unaware of the boats commuting between Norway and the Shetland Isles, taking refugees to Britain and ferrying volunteers, weapons and other material to Norway for use in the underground movement. Norwegian resistance fighters from the growing ranks of the Milorg helped in British attacks on German warships such as the *Bismarck* and the *Tirpitz*, while also destroying German vessels and disrupting not only supply routes but also industrial complexes vital to the armaments industry and, finally, carrying out assassinations of representatives of the occupying power. The most spectacular act of sabotage was the attack on the heavy water reactor at Vermork, which was crucial to the German nuclear research programme. Carried out in February 1943, it was the work of a Norwegian commando trained by the British Special Operations Executive.

The Germans responded to every act of resistance with drastic retaliatory measures, generally involving the execution of men and women who had not been directly involved. In one such retaliatory act in April 1942 the fishing village of Televåg was razed to the ground. It was here that two resistance fighters had hidden after returning to Norway from the Shetland Isles and killing two Gestapo agents. The men of the village were deported to the concentration camp at Sachsenhausen, where thirty-one of them died, while the women and children were sent to camps in the Norwegian interior. In the autumn of 1943 the German authorities closed the University of Oslo, having previously arrested 1,200 students and thirty members of the teaching staff. By the end of the war some 40,000 Norwegians were interned in camps that the Germans had built in the country. Among them were numerous policemen and army officers who had refused to declare their allegiance to the new state. Since April 1940 some 50,000 Norwegians had fled to neighbouring Sweden, including 900 Jews – more than half the number of Jews who had been living in Norway in 1940. Of the 700 Jews who remained in Norway, few survived the Second World War.

The Norwegians who succeeded in fleeing their native country and in reaching either Sweden or Great Britain formed the nucleus of an army of volunteers that was recruited by the Norwegian government in exile under the Social Democrat Johan Nygaardsvold. Comprising land troops, an air force and a navy, it numbered around 2,500 men by the winter of 1942/3 and took part in numerous Allied operations. When the German forces abandoned Norway without a struggle in May 1945, Terboven took his own life. King Haakon VII and his government returned to Oslo on 31 May, and Quisling handed himself over the Norwegian Home Guard. He was tried and sentenced to death, an execution carried out on 15 October 1945. Twenty-five Norwegian collaborators suffered a similar fate.

Denmark – the most southerly of the Scandinavian states – represented a special case in terms of Germany's occupation of foreign states. Here King Christian X remained in the country throughout the occupation, and the cabinet, which had been enlarged in 1940 to become what was effectively an all-party government under the Social Democrat prime minister, Thorvald Stauning, worked closely with the German authorities, a situation that continued under Stauning's successor, Vilhelm Buhl, after Stauning's death on 3 May 1942. German interests were represented by the Gestapo's former legal adviser and now SS group leader Werner Best, who replaced the diplomat Cécil von Renthe-Fink on 5 November 1942. As long as the Danish government accepted its political dependence on the German Reich and was able to dissuade the Danish people from engaging in any major acts of resistance, the occupying power respected the democratic system of government in Denmark, including the leading role of the Social Democrats.

For Werner Best – one of the SS's intellectuals – Germanic Denmark was one day destined to become a part of the Greater German Reich, which is why he felt the need to treat the country as considerately as possible. The kingdom was also of great strategic and economic significance for Germany, inasmuch as it provided a bridge to Norway and to a part of the Continental coastline that faced England. It also provided Germany with a sizeable proportion of its food needs – between 10 per cent and 15 per cent in 1941, representing 75 per cent of all Danish agricultural exports. In terms of its foreign policy, Denmark made important concessions to Germany by leaving the League of Nations in July 1940 and joining the anti-Comintern pact in November 1941. Moreover, the Danish government placed no obstacles in the way of a recruitment drive for volunteers for the Waffen-SS and, among the German minority in North Schleswig, for the Wehrmacht. The country's leaders in Copenhagen hoped that in this way they could avoid becoming directly involved in the war and maintain their autonomy.

Given the government's aims, it was inconceivable that the small Danish National Socialist Party would be interested in a place in government. Still less was it possible to install a government under the leadership of Frits Clausen, Denmark's leading National Socialist, which was the solution demanded by Hitler in the autumn of 1941. Soon after taking up his new appointment, Best was able to persuade Clausen to renounce all thought of his party's joining the government, thereby opening up the way for a constitutional solution that involved the appointment of the non-party foreign minister, Erik Scavenius, to lead a cabinet that continued to be made up of all the principal parties from the Social Democrats to the conservatives. In keeping with Hitler's demand, the Reichstag even passed an enabling act that granted the Danish government extensive powers in the field of legislation. But the way in which these powers were implemented continued to be decided by the parties that made up the cabinet. Scavenius's cabinet was more dependent on Germany than its Social Democrat predecessors, but it was still far from being a puppet government.

By the beginning of 1943 Best believed that the situation in Denmark was sufficiently stable for him to agree to the country's participation in the Reichstag elections that were due to take place by 3 April at the latest. In the event, the elections were held on 23 March, when the Social Democrats emerged as the largest party with 44 per cent of the votes cast. Together, the four coalition parties won 92 per cent of the vote. The Danish National Socialists polled only 2 per cent and remained a mere splinter group. Scavenius's government was rightly able to interpret the result as a plebiscite for its policy of *folkestyre*, or Danish self-determination.

The coalition government's domestic triumph was followed only a few months later by its worst crisis to date. The military defeats inflicted on Germany since the end of 1942 and the propaganda broadcast by the BBC on the basis of reports received from Danish politicians in exile in London led to growing unrest among the Danish population in the course of 1943 and even to the fear that Denmark might be regarded as a partner of the Axis Powers by the likely victors and punished accordingly. In the spring of 1943 the Special Operations Executive began to increase the number of its contacts with Danish resistance groups and to provide weapons and explosives for the agents who arrived in Jutland by sea or by air. The number of acts of sabotage grew from twenty-four in January to eighty in April 1943, and there was also a series of strikes and clashes between Danish civilians and soldiers from the Wehrmacht.

The German military commander in Denmark, General Hermann von Hanneken, was all in favour of punishing every act of sabotage and resistance with draconian severity, but Best preferred to continue to adopt his former, more tolerant approach, and it was his policy that prevailed until the summer of 1943. But then the situation changed. The fall of Mussolini and the devastating air raids on Hamburg by the Royal Air Force in July left many Danes believing that the war would soon end with Germany's defeat, and the gulf between the government parties and the population widened, while the Social Democrats and trade unions lost much of their influence on the workers. In early August unrest broke out in many parts of the country: in Esbjerg, for example, a wild-cat strike began on 6 August and lasted six days. On 21 August, Best was able to persuade the government parties to issue a further joint appeal against strikes and acts of sabotage, but it had no effect. Instead, there was an increase in the number of bombings, especially of transport links. Particularly unsettling for the occupying power was the spread of strikes to North Jutland, where an Allied invasion was currently expected.

On 24/5 August, Best met Hitler at the latter's headquarters in the Wolfsschanze near Rastenburg in East Prussia and reported on the tense situation in Denmark. He discovered that the Führer had already decided to adopt a much harsher policy towards the Danes: the days of the 'model protectorate' were over, and Best himself felt that his own days were numbered in spite of the backing of Himmler, Ribbentrop and the minister of food, Herbert Backe. Against his better judgement, Best was obliged to issue an ultimatum and impose conditions on Scavenius's government that it could not possibly meet, including the use of force against striking workers. Since the Social Democrats rejected the ultimatum outright, the government had no choice but to do so as well. The Germans reacted by declaring a state of emergency and replacing Scavenius's government with Hanneken on 29 August 1943. Hanneken was invested with executive powers. Although King Christian X refused to accept his ministers' resignation, their powers were now merely nominal and they were unable to perform their official duties.

The confrontational policies long demanded by Hitler and implemented by Hanneken were successful to the extent that the strikes and demonstrations ended very quickly, but there could no longer be any question of the two sides working together in any productive manner. Best was therefore able to persuade the authorities in Berlin to end the state of emergency as quickly as possible and to appoint an 'apolitical' cabinet or an administrative committee to run the country. But Best also felt that the state of emergency should be used to create a powerful German police force that would prosecute all attacks on German interests. The Danish negotiators accepted that as things stood it was no longer possible to form a constitutional government but only an administration made up of ministerial secretaries of state that would operate under strict German supervision.

In the meantime the occupying power had issued a series of draconian decrees against strikes and acts of sabotage. It was on this basis that a Danish resistance fighter was sentenced to death on 8 September. The small Danish army was disbanded, although the navy pre-empted the move by scuttling its own ships. On 8 September, Best sent a telegram to the Foreign Office demanding that the question of the country's Jews and Freemasons be resolved while the emergency legislation was still in force, since there would inevitably be unrest and possibly even a general strike if the Germans waited until the state of emergency had expired before acting against the 8,000 or so Jews living in Denmark. As Best's German biographer, Ulrich Herbert, has rightly noted, Best's concern – in spite of his later testimony – was not to solve the Jewish question by giving this order. Rather, he had always been eager to remove the Jews from the sphere of German influence in Europe, a position that had no practical consequences in Denmark only because in the present circumstances radical action would have run counter to the overriding German considerations, not least of which was the uninterrupted flow of Danish foodstuffs to the Reich.[62]

But the expectation that the state of emergency would allow the authorities to act swiftly without causing a stir proved mistaken. Once Hitler had approved the deportation of Danish Jews, Best instructed the Danish police to impound the Jewish community's list of members on 17 December, a move which, combined with the arrival of an additional German police presence from

Norway, spread alarm not only among Denmark's Jews but also among the public at large. From now on Best was forced to confront the fact that the step that he himself had demanded would result in violent opposition, a view that was shared by Hanneken. But it was Georg F. Duckwitz, the shipping expert at the German Embassy, who took the decisive step. When he was informed on 11 September – presumably by Best – that the raid would be carried out on 1/2 October, he informed two Social Democrat politicians of his acquaintance, Hans Hedtoft and Hans Christian Hansen, who in turn alerted representatives of the Danish Jewish community to the German plan.

This timely warning meant that the majority of the Jews in Denmark could make good their escape. The government in neutral Sweden was informed of developments by its ambassador in Copenhagen and passed word to the German government that it was prepared to accept the Danish Jews, an offer also broadcast on the radio in order to apprise the individuals concerned of what was happening and allow them to seek refuge with Danish friends and neighbours. The German navy had made no preparations to prevent the Jews from escaping via the Öresund, and so some 7,000 Jews, together with several hundred of their non-Jewish partners, were able to reach Sweden in Danish fishing boats and small ships. Back in Denmark, the German police were able to arrest a further 481 Jews on 2 October and in the days that followed. At Best's urging, they were sent not to any of Germany's extermination camps but to the concentration camp at Theresienstadt, where most of them survived the war. In his capacity as Hitler's plenipotentiary in Denmark, Best let it be known that in spite of the failure of the attempt to arrest the country's Jews, he had achieved his principal aim of ridding Denmark of its Jewish population.

The state of emergency came to an end on 6 October 1943, and after that date Best was required to confer on all policy matters with the secretary of state at the Foreign Office, Nils Svenningsen, who spoke on behalf of all the secretaries of state. Meanwhile the various Danish resistance movements had joined forces as a 'Freedom Council' that maintained close links with the British government and enjoyed growing support among the Danish population. It was the Freedom Council that carried out most of the acts of sabotage that were committed in increasingly large numbers after October 1943, including the murder of Danish spies who had been working for the Germans. Several saboteurs whom the German secret police had been able to arrest were tried by a German war tribunal and a number of them were sentenced to death. But in his attempt to avoid an escalation of the situation, Best refused to shoot hostages, which was one of the reprisals demanded by Hitler. He was equally steadfast in his refusal to liquidate members of the resistance as a response to assassinations and acts of sabotage.

Best was able to get his way in the case of the shooting of hostages, but the same was not true of what can only be described as the reign of 'counter-terror'. On 4 January 1944, the playwright and Lutheran pastor Kaj Munk was assassinated by

German secret agents in reprisal for the killing of a spy from the ranks of the Danish National Socialists. This was followed by many more acts of 'counter-terror' in a ratio of two to one – two Danes were killed for every dead German. Hitler had initially demanded a ratio of five to one.

The Danish resistance movement culminated in a 'people's strike' in Copenhagen at the end of June 1944, an action triggered by the partial destruction of the Tivoli amusement park and by a night curfew that represented Germany's response to an act of sabotage on a munitions factory. The strike by the city's workers was so successful that Best was left with no choice but to lift the curfew on 28 June. The following day eleven demonstrators were shot by the police and it was announced that eight resistance fighters had been executed. The strikes continued to spread until Best declared a state of siege in Copenhagen and shut down the service industries. Military patrols were also instructed to shoot on sight, and fighter aircraft were equipped with incendiary bombs. This last-named measure proved so intimidating that the strikes began to crumble after 1 July, and two days later the insurrection was over.

Hitler was furious at the events in Copenhagen, which he interpreted as a total failure of the tactics adopted by Best. On 5 July the latter received a severe reprimand from the Führer at the Berghof near Berchtesgaden, and the limited powers that he had enjoyed until then were without exception removed when Hitler's new decree of 30 July 1944 abolished the legal prosecution of resistance fighters and permitted only 'counter-terror'. Denmark's special status was over, and the Scandinavian kingdom was finally one more occupied country among many others.

Occupation, Collaboration, Resistance (II): France

At first sight Vichy France bore a striking similarity to occupied Denmark, initially enjoying a considerable degree of autonomy in terms of the country's domestic policies and politics. On a deeper level, however, it differed fundamentally from Denmark, for whereas the Social Democrat-led government in Copenhagen met the Third Reich halfway in all matters relating to foreign policy in order to be able to retain its democratic system, the Pétain regime in Vichy used the country's military defeat and exploited German rule to do away with the Third Republic's parliamentary democracy. The 'national revolution' proclaimed by the elderly marshal in his capacity as head of state was not aimed at establishing a Fascist dictatorship, however, but at creating an authoritarian regime that most clearly resembled the *estado novo* of Salazar's Portugal.

The *état français* drew on various traditions of the French right, traditions extending from the ideologues of the counterrevolution such as Louis de Bonald and Joseph de Maistre to Bonapartism and Boulangism and including present-day representatives such as the Croix de Feu and Action Française. The last-named of these groups benefited from the fact that in July 1939, shortly after his election as pope, Pius XII had lifted the order of excommunication placed by his predecessor, Pius XI, in 1926 on all those French men and women who read the group's newspaper, *Action Française*. One of the organization's most prominent representatives in Vichy France was Raphaël Alibert, the first minister of justice and author of the constitutional decrees of July 1940 to which we have already referred. The motto of the *état français* – 'Labour, family, fatherland' – had been coined in 1934 by Colonel Casimir de la Rocque, the leader of the Croix de Feu. It was young right-wing groups who in the interwar years had drawn up the ideas on a planned economy that Darlan's government now adopted, although it was Italian Fascism that provided the model in terms of professional groupings, the wearing of uniforms by members of paramilitary organizations close to the government, the use of propaganda and the stigmatization of real or imagined enemies of the state such as Communists, Freemasons, foreigners and Jews. National Socialist Germany's Reich Labour Front inspired the creation of youth work camps ('chantiers de jeunesse'), while the systematic glorification of Pétain as the 'hero of Verdun' recalled the lionization of Marshal Piłsudski in Poland, Admiral Horthy in Hungary, Marshal Antonescu in Romania and Generalissimo Franco in Spain. In every one of these countries it was the best-known military leader who was called upon to embody the unity of the nation and to symbolize the new order.

When Pétain dismissed Laval in December 1940, he was far from abandoning the idea of collaboration with Germany, an idea that he had publicly endorsed on 30 October 1940, barely a week after his meeting with Hitler in Montoire. If Laval had to go, it was because Pétain did not trust him or his closest advisers. François Darlan, who as vice-president of the Council of Ministers and foreign minister, home secretary, minister of information and minister of the navy all rolled into one had become the government's new strong man, issued a series of protocols in May 1941 that were designed to reduce by a quarter the cost of the country's occupation as well as agreeing to the release of 100,000 prisoners of war and offering the Germans tacit support in their war with Great Britain in Iraq, Syria and North Africa. But the protocols encountered such stiff resistance on the part of the German and French governments that in the end they remained unsigned. On 18 April 1942, Pétain, bowing to tremendous pressure from Germany, reappointed Laval as the head of his government, while also investing him with extraordinary powers. On 22 June 1942 – the first anniversary of the German invasion of the Soviet Union – Laval addressed the nation. His speech contained a sentence which in the eyes and ears of most of his radio listeners defined him as a mere agent of the occupying power: 'I wish a German victory, because, without it, bolshevism to-morrow would settle everywhere.'[63]

Vichy France revealed many romantic and backward-looking features. Among them was the exclusion of women from public service, the emphasis placed on the father as the head of the family, the subsidized 'return to the soil' that was meant to stop the mass exodus from the countryside and the attempt to combat Freemasonry and the ideas of the Enlightenment, an attitude that in many cases went hand in hand with a demonstrative clericalism. The regime pandered to the political right by forcing farmers and many freelance professionals such as doctors, chemists and architects to form their own organizations, and the same was true of the disbandment of trade unions and of the employers' umbrella organization in favour of purely professional unions. The Italian Carta del Lavoro of 1926 found its counterpart – and namesake – in the Charte du Travail of 4 October 1941, which created a legal framework for relations within business and industry and consolidated the power of the head of each firm behind the façade of good working relations between unions and management.

Vichy revealed its reactionary and repressive aspect particularly clearly in the aforementioned Jewish decrees of October 1940 and June 1941 but also by purging the civil service and judiciary of supporters of the Third Republic. The law preventing the removal of judges was repealed, and with it went the independence of the judiciary. There followed the creation of a whole series of special courts, including ones set up to prosecute those French men and women 'responsible for the country's defeat' as well as to suppress Communists and combat the black market. But the Supreme Court trial in Riom of those blamed for the defeat of 1940, including Léon Blum and Édouard Daladier, turned into a complete debacle, and the proceedings were adjourned on 11 April 1942 after Hitler had publicly complained that the trial was not about responsibility for the war but merely about the inadequate preparations for war.

In addition to its constraints, its repression and its reactionary policies, however, the *état français* also contained within it a number of modernizing tendencies. René Rémond has argued that it harboured a handful of economic and financial theorists aware of France's financial backwardness and determined to transform the country into a powerful industrial nation:

> These technocrats, who were relatively indifferent to the political situation, were the heirs of the pre-war generation of technicians [. . .] and at the same time the precursors of the future generation of high-ranking officials who were successful in modernizing France after 1945, a process that would not have been so swift if Vichy had not laid the foundations for it.[64]

Germany's invasion of the Soviet Union proved to be a turning point in France just as it was elsewhere. In the wake of the Hitler–Stalin Pact, the outlawed French Communist Party had sought to reach an agreement with the occupying power and even to revive *L'Humanité* and other party newspapers, a request that was immediately turned down. But after 22 June 1941 the situation changed completely, and the Communists began a campaign of active resistance designed to oust the Germans and their French lackeys. On 21 August the Communist Party member Pierre Georges, who was later to play a leading role in the French Resistance as Colonel Fabien, shot a random member of the Wehrmacht, the naval adjutant Alfons Moser, at the Barbès-Rochechouart underground station. The Germans reacted to this and similar acts with unprecedented severity, and at the end of October ninety-eight French hostages were shot. In the autumn of 1944 the Vichy government's home secretary, Pierre Pucheu, gave orders for around 100 prisoners to be executed.

The murder of Alfons Moser came at a time when Pétain, addressing the nation in a radio broadcast on 12 August, claimed that an 'ill wind' was sweeping through the country. He and his prime minister, Édouard Daladier, were unsettled less by the increasing impact of the BBC's French-language broadcasts that could be heard all over France and that included the propaganda put out by de Gaulle's France Libre than by strikes such as the miners' walkout in the *département* of Pas-de-Calais in May 1941, an action designed to protest at the closeness of the relationship between the pits' managers and the occupying power.

The Vichy government responded to the unrest by banning all political gatherings and undertaking a new wave of purges aimed chiefly at the country's Freemasons. They also doubled the strength of the police force and actively encouraged the Légion Française des Combattants, which in November 1941 became the Légion Française des Combattants et des Volontaires de la Révolution Nationale. Its final nucleus was formed in January 1943 by the uniformed Service d'Ordre Légionnaire, or SOL, which under its leader, the philo-Fascist Joseph Darnand, waged a bitter war on Gaullists, Bolsheviks, Freemasons and, last but not least, the country's Jews.

When the *état français* was created in July 1940, there were some 330,000 Jews living in France, excluding Algeria. Of these, 200,000 were French citizens. The remainder were foreigners made up of 90,000 Poles, Russians, Germans, Austrians and Romanians and 40,000 refugees from the Netherlands, Belgium and Luxembourg. They were joined in October 1940 by almost 7,000 Jews from Baden and the Saarland Palatinate who had been deported to unoccupied France by the Reich Main Security Office without any attempt at prior consultation with the government in Vichy.

France had already started to intern foreign Jews and other undesirable aliens in improvised camps in the autumn of 1939. Conditions in camps such as those at Gurs, Les Milles and Rivesaltes were so appalling that many inmates died of illness, hunger and exhaustion. The writer Arthur Koestler was interned at Gurs during the winter of 1939/40 and claimed that it was worse than a 'Nazi concentration camp in terms of its food, amenities and hygiene'.[65] By 1942 the number of camp inmates in the German-occupied parts of France was 15,000 and in the unoccupied parts as many as 50,000. They included not only Jews and non-Jewish immigrants but also Sinti and Roma who had no French passports.

In late March 1942 the occupying power deported 1,000 Jews, mostly French citizens, from Le Bourget to the concentration camp at Auschwitz. Starting on

7 June 1942, all Jews in the occupied regions of France were required to wear the Jewish Star. For the present the Jews in the rest of the country were spared this measure because the government – once again headed by Pierre Laval since 18 August – was afraid of negative reactions on the part of the population at large. The new director general of the French police, René Bousquet, whom Laval himself had personally appointed, assured his German colleagues that the police under his command would take part in any anti-Jewish measures in return for the promise that it would be foreign Jews who would be the first to be affected.

It was Laval who proposed that children under the age of sixteen could also be deported, even though the Germans had made no such demand: he did not want his government to be responsible for the welfare of the underage Jews who would otherwise have been left behind, thereby placing a further burden on the state. The biggest raid was organized by the French police in the middle of July 1942, when 12,800 foreign Jews were held for several days in the Vélodrome d'Hiver – the capital's winter cycling track – until they could be deported. Here they were herded together in extremely cramped conditions, even though the authorities had made no plans to accommodate and feed so many people. By October 10,500 foreign Jews had been transported from internment camps in unoccupied France to Drancy, from where they were taken by train to occupied Poland. By the end of 1942 the number of Jews deported from France totalled 42,000, more than half of all the Jews arrested in France who were victims of National Socialist genocide.

The raids that took place in several French cities during the summer of 1942 could not be kept secret and gave rise to nationwide protests: prefects reported anger among the population at large; and several Catholic bishops took issue with the injustice done to the Jews, expressing their outrage in pastoral letters read out in church – on 23 August the archbishop of Toulouse, Jules Saliège, described Jews as people whom Christians should treat as their brothers. Until then the Vichy regime had been able to rely on the support of the Catholic clergy. It now responded by quoting anti-Jewish remarks by popes and scholastics and by speaking of political agitation fomented by enemies of the 'national revolution'. In early September, using the official news service, the government called on all Catholics to direct their feelings of sympathy to the 1.2 million French prisoners of war who at least were 'genuine sons of France'.[66]

French prisoners of war also played a role in the Vichy government's attempts to meet German demands for a great commitment on France's part to Germany's wartime economy. When Hitler's general plenipotentiary for labour deployment, Fritz Sauckel, demanded that 350,000 French workers be made available for the second half of 1942, Laval managed to lower that figure to 150,000 and arranged for three workers to be exchanged for every one prisoner of war, an exchange known as the *relève*. But by the end of July 1942 only 40,000 workers had volunteered for the programme in response to Laval's appeal of

22 June, with the result that the Reich forced most of its 1.2 million prisoners of war to undertake the work against their will.

In September 1942 the government passed a law allowing all men between eighteen and thirty-five to be mobilized for tasks deemed to be in the national interest. Under its terms a further 240,000 French workers were sent to Germany between then and the end of 1942. Sauckel's demand for an extra 250,000 foreign workers from France led to the introduction of further legislation whereby all men born between 1920 and 1922 were forced to work in Germany for a two-year period – the Service de Travail Obligatoire, or STO. All those affected by this measure, together with their families and the Church, reacted with outrage, and many young men joined the French Resistance in order to avoid having to undertake forced labour in the Reich. Within the administration and in the police force and gendarmerie, there were many who, in spite of the threat of severe penalties, showed no interest in making the STO work.

In November 1942, between the law mobilizing large sections of the French workforce and the introduction of the STO, came two major events in the history of the Vichy regime, when Allied troops landed in North Africa and Germany occupied the rest of France. Until then the government had had a certain political leeway, but it now became a satellite state entirely dependent on the will of the Reich, a state of affairs that Laval repeatedly tried to deny. On 30 January 1943 – the tenth anniversary of Hitler's seizure of power in Germany – Laval replaced the Service d'Ordre Légionnaire with the Milice Française and appointed the former organization's head, Joseph Darnand, its successor's secretary general. The paramilitary militia was made up of volunteers whose task was to maintain order and to track down and hand over to the police all who refused to work or opposed the regime and all Jews who had gone into hiding. The militia was intended to strengthen Laval's personal power over his political rivals in Vichy and Paris and also over the German occupiers. But this last-mentioned task proved increasingly impossible for Darnand to perform when he began to pursue his own policies, formed alliances with Pétain's enemies and forged ties with the German secret service and police.

Like Pétain, Laval was a collaborator in the sense of a *collaboration d'état*, but he was not a *collaborationniste*. French historians define *collaboration d'état* as collaboration between the Vichy government and the occupying power undertaken in the interests of the state but not necessarily based on any ideological ties with the Third Reich, being aimed in the main at progressively increasing France's scope for action and restoring its sovereignty at the first available opportunity. *Collaborationnistes*, conversely, were those politicians and intellectuals who openly admitted their support of Fascism and regarded National Socialists as kindred spirits and Hitler's Germany as the only power capable of preserving Europe from both 'Jewish Bolshevism' and the overwhelming influence of Anglo-Saxon democracies, foremost among which was the United States of America. Since *collaborateurs* were mostly ardent anti-Communists and anti-Semites, there were not only differences between them and the *collaborationnistes* but also important points that the two groups had in common.

Two of the most prominent *collaborationnistes* were the former Socialist politician Marcel Déat and the erstwhile leader of the Communists, Jacques Doriot. By July 1940 Déat, who in May 1939 had coined the defeatist slogan 'Mourir pour Dantzig?', was already championing the idea of a single great unity party led by Pétain and modelled on the parties of the Italian Fascists and German National Socialists, but he was unable to persuade Pétain to accept this suggestion. He then approached the German occupying power and in February 1941 formed his own movement, the Rassemblement National Populaire, or RNP, whose party newspaper, *L'Œuvre*, attacked the Vichy regime as nationalist, capitalist and reactionary. In the summer of 1941 he joined forces with Doriot and Eugène Deloncle, the leader of the pro-Fascist Mouvement Social Révolutionnaire, and founded the Légion des Volontaires Français contre le Bolshévisme, which in 1943 was to provide the nucleus of the French unit of the Waffen-SS, later to become known as the SS Division Charlemagne.

Unlike the intellectual Déat, the people's tribune Doriot, who was the leader of the radical right-wing Parti Populaire Français (PPF) of 1936, took his anti-Communism to such extreme lengths that for a time he saw active service in the war against the Soviet Union, fighting as a French legionary and wearing a Wehrmacht uniform. While the Foreign Office in Berlin and the German ambassador in Paris, Otto Abetz, banked on Déat, the more radical Doriot enjoyed the backing of the SS, but neither man was able to command mass support. As a *collaborationniste*, Doriot lost most of the followers that he had had before the war, although his party continued to have more members than Déat's. Together with other Fascist organizations, including Deloncle's, the RNP and PPF are believed to have had a little over 14,000 members in fifty-two *départements* between 1942 and 1944. The total number of members of all Fascist and pro-German organizations during the second half of 1943 has been estimated as being 50,000 at the very most.

Among the intellectual *collaborationnistes* were the journalist Alfred Fabre-Luce and the writers Louis-Ferdinand Céline, Robert Brasillach, Pierre Drieu la Rochelle and Henry de Montherlant, all of whom were eloquent advocates of a struggle spearheaded by National Socialist Germany and designed to save Europe from Bolshevism. The spokesmen for the *collaborationnistes* were based in Paris, but they also had influential allies in Vichy, including the former Communist Paul Marion, who became minister of information and propaganda in February 1941; Jacques Bénoist-Méchin, the secretary of state to the vice-president of the Council of Ministers; and Joseph Darnand, the head of the Milice Française, who, with the active support of his closest colleague Philippe Henriot, came to embody the Vichy regime's increasingly rapid slide into Fascism after 1943.

The year 1943 marked the high point of the French Resistance. With the introduction of forced labour in January 1943, the number of fighters grew, as did the number of their armed attacks on policemen associated with the Vichy regime as well as on militia members, well-known collaborators and members of the occupying power. The occupiers responded with mass deportations to German concentration camps: of the 87,000 French men and women affected by this measure, two-thirds belonged to the resistance movement. The remainder were made up for the most part of hostages, prisoners and homosexuals.

The various resistance groups were originally divided both regionally and politically, but under the impact of the regime's increasingly repressive measures they forged closer links among themselves, and in January 1943 de Gaulle's personal representative in France, Jean Moulin, who was the former prefect of the *département* of Eure-et-Loire, succeeded in bringing together the leading left-wing resistance groups in the east of the country, namely, 'Combat', 'Libération-Sud' and 'Franc-Tireur'. On 27 May he formed the Conseil National de la Résistance (CNR) in Paris. It included not only the outlawed fighting units of the moderate left and right and the Republican parties but also the largest and most active of all the resistance organizations, the Communist-led Front National. Four and a half weeks later Jean Moulin was arrested by the Gestapo. Brutally tortured by the head of the Gestapo in Lyons, Klaus Barbie, he died of heart failure two and a half weeks later, on 8 July. It was a serious blow for the French resistance movement but no more than a temporary setback, for the *maquisards* – named after the *maquis*, or scrubland, in the Massif Central and other regions suitable for guerrilla fighting – continued to attack the occupying Germans and their French supporters with unrelenting resolve.

The amalgamation of the different resistance groups in France lent new impetus to attempts to bring together the anti-Vichy forces outside France. In the spring of 1943, General Henri Giraud, the civilian and military high commissioner in North Africa, responding to pressure from his close adviser Jean Monnet, formally broke with Pétain's government, prompting de Gaulle to give in to British demands and form an alliance with Giraud. On 3 June 1943 the two generals met in Algiers and founded the Comité Français de Libération Française, or CFLN. But the dual presidency of Giraud and de Gaulle proved to be short-lived, and under pressure from those members of the French Resistance in Algeria who set the tone in the Advisory Assembly that met in September, Giraud was forced to stand down in early October, leaving de Gaulle as sole leader of the CFLN and at the same time the representative of French power in Algeria. Since the Allies had already recognized the CFLN as representing French interests in July, the leader of France Libre was from now on able to rely on the support of a power which until 8 November 1942 had maintained diplomatic relations with Vichy and banked on Giraud in North Africa: the country in question was the United States of America.

With Giraud gone, the rift between the members of the French military active outside France came to an end. It was a rift that had already cost many lives: those lost during de Gaulle's attempt to land his troops, with British help, in Dakar in September 1940; those lost in the fighting in Syria in the summer of 1941 between the forces of Vichy and those of Britain and France Libre; and, later, those lost in the battle for North Africa on the occasion of the Allied landings there in November 1942. Within France, too, de Gaulle's authority increased. Following his arrest, Moulin was replaced by another of the general's confidants, Georges Bidault. Meanwhile the resistance movement continued to attract new members thanks not only to the increasingly harsh repressive measures adopted by the Vichy regime and the occupying power but also to a factor over which the French had little influence, no matter what their political affiliations: the military successes of the Allies, who were already inflicting heavy defeats on the Germans on every front. As a result, the belief in an ultimate victory by the Reich and its allies began to fade in France just as it did elsewhere.

Within the Vichy regime, there was renewed friction between Pétain and Laval in the summer of 1943, when the former refused to accept a German proposal to strip of their French citizenship all Jews who had become French nationals since 1927, thereby making it easier for the Germans to arrest them. Laval, who had already agreed to the German plan, had to back down, a step that delayed, while not preventing, the deportation of Jews holding French passports. A few months later a serious crisis blew up between the occupying power and the French state, when Pétain, eager to prevent Laval from stripping away even more of his powers, took a step that has been described by the historian Marc-Olivier Baruch as a 'constitutional *coup d'état*': on 11 November the marshal signed a constitutional act by which the two chambers of the National Assembly that had been suspended in July 1940 were reconvened. Their task was to work out the new constitution and appoint Pétain's successor. The occupying power intervened at once and prevented Pétain from addressing the nation by radio. Pétain protested but was forced to give in and henceforth accept his permanent supervision by the German diplomat Cécil von Renthe-Fink, the Reich's former plenipotentiary in Denmark. It was Laval who emerged victorious from this power struggle in France's domestic politics.

At the beginning of 1944 the Germans insisted on the dismissal of a number of Pétain's closest advisers as well as numerous prefects and sub-prefects, some of whom were deported to Germany. At the same time the occupying power was able to ensure the appointment of dyed-in-the-wool *collaborationnistes* to government posts: on 1 January 1944 Joseph Darnand, the secretary general of the Milice Française, became the secretary general responsible for maintaining law and order and, hence, effectively chief of police, while his colleague Philippe Henriot, who like Darnand was a fanatical anti-Semite, became minister for information and propaganda five days later. With the appointment of Marcel

Déat as minister of labour on 17 March, three declared Fascists were now in key positions in the French government. All, moreover, could rely on the Milice Française, which had long been the principal instrument in the struggle with the French Resistance. Darnand appointed its members prefects, police chiefs, prison wardens and leading officials in the secret service. The new courts set up by Darnand in January 1944 were given the task of sentencing resistance fighters who had prepared or carried out assassinations. Since appeals were not allowed, a guilty verdict was followed by the accused's immediate execution.

As the Milice Française gained in power, so the police grew more ineffectual and at the same time drifted away from the *état français*, leading to increased support for the resistance movement both from disenchanted members of the police force and from the ranks of the civil service. In turn this meant that for a time the dividing line between collaboration and resistance became blurred. There were particularly violent clashes between the Résistance and the Milice in early 1944 in the scrubland around Glières in the *département* of Haute-Savoie. Here the forces loyal to the Vichy regime were able to prevail only with German help. In the wake of these clashes many resistance fighters were executed without trial. In the population at large Laval was held responsible for the Milice's reign of terror, Pétain escaping relatively lightly thanks to his considerable personal standing. On 26 April, on his only visit to Paris since the ceasefire, Pétain was greeted with an ovation, a reception repeated in other French towns and cities through which he passed in the spring of 1944. And yet there was no longer any broad support of the kind that the *état français* had initially enjoyed: most French men and women were by now waiting impatiently for their country's liberation from foreign rule, a state that came perceptibly closer with the Normandy landings on 6 June 1944.

It was shortly after this that the occupying power and the Milice Française committed some of the worst atrocities of the whole of the Vichy era. On 7 June German troops recaptured Tulle from the Franc-Tireurs et Partisans resistance group and on the 8th hanged ninety-nine of the town's inhabitants from the balconies of local buildings. Two days later an SS division known as 'Das Reich' wiped out an entire village, Oradour-sur-Glane: 642 men, women and children were herded into a barn and into the village church and either shot or burnt alive. On 20 June members of France-Garde, the billeted militia, abducted the former Radical Socialist minister Jean Zay from his prison cell at Riom. His body was not found until 1946. On 7 July members of the Milice Française murdered another Radical Socialist politician, Georges Mandel. His death was intended as retribution for the murder of the minister of propaganda, Philippe Henriot, who had been killed by resistance fighters on 28 June.

On 20 August, by which date the Germans had already begun to retreat from France, Pétain was taken against his will from Vichy to Belfort and from there to Sigmaringen in Swabia. He was followed by Laval and his ministers, also against their will. The new government in exile, which included Darnand

and Déat, was headed by Fernand de Brinon, the Vichy government's former representative with the German High Command in Paris and later secretary of state. His appointment had Pétain's approval. The Sigmaringen cabinet no longer had any real power; this now lay in the hands of the French Resistance movement. On 25 August, three days after the last Jews had left for Auschwitz, troops from France Libre under General Jacques-Philippe Leclerc liberated Paris with the help of fighters from the French Resistance. Within hours de Gaulle had entered the capital and addressed the waiting crowds from the Hôtel de Ville. The following day, to tempestuous acclaim, he marched at the head of his loyal supporters along the Champs-Élysées to the Place de la Concorde.

As long as the Germans had the final word in France, it had remained unclear what would become of the country in the event of a German victory. All that was certain was that Alsace-Lorraine would remain in German hands. Since 1941 there had no longer been any talk of Burgundy becoming German, although this had occupied the thoughts of Hitler, Himmler and Goebbels both before and after the campaign in the west. But Hitler had never envisaged the rest of France as part of a Greater German Reich. Presumably a territorially reduced France would have had a role to play as a vassal state of a victorious Germany. The fact that Hitler felt a certain respect for French culture and that the German ambassador in Paris, Otto Abetz, and many German officers held France in even higher esteem meant that the French were not treated as a helot race and thus avoided the fate suffered by the White Russians, Ukrainians and Poles.

On the other hand, many of the French artists and intellectuals courted by Abetz simply came to terms with the realities of the situation, if they did not actively collaborate with the enemy. Between 1940 and 1944 a number of important plays were premièred in Paris, including Sartre's Les Mouches and Claudel's Le Soulier de satin. With German approval books continued to be published, including works by Camus, Duhamel and even François Mauriac, who was a member of the Résistance and who also wrote for an underground publishing house, Éditions de Minuit. Painters and sculptors remained unmolested as long as they did not attack the occupying power. Describing the cultural life of Paris between 1940 and 1944, Marc-Olivier Baruch has even spoken in this context of a 'period of efflorescence'.[67]

With the liberation of France came the mythical transfiguration of the French Resistance. In his speech to the crowd outside Paris's Hôtel de Ville on 25 August 1944 de Gaulle declared that France had been liberated by its own people with the help of its armies and the support of 'fighting France, in other words, the only true and eternal France'.[68] In making this claim, de Gaulle turned the achievements of a small minority of a million or so French men and women into the exploits of an entire nation, while collaboration was ascribed to a finite number of individuals whom it was now a question of ruthlessly calling to account. Both in the weeks before the Allied invasion and in the months that followed it, some 10,000 men and women fell victim to this process of *épuration*. None was ever tried in a court of law. Their number included politicians, members of the Milice Française and gendarmes. Women who had had intimate relations with German soldiers were indiscriminately accused of collaboration, just as they were in other occupied countries. All were ostracized and in many cases their hair was shaved off. Children who were the offspring of such liaisons were never allowed to forget their origins.

Informal retribution was followed by its formal counterpart. Of the Vichy regime's ministers and secretaries of state, twenty-two were sentenced to varying terms of imprisonment or forced labour in 1945, while eighteen were sentenced to death – ten of them in their absence. Among those who received the death sentence was Pétain, although in view of his age the sentence was not carried out: instead, he was banished to the island of Yeu off the Vendée, where he died on 23 July 1951. Laval, Brinon and Darnand were executed. Doriot was killed in an air raid on Germany in February 1945, while Déat managed to escape to Italy, where he hid in a monastery and died in 1955. Of the senior figures in the Milice and other high-ranking officials of the Vichy regime, some 1,500 were sentenced to death and executed; 38,000 served terms of imprisonment.

Not a few collaborators were helped by the fact that they had maintained links with the resistance movement. Among them was René Bousquet, who until the end of 1943 had been secretary general of the French police and, as such, had been at the very top of his country's repressive regime. He had even played a substantial role in the deportation of Jews living in France, all of whom were taken to the extermination camps to the east. His sentence was limited to a five-year ban on holding public office. Only when new incriminating evidence came to light much later, including his complicity in the deportation of 194 Jewish children, was he tried again in 1991, but the trial was repeatedly postponed thanks to Bousquet's friendship with François Mitterrand, who was president of France from 1981 to 1995. Bouquet was shot on 8 June 1993 by an assailant who was said to have been of unsound mind.

'To cause this nation to vanish from the face of the earth': The 'Final Solution' (II)

The first country to report that all of its Jews had been exterminated was Serbia. Thousands of Jewish men were shot in the wake of the 'atonement measures' undertaken in the summer and autumn of 1941. These deaths were followed between March and May 1942 by the murders of some 8,000 Jewish women and children in the concentration camp at Sajmište and afterwards by the killing of patients and staff at the Jewish Hospital in Belgrade and of Jews from the nearby camp, all of whom perished in a gas van sent from Berlin. A similar fate was suffered by Sinti and Roma, who both here and in others parts of Europe occupied by the Germans were regarded as racially and socially inferior and as unnecessary mouths to be fed. In August 1942, the head of the civilian administration in Belgrade, SS group leader Harald Turner, reported on the completion of his murderous actions, striking a note of pride in his telegram: 'Serbia is the only country in Europe where the Jewish problem has been solved.'[69]

On the strength of the experiences gleaned during the murder of the mentally ill, gas vans were also used to exterminate Jews in the Baltic States, White Russia, the Ukraine and in the camp at Chelmno (Kulmhof). Not until November 1941 were Jews murdered in large numbers in gas chambers in Belzec in the General Government of Poland. Along with Sobibór, Treblinka and, after July 1942, Majdanek, Belzec was one of the extermination camps supervised by the Lublin district SS group leader, Odilo Globocnik. 'Action Reinhard' was presumably so called in memory of Reinhard Heydrich. By the end of 1942 some 434,000 Jews had been murdered at Belzec, while the figure for Sobibór for March to June 1942 – the first three months during which it was operational – was between 90,000 and 100,000, most of them from Lublin, Austria, the Old Reich and the Protectorate of Bohemia and Moravia. Systematic killings in the gas chambers at Treblinka began in July 1942. Majdanek was originally intended for Soviet prisoners of war but soon became both a concentration camp used for slave labour and an extermination camp. The same was true of Auschwitz. Here the Economic and Administrative Main Office ensured that inmates were killed through overwork, while direct physical annihilation by gassing was carried out by the Reich Main Security Office.

The extermination camp at Auschwitz-Birkenau opened in September 1941 with the killing of some 600 Russian prisoners of war and 200 other inmates who were either ill or unable to work. All were murdered using Zyklon B gas. By the middle of February 1942 the mass killings in gas chambers had started. Early victims included Jews from the labour camps in Upper Silesia who were declared unfit for work. In 1943 a separate camp was built at Birkenau for women, families and gypsies and a 'family camp' for Jews from the concentration camp at Theresienstadt. Jews who were to be killed had to strip naked before being gassed. Death was by suffocation and was painful. The bodies were then processed: gold teeth were removed, the women's hair was cut off, artificial limbs were removed and items of value such as wedding rings and spectacles were collected in piles. This task was performed by Jewish *Sonderkommandos*, or special commandos. Initially the bodies were buried, but from 1943 onwards they were burned in large ovens produced by the Erfurt firm of Topf & Sons. The bones were crushed in special machines. In Saul Friedländer's words, 'the ashes were used as fertilizer in the nearby fields, dumped in local forests, or tossed into the river, nearby. As for the members of the *Sonderkommandos*, they were periodically killed and replaced by a new batch'.[70] The number of men, women and children murdered at Auschwitz has been put at 1.3 million, a figure made up of 1.1 million Jews, 140,000 Poles, some 20,000 Sinti and Roma and 10,000 Soviet prisoners of war.

Those who were murdered in this way came from every part of Europe that was either occupied or controlled by Germany. The Jews were rarely offered assistance by the local population. Nowhere was that help as successful and as comprehensive as it was in Denmark. In the Netherlands, by contrast, the displays of solidarity in Delft, Leiden and Amsterdam in 1940–41 were soon replaced by cooperation between the police and civil servants on the one hand and the occupying power on the other whenever it was a question of deporting Jews to the extermination camps to the east. The same was true of Belgium, where, unlike its neighbour to the north, the overwhelming majority of the Jews who were living in the country were of foreign extraction. In France, collaboration encountered resistance when it was a question of deporting Jews who had long been established in the country. Of the Jews who were deported from France, 68 per cent were of foreign extraction. Of the foreign Jews who had been living in France, 39 per cent fell victim to the Holocaust, whereas the figure for French Jews was small by comparison: 12 per cent. In France 23 per cent of the country's Jewish population were deported or killed, whereas the proportion in Belgium was around 50 per cent, in the Netherlands as high as 75 per cent.

The first 10,000 Jews to be transported from Belgium to the extermination camps in the east left in August 1942. They were Poles, Czechoslovaks, Russians and other foreign Jews, but as yet their number did not include any Belgian nationals. In a report that he sent to Berlin on 9 July, Werner von Bargen, the Foreign Ministry representative with the German military high command in Belgium, attributed this situation to the fact 'that the understanding of the Jewish question is not yet very widespread here [in Belgium]', while 'the Jews here are integrated into economic life, so that one could be worried about difficulties in the labor market'.[71] Those Belgian and foreign Jews who survived the Holocaust owed their survival to spontaneous help from the local population and to the support of resistance groups. The last train to take Jews from the collection camp at Mechelen left for Auschwitz on 31 July 1944 and included the artist Felix Nußbaum, whom the National Socialists deemed a representative of 'degenerate art'. He was gassed at Auschwitz, probably on 2 August 1944.

In the Netherlands the leaders of all the country's Christian Churches protested at the deportation of Jews in July 1942. When the Reich commissar, Arthur Seyß-Inquart, agreed to exclude baptized Jews who had converted to Christianity before the German occupation, the Protestant bishops backed down, but the Catholic bishops continued to voice their objections and to inform their congregations of their anger. The authorities responded by arresting the majority of Catholic Jews in the Netherlands and deporting ninety-two of them to Auschwitz, where they were immediately gassed. One of the victims was the Carmelite nun and philosopher Edith Stein, a native of Breslau who had converted to Catholicism in 1922.

Among the German Jews who fled to the Netherlands and did not convert to Christianity was Anne Frank, who had been born in Frankfurt in

June 1929. For two years from 6 July 1942 to 4 August 1944, she and her family were able to hide in a building at the rear of a house in Amsterdam's Prinsengracht thanks to the help of a number of Dutch neighbours. She described this period in the pages of her now famous diary. She and the other Jews who were hiding in the secret annexe were denounced and arrested on 4 August 1944. Only her father, Otto, who was deported to Auschwitz, survived the war. Anne herself and her sister Margot were taken to the concentration camp at Bergen-Belsen, where they both died of typhoid fever in March 1945, shortly before the camp was liberated.

Jews living in countries occupied by the Germans could survive only by escaping – which became almost impossible in southern France, too, after that part of the country had been overrun in November 1942 – or by going underground, a move that presupposed the active assistance of non-Jews. In all the occupied countries and even in Germany itself there were individuals willing to risk life and limb by protecting Jews from their persecutors. But nowhere were there as many such individuals as in Poland, a country that had traditionally been anti-Semitic. Money and extortion also played a role here, and there is no doubt that there were many more Poles who sympathized with the extermination of the Jews and who denounced Jews who had gone into hiding than ones who helped assimilated Jews to conceal their identity, and still fewer who offered Jews somewhere to hide. Of the 3.3 million Jews who had been living in Poland in 1939, some 300,000 survived the war. Of these, 40,000 at most had remained in Poland itself.

Most of the countries that were allied to National Socialist Germany adopted an inconsistent and contradictory attitude to the extermination of the Jews, and this is even true of Fascist Italy. In the occupied parts of Greece, Croatia and southern France, Italian diplomats and army officers saved thousands of Jews from certain death by preventing them from being deported to extermination camps. In Croatia, this put them at odds not only with the Germans but also with the radically anti-Semitic Ustaše, who had already exterminated most of the Jews in those areas that were under German control or influence. On 21 August 1942 Mussolini informed his military and civilian subordinates that he supported Germany's claim to the Jews living in those parts of Croatia that were under Italian occupation. Italy's Foreign Ministry had been told shortly beforehand about the purpose of the deportation demanded by the Germans in a letter sent by the second-in-command at the German Embassy in Rome, the envoy Otto von Bismarck, who was a grandson of the founder of the Reich and whose language was unusually candid: that aim was 'the dispersal and total elimination' of all the Jews whom Germany wanted to see deported.[72]

If leading Italian military figures on the other side of the Adriatic under General Mario Roatta, the commander in chief of the Second Army in Slovenia, Dalmatia and Croatia, were unwilling to bow to Rome's directive, their reluctance was due less to humanitarian considerations than to their concern for political reality: for all their horror of the murderous racism of their German allies, they were also worried that if Germany were to be defeated, they would be regarded by the victorious powers as complicit in an appalling crime. But in spite of Roatta's objections, Mussolini ordered all Jews living in the Italian-occupied part of Croatia to be interned in the middle of October and then to be handed over to Croats and Germans. But although they were interned in a camp on the island of Rab, they were not handed over, Roatta having prevailed on the Duce to issue further instructions and defer any decision on the fate of the camp's inmates until the spring of 1943. Only after the fall of Mussolini in July 1943 and the signing of an armistice between Italy and the Western Allies on 8 September were the Germans able to seize at least some of the Jews living in those parts of Croatia that had been under Italian occupation and deport them to Auschwitz – another group had in the meantime joined Tito's partisans.

Until the summer of 1942 it looked as if another of Hitler's loyal allies, the Romanian leader Ion Antonescu, would support Germany in its quest for a 'final solution to the Jewish question', just as he had supported the Reich in its war on the Soviet Union. During the first twelve months of the war in the east, Romania's army and gendarmerie murdered between 280,000 and 380,000 Jews in the recaptured regions of Bessarabia and Northern Bukovina. And in October 1941 Romanian troops killed between 45,000 and 50,000 Jews in Odessa after marching into the city. But in the autumn of 1942, Antonescu, presumably reacting to the military defeats sustained by the Axis Powers, began to rethink his policy, and in October he postponed to the following spring the deportation of the remaining 300,000 Romanian Jews to which he had already agreed, informing one of Himmler's representatives in November that Romania disap-proved of Germany's attitude to the Jews. It is clear that the pressure exerted by Berlin on Bucharest had the opposite effect to the one intended. In the light of the military situation on the eastern front, Hitler was unable to use military force against the recalcitrant *conducator* and as a result he was obliged to accept Romania's refusal to continue with its programme of extermination.

Under Miklós Horthy, Hungary was scarcely less anti-Semitic than the Romania of Ion Antonescu. The anti-Jewish racist legislation of May 1939 was followed in the spring of 1942 by the nationalization of land under Jewish ownership. Jews were sent to the eastern front as part of a forced labour programme, resulting in countless deaths. But this period also witnessed a significant shift in Horthy's foreign policy. In March 1942, convinced that in the end the Third Reich would be defeated by the Allies, he replaced his unequivo-cally pro-German prime minister, László Bárdossy, by a landowner, Miklós Kállay. Regarded as an outspoken foe of both Hungarian National Socialism in the form of Ferenc Szálasi's Arrow Cross Fascists and of German National Socialism, Kállay sought closer ties with the Western Powers in keeping with Horthy's wishes.

Kállay initially refused to bow to Germany's demands that the Jewish Star be introduced into Hungary, too, and that he begin to deport the country's 800,000 or so Jews. Hitler met Horthy at Schloß Kleßheim near Salzburg in April 1943, but their meeting resulted in no closer agreement between the two sides. The following month Kállay insisted in an official speech that all European Jews should without exception be deported from the Continent but at the same time conceded that the most important precondition for such a policy did not exist and would not exist until a solution had been found to the problem of where the Jews should be resettled. Moreover, Kállay also professed his faith in an ideal that could hardly have been further removed from National Socialist ideology: 'Hungary will never deviate from those precepts of humanity, which, in the course of history, it has always maintained in racial and religious questions.'[73]

Barely a year later, Hitler decided to act. In order to pre-empt Hungary's switch of allegiance to the Allied camp, he gave Horthy an ultimatum when the two men met again at Schloß Kleßheim on 18 March 1944: threatening to use military force against Hungary, he compelled Horthy to agree to his country's occupation, to install a pro-German government and to make available 100,000 Jews whom he claimed were needed to work in Germany. The very next day Hungary was occupied by German troops. The former ambassador in Berlin, Döme Sztójay, was placed in charge of the government, and a number of Horthy's closest colleagues were arrested and sent to German concentration camps.

Adolf Eichmann, the head of the department responsible for Jewish affairs at the Reich Main Security Office, arrived in Budapest on 20 March and opened the final chapter in the Third Reich's attempts to deal with Hungary's Jews as part of the 'final solution of the Jewish question'. The first arrests were made in the Hungarian provinces on 7 April, a move undertaken with the active support of the gendarmerie and with the enthusiastic acclaim of sections of the local population. The first deportations to Auschwitz took place in May, with between 12,000 and 14,000 Jews setting out for the extermination camp on a daily basis.

Slovakia was already involved in this development and had been since late March 1942, when the first train left for Auschwitz carrying 999 young women. The deportation took place not in response to German demands but according to the wishes of the government under its prime minister, the fiercely anti-Semitic Vojtěch Tuka: in the wake of the large-scale 'Aryanization' of Jewish property, the government had no desire to be saddled with the welfare of impoverished Jews. Slovakia had already sent 20,000 Jews to Germany at the beginning of 1942 to work on forced labour projects – in the event they all helped to build the camp at Auschwitz-Birkenau. By the end of June 1942 some 52,000 Jews had been deported to Auschwitz and other extermination camps. At this juncture the country's president, Josef Tiso, a Catholic prelate, responding to warnings from the Vatican, raised doubts about the policy with the result that the deportations were briefly suspended, leading in turn to a muted protest from Ernst von Weizsäcker, the secretary of state at the Foreign Office. By September 1943, however, three transports again left for Auschwitz in response to German demands.

By March 1943 only around 20,000 Jews were still living in Slovakia, most of them baptized. When Tuka raised the possibility of their being deported to Germany, too, the Catholic clergy protested, as did the population at large, persuading the prime minister, Vojtěch Tuka, to abandon the idea. When Tiso met Hitler on 22 April 1943, he showed no inclination to deport the converted Jews, a position he was able to maintain largely because, given the relatively small number of Jews still living in Slovakia, Berlin had little reason to exert pressure and force the country to act.

Like Slovakia, Bulgaria was initially willing to cooperate with Germany by deporting the region's Jews, and in June 1942 parliament empowered the government of Bogdan Filov to deal with the problem. With the agreement of Tsar Boris III, the 1,100 or so Jews living in the two areas that Bulgaria had been able to annex in April 1941 on the strength of its involvement in the two German campaigns in the Balkans – the former Greek Thrace and the hitherto Yugoslav Macedonia – were handed over to the Germans in the spring of 1943 and deported to the extermination camp at Treblinka. Those Bulgarian Jews who, unlike the ones from Thrace and Macedonia, were not regarded as foreigners were to be deported soon afterwards in keeping with an agreement made between Tsar Boris and representatives of the SS, but in the wake of protests on the part of parliament and of the Orthodox Church, Boris went back on his word, with the result that Bulgaria's remaining 25,000 Jews were left in the country and in that way survived the Holocaust.

Even in Finland, where only 150 to 200 Jews of foreign extraction were living, Germany demanded a contribution to the 'final solution'. In July 1942 Himmler visited Helsinki and insisted on this demand, whereupon the country's secret police began to compile lists of names and addresses of all the individuals who were to be handed over. But the affair could not be kept quiet and there were protests both in parliament and from the public at large, with the result that of the thirty-five foreign Jews originally believed to have been on the secret police's list, just eight remained there and were deported to German-occupied Estonia in November. Only one of them survived the end of the war.

Even those European countries that remained neutral were indirectly affected by the persecution and extermination of the Continent's Jews. Although tens of thousands of Spanish volunteers from the 'Blue Division' fought on the eastern front until December 1943, Spain tried to keep its distance from the conflict and not compromise its neutrality by consorting with the dictators in Berlin and Rome or with the Anglo-Saxon democracies. As part of this balancing act, Madrid replaced its Axis-friendly foreign minister Ramón Serrano Suñer with the Anglophile Count Francisco Gómez-Jordana in September 1942, while at the same time allowing Jews who hoped to reach the West from those parts of

France that were still unoccupied to pass through Spain and Portugal. Although Portugal's dictator, Antonio Oliveira Salazar, insisted that transit visas be issued on only the most restrictive basis, many Portuguese consuls ignored Lisbon's instructions, allowing as many as 50,000 Jews to escape in this way.

Among those who sought their freedom by crossing the Pyrenees was the literary scholar and philosopher Walter Benjamin, who had emigrated to France in 1933. He was granted a visa by the American consulate in Marseilles and had also obtained transit visas for Spain and Portugal, but when he and other Jewish refugees were on the point of crossing the border at Port Bou on 26 September 1946, the Spanish border police refused to recognize the visa provided for him in Marseilles. In his despair, Benjamin abandoned his attempts to cross into Spain and took his own life that same day.

Unlike Spain and Portugal, Switzerland and Sweden remained democratic countries. In response to Swiss demands in November 1938, Germany had stamped all Jewish passports with an indelible red J, a move that Sweden adopted a little later. After this date it was practically impossible, therefore, for Jews to enter Switzerland legally. Border controls were greatly increased in 1942, and in the August of that year the cantonal authorities were instructed to send back all foreign Jews to the country's borders on the grounds that they were not political refugees: directly or indirectly such Jews would in this way fall into German hands. Until the end of 1943 this directive was more or less rigorously upheld. After that date, occasional, if rare, exceptions were made.

Until the end of 1942, Sweden adopted a similarly restrictive approach to Jewish refugees, but the country changed its policy when it became clear from news reports that Jews were being systematically exterminated in vast numbers. In response Sweden opened up its borders to Norwegian and Danish Jews. Sweden also veered from its policy of neutrality by supporting the Norwegian resistance movement, providing equipment and training its members in camps that lay close to the border. At the same time, however, the Social Democrat government helped Germany's wartime economy by means of ore and ball bearings exports. Here too there were parallels with Switzerland, which allowed Germany to transport material over the Alps to Italy, while its industry worked for the Axis Powers. On the other hand, Switzerland was dependent on coal imports from Germany. Neither Sweden nor Switzerland would have been able to maintain its independence without making concessions to Germany. But their cooperation not only helped – albeit unwittingly – to prolong the war, it also contributed indirectly to that aspect of National Socialist policy that was taken in hand only once the war had started: the final solution to the Jewish question.

Neutral countries like Sweden and Switzerland were aware from an early date that Germany was systematically murdering the Continent's Jews. In the summer of 1942, Kurt Gerstein, a devout Protestant who was a disinfection expert in the hygiene service of the Waffen-SS in Berlin and who had presumably had a subversive agenda when joining the organization, was ordered by the Reich Main Security Office to obtain around 220 pounds of Zyklon B (prussic acid) and deliver it to Lublin. In Belzec he witnessed the mass gassing of Jews and on the train journey from Warsaw to Berlin he spoke about what he had seen to an attaché at the Swedish Embassy in Berlin, Göran von Otter. He also informed the Evangelical bishop in Berlin, Otto Dibelius. Shortly afterwards, another Swedish diplomat, Karl Ingve Vendel, who was the Swedish consul in Stettin, was told about the mass killing of Jews. His informant was almost certainly Henning von Tresckow, the chief operations officer of Army Group Centre and a leading member of the military resistance to Hitler. Both of these Swedish diplomats informed the government in Stockholm about what they had learnt, but Stockholm failed to pass on their reports to the Western Allies.

Similar news reached Switzerland in the summer of 1942. The German industrialist Eduard Schulte was well connected to high-ranking figures in the National Socialist regime and in the course of a visit to Zurich told a Jewish business friend that Germany was planning to wipe out all the Jews in Europe. The business friend informed the director of the Geneva office of the World Jewish Congress, Gerhart Riegner, who in turn sent a cable to the World Jewish Congress headquarters in New York and London via the American and British legations in Berne, while at the same time questioning the reliability of the information contained in the report. In this way not only the World Jewish Congress but also the foreign ministries in London and Washington learnt about the 'final solution'. The American undersecretary of state, Sumner Welles, agreed with the president of the World Jewish Congress that they would not publish the report until they had received independent confirmation. The International Red Cross and the Swiss government reacted with similar reserve.

News of the 'final solution' became more widely known in Great Britain at the end of June 1942. In the United States the State Department saw itself compelled in November to confirm to the World Jewish Congress that Riegner's telegram was based on fact. On 10 December the British government received a detailed report from the foreign minister of the Polish government in exile, Count Edward Raczyński, spelling out all that was happening in the extermination camps. A week later the Allied governments and the National Committee of France Libre issued a declaration informing the world that the Jews of Europe were being systematically exterminated and that those responsible for these crimes would not escape retribution.

In October 1942, a Polish underground militant, Jan Karski, who had previously been able to visit the Warsaw ghetto with Jewish help, disguised himself as a Ukrainian guard and witnessed a mass execution of Jews in one of the outposts of the extermination camp at Belzec. Shortly afterwards Karski managed to escape via Germany, Vichy France, Spain and Gibraltar to London, where the Polish government in exile had summoned him to appear. His reports were initially greeted with scepticism not only in Polish and British circles but even among the Jews to whom he spoke. In July 1943 he travelled to Washington as the courier of the Polish government in exile and met Catholic archbishops, leaders of local Jewish organizations, the associate justice of the United States Supreme Court, Felix Frankfurter, and even President Roosevelt, informing them all about the situation in Poland and about the extermination of the Jews, but his first-hand reports had no practical consequences. The representatives of America's Jews were emphatic in their support for the war on National Socialist Germany but had no wish to place the president under any additional pressure where their own particular cause was concerned.

By the end of April 1944 the Allies were fully apprised of the activities of the largest of the extermination camps thanks to the Auschwitz Protocols of Rudolf Vrba and Alfréd Wetzler, two Jewish inmates who had escaped to Slovakia and whose reports reached Great Britain and America via Switzerland. But all attempts by individual Jews to persuade American leaders to bomb the gas chambers at Auschwitz or to destroy the railway line leading to the camp foundered on the lack of interest evinced by the State Department and on the resistance of the War Department. The standard argument of the opponents of the plan was that in this way resources would be diverted from areas where they were more urgently needed. In August 1944 the assistant secretary of war, John J. McCloy, offered a further objection, arguing that such an action would merely serve to encourage the Germans to commit even greater atrocities.

British reactions were equally negative. On both sides of the Atlantic, leading military figures and politicians were afraid that any increase in their commitment to the Jews would lead to greater anti-Semitic resentment at home. In certain cases anti-Jewish prejudice on the part of individual politicians may also have played a role here. At no time were there any military actions on the part of the Allies specifically designed to save the Jews. Technically speaking, it would have been possible to bomb the railway lines leading to Auschwitz: after all, industrial plants only a few miles away from the gas chambers and ovens were repeatedly attacked by Allied bombers between July and November 1944.

The Vatican, too, was well aware of what the Germans were doing to the Jews, having received reports of the mass executions in the Baltic States in early 1942 and, shortly afterwards, learning about the events in Poland and the Ukraine. But Pope Pius XII was unwilling to criticize the Third Reich publicly since he feared reprisals against Catholics in Germany and in other German-controlled parts of Europe. Like so many others, he also regarded Bolshevism as a greater danger than National Socialism. In his 1942 Christmas message he expressed his sympathy for those who had been condemned to death on national or racial grounds and for those others who had been 'consigned to a slow decline' but he reduced the impact of his criticism by referring in the same breath to the victims of air raids.

Pius passed no comment on the deportation of Rome's Jews in October 1943, and when the bishop of Berlin, Count Konrad von Preysing, wrote to him in March 1943 and asked him to speak out against the deportation of Jews elsewhere and pointed out that there were many Catholics among those who were being deported, the pope contented himself with thanking Berlin's Catholics for the love that they had shown 'so-called non-Aryans' in their time of need.[74] Throughout the war the pope behaved exactly like a diplomat for whom the interests of the Catholic Church – at least as he himself interpreted those interests – took precedence over all humanitarian considerations that others might have derived from the Christian message. The extermination of European Jews could thus proceed without any public protest from the Vatican.

In late July 1942, at more or less the same time that news of the mass gassing of Jews was reaching the West, a Jewish resistance group – the Żydowska Organizacja Bojowa, or ŻOB – was being established in the Warsaw ghetto. Its 200 or so activists obtained pistols and hand grenades from the Communist underground movement. Its activities were initially aimed at Jewish collaborators on the Jewish Council but it made little progress, and in August and September its leading members were arrested by the Germans. In spite of this setback, the organization had not been crushed, and in January 1943 its members attacked an SS escort, whereupon between 5,000 and 6,000 Jews were arrested. The ŻOB reacted by killing Jews who had been working for the Germans, including the assistant head of the Jewish ghetto police. The ŻOB's work with the Polish home guard was made more difficult by the fact that the latter had little time for the Communist tendencies of some of the Jewish resistance fighters and their links with the Communist underground. In spite of this, weapons continued to reach the ghetto.

Himmler had given orders for the Warsaw ghetto to be destroyed, starting on 19 April 1943. Its inhabitants were to be deported to the extermination camps. The ŻOB and its military arm, the Żydowski Związek Wojskowy, or ZZW, were prepared for this operation and began an armed struggle against the SS. The fighting lasted for nine days, initially in the streets, then from underground bunkers. A handful of activists avoided death by tunnelling through into the non-Jewish part of the capital. The SS used flamethrowers, machine guns, hand grenades, dynamite and tear gas. It was with some pride that SS brigade leader Jürgen Stroop was able to report on the results of his actions on 16 May 1943: 'The Jewish quarter in Warsaw exists no more.'[75] The SS claimed to have killed as many as 60,000 Jews.

The uprising in the Jewish ghetto in Warsaw was not the only act of self-defence on the part of the Jews, for armed clashes also took place in the ghettos in Bialystok and Vilnius when attempts were made to clear them. There was even a riot in the camp at Treblinka in August 1943. This was preceded by the exhumation and burning of bodies – a clear sign that the Germans were keen to remove all trace of their crimes and that the camp was being closed down in advance of the Red Army's expected arrival. Of the 850 'working Jews' who were still living in Treblinka at this time, all were killed during or soon after the uprising, the only survivors being the 100 or so who had been able to escape.

The Jews in the camp at Sobibór rose up in mid-October 1943. This camp, too, was scheduled for closure. The inmates succeeded in killing the SS guards and some 300 Jews escaped across the River Bug and sought refuge in the nearby woods, where they joined the local partisans. The SS struck before similar uprisings could take place at Majdanek and in the camps at Trawniki and Poniatowa. As part of Operation Harvest Festival some 42,400 Jews were executed in early November 1943. In order to drown out the sounds of shooting and the cries of the dying prisoners, deafening music was played over the camps' loudspeakers.

The extermination of the Sinti and Roma was relatively unsystematic when compared to that of the Jews. Although they came originally from north-west India and were therefore 'Aryan', the Sinti and Roma were still regarded as 'subhuman' by the National Socialists. Gypsies living in Germany were sent to concentration camps from as early as 1936. Within two years they were being used as forced labourers. The first mass shootings took place in 1941. By the following year gypsies were being gassed at Chelmno. In Vichy France some 30,000 Sinti and Roma were interned before being handed over to the Germans. In Poland, the Soviet Union and Serbia thousands of gypsies were murdered during the German occupation. The Ustaše regime in Croatia and Antonescu's government in Romania likewise murdered tens of thousands of gypsies. Of the 22,600 men, women and children interned in the gypsy camp at Auschwitz, 19,300 perished. Of the gypsies and 'gypsy half-castes' living in the Old Reich, around 15,000 were killed, while the figures for Austria and Czechoslovakia are 8,000 and 35,000 respectively. Estimates of the total number of gypsies murdered under German rule range from 220,000 to 500,000.

At the end of 1942 the SS decided to distinguish between the Sinti, who they argued could be traced back to their Aryan roots and who were therefore 'racially pure', and the Roma, who were said to be racially impure. As a result, the SS stopped deporting both groups to extermination camps with the immediate aim of murdering them. In 1944 as many as 2,500 half-gypsies who were described as 'non-conformist' were sterilized in Germany. The National Socialists' policy towards gypsies was riven by contradictions, motivated, as it was, by a mixture of biological racism and socio-political utilitarianism. If the desire to exterminate gypsies was less intense and less all-encompassing than was the case with the Jews, then this was due to the fact that while they were regarded as less deserving members of society, they were not held responsible for an international conspiracy. The Jews alone fell into this last-named category.

On 4 October 1943, the leader of the SS, Heinrich Himmler, addressed SS group leaders in Poznan and spoke more openly than ever before about the extermination of the Jews:

> 'The Jewish people is being exterminated,' says every party comrade, 'that's clear, it's in our party's programme, eliminating the Jews, exterminating them, that's what we're doing.' And then they all turn up, the eighty million good Germans, and each of them knows at least one decent Jew. It's clear that the others are bastards, but this one is a first-rate Jew. Of all who talk like this, not one has looked on, not one has survived it. Most of you will know what it means when one hundred corpses lie side by side, when five hundred are lying there and when one thousand are lying there. To have endured this and at the same time – always excepting the odd case of human weakness – to have remained decent: it is this that has made us strong. This is a glorious chapter in our history that has never been written and that can never be written.[76]

Two days later Himmler addressed a meeting of NSDAP Gauleiters in the city. Once again he addressed the subject of the extermination of European Jewry:

> The question has been asked of us, how it is with the women and children? I have taken the decision to achieve a clear solution also in this matter. I did not consider that I had the right to eliminate the men – that is to kill them or have them killed – and let their children grow up to become the avengers against our own sons and grandsons. The difficult decision had to be taken to have this people disappear from the face of the earth.[77]

Goebbels, too, attended the meeting of Gauleiters in Poznan and afterwards noted in his diary that Himmler had provided 'a very unvarnished and frank account' of the problem:

> He is convinced that we can solve the Jewish question throughout Europe by the end of this year. He proposes the harshest and most radical solution: to exterminate the Jews root and branch. It is certainly a logical solution, even if it is a brutal one. We have to take the responsibility of completely solving this issue in our time. Later generations will certainly not handle this problem with the courage and the ardor that are ours.[78]

Of the two great goals of National Socialism, one of them – creating more Lebensraum in the east – seemed no longer to be attainable by the autumn of 1943. Hitler had been forced to abandon Operation Citadel in the Kursk salient in the middle of July, after which the Red Army continued its western advance more or less unchecked. In August and September 1943 the Germans had to abandon the Donets Basin and the Kuban bridgehead, and in November the Dnieper Line was lost. But it still seemed as if the other great aim – the final solution of the Jewish question – might yet be achieved. That being so, the National Socialist leadership addressed this question with all the greater determination. Its ultimate aim was not the physical eradication of all Jews: after all, Hitler was convinced that Jewry had left its mark on early Christianity in such a way that the spirit of Judaism lived on in Christianity and was therefore ultimately to blame for the fact that the Aryan nations' desire to assert themselves had been fatally impaired, with the result that the struggle to defeat the Jewish spirit could be won only if Christianity was defeated first.

In his monologues in his headquarters, Hitler repeatedly returned to the idea that Jesus was an Aryan or at least a half-Aryan and that it was Paul who as a Jew had set early Christianity on a course that had led it irrevocably in the direction of Bolshevism, as Hitler explained on 21 October 1941:

> If the Jew has succeeded in destroying the Roman Empire, that's because St. Paul transformed a local movement of Aryan opposition to Jewry into a supra-temporal religion, which postulates the equality of all men amongst themselves, and their obedience to an only god. This is what caused the death of the Roman Empire. [. . .] Rome was Bolshevised, and Bolshevism produced exactly the same results in Rome as later in Russia. [. . .] Saul has changed into St. Paul, and Mardochai [the birth name of Karl Marx's grandfather] into Karl Marx. By exterminating this pest, we shall do humanity a service of which our soldiers can have no idea.[79]

Three years later, on 30 November 1944, Hitler expressed his views on the Jewish character of Christianity in the following terms:

> Jesus fought against the materialism of His age, and, therefore, against the Jews. [. . .] Paul [. . .] realised that the judicious exploitation of this idea among non-Jews would give him far greater power in the world than the promise of material profit to the Jews themselves. It was then that the future St. Paul distorted with diabolical cunning the Christian idea. Out of this idea, which was a declaration of war on the golden calf, on the egotism and the materialism of the Jews, he created a rallying point for slaves of all kinds against the élite, the masters and those in dominant authority. The religion fabricated by Paul of Tarsus, which was later called Christianity, is nothing but the Communism of to-day.[80]

Hitler's hatred of the Jews was not simply an expression of racism. The 'Negroes', whom he despised most of all, were not to be wiped out but only reduced to the status of slaves. Gypsies, whom he defined as 'foreign to the species', were persecuted and murdered because they were 'asocial'. But he felt increasing respect for the 'non-Aryan' Japanese and Chinese. The racist Hitler was aware that strictly speaking the Jews were not a race. On 3 February 1945 he dictated the following statement to Martin Bormann, the director of the party chancellery; the authenticity of the remark has been questioned:

> Spiritual race is of a tougher and more enduring kind than natural race. The Jew remains a Jew wherever he goes. He is by nature a creature who cannot be assimilated. And it is this quality of non-assimilability that determines his race and that is bound to offer us sad proof of the superiority of the 'spirit' over the 'flesh'![81]

But the physical annihilation of the Jews did not mean that the Jewish 'spirit' had been defeated once and for all. Since this spirit had been taken over into Christianity, the 'Nordic race' would still face a difficult fight even after the 'Jewish question' had been solved. As a result, the 'final military victory' would have to be followed in Hitler's view by an unprecedented cultural revolution whose aim was to rectify a historical mistake that had been committed almost 2,000 years earlier, when the Jewish spirit in Christian form had set about conquering Europe and breaking the back of the Aryan nations by robbing them of their true nature as a master race and shackling them to the alien Jewish commandment of 'Thou shalt not kill'.

Towards the end of the nineteenth century, German anti-Semites like Paul de Lagarde had commented on St Paul's alleged falsification of Jesus's teachings. Hitler took up their ideas and thought them through to their logical conclusion: the 'final solution of the Jewish question' was the necessary precondition for the removal of the influence that the Jews and Jewish Christianity continued to exert on European and world history. Only then would the true Aryan nature, no longer inhibited by the morality of compassion, be able to develop to its full extent and enable Aryan man to assert himself permanently in the struggle for existence. To achieve this goal, or at least to come as close to achieving it as possible, was the mission of the man who saw himself merely as the agent of the will of history.

Collapse of a Dictatorship: Italy 1943–4

Mussolini's Italy could not hold a candle to National Socialist Germany in terms of the intensity of its hatred of the Jews, but in terms of their domination as an occupying power the Italian Fascists did all they could to compete with their most ruthless ally. In Abyssinia Italian troops managed to kill 75,000 guerrillas before having to surrender to the British in May 1941, while the number of individuals summarily shot has been estimated at 24,000, those who died in concentration camps at a further 35,000. The Swiss historian Aram Mattioli has described the regime established by the Italians in Abyssinia between 1936 and 1941 as a 'reign of terror for which there were few precedents in the colonial history of either Africa or Asia'.[82]

The Italians were so ill prepared for their occupation of Greece that some 5 per cent of the civilian population died from starvation during the winter of 1941/2. In Croatia and Montenegro the Italian forces reacted to attacks by Tito's partisans with methods all too reminiscent of those used by the SS: torture, the shooting of hostages, the burning down of entire villages and mass deportations to concentration camps were the norm. Whenever hostages were executed, the general rule was to shoot ten of them for every officer killed or injured. In total, 100,000 Slovenians and Croats were deported in order to 'Italianize' the annexed areas as quickly and as comprehensively as possible. In this regard a particularly radical solution was found by the commander in chief of the Second Royal Army, General Mario Roatta, the same man who, as we have already observed, successfully opposed the handing over of Jews to the German authorities in the autumn of 1942.

For ideological and economic reasons as well as on the grounds of prestige, Mussolini insisted on Italy's taking part in the Germans' campaign against the Soviet Union, but the 200,000 men from the Armata Italiana in Russia (ARMIR) were ill prepared for their deployment in the east. Above all, they lacked winter clothing and heavy weapons. By the time that the Red Army recaptured Stalingrad in early February 1943, the Italians had lost 95,000 men, almost 70 per cent of their vehicles and practically all of their artillery. The number of wounded Italian soldiers ran into the tens of thousands. The Italian retreat from the eastern front in the spring of 1943 was chaotic in the extreme, and only around 10,000 of the ARMIR's soldiers ever saw their homeland again.

The fall of Stalingrad was preceded in November 1942 by the lost Battle of El Alamein. For the Italians the Axis Powers' worst defeat to date in North Africa had a similar significance to the Germans' defeat at Stalingrad and marked the beginning of the end. German and Italian forces in North Africa were obliged to capitulate in May 1943. On 10 July British and American troops under the command of General Eisenhower landed in south-east Sicily and, as the historian Jens Petersen has noted, destroyed at a stroke the National Socialist 'myth of the impregnability of Europe as a fortress'.[83] Augusta and Syracuse were left with no choice but to capitulate. Only in the north-eastern corner of the island, opposite the Strait of Messina, were German troops able to resist, at least for a time. The Allies' advance on Sicily was the main reason why Hitler abandoned Operation Citadel on 13 July and moved his Second SS Panzer Division from Russia to Italy.

Even before the Allies had invaded Sicily, Italian discontent and war-weariness had found expression in hunger strikes and, in March 1943, in major strikes that started in the Fiat Works in Turin and quickly spread to other parts of northern Italy. These were the first strikes for almost twenty years and involved up to 300,000 workers. Their primary aim was higher wages and increased food rations, but there were also calls for an immediate end to the fighting. The employers entered into negotiations with the strikers and as far as it was in their power to do so they met their demands. The state apparatus, the Fascist Party and the official corporations, conversely, remained conspicuous by their absence. The *stato corporativo* proved to be no more than a façade – a clear sign that the Fascist system was already losing its authority.

The social unrest lent moral and political support to the forces of opposition that had begun to regroup by the winter of 1942/3. The agents of the regime noted an increase in support for the Communists, but by the summer of 1943 it was a group of politicians from parties to the right of the Communists who were gaining in importance and whose figurehead was the former Reform Socialist Ivanoe Bonomi, who had been prime minister in 1921–2. Bonomi was in contact with the group of supporters associated with the daughter-in-law of the king, Princess Marie José of Piedmont, a daughter of the late king of the Belgians, Albert I. By the summer of 1942 this group was already planning a *coup d'état* against Mussolini, the aim being to topple the Duce and lock him up, after which a general would head a temporary military regime prior to the formation of a cabinet made up of older politicians whose task it would be to negotiate with the Allies in the hope of extricating Italy from the war.

By now there was also opposition to Mussolini in the Fascist Party itself. The leader of the conspirators was the president of the Chamber of Deputies, Count Dino Grandi, who was convinced that the Axis Powers were facing defeat and who also bore a personal grudge against the Duce following his dismissal as minister of justice in early February 1943. Grandi's closest allies were the former leader of the Senate, Luigi Federzoni, the corporation minister Giuseppe Bottai and Mussolini's son-in-law, the former foreign minister, Gian Galeazzo Ciano, who had been dismissed in February 1943. All three men were united by the fact that they had opposed Italy's entry into the war in 1940. In the summer of 1943 Grandi sought a reconstitutionalization of the Fascist regime under the terms of which the monarch, Senate and Chamber would be restored to their constitutional roles. A new government would be re-established on this basis and begin peace talks with the Western Allies. From 1932 to 1939 Grandi had been the Italian ambassador in London, where he had built up a good personal relationship with Churchill. By 1943 he evidently felt that he was ready to shoulder a greater challenge and, like his political friends, he was convinced that his plans could be achieved not with Mussolini but only with the Duce's removal from power.

Within the military it was the chief of the army's general staff, Vittorio Ambrosio, who was the driving force behind a faction that had grown increasingly sceptical about the Duce's leadership. From Ambrosio's standpoint, Mussolini could remain the head of the government only if he were able to persuade Hitler to accept a fundamental shift in his strategic priorities and, by ending the war in the east, concentrate the Axis Powers' military strength on the struggle with the Western Allies, especially in the Mediterranean. Alternatively, Mussolini would have to agree to Italy's complete withdrawal from the war. If Mussolini were unwilling to do this or if his approach to Hitler were unsuccessful, the Duce would have to be removed from the equation. And for this, the king's involvement would be required.

As for Victor Emanuel III, he too had good reason to distance himself from Mussolini, for if Italy was defeated, the monarchy would almost certainly be toppled. And so he needed to break off all relations with the man who had led his country into war. It seems to have been in early July 1943 that Victor Emanuel declared his willingness to have Mussolini removed by the army and the carabinieri and to replace him with a provisional government under Pietro Badoglio, the former chief of the general staff whom Mussolini had dismissed in December 1940. The more support such a move enjoyed on the part of the Fascist Party, the greater its chance of succeeding without bloodshed or a civil war. But Victor Emanuel was keen to await the outcome of a meeting between Hitler and Mussolini that was due to take place in Feltre in northern Italy on 19 July. In delaying his decision, the king still hoped that Italy's withdrawal from the war might be achieved by diplomatic means and with Germany's agreement.

The meeting between the Führer and the Duce that took place in Feltre consisted for the most part of an interminable monologue on the part of Hitler, who expatiated for hours on the importance of the Ukraine and the Balkans to Germany's wartime economy. Mussolini, who was in particularly poor health by this date, demanded increased military support from Germany but otherwise was essentially content to listen, in which regard he disappointed the hopes of the army's leaders, notably Ambrosio himself, who had travelled to Feltre with Mussolini and who urged the latter to draw attention to Italy's desperate plight and to the need to end the war in the shortest possible time. While the two dictators were conferring in Feltre, the Allies were bombing Rome. Although it was only one of many air raids that helped to depress the mood and morale of the Italian people in the course of 1943, it was the first attack on the Italian capital and, as such, it had a particular political and symbolic significance.

That same day the conspiracy against the Duce assumed a more concrete form when the king agreed to Mussolini's dismissal. Grandi drew up various documents spelling out his ideas on Italy's return to constitutional rule and the abolition of the Duce's dictatorship. He submitted his plans to Mussolini on 21 July, plans proposed not only by Grandi and his allies but also by more moderate Fascists, including those well disposed to the monarchy. Mussolini was in fact already aware of them thanks to Roberto Farinacci, the Fascist Party's radical leader in Cremona. Mussolini agreed to Farinacci's suggestion that his enemies be called to account at a meeting of the Gran Consiglio del Fascismo, the party's supreme committee, which had not been convened for many years. Mussolini proposed the time and place of the meeting: late in the evening of 24 July at his own official headquarters, the Palazzo Venezia.

Mussolini committed a serious error at the meeting, for although the Gran Consiglio was merely an advisory body with no decision-making powers, he ordered a vote on Grandi's proposal. Twenty-eight members voted for it, nineteen against, amounting to a vote of no confidence in the dictator. Mussolini still hoped for the support of the king and the military, with the result that he attributed little importance to his defeat. But Victor Emanuel III was resolved to seize his chance. The vote in the Gran Consiglio made it unlikely that the Fascist Party and its supporters would oppose the dismissal of the prime minister. But he needed to act swiftly.

When Mussolini turned up for an audience with the king at the Villa Savoia on the afternoon of 25 July, he planned merely to hand back to the king his supreme military control of the war, which had been conferred on him on 10 June 1940 without any urging on his part. But the king asked Mussolini simply for his resignation and informed him that to all intents and purposes Badoglio had already taken over the reins of government. On leaving the Villa Savoia, Mussolini was arrested by carabinieri. After being held briefly against his will on the islands of Ponza and La Maddalena off Sardinia, the disempowered Duce was taken to a hotel on the Gran Sasso in the Abruzzi mountains on 28 August.

The bloodless coup on 24/5 July 1943 was possible only because Fascist Italy was less totalitarian than the regime claimed to be. There was a legitimate force alongside and above Mussolini, namely, the monarchy, and the crisis that overtook Italy in the summer of 1943 demonstrated that the representative of the crown, not least as a result of the support that he enjoyed among army leaders, still had the ability to assume the role of a counterforce. And there was another way in which Fascist Italy was less of a Führer state than National Socialist Germany: the Third Reich had no committee comparable to the Gran Consiglio, which could be used by the country's internal opposition to subvert the man at the top. Ultimately, control over the country's population was far less tight and far less comprehensive than was the case with Italy's ally to the north of the Alps. Had it been otherwise, the strikes in the industrial areas of Turin, Milan and Genoa could not have taken place in the spring of 1943 and the Duce's dictatorship could not have imploded so unresistingly only a few months later.

Badoglio's government was no alternative Fascist regime as Grandi and his friends had envisaged, but was essentially a military cabinet that filled a handful of posts with civilian commissioners, including past and present prefects. One such portfolio was that of the minister of the interior. Until his dismissal as the chief of the general staff in 1940, Badoglio had been a loyal follower of Mussolini and had committed a number of serious war crimes in Libya and elsewhere. The jubilation that greeted the change of government and that found expression in the streets of several Italian cities on 25 July was aimed not at Badoglio but at the assumption that a peace treaty would soon be signed with the Allies.

Whenever the authorities felt that the demonstrations and strikes had gone too far, those uprisings were brutally suppressed by the police, most notably in Reggio Emilia and Bari. In the course of the clashes that took place between the state and the population all over Italy between 25 July and 8 September 1943, there were 105 fatalities, 572 injuries and 2,455 arrests. The new government made no attempt to repeal or alter the Fascists' anti-Semitic legislation but contented itself with disbanding the Fascist Party, the Gran Consiglio and the politically inspired Special Court and with incorporating the militia into the army. On 25 July Badoglio tried to reassure his country's German allies by publicly declaring that the war would continue and that Italy would keep its word.

Hitler refused to believe such assurances, which were in any case at odds with the true facts of the matter, for while Badoglio was officially seeking to persuade the Germans to allow Italy to withdraw from the war by common consent, he had secretly made contact with the Western Allies in Lisbon. In responding to Badoglio's approach the Allies were in fact flouting an agreement of 1 January 1942 in which all the Western Powers involved in the war had promised not to sign a special peace deal with any of the Axis Powers. The Americans and British insisted on Italy's unconditional surrender in keeping with the agreement reached in Casablanca in January 1943, but this was a demand that Badoglio and his government resisted for several weeks. A secret armistice was finally signed in Cassibile on the island of Sicily on 3 September. Not even Italy's own troops were informed about this treaty. That same day two British divisions landed in Calabria, and on 8 September Eisenhower in his capacity as commander in chief of the Allies announced the truce to the world. The following day American troops landed at Taranto and Salerno.

At the time of the coup, German troops were stationed not only in Sicily, where they were engaged in fighting the Allies, but also in Calabria and Sardinia, where they were supposed to establish a second front. Other German soldiers were stationed in central Italy with the aim of defending the Gulf of Genoa. When Mussolini was ousted from power, Hitler massively increased the Reich's military presence in Italy. The king and his government no longer felt safe in the capital and fled via Pescara to Brindisi on 9 September, the day after the armistice came into force. Once in Brindisi, they sought refuge with the Allies who had landed there. The Germans spoke of 'treachery' and occupied Rome on 10 September, the capital having been declared an 'open city' on 31 July.

On 12 September a unit of German paratroopers managed to free Mussolini from prison on the Gran Sasso. That same day he was flown to Vienna on Hitler's orders and on the 13th he met the Führer at the latter's headquarters at Rastenburg. Hitler informed him of his future role: he was to head the 'Fascist National Government' that had been formed by a number of Radical Fascists, including Roberto Farinacci, at the Germans' bidding during the night of 8/9

September. By now Mussolini regarded the term 'Fascist' as so ineffectual that he rejected it when choosing a new name for the state, the Repubblica Sociale Italiana, or RSI. The new government established its headquarters in the small town of Salò on Lake Garda, with the result that Italy's second Fascist regime has gone down in history as the 'Repubblica di Salò'.

Following the armistice, all Italian troops, no matter where they were based in Europe, were regarded as traitors and as enemy combatants by the Germans and disarmed, so that around half a million Italian soldiers now had to undertake forced labour for the Reich as prisoners of war either in Germany itself or in the occupied areas to the east. In the Balkans and especially in Greece armed conflict broke out between the Italians and their former allies in consequence of the brutal behaviour of the Wehrmacht and Waffen-SS. Some 25,000 Italian soldiers died in these clashes or perished while being transported to German-held areas. A similar number of military internees died in German camps. On the Greek island of Cephalonia 5,000 soldiers of the Divisione Acqui were shot after being taken prisoner, an unprecedented war crime committed against members of a state that until very recently had been the Reich's closest ally. In Italy itself not a few soldiers were able to avoid being disarmed and transported to Germany by going into hiding among the civilian population.

In the Balkan peninsula it was the local partisans who were the principal beneficiaries of Italy's capitulation. In Greece, Albania and Yugoslavia they captured large quantities of weapons and ammunition and in many cases were able to establish a base in those regions that had been vacated by the Italians. In Croatia the Second Italian Army surrendered to Tito's partisans. The war materials that fell into the latter's hands helped them in their struggle with their remaining enemies, the Germans, the Chetniks and the Ustaše. The Ustaše likewise benefited from Italy's withdrawal from the Axis alliance, for the Ustaše state was able to rid itself of a troublesome protector and annex the coastal region along the Adriatic that the Italians had overrun in 1940.

By the autumn of 1943 Italy was no longer under a single rule. The royalist government under Badoglio set up its headquarters in Salerno but enjoyed limited authority only in those areas in the south of Italy that were occupied by the Allies. To the north of the Gulf of Gaeta, where the Allied offensive became bogged down for some time, Mussolini's Repubblica Sociale Italiana was in theoretical control but in practical terms, central Italy, with the exception of Rome, was largely administered by the German military under General Field Marshal Albert Kesselring. In the north two operational zones were created as separate entities cut off from the rest of Italy, namely, the foothills of the Alps and the Adriatic coast, which were administered by the Gauleiters of the Tyrol and Carinthia respectively. In consequence the Salò government was effectively left with only the areas to the north and south of the Po, including Romagna, which it administered under the watchful eye of the plenipotentiary of the Greater German Reich, the diplomat Rudolf Rahn.

Mussolini's RSI presented a socialist image to the world and announced comprehensive plans for nationalization that seemed to reflect the Duce's desire to return to his roots. At the same time, however, the Partito Fascista Repubblicano that was reconstituted in November 1943 pinned its colours to the mast of a radical anti-Semitism in its 'Verona Manifesto': the Jews were excluded from the Italian nation and stripped of their last remaining rights, the others having already been removed under the race laws of 1938. Some 7,000 Jews were handed over to the Germans by Mussolini's regime and deported to extermination camps, mostly to Auschwitz. Of them, only 830 lived to see the end of the war. In Rome the Germans ensured that the 1,030 Jews living in the city were rounded up in the middle of October 1943 and sent to Auschwitz. Of them, only fifteen survived the genocide. In total, around a fifth of the 43,000 Jews who were still living in Italy in 1942 fell victim to the Holocaust.

The Salò regime held its first show trial against five defendants in Verona in early 1944. All were accused of betraying the Fascist ideal. The most prominent of the 'traitors' who came before the court was the country's foreign minister of many years' standing, Count Gian Galeazzo Ciano, Mussolini's son-in-law. Like the other defendants, he was sentenced to death and executed on 11 January 1944. The Republican National Guard and the Black Brigades that were summoned into existence in the summer of 1944, and that all party members aged between sixteen and sixty were required to join, conducted a reign of terror against all who held divergent views. Mention should also be made in this context of the Decima Mas under Prince Valerio Borghese, which was a former elite division from the marines and specialized in fighting against the partisans.

The Germans were reluctant to accept the formation of a regular army by the RSI. In the end around 43,000 men served in the Republican armed forces, while a further 70,000 fought as volunteers in the Waffen-SS or in units under the direct orders of the German High Command. Among those who remained loyal to Mussolini to the very end were not only old Fascists for whom the coup of July 1943 was an expression of opportunism, cowardice and treachery but also many younger Italians for whom the fight against Bolshevism was in itself a good enough reason to side with the Duce and, hence, with the Germans.

Of course, the Salò regime was incapable of winning over the masses with its socialist rhetoric and anti-Bolshevist propaganda. The attitude of the workforce emerged in November 1943 from a new strike at the Fiat works in Turin that on this occasion was called by the Communists and involved 50,000 workers. The proposed programme of nationalization was frustrated from the outset by the Germans, its failure contributing in no small measure to the contempt felt by the proletarian masses for the satellite regime in Salò that was entirely dependent on the Reich.

The alternative Italian government – that of Marshal Badoglio in Salerno – was in its own way no less dependent on foreign rule: formed by the Western Allies, his military regime was obliged to work with those anti-Fascist parties and groups who had merged to form the Comitato di Liberazione Nazionale in late January 1944. Among the members of this heterogeneous alliance were Communists, Socialists, left-wing Liberals and Catholics. All were initially fiercely opposed to the king and to the prime minister he had appointed, but in the spring of 1944 the leader of the Communists, Palmiro Togliatti, who had only recently returned from exile in Moscow, brought about a change of direction that reflected Stalin's orders: to free Italy from 'Nazifascismo' was to take precedence over all other goals, with the result that internal disputes now had to wait to be resolved. Joining forces with the left-wing Socialist Pietro Nenni, Togliatti aimed to bring the political left to power by democratic means and on 15 April 1944 even entered Badoglio's cabinet as a minister without portfolio. Two other eminent figures who took the same step at this time were the philosopher Benedetto Croce and Count Carlo Sforza, who had held the post of minister of the interior under Giovanni Giolitti in 1920–21 and who returned from exile in America to resume his political career.

Italy's Communist Party, the PCI, had undergone a period of reorganization during its exile in France and since 1942 had been active in the Italian underground movement. Its members were behind not only a number of strikes, including the one in Turin in November 1943, but also countless attacks on Fascist officials and collaborators as well as on landowners and employers. The PCI was by far the most powerful group within the Resistenza, which by 1943/4 had developed into a military force to be reckoned with. Meanwhile, the Socialists who were active as a guerrilla group came together in Rome in the autumn of 1943, forming the Partito Socialista di Unità Proletaria under the leadership of Pietro Nenni, Giuseppe Saragat and Lelio Basso. On the bourgeois side, the most active group in the Resistenza was the Partito d'Azione under Ferruccio Parri. The Liberals formed the Partito Liberale Italiano in July 1942, while the Freemasons, whom the Fascists had tried to suppress, were behind the Partito della Democrazia del Lavoro. The Democrazia Cristiana rose from the ashes of the Catholic Partito Popolare Italiano and the Azione Cattolica in October 1942. After 1945 the Democrazia Cristiana was to become the principal government party under the leadership of Alcide de Gasperi.

The Resistenza was fighting two enemies: the German occupiers and the Italian Fascists. It has been calculated that in the summer of 1944 there were 80,000 armed resistance fighters and that that number rose to more than 200,000 at the height of the movement's activities in the spring of 1945. Most of these *partigiani* were former members of the Royal Army who had been able to avoid being disarmed by the Germans in September 1943. Between 30,000 and 40,000 partisans are believed to have been killed in action, while around 12,000 Fascists and collaborators fell victim to the anti-Fascist vendetta. The Germans retaliated with their usual brutality whenever members of the Wehrmacht, Waffen-SS and German military police were attacked. On 24 March 1944, for example, 335 hostages were shot by an SS unit under Herbert Kappler in the

Fosse Ardeatine near Rome. Among those murdered on this occasion were leaders of the Jewish community in Rome and members of the anti-Fascist parties. And on 29 September 1944, at the village of Marzabotto to the south of Bologna, 770 civilians were executed by the SS and Wehrmacht on the orders of Major Walter Reder. A total of 9,200 men, women and children were killed by the Germans in their attempts to combat the partisans and to intimidate them by shooting hostages.

The Kingdom of Italy had already declared war on Germany on 13 October 1943. Units of the Royal Army that had been restored to combat strength were deployed by the Allies as Badoglio Divisions. But the main burden of the fighting fell on the shoulders of the Americans and of British Commonwealth troops. By the middle of August the Wehrmacht had already retreated from Sicily and, following the Allies' landing at Salerno, they withdrew to the Gustav Line at Monte Cassino and Ortona, a line they were able to defend until early 1944. At the end of January an American corps established a bridgehead at Anzio and Nettuno to the south of Rome. Finally, on 18 May, troops from New Zealand, India and Poland succeeded in taking the fortress at Monte Cassino. During the weeks that followed, the Germans were forced to retreat not only from southern Italy but from central Italy as well.

The Allies entered Rome on 4 June and once again declared it an 'open city'. Five days later, in an attempt to salvage the monarchy, Victor Emanuel III appointed his son Umberto the 'general governor of the kingdom'. Badoglio's cabinet stepped aside in order to make way for a coalition government made up of anti-Fascist parties and once again including Togliatti. Although the struggle to liberate Italy was still far from over, there could no longer be any serious doubts about its outcome in the early summer of 1944.

The Allies Advance: Eastern Asia and Europe 1943–4

The year 1943 was a decisive one not only for Germany but also for the Reich's Axis ally in the Far East, for in January the Chinese government that had been installed by the occupying power in Nanking in March 1940, as an alternative to the nationalist government of Chiang Kai-shek in Chungking, declared war on the United States and Great Britain. Yet this did little to improve Japan's strategic position vis-à-vis the Anglo-Saxon powers. In the spring of 1943 the new foreign minister in Tojo Hideki's government, Shigemitsu Mamoru, began what was from the outset an illusory attempt to use his relations with the Soviet Union to bring about a special peace between Germany and Russia in order to be able to concentrate all of his country's forces on its conflict with the Western Allies. Not quite so hopeless was the attempt to change Japan's policy in the countries it was currently occupying in south-east Asia and to shift the emphasis from the brutal exploitation of the occupied regions to the deliberate encouragement of anti-colonial movements, especially in Burma and the

Philippines. In both cases this policy led to unilateral declarations of independence: in Burma on 1 August and in the Philippines on 14 October.

A week later, on 21 October, the Indian nationalist Subhas Chandra Bose, who, as we have already noted, had escaped to Singapore on board a German submarine in June 1943 and made his way from there to Tokyo, placed himself at the head of a Free India government in the Japanese capital. On 30 October a friendship treaty was signed with the Nanking government in which Japan relinquished the special rights that it had enjoyed under the terms of the Boxer Protocol of 1901. A Greater East Asia Conference was held in Tokyo on 5 and 6 November 1943, its participants including not only Japan itself but also Manchukuo, Nanking China, Thailand (an ally of Japan), the Philippines, Burma and Bose's Free India. The results remained largely rhetorical, the participants merely agreeing to work together more closely in order to develop a common sphere of affluence in eastern Asia and to respect each other's sovereignty. Japan's new commitment to its allies and to those states that were dependent on it was a reaction not only to Italy's departure from the Axis camp but also to the defeats that it had suffered in its war with the Western Powers: in late June American forces had landed on New Guinea and on the Solomon Islands, marking the launch of a major Allied offensive in the South Pacific. On 30 September Japan moved its main line of defence back to the Mariana and Western Caroline Islands.

Tokyo's hopes that its new slogans would win massive support for Japan as a major power in the occupied countries foundered not least on the fact that its repressive policies remained largely unchanged. Forced labourers continued to be deported to Japan from China, Taiwan, Korea and most of the regions that it subsequently overran, while women were forced into prostitution within the armed forces. According to reliable estimates, one million men, women and children died from overwork in the occupied regions. A further 540,000 prisoners of war succumbed to starvation, poor hygiene and lack of medical care. In addition, 3.6 million Chinese and one million Filipinos were massacred by Japanese soldiers. 550,000 were killed by carpet bombing and by chemical and biological weapons, 250,000 by artificially induced famine. The total number of civilians killed by the Japanese in the context of their belligerent Lebensraum policy has been estimated at six million.

The harshness of Japan's colonial policy led to the formation of resistance movements in almost all of the countries that it occupied after the end of 1941. A people's army, or Hukbalahap, was created in the Philippines in 1943. Made up for the most part of impoverished peasants, it directed its activities both at the Japanese and at the upper stratum of society that was guilty of collaborating with the country's invaders. In the Malay Peninsula, it was above all ethnic Chinese who joined the anti-Japanese people's army. In French Indochina, the League for the Independence of Vietnam – the Vietminh that was formed by the Communist Party under Ho Chi Minh – resisted the foreign rule of both

Japan and France, which with Tokyo's consent maintained its administrative grip on the country until March 1945. In Burma, the Burma National Army under General Aung San, which had initially sided with Japan against the British, began its armed struggle against the occupying power in March 1945. The Anti-Fascist Freedom League that was created in August 1944 also included Communists. In the Dutch East Indies, by contrast, the independence movement under Ahmed Sukarno continued to the end to work with the Japanese, believing, as it did, that its aim of an independent Indonesia would be achieved only when the Japanese imperial armies had defeated the European colonial powers.

Between 22 and 26 November 1943 – only weeks after the Greater East Asia Conference had ended – Churchill, Roosevelt and Chiang Kai-shek met in Cairo, where they agreed on a campaign to recapture Burma, to restore Korean independence and to hand back Taiwan, the Pescadores Islands and Manchuria to the Chinese. Japan was to lose the German islands in the Pacific that it had captured after 1914, and the war with both Japan and with National Socialist Germany was to end with their unconditional surrender. Chiang Kai-shek could be satisfied with this outcome, for in Cairo the Anglo-Saxon powers had effectively acknowledged him not only as China's main representative but as the leader of a major international power.

At more or less the same time that the Cairo Conference was taking place, American troops under Chester Nimitz were landing on the Gilbert Islands, a move that triggered the legendary strategy known as 'island-hopping' or 'leap-frogging'. In December British Indian forces began their attempt to regain control of Burma, an objective in which they were soon joined by American and Chinese troops. The month of January 1944 saw the American invasion of the Marshall Islands, followed in the summer by the Mariana Islands, starting with the capture of Guam. The fall of one of the Mariana Islands, Saipan, triggered a political earthquake in Japan, forcing Tojo Hideki's government to step down on 18 July. It was replaced by a cabinet under the retired general Koiso Kuniaki, whose first action in office was to lower the age of conscription to seventeen.

The capture of the Mariana Islands also had a major strategic significance, for American bombers could now reach Japan from their new base there. Carpet bombing raids began in November 1944 and culminated on the night of 9/10 March 1945, when more than 85,000 men, women and children were killed in a single night in Tokyo, more than in any other air raid during the whole of the Second World War. American troops under General Douglas MacArthur landed on the Philippine island of Leyte in October 1944, prompting Japan to deploy most of its fleet and turning the fighting there into the biggest naval battle of the Second World War. Not even the first kamikaze attacks by Japanese pilots who packed their planes with explosives and crashed them on to the enemy warships proved effective in the longer term, for the Americans emerged victorious, albeit after suffering heavy losses.

The Philippine capital, Manila, fell to American forces in February 1945, but only after the Japanese had massacred members of the civilian population. That same month United States troops captured their first Japanese island, Iwojima, again only after sustaining many casualties. At least 7,000 American servicemen fell, while the equivalent number for the Japanese was over 20,000.

The battle for Okinawa began on 1 April, when thousands of kamikaze pilots were deployed. Four days later the Soviet Union unilaterally ended its neutrality agreement of 13 April 1941 and in doing so came closer to fulfilling a promise that it had given to the Western Allies in Yalta in early February, when it had agreed to enter the war on Japan within two or three months of Germany's capitulation. At this date there were still Japanese forces in Manchuria, Korea, large parts of China, the Dutch East Indies and Indochina. The Japanese leadership still had at its disposal some three million soldiers who had yet to see active service. Everything seemed to indicate that Japan would draw on these untapped resources in the hope of averting a military defeat.

Meanwhile, back in Europe, the Red Army succeeded in driving the Germans out of the Ukraine in March 1944 and by April had crossed the Dniester and entered Romania. The Crimea was in Soviet hands by the middle of May. In early June an offensive was launched against Finland on the Karelian Isthmus, ending with the Finns' defensive victory in the middle of July. On 31 July the Finnish prime minister, Risto Ryti, was forced to resign after he had assured Ribbentrop the previous month that he would not sign a separate peace treaty with the Soviet Union. The Finnish president, Field Marshal Carl Gustav Mannerheim, took over the running of the country and on 2 September met one of the Soviet Union's principal demands by breaking off all contact with Germany. Two days later the fighting ended. Under the terms of the truce signed in Moscow on 17 September, Finland renounced all claims to those parts of Western Karelia that it had had to cede to the Soviet Union in 1940. It also renounced the Petsamo region. The Soviet Union acquired a military base in Porkalla and received reparations amounting to $300 million, a sum that had to be paid within the space of six years.

In south-east Europe, too, the Germans lost two former allies at this time. On 20 August the Red Army advanced as far as the Romanian heartlands. Three days later King Michael dismissed his prime minister, Ion Antonescu, who was immediately arrested. And he gave orders for the fighting to stop. A German air raid on Bucharest prompted Romania to declare war on Germany on 25 April. At the end of August the Red Army occupied Bucharest and the oilfields at Ploieşti. An armistice was signed in Moscow on 12 September. Romania's southern neighbour, Bulgaria, tried to appease the Soviet Union by announcing that it was leaving the anti-Comintern pact on 2 September, an announcement precipitated by the fact that the Red Army had reached the Danube at Giurgiu. But this was insufficient to prevent the Soviet Union from declaring war on Sofia on 5 September. On 8/9 September a coup brought to power a pro-Soviet, Communist-dominated government under Kimon Georgiev. Shortly afterwards Bulgaria was overrun by the Red Army. On 11 October Sofia formally renounced those parts of Greece and Macedonia that it had captured in 1940. An armistice was signed in Moscow on 28 October between Bulgaria on the one hand and the Soviet Union, Great Britain and the United States on the other.

The Red Army's advance was everywhere accompanied by the ruthless persecution of political enemies and by a comprehensive resettlement programme. In the run-up to the summer offensive of 1944 some 300,000 Poles pre-empted the Soviet advance by fleeing from Volhynia and Eastern Galicia to the Polish heartlands. Between 1944 and 1946 a total of 800,000 Poles were relocated from the Ukraine to Poland, while 500,000 Ukrainians were moved from Poland to the Ukraine. Even before the return of the Red Army, the virulently nationalist and anti-Semitic Ukraińska Povstanska Armija – the Ukrainian Insurgent Army, or UPA – had been committing acts of terror against Polish settlers: some 80,000 Poles, including women and children, were murdered by them. The counter-terror of the Polish Home Army, or Armia Krajowa, is believed to have cost the lives of around 20,000 Ukrainians.

The Red Army launched Operation Bagration on 22 June 1944, the third anniversary of Germany's invasion of the Soviet Union. Named after a tsarist general at the time of the Napoleonic Wars, this major offensive was aimed at Army Group Centre, which was currently occupying the front line between Vitebsk and Bobruisk. Within days the Wehrmacht had sustained losses far in excess of those incurred during the Stalingrad debacle. Soviet troops took the White Russian capital Minsk on 3 July. Since the start of the offensive twenty-eight German divisions had been crushed and around 350,000 men killed. Shortly afterwards a second major Soviet offensive was launched in Galicia, allowing the Red Army to continue its western advance. Soviet troops crossed the River Bug on 20 July, and by the end of the month their leading tank divisions had reached the eastern suburbs of Warsaw.

During their summit meeting in Teheran between 28 November and 1 December 1943, Stalin, Roosevelt and Churchill had already agreed in principle to move Poland further to the west. The country's eastern border was essentially to be the one proposed by Britain's foreign secretary, Lord Curzon, in 1912, while the area around Bialystok was to fall to Poland, the northern section of East Prussia, including Königsberg, to the Soviet Union. The modified Curzon Line secured for the Soviet Union nine-tenths of the spoils of war that it had already received under the terms of the Molotov–Ribbentrop Pact of 1939. As for Poland's western border, Stalin and Churchill agreed in Teheran that it should be the River Oder. In order not to antagonize Polish voters at home, Roosevelt preferred not to be so specific. But the Allies were in no doubt that any territorial losses to the Soviet Union in the east of Poland should be counterbalanced by gains in the west at the expense of Germany. On 22 February 1944 Churchill told the House of Commons that this agreement was the best solution possible to the Polish question.

The Polish government in exile in London was now headed by Stanisław Mikołajczyk, the successor of Władisław Sikorski who had been killed in a plane crash at Gibraltar on 4 July 1943. He agreed to his country's western expansion but in spite of the accord reached in Teheran he was keen to retain the eastern border laid down by the Peace of Riga that had been signed in March 1921. This placed the frontier some 150 miles to the east of the Curzon Line. Diplomatic relations between Moscow and the government in exile had been broken off in April 1943 in the wake of the murder of thousands of Polish officers by the GPU at Katyn. On 1 January 1944 a National Council was established in Warsaw under the leadership of the Communist Bolesław Bierut and immediately formed an Armia Ludowa (People's Army) to counteract the Armia Krajowa. On 22 July Moscow Radio announced the formation of a Polish Committee for National Liberation – also known as the Lublin Committee – under the Socialist Edward Osóbka-Morawski. It was nothing less than a Communist-run alternative to the government in exile in London.

The Armia Krajowa, which had played a part in the liberation of Vilnius in July 1944, was offered an alternative by the Red Army: either it should join the Polish Army in exile under Zygmunt Berling that was now fighting on the Soviet side or it should disarm. Officers from the underground army who rejected both options were taken prisoner and either deported to the east or shot. Many of those who were able to escape from Soviet clutches later joined the Communist underground.

For the Polish Home Army, the Red Army's military successes in Poland were arguably the main reason why its members finally felt able to launch a long-planned operation in Warsaw on 1 August 1944 and rise up against the German occupiers. The capital was to be liberated by Poles before the Soviet troops arrived. The Armia Krajowa's decision was also motivated by Claus Schenk von Stauffenberg's failed attempt to assassinate Hitler on 20 July 1944, an event that was widely seen as a harbinger of the imminent collapse of National Socialist Germany. The Home Army had received weapons and munitions by air from the Western Allies, albeit on a much smaller scale than had been the case with the French Resistance. It is reckoned that 40,000 armed fighters took part in the Warsaw Uprising. They were led by the commander of the Home Army, General Tadeusz Bór-Komorowski.

Two days after the uprising began, the prime minister, Stanisław Mikołajczyk, responding to an invitation from Stalin and at the urging of the British, opened talks with representatives of the Lublin Committee in Moscow, but by the time the negotiations ended on 10 August, the two sides were no closer together. Meanwhile the rebels, cheered on by the local population, had liberated large sections of the capital. By 4 August, however, the

Germans had launched a counterattack. Both Hitler and Himmler were keen to see Warsaw razed to the ground as the home of the Polish intelligentsia and of the national resistance movement. The rebels were to be shot on sight, no matter whether they were engaged in fighting or not. And the non-combatant population, too, was to be gunned down. The German counteroffensive was placed in the hands of Erich von dem Bach-Zelewski, an SS group leader. The street fighting was accompanied by artillery fire and flamethrowers, while the Luftwaffe rained down bombs on the city. One of the worst atrocities, involving the murder of 40,000 men, women and children, including wounded fighters and the doctors and nurses caring for them, was committed on 5 and 6 August by the Dirlewanger Brigade that had previously massacred large numbers of civilians in White Russia. Members of another special unit raped thousands of Polish women.

By the time the Warsaw Uprising ended on 2 October with the capitulation of the Home Army, the number of Polish victims was somewhere between 150,000 and 180,000, nine-tenths of whom were civilians. Those of the city's inhabitants who had survived were driven out of Warsaw, after which the Germans began systematically to destroy the capital and its cultural treasures. The mass murders committed in Warsaw between August and October 1944 were perpetrated not only by Germans and by their hired thugs, including Red Army deserters from Azerbaijan, but also by 'a passive accomplice in the form of the Soviet Union', to quote the Polish historian Włodzimierz Borodziej.[84] Soviet troops lay to the east of the city but did nothing to help the rebels. Stalin also refused to allow the Western Allies to intervene. Until 10 February American aircraft were prevented from using Soviet airports. A single aid flight to the Polish capital was the only concession that Russia was willing to make.

If the rebels had triumphed, then from Stalin's point of view the 'wrong' Poles would have won – not his own Poles, but those who sympathized with the Western Allies. In turn this meant leaving the Germans to deal with the most active section of the Polish population, a section that Stalin fully expected would become his enemies in the future. Once Hitler's Germany was defeated, the 'right' Poland – that of the Lublin Committee – would be in a far better position than it had been before the Warsaw Uprising. Stalin was perfectly willing to accept that the Western Allies would regard his country's attitude to the Polish uprising as a deliberate slap in the face.

On 9 October, just under a week after the Warsaw Uprising had been suppressed, an Anglo-Soviet conference opened in Moscow. It was attended by Churchill and Stalin and, as an observer, the American ambassador Averell Harriman. In his capacity as head of the Polish government in exile, Stanisław Mikołajczyk was asked to attend in an advisory capacity but he continued to refuse to recognize the Curzon Line as Poland's eastern border or to concede that the Lublin Committee, which was also represented at the conference and which had in the meantime assumed an executive function in the area between the Bug and the Vistula, should provide the majority of ministerial posts in a post-war cabinet. When Churchill repeated the Soviet demands regarding Poland's borders and Roosevelt, following his re-election on 7 November 1944, refused to guarantee the borders of an independent Poland, Mikołajczyk and his cabinet in exile resigned on 24 November. The new prime minister was the staunchly anti-Communist Socialist Tomasz Arciszewski. The last Polish government in exile no longer had a role to play on the international stage. In terms of Poland's domestic policies, the main beneficiaries of the Allied stance were the Lublin Committee and the National Council that was equally loyal to Moscow and that had already appointed its leader, the Communist Bolesław Bierut, as the new president of Poland.

During the initial part of the Warsaw Uprising, the Red Army had been held up by a German counterattack near the Polish capital, as well as being detained further north, close to the border with East Prussia. A new Soviet counteroffensive began on the German-Romanian front on 20 August. A few days later there was an uprising against the Germans in Slovakia, where the Red Army had in the meantime reached the Dukla Pass in the Carpathian Mountains, but by early October the Germans had succeeded in putting it down in spite of support from Soviet paratroopers. On 13 October the German Army Group North was driven from Riga and forced to retreat to Courland, where it was surrounded and continued to resist until May 1945. On 16 October Soviet troops attacked East Prussia, and although the Wehrmacht was able to recapture most of the towns taken by the Red Army, including Goldap, by early November, the eastern front had shifted, with a section of it now lying in the territory of the Old Reich.

Militarily speaking, the main event of 1944 was the formation of a second front in France, which Stalin had been demanding since 1942 but which the British and the Americans had repeatedly postponed. The Western Allies finally landed in Normandy on 6 June. Hitler and the leaders of the Wehrmacht had long been reckoning on such an offensive by the Americans and British, albeit further north than was actually the case: they had assumed that the Allies would land their troops in the Pas-de-Calais at the narrowest point of the English Channel. As a result, the Germans believed that they were relatively secure with their Atlantic Wall which they had systematically constructed along the Belgian and French coastline and which included almost 15,000 bunkers and nearly 2,700 gun emplacements. Hitler, at least, refused to believe in the possibility that the Western Powers could launch a successful invasion of France.

The Anglo-American Combined Chiefs of Staff had been set up in early 1942 and had planned Operation Overlord for 1943, then, following an agreement reached by Roosevelt and Churchill in Quebec in August 1943, set D-Day – the D stands for 'disembarkation' – as 1 May 1944 but finally delayed it until June because of bad weather. The landings were preceded by the systematic bombing of the enemy's transport links and of the missile launch sites that were currently being built in northern France.

Under Eisenhower's overall command were twenty-three infantry divisions, ten tank divisions and four air landing divisions, making a total of three million soldiers from America, Britain and the Commonwealth as well as Gaullist, Polish, Czech and Dutch volunteers. The German forces comprised 1.87 million soldiers under the supreme command of Field Marshal Gerd von Rundstedt. Three Allied air landing divisions were dropped behind the German lines on the morning of 6 June before the landing itself began. This move resulted in serious losses for the Allies. And yet even on the first day of the operation, Allied forces were able to break through the German lines at three points, allowing them to establish bridgeheads in France and in the course of the following days to create a larger area of operations.

The First American Army under General Omar Bradley succeeded in crossing the Cotentin Peninsula on 18 June. The previous day the commander of Army Group B, Field Marshal Rommel, in whom the Germans had placed their greatest hopes, was badly injured in a low-flying aircraft attack. By the end of July some 116,000 men had fallen on both sides. The Seventh German Army and parts of the Fifth Army – a total of 125,000 men – were surrounded at Falaise on 19 August, and only a fraction of them managed to escape, with 45,000 being taken prisoner. With that the Allies had effectively won. The road to Paris was now open and the actual battle for France could begin. Six months were to pass before it reached its successful conclusion.

By the end of August the Germans had lost around 250,000 men. In the course of the weeks that followed, they were able to delay the Allies' advance in several places but they could not prevent troops from the United States and France Libre from landing on the Mediterranean coast between Toulon and Cannes on 15 August. Nor could they stop de Gaulle from entering Paris on 25 August. The first German city to fall into American hands was Aachen on 21 October, and by the end of November American troops had taken Metz and Strasbourg. But then the Allied advance ground to a standstill. Since Roosevelt felt no reason to mistrust Stalin, he did not insist on his own troops entering Berlin before the Red Army. Had he done so, the post-war era would have taken a different turn.

In general the Western Allies banked on their aerial supremacy. Starting in the summer of 1943, they had increased the frequency of their air raids on German towns and cities. In late July 1943, 35,000 men, women and children in Hamburg were killed as part of Operation Gomorrah. A further 2,700 died in Berlin in November and December. In August the air raids on Peenemünde, where Germany's V-2 rockets were made, had particularly serious repercussions for the country's war effort, but even more devastating were the raids on the ball-bearing factories at Schweinfurt in October 1943. In May 1944 the Allies' combined air forces concentrated their efforts on destroying factories in the Reich and in the Protectorate of Bohemia and

Moravia where Germany was producing synthetic fuel. In July 1944 large parts of Stuttgart were bombed, and at the end of August the inner town of Königsberg was destroyed.

The Germans responded with renewed air raids on London between January and April 1944, but they were unable to break the fighting spirit of the British any more than the unmanned V-1 and V-2 missiles that were used to attack the capital from June 1944 onwards. But nor did the Allies' nightly bombing raids on larger and medium-sized German towns and cities have the desired effect, for the Germans showed no sign of rebelling against their leaders. While the majority of Germans no longer believed in an 'ultimate victory' following the military disasters at El Alamein and Stalingrad and in the wake of the landings in Sicily and of the collapse of Fascism in Italy, they had acclaimed their Führer for far too long to break with him now that the Reich's future was looking increasingly bleak. The Allies' watchword of 'unconditional surrender' had generated a sense of fatalism along a broad front: by 1943, most Germans, with the exception of only the most fanatical National Socialists, must have reckoned that their country was heading for defeat and yet they still preferred that prospect to a terror without end.

The twentieth of July 1944: German Resistance to Hitler

Between committed National Socialists and those 'party comrades' who vacillated between the cult of Hitler and a feeling of fatalism, there was a third group of Germans: those who were emphatically opposed to the Führer. To the extent that their opposition turned to active resistance, they differed from the resistance movements of other countries in that they were fighting not a foreign government or a regime installed by a foreign power but their own government: to attempt to overthrow their own leaders during the war was tantamount to breaking with traditional ideas of national loyalty, and this was a notion that gave rise to a serious crisis of conscience on the part of many Germans, especially those of a conservative frame of mind.

If organized resistance to Hitler and to his regime was to be effective, then it presupposed that those who carried it out were close to power, a paradox that became true once the National Socialists could rely on solid support among the population at large, namely, after the summer of 1933 at the latest. Among Hitler's earliest opponents were members of the country's labour movement, but they were too divided and not close enough to him to be effective in this regard. Closer to power and yet not synonymous with the innermost circle of power, conversely, were those members of the officer corps and high-ranking bureaucrats who had maintained a certain distance from National Socialist ideology or who had even turned their backs on it. Among the first group were older conservatives (in the widest sense of the term), while the second group included some of Hitler's younger opponents.

Among those who had access to the means of power were others who exercised particular authority or who had specialist knowledge. They included the former chief of the general staff, Ludwig Beck, and the former mayor of Leipzig, Carl Goerdeler; theologians of both the major denominations such as the Evangelical pastor Dietrich Bonhoeffer and, on the Catholic side, the Jesuit priest Alfred Delp; former Social Democrat politicians such as Julius Leber, Carlo Mierendorff and Theodor Haubach; and former trade union leaders such as Wilhelm Leuschner and Jakob Kaiser. (Leuschner had been a member of the free trade unions, Kaiser of their Christian counterpart.) The active officers, diplomats and civil servants who were resolved to bring down Hitler needed the assistance of experts and links to the most important groups in society. And if they were to achieve anything, the advisers and planners were dependent on the cooperation of oppositional forces in the military and civilian apparatus of state.

Politically speaking, the alliance of convenience that was forged by Hitler's enemies was a coalition extending from the Social Democrats to the German nationalists. On its right wing were convinced monarchists and the supporters of an authoritarian system, while on the left were those who advocated a single trade union and the nationalization of key industries. What united them was their conviction that tyranny must be replaced by a state under the rule of law. But the notion that bound them together could not be a return to a state like the Weimar Republic. Those Germans, including conservatives, who had opposed the first German democracy to have existed in their own lifetimes were no more likely to hanker after it after 1933 than they had welcomed it prior to that date. But even those who had once defended the Weimar Republic no longer felt that it was responsible of them to reintroduce a system that had ultimately foundered on the shortcomings inherent in its very constitution.

The aim of the Kreisau Circle associated with the lawyer Helmuth James von Moltke was to create a synthesis out of all these opposing traditions. Both on Moltke's Silesian estate at Kreisau and in the Berlin apartment of his friend Peter Yorck von Wartenburg, a government adviser with the Economic Staff East of the Wehrmacht's supreme command, conservatives and socialists pondered the question of a post-war Germany in which the opposition between 'left' and 'right' would be abolished and replaced by an order based more on smaller communities such as family, parish, homeland, profession and business than on parties and other large organizations, while self-government and federalism would provide a counterbalance to the Reich as the principal guiding force. Right up to district level, the Germans were to be allowed to vote for their representatives directly, the head of each household receiving an additional vote for every child who was not entitled to vote. Above the district level, the voting would be indirect, so that the regional assemblies would emerge from the parish and district councils, the Reichstag from the regional assemblies. In terms of their foreign policy, the members of the Kreisau Circle opposed traditional nationalism and championed a united Europe, not that this prevented their principal spokesman, Adam von Trott zu Solz, an adviser in the Information Department at the Foreign Office, from arguing for a time that parts of West Prussia and the whole of the Sudetenland should remain in German hands.

The older conservatives such as Carl Goerdeler, who was regarded as a future chancellor; the former ambassador in Rome, Ulrich von Hassell, who was seen as a prospective foreign secretary; and the Prussian finance minister Johannes Popitz were all major politicians in the Wilhelmine mould, in which regard they differed markedly from the members of the Kreisau Circle. The lands that Hitler had conquered up to 1940 were to remain German, the only exceptions being the General Government and the Protectorate of Bohemia and Moravia. Like the academics who supported National Socialism, Goerdeler, Popitz and Hassell regarded the Reich as an instrument of law and order in Europe. They rejected the methods with which Hitler planned to subjugate the lands to the east of Germany but at least until the winter of 1941/2 they felt that the war on the Soviet Union had a positive aspect to it, since the overthrow of Bolshevism and the consolidation of German hegemony could in their view be fully reconciled with their ideas on a new order in Europe.

With regard to their domestic policies, the older conservatives differed markedly from the members of the Kreisau Circle in that they were far more emphatic in their rejection of western democracy. Popitz, for example, envisaged a rigorously centralized state. In his draft version of a provisional Grundgesetz that he drew up in January 1940 Popitz granted the country's head of state an altogether dictatorial range of powers. Only in the definitive constitution was the nation to be offered the chance to exert any influence on politics through professional representation.

Goerdeler, too, sought a largely independent executive with no effective parliamentary control. The government could at any time issue decrees that would take the place of laws. To abolish them or to topple the government would require a two-thirds majority in the Reichstag. A simple majority would be sufficient if the Reichstag and the Reichsständehaus – the first chamber made up of representatives of professional organizations, the Churches and the universities – were jointly to demand that the existing government be prorogued. Half of the members of the Reichstag would be elected by the Gau councils, the other half directly by the people. Heads of households with at least three legitimate children would receive an additional vote. Laws would come into force only with the assent of the first chamber. As head of state, Goerdeler proposed a governor general, who might later step down in favour of a hereditary monarch.

Goerdeler's objections to the whole idea of the people's right of self-determination had always been a part of the conservative tradition, but this was by no means their only rationale. It was not necessary to be a conservative to conclude from the experience of Weimar that the majority could be wrong and that the majority principle should not be allowed free rein. Although Hitler did not owe his position as chancellor to free elections, his political rise was certainly the result of a choice on the part of voters who had made his party by far the largest in Germany. His abiding popularity justified mistrust in the masses' powers of judgement, a view held not only by conservatives but also by many Social Democrats. But an authoritarian system like the ones proposed by Popitz or, in a milder form, by Goerdeler could have been maintained only with the help of the military. Hitler's conservative enemies were deluding themselves if they believed that the people would settle for far fewer political rights than they had enjoyed before 1933.

In short, those conservatives who were hoping to topple Hitler from power did not need to be committed opponents of anti-Semitism since misgivings about the Jews had long been a part of the conservative tradition in Germany. Both before and after 1933 it was a part of the conservative credo that the influence of the Jews on the country's economy and culture needed to be reduced, with the result that the Nuremberg Laws struck many conservatives as an essentially valid attempt to deal with Jewish presumption. In a memorandum that he drafted in early 1941, Goerdeler, for example, expressed his desire to repeal a whole series of discriminatory measures against the Jews and to make ghetto conditions in countries occupied by Germany 'more humane', but he also thought that if the international community were to be successful in establishing a Jewish state 'in parts of either Canada or Latin America under conditions that would make life worth living', then Germany's Jews should be automatically relocated there. The only exceptions would be those Jews who had fought in the First World War, who could prove that their families had been naturalized before 1871 or who could show that they had been baptized. Other exceptions were the Christian descendants of 'mixed marriages' that predated 1933. Goerdeler was scarcely exaggerating when he claimed that these new measures would completely invalidate the Nuremberg Laws. Nor did his comment that it was a 'truism' that 'the Jewish people belong to another race' represent a departure from conservative thinking.[85]

Goerdeler's memorandum was written before the country embarked on its systematic destruction of the Jews. The members of the resistance movement spoke as one in condemning this crime. In another memorandum dating from 1944, Goerdeler wrote of the 'monstrous nature of the systematically planned and bestially executed elimination of the Jews'.[86] A young officer from the legendary Ninth Potsdam Infantry Regiment, Axel von dem Bussche, witnessed a mass execution of Jews in the Ukraine in the autumn of 1942 and decided to offer to assassinate the man responsible for ordering this atrocity. After speaking to like-minded members of the military, including Claus Schenk von Stauffenberg of the general staff, he planned to blow up both Hitler and himself during a presentation of a new army uniform, but before he could do so, he was seriously injured on the front and unable to play an active role in the conspiracy. An attempt by another young officer, Ewald Heinrich von Kleist-Schmenzin, to kill Hitler in a similar way in February 1944 was thwarted when the planned presentation was cancelled at very short notice.

Bussche and Kleist were not the only officers willing to blow themselves up with Hitler. Another member of the general staff, Colonel Rudolf-Christoph von Gersdorff, who hailed from an old Prussian family of aristocrats, began planning a similar attack in the summer of 1942 and by 21 March 1943 was ready to put it into action when showing Hitler captured enemy war material in the course of celebrations marking Heroes' Memorial Day in the Arsenal in Berlin. His plan was to explode two English limpet mines, but Hitler rushed through the exhibition so quickly that the attack could not take place. Gersdorff had already lit one of the mines but managed to prevent it from exploding. The 'Providence' so often invoked by Hitler seemed to be on his side once again.

Gersdorff had planned this attack at the urging of Colonel Henning von Tresckow, the first general staff officer of Army Group Centre and a key figure in the military resistance movement. He knew exactly what atrocities had been committed by the SS in the east since he received and signed orders to destroy alleged or real partisans, both Jewish and non-Jewish, together with members of their families, including women and children. He evidently regarded extreme measures as an unavoidable military necessity in combating partisans, and initially at least the war on Bolshevism was also his war. Not until the autumn of 1941 did he decide to resist the regime that was fighting this war: by then he was no longer in any doubt about the genocidal intentions of the National Socialists towards the Jews and, hence, about the fundamentally criminal character of the Third Reich. From then on it was clear to Tresckow that only the removal of Hitler could put an end to the murders.

The man who planned to kill Hitler in the Wolfsschanze – the Führer's headquarters at Rastenburg in East Prussia – on 20 July 1944 came from a family of Catholic aristocrats in Swabia. Like his brother Berthold, Colonel Claus Schenk von Stauffenberg had been one of the disciples of the poet Stefan George and shared the latter's dream of an aristocracy of the mind as well as of a 'new Reich' and of a Germany that was more inward-looking. Both brothers initially regarded National Socialism as an opportunity to create a national community that overcame all divisions, and even racism seemed to them to be a healthy phenomenon, although both of them regarded the racial policies of National Socialism as a dangerous exaggeration of a basically sound idea.

When Helmuth von Moltke put out feelers in 1941 or early 1942 to see if Stauffenberg was willing to join the resistance movement, Stauffenberg's initial answer was no: Germany first had to win the war, for not until after the war on Bolshevism was it possible to deal with the 'Nazi plague'. Only during 1942 did Stauffenberg change his mind and realize that Hitler must be removed from power while the war was still in progress. By now he was convinced that

Germany could no longer win the war but that a defeat in the east could still perhaps be averted. In October 1943 he was appointed chief of staff to the commander of the Replacement Army that was charged with training soldiers to reinforce first-line divisions at the front, a position that had considerable strategic significance for the conspiracy and that granted him access to Hitler.

Stauffenberg's bomb exploded only after he had left Hitler's headquarters at Rastenburg and was already on his way back to Berlin. The actions carried out by the conspirators from the Wehrmacht's high command on 20 July 1944 in their attempt to topple the National Socialist regime were doomed in advance to failure since their basic assumption was flawed: Hitler was not dead but had survived the attack with only minor injuries.

That same evening Stauffenberg and his fellow conspirators – Friedrich Olbricht, Albrecht Mertz von Quirnheim and Werner von Haeften – were shot in the courtyard of the Wehrmacht's high command on the orders of General Friedrich Fromm, the commander of the Replacement Army. Ludwig Beck, who was to have become head of state if the coup had succeeded, was already dead at this point. At Fromm's insistence he had tried to shoot himself but, having failed, was then shot dead by a sergeant. The following day Henning von Tresckow took his own life on the eastern front at Ostrów in Poland, where he faked an enemy grenade attack, a move dictated by the fear that he would be tortured into revealing the names of his fellow conspirators.

Hitler wrought terrible revenge on all who were directly or indirectly implicated in the plot, but he was unable to prevent one defendant after another from admitting to his guilt at the People's Court in Berlin and openly defying the tyrannical court president, Roland Freisler. Ulrich Wilhelm Schwerin von Schwanenfeld, who worked in the quartermaster general's office, gave 'the many murders in Poland' as his reason for acting as he did. Count Peter Yorck declared that 'what matters is what links all these questions together, the state's totalitarian claims on the citizen to the exclusion of his religious obligation to God'. Hans-Bernd von Haeften, an adviser to the Foreign Office and the elder brother of Werner von Haeften, was also speaking for his friends when he said that 'my view of the Führer's role in world history is that he is a great agent of evil'.[87]

Of those whom Freisler sentenced to death, the first eight, including Field Marshal Erwin von Witzleben, General Erich Hoepner and Yorck, were hanged at Plötzensee Prison immediately after the sentence was handed down on 8 August. The others had to wait. Julius Leber, whom the Gestapo had arrested on 5 July on the strength of his contacts with the illegal German Communist Party, was sentenced to death on 20 October and executed on 5 January 1945. Goerdeler was sentenced on 8 September, though it was not until 2 February 1945 that he was executed. Moltke was sentenced and executed in January 1945. The same fate befell Father Alfred Delp on 2 February. Dietrich Bonhoeffer, who had been arrested in early 1943, was sent to the Flossenbürg concentration camp in February 1945 and after a summary trial was executed on 9 April. The total number of executions related to the events of 20 July 1944 was around 200.

But even if Hitler had been killed in the assassination attempt, this would not have meant that the conspirators would have won, for they had little support in the population at large. According to official reports, most Germans were outraged by the attack, and there was much joy at the news that Hitler had suffered only minor injuries. The president of the Nuremberg Court of Appeal observed that the attempted assassination was

> repudiated even by those who are not outspoken National Socialists, not only because of their repugnance at the crime itself but also because they are convinced that the Führer alone can control the situation and that his death would result in chaos and civil war.[88]

This was by no means an unrealistic assessment of the situation, for a power struggle among leading National Socialists in the wake of Hitler's death was entirely predictable. Through his contacts with Popitz even Himmler was implicated in the conspiracy, although there was no evidence that the Wehrmacht as a whole would side with the conspirators. Stauffenberg and his friends were convinced that they would have been accused of stabbing the troops in the back. The National Socialists' claim that the conspiracy was the work of a small and reactionary minority fell on fertile ground. Although the 'Hitler myth' may now have been fatally undermined, it had still not been definitively scotched. Indeed, the failed attempt to kill Hitler on 20 July 1944 even led to a brief revival of the myth, with many Germans believing that Hitler was really in league with 'Providence' and that only through him could Germany still be saved.

Those who had been involved in the events of 20 July 1944 could not be in any doubt that Hitler was more popular than they were. It was also highly unlikely that they would ever have been able to convince the German people of the need for an act of tyrannicide by subsequently exposing the crimes of the National Socialists. And once Churchill and Roosevelt had demanded the Germans' unconditional surrender at their conference in Casablanca in January 1943, the conspirators could not even be certain that the Allies would impose more lenient terms on Hitler's enemies than they would on a Germany led by the National Socialists. But for the core group of the resistance, the success of their action in the summer of 1944 was not what mattered. What mattered to them above all was that the world and coming generations of Germans should know that Hitler was not Germany but that there was another, better Germany.

For all those who thought along these lines it was a question of honour to act in the way that the conspirators of 20 July had done. Most of them had become active members of the resistance movement only at a relatively late date. Their outlook was 'nationalist' and so there was much about National Socialism that was not at all alien to their thinking. For them, the war was by no means only Hitler's but also their own, its aim being not only to assert Germany's leading role in the world but also, after the summer of 1941, to combat an aggressive and criminal system in the form of Bolshevism. The realization that they themselves were serving an aggressive and criminal system finally came to them all, in some cases sooner than others. Whether they were willing to admit it or not, all of them were guilty to varying degrees. To risk their lives in rebelling against Hitler was a way of atoning for that guilt.

A different Germany was arraigned before Roland Freisler's court, for its finest representatives had been acting according to a tradition that was marked by Christian, humanitarian, Kantian and Prussian ideals. This was a tradition that acknowledged an authority higher than the state and the man in charge of that state, namely, the individual conscience. Inasmuch as the conspirators had been following the dictates of their conscience, 20 July 1944 was a great day in recent German history. Two other dates that have gone down in the annals of the German resistance to Hitler have an equally high moral status: 8 November 1939, the day on which the Württemberg carpenter Johannes Georg Elser tried to kill Hitler with a homemade bomb during the Führer's anniversary visit to the Bürgerbräukeller in Munich; and 18 February 1943, when Hans and Sophie Scholl, the founders of the White Rose student organization, responded to the defeat at Stalingrad by distributing hundreds of leaflets in the courtyard at Munich University, protesting in that way at Hitler's unconscionable leadership.

Elser, who was a simple man acting alone, and Hans Scholl and his sister, together with their fellow students Christoph Probst, Alexander Schmorell and Willi Graf and their academic mentor Kurt Huber, all suffered the same fate as the conspirators of 20 July 1944: they were all executed. If they and others had not risen up against Hitler, the Germans would have had little to look back on after the end of the National Socialists' rule that could have given them cause for hope as they contemplated the events of the years from 1933 to 1945.

The Partition of Europe (I): The Allies' Post-war Plans

Right until the very end a number of Hitler's principal enemies, most notably Carl Friedrich Goerdeler, still hoped that the overthrow of the National Socialist regime would place Germany in a position to conclude a peace treaty with the Allies that would be based on mutual understanding. But once Churchill and Roosevelt had referred to the Axis Powers' 'unconditional surrender' in Casablanca, this was no longer a realistic expectation. The Normandy landings in June 1944 merely served to stiffen London's and Washington's resolve. Churchill, who was fully informed about the aims of the conspirators in Berlin, while at the same time feeling a profound distrust of all things Prussian, believed that he needed to speak dismissively of the group of individuals associated with the events of 20 July when he addressed the House of Commons on 2 August 1944:

the attack on Hitler, he insisted, was no more than an example of infighting among the leading figures in the Reich.

Central to Allied plans for a post-war Germany was the 'dismemberment' of the Reich. One of the first leaders to propose this idea was Stalin in talks with the British foreign secretary Anthony Eden in December 1941, when the Soviet leader had suggested that the Rhineland be taken out of Prussian hands and that East Prussia be ceded to Poland, while Bavaria was to become an independent state. In October 1943 the foreign ministers of the United States, Great Britain and the Soviet Union – Cordell Hull, Eden and Vyacheslav Molotov – met in Moscow and agreed that the borders of an independent Austria should return to what they had been in 1938 and that East Prussia should be ceded to Poland. Details were to be drawn up by the European Advisory Commission, which had its headquarters in London.

As we have already noted, Roosevelt, Stalin and Churchill met in Teheran between 28 November and 1 December 1943 and agreed that Poland should be moved further west and that the northern part of East Prussia should pass into Soviet hands. They also agreed, in principle at least, that Germany should be dismembered. At the final session of the talks, Churchill demanded that Prussia be isolated and treated more harshly than the rest of Germany, which was to form a separate state. He also proposed the formation of something like a Danube Federation comprising Bavaria, Austria and possibly also Hungary. Roosevelt was in favour of five autonomous German states: first, Prussia; second, Hanover and north-west Germany; third, Saxony; fourth, Hessen; and, fifth, Bavaria, Baden and Württemberg. The Ruhr and the Saarland should no longer be under German sovereignty but governed by the United Nations. Although Stalin was more inclined to side with Roosevelt than with Churchill, no binding decisions were taken in Teheran, and the three leaders left it to the European Advisory Commission to discuss all remaining aspects of Germany's partition.

In terms of Germany's treatment in the future, opinions differed greatly even within the American government. Cordell Hull advocated a voluntary fragmentation of Germany, a view based on his belief that there were powerful separatist movements in the west and south of the country. The assistant secretary of state, Sumner Welles, on the other hand, was emphatically in favour of force to implement Germany's dismemberment. The treasury secretary Henry Morgenthau went even further: he wanted the southern part of East Prussia and the whole of Silesia to pass to Poland, while France was handed the Saarland and all the territories to the west of the Rhine and Mosel. He also wanted the Ruhr to be placed under international control and the rest of Germany to be divided into two autonomous states: a northern half and a southern half. In order that Germany would never again pose a threat to the rest of the world, the country was to be radically de-industrialized and turned back into an agrarian economy.

When they met in Quebec in September 1944, Roosevelt and Churchill expressed their support for Morgenthau's plan. But by 22 September Roosevelt had withdrawn his imprimatur, a move influenced by the objections of Hull as secretary of state, of Stimson as secretary of war and of Stimson's assistant, John McCloy, all of whom had persuaded him that Morgenthau's ideas for a re-agrarianized Germany were the product of backward-looking wishful thinking and would be fatal for Europe's economic revival. Shortly afterwards Churchill, too, distanced himself from the Morgenthau Plan.

Of course, the Allies' agenda continued to include the partition of Germany. On 27 October 1944 Churchill cabled Roosevelt, informing him about his talks with Stalin in Moscow and noting that the Soviet leader had given his approval to the idea of separating the Ruhr and the Saarland from Prussia and of creating an independent Rhineland and a southern German state that would include Austria and have its capital in Vienna. Yet another set of ideas was proposed by the new provisional government of the French Republic that had been formed under de Gaulle on 10 September 1944 and that the Allies recognized on 23 October: the left bank of the Rhine was to be removed from German control, while the Rhine as far as a point to the north of Cologne was to become the new permanent French border; the Ruhr was to become international and the Saarland would be annexed by France; there would also be a French-occupied zone in south-west Germany. Germany would henceforth be a collection of states that would at best be loosely held together. During a visit to Moscow in December 1944, when a twenty-year pact of alliance was signed between France and the Soviet Union, de Gaulle expressed his agreement with the proposed relocation of the German-Polish border along the Oder–Neiße Line, but Stalin declined to agree to French demands that the Rhine should become the new border between Germany and France.

The American presidential elections on 7 November 1944 provided Roosevelt with a domestic distraction between Churchill's visit to Moscow in October 1944 and the planned summit of the three leaders in early 1945. The Republican candidate was the governor of New York, Thomas E. Dewey, one of the most active politicians of the younger generation, while the Democrat candidate was Roosevelt, hoping to enter the White House for the fourth time in his career. As Roosevelt's running mate the party passed over the present incumbent as vice-president, the New Dealer Henry Wallace, and instead chose the Missouri senator, Harry S. Truman, who was regarded as relatively conservative. Although Roosevelt was by now in poor health, not least as a result of progressive arteriosclerosis, his campaign proved effective and he again triumphed at the polls, winning 53.5 per cent of the vote, while his rival won 46 per cent. In the Senate the Democrats lost one seat but won twenty more seats in the House of Representatives, with the result that the president's party was able to maintain its majority in both houses of Congress.

On 4 February 1945, three months after the presidential elections, Roosevelt, Churchill and Stalin met at Yalta in the Crimea, whither they were accompanied by their foreign ministers, leading members of their armed forces and their principal political advisers. The conference took place at a time when the American military was reckoning on having to fight a lengthy war in the Far East, possibly lasting until 1946 and involving the loss of a further one million American soldiers. It seemed to Roosevelt to be all the more important, therefore, to persuade the Soviet Union to build up a second front against Japan.

Stalin was willing in principle not only to end the neutrality agreement that he had signed with Tokyo in April 1941 and which was due to last five years but also to enter the war against Japan within three months of Germany's surrender. However, he attached rigorous conditions to this second step: Russia was to be handed back both the Kuril Islands that the tsarist empire had ceded to Japan in 1875 and southern Sakhalin, which Russia had lost to Japan in 1904/5. Russia's old rights to railways and ports in Manchuria were also to be restored. Roosevelt agreed to these demands on condition that he also had the backing of Chiang Kai-shek and in this way he made it possible for Moscow to end the Soviet-Japanese neutrality agreement, which was done on 5 April 1945, albeit initially purely as a symbolic gesture.

The desire to end the war in East Asia and in the Pacific as quickly as possible with Soviet help was not the only reason why Roosevelt was far more willing than Churchill to accommodate Stalin's wishes in Yalta. Ever since the summit in Teheran, Roosevelt had regarded the United States and the Soviet Union as the two world powers on whose close cooperation the preservation of world peace would primarily depend in the future. Such a joint agreement presupposed mutual trust, and Roosevelt was willing to place that trust in Stalin if the Soviet leader was prepared to do the same.

When, in Yalta, the Soviet dictator repeated his demand that Germany be dismembered, Roosevelt did not contradict him. But Churchill and above all Eden now had misgivings about such a policy, since they believed that the Soviet Union would derive the principal benefit from it. The outcome of their discussions was a compromise: although Germany's dismemberment was formally agreed, a new committee was set up with the aim of advising on the matter. In this way a decision was deferred.

All three leaders agreed that absolute power over Germany should be placed in the hands of the Allies, who committed themselves only to 'take such steps, including the complete disarmament, demilitarization and dismemberment of Germany, as they deem requisite for future peace and security'.[89] In keeping with a promise that Stalin had given to Churchill in October 1944 France was to have a seat on the Allied Control Council and was to be given an occupied zone in south-west Germany, which would be created at the expense of the American and British zones. But France did not have a seat on the Committee on Dismemberment of Germany.

In every other respect the division into zones reflected the one agreed to by the European Advisory Commission between September and November 1944: the south of Germany, including Hessen, was to be a part of the American zone, to which Bremen and Bremerhaven were added as an enclave in early 1947; the British zone comprised north-west Germany; and the Soviet zone was made up of eastern and central Germany, its border running to the west of Lübeck and along the Elbe to the north of Wittenberge, after which it followed the western borders of the Prussian province of Saxony and of the Länder of Thuringia and Saxony, ending at the western border of Czechoslovakia. Berlin was to be divided into four sectors. Similar provisions were made for Vienna and Austria. The question of reparations remained unresolved. Like the problem of Germany's dismemberment, it was passed on to a special commission that would examine the matter more closely and that would be set up in Moscow.

Germany's future was only one of the subjects that exercised the Big Three during their week-long summit in Yalta. The modified Curzon Line was recognized as Poland's eastern border. Neither Britain nor America wanted to extend the country as far as the River Oder. Churchill turned down Stalin's demand that the Oder–Neiße Line should be its western border, famously commenting that 'It would be a great pity to stuff the Polish goose so full of German food that it died of indigestion.'[90] In view of these differences of opinion the three leaders merely promised to ensure that Poland would receive a considerable increase in its territory in the north and west but without committing themselves to solving the question of where its border should lie.

All the participants were well aware that if Poland were to be moved further west, this would involve the enforced resettlement of millions of men, women and children. Churchill had already told the House of Commons on 15 December 1944 that 'a clean sweep' was necessary and that the 'expulsion' of the Germans living in the eastern parts of the Reich was 'the most satisfactory and lasting' way of achieving that goal. He refused to accept that there was no room in Germany for the population of those areas that were to be ceded to Poland (and in the case of the northern part of East Prussia, to the Soviet Union): 'After all, 6,000,000 or 7,000,000 Germans have been killed already in this frightful war. [. . .] Moreover, we must expect that many more Germans will be killed in the fighting which will occupy the spring and summer.'[91]

The leaders of the Western Powers showed rather more qualms when it came to Stalin's demand that they all recognize the Polish provisional government, the former Lublin Committee that had been installed by the Communists on Soviet instructions. Churchill pointed out that the sovereign independence and freedom of Poland were a question of honour for Great Britain, although he was willing to compromise in this regard. Both Churchill and Roosevelt agreed that the provisional government should be expanded by the inclusion of 'democratic leaders' currently living in exile and in Poland itself, after which it would gain general acceptance. But in fact both leaders had by this point already withdrawn their support for the government in exile in London, whose prime minister, the Socialist Tomasz Arciszewski, was unwilling to make any compromises. Instead, they accepted Stalin's promise that free elections would be held in Poland, perhaps within a month, and in that way – without being conscious of what they were doing – they sealed the fate of the country for whose sake Great Britain had declared war on Germany in September 1939.

Churchill's willingness to abandon Poland was part of a wider strategy that involved the division of south-east and eastern central Europe into zones of interest. In May 1944 Great Britain had proposed to the Soviet Union that Romania be treated as a Soviet zone of operation, Greece as a British zone. In the course of the ensuing talks the operational zones of both powers were extended, so that Britain's came to include Yugoslavia and Russia's Bulgaria. Roosevelt agreed to this arrangement on 12 June. These spheres of influence appeared to be more clearly defined at the talks between Stalin and Churchill that were held in Moscow in October 1944 and that were also attended by the American ambassador to the Soviet Union, Averell Harriman, as an observer. According to this definition, Soviet influence in Romania was to be 90 per cent and in Bulgaria 80 per cent, while Britain ensured that it had 90 per cent control over Greece, a country it viewed as strategically very important. In the case of Hungary and Yugoslavia, they agreed on a ratio of 50:50, although in the case of Hungary this was soon altered to 80:20 in favour of the Soviet Union.

By the time the Big Three met in Yalta, there was no longer any talk of this kind of division along percentage lines. By now the Red Army had overrun Romania and Bulgaria and driven the Germans from Poland, Belgrade had been taken on 20 October 1944, and while the Allies were meeting in the Crimea, Budapest was about to fall. The Big Three welcomed the agreement between the exiled Yugoslav prime minister, Ivan Šubašić, and the leader of the Anti-Fascist Council, Marshal Tito, on forming a coalition government, although when it was constituted on 17 March 1945, the actual power lay with the Communists. In a 'Declaration on Liberated Europe', Stalin, Roosevelt and Churchill specifically referred to the Atlantic Charter when assuring all nations of the right to 'form interim governmental authorities broadly representative of all democratic elements in the population and pledged to the earliest possible establishment through free elections of governments responsive to the will of the people'.[92]

This final promise was not worth the paper it was written on, for the Western Powers handed over large tracts of south-east and eastern central Europe to the Soviet Union, a power that already had a military say in those areas following the advance of its armies and that could no longer be expelled from its new area of influence, the former anti-Bolshevik cordon sanitaire of the interwar period – or at least it could not be removed without unleashing another war. Poland was just one of the countries that had to adapt to the dictates of the new political reality.

Three formerly independent states – the Baltic republics of Estonia, Latvia and Lithuania – had not been discussed at all in either Teheran or Yalta. Stalin managed to persuade the Western Powers to agree to these countries' remaining a part of the Soviet Union, which was itself one of the outcomes of German-Soviet cooperation from 1939 to 1941. Even as early as March 1942 Churchill had demonstrated his willingness to allow the Soviet Union to retain its borders of June 1941. In August 1942 the embassies of the three Baltic States in London were removed from its list of diplomatic representatives. And although the United States continued to accept the de jure existence of the Baltic States, it accepted their de facto annexation by Soviet Russia, just as it accepted one of the consequences of the Sovietization of the Baltic region: the deportation to Siberia of large sections of the bourgeois elites and of hundreds of thousands of peasants who had opposed the enforced collectivization of agriculture. Getting into bed with Stalin demanded a high moral price in the form of a disavowal of the principles of the Atlantic Charter of August 1941, to which the Soviet Union, too, officially subscribed since signing the United Nations Charter on 1 January 1942.

At this date in its history the term 'United Nations' referred to the twenty-six states that had already declared war on Germany. But for Roosevelt the phrase meant much more, standing, as it did, for his vision of a just order of world peace or a global 'New Deal', a vision very similar to that of Woodrow Wilson in 1917/18 but one that now had a good chance of not being undermined by his enemies at home. The president hoped that the League of Nations, which had had no real significance since 1939, would be replaced by a new organization based on universal principles, responsibly led by the great powers and capable of acting in the interests of collective security: the United Nations Organization, or UNO.

Since the United States had no desire to be outvoted, it needed to have an extensive right of veto in the United Nations' most important committee, the Security Council, a right that it would share with all the other major powers. It also needed to reach a fundamental agreement with the other major power, the Soviet Union, that would guarantee lasting peace in the world. The League of Nations had been created in 1919 with the aim of safeguarding the status quo that had emerged at the end of the First World War. As envisaged by Roosevelt, the United Nations was in an even more difficult situation in 1945. As the historian and political scientist Waldemar Besson has aptly noted, it 'represented a world government designed to preserve a status quo that had not yet been established'.[93]

Stalin had initially been sceptical and even dismissive about the American project but had begun to shift his ground in 1943. At the conference of foreign ministers in Moscow in the October of that year, Molotov agreed to the proposal that once the Axis Powers had been defeated, an international organization should be set up with the aim of maintaining peace. At the talks that were held by inter-Allied experts in Dumbarton Oaks, DC, between 21 August and 7 October 1944 the structure and function of the United Nations were discussed, including a future International Court. The two Anglo-Saxon powers negotiated first with the Soviet Union, and then with the China of Chiang Kai-shek, which enjoyed the backing of the United States as the fourth major power.

The result of these discussions provided the basis for the United Nations' future charter. The Security Council could be convened at any time, in which regard it differed from the Council of the League of Nations; France was offered a permanent seat on the Council; and the major powers would all have the right of veto. No less important to the United States was the fact that in the event of an attack all member states should have the 'inherent right' to defend themselves individually and collectively until the Security Council had taken whatever steps were deemed necessary. No agreement was reached on the particular form that the right of veto should take or on the Soviet demand that all sixteen Soviet republics should have a seat and a vote in the general assembly by analogy with the Dominions of the British Commonwealth. Discussion of both of these contentious issues was deferred, with the result that both of them were again on the agenda at Yalta.

At Yalta, Roosevelt, Stalin and Churchill agreed that two of the Soviet Union's republics, the Ukraine and White Russia, should be accepted into the United Nations alongside the Soviet Union itself. The right of veto was accepted in the absolute form on which Stalin had insisted: a major power could make use of this right even when it was itself involved in a dispute. All of those states that had been at war with Germany or that had declared war on their common enemy before 1 March 1945 were to be allowed to become members of the United Nations. This second possibility was used not only by a number of Latin American republics but also by Egypt, Syria, the Lebanon and Saudi Arabia, as well as by a country that had remained neutral throughout the Second World War and broken off diplomatic relations with Germany on 2 August 1944 only in response to massive pressure from the Allies: Turkey had declared war on Germany on 23 February 1945, almost the last possible moment that it could have done so and still qualified as a member of the United Nations.

Just eight weeks later, on 25 April 1945, the inaugural conference of the United Nations met in San Francisco at the invitation of the five major powers: the United States, the Soviet Union, Great Britain, China and France. The representatives of fifty-one nations signed the UNO Charter at their first plenary session on 26 June, the same day as that on which the statute of the International Court was passed. Once the five major powers and the majority of the other signatory states had left the ratification documents with the American government, the charter could come into force on 24 October 1945.

Among the organization's primary aims were the preservation of international peace and security by means of effective collective measures; the development of friendly relations between states based on the principle of equality and the right of self-determination; international cooperation designed to solve international problems of an economic, social, cultural and humanitarian kind; and respect for human rights and basic freedoms for all without regard for race, gender, language or religion.

The dominance of the five great powers may well have instilled in the other members of the United Nations the feeling that they were second-class states, but their privileged status was essential if the new organization was to operate efficiently, for only if they backed a Security Council resolution could that resolution be implemented. It was the colonies that had far more reason to complain, for the mandated regions of the League of Nations were placed under the supervision of the UN's Trusteeship Council and as a result had neither a seat nor a vote in the general assembly. For their subsequent fate they could hope for the support of the two remaining major powers, the United States and the Soviet Union, both of which regarded themselves as anti-colonial. But in the immediate wake of the Second World War neither Washington nor Moscow could think of creating a new world order without their most important ally, Great Britain, which itself stressed the fact that it was not the only colonial power among the major powers. This also explains why Britain was so keen to see France return to the group of major powers.

The United Nations was only one of two projects with which the United States sought to place its seal on the post-war world. The other was discussed at Bretton Woods in New Hampshire between 1 and 22 July 1944. This conference was attended by members of forty-four governments in the anti-Hitler coalition and addressed questions of currency, payments and trade in the post-war period. The result bore the imprint of the American financial expert Harry Dexter White rather than that of the chief British delegate, John Maynard Keynes, and established the Bretton Woods system, which initially had two pillars to it: the International Monetary Fund, or IMF, and the World Bank. (The third pillar was to be introduced in 1947 in the form of the General Agreement on Tariffs and Trade, or GATT.) In order to ensure the free convertibility of their currencies, the member states of the IMF agreed on fixed gold and dollar parities: the dollar standard, which was initially set at \$35 per ounce of gold.

The American Central Bank was required to redeem dollars for gold whenever it was asked to do so. The other members of the Bretton Woods system were tied to the dollar by fixed exchange rates. Revaluations and devaluations within a margin of up to 20 per cent were possible only in the case of lasting imbalances and only within the context of international agreements. As a result, only the United States was genuinely independent in terms of its monetary and currency policy. The mixed gold–dollar standard was less rigid than the previous pure gold standard or the gold currency standard that had existed between 1925 and 1931: the possibility of altering the parity of all currencies in relation to gold provided a considerable degree of flexibility, as did the possibility of a limited revaluation or devaluation of individual currencies. But the Bretton Woods system could function only as long as the United States had no sizeable foreign trade deficit and pursued a policy of controlling the money supply, two preconditions that obtained only until the early 1960s.

The principal aims of the International Monetary Fund, which was a special organization of the United Nations, were international cooperation in the field of currency policy; facilitating international trade; safeguarding currency relations; creating a multilateral payment system; removing exchange controls; and making it easier to achieve a balance of payments by granting credit to member states. The task of the bank – originally called the International Bank for Reconstruction and Development – was to foster the economic development of member states by means of loans to governments and private business.

From an American perspective, the Bretton Woods initiative finally allowed the United States to take on the leading economic role that it had effectively inherited at the end of the First World War but from which it had subsequently withdrawn with catastrophic consequences for the world economy. The architects of the new currency agreement saw the United States as the new global stabilizer, a world power which in a spirit of self-interest had drawn the right conclusions from the economic and financial crises of the interwar years and placed its material resources in the service of a world economy geared to lasting, uninterrupted growth, in that way making a decisive contribution to ensuring world peace in the guise of a kind of global New Deal.

Stalin's perspective was very different: for the Soviet dictator, making the dollar the world reserve currency was clear proof of the United States' imperialist intentions, with the result that neither Soviet Russia nor the countries dependent on it signed the Bretton Woods agreement in 1945. In turn, this meant that only 'capitalist' countries were able to draw on the IMF in the case of problems with their balance of payments and to intervene in the case of major fluctuations in the value of the dollar. Tied as they were to the dollar and to gold, international exchange rates brought these nations substantial advantages over a long period of time, while the Soviet-dominated Eastern Bloc that began to emerge at that time cut itself off from everything that might serve to consolidate the United States in its hegemonic role. The outlines of the East–West confrontation of the post-war period were already clearly visible in the field of international currency even as early as 1945.

The man who had played a leading role in overcoming American isolationism did not live to see the end of the war and the foundation of the United Nations. Franklin Delano Roosevelt died of heart failure on 12 April 1945 at the age of sixty-three. It had taken him a long time to realize that his country could have a future as a world power only if it spearheaded the fight against Hitler. His attitude to Stalin and to the latter's long-term goals was marked by extraordinary naivety.

When he announced in Yalta that the United States planned to leave its troops in Europe for no more than two years after the end of the war, he unwittingly risked everything for which the American armed forces had been fighting and for which they would continue to fight.

But it was above all his charisma and his strength of will that helped America to overcome the deep depression of the 1930s and brought his country to the point at which it stood in the spring of 1945. His successor, Harry S. Truman, was a failed shopkeeper but a highly successful senator for his home state of Missouri. He lacked much of what had made FDR one of the great presidents of the United States and he had no experience in the field of foreign policy. But he was willing to learn and, as was soon to become clear, he had enough intelligence and instinct to deal with the challenges that he faced on becoming the thirty-third president of the United States on 12 April 1945.

Completion of a Mission: The 'Final Solution' (III)

While the Allies were preparing for the new world order that they wanted to see established in the wake of the Second World War, National Socialist Germany was attempting to complete what it saw as its historic mission of rooting out and destroying European Jewry. The few German Jews who had not yet been deported by the winter of 1944/5 were either living in what were described as 'privileged mixed marriages' with an 'Aryan' partner or, more rarely, they had managed to conceal their Jewish origins or were living in hiding among non-Jewish Germans. The Jewish partners in a 'mixed marriage' were stripped of all their rights. They had to wear the Jewish Star, to live with their spouses in special 'Jewish houses' and to face the constant threat of being sucked into the maelstrom of the extermination process.

Many 'mixed breeds' also felt threatened, especially those 'of the first degree', namely, 'half-Jews', even if they were not officially numbered among Geltungsjuden, i.e. those persons who were legally considered to be Jews in National Socialist Germany and who were 'mixed breeds' with two Jewish grandparents or were married to a Jew or were members of the Jewish faith. 'Half-Jews' and 'quarter-Jews' were subjected to discrimination and harassment – after 1941 they were dismissed from the armed services, pensioned off as civil servants and banned from pursuing certain professions. After March 1944 'half-Jews' were obliged to undertake forced labour in the Todt Organization's special units. In December 1942 the Ministry of Education decreed that 'mixed breeds of the second degree' could study medicine, dentistry and pharmacy, but not veterinary medicine. Behind this decree lay the assumption that 'Aryan' Germans might be willing to allow themselves to be treated by a 'quarter-Jew' but that they would not permit their pets to receive treatment in this way. Questions relating to the special treatment of 'mixed breeds' were to be settled by the party chancellery, which ultimately meant

Hitler himself. For its part, the Reich Main Security Office was keen to see as many 'mixed breeds' exterminated as possible.

Among the concentration camps built outside Germany itself, one of them had special status: Theresienstadt lay in the Protectorate of Bohemia and Moravia. It was in part a concentration camp and in part a transit station on the way to one of the death camps. Saul Friedländer has described this 'dual face' as follows: 'On the one hand, transports were departing to Auschwitz and Treblinka, on the other, the Germans set up a "Potemkin village" meant to fool the world.'[94] Among the camp's 'amenities' were a coffee house, concerts, performances of plays, a reading room and a bank. It was to Theresienstadt that Leo Baeck was deported in January 1943, together with other leading members of the Reich's Association of Jews in Germany. The following October saw the arrival in the camp of the few Danish Jews whom the Gestapo had been able to arrest. In June 1943 a commission from the International Committee of the Red Cross was allowed to visit the camp. In case the commission asked to see where the Jews deported from Theresienstadt would ultimately be taken, Adolf Eichmann in his capacity as head of the Jewish Department at the Reich Main Security Office ordered a 'family camp' to be built at Auschwitz-Birkenau. For the time being, its inmates were not exterminated, but as soon as it became clear that the Red Cross commission would not ask to see Auschwitz, all of the inmates in the 'family camp' were immediately sent to the gas chambers.

In the autumn of 1944 a propaganda film was made in Theresienstadt. Its official title was *Theresienstadt: A Documentary Film from the Jewish Settlement Area*, though the prisoners referred to it under the ironical title of *The Führer Gives a Town to the Jews*. It presented Theresienstadt as an almost luxurious resort with schools, parks, swimming pools, football competitions and endless cultural activities. Its director was the well-known Jewish actor Kurt Gerron, one of the most prominent of the camp's inmates. Shortly after the film was completed, he was taken to Auschwitz on the last transport and murdered there on 8 October 1944.

The film was never shown in public. Its only audience was a second commission from the International Committee of the Red Cross which visited the camp in April 1945 and reported back to Geneva with an account of the 'small Jewish state' that they had seen. Since November 1941 more than 140,000 Jews and 'mixed breeds' were transported to Theresienstadt. Some 33,000 died there, while a further 88,000 were deported to the extermination camps. By the time they were liberated by the Red Army on 8 May 1945, only 17,000 Jews were still living in the camp. Among them was the former head of the Reich's Association of Jews in Germany, Leo Baeck.

The 'final solution' took a particularly dramatic turn in Hungary, which was overrun by German troops in March 1944. By 9 July Adolf Eichmann and his colleagues had managed to deport 438,000 Hungarian Jews from the Hungarian provinces to Auschwitz, starting in the Carpathian Ukraine and northern Transylvania. Around 394,000 were gassed on their arrival in the camp. By this date there were still some 200,000 Jews living in the Hungarian capital. Since the spring of 1944 the Jewish Relief and Rescue Committee had been trying to buy the lives of Jews who had not yet been deported. Acting on Himmler's orders, Eichmann agreed to this deal, and in April 1944 the lives of one million Jews were exchanged for 10,000 winterized trucks that were made available by the Western Allies for use on the eastern front. The exchange was negotiated by the Jewish dealer Joel Brand.

Hitler was presumably hoping to drive a wedge between the Western Allies and the Soviets and, if possible, to persuade the Anglo-Saxon powers to enter into separate peace negotiations prior to a joint assault on the Soviet Union. In order to achieve this objective, the head of the SS would presumably even have been willing to delay the extermination of European Jewry or at least to accept a reduction in the numbers murdered. But the Western Allies had no intention of agreeing to such a realignment of their allegiances, quite apart from the fact that Himmler did not have the power to implement it without Hitler's approval. The Jewish middlemen travelled from Vienna to Istanbul, from where they were taken to Cairo, where they were interrogated and interned by the British authorities. As a result, Eichmann's proposed deal did not take place.

Another deal proved more successful, when another of the leaders of the Jewish Relief and Rescue Committee, Rudolf Kastner, obtained permission for 1,684 Jews to travel from Budapest to Switzerland, their journey taking them – unexpectedly – via Bergen-Belsen. The price paid was $1,000 for each of the Jews who were saved in this way. Switzerland was willing to accept this group of Hungarian Jews and, indeed, had little choice in the matter if its international reputation was not to suffer. By now the whole world knew what was happening in the extermination camps, and by the time the two transports from Bergen-Belsen arrived in Switzerland in the autumn of 1944, images of the gas chambers at Treblinka had been circulated all round the world. The camp had been liberated by the Red Army at the end of July before the Germans had been able to destroy all trace of their crimes there.

For the Hungarian regent, Miklós Horthy, there was no longer any doubt about the outcome of the war by the summer of 1944, and on 6 July he ordered an end to the deportation of Jews, dismissing his prime minister, Döme Sztójay, who had been markedly loyal to the Reich, and replacing him on 25 August with Géza Lakatos, an army general colonel who enjoyed his confidence and who immediately ordered the reopening of all the Jewish shops and businesses that had been closed in April, at least to the extent that their owners or managers were not Jewish. When the Red Army entered Hungary from Romania in early October, Horthy began secret talks in Moscow with the aim of reaching an agreement with the Soviet Union, and on 11 October a provisional armistice was signed in the Soviet capital. Four days later, in a radio address, Horthy ordered his troops to lay down their weapons. By now, however, the radically anti-Semitic Arrow Cross under Ferenc Szálasi had so comprehensively infiltrated the army that Horthy's orders were ignored. The SS arrested Horthy and threatened to shoot his son if he did not appoint Szálasi his prime minister and resign as his country's regent. He was then interned in Germany.

During the weeks that followed, around 50,000 Hungarian Jews, both men and women, were forced to make the journey to Austria on foot. Many of them died on the way. Of the survivors, thousands perished building fortifications around Vienna, while 35,000 were used for a similar project near Budapest. By December Soviet troops were drawing ever closer, making it inevitable that the Hungarian army would retreat to the capital, whereupon 'Nyilas' – thugs affiliated to the Arrow Cross Party – butchered large numbers of Jewish workers, causing terrible carnage on the banks of the Danube and on the bridges spanning the river. The bodies were dumped in the river.

There were two ghettos in Budapest at this time, the first and smaller of which was 'international' and under the protection of neutral countries such as Switzerland and Sweden. After the Hungarian government had bowed to foreign pressure and agreed to let 8,800 Jews emigrate to Palestine, the Jewish Relief and Rescue Committee succeeded in turning the individual exit permits into family permits. Carl Lutz, the head of the 'Foreign Interests' section at the Swiss Embassy, provided 'protection papers' for 40,000 Jews. Almost 35,000 of these papers were recognized by Szálasi's government, but the plans to allow some 40,000 Hungarian Jews to emigrate to Palestine were thwarted in the end by the SS. At that point Lutz joined forces with the first secretary at the Swedish Embassy, Raoul Wallenberg, and with the German diplomat Gerhart Feine, who was critical of the regime, and rented around thirty large apartment blocks, where 30,000 of Budapest's Jews found a safe haven between then and the end of the war. In addition to Lutz and Wallenberg, the papal nuncio and a number of diplomats from Spain and Portugal were also involved in saving thousands of Hungarian Jews. The best-known of them, Raoul Wallenberg, was taken to the Soviet Union by the NKVD in 1945. All trace of him disappears after 1947.

The Nyilas continued their brutal killings even while the diplomats were saving lives. Their last great massacre took place on the banks of the Danube in the middle of January 1945, when the majority of their victims were Jewish, including women and children. Between 10,000 and 20,000 Jews were murdered by anti-Semitic gangs during the winter of 1944/5, before the Red Army took the city on 13 February. Barely half of the capital's 200,000 Jews survived the war.

It was also during the winter of 1944/5 that Himmler redoubled his efforts to reach out to the Western Allies by making concessions on the Jewish question, authorizing contacts between his inferiors and the representatives of Jewish organizations in Switzerland and also forging links with possible mediators in both Sweden and Switzerland. Among his personal acquaintances was the Swiss politician Jean-Marie Musy, and it was to Musy that he proposed the release of 10,000 Jews in order to lay the foundations for his negotiations with Britain and America. In January 1945 a train bringing 1,200 Jews from Theresienstadt did indeed reach Switzerland. The following month the vice-president of the Swiss Red Cross, Count Folke Bernadotte, travelled to Berlin to confer with Himmler on the release of Scandinavian internees from the concentration camp at Neuengamme and of Jews at both Theresienstadt and Bergen-Belsen. Himmler proved highly cooperative, and on 21 April he even received a representative of the World Jewish Congress, Norbert Masur, who travelled to Berlin from Sweden. But the outcome of the talks was only modest: Himmler agreed to the release of 1,000 Jewish women and a number of prominent foreigners among the Jewish inmates at Ravensbrück, all of whom were allowed to travel to Sweden.

But there could be no talk of a radical change of policy with regard to the implementation of the 'final solution', for the killings continued until the final weeks of the war. In November 1944, under the impact of the advancing Soviet troops, Himmler ordered an end to the gassings at Auschwitz. All the gas chambers and crematoria were to be blown up in order to destroy all trace of the genocide. As far as possible, the SS had already adopted a similar approach to the extermination camps further to the east. Here the bodies were dug up from the mass graves and burnt. As we have already noted, attempts to cover up the crimes that had been committed at Treblinka were thwarted by the arrival of the Red Army in July 1944.

Even before the camp at Auschwitz had been closed, the SS had responded to a request from Albert Speer and sent able-bodied Jews to work in the armaments industry in Germany. Some were dispatched to Dachau, others to the Dora-Mittelbau tunnels in the Harz, where they were employed under barbaric conditions in the manufacture of V-2 rockets, a scheme operated by the Todt Organization. In January 1945 all the camps in the east were evacuated on Himmler's orders, and between 700,000 and 800,000 prisoners, most of them Jews, were forced to march westwards. At least a quarter of a million of them died of exhaustion or cold or were shot or burnt alive. In many places civilians, including members of the Hitler Youth movement, joined in the killings.

Elsewhere, over 5,000 Jewish prisoners from outposts of the Stutthof concentration camp were shot near Palmnicken in the second half of January on the orders of the Gauleiter of East Prussia, Erich Koch, after their progress had been stalled in the course of their march along the Baltic coast. A similar fate befell the majority of the 3,000 prisoners from Buchenwald, whom the SS dispatched on foot to Theresienstadt in April 1945. Of the 45,000 inmates at Buchenwald around one-third did not live to see the end of the war. Prisoners who were too ill to travel were left behind. At Auschwitz 200 sick women were killed by the SS before they left. The Red Army captured the largest German extermination camp on 27 January 1945 and freed the 7,000 or so survivors. The total number of men, women and children murdered there has been put at 1.3 million. The total number of victims of the Holocaust has been estimated to be between five and six million.

It was not only Germans who took part in the murder of European Jews. So, too, did anti-Semites and willing helpers of the SS in every part of Europe under German rule. But it was National Socialist Germany that planned and put into operation this unprecedented act of genocide. Without their determination to exterminate the Jews, without the discipline of the officials entrusted with its implementation and without the capacity of Germany as a highly developed industrialized nation, the project could never have been realized. Even by the spring of 1945 many Germans must have suspected that they would be called to account by the Allies for this crime against humanity, but it was only much later that they became aware of a far more radical consequence of their elimination of European Jewry, for in the wake of what they had done to the Jews, they would never again be able to see themselves in the same way as they had before the greatest turning point in German history: Hitler's seizure of power in 1933.

The End of the War (I): The Fall of the Third Reich

By the end of 1944 Hitler's final major advance on the western front – the Ardennes Offensive – had to all intents and purposes failed. The Allies lost over 70,000 men, the Germans more than 80,000. All that Hitler had achieved was to delay by six weeks the British and American invasion of Germany. After heavy fighting, the still undamaged bridge over the Rhine at Remagen fell into American hands on 7 March 1945. Here American forces established their first bridgehead on the right bank of the Rhine and now had a position from which to launch their attacks on the Bergisches Land and the Ruhr.

The last large-scale offensive by the Red Army began on 12 January 1945 along a front running from the Memel to the Carpathians. To the east, German troops were still surrounded in Courland, an area that Hitler obstinately refused to leave. Since the Ardennes Offensive in the west meant that the Wehrmacht no longer had any reserves that it could call up, the Soviet troops were able to advance westwards within a matter of days. At the end of January 1945 they overran the industrial region of Upper Silesia that had escaped any wartime destruction. The implications of this move prompted Speer, in his capacity as minister of armaments, to draft a memorandum to Hitler, culminating in the observation that the Reich's ability to fight the war and to produce any further weapons was practically over. On 31 January Marshal Georgi Zhukov established a bridgehead at Küstrin an der Oder (now Kostrzyn nad Odrą). That same day Königsberg (Kaliningrad) was surrounded, albeit only temporarily. And on 4 March the Red Army pushed forward to the Baltic and cut off East Prussia from the rest of the Reich.

The area's Gauleiter, Erich Koch, had repeatedly prevented the local population from evacuating the region in good time, with the result that the precipitate flight of tens of thousands of East Prussians proved little short of disastrous. Many convoys of people were crushed by Soviet tanks or shot at by Soviet fighter planes, while horse-drawn vehicles fell through the ice on the Vistula Lagoon. Not even those who found a boat in the small port at Pillau (Baltiysk) were safe, for several of the vessels sent to East Prussia by the navy were sunk by enemy fire, including the former Kraft durch Freude steamer *Wilhelm Gustloff*. At least 25,000 men, women and children were killed while fleeing across the Baltic to Schleswig-Holstein or Denmark. No less terrible was the fate of those East Prussians who were unable to escape from the advancing Soviet troops. Countless women and girls were raped, and men and women who were capable of working were abducted to the Soviet Union. Men and women of all ages were indiscriminately killed. The number of German civilians who were killed because old age or illness prevented them from fleeing has been put at over 100,000.

Tens of thousands of refugees travelling westwards stopped in and around Dresden in the middle of February, a state of affairs which, although well known to the Allies, did not prevent them from transforming a city famous not only as 'Florence on the Elbe' but also as an industrial centre into a burning inferno on the night of 13/14 February. Two waves of attacks by British Bomber Command involving more than 7,000 aircraft were followed at midday on the 14th by an American bombardment. In all, between 20,000 and 25,000 people lost their lives.

Apart from Hamburg, where 35,000 people had died in Operation Gomorrah in July 1943, Dresden has been seared into the German consciousness with particular intensity as a result of its destruction in Allied air raids. The carpet bombing of German towns and cities was an integral part of the Allies' campaign, having been specifically sanctioned at the conference in Casablanca in January 1943. Among the targets chosen were not only centres of German industry and of arms production but also important traffic hubs and ports that were regarded as strategically vital. These raids were also designed to undermine the morale of the civilian population and were described by the Royal Air Force as 'moral bombing' in contradistinction to 'strategic bombing'.

This aim of destroying morale was not achieved, for, far from persuading 'national comrades' to rise up and overthrow Hitler and his regime, the enemy air raids merely served to encourage the feeling that the Germans belonged to a community fated to suffer a single destiny that involved holding out against all the odds. There was nothing 'moral' about the bombs that were used to terrorize women, children and the elderly. Rather, the carpet bombing was a sign that the inhumanity of the aggressor can also change the person who gets in his way to the point of denying the very humanity of those who are fighting a defensive war. It was this insight that persuaded the bishop of Chichester, George Bell, to protest at 'moral bombing' from 1941 onwards. This and other objections were finally heard, and in the wake of the destruction of Dresden, even Churchill came to the conclusion that to continue this kind of carpet bombing was harming Britain's war aims more than it was helping them and that it could not be justified in the longer term.

At the same time as the Red Army was overrunning the eastern half of Germany, there were still German troops in Norway, Denmark, the northern part of the Netherlands, Courland, the Protectorate of Bohemia and Moravia, northern Croatia, Slovenia and northern Italy. A major Allied offensive began in Emilia-Romagna on 9 April, leading to the liberation of Bologna twelve days later. The Americans took Genoa on 27 April, the same day that Communist partisans captured Mussolini near Dorio on Lake Como. He had been trying to escape disguised as a Wehrmacht soldier. The following day he and his mistress, Clara Petacci, were shot, after which they were hung upside down from the roof of a filling station on the Piazzale Loreto in Milan, where their bodies were displayed with those of twenty of Mussolini's followers, including the former party secretary, Achille Starace. The last stage of Fascist rule in Italy, the Repubblica di Salò, was definitely over. In its place came a wave of bloody anti-Fascist purges that culminated in the early summer of 1945.

On 29 April, a day after Mussolini had been shot, the German forces in Italy surrendered unconditionally at a ceremony in the Allies' headquarters at Caserta in the presence of a group of Soviet officers. The armistice came into force at two o'clock on the afternoon of 2 May. It had been preceded by secret talks that the German military governor in northern Italy, SS group leader Karl Wolff, had entered into on his own initiative with Allen Dulles, the head of America's Office of Strategic Services, in Zurich. These talks were continued in Ascona on 19 March in the presence of two high-ranking American generals.

For Stalin, these contacts between their common foe and the Western Allies were a source of deep mistrust, and in a telegram that he sent to Roosevelt on 3 April he voiced his suspicion that with German agreement the British and Americans were planning to advance into the very heart of Germany while Soviet troops would continue fighting the Wehrmacht, a claim that Roosevelt emphatically rejected two days later. There was no such intention in the Allied camp. After all, both Roosevelt and Churchill knew very well that they owed their imminent victory to the military efforts of the Soviet Union, and so they repeatedly stressed that there was complete agreement between the three Allies in terms of Germany's unconditional surrender.

In fact, there could no longer be any talk of an agreement between the Allies with regard to the fate of eastern central and south-east Europe at this time. On 6 March the Soviet Union forced Romania to install a government that may have appeared on the surface to be a multi-party cabinet but which was in fact effectively dominated by Communists. Even more unsettling in the view of both Roosevelt and Churchill were the developments currently taking place in Poland, where the Soviet Union, aided and abetted by the Provisional Government, was in the process of building a Communist satellite regime and preventing the Americans and British from sending representatives into the country that had been 'liberated' by the Red Army.

'An impenetrable veil has been drawn across the scene,' Churchill wrote to Roosevelt on 16 March 1945. Eleven days later he drew the president's attention to the fact that 'Eastern Europe will be shown to be excluded from the terms of the Declaration on Eastern Europe, and you and we will be excluded from any jot of influence in that area.' And yet the agreements reached at Yalta allowed precisely the outcome with which Churchill now saw himself confronted: the 'Russian form of democracy' would be imposed on Poland and other states in eastern and south-east Europe.[95]

During the weeks that followed, Churchill's concerns regarding Poland continued to increase. In April he persuaded the former head of the Polish government in exile, Stanisław Mikołajczyk, who had stepped down in November 1944, to acknowledge his friendship with the Soviet Union, to recognize the modified Curzon Line as Poland's eastern border and to withdraw all claims to Lemberg (L'viv). In spite of this, non-Communist forces in Poland continued to be driven back. At the end of March sixteen leading representatives of the non-Communist underground movement were invited to Moscow, ostensibly to take part in talks on the formation of a Polish government of national unity, only to be arrested on their arrival and held in detention. When Churchill protested to Stalin on 29 April, the Soviet dictator replied by claiming that the accused had planned and carried out acts of sedition behind the back of the Red Army. In a show trial that began on 18 June, thirteen of the accused were sentenced to terms of imprisonment ranging from four months to ten years. Three of them were acquitted.

On 4 May 1945 Churchill drew up a paper in which he sketched out the situation on which the Western Powers needed to take a stand. If Germany were to be divided into zones, as the Allies had agreed, and if Poland were occupied by the Russians, then

> Poland would be completely engulfed and buried deep in Russian-occupied lands. What would in fact be the Russian frontier would run from the North Cape to Norway, along the Finnish-Swedish frontier, across the Baltic to a point just east of Lübeck, along the at present agreed line of occupation and along the frontier between Bavaria and Czechoslovakia to the frontiers of Austria, which is nominally to be in quadruple occupation, and half-way across that country to the Isonzo river, behind which Tito and Russia will claim everything to the east. Thus the territories under Russian control

would include the Baltic provinces, all of Germany to the occupational line, all Czechoslovakia, a large part of Austria, the whole of Yugoslavia, Hungary, Roumania, Bulgaria, until Greece in her present tottering position is reached. It would include all the great capitals of Middle Europe, including Berlin, Vienna, Budapest, Belgrade, Bucharest, and Sofia. The position of Turkey and Constantinople will certainly come immediately into discussion.

In Churchill's view, this was 'an event in the history of Europe to which there has been no parallel, and which has not been faced by the Allies in their long and hazardous struggle'. Even Soviet demands on Germany for reparations

> will be such as to enable her to prolong the occupation almost indefinitely, or at any rate for many years, during which time Poland will sink with many other States into the vast zone of Russian-controlled Europe, not necessarily economically Sovietised, but police-governed.

The conclusions were obvious:

> We have several powerful bargaining counters on our side, the use of which might make for a peaceful agreement. *First, the Allies ought not to retreat from their present positions to the occupational line until we are satisfied about Poland, and also about the temporary character of the Russian occupation of Germany, and the conditions to be established in the Russianised or Russian-controlled countries in the Danube valley, particularly Austria and Czechoslovakia, and the Balkans.* Secondly, we may be able to please them about the exits from the Black Sea and the Baltic as part of a general statement. All that matters can only be settled before the United States armies in Europe are weakened. If they are not settled before the United States armies withdraw from Europe and the Western World folds up its war machines there are no prospects of a satisfactory solution and very little of preventing a third World War. It is to this early and speedy showdown and settlement with Russia that we must now turn our hopes. Meanwhile I am against weakening our claim against Russia on behalf of Poland in any way.[96]

Churchill noted his concerns and demands at a time when the new president of the United States, Harry S. Truman, had yet to give any firm commitment or sense of direction to his country's policies. As far as ending the war in Europe was concerned, the actual running of the country seemed for a time to lie in the hands of Dwight D. Eisenhower as the supreme commander of the American and Western Allied troops in Europe. Unlike Churchill, Eisenhower appeared to have no interest in ensuring that the Western Allies reached Berlin as quickly as possible in order to prevent the capital from falling into the hands of the Red Army. Eisenhower regarded even his advance on Prague as less urgent than

Churchill believed to be necessary. The American general's prime concern was to occupy southern Germany as far as the Czechoslovak border of 1937, a concern guided by the fear that the Americans would encounter massive resistance from German troops holed up in what he regarded as the 'fortress' of the Alps. Churchill tried to persuade Eisenhower to change his priorities but was unsuccessful, not least because Truman backed his commander in chief. The overall interests of the western world to which Churchill referred in his memorandum of 4 May had only a single clear-sighted and eloquent advocate in the final weeks of the Second World War, and that was Churchill himself.

Of course, he, too, was partly to blame for the situation in which he found himself, even though he was by no means as trusting of Stalin as Roosevelt had been. Great Britain and the United States had left the Soviet Union to shoulder much of the burden of the Allies' military confrontation with National Socialist Germany and repeatedly delayed opening up a second front in France, as Stalin had demanded. There had invariably been compelling military reasons for such a delay. And in this way the two great Western Powers managed to ensure that the losses sustained by their armies remained within reasonable bounds, an attitude that they hoped would be shared by their countries' voters. An additional factor was Great Britain's imperial interest in the Mediterranean and in the survival of the Commonwealth. It was these interests that meant that the Western Powers invaded North Africa before they attempted to land their troops on the European mainland.

But the price of this policy was the western democracies' abandonment of a large part of Germany to the Soviet Union and effectively a willingness to hand over the whole of eastern central and south-east Europe without a struggle. The promises that Roosevelt and Churchill had made to Stalin in Teheran and Yalta could no longer be taken back. Moreover, the end of the war in Europe was by no means the end of the Second World War, and both Washington and London believed that they needed Soviet help to defeat Japan. In the circumstances there could be no talk of a major confrontation with Stalin in the spring of 1945.

While Churchill's warnings about the danger in the east grew ever more urgent, the Red Army continued its advance westwards, an advance accompanied by hundreds of thousands of rapes and instances of looting, to say nothing of the murder of countless civilians. Danzig (Gdańsk) fell on 30 March, Königsberg (Kaliningrad) on 9 April, the day on which Hungary capitulated to the Soviets. By 13 April the Red Army had moved into Vienna. Three days later the major Soviet offensive against Berlin was launched from the Oder-Neiße Line.

Meanwhile, the British and Americans were advancing through Germany from the west. On 18 April American troops took Magdeburg and the following day they captured Leipzig. Bremen fell into British hands on 26 April, and four days later the American Seventh Army occupied Munich, the former 'capital of the movement'. In the course of April the Western Allies not only overran German towns and cities, they also liberated three German concentration camps: Buchenwald on the 11th, Bergen-Belsen on the 15th and Dachau on the 29th. The photographs and film recordings of the starving inmates and mountainous piles of bodies were circulated all round the world and left an indelible mark on the minds and memories of shocked contemporaries.

By the final weeks of the war only a tiny minority of fanatical National Socialists still believed in a 'final victory' by the Third Reich. 'The nation has completely lost its nerve and is terribly agitated and afraid,' we read in an official report of the mood in Bad Aibling in Bavaria in March 1945. According to a report filed by the secret service on 7 March and relating to Berchtesgaden,

> the broad mass couldn't care less what a future Europe looks like. It can be gathered from every conversation that the people's comrades from all walks of life want a return to the living standard of the pre-war era as soon as possible, and don't lay the slightest value on going down in history.

One local inhabitant was quoted as saying: 'If we'd have imagined in 1933 how things would turn out, we'd never have voted for Hitler.' According to another report, the following opinion was also being expressed at around this time: 'The Führer was sent to us from God, though not in order to save Germany, but to ruin it. Providence has determined the destruction of the German people, and Hitler is the executor of this will.'[97]

Hitler was determined to drag down Germany and the German people and take them with him into the abyss if the war was to end with the Reich's defeat. On 19 March he issued instructions that whenever a region had to be surrendered to the enemy, all military installations were to be destroyed, as were all transport links, newspaper offices, industrial plants and public utilities. (Not until five weeks later did he learn from Albert Speer that not only were his orders not being carried out but that every effort was being made to prevent them from being implemented.) Until April Hitler continued to hope that the alliance between the western democracies and Bolshevik Russia would fall apart. When he received the news that Roosevelt was dead, he thought that the alliance would collapse within weeks, if not days, an assessment in which he was confirmed by Goebbels. And when this expectation failed to be met, he expressed the confident hope that the decisive battle would be fought in Berlin and that he would win.

Soviet tanks reached the eastern suburbs of the capital on 20 April, Hitler's fifty-sixth birthday, and began to shell the city. This was the day on which most of the Third Reich's dignitaries saw the Führer for the last time. Shortly after coming to his bunker and lining up to congratulate him on his birthday, Göring, Himmler and most of the country's ministers left Berlin. (Speer also left the city, but in his case it was not for good.) Two days later Goebbels announced that Hitler had decided to remain in the capital.

Many of the Führer's vassals interpreted this decision as a gesture of resignation and were convinced that he would resign as chancellor. On 23 April, Göring, who since 1941 had been Hitler's designated successor, sent a telegram from the Obersalzburg near Berchtesgaden, announcing that if he received no word from Berlin by ten o'clock that evening, he would take Hitler's place at the head of the Reich. In Berlin there was no doubt about Göring's aim, which was to start talks with the Western Powers and negotiate the terms for Germany's surrender. Hitler forced Göring to resign from all his positions and ordered him to be placed under house arrest.

Hitler's reaction was far less muted when he discovered on the 28th that five days earlier Himmler had met the vice-president of the Swedish Red Cross, Count Folke Bernadotte, in Lübeck and through him offered to surrender to the Western Allies. Hitler spoke of 'the most shameless betrayal in human history'[98] and ordered Himmler's immediate arrest and liquidation, but to no effect.

By this time Soviet troops were already fighting their way through to the Potsdamer Platz in the immediate vicinity of the Chancellery and of the Führer's bunker. The city's defence lay in the hands of regular soldiers, members of the Hitler Youth movement and older members of the Volkssturm, or People's Militia. They did not have the slightest chance of defeating the Red Army. In the course of the 'Battle for Berlin', which was by now drawing to a close, the Soviets lost a further 100,000 soldiers – almost as many as the Americans lost in the whole of the European theatre of war.

It was during the night of 28/9 April 1945 that Hitler took the decision to draw from Germany's defeat the conclusion that he had repeatedly announced would be taken in this case and one to which all his policies had been geared, even if he himself was only subconsciously aware of that fact: he would take his own life. He dictated his political testament early on the morning of 29 April, blaming international Jewry for the war and 'charging the leadership of the nation and their subjects with the meticulous observation of the race-laws and the merciless resistance to the universal poisoner of all peoples, international Jewry'.[99] He named Karl Dönitz the new head of state and the new commander in chief of the country's armed forces – until then Dönitz had been the commander in chief of the navy and had established his headquarters at Plön in Holstein. Goebbels was appointed the new chancellor.

Hitler killed himself at around four o'clock on the afternoon of 30 April with a single gunshot to his right temple. His companion of many years' standing, Eva Braun, whom he had married the previous day, took poison. The news of Hitler's death was broadcast on the radio the following evening at 22:26: he had, it was claimed, died that afternoon 'in combat at his post in the Reich Chancellery, while fighting to his last breath against Bolshevism'.[100] His successor as chancellor was already dead, Goebbels having committed suicide several hours earlier, together with his wife, after the two of them had first killed their six children by administering prussic acid. Like those of Hitler and

Eva Braun, the bodies of Joseph and Magda Goebbels were soaked in petrol and burned in the Chancellery gardens in keeping with the instructions that they had left. There they were discovered on 2 May by the first Soviet troops to reach the former power centre of the German Reich after the soldiers defending the city had surrendered to the Red Army earlier that same day.

Few mourned Hitler's passing. Most Germans received the news with a mixture of apathy and relief. With the approach of the Allied troops, the former 'people's comrades' did everything they could to hide symbols of the Third Reich, such as photographs of the Führer, swastika flags, National Socialist uniforms and party badges.

It was his compatriots' faith in the charisma of their Führer that had allowed Hitler to remain in power for twelve years, and it was only the belated realization that his rule had turned out to be a disaster for Germany that finally broke the spell that he had cast on the majority of his fellow Germans. This spell had been the precondition for the role that Hitler had played in the history of the world since 1933. No other individual has influenced the course of twentieth-century history as much as he did, and few of the major events that have taken place in the world since 1945 have not been connected, directly or indirectly, with his rule.

Hitler has gone down in history as the man who, more than any other, destroyed traditions and values that until then had been regarded as self-evident in the whole of the western world, including Germany itself. To the extent that anti-colonial freedom movements were fuelled by the world war that he himself fomented, then this was a collateral benefit of his impact. Posterity's memory of him rests for the most part on the millions of people, mainly Jews, whose lives were sacrificed to his obsessions. When his empire finally crashed to the ground, most Germans were left feeling numb, so much so that in 1945 few of his compatriots were willing to accept the idea that their former enthusiasm for their leader had made it possible for their country to commit the crimes with which the victorious Allies were now about to confront them.

The new government that Hitler's successor, Karl Dönitz, formed on 2 May transferred its seat of power to Flensburg. Its main goal was to ensure that as many German troops as possible surrendered to the Allies before they could be taken prisoner by the Soviets. The first regional surrender took place in Italy and, subsequently approved by Dönitz, came into force on 2 May. It was followed by a second surrender on the evening of the 2nd at Ludwigslust Castle in Mecklenburg. On the 3rd a further surrender was signed at Stendal to the west of the Elbe. Both of these last two treaties were made with the Americans.

On 4 May Admiral Hans Georg von Friedeburg, acting on Dönitz's instructions, signed a regional partial surrender of all German troops in the Netherlands, north-west Germany and Denmark. It was concluded in Montgomery's headquarters on the Lüneburg Heath. In return, Montgomery gave his verbal assurance that German soldiers still fighting the Red Army would be allowed to serve time as British prisoners of war. Around 1.85 million German soldiers were able to escape from Soviet detention and surrender to the British and to the Americans during the first week of May, their flight more or less disorganized and individually undertaken. Between 2 and 8 May hundreds of thousands of refugees reached those parts of Germany where they were safe from rape and harassment at the hands of members of the Red Army.

At the same time, the fighting continued in many other places, notably northern Yugoslavia and the Protectorate of Bohemia and Moravia. The Czech resistance movement organized an uprising in Prague on 5 May that was put down by units of the SS and, initially at least, by a division of the Vlasov Army that shortly afterwards defected to the Czechs. The American troops under Patton had in the meantime occupied the western part of Czechoslovakia as far as the agreed demarcation line running from Karlsbad (Karlovy Vary) to Pilsen (Plzeň) and Budweis (České Budějovice) and played no part in the fighting. Not until 9 May did the Red Army march into Prague and bring an end to German rule in the Protectorate of Bohemia and Moravia.

Four days earlier General Field Marshal Albert Kesselring had completed the surrender of German troops in southern Germany and western Austria in Munich. That same day Dönitz's representative, Admiral Hans Georg von Friedeburg, arrived at Eisenhower's headquarters in Reims. His attempts to ensure that German troops fighting in Yugoslavia and Bohemia had time to make their way into American captivity proved futile, Eisenhower insisting on unconditional surrender on all fronts during the night of 8/9 May. Dönitz had no choice but to accept this condition. With his agreement and on his orders Alfred Jodl, the chief of the operations staff of the Wehrmacht's High Command, signed the surrender in Reims early on the morning of 7 May.

On Stalin's insistence the act of surrender was repeated in the Soviet head-quarters in Berlin shortly after midnight on 9 May. The German signatories were representatives of all three branches of the armed forces: the chief of the Wehrmacht's Supreme High Command, Field Marshal Wilhelm Keitel, for the army; Admiral Hans Georg von Friedeburg for the navy; and Colonel General Hans-Jürgen Stumpff for the air force. The armistice had come into force shortly beforehand at 00:01, marking the end of the Second World War in Europe.

Dönitz's government in Flensburg survived for another two weeks, but on 23 May Eisenhower, responding to pressure from the Russians and from the French, ordered the arrest of all of its members, whose shadowy existence had been tolerated only by the British. The German Reich that had been established in 1871 was finally at an end.

That same day Heinrich Himmler, the man primarily responsible for the genocide of European Jewry, took his own life by swallowing a capsule of poison hidden in his mouth: he had gone underground using a false name, but had been captured by the British military on 21 May. The highest-ranking of Hitler's followers who was still alive at this time was Hermann Göring, who was arrested by members of the American armed forces at Berchtesgaden on 9 May. He too managed to evade responsibility for his crimes, for although he was one of the twelve accused in the trial of the principal war criminals at the International Military Tribunal in Nuremberg who on 30 September and 1 October 1946 were sentenced to be hanged, he killed himself by swallowing poison on the evening of 15 October, the day before his planned execution.

The Partition of Europe (II): Radical Changes and Deportations

Churchill addressed the British nation in a radio broadcast on 13 May, praising the Allies' victory in Europe and thanking the soldiers of Great Britain and the Commonwealth as well as their American allies for defeating Hitler's and Mussolini's military might. Towards the end of his broadcast he reminded his listeners not only that Japan had not yet been defeated but also that the ideals of the Western Allies were still under threat in Europe:

> On the continent of Europe we have yet to make sure that the simple and honourable purposes for which we entered the war are not brushed aside or overlooked in the months following our success, and that the words 'freedom', 'democracy', and 'liberation' are not distorted from their true meaning as we have understood them. There would be little use in punishing the Hitlerites for their crimes if law and justice did not rule, and if totalitarian or police Governments were to take the place of the German invaders.[101]

In a telegram sent to Truman the previous day, Churchill had expressed himself even more clearly. For the first time he referred to what he called an 'iron curtain' that was being 'drawn down upon their front':

> There seems little doubt that the whole of the regions east of the line Lübeck–Trieste–Corfu will soon be completely in their [i.e. Soviet] hands. To this must be added the further enormous area conquered by the American armies between Eisenach and the Elbe, which will, I suppose, in a few weeks be occupied, when the Americans retreat, by the Russian power. [. . .] Meanwhile the attention of our peoples will be occupied in inflicting severities upon Germany, which is ruined and prostrate, and it would be open to the Russians in a very short time to advance if they chose to the waters of the North Sea and the Atlantic.

It was vitally important, therefore, 'to come to an understanding with Russia, or see where we are with her, before we weaken our armies mortally or retire to the zones of occupation'.[102]

Churchill knew what he was talking about, for he was describing a process made possible by his own and Roosevelt's concessions to Stalin with regard to south-east and eastern central Europe. In Bulgaria a putsch by the newly formed Patriotic Front on 9 September 1944 had brought to power a pro-Soviet government under the former prime minister Kimon Georgiev in which Communists held key positions, including the ministries of the interior and of justice. In the winter of 1944/5 the new regime began a rigorous policy of persecuting former members of the government. The trial of 162 men accused of high treason ended with death sentences on ninety-six of them in early February 1945. Those sentenced to death, including all of the members of the new government council that functioned as the head of state on behalf of Simeon II, (who had mounted the throne of his father, Boris III, in August 1943, when he was only six) were executed immediately afterwards. In Romania, meanwhile, the pro-Soviet Communist government that was installed on 6 March under Petru Groza began to reduce the influence of the non-Communist forces headed by King Michael. As in Sofia, so in Bucharest, the posts of minister of the interior and of justice were filled by Communists.

In Hungary, by contrast, the Soviet Union proceeded more cautiously. Here, in December 1944, a number of Communists, returning from their self-imposed exile in Moscow, had formed a National Independence Front in Szeged, which had recently been recaptured by the Red Army. A provisional national government whose members were elected by acclamation was formed in Debrecen on 21 December 1944. The following day it appointed Colonel General Béla Miklós Dálnoki its prime minister following his defection to the Red Army. Communists held four ministerial appointments in his government, including the Ministry of the Interior, granting them control of the police. Under Soviet supervision National Committees were set up in every town and city with the power to pass laws, annul court decisions and order arrests. In March 1945 the Communist Party forced through a series of agricultural reforms designed to do away with larger and medium-sized estates and to create a new class of peasants that was scarcely viable in economic terms but which the Communists hoped would later agree to promote agricultural cooperatives: in other words, collectivization.

As Czechoslovakia returned to life in the final months of the war, the Soviet government took advantage of the fact that Edvard Beneš's government in exile had drawn closer to Moscow after 1943 and signed a friendship and mutual assistance treaty with the Soviet Union in the December of that year. Even though the Soviet Union annexed Carpatho-Ukraine – a part of the former Czechoslovakia – in December 1944, Beneš continued on his chosen course, not deviating from it for a moment. At the end of January 1945 his government broke off all relations with the Polish government in exile in London and recognized the pro-Soviet Lublin Committee as Poland's provisional government. No other country had proved as accommodating towards Stalin with regard to Poland.

In March 1945 the various Czech groups living in exile agreed on a joint programme with the Communists in Moscow. This was the basis of the National Front government of Czechs and Slovaks that was formed in Košice in Slovakia on 5 April under the leadership of the Social Democrat Zdenek Fierlinger. It included the Communist Party leader Klement Gottwald as one of the deputy prime ministers and the Communist sympathizer General Ludvík Svoboda as minister of the interior. Beneš once again took over the post of state president. It agreed to nationalize heavy industry, mining and banking and to undertake extensive land reforms. Slovakia was granted a considerable degree of autonomy. Germans and Hungarians who had not actively fought against the separatist forces were stripped of their citizenship. The Munich Agreement of September 1938 that had obliged Czechoslovakia to cede the Sudetenland to Germany had already been annulled by the British war cabinet in July 1942 following representations from Beneš. At the same time London had declared its willingness to agree to the resettlement of the region's German minority.

The Beneš Decrees – presidential orders from the period between May and October 1945 and retrospectively approved by the Provisional National Assembly on 28 March 1946 – provided the quasi-legal basis for denying citizenship to the majority of Germans and Magyars, who were dispossessed with no recourse to compensation. Their savings were confiscated, and they were forced to work on repairing the damage caused by the war. National Socialist criminals were punished, as were traitors and their accomplices. During the weeks between these unauthorized deportations and the practical implementation of the decrees of the Potsdam Three-Power Conference at the end of January 1946, some 800,000 Germans were expelled from the country, their deportation accompanied by the most terrible atrocities committed by the troops who were returning from exile, including revolutionary guards and in some cases civilians, too. Between May and July 1945 massacres took place in Landskron (Landskroun), Postelberg (Postoloprty), Saaz (Zatec) and Aussig (Ústí nad Labem). Hundreds of Germans died while being deported from Brno to the Austrian border, most of them from illness and lack of the most basic medical care. Countless Sudeten Germans took their own lives in work camps and internment camps, where they were held prior to their actual removal.

Cautious estimates of the number of Germans who died during these unofficial expulsions from Czechoslovakia amount to between 13,000 and 30,000. A law passed by the Provisional National Assembly on 8 May 1946 provided for the retroactive immunity from prosecution of those who had infringed any rules in the wake of this *odsun*, or deportation. The government adopted a far more lenient approach to Magyars than to Germans, a situation due in the main to the fact that the government in Budapest was opposed to these deportations. On the strength of the resettlement treaty of February 1946, 68,000 ethnic Hungarians from the Slovak region of the country were exchanged for 77,000 Slovaks living in Hungary. The majority of the country's half a million

Magyars remained where they were. Out of a total of more than 2.8 million Sudeten Germans, only around 200,000 were still living in Czechoslovakia by 1950.

After all that the Germans had done to the Czechs in the Protectorate of Bohemia and Moravia during the war, there can have been very few Czechs who in 1945 thought it possible or even desirable to live together in peace and harmony with the Germans in the new Czechoslovak state. Moreover, the vast majority of Sudeten Germans had opposed Czechoslovakia through their support for Konrad Henlein's party and actively agreed to the country's dismemberment in 1938/9. The backing of the Allies gave the whole idea of *odsun* an international legitimacy even if this policy was incompatible with the principles of the Atlantic Charter and of the United Nations Charter. But the violence that had accompanied the unofficial deportations made it clear yet again that the dehumanization of politics and warmongering under Hitler had set in train a disastrous series of events that acquired its own momentum: in their attempt to combat National Socialist aggression, even Hitler's democratic enemies resorted to methods that were profoundly inhumane.

In Poland the Communists already wielded far more power at the end of the war than they did in Czechoslovakia. General Leopold Okulicki disbanded his Home Army on 19 January 1945, even though he was under no illusions that German foreign rule would not be replaced by its Soviet equivalent. His soldiers were freed from their oath of allegiance. Okulicki's final command to his followers was to begin to rebuild their country, no matter how difficult the circumstances, and most of his soldiers responded to his orders, but by no means all of them. More than 10,000 went underground, from where they organized resistance to the Sovietization of Poland.

The Communist-dominated provisional government of the Socialist Edward Osóbka-Morawski transferred its seat of power from Lublin to Warsaw on 1 February. In spite of the many arrests and deportations of the opponents of the Communists, the former head of the Polish government in exile, Stanisław Mikołajczyk, who had resigned in November 1944, responding to pressure from Churchill, declared his willingness in June 1945 to travel to Moscow and discuss with two Polish Communists, Bolesław Bierut and Władisław Gomułka, the formation of a Polish government of national unity. Since the Western Powers did not recognize Osóbka-Morawski's government and since the Soviet Union did not recognize Tomasz Arciszewski's government in exile in London, Poland was prevented from attending the first conference of the United Nations in San Francisco and from signing the UNO Charter on 26 June. The enlarged cabinet of national unity was finally formed two days later, on 28 June. Mikołajczyk – formerly the secretary general of the Peasants' Party – was appointed deputy prime minister and minister of agriculture, while the Socialist Jan Stańczyk took over as labour minister and minister of welfare. The important Ministry of Public Safety remained in the hands of the

Communist Stanisław Radkiewicz. This largely symbolic cabinet reshuffle was followed between 29 June and 5 July by the official recognition of the Provisional Government of National Unity by France, Great Britain and the United States. Poland signed the United Nations Charter on 15 October and in that way was finally accepted as one of the organization's founder members.

By the date in question, the largest of the country's political parties, the Communist Polish Workers' Party, had some 190,000 members, while the two parties that were dependent on it, the Socialists and the new Peasants' Party, had 124,000 and 150,000 members respectively. The former right-wing parties – the National Democrats and the Sanacja parties associated with Józef Piłsudski – were regarded as 'Fascist' and, as such, were excluded from political life. The privileged position of the Communists rested on the fact that they had come to occupy all of the country's key posts within a short space of time, and their protector, the Soviet Union, still controlled many military bases even after the Red Army had left in the summer of 1945. Moreover, the NKVD continued to maintain powerful regiments of special troops that were able to help the government in its ruthless attempts to suppress the anti-Communist underground movement.

The outcome of the Second World War left Poland radically transformed. Around six million Poles had lost their lives as a direct result of the conflict. Of these, between 80 per cent and 90 per cent were Jews, while 12 per cent were ethnic Poles. The material losses have been estimated to be $49,000 million at 1939 prices. In eastern Poland the country lost 47 per cent of its pre-war territory and 23 per cent of its 1939 population. Vilnius and L'viv, both of which had played a major role in the history of Poland, were now a part of the Soviet Union. Gdańsk and Wrocław, two cities with powerful links with Germany, now belonged to Poland.

Describing the events of 1944 to 1947, the Polish historian Włodzimierz Borodziej has spoken of 'the greatest migration of peoples' ever witnessed by Poland:

The newly drawn border in the east left the vast majority of Belorussians and Ukrainians in the Soviet Union. From the autumn of 1944 an exchange of populations began to take place along the new eastern border, an exchange designed to bring national identity into line with state identity. Partly under constraint, around half a million Ukrainians and 36,000 Belorussians were resettled in the Soviet Union. According to official estimates at least 1.1 million crossed the eastern border from former Polish regions to the east and from camps and settlement areas. Of these, 250,000 were Jews. Whereas those who were deported in 1940/41 travelled voluntarily to the west, those who were 'evacuated' from the former areas in the east of the country left their own homeland out of fear of the new occupying regime. The great majority of eastern Poles and Jews settled in the new regions in the west and north of the country.[103]

The four to five million German citizens who in May 1945 were still living to the east of Poland's future western border were largely expelled from the region before the border was defined at the Potsdam Conference in July and August 1945. In many cases violence was used to resettle them, although the brutality was nowhere as extreme as it was in the case of Czechoslovakia. Conditions in the work camps and internment camps, including former concentration camps, where the Germans had to wait before leaving the region, were so appalling that according to later Polish estimates the death rate among the inmates was between 20 per cent and 50 per cent. Germans were allowed to remain in Poland if it was thought that they could be won back to the Polish cause or if they might consider converting to it. This was the case chiefly with Germans from Upper Silesia, Kashubia and Masuria.

Ethnically speaking, the new Poland was far more homogeneous than the older one had been and in consequence it was far more of a nation state than its predecessor. And, as Borodziej has noted, it was incomparably more 'proletarian' than pre-war Poland. As a result of the war and of German and Soviet occupation, it had lost 57 per cent of its lawyers, 39 per cent of its doctors, 27 per cent of its Catholic clergy and 29 per cent of its university teachers. Many of those who had emigrated and who included intellectuals, artists, politicians, civil servants and army officers never returned. Post-war Communist-led Poland was far from being the same country as the one for which these men and women had fought since 1939 by means of either weapons or words.

The Red Army's presence in a country was by no means the only way to bring a Communist party to power or to ensure that it played a decisive role in government. In Yugoslavia, for example, it was not Soviet troops who liberated the country from German rule but Tito's partisans, who were able to achieve their objective not least as a result of massive support from the Western Allies. In no other country was the Second World War a civil war to the extent that it was here, and it was far from over when Germany capitulated on 8/9 May 1945. During the weeks that followed, Tito's Communist partisans delivered their final devastating blows against their internal Yugoslav foes, who included the followers of Milan Nedić's Serbian satellite regime that was swept from power in the autumn of 1944, to say nothing of its collaborators, the Greater Serbian Chetniks under Draža Mihajlović and the Fascist Ustaše in Ante Pavelić's Croatia.

Tito's partisan army marched into Zagreb on 8 May 1945. The task of meting out retribution to the Ustaše and the Slovenian anti-Communists in those parts of the country that had been annexed by the German Reich was made simpler by the fact that the British troops that were by now stationed in Carinthia and Styria handed over more than 100,000 Croat soldiers and members of the Ustaše militia, as well as around 20,000 Slovenes, to Tito's units, leading to mass executions beginning with the one in Maribor (Marburg) on the Drau in May 1945, when thousands of Tito's political enemies were killed. In Slovenia tens of thousands of men, women and children were shot or clubbed to death, their bodies burnt in pits, mineshafts and karst caves. Half a century later, following the breakup of Yugoslavia, the dead were registered by Slovenia's post-Communist government in around 600 mass graves and found to include tens of thousands of Croats, Slovenes, German soldiers and members of the German minority as well as numerous Serbs, Montenegrins, Italians and Hungarians.

Of the anti-Communist leaders, Milan Nedić, who had been arrested in Austria, was able to avoid a trial by taking his own life in February 1946. Mihajlović hid for a whole year in Bosnia before being captured in March 1946. Together with other leaders of the Chetniks, he was subjected to a show trial that ended in guilty verdicts and the execution of the accused. A similar fate was suffered in June 1947 by the Croat marshal Slavko Kvaternik, who had been his country's head of state in 1941–2 before being stripped of all his powers by Pavelić in October 1942. With the help of the Church authorities, Pavelić escaped from Croatia to Italy in 1945, finally reaching Buenos Aires in late 1948 as the guest of the Argentine dictator Juan Peron. When Peron was deposed in 1955, Pavelić fled to Spain, dying in Madrid's German Hospital in December 1959.

The murder of members of the German minority was part of a plan to put an end once and for all to the peaceful coexistence of Croats and Danubian Swabians who had been living in this region for centuries. Most of the ethnic Germans were housed in camps where tens of thousands of them died as a result of mistreatment, illness and lack of medical care. The survivors were able to leave only gradually following the foundation of the German Federal Republic in 1949. But Tito's state not only wanted to get rid of the Germans living in Yugoslavia but also to annex the largely German-speaking areas of Austria and provide troops that would be used to occupy Austria, a demand that the Allies rejected. In the middle of May 1945 partisans who had marched into southern Carinthia occupied Klagenfurt but by the end of the month they were forced to leave. For the present Yugoslavia continued to lay claim to parts of Carinthia and Styria, where there was a powerful Slovenian minority.

A far more serious international problem arose from Yugoslavia's attempts to revise the border laid down in the Treaties of St-Germain and Rapallo in 1919–20 and to do so, moreover, at the expense of Italy. Even before the arrival of the Western Allies at the end of April 1945, Yugoslav units had occupied the whole of Istria before moving on to Trieste, Fiume (Rijeka) and Gorizia (Görz) in early May, forming 'National Liberation Committees' and organizing a popular movement for the annexation of these regions by Yugoslavia. The occupation of Trieste and Gorizia by British and American units in May marked the start of a conflict that soon became focused on the future of Trieste. On 9 June the military administration of Istria was entrusted to Yugoslavia by a three-power agreement, but Tito's troops were required to leave Trieste, Pola (Pula) and the Isonzo Valley. A line of demarcation was agreed upon in Duino eleven days later: Pola, Trieste and the Isonzo Valley remained under the provisional military rule of the Allies, while Yugoslavia was offered the prospect of acquiring Fiume, Zara (Zadar), the greater part of Istria and the islands along the Dalmatian coast that had until then belonged to Italy, in other words, regions with largely Slovene and Croat populations.

The question of who held the reins of power in Yugoslavia in 1945 was very quickly settled. The Red Army left the country in the May of that year, and by August, in response to an Allied recommendation, the Anti-Fascist Council for the National Liberation of Yugoslavia had been enlarged to include a further 121 politically active individuals, including thirty-nine former parliamentarians, ensuring that the Communists and their allies had a two-thirds majority. This enlarged Council declared itself the provisional parliament of a democratic and federal Yugoslavia and passed an electoral law preventing 'collaborators' from voting and lowering the voting age from twenty-one to eighteen.

Even during the electoral campaign the former prime minister in exile, Ivan Šubašic, who had been the foreign minister in Tito's coalition cabinet, resigned from the government in October, so disillusioned was he at the ruthlessness of the Communists. The elections to the two chambers of the Constituent Assembly on 11 November 1945 resulted in a majority of more than 90 per cent for the Communist People's Front in the Federal Council and 89 per cent in the Council of Nationalities. Among its first decrees, the Constituent Assembly proclaimed Yugoslavia a republic and declared that all the laws passed by the Anti-Fascist Council were legally binding. On 31 January 1946 a constitution came into force based on the Soviet constitution of 1936 and making Yugoslavia a Federal People's Republic comprising six regions: Slovenia, Croatia, Serbia, Bosnia-Herzegovina, Montenegro and Macedonia.

In Albania the Communists were able to seize power even more swiftly than in Yugoslavia. The small Communist Party that Tito had founded in 1941 established an apparently all-party Anti-Fascist Council for National Liberation with his active support in May 1944. Like its Yugoslav counterpart, it received material and military support from the Western Allies, especially Great Britain. The chairman of the Communist Party's Central Committee, the grammar school teacher Enver Hoxha, had himself elected leader of the Council's executive organ, the National Liberation Committee. The National Front – a rival organization active in the south of Albania – had fought the Italian troops occupying the region and opposed the satellite regime installed by the Italians in Tirana, but it also collaborated with the Germans who marched into Albania following the Italian surrender in September 1943 and nominally re-established the region's independence.

The Communist-led National Liberation Army took up the fight against the Germans and enjoyed considerable success, its actions helping to speed up the withdrawal of the Wehrmacht from central and northern Albania in the autumn of 1944. On 22 October, even before Tirana had been captured, the National Liberation Committee had itself declared Albania's democratic government by an ad hoc assembly in the form of the Second Anti-Fascist Congress for National Liberation. As a result, the Communists were now the country's de facto rulers. By rigging the elections on 2 December 1945, Hoxha's Democratic Unity List gave itself a semblance of parliamentary legitimacy. The newly elected National Assembly proclaimed the Albanian People's Republic on 11 January 1946, allowing the Communist revolution to proceed in a pseudo-legalistic form.

There were good reasons why Stalin, unlike Tito and Hoxha, took his time in establishing Communist regimes in the countries of eastern central and south-east Europe that were under the direct influence of the Soviet Union. In 1945 the secretary general of the Soviet Communist Party was keen to ensure that a democratic façade was maintained in those countries occupied by the Red Army and, where possible, to set up coalition governments in which the Communists were not obviously in the ascendant. If he adopted this course, it was not simply to take the sting out of any potential criticism of these burgeoning 'people's democracies' on the part of the Western Powers, he also did so in the interests of the Communist Parties that were involved in government in four countries in western Europe: France, Italy, Belgium and Denmark.

In France the Communists had joined the National Liberation Committee in April 1944 at the repeated request of de Gaulle. Communists held the posts of minister of health and of aviation in de Gaulle's provisional government that was formed on 10 September 1944. In Italy the Communist leader Palmiro Togliatti was deputy prime minister under Ivanoe Bonomi, a post he retained until 8 June 1945, when he became minister of justice under Ferruccio Parri. The finance ministers in both Bonomi's and Parri's cabinet were also party members. In Belgium, too, the Communists were active in government, sitting in cabinet alongside Christian Democrats and Liberals in the coalition government of the Socialist Achille van Acker. In Denmark the transport minister in the Liberation Ministry under the Social Democrat Vilhelm Buhl was also a Communist. In all four countries the Communist ministers remained loyal and did nothing that might be construed as preparations for a violent overthrow of the existing regime.

In 1945 Stalin had no ambitions in this regard: his principal interest was to consolidate and build up Soviet influence wherever the Red Army had the means by which to steer governments and political life in whatever direction it wanted. And nowhere were these conditions as well defined as in the Soviet-occupied part of Germany. In Stalin's eyes, this region was not only the jewel in the Soviet crown following the defeat of National Socialist Germany, it was also the guarantee of a further increase in Soviet power in Europe. As long as the

United States maintained a powerful military presence in Europe, Stalin was keen not to provoke America unnecessarily. But once the United States had withdrawn its troops, the balance of power in Europe would shift, a prospect that the Soviet Union found gratifying in the extreme.

New Beginnings and Traditions: Germany after Capitulation

Even before Germany surrendered, the Soviet Union had already begun to implement political changes in the part of the country that it occupied. On 2 May 1945 – the day on which the troops defending Berlin laid down their weapons – a group of émigré German Communists under the leadership of Walter Ulbricht, a former member of the Saxon Reichstag and of the Communist Party's Politburo since 1927, arrived in the capital. Their task was to provide systematic support for the Soviet Union in its attempts to reform the region in the spirit of Communism. On 17 May the Soviet commander of Berlin, General Nikolai Bersarin, established a municipal authority for Greater Berlin under a non-party mayor, placing all of the key positions in the hands of Communists. A similar policy was adopted by the Soviet occupying powers in the other towns and cities that were a part of the Soviet zone.

The victory speech that Stalin delivered in Moscow on 9 May left the world in no doubt about his aims with regard to Germany: the Soviet Union was celebrating victory, he declared, but it had no intention of either dismembering or destroying Germany. This was a clear rejection of the plans for Germany's dismemberment that he had proposed in Teheran and Yalta. In the meantime he had evidently convinced himself that, having gained the northern part of East Prussia and pushed Poland westwards at Germany's expense, the Soviet Union could best safeguard its own interests by using its zone of occupation to influence the whole of Germany. In order to do this, it was important to ensure that what remained of the Reich was not broken down into independent states.

On 5 June the four victorious powers drew the logical consequence from Germany's unconditional surrender and assumed overall control of the areas they occupied. The Declaration Regarding the Defeat of Germany and the Assumption of Supreme Authority in Germany was issued in Berlin in the joint names of the four commanders in chief of the Allied forces: Dwight D. Eisenhower for the United States; Georgi Zhukov for the Soviet Union; Bernard Montgomery for the United Kingdom; and Jean de Lattre de Tassigny for France. It included the general terms of Germany's surrender as enshrined in its military capitulation of 8/9 May, its preamble specifically stating that 'there is no central Government or authority in Germany capable of accepting responsibility for the maintenance of order, the administration of the country and compliance with the requirements of the victorious Powers'. The assumption of supreme authority by the four Allies included 'all the powers possessed by the German Government, the High Command and any state, municipal, or local government authority'. Specifically excluded from this declaration was any mention of 'the annexation of Germany'.[104]

Supreme authority was exercised by the commanders in chief in the occupied zones under their control and by the Allied Control Council in all matters affecting Germany as a whole. The same was true of Berlin, which was divided into four sectors. Here all matters pertaining to the city as a whole were the responsibility of Allied Command. Between 1 and 4 July Soviet troops occupied the western parts of Saxony, Thuringia and Mecklenburg that had recently been vacated by the Americans and British. At the same time the Americans, British and French moved into their allocated sectors in Berlin. As agreed in Yalta, the French-occupied zone in the south-west of Germany was taken from what had been planned as the American and British zones.

The Allies adopted a similar procedure in Austria, except that in Vienna, unlike Berlin, the inner city was administered jointly by the four Allies, and, unlike Germany, Austria already had its own government by the summer of 1945. The Soviet Union had installed a provisional coalition government under the former chancellor Karl Renner on 27 April. It included not only Renner's Socialists but also Christian Socialists and Communists and reintroduced the 1929 version of the 1920 constitution on 1 May and a week later permitted the formation of regional governments in the restored regions. The provisional government in Vienna was formally recognized by the Western Powers on 20 October.

The first signs of a new political beginning in Germany were already making themselves felt in what would later be the British zone even before the country's military surrender. Here the driving force was a former Social Democrat member of the Reichstag, Kurt Schumacher, who had been released from Dachau in March 1943 after a ten-year martyrdom. On 19 April – nine days after the Americans had captured Hanover – he convened a meeting in the city intended to re-establish the Social Democrats as a political party. The first local association was formed in Hanover on 6 May, becoming the provisional party headquarters – the Schumacher Bureau – in the British and American zone.

The first party to regroup after the collapse of Germany was the Communist Party, which was re-founded in Berlin on 11 June, the day after the Soviet Military Administration had allowed the formation not only of 'anti-Fascist and democratic' parties but also of trade unions. In calling for new members, the party struck an emphatically nationalist and reformist note, professing its belief in free trade and private initiatives in business on the basis of private property. It also expressed the view that it would be wrong 'to impose the Soviet system on Germany', since such a course of action did not take account of the present conditions in the country. Rather, the decisive interests of the German people suggested an alternative course in the form of the establishment of 'an anti-fascist, democratic regime in a parliamentary-democratic republic with all democratic rights and liberties for the people'.[105]

It was by no means clear in the summer of 1945 how relations would develop between the Communists and the Social Democrats. In both parties there were many who thought that Hitler would never have come to power if there had not been a deep split within the 'Marxist' workers' movement and that it was therefore imperative that they overcome their historical differences. Acting in complete agreement with Stalin, the 'Ulbricht Group' gave absolute priority to rebuilding the Communist Party: once the party was effectively organized, it could – and must – make the unity of the working class one of its principal objectives. Schumacher was emphatically opposed to all plans to unite the workers' movement, and in August 1945, in his 'Political Guidelines for the Social Democrats in their Relations to Other Political Factors', he made his views clear in no uncertain terms: 'The Communist Party is indissolubly tied to one, and only one, of the victorious powers, to nationalist and imperialist Russia and to its foreign policy aims.'[106] As Schumacher was increasingly able to consolidate his position within the Social Democrat movement in the western-occupied zones, then this position also became that of the Social Democrats in the western parts of Germany.

The first 'bourgeois' party to be formed after the war was the Christian Democratic Union, or CDU, which represented an attempt to overcome the denominational divide in Germany and bring together Catholics and Protestants in a people's party that could appeal to every social class. Branches were founded in Cologne, Berlin and Frankfurt, and it was here that the first meetings were held in June 1945. Konrad Adenauer, whom the Americans restored to his former post as mayor of Cologne on 4 May 1945 and who went on to become federal chancellor, was not one of the CDU's founding members, for he spent the early months after the end of the war vacillating over whether to revive the Catholic Centre Party or to join the new interdenominational party. Not until the end of August did he join the CDU. German liberals also began to regroup in July 1945. Although they may have adopted a variety of names, their common goal was to avoid the old split between a left- and a right-wing liberal party.

The Americans initially kept their distance from these new political groupings. Directive 1067 of the Joint Chiefs of Staff that Truman ratified on 10 May stated that American policy was aimed not at the liberation of Germany as a defeated enemy state but at its occupation. It also included a ban on all political activity. In practice, of course, this ban could no more be maintained than the slogan 'No fraternization' that was a part of the same directive. If Americans wanted to re-educate the Germans and turn followers of National Socialism into democrats, then the latter had to be given the chance to act in politically responsible ways. Since this was impossible on a higher level in 1945, it was necessary to make a start on a lower level among the country's parishes and communes. The Americans placed far too much trust in 'grass-roots democracy' for them to be able to ignore this insight in the longer term.

In parishes and towns in the American zone, especially those in Bavaria, it was often local Catholic priests and, later, former trade union leaders whose opinions were sought by the officials representing the occupying power and whom they consulted whenever they wanted to know which Germans could be trusted with administrative tasks. Equally important were the expertise and personal experience of German émigrés, some of whom had been smuggled back into Germany in May 1945 with the agreement of the Social Democrats' executive committee in London and with the help of the American Office of Strategic Services. On their return to Germany a number of them played an active role in forming anti-Fascist workers' initiatives. German émigrés also featured in the 'White Lists' of Germans who, politically speaking, had not been compromised or who were known to have opposed Hitler. The support that the Soviet occupying power offered to Germans eager to found their own parties also helped to undermine the ban on political activities as early as the summer of 1945. If the democratic principles espoused by the Western Powers were to prosper in Germany, then it was necessary to rely on the people and institutions that had helped to sustain the first German democracy, the Weimar Republic.

And there was another German tradition, older than the country's democratic legacy, that the Western Allies sought to use for their own ends. This was the federalist tradition, which seemed well suited to preventing the resurgence of a powerful central force. In the light of their experience of the totalitarian single-party state that the Third Reich had been, many Germans might be expected to feel a certain sympathy for a federalist system. And even the Soviet occupying power struck a federalist note by dividing its zone into five regions on 9 July: Thuringia, Saxony, Mecklenburg, Brandenburg and Saxe-Anhalt. Even so, these regional governments had only limited powers when compared with the eleven central authorities under the Soviet Military Administration which, largely Communist-controlled, had been established only a short time earlier.

In the western zones, it took much longer to establish regional administrations. This was a process that began on 28 May 1945, when the Americans installed a new government in Bavaria under the former leader of the Bavarian People's Party, Fritz Schäffer, and that ended on 1 November 1946 with the formation of the region of Lower Saxony that was ordered by the British authorities. The Saarland enjoyed special status, for although the Allies had all agreed that it would be a part of the French zone, it was in fact annexed by France as a separate economic region cut off from the rest of Germany.

The occupying powers agreed in principle that the danger that had been posed by National Socialism and by German militarism needed to be removed once and for all. The Berlin Declaration of 5 June ordered the arrest of leading Nazis and of all 'the war criminals and all persons who have participated in planning or carrying out Nazi enterprises involving or resulting in atrocities or war crimes'.[107]

But from the very outset there were clear differences between the Allies in terms of the thrust and methods that should be used in combating the legacy of National Socialism – or, as the Soviet and German Communists called it, 'Fascism'. The western democracies were keen above all to punish all guilty individuals, while the Soviet Union additionally wanted to remove the 'class distinctions' that in the Marxist-Leninist view of history had produced 'Fascism' in the first place, hence the Russian desire to destroy the basis on which the Junker class and the capitalist bourgeoisie had built up their power. In Soviet eyes, the principal aim of 'anti-Fascism' was to secure the hegemony of the Communists. On 14 July 1945 – the twelfth anniversary of Germany's ban on all political parties with the exception of the NSDAP – the United Front of Anti-Fascist and Democratic Parties (Antifa) was founded in the Soviet-occupied zone. It comprised the German Communist Party, the German Social Democrats, the Christian Democratic Union and the German Liberal Democrat Party. The Communists' leading role was not spelt out in detail but was already guaranteed even at this early date.

The country in which the four occupying powers were to exercise supreme authority for the most part lay in ruins. The largest cities and many of the larger towns had been turned into a wasteland by the Allies' bombing campaign. Many transport links, including nine-tenths of the railway network, were destroyed or disrupted. And millions of men, women and children, including those whose homes had been bombed, refugees from the east, survivors of the Holocaust and displaced persons from eastern, eastern central and south-east Europe, were either housed in the most primitive conditions or had nowhere at all to live. The Reichsmark had lost most of its value; German savings had been largely destroyed by the National Socialists' method of financing the war; food was in such short supply that many people, especially those living in the towns and cities, were suffering from hunger; and with the approach of winter the lack of fuel was a cause for serious concern. Many of the 'middle-class' ideas on morality that had been accepted until then had been radically undermined, especially respect for the property of others, be it in private or public hands.

On paper at least, JCS 1067, the Joint Chiefs of Staff directive that was inspired by the Morgenthau Plan and that had been issued in May 1945, was still in force in early July: under its terms no measures could be undertaken that might be 'designed to maintain or strengthen the German economy'.[108] But if the United States had stuck to this maxim, Germany would have been engulfed in an unimaginable catastrophe that would not only have affected the occupying troops but caused the men and women living in western democracies, notably the American people, to rise up against their leaders. The United States could not afford to contemplate such a conflict with its own people and with its own values, with the result that when the three victorious powers – the United States, the Soviet Union and Great Britain – met in Potsdam between 17 July and 2 August July 1945, there was every likelihood that Truman would use the opportunity to call for a change of heart.

Potsdam: The Decision of the Three Great Powers

In the wake of Germany's surrender the question of a further summit between the three main powers was left hanging in the air. In both Teheran and Yalta the leading statesmen of the United States, the Soviet Union and Great Britain had agreed on certain basic principles concerning the post-war world order. Now that National Socialist Germany had been defeated by their troops, they needed to work out in detail how to proceed in Germany and central Europe. There was no thought of including a fourth power in their deliberations, for although France had once again been recognized as a major power and been given a zone to occupy in both Germany and Austria, Stalin had no interest in negotiating with three, rather than two, other western powers, and neither Truman nor Churchill saw any reason to give the headstrong General de Gaulle a chance to make agreement among the Allies even harder to achieve than it already promised to be. After all, de Gaulle had provoked Britain and America in the spring of 1945 by occupying the Aosta Valley in Italy and by sending troops to the Lebanon and Syria. In both cases the Anglo-Saxon powers had been driven to the brink of military conflict as a result of his high-handed actions.

It was Churchill who was the first to insist on a further meeting with Truman and Stalin, a conference he proposed to Roosevelt as early as 11 May, so afraid was he that Stalin was planning to extend Soviet influence in Europe. In Churchill's view only a powerful Anglo-Saxon West whose members acted together had any chance of placating the 'imperialistic demands of Soviet Communist Russia',[109] which is why at the end of May he roundly condemned the plan put forward by Truman's pro-Soviet special envoy, Joseph E. Davies, that any summit attended by all three world leaders should be held only after a meeting between the American president and the Soviet party leader. Such conditions, he explained, were demeaning for Great Britain and the Commonwealth, and the British government would not attend an Allied conference that was held in these circumstances. Britain, Churchill insisted, must be treated as an equal partner from the very outset.

In a memorandum that he handed to the American diplomat at the end of May, Churchill raised his objections to the idea of an American-Soviet summit to the level of a point of principle:

> It must be remembered that Britain and the United States are united at this time upon the same ideologies, namely, freedom, and the principles set out in the American Constitution and humbly reproduced with modern variations in the Atlantic Charter. The Soviet Government have [sic] a different philosophy, namely, Communism, and use to the full the methods of police government, which they are applying in every State which has fallen a victim to their liberating arms. The Prime Minister cannot readily bring himself to accept the idea that the position of the United States is that

Britain and Soviet Russia are just two foreign Powers, six of one and half a dozen of the other, with whom the troubles of the late war have to be adjusted. [...] The great causes and principles for which Britain and the United States have suffered and triumphed are not mere matters of the balance of power. They in fact involve the salvation of the world.[110]

Although Truman immediately denied that he had been planning a preliminary conference involving only America and the Soviet Union, he was unable to allay Churchill's fears that the new president was intending to pursue a policy of appeasement towards the Soviet Union. During the initial months of his presidency, Truman was influenced by his country's foreign minister, James F. Byrnes, as well as by Joseph Davies and by Harry Hopkins, who had been Roosevelt's closest adviser, with the result that he tended to regard Stalin as a pragmatic leader whose lust for power was already sated, while he was convinced that Churchill was guilty of seriously exaggerating the Russian dictator's expansionist ambitions to the point of becoming a hysterical anti-Communist. It was during the negotiations that took place in Moscow in late May and early June 1945 between Hopkins and Stalin that the die was cast with regard to Poland's future fate, when Hopkins agreed to the enlargement of the Communist-dominated Warsaw cabinet through the inclusion of a number of former exiles and 'bourgeois' politicians, a move which, purely symbolic in character, persuaded both Washington and London to recognize Osóbka-Morawski's government in early July. At this juncture Truman was keen above all to persuade the Soviet Union to enter the war with Japan as soon as possible and to maintain Soviet-American cooperation beyond the end of the war.

Soviet policies were not the only reason why Churchill was keen to convene a three-nation summit as quickly as possible. By the time he drafted his memorandum to Davies at the end of May, he was no longer the head of a national government but only of a purely Conservative cabinet. At its party conference in Blackpool, the Labour Party had decided to leave what had effectively been an all-party government, prompting Churchill to ask King George VI to accept his resignation on 23 May and to form a new government. One of his first official acts on being reappointed prime minister was to dissolve the House of Commons that had been elected in November 1935 and whose term in office had twice been extended on account of the war, most recently in December 1944. New elections were set for 5 July, an early date thought to favour the Tories, who hoped that Churchill's popularity as wartime prime minister would benefit them so soon after their country's victory over Germany. Since most British soldiers could vote only while they were still abroad and it would need time to bring their ballot boxes back to England, the lower house decided to seal these boxes for a period of three weeks. Until then the outcome of the elections remained uncertain. Insofar as it was in Churchill's power to influence matters, the planned summit had to take place before the election results were known, in other words, at a time when no one could doubt whether or not he was still the British prime minister.

At the end of May Truman, Churchill and Stalin agreed to hold their summit in Berlin on 15 July. In fact the conference began two days later than planned and not in the ruins of the former capital, but in Potsdam, which had suffered slightly less badly. The main topic on the agenda during the first eight days of the conference was Poland's western border. Appealing to the wishes of the Polish government, Stalin demanded that the border be the Oder–Neiße Line, while Churchill and – far less forcefully – Roosevelt had insisted that it be further to the east. Churchill's main argument was that the population between the Lausitz Neiße and the Glatz Neiße was purely German and that Germany already had enough problems trying to house and care for millions of refugees from the east. The food and fuel available within the 1937 borders had to be available to all Germans, regardless of the zone in which they were living. On this point Churchill refused to be moved even by the Polish delegation under Bolesław Bierut that was able to explain its position to the three powers on 24 July.

The following day Churchill flew back to London in order to be present when the elections results were announced on 26 July. To the surprise of most observers, the overwhelming victor was the Labour Party, which returned 393 members to the lower house, while the Conservatives held on to only 197 seats. (The Labour Party won 49.7 per cent of the vote, the Conservatives 36.2 per cent and the Liberals 9 per cent, resulting in twelve seats.) The brief campaign had concentrated on the economy and on social policy rather than the merits of the wartime premier and his party. The majority of the British population wanted to see the implementation of the reforms that had been promised to them by the Beveridge Report of 1942 but which had yet to be put into operation. (The one exception was the Education Act of August 1944, which raised the school-leaving age to fifteen and introduced free lessons at secondary as well as primary schools.) The Labour Party's slogan – 'Let us face the future' – had proved more attractive than the Tories' patriotic appeal to keep Churchill in office as a tried and tested statesman. Churchill could comfort himself with the knowledge that even those of his compatriots who had voted for the Labour Party recognized his historic achievement: no other western leader had contributed as much to the Allies' victory over National Socialist Germany and to the preservation of free democracy as the now seventy-year-old Churchill.

His successor as prime minister was Clement Attlee, the country's former deputy prime minister and until then the leader of the opposition in the House of Commons. At Churchill's insistence he had been a member of the British delegation at the Potsdam Conference, but he and his new foreign secretary, Ernest Bevin, who had replaced Anthony Eden, were far less familiar than their predecessors with the problems that needed to be resolved in Potsdam. In the case of Poland's disputed western border with Germany, neither of them felt bound to Churchill's implacable rejection of the Oder–Neiße Line that was demanded by

Poland and the Soviet Union. After 26 July the political weight that Great Britain could add to the scales at the Potsdam Conference was reduced, while that of the Americans increased. This was the first example of the way in which the change of government in London was to affect British foreign policy.

Truman's opposition to the more westerly border was less resolute than Churchill's even during the first few days of the conference. After 26 July the Americans and especially their secretary of state, James F. Byrnes, came to hold the view that they could reasonably go more than halfway in meeting Soviet demands with regard to Poland's western border if Stalin were to agree to a compromise on another controversial matter, the question of reparations. Here the parties additionally felt pressed for time, for Truman wanted to return to the United States as quickly as possible in order to devote himself fully to a victorious conclusion to the war with Japan. In turn this meant that he was eager to withdraw most of his American troops from Europe and deploy them in the Far East.

The agreement on Poland's western border that was reached in Potsdam was only apparently a compromise. The border was to begin in the north at a point just to the west of Swinemünde (Świnoujście), so that Stettin (Szczecin) became a part of Poland. After that it followed the Oder and the western Neiße as far south as the Czechoslovak border. With the exception of the northern part of East Prussia, the German regions in the east were to be administered by Poland. A definitive ruling on the border was left to a peace treaty to resolve. Northern East Prussia, including Königsberg (Kaliningrad), was placed under Soviet control, the Western Powers agreeing to support the Soviet Union's claims to this region in any peace treaty that was still to be negotiated.

Polish administration in the German regions in the east did not mean that Poland became a fifth occupying power with a representative on the Allied Control Council. In terms of international law the administrative authority in these territories was merely provisional, but in practice Poland exercised sovereign control over its new regions in the west. In this regard the United States and Great Britain had been faced with a fait accompli: in the light of the Red Army's conquest of the areas in question and in view of the continuing deportation of Germans from these eastern regions, everything suggested that the provisional nature of the governance of these areas to the east of the Oder–Neiße Line, which represented a quarter of the land mass of the German Reich before 1937, would prove to be worth no more than the paper on which it was written. Germany as defined by its 1937 borders, which was the starting point of the Potsdam Conference and, as such, agreed to by Stalin, became a legal fiction thanks to this very same conference. In reality, Germany consisted of the area occupied by the four Allies and governed by the Allied Control Council. This was the Germany that emerged from the Second World War, a Germany that no longer included East Prussia, Farther Pomerania, East Brandenburg and Silesia.

On the question of reparations, too, the Allies sought to accommodate Stalin's wishes, even if they were reluctant to go as far as they did with regard to Poland's western border. Although the Soviet Union failed to achieve partial control over the Ruhr, as it had hoped to do, it did receive assurances that its claims to reparations payments from the three occupied zones in the west would be met. The three major powers agreed in principle that over the next two years reparations could come both from the dismantling of German industrial plants – a move designed to destroy Germany's potential for waging another war – and from Germany's foreign assets. The Potsdam Agreement did not include any provisions for reparations payments from current production of a kind that the Soviet Union had already implemented in its own occupied zone.

In keeping with a recommendation from the Allied Reparations Committee that had been set up at Yalta, the Soviet Union, which had suffered the most from the war that Hitler had unleashed, received 56 per cent of the reparations from all the occupied zones as well as 10 per cent from the industrial plants that were to be dismantled in the western zones. In addition, Moscow received a further 15 per cent from these plants in return for Soviet supplies of food-stuffs, coal, potash, zinc, timber, clay and petroleum products from its own occupied zone. Poland's claims were to be met from the Soviet quotient. In response to American demands, Austria was spared any reparations payments on the grounds that it had been Hitler's first victim. With regard to German assets abroad, Britain and the United States agreed not to make any claims on Bulgaria, Romania, Hungary, Upper Austria and Finland if, for its part, the Soviet Union forfeited the right to any claims on German assets to the west of the aforementioned regions or to the gold that the Western Powers had taken from those parts of the Soviet-occupied region that had been temporarily under their control.

The Potsdam reparations ruling was a provisional measure riven by contra-dictions and conflict. In response to British demands, there was no attempt to set an upper limit of $20,000 million on the total cost of reparations, a figure that the Soviet Union had asked for. Since every occupying power could collect reparations from its own zone, everything depended on the Allies' ability to work together. But it soon became clear that in spite of the agreements reached in Potsdam the Soviet Union was continuing to draw the bulk of its reparations from current production, not only jeopardizing the welfare of the German population in its own occupied zone but also flying in the face of its promise to provide food and other goods to the western zones by way of exchange. In the circumstances it was impossible to achieve the declared aim of Truman, Attlee and Stalin to treat Germany as a single economic entity within its 1945 borders.

But the practical implementation of this maxim was thwarted by one of the western occupying powers, too, when France, which had not attended the Potsdam Conference, announced in no uncertain terms on 7 August 1945 that it was vetoing the establishment of German central administrative units that the

Allies were supposed to support in order to maintain Germany's economic unity. France retained the right to decide as it thought fit with regard to the Potsdam reparations agreement even though it was a member of the Allied Reparations Commission. In general Paris regarded as binding only those decisions to which it subsequently gave its explicit approval.

Truman, Churchill and Stalin had evidently not thought through to their logical conclusion the possible consequences of excluding France from the Potsdam Conference. Quite apart from the dilatory character of the reparations compromise, the French objections to central administrative offices in Germany played a significant part in ensuring that Germany's economic unity remained a mere postulate. Although the three major powers had shelved the idea of 'dismembering' Germany that had been raised at their conferences in Teheran and Yalta, they had not completely ruled out a partition of the country. In the summer of 1945, therefore, it was impossible to predict whether or not Germany would ever constitute a single economic and national entity.

The question of Poland's western border and the problem of reparations remained intractable, but most of the other issues relating to Germany were relatively uncontroversial. According to its opening statement, the Potsdam Declaration's principal aim was to ensure that 'German militarism and nazism will be extirpated and the Allies will take in agreement together, now and in the future, the other measures necessary to assure that Germany never again will threaten her neighbors or the peace of the world'. At the same time, the Allies offered an assurance that it was not their intention 'to destroy or enslave the German people'. Rather, they wanted to give the German people the opportunity

> to prepare for the eventual reconstruction of their life on a democratic and peaceful basis. If their own efforts are steadily directed to this end, it will be possible for them in due course to take their place among the free and peaceful peoples of the world.

The occupation of Germany was to be guided by the following aims: 'The complete disarmament and demilitarization of Germany and the elimination or control of all German industry that could be used for military production'. The NSDAP was to be destroyed, as were subsidiary organizations such as the SS, SA, secret service and Gestapo, together with the country's land forces, its navy and its air force, including its general staff. All National Socialist laws that discriminated against people on the basis of their race, religion or political beliefs were to be repealed. War criminals and their agents were to be detained and brought to trial, and all National Socialist party leaders were to be arrested and interned, as were all those persons deemed to pose a threat to the Allied occupation and its aims. An initial list of the principal war criminals was to be published on 1 September. The three great powers wanted to decide as soon as possible on the best way of proceeding against this group of war criminals.

'To prepare for the eventual reconstruction of German political life on a democratic basis and for eventual peaceful cooperation in international life by Germany', it was necessary to reorganize the country's educational and legal systems as well as its administration, beginning on a local level. All democratic political parties were to be permitted and encouraged. All of them were to have the right to call meetings and hold public discussions. Elected assemblies were to be set up as soon as possible on a local, provincial and regional level. As far as the need for military security allowed it, there should be freedom of speech, freedom of the press and freedom of religion. Religious institutions must be respected, and free trade unions should be established. But before the Allies could make good their promises, the German people must accept that

> they have suffered a total military defeat and [...] they cannot escape responsibility for what they have brought upon themselves, since their own ruthless warfare and the fanatical Nazi resistance have destroyed [the] German economy and made chaos and suffering inevitable.

Under the heading 'Economic Principles' Germany was given the task of destroying its potential for fomenting a new war and of introducing a rigorous policy of decentralization, the aim of which was to be achieved by 'eliminating the present excessive concentration of economic power as exemplified in particular by cartels, syndicates, trusts and other monopolistic arrangements'. In reorganizing the economic life of the nation particular emphasis was to be placed on the development of agriculture and 'peaceful domestic industries'. Allied controls were to be imposed on Germany 'only to the extent necessary'. Reparations should leave the German people with sufficient means to subsist without the need to rely on external assistance. The proceeds of exports from current production and from existing supplies were to be available in the first instance to pay for imports for which the necessary means were to be made available when drawing up a budgetary plan. In this context German administrative centres were required to play a significant role, except that the French veto prevented such an apparatus from ever being established.

There was no argument among the Allies concerning the vast movement of peoples that resulted from the redrawing of the map of Europe. Throughout the war, Churchill had repeatedly drawn attention to the example of the Greek-Turkish population transfer that had been carried out under the terms of the Treaty of Lausanne of 1923. On the basis of this agreement 1.2 million Greeks had been deported to Greece from Asia Minor, from the Pontus region and from Eastern Thrace, while 400,000 Turks from Macedonia, Thessaly and the Epirus were resettled in Turkey. A similar population exchange between Turkey and Bulgaria had been envisaged in November 1919 under the terms of the Treaty of Neuilly. In the light of these precedents, neither Britain nor America felt any misgivings that might have militated against forced resettlements as long as these were regulated under international law.

In the specific case that was to be decided in Potsdam, the experience of German policies of the last decade suggested a population transfer. After all that the Germans had done to their neighbours, no one could think that Poles, Czechs and Germans would live together harmoniously in the territories that lay beyond the new border with Germany. If the three great powers had left millions of Germans to live in these parts of Poland and Czechoslovakia, then from an Allied point of view this could merely encourage an aggressive German irredentism and hence pose a further threat to peace in Europe.

In response to demands from Soviet Russia, Poland and Czechoslovakia, the Allies recognized, therefore, that 'the transfer to Germany of German populations, or elements thereof, remaining in Poland, Czechoslovakia and Hungary, will have to be undertaken. They agree that any transfers that take place should be effected in an orderly and humane manner.'[111] This humanitarian provision was not legally enforceable, but it was included in an attempt to reassure the general public in all the western democracies: they had all been fully aware of the atrocities committed during the unofficial deportations during the war. But the notion of dividing the refugees among the different occupied zones in a way envisaged by the Potsdam Declaration proved to be illusory, for in August 1945 France refused to open up its borders to refugees and displaced persons.

By the time the Potsdam Conference ended on 2 August 1945, there was a further committee on which the three major powers had agreed, at least on paper: the Council of Foreign Ministers. Its members were representatives of the United States, the Soviet Union and Great Britain in addition to France and China. Its most important function was to draw up peace treaties for Italy, Romania, Bulgaria, Hungary and France and then submit these to the United Nations. (France and China were to advise on these treaties to the extent that they had signed armistice agreements with the states in question.) The Council was also to work towards a peaceful settlement in Germany so that the document in question could be accepted by a German government suitable for this purpose, once such a government had been formed.

Some of the agreements made by the Three Powers were initially not intended for publication, although they were not officially secret. They included agreements to begin the withdrawal of British and Soviet troops from Iran by withdrawing Allied troops from Teheran with immediate effect and to revise the Black Sea Straits Agreement signed in Montreux in 1936, which restored to Turkey full sovereignty over the Dardanelles, the Sea of Marmara and the Bosporus. This last-named point amounted to western support for the Soviet demand to be allowed to control the straits in question, a demand to which Turkey would of course have had to agree – which it did not in fact do.

None of the countries that attended the Potsdam Conference had pursued the aim of dividing Germany. Unlike France, all three were keen – albeit for different reasons – to treat the occupied country as an economic and, as far as possible, a future political unit. For the United States and Great Britain this was their only way of exerting influence on the Soviet zone and of receiving a share of the supplies to their own zones that the Soviets had agreed in Potsdam to provide. For their part, the Soviets banked on being able to influence the western-occupied zones and hoped to have the Ruhr – Germany's industrial heartland – placed under the control of all four powers, a suggestion that had not been rejected out of hand in Potsdam. If no agreement could be reached on these contentious issues, then there was no mistaking the geographical line along which the occupied area would be divided in two: it was the border that ran between the British and American zone on the one hand and the Soviet zone on the other.

At first blush, it was Stalin who emerged the victor from the Potsdam Conference. He had managed to have Poland moved further west, just as he had wanted, and on the question of reparations his demands had been met with the exception of an upper limit of $20,000 million and the internationalization of the Ruhr. If he had succeeded in asserting his demands with regard to the industrial region on the Rhine and in the Ruhr, the Soviet Union would have acquired decisive influence in the western half of Germany and also substantially strengthened its position in western Europe. But this triumph was denied to Stalin. His claims on the Ruhr encountered stiff resistance not only from the British in whose zone the industrial region lay but also from the United States, which was unquestionably the leading power in the West. Truman drew a far-reaching conclusion from the course of the Potsdam negotiations: even if the Soviet Union were to enter the war in the Far East, he had no desire to accord it the right to play a part in the occupation of Japan. Haggling with Stalin over the German question and the closely related Polish question had been unavoidable, but he was not willing to conduct similar negotiations with the Soviet leader following what he hoped would be the Allies' victory over Japan.

For Germany the results of the Three Powers' summit in Potsdam were mixed. The Potsdam Declaration was not a peace treaty but was intended to replace one for the foreseeable future. In terms of the territorial losses that it enshrined, to say nothing of the economic burdens that it imposed and the political obligations that it placed on Germany, it was far harsher than the Treaty of Versailles. But Potsdam also represented the United States' definitive abandonment of the spirit of the Morgenthau Plan. By now Morgenthau was no longer a member of the American government, Truman having accepted his treasury secretary's verbal resignation without further ado on 5 July – Morgenthau had resigned in response to Truman's refusal to allow him to attend the Potsdam Conference. The Declaration's demands on dismantling German industry may have been hard to meet but they were far from being a programme designed to deindustrialize the country or return it to an agrarian economy.

Politically, too, the outcome of the conference gave the Germans modest cause for hope. They received the assurance of individual rights and democratic participation in any decision-making process, marking a repudiation of JCS 1067 that had remained in force until then. Only in the western-occupied zones and in the western sectors of Berlin, of course, were there any real grounds for political optimism on the part of the Germans, for Stalin's interpretation of the word 'democracy' differed fundamentally from that of the Americans, the British and the French, a point he had proved not only in the Soviet Union but in all of those countries where with Soviet help Communists had gained key positions in 1944 and 1945.

Everything that the Western Powers noted on this subject in Potsdam confirmed Stalin in his conviction that they had finally come to accept as a fait accompli the events that had unfolded in south-east and eastern central Europe. Although the German question might still be unresolved, there was no longer any doubt that Europe was now divided into an eastern and a western sphere of influence and that it would remain so divided for the foreseeable future. By the time the Potsdam Conference ended, Churchill's reference to an 'iron curtain' summed up the reality of the old Continent even more aptly than it had before.

The End of the War (II): The Atom Bomb and Japan's Capitulation

Early on 16 July 1945 – the day before the start of the Potsdam Conference – a team of American and British nuclear physicists at Alamogordo in the New Mexico desert conducted an experiment that was to change the world, when they successfully exploded the first atom bomb. The experiment was the result of years of research that had been massively funded by the United States government in the form of what had become known as the Manhattan Project.

American efforts were driven in particular by the fear that thanks to the research of three German nuclear physicists, Otto Hahn, Werner Heisenberg and Carl Friedrich von Weizsäcker, Hitler's Germany might be able to produce and use the new means of mass destruction even before the United States. The fear proved to be unfounded, for Hitler was interested solely in 'miracle weapons' that could be used only in the shorter term and gave no thought to investing huge resources in a technology that might never even be used for military purposes. In consequence, German nuclear research lagged far behind its Anglo-Saxon counterpart and by 1944 had still only reached the stage at which Roosevelt's Uranium Committee had begun its work in July 1941. Although nuclear experiments were conducted in Germany – on the island of Rügen in October 1944 and at Ohrdruf, an outpost of the Buchenwald concentration camp, in early March 1945, the latter supervised by the SS – Germany was nowhere near having the capability of deploying atomic weapons by the end of the war.

The destructive force of 'Trinity' – the code name for the bomb exploded in New Mexico – far exceeded the expectations of J. Robert Oppenheimer, the man in charge of the team at Los Alamos. The science editor of the *New York Times*, William L. Laurence, was able to observe the clandestine event from a distance of some twenty miles and reported seeing

> a burst of flame such as had never before been seen on this planet, illuminating earth and sky, for a brief span that seemed eternal, with the might of many super-suns. [. . .] Then out of the great silence came a mighty thunder. For a brief interval the phenomena we had seen as light repeated themselves in terms of sound. It was the blast from thousands of blockbusters going off simultaneously at one spot. [. . .] The ground trembled under our feet as in an earthquake.[112]

Truman had arrived in Potsdam on 15 July and immediately after the experiment had taken place, he was told that it had been a success. Even before that, he had resolved that if there was no prospect of a rapid end to the war in the Far East, he would deploy the new weapon as soon as it had been tested. On 18 June, his chief of staff, Admiral William Leahy, had reckoned that based on the experiences of the Battle of Okinawa between April and June 1945, an invasion of the principal islands of Japan would cost the lives of some 268,000 American soldiers – approximately as many as had already lost their lives on every front in the Second World War. Together with his secretary of war, Henry Lewis Stimson, and his secretary of state, James F. Byrnes, Truman believed that if the war were to continue using conventional weapons, it would be several months – possibly as late as the autumn of 1946 – before Japan surrendered. Since the atom bomb offered a chance to save the lives of hundreds of thousands of GIs, it would have to be dropped on a Japanese city. Not only Truman and his closest advisers were in agreement on this point, so, too, was Churchill. Truman and Byrnes – he, too, a former senator – were essentially domestic politicians in the summer of 1945, and both thought invariably of home voters, who would not forgive their own leaders if they continued a bloody and costly war even though they had the technical means to bring it to an early end.

After he had been informed of the results of the experiment in the New Mexico desert, Truman spoke to Stalin on the margins of the eighth plenary session of the Potsdam Conference on 24 July and mentioned in passing that the United States now had at its disposal a new and unusually destructive weapon. Stalin reacted calmly and said only that he hoped that the United States would use it to good effect against Japan. In fact Stalin had long known about the experiment at Alamogordo thanks to a Soviet spy, the nuclear physicist Klaus Fuchs, who had emigrated to Britain from Germany in 1933 and had worked on the Manhattan Project.

At this stage no decision had been taken to drop a nuclear bomb on Japan. Before such a step was taken, Japan was to be given a chance to end the war. In an ultimatum dated 26 July, Truman, Churchill and the president of the National Government of the Republic of China, Chiang Kai-shek, who was not in fact present in Potsdam, demanded that Japan lay down its arms by 3 August at the latest and in that way avoid the total destruction of its armed forces and devastation of the country's islands.

The Allies' conditions were non-negotiable. All of those deemed involved in the country's 'irresponsible militarism' and policy of aggressive expansionism must be removed from power and Japanese war criminals called to account. As set forth in the Cairo Declaration of November 1943, the territories and sovereignty of Japan were to be limited to the areas that it held before it embarked on its expansionist policy. And Japan would be occupied until such time as a new, democratic and peaceful order had been established. The Potsdam Declaration said nothing about the *Tenno* (emperor), demanding neither his abdication and condemnation nor the transition from a monarchy to a republic. Nor did the Declaration indicate the Allies' willingness to leave Emperor Hirohito on the throne. Finally, there was no direct threat to use the atom bomb.

Since 7 April 1945 the Japanese government had been headed by Admiral Suzuki Kantaro, who, now in his late seventies, enjoyed the emperor's trust. He owed his appointment to forces eager for peace. At the urging of the Japanese foreign minister, Togo Shigenori, the former prime minister Konoe Fumimaro began talks in Moscow in July in the hope of persuading the neutral Soviet Union to intervene with the Western Powers, but the Soviet negotiators reacted with extreme reserve and prevaricated. Konoe's actions were discussed in Potsdam and were not without result, for the Potsdam Declaration demanded only the unconditional surrender of the Japanese armed forces, not of the country as a whole, as had been the case with Germany, leaving the Japanese the right of political self-determination and holding out the prospect of access to raw materials and participation in world trade relations. All of these points were intended as a signal to those forces in Tokyo that were keen to see a rapid return to peace.

But the Japanese leadership was deeply divided. The moderate forces associated with the foreign minister saw positive points in the Potsdam Declaration but felt that they needed to clarify the question as to the Allies' future attitude to Emperor Hirohito, whereas the radical militarists associated with the minister of the army, Anami Korechika, and with the chief of the army's general staff, General Umezu Yoshijiro, regarded the acceptance of an ultimatum as incompatible with Japanese honour. On 28 July, at the end of lengthy discussions within the Supreme War Council, Togo recommended that they wait for the Soviet response to Konoe's mission. In a subsequent press conference, the prime minister explained that they had decided on a policy of *mokusatsu*, which, although difficult to translate, amounted to a refusal to acknowledge the situation and to treat it with silent contempt, prompting the minister for the army to coin the phrase that dominated the headlines of the nationalist press the following day: 'Rejection Through Ignorance.' From an American perspective this was an unambiguous no and, as such, a signal that the United States should begin preparations to drop the first atom bomb.

As the city chosen to be bombed, the planners opted for an industrial and military centre, the port of Hiroshima. At 08:15 on the morning of 6 August 1945, acting on the orders of President Truman, the crew of the *Enola Gay* bomber dropped the first atom bomb to be used as a military weapon from a height of approximately 2,000 feet. The bomb bore the name 'Little Boy'. Some 80,000 of the city's 355,000 inhabitants were killed outright, and a further 60,000 were dead by the end of 1945. Over the coming months and years a further 60,000 died from radioactive poisoning. Four-fifths of the city's build-ings were destroyed or severely damaged on 6 August 1945.

On 8 August, two days after the bombing of Hiroshima, the Soviet Union declared war on Japan. At this date the Americans had still not received a formal offer of surrender from Japan even though Truman had threatened only the previous day that he would order further air raids if Japan did not sue for peace forthwith. The reason for Tokyo's silence was the continuing divisions among the country's leaders: the Supreme War Council could take only unanimous decisions, and these were impossible to achieve because of the differences between the moderates and the radicals. And so Truman ordered a second atom bomb to be dropped, the last of the three produced within the framework of the Manhattan Project. 'Fatman' was dropped on the port of Nagasaki at 11:00 on the morning of 9 August, landing on an armaments factory operated by Mitsubishi. Of the city's 270,000 inhabitants, 39,000 died as a direct result of the attack, and a further 31,000 had perished by the end of the year. Some 40 per cent of the city's buildings were destroyed.

Even after the second bomb had been dropped, those advocating a hard line in Tokyo were still unwilling to accept the terms of the Potsdam Declaration. But just before midnight on the evening of 9 August Emperor Hirohito himself intervened in the Council's deliberations. His prime minister asked him to decide between the positions of the moderates and the radicals, whereupon Hirohito sided with his foreign minister, who advised acceptance of the ulti-matum. Shortly afterwards the Foreign Ministry sent word via the Japanese Embassy in Berne that Japan was ready to surrender as long as the victorious powers made no demands that would jeopardize the rights of the emperor as the country's supreme ruler.

After consulting with Great Britain, China and the Soviet Union, the United States government agreed to this demand but only to the extent that it promised to leave the decision about the country's ultimate form of state to the free will of the Japanese people and to occupy Japan only until such time as the aims of the Potsdam Declaration had been met. The note signed by Byrnes in his capacity as secretary of state arrived in Tokyo early on the morning of 12 August. Two days later, the Supreme War Council accepted it at the emperor's insistence. That same evening an attempt to mount a coup by a number of rebellious army units was quickly put down. A handful of radical nationalists among the military and political leaders committed hara-kiri.

On 15 August Hirohito addressed the nation and informed his listeners that Japan had accepted the American note. At no point did he use the words 'defeat', 'surrender' or 'capitulation'. He condemned the bombing of Hiroshima and Nagasaki but also declared in unambiguous terms that to have continued the war would have meant the collapse and extinction of the Japanese nation. The following day he ordered a ceasefire on every front. Shortly after 09:00 on the morning of 2 September 1945 the unconditional surrender of the Japanese armed forces was accepted by the commander in chief of the American troops, General Douglas MacArthur, on board the battleship *Missouri* that was anchored in the Bay of Tokyo. The agreement was signed in the presence of representatives of the Soviet Union, China, Great Britain, Australia, New Zealand, Canada and France. The Japanese signatories were the new foreign minister, Shigemitsu Mamoru, and the chief of the general staff, General Umezu Yoshijiro. With that the war in Asia was over.

Truman was returning home by sea from the Potsdam Conference when he heard that Hiroshima had been bombed. His reaction was one of relief and even delight. He had had no moral scruples about deploying the weapon. From his point of view, it was a legitimate and even necessary means by which to end a terrible war at the earliest available opportunity with the least possible number of American casualties. Washington was happy to accept that this action would result in the deaths of an incalculable number of Japanese civilians, including women and children. Hundreds and thousands of civilians had already been killed in conventional bombing raids – in Tokyo alone more than 85,000 had died on the night of 9/10 March 1945. Every western democracy was by now so inured to the mass killing of civilians that any moral inhibitions on the part of those responsible for such actions were already beginning to fade. The atom bomb permitted a tremendous increase in the capacity for destruction, and it was this that made it strategically useful. The long-term consequences of radiation poisoning were barely taken into account.

There is no evidence to support the view that Truman and his closest advisers were guided by widespread racist prejudice against the 'Japs' when they decided to bomb Hiroshima and Nagasaki. The new weapon of mass destruction would presumably have been used in the war on Germany, too, if it had been available in time. Nor is there any indication that Truman was influenced by the consideration that it was necessary to have made practical use of the atom bomb on at least a single occasion in order to show the world once and for all that in the future war could no longer be the recourse of politicians. This idea was, however, represented by two leading scientific advisers to the American government, the presidents of the Massachusetts Institute of Technology and of Harvard University, Karl T. Compton and James B. Conant. Compton wrote to the secretary of war, Henry Lewis Stimson, on 11 June 1945 to state that if the weapon was not used in the present conflict, 'the world would have no adequate warning as to what was to be expected if war should break out again'.[113] This was a consideration that was exceptionally far-reaching in its implications, which perhaps helps to explain that it was beyond the remit of those whose task it was in the summer of 1945 to decide on whether or not to deploy the atom bomb at all.

The keenest scientific criticism of the decision to drop the first atom bombs was voiced in 1965 by the historian Gar Alperovitz, the spokesman of a 'revisionist' school of thought in American historiography. His central thesis was that by the summer of 1945 Japan was on the point of military collapse and it was unnecessary to use atomic weapons to shorten the war. Alperovitz believed that Truman and his advisers had been following a very different agenda, which was to intimidate the Soviet Union. The American leadership was convinced that a display of nuclear strength in the Far East would have a positive effect on Soviet policies in Europe, and once he knew that the experiment at Alamogordo had been a success, Truman had adopted a far less accommodating stance towards Stalin even at the Potsdam Conference.

In point of fact, the Japanese leadership was far from accepting the inevitability of surrender before 6 August 1945. If the bombs had not been dropped on Hiroshima and Nagasaki, the war would have lasted very much longer: Truman and his closest advisers were entirely right on this point. As for the Soviet Union, Byrnes had come to the conclusion by 21 July – the day on which he and Truman were informed in detail about the nuclear explosion at Alamogordo – that Russia no longer needed to enter the war with Japan. Byrnes, too, initially hoped that the United States' new military strength might have a positive influence on Soviet policy in Europe, but he was the only member of the American delegation in Potsdam to hold this view. After 21 July Truman no longer attached any importance to the Soviet Union's declaration of war on Japan but at the same time he did nothing to prevent Russia from taking that step. We may also infer a further political effect of the events in the New Mexico desert: the atomic bomb will have confirmed Truman in his intention of refusing to allow the Soviet Union to assist in occupying Japan and in that way of preventing the country from causing him the same sort of difficulties as those he had already had to endure in the case of Germany.

As far as Europe was concerned, the United States was able to avoid an anti-Soviet volte-face in the summer of 1945. Even the planned cooperation on arms control that was advocated above all by Stimson survived this strain on their relations. In short, there could be no talk of a hardening of Washington's position towards Moscow at the Potsdam Conference after 21 July. Rather, the

United States continued to count on working together with the Soviet Union and accepted as a fait accompli the existence of a Soviet sphere of influence in south-east and eastern central Europe. The nuclear bomb represented a military and technological revolution that shifted the balance of political power between Soviet Russia and the United States in favour of America. But in 1945 the United States did not pursue a policy of 'atomic diplomacy' in the sense understood by Alperovitz. The Cold War began only later.

In declaring war on Japan on 8 August, the Soviet Union may have entered the conflict only at the very last moment, but it was far more than merely a symbolic act. As soon as war was declared, the Red Army advanced into Manchuria and sent troops to the northern part of Korea as well as to the Kuril Islands and to Sakhalin, both of which were annexed by Soviet Russia. (In the case of the four southernmost Kuril Islands that had not been among the group of islands ceded by Russia to Japan in 1875, this meant the annexation of territory inhabited by Japanese nationals, which in turn resulted in the deportation of the islands' population.) In Korea the fighting lasted until 26 August. In keeping with an agreement made with the United States, the Japanese troops surrendered to the Soviets north of the thirty-eighth parallel, while to the south it was the Americans who accepted the Japanese surrender, marking the birth of a line of demarcation that was very soon to prove extremely contentious.

In China the Japanese troops surrendered to Chiang Kai-shek on 9 September. The Soviet Union and Chiang had signed a friendship and alliance treaty only eight weeks earlier, on 14 August, when Soviet Russia had confirmed various rights agreed to by the Western Powers in Yalta and including Manchuria, a naval base in Port Arthur (Lüshunkou) and additional privileges on the Liaotung Peninsula. The National Chinese government also recognized the independence of Outer Mongolia. In terms of China's domestic policies, the treaty resulted in a strengthening of the position of Chiang's party, the Kuomintang, in its struggle with the Chinese Communists under Mao Zedong, who inevitably interpreted such a move as a serious affront.

Throughout the previous period Mao had waged a tenacious guerrilla war on the Japanese in northern China, and in August 1945 he and his troops took part in the Soviet invasion of the region. At Soviet insistence and through the intermediary of the Americans Mao began talks with Chiang Kai-shek in Chungking, the provisional headquarters of the Chinese National government. Starting in late August, they ended on 10 October with a joint declaration in which both sides recorded their readiness to work together in peaceful coexistence. The communiqué was to be worth no more than the paper on which it was written and produced no real agreement between the two opposing camps. No more successful was a subsequent agreement more or less imposed by the Americans on 25 February 1946 and relating to troop numbers and troop distribution. Violent fighting broke out between the Nationalists and the

Communists in April, and by the spring of 1947 there was open civil war, a conflict that ended only two years later with the victory of the Communists and the expulsion of the Kuomintang from the Chinese mainland to Taiwan.

Following Japan's surrender, many of the colonies of the European powers that had been occupied by Japan attempted to prevent a return to the status quo. In Java, which was part of the Dutch East Indies, two leaders of the independence movement, Ahmed Sukarno and Mohammad Hatta, proclaimed the Republic of Indonesia on 17 August 1945. The armed forces of Sukarno and Hatta were able to bring under their control not only Java itself but also Sumatra and the island of Madura to the south of Sumatra and would probably have continued their triumphal advance if Anglo-Indian troops, supported by units of Japanese soldiers who had been released from prisoner-of-war camps for this very purpose, had not offered them stout resistance. Dutch troops replaced the British soldiers in October 1946. Attempts by the colonial power to reach an agreement with the new republic proved unsuccessful in the longer term, and after several bloody interventions by the police between 1947 and 1949 the government in The Hague was finally forced to bow to international pressure, more especially from the United States, and offer Indonesia its independence in December 1949.

Among the French colonies occupied by the Japanese, Vietnam was the one where news of the Japanese surrender triggered the biggest pro-independence demonstrations. Installed by the Japanese in March 1945, Emperor Bao Dai abdicated on 25 August 1945, and on 2 September the Communist leader Ho Chi Minh proclaimed the Democratic Republic of Vietnam in Hanoi. In the north of the country the Japanese were replaced by a National Chinese army, while the south was occupied by Anglo-Indian troops who, as in the Dutch East Indies, were able to rely on the support of units of former Japanese prisoners of war. The month of September witnessed the first clashes between the forces of Ho Chi Minh – the Viet Minh – and French soldiers whom the British had rescued from Japanese prisoner-of-war camps. General Jacques-Philippe Leclerc – the liberator of Paris – leading 35,000 French colonial troops arrived in the south of Vietnam in October. Some twelve months later, following the failure of all attempts by Ho Chi Minh to reach a settlement with France, the First Indochina War broke out.

Like the Dutch and the French, the British, too, found themselves facing independence movements in many of their south-east Asian colonies in the wake of Japan's capitulation. There were powerful anti-colonial forces in Singapore, Malaya and above all Burma, where the attempt to restore colonial rule provoked determined resistance. As in other occupied countries, Japanese rule had strengthened the resolve of those who opposed every form of colonial control. If there was a positive side to Japanese imperialism, then this was it.

It was easiest for the United States to adapt to the new situation, for as long ago as 1935 it had already promised its quasi-colony, the Commonwealth of the Philippines, national independence in 1945. As a result of the war, it was not until July 1946 that America belatedly kept its word, while at the same time ensuring that it maintained a number of trading privileges and several military bases in the Philippines. The European colonial powers needed more time to realize that the Second World War had permanently undermined the foundations of their rule in Asia. The longer it took them to reach this understanding, the harder it would be for them to abandon their illusions, a process that would turn out to be as costly as it was bloody.

Guilt and Atonement: The Caesura of 1945 (I)

The number of people who perished directly or indirectly as a result of the Second World War has been put at sixty million. More civilians than soldiers died, although estimates of the number of civilian deaths vary wildly. Among the civilian deaths were the Jews, Poles, Russians, White Russians, Ukrainians, Sinti and Roma murdered by the National Socialists; the civilian victims of the civil wars in Yugoslavia and Greece; and the murdered hostages, the refugees, the victims of air raids and the millions who died of starvation and who are not even included in many sets of statistics.

The number of soldiers who fell in combat or who died in prisoner-of-war camps was at least twenty-seven million and as such was more than three times higher than the equivalent figure for the First World War, when an estimated 8.5 million soldiers perished. The greatest losses were sustained by the Soviet Union and China, with twenty-seven million and 13.5 million fatalities respectively. Next came Germany with 6.35 million, India with more than three million and Japan with more than two million deaths. In every case the number includes both fallen soldiers and dead civilians.

With the exception of those conflicts that were purely civil wars, there had been no European war since the Thirty Years War in which the distinction between combatants and civilians was as blurred as it was in the Second World War. Even though it was not a total war that involved every corner of the world, it was certainly far more 'total' than the First World War had been. The Hague Regulations Respecting the Laws and Customs of War on Land (1907) had stipulated that only military targets should be attacked and that the civilian population should as far as possible be spared. These regulations were ignored not only by the dictator-ruled aggressor nations but increasingly by western democracies. By their own admission, the Allies' 'moral bombing' was intended to break the will of the civilian population and in that way to rob the aggressor states of their mass support.

But the carpet bombing of German and Japanese cities was not the only way in which the democratic Western Powers came closer to the brutal fighting methods of their enemies. The mass expulsions sanctioned by the Western Powers in 1945 would not have happened if Germany had not already undertaken extensive ethnic cleansing operations in those parts of Europe that it controlled. In the words of the historians Jörg Baberowski and Anselm Doering-Manteuffel: 'The extermination of the German armies and the expulsion of the German population from the regions to the east of the Oder-Neiße Line as well as from Bohemia were the consequence of the German conquest and occupation of those areas.'[114]

According to the understanding of the time, neither carpet bombing nor mass deportations were war crimes. In the case of the Allied bombings, those responsible saw their actions as an appropriate response to German and Japanese aggression, and in the case of forced migration, the Western Powers were able to point to contractually agreed precedents from the period after the First World War, especially the Greek-Turkish population exchange that was made on the basis of the Treaty of Lausanne of 1923.

It may be added that war crimes were not a new feature of the Second World War. Nor were they committed only by the dictatorial regimes that had unleashed the war and that were responsible for most of the atrocities. The list of Soviet war crimes was equally long, and it did not begin with the murder of thousands of Polish officers at Katyn in the spring of 1940. The Western Allies felt more firmly committed to international law than their Communist allies, but even they were guilty of actions that come under the heading of war crimes. In the spring of 1945 the first wave of occupation in the western part of Germany brought with it lootings, rapes and violent excesses on the part of Allied troops. Among Allied war crimes was the inhuman treatment meted out to several hundred thousand German prisoners of war in some twenty 'camps' in fields on the left bank of the Rhine, where the 'accommodation' consisted of holes in the ground dug by the inmates themselves and where at least 8,000 prisoners died.

In 1945 the term 'war crime' struck many legal scholars and politicians in western democracies as too weak adequately to describe what National Socialist Germany and its allies had done to humankind. Three decades earlier, on 24 May 1915, Great Britain, France and Tsarist Russia had jointly signed a note protesting at the massacre of Armenians and accusing the Ottoman Empire of a 'crime against humanity and against civilization'. The victorious powers returned to this expression at the end of the Second World War and on 8 August 1945 the representatives of the three major powers and France, in keeping with an agreement reached at the Potsdam Conference, accepted the London accord whereby the legal authority of the International Military Tribunal in Nuremberg that was still to be set up should be extended to crimes against peace in the sense of planning, preparing, unleashing or carrying out a war of aggression as well as committing war crimes and crimes against humanity.

The law on whose basis sentences were passed in Nuremberg and shortly afterwards in Tokyo, too, was a newly created international law. Experts on international law in the western democracies did not feel bound to the principle of '*nulla poena sine lege*' (no punishment without a law) that banned all retroactive penal legislation and that had been constitutive for all states under the rule of law, their response being based on a consideration that they felt could be justified only under natural law. The National Socialists' crimes were punishable simply because they were fundamentally at odds with the legal principles universally recognized by civilized peoples. The reprehensibility of the crimes that were detailed in Nuremberg was so great that contemporaries' sense of justice would have been violated in a far more flagrant manner if these crimes had not found a condign punishment. For this reason the Western Powers were willing to accept a further shortcoming: one of the victorious powers that was sitting in judgement had itself committed war crimes and crimes against humanity on a vast scale and was now ensuring that these actions were not discussed in Nuremberg.

After a trial lasting almost eleven months, the first sentences were handed down on the principal defendants on 1 October 1946. Twelve of the highest-ranking officials of the Third Reich, including Göring, Ribbentrop, Frick, Rosenberg, Keitel and Jodl, were sentenced to death by hanging; others, such as Hitler's deputy Rudolf Heß and his armaments minister Albert Speer, received lengthy prison sentences. As we have already noted, Göring was able to avoid execution on 16 October by taking his own life. The country's former vice-chancellor, Franz von Papen, and the president of the Reichsbank and minister of finance, Hjalmar Schacht, who had smoothed Hitler's path to the Chancellery but who had committed no crimes in the sense of the indictments made at the Nuremberg War Trials, were both acquitted.

The trial of the principal war criminals was followed by proceedings against doctors, lawyers, prominent industrialists and businesses, including Flick, Krupp and IG Farben, members of the Foreign Office, the Wehrmacht high command and individual military figures and SS leaders. (The SS had previously been declared a 'criminal organization' together with the leaders of the NSDAP, the Gestapo and the secret service.) These trials ended in a further thirty-six death sentences. The total number of individuals sentenced by their former enemies for war crimes and crimes against humanity has been reckoned to be between 50,000 and 60,000. Of those who were sentenced in the Soviet zone, around one-third were deported and made to take part in forced labour programmes inside the Soviet Union. In the western zones, 806 death sentences were handed down and 486 of these were carried out. (This figure includes the defendants in the Nuremberg Trials.) It is not known how many death sentences were handed down and carried out in the Soviet zone.

The 'denazification' of the millions of members of National Socialist organizations was a random, more or less mechanical, process that varied from zone to zone, but the procedures adopted by the Soviet Union were by far the most rigorous and arbitrary. Those National Socialists who were not deported to the Soviet Union were sent to 'special camps', as were unpopular bourgeois democrats and Social Democrats and even Communists who opposed the new regime.

Of the 120,000 or so prisoners in these camps, which remained in existence until 1950, 42,000 are said to have perished. One of them was the former concentration camp at Buchenwald. When Thomas Mann delivered a lecture in the National Theatre in Weimar on 1 August 1949, marking the bicentenary of Goethe's birth, he declined to comment on the continuing nature of the terror, a silence that left many of his admirers feeling disappointed.

The counterpart to repression was privilege. The administration, police and schools were thoroughly purged, and, wherever possible, reliable Communists were smuggled into leading positions. 'People's judges' and 'new teachers' who had received only the most rudimentary training replaced their politically compromised predecessors. Criteria such as professionalism and efficiency played no part in these appointments: denazification and politics pursued by men and women chosen for their Communist sympathies fitted together entirely seamlessly.

The mirror image of the Soviet zone was the French-occupied zone, where France adopted a relatively generous attitude to former National Socialist officials, whose past transgressions as party comrades were used from the outset to exert pressure and compel loyalty to the new regime. Here, too, of course, there were dismissals, arrests and internments. In all four zones these formed the first phase of the denazification process that lasted until well into 1946. The second phase began in the American zone in March 1946 and in the British and French zones six months later and involved court-like appearances before tribunals that divided into five groups those Germans who on the basis of questionnaires were arraigned before them: major offenders, offenders, lesser offenders, followers and, finally, those who were acquitted. The Americans were the most rigorous, acquitting only a small minority and initially banning all of those who were classed as 'followers' from pursuing their professional careers. The British dispensed with this expedient and declared more than half of those whom they examined to have been 'exonerated'.

The more clear-cut the contrast between east and west became in the course of 1947, the more tolerant the Americans grew towards former National Socialists. For years Hitler had been a national hero, his party a mass movement. To have pursued with ruthless rigour all of his former followers risked creating a reservoir of social discontent and political radicalism. Better results were expected from leniency and re-education in the form of the rapid acceptance of democracy and resistance to extremist slogans from both right and left. All in all, denazification proved to be a mistake. In the western half of Germany, those who were not guilty of a criminal offence could return to their former professional lives after 1949. After a few years had gone by, not only 'followers' and 'lesser offenders' could hope to escape their political past, so, too, could 'offenders'.

The Soviet Union proceeded in much the same way against lesser National Socialists, who were expected to undergo a process of re-education and learn to be honest 'anti-Fascists'. From the standpoint of the Soviet Military Administration, the most important part of the denazification process was not individual sanctions but structural changes, including breaking the power of those classes which according to Marxist and Leninist thinking had helped the Fascists come to power in the first place. This approach also found expression in the land reforms of September 1945 that were designed to do away once and for all with the Junker class to the east of the Elbe. Some 7,000 landowners were dispossessed without recourse to compensation, their lands passing into peasant hands. Of the half a million individuals who received lands in this way, 83,000 had been driven from their former homes in the regions to the east.

Dispossession affected not only former supporters of National Socialism but even those who had opposed it. Even so, it is impossible to describe this radical policy as specifically Communist. Middle-class agrarian reformers had for decades been demanding a change to the way property was distributed in the area to the east of the Elbe, but what they had had in mind was certainly not expropriation without compensation. And yet this did nothing to detract from the popularity of 'land reform', many members of the middle classes welcoming the redistribution of these landed estates as justified and, indeed, long overdue.

The same cannot be said of the industrial reforms that were ushered in shortly afterwards, in October 1945. These affected not only war criminals and National Socialists but big business in general. By the spring of 1948 almost 10,000 businesses had been taken over by the state without any compensation. As a result, 40 per cent of industrial production was in the public sector by this date. To these businesses may be added the Soviet corporations in heavy industry that the occupying power ran under its initiative. Banks and building societies had been nationalized even earlier, in July 1945. By the autumn there could no longer be any doubt about the Soviets' goal: the capitalist social order was to be systematically dismantled and replaced by a socialist order.

In the western zones the social changes undertaken by the occupying powers remained relatively limited. Although there were tentative moves in the direction of land reform, these failed to produce any results. In industry, conversely, a number of major companies and banks whose role under National Socialism had been particularly incriminating and that included IG Farben, the iron and steel industry in the British zone, the Commerzbank, the Dresdner Bank and the Deutsche Bank were seized and placed in trusteeship. The twelve largest coal and steel companies were turned into twenty-eight independent companies by the British occupying power after it had seized control of them in December 1945. No compensation was paid. Although the Labour Party introduced a policy of nationalization of major industries following its election victory in July 1945, this failed to meet the approval of the American military governor, General Lucius D. Clay, whose own policy prevailed, and the question of nationalization was postponed on the grounds that it was too important to be decided in one particular region or a single occupied zone but must be left to a later German legislator to resolve.

The scissure in German social history represented by the year 1945 can be best appreciated by a comparison with the situation in Germany at the end of the First World War, when the German government – in the form of the Council of People's Deputies – enjoyed a legitimacy that was not questioned by the Allies. The Reich was not occupied, and none of the old power elites was forced to step down. Although the landowners on the right bank of the Elbe temporarily lost some of their political influence, they were able to hold on to the social bases of their power. And heavy industry was able to defy the nationalization movement. The civil service was not substantially shaken by the revolution of 1918/19, while the judiciary remained entirely untouched by it. The military was obliged to respect the limits placed on it by the Treaty of Versailles, but throughout the years of the Weimar Republic it remained exactly what it had been in the old Reich: a state within a state. It was also a factor in the country's internal politics and in the case of a national emergency it could assume an executive function.

In keeping with the terms of the Potsdam Declaration there was initially no German state and no German military after the Second World War. After the 'land reforms' had been completed, there were no longer any landed estates to the east of the Elbe. Under Decree 46, the state of Prussia that had been domi-nated by these estates was disbanded by the Allied Control Council on 25 April 1947 with the blanket justification that Prussia had 'always been the upholder of militarism and reaction in Germany' and that it had therefore ceased to exist.[115] Heavy industry was expropriated in the east, while in the west it was broken up by the occupying powers and later, after the foundation of the Federal Republic, handed over to the workers according to a system of equal representation. As a result, none of the power elites that had resisted demo-cratic change in the years before 1933 was able to play a similar role after 1945.

As far as the western zones were concerned, there was a far greater sense of continuity in the public services. American and British attempts to do away with the German civil service and replace it with an English-style system proved inef-fectual. No judge who had been complicit in the sentencing crimes of the Third Reich was himself sentenced on that score. A number of university teachers such as Martin Heidegger and Carl Schmitt who had compromised their reputa-tions in particularly flagrant ways between 1933 and 1945 lost their positions, but many who with hindsight appear to have been scarcely less culpable were able – after an involuntary break – to resume their careers at the point they had reached in 1945. Political checks on civil servants served to keep them in line, much as the experience of the country's 'collapse' had had a sobering effect. Open hostility to democracy was now discredited, and this was as true of civil servants as it was of the judiciary.

Following the fall of the Third Reich, there was no new beginning, and yet the term often used by the Germans in this context – 'die Stunde Null', or 'Zero

Hour' – is an accurate reflection of contemporaries' perceptions. Never had the future been so hard to predict in Germany, never had chaos been so omnipresent as it was in the spring and early summer of 1945. There was no longer any sense of security, and this feeling left its mark on memories of this period, albeit in different ways – it was far more brutal in the Soviet zone, for example, than it was elsewhere. In all four zones, society lay in ruins and proved to be extremely mobile. Hungry city dwellers undertook foraging expeditions into the countryside, where they were able to barter goods and obtain the food they needed, while many of those who had been better off but who now had no salaries or pensions or other regular income had for a time to take on primitive jobs. The women who scoured bombsites, removing rubble and salvaging building bricks and other valuable kinds of building material, came to embody the radical change that had taken place in society, with women now performing the roles traditionally taken by men.

During the years of National Socialist domination the claims of the traditional upper class to greater social prestige had been systematically opposed in the spirit of a 'national community', and yet the actual structure of German society had not been revolutionized. Only in the wake of the air raids, the deportations and social breakdown did German society undergo a change far more radical than anything it had known during the first ten years of the Third Reich. Even so, few of the changes that took place in 1945 proved longlasting. This was an exceptional period, and one that gave rise to no new order but only to a profound desire to return to some kind of normality as quickly as possible.

The shock sustained by the Germans was moral rather than social and, in spite of all their attempts to apologize for the war, it was to leave a lasting impression. After 1918, the myth that the Germans were innocent and that they had been stabbed in the back met with the approval of the country's elites and also of the broad mass of the population, but this was no longer the case after 1945, for it was all too obvious that the man at the top had unleashed the Second World War and that he bore most of the responsibility for what had happened. The ruined cities, the plight of those whose homes had been bombed and who had been evacuated, the misery of the refugees and of the displaced and, finally, the increasing awareness of the concentration camps and of the murder of the Jews: all of these factors were an indictment of Hitler and an argument against any reversion to National Socialism. Even so, there was for a long time the popularly held view that the party leaders and the SS were solely to blame for the crimes that had been committed, while the Wehrmacht and the mass of Germans were routinely said to have remained 'decent'. It was one thing for the Germans to distance themselves from their Führer and his fanatical helpers but another to acknowledge the German traditions that National Socialism had tapped into and accept responsibility for all that had happened in and through Germany since 1933.

The philosopher Karl Jaspers, whose writings were banned by the National Socialists in 1937/8, triggered a wave of positive and negative reactions with his essay *The Question of German Guilt* when it appeared in print in 1946. (It was based on a lecture that he had given at Heidelberg University during the winter of 1945/6.) Jaspers spoke of a 'collective' and 'moral guilt' in the sense that the Germans were responsible for political conditions between 1933 and 1945. 'That the spiritual conditions of German life provided an opportunity for such a régime is a fact for which all of us are co-responsible.' The term 'collective guilt' was enough for many to criticize Jaspers for adopting an arbitrary approach to the Allies. The fact that Jaspers disputed that the Germans were solely to blame for National Socialism and that he claimed that the rest of the world was complicit in Hitler's success, and that, quoting from a recent study, *The German Question*, by the émigré economist Wilhelm Röpke, he referred to the Germans as Hitler's 'first victims' and even argued that 'German anti-Semitism was not at any time a popular movement' did little to reduce the anger felt by those who reacted unfavourably to Jaspers's views.[116]

No less divisive was the response to a manifesto that sought to break with the nationalist legacy of German Protestantism: the 'Stuttgart Admission of Guilt' by the Provisional Council of the Evangelical Church in Germany was published in October 1945 and written mainly at the instigation of the bishop of Württemberg, Theophil Wurm, and of the former concentration camp victim Martin Niemöller, who had been president of the Church of Hessen-Nassau. It spoke of a 'solidarity of guilt' between Church and nation and encountered considerable opposition within the Church itself. Particular offence was caused by the sentence: 'Through us endless suffering has been caused to many nations and countries.' The phrase was thought to reflect the Allied view that the Germans bore collective responsibility for the war. For conservative Protestants, there was something excessive about the self-reproach that 'we did not profess our faith more courageously, that we did not pray more ardently, did not believe more joyfully and did not love more fervently'.[117] But it was also these words that seared themselves into the collective memory of German Protestants and played a decisive role in providing Protestant churches outside Germany with a starting point for their attempts to deal in a spirit of reconciliation with the country that had given rise to the Reformation.

The Stuttgart statement did not refer specifically to the greatest and most terrible of the crimes committed by National Socialism: the murder of European Jewry. And decades were to pass before the Germans acknowledged the central significance of the Holocaust in their country's history. This act of genocide was described by the historian Dan Diner as a 'break in civilization':

> As an event, Auschwitz touches on every level of civilizatory certainty that is a part of the basic conditions of the way we behave towards one another. This bureaucratically organized and industrially enforced mass destruction

represents something amounting to a denial of a civilization whose thoughts and actions obey a rationality that presupposes a minimum of anticipatory trust, a trust marked by utilitarianism that precludes groundless mass killing, especially in the form of rational organization, and precludes it, moreover, on the grounds of calculated interest and self-preservation on the part of the perpetrators. A socially developed trust in social rules that determine life and survival was turned into its opposite: the mass killing became the rule, while survival was owed to mere chance.[118]

The murder of European Jewry was the quintessential breach in civilization that the National Socialists pursued most systematically and most rigorously of all. It began with mass shootings and ended with mass gassings. In parallel with the Holocaust other mass murders were committed by the Germans and these too can be described as 'breaches in civilization', assuming that we do not stress the element of 'industrial' killing as much as Diner does. In addition to the murder of the mentally ill that Hitler himself ordered, there was also the extermination of a large section of the Polish elites and the de facto condemnation to death by starvation of millions of White Russians, Ukrainians, Russians and members of other nations that made up the Soviet Union. The number of victims among Russia's civilian population has been reckoned to be fifteen million. According to the calculations of the American historian Timothy Snyder, one Soviet citizen in twenty-five was killed by German hands, while the figures for the Ukraine and Poland were one in ten, that for White Russia one in five.[119] At the same time the National Socialists murdered hundreds and thousands of Sinti and Roma, an act of genocide that may not have been carried out with the same systematic ruthlessness as that of the Jews, but which was no less industrial in its scale.

Breaches in civilization before 1939 include the Turkish massacre of Armenians in the First World War and Stalin's collective murders, including those of the Kulaks and, during the great famine of 1932–3, the peasants in the Ukraine. Others that fall under this heading are Stalin's condemnation of large sections of the non-Russian population of the Soviet Union during the Second World War, all of whom were regarded as unreliable from a nationalist point of view. Common to all these actions – whether or not they count as genocide in the sense defined by the United Nations Convention on the Prevention and Punishment of the Crime of Genocide of 1948 – is that they reflect a 'utopia of unambiguity'. The phrase is that of Jörg Baberowski and Anselm Doering-Manteuffel citing the sociologist Zygmunt Bauman and describes the belief in a racist, ethnic, national or class-based homogeneity in whose name all those elements must be liquidated that fly in the face of this notion. Bauman himself draws attention to a further characteristic bound up with the postulate of 'unambiguity' and useful in distinguishing the 'modern' mass murders practised by totalitarian regimes from the older type of atrocity: 'Contemporary mass murder is distinguished by a virtual absence of all spontaneity on the one hand, and the prominence of rational, carefully calculated design on the other.'[120]

But if the Germans' attempts to exterminate European Jewry differed from other acts of genocide, then the difference lay not in bureaucratic routine or the technical perfection with which the victims – men and women, the elderly and the very young – were swept away and mechanically killed at Belzec, Sobibór, Treblinka and Auschwitz, for there were also a number of other distinguishing features that deserve to be mentioned here. The Jews were not a 'nation' as such but were the citizens of many other states, and in many countries they regarded themselves as fully integrated members of the nation in question. In the eyes of their enemies, conversely, the Jews were to be found everywhere in the world and, as a result, there was nowhere where they could be said to be at home. For radical anti-Semites – unlike those who advocated the older kind of religious anti-Judaism – it mattered little whether the Jews continued to hold their traditional religious beliefs or whether they had forsworn the religion of their forefathers. If Jews were the Germans' mortal enemy, this was because Jewry strove for world dominion, whether in a capitalist and plutocratic form or in a Marxist, Bolshevist guise. On their way to achieving this goal, the Jews would allegedly stop at nothing in order to subvert the 'Aryan' race from the inside and turn its members against one another.

This belief was shared by minorities in many European countries, but only in Germany had extreme anti-Semitism come to power on its own terms. Only here was the country headed by a man who believed that he was called upon by Providence not only to destroy Jewry but the Jewish spirit, too, a spirit that had permeated Christianity and in that way infiltrated the 'Aryan' nations as well. Culturally speaking, Germany was a western country and had taken part in the great processes of European emancipation that had swept across the Continent since the Middle Ages and in the case of the Reformation had even set that movement in train. Germany had contributed to the European Enlightenment and in the nineteenth century had produced a state under the rule of law that reflected western standards. As a social state, it had been a model for others, and by the beginning of the twentieth century it was a highly developed industrial country and one of the world's leading scientific nations. This helps to explain why the extermination of European Jewry gave rise to such incomprehension and horror in western democracies. 'There is no doubt', Churchill wrote to Anthony Eden on 11 July 1944, that the persecution of the Jews in Hungary and their expulsion from enemy territory

is probably the greatest and most horrible crime ever committed in the whole history of the world, and it has been done by scientific machinery by nominally civilised men in the name of a great State and one of the leading races of Europe.[121]

The Holocaust was a crime against humanity committed by a country in the old West whose traditional elites were none the less different from those of the nations of the transatlantic West, for at least until 1918 Germany had only partially assimilated the 'normative project of the West' in the form of the ideas of 1776 and 1789. Inalienable human rights and the principles of national sovereignty and of representative democracy were not part of the political culture of the Kaiserreich. In the minds of the German bourgeoisie, obeying a state which, as a state under the rule of law, could by definition do no wrong was more important than the idea of political responsibility for the community. During the First World War Germany's war ideologues contrasted the ideas of 1789 with those of 1914 and in that way presented the German state – a powerful cultural and authoritarian entity – as a superior answer to the universal values associated with all of the western democracies.

Following the defeat of 1918, Weimar's parliamentary democracy seemed to many members of the various elite groups who shaped public opinion to be a form of state that had been imposed on them by their victors and, hence, as 'un-German' – an interpretation shared by Hitler, among others. National Socialism was the most extreme expression of the Germans' anti-western resentment. All of those features of the Third Reich that were 'modern' were a reflection of normative deficiencies in the process of German modernization. Without the support of the pre- and anti-democratic traditions on which he was able to draw, Hitler would never have been able to subject Germany to his tyranny in 1933, and only because he held the reins of state was he able to implement a radical solution to the Jewish question, which was a central element in the National Socialist project. The Holocaust had a prehistory that went beyond the history of anti-Semitism and racism and that cannot be separated from German history in general, the history of a largely western country whose traditional elites had until 1945 obstinately refused to open themselves up to the political culture of the West and which now had to suffer the consequences of this catastrophic policy.

By the time the sentences were passed on the principal defendants in Nuremberg in October 1946, Italy had long since ceased to be an occupied country. The Anglo-American military government had remained in office until 31 December 1945, during which time it had had the final say on all legislative matters. No law came into force without its agreement, and no changes to the law could be made. The Western Allies exerted a decisive influence on the purging of the civil service, on restructuring the press and on shaping cultural politics.

Attempts to wreak vengeance on Italy's Fascists had begun as early as 1943 in those parts of the country that were not occupied by German troops – most brutally in the form of the unofficial purges that cost the lives of some 1,200 Fascists between 1943 and 1946. In parallel to this, an official political purge – *epurazione* – was conducted by committees installed by the Allied military government as well as by liberation committees and state commissions. Most of the mayors who had served under Mussolini were dismissed from their posts, and the same was true of those who had held leading positions in the country's administrative apparatus. In northern Italy commissions set up by the Communists to purge the country of Fascists went much further and in many factories not only dismissed former Fascists but also removed all of those individuals whom they regarded as hostile to the workers.

In Italy, unlike Germany, it was left to the country's judiciary to deal with the legal fallout from the years of Mussolini's dictatorship. In those cases where the existing penal code of 1931 proved inadequate, the newly created Alta Corte di Giustizia and the International Military Tribunal in Nuremberg fell back on universally recognized legal principles and in doing so consciously departed from the principle of *nulla poena sine lege*, and the same was true of the special courts that tried between 20,000 and 30,000 politically compromised Fascists and their collaborators between 1945 and 1947, passing around 1,000 death sentences and handing down a large number of lengthy terms of imprisonment. According to the historian Hans Woller, 'In no European country – with the possible exception of France – did the courts proceed so quickly and so brutally against discredited Fascists. Nowhere else did so many representatives of the old regime have to atone for their shameful acts in 1945 as they did in Italy.'[122]

At the end of 1945 the Italian governments were under massive pressure from the Allies to rid the country of all Fascist elements, but once the occupying troops had left, this was no longer a factor. The Christian Democrats who since 4 December 1945 were part of an all-party government under Alcide de Gasperi were markedly less interested in continuing these purges than their left-wing coalition partners, namely, the Socialists under the deputy prime minister Pietro Nenni and the Communists under the justice minister, Palmiro Togliatti. In June 1946 Togliatti underwent a change of heart with regard to the country's Fascist past, a volte-face that provoked dissent even among his party colleagues. He proposed an amnesty that weakened or abolished many of the sanctions that had been imposed prior to that date and that came into force on 22 June. Three weeks earlier the first post-war parliament had been elected on 2 June. The left-wing parties polled far fewer votes than expected – the Communists won 18.9 per cent of the total, the Socialists 20.7 per cent – while the Christian Democrats won 35.2 per cent, registering a victory that was felt to be little short of sensational.

On the same day as the elections, a plebiscite was held to decide the future type of state that Italy would be. Some 54.3 per cent voted for a republic, 45.2 per cent for the retention of the monarchy. Victor Emanuel III, who had appointed Mussolini his prime minister in October 1922 and who had dismissed him in October 1943, was no longer on the throne by this date in the country's history, having abdicated in favour of his son, Umberto II, on 9 May 1946 and gone into exile in Egypt. A few days after the referendum, Umberto, too, left the country, choosing Portugal as his new home.

Apart from the king, the military, too, had provided reliable support for the Duce and his Fascist regime, at least until 1943. Its leaders felt that the country owed them a debt of gratitude for their role in the dictator's overthrow and as the Western Powers' ally and in this they enjoyed the support of the Christian Democrats and the latter's governments, which consistently refused to heed a United Nations demand and hand over some 1,700 members of the Italian armed forces who were accused of serious war crimes.

Since Italy, for its part, was demanding the extradition of German war criminals, it was obliged to give at least the impression that it took seriously its announcement that it would deal with its own war criminals. The military prosecutor's office did indeed initiate more than 2,000 preliminary proceedings affecting not only Germans but also Italian collaborators and members of the armed forces. But the determination not to indict any Italian war criminals meant that practically no charges were ever brought before the courts. The vast majority of Italians saw nothing untoward in this development: their own officers and simple soldiers continued to be regarded as 'decent people' who, unlike the Germans, were incapable of carrying out atrocities. As a result, the war crimes that Italians had committed most notably in Ethiopia, Greece and Yugoslavia for the most part went unpunished.

The suppression of the wrongs that Italy had inflicted on other countries under Fascist rule went hand in hand with the tendency to draw such a clear distinction between Italian Fascism and German National Socialism that it became almost impossible to see any similarities between the two regimes. At the same time the Italian left promoted the myth that there had been widespread resistance to Fascism – it was a myth that allowed the Communists to appeal to the common legacy of all anti-Fascist forces after they became the party of opposition in 1947.

According to Wolfgang Schieder, this process allowed the 'ritualized history of the "Resistenza" ' to be 'raised to the level of a masterly narrative in Italian politics', deliberately reducing the story of Fascism to a tale of anti-Fascism. Whereas the political left was reluctant to be reminded of its impotence and defeat before and under Fascism, the political right had no interest in reminding the world of the part that it had played in the rise of the Fascist dictatorship and the support that it had given Mussolini's regime. In Schieder's estimation, the result was two decades of 'shared uninterest in Fascism' after 1945.[123]

During the early post-war period, a further point in common was the attempt to negotiate a peace treaty that kept the country's borders more or less unchanged and that left Italy as materially unencumbered as possible. There were no peace talks in the narrower sense of the term: the Italians were merely able to state their position in Washington, Moscow, London and Paris. In every case the central argument was that Mussolini had forced Italy into war on the side of Germany, that it had fought a decent war and that it had broken free from the Duce's tyranny in 1943 of its own accord, before making an important contribution to the Allies' victory over Germany. As Woller has noted, the Italian representatives portrayed Italy as 'the principal victim of Fascism', an interpretation of the true facts of the matter so wayward that it failed to find acceptance in any of the four capitals where it was proposed.[124]

The conditions imposed on Italy under the terms of the Paris Peace Treaty of 10 February 1947 were entirely acceptable. The former Axis Power was required to cede the Dodecanese to Greece (it had captured the islands in 1912), to return Istria to Yugoslavia and to renounce all claims to its colonies, although this did not prevent it from receiving a mandate from the United Nations in November 1949, offering it trusteeship over its former colony of Somalia in order for the region to prepare for independence. Trieste initially became a free state but reverted to Italy in 1954. South Tyrol remained Italian and in January 1948 received its first autonomous statute. The reparations that Italy was required to pay were modest: Yugoslavia was promised $125 million, Greece $105 million, the Soviet Union $100 million, Ethiopia $25 million and Albania $5 million. The Italian armed forces had to accept reductions in their manpower and equipment. The bulk of the Italian navy was acquired by France, Greece, Yugoslavia and the Soviet Union.

The peace treaty proved hugely controversial at home: not only the extreme right in the guise of the neo-Fascists and the monarchists but also the liberals made common cause against what they viewed as a brutal imposition. The truth of the matter is that Italy emerged practically unscathed from the Paris talks. In Ethiopia it had waged a racist war under Mussolini's leadership and used methods of mass execution for which there were few parallels in European colonial history. It had fought alongside the Germans in North Africa, in the Balkans and in the Soviet Union and increased its territory at the expense of other European nations. And it had contributed to the persecution and extermination of European Jewry. In 1947 the majority of Italians refused to acknowledge any of this. For them, it was reassuring to think that everything for which Fascist Italy might be reproached was overshadowed by the far greater and more terrible crimes committed by its former ally, National Socialist Germany.

In Japan, conversely, the monarchy may have been retained, but its character changed irrevocably. On 1 January 1946 Emperor Hirohito expressly rejected the idea that he was a god in human form. Ten months later, on 3 November 1946, he announced a new constitution, which had been produced by a commission set up by the American occupying power and which had been approved by an overwhelming majority by the newly elected parliament in October 1946. It came into force six months later, on 3 May 1947. The emperor was no longer the sovereign ruler of the nation but the symbol of the state and of the unity of the nation. The aristocracy was abolished. Japan was henceforth a parliamentary democracy with an independent authority to administer justice. The state and religion were separate entities and Shinto no longer the privileged religion. The constitution guaranteed the classical basic rights, including freedom of religion, and acknowledged that men and women enjoyed equal rights. Under Article 9 Japan renounced the right to maintain a military force and to wage war, a radical innovation whose origins remain unclear: whether it stemmed from a Japanese initiative or whether it was due to pressure exerted by the occupying power is a question that has never been fully resolved.

Unlike Germany, Japan continued to have its own government even after it had surrendered. The commander in chief of the Allied troops, General Douglas MacArthur, headed what was effectively the only occupying power. Within hours of Japan's surrender he had ensured that all state control was placed in the hands of the occupying power, but in the light of Japanese protests and a directive from the State Department, he was very soon obliged to revise this arrangement: from then on, MacArthur issued his orders through the Japanese government, which in this way became the executive organ of the occupying power.

MacArthur's orders were all aimed at the systematic westernization of Japan. He repealed the country's repressive security laws and ordered the release of political prisoners and the arrest of others who were suspected of war crimes. He allowed the creation of free trade unions and the right to strike, banned child labour, legislated for equality between the sexes, broke up major businesses (*zaibatsu*), introduced land reform and liberalized education. As a result, many of the changes enshrined in the new constitution of 1947 merely enacted innovations that had already been ordered by the occupying power.

One of the United States' principal aims was to punish war criminals, but this was made more difficult by the fact that in the brief period between the country's surrender and the American occupation much of the incriminating material was destroyed by the Japanese authorities. Not until May 1946 could a Nuremberg-style International Military Tribunal begin its work in Tokyo. Some of those accused, including the former prime minister, Konoe Fumimaro, and the former army minister and chief of the general staff, Sugiyama Gen, committed suicide and in that way avoided arrest. The wartime prime minister, General Tojo Hideki, who was another of the principal war criminals, survived an attempt to take his own life that left him seriously injured.

Tojo was one of seven defendants sentenced to death at the International Military Tribunal in November 1948. Six of them were members of the military. The only civilian was the former prime minister and foreign minister, Hirota Koki. In sixteen cases the judges passed life sentences, in two cases long terms of imprisonment, although all of those who were still alive were released in 1956. As in Germany, the trials of the principal war criminals were followed by others against individuals accused of war crimes. There were also trials of Japanese war criminals in the Philippines, China and the Soviet Union.

The United States also wanted to see a process of political purges similar to the denazification trials that had taken place in Germany, but this demand was thwarted by resistance on the part of Japanese civil servants. Of the structural changes ushered in by the occupying power, land reform was probably the most successful. Some five million smallholders profited from the fact that between 1946 and 1949 the state bought up land from the larger landowners and then redistributed it. After that, no one was allowed to own more than three hectares of land or to farm it as a tenant farmer. Only on the barren island of Hokkaido were larger farms of up to twenty hectares allowed.

Reform of the educational system also had a lasting impact. Pupils were now required to attend school for nine, rather than six, years, with the introduction of a three-year period of secondary education similar to that provided by American colleges. The teaching staff was 're-educated' and the syllabus demilitarized. The Americans were less successful in their attempts to break up the country's larger businesses, for although the requisite laws were passed, they did not prevent new mergers from being formed and new amalgamations from coming into existence. In the view of the historian Gerhard Krebs, the American reformers ultimately achieved the opposite of what they had set out to do: thanks to the modernization of its industrial and financial institutions, Japan became a more powerful rival to the United States than it had been before the Second World War.[125]

In post-war Japan there was no debate on the subject of war guilt similar to the one conducted in Germany, where it was no accident that the discussion was prompted by Protestant figures: humanity's guilt as a result of our inherent sinfulness has always been a central topic of all Christian religions, especially Lutheranism. In the Shinto religion, conversely, there is no such tradition and as a result there was no 'guilty conscience' with regard to Tokyo's aggressive policies during the 1930s and 1940s or to the terrible suffering that the Japanese military and especially the military police – the Kempeitai – had inflicted on the civilian population and, above all, on the 100,000 women and girls forced into prostitution in China, Manchuria, Korea and many of the other regions overrun by Japan. Any admission of guilt was seen as incompatible with the Japanese sense of 'honour' in large sections of the population, an attitude as true today as it was in 1945. A deeply rooted feeling of shame means that any admission of guilt is seen as a loss of face, and this is something that has to be avoided at all costs.

From the standpoint of Japan's political right, the war criminals who were executed continue to be seen as patriots and martyrs. They are still commemorated at the Yasukuni Shrine, a Shinto sanctuary established by Emperor Meiji in 1869. Between 1975 and 2009 prominent members of the Liberal Democratic Party regularly took part in the nationalist ceremonies that were held here every year on 15 August, the official anniversary of Japan's surrender. The atomic bombs that were dropped on Hiroshima and Nagasaki confirmed the Japanese in their belief that they had been victims, rather than perpetrators, in the Second World War, a view that continues to affect the country's relations with its neighbours and that sets it apart from western democracies of the post-war era.

On 8 September 1951, four and a half years after Italy, Japan finally signed a peace treaty in San Francisco. Notable absentees among its other signatories were Communist China and the Soviet Union. In it Japan declared its willingness to abandon all territories that it had gained or conquered after 1895. The United States gained limited administrative authority over a number of smaller but strategically important islands and signed a security treaty with Japan that allowed the country to form 'self-defence units', effectively allowing it to rearm. In return for America's concession, Japan reluctantly agreed to sign a peace treaty with the Kuomintang government in Taiwan, recognizing it as the only legitimate Chinese government.

Japan's extreme militarism now belonged to the country's past. But many of those who had been partially responsible for the policies pursued by Japan during the war again had a political future once the occupying troops had left in 1951. The former foreign minister, Shigemitsu Mamoru, who had in the meantime served a term of imprisonment, returned to his old post in 1954, and three years later the outspokenly anti-Communist Kishi Nobusuke, who had been a member of Tojo's war cabinet, returned to lead the government. In Japan this was regarded as a sign of normalization, and not even the United States was shocked by such a development any longer.

Japan, Italy and Germany: the period between 1943 and 1945 was a time of catastrophic failure by three countries attempting to create an empire in the twentieth century. The regimes in Tokyo, Rome and Berlin hoped to achieve what older powers had managed to do in previous centuries and expand their rule to foreign countries that they preferred to be less well developed. It was not imperialism as such that produced these aggressive regimes during the interwar period. Rather, these systems emerged in countries that felt they had come off badly when the world had been divided up at an earlier date. If there is a common origin for the global catastrophe of the first half of the 1940s, then it is to be found in the compulsively compensatory attempt on the part of three powers that believed themselves disadvantaged by destiny and that were determined to change the international and political status quo in their favour, in that way securing for themselves the place in the world to which they believed they were entitled.

West, East, Third World: The Caesura of 1945 (II)

The three major powers had met in Potsdam in July and August 1945, and yet even at this early date many Britons were already beginning to ask themselves whether they were really members of the 'Big Three' any longer. Almost five million Commonwealth soldiers had fought alongside United Kingdom troops in the course of the Second World War: 2.5 million from India, more than one million from Australia and New Zealand, 725,000 from Canada, almost 500,000 from the colonies in East and West Africa and 200,000 from South

Africa. For their mother country this military help was just as important as the loans that Great Britain received from India and from the old Dominions of Canada, Australia and New Zealand. Added to these were the generous supplies of American materials made available under the Lend-Lease Program. Without this support the United Kingdom would not have been able to fight the Axis Powers or to emerge victorious from the conflict. Materially speaking, this historic victory was based on tick.

Once the war was over, bills would be presented: the government in London was in no doubt on this score. Supplies from the United States ended abruptly on 2 September 1945. In the course of lengthy negotiations in which John Maynard Keynes again played a leading role, the British managed to obtain a considerable amount of debt relief: the United States reduced its demands under the Lend-Lease Program from $22,000 million to $650 million, just 3 per cent of the sum that Britain owed. The Commonwealth countries that had helped Britain with loans ultimately demanded only 1 per cent of the amount that was due to them, meaning that they voluntarily wrote off £38,000 million, or $152,000 million.

This counteroffer came as a huge relief to London, but it was not enough to restore the United Kingdom's ability to act in a financially responsible way. The Second World War had destroyed around 28 per cent of the national wealth at home and abroad. Financial ruin threatened if Britain could not borrow from abroad. Difficult talks were again necessary before the required loans could be obtained: $125,000 million from Canada and three times that amount – £375,000 million – from the United States.

There was fierce opposition to the requested loan in Congress, but the Senate finally agreed to the proposal in May 1946 by forty-six votes to thirty-four, the House of Representatives in July by 219 votes to 155, allowing Truman to sign the new law on 15 July 1946. The agreement of the two houses was ultimately the result of their realization that Great Britain was an important and, indeed, their most important ally in their attempts to prevent the Soviet Union from extending its influence yet further in Europe. Now the leader of the opposition, Winston Churchill had delivered a historic speech in Truman's presence in Fulton, Missouri, on 5 March 1946, when he had spoken for the first time in public of the 'Iron Curtain' that had descended on Europe from Stettin in the north to Trieste in the south. Against this sombre background he had invoked the 'special relationship' between the two great English-speaking democracies, the United States and Great Britain. Churchill's words served as a wakeup call.

The widespread misgivings provoked in both of the biggest American parties by the British request for a loan were due in no small part to the United Kingdom's policy towards Palestine. In a White Paper published in May 1939, the government in London had explicitly stated that the Balfour Declaration of November 1917, promising a national home for the Jews in Palestine, had never been intended to imply the foundation of a Jewish state against the will of the Arab population. Palestine was to be given its independence within ten years, when Arabs would continue to be in the majority in the new state. For the next five years – from 1940 to 1944 – the White Paper established a limit of 75,000 Jewish immigrants – a regular yearly quota of 10,000 and a flexible supplementary quota of 25,000. For Zionists, this ruling represented the worst setback in their history.

Immediately after the end of the war Jewish and Arab interests clashed in the mandated region. For the Jews, Palestine had become their primary place of refuge in the wake of the National Socialists' policy of persecution and extermination, while the resident Arabs were emphatically opposed not only to any further Jewish immigration but also to any partition of Mandated Palestine into a Jewish and an Arab sector, a solution advocated by Chaim Weizmann as head of the Jewish Agency and president of the World Zionist Organization. The Mandate's British administration was also opposed to any further influx of Jews from Europe but was unable to prevent illegal immigration: by the beginning of 1946 the number of illegal immigrants was exceeding 1,000 every month and the number of Jews living in Palestine already amounted to 608,000, making up two-fifths of the region's overall population.

In the United States – which itself had no intention of taking in any more Jews from Europe – the British attitude was harshly criticized. Washington demanded that Mandated Palestine should immediately open up its borders to 100,000 Holocaust survivors, a demand that the British resisted. In order to end the arrival of 'illegal' immigrants, London imposed a naval blockade and interned a total of 26,000 refugees in camps on the island of Cyprus. A ship with 4,500 Jewish displaced persons, the *Exodus 1947*, was sent back to Europe in the late summer of 1947. In Palestine itself, the mandated power found itself fighting an increasingly bitter war against Zionist underground groups such as the right-wing Irgun under the later prime minister Menachem Begin and the Stern Group under Avraham Stern. Starting on Black Sabbath, 29 June 1946, both groups carried out multiple attacks on British institutions. The Zionist reign of terror culminated on 22 July 1946 in a bomb attack by Irgun on the King David Hotel in Jerusalem that was used by the British Mandate administration. Ninety-one people lost their lives in the attack.

The radicalization of the Jewish protest contributed in no small way to the fact that in Great Britain public opinion was turned against the country's existing policy on Palestine, with the result that in February 1947 the Labour government under Clement Attlee was persuaded to leave the United Nations to solve the Palestine problem – the United Nations was the successor of the League of Nations that had entrusted Great Britain with the Mandate in 1922. But Britain refused to play any part in the division of Palestine that a plenary session of the United Nations Organization resolved to implement by a two-thirds majority on 29 November 1947, even declining to allow the United Nations' Palestine Commission to travel to the mandated region.

By the winter of 1947/8 the fighting between Arabs and Jews had escalated to the point of open civil war. On 14 May 1948 – the day before Great Britain unilaterally ended its mandate – the prime minister of the provisional Israeli government, David Ben-Gurion, proclaimed the state of Israel. The following day troops from Arab neighbour states marched into Palestine. The war ended in July 1949 with the victory of the Israeli army and a sizeable increase in the size of the state of Israel.

By this date a historic decision with regard to India had already been taken in London, for on 20 February 1946 Attlee's government had announced its firm intention of taking all the necessary steps to ensure that by June 1947 power would have been transferred to a responsible Indian government. But London's desire to turn India into a loose federation ran into difficulties both with the centralist Congress Party under Jawaharlal Nehru and with the Muslim League under Muhammed Ali Jinnah, an outspoken advocate of a partition of British India. In August 1946 bloody fighting broke out in Calcutta and the Punjab between Hindus and Muslims, leading to the deaths of more than 4,000 members of the two communities. The last viceroy of India, Lord Mountbatten, and Attlee's cabinet finally realized that there was only one viable solution to the chaos that threatened, and on 3 June 1947 the government in London announced a plan to divide the subcontinent into a largely Hindu and a predominantly Muslim state. The relevant law was passed by parliament on 18 July and came into force on 15 August. British rule in India was over.

Churchill and other Conservative diehards had repeatedly warned that Britain's withdrawal from India would mark the beginning of the end of the Empire, but the Labour government refused to be deterred from taking a step that it regarded as unavoidable and one that the United States expected not only of Britain but also, in principle, of all the other European colonial powers: their willingness to give up colonies that wanted their independence. In the case of India there had in the meantime been a shift in the material balance between the colonial power and its colony, for Britain was now the debtor, India the creditor. Its credit balance in London amounted to £1,300 million, while British exports to India, which in 1914 had made up two-thirds of Indian imports, had sunk to a mere 8 per cent of the total by 1940.

As the German historian Peter Wende has written in his book on the British Empire, it was by now clear that

Britons no longer had sufficient resources to be able to hold on to power by force if a crisis were to arise in the future. In the light of experiences gleaned during the war, the British government no longer regarded the Indian Army as a reliable tool with which to suppress a possible uprising. Moreover, the growing participation of Indians in the administration of their country reduced the chances of Britons making a career for themselves in the Colonial Office. For a long time the Indian Civil Service had been the preserve of graduates from English universities, but by 1947 it numbered among its ranks 510 officials of Indian origin alongside 429 of British stock. [. . .] It was no spectacular military defeat but a progressive erosion of power that made the withdrawal of the British from India a political necessity.[126]

Great Britain was so weakened by the Second World War that it could no longer afford to wage a series of lengthy and costly colonial wars, quite apart from the lack of desire on the part of the population at large to support such conflicts. At the beginning of 1948 the emergence of the new states of India and Pakistan from fighting of particular ferocity was followed by the independence of two other colonies in Asia: Burma and, far less fraught with conflict, Ceylon. Like India and Pakistan, Ceylon (Sri Lanka) became a member of the Commonwealth, whereas Burma eschewed that honour. But this did not mean the end of British rule in Asia, for Malaya, Singapore and North Borneo remained British colonies, at least in the shorter term: Malaya gained its independence in 1957, Singapore in 1963 and Brunei in 1984. The crown colony of Hong Kong was handed back to China in 1997 at the end of a ninety-nine-year lease signed in 1898. In Africa there was a bloody uprising against British rule in Kenya in the 1950s. By the 1960s one British colony after another was gaining its independence in Africa. Only in Southern Rhodesia (Zimbabwe) were white settlers able to delay this step until 1980.

The United Kingdom was undoubtedly one of the victorious powers in the Second World War, which is why it was easier for it to bid farewell to its colonies than was the case with France. The Fourth Republic did everything in its power to retain its overseas possessions, which it had inherited from the Third Republic and, in the case of Algeria, from the restored Bourbon monarchy of 1814–15 and the July Monarchy of 1830. There was a marked sense in which these possessions represented a form of compensation for France: the colonies, protectorates and Algeria, which had been incorporated into Metropolitan France in 1848, seemed to provide something of the *gloire* that France felt it needed after the dramatic defeat of 1940 and the German occupation. It was an expensive illusion that cost many human lives but one that a whole series of post-war governments continued to harbour in France. Ironically, it required the return to power of the national war hero Charles de Gaulle in 1958 to reconcile France to the fact that it had no other future except that of a purely European nation. When Algeria was granted its full independence in 1962, French colonial rule finally came to an end in Africa.

The Belgian Congo gained its independence in 1960, the same year as most of the French colonies in sub-Saharan Africa. This move marked the beginning of one of the most terrible chapters in Africa's post-colonial history. Portugal, which had remained neutral in the Second World War, proved to be the most unwilling European country to bid farewell to its past greatness. Its armed forces finally ended the bloody colonial wars in its African possessions of

Angola and Mozambique. In 1975, a year after its Lisbon putsch – the Carnation Revolution of 25 April 1974 – the army drew a line under Portugal's colonial history in Africa. In 1999, two years later than Hong Kong, Portugal's last colony in Asia, Macao, was handed back to the People's Republic of China.

During the Second World War the colonial question had been a bone of contention between the United States and Great Britain, for, unlike Wilson, Roosevelt was an outspoken anti-colonialist. He was also keen to interpret the concept of self-determination as the right of Asian and African colonies to enjoy their independence: the promises enshrined in the Atlantic Charter of August 1941 were to apply to them as well. In this regard nothing changed under Truman. But, unlike Roosevelt, Truman had no need to exert any pressure on London on this point, for Attlee's Labour cabinet granted India – a particularly pressing case – its independence even more quickly than Washington had expected. The Netherlands, by contrast, needed considerable persuasion to end their colonial rule in Indonesia.

During the Cairo Conference in November 1943 Roosevelt had offered control of French Indochina to the National Chinese government of Chiang Kai-shek, which sent troops into North Vietnam in the summer of 1945. But the United States had no thoughts of supporting the Communist Viet Minh, and following the Communist victory in China Washington reined in its anti-colonial policies in south-east Asia, too. Where necessary, they preferred to support French colonial power rather than an independence movement whose successes were threatening to shift the political balance in favour of the Soviet Union. In Africa the problem of colonialism was not yet an immediate cause for concern in American eyes in the 1940s: not until the following decade did the Black Continent command Washington's attention to any greater extent.

In 1945 the United States was by far the most powerful country in the world from an economic, financial, military and political point of view, and it clearly relished the significance of this state of affairs in its dealings with its closest ally, Great Britain. The United Kingdom was so financially dependent on the goodwill of the United States that it felt the need to toe Washington's line in terms of British foreign policy. Conversely, the United States set store by according Great Britain a privileged place in the post-war order and in that way compensating it for the loss of its standing in the world. On 15 November 1945, responding to an American initiative on Truman's part, Attlee and the Canadian prime minister, William Mackenzie King, visited Washington to sign a joint declaration on closer cooperation in the field of the peaceful use of nuclear energy. Other countries were invited to sign as soon as there were reliable guarantees that they would not use fissionable material for military purposes. The signatories also expressed their support for an international ban on atomic weapons and on all other weapons of mass destruction. The United States had no intention, of course, of relinquishing its monopoly on nuclear weapons.

By the autumn of 1945 there were already signs that relations between the Western Powers and the Soviet Union were beginning to deteriorate. At the meeting of the Council of Foreign Ministers set up in Potsdam and held between 10 September and 2 October 1945, Vyacheslav Molotov responded to the refusal of Byrnes and Bevin to recognize the Communist-dominated government of Romania by agreeing to accept the Anglo-American proposal that France and China be allowed to take part in the preparatory peace talks only if they had first signed armistice agreements with the country in question. (This applied in the case of Romania.)

The Western Powers were far more troubled by the clear violation of an agreement reached in Potsdam, namely, the reinforcement of Soviet troops stationed in northern Iran and the separatist movement led by the Communist Tudeh Party in those Iranian parts of Azerbaijan and Kurdistan where autonomous republics had been proclaimed in December 1945. Only when, with the backing of the United States and of Great Britain, Iran complained to the Security Council of the United Nations about Soviet aggression in March 1946 did Moscow promise to withdraw its troops within six weeks. But at the same time the Soviet Union increased its pressure on Turkey, demanding that Ankara not only grant it joint control over the Bosporus but also that it return the southern Caucasian areas around Kars, Ardahan and Artvin that it had ceded in 1921. In March 1946 it also announced that it was ending the Soviet-Turkish non-aggression and neutrality pact that it had signed in 1925. In order to lend military weight to his demands Stalin ordered massive troop concentrations on the border with Turkey.

In the summer of 1946 the tensions between the Soviet Union and Turkey led to a fundamental rethinking of American policy towards Soviet Russia and played a significant part in the outbreak of the Cold War. But in the early months of 1946 there could as yet be no talk of a definitive breach between East and West. The United States did not question Soviet dominance in eastern central and south-east Europe. In February 1946, after hesitating for a long time, Washington recognized the government in Romania that had been installed by the Soviet Union. By this date Communists loyal to Moscow had long since taken up key positions in government and in the state apparatus in Sofia, Bucharest and Warsaw, while they were also actively involved in the governments in Budapest and Prague. In the Soviet zone in Germany the Communist Party and the Social Democratic Party had merged to form the Socialist Unity Party of Germany in April 1946, albeit only after massive pressure was exerted on them by the occupying power. In this way the foundations were laid for the hegemony of the Communists and for the alignment of all the other parties. Churchill was not exaggerating when in the speech that he delivered in Fulton in March 1946 he referred to an 'Iron Curtain' dividing Europe in two.

But the line of demarcation that had been drawn in Yalta did not simply divide the Continent into 'East' and 'West', for it ran right through the heart of the old West. The new East encompassed not only two countries marked by Byzantine Orthodoxy, Bulgaria and Romania, but also countries whose religious thinking was influenced by the western Christian Church, including the Baltic, Poland, Czechoslovakia, Hungary and the Soviet-occupied part of Germany. And the new transatlantic West included not only countries of the Occident but also – following the defeat of the Communists in the civil war that ended in 1949 – Orthodox Greece and Islamic Turkey. During the Cold War, the historic concepts of the 'West' and of the 'East' were so overlaid by the new opposition between East and West that the older reality and its semantic associations were increasingly lost from sight.

After 1945 there were no longer any purely European world powers. By then the two world powers were the United States and the Soviet Union, both of them key players in the anti-Hitler coalition. And both acquired a position of hegemony within their respective spheres of influence. Initially, at least, the 'bipolarity' that began to emerge in 1945 was asymmetrical, for as long as only one of them could produce nuclear weapons, it continued to enjoy a decisive advantage over its international rival. Economically and financially, too, the United States was superior to the Soviet Union. It was the new world banker, with the dollar as the leading global currency. During the immediate post-war era there could be no talk of any equality or balance of power between the United States and the Union of Soviet Socialist Republics.

After 1945 most European countries fell under the influence of one or other of the two remaining world powers. With the exception of the Korean peninsula, the United States and the Soviet Union were nowhere in such immediate proximity to one another as they were in the old Continent of Europe. But Europe was only a small part of the world, and countries that the European powers had subjected to their rule in other continents were no longer guaranteed to remain theirs after 1945. In the immediate aftermath of the Second World War, there was not yet a 'Third World', but two of the states that had been reborn between 1945 and 1949 – India and Indonesia – were so large that they were clearly predestined to assume a leading role when the countries outside the sphere of influence of the two superpowers finally became aware of their own common interests.

The Soviet Union had always seen itself as an anti-imperialist power – not that this prevented it from pursuing a policy towards China in Manchuria that was little more than a continuation of the policies of the imperialist Russia of the tsars. After 1945 Moscow could count increasingly on being able to recruit fighters from national liberation movements who would commit themselves to the global class war and hence to the world revolution. The United States, which owed its existence to an anti-colonial revolution, was obliged to distance itself from colonialism in order not to expose itself to criticism on the part of the Soviet Union.

The Second World War advanced the cause of emancipation for all the colonial nations – not because this was the intention of the man who had unleashed the war, but because the war left all of the old colonial powers permanently weakened. By the end of the hostilities the days of the British Empire that Hitler had always admired were numbered, as were those of the French colonial empire. Paradoxically, the post-war world order whose outlines could already be dimly discerned in 1945 continued to bear a German stamp in both Europe and Asia, for this order was largely the result of the second attempt of the German Reich to turn itself into a world power and, indeed, into the foremost world power. It was an attempt that had ended in catastrophic failure.

From World War to World War:
Retrospective of an Exceptional Period

O N 18 SEPTEMBER 1941, General de Gaulle spoke to the French nation in his capacity as the head of France Libre and sought to place contemporary events within a broader historical context. 'The war on Germany began in 1914,' he declared:

> The Treaty of Versailles certainly did not end that war but merely signalled an armistice in the course of which the enemy rebuilt his forces of aggression. German aggression began again in March 1936, initially with the occupation of the Rhineland, then against Austria and Czechoslovakia, followed by preparations for the campaigns against Poland, Belgium and France, which for their part were merely a prelude to the invasion of Russia and to the present concentration of the war effort on the Anglo-Saxon nations. In reality, therefore, the world is fighting a thirty years war either for or against the universal domination of Germany.[1]

Two and a half years later Winston Churchill took this interpretation of history as his own, writing to Stalin on 27 February 1944 to say that he regarded 'this war against German aggression as all one and as a thirty years' war from 1914 onwards.'[2]

This reference to a second Thirty Years War may have been an example of psychological warfare but it was not without historical substance. Germany was not solely to blame for unleashing the First World War, but it was a major power that bore the greatest responsibility for the escalation of the July crisis and, hence, for ensuring that the Austro-Serbian conflict developed into a major European war. After 1918 Germany was unable to come to terms with its defeat, and if the country was in agreement on any single point, it was what it regarded as the injustice of the Treaty of Versailles, which it insisted required revising. Hitler was resolved from the outset on belligerent expansionism, but unlike the majority of the revisionists, he never had any intention of accepting the borders of the pre-war period. Even so, there was a sense of continuity in terms of

Germany's questioning the status quo, and once Hitler had come to power, this aspiration became the single most unsettling factor in European politics. With hindsight, it became tempting, therefore, to regard the interwar period as no more than a fragile peace and to accuse German politics since 1918 of a single-mindedness that made the Second World War seem inevitable.

If we extend our field of vision beyond Europe to Asia, we shall find further reasons to question the view that the two decades after 1918 were a time of untroubled peace. Japan, which was later to become an Axis partner of National Socialist Germany, had begun to expand its own power base as early as 1931, when it had established the protectorate of Manchukuo. By July 1937 it had triggered the Sino-Japanese War with an incident on the Marco Polo Bridge in Beijing, a conflict which by the end of 1941 had become a part of the Second World War. Germany's other Axis partner, Italy, had invaded Ethiopia in 1935 and begun a war that was more than the traditional colonial conflict but, rather, a racially motivated war of extermination and to that extent a harbinger of what the world was to experience on a far larger scale after 1939, initially in eastern central Europe, thereafter in eastern Europe. The Spanish Civil War, too, bore all the hallmarks of a prelude to the Second World War, with the Axis powers of Germany and Italy fighting on one side, while the Soviet Union was actively involved on the other. This was the first time that 'Fascism' and 'Bolshevism' had clashed militarily, two ideological opposites that were to cooperate with each other only a short time afterwards as part of the Hitler–Stalin Pact, only for them to become embroiled in a life and death struggle following the German invasion of the Soviet Union on 22 June 1941.

After 1945 references to a second Thirty Years War are also found in the writings of historians, most vividly and most emphatically in a 1988 study by the American historian Arno J. Mayer, *Why Did the Heavens Not Darken? The 'Final Solution' in History*, where the author describes the Second World War as a German crusade against Jewish Bolshevism. In Mayer's view, there were several significant parallels between the Thirty Years War of 1618–48 and the 'thirty years war' of 1914–45:

> In terms of the international system, the issue in both cases was the bid of a major power for continental hegemony, a bid which was opposed by ideologically inconsistent military coalitions. As champions of the balance of power, Richelieu and Gustavus Adolphus were as incongruous a pair as Winston Churchill and Joseph Stalin. In one case central Europe was in the eye of a hurricane; in the other case eastern Europe was. Both times the bloodletting was enormous and there were more civilian than military casualties. [. . .] In 1648 the checkmate of the Habsburgs' hegemonic and centralizing pretensions was translated into the continuance of Germany as a collection of over two hundred virtually autonomous territorial states whose rulers wielded authority on the principle of *Cuius regio, eius religio*.

In 1945 the defeat of the drive for European mastery by a belatedly united Germany resulted in its being divided in two halves, each of which had its own inviolable civil religion.

According to Mayer, in both cases

the traditional foundations of Europe were shaken by a general crisis in civil and political society which was at once cause and effect of total and monstrous war. The first half of the seventeenth century had the dubious distinction of being the bloodiest and most destructive half century on record, until it was surpassed by the first half of the twentieth. [. . .] Whereas the General Crisis and Thirty Years War of the seventeenth century marked the last phase of the ideological struggle between Catholicism and Protestantism, the General Crisis and Thirty Years War of the twentieth century marked the climacteric of the ideological struggle between fascism and bolshevism. [. . .] In the seventeenth century Europe simultaneously reordered and enlarged its imperial reach; in the twentieth century it lost its world primacy and overseas empire.[3]

The comparison between the first half of the seventeenth century and the first half of the twentieth century, both of which could be described as exceptional periods, is illuminating. Like the Thirty Years War, the First and Second World Wars were not just conflicts between states but were also waged on the level of ideological confrontations and for a time assumed the form of a civil war. Like 1648, 1945 signified a profound break in the state system and in the internal order of the states involved in the conflict. If the Thirty Years War ended in the victory of the principle of *cuius regio, eius religio*, then the outcome of the Second World War could be encapsulated in the phrase coined by the German international lawyer Hans Peter Ipsen, '*cuius occupatio, eius constitutio*' (the occupier chooses the constitution). The 'Westphalian System' was based on the maxim that all states should determine their own internal order and that other states had no right to intervene in their sovereign affairs. The system proposed at Yalta and Potsdam transferred this maxim to the sphere of influence of the major powers: what happened within the gradually emerging blocs did not justify any violent intervention by the other side, not even if the hegemonic power threatened the sovereignty of a state within its own sphere of influence. Conflicts might break out between the leading powers if the spheres of influence intersected, as was the case with the treatment of Germany as a single economic entity, or if the formally agreed demarcation line was ignored and crossed by one side, as was the case with Korea in 1950.

But alongside the parallels there are also fundamental differences between the seventeenth and twentieth centuries. In spite of its different phases and shifting coalitions, the Thirty Years War struck contemporaries as a single war, whereas the majority of Europeans and North Americans did not feel that they were at war during the two decades that separated the First and Second World Wars. The peace that was produced by the treaties signed in Versailles and in the other Paris suburbs would presumably have lasted much longer if the Weimar Republic had not been fatally buffeted by the storms of the world economic crisis and if it had not been replaced by Hitler's Führer state. The term 'second Thirty Years War' suggests an inevitability to the way in which events unfolded between 1914 and 1945 and turns the years of peace into an optical illusion, a teleological and deterministic view of history that no longer allows us to distinguish between the situation that might have developed at the end of the First World War and the one that actually emerged under the impact of a global economic catastrophe.

For the French and the British, the First World War continues to be the 'Grande Guerre' and the 'Great War'. And war remains 'the father of all and king of all' in the sense defined by Heraclitus of Ephesus. Writing in 1925, the German economist Moritz Julius Bonn noted that 'The Great War meant the triumph of the theory of violence':

> The Great War differed from other wars in one respect: it was not a mere professional war. Most wars in days gone by have been fought by people whose business it was to deal with the enemy in accordance with approved military rules. The Great War was a war of nations. The activities deciding it were not restricted to the front. Its consequences, not only its direct consequences, were daily felt in every home. In this respect it must be compared with organized civil war, which is bound to shake the relations of society wherever it is raging. [. . .] War denies the principles on which our civilization is really based; it denies the sacredness of human life; it denies the inviolability of private property; it tears up treaties. [. . .] Now this spirit of violence developed by a four years' uninterrupted practice cannot suddenly be transformed into one of gentleness when the word 'disband' is spoken.[4]

After 1918 paramilitary violence became a feature of the internal politics of many states, especially those that had been defeated. Russia was the first country to see war turn into civil war. As early as November 1914 Lenin had spoken of 'the conversion of the present imperialist war into a civil war' as being 'the only correct proletarian slogan'.[5] After the October Revolution of 1917 Lenin had had a chance to put his theory into practice, at the same time hoping that the Russian example would spark a revolution in Europe as a whole.

In fact the Communist revolution was confined to Russia, but as a threat it was soon a constant presence in Europe thanks to the Communist International and its affiliated parties. The civil wars of the immediate post-war period remained restricted to the regions where they broke out and failed to merge as a single great civil war in the way that the Bolsheviks had hoped. But the whole of Europe was gripped by the fear of civil war and of Red revolution, and nowhere more so than in the country without whose active help Lenin and the Bolsheviks would never have come to power: Germany. The deeper reason for this state of affairs was a national trauma: the experience of the breakdown of the old order and the exposure to chaos, blind violence and the rampages of foreign soldiers in the Thirty Years War of 1618–48. This was the quintessential negative experience of the earlier period of German history, the German seminal catastrophe.

Like Bolshevist Russia, the United States of America first became actively involved in European politics in 1917. Woodrow Wilson, who was instrumental in taking his country into the war, spoke of a nation's right of self-determination and in doing so created a slogan more powerful than Lenin's call for world revolution. The states that succeeded the Russian and Habsburg Empires in eastern central and south-east Europe became the beneficiaries of two archetypal western principles, national sovereignty and democratic majority decisions, both of which were inextricably linked to the American Revolution of 1776 and to the French Revolution of 1789.

But the application of these principles to regions of mixed nationality naturally led from the outset to conflicts with other western traditions, namely, respect for the human and civic rights of all citizens and, hence, tolerance of minorities. The new states felt that they were nation states, although none was a nation state in the strict sense of that term: Yugoslavia, Czechoslovakia and Poland, in particular, were all states made up of multiple nationalities. The agreements designed to protect minorities and foisted on these countries by the League of Nations rarely proved satisfactory, and with the exception of Finland and Estonia, none of the new states could be held up as an example of a successful relationship between the titular nation and its ethnic minorities.

The problems associated with these nationalities made it more difficult to form stable political majorities and in that way contributed to the fact that western democracy failed to put down any permanent roots in most of these young states. Other typical burdens on democracy were the peasants' lack of land, widespread illiteracy, the distrust of the clergy, of the military and of the privileged classes, especially the major landowners, vis-à-vis the parliamentary system, and the radical protest of peasants, members of the petty bourgeoisie and workers at existing conditions. Those in power generally responded to the signs of an internal crisis with a forced nationalism that often included anti-Semitism. And they also fell back on repressive measures. In the end the self-determination of the leading nation invariably triumphed over the democratic self-government of its citizens. It was a development that took to its most absurd extreme Woodrow Wilson's attempt to equate these two principles.

The first new state to turn itself into one based on an authoritarian system was Hungary in 1919–20. Hungary was one of the nations that had lost out in the war and now mourned for the frontiers that it had forfeited under the terms of the Treaty of Trianon. It was also the only country in central Europe to witness a Communist revolution in 1919. A decade after the end of the First World War there were few new states that could be described as democracies, and by the middle of the 1930s all but two were governed by more or less authoritarian regimes. The exceptions were Czechoslovakia, the most heavily industrialized and secularized country to emerge from the Austro-Hungarian Empire, where the majority of the population was middle-class, and Finland, which numbered itself among the Scandinavian democracies and was power-fully influenced by their political culture. Finland's southern neighbour, Estonia, occupied an intermediate position with its 'state-run democracy'.

Not only most of the new states in eastern central and south-east Europe were ruled by dictators by the first half of the 1930s, so, too, were many of the older European states. In the Balkans and on the Iberian peninsula there were no longer any democracies by 1938. By then western democracy had retreated to Scandinavia, Great Britain, Ireland, the Netherlands, Belgium, Luxembourg, France and Switzerland. Czechoslovakia remained a part of this group of states only until it was destroyed by National Socialist Germany in March 1939.

Any attempt to identify a common factor that would explain the gradual disappearance of democratic governments during the interwar period will find that in almost every case it was the social and mental backwardness of the countries in question. Authoritarian right-wing dictatorships gained a foot-hold in countries that were still predominantly agrarian in character, countries in which, with the obvious exceptions of the Baltic States and Austria, large sections of the population were unable to read and write, and the Orthodox Church formed a powerful cartel with the country's traditional upper class.

But in two cases the term 'backwardness' is inadequate to explain the situa-tion, namely, in Italy and even more so in Germany. Both countries had much in common. Both had achieved national unity only relatively recently, in the second half of the nineteenth century, and both had become colonial powers only at an even later date. In both countries, moreover, there were striking differences in the way in which their regions had developed: in Italy, there was a north–south divide, whereas in Germany the divide was between the west and east of the country. Before 1914 both countries had been only partially democratized. And although Italy was a parliamentary monarchy, it had adopted something close to universal franchise only in 1912. Moreover, the electoral boycott imposed by the Vatican in 1870 in response to the abolition of the Papal States was still in force. In Germany there had been universal male suffrage since 1871, but the country became a parliamentary monarchy only in October 1918, when the prospect of its imminent military defeat could no longer be ignored.

This lack of synchronicity in Germany's democratization process – the early democratization of the right to vote and the belated introduction of a parliamentary system of government – continued to affect the country in the wake of the First World War, when the revolution of 1918/19 could involve only *more* democracy in the form of the introduction of women's suffrage, the democratization of the right to vote in the individual states and the full implementation of the parliamentary system of government. Attempts on the part of the extreme left to establish a 'dictatorship of the proletariat' on the Soviet model had the backing of only a minority of the proletariat and were brutally suppressed in 1919–20. Italy witnessed no revolution after 1918, although it did experience revolutionary unrest in the form of the *biennio rosso* of 1919–20, when the parliamentary system of government was subjected to a stern test. In the Germany of the Weimar Republic western democracy struck large sections of the middle classes as a form of government imposed on them by the victorious nations and, hence, as an 'un-German' product of their defeat. In Italy the West fell into disrepute because the political right blamed it for the country's ostensible *vittoria mutilata*, when it had been robbed of the fruits of its heroic struggle. In this way anti-western resentment marked the beginning of each country's rebellion against democracy as an institution.

Fascism came to power in Italy in October 1922 with the active help of the monarchy and the willing indulgence of the liberals who set the political tone at this time. It created a system hitherto unknown in Europe, a system that relied for its support on paramilitary forces that had previously acted with extreme violence against the divided left and that had received financial backing from the country's major landowners. When Mussolini came to power, this was far from spelling the end of the reign of terror. Instead, it gave state approval to that terror.

Italian Fascism was the most radical response to Bolshevism that had been witnessed up to that time, while in certain respects modelling itself on the Russian movement. In terms of their intolerance of political and ideological opponents, Fascists and Communists were practically indistinguishable. Both regimes appealed to the whole man and promised that the future would give rise to a 'new man' shaped by their own ideas. The comprehensive nature of this claim set the new dictatorships in Italy and the Soviet Union apart from traditional authoritarian regimes such as earlier military dictatorships. Italy was the first country in which the new type of regime was described as 'totalitarian' by its liberal and socialist critics. It was a term that was taken over by Mussolini and later applied by academic writers to characterize the features that Fascism, National Socialism and Bolshevism all had in common: the monopoly on power and on propaganda that was enjoyed by a single party, the rigorous elimination of each and every form of division of power, the suppression of all forms of opposition, the omnipresence of the secret police and of terror, the disfranchisement of the individual, the mobilization of the masses and the cult of the country's leader.

In 1922 Italy had only partly been industrialized and was still largely a rural economy. In many parts of the Mezzogiorno, including Calabria, the population was still largely illiterate in the early 1920s. (The national average in 1921 was 27 per cent.) If backwardness in Italy was one of the reasons for the failure of democracy and for the emergence of a right-wing dictatorship, then it was also one of the reasons why a similar development was relatively unlikely in Germany. Germany was a highly developed industrial country where all children had long been required to attend school. Those regions that were regarded as 'backward' included the countryside to the east of the Elbe that was dominated by major landowners and, more especially, East Prussia, which was cut off from the rest of Germany and able to survive only with generous financial help from Prussia and the Reich. But unlike Italy there was no part of Germany where the level of education was strikingly lower than elsewhere.

The fact that a single movement, modelled on the Italian Fascists, could become the most powerful party in Germany after 1930 was due in no small part to the lack of synchronicity within the process of democratization in the country. Once the parliamentary system had foundered on the lack of any willingness to compromise on the part of the moderate parties, Hitler's National Socialists were presented with a unique chance that allowed them to appeal not only to the wide-spread resentment at western democracy but also to the nation's claims to have a share in power in the form of universal suffrage, a claim documented since Bismarck's day and one that was largely robbed of its political impact by the semi-authoritarian presidential cabinets that ruled the country from 1930 onwards.

It was a pseudo-democratic appeal to the people that distinguished Hitler's radical rejection of Weimar from that of the traditional right. Until then the political right had for the most part sought an authoritarian solution to the crisis that threatened to plunge the country into a bloody civil war. By the winter of 1932/3 a number of conservatives had come to believe that in a country with a long tradition of democratic suffrage the planned change of regime needed broad support among the masses. Since Hitler, as the leader of the largest 'nationalist' party, seemed a suitable candidate to guarantee this support and since he was willing to share power with the conservatives, the right-wing establishment, headed by Hindenburg as the country's president, was instrumental in helping him to win the chancellorship on 30 January 1933.

Italian Fascism and German National Socialism had many points in common. Both movements subscribed to an extreme nationalism. Both were radically anti-Marxist and anti-liberal. Both of them inflicted unprecedented brutality on their political opponents, and both of them idolized their leaders and glorified their nation's youth as well as admiring virility and military virtues. Once they had come to power, they systematically eliminated all of the forces and institutions that stood in their way and by dint of a mixture of prop-aganda and terror created an acclamatory pseudo-public that brooked no opposition and offered the regime the semblance of legitimacy.

As far as the gradual suppression of the country's traditional elites was concerned, the National Socialists were far more ruthless and successful than the Italian Fascists, who were obliged right up until the end to reach an agreement with both the monarchy and the military. In spite of the constant internal power struggles associated with the country's leader, National Socialism was far more totalitarian and far closer to enjoying a monopoly of absolute power than Italian Fascism. Another difference was the fanatical anti-Semitism that was integral to Hitler's movement. Not until the end of 1938 did Mussolini's regime adopt anti-Jewish policies inspired by the Nuremberg Laws of 1935 but never implemented with the same degree of bureaucratic ruthlessness as was the case in Germany. Of course, Italian Fascism, too, was racist, a point abundantly clear from the country's colonial wars in Libya and, later, in Ethiopia. In Africa the Duce revealed just how ruthlessly aggressive towards the outside world his regime was capable of being. But in spite of his repeated claims to be anti-Bolshevist, he never considered waging war on the Soviet Union, a reluctance due in the main to his realization that Italy lacked the material resources for such a conflict. If, in 1941, he took part in the German campaign in the east – a late colonial land grab that was also an ideological war of extermination – then this was because Fascist Italy had no wish to come away empty-handed from the expected new world order.

The similarities between Italian Fascism and German National Socialism were so self-evident that even contemporaries bundled them together under the catch-all term 'Fascist'. National Socialism was indeed the German expression of Fascism, while at the same time diverging from its Italian model on so many essential points that it would be wrong to see in it merely a form of 'German Fascism'. There were many Fascist movements in Europe during the interwar years, including the Spanish Falangist movement, the Croatian Ustaša, the Romanian Iron Guard and the Hungarian Arrow Cross. But only in Italy and Germany did Fascist parties come to power without outside help, and only in these two countries did autonomous Fascist regimes come into existence.

Attempts to turn European Fascist movements into international organizations were doomed from the outset to failure, for their exclusive nationalism made it impossible for Fascist regimes to create a sense of international solidarity comparable to that enjoyed by the Communist International. Thanks to its anti-Semitism and anti-Bolshevism, the Third Reich succeeded in persuading a handful of intellectuals, politicians, parties and groupings to collaborate with it in the countries that it occupied, but it was never able to mobilize the masses. Fascist or National Socialist internationalism would have been a contradiction in terms.

The most extreme opponents of the far right were the Russian Bolsheviks, who had always seen themselves as the vanguard of a new, classless society, with the result that following their seizure of power they immediately set about eliminating the ruling classes and, where possible, destroying them root and branch. The Italian Fascists and the German National Socialists had no desire to destroy their countries' economic, military, bureaucratic and intellectual elites but wanted to make them compliant to their own particular needs, an aim in which they succeeded to varying degrees. For Stalin, it was crucial to his rule to deal with Russia's backwardness once and for all, and thanks to the brutal means that he employed he came closer to this goal than any politician before him. Conversely, it is only with considerable reservations that we can speak of a modernization of Italian society by Fascism. Only in the case of the attempt to do away with illiteracy can we speak of any real success, and yet even here Mussolini was merely pursuing a policy already introduced by Giolitti. In National Socialist Germany industrialization proceeded apace in spite of the agrarian romanticism of the party's ideological outlook. And yet this, too, was not because Hitler wanted to modernize Germany but because he would not have been able to pursue his war aims if he had not forced the pace of growth in the country's arms industry. National Socialist Germany and Fascist Italy were not dictatorships bent on modernization but an expression of a modernization crisis in two nations that had achieved national unity only at a very late date, that were unable to solve their social problems by democratic means and that were profoundly dissatisfied with their place in the new post-war world order.

The crisis in European democracy during the interwar years was not confined to those countries that had been turned into authoritarian or Fascist dictatorships, for it also affected most of the countries that could look back on older democratic traditions. The First World War had dealt a severe blow to contemporaries' faith in reason and fuelled nationalist passions that continued to burn even after the weapons had fallen silent. But the war had also produced a feeling of hatred directed at all who were held responsible for the killings, including those who had justified the millions of deaths or who had profited from them. After 1918 a return to normality was difficult even in those countries where there was a long tradition of solving political conflicts on the parliamentary stage through a peaceful exchange of ideas. The propertied classes were everywhere afraid of the increased power of the workers' movement and of its trade unions and affiliated parties. After 1918 it seemed more likely that the bourgeoisie would be outvoted by the political left than had been the case before 1914.

At the same time, parliamentary democracy foundered only in those countries where it had not been introduced until 1918 and 1919 or where it did not enjoy broad support within society at large. In older democracies, Fascist movements were unable to establish the sort of mass base for their activities that they enjoyed in Germany and in Italy. Even in a country like France, where the Communists managed to unite a large section of the working class, they were still not in a position to force the Socialists into second place. Even in France and Great Britain there was right-wing criticism of the parliamentary system and of democracy, and there was also a responsive audience willing to listen to such concerns. But in contrast to the Conservative Revolution in Germany, young right-wing intellectuals in neither France nor Great Britain ever succeeded in defining public opinion but merely represented one line of thinking among many.

The world economic crisis that saw Germany abandon its parliamentary system and embrace a right-wing totalitarian dictatorship left Great Britain and the United States scarcely less badly affected than the Reich, but in both of these Anglo-Saxon countries democracy survived, economic and social reforms allowing it to reconstitute itself on a new and more solid basis. During the Great Depression all of the old expressions of freedom demonstrated their resilience. Wherever the normative project of the West had put down roots and left its mark on the political thinking of the rulers and of the ruled, it proved its worth in the great crisis that affected the world from 1929 onwards, a crisis that represented the most serious challenge the West had faced until then.

If there was anything about Adolf Hitler's Reich that earned the sympathy of conservative circles in the West after 1933, it was its militant anti-Bolshevism. Britain's policy of appeasement during the second half of the 1930s rested in no small part on the assumption that this hostility was unshakeable and that it could therefore serve as the basis for limited cooperation between London and Berlin. The German-Soviet Non-Aggression Pact of 23 August 1939 revealed this estimation to be no more than an example of wishful thinking. On the other hand, it was not hard to predict that the arrangement between Hitler and Stalin would not last, and the German invasion of the Soviet Union on 22 July 1941 gave Great Britain the chance to continue its war on National Socialist Germany with a powerful ally at its side. The fact that the Conservative Churchill was an outspoken opponent of revolutionary Bolshevism was of no importance in this context. As long as the future of Great Britain and of the British Empire was at stake, any ideological differences were bound to fade into insignificance next to the common interest in defeating the German aggressor as swiftly and as comprehensively as possible.

Roosevelt seems to have had no ideological scruples about working with Stalin to overthrow Hitler and for a time he regarded the Soviet Union as a calculable entity whose anti-colonialism was very much after his own heart and, as such, in welcome contrast to Churchill's imperialism. Hitler was the enemy *tout court*: there was nothing about him or his regime or his view of the world that offered a point of contact for American policy-makers. With Stalin, conversely, it was possible to act in concert and, indeed, there seemed every likelihood that this spirit of cooperation would extend beyond the war. The United States and the Soviet Union would emerge from the Second World War as the two most powerful nations of the post-war era, and in Roosevelt's eyes the ability to maintain world peace would depend in future on their ability to agree and to work together.

The sociologist M. Rainer Lepsius has described Communism and Fascism as 'the two great twentieth-century movements against parliamentary democracy and against the project of civil society'.[6] In fact it was not only Italian Fascism and German National Socialism but also Russian Bolshevism that represented a radical negation of the normative project of the West that had emerged from the Atlantic revolutions of the late eighteenth century. But there was something distinctly asymmetrical about the stance that these two ideological opposites adopted towards this project. The Fascists rejected every aspect of the legacy of 1789 and to that extent were part of a tradition linking them to the Catholic and romantic counterrevolution of the early nineteenth century, whereas the Bolsheviks saw themselves as the heirs of the extreme left wing of the French Revolution, the 'conspiracy of equals' associated with François-Noël ('Gracchus') Babeuf, who was the first to demand the complete abolition of private property and the creation of a Communist society. Within this tradition of revolutionary thinking, there was no room for individual freedom.

For four years, from 1941 and 1945, it proved possible to neutralize the ideological conflict between western democracies and the totalitarian Soviet system, but only because of their shared opposition to another totalitarian regime, that of National Socialist Germany. Throughout this period the Anglo-Saxon powers were obliged to abandon positions that they had solemnly championed in the Atlantic Charter of 14 August 1941. Even without being conscious of what they were doing, they sacrificed the right of self-determination of the peoples of eastern central and south-east Europe on the altar of a partnership forced upon them by Hitler. When Churchill became aware of the fatal consequences of this policy during the final weeks of the war, he protested at what had happened but was unable to effect any changes. The fault lines in the post-war world were clearly identifiable in the spring of 1945, Europe being divided into one part that was able to keep the promises enshrined in the Atlantic Charter and another part that was denied this opportunity.

With their joint victory over National Socialist Germany, there was no longer any need for the western democracies to work together with the Soviet Union, and it was only a question of time before the ideological conflict between these two different worlds flared up anew. The historian Dan Diner has seen in the clash between 'freedom' and 'equality' the central key to our understanding of the twentieth century, whereby 'equality', according to the Soviet understanding of that term, has nothing to do with the liberal equality before the law or with the socio-democratic belief in equal opportunities but presupposes absolute equality in the sense of the radical elimination of the inequalities that are due to the class system.

To express this antithesis, Diner draws on the metaphor of a 'universal civil war':

> On a vertical plane, the confrontation cut through previous state and national loyalties, corresponding in this way to the nineteenth-century

antinomies of freedom and equality, bourgeoisie and proletariat, revolution and counterrevolution. Decolonization also appropriated the political terminology of 1789: in the second half of the twentieth century, entire continents were raised to the status of revolutionary subjects, with commentators now beginning to speak of a *tiers monde* in analogy to the *tiers état*.[7]

As a metaphor, the term 'universal civil war' encapsulates the basic ideological conflict that was to leave its mark on the twentieth century up to the end of the Communist regime in Europe between 1989 and 1991. This conflict had begun with the Russian Revolution of October 1917. There were three reasons why this conflict failed to break out fully during the interwar years. First, a whole series of setbacks in terms of its efforts to export its own particular brand of revolution meant that the Soviet Union was forced to postpone the 'world revolution' and to concentrate instead on Stalin's slogan about 'building socialism in *one* country'. Second, the democratic messianism of the United States was thwarted by American isolationism, which prevented any lasting transatlantic or global commitment on the part of what was potentially the leading western power. And, third, a third force emerged with the Fascists and, more especially, with the National Socialists and their seizure of power that made it impossible for East and West to confront one another as part of a conflict between 'freedom' and 'equality' or between 'democracy' and 'dictatorship'.

The victory of the anti-Hitler coalition led to a radical simplification of the international situation, for now there were only two world powers, the United States and the Soviet Union. And the United States was by far the more powerful of the two as a result of its superior technological know-how and its monopoly on atomic weapons. If we define a major power by whether it has a permanent seat on the Security Council of the United Nations, then China was paralysed by its internal power struggle between the Kuomintang and the Communists, and Great Britain and France, the two greatest colonial powers in Europe, had been so weakened by the war that it was questionable if they would ever be able to recover from it.

By now the United Kingdom was so materially dependent on its former colony, the United States, that we may agree with Dan Diner when he speaks of the transfer of the 'imperial baton' from Great Britain to the United States and of a '*translatio imperii* of our time'.[8] For the present it remained unclear what would become of the two former world powers, Germany and Japan. At least in Europe the age of the classic, sovereign nation states was drawing to a close, a realization that naturally needed time to sink in. The fate of the old Continent no longer lay in its own hands but in those of the two world powers that between them had decided the outcome of the Second World War.

The year 1945 marked the end of one particular type of totalitarian dictatorship but not the end of totalitarian rule as such. Germany's surrender drew a line not only under the twelve-year history of the Third Reich but also under the seventy-four-year history of the German Reich. The year brought an end to Germany's revolt against the normative project of the West, an act of rebellion that had started long before 1933. By unleashing the Second World War, Germany destroyed the foundations of all that had retained its universal validity in Europe in the wake of the First World War. The Holocaust made it clear to the world what ideological blindness could accomplish when harnessed to modern technology and when a country like Germany abandoned the rule of law, as it did in 1933. If the murder of European Jewry has left deeper scars on the collective conscience of the West than the millions of murders carried out by Stalin, then this is not only because the Shoah was unique in its chilling and mechanical efficiency but for another reason, too: this crime against humanity was committed by a nation that was a part of western culture and that was judged, therefore, by western standards. This was at the heart of the 'German catastrophe' of which the historian Friedrich Meinecke spoke in the title of a widely read book that was first published in Germany in 1946.[9]

In Europe western values survived the Second World War because the new West in the guise of America and the British Dominions came to the aid of the libertarian forces in the old Continent. But the cause of freedom continued to be threatened. The ability of the West to maintain a coherent and cohesive stance on both sides of the North Atlantic depended on whether the ideas of 1776 and 1789 would continue to shine as a beacon of light in the post-war world.

LIST OF ABBREVIATIONS

AAA — Agrarian Adjustment Administration
ACA — Army Comrades Association
ADGB — Allgemeiner Deutscher Gewerkschaftsbund (= Confederation of German Trade Unions)
AEG — Allgemeine Elektrizitäts-Gesellschaft (= General Electric Company)
AFL — American Federation of Labor
ARMIR — Armata Italiana in Russia
BBC — British Broadcasting Corporation
BBWR — Bezpartyjny Blok Współpracy z Rządem (= Non-Partisan Bloc for Cooperation with the Government)
BEF — Bonus Expeditionary Force
BUF — British Union of Fascists
BVP — Bayerische Volkspartei (= Bavarian People's Party)
CCC — Civilian Conservation Corps
CDU — Christlich-Demokratische Union (= Christian Democratic Union)
CEDA — Confederación Española de Derechas Autónomas (= Spanish Confederation of Autonomous Right-Wing Groups)
CFLN — Comité Français de Libération Nationale (= French Committee of National Liberation)
CFTC — Confédération Française des Travailleurs Chrétiens (= French Confederation of Christian Workers)
CGPF — Confédération du Patronat Français (= General Confederation of French Employers)
CGT — Confédération Générale du Travail (= General Confederation of Labour)
CGTU — Confédération Générale du Travail Unitaire (= General Confederation of Unitary Labour)
Cheka — All-Russian Extraordinary Commission for Combating Counterrevolution and Sabotage (the first of the Bolshevik state secret-police organizations)

CIK	Central'nyj Ispolnitel'nyj Komitet (= Central Executive Committee)
CIO	Congress of Industrial Organizations
CNPF	Confédération Nationale de la Production Française (= National Confederation of French Production) later the CGPF
CNR	Conseil National de la Résistance (= National Council for the Resistance)
CNT	Confederación Nacional de Trabajadores (= National Confederation of Workers)
CORE	Congress of Racial Equality
CPA	Communist Party of the United States of America
CWA	Civil Works Administration
DAF	Deutsche Arbeitsfront (= German Labour Front)
DC	Deutsche Christen (= German Christians)
DDP	Deutsche Demokratische Partei (= German Democratic Party)
DNVP	Deutschnationale Volkspartei (= German National People's Party)
DVP	Deutsche Volkspartei (= German People's Party)
EAM	Ellenion Apelevtherikon Metopon (= National Liberation Front)
ECCI	Executive Committee of the Communist International
EDES	Ethnikos Dimokratikós Ellenikós Sýndesmos (= National Republican Greek League)
ELAS	Ethnikós Laikós Apelevtherotikós Stratós (= National Liberation Army)
FAI	Federación Anarquista Iberica (= Iberian Anarchist Federation)
FBI	Federal Bureau of Investigation
FERA	Federal Emergency Relief Administration
FNTT	Federación Nacional de Trabajadores de la Tierra (= National Federation of Agricultural Workers)
FVP	Fortschrittliche Volkspartei (= Progressive People's Party)
GATT	General Agreement on Tariffs and Trade
Gosplan	Gosudarstvenniy Komitet po Planirovaniyu (= State Planning Committee)
GPU	Gosudarstvennoye Politcheskoye Upravleniye (All-Union State Political Administration)
ICRC	International Committee of the Red Cross
IGB	Internationaler Gewerkschaftsbund (= International Confederation of Trade Unions)
IKL	Isänmaallinen Kansanliike (= Patriotic People's Movement)
ILP	Independent Labour Party
IMF	International Monetary Fund
IMRO	Internal Macedonian Revolutionary Organization
IRA	Irish Republican Army
IRI	Istituto per la Ricostruzione Industriale (= Institute for Industrial Reconstruction)

IWW	Industrial Workers of the World
JCS	Joint Chiefs of Staff
JONS	Juntas de Ofensiva Nacional-Sindicalista (= Unions of the National-Syndicalist Offensive)
JP	Jeunesses Patriotes (= Patriotic Youth)
KdF	Kraft durch Freude (= Strength Through Joy)
KPD	Kommunistische Partei Deutschlands (= German Communist Party)
LIPA	League for Independent Political Action
MSPD	Mehrheitssozialdemokratische Partei Deutschlands (= Majority Social Democratic Party of Germany)
NAACP	National Association for the Advancement of Colored People
ND	Nationaldemokraten (= National Democrats)
NEP	Novaya Ekonomicheskaya Politika (= New Economic Policy)
NKVD	Narodniy Komissariat Vnutrennikh Del (= People's Commissariat for Internal Affairs)
NRA	National Recovery Administration
NSB	Nationaal-Socialistische Beweging (= National Socialist Movement)
NSDAP	Nationalsozialistische Deutsche Arbeiterpartei (= National Socialist German Workers' Party)
NUWM	National Unemployed Workers Movement
OGPU	Obyedinyonnoye Gosudarstvennoye Politicheskoye Upravleniye (= Joint State Political Directorate)
OND	Opera Nazionale Dopolavoro (= National Recreation Club)
ONR	Obóz Naradowo-Radykalny (= National Radical Camp)
OUN	Organizacija Ukrajinskih Nacionalista (= Association of Radical Ukrainian Nationalists)
OVRA	Organizzazione di Vigilanza e Repressione dell'Antifascismo (= Organization for Vigilance and Repression of Anti-Fascism)
OZN	Obóz Zjednoczenia Narodowego (= Camp of National Unity)
PC	Parti Communiste (= Communist Party)
PCE	Partido Comunista de España (= Communist Party of Spain)
PCF	Parti Communiste Français (= French Communist Party)
PCI	Partito Comunista Italiano (= Italian Communist Party)
PNF	Partito Nazionale Fascista (= National Fascist Party)
PNV	Partido Nacional Vasco (= Basque Nationalist Party)
POLPOL	Divisione Polizia Politica (= Political Police Division)
POUM	Partido Obrero de Unificación Marxista (= Workers' Party of Marxist Unification)
POW	Polska Organizacja Wojskowa (= Polish Military Organization)
PPD	Parti Démocrate Populaire (= People's Democratic Party)
PPF	Parti Populaire Français (= French People's Party)

PPR	Polska Partia Robotnicza (= Polish Workers' Party)
PPS	Polska Partia Socjalistyczna (= Socialist Party of Poland)
PSF	Parti Social Français (= French Socialist Party)
PSOE	Partido Socialista Obrero Español (= Spanish Socialist Workers' Party)
PSU	Partito Socialista Unitario (= United Socialist Party)
PSUC	Partit Socialista Unificat de Catalunya (= United Socialist Party of Catalonia)
PWA	Public Works Administration
RAD	Reichsarbeitsdienst (= Reich Labour Service)
RFC	Reconstruction Finance Corporation
RGI	Rote Gewerkschaftsinternationale (= Red Trade Union International)
RNP	Rassemblement National Populaire (= Popular National Party)
RSHA	Reichssicherheitshauptamt (= Reich Main Security Office)
RSI	Repubblica Sociale Italiana (= Italian Social Republic)
SA	Sturmabteilungen (= Storm Troopers)
SAP	Sozialistische Arbeiterpartei Deutschlands (= Socialist Workers' Party of Germany)
SD	Sicherheitsdienst (= Security Service)
SdP	Sudetendeutsche Partei (= Sudeten German Party)
SEC	Securities and Exchange Commission
SFIO	Section Française de l'Internationale Ouvrière (= French Section of the Workers' International)
SMAD	Sowjetische Militäradministration in Deutschland (= Soviet Military Administration in Germany)
SNCF	Société Nationale des Chemins de Fer (= National Company of Railways)
SNK	Sovet Narodnych Komissarov (= Council of People's Deputies)
SOE	Special Operations Executive
SPD	Sozialdemokratische Partei Deutschlands (Social Democratic Party of Germany)
SPÖ	Sozialdemokratische Partei Österreichs (= Social Democratic Party of Austria)
SS	Schutzstaffeln (= Protections Squadrons, or Defence Corps)
STAB	Svenska Tändsticks Aktiebolaget (= Swedish Match)
STO	Service de Travail Obligatoire (= Compulsory Work Service)
TUC	Trades Union Congress
TVA	Tennessee Valley Authority
UAW	United Automobile Workers
UGT	Unión General de Trabajadores (= General Workers' Union)
UME	Unión Militar Española (= Spanish Military Union)
UN	United Nations

UNO	United Nations Organization
UPA	Ukraińska Povstanska Armija (= Ukrainian Insurgent Army)
USA	United States of America
USPD	Unabhängige Sozialdemokratische Partei Deutschlands (= Independent Social Democratic Party of Germany)
USR	Union Socialiste Républicaine (= Republican Socialist Union)
USSR	Union of Soviet Socialist Republics
WPA	Works Progress Administration
ŻOB	Żydowska Organizacja Bojowa (= Jewish Combat Organization)
ZWZ	Związek Walki Zbrojnej (= Union of Armed Struggle)
ŻZW	Żydowski Związek Wojskowy (= Jewish Military Union)

NOTES

Chapter 1. The Twentieth Century's Seminal Catastrophe: The First World War

1. John Horne and Alan Kramer, *German Atrocities, 1914: A History of Denial* (New Haven, CT, and London, 2001), 209.
2. Klaus Böhme (ed.), *Aufrufe und Reden deutscher Professoren im Ersten Weltkrieg* (Stuttgart, 1975), 49.
3. Fritz Fischer, *Griff nach der Weltmacht: Die Kriegszielpolitik des kaiserlichen Deutschland 1914/1918* (Düsseldorf, 1961), 111–12.
4. Heinrich August Winkler, *Der lange Weg nach Westen*, vol. 1: *Vom Ende des Alten Reiches bis zum Untergang der Weimarer Republik*, 6th edn (Munich, 2005), 342–3; trans. Alexander J. Sager as *The Long Road West, 1789-1933* (Oxford, 2006), 307.
5. Johann Plenge, *Eine Kriegsvorlesung über die Volkswirtschaft: Das Zeitalter der Volksgenossen* (Berlin, 1915), 73, quoted in Winkler, *Der lange Weg* (note 4), 336; Engl. trans. 303–4.
6. Max Scheler, *Der Genius des Krieges und der Deutsche Krieg* (Leipzig, 1915), 73, quoted in Winkler, *Der lange Weg* (note 4), 339; Engl. trans. 304.
7. Werner Sombart, *Händler und Helden: Patriotische Besinnungen* (Munich, 1915), 84–5, quoted in Winkler, *Der lange Weg* (note 4), 339; Engl. trans. 305 (emended).
8. Quoted by Winkler, *Der lange Weg* (note 4), 340; Engl. trans. 305–6; for an alternative translation, see Thomas Mann, *Reflections of a Nonpolitical Man*, trans. Walter D. Morris (New York, 1983), 229.
9. L. T. Hobhouse, *The World in Conflict* (London, 1915), 101.
10. Quoted by Gerd Krumeich, 'Ernest Lavisse und die Kritik der deutschen "Kultur", 1914–1918', in Wolfgang J. Mommsen (ed.), *Kultur und Krieg: Die Rolle der Intellektuellen im Ersten Weltkrieg* (Munich, 1996), 149, 153.
11. Émile Durkheim, *'L'Allemagne au-dessus de tout': La mentalité allemande et la guerre* (Paris, 1915), 44.
12. Ibid., 47.
13. Thorstein Veblen, *Imperial Germany and the Industrial Revolution* (New York, 1915), 86.
14. Ibid., 162.
15. Ibid., 249.
16. Ibid., 270.
17. Vladimir Ilyich Lenin, 'Imperialism, the Highest Stage of Capitalism', *Collected Works*, 45 vols (Moscow, 1964–74), xxii.276.
18. Lenin, 'The War and Russian Social-Democracy', *Collected Works*, xxi.34.
19. Ibid., xxi.29.
20. Ibid., xxi.30.
21. Julius Braunthal, *Geschichte der Internationale*, 3 vols (Hanover, 1961–71), ii.64–5; trans. John Clark as *History of the International*, 2 vols (London, 1967), ii.27.

22. G. D. H. Cole, *A History of the Labour Party from 1914* (London, 1948), 18.
23. Heinrich Schulthess, *Europäischer Geschichtskalender*, New Series, xxxiii (1920), 672.
24. Ibid., 678–9.
25. Dietrich Geyer, *The Russian Revolution: Historical Problems and Perspectives*, trans. Bruce Little (Leamington Spa, 1987), 74–5.
26. Lenin, 'Letters from Afar', *Collected Works* (note 17), xxiii.325–6.
27. Lenin, 'The Tasks of the Proletariat in the Present Revolution', *Collected Works* (note 17), xxiv.23.
28. Ibid., xxiv.24.
29. Lenin, 'The Tasks of the Proletariat in Our Revolution', *Collected Works* (note 17), xxiv.87.
30. Lenin, 'The Dual Power', *Collected Works* (note 17), xxiv.40.
31. Lenin, 'Marxism and Insurrection: A Letter to the Central Committee of the R.S.D.L.P.', *Collected Works* (note 17), xxvi.24–5.
32. Lenin, 'The State and Revolution', *Collected Works* (note 17), xxv.412.
33. Ibid., xxv.424.
34. Ibid., xxv.461–2.
35. Ibid., xxv.468.
36. Ibid., xxv.472.
37. Lenin, 'The Tasks of the Proletariat in the Present Revolution', xxiv.22.
38. Zbyněk A. B. Zeman, *The Break-Up of the Habsburg Empire, 1914–1918: A Study in National and Social Revolution* (London, 1961), 113.
39. Arthur S. Link (ed.), *The Papers of Woodrow Wilson*, 69 vols (Princeton, NJ, 1966–94), xl.533–9.
40. Quoted by J. W. Schulte Nordholt, *Woodrow Wilson: A Life for World Peace* (Berkeley, CA, 1991), 289.
41. Link, *The Papers of Woodrow Wilson* (note 39), xli.519–27.
42. See Winkler, *Der lange Weg* (note 4), 343; Engl. trans. 314–15.
43. See ibid., 344; Engl. trans. 316.
44. Ibid.; Engl. trans. 309.
45. Sir Llewellyn Woodward, *Great Britain and the War of 1914–1918* (London, 1967), 483.
46. Christoph Jahr, *Gewöhnliche Soldaten: Desertion und Deserteure im deutschen und britischen Heer 1914–1918* (Göttingen, 1998), 250.
47. Lenin, 'Report on Peace', *Collected Works* (note 17), xxvi.251–2.
48. Lenin, 'Draft Decree on the Dissolution of the Constituent Assembly', *Collected Works* (note 17), xxvi.435–6.
49. Hans-Jürgen Mende (ed.), *Soziales Denken*, 2 vols (Berlin, 1990), i.33.
50. Ibid., i.37–9.
51. Clara Zetkin, 'Mit Entschiedenheit für das Werk der Bolschewiki! Aus einem Brief an eine Konferenz des Reichsausschusses und der Frauenkonferenz der USPD (Frühsommer 1919)', *Ausgewählte Reden und Schriften*, 3 vols (Berlin, 1960), ii.26.
52. Rosa Luxemburg, 'Die russische Revolution (1918)', *Politische Schriften*, 3 vols, ed. Ossip K. Flechtheim (Frankfurt, 1966–8), iii.134.
53. Lenin, 'Speech to the Seventh Congress of the Russian Communist Party on the Brest-Litovsk Peace', www.marxists.org/history/ussr/government/foreign-relations/1918/March/7.htm.
54. Lenin, 'The Socialist Fatherland is in Danger!', *Collected Works* (note 17), xxvii.80.
55. Karl Marx, 'Moralising Criticism and Critical Morality', *Deutsche-Brüsseler-Zeitung*, xc (11 November 1847), *Marx/Engels Collected Works*, 50 vols (London, 1975–2005), vi.319.
56. Schulthess, *Europäischer Geschichtskalender* (note 23), xxxiv (1922), 142–7.
57. Link, *The Papers of Woodrow Wilson* (note 39), xlv.534–9.
58. Quoted by Winkler, *Der lange Weg* (note 4), 361; Engl. trans. 326.
59. Ibid., 365; Engl. trans. 328. There was nothing remotely anti-Jewish about Kleist's play, *Die Hermannsschlacht* (1808–9), which describes the battle between the German national hero Hermann and the invading Romans in AD 8.

60. Ibid., 366; Engl. trans. 329.
61. Ibid., 372-3; Engl. trans. 335.
62. Ibid., 374-5; Engl. trans. 336.
63. Ibid., 376; Engl. trans. 337.
64. Max Weber, *Economy and Society: An Outline of Interpretive Sociology*, trans. Ephraim Fischoff and others and ed. Guenther Roth and Claus Wittich, 2 vols (Berkeley, CA, 1978), i.265.
65. Ibid., i.37.
66. Zeman, *The Break-Up of the Habsburg Empire* (note 38), 117.
67. Ibid., 123.
68. Ibid., 126.
69. Ibid., 141.
70. Gotthold Rhode, 'Die Tschechoslowakei von der Unabhängigkeitserklärung bis zum "Prager Frühling" 1918-1968', in Theodor Schieder (ed.), *Handbuch der europäischen Geschichte in 7 Bänden* (Stuttgart, 1979), vii.920-77, esp. 926.
71. Adam Wandruszka, 'Österreich-Ungarn vom ungarischen Ausgleich bis zum Ende der Monarchie (1867-1918)'; Schieder, *Handbuch der europäischen Geschichte* (note 70), vi.354-400, esp. 399.
72. Zeman, *The Break-Up of the Habsburg Empire* (note 38), 231.
73. Ibid., 232.
74. Hans Roos, *A History of Modern Poland from the Foundation of the State in the First World War to the Present Day*, trans. J. R. Foster (London, 1966), 9.
75. Ibid., 14.
76. Ibid., 30.
77. Ibid., 39.
78. Wolfram Fischer, 'Wirtschaft, Gesellschaft und Staat in Europa 1914-1980', *Europäische Wirtschafts- und Sozialgeschichte vom Ersten Weltkrieg bis zur Gegenwart*, ed. Wolfram Fischer and others (Stuttgart, 1987), 1-221, esp. 173-4.
79. Rudolf Hilferding, 'Arbeitsgemeinschaft der Klassen?', *Der Kampf*, viii (1915), 321-9, esp. 322.
80. Ibid.
81. Franz Marc, 'Das geheime Europa', *Das Forum*, i (1914/15), 630-36.

Chapter 2. From the Armistice to the World Economic Crisis: 1918-33

1. Heinrich August Winkler, *Der lange Weg nach Westen*, vol. 1: *Vom Ende des Alten Reiches bis zum Untergang der Weimarer Republik*, 6th edn (Munich, 2005), 380-1; trans. Alexander J. Sager as *The Long Road West, 1789-1933* (Oxford, 2006), 342 (emended).
2. Ibid., 388; Engl. trans. 344.
3. Ibid., 384; Engl. trans. 345.
4. Eberhard Jäckel and Axel Kuhn (eds), *Hitler: Sämtliche Aufzeichnungen 1905-1924* (Stuttgart, 1980), 88-90 (letter from Hitler to Adolf Gremlich, 16 September 1919).
5. Hermann August Winkler, *Weimar 1918-1933: Die Geschichte der ersten deutschen Demokratie*, 4th edn (Munich, 2005), 87.
6. Vladimir Ilyich Lenin, 'Greetings to the Hungarian Workers', *Collected Works*, 45 vols (Moscow, 1964-74), xxix.390.
7. Stéphane Courtois and others, *Das Schwarzbuch des Kommunismus: Unterdrückung, Verbrechen und Terror* (Munich, 1998), 88-90.
8. Ibid., 114.
9. 'Hanging Order', *Revelations from the Russian Archives*, ed. Diane P. Koenker and Ronald D. Bachman (Washington DC, 1997), 1-2 (1992 Library of Congress exhibition).
10. Julius Braunthal, *Geschichte der Internationale*, 3 vols (Hanover, 1961-71), ii.184-5; trans. John Clark as *History of the International*, 2 vols (London, 1967), ii.167.
11. Arno J. Mayer, *Politics and Diplomacy of Peacemaking: Containment and Counterrevolution at Versailles, 1918-1919* (London, 1968), 409.

12. Ibid., 157.
13. Ibid., 222.
14. Winkler, *Der lange Weg* (note 1), i.399–400; Engl. trans. i.358.
15. Klaus Schwabe, *Weltmacht und Weltordnung: Amerikanische Außenpolitik von 1898 bis zur Gegenwart* (Paderborn, 2006), 652.
16. Mayer, *Politics and Diplomacy* (note 11), 771–4.
17. John Maynard Keynes, *The Economic Consequences of the Peace* (London, 1920), 29.
18. Ibid., 33.
19. Ibid., 211–12.
20. Ibid., 233.
21. Ibid., 135.
22. Hermann Weber, *Die Kommunistische Internationale: Eine Dokumentation* (Hanover, 1966), 44–7.
23. Gotthard Jäschke, 'Die Türkei als Nationalstaat seit der Revolution Mustafa Kemals (Atatürk), 1920–1974', in Theodor Schieder (ed.), *Handbuch der europäischen Geschichte in 7 Bänden* (Stuttgart, 1979), vii.1339–51, esp. 1341.
24. Samuel P. Huntington, *The Clash of Civilizations and the Remaking of World Order* (London, 1997), 177.
25. Hans Roos, *A History of Modern Poland from the Foundation of the State in the First World War to the Present Day*, trans. J. R. Foster (London, 1966), 96.
26. Theodor Schieder, 'Europa im Zeitalter der Weltmächte', in *Handbuch der europäischen Geschichte* (note 23), vii.125.
27. Winkler, *Der lange Weg* (note 1), i.127; Engl. trans. i.114.
28. Robert K. Murray, *Red Scare: A Study of National Hysteria, 1919–1920*, 2nd edn (New York, 1964), 132.
29. Ernst Fraenkel, *Das amerikanische Regierungssystem: Eine politische Analyse*, 2nd edn (Cologne, 1962), 77.
30. Gary Gerstle, *American Crucible: Race and Nation in the Twentieth Century* (Princeton, NJ, 2001), 107.
31. William E. Leuchtenburg, *The Perils of Prosperity 1914–1932* (Chicago, 1958), 188.
32. Vladimir Ilyich Lenin, 'Our Foreign and Domestic Position and Party Tasks', *Collected Works* (note 6), xxxi.415.
33. Heiko Haumann, 'Sozialismus als Ziel: Probleme beim Aufbau einer neuen Gesellschaftsordnung (1918–1928/29)', *Handbuch der Geschichte Russlands*, iii: *Von den autokratischen Reformen zum Sowjetstaat*, ed. Gottfried Schramm (Stuttgart, 1983), 711.
34. Lenin, 'The Tax in Kind', *Collected Works* (note 6), xxxii.340.
35. Manfred Hildermeier, *Geschichte der Sowjetunion 1917–1991: Entstehung und Niedergang des ersten sozialistischen Staates* (Munich, 1998), 231.
36. Lenin, 'Left-Wing Communism: An Infantile Disorder', *Collected Works* (note 6), xxxi.25.
37. Braunthal, *Geschichte der Internationale* (note 10); Engl. trans. ii.536–42.
38. Andrew Lambirth, *Literacy on the Left: Reform and Revolution* (London, 2011), 108–9.
39. Braunthal, *Geschichte der Internationale* (note 10), ii.208; Engl. trans., ii.190–91.
40. Ibid.; Engl. trans. ii.250.
41. Lenin, 'We Have Paid Too Much', *Collected Works* (note 6), xxxiii.332 (originally published in *Pravda*, 11 April 1922).
42. Weber, *Die Kommunistische Internationale* (note 22), 91–6.
43. Lenin, 'Five Years of the Russian Revolution and the Prospects of the World Revolution', *Collected Works* (note 6), xxxiii.420.
44. Heinrich August Winkler, 'Demokratie oder Bürgerkrieg: Die russische Oktoberrevolution als Problem der deutschen Sozialdemokraten und der französischen Sozialisten', *Vierteljahrshefte für Zeitgeschichte*, xlvii (1999), 1–23, esp. 6–7.
45. Denis Mack Smith, *Italy: A Modern History*, 2nd edn (Ann Arbor, MI, 1969), 348.
46. Hans Woller, *Geschichte Italiens im 20. Jahrhundert* (Munich, 2010), 93.
47. Winkler, *Der lange Weg* (note 1), i.426; Engl. trans. i.381 (emended).

48. Ibid., i430; Engl. trans. i.385 (emended).
49. David Clay Large, *Where Ghosts Walked: Munich's Road to the Third Reich* (New York, 1997), 145.
50. Winkler, *Der lange Weg* (note 1), i.436; Engl. trans. i.389-90 (emended).
51. Ibid., i.445; Engl. trans. i.397.
52. Ibid., i.447; Engl. trans. i.399.
53. Ibid., i.450; Engl. trans. 401-2.
54. Peter Gay, *Weimar Culture: The Outsider as Insider* (New York, 1968).
55. Winkler, *Der lange Weg* (note 1), i.461; Engl. trans. i.412.
56. Martin Heidegger, *Being and Time*, trans. John Macquarrie and Edward Robinson (Malden, MA, 1962), 165.
57. Carl Schmitt, *The Crisis of Parliamentary Democracy*, trans. Ellen Kennedy (Cambridge, MA, 1985), 4 (preface to the 2nd edn).
58. Heinrich August Winkler, *Der lange Weg nach Westen*, vol. 2: *Deutsche Geschichte vom 'Dritten Reich' bis zur Wiedervereinigung*, 5th edn (Munich, 2010), 6-7; trans. Alexander J. Sager as *The Long Road West, 1933-1990* (Oxford, 2007), 8.
59. Winkler, *Der lange Weg* (note 1), i.463; Engl. trans. i.414.
60. Ibid., i.464; Engl. trans. i.415 (emended).
61. Heinrich August Winkler, *Von der Revolution zur Stabilisierung: Arbeiter und Arbeiterbewegung in der Weimarer Republik 1918 bis 1924*, 2nd edn (Bonn, 1984), 704.
62. Heinrich August Winkler, *Der Schein der Normalität: Arbeiter und Arbeiterbewegung in der Weimarer Republik 1924-1930* (Berlin, 1985), 679.
63. Heinrich August Winkler, 'Von Weimar zu Hitler: Die gespaltene Arbeiterbewegung und das Scheitern der ersten deutschen Demokratie', *Streitfragen der deutschen Geschichte: Essays zum 19. und 20. Jahrhundert* (Munich, 1997), 71-93, esp. 81.
64. Winkler, *Der lange Weg* (note 1), i.467; Engl. trans. i.416 (emended).
65. Ibid., i.468; Engl. trans. i.417 (emended).
66. Ibid., i.469; Engl. trans. i.417 (emended).
67. Roos, *A History of Modern Poland* (note 25), 112.
68. Walther L. Bernecker, *Spanische Geschichte: Von der Reconquista bis heute* (Darmstadt, 2002), 136.
69. Bernd Henningsen, *Der Wohlfahrtsstaat Schweden* (Baden-Baden, 1986), 313-14.
70. Ibid., 317.
71. Ann-Judith Rabenschlag, 'Für Rasse und Volkstum: Bevölkerungspolitische Konzepte, Rassenbiologie und soziale Ingenieurskunst in Schweden in der Zwischenkriegszeit. Brüche und Kontinuitäten' (diss., Humboldt-Universität zu Berlin, 2007), 85.
72. Michael Maurer, *Kleine Geschichte Irlands* (Munich, 1998), 284-5.
73. Giovanni Zibordi, 'Towards a Definition of Fascism', *Marxists in Face of Fascism*, ed. David Beetham (Manchester, 1983), 88-93.
74. Jens Petersen, 'Wählerverhalten und soziale Basis des Faschismus in Italien zwischen 1919 und 1928', *Faschismus als soziale Bewegung: Deutschland und Italien im Vergleich*, ed. Wolfgang Schieder (Hamburg, 1976), 119-56, esp. 131.
75. Renzo De Felice, *Mussolini il fascista*, i: *La conquista del potere 1921-1925* (Turin, 1966), 624.
76. Stanislao G. Pugliese, *Fascism, Anti-Fascism, and the Resistance in Italy: 1919 to the Present* (Lanham, MD, 2003), 71-3.
77. Wolfgang Schieder, 'Der Strukturwandel der faschistischen Partei in der Phase der Herrschaftsstabilisierung', in *Faschistische Diktaturen: Studien zu Italien und Deutschland* (Göttingen, 2008), 93.
78. Wolfgang Schieder, 'Rom - die Repräsentation der Antike im Faschismus', in *Faschistische Diktaturen* (note 77), 125-46, esp. 145-6.
79. Jeffrey T. Schnapp (ed.), *A Primer of Italian Fascism* (Lincoln, NE, 2000), 301.
80. Ibid., 305.
81. Pugliese, *Fascism* (note 76), 87-90.
82. Ibid.

83. Ernst Nolte, *Der Faschismus in seiner Epoche: Action française – Italienischer Faschismus – Nationalsozialismus* (Munich, 1963), 635.

84. Heinrich August Winkler, *Geschichte des Westens: Von den Anfängen in der Antike bis zum 20. Jahrhundert*, 2nd edn (Munich, 2010), 640.

85. August Thalheimer, 'Über den Faschismus', *Faschismus und Kapitalismus: Theorien über die sozialen Ursprünge und die Funktion des Faschismus*, ed. Otto Bauer and others (Frankfurt, 1967), 19–38, esp. 31. The quotation from Marx's 1852 essay, 'The Eighteenth Brumaire of Louis Bonaparte', is taken from *Marx/Engels Collected Works*, 50 vols (London, 1975–2005), xi.195.

86. Mary Soames (ed.), *Speaking for Themselves: The Personal Letters of Winston and Clementine Churchill* (New York, 1998), 303 (letter from Winston to Clementine Churchill, 6 January 1927).

87. 'Churchill Extols Fascismo for Italy', *New York Times* (21 January 1927).

88. Wolfgang Schieder, 'Das italienische Experiment: Der Faschismus als Vorbild in der Krise der Weimarer Republik', in *Faschistische Diktaturen* (note 77), 149–85, esp. 157.

89. Ibid., 158.

90. Braunthal, *Geschichte der Internationale* (note 10), ii.326; Engl. trans. ii.304.

91. Susan Kingsley Kent, *Aftershocks: Politics and Trauma in Britain, 1918–1931* (Basingstoke, 2009), 122–3.

92. Ibid., 132.

93. Ibid., 134.

94. Martin Pugh, *'Hurrah for the Blackshirts!' Fascists and Fascism in Britain Between the Wars* (London, 2005), 106.

95. Quoted by Bernhard Dietz, 'Neo-Tories: Britische Konservative im Aufstand gegen Demokratie und politische Moderne (1929–1939)' (diss., Humboldt-Universität zu Berlin, 2010), 50.

96. Wolfram Fischer, *Deutsche Wirtschaftspolitik 1918–1945* (Opladen, 1968), 31.

97. See Winkler, *Weimar* (note 5), 329–30.

98. Knut Borchardt, 'Wirtschaftliche Ursachen des Scheiterns der Weimarer Republik', *Wachstum, Krisen, Handlungsspielräume der Wirtschaftspolitik: Studien zur Wirtschaftsgeschichte des 19. und 20. Jahrunderts* (Göttingen, 1982), 183–203.

99. Winkler, *Der lange Weg* (note 1), i.457; Engl. trans. i.409 (emended).

100. Ibid., i.460; Engl. trans. i.410 (emended).

101. Ibid., i.469; Engl. trans. i.418 (emended).

102. Ibid., i.470; Engl. trans. i.419 (emended).

103. Ibid., i.475; Engl. trans. i.423.

104. Ibid., i.477; Engl. trans. i.425 (emended).

105. This is the translation of *Deutschnationale Arbeitsgemeinschaft* offered by Hermann Beck in his study *The Fateful Alliance* (New York, 2008). In his translation of Heinrich August Winkler's *Der lange Weg nach Westen*, Alexander J. Sager proposes 'German Nationalist Cooperative Union'.

106. Winkler, *Der lange Weg* (note 1), i.487; Engl. trans. i.434 (emended).

107. Ibid., i.487; Engl. trans. i.434 (emended).

108. Ibid., i.488; Engl. trans. i.435 (emended).

109. J. V. Stalin, 'Questions and Answers', *Works*, 13 vols (Moscow, 1952–5), vii.

110. Lenin, 'On the Slogan for a United States of Europe', *Collected Works* (note 6), xxi.343.

111. David Shub, *Lenin: A Biography* (London, 1966), 435.

112. Leonard Schapiro, *The Communist Party of the Soviet Union* (London, 1970), 296.

113. Winkler, *Der Schein der Normalität* (note 62), 661.

114. Ibid., 661–5.

115. Stalin, 'Concerning Questions of Agrarian Policy in the USSR', *Works* (note 109), xii.147–78, esp. 172.

116. Helmut Altrichter, *Kleine Geschichte der Sowjetunion 1917–1991* (Munich, 1993), 70.

117. Nicolas Werth, 'A State against Its People: Violence, Repression, and Terror in the Soviet Union', in Stéphane Courtois (ed.), *The Black Book of Communism: Crimes, Terror, Repression*, trans. Jonathan Murphy (Cambridge, MA, 1999), 33–268.

118. Stalin, 'The Tasks of Business Executives', *Works* (note 109), xiii.
119. Stalin, 'Concerning Questions of Leninism', *Works* (note 109), viii.13–96, esp. 18.
120. Ibid.
121. Jörg Baberowski, *Der rote Terror: Die Geschichte des Stalinismus* (Munich, 2003), 107.
122. Ibid., 112.
123. Hildermeier, *Geschichte der Sowjetunion* (note 35), 404.
124. Sobhanial Datta Gupta (ed.), *The Ryutin Platform: Stalin and the Crisis of Proletarian Dictatorship* (Parganas, India, 2010).
125. Heinrich August Winkler, *Der Weg in die Katastrophe: Arbeiter und Arbeiterbewegung in der Weimarer Republik 1930 bis 1933*, 2nd edn (Bonn, 1990), 277.
126. François Furet, *The Passing of an Illusion: The Idea of Communism in the Twentieth Century* (Chicago, 2001), 155.
127. Ibid., 147; see also Robert Conquest, *The Harvest of Sorrow: Soviet Collectivization and the Terror-Famine* (London, 2002), 314–15.
128. Furet, *The Passing of an Illusion* (note 126), 155.
129. On Sombart, see Winkler, *Geschichte des Westens* (note 84), 951–2.
130. Richard H. Pells, *Radical Visions and American Dreams: Culture and Social Thought in the Depression Years* (New York, 1973), 66.
131. Ibid., 64.
132. Arthur M. Schlesinger, Jr, *The Age of Roosevelt*, i: *The Crisis of the Old Order 1919–1933* (Boston, 1957), 149.
133. David F. Schmitz, *The United States and Fascist Italy 1922–1940* (Chapel Hill, NC, 1988), 112.
134. John Kenneth Galbraith, *The Great Crash 1929*, 3rd edn (Boston, 1961), 6.
135. Wilhelm G. Grewe, *Epochen der Völkerrechtsgeschichte*, 2nd edn (Baden-Baden, 1988), 729–31.
136. Henry Steele Commager (ed.), *Documents of American History*, 3rd edn (New York, 1943), 222–5.
137. Galbraith, *The Great Crash* (note 134), 79.
138. Alan Brinkley, *The Unfinished Nation: A Concise History of the American People*, 5th edn (Boston, 2008), 652–3.
139. Joseph Schumpeter, *Business Cycles: A Theoretical, Historical and Statistical Analysis of the Capitalist Process* (New York, 1939).
140. Leuchtenburg, *The Perils of Prosperity* (note 31), 249.
141. Schlesinger, *The Age of Roosevelt* (note 132), 313–14.
142. Ibid., 436.
143. Commager, *Documents of American History* (note 136), 239–42.
144. Winkler, *Der Weg in die Katastrophe* (note 125), 35.
145. Winkler, *Der lange Weg* (note 1), i.490–91; Engl. trans. i.437 (emended).
146. Ibid., i.495; Engl. trans. i.441 (emended).
147. Ibid., i.496; Engl. trans. i.442 (emended).
148. Ibid., i.497; Engl. trans. i.442 (emended).
149. Ibid., i.497; Engl. trans. i.442 (emended).
150. Ibid., i.497; Engl. trans. i.442–3 (emended).
151. Ibid., i.498; Engl. trans. i.443–4 (emended).
152. Ibid., i.502; Engl. trans. i.447 (emended).
153. Ibid., i.502; Engl. trans. i.447 (emended).
154. Ibid., i.503; Engl. trans. i.448 (emended).
155. Ibid., i.503; Engl. trans. i.448 (emended).
156. Ibid., i.504; Engl. trans. i.448–9 (emended).
157. Ibid., i.507; Engl. trans. i.451 (emended).
158. Ibid., i.508; Engl. trans. i.452 (emended).
159. Serge Berstein and Pierre Milza, *Histoire au XXᵉ siècle* (Paris, 1950), ii.412–13.
160. Hans Wilhelm Eckert, *Konservative Revolution in Frankreich? Die Nonkonformisten der Jeune Droite und des Ordre Nouveau in der Krise der 30er Jahre* (Munich, 2000), 63.

161. Heinrich August Winkler, 'Klassenkampf versus Koalition: Die französischen Sozialisten und die Politik der deutschen Sozialdemokraten 1928–1933', *Geschichte und Gesellschaft*, xvii (1991), 182–219, esp. 198.
162. Adam Tooze, *The Wages of Destruction: The Making and Breaking of the Nazi Economy* (London, 2006), 20.
163. G. D. H. Cole, *A History of the Labour Party from 1914* (London, 1948), 261.
164. Dietz, 'Neo-Tories' (note 95), 218.
165. Ibid., 142.
166. Winkler, *Der lange Weg*, i.520; Engl. trans. i.461 (emended).
167. Ibid., i.521; Engl. trans. i.462 (emended).
168. Ibid., i.522; Engl. trans. i.462 (emended).
169. Ibid., i.527; Engl. trans. i.466 (emended).
170. Ibid., i.528; Engl. trans. i.467 (emended).
171. Ibid., i.530; Engl. trans. i.469 (emended).
172. Ibid., i.533; Engl. trans. i.471–2 (emended).
173. Ibid., i.533; Engl. trans. i.472 (emended).
174. Ibid., i.536; Engl. trans. i.475 (emended).
175. Ibid., i.538; Engl. trans. i.477 (emended).
176. Ibid., i.543; Engl. trans. i.482.
177. Ibid., i.544; Engl. trans. i.483.
178. Ibid., i.545; Engl. trans. i.483 (emended).
179. Ibid., i.547; Engl. trans. i.485 (emended).
180. Ibid., i.550; Engl. trans. i.487 (emended).
181. Ibid., i.550; Engl. trans. i.487 (emended).
182. Ibid., i.551; Engl. trans. i.487 (emended).
183. Ibid., i.552; Engl. trans. i.488 (emended).
184. Max Weber, *Economy and Society: An Outline of Interpretive Sociology*, trans. Ephraim Fischoff and others and ed. Guenther Roth and Claus Wittich, 2 vols (Berkeley, 1978), i.265.
185. Winkler, *Der lange Weg* (note 1), i.555; Engl. trans. i.490 (emended).
186. Ibid., i.555; Engl. trans. i.490 (emended).
187. Winkler, *Der lange Weg nach Westen*, vol. 2: *Deutsche Geschichte vom 'Dritten Reich' bis zur Wiedervereinigung* (note 58), 8; Engl. trans. 10 (emended).
188. Ibid., ii.8; Engl. trans. ii.10 (emended).
189. W. G. Beasley, *The Modern History of Japan* (London, 1978), 235.
190. Quoted by Reinhard Zöllner, *Geschichte Japans: Von 1800 bis zur Gegenwart* (Paderborn, 2006), 354–5.
191. Sean Langdon Malloy, *Atomic Tragedy: Henry L. Stimson and the Decision to Use the Bomb Against Japan* (Ithaca, NY, 2010), 36.
192. Ray Lyman Wilbur and Arthur Mastick Hyde, *The Hoover Policies* (New York, 1951), 600–601.

Chapter 3. Democracies and Dictatorships: 1933–9

1. Robert Pasquill, *The Civilian Conservation Corps in Alabama, 1933–1942: A Great and Lasting Good* (Tuscaloosa, AL, 2008), 12.
2. Arthur M. Schlesinger, Jr, *The Age of Roosevelt*, iii: *The Politics of Upheaval, 1935–1936* (Boston, 1960), 84.
3. Ibid., 86.
4. Heinrich August Winkler, 'Die Anti-New-Deal-Bewegungen: Politik und Ideologie der Opposition gegen Präsident F. D. Roosevelt', *Die große Krise in Amerika: Vergleichende Studien zur politischen Sozialgeschichte 1929–1939*, ed. Heinrich August Winkler (Göttingen, 1972), 216–35, esp. 225.
5. Schlesinger, *The Politics of Upheaval* (note 2), 326.
6. Ibid., 329.

7. William E. Leuchtenburg, *Franklin D. Roosevelt and the New Deal 1932–1940* (New York, 1963), 154.
8. Schlesinger, *The Politics of Upheaval* (note 2), 585.
9. Ibid., 190.
10. Leuchtenburg, *Roosevelt and the New Deal* (note 7), 67.
11. Arthur M. Schlesinger, Jr, *The Age of Roosevelt*, ii: *The Coming of the New Deal* (Boston, 1958), 254.
12. Ibid., 480.
13. Wolfgang Schivelbusch, *Entfernte Verwandtschaft: Faschismus, Nationalsozialismus, New Deal 1933–1939* (Munich, 2005), 27.
14. Ibid., 24.
15. Ibid., 14.
16. Adolf Hitler, *Mein Kampf* (Munich, 1942), 69–70; trans. Ralph Manheim as *Mein Kampf* (London, 2002), 60. It is a foolhardy translator who questions Ralph Manheim, but I cannot help thinking that he has misread Hitler's 'Totentanz' as 'Totenkranz' and that the first sentence should read 'his crown will be the dance of death of humanity'.
17. Ibid., 738–42; Engl. trans. 595–8.
18. Ibid., 742; Engl. trans. 598.
19. Adolf Hitler, *Hitlers Zweites Buch: Ein Dokument aus dem Jahr 1928* (Stuttgart, 1961), 52; trans. as *Hitler's Second Book: The Unpublished Sequel to 'Mein Kampf'*, ed. Gerhard L. Weinberg (New York, 2006), 34.
20. Ibid., 64; Engl. trans. 47.
21. Ibid., 132; Engl. trans. 105.
22. Ibid., 94; Engl. trans. 73.
23. Heinrich August Winkler, *Der lange Weg nach Westen*, vol. 2: *Deutsche Geschichte vom 'Dritten Reich' bis zur Wiedervereinigung*, 5th edn (Munich, 2010), 5; trans. Alexander J. Sager as *The Long Road West, 1933–1990* (Oxford, 2007), 7 (emended).
24. Adolf Hitler, *Monologe im Führerhauptquartier 1941–1944: Die Aufzeichnungen Heinrich Heims*, ed. Werner Jochmann (Hamburg, 1980), 155; trans. Norman Cameron and R. H. Stevens as *Hitler's Table Talk 1941–1944*, ed. H. R. Trevor-Roper (London, 2000), 149. There are a number of puzzling discrepancies between the original German, as edited by Werner Jochmann, and the translation by Norman Cameron and R. H. Stevens. A more literal translation of the German would read: 'It was a decisive moment for me when we first took power: should we continue to use the existing calendar? Or should we take the new world order as the signal to start a new calendar? I told myself that the year 1933 was nothing less than the restoration of a state that had lasted one thousand years. At that time the notion of the Reich had been almost entirely eradicated, but it has now victoriously reasserted itself both at home and in the wider world. When people speak of Germany nowadays, no matter where they may be, they speak only of the Reich.'
25. Winkler, *Der lange Weg* (note 23), ii.8; Engl. trans., ii.10.
26. Ibid., ii.10; Engl. trans. ii.12 (emended).
27. Heinrich August Winkler, *Der Weg in die Katastrophe: Arbeiter und Arbeiterbewegung in der Weimarer Republik 1930–1933*, 2nd edn (Bonn, 1990), 904.
28. Winkler, *Der lange Weg* (note 23), ii.13; Engl. trans. ii.15 (emended).
29. Ibid., ii.19; Engl. trans. ii.21 (emended).
30. Ibid., ii.20; Engl. trans. ii.22.
31. Ibid., ii.20; Engl. trans. ii.22 (emended).
32. Ibid., ii.22; Engl. trans. ii.24 (emended).
33. Adam Tooze, *The Wages of Destruction: The Making and Breaking of the Nazi Economy* (London, 2006), 52.
34. Winkler, *Der lange Weg* (note 23), ii.32; Engl. trans., ii.34 (emended).
35. Ibid., ii.32; Engl. trans. ii.34 (emended).
36. Ibid., ii.33; Engl. trans. ii.35 (emended).
37. Ibid., ii.35; Engl. trans. ii.37 (emended).
38. Ibid., ii.35; Engl. trans. ii.37 (emended).

39. Ibid., ii.37; Engl. trans. ii.39 (emended).
40. Ibid., ii.37; Engl. trans. ii.39.
41. Ibid., ii.38; Engl. trans. ii.39 (emended).
42. Jens Petersen, *Hitler – Mussolini: Die Entstehung der Achse Berlin – Rom 1933–1936* (Tübingen, 1973), 114–15.
43. Ibid., 378.
44. Ibid., 400.
45. Hans Woller, *Geschichte Italiens im 20. Jahrhundert* (Munich, 2010), 144.
46. Aram Mattioli, 'Ein vergessenes Schlüsselereignis der Weltkriegsepoche', *Der erste faschistische Vernichtungskrieg: Die italienische Aggression gegen Äthiopien 1935–1941*, ed. Asfa-Wossen Asserate and Aram Mattioli (Cologne, 2006), 24–5.
47. Aram Mattioli, 'Entgrenzte Kriegsgewalt: Der italienische Giftgaseinsatz in Abessinien 1935–1936', *Vierteljahrshefte für Zeitgeschichte*, li (2003), 334.
48. Ibid., 336.
49. Renzo De Felice, *Mussolini il duce: Gli anni del consenso 1929–1936*, 2nd edn (Turin, 1996), 745.
50. Aram Mattioli, *Experimentierfeld der Gewalt: Der Abessinienkrieg und seine internationale Bedeutung 1935–1941* (Zurich, 2005), 131–2.
51. Woller, *Geschichte Italiens* (note 45), 149–50; Engl. trans. from MacGregor Knox, *Mussolini Unleashed, 1939–1941: Politics and Strategy in Fascist Italy's Last War* (Cambridge, 1982), 4.
52. Woller, *Geschichte Italiens* (note 45), 13.
53. J. V. Stalin, 'Report to the Seventeenth Party Congress on the Work of the Central Committee of the C.P.S.U.(B.)', *Works*, 13 vols (Moscow, 1952–5), xiii.
54. Hermann Weber (ed.), *Die Kommunistische Internationale: Eine Dokumentation* (Hanover, 1966), 279.
55. Ibid., 279.
56. Theo Pirker (ed.), *Komintern und Faschismus 1920–1940: Dokumente zur Geschichte und Theorie des Faschismus* (Stuttgart, 1965), 187–8.
57. Jörg Baberowski, *Der rote Terror: Die Geschichte des Stalinismus* (Munich, 2003), 174–5.
58. Ibid., 204–7.
59. Robert Gellately, *Lenin, Stalin and Hitler: The Age of Social Catastrophe* (New York, 2007), 359.
60. François Furet, *The Passing of an Illusion: The Idea of Communism in the Twentieth Century* (Chicago, 2001), 278.
61. Ibid., 289.
62. Ibid., 300.
63. Karl Schlögel, *Moscow, 1937*, trans. Rodney Livingstone (Cambridge, 2012), 127–8.
64. Winkler, *Der lange Weg* (note 23), ii.27; Engl. trans. ii.28 (emended).
65. Michael Wildt, *Generation des Unbedingten: Das Führerprinzip des Reichssicherheitshauptamtes*, 2nd edn (Hamburg, 2003); trans. Tom Lampert as *An Uncompromising Generation: The Nazi Leadership of the Reich Security Main Office* (Madison, WI, 2010).
66. Winkler, *Der lange Weg* (note 23), ii.47; Engl. trans. ii.47 (emended).
67. Ian Kershaw, *The 'Hitler Myth': Image and Reality in the Third Reich* (Oxford, 2001), 82.
68. Ibid.
69. John Maynard Keynes, *The General Theory of Employment, Interest and Money* (London, 1936), 378.
70. Tooze, *The Wages of Destruction* (note 33), 206–7.
71. Wilhelm Treue, 'Hitlers Denkschrift zum Vierteljahresplan 1936', *Vierteljahrshefte für Zeitgeschichte*, iii (1955), 184–210, esp. 204.
72. Ibid., 205.
73. Ibid., 210.

74. Timothy W. Mason, *Arbeiterklasse und Volksgemeinschaft: Dokumente und Materialien zur deutschen Arbeiterpolitik 1936–1939* (Opladen, 1975), 1–3.
75. Ibid., 163–4.
76. Ibid., 124. The phrase *le plébiscite de tous les jours* is associated with the French thinker Ernest Renan (1823–92).
77. Ibid., 169.
78. Klaus Hildebrand, *Das vergangene Reich: Deutsche Außenpolitik von Bismarck bis Hitler* (Stuttgart, 1995), 607.
79. Winkler, *Der lange Weg* (note 23), ii.50–51; Engl. trans. ii.49–50 (emended).
80. Hildebrand, *Das vergangene Reich* (note 78), 631.
81. Hans-Ulrich Thamer, *Verführung und Gewalt: Deutschland 1933–1945* (Berlin, 1986), 552.
82. 'Das Hoßbach-Protokoll', *Internationaler Militärgerichtshof: der Prozeß gegen die Hauptkriegsverbrecher* (Nuremberg, 1947–9), xxv.403–5.
83. Anne Perkins, *Baldwin* (London, 2006), 100.
84. Hildebrand, *Das vergangene Reich* (note 78), 699.
85. Perkins, *Baldwin* (note 83), 105.
86. René Rémond, *Frankreich im 20. Jahrhundert* (Stuttgart, 1994), 203.
87. Jacques Kergoat, *La France du Front Populaire* (Paris, 1986), 86.
88. Rémond, *Frankreich im 20. Jahrhundert* (note 86), 234.
89. Charles Bloch, *Die dritte französische Republik: Entwicklung und Kampf einer parlamentarischen Demokratie (1870–1940)* (Stuttgart, 1972), 457.
90. Kergoat, *La France du Front Populaire* (note 87), 105.
91. Pierre Broué and Émile Témime, *Revolution und Krieg in Spanien* (Frankfurt, 1968), 328–9.
92. Ibid., 480. Koltsov was *Pravda*'s official correspondent.
93. Ibid., 359.
94. Ibid., 367.
95. Willy Brandt, *Hitler ist nicht Deutschland: Jugend in Lübeck – Exil in Norwegen 1928–1940*, ed. Einhart Lorenz (Bonn, 2002), 329.
96. John Whitaker, 'Prelude to World War: A Witness from Spain', *Foreign Affairs*, xxi (October 1942–July 1943), 108.
97. Franz Borkenau, *The Spanish Cockpit* (London, 1986), 281–2. The year 1707 refers to the War of the Spanish Succession, while 1808 is a reference to the guerrilla war waged against Napoleon.
98. Ibid., 287.
99. Ibid., 288.
100. Ibid., 297.
101. Ibid., 297–8.
102. Woller, *Geschichte Italiens* (note 45), 153–4.
103. Boris Celovsky, *Das Münchner Abkommen 1938* (Stuttgart, 1958), 93–4.
104. Ibid., 116.
105. Ivan Pfaff, 'Stalins Strategie der Sowjetisierung Mitteleuropas 1933–1938', *Vierteljahrshefte für Zeitgeschichte*, xxxviii (1990), 543–88, esp. 549.
106. Alice Teichova, 'Die Tschechoslowakei 1918–1980', *Europäische Wirtschafts- und Sozialgeschichte vom Ersten Weltkrieg bis zur Gegenwart*, ed. Wolfram Fischer (Stuttgart 1987), 598–639, esp. 617 (= Handbuch der europäischen Wirtschafts- und Sozialgeschichte, vol. vi).
107. Włodzimierz Borodziej, *Geschichte Polens im 20. Jahrhundert* (Munich, 2010), 177.
108. Ronald Modras, *The Catholic Church and Antisemitism in Poland, 1933–1939* (Abingdon, 2004), 346–7.
109. Borodziej, *Geschichte Polens* (note 107), 178.
110. Leuchtenburg, *Roosevelt and the New Deal* (note 7), 225.
111. *The Public Papers and Addresses of Franklin D. Roosevelt: 1937* (New York, 1941), 406–11.
112. Winkler, *Der lange Weg* (note 23), ii.54; Engl. trans. ii.52.

113. Ibid., ii.54; Engl. trans. ii.53.
114. Ibid., ii.55; Engl. trans. ii.53.
115. Ibid., ii.55; Engl. trans. ii.54 (emended).
116. Ibid., ii.55; Engl. trans., ii.55 (emended).
117. Ibid., ii.58; Engl. trans. ii.56 (emended).
118. Ibid., ii.58–9; Engl. trans. ii.56–7 (emended).
119. Celovsky, *Das Münchner Abkommen* (note 103), 337.
120. Winkler, *Der lange Weg* (note 23), ii.60–61; Engl. trans. ii.58.
121. Ibid., ii.61; Engl. trans. ii.58 (emended).
122. Keith Feiling, *The Life of Neville Chamberlain*, 2nd edn (London, 1947), 381.
123. Celovsky, *Das Münchner Abkommen* (note 103), 469.
124. Ibid., 468.
125. Saul Friedländer, *The Years of Persecution: Nazi Germany and the Jews 1933–39* (London, 2007), 241–2.
126. Ernest Jones, *Sigmund Freud: Life and Work*, 3 vols (London, 1957), iii.241.
127. Friedländer, *The Years of Persecution* (note 125), 264.
128. Winkler, *Der lange Weg* (note 23), ii.48; Engl. trans. ii.47–8 (emended).
129. Leuchtenburg, *Roosevelt and the New Deal* (note 7), 285.
130. Winkler, *Der lange Weg* (note 23), ii.49; Engl. trans. ii.48 (emended).
131. Ibid., ii.50; Engl. trans. ii.49 (emended).
132. Ibid., ii.63–4; Engl. trans. ii.59–60 (emended).
133. Hermann Graml, *Europas Weg in den Krieg: Hitler und die Mächte 1939* (Munich, 1990), 139.
134. Winkler, *Der lange Weg* (note 23), ii.63–4; Engl. trans. ii.61 (emended).
135. Ibid., ii.64; Engl. trans. ii.62 (emended).
136. Ibid., ii.65; Engl. trans. ii.62 (emended). Hugelmann's book, *Volk und Staat im Wandel deutschen Schicksals*, was published in Essen in 1940.
137. Winkler, ii.66; Engl. trans. ii.63 (emended). Schmitt's *Völkerrechtliche Großraumordnung mit Interventionsverbot für raumfremde Mächte* appeared in 1940. Its title is almost impossible to translate. (No previous translator has tried to tackle it.) More or less literally, it means 'Large-scale territorial order under international law with a ban on intervention by powers that are alien to that space'.
138. Ibid., ii.66; Engl. trans. ii.63 (emended).
139. Frank McDonough, *Hitler, Chamberlain and Appeasement* (Cambridge, 2002), 74.
140. Borodziej, *Geschichte Polens* (note 107), 189.
141. Stalin, 'Report on the Work of the Central Committee to the Eighteenth Party Congress of the C.P.S.U.(B.)', *Works* (note 53), xiv.
142. Winkler, *Der lange Weg* (note 23), ii.67; Engl. trans. ii.64 (emended).
143. Woller, *Geschichte Italiens* (note 45), 169.
144. Winkler, *Der lange Weg* (note 23), ii.68; Engl. trans. ii.65.
145. Robert Gellately, *Lenin, Stalin and Hitler: The Age of Social Catastrophe* (London, 2008), 358.
146. Heinrich August Winkler, *Geschichte des Westens: Von den Anfängen in der Antike bis zum 20. Jahrhundert*, 2nd edn (Munich, 2010), 448 and 718–19.
147. Mao Tse-tung, 'Interview with a *New China Daily* Correspondent', *Selected Works of Mao Tse-tung* (Beijing, 1965), ii.263–5.
148. Winkler, *Der lange Weg* (note 23), ii.69; Engl. trans. ii.66 (emended).
149. Ibid., ii.69; Engl. trans. ii.66.
150. Ibid., ii.69; Engl. trans. ii.66.
151. Ibid., ii.70–71; Engl. trans. ii.67 (emended).
152. Ibid., ii.71; Engl. trans. ii.67 (emended).
153. Ibid., ii.72; Engl. trans. ii.68 (emended).
154. Ibid., ii.72; Engl. trans. ii.68 (emended).
155. Ibid., ii.72; Engl. trans. ii.69 (emended).

Chapter 4. Fault Lines in Western Civilization: The Second World
War and the Holocaust

1. Archiv des Auswärtigen Amts (ed.), *Akten zur Deutschen Auswärtigen Politik 1918–1945*, Serie D (1937–1945) (Baden-Baden, 1950–), vii.171–2; see also Winfried Baumgart, 'Zur Ansprache Hitlers vor den Führern der Wehrmacht am 22. August 1939', *Vierteljahrshefte für Zeitgeschichte*, xvi (1968), 120–49.

2. Christian Hartmann and Sergej Slutsch, 'Fritz Halder und die Kriegsvorbereitungen im Frühjahr 1939: Eine Ansprache des Generalstabschefs des Heeres', *Vierteljahrshefte für Zeitgeschichte*, xlv (1997), 467–95, esp. 482–3. Cannae was the scene of Hannibal's comprehensive victory over Rome and its allies in 216 BC.

3. Jochen Böhler, *Auftakt zum Vernichtungskrieg: Die Wehrmacht in Polen 1939* (Frankfurt, 2006), 36.

4. Klaus-Michael Mallmann, Jochen Böhler and Jürgen Matthäus, *Einsatzgruppen in Polen: Darstellung und Dokumentation* (Darmstadt, 2008), 57.

5. Martin Broszat, *Nationalsozialistische Polenpolitik 1939–1945* (Stuttgart, 1961), 31.

6. Heinrich August Winkler, *Der lange Weg nach Westen*, vol. 2: *Deutsche Geschichte vom 'Dritten Reich' bis zur Wiedervereinigung*, 5th edn (Munich, 2010), 74; trans. Alexander J. Sager as *The Long Road West, 1933–1990* (Oxford, 2007), 71 (emended).

7. Ibid., ii.74–5; Engl. trans. ii.71 (emended).

8. Seppo Hentilä, 'Von der Erringung der Selbstständigkeit bis zum Fortsetzungskrieg 1917–1944', in Osmo Jussila and others, *Vom Großfürstentum zur Europäischen Union: Politische Geschichte Finnlands seit 1809* (Berlin, 1999), 115–235, esp. 207.

9. Ian Kershaw, *Fateful Choices: Ten Decisions that Changed the World, 1940–1941* (London, 2007), 23.

10. David Cannadine (ed.), *The Speeches of Winston Churchill*, 2nd edn (Harmondsworth, 1990), 147–9.

11. Charles de Gaulle, *Discours et messages: Pendant la guerre 1940–1946* (Paris, 1970), 3–4.

12. Karl-Heinz Frieser, *Blitzkrieg-Legende: Der Westfeldzug 1940*, 2nd edn (Munich, 1996), 435–9.

13. Winkler, *Der lange Weg* (note 6), ii.76; Engl. trans. ii.73 (emended).

14. Karl Richard Ganzar, *Das Reich als europäische Ordnungsmacht* (Hamburg: Hanseatische Verlagsanstalt, 1941), 86.

15. Winkler, *Der lange Weg*, ii.77–8; Engl. trans. ii.74 (emended).

16. Ibid., ii.78; Engl. trans. ii.74 (emended).

17. William E. Leuchtenburg, *Franklin D. Roosevelt and the New Deal 1932–1940* (New York, 1963), 321.

18. Ibid., 322.

19. Robert Dallek, *Franklin Delano Roosevelt and American Foreign Policy 1932–1945*, 2nd edn (New York, 1995), 255.

20. Henry Steele Commager (ed.), *Documents of American History*, vol. 2: *Since 1898* (New York, 1973), 447–9.

21. Joachim C. Fest, *Hitler*, trans. Richard and Clara Winston (London, 1974), 637.

22. Generaloberst [Franz] Halder, *Kriegstagebuch: Tägliche Aufzeichnungen des Chefs des Generalstabs des Heeres, 1939–1942*, 3 vols (Stuttgart, 1962–4), ii.49; partial trans. from John Lukacs, *June 1941: Hitler and Stalin* (New Haven, CT, 2006), 27; Engl. trans. from Ian Kershaw, *Hitler 1936–1945: Nemesis* (London, 2001), 308.

23. Andreas Hillgruber, *Hitlers Strategie: Politik und Kriegsführung 1940– 1941*, 2nd edn (Munich, 1982), 225.

24. Kershaw, *Hitler* (note 22), 335.

25. Winkler, *Der lange Weg* (note 6), ii.80; Engl. trans. ii.76 (emended).

26. Ibid., ii.80; Engl. trans. ii.77 (emended).

27. Max Domarus (ed.), *Hitler: Reden und Proklamationen 1932–1945*, Vol. 2/2: *Untergang 1941–1945* (Munich, 1965), 1726–32.

28. Winkler, *Der lange Weg* (note 6), ii.82–3; Engl. trans. ii.78 (emended).

29. Hans-Ulrich Thamer, *Verführung und Gewalt: Deutschland 1933–1945* (Berlin, 1986), 662.

30. Adolf Hitler, *Monologe im Führerhauptquartier 1941–1944: Die Aufzeichnungen Heinrich Heims*, ed. Werner Jochmann (Hamburg, 1980), 91; trans. Norman Cameron and R. H. Stevens as *Hitler's Table Talk 1941–1944*, ed. H. R. Trevor-Roper (London, 2000), 69.

31. Kershaw, *Fateful Choices* (note 9), 381.

32. Commager, *Documents of American History* (note 20), 451.

33. Domarus, *Hitler: Reden und Proklamationen* (note 27), 1794–811.

34. Ibid., 1808.

35. Winkler, *Der lange Weg* (note 6), ii.86; Engl. trans. ii.82 (emended).

36. Ibid., ii.90–91; Engl. trans. ii.83 (emended).

37. Christian Streit, *Keine Kameraden! Die Wehrmacht und die sowjetischen Kriegsgefangenen* (Stuttgart, 1978), 115; Engl. trans. from Winkler, *Germany: The Long Road West*, ii.84 (emended).

38. Saul Friedländer, *The Years of Extermination: Nazi Germany and the Jews 1939–1945* (London, 2008), 185.

39. Alexander Dallin, *German Rule in Russia 1941–1945* (New York, 1957), 206.

40. Domarus, *Hitler: Reden und Proklamationen* (note 27), 1663.

41. Ibid., 1820–21.

42. Winkler, *Der lange Weg* (note 6), ii.90–91; Engl. trans. ii.85–6 (emended).

43. Ibid., ii.91–2; Engl. trans. ii.86–7 (emended).

44. Ibid., ii.92; Engl. trans. ii.87.

45. Ibid., ii.92; Engl. trans. ii.87 (emended).

46. Ibid., ii.93; Engl. trans. ii.88 (emended).

47. Ibid., ii.93; Engl. trans. ii.88.

48. Ibid., ii.94; Engl. trans. ii.88 (emended).

49. L. J. Hartog, *Der Befehl zum Judenmord: Hitler, Amerika und die Juden* (Bodenheim, 1997), 65–6.

50. Domarus, *Hitler: Reden und Proklamationen* (note 27), 1828–9; Engl. trans. from Winkler, *Germany: The Long Road West* (note 6), ii.90 (emended).

51. Friedländer, *The Years of Extermination* (note 38), 190.

52. Richard J. Overy, ' "Blitzkriegwirtschaft"? Finanzpolitik, Lebensstandard und Arbeitseinsatz in Deutschland 1939–1942', *Vierteljahrshefte für Zeitgeschichte*, xxxvi (1988), 379–435, esp. 401. (This article appears not to have been published in English.)

53. Christoph Buchheim, 'Der Mythos vom "Wohlleben": Der Lebensstandard der deutschen Zivilbevölkerung im Zweiten Weltkrieg', *Vierteljahrshefte für Zeitgeschichte*, lviii (2010), 299–328, esp. 327.

54. Marie-Luise Recker, *Nationalsozialistische Sozialpolitik im Zweiten Weltkrieg* (Munich, 1985), 130.

55. Rolf-Dieter Müller, *Der letzte deutsche Krieg 1939–1945*, 10th edn (Stuttgart, 2004), 289.

56. Ian Kershaw, *The 'Hitler Myth': Image and Reality in the Third Reich* (Oxford, 2001), 189.

57. Malcolm Pearce and Geoffrey Stewart, *British Political History 1867–1995: Democracy and Decline* (London, 1996), 439–40.

58. Alexander Werth, *Russia at War: 1941–1945* (New York, 1964), 213–16.

59. Ibid., 414.

60. Jörg Baberowski, *Der rote Terror: Die Geschichte des Stalinismus* (Munich, 2003), 231.

61. Josef Ackermann, *Heinrich Himmler als Ideologe* (Göttingen, 1970), 273.

62. Ulrich Herbert Best, *Biographische Studien über Radikalismus, Weltanschauung und Vernunft, 1903–1989*, 2nd edn (Bonn, 1996), 370.

63. Yves Beigbeder, *Judging War Crimes and Torture: French Justice and International Criminal Tribunals and Commissions (1940–2005)* (Leiden, 2006), 193.

64. René Rémond, *Frankreich im 20. Jahrhundert* (Stuttgart, 1994), 357.

65. Henry Rousso, *Vichy: Frankreich unter deutscher Besatzung 1940–1944* (Munich, 2009), 84.
66. Marc-Olivier Baruch, *Das Vichy-Regime: France 1940–1944* (Stuttgart, 1999), 108–9.
67. Ibid., 162.
68. Charles de Gaulle, *Discours et messages: Pendant la guerre 1940–1946* (Paris, 1970), 441–2.
69. Friedländer, *The Years of Extermination* (note 38), 364.
70. Ibid., 503.
71. Ibid., 422.
72. MacGregor Knox, 'Das faschistische Italien und die "Endlösung", 1942/43', *Vierteljahrshefte für Zeitgeschichte*, lv (2007), 53–92, esp. 53.
73. Friedländer, *The Years of Extermination* (note 38), 484.
74. Ibid., 570.
75. Ibid., 524.
76. Thamer, *Verführung und Gewalt* (note 29), 703.
77. Friedländer, *The Years of Extermination* (note 38), 543.
78. Ibid.
79. Winkler, *Der lange Weg* (note 6), ii.107; trans. Norman Cameron and R. H. Stevens as *Hitler's Table Talk 1941–1944*, ed. H. R. Trevor-Roper (London, 2000), 78–9.
80. Winkler, *Der lange Weg* (note 6), ii.107; Engl. trans. from *Hitler's Table Talk* (note 79), 721–2.
81. Winkler, *Der lange Weg* (note 6), ii.107; Engl. trans. ii.101 (emended).
82. Aram Mattioli, 'Ein vergessenes Schlüsselereignis der Weltgeschichte', *Der erste faschistische Vernichtungskrieg: Die italienische Aggression gegen Äthiopien 1935–1941*, ed. Asta-Wossen Asserate and Aram Mattioli (Cologne, 2006), 9–25, esp. 17.
83. Jens Petersen, 'Sommer 1943', *Italien und die Großmächte 1943–1949*, ed. Hans Woller (Munich, 1988), 23–48.
84. Włodzimierz Borodziej, *Geschichte Polens im 20. Jahrhundert* (Munich, 2010), 251.
85. Winkler, *Der lange Weg* (note 6), ii.98; Engl. trans. ii.95 (emended).
86. Ibid., ii.98; Engl. trans. ii.95 (emended).
87. Ibid., ii.100; Engl. trans. ii.97 (emended).
88. Ibid., ii.101; Engl. trans. ii.98 (emended).
89. Derek W. Unwin, *A Political History of Western Europe since 1945*, 5th edn (New York, 1997), 62.
90. Winston S. Churchill, *The Second World War*, 6 vols (London, 2000), vi.295.
91. Hansard for 15 December 1944 (clvi.1484).
92. *Die offiziellen Jalta-Dokumente des US State Departments* (Vienna, 1955), 355.
93. Waldemar Besson, *Von Roosevelt bis Kennedy: Grundzüge der amerikanischen Außenpolitik 1933–1963* (Frankfurt, 1964), 96.
94. Friedländer, *The Years of Extermination* (note 38), 354.
95. Churchill, *The Second World War* (note 90), vi.338–41.
96. Ibid., vi.394–5.
97. Kershaw, *The 'Hitler Myth'* (note 56), 223 and 221.
98. Kershaw, *Hitler* (note 22), 819.
99. Ibid., 823.
100. Ibid., 832.
101. Churchill, *The Second World War* (note 90), vi.431.
102. Ibid., vi.450–51.
103. Borodziej, *Geschichte Polens* (note 84), 260.
104. Ernst Deuerlein (ed.), *Die Einheit Deutschlands*, i: *Die Erörterungen und Entscheidungen der Kriegs- und Nachkriegskonferenzen 1941–1949*, 2nd edn (Frankfurt, 1961), 241–2.
105. Winkler, *Der lange Weg* (note 6), ii.117; Engl. trans. ii.116.
106. Ibid., ii.116; Engl. trans. ii.115 (emended).
107. Deuerlein, *Die Einheit Deutschlands* (note 104), 243.
108. Ibid., 245.

109. Churchill, *The Second World War* (note 90), vi.456.
110. Ibid., vi.455.
111. Ernst Deuerlein (ed.), *Potsdam 1945: Quellen zur Konferenz der 'Großen Drei'* (Munich, 1963), 350–70.
112. William L. Laurence, *Dawn Over Zero: The Story of the Atomic Bomb* (London, 1947), 3 and 10.
113. Martin J. Sherwin, *A World Destroyed: The Atomic Bomb and the Grand Alliance* (New York, 1975), 213.
114. Jörg Baberowski and Anselm Doering-Manteuffel, *Ordnung durch Terror: Gewaltexzesse und Vernichtung im nationalsozialistischen und im stalinistischen Imperium* (Bonn, 2007), 15.
115. Hugo von Münch (ed.), *Dokumente des geteilten Deutschland* (Stuttgart, 1976), 54–5.
116. Karl Jaspers, *The Question of German Guilt*, trans. E. B. Ashton (New York, 2000), 73 and 89–90.
117. Winkler, *Der lange Weg* (note 6), ii.110–11; Engl. trans. ii.103 (emended).
118. Dan Diner, 'Vorwort des Herausgebers', *Zivilisationsbruch: Denken nach Auschwitz* (Frankfurt, 1988), 9.
119. Timothy Snyder, *Bloodlands: Europe Between Hitler and Stalin* (New York, 2010), 155–7.
120. Baberowski and Doering-Manteuffel, *Ordnung durch Terror* (note 114), 83; and Zygmunt Bauman, *Modernity and the Holocaust* (Cambridge, 1989), 90.
121. Churchill, *The Second World War* (note 90), vi.543.
122. Hans Woller, *Geschichte Italiens im 20. Jahrhundert* (Munich, 2010), 218.
123. Wolfgang Schieder, *Der italienische Faschismus 1919–1945* (Munich, 2010), 112–13.
124. Woller, *Geschichte Italiens* (note 122), 222.
125. Gerhard Krebs, *Das moderne Japan 1868–1952: Von der Meji-Restauration bis zum Friedensvertrag von San Francisco* (Munich, 2009), 94–5.
126. Peter Wende, *Das britische Empire: Geschichte eines Weltreichs* (Munich, 2008), 274.

From World War to World War: Retrospective of an Exceptional Period

1. Charles de Gaulle, *Discours et messages: Pendant la guerre. Juin 1940 – Janvier 1946* (Paris, 1970), 102–3.
2. *Briefwechsel Stalins mit Churchill, Roosevelt und Truman 1941–1945* (Berlin, 1961), 254.
3. Arno J. Mayer, *Why Did the Heavens Not Darken? The 'Final Solution' in History* (London, 2012), 31–2.
4. Moritz Julius Bonn, *The Crisis of European Democracy* (New Haven, CT, 1925), 30 and 35–6.
5. Vladimir Ilyich Lenin, 'The War and Russian Social-Democracy', *Collected Works*, 45 vols (Moscow 1964–74), xxi.25–34, esp. 33.
6. M. Rainer Lepsius, 'Das Legat zweier Diktaturen für die demokratische Kultur im vereinigten Deutschland', *Aufhebung der Bipolarität: Veränderungen im Osten, Rückwirkungen im Westen*, ed. Everhard Holtmann and Heinz Sahner (Opladen, 1995), 25–39, esp. 30.
7. Dan Diner, *Cataclysms: A History of the Twentieth Century from Europe's Edge*, trans. William Templar and Joel Golb (Madison, 2008), 47.
8. Ibid., 200.
9. Friedrich Meinecke, *Die deutsche Katastrophe: Betrachtungen und Erinnerungen*, 3rd edn (Wiesbaden, 1947); an Engl. trans. was published by Harvard University Press in 1950 as *The German Catastrophe: Reflections and Recollections* and reprinted in 1963.

INDEX

NOTE: Ranks and titles given here are generally the highest mentioned in the text